AF695694

OFCCP

Federal Contractor Compliance Manual

And

Regulatory Documents

2016

OFCCP Federal Contractor Compliance Manual and Regulatory Documents

ISBN: 978-1-937299-26-2

All of our books are available from the publisher at special quantity discounts for use as premiums, sales promotions, or for training programs. Please contact the publisher at info@datamotionpublishing.com

DataMotion Publishing, LLC
1019 Fort Salonga Road, Suite 10-333
Northport, NY 11768-2209

DISCLAIMER

This document contains information publicly available and was created in order to provide readers with print documents of important regulatory information. This service is not intended as a substitute for competent legal or other professional advice and the publisher has made every effort to compile the most current information as of the date of publication. However, as the regulatory environment is a highly dynamic one, no guarantee is made as to the currency or accuracy of the information contained herein. The reader is advised to consult with appropriate counsel prior to acting on any information contained herein. No attorney client relationship exists between the reader and the publisher.

OFCCP
Federal Contractor Compliance Manual
And
Regulatory Documents

2016

CONTENTS

Executive Order 11246, As Amended

Office of Federal Contract Compliance Programs (OFCCP)

Executive Order 11246, As Amended

Executive Order 11246 — Equal Employment Opportunity

SOURCE: The provisions of Executive Order 11246 of Sept. 24, 1965, appear at 30 FR 12319, 12935, 3 CFR, 1964-1965 Comp., p.339, unless otherwise noted.

Under and by virtue of the authority vested in me as President of the United States by the Constitution and statutes of the United States, it is ordered as follows:

Part I — Nondiscrimination in Government Employment

[Part I superseded by EO 11478 of Aug. 8, 1969, 34 FR 12985, 3 CFR, 1966-1970 Comp., p. 803]

Part II - Nondiscrimination in Employment by Government Contractors and Subcontractors

Subpart A - Duties of the Secretary of Labor

SEC. 201. The Secretary of Labor shall be responsible for the administration and enforcement of Parts II and III of this Order. The Secretary shall adopt such rules and regulations and issue such orders as are deemed necessary and appropriate to achieve the purposes of Parts II and III of this Order.

[Sec. 201 amended by EO 12086 of Oct. 5, 1978, 43 FR 46501, 3 CFR, l978 Comp., p. 230]

Subpart B - Contractors' Agreements

SEC. 202. Except in contracts exempted in accordance with Section 204 of this Order, all Government contracting agencies shall include in every Government contract hereafter entered into the following provisions:

During the performance of this contract, the contractor agrees as follows:

1. The contractor will not discriminate against any employee or applicant for employment because of race, color, religion, sex, sexual orientation, gender identity, or national origin. The contractor will take affirmative action to ensure that applicants are employed, and that employees are treated during employment, without regard to their race, color, religion, sex, sexual orientation, gender identity, or national origin. Such action shall include, but not be limited to the following: employment, upgrading, demotion, or transfer; recruitment or recruitment advertising; layoff or termination; rates of pay or other forms of compensation; and selection for training, including apprenticeship. The contractor agrees to post in conspicuous places, available to employees and applicants for employment, notices to be provided by the contracting officer setting forth the provisions of this nondiscrimination clause.
2. The contractor will, in all solicitations or advancements for employees placed by or on behalf of the contractor, state that all qualified applicants will receive consideration for employment without regard to race, color, religion, sex, sexual orientation, gender identity, or national origin.
3. The contractor will not discharge or in any other manner discriminate against any employee or applicant for employment because such employee or applicant has inquired about, discussed, or disclosed the compensation of the employee or applicant or another employee or applicant. This provision shall not apply to instances in which an employee who has access to the compensation information of other employees or applicants as a part of such employee's essential job functions discloses the compensation of such other employees or applicants to individuals who do not otherwise have access to such information, unless such disclosure is in response to a formal complaint or charge, in furtherance of an investigation, proceeding, hearing, or action, including an investigation conducted by the employer, or is consistent with the contractor's legal duty to furnish information.
4. The contractor will send to each labor union or representative of workers with which he has a collective bargaining agreement or other contract or understanding, a notice, to be provided by the agency contracting officer, advising the labor union or workers' representative of the contractor's commitments under Section 202 of Executive Order No. 11246 of September 24, 1965, and shall post copies of the notice in conspicuous places available to employees and applicants for employment.

5. The contractor will comply with all provisions of Executive Order No. 11246 of Sept. 24, 1965, and of the rules, regulations, and relevant orders of the Secretary of Labor.
6. The contractor will furnish all information and reports required by Executive Order No. 11246 of September 24, 1965, and by the rules, regulations, and orders of the Secretary of Labor, or pursuant thereto, and will permit access to his books, records, and accounts by the contracting agency and the Secretary of Labor for purposes of investigation to ascertain compliance with such rules, regulations, and orders.
7. In the event of the contractor's noncompliance with the nondiscrimination clauses of this contract or with any of such rules, regulations, or orders, this contract may be cancelled, terminated, or suspended in whole or in part and the contractor may be declared ineligible for further Government contracts in accordance with procedures authorized in Executive Order No. 11246 of Sept. 24, 1965, and such other sanctions may be imposed and remedies invoked as provided in Executive Order No. 11246 of September 24, 1965, or by rule, regulation, or order of the Secretary of Labor, or as otherwise provided by law.
8. The contractor will include the provisions of paragraphs (1) through (8) in every subcontract or purchase order unless exempted by rules, regulations, or orders of the Secretary of Labor issued pursuant to Section 204 of Executive Order No. 11246 of September 24, 1965, so that such provisions will be binding upon each subcontractor or vendor. The contractor will take such action with respect to any subcontract or purchase order as may be directed by the Secretary of Labor as a means of enforcing such provisions including sanctions for noncompliance: Provided, however, that in the event the contractor becomes involved in, or is threatened with, litigation with a subcontractor or vendor as a result of such direction, the contractor may request the United States to enter into such litigation to protect the interests of the United States." [Sec. 202 amended by EO 11375 of Oct. 13, 1967, 32 FR 14303, 3 CFR, 1966-1970 Comp., p. 684, EO 12086 of Oct. 5, 1978, 43 FR 46501, 3 CFR, 1978 Comp., p. 230, EO 13665 of April 8, 2014, 79 FR 20749, EO 13672 of July 21, 2014, 79 FR 42971]

SEC. 203.

a. Each contractor having a contract containing the provisions prescribed in Section 202 shall file, and shall cause each of his subcontractors to file, Compliance Reports with the contracting agency or the Secretary of Labor as may be directed. Compliance Reports shall be filed within such times and shall contain such information as to the practices, policies, programs, and employment policies, programs, and employment statistics of the contractor and each subcontractor, and shall be in such form, as the Secretary of Labor may prescribe.
b. Bidders or prospective contractors or subcontractors may be required to state whether they have participated in any previous contract subject to the provisions of this Order, or any preceding similar Executive order, and in that event to submit, on behalf of themselves and their proposed subcontractors, Compliance Reports prior to or as an initial part of their bid or negotiation of a contract.
c. Whenever the contractor or subcontractor has a collective bargaining agreement or other contract or understanding with a labor union or an agency referring workers or providing or supervising apprenticeship or training for such workers, the Compliance Report shall include such information as to such labor union's or agency's practices and policies affecting compliance as the Secretary of Labor may prescribe: Provided, That to the extent such information is within the exclusive possession of a labor union or an agency referring workers or providing or supervising apprenticeship or training and such labor union or agency shall refuse to furnish such information to the contractor, the contractor shall so certify to the Secretary of Labor as part of its Compliance Report and shall set forth what efforts he has made to obtain such information.
d. The Secretary of Labor may direct that any bidder or prospective contractor or subcontractor shall submit, as part of his Compliance Report, a statement in writing, signed by an authorized officer or agent on behalf of any labor union or any agency referring workers or providing or supervising apprenticeship or other training, with which the bidder or prospective contractor deals, with supporting information, to the effect that the signer's practices and policies do not discriminate on the grounds of race, color, religion, sex, sexual orientation, gender identity, or national origin, and that the signer either will affirmatively cooperate in the implementation of the policy and provisions of this Order or that it consents and agrees that recruitment, employment, and the terms and conditions of employment under the proposed contract shall be in accordance with the purposes and provisions of the order. In the event that the union, or the agency shall refuse to execute such a statement, the Compliance Report shall so certify and set forth what efforts

have been made to secure such a statement and such additional factual material as the Secretary of Labor may require.

[Sec. 203 amended by EO 11375 of Oct. 13, 1967, 32 FR 14303, 3 CFR, 1966-1970 Comp., p. 684; EO 12086 of Oct. 5, 1978, 43 FR 46501, 3 CFR, 1978 Comp., p. 230, EO 13672 of July 21, 2104, 79 FR 42971]

SEC. 204

a. The Secretary of Labor may, when the Secretary deems that special circumstances in the national interest so require, exempt a contracting agency from the requirement of including any or all of the provisions of Section 202 of this **Order** in any specific contract, subcontract, or purchase **order**.
b. The Secretary of Labor may, by rule or regulation, exempt certain classes of contracts, subcontracts, or purchase orders (1) whenever work is to be or has been performed outside the United States and no recruitment of workers within the limits of the United States is involved; (2) for standard commercial supplies or raw materials; (3) involving less than specified amounts of money or specified numbers of workers; or (4) to the extent that they involve subcontracts below a specified tier.
c. Section 202 of this **Order** shall not apply to a Government contractor or subcontractor that is a religious corporation, association, educational institution, or society, with respect to the employment of individuals of a particular religion to perform work connected with the carrying on by such corporation, association, educational institution, or society of its activities. Such contractors and subcontractors are not exempted or excused from complying with the other requirements contained in this**Order**.
d. The Secretary of Labor may also provide, by rule, regulation, or order, for the exemption of facilities of a contractor that are in all respects separate and distinct from activities of the contractor related to the performance of the contract: provided, that such an exemption will not interfere with or impede the effectuation of the purposes of this **Order**: and provided further, that in the absence of such an exemption all facilities shall be covered by the provisions of this **Order**."

[Sec. 204 amended by EO 13279 of Dec. 16, 2002, 67 FR 77141, 3 CFR, 2002 Comp., p. 77141 - 77144]

Subpart C - Powers and Duties of the Secretary of Labor and the Contracting Agencies

SEC. 205. The Secretary of Labor shall be responsible for securing compliance by all Government contractors and subcontractors with this Order and any implementing rules or regulations. All contracting agencies shall comply with the terms of this Order and any implementing rules, regulations, or orders of the Secretary of Labor. Contracting agencies shall cooperate with the Secretary of Labor and shall furnish such information and assistance as the Secretary may require.

[Sec. 205 amended by EO 12086 of Oct. 5, 1978, 43 FR 46501, 3 CFR, 1978 Comp., p. 230]

SEC. 206.

a. The Secretary of Labor may investigate the employment practices of any Government contractor or subcontractor to determine whether or not the contractual provisions specified in Section 202 of this Order have been violated. Such investigation shall be conducted in accordance with the procedures established by the Secretary of Labor.
b. The Secretary of Labor may receive and investigate complaints by employees or prospective employees of a Government contractor or subcontractor which allege discrimination contrary to the contractual provisions specified in Section 202 of this Order.

[Sec. 206 amended by EO 12086 of Oct. 5, 1978, 43 FR 46501, 3 CFR, 1978 Comp., p. 230]

SEC. 207. The Secretary of Labor shall use his/her best efforts, directly and through interested Federal, State, and local agencies, contractors, and all other available instrumentalities to cause any labor union engaged in work under Government contracts or any agency referring workers or providing or supervising apprenticeship or training for or in the course of such work to cooperate in the implementation of the purposes of this Order. The Secretary of Labor shall, in appropriate cases, notify the Equal Employment Opportunity Commission, the Department of Justice, or other appropriate Federal agencies whenever it has reason to believe that the practices of any such labor organization or agency violate Title VI or Title VII of the Civil Rights Act of 1964 or other provision of Federal law.

[Sec. 207 amended by EO 12086 of Oct. 5, 1978, 43 FR 46501, 3 CFR, 1978 Comp., p. 230]

SEC. 208.

a. The Secretary of Labor, or any agency, officer, or employee in the executive branch of the Government designated by rule, regulation, or order of the Secretary, may hold such hearings, public or private, as the Secretary may deem advisable for compliance, enforcement, or educational purposes.

b. The Secretary of Labor may hold, or cause to be held, hearings in accordance with Subsection of this Section prior to imposing, ordering, or recommending the imposition of penalties and sanctions under this Order. No order for debarment of any contractor from further Government contracts under Section 209(6) shall be made without affording the contractor an opportunity for a hearing.

Subpart D - Sanctions and Penalties

SEC. 209. In accordance with such rules, regulations, or orders as the Secretary of Labor may issue or adopt, the Secretary may:

1. Publish, or cause to be published, the names of contractors or unions which it has concluded have complied or have failed to comply with the provisions of this Order or of the rules, regulations, and orders of the Secretary of Labor.
2. Recommend to the Department of Justice that, in cases in which there is substantial or material violation or the threat of substantial or material violation of the contractual provisions set forth in Section 202 of this Order, appropriate proceedings be brought to enforce those provisions, including the enjoining, within the limitations of applicable law, of organizations, individuals, or groups who prevent directly or indirectly, or seek to prevent directly or indirectly, compliance with the provisions of this Order.
3. Recommend to the Equal Employment Opportunity Commission or the Department of Justice that appropriate proceedings be instituted under Title VII of the Civil Rights Act of 1964.
4. Recommend to the Department of Justice that criminal proceedings be brought for the furnishing of false information to any contracting agency or to the Secretary of Labor as the case may be.
5. After consulting with the contracting agency, direct the contracting agency to cancel, terminate, suspend, or cause to be cancelled, terminated, or suspended, any contract, or any portion or portions thereof, for failure of the contractor or subcontractor to comply with equal employment opportunity provisions of the contract. Contracts may be cancelled, terminated, or suspended absolutely or continuance of contracts may be conditioned upon a program for future compliance approved by the Secretary of Labor.
6. Provide that any contracting agency shall refrain from entering into further contracts, or extensions or other modifications of existing contracts, with any noncomplying contractor, until such contractor has satisfied the Secretary of Labor that such contractor has established and will carry out personnel and employment policies in compliance with the provisions of this Order.

(b) Pursuant to rules and regulations prescribed by the Secretary of Labor, the Secretary shall make reasonable efforts, within a reasonable time limitation, to secure compliance with the contract provisions of this Order by methods of conference, conciliation, mediation, and persuasion before proceedings shall be instituted under subsection (a)(2) of this Section, or before a contract shall be cancelled or terminated in whole or in part under subsection (a)(5) of this Section.

[Sec. 209 amended by EO 12086 of Oct. 5, 1978, 43 FR 46501, 3 CFR, 1978 Comp., p. 230]

SEC. 210. Whenever the Secretary of Labor makes a determination under Section 209, the Secretary shall promptly notify the appropriate agency. The agency shall take the action directed by the Secretary and shall report the results of the action it has taken to the Secretary of Labor within such time as the Secretary shall specify. If the contracting agency fails to take the action directed within thirty days, the Secretary may take the action directly.
[Sec. 210 amended by EO 12086 of Oct. 5, 1978, 43 FR 46501, 3 CFR, 1978 Comp., p 230]

SEC. 211. If the Secretary shall so direct, contracting agencies shall not enter into contracts with any bidder or prospective contractor unless the bidder or prospective contractor has satisfactorily complied with the provisions of this Order or submits a program for compliance acceptable to the Secretary of Labor.
[Sec. 211 amended by EO 12086 of Oct. 5, 1978, 43 FR 46501, 3 CFR, 1978 Comp., p. 230]

SEC. 212. When a contract has been cancelled or terminated under Section 209(a)(5) or a contractor has been debarred from further Government contracts under Section 209(a)(6) of this Order, because of noncompliance with the contract provisions specified in Section 202 of this Order, the Secretary of Labor shall promptly notify the Comptroller General of the United States.

[Sec. 212 amended by EO 12086 of Oct. 5, 1978, 43 FR 46501, 3 CFR, 1978 Comp., p. 230]

Subpart E - Certificates of Merit

SEC. 213. The Secretary of Labor may provide for issuance of a United States Government Certificate of Merit to employers or labor unions, or other agencies which are or may hereafter be engaged in work under Government contracts, if the Secretary is satisfied that the personnel and employment practices of the employer, or that the personnel, training, apprenticeship, membership, grievance and representation, upgrading, and other practices and policies of the labor union or other agency conform to the purposes and provisions of this Order.

SEC. 214. Any Certificate of Merit may at any time be suspended or revoked by the Secretary of Labor if the holder thereof, in the judgment of the Secretary, has failed to comply with the provisions of this Order.

SEC. 215. The Secretary of Labor may provide for the exemption of any employer, labor union, or other agency from any reporting requirements imposed under or pursuant to this Order if such employer, labor union, or other agency has been awarded a Certificate of Merit which has not been suspended or revoked.

Part III - Nondiscrimination Provisions in Federally Assisted Construction Contracts

SEC. 301. Each executive department and agency, which administers a program involving Federal financial assistance shall require as a condition for the approval of any grant, contract, loan, insurance, or guarantee thereunder, which may involve a construction contract, that the applicant for Federal assistance undertake and agree to incorporate, or cause to be incorporated, into all construction contracts paid for in whole or in part with funds obtained from the Federal Government or borrowed on the credit of the Federal Government pursuant to such grant, contract, loan, insurance, or guarantee, or undertaken pursuant to any Federal program involving such grant, contract, loan, insurance, or guarantee, the provisions prescribed for Government contracts by Section 202 of this Order or such modification thereof, preserving in substance the contractor's obligations thereunder, as may be approved by the Secretary of Labor, together with such additional provisions as the Secretary deems appropriate to establish and protect the interest of the United States in the enforcement of those obligations. Each such applicant shall also undertake and agree (1) to assist and cooperate actively with the Secretary of Labor in obtaining the compliance of contractors and subcontractors with those contract provisions and with the rules, regulations and relevant orders of the Secretary, (2) to obtain and to furnish to the Secretary of Labor such information as the Secretary may require for the supervision of such compliance, (3) to carry out sanctions and penalties for violation of such obligations imposed upon contractors and subcontractors by the Secretary of Labor pursuant to Part II, Subpart D, of this Order, and (4) to refrain from entering into any contract subject to this Order, or extension or other modification of such a contract with a contractor debarred from Government contracts under Part II, Subpart D, of this Order.

[Sec. 301 amended by EO 12086 of Oct. 5, 1978, 43 FR 46501, 3 CFR, 1978 Comp., p. 230]

SEC. 302.

a. "Construction contract" as used in this Order means any contract for the construction, rehabilitation, alteration, conversion, extension, or repair of buildings, highways, or other improvements to real property.
b. The provisions of Part II of this Order shall apply to such construction contracts, and for purposes of such application the administering department or agency shall be considered the contracting agency referred to therein.
c. The term "applicant" as used in this Order means an applicant for Federal assistance or, as determined by agency regulation, other program participant, with respect to whom an application for any grant, contract, loan, insurance, or guarantee is not finally acted upon prior to the effective date of this Part, and it includes such an applicant after he/she becomes a recipient of such Federal assistance.

SEC. 303.

a. The Secretary of Labor shall be responsible for obtaining the compliance of such applicants with their undertakings under this Order. Each administering department and agency is directed to cooperate with the Secretary of Labor and to furnish the Secretary such information and assistance as the Secretary may require in the performance of the Secretary's functions under this Order.
b. In the event an applicant fails and refuses to comply with the applicant's undertakings pursuant to this Order, the Secretary of Labor may, after consulting with the administering department or agency, take any or all of the following actions: (1) direct any administering department or agency to cancel, terminate, or suspend in whole or in part the agreement, contract or other arrangement with such applicant with respect

to which the failure or refusal occurred; (2) direct any administering department or agency to refrain from extending any further assistance to the applicant under the program with respect to which the failure or refusal occurred until satisfactory assurance of future compliance has been received by the Secretary of Labor from such applicant; and (3) refer the case to the Department of Justice or the Equal Employment Opportunity Commission for appropriate law enforcement or other proceedings.

c. In no case shall action be taken with respect to an applicant pursuant to clause (1) or (2) of subsection (b) without notice and opportunity for hearing.

[Sec. 303 amended by EO 12086 of Oct. 5, 1978, 43 FR 46501, 3 CFR, 1978 Comp., p. 230]

SEC. 304. Any executive department or agency which imposes by rule, regulation, or order requirements of nondiscrimination in employment, other than requirements imposed pursuant to this Order, may delegate to the Secretary of Labor by agreement such responsibilities with respect to compliance standards, reports, and procedures as would tend to bring the administration of such requirements into conformity with the administration of requirements imposed under this Order: Provided, That actions to effect compliance by recipients of Federal financial assistance with requirements imposed pursuant to Title VI of the Civil Rights Act of 1964 shall be taken in conformity with the procedures and limitations prescribed in Section 602 thereof and the regulations of the administering department or agency issued thereunder.

Part IV - Miscellaneous

SEC. 401. The Secretary of Labor may delegate to any officer, agency, or employee in the Executive branch of the Government, any function or duty of the Secretary under Parts II and III of this Order.
[Sec. 401 amended by EO 12086 of Oct. 5, l978, 43 FR 46501, 3 CFR, 1978 Comp., p. 230]

SEC. 402. The Secretary of Labor shall provide administrative support for the execution of the program known as the "Plans for Progress."

SEC. 403.

a. Executive Orders Nos. 10590 (January 19, 1955), 10722 (August 5, 1957), 10925 (March 6, 1961), 11114 (June 22, 1963), and 11162 (July 28, 1964), are hereby superseded and the President's Committee on Equal Employment Opportunity established by Executive Order No. 10925 is hereby abolished. All records and property in the custody of the Committee shall be transferred to the Office of Personnel Management and the Secretary of Labor, as appropriate.

b. Nothing in this Order shall be deemed to relieve any person of any obligation assumed or imposed under or pursuant to any Executive Order superseded by this Order. All rules, regulations, orders, instructions, designations, and other directives issued by the President's Committee on Equal Employment Opportunity and those issued by the heads of various departments or agencies under or pursuant to any of the Executive orders superseded by this Order, shall, to the extent that they are not inconsistent with this Order, remain in full force and effect unless and until revoked or superseded by appropriate authority. References in such directives to provisions of the superseded orders shall be deemed to be references to the comparable provisions of this Order.

[Sec. 403 amended by EO 12107 of Dec. 28, 1978, 44 FR 1055, 3 CFR, 1978 Comp., p, 264]

SEC. 404. The General Services Administration shall take appropriate action to revise the standard Government contract forms to accord with the provisions of this Order and of the rules and regulations of the Secretary of Labor.

SEC. 405. This Order shall become effective thirty days after the date of this Order.

FEDERAL CONTRACT COMPLIANCE MANUAL

OCTOBER 2014

Federal Contract Compliance Manual

October 2014

OFFICE OF FEDERAL CONTRACT COMPLIANCE PROGRAMS

OFCCP

U.S. DEPARTMENT OF LABOR

www.dol.gov/ofccp

TABLE OF CONTENTS

INTRODUCTION

At the Office of Federal Contract Compliance Programs (OFCCP), we protect workers, promote diversity through equal opportunity, and enforce the law. We hold those who do business with the Federal Government, contractors and subcontractors, to the fair and reasonable standard that they take affirmative action and not discriminate based on sex, race, color, religion, national origin, disability or status as a protected veteran.

It is estimated that nearly one in four American workers is employed by a company receiving federal funds for contracted work. That is nearly more than 200,000 businesses with contracts totaling almost $700 billion based on 2011 data from the Division of Program Operations. Among the several ways OFCCP protects employees of companies doing business with the Federal Government, and educates these companies about their rights and obligations, is conducting quality compliance evaluations and complaint investigations.

This revised Federal Contract Compliance Manual (hereafter referred to as the "FCCM" or the "Manual") provides new and experienced compliance officers (COs) the procedural framework for executing quality and timely compliance evaluations and complaint investigations. It provides procedural and technical guidance on compliance issues based on current agency procedures and processes, and improves consistency across the agency's regional and field offices. It may also provide our contractors and subcontractors more transparency and clarity about basic OFCCP procedures and processes. That said, there might be slight differences between regions and offices because some discretion remains with COs and their supervisors as to the best way to manage individual compliance evaluations and investigations within the framework created by the Manual. Remember, these differences should be minor and should occur infrequently because one of the goals of the Manual is standardization. All references to the terms "compliance officer" and CO in this Chapter and throughout the Manual include any OFCCP employee that is responsible for the tasks or activities described.

The FCCM does not establish substantive agency policy. Therefore, if there is an inconsistency between material in the Manual and other OFCCP policies and its implementing regulations, the latter are controlling. OFCCP continues to use directives and other issuances to communicate substantive policy guidance, procedures, and agency enforcement priorities to its COs and those we regulate. This Manual is subject to change without public notice. The FCCM does not create new legal rights or requirements or change current legal rights or requirements for federal contractors. The official sources for contractors' compliance obligations remain Executive Order 11246, as amended; Section 503 of the Rehabilitation Act of 1973, as amended; the Vietnam Era Veterans' Readjustment Assistance Act of 1974, as amended; OFCCP's regulations at 41 CFR Part 60; and applicable case law.

The Manual has eight chapters, a list of key words and phrases, a glossary and several attachments, including sample forms and letters. The chapters cover how OFCCP's COs, and others responsible for conducting the activities covered in the Manual, conduct a desk audit, an onsite review, a construction industry compliance evaluation, a corporate management compliance evaluation and a complaint investigation. It also covers the agency's functional affirmative action program (FAAP), the various types of discrimination remedies and ways to resolve noncompliance issues.

The National Office wishes to acknowledge the contributions of our regional and field staff during the development of this revised Manual. Their insight and experience greatly enriched this Manual. The agency is dedicated to providing its COs ongoing support and training because we believe that a well-trained workforce is an effective workforce. We will continue supplementing the processes and procedures in this Manual with uniform staff training and by providing other appropriate resources.

CHAPTER 1
DESK AUDIT

1A INTRODUCTION

The regulations implementing Executive Order 11246 (EO 11246), as amended, authorize OFCCP to conduct compliance evaluations of federal contractors.[1] Compliance evaluations determine whether federal contractors maintain nondiscriminatory hiring and employment practices.[2] OFCCP also uses them to determine whether contractors are taking affirmative action to ensure that applicants and employees are treated without regard to race, color, religion, sex or national origin.[3] Other regulations permitting OFCCP to conduct compliance evaluations are 41 CFR 60-250.60 and 60-300.60 implementing provisions of the Vietnam Era Veterans' Readjustment Assistance Act of 1974, as amended, 38 U.S.C. 4212 (Section 4212 or VEVRAA); and the regulations at 41 CFR 60-741.60 implementing Section 503 of the Rehabilitation Act of 1973, as amended, 29 U.S.C. 793 (Section 503). These evaluations are to determine whether federal contractors are complying with their obligations to ensure nondiscrimination. They also determine whether contractors are taking affirmative action to employ, promote, train, retain and provide reasonable accommodation to certain protected veterans and individuals with disabilities, respectively.

1A00 TYPES OF COMPLIANCE EVALUATIONS

OFCCP may conduct a compliance evaluation that consists of one, or any combination of, the following investigative procedures:

- compliance review,
- offsite review of records,
- compliance check, and
- focused review.

Each of the investigative procedures is discussed in this chapter, the first is compliance review procedures. A compliance review is a comprehensive analysis and evaluation of the employment practices of the contractor, including the contractor's written affirmative action program (AAP), and the results of the contractor's affirmative action efforts. A compliance review may proceed in three stages:

- desk audit,

---

[1] 41 CFR 60-1.20. The term "contractor" as used in the Manual includes "subcontractors" unless otherwise noted.
[2] Ibid.
[3] Ibid.

- onsite review, and
- offsite analysis.

However, the regulations do not require an onsite review or offsite analysis in all cases. Depending on the circumstances or the results of the desk audit, a compliance review may:

- close after the desk audit,
- continue with an onsite review, or
- continue with an offsite analysis of the information gathered during or pursuant to the onsite review.

An offsite review of records is an analysis and evaluation of the all or some portion of the AAP and supporting documentation, and other documents related to the contractor's personnel policies and employment actions that may be relevant to a determination of whether the contractor complied with the requirements of EO 11246, Section 503 and Section 4212, as appropriate. COs must use the desk audit procedures outlined in this chapter when conducting an offsite review of records.

A compliance check is an examination to determine whether a contractor maintained certain records as required by the regulations at 41 CFR 60-1.12, 41 CFR 60-250.80, 41 CFR 60-300.80, and 41 CFR 60-741.80. The contractor has the option of providing the documents either onsite or offsite. Therefore, COs must contact the contractor to determine whether the requested records will be provided onsite or offsite.[4] COs will also need to contact the contractor during the course of the review if they need specific issues clarified. A compliance check need not include an onsite review. If a contractor provides records offsite, but a CO finds that it may be appropriate to conduct a physical, onsite inspection, the CO must discuss the matter with his or her supervisor.[5]

Finally, a focused review is an onsite review focused on one or more components of the contractor's organization, or on one or more aspects of the contractor's employment practices. OFCCP will identify the subject of the focused review and inform the contractor prior to the start of the review.

1A01 CONTENTS OF CHAPTER

This chapter outlines the procedures COs use to conduct a desk audit during a compliance evaluation, whether it is conducted in the office or onsite. The elements of this chapter also apply when COs are conducting compliance evaluations using the investigative procedures for

---

4 All references to the term Compliance Officer (CO) in this Chapter and throughout the Manual include any OFCCP employee that is responsible for the tasks or activities described.

5 See Chapter 2 – Onsite Review. This chapter covers onsite review procedures, including any required supervisory approvals.

the offsite review of records. Additionally, this chapter references the relevant sections of the Standard Compliance Evaluation Report (SCER) that COs must complete during the desk audit stage of compliance evaluations.

1A02 PURPOSE OF THE DESK AUDIT

By conducting a desk audit of the AAP and supporting documentation provided by contractors, a CO begins to determine whether a contractor is complying with all relevant provisions of 41 CFR Chapter 60; specifically:

- complying with applicable nondiscrimination provisions, and
- complying with the applicable affirmative action provisions to ensure equal employment opportunity without regard to race, color, religion, sex, national origin, disability or status as a protected veteran.

1A03 PRINCIPLES AND FOCUS OF DESK AUDITS

A desk audit typically enables COs to review a contractor's compliance with its affirmative action and equal opportunity obligations at a particular establishment. COs must conduct desk audits in accordance with the following general principles:

a. *Equal Employment Opportunity*. A contractor's personnel policies and practices must not have the purpose or effect of discriminating against anyone because of race, color, religion, national origin, sex, disability or status as a protected veteran. Contractors must eliminate and remedy discrimination that, for example, limits a job applicant's or an employee's ability to engage in open and fair competition for a job or position, or that results in paying employees differently based on race, sex or membership in other protected classes.

b. *Affirmative Action Program*. An affirmative action program is a management tool. The written affirmative action program includes diagnostic and self-monitoring components as well as a set of specific and result-oriented policies and procedures designed to achieve equal employment opportunity.

c. *Inclusion and Acceptability*. An affirmative action program is assessed for "inclusion" and "acceptability." This chapter discusses these concepts more fully in Sections 1E – 1H.

When conducting the desk audit, COs focus on a review of the following areas:

a. *Workforce Structure, Personnel Policies and Procedures*. COs examine a contractor's personnel policies and procedures to determine if they warrant in-depth investigation such as an onsite review. Likewise, an examination of a contractor's basic organizational or workforce structure may reveal irregularities that merit investigating.

b. *Good Faith Efforts*. COs examine a contractor's good faith efforts to achieve established goals. In doing so, they should seek to determine at least three specific things:

- Whether there are any areas where there is a lack of progress toward established goals;
- Whether further information is needed in any area; and
- Whether an onsite visit is needed to evaluate the contractor's good faith efforts to develop and implement affirmative action programs designed to improve opportunities for minorities, women, people with disabilities and protected veterans.

c. *Potential Discrimination.* COs must be aware of the signs of potential discrimination. Being alert to these signs allows a CO to assess when additional investigation in required. Below are examples of signs of potential discrimination:.

- Individuals in a particular protected class are significantly overrepresented or underrepresented in a particular area of the workforce.
- Indications exist that an employment practice or procedure has adversely affected individuals based on their race, sex or ethnicity.
- Compensation practices of a contractor result in differences in pay that appear to be based on race, sex or ethnicity.
- Indications exist that leave for family caregiving is applied differently for men and women.

1A04 USE OF THE STANDARD COMPLIANCE EVALUATION REPORT

The SCER is a tool used by COs to conduct and document desk audits. The SCER and its instructions, found in Appendices A-1 and A-2, establish a framework for conducting the desk audit, and assisting in the development and implementation of the onsite investigative plan. COs use the SCER, either in whole or in part, when conducting a compliance evaluation using the compliance review, offsite review of records or focused review investigative procedures discussed in subsection 1A00 of this chapter. Compliance checks require the completion of the Compliance Check Control Sheet, rather than the SCER.[6]

The SCER has a Compliance Evaluation Summary section which is followed by three main parts.[7]

a. *Part A: Preparation.* Part A includes general information about the contractor, such as the contractor's past review history, overall EEO trends in its workforce and its organizational structure. It also documents a CO's initial review of the contractor's AAP(s) and support data for inclusion and acceptability.

---

[6] See Figure F-3 – Compliance Check Control Sheet.

[7] The SCER also has three other parts: Part D is for corporate management evaluation narratives, Part E is the Compliance Check Control Sheet, and Part F is a summary of the findings.

b. *Part B: Affirmative Action.* Part B summarizes any problems with the AAP(s) and support data. It provides for analysis of affirmative action progress and identifies any areas where a CO needs additional information to determine the extent of a contractor's good faith efforts. This Part also includes an assessment of a contractor's implementation of any other affirmative action obligations. For each affirmative action problem unresolved at the conclusion of the desk audit, the SCER requires the development of an onsite plan.

c. *Part C: Problems Identified.* Part C identifies problems found during the compliance evaluation, including the nature of the problem, relevant evidence reviewed, actions taken to resolve the problem, and whether and how the problem was resolved. For each potential discrimination problem unresolved at the conclusion of the desk audit, the SCER requires the development of an onsite investigative plan.

1A05 CASE MANAGEMENT SYSTEM

The Case Management System (CMS) is the data collection component of the OFCCP Information System (OFIS) COs use to record basic information about the contractor, to track major events encountered throughout the evaluation, and to summarize any violations found and remedies obtained. COs must ensure that all relevant dates, information and occurrences are promptly entered into CMS, beginning with the initial scheduling of the compliance evaluation and ending with the closure of the review, including the Conciliation Agreement (CA) monitoring period, if applicable. COs should refer to the CMS Manual for further instruction on how and when to enter case status information. The reporting component of OFIS is the Executive Information System (EIS).

1A06 CONFIDENTIALITY OF INFORMATION

Under the regulations at 41 CFR 60-1.20(g), *Public Access to Information*, COs must treat information obtained during the compliance evaluation as confidential to the maximum extent the information is exempt from public disclosure under the Freedom of Information Act, 5 U.S.C. 552. This applies to confidential information as well as sensitive information such as personnel records, medical information and salary data. During the course of a compliance evaluation, a CO will handle contractor information that is both sensitive and non-sensitive in nature.

1A07 NOVEL ISSUES

Novel issues are those that are unfamiliar, unique or fall outside the norm. COs may encounter novel issues in the course of a compliance evaluation and when this occurs they must, in coordination with their supervisor and Regional Office (RO), contact the Division of Program Operations (DPO) in the National Office before recommending a finding of compliance or non-compliance. Examples of novel issues include issues not routinely addressed or that involve coordination with the Statistical Analysis Unit (SAU) or DPO such as testing, multi-establishments, complex or unusual compensation issues and fetal protection. Chapter 6 of this Manual includes a brief discussion of other novel issues as they may arise in the context of complaint investigations.

1A08 CORPORATE MANAGEMENT COMPLIANCE EVALUATIONS

Under the regulations at 41 CFR 60-2.30 on corporate management compliance evaluations (CMCEs), COs may conduct a CMCE to ascertain whether individuals are encountering artificial barriers to advancement into mid-level and senior corporate management. The desk audit procedures outlined in this chapter apply to CMCEs. We discuss CMCEs in Chapter 4 of this Manual.

1A09 FUNCTIONAL AFFIRMATIVE ACTION PROGRAMS

Under the regulations at 41 CFR 60-2.1(d)(4), a contractor can seek the agency's agreement to develop and use an AAP that is based on a functional or business unit instead of an establishment. This type of AAP is called a functional affirmative action program (FAAP). The desk audit procedures outlined in this chapter apply to both traditional and functional AAPs. Chapter 5 fully covers FAAPs.

1A10 PREAWARD COMPLIANCE EVALUATIONS

Under the regulations at 41 CFR 60-1.20(d) and 60-1-29 on preaward compliance evaluations, an agency is required to notify OFCCP, and request a preaward evaluation when a nonconstruction contract or first tier subcontract of $10 million or more is awarded. Within 15 calendar days of the notice, OFCCP will inform the awarding agency of its intent to conduct a preaward compliance evaluation. If OFCCP informs the agency of its intent to conduct a preaward evaluation, OFCCP is allowed an additional 20 calendar days after that date to provide a conclusion relative to the contractor's compliance. A preaward compliance evaluation of a supply and service contractor only covers the contractor's compliance with EO 11246

1B PRE-DESK AUDIT ACTIONS

This section discusses the various steps and actions that COs must take prior to starting a compliance evaluation of a contractor establishment. These steps include:

- contacting the contractor,
- setting up appropriate case files and logs, and
- obtaining relevant information about the contractor from other EEO and Department of Labor enforcement agencies.

1B00 INITIAL CONTACT WITH THE CONTRACTOR

This subsection covers the information COs gather through their initial contact with the contractor; specifically: the contractor's information, the contractor's representative's confirmation information, and information that may preclude the evaluation.

a. *Contractor Information.* Prior to issuing a Scheduling Letter and Itemized Listing, COs must verify the following information:

- the name of the highest ranking management official at the establishment,
- the legal name of the company,
- the name and e-mail of the person responsible for the preparation and implementation of the AAP, and
- the correct mailing address for the establishment.

If an establishment is part of a larger entity, the CO must obtain the name of the corporate chief executive officer (CEO), the name of the corporate person responsible for Equal Employment Opportunity and Affirmative Action matters, and the correct corporate mailing address. COs enter this basic identifying information on the Compliance Evaluation Summary, in the Background Information section of the SCER.

b. *Representation.* A contractor's statement about representation can come during the initial contact or at some later point. When a contractor indicates that it is or will be represented by counsel or a consultant company, a CO must ask the contractor to provide written confirmation of the representation, including:

- the contact information for the representative that includes the representative's name, address, e-mail, and phone number, and
- the scope of the representative's authority, including whether the authority granted to the representative extends to negotiating a settlement, if necessary, on behalf of the contractor.

A CO must also ask the contractor to clarify in writing as a part of the representation confirmation whether:

- all contacts, including routine ones to make appointments or to clarify data or other information, should be made through the representative, and
- all correspondence is only provided to the representative or if a copy is to be provided to the contractor.

The CO obtains the same written confirmation if a person indicates to the CO or other representative of OFCCP that he or she represents the contractor. After receiving written confirmation of representation, a CO must handle contacts and correspondence according to its terms for the duration of the evaluation. The handling of contacts and correspondence will change if the contractor specifies a different period or subsequently alters its instructions. Alterations of representation instructions must be in writing.

COs provide the contractor's highest-ranking management officials copies of all substantive documents that they mail. For these purposes, we define substantive documents as documents that this Manual requires a CO to mail. This would include, for example, any Predetermination Notice (PDN), Notice of Violation (NOV), Show Cause Notice (SCN), and Conciliation Agreement (CA).

c. *Circumstances Precluding Evaluation.* Prior to beginning a compliance evaluation, a CO in coordination with his or her supervisor must determine whether circumstances exist that preclude conducting the compliance evaluation of the contractor. Several resources are available to a CO that assist with reaching this determination, including EIS and the Excluded Parties Listing System (EPLS).[8] EPLS is the electronic version of the Lists of Parties Excluded from Federal Procurement and Nonprocurement Programs. This database identifies entities and individuals excluded from receiving federal contracts, certain subcontracts and from certain types of federal financial and nonfinancial assistance and benefits. Other factors that could preclude selecting the contractor include closure of the establishment selected for review, review of the establishment selected within the last 24 months[9], and the existence of an approved FAAP agreement.

Additionally, a CO will gather information about contract coverage, single entity status and other coverage issues. If circumstances arise that could preclude the compliance evaluation COs must discuss the matter with their supervisor.

1B01 PREPARATION AND MAINTENANCE OF THE CASE CHRONOLOGY LOG

COs must prepare and maintain a case Chronology Log for each compliance evaluation. This log is an integral part of the case file and is an invaluable tool in tracking the progress and the status of the case.[10] It is, therefore, important that COs keep the case Chronology Log current. A case Chronology Log includes:

- Event summaries that begin with the initial contact with the contractor and continue through to the approval of case closing documents.
- Documentation of all telephone conversations, e-mails, correspondence and meetings associated with the evaluation, indicating the date, nature of the contact, person contacted, summary of discussion or actions taken, and the CO's name.

Records of telephone calls in the log should include the time of the call. All meetings must include the date, location, and names of the people in attendance. In addition, record in the log all requests for data and records, and the dates the CO received these items. COs must record all events and actions as they occur.

[8] EPLS is located at https://www.epls.gov/ (last accessed in Sept. 2011). EPLS is migrating to the System for Award Management (SAM) in 2012. EPLS users will have access to SAM.

[9] The establishment is not currently being monitored by OFCCP as the result of a Conciliation Agreement or Consent Decree and receivd a notice of review closure in the last 24 months.

[10] See subsection 1B02 – Creation and Maintenance of the Case File; Figure F-1 – Case Chronology Log (CC-53).

Many COs print a hardcopy of the case Chronology Log to facilitate their ability to write in the day-to-day events and activities as they occur. This practice is acceptable, as long as the final case Chronology Log included in the case file is typed, legible and maintained electronically.

1B02 CREATION AND MAINTENANCE OF THE CASE FILE

COs must create and maintain a case file for each scheduled compliance evaluation. The case file generally consists of various folders so, in order to create a case file, COs must create individual folders using the below headings.[11]

- Folder 1: Standard Compliance Evaluation Report (SCER) and Data Pertaining to SCER Findings
- Folder 2: Case Chronology Log, Correspondence and Meeting Notes
- Folder 3: Collective Bargaining and Other Agreements, and Miscellaneous Items
- Folder 4: SOL Opinions, JRC Memoranda and Post SCER Update
- Folder 5: Progress Reports and Quality Audit
- Folder 6: Historical Review Results
- Folder 7: AAP and AAP Support Data

COs add information and documents to the appropriate folder throughout the course of the compliance evaluation. If enforcement becomes necessary, COs provide the compliance evaluation case file to the Solicitor's Office for further action. It is critically important that all information obtained, observed or reported be part of the case file and remain there through case closure.

Once again, maintaining these files is crucial. This includes labeling the folder and any additional folders or subfolders needed (e.g., Folder 1A, 1B). This is especially useful when the material in a folder is voluminous. COs must arrange the documents in each folder by date, with the most recent document on top. COs are required to attach certain documents in each folder to the left or right side of the folder, as indicated below. Generally, whenever there are ten or more separate documents in a folder, the CO must prepare an index and place it in the front of that folder.

A complete and thorough case file is critically important, especially in the event that enforcement becomes necessary. Therefore, COs must be sure that the case file contains all documents obtained or generated during the compliance evaluation, not just the material that

[11] Though the case file folder numbers and titles do not change, the case file contents may vary based upon the investigative procedures used in the compliance evaluation, and the availability and existence of specific documents.

supports the conclusions reached. This means, for example, that the file includes both evidence that supports the CO's violation findings, as well as evidence that supports the contractor's rebuttal. The case file must contain all contractor records and unaltered copies of all e-mail correspondences in paper or electronic format. Drafts of OFCCP memoranda are not included in the case file; COs retain only final versions of agency memoranda.

If a CO is submitting a case for enforcement a Transmittal Memorandum, as discussed in Chapter 8 of this Manual on the resolution of noncompliance, must accompany the case file. A copy of at least one contract or subcontract establishing coverage during the period at issue is also required. Additionally, the enforcement submission includes copies of all relevant analyses, properly labeled, in electronic format. Remember to keep a copy of all files submitted for enforcement in the appropriate field office.[12] Below is a list of the folders and their content.

Folder 1: Standard Compliance Evaluation Report (SCER) and Data Pertaining to SCER Findings. This folder contains the SCER and data pertaining to SCER findings such as:

- compliance officer notes, worksheets and analyses, including any regression analyses,
- witness statements that are appropriately labeled,
- contractor records, and
- other information and records pertinent to the issues investigated.

COs organize the material according to the relevant SCER issue, and tabs and labels them accordingly. Documents must cross-reference other folders, as appropriate. For example, if a SCER document in Folder 1 also involves or is relevant to a union contract matter, the document in Folder 1 will refer to the union contract placed in Folder 3. COs attach certain documents to the left side of this folder. They place CMS Form CC-100a on top and place underneath it the following items:

- contract coverage results,
- CMS forms associated with the review,
- contractor extension requests for the AAP and OFCCP responses, including extensions of time frames in a consent decree, and
- Preaward Clearance Request letter and other related materials.

[12] See Appendix A-4 – Index for a Supply and Service Review.

Folder 2: Case Chronology Log, Correspondence and Meeting Notes. This folder contains all correspondence and e-mails, both internal and external, as well as meeting notes associated with the review. File these items chronologically. CO's must preserve all communications related to the compliance evaluation or complaint investigation, data and record submissions, information gathering and interviews in this folder. This includes any material resulting from contacts with third parties such as other government agencies, local interest groups.

For ease of reference, the folder must have a tab for the closure document.[13] A CA is the closure document if violations were identified and resolved, in the absence of violations a closure letter is the closure document. Place the original of the closure document in Folder 6, Historical Review Results. COs must attach a typed copy of the Case Chronology Log to the left side of this folder.

Folder 3: Collective Bargaining and Other Agreements, and Miscellaneous Items. This folder contains a copy of any collective bargaining agreements, fringe benefits and leave policy booklets, employee handbooks, apprenticeship or training agreements and any other similar contractor documents relevant to the establishment reviewed. COs place relevant documents that do not fit the description of documents contained in other folders into this folder.

Folder 4: SOL Opinions, JRC Memoranda and Post-SCER Update. This folder contains Solicitor's Opinions and Joint Review Committee memoranda associated with the review. It also includes any material, other than progress reports,[14]generated after a CO submits the review report such as transmittal memoranda, additional conciliation efforts. This includes, for example, a record of any later conciliation efforts by the District Office, Regional Office and National Office, as appropriate, along with the results of those efforts.

Folder 5: Progress Reports and Quality Audit. This folder contains progress reports the contractor submitted under a CA, along with OFCCP's evaluation of those reports. COs enter the results of these evaluations on the "Summary of Progress Reports" form. After entering the last report, COs place a copy of the referenced summary in Folder 6, Historical Review Results. They also log all progress reports in the Chronology Log, and attach the Quality Audit form (CC-73) to the left side of this folder with relevant quality audit documents underneath it. This folder also includes consent decrees or other court orders.

Folder 6: Historical Review Results. This folder contains a copy of closure letters and documents, including any previous CA, generated by any past reviews of this establishment, as well as a copy of the closure letter and document for the current review. If a contractor must file progress reports under a current CA, when the CO evaluates the

---

[13] Copies of these letters are in the Manual at Letters L-4 - Notice of Closing: Compliance Evaluation (No Violations Found), and at L-33, Closure Letter for Substantive Violations.

[14] Progress reports are filed in Folder 5, Progress Reports and Quality Audit.

last report, the CO will add a copy of the "Summary of Progress Reports" to this folder on top of the original CA.

It is important that the field office retains the historical folder indefinitely. If OFCCP schedules another review of this establishment before this case file is retired and archived, the field office will pull the historical folder from the old case file and move it to the new one. If OFCCP does not schedule another review by the time the case file must be retired, the field office will pull the historical folder and retain it before retiring the rest of the case file.

Folder 7: AAP and Support Data. This folder contains the contractor's AAP(s) and AAP support data evaluated in this review. Place this material at the end only because it is often the most voluminous.

1B03 SENDING THE SCHEDULING LETTER AND ITEMIZED LISTING

OFCCP uses the Scheduling Letter and Itemized Listing to schedule a compliance evaluation and request the Affirmative Action Program (AAP) and supporting data from the contractor. Copies of these two items are Figures F-2 in the Manual. The Scheduling Letter and Itemized Listing are reauthorized for the agency's use every three years by the Office of Management and Budget (OMB), if not earlier should the agency seek it. Therefore, COs must review the most recently authorized Scheduling Letter and Itemized Listing to ensure that they are familiar with the documents and information requested from the contractor.[15]

This Scheduling Letter and Itemized Listing are sent by certified mail, return receipt requested, to the highest ranking official at the contractor's establishment or functional unit, with a copy to the CEO at the contractor's corporate headquarters unless the establishment and corporate headquarters are the same. The appropriate field office official signs the Scheduling Letter, the letter must include the name and telephone number of the CO who will receive the AAP and supporting data or the CO's appropriate supervisor.

1B04 FOLLOW-UP CONTACT WITH CONTRACTOR

COs must contact the contractor within 15 calendar days after sending the Scheduling Letter and Itemized Listing to ensure that the contractor or the contractor's representative, or both, fully understand the requests contained in the letter. If the contractor has questions, COs will provide technical assistance to clarify the contractor's obligations and the compliance evaluation process.

If the contractor challenges the agency's jurisdiction and the CO, in coordination with his or her supervisor and regional office, is unable to establish jurisdiction, the issue must be elevated to the attention of DPO. Once jurisdiction is established, and yet the contractor continues to

[15] Discussions of the content of the Scheduling Letter and Itemized Listing are based on existing requirements as of September 2011. As of the completion of this Manual, the OMB reauthorization process for these two documents was still underway. The documents under OMB review propose several substantive changes and they are not reflected in this Manual.

dispute OFCCP's jurisdiction, the CO will recommend issuance of an Show Cause Notice (SCN). More on resolving noncompliance issues is in Chapter 8 where the focus is on resolving noncompliance issues.

1B05 CONTACTING EEOC, VETS AND OTHER AGENCIES

Simultaneous with the mailing of the Scheduling Letter, COs will seek information regarding the employment policies and practices of the contractor being scheduled from the Equal Employment Opportunity Commission (EEOC), Veterans Employment and Training Service (VETS) and other EEO and labor law enforcement agencies. Such information provides a better understanding of the contractor's workforce and operations, and may indicate potential problem areas.

a. *EEOC and State and Local Fair Employment Practices (FEP) Agencies.* The CO sends an Inquiry Letter simultaneous with the mailing of the Scheduling Letter.[16] The Inquiry Letter goes to the appropriate district office of the EEOC, and to the appropriate state and local FEP agencies. It requests information on discrimination complaints filed against the contractor, and any other information that may be pertinent to assessing the contractor's EEO posture. After 15 calendar days, COs must follow-up by telephone with any agency that failed to respond or from which additional information is needed.

   OFCCP has a Memorandum of Understanding (MOU) with EEOC that includes provisions about complaint referrals, coordination and consultation. COs are urged to review and become familiar with the provisions of this MOU.

b. *Veterans Employment and Training Service and Other DOL Enforcement Agencies.* COs must contact the VETS representative at the appropriate local employment delivery system to request any information that could be pertinent to the pending review, including information regarding the contractor's compliance with the mandatory job listing requirements of 41 CFR 60-250.2(a) and 60-300.5(a).[17] When conducting compliance evaluations and complaint investigations, COs must query the VETS-100 database to verify that a federal contractor completed the annual reporting requirements for the appropriate reporting year. Moreover, the information in this database may be useful when analyzing an employer's recruitment and hiring practices. OFCCP has a MOU with VETS that includes provisions related to the VETS database and agency coordination and consultation. COs are urged to review and become familiar with the provisions of this MOU.

   Additionally, COs must check the DOL Enforcement Database at www.dol.gov/enforcementdata for closed complaints and compliance evaluations of the contractor's establishment, and contact other DOL enforcement agencies to identify the number, types and status of any complaints filed against the contractor. For example, the

---

[16] A sample of this letter is in this Manual as Letter L-1, Sample Inquiry Letter for Requesting Complaint Data from EEOC and State and Local FEPs.

[17] Sample letters are in this Manual at Letters L-2, Sample Inquiry Letter for Requesting Compliance with Mandatory Job Listing Requirements from Employment Service Delivery Systems, and L-3, Sample Inquiry Letter for Requesting Information on Pending Review from Veterans Employment and Training Service.

Wage and Hour Division may have filed Family and Medical Leave Act (FMLA) violations related to the contractor that is the subject of a compliance evaluation.

1B06 INFORMATION ON EEO COMPLAINTS FILED WITH OR BY OTHER AGENCIES

COs must carefully examine all information regarding complaints against a contractor that they receive from federal, state, and local agencies in response to a letter of inquiry. COs enter basic information about these complaints in Part A.I of the SCER, including:

- the agency with which the complaint was filed,
- the jurisdictional or legal basis (e.g., race, sex) of the complaint,
- the current status of the complaint, and
- the area of the contractor's workforce involved in the complaint.

COs will note any patterns in the types of complaints filed and any discrimination findings made on them. For example, there may be a clustering of complaints filed by employees in certain job areas, or by applicants or employees from a particular race, religion, ethnic group or sex; by covered veterans; or by individuals with disabilities. As the review progresses, COs must cross-reference complaints to any potential problem areas they identify. There may be, for example, indications of a lack of good faith efforts, adverse impact ratio analyses (IRAs), or concentration or underrepresentation in areas where complaints were filed.

When appropriate, COs will contact the appropriate EEOC office or state or local FEP agency to arrange to review relevant discrimination complaint files as part of the compliance evaluation. This can be particularly useful when, based on as the result of the desk audit, a CO identifies potential systemic problems in complaint areas.

Upon receipt of the AAP and supporting data, COs must compare any information a contractor provides with respect to current or past complaints to the information received from other agencies. COs will note discrepancies and information not provided by the contractor for possible further investigation during the review, and will seek an explanation and additional information from the contractor.

1B07 RELATIONSHIP OF OFCCP COMPLIANCE ACTIVITIES TO EEO LITIGATION OR COURT ORDERS

If, during the conduct of a compliance evaluation, a CO finds that the contractor is involved in litigation or is under a court order on EEO matters, then the CO must identify:

- the EEO issues involved,
- the court and the parties, and

- the case name and number.

The CO must bring the matter to the attention of his or her supervisor. The field office, in consultation with the Regional Solicitor's Office, will determine whether the litigation or court order imposes limitations on the compliance evaluation.

1B08 REVIEW OF COMMUNITY RESOURCE FILES

Each field office must maintain resource files on the communities within its geographic area. For each community, these files should identify local organizations that represent or provide services to protected groups. These would include groups and organizations representing or servicing women, racial and ethnic minorities, veterans and individuals with disabilities. Some COs may not be knowledgeable about the local organizations in the area. In these instances, they must review the resource files and introduce themselves to representatives from the various organizations. The Communications Team in the National Office and Regional Office Outreach Coordinators (ROCs) may also be useful resources.

If a contractor is located near an Indian Reservation with a Tribal Employment Rights Organization (TERO) or other employment organization on the reservation, COs must contact these organizations. Chapter 2 of this Manual discusses the importance of linkages and how a CO can establish relationships with local organizations representing covered group members.

1B09 REVIEW OF PREVIOUS COMPLIANCE ACTIONS

COs must determine whether another OFCCP office reviewed the same contractor when scheduling contractor establishments for compliance evaluations. If another OFCCP office is currently reviewing a contractor proposed for an evaluation, the CO or the supervisor must contact the supervisor of the other OFCCP office to discuss what issues, if any, are present in their ongoing case. This is particularly important for detecting company-wide practices that result in discrimination. An example of this may be a test that is not validated and has an adverse impact on specific groups.

COs may also examine closed case files to identify issues relevant to the current evaluation. They will also note the terms of any CA or Consent Decree, including back pay, hires and other remedial measures contained in the CA or Consent Decree. In addition, COs must determine whether a contractor has been subject to an OFCCP complaint investigation and, if so, review the complaint file for any violations or problems identified.[18] Any violations found in these past compliance actions must be recorded in Part A.I of the SCER. While the existence of a past problem is not considered evidence of the existence of present problems, COs must be alert to any indications that past problems remain unresolved, have recurred or that similar problems have arisen.

[18] See subsection 1B06 – Information on EEO Complaints Filed with or by Other Agencies.

1C RECEIPT OF AAPs AND SUPPORT DATA FOR DESK AUDIT

The appropriate field office will receive copies of a contractor's current EO 11246 AAP within 30 calendar days of the contractor's receipt of the Scheduling Letter and Itemized Listing. It should also receive the AAPs for Section 503 or Section 4212, or both, within this same timeframe. If the field office does not timely receive the current AAPs, the CO calls the contractor to determine the status of the AAPs submission. If the AAPs were not submitted, the CO's supervisor has the discretion to determine whether to grant the contractor a reasonable extension and the length of time of any extension.

1C00 NON-RECEIPT OF EXECUTIVE ORDER AAP

If the contractor fails to request an extension, or if the request is denied, or if the contractor fails to submit the Executive Order AAP within the established timeframe, COs recommend issuance of an SCN. However, the regulations at 41 CFR 60-1.26(b)(1) give the director of OFCCP the discretion to go directly to administrative enforcement when a contractor refuses to submit an AAP and efforts to conciliate the matter are unsuccessful. COs must inform their supervisor of a contractor's failure to submit an AAP to determine if they should ask the director to exercise that discretion.

1C01 NON-RECEIPT OF EXECUTIVE ORDER SUPPORT DATA

If, in response to the Scheduling Letter, a contractor does not submit personnel activity data[19] or submits incomplete data, the COs must contact the contractor and request that the information be submitted promptly. Examples of incomplete data include not submitting data for one or more personnel activity elements, such as applicant flow, hires, compensation, promotions or terminations. If the contractor fails to submit the personnel activity data promptly, the CO must recommend that the contractor be issued an SCN.

If the field office is issuing an SCN at the desk audit stage for reasons other than failure to submit the activity data,[20] the SCN will include the failure to submit the activity data. If, however, the only reason the field office is issuing an SCN at the desk audit is for the failure to submit the activity data, the CO will use the procedures outlined in Chapter 8 on resolving noncompliance issues to recommend issuance of the SCN.

If a contractor fails to submit personnel activity data because it did not maintain appropriate records, one or more of the following regulatory sections may be applicable and COs will cite it in the SCN:

- *General Data Requirements under the Uniform Guidelines on Employee Selection Procedures (UGESP).* 41 CFR 60-3.4(A) requires that each contractor "...maintain and have available for inspection records or other information which will disclose the impact

[19] Unless otherwise specified, all references to "personnel activity" include determinations related to rates of pay or other forms of compensation.

[20] See subsection 1C00 – Non-Receipt of EO 11246 AAP.

which its . . . selection procedures have upon the employment opportunities of persons by identifiable race, sex, or ethnic groups. . ." The identifiable groups are defined by 41 CFR 60-3.4(B) as black, Hispanic, Asian/Pacific Islander, American Indian/Alaskan Native and white.

- *Data Requirements under UGESP for Contractors with 100 or More Employees.* 41 CFR 60-3.15(A)(2) requires contractors with 100 or more employees to maintain and have available records for each job on all applicants, hires, promotions, terminations and any other selection decisions by sex and by each race and/or national origin group identified above.

- *Data Requirements under UGESP for Contractors with less than 100 Employees.* 41 CFR 60-3.15 (A)(1) requires contractors with less than 100 employees to maintain and have available records for each job on all applicants, hires, promotions, terminations and any other selection decisions by sex and by race and/or national origin for any race and/or national origin group constituting more than 2% of the labor force in the relevant labor area. However, it is not necessary to maintain records by race and national origin if one race or national origin group in the relevant labor area constitutes more than 98% of the labor force in that area.

- *Record Retention Requirements under 41 CFR 60-1.12.* Part 60-1.12 sets forth the required document retention periods and identification requirements for all employment and personnel records and AAPs.

- *Recordkeeping Violations and AAP Requirements under 41 CFR Part 60-2.* 41 CFR 60-2.17(b) requires that the AAP identify problem areas and 41 CFR 60-2.17(d) requires that the AAP include internal audit and reporting systems. COs can cite these requirements for recordkeeping violations because they cannot be appropriately implemented without maintaining and analyzing basic data on employment activity as required by 41 CFR 60-3.4 and 60-3.15.

1C02 NON-RECEIPT OF SECTION 503 AND SECTION 4212 AAPs

Section 503 and Section 4212 AAP(s) may be included in an Executive Order AAP, combined in one document separate from the Executive Order AAP or submitted as individual documents. If the contractor fails to submit the AAP within the established timeframe or request, or does not receive an extension, the field office generally issues an SCN.

1C03 EVALUATION PERIOD

COs must evaluate the contractor's performance for at least the last full AAP year. Contractor performance includes, for example, goals progress, good faith efforts and personnel activity. COs must also examine the current year performance if the contractor is six months or more into its current AAP year. For example, if the AAP is established on a calendar year basis, and the compliance evaluation is scheduled in August, a CO would evaluate the contractor's performance of the prior year from January through December under the prior AAP, and the preceding January through July under the current AAP.

Special circumstances or exceptions can exist that warrant a CO extending the analysis of a contractor's AAP(s), personnel activity, policy implementation and supporting documentation to cover a period beginning two years prior to the date the contractor received the Scheduling Letter. The appearance of potential discrimination is a special circumstance or exception. In order to fully investigate and understand the scope of potential violations the CO may need to examine information after the date of the Scheduling Letter in order to determine, for example, if violations are continuing or have been remedied. This assumes, however, that the CO can establish coverage for the entire period. If the CO believes it necessary to request information related to periods after the date of the scheduling letter the CO must discuss the issue with his or her supervisors.

The CO will request data relevant to the potential discrimination issues identified at the desk audit to determine how far into the evaluation period the violation extends and whether the violation continues to the present day. This information is necessary to ensure that any discriminatory practices have ended and to ensure that all victims of discrimination receive appropriate remedies.

1D INITIAL REVIEW OF AAPs

After receiving a contractor's AAP(s) and supporting data, COs must ensure that it is complete and acceptable. There are three types determinations: inclusion, missing items, and acceptability; each is described below.

- *Inclusion.* Immediately review the material to ensure that the contractor provided all of the materials identified in the Scheduling Letter and accompanying Itemized Listing.
- *Missing Items.* Create an inventory list of every document that the contractor provided, including the date requested, if any, and date received. Also record on the list the items requested but not provided by the contractor.
- *Acceptability.* Determine whether the AAP(s) and supporting data are current, complete and acceptable.

These determinations are discussed further in following Section 1E-1I.

The results of this initial review for inclusion and acceptability, as outlined below in Sections 1E through 1H, are documented on Part A.II of the SCER. Each specific problem a CO identifies is described in Part A.III of the SCER, along with the corrective actions the CO plans to take to resolve them.

1E REVIEW OF AAPS FOR CURRENTNESS AND INCLUSION FOR EO11246, SECTION 503 AND SECTION 4212

This Section covers CO actions and responses when the AAP(s) is not current or is missing information requested in the Scheduling Letter and Itemized Listing. The first subsection, 1E00, is devoted to the AAP(s) that are not current while the subsequent two subsections cover the issue of inclusion and the actions that can be taken when the AAP(s) is missing elements, respectively.

1E00 ACTION WHEN AAP IS NOT CURRENT

After receiving the AAP(s) for a desk audit, a CO first determines whether the AAP is current, that is, whether the AAP is still effective either by the date of the Scheduling Letter or the data actually submitted. If it is not, the CO will contact the contractor and request immediate submission of the current AAP. If the contractor still fails to submit the AAP, the CO will recommend issuance of an SCN.[21]

1E01 INCLUSION

If the contractor's AAP(s) is current, the CO will review the AAP and support data to determine whether the contractor's submission includes all requested information. To do so, the CO must first determine whether the contractor submitted all materials requested in the Scheduling Letter and Itemized Listing, including the Section 503 and Section 4212 AAPs. Next, the CO must determine if the Executive Order, Section 503 and Section 4212 AAPs contain all the elements required by the regulations.

The elements of the required Executive Order AAP are listed in 41 CFR 60-2.10(b) while the required Section 503 and Section 4212 AAP elements are found in 41 CFR 60-741.44 and 41 CFR 60-250.44 and 60-300.44, respectively. Executive Order support data are also required.

1E02 MISSING AAP ELEMENTS

Actions that must be taken when an AAP is missing or inadequate under the legal authorities enforced by OFCCP are discussed in this subsection. First is the discussion of the Executive Order AAP, followed by AAPs under Section 503 and Section 4212.

a. *Executive Order AAP*. If one or more of the below listed Executive Order AAP elements is missing, COs must automatically consider the submission unacceptable.

- Organizational Profile (workforce analysis or organizational display).
- Job group analysis, including a list of the job titles that comprise each job group.
- Utilization analysis, including its component parts of job group formation, availability estimates and, as appropriate, identification of underutilization.

---

[21] See subsections 1C00 – Non-Receipt of EO 11246, and 1C02 – Non-Receipt of Section 503 and Section 4212 AAPs.

- Comparison of incumbency to availability.
- Placement goals at least equal to the availability figure derived for women or minorities, as appropriate for job groups where minorities or women employed is less than would be reasonably expected given their availability.
- Designation of a responsible official.
- Identification of problem areas.
- Action-oriented programs.
- Internal audit and reporting system.

A CO may contact the contractor and request that it immediately provide the information. The CO may provide the contractor with compliance assistance, if needed. If the contractor does not comply, the CO must suspend the desk audit and recommend issuance of an SCN. If the contractor includes all of these elements, the CO will then evaluate them for acceptability.

b. *Section 503 and Section 4212 (or VEVRRA) AAPs.* If one or more of the below listed Section 503 and Section 4212 AAP elements is missing, COs automatically consider the submission unacceptable.

  - Equal employment opportunity policy statement.
  - Review of personnel processes to ensure full consideration of individuals with disabilities and protected veterans for available opportunities.
  - Review of physical and mental job qualifications to ensure they are job-related and consistent with business necessity.
  - Reasonable accommodation policy.
  - Harassment policy prohibiting harassment based on disability or veteran status.
  - External dissemination of the contractor's EEO policy.
  - Internal dissemination of the contractor's EEO policy.
  - Description of the contractor's audit and reporting system.
  - Identification of the person(s) responsible for implementation of the AAP.
  - Training policy that provides training for all personnel involved in the recruitment, screening, selection, promotion, disciplinary and related processes to ensure that the commitments in the contractor's AAP are implemented.

COs may contact the contractor to request that the contractor provide the information immediately. The CO may provide the contractor with compliance assistance, if needed. If the contractor does not comply, the CO will suspend the desk audit and recommend issuance of an SCN. If the contractor included all of these elements, the CO will evaluate them for acceptability.

1F REVIEW OF AAPs FOR ACCEPTABILITY

The next three subsections discuss a CO's review of a contractor's AAP(s) for acceptability. Because the requirements for acceptability are not the same under all of the laws that OFCCP enforces, the acceptability requirements for the Executive Order AAP are not reviewed along with those from Section 503 and Section 4212. Section F reviews the acceptability requirements for the Executive Order AAP and Section G discusses the acceptability requirements for the Executive Order AAP support data. Lastly, Section H discusses the acceptability requirements for Section 503 and Section 4212 AAPs.

1F00 REVIEW OF EXECUTIVE ORDER AAP FOR ACCEPTABILITY

The regulations at 41 CFR 60-2.10 through 60-2.17 prescribe the required elements of an Executive Order AAP, and specify what a contractor must include in a written AAP. Once a CO determines that the contractor's submission includes the elements necessary to proceed with the desk audit, the desk audit proceeds with an evaluation of the acceptability of each required element. This means that the CO examines the AAP to determine if the information the contractor provided in each element is sufficient to satisfy the regulatory requirements. The determination of the *acceptability* of the items listed in Part A.II of the SCER is limited to the evaluation that the CO can conduct during the desk audit. This is different from an evaluation of a contractor's *implementation* of its AAP and regulatory requirements, which in most instances the CO cannot determine without further investigation onsite. Onsite reviews are discussed in Chapter 2.

We address the acceptability assessment of each required element below.

1F01 ORGANIZATIONAL PROFILE

An organizational profile is a depiction of the staffing pattern within an establishment. Contractors must use either a workforce analysis or an organizational display as its organizational profile.

a. *Workforce Analysis.* Pursuant to 41 CFR 60-2.11(c), a workforce analysis is acceptable if it:

- contains a listing of each job title, as it appears in applicable collective bargaining agreements or payroll records, within each department or other similar organizational unit, including the unit supervisor, ranked from lowest paid to highest paid (or highest to lowest); and

- provides a separate listing for each work unit or line of progression, including the unit supervisor when there are separate work units or lines of progression within the department or organizational unit.

In addition, the workforce analysis must include information by job title, wage rate, department and/or organizational unit, and lines of progression. Below is a description of each of these elements.

- *Information by Job Title.* Each job title listed shows the total number of people in the job title, the total number of men and women, and the total number of men and women in each of the following groups: whites, blacks, Hispanics, Asian/Pacific Islanders and American Indians/Alaskan Natives.[22] The list must include all job titles, including managerial job titles. Upper management positions located in the establishment must be included in an establishment's workforce analysis even though the managers may have been chosen by those outside the establishment and included for goal-setting purposes in a corporate or mid-level AAP. [23]

- *Wage Rate.* The wage rate or salary range for each job title is provided, although this information may be coded as discussed in the following bullet. Titles must be listed from lowest paid to highest paid.[24] Contractors must provide the key to wage rate or salary range codes if they are used. The codes must be consistent across department or unit lines. For example, a job with a salary code 1157 in Department A pays the same as one coded 1157 in Department B. The codes must also be consistent in wage rate or salary range order within each department or other similar organization unit. Finally, the contractor's submission should include a list of the codes used in wage and salary order with the lowest and highest codes labeled appropriately.

- *Departments or Organizational Units.* The departments or organizational units, or both, used in the workforce analysis are identifiable and should reflect the contractor's organizational structure. If the contractor provides an organizational chart as part of the supporting documentation, the CO will compare it to and match it with the units used in the workforce analysis.

- *Lines of Progression.* Lines of progression or usual promotional sequences show the order of jobs in the line through which an employee moves to reach the top of the line. Lines of progression or promotional sequences can be identified from collective bargaining agreements as well as from organizational charts. If the CO determines that lines of progression exist, but adequate information is not provided at the desk audit, the CO will contact the contractor to request a prompt submission of the information.

---

[22] For purposes of complying with OFCCP requirements, contractors choosing to follow the current EEO-1 categories may count applicants and employees identifying as "two or more races" as minorities. (*Interim Guidance on the Use of Race and Ethnic Categories in Affirmative Action Plans*, OFCCP Directive, Transmittal 283 (Aug. 14, 2008).) This guidance indicates that OFCCP will accept AAPs and supporting records that reflect the race, ethnicity and job categories outlined in either 41 CFR Part 60-2 or the current EEO-1 Report.

[23] 41 CFR 60-2.11(c)(3) and (c)(4).

[24] Ibid.

b. *Organizational Display*. An acceptable organizational profile is one that meets the requirements of 41 CFR 60-2.11(b). It must contain the following elements for each unit:

- name of the unit;
- job title, gender, race and ethnicity of the unit supervisor (if the unit has a supervisor);
- total number of male and female employees in the unit; and
- total number of male and female employees in each of the following groups: black, Hispanic, Asian/Pacific Islander and American Indian/Alaskan Native.[25]

1F02 JOB GROUPS

A job group analysis is acceptable if it meets the requirements of 41 CFR 60-2.12. Job groups must be comprised of a group of jobs and/or job titles within a particular establishment having similar content, wage rates and opportunities. Similarity of content refers to duties and responsibilities of the job titles that make up the job group. Similarity of opportunities refers to training, transfers, promotions, pay, mobility and other career enhancement opportunities offered by the jobs within the job group.

a. *List of Titles in Each Group*. In order for COs to assess job group acceptability, the AAP must include, for each job group, a listing of the job titles that make up that group. If a contractor did not provide the lists, the CO must immediately contact the contractor and request that the lists be promptly provided for the desk audit.

b. *Criteria for Acceptability*. The following criteria are to be used in assessing the acceptability of job groups:

- *Similar Work Content*. Similarity of work "content" refers to the duties and responsibilities of the job titles that make up the job group.
    - *Appropriate EEO Category*. The CO will review the establishment's job titles that make up each of the job groups to verify they are within the proper EEO-1[26] job categories. Job titles in each job group must, as a general rule, be within the same EEO-1 job category.[27]

[25] For purposes of complying with OFCCP requirements, contractors choosing to follow the current EEO-1 categories, may count applicants and employees identifying as "two or more races" as minorities. (*Interim Guidance on the Use of Race and Ethnic Categories in Affirmative Action Plans*, OFCCP Directive, Transmittal 283 (Aug. 14, 2008).)

[26] Higher education institutions are required to submitthe Integrated Post Secondary Education System Survey (IPEDS).

[27] Contractors that employ fewer than 150 employees are permitted to use the job categories listed in OFCCP's regulations or the current EEO-1 job categories which subdivide the Officials and Managers category into two categories: Executive and Senior Level Officials & Managers and First and Mid-Level Officials & Managers.

  - *Use of Occupational Information Network (O*NET).* The CO may refer to the Department of Labor's Employment Training Administration's O*NET database, as well as collective bargaining agreements, organizational charts and other data provided by the contractor to evaluate how the contractor formulated its job groups. O*NET lists standard job titles for most positions and codes them based on their duties, requirements and other factors. O*NET also gives descriptions of job duties and commonly required qualifications.

- *Similar Rates of Pay.* COs must review pay rates in conjunction with job content. Large apparent differences in pay, when associated with different job titles within a job group or different locations within an organization, or both, suggest an unacceptable job grouping. They may also indicate areas where compensation or job assignment practices need further review.

- *Similar Opportunities.* "Opportunity" refers to the ability to take advantage of training opportunities, transfers, promotions, mobility to desirable wage or salary situations and other employment benefits. Most often, it refers to upward mobility. Ideally, each job within a job group should offer the same opportunities as any other job title within that job group.

  - *Jobs in Separate Unions.* Jobs groups should not group together jobs from separate unions, or jobs from different departments where interdepartmental mobility is not available. For example, job groups should not normally group together nonunion clerical jobs and clerical jobs that are covered by a collective bargaining agreement.

  - *Jobs in Lines of Progression.* Contractors should separate jobs that are in lines of progression (LOP) from those that are not. When transferring or hiring into jobs above entry level is rare, COs must analyze each LOP separately. When there are LOP governed by strict seniority, the contractor should consider the job titles in the progression as a single job group.

c. *Job Groups Must Not Obscure Underutilization.* Job groups that combine jobs with different content, wages or opportunities may obscure underutilization and OFCCP does not accept them.

d. *Effect of Size of Contractor's Workforce.* While assessing the acceptability of a contractor's job groups, COs must remember that the size of the contractor's workforce is a major factor in determining how well the contractor meets the three criteria for acceptability of job groups.

  - *Job Groups Must Permit Meaningful Analyses.* Job groups should have enough incumbents to permit meaningful utilization analyses and goal setting. Optimally, when COs identify underutilization in a job group, the job group should be large enough so that a goal of at least one whole person can be established. No minimum size is established for this purpose because the goal is dependent on the size of the job group and the percentage and the number of minorities or women already in the job group.

- *Job Groups Should Not Normally Cross EEO-1 Job Categories.* A contractor's job groups should not ordinarily cross EEO-1 job categories. This means, for example, that a job group should not consist of a mixture of job titles from the "Professional" category and the "Technicians" category. COs should note that larger contractor establishments may have multiple job groups that fall into the same EEO-1 job category. Also, COs should note that smaller establishments (less than 150 employees) may use the EEO- 1 job categories as their job groups.

e. *Relationship Between Job Groups and Availability.* The organization of jobs into groups should allow contractors to tie specific jobs to availability statistics in order to assess the degree to which their own workforce representation approximates availability.

1F03 UTILIZATION ANALYSIS

The utilization analysis is a series of separate but interrelated analyses COs use to identify whether a contractor employs minorities or women in the workforce at a rate that would be expected based upon their availability for employment. Contractors must perform a utilization analysis that includes the placement of the contractor's employees into job groups, the determination of the availability for employment of minorities and women and a comparison of their incumbency in the job groups to their availability. If a contractor's utilization analysis reveals underutilization of minorities or women, or both, in any of the job groups the contractor must establish placement goals designed to cure the underutilization.

a. Placement of Incumbents in Job Groups. Having combined the job titles for the job group analysis, the contractor must separately state the percentage of minorities and the percentage of women employed in each job group.

b. Determining Availability. After aggregating individual job titles into job groups, the contractor must determine the availability of women and minorities for those job groups. "Availability" is a percentage estimate of the women and minorities in the reasonable recruitment area who have the skills required to perform the jobs within the job groups compared to all. When determining availability, the contractor must separately determine the availability of minorities and women for each job group and consider at least the following factors:

- The percentage of minorities and women with the requisite skills in the "reasonable recruitment area." We define "reasonable recruitment area" as the geographical area from which the contractor usually seeks, or reasonably could seek, workers to fill the positions in question. When selecting the reasonable recruitment area, the contractor must not select an area in such a way that it would exclude minorities or women. For each job group, the contractor must identify and provide a brief explanation of the rationale for selection of that recruitment area.

- The contractor should utilize the most current and discrete statistical information available to derive availability figures (such as census data, data from local job service offices, colleges and other training institutions). When evaluating the contractor's availability information, COs must utilize the most recent Federal Consortium Census Special EEO File located on the Census Bureau's Web site under the "Access to Data from the Special EEO Tabulation" link.

- The percentage of minorities and women among those promotable, transferable or trainable within the contractor's organization. The contractor must not define the pool of promotable, transferable and trainable employees in such a way as to exclude minorities or women. For each job group, the contractor must identify the pool of promotable, transferable and trainable employees and provide a brief explanation of the reason for selection of that pool.

c. *Comparing Incumbency to Availability.* The contractor must compare the utilization of minorities and women in each job group with their estimated availability, and identify job groups where the percentage employed is less than would be reasonably expected given their availability.

We use the term "underutilization" to refer to the presence of fewer minorities or women in a particular job group than would reasonably be expected given their availability. Contractors use a number of methods to determine whether the actual representation rates of minorities and women are lower than would reasonably be expected. Some contractors declare underutilization when there is any difference between the availability percentage and the utilization percentage, while others conclude that underutilization exists when the number of minority or women incumbents in a particular job group is at least one whole person lower than the number predicted by the availability percentages. Other contractors use an "80 percent" rule of thumb and declare underutilization only when the actual representation of minorities or women is less than 80 percent of availability (which is the expected representation). Still others test whether the difference between the actual and expected representation of minorities and women is statistically significant.

While contractors may choose any of these methods for comparing incumbency and availability, they must uniformly apply the same standard to all job groups, as appropriate. Occasionally a different method may be more appropriate to determine underutilization. For example, in some instances it may not be reasonable for contractors to use the 2 standard deviation method. No matter the method used, the contractor should be able to explain why it selected that method. Contractors should not use more than one method so as to mask underutilization.

The contractor must establish a placement goal if the percentage of women or minorities, or both, employed in a specific job group is less than would be reasonably expected, given their availability percentage in that particular job group.

1F04 PLACEMENT GOALS

Regardless of the method employed to determine underutilization, the contractor must establish a placement goal for those job groups where minorities or women, or both, are underutilized.[28] The placement goal established must be at least equal to the availability percentage of the underutilized minorities and women for the specific job group.[29] If a contractor establishes a goal higher than required under the Executive Order, failure to meet this higher goal does not constitute noncompliance. Placement goals are not rigid and are not quotas.

In the event of a substantial disparity in the utilization of a particular minority group or in the utilization of men or women of a particular minority group, the contractor may be required to establish separate goals for those groups. We refer you to 41 CFR 60-2.16(d) for additional information.

1F05 ADDITIONAL REQUIRED ELEMENTS OF AAPs

This subsection, focusing on 41 CFR 60-2.17, covers the designation of responsibility for the AAP(s), identification of problem areas, creation of action-oriented programs, reporting system and internal audit, and reviewing the results of the report.

a. *Designation of Responsibility.* Under 41 CFR 60-2.17(a), contractors must provide for the implementation of equal employment opportunity obligations and the affirmative action program by assigning responsibility and accountability to an official of the organization. These officials must have sufficient authority and resources, and must also have the support of, and access to, top management to ensure the effective implementation of the contractor's EEO obligations and affirmative action program. To be acceptable, the AAP(s) should contain, at a minimum, a narrative description of the positions or job titles, or both, that the contractor designates to direct or manage its affirmative action program and a description of the incumbent's duties.

b. *Identification of Problem Areas.* 41 CFR 60-2.17(b) requires that contractors perform an in-depth analysis of their total employment process to determine whether or where impediments to equal employment opportunity exist. They must evaluate the following:

   - *Organizational Structure.* The contractor must examine its workforce by organizational unit and job group to determine whether there are problems of minority or female utilization, or of minority or female distribution;

   - *Personnel Activity.* The contractor must examine applicant flow, hires, recruitment, referral, terminations, promotions, transfers and other personnel activities to determine whether there are selection and termination disparities;

---

[28] See 41 CFR 60-2.15.
[29] See 41 CFR 60-2.16(b).

- *Compensation*. The contractor must determine whether there are gender, race or ethnicity disparities in its compensation system;

- *Personnel Procedures*. The contractor must determine whether its selection, recruitment, referral, and other procedures result in disparities in the employment or advancement of minorities or women and their resulting pay; and

- *Other Areas*. The contractor must evaluate any other areas that might affect the success of the affirmative action program. Examples include things that might affect the AAP include seniority practices, leave policies, time off policies, policies regarding part-time work, conduct of company sponsored social events, apprenticeship program practices, workforce environment, compliance with posting and union notification requirements.

These procedures should be consistent with the Sex Discrimination Guidelines at 41 CFR Part 60-20 in that the procedures should not create conditions of employment differentiated on the basis of sex and should not discriminate on the basis of sex. Sex discrimination can take several forms. One form may include treating a female employee or job applicant unfavorably because of pregnancy, childbirth, or medical issues related to her pregnancy or childbirth. It may also take the form of policies and practices that discriminate based on marital status or care giving responsibilities.

c. *Action-Oriented Programs*. 41 CFR 60-2.17(c) requires that contractors develop and execute action-oriented programs designed to correct problem areas and to attain established goals and objectives. To be effective, contractors must ensure that their action-oriented programs are something other than following the same procedures that previously produced inadequate results. Action-oriented programs should be "specific" and "result-oriented."

By "specific" we mean that the programs describe in some detail what action the contractor will take, who is responsible for taking the action, and when the action will be accomplished. "Result-oriented" programs are those where proper execution of the program will likely lead to an increase in minority or female participation, or both, in the department, job group, training program or other identified problem area. The action-oriented programs must be sufficient, if successfully implemented, to achieve their stated objectives. Contractors must describe these programs in the AAP(s).

For example, if a contractor identifies a lack of women in a job as a problem area the contractor should also identify the reasons for the absence of women. The reasons identified may include the rigid work hours, the impact or application of leave policies, the lack of recruitment, the lack of training, and the absence of a career path or ladder leading to the job, a working environment hostile to women, or hiring discrimination. Whatever the reasons contributing to the absence of women, the contractor should establish action-oriented programs to eliminate or minimize the reasons women are adversely affected. The action-oriented programs, when fully implemented, should result in an increase in the representation of women in the job identified as a problem area. Similarly, a lack of representation of minorities may result from the unwarranted screening out of applicants based on criminal records, credit history, or unemployment status that requires action-oriented programs.

d. Internal Audit and Reporting System. 41 CFR 60-2.17(d) requires contractors to design and implement an internal auditing system that periodically measures the effectiveness of its total affirmative action program. This system must be detailed in the AAP(s) and the internal audit and reporting system must:

- *Monitor Records.* The internal audit and reporting system must monitor records of all personnel activity, including referrals, placements, transfers, promotions, terminations and compensation, at all levels.
- *Require Internal Reporting.* The contractor produces an internal report on the effectiveness of the AAP(s) on a regularly scheduled basis.
- *Review Report Results.* Top management is advised of the program's effectiveness and any deficiencies, and management at all levels reviews the results of these reports.

The AAP(s) should contain a narrative description of every aspect of the internal audit and reporting system. This description should specify the frequency of reports and audits. It should also state that, as problems are discovered, the contractor is taking the necessary corrective actions. The description should also designate the contractor officials responsible for taking these corrective actions. Lastly, the contractor should state how and when it reviews program results and effectiveness with management at all levels of the company.

1G REVIEW OF EXECUTIVE ORDER SUPPORT DATA FOR ACCEPTABILITY

Contractors must prepare a report on the results of their prior year AAP and the current year AAP, if they are six months or more into the current year by the time they receive their Scheduling Letter.[30] This report is part of the support data for the AAP(s) that COs request in the Itemized Listing that accompanies the Scheduling letter. The Itemized Listing requests data and information indicating the numerical and other results of contractors' affirmative action goals for each job group for the current and preceding AAP years. For each goal not attained, or not currently being attained, contractors must describe the good faith efforts they undertook to achieve the goal. Contractors should always submit prior year data, unless they were not federal contractors covered by 41 CFR Part 60-2.

a. Data Required. As noted above, the contractor must provide summary data indicating the numerical results of affirmative action goals for each job group.

- *Information on Job Groups with Goals.* COs, in order to measure the results of goals, must first know whether a contractor established goals for its job groups and what the goals are. The contractor's current AAP submitted for desk audit will have this information for the current year. The contractor's report on prior year goals should

[30] See 41 CFR 60-1.12(b), 60-2.16 and 60-2.17(c).

specifically state the goals for the prior year; however, when it does not, the CO must request a copy of the goals section of the contractor's prior year AAP.

- *Information on Placements into Job Groups with Goals.* Since contractors establish annual goals in terms of a percentage placement rate, evaluation of progress toward the these goals requires knowledge of the total number of placements into the job groups (hires, promotions and transfers) and the number of minority and female placements, as appropriate. If a contractor's progress report does not include this information or if it includes incomplete information (e.g., the number of minorities and females but not total placements), the CO will determine if the missing information can be obtained from the contractor's submission of personnel activity data. If the information cannot be obtained from the personnel activity data, the CO must ask the contractor to forward a copy of the report on the progress made toward its goals as prepared under its internal audit and reporting system.[31] If the contractor employs 100 or more people, a copy of the underlying data it used for its adverse impact determinations on hires, promotions and any other placements into job titles within the job group should be requested.[32]

b. *Good Faith Efforts.* When a contractor's goals report does not describe its good faith efforts to achieve the goals that it failed to meet, or does not describe those efforts in sufficient detail for a CO to evaluate their adequacy, the CO must request additional information to review during the desk audit.[33] The CO must also include this request for more information in the onsite plan for evaluation of good faith efforts. Even if the contractor corrects the goals report, the closure letter may identify the incorrect or incomplete report as a technical violation that was corrected during the review.[34]

The Itemized Listing requests support data regarding the contractor's employment activities such as applicants and hires, promotions, and terminations for the prior and current AAP years; and compensation data for all employees.[35]

a. *Review of Support Data for Acceptability*

- *Data Format.* To be acceptable for the desk audit, the contractor must present support data either by job group or by job title. For example, data by total workforce is not acceptable; nor is data by EEO-1 job category, unless a category legitimately constitutes a job group at the particular establishment.

- *Information Included.* For each job group or job title, support data in each major personnel activity area (e.g., applicant flow, hires, promotions and terminations) must, at least, include the total number of actions, the total number of actions for women and the total number of actions for minorities. For example, applicant flow for a job group or job

---

[31] See subsection 1F05(d)-Additional Required Elements of AAPs: Internal Audit and Reporting System.

[32] See Section 1G – Review of Executive Order Support Data for Acceptability.

[33] See Part B.I of the SCER.

[34] See Letter L-4 – Notice Closing Compliance Evaluation No Violation Found.

[35] For most current and detailed information on the content of the Itemized Listing you should refer to a copy of the most current Itemized Listing authorized by OMB for the agency's information collection.

title must include at least the total applicants, total female applicants and total minority applicants; hires for a job group or job title must include at least the total hires, total female hires and total minority hire.

- *Evaluation Period Covered.* Generally, it is better to have the longest possible period because the data are more likely to reflect the contractor's usual way of operating. At a minimum, however, the support data must cover the prior AAP year and, if the contractor is six months or more into its current AAP year when it receives the Scheduling Letter, the current AAP year. If there are indicators of a violation, the evaluation period will extend to cover the two years prior to the contractor's receipt of the Scheduling Letter. In order to fully investigate and understand the scope of potential violations, the CO may need to examine information relating to periods after the date of the Scheduling Letter in order to determine, for example, if violations are continuing or have been remedied. If the CO believes it is necessary to request information for periods after the date of the Scheduling Letter the CO must discuss the issue with his or her supervisor.

- *Source of Applicant Data.* COs must determine if a contractor used the Internet to recruit for any job group(s). When the AAP does not readily specify the applicant pool for job groups in which individuals applied through the Internet, the CO must contact the contractor to request the criteria used by the contractor in defining applicants for the job position(s) in question. The contractor's submission should address the following four questions:

  - Did the individual express an interest in employment through the Internet or related electronic data technologies?

  - Did the contractor consider the individual for employment in a particular position?

  - Did the individual's expression of interest indicate that the individual possesses the basic qualifications for the position?

  - Did the individual at any point in the contractor's selection process prior to receiving an offer of employment from the contractor, remove himself or herself from further consideration or otherwise indicate that he or she was no longer interested in the position?

To be acceptable, the contractor must identify the electronic data technologies used to collect expressions of interest, the specific job positions for which the contractor considered applications through the Internet and the basic qualifications for these positions. COs will note unacceptable submissions in Part A.III of the SCER, and investigate during the onsite review.

b. *Action When Data Are Unacceptable.* If employment activity data is submitted, but is not acceptable, COs must call the contractor and request that the appropriate changes be promptly made and the data resubmitted within the timeframe specified by the OFCCP field office. If, at the end of the allotted timeframe, the data are not received in a form that is acceptable, COs will recommend issuing an SCN specifying the regulatory sections the contractor violated.

Examples of unacceptable data submissions include, but are not limited to, instances where the data are in aggregations larger than job group or are not provided by sex or by minority versus non-minority.

1H REVIEW OF SECTION 503 AND SECTION 4212 AAPs FOR ACCEPTABILITY

As with an Executive Order AAP, the determination of the *acceptability* of items listed in Part A.II of the SCER for Section 503 and Section 4212 AAPs is limited to an evaluation conducted at the desk audit. This is different from an evaluation of the contractor's *implementation* of these items, which usually is done onsite. Additionally, the Section 503 and Section 4212 regulations require the contractor to take a number of actions even though the contractor does not address them in the AAP(s). Part B.III of the SCER covers the additional requirements, most of which are completed onsite.

1H00 ITEMS INCLUDED

The regulations at 41 CFR 60-741.44 identify the required elements of a Section 503 AAP. Similarly, the regulations at 41 CFR 60-250.44 and 60-300.44 list the required elements of a Section 4212 AAP. Therefore, to be acceptable, a contractor's Section 503 and Section 4212 AAPs must include the below items listed in 41 CFR 60-741.44(a) through (j), 41 CFR 60-250.44 (a) through (j), or 60-300.44 (a) through (j), as appropriate.

- Policy Statement
- Review of Personnel Processes
- Review of Physical and Mental Job Qualifications
- Reasonable Accommodations of Physical and Mental Limitations
- Harassment Prevention
- External Dissemination of EEO Policy and Outreach
- Internal Dissemination of EEO Policy
- Audit and Reporting System
- Responsibility for AAP Implementation
- Training

Since these items are similar in all three regulations, we discuss them together below. When there are differences, we expressly identify them. It is the responsibility of COs to determine whether the contractor included all of the required items in the contractor's Section 503 and Section 4212 AAPs. We describe the acceptability assessment of each required element below.

1H01 POLICY STATEMENT

Contractors are required to take affirmative action to employ and advance in employment qualified individuals with disabilities and protected veterans. The contractor must affirm its commitment to this affirmative action requirement by incorporating it in a policy statement included in its AAP(s).[36] The contractor must also post this policy statement conspicuously at the workplace and communicate the policy to all employees and applicants.

At a minimum, to be acceptable, the policy statement must include:

- a statement indicating the top establishment official's support for the EEO policy;
- a statement identifying the EEO official responsible for the implementation of the AAP;
- a statement that the contractor hires, recruits, trains and promotes without discrimination on the basis of disability or status as a protected veteran;
- a statement providing for an audit and reporting system;
- a statement that the contractor bases all employment decisions only on valid job requirements; and
- a statement that the contractor will not subject employees and applicants to harassment, intimidation, threats, coercion or retaliation because they engaged or may engage in filing a complaint or assisted in a review, investigation or hearing related to any federal, state or local law requiring EEO for individuals with disabilities or protected veterans; or because they opposed any act deemed unlawful by any of the above referenced laws; or because they exercised any other right under Section 503 or Section 4212.

1H02 CONTRACTOR REVIEW OF PERSONNEL PROCESSES

An AAP, to be acceptable, must affirm that the contractor reviewed its personnel processes. These processes must provide for the careful, thorough, and systematic consideration of the job qualifications of applicants for hiring or promotion, and all training opportunities offered or available and employees who are known individuals with disabilities and protected veterans.[37] A contractor's AAP(s) must describe its review and any modifications made or new procedures implemented because of that review.

---

[36] See 41 CFR 60-250.44(a); 300.44(a); 741.44(a).
[37] See 41 CFR 60-250.44(b); 300.44(b); 741.44(b).

a. *Use of Appendix C.* Contractors may utilize the procedures described at Appendix C in 41 CFR Parts 60-250, 41 CFR 60-300, and 41 CFR Part 60-741, as appropriate, to fulfill this requirement. These procedures describe how contractors annotate applications or personnel forms of protected veterans and individuals with disabilities when considering them for employment opportunities.

b. *Adequacy of Present Procedures.* Contractors may assert that their present personnel procedures are adequate and indicate that modifications to the procedures are unnecessary, COs must determine whether the information received during the desk audit supports that assertion in order to determine acceptability. COs must request additional information during the desk audit or onsite review if they are unable to make an acceptability determination.

c. *Additional Section 4212 Requirement.* 41 CFR 60-250.44(b) and 60-300.44(b) also require contractors to limit any consideration of a disabled or other protected veteran's military record to only those portions of the record that are relevant to the specific job or promotion for which the veteran is being considered.[38]

1H03 CONTRACTOR REVIEW OF PHYSICAL AND MENTAL QUALIFICATIONS

An AAP must contain the contractor's schedule for the review of all physical and mental job qualification requirements to ensure that, to the extent they tend to screen out qualified individuals with disabilities, they are job-related and consistent with business necessity.

a. *Scheduled Review.* To be acceptable, an AAP must affirm that the contractor completed a review of the physical and mental job qualification requirements. If it is a newly covered contractor, the AAP must provide a specific and reasonable time by which the contractor will review the jobs qualifications. When the AAP indicates that the contractor completed the review and the qualification standards remain unchanged, the contractor is not required to review those physical and mental job qualification requirements again unless there is a change in working conditions. The AAP should state, however, that when there is such a change in working conditions the contractor will reevaluate the requirements.

b. *Confidentiality of Medical Information.* To be acceptable, the AAP must affirm that any inquiries or medical examinations regarding an applicant's or employee's medical condition that are made by, or at the behest of, the contractor are conducted only in accordance with the law, and that all medical information the contractor obtains as a result of such inquiries or exams is kept confidential, except as otherwise provided for in the regulations. The CO may consult the EEOC's *Enforcement Guide: Preemployment Disability-Related Questions and Medical Examinations* (http://www.eeoc.gov/policy/docs/preemp.html) for more information on this subject matter.[39]

---

[38] The contractor should confirm compliance with this requirement in the AAP.

[39] See 41 CFR 60-250.23(d) and 60-300.23(d); and 41 CFR 60-741.23(d).

1H04 REASONABLE ACCOMMODATION TO PHYSICAL AND MENTAL LIMITATIONS

Contractors must make reasonable accommodation to the physical and mental limitations of qualified individuals and veterans with disabilities unless they can demonstrate that such accommodation would impose an undue business hardship. In assessing undue hardship, contractors may consider factors such as financial costs and interference with the ability of other employees to do their jobs. To be acceptable, this section of the AAP must contain the contractor's policy with respect to reasonable accommodation. This policy must be consistent with the requirements of the regulations.

1H05 HARASSMENT PREVENTION

Contractors must develop and implement a policy prohibiting harassment based on disability or veteran's status. A contractor should include a copy of this policy and its implementation procedures in the AAP(s). This statement may be part of a broader anti-harassment policy that also prohibits harassment on other bases, such as race and sex.

1H06 EXTERNAL DISSEMINATION OF EEO POLICY AND OUTREACH

An acceptable AAP must affirm that the contractor periodically reviews its employment practices, and that the contractor undertakes appropriate outreach and positive recruitment activities when indicated by the findings of such reviews. The AAP may also describe in some detail the steps taken by the contractor in its review of employment practices and the resulting outreach and recruitment activities.

1H07 INTERNAL DISSEMINATION OF EEO POLICY

The contractor must disseminate its EEO policy internally. An acceptable AAP must address the contractor's internal procedures to foster understanding, acceptance and support of the contractor's obligation to promote equal employment opportunity for individuals with disabilities and protected veterans. The scope of the contractor's efforts will depend upon all the circumstances, including the contractor's size and resources and the extent to which its existing practices are adequate. The regulations at 41 CFR 60-250.44(g) and 60-300.44 (g), and 41 CFR 60-741.44(g) provide examples of the types of activities contractors may undertake in this area. For example, contractors may conduct meetings with executive, managerial and supervisory personnel to explain the intent of the policy and to delineate individual responsibility for its implementation.

1H08 AUDIT AND REPORTING SYSTEM

The AAP should contain a narrative description of every aspect of its internal audit and reporting system. The description should specify the frequency of reports and audits, and state that the contractor will take corrective actions, if necessary, as problems are revealed. The description should also designate the contractor official responsible for taking corrective actions. Lastly, contractors should indicate how and when their program results and effectiveness will be reviewed with the various levels of management in the company. An acceptable internal audit system should also include a review of a contractor's online and electronic application systems to determine if they are accessible to individuals with disabilities, to ensure that procedures to request reasonable accommodation for the application process are prominently displayed and to ensure that individuals with disabilities can readily obtain needed accommodations.

1H09 ESTABLISHMENT OF RESPONSIBILITY FOR AAP IMPLEMENTATION

The AAP(s) should identify the person responsible for implementing the contractor's affirmative action activities with respect to individuals with disabilities and covered veterans and should describe his or her responsibilities. Management must give this official necessary support and staff to manage the implementation of the program. The AAP should also describe the responsibilities of line management in carrying out the program.

1H10 TRAINING TO ENSURE AAP IMPLEMENTATION

Contractors are required to train their personnel involved in recruitment, screening, selection, promotion, disciplinary and related processes about the company's EEO obligations and, if appropriate, about the contractor's affirmative action commitments under Section 503 and Section 4212. To be acceptable, this section of the AAP must contain the contractor's training policy.

1H11 NO REDUCTION IN COMPENSATION

COs must note that in offering employment or opportunities to individuals with disabilities and protected veterans, it is unlawful for a contractor to reduce the amount of compensation offered because of any income based upon a disability-related pension or other disability-related benefit the applicant or employee receives from another source. The CO must evaluate the contractor's implementation of this requirement onsite. Chapter 2, Section 2L provides detailed guidance on conducting this aspect of the onsite review.[40]

1I SUMMARY OF ACCEPTABILITY PROBLEMS WITH AAPs AND SUPPORT DATA

COs identify problems with the completeness and acceptability of a contractor's AAPs under EO 11246, Section 503 and Section 4212 and support data in Part A.III of the SCER. For each problem, COs must use Part A.III of the SCER to describe the specific problems and actions taken at the desk audit to resolve it and actions planned for onsite review.

A CO may resolve some problems with the AAP(s) and support data at the desk audit after additional contact with the contractor. For example, if the CO's problem is that he or she cannot evaluate job group acceptability because there is no information on what job titles are in each group, that CO may be able to resolve the problem by obtaining the missing information from

[40] See 41 CFR 60-250.21(i), 60-300.21(i) and 60-741.21(i).

the contractor. The CO will note this follow-up contact and receiving the additional information on the SCER. Such a notation could be written like this: "Called J. Smith May 1, 2011 and asked him to send a list of titles in each group. List received May 8, 2011."

If a CO determines that the Executive Order, Section 503 or Section 4212 AAP(s) does not meet one or more of the standards for acceptability as discussed previously in this chapter, the CO will suspend the desk audit and recommend issuance of an SCN in most cases.

1J ANALYSIS OF SECTION 503 AND SECTION 4212 AAPs: REVIEW OF ONLINE APPLICATION PROCESS

In addition to reviewing a contractor's Section 503 and Section 4212 AAP(s) as part of the desk audit, COs will review the contractor's online application system (electronic or Web-based) to:

- assess whether individuals with disabilities can access the application system, and
- determine whether the contractor is providing reasonable accommodation, when requested and otherwise appropriate.

If a contractor uses an online application system to accept applications for employment, the contractor must ensure that potential applicants with disabilities can use the system (with or without reasonable accommodation) or can submit an application in an equally effective and timely manner through alternative means. This includes providing a means for contacting the contractor, other than through the online system, to request a reasonable accommodation.[41]

The contractor must provide information on how to obtain reasonable accommodations on its online application system, as well as on its paper applications and job announcements. Ideally, the contractor should prominently display such notices, and include them at the beginning of the online application process. At a minimum, this information must include the name and contact information of the person to whom a request for an accommodation should be made and the process for requesting an accommodation. COs must check the contractor's online application system to determine if this information is readily displayed. COs will document the results of this analysis in Part B.III of the SCER.[42]

---

[41] The accommodation should give the applicant with a disability an equal opportunity to apply and be considered for the contractor's jobs.

[42] OFCCP retains and investigates discrimination complaints involving federal contractors' online application systems rather than referring them to the EEOC or some other agency. This includes all Section 503 and VEVRAA complaints alleging failure to accommodate in the application process where an electronic process is used. It also includes failure to hire complaints based on an individual's status as a protected disabled veteran or disability where an online application system was used.

1K ANALYSIS OF EO 11246 AAP: OVERVIEW OF SUPPORT DATA, EEO TRENDS, WORKFORCE STRUCTURE AND PERSONNEL PRACTICES

The review of the personnel activity data such as hires, promotions and terminations provides a broad framework for the detailed review by job group of affirmative action progress, or placement goals, and the assessment of any potential discrimination in employment activity. COs will review personnel activity data to gain an understanding of the specific kinds of employment activity that took place, including where or in which job groups, during the contractor's current and prior AAP years. COs must use Part A.III of the SCER to describe the specific problems and actions taken at the desk audit to resolve issues with the contractor's support data.

1K00 EEO TREND ANALYSIS

COs must make an initial assessment of a contractor's workforce and utilization trends by reviewing the contractor's EEO-1 reports in Part A.IV of the SCER.

a. *Long-Term and Short-Term Trends.* A CO must compare data from the contractor's most recent EEO-1 Report to data from its earlier EEO-1 reports. For example, if the contractor provides EEO-1 reports for 2010, 2009 and 2008, then the CO compares the 2010 data to the 2008 data to look at the long-term trends, and compares the 2010 and 2009 data for short-term trends. This information provides an overview of:

   - the distribution of jobs within the contractor's workforce (white-collar, blue-collar, predominant EEO job categories);
   - the direction of change in the total workforce and particular workforce categories (expanding, contracting, stable); and
   - the increases and decreases in minority and female representation in various areas.

b. *Changes Due to Reclassifications.* If a CO observes significant changes in the size of EEO job categories with little or no corresponding personnel activity, the CO must investigate further to determine if the changes are due to the reclassification of jobs with concentrations of minorities or women from one EEO-1 job category to another. For example, suppose the total number of positions in the Craft category increases from one year to the next and indicates an increase in women. Over the same period, however, both the total number of Operative positions and the total number of women listed as Operatives decreases by nearly the same amount. The CO may then infer that the increase in Crafts may have resulted from the contractor changing the EEO-1 job category of the women's jobs, rather than from genuine hires or promotions.

c. *EEO Category Patterns.* EEO trend analysis allows COs to identify broad areas where minorities and women have been persistently underrepresented or concentrated, setting a framework for the detailed review of the workforce analysis for potential discrimination problems, and the review of the contractor's goals progress by job group.

d. *Particular Minority Group.* This analysis permits the CO to identify any substantial disparity in the representation of a particular race or ethnic group when compared with the distribution of those same groups in the contractor's labor area and in possible internal feeder categories. The disparity may exist in the contractor's workforce as a whole or in certain categories. When a CO identifies such a disparity, the CO must plan to conduct an IRA of the particular group, at least in those workforce areas where the disparity exists and for the type of activity most likely to have created the disparity.

For example, if Hispanics are well represented in the labor area but have historically been absent from the contractor's workforce, the CO will plan to conduct hiring IRAs separately for Hispanics. If blacks have historically been concentrated in Laborers category, but poorly represented in Operatives and Crafts, the CO's review of the workforce analysis should focus on the types of jobs held by blacks and any structural impediments to upward mobility from those jobs. In addition, the CO's IRA of blue-collar job groups, particularly for promotions and hires into jobs above Laborers, should be conducted separately for blacks. Sections 1O00 and 1O02 below further discuss separate discrimination analyses for particular groups. The CO will also note if investigation of such a disparity does not show discrimination. The CO will consider whether goals and/or specific affirmative action steps for the particular group are warranted.

1K01 WORKFORCE STRUCTURE AND PERSONNEL PRACTICES

In the initial review of the AAP and support data, COs evaluated the workforce analysis for acceptability. As a result, they have a basic understanding of the contractor's organization and operations. For example, the workforce analysis should show:

- whether the contractor organizes the facility by department or other unit (e.g., division),
- whether lines of progression exist, and
- how the contractor structures pay and other characteristics that may prove useful for subsequent analyses of both affirmative action and potential discrimination issues.

Other supporting data that the contractor may provide with the AAP, such as copies of labor agreements, should contain additional information such as pay rates, work performed, organizational structure and rules for internal mobility. COs must enter this information, to the extent that it is available during the desk audit, in Part A.III of the SCER.

1L ANALYSIS OF EO 11246 AAP: GOALS PROGRESS AND GOOD FAITH EFFORTS

The effectiveness of a contractor's overall affirmative action program is not measured by whether the contractor met all its goals, but rather by whether the contractor made good faith efforts to do so. Generally, if the contractor met properly determined goals in a job group, further examination of good faith efforts with respect to that job group is unnecessary. Therefore, to focus the investigation on good faith efforts, COs must take the following steps:

- measure the degree of progress in job groups where the contractor established goals and opportunities occurred;
- evaluate the contractor's resulting overall goals performance; and
- identify areas where specific additional information is needed to evaluate good faith efforts.

COs will evaluate both prior year and current year, if applicable, and address any goal issues in Part B.I of the SCER.

1L00 ANALYSIS OF GOALS PROGRESS

As noted earlier, to be acceptable, AAP support data must include a report of progress on prior AAP year goals. In addition, the contractor should include a report of progress on current goals if the contractor is at least six months or more into its current AAP year when it receives the Scheduling Letter. COs will use this progress report to conduct the analysis of goals progress.

a. *Data Needed.* To conduct this analysis, COs must first identify the job groups for which the contractor established goals at the beginning of the period under review. Second, COs must determine the percentage placement goal for each job group and the protected class to which it applies. Third, for each such job group, the number of total placements including hires and promotions, and the number of minority and/or female placements must be determined. If a contractor does not submit this information at the desk audit, COs will conduct the analysis below at whatever point in the review they obtain sufficient information.

b. *Analysis.* The analysis takes into consideration the number of opportunities the contractor provided in relationship to the goal. More specifically, to determine how many minorities or women the contractor would have placed if the goal were met, COs multiply the percentage placement goal by the number of placements that actually occurred. The CO then compares this result with the number of minorities or women actually placed.

If a contractor established a goal for a particular race or ethnicity, or for men or women of a particular race or ethnicity, then the CO conducts the evaluation of progress on that goal in the same fashion as in the above example. You can find additional examples in Part B.I of the SCER.

1L01 EVALUATION OF GOOD FAITH EFFORTS

An evaluation of good faith efforts includes a review of the contractor's overall performance toward goals, the identification of areas requiring additional examination, and ensuring that adequate information is available to determine good faith. Each is discussed in this subsection.

a. *Overall Performance*. In evaluating a contractor's good faith efforts, COs must first make an overall assessment of its goals and affirmative action performance.[43] For example, were there areas where goals were established but not met? This evaluation should also take into account fulfillment of AAP commitments and the quality of those commitments in terms of creative problem-solving to remove any impediments to minority and female utilization.

b. *Goal Areas Needing Further Examination for Good Faith Efforts*. Because of the analysis on goal progress, COs must identify goal areas needing further evaluation for good faith efforts.[44] For each such goal area, the COs will review any contractor description of good faith efforts pertinent to the area. This should be included as part of the contractor's report on goals. COs will also use the AAP and support data to identify the reasons for lack of progress and the type of AAP action items that would be pertinent. The below are some examples of the types of inquires a CO could pursue.

   - Do the support data on employment activity show that the jobs were filled predominantly by hires or by promotions? If by hires, was there low applicant flow?
   - What AAP commitments did the contractor make about recruitment efforts? Is there any evidence they were fulfilled?
   - Was there an adequate representation of minorities and women in probable feeder groups if the contractor filled jobs primarily by promotion?
   - What AAP commitments did the contractor make concerning the promotion process (e.g., job posting, encouraging bidding, and training)? Is there any evidence the contractor fulfilled these commitments?

1L02 PLAN FOR EVALUATION OF GOOD FAITH EFFORTS

For each goal area without sufficient information to determine good faith efforts, the CO will list the additional information needed on SCER Part B.I. For example, the contractor did not meet its goal for minorities in the Clerical I job group. However, in reviewing the data, it appears that low applicant flow is the cause. The AAP may state that the contractor will use a particular agency with a significant minority clientele to aid in the recruitment of minority applicants for the Clerical 1 job group. The additional information needed here may include contact with the agency to confirm its use by the contractor, as well as other action such as identifying additional recruitment sources while onsite.

1M BASIS FOR POTENTIAL DISCRIMINATION ANALYSES

It is OFCCP's policy, in conducting analyses of potential discrimination issues based on race, color, religion, sex or national origin under the Executive Order, to follow the principles of Title

[43] See SCER Part B.I

[44] Ibid.

VII of the Civil Rights Act of 1964, as amended, which the U.S. Equal Employment Opportunity Commission (EEOC) enforces.

When conducting analyses for minorities versus non-minorities, the term "minorities" means blacks, Hispanics, Asians/Pacific Islanders and American Indians/Alaskan Natives.[45] As used in the instructions for potential discrimination analyses that follow, "minorities" may mean those groups taken together or individually, depending on the characteristics of the labor area and patterns in the contractor's workforce. In general, when COs observe a disparity in the representation of a particular group, they conduct standard desk audit potential discrimination analyses separately for that group.[46]

a. *Guidelines on Discrimination Because of Religion or National Origin.* These Guidelines, at 41 CFR Part 60-50, are not a required AAP element under 41 CFR 60-2.10. Therefore, COs must evaluate them onsite. Chapter 2, Section 2G provides detailed guidance on conducting this aspect of the onsite review.

b. *Sex Discrimination Guidelines.* These Guidelines, at 41 CFR Part 60-20, are not a required AAP element under 41 CFR 60-2.10. The contractor's implementation of them, therefore, must be evaluated onsite. Chapter 2, Section 2H provides detailed guidance on conducting this aspect of the onsite review.

c. *Desk Audit Observation.* While the implementation of these Guidelines can only be evaluated onsite, COs must pay particular attention to any problem area identified during the desk audit for women or religious or national origin minorities. Additional information should be gathered onsite and directed to those portions of both Guidelines that are not addressed elsewhere in the regulations; for example, leave for religious purposes and maternity leave.

1N ANALYSIS OF EO 11246 AAP: AUDIT OF THE WORKFORCE ANALYSIS OR ORGANIZATIONAL PROFILE

The workforce analysis and organizational profile essentially reflect employment activity over an extended period. COs review the workforce analysis or organizational profile to determine whether minorities and females are present throughout the workforce. This review permits COs to look at individual work units or departments, or both. COs must closely examine patterns of minority and female employment in each department or work unit to identify disparities for further investigation onsite. One example of a disparity that may warrant further investigation is departments or job titles where women or minorities are either significantly over or underrepresented based on their representation in the overall workforce. COs must pay

[45] For purposes of complying with OFCCP requirements, contractors choosing to follow the current EEO-1 categories may count applicants and employees identifying as "two or more races" as minorities. (*Interim Guidance on the Use of Race and Ethnic Categories in Affirmative Action Plans*, OFCCP Directive, Transmittal 283 (Aug. 14, 2008).)

[46] See subsection 1O01 – Specific Race/Ethnic Group Analysis.

particular attention to departments and work units where minorities or women are absent or comprise nearly the entire department or unit.

1N00 UNDERREPRESENTATIONS AND CONCENTRATIONS

When examining patterns of minority group and female employment within the contractor's workforce, COs look for evidence of concentration and underrepresentation.

a. *Concentration.* The term *concentration* refers to any job titles where there are significantly high representations of a minority group or women than would be expected in consideration of their overall representation in the contractor's workforce or in a relevant unit of that workforce.

b. *Underrepresentation.* The term *underrepresentation* is the opposite of "concentration." It exists when a minority group or women are found in a particular department, job group or job title in numbers significantly lower than would be expected in light of their overall representation in the contractor's workforce or in a relevant unit of that workforce.

It is important to note that the identification of a concentration or underrepresentation does not mean that there is discrimination. It is only an indicator that further investigation is warranted.

COs must document areas of underrepresentation and concentration on Part B.II of the SCER and investigate further.

1N01 DETERMINING THE RELEVANT WORKFORCE SECTOR AND JOB AREAS

COs must review a contractor's workforce analysis to identify the concentration and underrepresentation of minorities and women. Under certain conditions, COs may reasonably expect that the contractor would evenly employ minorities or females throughout a particular job area. A "job area" is a sub-unit (e.g., department, job group, line of progression (LOP)) of the blue-collar or white-collar sectors of the contractor's workforce. The conditions for such a "reasonable expectation" are that:

- the jobs in the area have similar entry-level qualification requirements, and
- the jobs above entry-level are filled primarily by promotion.

Where these conditions exist, COs may use the Job Area Acceptance Range (JAAR) Analysis to measure job area distribution patterns. The JAAR assesses the representation of minorities and women in a particular job area in comparison with the relevant base workforce sector. A workforce sector is the total workforce of a particular job area. For example, if a contractor has 1000 employees at an establishment, and its production division is composed of four departments with a total workforce of 400 employees, then the production division is the job area and 400 employees is the workforce sector. In order for COs to conduct this analysis appropriately, they must determine the relevant workforce sectors or job areas to analyze.

a. *Relevance of Other Information.* To determine the relevant workforce sector and job areas for the analysis, COs are guided by the findings of the desk audit up to this point. For example, the information a CO obtains from the earlier analysis of EEO trends[47] may show persistent minority or female representation above or below comparable availability; or a CO may identify a substantial disparity in the representation of a particular minority group. Information the CO derived from the earlier review of the organization of the contractor's workforce and personnel practices (e.g., internal mobility, pay structure) informs the CO's analysis of workforce sector and job areas.

   The CO must conduct the Impact Ratio Analysis (IRA) on the personnel activity data provided for each job group or job title by race/ethnicity and gender.[48]

b. *Workforce Sector and Job Area.* COs must determine the appropriate sector of the contractor's workforce with which to compare minority group and female representation in the particular job(s) being examined (e.g., blue-collar, white-collar, clerical, the entire workforce, job group). To do so, COs must remember that there is a reasonable expectation that absent discrimination minorities and women will be more or less evenly distributed among the job areas within the sector. This expectation is highest when:

   - entry-level jobs in the sector require similar qualifications, and
   - the contractor primarily fills jobs above entry-level in the sector by promotion.

   The expectation may be lower if entry-level jobs in the sector are more differentiated in skill requirements. This is so because it may become more likely that minority or female availability will differ, or the contractor fills jobs above entry-level predominantly by hires.

c. *Relationship to Particular Contractor.* An appropriate definition of the workforce sector depends on the particular contractor's structure, and legitimate skill needs and personnel practices. In general, analyses that focus on where minorities and women are located organizationally,[49] and analyses that focus on the level at which minorities and women are employed[50] tend to identify potential promotion problems. These problems may be related to placement. Examples of some problems in placement, concentration or underrepresentation of employees include:

   - *Workforce as Sector or Departments as Job Area.* When there are departments or organizational units with largely similar qualifications for entry-level positions (e.g., unskilled and, to a more limited extent, semi-skilled, in blue-collar; undifferentiated trainee jobs in white-collar), COs must compare representation of women and minorities in each department with representation in the total workforce of all such departments.

---

[47] See SCER Part A.IV.

[48] See Section 1O, below.

[49] Examples include which departments, units, or lines of progression tend to identify potential placement problems.

[50] Examples include concentrations in lowest level jobs within a line of progression department.

- *Workforce as Sector or Lines of Progression as Job Area.* When there are LOP or usual promotional sequences that cut across department lines and have similar entry-level requirements, CO may compare representation of minorities and women in each LOP with representation in the total workforce of all LOPs.

- *Department as Sector or Lines of Progression within Department as Job Area.* When there are separate LOP and/or usual promotional sequences within a department or similar organizational unit, COs may compare representation in each LOP with the representation in the department as a whole.

- *Department as Sector or Jobs within Department as Job Area.* In the absence of LOPs or usual promotional sequences, and where jobs within a department are usually filled by promotion from within or might reasonably be filled in such a manner based on the nature of the jobs and the training the contractor could reasonably be expected to offer, COs may compare representation in a particular job area within that department with representation in the department as a whole.

- *EEO-1 Job Category as Sector or Type of Job as Job Area.* It can be useful to compare representation in an EEO-1 job category or job group with the distribution within specific titles in that category or group, or both. For example, in an Office and Clerical category, women may be concentrated in General Clerical positions, but underrepresented in Production and Material Control clerical jobs.

- *Lines of Progression as Sector or Jobs in Lines of Progression as Job Area.* The CO may also treat a LOP or usual promotional sequence, particularly one with a large number of incumbents, as a comparative workforce sector. Minority or female, or both, representation in the LOP can be compared with their representation in jobs at different levels in the LOP.

- *Job Title as Sector or Job Title within Department as Job Area.* When a job title, particularly one with a large number of total incumbents, appears in several departments, COs can compare representation in the title as a whole with representation in the title in each department.

d. *Applicability to Both White-Collar and Blue-Collar Jobs.* COs can apply these analyses to white-collar and blue-collar situations. In all cases, COs must ensure that the sector of the contractor's workforce that they use as a basis for comparison with a particular job area is, in fact, relevant. Particularly in the white-collar area, differences with respect to factors such as the need for specialized education or skills may make establishing a basis for comparison difficult.

e. *Determining "Substantially."* Once COs select the job area and the relevant workforce sector, the next step is to perform the analysis and identify those job areas which have "substantially" more or fewer minorities and women than would reasonably be expected by their representation in the workforce sector selected. The COs will investigate these job areas, in addition to any other indicators identified, statistical or otherwise, onsite.

1N02 ANALYSIS BASED ON A PARTICULAR RACE OR ETHNICITY

If a CO's review of the contractor's EEO job category data (SCER Part A.IV) shows substantial disparities in the representation of a particular race or ethnic group in the workforce as a whole, or in their distribution among job categories, the review of the workforce analysis should include a focus on that race or ethnic group. This is especially the case in those job areas where a CO observed disparity.

For example, if category data show that American Indians were concentrated in the Laborers category, poorly represented in Operatives and absent in Crafts, the CO's review of the workforce analysis must:

- specifically identify the types of blue-collar jobs in which American Indians are employed, and
- determine whether these jobs fall into lines of progression or departments or units, or both, that tend to inhibit progression to Operatives and Crafts, etc.

Even when a CO does not observe these disparities in the initial category screen, the CO must be alert for indications of potential problems in the distribution of the particular racial or ethnic groups while reviewing the workforce analysis. This is especially necessary if the labor area has high representation of more than one race or ethnic group, or the general employment patterns in the industry involved differ among specific race or ethnic groups. It is worth noting that both situations may exist simultaneously and could give rise to indicators of a potential problem.

1O ANALYSIS OF EO 11246 AAP: AUDIT OF PERSONNEL ACTIVITY AND THE IMPACT RATIO ANALYSIS

Although related, a CO must not confuse adverse IRAs with the term "adverse impact."[51] The Impact Ratio Analysis (IRA) is a method for identifying personnel activity that should be investigated further onsite. The IRA is a ratio between two selection rates, one for minorities or women, and one for others. Generally, if the seletion rate for a particular group is less than 80% of the selection rate for the favored group for a particular personnel activity,[52] (e.g., the selection rate for minorities or women is less than 80% the selection rate for non-minorities or men for a particular personnel activity), a CO must investigate further during the onsite.

1O00 CALCULATING THE IRA

COs must ensure that contractors submit personnel activity data according to OFCCP's requirements as specified in Itemized Listing of the Scheduling Letter. They must conduct an IRA of the data of all job groups or job titles by gender and minority to non-minority.

---

[51] 41 CFR 60-3.4.

[52] Examples of activities are hiring, promotion and termination.

For analysis of gender and minority to nonminority, the impact ratio is the ratio between the selection rates for the favored and nonfavored groups. The favored group is whichever group has the highest selection rate for a positive personnel activity like hiring or promotion, or the lowest selection rate for a negative personnel activity. Examples of negative personnel activity include termination and layoff. When an analysis of the personnel activity data comparing race or ethnicity, or both, indicates that a group is selected at a substantially lower rate than the favored group, a subgroup analysis by individual race and ethnic categories is necessary.[53] The IRA is determined by:

- Calculating the selection rate for each group by dividing the number of people selected from a group by the number of applicants from that group.
- Observing which group has the highest selection rate.
- Calculating the impact ratios by comparing the selection rate for each group with that of the highest group. Do this by dividing the selection rate for a group by selection rate for the highest group.
- Observing whether the selection rate for any group is substantially less (i.e., usually less than four-fifths or 80 percent) than the selection rate for the highest group.

Below is an example using the appropriate formulas.

Step 1: Calculate the rate of selection for each group (round off to two decimal places).

$$\frac{10 \text{ (women selected)}}{100 \text{ (women applied)}} = .10 \text{ (10\% selection rate)}$$

$$\frac{30 \text{ (men selected)}}{100 \text{ (men applied)}} = .30 \text{ (30\% selection rate)}$$

Step 2: Observe which group has the highest selection rate.
Men are the most favored group because they have the highest selection rate (30% men is a higher rate than 10% women).

Step 3: Calculate the impact ratio for the two groups. Since this is a positive action, the most favored group's rate (in this case men) is in the denominator position.

$$\frac{.10 \text{ (selection rate for women)}}{.30 \text{ (selection rate for men)}} = 0.33 \text{ (impact ratio)}$$

Step 4: Observe whether the impact ratio in Step 3 is less than 80%. If the selection rate for one group is less than 80% of that for another, the CO considers the IRA adverse.

[53] See subsection 1O01 – Specific Race/Ethnic Group Analysis.

The CO will investigate adverse IRA(s) when analysis or evidence indicates that it is nececcsary. Prior to scheduling an onsite review, the CO should obtain from the contractor any additional data that are needed in order to conduct offsite analyses prior to the onsite visit. [54] During the onsite, the CO will ask the contractor to provide a breakdown of the personnel activity data by individual race or ethnic categories for the job groups or job titles at issue. This breakdown can also be done by both race and ethnicity. In examining data, the CO pays particular attention to IRAs in those areas where review of the workforce analysis showed marked underrepresentation or concentration of minorities or women, or both.

1O01 SPECIFIC RACE AND ETHNIC GROUP ANALYSIS

When the personnel activity data is provided by race or ethnicity, or both, COs must conduct individual IRAs for each race or ethnic group. For example, if data shows that Hispanics are persistently absent from the workforce, COs must calculate separate hiring IRAs for each job group for Hispanics. Similarly, if blacks were concentrated in the entry level Laborer group, but poorly represented or absent in the higher level Operatives and Crafts groups, COs must conduct separate IRAs for blue-collar job groups, particularly for promotions and hires into Operatives and Crafts.

Even when COs do not observe substantial disparities during the initial screen of a contractor's workforce, they must be alert for any indications of potential problems in the selection of particular racial or ethnic groups, or both. Such indicators include situations where the labor area has a high representation of more than one minority group, or the general employment patterns for racial or ethnic groups, or both, in the industry involved differ from the contractor's workforce.

1O02 PROPER USE OF THE IRA RESULTS

It is important to remember that an adverse IRA is only a preliminary indicator of a potential discrimination problem. It is not proof, in and of itself, of discrimination or of the existence of an affected class. For example, a CO may compute an adverse IRA in a job group using an insufficiently refined candidate pool. Only further statistical analysis or further investigation onsite, or both, can determine whether discrimination has occurred.

1O03 IRA, STATISTICAL ANALYSIS SUMMARY AND ONSITE PLAN

When COs identify adverse IRAs, they must request additional data from the contractor for further statistical analysis. If the statistical analysis confirms that the statistical disparities exist and further investigation is needed, COs must describe the problem on SCER Part B.II and indicate that the matter needs further investigation onsite to determine whether there is discrimination.

---

[54] The standard deviation represents the distribution of the responses or data around the mean, and is often used to measure the amount of confidence in statistical conclusions. COs may run standard deviation analyses to determine whether and what types of additional information they may need to establish potential discrimination.

a. *Contractor Adverse Impact Determinations (Contractors with 100 or More Employees).*

- *Maintenance of Records.* As noted earlier in the discussion of the acceptability of support data, the UGESP require contractors with 100 or more employees to maintain specific records by job title that are sufficient to disclose whether its selection procedures have an adverse impact on the employment opportunities of each sex, and each race or ethnic group, or both. The race and ethnic groups include blacks, American Indians/Alaskan Natives, Asians/Pacific Islanders, Hispanics and whites.[55]

- *Analysis of Impact.* UGESP also requires that contractors with 100 or more employees annually analyze this data to determine whether the total selection process for each job is having any adverse impact. These determinations are required by sex and for each race and ethnic group (e.g., black, Hispanic, Asian/Pacific Islander, American Indian/Alaskan Native, white) that constitutes 2% or more of the labor force in the relevant labor area or 2% or more of the applicable workforce for jobs filled internally.

b. *Requesting Contractor Determinations.* When a CO identifies a job group with an adverse IRA, and the contractor employs 100 or more people, the CO will ask the contractor to furnish the adverse impact determinations prepared during the evaluated period as a part of its in-depth analyses for the job titles that fall within the job group. This assumes, of course, that the contractor has not already provided this information. For example, if the adverse IRA is for female hires into a Professionals job group, the contractor should submit its adverse impact determinations for the hiring of women in each title within the Professionals group. This will assist the CO in determining whether the IRA and other statistical analyses need to be refined before investigating further. A CO may also request the contractor's adverse impact analyses in other areas. For example, a review of the workforce analysis showed a concentration or underrepresentation suggesting a potential placement problem. The contractor provided personnel activity data by job group and it does not show placements into the titles of concern. In response, a CO must request the contractor's adverse impact analyses for hires, promotions and transfers into the job titles at issue. When appropriate, the CO may also ask to review the contractor's adverse impact analyses and/or may ask the contractor to identify those jobs where its analyses showed adverse impact.

c. *Need for Information about the Selection Process.* When the hiring, promotion or termination IRA for a job group or job title indicates that further investigation is needed, the CO must ask the contractor to provide a description of how the employment selections are made for positions in the job group or job title at issue. The description should include the steps in the process. For each step, the contractor should provide the data for each selection step, the decision makers, the criteria used, a description of how the criteria are used, and the records maintained. In addition, when a job group is under investigation, the CO should ask whether the selection process as a whole or individual steps apply to all of the job titles in the job group, and whether the process was the same throughout the entire duration of the review period. It is also helpful for the CO to know whether the process applies to other job groups or titles in addition to the group or title at issue. Steps may include, for example, review of

---

[55] 41 CFR 60-3.4 and 41 CFR 60-3.15.

application forms by the human resources representative, written tests, formal or informal interviews, physical examinations and on-the-job tests. The CO will plan to verify the contractor's statements through review of records, interviews with applicants and employees and, if possible, observation of the process by which applicants are screened and selected.

d. *Multi-Component Selection Processes - Contractor Obligations.*

- *Adverse Impact in Total Selection Process.* When the contractor submits its adverse impact analyses for desk audit, if the analysis shows adverse impact in the total selection process for a job group or job title, UGESP requires the contractor to evaluate the individual components of the total selection process for adverse impact. Therefore, in a multi-step and/or multi-criterion selection process with adverse impact, the CO must plan to request the contractor's records showing at what step(s) and/or by what criteria members of non-favored race/ethnicity or gender group(s) the contractor is disproportionately screening out, as well as any validity studies the contractor conducted of its selection procedures.

- *No Adverse Impact in Total Selection Process.* Generally, if the total selection process for a job does not have an adverse impact, a contractor will not usually be expected to evaluate the individual components for adverse impact or to validate those individual components, and enforcement action will not usually be warranted based on a component.

There are, however, several exceptions: when enforcement appears warranted and with individual complaints of discrimination.

- *Exception 1: When Enforcement May Be Warranted.* In some circumstances, even though there is no adverse impact in the total selection process, further investigation and, possibly, enforcement action may nonetheless be appropriate when an individual component has an adverse impact (e.g., height and weight requirements) and its use is not justified as job-related and consistent with business necessity.

- *Exception 2: Individual Complaints of Discrimination.* The "bottom line" standard – that a contractor need not evaluate the individual components of a selection process if the process as a whole does not result in adverse impact – does not preclude the investigation of complaints alleging race, ethnicity or gender discrimination caused by a component of a selection process.[56] The standard does not preclude investigating complaints alleging that a selection process or criterion screened out one or more individuals on the basis of disability.

1P ANALYSIS OF EO 11246 AAP: AUDIT OF COMPENSATION DATA

[56] See Questions and Answers Nos. 25 and 26 in Adoption of Questions and Answers to Clarify and Provide a Common Interpretation of the Uniform Guidelines on Employee Selection Procedures.

The compensation analysis is an indispensable part of OFCCP's task to enforce the nondiscrimination requirements of Executive Order 11246. COs must make sure that the data submitted for such analysis satisfy OFCCP's requirements.

1P00 DATA FOR COMPENSATION ANALYSIS

Upon receipt of a contractor's AAP and supporting compensation data, COs must confirm that the submitted compensation data, regardless of format, satisfies the requirements of the Scheduling Letter.[57] COs must also make sure that the data identify whether or not the compensation is set pursuant to a collective bargaining agreement.

If the submitted data do not meet the requirements of the Scheduling Letter, COs must determine whether the data can still be analyzed using OFCCP's compensation procedures. If the provided data cannot be examined under OFCCP's procedures, COs will contact the contractor to discuss the deficiency and, if necessary, request that the compensation data be resubmitted in accordance with the requirements of the Scheduling Letter.

During the desk audit and any ensuing onsite review, CO will also consider "other information" such as:

- an explanation or description of the contractor's compensation systems, and
- a description of internal compensation pay practices and policies (e.g., policies and practices regarding setting wages or salaries at hire, additions to regular pay including overtime, guidance on employee performance, the administration of bonuses or commissions, market survey data analyses, collective bargaining pay requirements, job descriptions and self-audit results).

Upon receipt of the data, a desk audit is conducted. OFCCP may continue to request and review additional compensation data, and conduct an onsite review, before making a final determination regarding compliance. During the desk audit and at subsequent stages of the compliance evaluation, the CO should communicate with the contractor, as appropriate, to ask clarifying questions about the materials submitted, interpret codes or categories used in the data, identify any missing or incomplete information, and to request additional information as needed. The CO should obtain all such information as early in the process as possible.

If the contractor fails to comply with the requirements of the Scheduling Letter within the agreed upon timeframe, a SCN must be issued in most instances.[58]

1P01 ACTION BASED ON THE DESK AUDIT RESULTS

Once the contractor provides the appropriate pay data, COs will conduct the initial desk audit analysis of compensation data. COs may take one of two actions based on the desk audit results:

---

[57] See Figure F-2 – OFCCP Scheduling Letter and Itemized Listing.

[58] See Chapter 8 – Resolution of Noncompliance.

a. *Closing the Compensation Review.* If the CO determines that there is no evidence or indicators of potential compensation discrimination, and that no further data or information is needed to make that determination, the CO may recommend closing, the compensation review portion of the compliance evaluation.

b. *Continuing the Compensation Review.* If the desk audit indicates potential compensation discrimination, COs must record such findings in Part C of the SCER:

1P02 REQUESTING ADDITIONAL DATA OR INFORMATION

In cases where OFCCP begins a review with summary compensation data, the CO may request additional employee level data for the entire workforce for a more in-depth analysis. Situations where it is appropriate to request additional employee level data include, but are not limited to, indicators or evidence of potential compensation discrimination based on summary data, indicators or evidence of discrimination with respect to another employment practice, complaints or anecdotal evidence, data integrity issues, reviews for quality audit purposes, or any review where more data or information is needed to make a compliance determination.

A CO may also need to request additional information to understand how to analyze or interpret either summary or employee level data before determining whether to proceed with or close the desk audit.

1Q SCER SUMMARY OF POTENTIAL DISCRIMINATION AREAS AND ONSITE INVESTIGATIVE PLAN (ALL LAWS)

All potential discrimination problems that a CO identifies during the desk audit must be summarized on Part A.I (Past Problems/Known Complaints), Part B.II (Other Problems For Investigation), and Part C (Problems Identified) of the SCER. These include any problems the CO identifies in the review of the Section 503 and Section 4212 AAP(s), any problems the CO identifies by the review of the contractor's online application process and any problems the CO identifies during the review and analyses of the Executive Order AAP and support data.

For each potential discrimination problem a CO identifies an onsite investigative plan must be developed. If the CO finds indicators of what appears to be a single potential discrimination problem through more than one analysis such as an area of minority concentration with an adverse IRA for minority promotions out of the area, the CO only needs to describe the problem once in the onsite plan.

The onsite plan should be as specific as possible, and will set priorities for the documents to be gathered. For example, if the IRA indicates a potential problem in minority hires into a particular job group, the actions to be taken while onsite should include interviewing the people, reviewing applications and personnel files, and obtaining information.[59]

[59]Chapter 2, Subsection 2C03 – Onsite Plan.

1R CONCLUSION OF THE DESK AUDIT

If a CO completes the desk audit and no problem areas are found, no outstanding questions remain, and no violations are identified then the evaluation is closed at the desk audit stage. If the CO found non-substantive problems, such as an unacceptable AAP element, the CO may close the compliance evaluation after all the identified problems are adequately resolved.

In order to close the compliance evaluation after the desk audit, the CO must ensure that no outstanding substantive issues exist. As previously noted, the CO may need to request additional materials from the contractor for review during the desk audit. For example, the CO may need to ask for information on protected veterans to address the extent of affirmative action efforts on their behalf, substantive documentation of good faith efforts for job groups where the contractor has established goals, or an employee roster in order to conduct appropriate compensation analyses.

1R00 DOCUMENTS FOR CLOSING COMPLIANCE EVALUATION AFTER THE DESK AUDIT

When closing a compliance evaluation after a desk audit, the CO will use one of the following closure letters:

a. A finding of no violations leads to issuance of a closure letter.[60]

b. A finding of minor technical violations, but no indicators of potential discrimination or lack of good faith efforts, leads to issuance of a closure letter, referencing the violations and their remedies.[61]

The appropriate supervisor must sign the closure letter (e.g., District Director or his or her designee) and send the letter to the contractor by first-class mail.

1R01 REASONS TO PROCEED WITH ONSITE REVIEW

The CO must proceed with an onsite review if:

- the contractor provided insufficient data to conclude the review at the desk audit stage;
- there are indicators of potential discrimination, failure to provide a completed AAP, complaints or problems that merit an onsite review; or
- the contractor has been identified for a complete compliance review in accordance with specific OFCCP selection procedures.

---

[60] See Letter L-4 –Notice Closing Compliance Evaluation No Violations Found.
[61] Ibid.

An onsite review is required before a Notice of Violation is issued. In instances where problems are resolved through a document submission during the desk audit, the CO's onsite review may consist of technical assistance to ensure that the contractor is aware of its obligations.[62]

1R02 COMPLETING APPROPRIATE SCER PAGES

COs must complete a SCER for every compliance evaluation. The stage at which the compliance evaluation is closed and the type of investigative procedures used in the compliance evaluation will determine which sections of the SCER COs must complete. In some evaluations, they may not be able to complete certain sections of the SCER; however, they must complete as much of the SCER as possible.

[62] Chapter 2, Section 2I – Technical Requirements.

CHAPTER 2
ONSITE REVIEW

2A INTRODUCTION

This chapter describes the procedures COs follow when conducting the onsite review of a compliance evaluation for a supply and service contractor. During an onsite review, COs gather data and information from the contractor, employees, applicants and others to better assess the contractor's compliance with the regulations implementing EO 11246, Section 4212 and Section 503,[63] and with any other appropriate mandates.[64] This chapter provides guidance to COs on how to prepare for, conduct and conclude an onsite review.

The nature and scope of the onsite review in each instance will vary depending on the type of compliance evaluation a CO is conducting. They may also vary depending on whether the CO has already identified potential problems. As noted in Chapter 1, Desk Audit, a compliance evaluation may consist of any one or any combination of the following investigative procedures.[65]

- *Compliance Review.* A comprehensive analyses and evaluation of the hiring and employment practices of the contractor, the written AAP, and the results of their affirmative action efforts. This procedure may proceed in three stages: desk audit, onsite review, and offsite analysis.
- *Offsite Review of Records.* An analysis and evaluation of the affirmative action program (AAP), or any part thereof, and supporting documentation.
- *Compliance Check.* A determination of whether the contractor maintained appropriate records consistent with 41 CFR 60-1.12, 41 CFR 60-250.80, 41 CFR 60-300.80 and 41 CFR 60-741.80. At the contractor's option, the contractor may provide the documents onsite or offsite.

---

[63] The regulations implementing the EO 11246 applicable to supply and service contractors are at 41 CFR Part 60-1, Obligations of Contractors and Subcontractors; 41 CFR Part 60-2, Affirmative Action Programs; and 41 CFR Part 60-3, Uniform Guidelines on Employee Selection Procedures. Part 60-20 contains the Guidelines on Sex Discrimination; and Part 60-50 contains the Guidelines on Discrimination Because of Religion or National Origin. Section 4212 implementing regulations are at 41 CFR Parts 60-250 and 60-300, and the regulations implementing Section 503 are at 41 CFR Part 60-741.

[64] When onsite OFCCP is responsible for assessing a contractor's compliance with Executive Order 13496, if applicable.

[65] 41 CFR 60-1.20, 41 CFR 60-250.60, 41 CFR 60-300.60 and 41 CFR 741.60.

- *Focused Review*. An onsite review that is restricted to one or more components of the contractor's organization, or one or more aspects of the contractor's employment practices.

Of the four options, the compliance review is the most common and is typically the most comprehensive. For this reason, this chapter focuses on the specific procedures COs follow when conducting an onsite review as a part of a compliance review.[66] There are generally four major tasks in an onsite review:

- investigating potential problem areas the CO identified at a desk audit;
- verifying the contractor's implementation of its AAP(s) or its assertions regarding its personnel activity and employment practices, or both;
- investigating matters that cannot be fully examined at the desk audit; and
- initiating resolution of identified violations.

The onsite review principles discussed in this chapter also provide guidance for performing an onsite review as part of other types of reviews. If the compliance evaluation is of a contractor that maintains a FAAP then the evaluation will essentially be the same as the other processes. A possible addition is onsite visits to more than one location to address all of the components of the FAAP. Chapter 5 discusses FAAP reviews in more detail.

The onsite portion of a review, a preaward compliance evaluation of a supply and service contractor only covers the contractor's compliance with EO 11246 unless it is converted to a postaward review.[67] The purpose of a preaward compliance evaluation is to determine whether a bidder, prospective prime contractor or proposed subcontractor will be able to comply with the provisions of the EO 11246 equal opportunity clause. COs conduct a postaward review in the same manner as a compliance review under 41 CFR 60-1.20(a)(1), 41 CFR 60-250.60(a)(1), 41 CFR 60-300.60(a)(1) and 41 CFR 60-741.60(a)(1) and they must cover a contractor's compliance with EO 11246, Section 503 and Section 4212.

Lastly, complaint investigations include an onsite review that responds to the specific allegations raised in the complaint unless OFCCP converts a class complaint into a full compliance review. Complaint investigations are discussed in detail in Chapter 6, Complaint Investigations.

---

[66] In light of their more limited scope, focused reviews and compliance checks may not always include all of the elements discussed in this chapter.

[67] A preaward compliance evaluation is subject to specific timeframes and is conducted prior to the award of a nonconstruction contract of $10 million or more. See 41 CFR 60-1.20(d). The preaward review requirement applies to both current and prospective contractors and to their first-tier subcontractors with proposed subcontracts of $10 million or more. Directive 223, issued Apr. 15, 1998, provides additional detail on preaward clearance procedures.

2B DETERMINING THE NEED FOR AN ONSITE REVIEW

When OFCCP schedules a contractor for a compliance evaluation, the compliance evaluation may use any one or a combination of investigative procedures, including a full or a focused compliance review, an off-site review of records or a compliance check. Onsite reviews are a part of each full or focused compliance review. COs determine whether to conduct an onsite review in conjunction with an off-site review of records or a compliance check, based on the circumstances of the evaluation and the outcome of the initial review. For example, if a CO finds indicators of compliance problems during a limited compliance check, the CO may expand the compliance check to a full compliance review.

In some instances, an onsite review may not be necessary. One example exists when the desk audit findings are that the required AAPs are acceptable and, for other reasons, the CO is not conducting an onsite review. With the approval of a supervisor, the CO may conclude the compliance evaluation with an offsite review of records.

2C ONSITE REVIEW PREPARATION

When conducting an onsite review COs are neutral fact finders and official representatives of the Federal Government. Consequently, COs must be unbiased in the identification and examination of all data and information that contributes to the full understanding of the contractor's employment practices and affirmative action efforts. They must attempt to verify assertions made by the contractor regarding its affirmative action efforts, personnel activity and employment practices.

Before going onsite, COs must review a contractor's compliance evaluation and complaint history, develop an Onsite Plan, and provide advance notice of the onsite review to the contractor. A part of a CO's preparation includes sound information management and an awareness of employee concerns surrounding employee retaliation. The subsections below discuss these and other preparatory steps.

2C00 PROHIBITION AGAINST RETALIATION

COs must be concerned with gaining information that makes the onsite review useful to answering the question of whether the contractor complied with its obligations. If employees are afraid of cooperating for fear of retaliation, the onsite review could be compromised. COs should, therefore, take specific actions to notify and protect employees.

COs, when onsite, must inform the contractor's managers, employees and applicants that individuals exercising their rights under OFCCP's laws have protections from retaliation. Specifically, the regulations implementing EO 11246, Section 503 and Section 4212 prohibit interference and intimidation of any individual exercising his or her rights under OFCCP's laws. The CO must give this notice to the contractor at the entrance and exit conferences, and include it as a part of any interview conducted during the onsite review.

The prohibition against interference and intimidation includes threats, coercion, harassment and discrimination. Retaliation may take the form of adverse employment actions such as termination, demotion, failure to hire and harassment. As with interference and intimidation, contractors may not retaliate against an individual for exercising his or her rights under the laws enforced by OFCCP. Specific activities protected from contractor interference, intimidation and retaliation include:

- filing a complaint;
- assisting or participating in an investigation, compliance evaluation, hearing, or any other activity related to the administration of the EO 11246, Section 503 and Section 4212 or other EEO laws;
- opposing any act or practice that violates any of these EEO laws; and
- exercising any other right afforded them by these laws.

2C01 USE OF THE STANDARD COMPLIANCE EVALUATION REPORT AND INFORMATION MANAGEMENT

a. *The Standard Compliance Evaluation Report (SCER).* The SCER documents the scope, progress and results of an onsite review.[68] It also includes notes confirming that a contractor met its obligations or describing any problem areas the CO identified during the desk audit, offsite analysis and onsite review. A CO may not be able to complete the desk audit portion of the SCER because the quality of the desk audit data is inadequate or was insufficient. In this example, the CO's initial task during the onsite review is to complete the desk audit portion of the SCER. You will find a copy of the SCER and instructions for completing it in Appendices A-1 SCER and A-2 SCER Instructions.

   With a full understanding of the contractor's employment practices and affirmative action efforts, a CO may identify new problems or find that the contractor resolved previously identified problems. COs must describe problems identified during the onsite review and record any recommendations for corrective actions to resolved problems.

b. *Obtaining and Maintaining Records.* All communications and information COs gather during the compliance evaluation must remain in the case file. Examples of information or data a CO might gather are data and record submissions by the contractor; information gathered from other sources such as applicants and employees; and interviews with contractor officials, employees and others. This includes all information obtained during the onsite review. In addition, COs must document their activities and communications in

[68] COs will not use all the pages of the SCER in every evaluation. Rather, which sections of the SCER are appropriate to each review will depend on the type of compliance evaluation. However, COs must complete all relevant SCER pages and sections.

connection with the onsite review in the compliance evaluation or complaint Chronology Log.[69]

These are several of the general principles for properly maintaining records:

- Every document collected during the review, even if it does not support the ultimate finding, is included in the case file. This includes both paper and electronic documents.

- All e-mail and other written communications must be dated, identify the individuals participating in the communication, and accurately reflect any agreed upon commitments. For example, the e-mails in a CO and contractor e-mail exchange on possible dates for the onsite review would reflect the CO's name and position, the name and position of the contractor's representative, the dates discussed and the dates for the onsite review that were agreed on.

- Original documents submitted by contractors or otherwise obtained by COs must not be altered. Alterations, including notes made by a CO, should be made on working copies.

- Interview statements, whether obtained by a CO in person or by telephone, must remain in the case file. These statements must include the name and position of the person conducting the interview, the name of the person interviewed and his or her title or position, the date and time of the interview, and the location of the interview. COs must also note if other people were present during the interview like the legal counsel or a personal representative. Interviewees should review and sign the CO's interview notes and typed statement indicating that they are accurate. Section 2M of this chapter provides specific information on interviews.

- Information obtained during interviews and a CO's observations must be reduced to writing as soon as feasible. The CO must type handwritten notes, using MS Word, before placing them in the case file.

- Supporting evidence must be in a clearly labeled section of the case file. Supporting evidence may include the CO's notes, worksheets, contractor data and any other material related to specific problem areas identified by the CO.

2C02 HISTORICAL DATA AND COMPLAINT HISTORY

Prior to going onsite, COs must check the electronic Case Management System (CMS) and the Executive Information System (EIS) to obtain a list of prior compliance evaluations of the establishment and identify any issues found in the previous OFCCP reviews. This information

---

[69] See Chapter 1, subsections 1B01 – Preparation and Maintenance of the Case Chronology Log; 1B02 – Creation and Maintenance of the Case File and Figure F-1 Case Chronology Log for additional information regarding the case file and Chronology Log.

may be useful when determining what information a CO wants to obtain or examine during the onsite review. If the CO previously performed this task as part of a related desk audit, the CO must review this information as part of the preparation for the onsite review. If OFCCP obtained a CA in a prior review, the CO must use the onsite visit to confirm that the contractor took and maintained the required corrective actions. If the purpose of the onsite review is to address questions that arose as part of the monitoring of a CA, the CO must develop an investigative plan that addresses those specific questions.

If COs do not already have information regarding discrimination complaints filed against the contractor with other agencies, they must contact the Equal Employment Opportunity Commission (EEOC) and the appropriate state or local fair employment practice (FEP) agencies to ascertain the existence, nature and scope of any complaints. COs must include the replies or information obtained from these agencies in the case file and incorporate them, as appropriate, into the onsite plan.[70] In addition, COs must check the Department of Labor's enforcement database[71] for information on the compliance posture of the establishment and the VETS-100 database.

2C03 ONSITE PLAN

An onsite plan is an important step, and COs must develop one prior to each onsite review. Although the scope of the onsite review may change as a result of the onsite observations and evidence, the onsite plan serves as the initial outline or "road map" for conducting the onsite review.

The onsite plan must include each problem area identified during a desk audit and described on the SCER in Part A. For each problem area, the onsite plan must identify or describe the data and records the CO will obtain and review, interviews that the CO will conduct, and any other known relevant materials the CO will review while onsite. For example, additional information may include materials related to the desk audit findings like personnel records, payroll records, applications and resumes, and materials not included in the original submission like employment advertisements, position descriptions. Interviewees might include the human resources manager, selection officials andr applicants for promotion.

The onsite plan must also include a list of technical items, such as the posting of the equal employment opportunity poster, that the CO will verify while onsite. Additionally, the plan must identify field office staff who will participate in the onsite review, and their roles and responsibilities. The onsite plan must also include the projected dates for the onsite review, as discussed with the contractor.

If a CO is going onsite as part of a focused review, the onsite plan will reflect the more limited scope of this type of review. Similarly, if a CO is going onsite to conduct a compliance check the onsite plan will be narrower. This is because the plan will not encompass all of the elements

---

[70] See Letters L-1 for a sample letter requesting complaint data from EEOC and state and local FEPS.

[71] See http://www.dol.gov/enforcementdata (last accessed September 2011). Chapter 1, subsections 1B05 and 1B06 also include discussions on gathering information from the EEOC and other agencies.

of an onsite plan that the CO would develop for a full review. When conducting a compliance check, COs must use the Compliance Check Control Sheet to record whether the contractor maintained the appropriate records or whether the contractor needs to provide additional information and documentation.[72]

2C04 NOTICE OF THE ONSITE DATE AND REQUESTS FOR ADDITIONAL INFORMATION

In preparation for the onsite review, the CO must contact the contractor, or the contractor's representative, to schedule the onsite review, request any additional information, and identify the contractor officials who will need to be available during the onsite visit. The CO must also inform the contractor that he or she may need additional information and interviews as the onsite review progresses. Having such a discussion prior to the onsite visit provides the contractor with time to locate and make available requested information and interviewees. It also provides notice that the CO may make additional requests for data and interviews.

The CO must provide the contractor with written confirmation of the onsite date(s) and time(s) at least three business days prior to the onsite. This confirmation must also include requests for other data and information that the CO is aware of at that time. The confirmation is sent to the contractor by certified mail, return receipt requested; however, a courtesy copy may be sent by e-mail or facsimile.

2D ONSITE PROCESS

The onsite review typically includes three important phases: entrance conference, facility inspection, and access to contractor records. However, other information may also be gathered. Each phase has its own unique challenges for COs and those related to the entrance conference, facility inspection and access to contractor records are discussed in the following subsections.

2D00 ENTRANCE CONFERENCE

The onsite review typically begins with an entrance conference with the CEO or highest ranking official in charge of the facility, his or her representative, and senior officials who are responsible for implementing the AAP(s). The entrance conference will provide general information to the CEO and explain the purposes of the compliance evaluation. During this conference, a CO will provide:

- a summary of the contractor's obligations under the programs administered by OFCCP,
- a description of the scope of the onsite review and the length of time that the CO anticipates being onsite, and

[72] See Figure F-3 – Compliance Check Control Sheet.

- a description of the information needed while onsite.

A CO must also advise the contractor of the need to conduct confidential employee interviews. During the conference, the CO will inform the CEO of the need to meet again to discuss tentative findings of the investigation and any outstanding requests for data and information.[73]

2D01 FACILITY INSPECTION

The facility inspection is an opportunity for COs to observe and evaluate the working conditions in departments or other organizational units of a contractor's establishment. It is also an opportunity to observe the composition and concentration of groups by race or ethnicity, or both. In addition, COs all have an opportunity to observe the composition and concentration of groups by sex and disability within the workforce. COs also use the inspection process to observe work performed in different job titles and to conduct brief focused interviews with supervisors and employees in order to obtain information about the facility and the work performed there. The CO will also conduct more formal interviews of supervisors, employees and the top union official, as appropriate, during the onsite visit.

By observing how employees complete their work, particularly in any job titles identified as problem areas, COs develop a better understanding of the functions and conditions of the job positions. This contributes to a CO's ability to make decisions and assess matters such as the relationship of certain job criteria to selecting individuals for certain jobs. For example, if females are underrepresented in a particular job title for which "the ability to lift 50 pounds" is a selection criterion, a CO may observe that the job is done with the use of mechanical equipment that performs the lifting rather than the employee. Further, the CO may observe that employees rarely lift 50 pounds without assistance from another employee. This observation allows the CO to question the contractor regarding:

- the timing and nature of the development of the selection criterion,
- the assessment that the criterion is job-related and consistent with business necessity,
- the changes in the selection process since the criterion's development,
- the point in the selection process when the selection criterion is applied, and
- the contractor's assessment of the validity of the selection criterion as a measure of whether an applicant can perform the job.

A facility inspection also allows COs to make observations regarding possible physical accessibility issues. COs must note whether there are physical barriers to applicants and employees. The presence of physical barriers does not mean that disability discrimination exists. Rather, a CO may use this opportunity to provide compliance assistance on providing reasonable

[73] See also 2C00 – Prohibition Against Retaliation.

accommodation to individuals with disabilities and disabled veterans. The CO may also ask about the contractor's process for receiving and handling requests for accommodation.

During the inspection, COs must visually confirm the posting of equal employment opportunity (EEO) posters and policy statements. Contractors are required to conspicuously display the *Equal Opportunity is the Law* poster, and EO 13496 requires that covered contractors post the prescribed notice of employee rights under the National Labor Relations Act.[74] Additionally, COs must observe and question, as appropriate, how the contractor provides notice to employees of the location and hours of availability of Section 4212 and Section 503 AAPs.[75] A CO must take notes during the inspection to record his or her observations, or record the observations immediately following the inspection. The CO must type handwritten notes, using MS Word, before placing them in the case file. During the inspection or during off-site analysis, the CO may verify required electronic postings. The CO must document his or her observations and findings in the SCER.

In appropriate circumstances, COs may also take photographs. However, if a contractor objects to the CO taking photographs, the CO must contact the District Office to discuss the contractor's concern.

2D02 ACCESS TO CONTRACTOR RECORDS

The agency's regulations require contractors to provide COs access to the contractor's books, records and accounts for the purpose of determining the contractor's compliance with the laws administered by OFCCP. When a CO knows that he or she will likely need to obtain copies of materials, the CO must initiate a discussion with the contractor regarding the need to obtain copies of materials prior to the onsite review. Working out the logistics for obtaining copies of requested materials prior to the onsite review may help the CO avoid conflicts. This may also be useful when scheduling the time needed to obtain copies of requested materials. If requested materials are available electronically, in a compatible format, the CO must accept the materials in electronic form. The CO must ensure that all requested data is present within the various materials.

Some of the types of records a CO will request and obtain prior to or during the onsite visit include:

- job applications for every applicant for the jobs at issue,
- personnel files,
- relevant payroll and HRIS data,
- labor agreements,

---

[74] See subsections 2I00 – Technical Requirements of EO 11246, Section 4212, and Section 503; Chapter 2, subsection 2I01 – EO 13496 Requirements.

[75] See 41 CFR 60-250.41, 41 CFR 300.41 and 41 CFR 741.41.

- policy and compensation manuals,
- directives,
- company newsletters, and
- posted job opening announcements.

COs must photocopy, digitize, transcribe or summarize pertinent information, as appropriate. If summarizing, the CO must describe the source documents in detail and describe the summarizing process. Also, the CO must ensure that his or her handwriting is legible. Photocopied originals are preferable to document summaries.

If a contractor objects to providing photocopying facilities or if, for any other reason, the CO must use an offsite copying facility, the CO will take appropriate precautions in removing original documents from the premises. COs must assure the contractor that the originals will return in a timely manner. It may also be helpful for COs, in coordination with a contractor official, to make a written inventory of the documents and materials that are being provided by the contractor for copying.

If the contractor refuses to provide access to materials or denies the CO the ability to copy requested materials, the CO will contact his or her supervisor to discuss denial of access concerns. It may be necessary to prepare an SCN for denial of access following this discussion. Chapter 8, Resolution of Noncompliance, is a source of additional information on this particular point.

2E EO 11246 AAP REQUIREMENTS

This section discusses the onsite review of identified problems related to the EO 11246 AAP and support data submitted for desk audit; the contractor's implementation of additional required elements of the AAP, and the contractor's good faith efforts and goals attainment. For each of the EO 11246 AAP elements, COs must indicate on the corresponding SCER section any problem areas identified during the onsite review and confirmation of any corrective actions taken by the contractor. Be aware that the desk audit results will already be recorded in the SCER.

The SCER will also include references to relevant evidence COs obtained during the onsite review and recommendations for any appropriate corrective action. It is important to note that COs may need to conduct an offsite analysis of evidence gathered during the onsite review to ensure a full understanding of the contractor's personnel activities and practices, and to appropriately identify problem areas that may constitute a violation requiring corrective action.

2E00 EO 11246 AAP AND SUPPORT DATA SUBMISSIONS

During the desk audit, a CO examines the contractor's AAP and support data to determine completeness or whether they included all the required elements, and whether the Executive

Order AAP and support data are acceptable. Part A of the SCER is used to report any problems in these areas. Before going onsite, the CO develops an onsite plan that reflects how the CO will address the identified problem areas during the onsite review.

A CO must conduct an onsite review to assess the contractor's implementation of its AAP(s). Before going onsite, a CO schedules an entrance conference the content of which is informed, in part, by the CO's onsite plan. The entrance conference must include a discussion of unresolved AAP deficiencies, especially if the official responsible for preparing and implementing the AAP(s) is present. The CO also explains which aspects of the program are unacceptable during the desk audit, and why they were unacceptable. The CO will also request that the contractor provide any additional information or documentation that the CO needs that the contractor did not provide as a part of the onsite review.

2E01 ADDITIONAL REQUIRED ELEMENTS OF AN EO 11246 AAP

The onsite review must include an assessment of the additional elements required in the EO 11246 AAP. The additional elements COs must examine are the designation of a responsible person for the AAP, the identification of problem areas, the use of action-oriented programs, and the existence of an internal audit and reporting system. Each element is discussed below.[76]

- *Designation of Responsibility for the AAP.* The contractor's appointment of a person to be responsible for implementing the AAP must be an executive who has the authority and resources to ensure that the AAP is put into practice. COs must obtain a copy of the responsible official's position description to ensure that it includes implementing the AAP. During the interview, the official responsible for the AAP's implementation must describe how the specific provisions of the AAP are implemented. The roles of the interviewed officials in developing and implementing the AAP must be the same as specified in the written AAP. If they are not the same, COs must ask the contractor for an explanation.

- *Identification of Problem Areas by the Contractor.* To evaluate the contractor's in-depth analysis of its total selection process, by race, ethnicity and sex, COs must first review any problems the contractor identified in the AAP. The contactor's analysis of its total employment process should indicate whether and where impediments to equal employment opportunity exist based on its utilization, personnel activities, compensation analysis, and selection procedures. During interviews with individuals who contributed to the development of the AAP, implementation of the AAP, and who are involved in the hiring or selection process, COs must discuss the contractor's identified problem areas. COs must determine how the contractor identified each problem, the scope of the problem, what solutions the contractor implemented, and the effectiveness of the actions taken.

In its AAP, the contractor should identify concentrations and absences of any specific protected group within its workforce. During the onsite review, COs must seek to identify

[76] See Chapter 1, subsection 1F05, Additional Required Elements of AAPs.

any job titles for which there are significantly high or low representations of any protected group. COs must incorporate questions regarding these circumstances into the interviews with the contractor's supervisors and employees. Additionally, they must ask whether the company has disseminated and explained its EEO and harassment policies to employees, and whether the company has trained supervisors to understand their responsibility for carrying out the policies.

- *Action-Oriented Programs*. COs must ensure that the contractor took appropriate steps to eliminate impediments to, and disparities in, equal employment opportunity; to increase employment opportunities for underutilized groups; and to produce quantifiable outcomes. The contractor should design action-oriented programs to address any specific problems the contractor identified. The programs should specifically describe who is responsible for implementing the program, what actions the contractor will take and when and how the program will work. The onsite review often illustrates the contractor's compliance with this requirement when COs investigate other issues. For example, in requesting copies of position descriptions and discussing them with personnel, a CO can determine how recently the contractor reviewed the descriptions, if the descriptions are accurate and if the contractor's selection process screens for the knowledge, skills and abilities related to the position descriptions. Additionally, when the CO questions interviewees like the contractor officials, employees and third parties about the contractor's recruitment and outreach efforts, the CO can obtain information related to the action-oriented nature and relative success of these efforts.

- *Internal Audit and Reporting System.* The contractor must design and implement internal audit and reporting systems which measure the effectiveness of the total AAP. Beginning with the desk audit, COs evaluate the contractor's internal audit and reporting systems. COs must interview appropriate officials to gain an understanding of how the contractor conducts its audits and to request documentation of how the contractor reports the results of internal equal employment opportunity and affirmative action audits. COs must request documentation, in the form of copies of reports, or copies of minutes of meetings.

  Below are several examples of relevant questions COs should ask contractors about their auditing and reporting system.

  - What data does the contractor review as a part of the audits?
  - How and when does the contractor gather and analyze the data?
  - Does the contractor prepare written reports, other than the AAP? If so, how often?
  - Who prepares the other written reports, who receives and reads them, and what is done in response to them?

COs must remember to record either their confirmation or description of problem areas identified in Part B of the SCER. The SCER must also include a description of any identified or implemented problem resolutions.

2E02 EVALUATION OF GOOD FAITH EFFORTS

One purpose of the onsite review is to evaluate whether the contractor made good faith efforts to implement the action-oriented programs outlined in the AAP. COs must assess good faith efforts on a case-by-case basis, taking into account all of the relevant facts and circumstances. However, in most situations good faith efforts will produce positive results. When a contractor's efforts have not produced such results, COs must ask the contractor to explain the following:

- why it its efforts were not effective,
- why it did not make additional or alternate efforts, and
- why its additional or alternate efforts, or both, were not sufficiently effective.

During the desk audit, COs evaluate the contractor's past goal attainment and progress on meeting current goals, and identify any goal areas requiring further evaluation of good faith efforts. To make informed judgments about the quality of the contractor's good faith efforts, COs must be familiar with the local area's community resources, a list of which is maintained in each field office. The list of community resources may include non-profit groups, EEO organizations, faith-based groups and caregiver support groups that can assist contractors in attaining their goals. Chapter 1, subsection 1B, includes a discussion of community resources

During the onsite review, COs explore the contractor's good faith efforts through interviews with contractor officials, employees and other pertinent parties.[77] For each of the activities listed below, COs must identify and obtain documentation that provides evidence of the extent of the contractor's good faith efforts.

a. *Good Faith Efforts – Internal Placements.* For internal placements through actions like hiring and promoting current employees, good faith may include the contractor's efforts to address barriers to opportunities for women, minorities, people with disabilities, and protected veterans. Possible areas of inquiry on this point are listed below.

- *Disseminating Information About Internal Opportunities.* Are job openings posted? If so, are they posted where all potentially eligible employees would see them? Are all jobs posted, or only certain jobs or classes of jobs? Why? Are jobs posted promptly? Is there ample time to apply?
- *Providing Training Opportunities.* Does the contractor provide apprenticeship programs? On-the-job training? Tuition reimbursement? If so, for which employees are these opportunities available? Are employees in favored and nonfavored groups equitably represented?

---

[77] See also Chapter 1, Section L – Analysis of E0 11246 AAP: Goals Progress and Good Faith Efforts.

- *Providing Counseling and Encouraging Minority and Female Employees to Apply for Internal Openings.* How does this occur? How often? What does the counseling or encouragement consist of? Does the contractor periodically assess whether its efforts are successful? Is counseling and encouragement available for caregivers?

- *Recruiting Externally into Feeder Job Groups.* What recruitment efforts is the contractor making? What resources is the contractor using?

- *Reviewing Selection Criteria and Selection Procedures.* Did the contractor review its selection criteria and determine whether it is applying them in a nondiscriminatory manner? Whether the selection criteria might have a disparate impact? How does the contractor document the review? Did the contractor ensure that the officials and managers responsible for applying selection criteria and procedures are familiar with, and are implementing, the contractor's EEO policies? Is the contractor providing training? How frequently?

b. *Good Faith Efforts – External Placements.* For external placement opportunities, evaluation of the contractor's good faith efforts may include exploring the below areas.

- *Recruiting Sources in the AAP.* Does the contractor use the recruitment sources listed in its AAP to reach out to minorities and women? If so, when and how? This inquiry includes the CO contacting at least some of the listed organizations to confirm and assess the contractor's use of the organization as a recruitment source.

- *Using Other Recruitment Sources.* Does the contractor use other recruitment sources that are not listed in its AAP to reach out to minorities and women? Does the recruitment source provide assistance and support regarding caregiver issues? What are they? How useful have they been?

- *Using the Media.* How are job openings advertised? Does the contractor advertise in publications or other media that are targeted to minorities and women? If so, which ones?

- *Recruiting at Schools and Universities.* Does the contractor recruit at high schools, colleges, and universities that enroll large numbers of minorities and women? If so, which ones?

2E03 AUDIT OF EMPLOYMENT ACTIVITY TO ENSURE EQUAL EMPLOYMENT OPPORTUNITY

An essential part of the contractor's affirmative action program is that it audits its employment activity to ensure progress toward meeting its goals. COs must ask and consider the answers to these questions in order to begin understanding the contractor's audit process:

- Does the contractor audit its employment activity?

- Who is responsible for conducting the audit?

- What is involved in the audit?
- How frequently does the contractor conduct the audit?
- Does the contractor issue a report? What happens to the report?
- Do the CEO and other high ranking officials receive the report?

COs must also specifically examine records on the contractor's employment activity, and selection criteria and processes to understand the contractor's good faith efforts. Questions that may be useful to CO in these two areas of inquiry are provided below.

a. *Records of Employment Activities.* Applicant flow data may provide useful documentation about the effectiveness of the contractor's good faith efforts, as can internal bid lists and applications for posted job openings. Does either the applicant flow data or the bid lists, or both, show an increase in previously underrepresented groups in the applicant pool? If so, for what positions were the contractor's efforts effective? If there are no changes, or there are decreases in representation, what alternative actions has the contractor taken or proposed taking in the future?

b. *Review of Selection Criteria and Selection Procedures.* Did the contractor review its selection criteria? Did the contractor apply the criteria in a nondiscriminatory manner and determine whether the selection criteria might have an adverse impact? Did the contractor perform validity studies on any criteria found to have an adverse impact, and did the contractor properly determine the criteria to be job-related and consistent with business necessity? How frequently does the contractor review selection criteria? How does the contractor document the review? Do the contractor's efforts comply with the Uniform Guidelines on Employee Selection Procedures at 41 CFR Part 60-3? Did the contractor ensure that the officials and managers responsible for applying selection criteria and procedures are familiar with, and are implementing, the contractor's EEO policies? Does the contractor provide training? If so, how frequently is training provided?

COs must record findings on the contractor's good faith efforts in Part B of the SCER, and include supporting documentation and other relevant evidence in the case file. This includes materials such as copies of correspondence, job orders, bid lists for posted job openings, contractor recruiting manuals, relevant pages from labor agreements, employee manuals, and summaries of conversations and interviews with contractor representatives, employees, applicants and recruitment source contacts.

2F SECTION 503 AND SECTION 4212 AAPs, AND ADDITIONAL REQUIREMENTS

Contractors must prepare, maintain and update on an annual basis, an AAP for individuals with disabilities and an AAP for protected veterans. This section addresses the AAP requirements under Section 503 and Section 4212 together because they are similar.[78] The contractor has the option to prepare a combined Section 503 and Section 4212 AAP or to prepare separate Section 503 and Section 4212 AAPs. COs use the onsite review to investigate problem areas they identified during the desk audit, to gather further information regarding the AAPs and their implementation, and to learn more about the contractor's employment activities and personnel practices. To gather information related to the Section 503 and Section 4212 AAP obligations, COs must interview contractor officials, employees and others, as appropriate. They must also identify and obtain documentation that evidences the contractor's compliance efforts. CO must record the information they obtain in the SCER Part B and include it in the case file.

2F00 AAP(S) AND SUPPORT DATA SUBMISSIONS

During the desk audit, COs examine the AAP(s) and support data to determine whether all required elements are included (completeness), and whether the AAP(s) and support data are acceptable. During the onsite review, they interview contractor officials and others regarding their development and implementation of the AAPs, and obtain documentation evidencing the same. COs record any problems identified during the desk audit in the SCER Part A. Any problems COs identify during the onsite review are noted in the SCER Part B. COs must examine whether the contractor satisfied the following elements that are required parts of Section 503 and Section 4212 AAPs:

a. *Develop an Equal Opportunity Policy Statement.* COs must examine the contractor's written EEO policy statement, noting whether the contractor updates it annually and whether the information on the contractor's EEO Coordinator is current, including the coordinator's name, job title, location and phone number. Along with a statement that the contractor does not discriminate on the prohibited bases, the EEO statement must also reflect that the contractor will not subject employees and applicants to retaliation or reprisal. COs must verify that the EEO statement is clearly posted on bulletin boards in areas open to employees and applicants, and is communicated to employees and applicants.

b. *Review of Personnel Processes.* Several questions are relevant to a CO's review of personnel processes and they include, but are not limited to:

- Does the contractor's AAP provide for periodic review of personnel processes to ensure that the job qualifications of individuals with disabilities and protected veterans are considered? How is this done? When?

- Do the personnel files contain notes regarding consideration for opportunities? Are these notes ever destroyed or removed from the personnel files? If so, why or at what point?

- Does the contractor document its review of personnel processes and any actions it takes? How is that review conducted and by whom?

[78] See Chapter 1, subsection 1H – Review of Section 503 and Section 4212 AAPs for Acceptability.

All relevant documentation, including reports and personnel files, must be obtained and reviewed by the CO.

If the contractor asserts that its present personnel procedures are adequate, COs must confirm that the contractor gives individuals with disabilities and protected veterans hiring and promotional opportunities through a review of appropriate records and interviews with contractor officials and employees.

c. *Review of Physical and Mental Job Qualifications.* The contractor is obligated to periodically review the physical and mental qualifications of its jobs and to eliminate those qualifications that tend to screen out qualified protected veterans or other individuals on the basis of disability, and are not job-related and consistent with business necessity. The AAPs should contain a schedule for this periodic review. Changes in technology, manufacturing processes, labor agreements, and changes in the industry are a few changes that may also trigger the review.

   To begin to assess the contractor's review of its physical and mental job qualifications, COs must ask or consider the following questions:

   - When did the contractor write or last update the job descriptions? Do the job descriptions accurately reflect the duties of the job? Do the job descriptions require the employee or applicant to perform duties in a specific way?

   - Are there job qualifications that would tend to screen out individuals on the basis of disability or disabled veterans?

   - Are the contractor's job qualifications based on business necessity? If not, are there alternative qualifications that the contractor can use?

   - Are there positions that do not have written job descriptions? If so, how does the contractor identify and review job qualifications?

d. *Provide Needed Reasonable Accommodation to Qualified Individuals with Disabilities and Disabled Veterans.* Contractors must provide needed reasonable accommodation to the known physical and mental limitations of qualified individuals and disabled veterans unless the accommodation would cause an undue hardship. Accommodations may include, but are not limited to:

   - modifying work places and making work places and other contractor facilities used by employees accessible;

   - restructuring of marginal functions of jobs;

   - allowing essential functions to be performed in a different way;

   - assigning nonessential functions of the job to other employees;

- providing readers, sign language interpreters or assistive devices;
- providing part-time work, flexible hours, or telework; and,
- reassigning employees to a vacant position, if necessary.

COs must verify that there is a process in place by which individuals can request needed accommodations and procedures exist for promptly responding to requests and implementing accommodations. They must also verify that employees and applicants are aware of the process and that officials responsible for implementing the procedures are knowledgeable and appropriately trained. CO must interview contractor officials and employees to confirm that the contractor implemented the procedures and provided needed accommodations in a timely manner. A reasonable accommodation does not have to have been provided if the contractor demonstrates that the needed accommodation would have caused it undue hardship. COs must also review the contractor's accommodation request records to see that the contractor responds to requests promptly and appropriately. All accommodations made by the contractor must be effective. Generally, this means it must provide the person who needs the accommodation the ability to perform essential job duties or, in the case of an applicant to apply for employment opportunities. If requests for accommodation were denied, COs must obtain documentation reflecting these decisions and the basis for the decisions to ensure that the denials were proper.

As a part of the desk audit, COs must examine whether individuals with disabilities can access the contractor's online application system and determine whether the contractor is providing reasonable accommodation, when requested, unless such accommodation would cause an undue hardship. During the onsite review, COs must question contractor officials, employees and applicants regarding how the online application system works and whether any accessibility problems have occurred. The COs will determine whether the contractor is providing needed reasonable accommodation when requested, unless such accommodation would cause an undue hardship. This includes providing an alternate means for an applicant to contact the contractor and apply for jobs other than through the contractor's online system. If there are application or testing kiosks onsite, COs must ensure that individuals with disabilities can access them, that information regarding how to request accommodation is clearly displayed, and that the contractor promptly made needed reasonable accommodations.

e. *Develop and Implement Procedures to Prevent Harassment.* COs must confirm that the contractor developed and implemented policies and procedures for preventing harassment. Part of the process includes COs requesting a copy of the policies and procedures, interviewing the official responsible for implementation, and reviewing reports or internal investigations of alleged harassment and the contractor's response.

f. *Disseminate EEO Policy Externally and Perform Outreach and Positive Recruitment.* COs must verify during the onsite review that the contractor engaged in outreach and positive recruitment activities. To do this, COs must conduct interviews with contractor officials and third party organizations regarding outreach and recruitment efforts. Interviews with applicants and employees may also provide information regarding these efforts.

Outreach and positive recruitment may also include linkage agreements.[79] COs must be prepared to refer the contractor to groups that serve individuals with disabilities, including disabled and otherwise protected veterans.

g. *Disseminate EEO Policy Internally.* AAPs should clearly describe the methods the contractor used to disseminate its EEO policy internally. COs must verify that the contractor actually implemented these measures. They must also obtain documentation and verify through interviews that appropriate staff meetings were held to thoroughly discuss the policies. COs can also evaluate the effectiveness of the contractor's methods of internal dissemination, in part, from the participation of individuals with disabilities, and disabled and other protected veterans, in promotions and in training programs.

h. *Design and Implement an Audit and Reporting System.* COs must confirm that the contractor has an audit and reporting system, and that it measures the effectiveness of its total AAP. The audit system should periodically review all of the contractor's employment practices and policies, compensation systems, recruitment efforts, training programs, reasonable accommodation procedures, and other terms, conditions and privileges of employment. COs must obtain copies of past audits, determine the frequency of reports, and when corrective action was taken, determine the nature of the problem and the effectiveness of the action taken to remedy it. The COs will also conduct interviews with responsible officials and employees.

i. *Designate a Management Official to Assume Responsibility for Ensuring the Implementation of the AAP.* COs must obtain documentation regarding who the contractor appointed to serve as director or manager of the contractor's affirmative action activities. COs will seek an interview with the named individual to determine the specific responsibilities and authority assigned to that individual, how the official carries out those responsibilities, and how the official assesses the implementation of the AAP. COs must obtain documentation, such as a copy of the individual's position description, copies of reports the individual has prepared, and supporting documentation for any assessments the official conducted.

j. *Train Personnel to Ensure that the Contractor Implements EEO and AAP Commitments.* COs must interview contractor staff, managers and officials to confirm that the contractor's personnel involved in the recruitment, screening, selection, promotion, discipline and related processes are knowledgeable about its EEO obligations. Questions relevant to this determination include:

- Does the contractor provide training to personnel? What type of training does the contractor provide? When, how frequently, and by whom is this training provided?
- What are the trainer's qualifications?
- Did the trainer use training materials? What were they?

[79] See Section 2K – Linkage Agreements.

- If the trainer used written training materials, the CO must request a copy.

2F01 AVAILABILITY OF AAPs FOR INSPECTION

COs must confirm that the contractor posted a notice, available to both employees and applicants for employment, stating that the Section 503 and Section 4212 AAP(s) are available to any employee or applicant for employment to inspect, upon request. When the contractor conducts personnel related business through the Internet, such as recruiting and disseminating employment notices, COs should strongly encourage the contractor to post AAP notices electronically. The notice must include the location and hours during which the documents may be obtained. An example of possible acceptable language is, "The AAP is available in the personnel office during regular business hours."

2F02 INVITATION TO SELF-IDENTIFY

Contractors must offer applicants the opportunity to self-identify as an individual with a disability under Section 503 or as a disabled veteran under Section 4212 after they extend a job offer but before the applicant begins working.[80] A contractor may invite individuals with disabilities and disabled veterans to self-identify prior to making a job offer when:

- the contractor is actually undertaking affirmative action for individuals with disabilities or disabled veterans, or both, at the pre-offer stage; or
- the invitation is made pursuant to a federal, state or local law requiring affirmative action for disabled veterans.[81]

Contractors may invite all other applicants to self-identify as a veteran protected by Section 4212 anytime before the applicants begin working.[82] COs must confirm that the invitation to applicants to self-identify as an individual with a disability or as a disabled or protected veteran is voluntary. The contractor must keep information an employee provides regarding disability in response to the invitation to self-identify in a separate confidential file and not in the employee's personnel file. The contractor must not use an applicant's refusal to self-identify to subject the applicant to any adverse treatment. COs must confirm how the contractor used the information and ensure that the contractor used it only in accordance with the applicable regulations. A copy of the invitation must be obtained if it was not provided in the AAPs.

COs must examine the application or personnel file, or both, of each individual who self-identifies as having a disability. They must also review employment data indicating whether the contractor hired these individuals and, if not, the reason for nonselection. COs will also examine whether the individual requested a reasonable accommodation, and if so, review the appropriate accommodation records to determine whether the contractor handled the accommodation request

---

[80] See 41 CFR 60-741. 42(a), 41 CFR 60-250.42(a) and 41 CFR 60-300.42(a).
[81] See 41 CFR 60-250.42(a)(1)-(2) and 41 CFR 60-300.42(a)(1)-(2).
[82] See 41 CFR 250.42(b) and 300.42(b).

appropriately. If the contractor denied an accommodation request, COs must determine whether the denial was proper and whether, if needed, the contractor provided a suitable alternative accommodation without undue delay. If any concerns are identified, COs will also interview the affected applicants, employees and others, as appropriate.

2F03 ADDITIONAL REQUIREMENTS

a. *Disability-Related Questions and Medical Examinations.* Section 503 and Section 4212 prohibit contractors from asking applicants disability-related questions or questions that are likely to elicit information about a disability. These same laws also prohibit contractors from conducting medical examinations of applicants *until after a conditional job offer is made.* Once the contractor makes a conditional job offer, the contractor may ask disability-related questions and require medical examinations, regardless of whether they are related to the job, as long as this is done for all entering employees in the same job. COs must determine whether the contractor improperly made such inquiries on the job application itself or during the selection process, and whether the contractor administered medical examinations prematurely. The contractor needs to take corrective action to ensure the discontinuation of these unlawful practices.

   COs must also assess whether the contractor used lawfully obtained disability-related information, including information about an impairment that is not "transitory and minor", when withdrawing a conditional job offer.[83] If so, the contractor must show that the criteria used to withdraw the job offer from the individual with a disability or the disabled veteran are job-related and consistent with business necessity. This could possibly include showing that the individual would have posed a direct threat.[84]

   Disability-related inquires and medical examinations of *employees*, such as return to work exams and periodic physicals, are permissible only when, and to the extent that, they are job-related and consistent with business necessity. The contractor may not use information obtained as a result of such a lawful inquiry or exam in a way that discriminates on the basis of disability. Drug tests for the illegal use of drugs are not medical exams.

b. *Confidentiality Requirement.* Whenever a contractor makes a disability-related inquiry or conducts a medical examination of an applicant or employee, the contractor must keep any information obtained about the individual's impairments or health in a separate confidential medical file and not with personnel files. However, government officials investigating compliance with EEO laws may have access; the contractor may inform supervisors and managers of necessary restrictions or needed reasonable accommodations; and the contractor may inform first aid and safety personnel of any needs. COs must make an assessment of acceptability of the contractor's system for maintaining confidentiality of medical information, including inspecting where the records are kept, who has access to the records and why, and measures that ensure confidentiality of the records.

---

[83] An example of a transitory or minor injury is a simple sprain wrist expected to heal normally.
[84] For more information on direct threat see 41 CFR 60-741.2.

2G RELIGION AND NATIONAL ORIGIN REQUIREMENTS

COs must include assessment of the contractor's compliance with the *Guidelines on Discrimination Because of Religion or National Origin* as a part of the onsite review.[85] Although the Executive Order AAP does not require that the contractor include a reference to these guidelines, the contractor must still comply with them. COs must examine the contractor's policy statement to ensure that it references the contractor's obligation to provide equal employment opportunity without regard to religion and national origin. COs must also interview contractor officials and employees regarding implementation of the policy, including the provision of accommodation for religious observances and practices. COs include information obtained during the onsite review in the SCER in Part B III.

2G00 CONTRACTOR POLICY AND IMPLEMENTATION

A contractor must review its employment practices to determine whether members of various religious and ethnic groupsreceive fair consideration for job opportunities. COs must ask the contractor whether it conducted a review of its employment practices for this purpose, and if so, when, how, and whether they documented the review. If the contractor undertook a review, the CO must verify its results and the sufficiency of any corrective actions that the contractor implemented. In making this assessment, the CO will keep in mind that the scope of the contractor's efforts depends on a review of all circumstances, including the nature and extent of any problem areas, as well as the size and resources of the contractor. COs must take into consideration that contractors are not required to collect data on applicants' and employees' religious affiliation. Therefore, a contractor's self-analysis will not use employment records to identify employees' religious affiliations. If the contractor did not conduct a review, the contractor must take corrective action.

COs must verify that the contractor communicated the nondiscrimination policy to contractor officials, human resources personnel, employees and applicants, and that procedures implementing the policy are in place. A CO will also verify that the contractor has participated in recruitment and outreach efforts. A CO will review employment policies regarding nondiscrimination based on religion and the provision of religious accommodations. During interviews with contractor officials, employees, and applicants, a CO will ask about requests for religious accommodations and how the contractor responded to these requests. COs must obtain documentation regarding recruitment and outreach, and other affirmative action efforts.

2G01 RELIGIOUS ACCOMMODATION

The contractor must accommodate the religious observances and practices of its employees and prospective employees; unless it can demonstrate that making a particular accommodation would result in undue hardship on its business.[86] In interpreting the extent of the contractor's obligation to provide reasonable accommodations on religious grounds, COs must consider:

---

[85] 41 CFR Part 60-50.
[86] See 41 CFR 60-50.3.

- business necessity,
- financial costs and expenses, and
- resulting personnel problems.

The agency follows Title VII legal principles on religious accommodations.[87] COs should note that Title VII standards for religious accommodation are not the same as those for reasonable accommodation under Section 503 of the Rehabilitation Act. COs must ask the contractor whether and how it has made accommodation to the religious observances and practices of its employees.[88] COs must also ask whether the contractor denied any religious accommodation requests. If so, the CO will seek documentation and verification of the reasons for denial and ensure that they were proper. In reviewing employee files, COs must be alert for any pattern of discipline or terminations based on refusal to work on certain days based on religious observances. If the contractor reports that no requests were made, COs must review procedures available for evaluating such requests.

2G02 POTENTIAL HARASSMENT AND DISCRIMINATION

While conducting interviews and review of records, COs may obtain information regarding potential harassment or discrimination based on religion or national origin, or both. Like harassment based on race, sex or disability, harassment based on religion or national origin may take a number of forms, including name calling, negative treatment, derogatory speech directed at individuals of a specific religion, national origin, or ethnicity. If a CO obtains information about potential harassment or discrimination, the CO must investigate further to determine:

- whether the discrimination occurred in the past or is ongoing,
- whether the contractor knew or should have known of the discrimination,
- whether the contractor has internal discrimination and harassment complaint procedures in place,
- whether the contractor's internal discrimination and harassment complaint procedures are known to the employees, and
- whether the contractor has done anything to address the problem.

Additional information regarding harassment and hostile environment on the bases of race, color, sex, national origin, religion, disability or veteran status is discussed in Chapter 6, Complaint Investigation.[89]

---

[87] Title VII of the Civil Rights Act of 1964, as amended, (sections 701(j), 703 and 717).
[88] See 41 CFR 60-50.3 and http://www.eeoc.gov/laws/types/religion.cfm (last accessed September 2011).
[89] See also Subsection 2M03 – Issues that Arise During the Onsite Review.

Additionally, if the CO finds indicators of disparate treatment or disparate impact,[90] or both, the CO must fully investigate the issue. The CO must obtain copies of any documents reflecting these concerns, or indicating how the contractor dealt with the concern. The CO must also interview people knowledgeable about the matter. If the investigation identifies issues specific to religious or national origin discrimination that the *Guidelines* do not address, the CO must follow Title VII principles in determining whether a violation may have occurred.

2G03 COMMUNITY CONTACTS

As part of the onsite review, COs may identify organizations representing the interests of various nationalities and religious groups located in the labor area serving the contractor's facility. COs may find it useful to contact such groups for information about possible employment problems experienced by their members who have applied for employment with the contractor.

2H COMPLIANCE WITH SEX DISCRIMINATION GUIDELINES

It is unlawful for a contractor to discriminate against any employee or applicant for employment because of sex. The contractor may not make any distinction based on sex in recruitment, hiring, firing, promoting, training, paying, assigning hours, assigning jobs, determining benefits, or in other terms, conditions, or privileges of employment.[91] COs are reminded that discrimination on account of pregnancy, childbirth, childbearing capacity, or related medical condition is a form of unlawful sex discrimination. A few examples of unlawful pregnancy discrimination are:

- Refusing to hire pregnant women or women of childbearing capacity, or subjecting these women to adverse employment treatment because of their pregnancy or their capacity to bear children;
- Providing employees with health insurance that does not cover hospitalization and other medical costs for pregnancy, childbirth, and related medical conditions to the same extent that hospitalization and other medical costs are covered for other medical conditions;
- Denying an alternative job assignment or modified duties to a pregnant worker who is temporarily unable to perform some of her job duties because of pregnancy, childbirth, or related medical conditions when such assignments or modifications are provided to other workers whose abilities or inabilities to perform some of their job duties are similarly affected; and

---

[90] Disparate impact the theory of discrimination that focuses on the effect of a practice or policy. Disparate impact discrimination occurs when a contractor's use of a facially neutral policy or selection procedure (e.g., a test or degree requirement) disqualifies members of a protected class at a substantially higher rate than others and is not justified by business necessity and job relatedness. Discriminatory intent is not required. See definitions in the Key Words and Phrases section of the Manual.

[91] 41 CFR Part 60-20.

- Firing a woman or requiring her to go on leave because she becomes pregnant or begins to physically show that she is pregnant.

To ensure compliance, COs must request a copy of the contractor's policies covered by 41 CFR Part 60-20 and examine whether the contractor implemented its employment activities and decisions in a manner consistent with Part 60-20. COs must examine the contractor's policy statement to ensure that it references the contractor's obligation to provide equal employment opportunity without regard to sex. COs must also interview contractor officials and employees regarding the implementation of the policy. The CO must include information obtained during the onsite review in the SCER in Part B III.

2H00 REVIEW OF CONTRACTOR POLICIES AND IMPLEMENTATION

This section on a CO's review of contractor policies covers eight areas: conditions of employment, distinctions based on marital status or caregiving responsibilities, bona fide occupational qualifications, employment opportunities, wage discrimination, employment advertising, employment benefits, and family and pregnancy leave.

a. *Conditions of Employment.* COs must examine whether contractor policies make prohibited distinctions in conditions of employment based on sex, including the basis of pregnancy, childbirth or related medical conditions, or on the basis of sex-based stereotypes, including those related to actual or perceived caregiver responsibilities. Contractors must not make employment decisions based on stereotypes about how males and females are "supposed" to look or act. Such employment decisions are a form of sex discrimination prohibited by Executive Order 11246, as amended.

   Examples of discrimination based on sex stereotyping include, but are not limited to, adverse treatment of an employee or applicant for employment based on sex-based stereotypes about caregiver responsibilities. Adverse treatment of a female employee because of a gender-based assumption that she has family caretaking responsibilities and that these responsibilities will interfere with her work performance is an example of sex discrimination. Another common example is an employer paying a female employee less than a male employee for the same or similar job because the woman is married and the husband is presumed to be the "breadwinner" in the family. In contrast, decisions based solely on actual work performance are not generally discriminatory.

b. *Distinctions Based on Marital Status or Caregiver Responsibilities.* COs must examine written policies and conduct interviews with contractor staff and employees regarding the implementation of policies and practices to identify whether distinctions between married and unmarried people apply equally to both sexes, including distinctions between single parents and married parents based on gender. In addition, COs must assess contractor policies and practices to ensure that sex-based stereotypes about actual and perceived caregiving responsibilities are not in effect. For example, a CO may find a practice of male employees being given the opportunity to participate in high profile activities that could lead to promotion and that female employees are not given these assignments because of the stereotype that female employees must deal with day care and childrearing responsibilities.

c. *Bona Fide Occupational Qualifications (BFOQ).* As a part of most onsite reviews, COs examine job qualifications as stated by the contractor. Under Title VII, sex has been found to be a BFOQ in extremely rare instances. Among them are:

- *Authenticity.* Jobs involving a need for authenticity or genuineness, such as actors or models.

- *Personal Privacy.* Jobs where the performance of essential job elements would entail substantial invasion of personal privacy (e.g., a permanent restroom attendant). This is limited to situations where the normal operation of the contractor's business depends on the employee being the same sex as its employees or customers and there is no other way to ensure privacy. This is different from customer preference. For example, a contractor cannot refuse to hire female salespeople in the belief that male customers will not accept them as well.

d. *Employment Opportunities.*

- *Hazardous Jobs*: Contractors may not exclude women from jobs they may believe are dangerous or unsuitable for women to perform unless sex is a BFOQ.

- *Reproductive Hazards*: OFCCP follows Title VII principles when determining whether a policy excluding women from a job because of a concern about reproductive hazards is discriminatory. If a question relating to reproductive hazards arises during a compliance evaluation, COs must discuss the issue with their supervisors.

e. *Wage Discrimination. COs* must examine possible wage discrimination issues. Compensation discrimination encompasses discrimination in pay and benefits. It may also include discrimination in how employees earn or contractors distribute raises and bonuses. Contractors cannot make distinctions in pay, benefits, raises or bonuses, or access to earnings opportunities or better paying job opportunities on the basis of sex. Whether as a result of the desk audit analysis of compensation data or a focused review of compensation practices, if COs identify areas for investigation, they must gather additional information and conduct interviews regarding the contractor's compensation policies and practices. Section 2L has additional information on compensation.

f. *Employment Advertising.* COs must examine the contractor's advertisements in newspapers, online and in other media. The advertisements must not express a sex preference unless the job is one for which sex is a BFOQ. It is prohibited to place ads in columns headed "male" or "female" (or "male interest" or "female interest"), or that otherwise indicate a partiality with regard to sex, because that would be an expression of preference, limitation, or specification based on sex. For example, applicants or potential applicants may perceive an advertisement for a "craftsman," as opposed to "craftsperson," as seeking male applicants only and may have the effect of only male applicants applying for the position.

g. *Employee Benefits*. See Section 2H01, Discrimination and Harassment, for a discussion.

h. *Family Leave and Pregnancy Leave*. See Section 2H01, Discrimination and Harassment, for a discussion.

2H01 SEX DISCRIMINATION AND HARASSMENT

During the onsite review, COs gather information and conduct interviews to determine whether the contractor developed and implemented policy prohibiting sex discrimination in accordance with the *Sex Discrimination Guidelines*. As mentioned earlier, this type of discrimination may take many forms. OFCCP's policy is to interpret the nondiscrimination provisions of EO 11246 consistent with Title VII principles, including, of course, the nondiscrimination requirements related to pregnancy, childbirth, and related medical conditions. COs should be familiar with the applicable law in this area, such as the Family and Medical Leave Act, as well as understand how the application of policies and the absence of policies may result in discrimination and harassment.

a. *Family and Medical Leave Act*. The Family and Medical Leave Act (FMLA) was enacted in 1993.[92] In part the purpose of FMLA is to address the needs of families and caregivers as affected by the demands of the workplace, specifically addressing leave issues. OFCCP and the Department's Wage and Hour Division (WHD), which enforces FMLA, entered in a MOU.[93] Under this MOU, OFCCP incorporates a FMLA inspection into its compliance evaluation and complaint investigation procedures, as discussed below.

b. *Family Leave and Pregnancy and Disability Leave*. The CO will examine the contractor's policy regarding leave in light of the prohibition of discrimination based on sex, including pregnancy, and FMLA.

- Family Leave Required under the FMLA. During the course of a routine compliance evaluation or complaint investigation, the CO will determine whether the FMLA notice is posted and whether written guidance about the provisions of FMLA is provided in accordance with 29 CFR 825.300. Incidents of suspected noncompliance with these provisions are referred to WHD. In addition, the CO may examine the application or use of these policies by the contractor for any adverse treatment of, or adverse impact on, any specific group protected by OFCCP's legal authorities. This is distinct from enforcing violations of family leave requirements. The FMLA requires employers of 50 or more employees to provide up to 12 weeks of unpaid, job protected leave for qualified workers for a worker's pregnancy or own serious health condition, or when a worker becomes a new parent. Covered employers are also required to provide FMLA leave to employees caring for a covered family member with a serious health condition (e.g., a mother caring for a child with cancer). Additionally, various states have their own family and medical leave laws that may provide additional leave or additional coverage.

---

[92] Family Medical Leave Act, Pub. L. 103-3 (29 U.S.C. 2601).
[93] The MOU between OFCCP and WHD was signed in September 1993.

- Pregnancy Disability Leave. The CO must examine whether the contractor has a sick leave or disability leave policy (written or unwritten), and leave for conditions associated with childbirth.[94] The CO must also examine whether the contractor's leave policy, or lack thereof, has an adverse impact on employees of one sex and is not justified by business necessity.

These requirements apply regardless of whether the contractor is a covered contractor under the FMLA or whether the employee qualifies for FMLA leave.

c. *Employee Benefits*. The *Sex Discrimination Guidelines* state that a contractor complies with the Executive Order if its contributions for employee benefits, sometimes referred to as fringe benefits, are the same for men and women or if the resulting benefits are equal. Subsequent to the publication of the *Guidelines* in 1978, the Supreme Court has held that under Title VII an employer must provide equal contributions and equal benefits to men and women, even if doing so costs more for one sex than the other. OFCCP's policy is to interpret the nondiscrimination provisions of EO 11246 consistent with Title VII principles. COs must, therefore, obtain information to determine whether a contractor is providing equal employee benefits for men and women, regardless of cost.

d. *Sexual Harassment*. Although not specifically mentioned in the *Guidelines*, sexual harassment, as well as harassment based on race, color, national origin or religion, is a violation of the nondiscrimination provisions of EO 11246. During the onsite review, COs must be alert for any indications of such harassment. OFCCP follows Title VII principles when determining whether sexual harassment has occurred.

e. *Sex-Based Stereotyping and Caregiver Discrimination*. Differential treatment for an employment-related purpose based on sex-based stereotypes, including those related to actual or perceived caregiving responsibilities, is a violation of Title VII of the Civil Rights Act of 1964. For example, it is prohibited to deny advancement opportunities to similarly situated mothers that are provided to fathers or women without children, based on stereotypes about mothers in the workplace; it is also prohibited to deny to fathers access to family-friendly policies like workplace flexibility that employers provide to mothers, based on stereotypes about fathers' roles in care giving.

f. *Treatment of Pregnancy, Childbirth, or Related Medical Conditions*. Title VII, as amended, provides that women affected by pregnancy, childbirth or related medical conditions are to be treated the same for all employment-related purposes, including receipt of benefits under fringe benefit programs, as other persons not so affected but similar in their ability or inability to work.

[94] "Leave" as used here includes but is not limited to eligibility for leave, duration of leave, accrual of seniority and reinstatement rights.

2I TECHNICAL REQUIREMENTS

Contractors have an obligation to meet certain "technical" requirements such as notices and postings requirements. Although these requirements are referred to as "technical requirements," that does not mean that they are unimportant. On the contrary, some of these requirements are extremely important and crucial to ensuring that contractors meet equal employment opportunity obligations and that failure to meet these obligations does not result in discrimination. The affirmative action clauses of EO 11246, Section 503 and Section 4212 mandate these technical requirements. Additionally, the contractor may have posting and other requirements under EO 13496.

While COs may have adequately confirmed some of these requirements during the desk audit, they verify other requirements during the onsite review. COs can provide compliance assistance to the contractor at any time during the review process in order to expedite resolution of identified problems. However, the contractor's failure to comply with a technical requirement constitutes a violation.

If the contractor asserts that it fully corrected identified problems of a technical nature, COs must seek to confirm this assertion. For example, if a required posting under EO 11246 or EO 13496 was missing and the contractor agreed to correct this problem, the CO must conduct a visual inspection to determine that the required posting is now present. The CO must include any other outstanding technical violations in the Notice of Violations.[95]

2I00 TECHNICAL REQUIREMENTS OF EO 11246, SECTION 4212 AND SECTION 503

In addition to requiring that covered contractors not discriminate against, and take affirmative action on behalf of, covered group members, the laws enforced by OFCCP contain a number of other requirements that COs must verify the contractor has met. COs must inspect the appropriate contractor records and obtain copies of them, as needed. COs must record their observations and whether the requirements were met in the SCER in Part B.

a. Technical Requirements Applicable to the EO 11246, Section 503 and Section 4212.

- Contractors must advise subcontractors, including vendors who are subcontractors, of their obligation to comply with non-discrimination obligations and develop an AAP if they meet coverage thresholds. Contractors should also insert the Equal Opportunity (EO) Clause into contracts with covered subcontractors. The clause may be included, either in its entirety or by reference, in all covered contracts and subcontracts (including purchase orders). In the absence of the clause in covered documents, it is applicable by operation of law. COs must question contractor officials as to how, and when, such notification occurs and must review a sampling of sub-contracts to determine whether they include the required clause.

[95] See Chapter 8 – Resolution of Noncompliance.

- Contractors must post notice of their EEO and affirmative action obligations in conspicuous places, available and accessible to both employees and applicants for employment. For example, EEO posters should be in break rooms, common areas for employees and areas frequented by applicants for employment. COs must conduct a visual inspection to confirm the required posting.

- Contractors must inform any labor unions or worker representative organizations with which they have a collective bargaining agreement or other agreement of the contractor's EEO and affirmative action commitments under the regulations. COs must obtain documentation that indicates the contractor provided this notice and will confirm receipt of notice with union representatives.

- Contractors must develop and maintain an AAP for each establishment. COs must confirm that the contractor is meeting this obligation. Please note that this provision applies to Corporate Management Compliance Evaluations (CMCEs) only. For a full discussion of CMCEs review Chapter 4.

b. *Technical Requirements Applicable Only to EO 11246.*

- The contractor must have filed a current Employer Information Report EEO-1 (EEO-1 Report). This report identifies the race, national origin and sex of the contractor's employees, by job category. COs must confirm the EEO-1 Report filing.

- Contactors must notify subcontractors, including vendors who are subcontractors, of their obligation to file an EEO-1 Report annually. COs must confirm that the contractor met this obligation.

- Advertisements and solicitations for employment must state that the contractor will consider all qualified applicants, regardless of race, color, sex, national origin or religion. COs will review a sample of such advertisements and solicitations.

c. *Technical Requirements Applicable Only to Section 4212.*

- The contractor is required to submit a VETS-100A Report annually.[96] The report includes the numbers of disabled and other protected veterans in the contractor's workforce by job category and hiring location. Contractors must also collect data indicating the total number of employees and covered veterans hired during the reporting period. COs must confirm the contractor filed the VETS-100A Report.[97] If it was not, COs must notify the Veterans' Employment Training Services (VETS) office at DOL.

---

96 If the covered contract predates December 1, 2003, and was not modified after that date for a total contract value of more than $100,000, the contractor is required to submit the VETS-100 form annually.

97 Director's Alert 2011-1 creates the requirement that COs and others, as appropriate, obtain VETS-100 database user accounts and that the regions report the number of COs with active accounts to the national office.

- Under Section 4212, contractors must list employment openings with the appropriate employment service delivery system when the openings occur. Contractors must list all employment openings except for executive and top management positions, positions filled internally and jobs lasting three days or less. If possible, COs will contact the employment office (employment service delivery system) used by the contractor in advance of the onsite review and request confirmation that the contractor has listed its employment openings with that office. COs must obtain from the employment office a listing of the job orders the contractor placed, by job title and date. COs must then compare this list with the list of jobs the contractor has filled through new hires, identify any jobs not listed with the employment office, and determine whether they should have been listed.

2I01 EO 13496 REQUIREMENTS

Pursuant to Executive Order 13496 and its implementing regulations, 29 CFR. Part 471, federal contractors and subcontractors, beginning on June 21, 2010, must notify employees about their rights under the National Labor Relations Act (NLRA). Contractors with covered contracts must meet their obligations under Executive Order 13496.[98]

Executive Order 13496 requires that covered contractors post notices specifying employee rights under the (NLRA). The NLRA guarantees employees the right to organize and bargain collectively with their employer, and to be free from retaliation for so doing. Contractors must post the notice conspicuously in and around their establishments, work sites, and offices so that it is prominent and employees who are covered by the NLRA and directly or indirectly (e.g., maintenance, repair, personnel, payroll work) engaged in contract-related activity can readily see it. COs must inspect employee bulletin boards and areas frequented by applicants and employees, such as break rooms, personnel offices and common areas, for the required poster. If the contractor customarily posts employee notices regarding the terms and conditions of employment electronically, then the contractor must also post the EO 13496 notice electronically. COs must verify the contractor's compliance.

EO 13496 also requires that covered contractors ensure that each subcontract and purchase order related to their federal contract(s) contains a notice of this posting obligation. COs must review a sampling of subcontracts and purchase orders to ensure that a covered contractor complies with this requirement.

There are exceptions to the posting requirements so COs must consult with the regional SOL, their supervisors or the National Office if there are questions about coverage under EO 13496.[99] If a violation of EO 13496 is not corrected, the Director of OFCCP, or a designee, refers the matter to the Director of OLMS, who may take enforcement action, as appropriate, under 29 CFR 471.13.

---

[98] See OFCCP Directive Number 290, issued June 15, 2010.

[99] See Executive Order 13496 Frequently Asked Questions, http://www.dol.gov/ofccp/regs/compliance/EO13496_faqs.htm (last accessed Oct. 23, 2011).

2I02 RECORDKEEPING

COs must verify that the contractor has complied with all regulatory requirements regarding personnel records. If the contractor's recordkeeping is not in conformance with 60-1.12; Part 60-3; 60-250.80; 60-300.80 and 60-741.80, the CO must record the recordkeeping violations in the SCER in Part C. Failure to preserve complete and accurate records as required by these regulations constitutes noncompliance with the contractor's obligations. If the contractor has destroyed or failed to preserve records, the CO may presume that the information would have been unfavorable to the contractor. Additionally, if a contractor's case file has multiple citations for recordkeeping violations and there is evidence of a recurrence, the CO will treat it as a repeat violation.[100]

2J SUPPORT AND PERSONNEL ACTIVITY REQUIREMENTS

The CO's objective as a neutral fact finder is to gather data and information during the investigation to determine whether there are violations of the laws OFCCP enforces, and if so, what caused them. Once gathered, the CO must analyze the information. The CO will do this using any or all of a variety of methods, as appropriate. While the CO may choose to perform some analysis onsite, the CO will perform much of the analysis offsite, even though the onsite phase of the review is still open.

If the impact analysis conducted by the CO during the desk audit[101] indicates an adverse IRA, there is a need for further analyses and investigation with regard to each adverse IRA. Based upon any additional data obtained during the desk audit or the onsite review, the CO may conduct a refined IRA, adverse impact analysis, additional cohort analysis, and/or appropriate statistical analyses. If the analyses indicate evidence of disparate treatment or adverse impact, or both, resulting from the employment process, personnel activity or application of selection criteria, the CO must determine whether the problem constitutes unlawful discrimination. The CO does this by examining all of the relevant information gathered during the compliance evaluation (e.g., employment data, the CO's observations, anecdotal evidence obtained during interviews) and applying the appropriate discrimination proof model to the facts of the case. If the CO determines that the contractor engaged in unlawful discrimination, the CO will record this violation finding in the SCER in Parts C and F. If, on the other hand, the determination is that no violation exists the CO records that finding in the Case Summary and Recommendations section.

2J00 ANALYZING THE SELECTION PROCESS

---

[100] See Chapter 8 – Resolution of Noncompliance.
[101] See Chapter 10 – Analysis of EO11246 AAP: Audit of Personnel Activity and the Impact Ratio Analysis.

a. *Identifying and Mapping the Employment Process.* The CO must determine how the contractor's selection process for the job or opportunity under examination works, including identifying all of the steps and decision points involved. The employment process usually consists of decisions and actions an employee or applicant must take such as applying for the job, as well as qualification points such as passing a test or interview in order to move to the next stage of the process. Once the CO identifies the employer's process, he or she may find it helpful to "map" or create a diagram representing the process and the points or steps in the process where the contractor can eliminate an employee or applicant from further consideration. In addition to mapping the process, the CO will need to gather information to understand when the process was instituted, why, by whom, whether there have been changes in the process and if so, when and why.

b. *Identifying Pass/Fail Points.* If an individual must successfully navigate a certain step(s) in the process before proceeding on to the next, that step(s) is a "pass/fail point." Ideally, the CO can examine each pass/fail point to see if the contractor is disproportionately screening out members of any specific group. However, if the contractor does not eliminate individuals at separate steps throughout the process, but instead weighs their performance at each step to formulate a final decision, then the CO evaluates the process as a whole. To do this, the CO must ask the contractor to explain the importance and weight of each step in the selection decision. If an analysis of the entire selection process shows that the contractor disproportionately screens out members of a specific group the CO must attempt to determine the particular criteria that are the source of the problem.

c. *Lack of Data*: If the contractor failed to maintain adequate data as required by 41 CFR Part 60-3, the CO must cite the contractor for this violation. If the contractor's lack of data hinders the CO's ability to determine the step or criterion that disproportionately eliminated members of the nonfavored group, then the CO must conduct the analysis based upon the "bottom line effect" or the existence of an adverse impact due to the total selection process. However, under such circumstances the CO must obtain as much information as possible about the process and make every effort to identify the step or criterion causing the problem. Below is a very basic example of the concept.

    Example. A selection process consists of: 1) completing an application; 2) having a high school diploma; 3) taking a written test; and 4) participating in an interview during which the contractor accepts or rejects the applicant. In this example, applicants must demonstrate they have a high school diploma before taking the test, and must pass the test before participating in an interview. For each applicant, the CO must determine the applicant's race and/or ethnicity and sex, whether the applicant had a high school diploma, the test results, and the results of the interview including the interviewer's notes, if any. This information is used when determining the number of members within each group eliminated at each step of the process. The CO must conduct an adverse impact analysis at each stage of the selection process to determine whether adverse impact occurs.

If the contractor's application process, or any part of the process, is subject to the Internet Applicant Rule, the CO must obtain applicant data and information regarding the basic criteria used in determining applicants for the job.[102] The CO must discuss with his or her supervisor the appropriate analyses for Internet applicants.

d. *Relevant Pools*. The relevant pool for each step of the contractor's selection process includes the individuals who made it *to that step* in the selection process compared with those who made it *through to the next step*. In the example in (c), above, if the CO is analyzing disparity in hiring rates, he or she would first consider the pool of all applicants to determine whether the high school diploma requirement is the source of the adverse impact. If the high school diploma requirement does not fully explain the disparity in hiring, the CO would next determine whether the test disproportionately eliminated members of the nonfavored group. Finally, the relevant pool for evaluating the effect of the interview would be all applicants who have a high school diploma and passed the test. Therefore, any difference in their selection rates would be attributable to the interview.

2J01 DISTINGUISHING OBJECTIVE FROM SUBJECTIVE SELECTION CRITERIA

The contractor's selection criteria fall into two broad categories: "objective criteria" and "subjective criteria."

a. *Objective Criteria*. The central characteristic of an objective criterion is that it can be independently verified. With objective criteria, different people measuring the criteria will reach the same results because they are clearly defined or quantifiable in nature. For example, if the criterion is possession of a certain diploma or degree, whether the individual has the degree or not is an independently verifiable fact.

b. *Subjective Criteria*. Subjective criteria require judgment in their application. Therefore, people can differ in opinion on whether a particular candidate possesses and meets such a criterion. For example, two selecting officials may easily have differing opinions on whether a candidate "has good leadership skills." In this example, if disparities exist in the application of the subjective criteria between groups, the CO would gather information to determine if the contractor applied the subjective criteria based on stereotypes. An example of this might be a statement made by hiring official that men commonly display leadership qualities that women do not.

In most cases, the CO will first analyze a contractor's use of objective criteria and the resulting impact, followed by an analysis of the contractor's use of subjective criteria and the resulting impact. Decisions based on subjective criteria involve the use of "judgment calls" by the contractor. Clearly, it can be difficult to assess whether subjective criteria are applied equally to all similarly situated applicants or candidates are tainted by prohibited stereotyping of groups. Generally, when the CO cannot attribute an adverse impact to objective criteria it is likely attributable to the use of subjective criteria. This is most likely where the CO finds that the reasons for the decision are undocumented or the contractor characterizes the decision in a subjective manner like saying that the applicant was "a good fit."

---

[102] See Section 1G – Review of Executive Order Support Data for Acceptability.

In some instances, the CO will find that the contractor used multiple criteria when making the hiring decision. When this occurs, the CO must determine if the person selected was required to meet each criterion individually or whether the contractor balanced the criteria (e.g., assigns weight to each criterion) in reaching a decision. If meeting each criterion was a requirement, the CO must perform the appropriate analysis for each one. If the criteria are weighted, the CO must establish how they were weighted in order to determine how to conduct an analysis.

For example, a contractor gives each criterion a specific weight but one criterion is not met by a candidate. The contractor, however, selects that candidate. The CO must analyze each criterion independently to, among other things, determine the relevance of each criterion in the selection process. If, however, a contractor gives each criterion a score, and it is the cumulative score that determines whether a candidate is selected, the CO would analyze the cumulative criteria. The contractor may also refer to criteria as "minimum" or "preferred." Minimum qualifications are usually treated as "pass/fail" whereas preferred qualifications are those that the contractor may prefer but are not necessarily required. The CO must determine whether, and how, the contractor is using this criterion in making employment decisions.

2J02 ANALYSIS OF OBJECTIVE CRITERIA

The first step in analyzing the contractor's use of objective selection criteria is verifying that the criteria were actually used to make selections and that they were applied uniformly to all members of the favored and nonfavored groups. COs only need to consider the contractor's stated legitimate objective criteria.

a. *Single Criterion.* To examine the application of the criterion, the CO must determine whether the same criterion was applied to each individual and that data reflecting the application of the criterion are available for all individuals in the relevant pool.

b. *Multiple Criteria.* When there are multiple criteria, or there is no summary record available to determine whether the people selected met the criteria, the CO will need to create a summary record. The CO can do this by creating a spreadsheet or a database that contains all relevant data for each individual applicant or candidate, or both. Based on the example in subsection 2J01(a) above, the spreadsheet data for each applicant would include race/ ethnicity, sex, high school diploma or no diploma, test result and interview result. The spreadsheet will allow the CO to analyze the data more readily and determine whether the multiple criteria were applied uniformly to each applicant and the result of their application (e.g., the applicant or candidate was either selected or not selected).

c. *Interpreting the Results of Criteria Verification.*

- When the review of individuals selected is complete, the CO must review the spreadsheet data to see if each selectee actually met the criteria. The CO may conclude that the contractor used the criteria if everyone met the criteria.

- If a substantial number of individuals selected do not meet a particular criterion, the CO may discount the contractor's statement that the criterion was the basis for the decision.

- If the contractor used the criterion in a non-uniform manner. This means determining whether the contractor applied the criterion differently to members of the favored group when compared to the nonfavored group. This comparison will reveal any disparate treatment.

- If the contractor applied the criterion uniformly to members of the nonfavored group and favored group, then the CO must analyze the effect of the application of the criterion for adverse impact.

2J03 ANALYSIS OF OBJECTIVE CRITERIA FOR ADVERSE IMPACT

a. *Pool of Individuals Used for Statistical Calculation.* In an adverse impact calculation, the CO compares the number of individuals from each group (by race,/ ethnicity, and sex) who were assessed using the criterion at issue with the number from each group who met the criterion. This yields a "pass rate" or "selection rate" for each group, and the CO then tests the difference in pass rates between the groups for adverse impact.

b. *Performing the Adverse Impact Calculation.* First, the CO must determine whether each objective criterion is a pass/fail requirement, (i.e., it eliminates an individual from further consideration if it is not met), or whether it is considered along with other criteria in making a final decision.

    - For each pass/fail criterion, the CO must determine whether the difference in pass rates for members of each group (by race, ethnicity, and sex) shows adverse impact.

    - When the criteria are not considered singly but are considered together in reaching a decision, the CO must determine how the contractor weighted each criterion to make a selection. Using the weights used by the contractor, the CO must determine whether this is causing the adverse impact. If it is not possible to isolate the contribution of the individual criterion to the bottom line effect, the CO will calculate the cumulative effect of all the criteria. This calculation may be appropriate when the contractor did not keep records of the effects of the individual criteria.

c. *Measurement of Statistical Significance.* Measurement of the statistical significance of a difference in selection rates, whether by standard deviations or another method, indicates the probability that a particular disparity in those rates could or could not have occurred by chance. The greater the disparity between the percentage of a specific group (e.g., women) actually selected and the percentage of the group expected, the more likely the variation did not happen by chance but was a result of the selection factor used to screen. When there is a significant probability that the disparity in selection rates for members of a nonfavored group could not have happened by chance, this is strong evidence of adverse impact.

2J04 ANALYSIS OF SUBJECTIVE CRITERIA AND DETERMINATION OF ADVERSE IMPACT

The CO will generally undertake an analysis of subjective criteria only after first determining the effects of any objective qualifications used by the contractor. Subjective criteria are analyzed in essentially the same way as objective criteria: namely, the CO first makes a determination as to whether the contractor is actually using the stated subjective criteria (verification) and then whether the contractor is applying them to members of all groups (if not, disparate treatment may have occurred). If the contractor applied subjective criteria to all groups, then use of subjective criteria will be analyzed for adverse impact.

The CO determines this by comparing the selection rates of members of favored and nonfavored groups who met the subjective requirements to determine whether statistically significant differences exist. If the disparity in these selection rates is not significant, then it is highly unlikely that discrimination resulted from the use of the subjective criteria. If the disparity is significant, then adverse impact exists and disparate impact discrimination may have occurred. The adverse impact analysis here is the same as the analysis described in 2J03 for the objective criteria analysis.

2J05 JUSTIFICATION OF SELECTION PROCEDURES WHEN ADVERSE IMPACT IS IDENTIFIED

According to the *Uniform Guidelines on Employee Selection Procedures* (UGESP), the use of any selection procedure or criterion that has an adverse impact on hiring, promoting or other employment opportunities of members of any race, ethnic group, or sex is discriminatory unless the procedure is shown to be validated or otherwise job-related and consistent with business necessity.[103]

It is the contractor's responsibility to provide validity evidence sufficient to justify each selection procedure or criterion found to have adverse impact. Validation is the demonstration of job-relatedness by showing the relationship between the selection procedure and job performance. If in conducting the analyses of the contractor's selection procedures, COs find that a selection procedure or criterion had an adverse impact, they must ask the contractor to provide all available information regarding its validation of the criterion in question. The contractor should provide information regarding the following:

- Development of the procedure and criterion, including, if the procedure is a written test, whether the contractor developed it internally or purchased it from a vendor;

[103] See 41 CFR 60-3.3A for the UGESP.

- Validity studies it conducted, including the correlation coefficient (criterion and construct validation), or how the selection criterion or test content is linked with job requirements, that is, content validation;[104]
- Job analysis in the case of content validity studies and job information that describes how and why the selection criterion was chosen for criterion-related validity studies;[105] and
- Consideration given to alternative selection criterion, the reason for rejecting the alternatives considered, and any efforts made by the contractor to lessen the adverse impact.[106]

COs must analyze this information, along with the analysis finding adverse impact caused by the use of the selection procedure and any other relevant evidence, in accordance with UGESP. Further analysis of the selection procedure or criterion at issue, or both, and their validation, will be coordinated between the Regional Office and the National Office.[107]

2K LINKAGE AGREEMENTS

COs are required to make contact with community organizations and recruitment resources as part of their assessment of a contractor's recruitment efforts. This requires that the CO have knowledge of the resources available in the community to provide assistance to contractors in resolving employment deficiencies. OFCCP encourages and facilitates such "linkage" relationships between contractors and community recruitment resources.

2K00 LINKAGE OBJECTIVES

OFCCP's online Resources Directory may provide sources of potential linkages. The following are OFCCP's objectives with respect to facilitating and encouraging linkages:

- To increase employment opportunities available to minorities, identified race/ ethnic groups, women, individuals with disabilities and disabled and otherwise protected veterans;
- To enhance the effectiveness of OFCCP's compliance activities by providing contractors with additional recruitment sources;
- To assist federal contractors in meeting their affirmative action hiring and promotion goals; and

[104] See 41 CFR Part 60-3.5, 3.14 and 3.15.
[105] See 41 CFR Part 60-3.14A; 60-3.14B(2) and (3).
[106] See 41 CFR Part 60-3.3B.
[107] See OFCCP Directive 267 (Oct. 15, 2004) on the investigative procedures used when a test is one cause of adverse impact in hiring.

- To increase cooperation between private sector employers and community recruitment resources.

2K01 LINKAGE REQUIREMENTS

COs must seek to develop new linkages between community recruitment and referral sources and contractors that have made insufficient recruitment efforts to generate applicants that satisfy their affirmative action objectives. Before a CO urges contractors to use the resources, the CO must identify and contact organizations to affirm that they can be of assistance, and to explain what is expected of both parties.

2K02 IMPLEMENTATION UNDER EO 11246

When linkage is needed, a CO must take the following actions to establish linkage agreements during the course of the compliance evaluation:

a. Identify those job groups in the contractor's workforce where goals were established and there was employment activity, but the goals were not met.

b. Evaluate the contractor's good faith efforts to identify possible recruitment sources for those underutilized job groups.

c. Contact appropriate linkage resources to obtain specific information on availability of potential applicants and potential trainees for positions in the areas of underutilization. If possible, the CO must arrange a meeting between the resource organization(s) and the contractor.

d. When a resource appears to be a likely source of applicants or trainees, the CO will include the contractor's commitment to utilize the linkage source along with other actions in the CA.[108]

e. The CA will require progress reports at least semi-annually. With respect to linkages, these reports should contain:

  - Total hire activity by job group, broken out by sex, race, and other relevant covered group status; and

  - Total hire activity and number of people referred from each linkage source agreed to in the CA, and any other appropriate source, broken out by sex, race and other relevant covered group status.

2K03 WHERE LINKAGE AGREEMENTS ARE NOT REQUIRED (EO 11246 Only)

---

[108] See Chapter 8 – Resolution of Noncompliance.

The establishment of new linkages is not required if a CO finds that the contractor's utilization approximates availability for the given job group. If this is true, utilization does not appear to be a problem. Additionally, if it is determined that a current recruitment and referral source with which there is an existing linkage is no longer able to provide the needed assistance, it may be appropriate to discontinue the existing linkage. The CO will assist the contractor in establishing replacement linkages if they are needed.

2K04 LINKAGE AGREEEMENTS FOR INDIVIDUALS WITH DISABILITIES AND DISABLED AND OTHERWISE PROTECTED VETERANS

Linkage arrangements involving recruitment or referral sources for individuals with disabilities, and disabled veterans and otherwise protected veterans are necessary when either or both of the following exists:

- A review of employee records, job applications and applicant flow data shows that there are few applicants who are members of these covered groups; or,
- There are no applicants, and the outreach and recruitment for people from these groups is non-existent or ineffective.

If the contractor needs new linkage relationships, the CO will follow the same steps to establish appropriate linkages for these groups as he or she would when establishing linkages to meet affirmative action goals for other groups.

2K05 CONFIRMATION OF LINKAGE AGREEMENT

At the conclusion of the compliance evaluation, the CO will provide written notices to all of the linkage resources or partners in the agreement with the contractor. A sample of a linkage letter is at Letter L-5 – Sample Linkage Letter. The contractor must be provided a copy of the letter. The CO must document the notifications in the case file.

2L COLLECTING INFORMATION

It is likely that the CO will need to review and evaluate offsite at least some of the data collected during the onsite review. For example, the CO may need to conduct analyses to determine whether disparate treatment and/or disparate impact have occurred. Therefore, the CO must gather the data necessary to conduct a proper analysis for both favored and nonfavored groups. The CO will also need to obtain all available data necessary to secure a full understanding of the contractor's employment practices and processes, including how they apply to any actions or processes the CO is examining.

Generally, the review period begins two years prior to the contractor's receipt of the Scheduling Letter and ends when the violations that were identified are corrected and remedied. This, of course, assumes that coverage is established for the full review period. The CO may need updated records and data for the period following the start of the review to update the information initially submitted by the contractor or to investigate issues first identified onsite.

For example, the CO must request data relevant to the potential discrimination issues identified at the desk audit to determine how long the violation extends and whether the violations continue to the present day. Such information is necessary for the CO to ensure that the contractor stops any identified discrimination and to determine what remedies victims need if they are to be made whole. On the other hand, the CO may need to review information relating to periods more than two years prior to the contractor's receipt of the Scheduling Letter where the potential for continuing violations exists.

The data collected should include, but not be limited to, applications for all applicants, test results, all interview notes, personnel files, policies and procedures, employment data and other relevant contractor documentation. The CO must also request employment data that the contractor had not previously submitted. For example, if a review of information indicates that the contractor did not include its entire workforce in its AAP(s),[109] the CO should request data and information regarding this determination. The CO will examine whether the contractor's determination not to include these workers as employees was correct or whether that decision improperly omitted or misclassified workers. If the contractor misclassified the workers or otherwise should have included them in the contractor's AAP(s), the CO must consider the employment data for these workers in the analyses.

To ensure the CO obtains all needed information, he or she makes a list of the data and other information needed from the contractor prior to departure from the onsite review. The CO must update this list, adding new items as the CO becomes aware of them, and recording when he or she received the requested or needed items.

2L00 TYPES OF EVIDENCE

The CO will obtain, review and analyze employment data, documents, policies, procedures, interview statements and observations throughout the review. An example of an observation that might be significant is the absence of women working on the loading dock. The CO will examine all the information to assess whether sufficient evidence exists to determine whether prohibited discrimination or other violation occurred during the review period. If either did occur, the CO must determine whether the discrimination or other violation is ongoing.

There are two broad types of evidence: direct evidence and circumstantial evidence. Direct evidence is evidence that, if believed, directly proves a fact. For example, an e-mail from the contractor's director instructing supervisors not to hire women into certain jobs or a statement by a manager that "we don't hire women here" would constitute direct evidence of discrimination against women. In contrast, circumstantial evidence is evidence that creates an inference or presumption of a fact. For example, data showing that the difference between the selection rates for blacks and non-minorities in the laborer job group is 3 standard deviations is circumstantial evidence of discrimination against blacks. The statistics do not *directly* prove discrimination. But if there is no non-discriminatory reason for the statistical discrepancy, discrimination against blacks will be inferred.

---

[109] An example is a contractor excluding temporary workers or independent contractors for the AAP.

The CO may use direct evidence and circumstantial evidence, either alone or in combination, to prove discrimination. The key question when determining if the contractor has engaged in discrimination is assessing whether the evidence, direct or circumstantial or both satisfies the appropriate burden of proof of discrimination.

Anecdotal evidence often supports statistical evidence of discrimination in systemic cases. Anecdotal evidence may be either direct or circumstantial, and is first-hand accounts of personal experiences with discrimination by the contractor at issue that bring "the cold numbers convincingly to life." Documents the contractor submits may contain anecdotal evidence, or COs may obtain anecdotal evidence from interviews with managers, employees or applicants. In some cases, OFCCP may find systemic discrimination based only on anecdotal evidence that directly supports a pattern or practice of discrimination.

For example, the company president sends an e-mail to managers stating his concern that women are unable to lift heavy objects and that if women are hired for stockroom positions there will be a higher risk of on the job injuries that will impact the company's profitability. This anecdotal evidence could support a finding of discrimination against women applicants for stockroom positions at that establishment.

2L01 PERSONNEL ACTIVITY AND SELECTION PROCESS

During the onsite review, it is imperative the CO develop an understanding of the contractor's employment procedures and practices. This includes obtaining copies of selection policies and procedures related to areas where the CO identified potential discrimination during the desk audit. The CO can also garner crucial information from interviews of human resources personnel, selecting officials, employees (e.g., hired, promoted or terminated during the review period) and other individuals identified as participating in or being affected by the selection process such as those who were candidates for open positions but were not hired or promoted. The CO must also gather contact information from potentially knowledgeable individuals no longer employed by the contractor, if applicable.

The type of information the CO will gather depends on identified concerns; however, some examples are provided below.

- *Hiring Data.* This includes job group and/or job title identification, copies of personnel files, payroll records, job applications, job announcements, staffing requisitions, advertisements (internal and external postings), job descriptions, job status (e.g., permanent, temporary, full or part-time), minimum qualifications, preferences, applicant flow data, documentation created at each stage of the selection process (e.g., selecting officials' interview notes, computerized screening of Internet applicants), phone screen procedures and testing information.

- *Promotions.* This includes from and/or to promotion identification, copies of personnel files, payroll records, promotion policies and procedures, internal advertisements and bid sheets, candidate flow data for eligible candidates, payroll data, documentation created at each stage of the promotion process (e.g., officials' interview notes), phone screen procedures, and testing information.

- *Terminations*. This includes job group and/or title identification, copies of personnel files, payroll records, information regarding voluntary and involuntary terminations, termination policies and procedures, documentation of the reason for termination, exit interview notes and documentation, termination letters and contact information for terminated employees.

2L02 SELECTION PROCEDURES AND TESTING

As noted in subsection 2J05 above, the UGESP at 41 CFR 60-3.3A states that using any facially neutral selection procedure or criterion resulting in an adverse impact on hiring, promoting or other employment opportunities of members of any race, sex or ethnic group is discriminatory unless the contractor proves that its use is justified. Information that the CO will obtain to assess whether the contractor's selection procedures or criteria have an adverse impact may include:

- A written description of the selection steps and criteria applied;

- A copy of the job description(s);

- A copy of all records the contractor created to implement the selection procedures or criteria during the review period. Examples of these records include test results, individual test scores, instruction manuals related to testing or selection procedures, interview forms and interview results. When the selection process includes a battery of tests, the CO must be sure to collect the scores for each part of the battery, as well as the composite or overall scores and learn how the contractor determined them. If the contractor is administering a test at a specific location, it is often helpful to see the testing location;

- Obtain signed interview statements from the contractor representatives who administered the selection procedure during the review period. The interviews need to include information about how the contractor administered the selection procedure, when they initiated the procedure, whether the contractor made any changes to the procedure, and when and why the changes were made. Additional information would include whether the contractor validated the selection procedure;[110] and whether there were any efforts to minimize the adverse impact. If efforts were made, COs must determine what those efforts were; and

- A copy of all job analyses or job information describing how the contractor established job requirements, and

- Copies of any validation studies conducted by the contractor.

---

[110] Validation means demonstrating that using the selection procedure met the validation standards of the UGESP.

Example interview questions the CO will ask may include these areas of inquiry:

- What are the selection procedures and criteria?
- How does the contractor administer the selection procedures? Are interviews and tests conducted in similar settings? Are they conducted by multiple individuals? Who administers each procedure? Who is the decision maker for each procedure?
- How did the contractor score or rate each selection procedure or criterion, or both? Is there a passing score set for each one? Is it weighted? How was it weighed and why? Does the contractor score or rate the candidates cumulatively? If so, how?
- How does the contractor select or "pass" candidates on the selection procedure (e.g., total test score, based on performance during interview)?
- How did the contractor come to use the selection procedure? If the procedure was a test, did the contractor develop it internally or by an external contractor or vendor? Did the contractor purchase a pencil and paper test?
- If the CO has identified adverse impact at any stage of the selection process, is the use of the procedure or criterion responsible for that impact justified by business necessity? What has the contractor done to consider alternative procedures with less impact? What actions did the contractor take to validate the selection procedure or test? Are there any validation reports or studies? Did the contractor consider such reports or studies, or both?

2L03 COMPENSATION

Investigation of potential compensation discrimination presents complex and nuanced issues. The choice of the best approach for a case depends upon the underlying facts, the available data, and the contractor's compensation system and practices. As such, OFCCP takes a case-by-case approach to analyzing compensation issues. In every case there are three key questions to be addressed, and onsite review may provide data or information necessary to answer them:

- Is there a measurable difference in compensation on the basis of sex, race, or ethnicity?[111]
- Is the difference in compensation between comparative employees under the contractor's wage or salary system?
- Is there a legitimate explanation for the difference?

---

[111] In situations where there is sufficient data and analytic power to use regression analysis, a measureable difference generally means a statistically significant difference, two standard deviations. In the situation of disparities in small group and/or individual compensation, a measureable difference and sufficient evidence will be determined in conformance with Title VII principles.

An onsite review may include analysis of workforce data and contractor compensation policies and practices; interviewing personnel and employees; examining payroll and Human Resource Information Systems (HRIS); and any other information necessary to understand or analyze compensation data or practices. In conducting the onsite COs examine all employment practices that have the potential to lead to compensation disparities. Prior desk audit results may assist the CO in identifying particular practices or issues to investigate.

Compensation includes any payments made to, or on behalf of, an employee as remuneration for employment, including but not limited to salary, wages, overtime pay, bonuses, commissions, vacation and holiday pay, allowances, reimbursements for expenses, expense account, insurance and other benefits, stock options, profit sharing. Compensation discrimination includes unexplained and unmerited differences in these areas but may also include discrimination in how employees earn or contractors distribute raises and bonuses. So, in examining compensation issues, COs must be mindful to include how the contractor treats fringe benefits. For example, if the contractor is not providing equal fringe benefits and/or not making equal contributions to insurance plans or pensions for men and women, this may constitute discrimination.

The compensation a group of employees or an individual employee receives may be negatively affected by denial of equal access to certain earnings opportunities. COs must examine employee access to opportunities affecting compensation such as higher paying positions, job classifications, work assignments, training, preferred or higher paid shift work, and other such opportunities. COs should also examine policies and practices that unfairly limit a group's opportunity to earn higher pay such as "glass ceiling" issues and access to overtime hours, pay increases, incentive compensation, and higher commission or desired sales territories. Differences may be observed in these and other areas:

- base salary;
- job assignment or placement;
- opportunities to receive training, promotions, and other opportunities for advancement;
- earnings opportunities; and
- access to salary increases or add-ons such as bonuses.

CO's must focus the onsite review on the information and practices relevant to the employer, industry and types of workers. For example, overtime issues are relevant to hourly and non-exempt workforces, while high level salaried positions may involve substantial bonuses, stock options and other incentive compensation. For sales employees, both commission and account or territory assignment practices may be relevant.

In addition to reviewing potential evidence of systemic pay discrimination, COs may use onsite reviews to determine if there is evidence sufficient to support an inference that individual or cohort pay differences are due to discrimination. Absolute pay differences between comparators, without any other evidence of pretext or possible discrimination, generally are not sufficient to support an individual disparate treatment analysis.

For purposes of evaluating compensation differences, employees are similarly situated where it is reasonable to expect they should be receiving equivalent compensation absent discrimination. Relevant factors in determining similarity may include tasks performed, skills, effort, level of responsibility, working conditions, job difficulty, minimum qualifications, and other objective factors. In some cases, employees are similarly situated where they are comparable on some of these factors, even if they are not similar on others. For example, when evaluating a job assignment issue, workers are similarly situated when their qualifications are comparable, but they are assigned to jobs at different levels. Who is similarly situated for purposes of an individual analysis or review of a single specific employment decision may be determined based on different criteria than when conducting a systemic discrimination analysis. Onsite review allows COs to make assessments of similarly situated employees or jobs by observing, by conducting interviews and by reviewing documents.

OFCCP will evaluate, on a case-by-case basis, information from the contractor regarding the factors the contractor considered in making compensation decisions. A factor is an element that the contractor offers to explain differences in employee compensation under its compensation system and practices. Factors may include internal and external elements potentially affecting compensation. A factor may be a qualification or skill that the worker brings to the position such as education, experience, etc. It may also be an employment element such as position, level or function; tenure in position; performance ratings, etc.

COs will use information gathered at the onsite review to evaluate whether these factors actually explain compensation, whether they are implemented fairly and consistently, whether data regarding that factor is accurate, and whether they should be incorporated into the analysis to be conducted.

The CO must also confirm that the amount of compensation offered to individuals with disabilities and veterans with disablities is not reduced due to them receiving a reasonable accommodation or any disability income, pension, other benefit received from another source. To verify compliance with this requirement, the CO will request the files of identified individuals with disabilities and/or disabled veterans, along with those of people without disabilities in the same job titles, and compare their compensation

2M INTERVIEWS

Based on results of the desk audit, the CO will develop an onsite investigative plan that includes interviews of contractor personnel, employees and applicants, as appropriate. The CO must meet with the contractor's staff members who are knowledgeable about the contractor's employment policies and practices. During these interviews, the CO will clarify any questions he or she may have regarding the contractor's organization, structure, corporate culture and other issues identified during the desk audit. This is also the CO's opportunity to become more familiar with the contractor's informal or unwritten policies and practices, and to compare these to written materials and practices outlined in the AAP. Interviews with employees and applicants may provide further information regarding the application of the contractor's procedures.[112]

If reasonable accommodation for an interviewee is necessary, the CO will arrange for the interviewee to receive the accommodation. Additionally, if the interviewee needs a translator, the CO will arrange for this in advance of the interview or schedule the interview to ensure translation services are present.

2M00 GENERAL INTERVIEW PRINCIPLES AND PROCEDURES

Interviews may be informal or formal. An informal interview may occur during the facility inspection while a formal interview occurs during a scheduled meeting with a pre-planned list of questions.

As the onsite review proceeds, there will be continuing discussions between COs and contractor personnel. COs must document in writing the content of these discussions as soon as possible. It is a good practice for COs to review their notes of these discussions with the interviewee to ensure they accurately reflect the interviewee's statements.

a. *Reason for Interview.* CO initiated interviews are conducted with an identified purpose or goal. Reasons for interviews may include:

   - gaining understanding of contractor policies and procedures,
   - obtaining relevant general information,
   - corroborating information received from other sources, and
   - identifying additional areas for investigation.
   - Depending on the results of the desk audit, the CO will pay specific attention to the contractor's employment practices, including compensation, hiring, termination and promotion practices. The CO will also conduct interviews with managers and employees that focus on contractor practices with regard to equal employment opportunities for minorities and women, for individuals with disabilities and for disabled and other veterans protected by Section 4212.

b. *Interview Plan.* As a part of the onsite plan, the CO must develop appropriate questions and identify specific individuals to interview regarding each identified potential problem area or compliance issue. Each planned interview or group of interviews should have an interview plan that indicates the topics the interview will address and spells out the initial questions the CO plans to ask. Interview plans will vary depending on whether the interviewee is a manager, other employee, unsuccessful candidate for hire, etc. If there is an individual that

[112] See 2C01(d) – Obtaining and Maintaining Records.

the CO identified for interview but did not interview, the CO will make a note in the case file as to why the interview did not take place.

c. *Informing the Interviewee.* The CO will tell each interviewee, at the outset of a formal interview that:

- the CO will show the interviewee his or her statement containing the answers to the questions asked during the interview, and
- the CO will ask the interviewee to sign his or her statement.

The CO will inform each interviewee that knowingly providing false or inaccurate information is unlawful and will explain that the following phrase is included in the interview notes where the interviewee signs:

"I have read the above and it is a true and accurate to the best of my knowledge."

In addition, each time the CO speaks with someone who is not a member of management he or she must inform the individual that the interview is kept confidential to the extent possible. The CO must inform all individuals, regardless of their position with the contractor, that it is unlawful for the contractor to intimidate them or take retaliatory action against them for participating in an interview.

d. *Contractor's Presence at Interviews.* When the CO conducts onsite interviews with non-management personnel, the contractor does not have the right to have a representative present. When the CO conducts interviews with upper level managers and directors that speak for or make decisions on behalf of the company, the contractor may have an attorney or other representative present. The exception to this is when the manager is not speaking for management. An example may be when the manager is a member of a potentially affected group speaking about the potential discrimination or his or her personal experience or acting as a whistleblower.

e. *Employee Representative Present at Interviews.* An employee may request that a personal representative, such as a union representative or legal counsel, accompany him or her during the interview. This is generally acceptable; however, the CO must discuss the presence of the representative with the interviewee privately to determine whether there may be a conflict of interest or whether the interviewee feels pressured into having the person present. If the individual wants the representative to be present the CO will note the representative's name and title on the documentation of the interview.

COs must be aware that, in some instances, the presence of a representative may affect confidentiality or other privileges. The CO must consult with RSOL if there are any questions about the impact of the presence of a third party on confidentiality or privileges.

f. *Formal Interviews.* After a formal interview, the CO must ask each person to read, sign and date the CO's interview notes. At the conclusion of the interview, the CO will review the questions asked and the answers given, and obtain confirmation that any direct quotes are accurate and that all paraphrases convey the interviewee's intended meaning. The CO will promptly type the handwritten interview notes using MS Word in order to provide the interviewee with a hard copy to sign as soon as possible after the interview. The CO must enter the following phrase above the space where the interviewee will sign:

"I have read the above and it is a true and accurate to the best of my knowledge."

If the interviewee must receive a hard copy of the interview for signature later, the CO must obtain a personal mailing address from the interviewee and a contact phone number. The CO will mail the hard copy to the interviewee. If the interviewee wants corrections made, the CO must incorporate the corrections and send a hard copy of the interview to the interviewee to sign. The CO maintains records of both the original and the corrected interview in the case file. If an interviewee refuses to sign the notes, the CO will record this and the reason(s) for refusal to sign, if known.

g. *Informal (Unplanned) Interviews.* At any point in the review process, a potential witness may approach the CO to provide information related to the review. The CO must make every effort to meet or otherwise interview the potential witness. The CO will follow the interview procedures described in this section.

   If, however, the potential witness is unwilling to be interviewed and only wants to provide the information, the CO must document the conditions under which the employee provided the information. For example, the CO records that the employee provided the CO with a document, briefly describes and attaches the document to the memorandum, and indicates in the memorandum that he or she was unwilling to be interviewed. The CO must then use other means to verify the credibility of the information provided in this manner.

h. *Location of Interviews.* The CO normally conducts interviews during the onsite review phase of the compliance evaluation. However, the CO may conduct interviews via telephone, as appropriate. There may be situations when a contractor refuses to allow onsite interviews of non-managerial employees or where such employees want their interviews conducted away from the establishment. When possible, the CO will attempt to explore alternatives with the contractor or the employee, as appropriate. One possible alternative is conducting interviews during meal breaks. Other options might include interviewing an employee onsite prior to the start of work shifts, or at the end of his or her shift. A CO may also conduct interviews at an offsite location.

i. *Telephone Interviews.* The CO will conduct telephone interviews only when it is not feasible to conduct the interview in person, since the CO cannot observe the interviewee's demeanor during a telephone interview, making credibility determinations more difficult. However, when telephone interviews of employees or applicants are necessary, the CO must type the resulting notes and send a copy to the interviewee for review, revisions, as appropriate, and signature. The CO will ask whether there is anyone else present with the interviewee to address any concerns this may create.

2M01 MANAGEMENT INTERVIEWS

COs must identify the managers that played a role in making employment decisions that the COs determine, through the desk audit review or other onsite analysis, need clarification. Examples of the types of questions that a CO should ask are below.

- How did the contractor make the personnel or other decision? What procedures were used? Are these procedures customarily used? Are exceptions made to these procedures made? If so, under what circumstances or when are exceptions made?

- How were the qualification criteria evaluated?

- What was the decision process? What was your role in the process or personnel action? Were you the sole decision maker or part of a team of decision makers? What did you base the decision on and what information did you have when making the decision?

- Is the contractor making efforts to reach out to or establish linkages with groups representing veterans, individuals with disabilities, women and minorities? Describe those efforts.

2M02 EMPLOYEE INTERVIEWS

When onsite, COs must interview current employees, including those identified as possible members of an adversely affected class and members of the favored group who the contractor hired for the position at issue. The COs must also interview individuals who may have information that is relevant to potential problem areas. Examples of the types of questions that the CO should ask during these interviews are below.

- Do you know whether management uniformly applies [describe the practice or procedure under investigation]? Does management make exceptions to the process? If so, under what circumstances or when are exceptions made?

- Do you have first-hand experience with the practice or procedure? If so, explain when and under what circumstances?

- What are the duties associated with the job at issue? Are the qualifications for the job necessary or related to job performance?

- Are you aware of company policies and procedures related to EEO?

- Are you aware of any instances where the company violated EEO policies?

- Do you know anyone else who might have knowledge about this practice or procedure?

2M03 ISSUES THAT ARISE DURING THE ONSITE REVIEW

During the course of the onsite review, or while interviewing employees and managers, issues may arise that were not identified during the desk audit review. If this happens, the CO must appropriately follow-up on the new issues. For example, if the issue concerns a possible systemic violation by the contractor or is relevant to the compliance evaluation in progress, the CO must include the matter in the ongoing investigation. If the matter is one alleging an individual instance of discrimination, or if someone files a complaint during the ongoing compliance review, the CO must discuss the matter with his or her supervisor to determine how to best proceed.[113]

2N EXIT CONFERENCE

Upon completion of the necessary onsite review and evaluation of all information obtained, COs will discuss the tentative findings of the compliance evaluation with the contractor at the onsite exit conference. The onsite exit conference should be held with the contractor's CEO executive officer or designee at a mutually agreed upon location. The CO will reiterate to the contractor that EO 11246, Section 503, and Section 4212 prohibit intimidation or retaliation of anyone assisting or participating in the investigation.[114] An exit conference does not mean that the onsite review is complete; therefore, COs should avoid making any statements that could lead the contractor to believe that the CO is no longer able to request a follow-up onsite or to seek additional information.

2N00 AREAS TO COVER AT THE EXIT CONFERENCE

COs must schedule the exit conference for the final day of the onsite visit. At this conference, the CO must be prepared to describe the aspects of the investigation and to discuss the tentative findings of the compliance evaluation in general terms. The CO will inform the CEO, or designee, of the next steps in the compliance evaluation process, of any outstanding or additional requests for information, and of the possibility that a PDN or NOV could be issued.

2O RETURN ONSITE VISIT AND DENIAL OF ACCESS

After the initial onsite review, a return onsite visit may be necessary if the CO identifies the need for additional data or personnel interviews. The CO must discuss this possibility with his or her supervisor.

When a second onsite visit is needed, the CO will follow the onsite procedures as described in this chapter. However, if the contractor can timely submit additional data or information without an onsite visit, the CO does not need to conduct a return onsite visit, unless the contractor fails to provide the information.

---

[113] See also Chapter 6 – Complaint Investigations.
[114] See also 2C00 – Prohibition Against Retaliation.

If the contractor refuses to provide the requested data or information or does not allow a follow up onsite visit, the CO will prepare an SCN for denial of access. More information on this issue is in Chapter 8, Resolution of Noncompliance.

2P INVESTIGATION SUMMARY OR REPORT WRITING

Throughout the compliance evaluation, the CO will use the SCER Part C to record potential discrimination issues that the CO identified and investigated. The CO will also use the SCER worksheets to specify:

- whether a particular issue or problem needs analysis as an individual case or a pattern or practice case, and
- whether the particular issue or problem requires a disparate treatment analysis, a disparate impact analysis, or both.

After concluding the onsite review, the CO must complete any required analyses of the data and other information that was gathered. The CO must investigate problem areas and issues until the case file contains sufficient evidence to establish whether discrimination did or did not occur. The case file should retain all evidence the CO obtained and documents the CO created, including any evidence that does not support the CO's conclusions.

2P00 SUMMARY OF FINDINGS

After completing the compliance evaluation, including all onsite and offsite analyses of the information obtained and recorded in the SCER Part C, the CO must compile a summary of findings to include in the SCER in Part F. This summary includes the findings of the case, the bases for the findings, and the CO's recommendations. The summary of findings should also include the:

- name and description of the facility;
- problem area(s) identified, if applicable;
- description of the selection or other process or practice examined (e.g., for a hiring case, the steps in the application process);
- results of any analyses conducted such as IRAs, comparative (cohort) analysis, and regression analysis;
- summary of any interviews conducted;
- relevant anecdotal evidence obtained;
- description of any violations and their bases;

- recommended corrective actions, where the CO has identified violations; and
- recommended next steps.

The summary should logically lead to the CO's conclusion about whether or not a violation occurred. The CO submits the completed SCER to his or her supervisor for approval.

Depending upon the circumstances of a particular case, it may be a good practice to conduct a follow-up meeting or teleconference with the contractor. Below is an example of why this is a good practice.

- The CO held an exit conference with the contractor at the conclusion of the onsite review. However, following offsite analysis, the CO found additional issues that need to be discussed with the contractor. More specifically, at the conclusion of the onsite, the CO told the contractor that it would be cited for failing to track the race, ethnicity and gender of job applicants passing through various phases of the selection process. However, during offsite analysis, it became clear to the CO that the contractor also discriminated in its termination activity.

After advising the contractor of its compliance evaluation findings, the CO must provide formal notification through a Predetermination Notice or Notice of Violation. COs use certified mail, return receipt requested, to provide this notice to the contractor. If requested by the contractor, a courtesy copy is sent by e-mail or facsimile. We discuss the various forms of notice in more detail in Chapter 8, Resolution of Noncompliance.

If, prior to the issuance of the notice of compliance, the contractor provides new evidence, the CO must conduct any necessary investigation and analyses to determine if the new evidence changes any of the initial findings and to ensure that the final findings are fully supported. A basic part of any additional investigation is verifying the credibility of the new evidence.

CHAPTER 3
CONSTRUCTION INDUSTRY COMPLIANCE PROGRAM

3A GENERAL

This chapter contains procedures for conducting compliance reviews of construction contractors and subcontractors, including those involved in federally assisted construction projects. The purpose of the reviews is to determine whether contractors are complying with requirements prohibiting discrimination and requiring affirmative action to ensure equal employment opportunity without regard to race, color, religion, national origin, sex, disability or covered veteran status.

3B COVERAGE

Federal construction contractors, if they have a construction contract of the requisite amount with a federal agency, are covered by Executive Order 11246 (EO 11246), as amended; the Vietnam Era Veterans' Readjustment Assistance Act of 1974, as amended (Section 4212); and Section 503 of the Rehabilitation Act of 1973, as amended (Section 503). These authorities also cover construction contractors if they have a contract or subcontract with a nonconstruction contractor or another construction contractor, and:

- the contract or subcontract is necessary in whole or in part to the performance of the covered contract; or

- the contractor or subcontractor performs, undertakes or assumes any portion of the contractor's obligation under a covered contract.

The Executive Order and Section 503 cover a contractor if the contract amount exceeds $10,000; Section 4212 covers a contractor with a contract of $100,000 or more ,or $25,000 or more if the contract was entered into prior to December 1, 2003.

Federally assisted construction contracts and subcontracts in excess of $10,000 are only covered by the Executive Order and not Section 503 or Section 4212.[115]

The following subsections provide COs additional guidance on the requirements of these legal authorities.

3B00 REGULATIONS APPLICABLE TO CONSTRUCTION CONTRACTORS

Regulations applicable to the affirmative action requirements of construction contractors and federally assisted construction contractors under Executive Order 11246 are published primarily in 41 CFR Part 60-4. Specific provisions in other parts of 41 CFR Chapter 60 are also applicable

[115] Executive Order 11246, as amended, Sec. 301.

to federal and federally assisted construction contractors.[116] The regulations implementing Section 503[117] and Section 4212[118] apply to contractors and subcontractors with a Federal construction contract or subcontract covered under those laws. As mentioned earlier, the regulations implementing Section 503 and Section 4212 do not apply to federally assisted construction contracts and subcontracts.

3B01 REQUIRED CONTRACT CLAUSES

Each federal contracting agency must include the equal opportunity clauses found at 41 CFR 60-1.4(a), 60-250.5, 60-300.5 and 60-741.5, in all covered prime construction contracts. Each contractor and subcontractor must include the equal opportunity and affirmative action clauses in its covered construction subcontracts.[119]

Applicants for federal assistance involving a construction contract are required to include the equal opportunity clause found at 41 CFR 60-1.4(b) in all covered federally assisted construction contracts. Moreover, each administering agency must include this clause as a condition of any grant, contract, loan, insurance or guarantee involving federally assisted construction. Federally assisted construction contractors and subcontractors are to include only the Executive Order equal opportunity clause in subcontracts.

Nonconstruction contractors must include the appropriate clauses in construction subcontracts that are necessary, in whole or in part, to the performance of a covered nonconstruction contract.

The equal opportunity clauses may be expressly included in construction contracts and subcontracts, or incorporated by reference.[120] The clauses are, however, a part of the construction contracts even if the contractor does not physically incorporate them into the contract document[121] If contractors fails to include the required clauses in covered subcontracts and purchase orders, a CO shall cite this omission as a violation in the closure document.

3B02 CONSTRUCTION CONTRACT NOTICE AND SPECIFICATIONS

Bid solicitations for all federal and federally assisted construction contracts in excess of $10,000 must include the "Notice of Requirement for Affirmative Action to Ensure Equal Employment Opportunity (Executive Order 11246)," commonly referred to as the "Notice."[122] Among other things, the Notice sets forth the goals for minority and female participation in construction trades in covered areas, identifies the covered areas and requires that contractors provide OFCCP with specific information concerning construction subcontracts in excess of $10,000 awarded in connection with the covered contract. In addition, the Notice must be included in:

---

116 41 CFR Parts 60-1, 60-3, 60-20, 60-40, and 60-50.

117 41 CFR Part 60-741.

118 41 CFR Parts 60-250 and 60-300.

119 41 CFR 60-1.4(a) and (b) at paragraph (7); 60-1.4(c); 41 CFR 60-250.5, paragraph 11; 41 CFR 60-300.5, paragraph 11; and 41 CFR 60-741.5, paragraph 11.

120 41 CFR 60-1.4(d), 60-250.5(d), 60-300.5(d) and 60-741.5(d).

121 41 CFR 60-4.9, 41 CFR 60-250.5(e), 60-300.5(e) and 60-741.5(e).

122 41 CFR 60-4.2(d).

- grants, contracts, subcontracts, loans, insurance or guarantees involving federally assisted construction covered by Part 60-4 as a condition of these agreements; and

- construction subcontracts contracts that are necessary in whole or in part to the performance of a covered nonconstruction contract.

The Standard Federal Equal Employment Opportunity Construction Contract Specifications (Executive Order 11246), or what are commonly known as the "Specifications," describe the affirmative action obligations and detail the specific affirmative action steps construction contractors must implement in order to make a good faith effort to achieve the goals for minority and female participation that are listed in the bid solicitation. The Specifications must be included in:

- solicitations for offers and bids on all federal and federally assisted construction contracts in excess of $10,000 to be performed in geographical areas designated by the director of OFCCP, in accordance with 41 CFR 60-4.6;

- grants, contracts, subcontracts, loans, insurance or gurantees involving federally assisted construction covered by Part 60-4, as a condition of these agreements;

- federal and federally assisted construction contracts in excess of $10,000 to be performed in geographical areas designated by the director of OFCCP, in accordance with 41 CFR 60-4.6; and

- construction subcontracts in excess of $10,000 necessary in whole or in part to the performance of nonconstruction federal contracts and subcontracts.[123]

By operation of the Executive Order, the Notice and the Specifications discussed in this section are deemed incorporated in every solicitation or every covered contract and subcontract. This is true whether or not they are expressly incorporated in the solicitation or contract, and whether or not the contract is written.[124]

3B03 SUPPORT FROM OTHER AGENCIES RELATED TO CONSTRUCTION CONTRACTORS

The CO must identify the contract(s) on which the contractor's obligations are based. The CO records this information in the case file and related correspondence. Information on contract awards may be obtained from other federal agencies.

[123] 41 CFR 60-4.3(a).
[124] 41 CFR 60-4.9.

Various federal, state and local government contracting offices may be able to provide notice of contract awards and help ensure that the contractors include equal opportunity and affirmative action clauses in construction contracts. For example, OFCCP has a Memorandum of Understanding with the General Services Administration that provides for information sharing on construction contract awards.[125]

Other federal agencies may also have information not available from the contractor. For example, the Wage and Hour Division may be able to provide the number of employees of the contractor by reviewing payroll records certified under the Davis-Bacon Act. Other sources of interagency cooperation may include the Employment and Training Administration funded agencies, as well as employment referral and training organizations identified by DOL's Employment Training Administration Office of Apprenticeship and the Women's Bureau.

3C GENERAL PRINCIPLES APPLICABLE TO THE CONSTRUCTION INDUSTRY

The equal opportunity and affirmative action clauses prohibit discrimination based on race, color, religion, sex, national origin, disability or covered veteran status.[126] They also require that contractors take affirmative action to ensure equal employment opportunity. This section covers the use and application of goals for the participation of minorities and females by construction contractors, preconstruction conferences, and notice of subcontract awards.

3C00 GOALS

Goals serve as reasonably attainable objectives and allow contractors to measure progress toward achieving equal employment opportunity. They are not quotas. Contractors must demonstrate good faith efforts toward meeting their minority and female participation rate goals contained in the bid solicitation. These goals are determined by the Director of OFCCP and are issued in accordance with 41 CFR 60-4.6 by geographic area.

The participation rate goals are expressed as a percentage of the hours a contractor's aggregate workforce worked in each trade on all construction work performed in the geographic area. For this purpose, it does not matter whether or not the work was federal, federally assisted or non-federal. Where a contractor performs construction work in a geographic area located outside the geographic area in which it has a covered contract, the contractor shall apply the goals established for the geographic area where the work is actually performed. Goals in the second area also are applicable to federally involved and nonfederally involved construction work.

---

[125] As of the time the Manual was issued, the existing MOU between OFCCP and GSA was being renegotiated by the parties.

[126] 41 CFR 60-1.4(a) and (b), 41 CFR 60-250.5, 41 CFR 60-300.5 and 41 CFR 60-741.5.

a. *Goals for Women*. The current goal for the utilization of women is 6.9% of work hours and applies to all of a contractor's construction sites regardless of where the federal or federally assisted contract is performed.[127]

b. *Minority Group Goals*. The current goals for the utilization of minorities are formulated in terms of work hours performed in a specific Standard Metropolitan Statistical Area (SMSA) or Economic Area (EA).[128] For example, ABC Company has a federal contract for construction work in SMSA X. The goals for SMSA X apply to all of ABC's construction work in SMSA X, both the federally involved and the nonfederally involved construction work. In addition, if ABC Company performs construction work in SMSA Y, it would apply the SMSA Y goals to all its construction work in SMSA Y, whether or not it had a federal or federally assisted contract in SMSA Y.

3C01 PRECONSTRUCTION CONFERENCES

Contracting and administering agencies may use preconstruction conferences to discuss any aspect of the contractual requirements of a project. The EEO, regional, district, or area office staff may participate in these conferences at the invitation of the contracting agency. The contracting agency reviews the construction contractor's nondiscrimination and affirmative action obligations, including applicable minority and female participation rate goals for the geographical area in which work is to be performed, and the contractor's for reporting and recordkeeping requirements necessary to demonstrate compliance.

3C02 NOTICE OF SUBCONTRACT AWARDS

The notice at 41 CFR 60-4.2(d) requires the contractor to notify the Director of OFCCP of the name, address, telephone number and employer identification number of each subcontractor; the estimated dollar amount of the subcontract; its estimated starting and completion dates; and the geographic area (SMSA or EA) in which the work is to be performed. This notice must be in writing and provided within 10 business days of the award of a subcontract in excess of $10,000.

3D THE COMPLIANCE REVIEW PROCESS

COs will find that several stages are involved in a compliance review of a construction contractor. The four major stages are listed below and are discussed in detail in Sections 3E through 3R of this chapter.

- Pre-Review Preparation
- Onsite Review

---

[127] This goal was originally published in the Federal Register of April 7, 1978, 43 FR 14899, 14900, as Appendix A. This goal was extended indefinitely based on a notice published in the Federal Register on December 30, 1980. See 45 FR 85750, 85751 (Dec. 30, 1980).
[128] 45 FR 65979, 65984, Appendix B-80 (Oct. 3, 1980).

- Entrance Conference
- Review of Records
- Audit of Policies, Practices and Procedures
- Interviews
- Worksite Inspection
- Identification and Investigation of Discrimination
- Exit Conference

- Compliance Review Report
- Notification of Compliance Review Results

The major focus of a review of a construction contractor is the contractor's trade workforce within a particular geographical area. However, unless coverage is based solely on a federally assisted construction contract, the contractor's entire workforce may be the subject of the review under the EO 11246, Section 503 and Section 4212. As noted at Section 3B, federally assisted construction contracts are subject only to the EO 11246. In auditing a contractor's compliance with these clauses in nontrade as well as trade occupations, CO must focus on any indications of potential discrimination and lack of affirmative action.

Additionally, if the contractor has 50 or more employees and a federal contract of $50,000 or more, the compliance review will include implementation of the Section 503 AAP. If the contractor has 50 or more employees and a federal contract of $100,000 or more, the compliance review will include implementation of the Section 4212 AAP.

3E PRE-REVIEW PREPARATION: SCHEDULING AND COORDINATION WITH OTHER AGENCIES

COs should notify the senior official at the contractor's establishment by telephone of the scheduled review. The telephone contact will include a discussion of where the review will take place, set a date for the review to begin, indicate the need for an onsite work area and confirm the location and availability of books and records that contain relevant information on the contractor's aggregate workforce in the covered area.

COs must confirm the date and time of the review by letter, sent certified mail, return receipt requested, to the senior official at the contractor's establishment with a copy to the chief executive officer at the corporate address. Mailing to both addresses is required unless the establishment and corporate offices are the same. A CO must mail the letter sufficiently in advance of the date of the review to give reasonable notice. In addition, the notification should specify items that the contractor is to make available for inspection and copying during the review. Examples of some of the items are listed below.

- Handbooks, records, payroll records, and other relevant documents, including a list, separated by construction project, of all employees who worked during the period to be reviewed identified by race, ethnicity and sex;
- Personnel activity records on applicants, hires, promotions and separations during the period to be reviewed identified by race, ethnicity and sex;
- Payroll records for construction employees showing hourly wage, hours worked, overtime wages and overtime hours worked;
- Evidence documenting the implementation of each of the specific affirmative action standards set forth in the specifications;
- Evidence of compliance with 41 CFR Parts 60-250, 60-300 and 60-741 for covered construction contractors; and
- Evidence demonstrating that the contractor has complied with the applicable equal opportunity and affirmative action clauses.

Equally as important as scheduling is interagency coordination. OFCCP believes that interagency coordination and collaboration strengthen our enforcement efforts and maximizes the use of our resources. Consistent with this view, COs must contact the appropriate EEOC office and state and local fair employment practice agencies to notify them of the scheduled review and request any information they might have regarding complaints against the contractor.[129]

If the administering agency is the Federal Highway Administration, Department of Transportation (FHWA - DOT), a DOL-DOT Memorandum of Understanding requires that DOT be notified of the scheduled review. The CO should also review DOL's enforcement database for information available from other labor agencies such as OSHA and the Wage and Hour Division.[130]

To locate previous closure documents including conciliation agreements negotiated with the contractor, COs must review appropriate office files. These documents may provide useful information about potential or recurrent problem areas.

3F ONSITE REVIEW PROCESS

[129] See Letter L-1 – Sample Inquiry Letter for Requesting Complaint Data from EEOC and State and Local FEPs.
[130] U.S. Department of Labor, Data Enforcement, http://ogesdw.dol.gov/ (last accessed Oct. 31, 2011).

The second major stage in a compliance review of a construction contractor is the onsite review. The purpose of the onsite review is to determine if the contractor complied with the requirements of EO 11246 and, as applicable, Section 503 and Section 4212. In doing this, COs will examine personnel activity, compensation data and work hours. In addition, they will evaluate the contractor's affirmative action efforts to comply with the Executive Order, Section 503 and Section 4212, if applicable. There are several activities that take place during the onsite review process and they include:

- entrance conference,
- review of records such as personnel activity, compensation and work hours,
- audit of affirmative action specifications,
- employee and supervisor interviews,
- physical inspection of the contractor's worksites,
- identification and investigation of discrimination, and
- exit conference.

Each of the activities of the onsite review process are discussed in Sections 3G through 3I of this chapter.

3G ENTRANCE CONFERENCE

The entrance conference should be attended by the contractor's CEO or his or her designee. The entrance conference is intended to provide information to the CEO and explain the purpose of the compliance review. During this conference a CO may, as appropriate:

- provide a brief explanation of the compliance review process;
- provide information on OFCCP policies, practices, rules and regulations and determine whether the contractor includes the appropriate clauses in its covered construction subcontracts and purchase orders;
- provide an estimate of the amount of time the onsite review will require;
- confirm the availability and location of the contractor's records and documentation of compliance with the affirmative action specifications;
- request cooperation for employee and supervisory interviews;
- state the need for and arrange to inspect federal and nonfederal worksites; and

- establish a tentative date for the exit conference.

3H REVIEW OF RECORDS

During the process of reviewing records as a part of the onsite review, the CO must record any matters that appear questionable. The CO should follow-up on these matters by gathering additional documentation, interviewing employees and interviewing any other relevant people.

In this section are discussions on the review of various contractor records including items such as payroll records, employment activity records, collective bargaining agreements and personnel policies.

3H00 PAYROLL RECORDS

In reviewing the contractor's payroll records, the CO should determine at least three things:

- the number of months of payroll activity to review in order to evaluate progress toward work hour participation rate goals,
- the existence of uniformity in the assignment of employees to various project sites, and
- the equity or lack thereof in allowing or granting overtime, and other benefits.

a. *Number of Months to Review.* Review the contractor's payroll records for at least a six month period. This review is to evaluate progress toward attaining work hour participation rate goals for minorities and women in each trade. CO's must review payroll records to determine the percentage of work hours by minorities and women out of the total hours worked by the contractor's employees in each trade.

b. *Uniformity of Assignment.* Evaluate the records to determine whether there is uniformity in the assignment of employees to various project sites (federal and nonfederal; commercial and residential; urban and rural). COs will determine whether certain types of projects pay more than others, and if so, whether women and minorities are provided equal opportunities for assignment to the better paying jobs.

c. *Equitable Overtime.* Evaluate the records to determine whether overtime, incentives, bonuses and other job benefits (e.g., holiday bonuses, pay advances, loans, and profit sharing) are provided without regard to race, color, sex, religion or national origin.

3H01 EMPLOYMENT ACTIVITY RECORDS

COs must determine how the contractor processes applications, union referrals and walk-in applicants. They must determine if the contractor is disproportionately rejecting qualified minorities and women. COs must also determine the contractor's reasons for the rejections.

When selection procedures are found to have an adverse impact, COs should refer to the procedures discussed in Chapter 2 for additional guidance.[131]

COs will conduct an impact ratio analysis of the contractor's hiring, promotions and separations, as well as a compensation analysis when reviewing the contractor's employment activity. The findings of the analysis should be included in the Narrative Summary of the SCER, with supporting documents attached.

3H02 COLLECTIVE BARGAINING AGREEMENT (CBA)

When a contractor asserts that hiring is controlled through a union hiring hall in accordance with a CBA, the CO must review the agreement to verify the assertion. If the CBA is not clear, the CO should contact the union hall to determine the process. If the CBA does not support the contractor's claim, the CO must evaluate the contractor's good faith efforts without considering its relationship with the union hiring hall.[132]

3H03 PERSONNEL POLICIES

As in a supply and service compliance evaluation, COs will examine the contractor's personnel policies and practices. COs will determine whether contractor policies make prohibited distinctions in the conditions of employment based on sex. Below are some areas of inquiry for COs.

a. *Conditions of Employment.* COs must examine whether contractor policies make prohibited distinctions in conditions of employment based on sex, including on the basis of pregnancy, childbirth or related medical conditions, or on the basis of sex-based stereotypes, including those related to actual or perceived caregiver responsibilities. Contractors must not make employment decisions based on stereotypes about how males and females are "supposed" to look or act. Such employment decisions are a form of sex discrimination prohibited by Executive Order 11246, as amended.

b. *Distinctions Based on Marital Status or Caregiver Responsibilities.* A CO should examine written policies and conduct interviews with contractor staff and employees regarding the implementation of policies and practices to identify whether distinctions between married and unmarried people apply equally to both sexes, including distinctions between single parents and married parents based on gender. In addition, the CO should assess contractor policies and practices to ensure that sex-based stereotypes about actual and perceived care giving responsibilities are not in effect.

---

[131] COs should be aware, however, that the adverse impact guidance discussed in Chapter 2, section 2J, is based on the UGESP recordkeeping requirements for contractors with 100 or more employees. As most construction contractors have smaller workforces, they would instead be subject to the simplified recordkeeping requirements at 41 CFR 60-3.15(A)(1) that apply to contractors with less than 100 employees. COs should therefore modify their adverse impact analysis, as appropriate, depending on the size of the contractor.

[132] See Standard Federal Equal Employment Opportunity Construction Contract Specifications (Executive Order 11246), paragraph 5, as set forth at 41 CFR 60-4.3.

c. *Bona Fide Occupational Qualifications (BFOQ).* As a part of most onsite visits, the CO will examine job qualifications as stated by the contractor. Under Title VII, sex has been found to be a BFOQ in extremely rare instances. Among them are:

- *Authenticity.* Jobs involving a need for authenticity or genuineness, such as actors or models.

- *Personal Privacy.* Jobs where the performance of essential job elements would entail substantial invasion of personal privacy. This is limited to situations where the normal operation of the contractor's business depends on the employee being the same sex as its employees or customers and there is no other way to ensure privacy. This is different from customer preference.

d. *Employment Opportunities.* Contractors may not exclude women from jobs they may believe are dangerous or unsuitable for women to perform unless sex is a BFOQ. OFCCP follows Title VII principles when determining whether a policy excluding women from a job because of a concern about reproductive hazards is discriminatory. If a question relating to reproductive hazards arises during a compliance evaluation, the CO should discuss the issue with his or her supervisor.

e. *Wage Discrimination.* The CO will also examine possible wage discrimination issues. Compensation discrimination encompasses discrimination in pay and benefits. It may also include discrimination in how employees earn or contractors distribute overtime, raises and bonuses. Contractors cannot make distinctions in pay, benefits, raises or bonuses on the basis of sex. Chapter 2, subsection 2L03, provides additional information on this issue.

f. *Employment Advertising.* The CO will examine the contractor's advertisements in newspapers or other media. The advertisements must not express a sex preference unless the job is one for which sex is a BFOQ. For example, applicants or potential applicants may perceive an advertisement for a "craftsman," as opposed to "craftsperson," as seeking male applicants only and may have the effect of only male applicants applying for the position.

g. *Employee Benefits.* See Chapter 2, Section 2H01, Discrimination and Harassment, for a discussion.

h. *Family Leave and Pregnancy Leave.* See Chapter 2, Section 2H01, Discrimination and Harassment, for a discussion.

Several examples of the types of issues that COs may encounter related to a review of personnel policies are provided in Chapter 2, subsection 2H00, Review of Contractor Policies and Implementation, and subsection 2H01, Discrimination and Harassment.

3H04 DISCRIMINATION AND HARASSMENT

During the onsite review, COs will gather information and conduct interviews to determine whether the contractor developed and implemented policy prohibiting sex discrimination in accordance with the *Sex Discrimination Guidelines*. Below is a list of several legal authorities and the types of contractor policies that are relevant to a CO determining the contractor's compliance. A detailed review of these authorities and several examples are in Chapter 2, subsection 2H01, Discrimination and Harassment.

Applicable Legal Authorities:

- Pregnancy Discrimination Act
- Family and Medical Leave Act
- Affordable Care Act

Contractor Personnel Policies:

- Family Leave and Pregnancy and Disability Leave Policies
- Employee Benefits Policies
- Sexual Harassment Policies
- Sex-Based Stereotyping and Caregiver Discrimination Policies

3I AUDIT OF AFFIRMATIVE ACTION STEPS SET FORTH IN 41 CFR 60-4.3(a) 7

An audit of the contractor's compliance with the affirmative action steps is the third of a total of seven activities in an onsite review. The others are an entrance conference, a review of records, interviews, a worksite inspection, identification and resolution of discrimination, and an exit conference.

In auditing a contractor's compliance with the affirmative action steps, COs must verify that the records, interviews and other information provided by the contractor demonstrate the contractor's compliance. For compliance review purposes, the affirmative action specifications in 41 CFR 60-4.3(a)7 are grouped into the following five major audit categories:

- recruitment practices,
- training,
- EEO policy and implementation,
- personnel operations, and
- contracting activity.

Each of these auditing categories is discussed in subsections 3I00 through 3I04, below.

These categories correspond to the organization of the Form CC-40 Standard Compliance Evaluation Report (or the Construction SCER).[133] The CO will evaluate the veteran and disability affirmative action requirements from Section III of the Construction SCER. The discussion below provides instructions on completing the Construction SCER.

3I00 AUDIT OF RECRUITMENT PRACTICES

The following subsections pertain directly to Part III.A of the Construction SCER and set forth the procedures for evaluating the contractor's recruitment practices.[134]

a. Recruitment Sources. The contractor must establish and maintain a current list of recruitment sources, including sources for minorities and women. The contractor must provide written notification to these recruitment sources and to community organizations when it or its union(s) has employment opportunities available. The contractor must maintain a record of recruitment source responses. See Item III.A.l. of the Construction SCER. To evaluate the contractor's compliance with this specification, the CO will:

- Determine whether the contractor maintains a current list of recruitment sources.
- Determine whether the list is current (has been updated within the last year); whether it contains an adequate number of active, available sources; and whether the recruitment sources listed are in operation, i.e., active.
- Contact referral sources to verify that they received recruitment letters and e-mails, and to determine whether they actually made referrals.
- Interview employees and hiring supervisors to determine whether they use the list when vacancies occur.
- Review correspondence with recruitment sources. This review should:
    - Verify that the contractor sent and the recruitment sources received the letters, and that the contractor made follow-up contact.
    - Ensure that the letters contained a statement of the contractor's EEO policy and the nature of the employment opportunity.
    - Review the contractor's files, telephone logs or other evidence to determine if the contractor maintained copies or records of responses. Determine if the contractor followed-up on responses.

---

[133] See Appendix A-3 Standard Compliance Evaluation Report

[134] Refer to 41 CFR Part 60-20, Sex Discrimination Guidelines; 41 CFR Part 60-50, Religion/National Origin Guidelines; and 41 CFR 60-4.3(a) 7. b, c, d, i and j for more information.

b. *Applicant Records.* In addition to preserving any personnel and employment record as described at 41 CFR 60-1.12, the contractor should maintain a current file of the names, addresses, telephone numbers, sex, race and ethnicity of each minority and female walk-in applicant or referral from a union, recruitment source or community organization, and of the action taken with respect to each individual.[135] If an individual was sent to the union hiring hall for referral and was not referred back to the contractor by the union or, if referred, was not employed by the contractor, the documentation in the file should include the reason why the individual was not hired (or referred) and any action the contractor took.[136] The CO should fully investigate any indications of possible discriminatory practices. To evaluate the contractor's compliance with this specification, the CO should:

- Determine whether the contractor maintains a current file that lists the names, addresses, telephone numbers, sex, race and ethnicity of each walk-in applicant and each referral from a union or community source.
- Evaluate the file for active construction recruitment sources such as unions and community referral organizations.
- Interview supervisors responsible for hiring to determine the general hiring procedure and any specific procedures they use to recruit workers, including minorities and women.
- Determine what sources the contractor uses to obtain job applicants. Sources may include, for example, walk-ins, union hiring hall, newspaper advertisements, word of mouth, and recruitment and training programs.

c. *Failure of Union to Refer.* The regulations require the contractor to immediately notify the Director, in writing, when a union(s) with which it has a collective bargaining agreement has not referred to the contractor a minority or woman sent by the contractor or when the contractor has other information that the union referral process has impeded the contractor's efforts to meet its contractual EEO obligations.[137]

To evaluate the contractor's compliance with this specification, the CO should determine whether the contractor took any other actions to facilitate hiring the individual such as additional written contact with the union specifically requesting referral of that individual, or attempting to hire the individual directly, without union referral. Whenever the contractor states in writing that the union has not referred minorities and women or that other union actions have impeded its affirmative action efforts; or there are allegations that the union has committed unlawful discrimination; or the CO becomes aware that union actions impede or threaten to impede the contractor's affirmative action efforts, the CO should discuss the matter with his or her supervisor as soon as possible.

---

[135] 41 CFR 60-4.3(a) 7.c, 60-1.12(c), and 60-3.15A.
[136] See Item III.A.2. of the Construction SCER.
[137] 41 CFR 60- 4.3(a)7.d. See Item III.A.3. of the Construction SCER.

d. Directing Recruitment Efforts. In accordance with regulations, the contractor is required to engage in recruitment efforts that reach out to all demographic groups in the recruitment area, including minority, women's and community organizations, and schools with minority and female students; and engage in recruitment efforts that reach out to recruitment and training organizations for minorities and women serving the contractor's recruitment area and employment needs.[138]

Not later than one month prior to the date for the acceptance of applications for apprenticeship or other training by any recruitment source, the contractor should send written notification to organizations in the recruitment area, describing the openings, screening procedures and test(s) to be used in the selection process. (See Item III.A.4. of the Construction SCER.)

To determine whether the contractor is in compliance with this specification, the CO should:

- Request written documentation of the contractor's efforts to recruit applicants for training and employment opportunities.
- Review documentation that the contractor provided timely notice to recruitment sources, including minority, women's and community organizations, at least one month prior to acceptance of applications for apprenticeship or training opportunities. The CO should also verify that appropriate sources have been contacted.

e. Employee Referrals. The regulations require the contractor to encourage employees, including present minority and female employees, to recruit others for employment openings.[139] When reasonable to do so, as required by the regulations, the contractor must provide after-school, summer and vacation employment to minority and female youth both on the site and in other areas of its workforce.[140] To evaluate the contractor's compliance with this specification, the CO should:

- Interview minority and female employees to determine whether the contractor has encouraged them to recruit other minority individuals and women to apply for employment.
- Interview supervisors, minority and female employees to determine whether the contractor provides after-school, summer and vacation employment to minority and female youth.
- Review personnel records to verify employment of minority and female youths in after-school, summer and vacation job opportunities.

3I01 AUDIT OF TRAINING

---

[138] 41 CFR 60-4.3(a)7.i.
[139] 41 CFR 60-4.3(a)7.j.
[140] See Item III.A.5. of the Construction SCER.

The contractor shall develop on-the-job training opportunities and participate in training programs that are relevant to the contractor's employment needs and are intended to upgrade the skills of its workers. These programs and opportunties must expressly include minorities and women.[141] Examples of possible programs and opportunities include apprenticeships and trainee programs relevant to the contractor's employment needs, especially those programs the Department of Labor funded or approved.[142]

To evaluate the contractor's compliance with this specification COs must:

- Determine whether the contractor has developed and conducted any training programs, and if so, whether it has provided notice of these programs to its recruitment sources. Obtain copies of any letters informing recruitment sources or schools of training programs, including those to minority and women sources. Get the names of applicants that the contractor referred to the programs. Determine whether the contractor has employed and trained anyone below the journey level. If it has, describe what was done.

- Determine which trades are covered by formal apprenticeship programs (typically found in projects utilizing union labor) or other types of formal training programs not associated with trade unions. When either type of program is in place, a CO must determine the participation rate of minorities and women.

- When there are no formal programs for a particular trade, determine what, if anything, the contractor has done to provide on-the-job training, and the extent to which that training was made available to minorities and women.

- If the contractor provides on-the-job training, determine whether minorities and women have equal access to training in all trades. Determine whether minorities and women are performing all aspects of their trade or if the contractor is repeatedly assigning them to the same task.

- Determine whether the contractor has records of cash contributions, equipment supplied or contractor personnel provided as instructors for Office of Apprenticeship approved, or Department of Labor funded, or other training programs.

- Determine whether the contractor has records of specific hiring and training of workers from such programs. The CO should also determine the results of the contractor's efforts (e.g., number of workers trained identified by race, ethnicity and sex, hours worked, relative compensation, trade) and record the results in the report.

3I02 AUDIT OF EEO POLICY IMPLEMENTATION

---

[141] 41 CFR 60-4.3(a)7e.

[142] See Item III.B.1.of the Construction SCER. Refer to 41 CFR Part 60-20, 41 CFR 68-4.3(a)7.e and Part III.B of the Construction SCER.

This subsection draws from 41 CFR Part 60-20; 41 CFR Part 60-50; 41 CFR 60- 4.3(a)7, g, h, 1 and p and Part C of the Construction SCER for more information. It covers five areas:

- development of and dissemination of EEO policy,
- review of EEO policy,
- external dissemination of EEO policy,
- promotion policy, and
- supervisory performance.

a. *Development and Dissemination of Policy.* The contractor shall develop and disseminate its EEO policy by providing notice of its policy to unions and training programs and by requesting their help in meeting its EEO obligations. The contractor shall also include its EEO policy in any policy manual and collective bargaining agreement and publicize it in the company newspaper or annual report, if any. The contractor shall also specifically review the policy with all employees at least once each year and post it on bulletin boards accessible to all employees and applicants at each location where construction work is performed.[143]

   To evaluate the contractor's compliance with this specification, COs must determine whether the EEO policy contains at least the following items:

   - a statement that the contractor will not discriminate against employees and applicants for employment because of race, color, religion, sex or national origin, and that it will take affirmative action to ensure that employees and applicants for employment will be employed and treated during employment, without regard to race, color, religion, sex or national origin;
   - the name, telephone number and means of access to the contractor's EEO Officer;
   - an assurance that this policy will be followed in all personnel actions; and
   - the signature of the CEO and date.

COs must also determine whether the EEO policy is posted in conspicuous places available to employees and applicants. Several places may be appropriate for posting the EEO policy and some examples include company offices, project sites and project trailers, if applicable.[144]

Interviews of employees is important for determining if the contractor reviewed EEO policy at least annually with all employees and personnel responsible for hiring, assignments and other personnel actions. Other actions COs must take to evaluate the contractor's compliance include:

---

[143] See Item III.C.l. of the Construction SCER.

[144] 41 CFR 60-1.4 (a)(3) or (b)(3).

- determining whether unions, where applicable, and training programs have been notified and provided with a copy of the EEO policy. Obtain copies of correspondence, or other documentation of such notification; and

- reviewing as applicable, policy manuals, collective bargaining agreements, company newspapers and/or annual reports for inclusion of the contractor's EEO policy.

b. *Review of Policy*. The contractor shall review, at least annually, the company's EEO policy and affirmative action obligations with all employees having any responsibility for hiring, assignment, layoff, termination or other employment decisions, including specific review of these items with all onsite supervisory personnel prior to the initiation of work at any job site. The contractor must maintain a written record of the time and place of these meetings, people attending, subject matter discussed and disposition of the subject matter.[145] Disposition of the subject matter may include any further action to be taken by attendees and participants. In evaluating the contractor's compliance with this specification, COs should:

- substantiate that the contractor has conducted, at least annually, a review of the contractor's EEO policy and affirmative action obligations with all employees having any responsibility for hiring, job assignment, layoff, termination or other personnel decisions, including the transferring of employees to different job sites;

- identify each job site at which the contractor has initiated work within the 12-month period prior to the start of the compliance review. Verify the date prior to the commencement of work at each such job site on which the contractor met with onsite supervisory personnel to discuss the contractor's EEO policy and affirmative action obligations; and

- review the actions taken by the contractor to resolve any problems identified.

c. *External Dissemination of Policy*. The contractor shall disseminate its EEO policy externally by including it in any advertising in the media, including media directed at minorities and women. In addition, the contractor shall provide written notification to, and shall discuss its EEO policy with, other contractors and subcontractors with which it does or anticipates doing business.[146] In evaluating the contractor's compliance with this specification, the CO should:

- review copies of advertisements to determine whether the contractor included its EEO policy (e.g., the EEO tag line) and whether advertisements appeared in media announcements that reach all demographic groups in the recruiting area;

- determine whether the contractor's written notification to other contractors and subcontractors with which it does or anticipates doing business is accurate and timely (at least at the start of each major contract); and

---

[145] See Item III.C.2., of the Construction SCER.
[146] See Item III.C.3. of the Construction SCER.

- review and verify documentation such as telephone logs, file notes, etc., on the contractor's discussion(s) with other contractors and subcontractors to determine whether the contractor's EEO policy was discussed.

d. *Promotion Policy.* At least annually, the contractor shall inventory and evaluate all current minority and women employees for promotional opportunities.[147] The contractor shall encourage these employees to seek or to prepare for promotional opportunities through appropriate training.[148] To evaluate the contractor's compliance with this specification, COs must:

- review the contractor's policies and personnel procedures regarding upgrading and promotion; determine how first-line and other supervisors are selected and how collective bargaining agreements impact company policies;

- review all promotions and the employees whom the contractor could have or should have considered;

- obtain documentation of the contractor's annual inventory and evaluation of all employees for promotional opportunities; and

- verify through interviews and a review of documentation that the contractor encouraged all employees, including minorities and women, to seek or prepare for promotional opportunities through appropriate training.

e. *Supervisory Performance.* The contractor shall conduct a review, at least annually, of all supervisors' adherence to and performance under its EEO policies and affirmative action obligations.[149] To evaluate the contractor's compliance with this specification, the CO should review letters, reports, performance evaluations, EEO training courses and materials and minutes of meetings. Interviews of supervisory personnel should be conducted.

3I03 AUDIT OF PERSONNEL OPERATIONS

The CO should consider four areas during an audit of personnel operations: work environment, validation, effects of personnel practices and nonsegregation of facilities and activities.[150] Each is discussed in turn in this section.

a. *Working Environment.* The contractor must ensure and maintain a working environment free of harassment, intimidation and coercion at all sites and in all facilities at which the contractor's employees are assigned to work. Harassment, intimidation and coercion can take many forms on the job site. These actions may be directed to minority as well as female

---

[147] 41 CFR 60-4.3(a)7.1.

[148] See Item III.C.4., of the Construction SCER.

[149] Refer to Item III.C.5., of the Construction SCER.

[150] Refer to 41 CFR Part 60-20; 41 CFR Part 60-50; 41 CFR 60-4.3(a)7.a, k, m and n; and Part 1II.D of the Construction SCER for more information.

employees. They may consist of verbal, visual or written abuse, such as insults, graffiti, posters, suggestive comments and demands, racial slurs, leering or pressure for sexual activity. They may also include physical aggressiveness such as touching, pinching, patting and shoving, or the hiding or sabotaging of tools and equipment. Whatever the action, it can create a stressful working atmosphere which impairs job performance and work relationships and often results in the victim quitting the job. During the physical inspection of the contractor's worksites, the CO should:

- look for any physical evidence of intimidation, harassment, or coercion;
- interview female and minority employees to determine whether there have been any incidents of harassment, intimidation or coercion;
- determine whether such incidents were reported to the supervisor and if so, what action was taken to resolve the problem;
- interview supervisory staff to determine whether they are aware of the contractor's obligation under this specification;
- review contractor files (minutes of meetings, memoranda, etc.) to determine whether the contractor has discussed this specification with supervisors; and
- review discharges and terminations, and where possible, interview minorities and women recently terminated, to determine if harassment or intimidation was a factor in their leaving the job.

Where possible, the contractor will assign at least two women to each construction project.[151] The contractor shall specifically ensure that all supervisory personnel are aware of, and carry out, its obligation to maintain such a working environment, with specific attention to minorities and women working at such sites or in such facilities.[152]

b. *Validation.* The contractor must validate all tests and other selection requirements where there is an obligation to do so under 41 CFR Part 60-3.[153] COs should also refer to the discussion in Chapter 2 and to the "Questions and Answers to the Uniform Guidelines on Selection Procedures.[154] Procedures for identifying adverse impact resulting from employee selection procedures are in Chapter 1 and Chapter 2.

c. *Effect of Personnel Practices.* Contractors must ensure that seniority practices, job classifications, work assignments, opportunities for overtime and other personnel practices do not have a discriminatory effect on minorities and women by monitoring all personnel and

---

[151] 41 CFR 60-4.3(a)7.a.
[152] See Item III.D.l., of the Construction SCER.
[153] See Item III.D.2 of the Construction SCER. Under 41 CFR 60-3.15 contractors with fewer than 100 employees are not required to make adverse impact determinations or maintain validity evidence.
[154] See 44 FR 11996, 12009 (Mar. 2, 1979) supplemented by 45 FR 29350 (May 2, 1980).

employment related activities to ensure that the specifications are being carried out.[155] In evaluating the contractor's compliance with this specification, COs will:

- determine whether the contractor's personnel policies and practices have a discriminatory effect; and

- review personnel policies and practices such as transfers that create employment opportunities, seniority practices, job classifications, work assignments (e.g., minorities and women sent only to federally or state funded projects), layoff procedures, project locations, wage rates,[156] overtime hours for discriminatory effects.

d. *Nonsegregated Facilities and Activities.* The contractor must ensure that all job sites, facilities and company activities are nonsegregated, except for separate or single user toilets and changing facilities where necessary to assure privacy between the sexes.[157] In evaluating the contractor's compliance, during the worksite inspection, the CO should:

- determine whether the contractor provides and maintains adequate toilet and changing facilities to ensure privacy between the sexes; and

- interview management and employees to determine whether announcements of company social/recreational activities have been posted and are made available to all employees.

3I04 AUDIT OF CONTRACTING ACTIVITY

One element of a good faith commitment to equal employment opportunity is the use of small disadvantaged businesses or disadvantaged business enterprises as subcontractors.[158] These efforts must be documented.

Records of all solicitations of offers for subcontracts from construction contractors and suppliers that are small disadvantaged businesses or business enterprises, including circulations of solicitations to minority and women's contractor associations, must be maintained and produced upon request.[159] In assessing the contractor's efforts in this regard, the CO should:

- determine whether there are solicitations to small disadvantaged businesses or disadvantaged business enterprises, and minority and female contractor associations;

---

[155] 41 CFR 60-4.3(a)7.m. See Item III.D.3. of the Construction SCER.

[156] COs are reminded that wage rates may be specified in Collective Bargaining Agreements.

[157] 41 CFR 60-4.3(a)7.n. See Item III.D.4. of the Construction SCER.

[158] 41 CFR 60-4.3(a)7.o. Regulations in place as of the time of the publication of this version of the FCCM refer to solicitation of offers from minority and female construction contractors and suppliers. Affirmative action programs in federal procurement are, however, no longer reserved for minority and women-owned businesses. The Small Business Admininstration and the Department of Transportation procurement programs are for small disadvantaged busineeses disadvantaged business enterprises, including minority and women-owned businesses. Accordingly, the terms "small disadvantaged business" and "disadvantaged business enterpises" are used in this section.

[159] Both 41 CFR 60-4.3(a)7.o and Part III.E of the Construction SCER provide related information.

- verify that the solicitations to small disadvantaged businesses or disadvantaged business enterprises are made on the same basis as those to larger contractors.

3J INTERVIEWS

Conducting interviews is the fourth activity in a construction onsite review; interviews typically take place during the CO's worksite inspection of the contractor's federal and nonfederal projects. COs should conduct sufficient interviews of employees and supervisors to resolve any outstanding issues or questions. This includes interviewing these key groups:

- supervisors, to determine if they are aware of and adhere to the affirmative action specifications. Supervisory personnel are often the individuals to whom applicants speak concerning employment opportunities, and they are likely to make job and overtime assignments;
- current employees (non-minority males, as well as minorities and women);
- union officials, if applicable;
- applicants (nonminority males, as well as minorities and women); and
- former employees (non-minority males, minorities and women) to determine how the contractor and co-workers treated them on the job.

If the contractor has only a few women or minorities in its construction workforce, COs will make every effort to interview each one. If all the women and minority employees cannot be interviewed, COs should select a representative sampling from each trade for interview. These interviews should probe for any evidence of sexual or racial harassment.

COs will refer any complaints received from employees during these interviews related to the Davis-Bacon Act wage rates to the Department of Labor's Wage and Hour office.

3K PHYSICAL INSPECTION OF CONTRACTOR WORKSITES

The purpose of conducting an inspection of worksites is to obtain additional information regarding the contractor's compliance with the requirements including, requirements that must be implemented at such sites (e.g., posting of policy, EEO poster). In addition, a CO can document the type of work performed, the conditions under which it is performed and the makeup of the workforce performing that work, through the onsite inspection.

The CO should inspect at least one federal or federally assisted construction worksite that is related to the construction contract as a part of the compliance review and, whenever possible, nonfederally involved worksites should be inspected as well.

3K00 INVESTIGATION OF COMPLIANCE

a. *Technical Requirements*. The CO should review bulletin boards maintained onsite to ensure that contractor's EEO policy is posted and that the required notice at 41 CFR 60-1.42 is also posted. For contractors subject to the AAP requirements of 41 CFR 60-250, 60-300 and 60-741, the CO should determine whether notice of the location and hours of availability of the written AAP(s) should also be posted. Contractors may utilize onsite bulletin boards to disseminate the invitation to self-identify.[160]

b. *Working Conditions*. The CO should review working conditions to determine whether there is evidence of harassment, intimidation or coercion of women or minorities including, for example, a substantial difference in the conditions available to women or minorities. When feasible, at least two women should be assigned to the project(s). Also ensure that all facilities are nonsegregated, and that where appropriate, the contractor provided separate or single-user toilet and changing facilities to ensure privacy between the sexes.

c. *Interviews*. COs will conduct interviews with onsite supervisors and with members of each of the trades used by the contractor. Interviewees should include minorities and non minorities, men and women. They should focus interviews on determining whether or not the contractor has complied with those requirements involving interaction with minorities and women in its construction workforce. Examples are encouraging present employees, including minorities and women to recruit others;[161] conducting an annual inventory of employees for promotional opportunities;[162] and reviewing the contractor's EEO policy with management personnel and with employees.[163]

3K01 COMPLIANCE WITH EXECUTIVE ORDER 13496

Executive Order 13496 requires federal contractors and subcontractors to inform employees of their rights under the National Labor Relations Act (NLRA). The NLRA guarantees employees the right to organize and bargain collectively with their employer and to be free from retaliation for doing so. Contractors must post the notice conspicuously in and around their establishments, work sites and offices so that it is prominent and readily seen by employees who are covered by the NLRA and directly or indirectly (e.g., maintenance, repair, personnel, payroll work) engaged in contract-related activity. The Office of Labor-Management Standards (OLMS) and OFCCP share enforcement responsibilities for the notice requirements. OFCCP is responsible for investigation of complaints, compliance evaluations and conciliation, and will refer violations to the OLMS for enforcement. The CO will inspect the work sites for the requisite posting(s).

3L COMPLIANCE WITH 41 CFR PART 60-20

---

[160] See 41 CFR 60-250.5(a)9, 41 CFR 60-300.5(a)4 and 60-741.5(c).
[161] 41 CFR 60-4.3(a)7.j.
[162] 41 CFR 60-4.3(a)7.1.
[163] 41 CFR 60-4.3(a)7.f.

All construction contractors, whether involved in federal or federally assisted construction work, must be able to demonstrate compliance with 41 CFR Part 60-20, the *Sex Discrimination Guidelines*. COs will refer to Chapter 2 for procedures to follow in reviewing for compliance with these guidelines. The contractor's compliance with these guidelines must be described in Section III.F. of the Construction SCER.

3M COMPLIANCE WITH 41 CFR PART 60-50

All construction contractors, whether involved in federal or federally assisted construction work, must be able to demonstrate compliance with 41 CFR Part 60-50, *Guidelines on Religion and National Origin*. The CO will refer to Chapter 2 for procedures to follow in reviewing for compliance with these requirements; they must describe the contractor's compliance with these guidelines in Section III.G. of the Construction SCER.

3N COMPLIANCE WITH SECTION 4212 AND SECTION 503

Construction contractors with a federal contract or subcontract of $100,000 or more, ($25,000 or more if the contract or subcontract was entered into before December 1, 2003), must comply with the requirements of the Vietnam Era Veterans' Readjustment Assistance Act of 1974, as amended, and its implementing regulations.[164] Similarly, construction contractors with federal contracts or subcontracts in excess of $10,000 must comply with the requirements of Section 503 of the Rehabilitation Act of 1973, as amended, and its implementing regulations.[165]

The general requirements of these regulations require federal contractors to invite applicants for employment and employees to inform the contractor if he or she is an individual with a disability or a veteran belonging to one or more of the categories of veterans covered under Section 4212 who wishes to benefit under the contractor's affirmative action programs.[166] The invitation must state that the information is provided voluntarily, that it will be kept confidential, that refusal to provide it will not subject the applicant or employee to any adverse treatment, and that it will be used only in accordance with the laws OFCCP enforces. COs must refer to Chapters 1 and 2, for procedures on assessing contractor compliance with all requirements, they must also describe in detail the federal contractor's compliance with Section 4212 and Section 503 implementing regulations in Section III.H. of the Construction SCER.

3O IDENTIFICATION AND RESOLUTION OF EMPLOYMENT DISCRIMINATION

[164] 41 CFR Parts 60-250 and 60-300.
[165] 41 CFR Part 60-741.
[166] The categories of protected veterans are found at 41 CFR 60-250.1(a) and 60-300.1(a) as of the time of publication of the FCCM.

The CO may identify potential individual or systemic discrimination during the compliance review. Chapter 2 of this Manual contains a detailed description of the procedures the CO should use for gathering and analyzing facts to determine whether employment discrimination exists. These procedures are directed primarily at supply and service compliance evaluations, but the CO may adapt them for use in construction compliance reviews. The theoretical bases for proving discrimination are equally applicable to employment discrimination identified in construction compliance reviews. Remedies for employment discrimination are also found at Chapter 7.

3P EXIT CONFERENCE

The exit conference is the final activity in an onsite review. In coordination with his or her supervisor, the CO should conduct an exit conference for the construction firm's CEO and/or his or her designee at the conclusion of the onsite review. During this conference, the CO should:

- outline the preliminary results of the review;
- identify any violations and the corrective actions necessary to resolve the violations;
- inform the contractor that it will receive a written notice summarizing the violations and giving remedies required; and
- inform the contractor that he or she may resolve the violations with a Conciliation Agreement.

If the contractor disputes the violation finding, the CO should assure the contractor that OFCCP will consider any pertinent additional evidence submitted within a specified time before determining its compliance status.

3Q STANDARD CONSTRUCTION COMPLIANCE EVALUATION REPORT

The report includes a narrative summary that is organized as follows:

a. *Scope of Review*. The CO should briefly state those items covered in the pre-review, the onsite review and the project interviews.

b. *Analysis*. The CO must present an analysis of pertinent materials for each area examined including any indicators he or she identified from analyses of personnel activity and compensation. The CO must identify sources of information (e.g., interviews conducted, records examined, worksites inspected, and community contacts made). If a CO finds deficiencies, the explanation must be sufficient to permit a person who is unfamiliar with the case to understand the basis for each deficiency determination. The CO will also provide detailed narrative information on problem areas identified during the review of the contractor's below activities.

- Recruitment Practices
- Training
- EEO/AA Policy and Implementation
- Personnel Operations and Leave Policies
- Contracting Activity
- Discrimination Violations
- Implementation of Sex Discrimination Guidelines[167]
- Implementation of Guidelines on Discrimination Because of Religious or National Origin[168]
- Implementation of Section 503 and Section 4212

c. *Conclusions.* The CO must make a final assessment of the findings and how these relate to the contractor's compliance status.

d. *Resolution.* If the CO identifies violations, the CO must describe the corrective action necessary to consider the contractor in compliance. Both parties must agree to specific corrective actions that the CO will include in a Conciliation Agreement, as appropriate. Otherwise the CO must issue a Show Cause Notice. [169]

e. *Recommendations.* The CO must recommend that the contractor be found either in apparent compliance or noncompliance. Reasons to support the CO's recommendation must be documented in the case file.

COs must use the Construction SCER to report compliance evaluation results of construction contractors. The Construction SCER aims to provide objective measures of a contractor's efforts to implement the required affirmative action obligations specified in the regulations. During an investigation the CO should use appropriate pages and worksheets from the Construction SCER. See Part V of the Construction SCER for more information.

3R NOTIFICATION OF COMPLIANCE REVIEW RESULTS AND RESOLUTION OF VIOLATIONS

---

[167] 41 CFR Part 60-20.
[168] 41 CFR Part 60-50.
[169] 41 CFR 60-4.8.

When no violations are found, a CO prepares a letter of no apparent violations, to be issued and signed by the District Director.[170] However, when violations are found, a Predetermination Notice or a Notice of Violation is prepared.[171] Both are issued and signed by the District Director.

The Predetermination Notice includes full details of each deficiency and violation, including appropriate citations to the regulations, and the needed corrective actions. Contractors may voluntarily resolve violations through a Conciliation Agreement. See Sections 3S below, for a discussion of this resolution document.

3S USE OF CONCILIATION AGREEMENTS

Violations such as those listed below should be resolved in a Conciliation Agreement:

- *List of Recruitment Sources.* Failure to maintain a list of recruitment sources that includes recruitment sources for women and minorities, and failure to provide written notice to these sources and community organizations regarding job opportunities and to maintain records of their responses.[172]
- *List of Applicants.* Failure to maintain a file of the names, addresses and telephone numbers of each applicant and referral, identified by sex, race and ethnicity, and the actions the contractor took.[173]
- *Referrals to Unions.* If applicants are referred to a union, failure to document results of this referral and any additional action taken.[174]
- *Impeding AA Efforts.* Failure to notify OFCCP that a union is impeding the contractor's affirmative action efforts.[175]
- *Direction of Recruitment Efforts.* Failure to direct its recruitment to all demographic groups in the recruitment area, including women and minorities, and community organizations, schools and training organizations.[176]
- *Training Programs.* Failure to develop on-the-job training opportunities and participate in training programs that opportunities expressly include minorities and women.[177]

---

[170] See Letter L-4.
[171] See Chapter 8 – Resolution of Non-Compliance.
[172] 41 CFR 60-4.3(a)7.b.
[173] 41 CFR 60-4.3(a)7.c.
[174] 41 CFR 60-4.3(a)7.c.
[175] 41 CFR 60-4.3(a)7.d.
[176] 41 CFR 60-4.3(a)7.i.
[177] 41 CFR 60-4.3(a)7.e.

- *Annual Review of Specifications.* Failure to review, at least annually, the obligations under the specifications with all employees having responsibility for employment decisions.[178]

- *Annual Review of EO/AA Performance.* Failure to conduct an annual review of its supervisors' adherence to and performance under EO/AA obligations.[179]

- *Annual Inventory.* The contractor's failure to conduct an annual inventory and evaluation of at least the currently employed women and minorities for promotional opportunities.[180]

- *Intimidation or Harassment.* Evidence of intimidation, harassment or coercion.[181]

- *Validation.* Failure to validate tests and selection procedures when required under 41 CFR Part 60-3.[182]

- *Monitoring Personnel Activities.* Failure to monitor all personnel and employment activities to ensure nondiscriminatory effect.[183]

- *Segregated Facilities.* Evidence of segregated facilities except where separate facilities are necessary to provide privacy between sexes.[184]

- *Discrimination.* All investigations in which there is evidence of employment discrimination.

3T REVIEW COMPLETION LETTER

Letter L-4 provides a format for a Notice of Review Completion for the CO to use when he or she finds no violations. When the CO finds a violation, the CO refers to the sample Notice of Review Completion letters that are in Chapter 8. OFCCP uses Letter L-32 or Letter L-33 when major violations were voluntarily resolved in a CA. If OFCCP issued an SCN the CO should use Letter L-32. If no SCN was issued, use Letter L-33.

3U REFERRAL FOR ENFORCEMENT

If the contractor and OFCCP cannot resolve the violations through a CA, OFCCP will issue an SCN[185] and will recommend the case for enforcement.

---

[178] 41 CFR 60-4.3(a)7.g.
[179] 41 CFR 60-4.3(a)7.p.
[180] 41 CFR 60-4.3(a)7.1.
[181] 41 CFR 60-4.3(a)7.a.
[182] 41 CFR 60- 4.3(a)7.k.
[183] 41 CFR 60-4.3(a)7.m.
[184] 41 CFR 60-4.3(a)7.n.

[185] 41 CFR 60-4.8.

CHAPTER 4
CORPORATE MANAGEMENT COMPLIANCE EVALUATIONS

4A INTRODUCTION

This chapter outlines the procedures for COs conducting Corporate Management Compliance Evaluations (CMCEs) of multi-establishment contractors subject to Executive Order 11246, as amended (EO 11246); Section 503 of the Rehabilitation Act of 1973, as amended (Section 503); and the Vietnam Era Veterans' Readjustment Assistance Act of 1974, as amended (Section 4212).[186] The CMCE includes all aspects of a standard compliance evaluation but focuses predominantly on the corporate headquarters. In addition, the CMCE specifically evaluates a contractor's selection, development, and retention practices that affect advancement into middle and senior-level corporate management.

4A00 PURPOSE OF CMCEs

The purpose of a CMCE, as described at 41 CFR 60-2.30, is to determine whether individuals are encountering artificial barriers to advancement into middle and senior-level corporate management. During CMCEs, COs pay special attention to components of a contractor's employment process that affect advancement or promotion into middle and senior-level positions.

As in other compliance evaluations, the CMCE focuses on a contractor's efforts to ensure a discrimination free workplace. To ensure a thorough analysis of EEO compliance, CMCEs focus not only on personnel activity data at the corporate headquarters, but also on affirmative action policies and procedures that ensure equal employment opportunity leading to advancement throughout the organization.

Therefore, during a CMCE COs begin their analysis of middle and senior-level management positions by focusing on two areas:

- potential discrimination, and
- affirmative action.

a. Potential Discrimination. When focusing on the potential for discrimination COs are typically seeking answers to two questions:

- Does unlawful discrimination exist in the selection processes and practices for middle and senior-level management positions?
- Does unlawful discrimination exist in employee performance review procedures or in employee developmental assignments?

---

[186] Unless otherwise noted, the term "contractor" includes subcontractors.

In addition to these questions, COs are also seeking to determine whether individuals currently in these positions are treated in a nondiscriminatory manner in all aspects of their employment including assignments, total compensation, development opportunities, reasonable accommodation and any other benefits or privileges associated with their positions.

b. *Affirmative Action*. The obligation to ensure equal employment opportunity extends to all levels of a contractor's activities, including the recruitment, development and selection processes for middle and senior-level management positions. The contractor's efforts are particularly important when evaluating higher-level positions. This is so because the selection criteria for these positions often become more subjective. Moreover, the selection criteria at these levels are closely related to corporate culture and values. COs, therefore, must evaluate whether and to what extent the contractor:

- Examines its development and selection criteria and practices for middle and senior-level management positions,
- Identifies EEO problems or potential barriers to equal opportunity, and
- Devises and implements effective strategies to address identified problems within the context of its own particular corporate environment.

4A01 SCOPE OF CMCE

A CMCE is always a full review and COs use the Standard Compliance Evaluation Report (SCER), but with the addition of the CMCE-specific "Section III" which addresses those elements unique to a CMCE.[187] The evaluation of a corporate headquarters includes a review of the written affirmative action program (AAP) to ensure that it includes all jobs for which the headquarters has decision-making authority, regardless of where those jobs are physically located. For example, jobs for which the corporate headquarters retains decision making or approval and disapproval authority usually include senior managers of the various corporation establishments. Such jobs are often important contributors to feeder pools for middle and senior-level corporate management positions.

A CMCE can be expanded beyond the corporate headquarters if, during the course of the CMCE, the CO becomes aware that problems exist at establishments outside the corporate headquarters.[188] In this instance, the CO should discuss whether it would be appropriate to expand the compliance evaluation beyond the headquarters with his or her supervisor.[189] If they decide to expand the evaluation, the CO should contact the contractor, explain the reasons for and scope of the expansion, and request appropriate records and other evidence regarding the additional issues(s) to be investigated.

---

[187] See Section 4B – Pre-Desk Audit Actions.

[188] 41 CFR 60-2.30(b).

[189] The regional and national offices are consulted when determining whether to expand the scope of a CMCE.

For example, the CMCE may need to include an analysis of feeder pools at subordinate establishments. In determining whether to include such an analysis, the CO should consider the degree to which the contractor has historically and recently filled corporate headquarters management positions from elsewhere in the corporation and the degree to which corporate headquarters tracks and monitors the progress of key personnel in subordinate establishments. COs should refer to subsection 4H04.c, Cross-Establishment Movement, for additional information on feeder pools and related issues.

Likewise, the highest level management positions held by members of nonfavored groups may be outside the corporate headquarters. Therefore, when doing a CMCE, the CO must request data from the contractor related to other establishments, when necessary, to determine the existence and extent of a "glass ceiling" within the corporation.

Lastly, during the course of the compliance evaluation it may come to the CO's attention that other types of compliance problems exist at locations outside the corporate headquarters. If so, then the scope of the evaluation should be expanded, as appropriate, to investigate the identified problems.

4A02 CONFIDENTIALITY

Some of the data examined during a CMCE, such as human resource development plans and total compensation packages for higher management levels, may be considered particularly sensitive by the contractor. COs must consult with the appropriate OFCCP managing officials to ensure that the appropriate steps are taken to ensure contractor confidentiality. In many cases this will include consultation with the district director.

If the contractor's representatives express concerns about confidentiality, the CO must advise the representative that OFCCP is required to "treat information obtained during the compliance evaluation as confidential to the maximum extent the information is exempt from public disclosure under the Freedom of Information Act, 5 U.S.C. 552."[190] Exemption 4 of the FOIA at 5 U.S.C. § 522 (b)(4) protects "trade secrets and commercial or financial information obtained from a person [that is] privileged or confidential." When submitting data and records to OFCCP, contractors should clearly identify all trade secrets and commercial or financial information it believes are exempt from disclosure. Moreover, the CO may advise the contractor that under the Trade Secrets Act, 18 U.S.C. §1905 (2000), it is a criminal offense for a government employee to release trade secrets and other forms of confidential commercial and financial information to another business or to the public unless the law authorizes such disclosure.

Other information may be exempt e.g., personnel files under Exemption 6 of the FOIA.[191] Moreover, even if none of these exemptions apply, DOL regulations require OFCCP to notify the contractor of the FOIA request and give the contractor an opportunity to object to the

---

[190] 41 CFR 60-1.20(g).

[191] 29 CFR Part 70.

disclosure.[192] For additional information regarding the agency's treatment of confidential information review 41 CFR 60-1.20(f) and 41 CFR 60-1.20(g).

4B PRE-DESK AUDIT ACTIONS

Although several of the steps of the CMCE are common to all reviews, the actual execution and information gathering are unique to a CMCE. The CO must use the customary Supply and Service Scheduling Letter, with the attached Itemized Listing, to notify the contractor of the evaluation. When a CO is conducting a CMCE, the Regional Director or his or her designee must sign the Scheduling Letter and send it by certified mail, return receipt requested, to the corporation's CEO. The Scheduling Letter should include the name and telephone number of the CO receiving the AAP and supporting data or the appropriate supervisor if the supervisor is receiving this information.

This discussion focused on providing notice of a CMCE. The following subsections review other matters related to preparing for the desk audit.

4B00 FOLLOW-UP CONTACT WITH CONTRACTOR

Generally, within 15 calendar days after sending the Scheduling Letter, COs must contact the contractor's head of human resources to inform him or her that the compliance evaluation will be a CMCE and to explain what is involved in the evaluation. In addition, this initial contact should include:

- the identification of the CO who will be involved in the evaluation,
- the establishment of the lines of communication between the contractor and OFCCP,
- the answers to any questions the contractor may have about the information OFCCP requested in the Scheduling Letter, and
- the answers to any questions regarding the differences between a standard compliance evaluation and a CMCE.

COs should offer any technical assistance the contractor needs to ensure the efficient and effective completion of the evaluation. This may include advising the contractor of its recordkeeping requirements during the course of the evaluation.

4B01 CORPORATION BACKGROUND RESEARCH

Before starting the evaluation, the CO should gather appropriate background information about the corporation he or she will evaluate. Using an array of data sources, including the Internet, the CO should try to learn as much as possible about the corporation's operations, personnel

---

[192] 29 CFR 70-26.

procedures and EEO compliance history in order to facilitate the process of the CMCE. Other important information that may impact the evaluation includes the history of the corporation and its product/service line(s), the corporate leadership and business trends (with specific focus on how that may impact corporate employment).

4B02 SEARCH FOR PUBLISHED REPORTS

COs should learn as much about the contractor and its industry as possible. There are several resources available but only a few are listed below.

- Industry resources such as Hoover's, Standard and Poor's, and Moody's provide comprehensive industry information, company profiles, key contact data, financial research and analysis, and news.
- Publications such as the "International Directory of Company Histories" and the "Reference Book of Corporate Managements" are sources of information on corporate histories and the backgrounds, executive leadership, labor and management actions, NAICS codes, key dates, ticker symbol, principal subsidiaries, principal divisions, principal operating units, principle competitors and other significant milestones.
- Articles on the corporation within the past two years in business oriented newspapers and periodicals, such as *The Wall Street Journal*, and *Forbes* and *Fortune* magazines.
- Corporate Web sites may contain the most current information regarding the changes in corporate management, or other pertinent information.
- Public records, including court documents on discrimination lawsuits, settlements and findings.

Subsection 4B11, Evaluation and Analysis of Corporate Information, gives details on how to use this and other research information. If a CO does not have ready access to this or other research materials, he or she may send a Request for Literature Search Letter to the DOL Library.[193]

4B03 RETRIEVAL OF "FORM 10-K" REPORTS

In addition to the publication search, COs must retrieve the latest "Form 10-K" for corporations that are required to file. The Securities and Exchange Commission (SEC) requires all publicly held corporations to file a "Form 10-K" report annually. Domestic corporations must make their filings on EDGAR, SEC's Electronic Data Gathering, Analysis, and Retrieval system.
Filings maintained on EDGAR are found at the Web address listed below.

http://www.sec.gov/edgar/searchedgar/webusers.htm (last accessed Jan. 2011)

---

[193] See Letter L-6 – Request for Literature Search.

Use of this information is discussed in 4B11, Evaluation and Analysis of Corporate Information.

4B04 RETRIEVAL OF EEO-1 REPORTS

As discussed elsewhere in the Manual, EEO-1 reports are required of all private employers who are:

- subject to Title VII of the Civil Rights Act of 1964 (as amended by the Equal Employment Opportunity Act of 1972) with 100 or more employees excluding state and local governments, primary and secondary school systems, institutions of higher education, Indian tribes and tax-exempt private membership clubs other than labor organizations; or

- subject to Title VII with fewer than 100 employees if the company is owned by or affiliated with another company, or there is centralized ownership, control or management so that the group legally constitutes a single enterprise, and the entire enterprise employs a total of 100 or more employees.

All federal contractors who are private employers file the report if they are not exempt under 41 CFR 60-1.5, have 50 or more employees, and:

- are prime contractors or first-tier subcontractors, and have a contract, subcontract, or purchase order amounting to $50,000 or more; or

- serve as a depository of Government funds in any amount, or

- are financial institutions that are issuing and paying agents for U.S. Savings Bonds and Notes.

The filing deadline is set by EEOC and is generally in September each year. Only those establishments located in the District of Columbia and the 50 states are required to submit an EEO-1. No reports are filed for establishments in Puerto Rico, the Virgin Islands or other American Protectorates.

COs must retrieve a contractor's two most recent EEO-1 reports from the Equal Employment Data System (EEDS). The EEDS is designed to provide information annually on the EEO characteristics of supply and service contractors and other employers. The system contains EEO-1 data for the current fiscal year, plus the four previous fiscal years. The EEO-1 report includes the below three report types detailing various aspects of multi-establishment corporations.

- *Type 2 report.* A consolidated report that covers all employees corporate-wide, including those at headquarters and those in establishments too small to require a separate establishment report.

- *Type 3 report.* A headquarters report covering employees at the corporate headquarters location.

- *Type 4 report.* A separate report for each establishment employing 50 or more people.

Subsection 4B12, Evaluation of EEO-1 Reports, reviews the possible uses of this information. If the EEO-1 information is not available through the EEDS system, a CO should request these data from the contractor directly.

4B05 OFCCP COMPLIANCE HISTORY REPORTS

The CO must check the electronic CMS and EIS to obtain a list of prior compliance evaluations of the contractor's corporate headquarters and other establishments and to identify any issues in the reviews. This may be useful for identifying information that the CO should obtain or examine during the onsite review. If this task was a part of a previous related desk audit, the CO should review this information as part of the preparation for the onsite. If a conciliation agreement was obtained in a prior review, the onsite visit should provide an opportunity to confirm that the contractor took and appropriately maintained the corrective action. Subsection 5B03, OFCCP Compliance History Reports, reviews the use of this information.

4B06 CONTACTING EEOC, VETS AND OTHER AGENCIES

Before starting the evaluation, a CO must also seek information regarding the employment policies and practices of the contractor from the Equal Employment Opportunity Commission (EEOC), Veterans Employment and Training Service (VETS) and other EEO and labor law enforcement agencies. This information provides the CO with a better understanding of the contractor's workforce and operations, and may indicate potential problem areas.

a. *EEOC and State and Local Fair Employment Practices (FEP) Agencies.* Simultaneous with the sending of the Scheduling Letter, a CO must send the Standard Inquiry Letter to the appropriate district office of the EEOC, and to the appropriate state and local FEP agencies.[194] This letter requests information regarding discrimination complaints filed against the contractor, and any other information that may be pertinent to assess the contractor's EEO posture. After 15 calendar days the CO will follow-up by telephone with any agency that failed to reply or from which the CO needs additional information.

b. *Veterans Employment and Training Service and Other DOL Enforcement Agencies.* The CO must also check the VETS-100 database and contact the VETS representative at the appropriate local employment delivery service to request any information that could be pertinent to the pending review. Additionally, the CO must check the DOL Enforcement Database for closed complaints and compliance evaluations of the contractor's establishments, as well as contact other DOL enforcement agencies, such as the Occupational Safety and Health Administration (OSHA) and the Wage & Hour Division (WHD) to identify the number, types and status of any complaints that have been filed against the contractor.

---

[194] See Letter L-1 – Sample Inquiry Letter for Requesting Complaint Data from EEOC and State and local FEPs.

4B07 FOLLOW-UP AND USE OF INFORMATION ON COMPLAINTS FILED WITH OR BY OTHER AGENCIES

A CO must examine all the information regarding complaints against the contractor that he or she receives from federal, state, and local agencies in response to the Standard Inquiry Letter and enter the information on Part A, Section 1, Question 2 of the SCER. Any complaints involving management jobs or "glass ceiling" issues should also be addressed in the "Introduction" element on Part D of the SCER.

If the response does not provide enough information to determine whether a complaint involves a management job or "glass ceiling" issue, the CO should contact the responding agency for additional information.

When needed, the CO should contact the appropriate EEOC office or state or local fair employment practices agency to arrange to review relevant discrimination complaint files as part of the compliance evaluation. This can be particularly useful when, as a result of the desk audit, the CO identifies potential systemic problems in complaint areas.

After receiving the AAP and supporting data, any information the contractor provided with respect to current or past complaints must be compared with the information received from the agencies. The CO will note discrepancies and information that the contractor did not provide for possible further investigation during the review, if warranted. The contractor should be asked to explain discrepancies and to provide additional information. In conducting the desk audit, the CO should pay particular attention to any indication of a potentially broader problem in the type of activity and management area/level that was an issue in previous complaints.

4B08 RELATIONSHIP OF OFCCP COMPLIANCE ACTIVITIES TO EEO LITIGATION OR COURT ORDERS

If, during the conduct of a compliance evaluation, a CO finds that the contractor is involved in litigation or is under a court order for EEO matters, he or she should identify the EEO issues involved, the court, the parties, the case name and number and bring the matter to the attention of his or her supervisor. The field office, in consultation with the Regional Solicitor's Office, will determine whether the litigation or court order should impose any limitations on the conduct of the compliance evaluation.

4B09 REVIEW OF COMMUNITY RESOURCE FILES

If a CO is not knowledgeable about the local organizations in the area in which the corporate headquarters is located, he or she should review the field office's community resource files to become familiar with local community groups, and introduce himself or herself to the various organizations. If the contractor is located near an Indian reservation, the CO should contact the reservation's Tribal Employment Rights Organization (TERO). Chapter 2 discusses how COs can establish relationships with local organizations representing members of covered groups.[195]

---

[195] See Chapter 2K – Linkage Agreements.

4B10 REVIEW OF PAST OFCCP COMPLIANCE ACTIONS

Based upon the information gathered in Section 4B, Pre-Desk Audit Actions, the CO should review the contractor's compliance history to identify cases with violations involving a corporate-wide policy or practice. Examples would be violations for prior discriminatory acts, failure to conduct a self-audit, benefits, medical screening and testing. As appropriate, a CO can contact the OFCCP office that conducted the evaluation or investigation to obtain further information on the violations, their resolution, and whether they applied to management jobs. The purpose of obtaining this information is not to revisit closed compliance actions, but to determine whether the same problem could exist corporate-wide. If the information indicates a potentially corporate-wide problem, especially one that could affect management jobs, the CO should include a review of that area in the onsite plan.

4B11 EVALUATION AND ANALYSIS OF CORPORATE INFORMATION

After conducting research on the contractor as described in subsections 4B01 through 4B10 and receiving the results, COs must sort and analyze the material. Particular emphasis should be given to areas that could be relevant to the evaluation. For example, a recent acquisition or merger could have significant impact on feeder pools for management positions. While reviewing and sorting the data, COs should place the information into one of three categories:

- Corporate Organization;
- Corporate History and Trends; and
- Backgrounds of Top Corporate Officials.

The scope and purpose of each of these categories are described below.

a. *Corporate Organization*. This category includes information related to the organization of the entire corporation; rather than just the corporate headquarters facility. If a contractor uses an Organizational Display, as described at 41 CFR 60-2.11(b) as part of its AAP, COs should be able to compare the Organizational Display to the current corporate organizational chart. Industry directories and handbooks can provide an overview of this information, with detail often provided in the corporation's Annual Report and portions of its "10-K" filed with the SEC. Information and data related to the below questions would normally be in this category.

    - What are the corporation's major components, or businesses, groups and divisions, and its subsidiaries, both domestic and foreign?
    - What are the components' major functions and/or products?
    - Where are the corporation's major components located?

- What percentage of total corporate personnel does each component employ (e.g., the ADC Products Group accounts for about 40% of total corporate personnel)?

This information will be helpful in identifying such factors as potential feeder pools for rotational assignments and headquarters management jobs. Also, information on the corporate organization will help OFCCP determine the degree to which willingness to relocate may impact advancement.

After receiving the contractor's desk audit submission, COs will compare the corporate structure as shown in this information with that shown in any published corporate organization charts.

b. *Corporate History and Recent Trends.* There are several sources for this information including industry directories and handbooks, particularly Hoover's Directories, at www.hoovers.com; specialized publications such as the "International Directory of Company Histories"; annual corporate reports and SEC submissions; newspapers and periodicals; and the corporation's Web site. COs should review these and other appropriate resources to gather information that answers these and other relevant questions.

   - When was the corporation founded?
   - What was its initial main business? How has this changed over time?
   - Has the corporation undergone a recent merger or acquisition?
   - What are its most and least profitable components over the last several years?
   - Has the corporation recently undergone, or is it projecting, substantial growth or cutbacks in particular areas of its business? Is so, what are they?
   - Has the corporation recently been awarded or lost major contracts? What business area(s) did the award or loss affect and how?
   - What are its long-range projections for areas of business growth?

   This information is relevant to a preliminary understanding of the business and economic context within which the corporation operates, and also will assist in evaluating particular corporate management issues. For example, recent mergers or major acquisitions may have caused a substantial change in the overall business mix of the corporation and in top management. Such changes may correspondingly impact corporate culture, and the skills mix that the corporation seeks in middle and senior-level management staff.

   Sources of current profitability usually influence allocation of bonus pools among different business components and often indicate where growth in management opportunities is likely to occur.

c. *Background of Top Officials.* The corporation's Web site, annual report, Form 10-K or other sources such as the "Reference Book of Corporate Managements" may provide information on the backgrounds of top corporate officials. This information usually includes education background, time with the corporation and the positions held.

Such information can help verify past corporate practices like the degree to which the contractor traditionally filled top positions internally versus externally. It also may help identify shifts in the type of background that top management may value like differences in the backgrounds, experiences, educational fields and/or levels of more recent entries to top management versus others.

The CO should summarize the information in this section under Part D of the SCER titled "Introduction."

4B12 EVALUATION OF EEO-1 REPORTS

EEO-1 reports are valuable sources of information on changes in the workforce. Therefore, COs must review the total corporate-wide employment shown in the latest consolidated (Type 2) EEO-1 report. A CO should compare this with the corporate-wide employment in the preceding consolidated report to determine whether total employment is stable, growing or declining. This review also helps determine which EEO-1 categories have changed the most.

COs should use the corporate headquarters EEO-1 reports, i.e., the Type 3 reports, to conduct EEO trend analyses[196] on the direction of headquarters employment generally, and by EEO-1 category, including changes in nonfavored groups.

Comparisons of the participation of nonfavored groups in the two Officials and Managers (O&M) categories and the Professional category on the Type 3 report with their representation in the same categories on the Type 2 report should also be conducted by COs.

COs should review the latest individual establishment reports to identify major facility locations. A major facility is one that contains 150 or more employees, or in the case of smaller corporations where no individual facility reaches the 150 employees mark, a facility where the number of employees is at least 33% higher than the average of all facilities. COs will compare the participation of nonfavored group members in the two O&M categories and the Professional category on the headquarters' Type 3 report with their representation in the same categories on the individual Type 4 reports for the selected establishments. Although not definitive, this can often provide a general idea of whether there appears to be considerable movement to corporate headquarters from subordinate establishments, which can help approximate the broad pool of protected group members potentially available for such movement.[197] The COs will also compare individual establishments and note any significant differences in the participation of members of nonfavored groups in specific categories between establishments, as well as within a given establishment from one year to the next.

---

[196] See Part A.IV of the SCER.

[197] See subsection 4H04c, Cross-Establishment Movement.

In addition to using Part A.IV of the SCER, COs should discuss any areas of potential concern or interest resulting from these analyses under the "Focus Level and Areas" element of Part C.III of the SCER.

4C RELATIONSHIP TO THE STANDARD DESK AUDIT

After receiving the contractor's corporate headquarters facility AAPs, COs should review and analyze the AAPs and its support data using the desk audit procedures outlined in Chapter 1. If the contractor does not provide AAPs and/or support data on time, COs should follow the procedures outlined in Section 2C. However, in addition to the standard desk audit, the primary focus in a CMCE desk audit is analyzing professional and management level job groups to identify nonfavored groups, determine their representation, and assess the impact of policies and procedures of these groups. For example, COs must assess or determine:

- Whether there is a level(s) at which there is a marked decline in participation.
- If there is such a level(s) of decline, the types of jobs at that level(s), both generally and by major functional area (e.g., vice-president, director, senior analyst, finance, legal, sales).

Consideration is also given to the types of jobs held by nonfavored group members below that level at which there is a marked decline in participation. Whether nonfavored group members are located in likely feeder pools for the upper level jobs should also be determined. For example, COs may find that women are concentrated in office and clerical job groups. Two other areas of interest include:

- The employee development and selection policies and practices regarding jobs at the level at which participation declines, and the jobs in their probable feeder pools.
- The nature and amount of employment activity in job groups around that level.

The following sections discuss each of these considerations in detail. When conducting the analyses, it is important for the CO to remember that these considerations apply corporate-wide, not just to headquarters positions.

4D DESK AUDIT – REVIEW OF THE ORGANIZATIONAL PROFILE

For the purposes of this section, "organizational profile" is a general term encompassing the workforce analysis, organizational display, job group analysis and utilization analysis. The CO should review all of these to determine which, singly or in combination, will best provide the necessary data for these analyses.

In addition to addressing them under the appropriate regular areas of the SCER, the CO should also discuss results of the analyses conducted under this section in the "Focus Level and Areas" element of Part C.III of the SCER.

4D00 ANALYSIS OF NON-FAVORED GROUPS' MANAGEMENT LEVEL PARTICIPATION

In reviewing the organizational profile, a CO should determine whether there is a marked decline in the participation of specific groups of individuals. This section covers conducting an analysis and determining the participation rates for nonfavored groups in top and middle management.

As a general rule, a corporation selected for a CMCE should be large enough to have job groups extending beyond the standard EEO-1 categories. Therefore, the top management level may be immediately evident from a scan of the job group analysis. When this is not the case, actual job titles, in conjunction with reporting relationship to the CEO, are usually reliable indicators of the top management level.

Typical titles at top levels include Executive Vice-President, Senior Vice-President, Comptroller, Chief Financial Officer and Vice-President. Reporting relationships are usually reflected in the corporation's organizational charts. The very top level consists of individuals reporting directly to the CEO; the second level consists of those individuals who report directly to the top level managers. While the number of reporting levels regarded as "top management" varies with the size and structure of the particular corporation, more than three levels down at the headquarters establishment is usually considered middle management. People at that middle corporate level may, in turn, be top management at subordinate establishments.

Middle management is different. Again, the job group analysis may be the easiest way of determining what positions large corporations classify as middle management. However, when that is not the case, salary may be a more reliable determinant than title. It may be best for COs to use salary level, range or grade as reflected in the workforce analysis or organizational display, to identify where nonfavored group participation declines.

When management levels are still unclear, COs must obtain more information before proceeding by contacting corporate human resources and making a request for clarification. Assuming management levels are defined, COs would move to their analysis of nonfavored group participation at these levels.

a. *Analyzing Nonfavored Group Participation.* In addition to analyzing and utilizing the normal EEO trend data, COs must conduct a breakout analysis specifically of the O&M categories. COs should total the number of O&M jobs by grade, race and gender across department lines. In doing so, they must keep track of the departments in order to examine the functional distribution of jobs at a later stage. Subsection 4D01, Functional Areas, may be a useful supplement to this discussion.

b. *Identify Marked Decline.* COs must identify whether there is a level at which there is a marked decline in any group's participation. A marked decline is the highest level with proportionately fewer nonfavored group members than the level immediately below, but except in rare cases, not the level without any nonfavored group members. There may be a single level at which there is a marked decline for one or more nonfavored groups, or there may be multiple levels at which a marked decline exists for different groups (e.g., there may be one level at which there is a marked decline of the participation of Hispanics, another level where there is a sharp decline in the participation of females, and a third at which there is a marked decline of individuals with disabilities). Marked declines also may differ by various functional areas.

The determination that there is a marked decline in nonfavored group member management participation will focus further CMCE investigation in two areas:

- At and above the grade or level where nonfavored group participation declines. At this level the focus should be on whether the incumbent nonfavored group members are treated in a nondiscriminatory manner in all aspects of their employment.

- Below the grade or level where nonfavored group participation declines. At this level the focus will be on why nonfavored group members have not advanced further. Specifically, areas to explore or questions to ask are:

    - Whether unlawful discrimination kept group members from advancing beyond that grade, either because of discrimination in the selection practice itself or because of discrimination in employee development practices or in assignment to career paths or /feeder pools for higher-graded positions.

    - Whether the contractor identified and removed any impediments to equal employment opportunity in selection procedures for higher-level positions. Such impediments might include management review procedures or contractor actions regarding formal or informal career paths and feeder pools.

4D01 FUNCTIONAL AREAS

Functional analysis is essentially analyzing whether career paths and feeder pools are determined by participation in specific functional lines. Absences of a particular group, observed in EEO categories, can often be a direct result of a functional line progression that has barriers to employment at early stages of career development (e.g., at a major aircraft manufacturing contractor, upper management may almost exclusively come from the engineering functions where there may traditionally have been fewer women). A functional analysis may also reveal more general issues such as hiring/placement disparities into certain professional categories. To conduct the appropriate analyses COs must:

- identify major functional areas,

- identify absences and concentrations in functional areas of certain groups,

- determine whether the major functional areas are "line" or "staff,"

- identify feeder pools,

- compare feeder pools to higher-level jobs, and
- examine the disparity between nonfavored and favored groups.

a. *Identify Major Functional Areas.* COs should return to the workforce analysis or organizational profile and review departmental data to determine “major functions.”

Although what is a "major function" will vary within a given corporate structure, a major function is usually headed by a manager who has either a "direct" or "second level" reporting relationship to the CEO, and typically includes or covers several departments.

Common "major functions" at a corporate headquarters include: Finance (under a Comptroller or Chief Financial Officer), Legal (under a General Counsel or similar title), Personnel or Labor Relations (under a Vice-President for Human Relations or similar title), and Marketing, Sales and Research.

b. *Absence and Concentrations in Functional Areas.* In each major functional area, COs should analyze participation in exempt jobs (managerial, professional and, as applicable, sales) to determine if particular groups are excluded or concentrated.[198] They should also analyze exempt jobs in any other functional areas where nonfavored groups are absent, underrepresented, or concentrated.

c. *"Line" versus "Staff."* COs must identify whether the major functional areas are "line" or "staff." A line area is one that directly contributes to the corporation's profitability, and generally focuses on a specific area; a staff area is one that primarily supports line functions.

Line jobs will vary a great deal depending on the corporation's product or service, but will include jobs and functional areas that are essential to producing and selling the product or service.

For example, at a consumer products firm, manufacturing, marketing, and sales would be major line functions; at a consulting firm, the consultants would be line jobs; and at a high-tech firm, research and engineering would be line functions. Staff functions typically include personnel, labor relations, purchasing, finance, legal, and facilities management.

While line and staff jobs are often at the same base salary, line jobs are more likely to be eligible for significant bonuses making their total compensation considerably higher. Also, the corporation is generally more likely to have promoted top management from line positions, although it is not unusual for top managers to have experience in line and staff positions.

COs must analyze the proportion of line versus staff exempt jobs in the workforce, and determine whether there is a significant difference in the workforce composition of the line

---

198 Generally, exempt jobs are jobs or positions that are exempt from the overtime provisions of the Fair Labor Standards Act.

and staff functions. COs should note as an area requiring further investigation any concentration of a particular race or gender in staff functions. At the onsite review, the CO should then review personnel files and conduct interviews to ensure that the presence of any concentrated race/gender groups in staff positions despite having education/experience pertinent to the corporation's line functions, is not resulting from "steering" either at or after hiring.[199]

d. *Identification of Feeder Pools.* COs should examine the utilization analysis and the raw personnel activity data from the AAP to determine the most likely feeder pools for the jobs at and above the grades/levels where minority and female participation declines. However, it is important to remember that potential feeder pools are not necessarily limited to the headquarters workforce. Therefore, COs may need to request additional data.

The likely feeder pools are not limited to subordinate management jobs but may include professional jobs and or other positions at comparable exempt grades. Likewise feeder pools are not necessarily restricted to the functional area in which a particular management job is located, but they are most often related to them. For example, it is generally more common for someone in finance to move to a financial management position than it is for someone in engineering to do so. Consequently, for desk audit purposes, in each major functional area, COs should identify the:

- number of jobs, by favored and nonfavored group members, at and above the grades or levels where the participation of nonfavored group members declines; and

- number of exempt jobs, by favored and nonfavored group members, below that level.

e. *Comparison of Feeder Pool to Higher-Level Jobs.* If clustering of nonfavored groups appears at lower grade levels, COs should try to determine whether:

- *Nonfavored Group Members Hold Jobs with More Limited Advancement Potential.* There are several areas of inquiry or questions that are useful for COs when examining limited advancement potential issues. For example, COs should seek to determine whether nonfavored group members are concentrated in functional areas that have fewer higher graded jobs than those they hold? Are they underrepresented in functional areas with higher graded jobs? If so, there may be a placement problem.

- *Nonfavored Group Members Hold Jobs with Advancement Potential, but Do Not Advance at a Rate Comparable with their Peers.* There are several areas of inquiry or questions that are useful for COs to pursue when examining this apparent disparity. For example, COs should seek to determine whether nonfavored groups are in functional areas that have a grade distribution comparable to that in other functional areas? If so, COs will need to investigate further to determine the reason why proportionally more nonfavored group members are in lower-graded jobs than their peers.

---

[199] See Section 4H – Onsite: Filling of Management Jobs.

COs should also seek to determine whether the reason for the disparity is attributable to some legitimate nondiscriminatory factor such as developmental programs, performance appraisals, assignments or other factors that are related to promotions.

f. *Disproportion or Disparity.* As a general rule, COs should first examine the functional areas where there is the greatest disparity between the participation of nonfavored group members above the grade where nonfavored group member participation declines, as well as below the grade where nonfavored group member participation declines.

4E DESK AUDIT: AAP AND EMPLOYMENT ACTIVITY INFORMATION DURING A REVIEW OF SELECTION PROCESSES AND DEVELOPMENTAL PROGRAMS

COs must review the contractor's written AAP(s) to find information on the selection processes that may apply to positions above and below the grades/levels where participation by nonfavored groups declines. As an example, a CO would look for information on the contractor's promotion policy. If the policy is to limit management jobs to internal candidates, the corporation should also have policies and procedures for making these job openings known to potential internal candidates within corporate headquarters and outside of headquarters. Other areas where policies may indicate a problem might include the absence of employee development programs that apply to positions above and below the grades/levels where nonfavored group member participation declines. The absence of outreach efforts designed to improve access to management positions for nonfavored group members could also be a problem.

COs must also use personnel activity data from the contractor's AAP to identify the employment activities that include jobs above and below the level where nonfavored group member participation declines. This is in addition to conducting the standard impact ratio analyses (IRAs). The CO must identify the number of hires and applicants at, above and below the grade where nonfavored group member participation declines. Based on the available data, the CO will determine how jobs at and above that level are filled (e.g., hired from the outside, or promoted or transferred from within). Proper analysis may require requesting additional data and gathering information during the onsite review. Useful information related to this section is in Section 4F, Notice of Onsite Review and Follow-up Data Requests and Section 4H, Onsite: Filling of Management Jobs.

Now the CO must next compare the number of hires, promotions and transfers at, above and below the grade where nonfavored group representation declines. The CO must also identify terminations of nonfavored group members above and below the grade where their participation declines.

Once this is complete, COs must address all areas of potential concern in the "Focus Level and Areas" element of Part C.III of the SCER.

4F NOTICE OF ONSITE REVIEW AND FOLLOW-UP DATA REQUESTS

At the conclusion of a desk audit, COs should contact the contractor to schedule the onsite review and discuss any additional material they need for further analysis. The COs should include any unresolved issues identified during the desk audit in the SCER.

The CO will prepare a letter to the contractor reiterating that the evaluation is a CMCE, confirming the onsite date and listing any additional data needed. The notice will state that the onsite review will begin with an entrance conference to discuss those issues with the CEO or appropriately designated corporate officials.

The notification letter to the contractor should identify the additional information needed. When the needed information is regarding the jobs filled at or above the level where minority or female participation or both drops, the data requested should be sufficient to identify the specific jobs filled and how they were filled (e.g., by hire, by promotion, by transfer). COs should note in the data request that if the contractor filled such jobs by promotion or transfer from subordinate establishments within the corporation, the contractor should identify the originating establishment. As pertinent, COs should request any other needed activity data (such as applicant flow, and terminations) and general information (e.g., jobs in subordinate establishments included in the corporate AAP).

4G ONSITE REVIEW

A CMCE onsite review follows the same process as the standard onsite review:

- conduct entrance conference to discuss purpose of onsite review and areas of concern;
- review of documents provided by the contractor and interviews with employees and management to eliminate, revise and confirm identified areas of concern;
- identify additional information still needed for further review on areas remaining unresolved;
- conduct closing conference to address any unresolved areas of concern and discuss "next steps" in the evaluation process.

COs should review Chapter 2 for specific guidance on onsite reviews. One primary difference between the CMCE and standard onsite review is that a Regional Director may lead the opening and exit conferences in a CMCE onsite review. Another difference is that the main focus is on corporate management positions, though the scope may be broader than just the corporate headquarters facility.

4G00 ENTRANCE CONFERENCE

COs must coordinate the entrance conferences with top corporate officials and with the appropriate OFCCP Regional Office. Coordination with the regional office gives the Regional Director or his or her designee the opportunity to attend the meeting. During the entrance conference, COs must obtain any clarification needed from the corporate organization (e.g., any organization charts not obtained to date), and any missing corporate background information the corporation may be able to provide (e.g., annual reports) prior to the onsite review. For example, corporate officials should be asked to explain and provide any documentation regarding:

- What the contractor values in candidates for middle and senior-level management positions?[200]
- Whether the contractor has developed any special EEO programs that it would like for OFCCP to consider as part of its corporate evaluation.

As in any other evaluation, COs should address any questions contractors have concerning the onsite and any other part of the evaluation process. COs must remind contractors that the onsite closing conference will be only an informal, preliminary discussion, and that a formal exit conference will be scheduled when OFCCP is prepared to discuss evaluation findings after having conducted offsite analysis.[201]

4G01 CORPORATE CULTURE

Each corporation has distinct characteristics, not only in terms of how it conducts its major business and the skill backgrounds it needs, but also in terms of its management style and the behaviors it tends to foster and reward among its employees. The CO should gather information that indicates or describes the contractor's corporate culture. This, in turn, may help the CO understand how the corporation makes management selection decisions. While some of this information may be found through research, including corporate self-descriptions, a CO will usually get a better picture during the onsite through interviews and observation.

a. *Corporate Business.* The nature of a corporation's business will tend to determine which corporate components are most essential to its profitability. For example, at a corporation that produces a fairly simple consumer product, marketing and sales are likely to be most central to profitability. On the other hand, in a corporation engaged in advanced research, engineering or scientific expertise is likely to be central to profitability. And as a general rule, employees in those functional areas (which are also usually line rather than staff positions) will have better advancement potential.

b. *Other Factors.* There are usually meaningful differences in predominant management style and valued employee behavior between different corporations even in the same industry. For example, one employer may value somewhat egalitarian management, while another prefers a more authoritarian approach. Or, one employer may value employee initiative and

---

[200] See subsection 4G01, Corporate Culture and subsection 4H00 – General Qualification Standards.

[201] See Section 4K – Completion of Compliance Evalouation: Exit Conference, Report Writing and Ntoice of Evalulation; also Section 2N – Exit Conference.

creativity, while another may place a higher value on mastery of standard procedures. Or, one employer may require rotational assignments (with or without frequent relocations or international stints) to develop a broad knowledge of the business, while another may more heavily weigh depth of expertise in the business area to be managed. Such differences also can extend to matters such as acceptable dress, expectations concerning uncompensated overtime, socializing outside work hours, etc.

These and other differences are not necessarily conscious ones. However, the degree of "fit" between what a corporation values and what an employee values or learns to value can influence whether a person will advance to management and, if so, what management level he or she is likely to reach. The importance of such "fit" usually increases with management level.

4G02 INTERVIEWS

As with any review, a prime source of information will be interviews of both management and employees. Consistent with the guidance in Chapter 2, contractor representatives, including internal or external attorneys or external consultants, may be present during interviews of bona fide exempt management and supervisory employees.[202] However, if a CO is interviewing a management or supervisory employee who is also a complainant or potential complainant, or is being interviewed in his or her capacity as an employee rather than a management official, the CO must conduct the interview in private.

As always, there will be some common questions. However, COs should be sure to tailor interviews to the specific areas of concern being investigated. Likewise, a CO must take care to select individuals for interviews who are tailored or relevant to the areas of concern. However, one common element is that a CO should usually begin with key corporate personnel and human resources officials to discuss and develop an understanding of corporate policies and practices in the following major areas:

- the contractor's middle and senior-level management positions and how the contractor fills them;[203]
- the use of outside hiring to fill middle and senior management positions and how the contractor locates and screens candidates;[204]
- the use of internal hiring for these positions;
- the "pool" for these positions;[205]
- the mechanisms the contractor uses to identify and develop candidates for those positions, both at corporate headquarters and at subordinate establishments;[206] and

---

[202] Section 3J – Interviews.
[203] Subsection 4D00 – Analysis of Nonfavored Groups' Management Level Participation.
[204] Subsection 4H01 – External Hires.
[205] Subsections 4D01 – Functional Areas; Subsection 5H02- Internal Development.

- the reward systems, both monetary and non-monetary, the contractor uses to retain key personnel.[207]

The CO should also ask for all documentation, whether written or electronic, of policies and practices relevant to these areas that the contractor has not already provided. This includes any personnel and human resource manuals, supervisory and employee handbooks and any other internal publications that might be relevant.

4H ONSITE: FILLING OF MANAGEMENT JOBS

As previously indicated, COs will have requested data on the hires, promotions and transfers into jobs at, above and below the level where the participation of nonfavored group members declines. COs will review this data to determine which methods the corporation used to fill jobs at each grade/level during the data period, and then conduct the appropriate analysis. Although the process of analysis is essentially the same as for any review, there are certain elements that are unique to CMCEs. The following subsections discuss the CMCE-specific factors COs may need to incorporate into the analysis. These factors apply whether the contractor fills the positions in question externally or internally.

The basics of conducting a hire or promotion analysis are not re-addressed here. However, where additional clarification is needed, these subsections include sample questions and analytical guidance. These sample questions may be viewed as guides for COs on information to research and consider or as actual "questions" to be asked of the contractor and its employees.

4H00 GENERAL QUALIFICATION STANDARDS

Corporate officials may cite any number of factors in describing what background and characteristics they look for in candidates for management positions. Among them may be a degree in a particular subject area or having an advanced degree, tenure with the corporation, successful profit and loss experience, international stints, and broad knowledge of the business or corporation. Whatever factors the contractor cites, COs must ask sufficient follow-up questions during interviews to thoroughly define the factors and to determine why the corporation believes they are important to the specific jobs, and how the corporation believes people acquire or could acquire such characteristics. Below are some follow-up lines of questions for several common factors contractors use.

- If the contractor views advanced or specialized degrees as important for a specific management position or level of management COs could ask these follow-up questions:
    - What level or in what field(s) must the degree be? For which position(s)? Why ?

---

[206] Subsection 4H04 – Internal Development.
[207] Section 4I – Onsite: Retention.

- How important is a specific college or university? Why?
- Can a person earn an advanced degree while employed? After hours only? Are there any corporate sponsored degree or continuing education programs? How do these programs operate?

- If the contractor views time with the corporation as important COs could ask these follow-up questions:
  - How much corporate service is typical for employees at and above the management level where nonfavored group participation declines?
  - Do employees usually earn this corporate service in a specific sector(s) of the corporation? If so, why?
- If successful profit and loss responsibility is important COs could ask these follow-up questions:
  - Why is it important to the particular management job or group of jobs?
  - Are there particular areas of the business in which one is most likely to gain that experience? Least likely?
  - At what management level does one usually gain it? Does this differ among business areas?
  - Is the number of profit and loss centers increasing, decreasing or remaining about the same?
- If international stints are important COs could ask these follow-up questions:
  - What is the value of having a previous international assignment? Are the number of these assignments and their duration factors?
  - How are people selected for these opportunities?
- If the contractor views exposure to different facets of the business as critical COs could ask these follow-up questions:
  - Why is it important?
  - Does this requirement encompass particular business sectors and does the contractor consider exposure to certain sectors more valuable than others? How much "exposure" is required? Why?
  - How do employees learn that such exposure is important to advancement?

- How do employees obtain such exposure?

Likewise, interviewed employees may cite any number of factors as important to advancement, which may or may not match the factors cited by management. When disparities exist, COs must consider additional sources of information such as personnel files of individuals actually promoted into the position(s) in question. Beyond basic elements such as advanced degrees, COs should explore how employees acquire the characteristics needed to become managers, with particular attention to any corporate practices that may be informal such as mentoring, networking, high visibility special projects, or rotational assignments.

Whether formal or informal, COs must also consider selection procedures for these programs as part of the analysis. Again, COs must be sure to ask for any documentation regarding the qualification standards for the jobs he or she is examining, and any continuing education, mentoring or similar corporate program. This documentation may include, but is not limited to, personnel handbooks, job announcements, memos, participant lists and e-mails.

4H01 EXTERNAL HIRES

When externally filling management jobs, particularly higher level management jobs, contractors frequently opt not to use conventional recruitment sources, such as newspaper or trade publication advertising, but rather use executive search firms or informal referrals from current executive level employees or both.

While filling a job by hire rather than by promotion or transfer does not in itself violate any of the laws OFCCP enforces, COs must be alert to any evidence or external hiring patterns that indicate that the decision to hire from the outside discriminates on the basis of a prohibited factor.

4H02 SOURCES OF APPLICANTS AND CANDIDATES

Contractors may use various sources for hiring middle and senior-level managers. These sources may include executive search firms and referrals from employees.

a. *Executive Search Firms.* As part of the CMCE, COs must determine the sources of the applicants and candidates for the managerial position(s) they are evaluating, and examine the relationship the contractor has with these sources.

    - *Types of Search Firms.* A contractor may maintain several different types of arrangements with executive search firms. Below are just two examples.

        - *Firm on retainer.* In this arrangement, the employer usually has a contract with the search firm under which the contractor pays the firm a basic fee for its services, with that fee supplemented for each referral hired. This type of arrangement is more common for professional or entry-management positions, where the employer anticipates a continuing need for hires in certain fields or at certain levels where there is a skills shortage internally, externally or both.

- *Firm on contingency*. In this arrangement, the firm is usually paid a fee only if a candidate it refers is hired. This type of arrangement is more common for middle to upper-level management jobs, and contractors may prefer this when they only occasionally hire from outside.

- *Unsolicited Referrals*. Contractors may sometimes hire from among unsolicited referrals from an executive search firm. In this arrangement, the firm is paid a fee only if the candidate is hired.

- *Equal Employment Opportunity and Affirmative Action Obligations in Referrals*. Contractors, under the EEO clause in its contracts, retain responsibility for ensuring that solicitations for employees placed on its behalf by a search firm or other referral source comport with all of the contractor's equal employment opportunity and affirmative action obligations.[208]

  Consistent with that clause, as well as with its obligation to incorporate the EEO clause in its subcontracts, the contractor is urged to notify the search firm of its EEO obligations, including that the firm, in seeking candidates on its behalf, must actively seek to include qualified nonfavored group members among those recruited and referred for listed jobs.

- *Monitoring Referrals:* Contractors using search firms must monitor referrals received by gender, minority group and, when possible, protected veteran and disability status as part of its internal auditing and reporting systems under 41 CFR 60-2.17(d), 60-250.44(h), 300.44(h) and 60-741.44(h). A contractor should ask its search firm how it locates and selects candidates if the search firm fails to refer women, minorities, individuals with disabilities or protected veterans.

A contractor is not relieved of its obligations related to recruitment by using a search firm; it must ensure that any firm acting as its agent carries out the contractor's affirmative action and nondiscrimination obligations.

b. *Employee Referrals*: Contractors may use employee referrals as a source for new hires. However, as with search firms, the use of employee referrals does not relieve a contractor of its obligations related to recruitment. For example, if a contractor has established a goal for a job group and the contractor relies on employee referrals to recruit that group, the contractor could make clear to employees that it desires referrals of a diverse group of qualified candidates. The contractor might also supplement employee referrals with other sources of qualified applicants for the jobs involved, such as through linkages.

---

[208] See 41 CFR 60-1.4(a)(2); 41 CFR 60-3.10(a)("The use of an employment agency does not relieve an employer or labor organization or other user of its responsibilities under Federal law to provide equal employment opportunity [under UGESP].").

A contractor's exclusive use of employee referrals may be discriminatory where there is evidence that the intent behind that reliance is to exclude underrepresented group members from consideration for certain jobs. Reliance on employee referrals may also be discriminatory when such reliance has a disparate impact on a particular gender, race or ethnic group, and is not job-related and consistent with business necessity.

4H03 SAMPLE QUESTIONS AND ANALYSIS FOR VARIOUS SEARCH SOURCES

If, in the course of a CMCE, a CO finds that a particular search firm may be discriminating in its recruitment or referral practices, he or she must inform his or her supervisor. As appropriate, OFCCP coordinates with EEOC to investigate the executive search firm under Section 703(b) of the Civil Rights Act of 1964, as amended. This section covers the referral practices of employment agencies. Moreover, if a contractor knowingly uses a search firm that discriminates the contractor will be found in violation of the Executive Order.

A CO engaged with a contractor using an executive search firm may want to ask several questions to understand that relationship. Some sample questions for the contractor are below.

- Have you used executive or other search firms? When and how often? Which firms do you use most? Identify the positions or types of positions (e.g., fields, levels) for which you have used search firms?
- Have you informed those firms of your EEO/AA policy? How? When?
- Who is responsible for monitoring search firm referrals to ensure that the firm complies with equal employment opportunity and affirmative action requirements? How is monitoring accomplished?
- What is the racial, ethnic, and gender composition of those who the contractor hired from among search firm referrals? What efforts did the search firm make to ensure a diverse candidate pool?

COs must conduct an analysis of the information and data received from contractors on their sources of applicants and candidates. For each job filled with a referral from a search firm, the CO should determine, when possible:

- The qualifications the search firm used to refer a candidate.
- The extent to which the contractor approved these qualifications or the amount of input the contractor had in the process to refer a candidate.
- The total pool of candidates who met the requirements to be referred, by race, sex, known disability or protected veteran status, and the total number of applicants actually referred by race, sex, known disability or protected veteran status.
- The status of the selectee as a member of an underrepresented group.

- The presence of members of underrepresented groups among the referrals made by the search firm.

- The existence of members of underrepresented groups as applicants for the job from other external sources.

- The existence of internal candidates for the job identified by race, sex, known disability and protected veteran status.

A CO engaged with a contractor using employee referrals may want to ask several questions to understand that process. Some sample questions for the contractor are below.

- How much, or to what degree, do you rely upon employee referrals for middle and senior-level management positions? Is this practice formal or informal?

- What is the typical relationship between the employee making the referral and the person being referred (e.g., used to work together, went to the same school, met through a professional association, belong to the same club, a neighbor, a relative, a personal friend)?

- Do you receive employee referrals of nonfavored group member candidates, as well as others? How many were referred by race, gender, ethnicity, known disability or protected veteran status? To whom were the nonfavored group members referred? Were any of the individuals referred hired?

- Do you inform employees that the corporation is actively interested in referrals of underrepresented individuals? How are they informed? When are they informed?

- Do you provide a reward or bonus for referring a candidate that is ultimately hired?

When collecting and analyzing employee referral data, COs must remember that information on whether a person was an employee referral will not necessarily be in an applicant log. If no referrals are shown on a log, the CO needs to examine a sample of the files of people hired at the same level involved. Information on the employment application, interview notes may provide an indication of the source of the applicant or candidate. The CO may also be able to obtain relevant information through interviews of successful candidates (e.g., those hired or promoted into the job title at issue).

4H04 INTERNAL DEVELOPMENT

If not already provided, the CO must request documents on the contractor's promotion, training and transfer policies and procedures. With this information, the CO should discuss the procedures with human resources and other appropriate corporate officials. In particular, the CO must clarify how they apply to headquarters positions at, above and below the management level where nonfavored group member participation declines. The CO must also clarify how these procedures apply to movement from subordinate establishments to corporate headquarters and vice versa.

For most corporate management positions, particularly at the higher senior levels, placement through internal movement like promotions and transfers rather than by new hire is generally the rule. Therefore, in order to conduct a proper analysis, it is important that the CO fully understand the various elements that can affect internal placement, particularly those unique to a CMCE such as succession plans. Further, the higher the management level, the less likely it is that the contractor will include the jobs in any formal job announcement system the contractor may have, and the more likely it is that the contractor includes the jobs in some kind of formal or informal succession planning.[209] Below are several sample questions that COs may find helpful.

- How do you make promotion and transfer opportunities known to potential candidates? Is the process the same in all functional areas? Are there differences in the process for positions at the upper management levels?

- Do you make openings at corporate headquarters known to employees in subordinate establishments as well as to employees at headquarters? How? How do employees at subordinate establishments express an interest in being considered for an opening at corporate headquarters?

- Do you make openings at subordinate establishments known to employees at corporate headquarters? Who is responsible for doing so? How is it done? What is the process by which employees at the corporate headquarters express an interest in being considered for openings at subordinate establishments?

- How many employees applied for positions at the corporate headquarters? Identify these employees by race and sex, and identify how many were hired?

The CO should review promotion and transfer actions for conformity with the corporation's stated policies and practices. The CO should also interview the contractor's current, former and new employees regarding their understanding of, and experiences with, the corporation's promotion and transfer practices at the corporate, regional and subordinate establishment levels.

The CO should examine personnel files of managers at and above the level where nonfavored group member participation declines.

a. Succession and Related Planning

The vast majority of corporations engage in some form of planning for future management and personnel needs. These plans go under many different names, such as "human resource development plans," "succession plans," "business plans," "management reviews," "replacement tables," "developmental needs assessment," "high-potentials," "fast-track," and "promotion rosters." The scope and detail of the plans may vary considerably. Areas where there may be the greatest variance include:

---

[209] See subsection 4H04a – Succession Planning.

- The depth of the plan or how deep into the organizational structure the plan reaches.

- The degree of centralization or the degree of control exercised by corporate headquarters exercise compared to the regional headquarters or subordinate establishments.

- The degree of formality involved with the plan (e.g., the existence of a written plan, the use of regular plan reviews).

- The degree the plan is affected by standard performance appraisal or other personnel processes.

When succession planning is explicit or more formal there may be more specificity and several contingent options when implementing the plan. For example, an explicit plan may specify that a specific person is ready to step into the job or position as a permanent replacement for the incumbent, if necessary. It will also have contingencies should that person be unable or unavailable to assume the position. If no one is currently ready to assume the position permanently, most formal plans still provide a way forward by:

- designating a person who could take over until a permanent replacement is developed; or

- designating one or more persons who could be a permanent replacement, given additional developmental experiences or training or both. The plan would also identify needed training and experiences, how long it will take, and other appropriate detail.

In addition, to this level of specificity, a corporation may identify:

- A pool of employees (either specific, named individuals or a description of an employee group such as the number of employees currently in feeder jobs) the contractor considers to have a high-potential to develop into middle to senior-level managers; and

- A broader pool of employees the contractor considers promotable (either specific, named individuals or a description of an employee group such as the number of employees currently in feeder jobs).

The identification of employees, whether for a particular job or generally, is usually fluid, i.e., people may move onto or off of lists depending on shifting business needs, changes in personnel or individual job performance.

COs may want to ask specific questions about succession planning to determine if all qualified candidates are considered and whether employees with potential have access to training and other developmental opportunities. Several sample questions are below.

- Does the corporation have a succession plan to fill particular management positions should there be one or more vacancies?

- Which management jobs or management level are covered by a succession plan?

- What does the corporation's plan cover? Does the succession plan include both short and long-term planning, i.e., people who are currently ready to assume the position and those who may be ready after further developmental experiences and training?

- Are candidates in regional headquarters or other subordinate establishments considered when designating possible successors? If they are, explain how non-headquarters and headquarters candidates are identified?

- Are there written materials describing the plan and offering guidance on selection and development of candidates? Who developed the plan? Are employees advised of the plan?

- If the succession plan identifies specific individuals as potential successors for certain jobs, does the permanent successor most often come from among those identified? What are some examples?

- When is the plan reviewed and modified? Who is responsible for the review?

- What is the representation by race, gender, ethnicity, protected veteran status and individuals with disabilities, among those identified as potential permanent successors?

- How does the representation of members of protected groups who are identified as potential permanent successors for management jobs compare to their representation in the total candidate pool (e.g., in feeder jobs) for those jobs?

    - If the proportion of one or more of these groups in the succession plan is well below their proportion in the total candidate pool, what is the reason for this discrepancy?

    - What steps do you take to rectify the problem and recruit and/ prepare more group members to be manager successors? Who (by group member status) has graduated from a succession planning system into management?

- What, if any, developmental experiences does the corporation require or prefer (e.g., onsite training, offsite training, rotational assignments, special projects)? Are there any individual development plans?

- Does the corporation have any policies or practices for identifying people below the management level with a high potential for advancement?

- How does the process work? How are the individuals identified? What factors are used? Does a person need to be "sponsored" by a current manager? Why or why not?

- What is the lowest level at which an employee will be considered for succession?

- Are there any written materials describing the process, offering guidance on selecting and developing participants?

- How closely and how often does corporate headquarters monitor the process? Does the monitoring include ensuring that affirmative actions are taken to guarantee equal employment opportunity in all aspects of succession planning and management development?

- What is the representation by race, gender, ethnicity, protected veteran status and individuals with disabilities among those identified as "high-potential" versus those eligible to be so identified?

- If the proportion of representation by race, gender, ethnicity, protected veteran status and individuals with disabilities is well below their proportion of those eligible, what, if any, analysis was done and what were the findings?

When the contractor has succession planning programs and there is a disparity in the proportions of representation by race, gender, ethnicity, protected veteran status and individuals with disabilities included in the candidate pool, COs must determine the reasons for the disparity. In order to do so, COs must explore several areas and follow-up including:

- If there is EEO monitoring and an explanation is offered for a disparity, COs should verify the explanation in the course of examining data and files concerning internal mobility, and through interviews with selected employees and managers.

- If there is no EEO monitoring or no explanation is offered for a disparity, COs should analyze the disparity based on the information provided concerning the scope of the program and the criteria for inclusion. A few examples may be:

    - Where there is multi-establishment participation in the succession planning program, do any establishments have a particularly large gap between the percentage representation by race, gender, ethnicity, protected veteran status and individuals with disabilities in the program, as compared with the percentage of identified group members eligible for inclusion (e.g., in feeder jobs)?

    - Were the selection criteria for inclusion in the program uniformly applied?

b. Movement Within Headquarters

- *Transfers within Headquarters*. As with lateral cross-establishment moves, transfers within headquarters may represent planned rotational assignments. Based on information already gathered, COs should identify those moves within headquarters that appear to meet that definition. Also, if the data permits, COs should identify instances in which people transferring were subsequently promoted. When those transfers or promotions are into the level at, above or below the level where minority or female participation or both declines, COs should incorporate the information into the analysis and interview the employees and selecting officials involved to confirm the reason(s) for each move and how it was initiated.

- *Promotions within Headquarters*. When beginning to determine the frequency, types and paths to internal promotions within headquarters, COs must first make several determinations:

    - What is the typical grade increment involved (e.g., one grade increase, two)?

    - To what extent do promotions tend to remain within broad functional areas (e.g., finance, engineering, personnel)?

    - To what extent do promotions cross functional areas (e.g., from engineering into personnel)?

    - Are there any patterns that stand out regarding functional or cross-functional promotions (e.g., promotions are functional up to a certain level, then switch to cross-functional, or vice versa)?

When there is considerable cross-functional movement, a refined IRA may be useful for focusing the investigation. For example, if employees typically progress in one gradeincrements, promotions by favored and nonfavored group status at each relevant grade may be compared with incumbency by favored and nonfavored group status in the next lower grade.

When movement is predominantly within function the COs should identify functions where promotions occurred. COs should evaluate whether nonfavored group members were not promoted even though there was good participation of nonfavored group members in the source grade. COs should pay particular note to any functional areas they identified at the desk audit with the greatest disproportion between the participation of nonfavored group members above and below the grade where their participation declines in the workforce as a whole.

When some functions have concentrations of favored or nonfavored group members and other functions have underrepresentation of favored or nonfavored group members, these employees are likely to stay in these positions. This is most likely when movement is primarily within function. Contractors should examine a sample of their files on nonfavored group members in the concentrated personnel areas to identify for any placement problems.

For example, if nonfavored group members are heavily concentrated in staff positions in a "high-tech" firm, the contractor should determine whether any of them have technical backgrounds that would have qualified them for line functions? If so, did they start in staff or move into staff position later? In either case, the contractor should determine why?

- *Average Time in Grade or Corporate Service.* One way for COs to evaluate whether nonfavored group members are progressing in the managerial ranks is to look at the average time they spend in their current pay grade in comparison to members of the favored group in the same grade. COs can also extend this comparison to corporate service or tenure. COs should refine the focus their inquiry if nonfavored group members spend considerably more time in the same grade than their counterparts. To do so, COs may focus on the possible reasons for the differences. For example, they can seek to determine whether nonfavored group members hold the type of jobs that limit opportunities, or whether the contractor passes over nonfavored group members for promotion. Alternatively, the analysis may show that nonfavored group members have less time in a grade than their peers. If this is the case, service time may be an explanatory factor for nonfavored group members not advancing to higher positions.

- *"Typical" Career Paths.* COs should ask whether promotions show repetitive patterns that appear to represent "typical" career paths within major functional areas. For example, in the functional area of purchasing, COs may want to explore whether promotions tend to be from being a Buyer, to becoming a Purchasing Supervisor, and then to a Purchasing Manager. In sales, COs may want to determine whether the typical career path is from Account Executive III to II to I, to Area Sales Manager, and then to District Sales Manager. When these progressions appear, COs should compare the representation of nonfavored and favored group members with the feeder titles of the composition of those promoted.

c. *Cross-Establishment Movement*

- *Movement to Headquarters from Subordinate Establishments.* Early in the corporate management evaluation, COs must determine the degree to which the contractor fills management openings at corporate headquarters by promotion or transfer from subordinate establishments rather than from within headquarters itself. This balance may vary depending on the management level or functional area. For example, at lower management levels, promotions or transfers may be predominantly within headquarters, while at higher levels they may come predominantly from outside headquarters.

Such information will assist COs in identifying feeder pools for management jobs and, therefore, may influence whether COs expand the evaluation to include one or more subordinate establishments.[210]

---

[210] See Subsection 4A01 – Scope of CMCEs.

- *Movement from Headquarters to Subordinate Establishments.* Promotions and transfers out of headquarters to subordinate establishments also may be relevant, particularly in situations where the contractor views exposure to different operating business components as important to advancement to or above the level where nonfavored group member participation declines.

- *Rotational Assignments.* Cross-establishment transfers, whether into or out of headquarters, or between non-headquarters establishments, may represent planned rotational assignments as a part of a formal or informal development program.

As with the choice to fill a job by hire or promotion, the choice to fill it by transfer rather than promotion, or from a subordinate establishment rather than within headquarters, is itself a selection decision. While that decision may appear to be EEO neutral, COs should be alert for any pattern that suggests a correlation with a prohibited factor. Sample questions that may be helpful on this and related points are below.

- Is work experience in subordinate establishments important to advancing to corporate management positions? In what fields? Is working at corporate headquarters important to advancing to senior management at subordinate establishments?

- When during an employee's career is a cross-establishment move generally made?

- Are cross-establishment moves ever part of a formal career planning process? How does this fit into long-term succession planning?

- Are rotations through the corporation's overseas locations a 'preferred' or 'required' qualification for moving into senior management positions, either officially or unofficially?

- What happens if an employee refuses a job offer requiring relocation? Are the effects of refusing to relocate on career prospects the same for all employees who refuse to relocate?

COs must review any written material on corporate policies related to promotions and transfers, as well as the data requested earlier on promotions and transfers to management jobs at, above and below the level where nonfavored group member participation declines. At a minimum, the data in the sample analysis should include:

- the date of the promotion or transfer,

- the race and gender information,

- the disability or protected veteran status or both, when known,

- the job title, grade and department, and

- the establishment from which and to which the promotion or transfer occurred, if it is not within corporate headquarters.

d. *Promotions and Transfers into Headquarters versus within Headquarters.* COs must determine the extent to which feeder pools for headquarters positions are internal and external to headquarters. COs must separate promotions from subordinate establishments into headquarters from promotions within headquarters. COs should do the same with transfers.

   CO should ask or seek to determine how, at given grades or types of functions, the volume of promotions and transfers into headquarters compares with the volume within headquarters.

e. *Promotions and Transfers into Headquarters from Subordinate Establishments.* If subordinate establishments are an important feeder pool, COs must examine the participation of nonfavored group members in this pool. For promotions and transfers from subordinate establishments into headquarters, COs must note the grade level and originating establishment.

   COs should ask several questions related to promotions and transfers into headquarters to identify potential problems:

   - How does the majority of the movement into headquarters occur? Is it from only a few establishments? Are these establishments part of a particular intermediate business group?

   - How does the participation of nonfavored group members in exempt positions in establishments from which promotions or transfers, or both, occurred compare to their participation in exempt positions in other establishments?

f. *Performance Appraisals.* Performance appraisals are an important and essential management tool. This tool can inform promotion and other decisions. The vast majority of corporations have a formal performance appraisal process for exempt staff. These processes differ in a number of ways, among them:

   - The frequency performance appraisals are conducted, although most are conducted annually.[211]

   - The degree to which the employee being appraised contributes to the process. For example, in some instances, the process begins with the employee giving a written self-evaluation of his or her progress against performance goals established in the last appraisal cycle. Sometimes this includes indicating what his or her goals are for the coming year.

---

[211] If a regular appraisal cycle is supplemented by a "benchmark", a longer term career assessment process such as career reviews at the 3rd and 7th years of employment may take place. The career assessment processes may be a component of succession planning. More on succession planning is in subsection 4H04.

- The manner in which the appraisers express the evaluation ratings. Some use only numeric values and others may use a narrative.[212]

- The requirement that employees sign their appraisals and whether employee comments are permitted.

- The level of the individual responsible for reviewing the appraisal.

Corporations link appraisals to wage increases, bonuses and promotions. Section 4H touches on issues related to promotions and Section 4I reviews issues related to wages and bonuses. COs will want to know whether the corporation gives employees in the same grade level who receive a given rating the same percentage raise. COs will also want to know when a formula is used for determining raises and bonuses, and how heavily the rating is weighted. COs may find the below sample questions on performance appraisals useful.

- What is the corporation's performance appraisal process for exempt staff? Does the corporation use the same appraisal process for all exempt staff? Is the process different for the various levels or grades in the company?

- Does the corporation use a numeric or narrative appraisal rating? If neither of these is used, describe your rating method.

- What are the highest and lowest scores for the corporation's numeric rating system? What is the range of acceptable scores? How is the range of acceptable scores established? When was the range established and when was it last modified?

- What score or performance rating does an employee generally need for promotion?

- Are there any written guidelines or training on how to administer the appraisal? Describe the guidelines the corporation provides to the rating official. Is reference made to EEO? If so, explain.

- How often are your employees appraised? Who appraises them and who approves the ratings? What is the degree of employee input?

- Is career planning included in your process? Is this planning short term, long term or both?

- Are "benchmark" or career interval appraisals used?

---

[212] For example, an "outstanding" rating may be valued at 4 points or assigned the number 4, while an "unacceptable" rating may valued at zero. A narrative rating would consist of a brief overview summarizing an employee's level of performance and accomplishments to substantiate a particular rating. Still other corporations may use both numeric and narrative forms of evaluation. Be aware that appraisal factors for supervisors and managers typically differ from those for professionals and, the higher level the manager, the less likely it is that the appraisal is only numeric.

- Does the corporation monitor appraisal results for EEO? If so, how? What have been the results?

- Are raises, including bonuses and promotions, based on appraisals? If so, what is the relationship?

After gaining a better understanding to the appraisal system and the use of employee ratings, COs should analyze this information. For example, if a CO learns that a numeric system is used, the CO should determine the average rating for the nonfavored group at the grade level just below where nonfavored group member representation declines. If the average appraisal rating is substantially lower for nonfavored group members, the CO must determine if the contractor's EEO audit offers any reasons or explanations. Other areas of inquiry include determining:

- what actions the contractor took to eliminate the disparity, and

- whether the disparity is traceable to certain functional areas.

If the corporation uses a narrative system, then the CO would explore any differences in the tone between appraisals of nonfavored and favored group members.

g. *Visibility*. One element of career advancement can be the amount and type of exposure to senior corporate management through assignment to special projects, task forces, corporate committees or through appointment to special assistant and executive assistant type positions.

   Being assigned special projects and working on teams and group are ways employees gain increased visibility within the corporation. There is considerable variation in the degree to which corporations use special projects, working groups and teams. Some projects may be more desirable than others in terms of opportunities for skills development and visibility. In some industries, this difference will be fairly clear simply because of the nature of the industry, or the corporation may have a formalized structure. For others, COs may need to rely on employee and management interviews as well as any group award program maintained by the contractor that may reflect projects that were particularly desirable.[213]

   COs will want to compare the nonfavored and favored group composition of special project teams and task forces with the nonfavored and favored group composition of the jobs or functional areas from which members were or reasonably could be drawn. Below are several sample questions that can result in useful information on opportunity and participation of nonfavored group members on teams and groups.

   - Does the corporation make much use of special projects, and teams and working groups? If so, in what areas of the business?

   - How are members selected and by whom?

---

[213] See Section 4I01 – Recognition:Awards and Honors.

- What special projects, teams and working groups are currently operating? What is the favored and nonfavored group composition of each?

- Are selections monitored to ensure equal opportunity for all eligible nonfavored group members? If so, by whom? Have there been any cases where a concern was raised, and if so, how was it handled?

h. *Corporate Committees*. Most boards of directors appoint standing committees to monitor and keep the board informed on a specific subject area. In many cases, these committees may simply reflect functions. The appointment to these committees is usually non-discretionary and based solely on position. It can be useful for COs to know the composition of such committees in order to understand the nonfavored group composition corporate-wide of such positions.

There may also be special purpose committees that draw from a wider range of positions and levels within the corporation. Serving on these committees often provide members career enhancing opportunities through exposure to corporate leadership, networking, mentoring relationships and broadening knowledge of the corporation. COs should examine nonfavored group member participation. COs should compare the membership for each committee with those eligible for such membership. For functional and position-based committees, COs should ensure that all qualifying employees are included as members and determine the reasons for any discrepancies.

i. *Special Assistants and Executive Assistants*. People holding such positions, particularly ones reporting directly to senior corporate management regardless of actual title, may be on a "fast-track" to middle management positions by offering the incumbent enhanced developmental opportunities. In some cases there may not be formal guidance on the creation or appointment of employees to these positions, therefore, interviews can be critical to gathering useful information.

In addition to other sources of information on these positions COs should review the organizational profile for any special assistant and executive assistant type of positions. Note that if such titles are nonexempt, or relatively low-level exempt, the incumbents may be in support staff rather than "fast track" positions.

j. *Assignments in Particular Industries and Lines of Work*. In some industries a number of people may share the same or very similar titles and yet differ substantially in the career growth potential offered by their assignments. For example, in sales positions, some product lines may offer higher commission potential than others. Some territories may have been worked extensively, and thus offer primarily opportunities for renewal or upgrade of orders. Others may be relatively un-worked and thus offer much opportunity for new business. For account managers, the dollar volume and growth potential of accounts managed are important to advancement.

After identifying distinctions between favorable and less favorable assignments, COs should determine if nonfavored group members are underrepresented in the former and concentrated in the latter. COs should determine how the corporation makes assignments, particularly for the most and least valuable. They should ask if these assignments are monitored to ensure equal opportunity for all eligible employees. It is also important to know if there is a formal structure that defines the value of these assignments.

4H05 MANAGEMENT TRAINING AND EXECUTIVE DEVELOPMENT

A CMCE should cover both management training and executive development programs. The success of new and high potential employees is influenced by how quickly they learn people-oriented management skills that complement their expert or technical knowledge. Management training is a source of the key skills, best practices and behaviors of effective managers like leadership, delegation, motivation, empowerment, communication and vision. Possessing these skills and traits increase the likelihood of being promoted or transferred into corporate management or other leadership positions. If a corporation offers any management training, COs must determine how it is delivered, who is eligible to participate, who makes the decisions, and how the decisions are made by the corporation. Other relevant questions are:

- Is the training a requirement for a management position? Has the corporation placed any people directly into management without such training? If so, what is their nonfavored or favored group status?

- How does an employee learn of the training? How is an employee selected for it?

- Who monitors participation in training to ensure equal opportunity for all eligible employees?

- What is the composition of the nonfavored and favored groups based on the individuals participating in training over the last year (or evaluation period)?

- How does that composition compare with the nonfavored and favored group composition of those eligible to participate in training?

- If there is a substantial difference between the proportion of nonfavored group members eligible and those participating, what cause was found?

- Does the training include any segments on EEO or diversity management? Up to what level do managers attend?

Executive development programs can be internal, external or both. These programs represent a substantial investment by the corporation in the development of people viewed as potential senior executives. They generally prepare middle-management executives to become more effective leaders and change agents within the company. Because the number of participants is typically small, it may be most useful to look at who participated at some point in their career rather than only who participated during the evaluation period. COs may want to specifically ask the below questions.

- What level manager is eligible? Are there, or have there been, any exceptions to the eligibility level (e.g., have managers below the designated level ever been able to participate in the program)? If so, who authorized those exceptions and why?

- How are people selected for executive development programs? By whom? Are selections monitored to ensure equal opportunity for all eligible employees? Have there been any cases where someone raised a concern, and if so, how did the corporation handle it?

- Among the eligible managers, can you identify who participated in the executive development program by nonfavored and favored group status? If nonfavored group members participated were their training programs comparable in type, school, duration, and other relevant areas to those attended by their favored group peers?

- If nonfavored group members have not participated, are there plans to have them do so? Did their predecessor participate? At what point in his or her career? To what program?

4H06 MENTORING AND NETWORKING

In addition to formal management development programs, many senior managers report having had mentors, at some point in their career, who served as role models, translators of corporate culture or advocates. Because these relationships are generally informal, and may be initiated by either the potential mentor or "mentee", interviews may be the only way to determine if:

- mentoring exists at the management levels under review;

- mentoring is a informal or formal program with policies and guidelines; and

- mentoring carries weight or is value-added in the career advancement process.

COs should also find ways to determine if there are any potential concerns regarding participation of nonfavored group members.

In addition to examining the role and importance of mentoring in career advancement, COs must also consider networking. As used here, networking is the establishment of contacts beyond one's immediate work setting or level, or both, that confer a business benefit. Some corporations have established groups that provide a formal opportunity for managers at a given level to network across division and often establishment lines. If the corporation has such a group, COs should determine the level of managers eligible to join, and ensure that any nonfavored group member managers at that level or above are offered membership on the same basis as their peers. Other networking opportunities may be found in outside professional associations and/or social clubs. If the corporation supports membership in such outside organizations COs should ensure that eligible nonfavored group member managers receive such support on the same basis as their peers.

Unlike formal networking, informal networking is generally interacting across establishment or functional lines with peers and higher level managers. If a corporation does not formally disseminate information on job openings or does so only up to a certain level, networking may be the prime source of information about job openings, particularly those at other establishments. Also, contacts established over time can contribute to career enhancing assignments on work projects involving other departments or establishments.

Although the general assumption is that informal networking is a matter of employee initiative, some corporations affirmatively encourage the development of such contacts among groups not currently well represented in management jobs by, for example, sponsoring meetings or establishing committees that bring together group members from different functions, establishments or management levels.

COs do have certain things to consider when evaluating the role of networking such as:

- Do internal formal networking groups exist? How and by whom are they administered?

- Who is eligible for membership? How and by whom is membership extended or approved? Who monitors membership to ensure equal opportunity for all eligible employees?

- Have there been any potential concerns regarding participation of nonfavored group members? If so, how were they handled?

- Does the corporation encourage or sponsor participation in external networking groups? If so, which ones and what form does the corporate 'support' take?

- Does the corporation ensure that all eligible employees know about this option? How?

- Who monitors the program(s) to ensure all eligible employees have equal opportunity to participate and receive the same support? Have there been any potential concerns regarding eligible nonfavored group members? If so, how were they handled?

- Does the corporation promote informal networking opportunities? How? Are there specific target groups?

4I ONSITE: RETENTION

A major way a corporation retains key personnel at all levels of its workforce is by paying a competitive salary for the type of work involved and offering benefits at least comparable to those offered by other corporations in its industry. Corporations may additionally have honor and award systems to recognize, reward and thereby encourage high performance.

4I00 OVERVIEW OF TOTAL COMPENSATION PACKAGES

Fair pay is a critical issue for workers and their families, and a cornerstone of OFCCP's equal employment protections. As such, identifying and remedying compensation discrimination has long been an important goal of OFCCP compliance efforts. The Executive Order and the implementing regulations specifically require contractors to ensure pay equity. They place federal contractors under affirmative duties to maintain data, conduct internal review and monitoring of pay practices for potential discrimination, and comply with Title VII's ban on discrimination in the paying of wages, salaries, and other forms of compensation.[214] Nevertheless, Bureau of Labor Statistics data and numerous research studies indicate that unexplained disparities in compensation on the basis of sex and race continue to exist.

OFCCP follows Title VII principles in investigating and analyzing compensation discrimination, While the approach set forth above in chapters 1 and 2 for analyzing compensation applies, there are additional complexities in typical corporate compensation programs for high level jobs. As in any other compensation analysis, the objective is to ensure that eligible nonfavored group members receive compensation and benefits to the same extent, and under the same standards, as their similarly situated peers. If not already provided, the first step should be to request any formal policies the corporation has regarding each such type of compensation. In addition to reviewing the policies, the CO will probably need to use interviews to determine at what level employees become eligible to receive each type, and what if any, exceptions the corporation made for people below the specified level.

When investigating compensation cases at the corporate management level COs must have an understanding of the compensation structure. As management level increases, it is likely that total compensation goes well beyond the base salary typically reflected in a workforce analysis.

Similarly, COs will find that benefits go well beyond what is standard for other employees. At higher management levels base salary is often supplemented or, for top managers, exceeded by other forms of compensation like cash bonuses, stock awards and stock options. Standard benefits are usually supplemented by what are often referred to as perquisites or "perks". Perks are numerous and varied, some examples are the use of corporate cars, concierge service that offers discounted services, free trips, access to the corporate plane, and housing subsidies or allowances.

Upper level management compensation, benefits and perks are normally specialized and closely held within the corporation. Therefore, it is usually necessary to interview the person in charge of compensation and benefits at the corporate level, identify who maintains the data and, if necessary, interview the secretary or some official who may have recordkeeping responsibility for the corporation.

a. *Bonuses*. As used here, bonuses refer to those that are predominantly exclusive to the management level. An addition to base salary, bonuses may be granted in cash, stock or in some combination thereof. Corporations most often distribute bonuses annually, usually

[214] 41 CFR. §§ 60-1.4; 60-1.12; 60-2.17(b)-(d).

soon after the end of a corporation's fiscal year or performance appraisal cycle. Corporations may distribute bonuses as a lump sum, or over a specified period of time, in which case, COs should consider the totality of the award in the analysis. In a multi-establishment corporation, it is fairly typical for the bonus "pot" to be allocated to component business groups in some proportion to their contribution to corporate profitability over the bonus period. Those business groups, in turn, may similarly allocate their bonus "pot" to their component establishments. Bonuses thus provide an incentive for managers to improve profitability. This incentive tends to increase as a larger proportion of a manager's compensation comes from bonuses rather than from base salary or other forms of compensation.

Cash bonuses are most often a percentage of base salary. When reviewing potential compensation issues where cash bonuses are involved, some areas COs should consider include:

- the level or salary grade at which employees become eligible for cash bonuses;
- the history of bonuses being granted to employees below this level;
- the role of corporate headquarters in allocating cash bonuses;
- the role of intermediate headquarters and subordinate establishments in allocating bonuses;
- the standard the corporation uses to determine whether an employee receives a cash bonus;
- the individuals, including their specific roles, determining who is eligible, what standards to apply, and the amount of the bonus;
- the levels of review and approval in the process; and
- the existence of safeguards that ensure that all eligible employees are given equal consideration in the allocation of cash bonuses.

In addition to exploring these areas, COs should ask questions to gather information on the consideration and representation of members of nonfavored groups during the bonus process. Below are a few sample questions.

- What proportion of those eligible, separated by nonfavored and favored group status, received a cash bonus?
- If the proportion of eligible nonfavored group members receiving such bonuses is lower than that of eligible favored group members, did the contractor review these allocations to ensure nondiscrimination? What were the findings or results?

- What is the average cash bonus separated by nonfavored and favored group status?[215]

- If the average cash bonus nonfavored group members received is lower than what favored group members received, did the contractor review allocations to ensure nondiscrimination? What were the findings or results?

b. *Stock.* Corporate stock plans can be a particularly strong incentive to improve corporate performance, since such improved performance usually increases the stock's share price and thus increases the value of any given number of shares of corporate stock an employee holds.

   Employers may sometimes use company stock as a bonus but may also use it as a way to retain key employees or to provide an incentive for a given action. The corporation also may offer employees the option to purchase corporate stock on favorable terms. If the corporation has not already provided it, COs should request any written policies and procedures regarding use of stock as a management incentive.

   - *Stock Awards – One-time Bonuses*: Corporations occasionally pay bonuses, in whole or in part, in corporate stock. This may be an outright grant, usually annual, of a certain number of shares of stock at the market value at the time of the grant. More often, however, a stock award is vested over a number of years.

   - *Stock Awards – Vested.* The term "vested" is more commonly associated with time-in-company required to begin accruing retirement and/or health benefits, it can also be applicable in this content.

     A stock award is vested when an employee, instead of immediately receiving a given number of shares, receives those shares after a given number of years (the "vesting period"). For example, the corporation may award a person 300 shares of stock, with 100 shares allocated immediately, and the remaining 200 to be allocated at the end of three years. Such vested stock awards provide an incentive for the recipient to remain with the corporation, since he or she will not receive the remaining stock if he or she leaves.

     Vesting also may be for a specific limited purpose. For example, a stock award may be conditional on an employee action, such as completing a particular project by a given date. In this case, the stock is "awarded" but it is not allocated until the employee timely completes the project.

   - *Stock Options.* This non-cash form of compensation offers the employee the ability to choose to buy or not to buy a given number of shares of stock at a specified price within a specified period of time. Stock options are issued as a private contract between the employer and employee. Because they cannot be exercised immediately, employers use stock options as a way to retain employees. The option to purchase stock may have conditions or limitations such as limited transferability and vesting

[215] This may be expressed as the average percentage of base salary.

requirements. Unless the company performs poorly, employees generally expect to sell the stock at a higher market price and make a profit.

For example, an employee is offered an option to buy 100 shares of corporate stock at $30 a share (its current market price) at any time within the next five years. If the stock goes down, the employee simply does not exercise the option to buy. If it goes up, however, say to $50 a share, and the employee exercises his or her option and has an immediate profit of $20 a share or $2,000.

When evaluating stock as a part of compensation there are several things to consider. For any area of potential compensation concern where stock appears to be a factor, COs must determine, for each year:

- the form in which the corporation gave the stock;
- the eligibility criteria;
- the extent the same form of stock was given to all eligible employees in the same manner, at the same time and with the same value;
- the change in stock type between years; and
- the consistency, or lack thereof, in the change in stock type for all eligible employees.

In addition to the above considerations, COs must ask specific questions when reviewing stock given during the last award cycle:

- What proportion of those eligible, by nonfavored and favored group status, received stock?
- If the proportion of eligible nonfavored group members receiving such an award is lower than that of eligible favored group members, did the corporation review these allocations to ensure nondiscrimination? What were the findings or results?
- What is the average stock award by nonfavored and favored group status?
- If the average stock award received by nonfavored group members is lower than that received by favored group members, did the corporation review these allocations to ensure nondiscrimination? What were the findings or results?

Finally, if the corporation awarded vested stock to keep favored group members with the corporation, COs should review data on terminations to determine if there were any nonfavored group members in similar positions who left the corporation around the same time. If so, COs should determine whether this group received vested stock. If not, COs should then determine whether they should have under the corporation's criteria for receiving such stock. When there is a finding of discrimination in the awarding of stock, there are some special considerations to be applied to the remedy. These are identified in Appendix A-6, Special Remedial Considerations Applicable to Stock.

c. *Perquisites*. Called "perks," these are privileges that corporations may provide employees as they reach a certain management level. "Perks" generally are benefits that have cash value like a corporate car, that save time like accounting or tax services, that offer a convenience like the use of corporate plane, and that protect key personnel like paid medical exams.

As with other compensation elements, COs must determine whether the corporation offers perks, what they offer, how it decides who is eligible for a given perk, and if the proportion of eligible nonfavored group members receiving each perk is lower than that of eligible favored group members. COs must also ask if the corporation reviews its allocations of perks to ensure nondiscrimination and obtain the findings or results of the reviews.

4I01 RECOGNITION: AWARDS AND HONORS

Corporations may offer any number of incentive awards or honors, with or without accompanying money. Often these are for meritorious achievement, whether individually or as part of a team on a particular project during a year. They also can be for superior performance generally, and be granted in conjunction with an annual performance appraisal. In the latter case, when people have reached the top of the salary range for their jobs, cash awards may be used instead of a permanent increase to base salary to reward high performance.

There are several things to consider when reviewing awards and honors. If not already provided, COs must request written policies and procedures covering all such programs. For each existing program, COs must determine:

- Who is eligible to receive an award or honor, or both? What eligibility criteria were used?

- Who, listed by favored and nonfavored group status, received an award or honor? What are the reasons each person received the award or honor? Were any nonfavored group members recommended for an award or honor, or both, who did not receive one? Why?

- If the proportion of eligible nonfavored group members receiving the honor or award, or both, was lower than that of favored group members, were the awards reviewed to ensure nondiscrimination? What were the findings or results?

- If the award was accompanied by money, and the amount of money varied, what was the average amount received by the favored group and the nonfavored group? If the average amount was lower for nonfavored group members than for favored group members, did the corporation review these awards to ensure nondiscrimination? What were the findings or results?

4J ONSITE: TERMINATIONS

Generally, the higher the job level, the less likely it is that a person's separation from the corporation is recorded as an involuntary termination, regardless of the circumstances surrounding his or her departure. Above a certain management level, if a corporation determines that an employee is not performing as expected, he or she may be offered the opportunity to resign. Therefore, it would not be unexpected to find that the records show all middle and senior-level management terminations as voluntary.

Many terminations, of course, will be genuinely voluntary, some for reasons such as "better job opportunity," "to spend more time with my family." Such departures, however, may have been influenced by any number of factors, such as a perception of lack of promotion prospects, that may or may not have EEO implications.

Even absent statistical disparity, COs should review involuntary terminations of nonfavored group member managers as well as a sample of voluntary ones. COs must conduct the analysis itself in the same manner as any termination analysis, complete with interviews.

4K COMPLETION OF COMPLIANCE EVALUATION: EXIT CONFERENCE, REPORT WRITING AND NOTICE OF EVALUATION

In a CMCE, the Regional Director or Deputy Regional Director, or both, will conduct an exit conference with top corporate officials. The purpose of the meeting is to:

- present and discuss any violation findings and required remedies to be incorporated in a Notice of Violations; and
- identify and discuss any particularly creative or innovative efforts the corporation made to ensure equal opportunity for nonfavored group members to advance to middle and senior-level management positions.

As noted in subsection 4A00, a CMCE includes all elements of a standard compliance evaluation, but with a special emphasis on the issues discussed in this chapter. Accordingly, COs must complete the SCER to document their evaluation findings but they must pay particular attention to the CMCE-specific supplemental Part D of the SCER that addresses issues unique to a CMCE.

4K00 NOTICE OF EVALUATION COMPLETION

As in any other compliance evaluation, COs send the corporation a notice of compliance evaluation completion, using the evaluation completion notices and procedures found at Letter L-4, Notice of Closing Compliance Evaluation No Violations Found.

Note that if the CO finds violations and an agreement that addresses a corporate-wide issue is necessary to bring the corporation into compliance, that agreement should require that the corporation implement the appropriate remedial action at all corporate establishments. If, during an evaluation of a subordinate establishment conducted after the effective date of that agreement, OFCCP discovers that this establishment has not fully implemented the agreement, a follow-up of the corporate evaluation may be necessary.

CHAPTER 5
FUNCTIONAL AFFIRMATIVE ACTION PROGRAM COMPLIANCE EVALUATIONS

5A INTRODUCTION

Multi-establishment federal supply and service contractors are allowed to develop affirmative action programs (AAPs) organized around distinct business functions or lines of business, rather than AAPs based on the contractor's establishments.[216] A contractor is permitted to develop AAPs for its functional or business units, referred to as functional affirmative action program or FAAP, only after reaching an agreement with OFCCP.[217]

This chapter provides guidance on evaluating a multi-establishment contractor's compliance with its nondiscrimination and affirmative action obligations under FAAPs.

5A00 APPLICABILITY OF CHAPTER

This chapter applies only to multi-establishment contractors with approved FAAP Agreements. Implementation of a FAAP Agreement occurs only with the written approval of the OFCCP Director, or his or her designee. Ongoing compliance evaluations of establishments will not be affected by a contractor's request to enter into a FAAP Agreement. If a contractor's establishment is selected for evaluation prior to the finalization of a FAAP Agreement, OFCCP will still move forward with the establishment-based compliance evaluation.

5A01 PURPOSE OF THE FAAP

Functional AAPs are designed to provide contractors the option of creating an AAP that better fits their business needs. Any multi-establishment supply and service contractor subject to AAP requirements may request an agreement with OFCCP that allows for the development and use of a FAAP. Some multi-establishment contractors may find it appropriate to develop AAPs based solely on functional or business units, while others may elect to use a combination of functional and establishment based AAPs. Participation in the FAAP program is optional for contractors. The FAAP Agreement cannot be construed to limit or restrict how the OFCCP conducts its compliance evaluations.

5A02 RELATIONSHIP TO STANDARD COMPLIANCE EVALUATIONS

A FAAP compliance evaluation is a full compliance review that includes all aspects of a standard compliance evaluation.[218] However, all AAP components are based on functional or

---

[216] This is in accordance with 65 Fed. Reg. 68022 (published Nov. 13, 2000). This notice added 41 CFR 60-2.1(d)(4), a new regulatory provision.

[217] A FAAP agreement addresses only the development of AAPs along functional lines. It does not address how OFCCP will conduct its compliance evaluations.

[218] A FAAP must include the components that are prescribed in 41 CFR Part 60-2.

business units rather than an establishment. If OFCCP selects the corporate headquarters unit for review, the FAAP compliance evaluation may be designated a CMCE. COs responsible for conducting FAAP compliance evaluations follow the procedures in Chapter 1 of this Manual on the procedures for conducting a desk audit, Chapter 2 on conducting an onsite review, and Chapter 4 on conducting a CMCE but with only a few differences. These differences are explained below in Sections 5B through 5E.

5A03 RELATIONSHIP TO THE STANDARD COMPLIANCE EVALUATION REPORT (SCER)

In conducting a compliance evaluation, including a desk audit and onsite review, COs complete the applicable sections of the SCER. It may be necessary for COs to indicate the functional unit for which the finding is made. Some sections of the SCER may not be applicable in every compliance evaluation.[219]

5A04 OFCCP PARTICIPANTS IN FAAP COMPLIANCE EVALUATIONS

OFCCP conducts FAAP reviews under the National Office's direction and oversight. The National Office compliance evaluation team schedules FAAP reviews and may coordinate data gathering and onsite activities with regional offices, as needed. Regional office staff members may participate in the compliance evaluation as agreed upon with the Director of DPO.

5B PRE-DESK AUDIT ACTIONS

COs will follow the same steps as required in Chapter 1, Section 1B – Pre-Desk Audit Actions. This section explains the various steps and actions that COs must take prior to starting a compliance evaluation. The steps include contacting the contractor, setting up appropriate case files and logs and obtaining relevant information about the contractor from other EEO and Department of Labor enforcement agencies such as WHD and OSHA. The following sections review the necessary variances in these steps when COs are conducting a FAAP compliance evaluation.

5B00 CREATION AND MAINTENANCE OF THE CASE FILE

COs must prepare and maintain an electronic case Chronology Log for each FAAP compliance evaluation.[220] They complete the Chronology Log as directed in Chapter 1, Section 1B01, of this Manual.

COs must create and maintain a case file for each scheduled compliance evaluation. The case file should generally consist of the items detailed in subsection 1B02 on creating a case file and possibly a complaint form. For a FAAP compliance review, the case file should also include a copy of the approved FAAP Agreement as signed by the Director of OFCCP. This information

---

[219] See Appendices A-1 – SCER and A2 – SCER Instructions.
[220] See Figure F-1 – Case Chronology Log.

should be included in the case file in Folder 1. COs will provide a cross reference in the case file for the location of the documentation supporting the FAAP Agreement.

5B01 SENDING THE SCHEDULING LETTER AND ITEMIZED LIST

The Director of the FAAP Unit signs the Scheduling Letter and Itemized Listing for a FAAP compliance evaluation and sends it by certified mail to the corporate CEO.[221] The Director also mails a copy of the Scheduling Letter and Itemized Listing to the managing official of the functional or business unit selected for review and the contact person the FAAP Agreement identifies. The Itemized Listing requests only data supporting the functional or business unit selected for review. Prior to sending the Scheduling Letter notifying a functional or business unit of a scheduled compliance evaluation, COs must contact the managing official identified in the FAAP Agreement to ensure that the functional or business unit still exists and to verify the name, title, mailing address and phone number of the managing official. The National Office must also be notified if the functional or business unit no longer exist because the FAAP agreement can be terminated in this instance.[222]

It is important to note that the contractor may also have standard establishment-based AAPs covering the remainder of its workforce. OFCCP will schedule compliance evaluations in accordance with the standard scheduling system for those areas of the workforce that are subject to establishment-based AAPs.

5B02 FOLLOW-UP CONTACT WITH CONTRACTOR

Within 15 calendar days after sending the Scheduling Letter and Itemized Listing, a CO must contact the contractor's representative to ensure that the contractor understands the requirements outlined in these items. If there are questions, the CO will provide technical assistance to clarify the requirements and the compliance evaluation process.

5B03 OFCCP COMPLIANCE HISTORY REPORTS

COs must check OFCCP's Case Management System (CMS) and Executive Information System (EIS) to obtain a list of prior compliance evaluations of the functional or business unit, corporation and its other related establishments. They should also review historical files contained in Folder 6 of the case file located in their respective field offices. Checking to determine if the prior evaluations identified any issues is an important preparatory step. If issues are identified in the historical files, COs must review the record to determine how they were resolved. These previously identified issues may provide useful information and possible indicators of current problem areas. If a prior review of this unit resulted in a Conciliation Agreement (CA), the onsite visit should provide an opportunity to confirm that the contractor took, and appropriately maintained, the required corrective action.

---

[221] See Figures F-2 – OFCCP Scheduling Letter and Itemized Listing.

[222] Directive 305, Functional Affirmative Action Programs (December 17, 2012). This Directive rescinded Directive 296 issued on June 14, 2011.

5B04 CONTACTING EEOC, VETS AND OTHER AGENCIES

As discussed in Chapter 1, simultaneous with the mailing of the Scheduling Letter, COs will also seek information on the contractor's employment policies and practices from the Equal Employment Opportunity Commission (EEOC), Veterans Employment and Training Service (VETS), state employment services, and other EEO and labor law enforcement agencies. Such information helps to provide a better understanding of the contractor's workforce and operations, and may indicate potential problem areas.

Because of the nature of a FAAP compliance evaluation the job groups or titles, or both, that are under review may be located in multiple establishments and in different locations. COs should determine the extent to which they need to establish contacts with the identified agencies in each location to ensure that he or she obtains enough information to assist in assessing the contractor's compliance and affirmative action efforts.

5B05 GATHERING EEO INFORMATION

COs will gather information to determine the scope of the information needed to establish whether there are any contractor employment practices that are relevant to the FAAP compliance evaluation. Additionally, COs should be aware of local and national community resources available to establish linkages, if required.

5C DESK AUDIT

Initially, COs will determine whether the Functional AAP is in accordance with the FAAP Agreement. This assessment should include, but is not limited to, determining if:

- the appropriate functional or business unit is covered,
- the functional or business unit continues to be a discrete autonomous function, and
- the functional or business unit includes the number of employees covered by the FAAP Agreement.

If a CO conducting a FAAP compliance evaluation finds problems, he or she should contact the contractor for clarification or additional information before proceeding with the desk audit. If significant changes have occurred, such that the functional or business unit scheduled for review no longer exists or has substantially decreased or increased in size, the CO should notify his or her supervisor to discuss the issue. The National Office must also be notified.

COs will conduct the desk audit as described in Chapter 1 of this Manual in Sections 1C through 1R with the exception that COs will organize the data by functional or business units. In some instances, during a FAAP compliance evaluation, COs will not have sufficient data to perform a trend analysis in accordance with subsection in Chapter 1 on EEO trend analysis. However, they should conduct all other analyses required in a desk audit. COs should complete all applicable sections of the SCER and further investigate identified problems areas and indicators of adverse impact during the onsite review.

In conducting analyses of employment decisions like hiring, terminations, promotions and compensation, COs should examine the data by function and business unit and job group and job title or any combination thereof.

5D ONSITE

When conducting a FAAP compliance evaluation it may be necessary to conduct onsite visits to more than one location to evaluate the business functions or lines of business under review. In such circumstances, COs and their supervisors will determine the onsite visits that will be conducted and the composition of each onsite team. COs will conduct the onsite review as described in Chapter 2 of this Manual using the SCER to record investigative findings and conclusions.

5E COMPLIANCE EVALUATION COMPLETION

If the offsite analysis of the data that the COs obtained during the desk audit and onsite review result in no violations being found, the COs should close the FAAP compliance evaluation. However, if there are findings of discrimination or other violations, COs should proceed in accordance with Chapter 8 and the issuance of a Predetermination Notice (PDN) or Notice of Violation (NOV), as warranted.[223]

COs must follow Chapter 8 in each FAAP compliance evaluation that results in a finding of a violation. If a CO issues a Conciliation Agreement to correct identified violations, then the CA, closing documents and letters must clearly reflect that the CO conducted a compliance evaluation of a FAAP and support data, and indicate the limited scope of the evaluation. As previously noted, the contractor may also have a standard AAP(s) covering the remainder of its workforce and employment actions that OFCCP did not review as a part of the FAAP review.[224]

[223] See Chapter 8 – Resolution of Noncompliance.

[224] See Chapter 7 – Employment Discrimination Remedies; Chapter 8 – Resolution of Noncompliance; and Letters L-27 – Pre-determination Notice and L-28 – Notice of Violation.

CHAPTER 6
COMPLAINT INVESTIGATION

6A INTRODUCTION

This chapter outlines the procedures for processing and conducting investigations of complaints alleging discrimination in employment by federal contractors. Preparing for and investigating a complaint differs from conducting a compliance evaluation as discussed in Chapter 2. The difference is that this investigation is primarily focused on the specific allegations in the complaints. This chapter includes the general principles of complaint processing and investigation planning. It, therefore, focuses on the CO's responsibilities related to investigating and resolving complaints. It describes the CO's responsibility to evaluate the allegations in a complaint to determine the legal and analytical framework for addressing each allegation, to identify data and information to obtain during an investigation, to conduct appropriate analyses and to develop and provide notification of findings. The chapter also discusses conciliation efforts and enforcement actions.

6B BASES OF COMPLAINT ALLEGATIONS

Employees and applicants may file complaints with OFCCP under any of the laws OFCCP enforces. However, OFCCP processes some complaints in coordination with the Equal Employment Opportunity Commission (EEOC). Specifically, the EO 11246 regulation at 41 CFR Part 60-1.24(a) states that OFCCP may refer appropriate complaints to the EEOC for processing under Title VII of the Civil Rights Act of 1964, as amended. In keeping with a Memorandum of Understanding (MOU)[225] between OFCCP and the EEOC, OFCCP will generally refer individual complaints alleging employment discrimination in violation of EO 11246 to the EEOC.

OFCCP retains EO 11246 *class and systemic* discrimination complaints. Whenever a complainant files a complaint of employment discrimination with OFCCP under EO 11246 and the allegations in the complaint also fall within the jurisdiction of Title VII, the complaint is dual filed. OFCCP acts as EEOC's agent for the purposes of receiving, investigating and processing the Title VII component of dual filed complaints. OFCCP processes these complaints in a manner consistent with Title VII principles of liability and relief.

---

[225] The MOU between OFCCP and the EEOC was first entered into on May 20. 1970, it was revised in 1974, and revised again in 1981 as published at 46 FR 7435 (Jan. 23, 1981). The 1981 MOU was revised in 1999 as published at 64 FR.17664 (Apr. 12, 1999), and most recently updated in November 2011 as published at 76 FR 71029 (Nov. 7, 2011).

OFCCP investigates individual and class complaints filed under Section 4212 and Section 503. In 41 CFR Part 60-742,[226] the regulation describes procedures applicable to complaints of employment discrimination based on disability filed against contractors when the complaints fall within the jurisdiction of both Section 503 and Title I of the Americans with Disabilities Act of 1990, as amended (ADA). If a complaint is dual filed under both Section 503 and the ADA, OFCCP uses legal standards for determining liability, as well as damages and remedies, consistent with those applied under the ADA in determining whether a contractor committed an unlawful employment practice. When proceeding with an investigation and resolution of a dual filed complaint, OFCCP is acting as EEOC's agent. OFCCP also follows ADA principles when investigating Section 503 allegations that are not dual filed.

Complainants may also file complaints alleging retaliation or interference. OFCCP's regulations prohibit interference and intimidation, including threats, coercion, harassment and discrimination of any individual exercising his or her rights under OFCCP enforced laws and any other federal, state or local law requiring equal opportunity. OFCCP investigates all such allegations.

OFCCP also investigates complaints filed under Executive Order 13496, which requires contractors to provide notice to their employees of their rights under federal labor laws. OFCCP and the Office of Labor-Management Standards (OLMS) share enforcement authority for EO 13496.[227]

6C COMPLAINT PROCESSING

The OFCCP's regional offices are responsible for implementing complaint intake procedures and policies.[228] These offices "perfect" the complaint for investigation. COs investigating a complaint may also assist with perfecting complaint allegations. This chapter does not cover regional or other administrative matters except as they may directly involve COs.

6C00 RECEIPT OF COMPLAINTS

If a regional office receives a complaint regarding a contractor or contractor's establishment that is in a different geographic jurisdiction, that office will immediately send the complaint to the appropriate office. Complainants filing under Section 4212 may also file through the Department of Labor's Veteran's Employment and Training Service (VETS) or through the Local Veterans' Employment Representative (LVER) at the local employment service office,

---

[226] If a complaint that alleges a violation of Section 503 (which does not include affirmative action obligations) and also raises an allegation of individual discrimination based on race, color, religion, sex, national origin or age (over which OFCCP does not have jurisdiction), the complaint will be referred to the EEOC.

[227] See Directive, Verification Procedures Under E.O. 13496: Notification of Employee Rights under Federal Labor Laws, Number 290 (June 15, 2010).

[228] The regulations at 41CFR 60-1.21 to 60-1.24; 60-250.61; 60-300.61; 60-741.61 and 60-742.5 address timeliness issues and the initial processing of a complaint. Further discussion of regional office processing of complaints is in the Administrative Practice Binder.

who will transfer the complaint to OFCCP.[229] The OFCCP office receiving the complaint will immediately date stamp the complaint and enter the date and time it arrived into office records before forwarding it to the appropriate regional office. COs use this date to determine whether the complainant filed on time.

Regional offices should encourage complainants to complete a Form CC-4.[230] Complainants can find the form on the OFCCP Web site where it is available in several languages. COs, if after reviewing a complaint, need clarification or additional information from the complainant they should contact the complainant immediately.

6C01 WHO MAY FILE A COMPLAINT

Any individual, group or third party may file a complaint. In some instances, complainants may file anonymously. Depending on the specificity or individual nature of a complaint, the regional office will determine whether OFCCP will proceed with an investigation or whether additional information regarding the complainant or alleged victim is needed in order to proceed.

When it is not necessary to identify an individual complainant or alleged victim, OFCCP will take appropriate action to protect the identity of the complainant or alleged victim. For example, if a complainant alleges that the application of a specific policy disparately impacts women, it may not be necessary to share the complainant's identity with the contractor.

6C02 COMPLAINT PERFECTION

The regional office will completely perfect the complaint within 10 calendar days of receiving the complaint, unless the regional office shows good cause. The regional office will conduct the perfecting of the complaint to determine timeliness, contract coverage and which allegations fall within the agency's jurisdiction. The regional office must determine jurisdiction as expeditiously as possible. As noted above, COs investigating a complaint may contribute to the perfection process.

A complaint shall include certain basic information such as:

- the name, address and telephone number of the complainant;
- the name and address of the contractor allegedly committing the discrimination;
- the description of the alleged discriminatory acts; and
- the information pertinent to the investigation and resolution of the complaint.

---

[229] If the complainant files with VETS or the LVER and alleges discrimination prohibited by Section 4212, OFCCP will use the date the complaint arrived at that office.

[230] See Figure F-4 – Complaint Form.

The complainant or his or her representative must sign the complaint.[231] Section 503 also requires the alleged victim to submit evidence proving he or she is disabled, has a history of a disability or is regarded as having a disability. Section 4212 requires the alleged victim to submit evidence that he or she is a veteran protected under 41 CFR 60-250.1(a) or 41 CFR 60-300.1(a).

The scope of complaints under EO 11246 is different from complaints filed under Section 503 and Section 4212. EO 11246 complaints must allege discrimination. Complainants filing under Section 503 or Section 4212 may allege a violation of the law or its implementing regulation. For example, a complainant could allege affirmative action or recordkeeping violations as well as discrimination under one or both of these authorities.

Upon perfecting a complaint, the regional office will assign the complaint to the field office in the jurisdiction of the establishment where the alleged discrimination occurred.

6C03 CASE FILE

a. *Maintenance of the Case File.* Upon receiving a complaint to investigate, a CO establishes a case file. COs should maintain all documents, correspondence, interview notes and records of contact, including e-mails and telephone calls, pertaining to the complaint in this file. When the investigation is complete, the case file should contain sufficient documentation to support either an enforcement recommendation based on a finding of a violation(s) or a decision to close the complaint investigation based on a finding of no violation. Regarding the maintenance of records, COs should follow the general principles below:

    - Date all telephone, e-mail and written communications; identify who participated in the communication by name and position; and accurately reflect any agreed upon commitments.

    - Keep documents from the complainant, contractor or others in their original condition. COs should make copies and label documents as copies if they need to make alterations to or notes on a document.

    - Use the case file to document and maintain interview statements, whether the interview is conducted in person or by telephone or some other electronic means. COs should record statements or observations as soon as possible after the conclusion of the interview or observation. The interview statement must note the name and title or position of the person conducting the interview, the name and position of the person interviewed, when and where the interview took place and the names of any other people who may have been present (e.g., legal counsel, a personal representative).

    - Record newly obtained information or observations in clearly legible writing or, preferably, in an electronic format. COs should type handwritten notes for the case file.

[231] See 41 CFR 60-1.23, 60-250.61, 60-300.61 and 60-741.61.

- Create and clearly label a section in the case file for supporting evidence for any conclusions the CO draws regarding the complaint allegations. Supporting evidence may include CO notes, worksheets, contractor data and any other materials relating to an allegation.

- Keep all records and information regarding a complaint investigation confidential.

b. *Case File Contents.* The case file will contain seven separate files labeled as follows and containing the listed contents.[232] COs should cross reference the files as appropriate.

1. *Complaint and Data Submitted by the Complainant.* This file will contain the CC-4 Form and any documentation or information the complainant submitted, including the envelope used to mail the complaint form. Documents may include: letter of complaint, list of witnesses, supporting documents, etc. These items should be on the right side of the file folder.

   On the left side of the file folder, the CO should place a copy of the CC-58 report for the establishment that he or she obtained from Case Management System (CMS). Underneath this form, the CO should include any CMS extension requests and responses.

2. *Case Chronology, Correspondence and Meeting Notes.* This file contains all correspondence and any attachments. This includes any materials from contacts with the contractor, union, witnesses, consultants, etc. It may also include memos to file, but not investigative notes the CO prepared and used in reaching factual and legal determinations. Correspondence should be in chronological order with the most recent on top.

   The Chronology Log CC-53 will be attached to the left side of the file and placed on top. The CO shall maintain the Case Chronology Log electronically, as described in subsection 1B01 of this Manual.[233] The CO should place the Quality Assurance Complaint Investigation Form CC-75 on the left side under the log.

3. *Investigative Material.* This file will contain the investigative materials. The CO should index and tab the materials. The file should contain the following materials:

   - investigative plan;

   - investigative report;

   - interview statements;

   - investigative notes;

---

[232] See Appendix A-8 – Complaint File Index.
[233] See Figure F-1 Case Chronology Log.

- statistical evidence;
- comparative evidence; and
- anecdotal evidence.

These materials may be voluminous. If so, the CO may appropriately label, tab and index separate folders to contain the materials.

4. *Medical/Veteran Documentation*: This file, organized with an index and tabs, will contain the medical and veteran documentation. The documents should have labels clearly stating the source of the information (e.g., complainant, contractor third party). The file should contain:

- Medical releases;
- Medical and/or disabled veteran status (e.g., DD-214);
- Medical coverage information;
- Diagnosis or medical description of disabling condition;
- Work restrictions; and
- For veterans, coverage information as needed (e.g., Armed Forces campaign badge information).

The CO must label and treat File 4 Medical/Veteran Documentation as "confidential."

5. *Legal*: This file will contain any documents related to legal activity, including:

- Notice of Investigation Report (place on top);
- Conciliation Agreement (on top of report, when complete);
- Solicitor's Opinion;
- Joint Review Committee meeting notes and reports; [234]
- Freedom of Information Act and Privacy Act determinations;

[234] The Joint Review Committee (JRC) is a committee – consisting of District Office staff members working on the complaint, Regional Office staff members and representative(s) of the Solicitor's Office – that discusses the complaint investigation and findings.

- Enforcement recommendations; and

- Jurisdictional and contract coverage information (on the bottom).

6. *Employment Handbooks, Collective Bargaining Agreement (if applicable) and Miscellaneous.* On the right side of this file, organized by an index and tabs, will be copies of any relevant collective bargaining agreements, employee handbooks, fringe benefits and leave policy materials and any similar contractor materials. The CO should place any items that are not otherwise listed and contained in other case file sections here.

7. *Historical Review Results.* This file will contain copies of any available closure letters and documents from previous complaint investigations of this establishment. The CO should note pertinent information regarding compliance evaluations of the establishment here as well as include the closure letter for the current investigation.

   The District Office should maintain the historical file indefinitely. If the District Office conducts another investigation of the establishment, this file becomes a part of the new investigative file. If the District Office is going to retire the case file, the District Office should remove and retain the historical file while filing the remainder of the case file.

c. *Applies to Enforcement and Non-Enforcement Cases.* The CO should maintain this case file format for enforcement and non-enforcement cases. For enforcement cases, the CO should transmit the file with a Transmittal Memorandum as described in Chapter 8. I t is particularly important that the CO maintain all records, except drafts, in the case file in enforcement cases. The CO should not include drafts of OFCCP memoranda, for example, Notification of Results of Investigation (NORI), Conciliation Agreement (CA), that have a later version.

6C04 CORRESPONDENCE

The CO should address all letters concerning a complaint to the senior official at the appropriate contractor establishment with a copy for the CEO at the corporate address, except when the contractor is a single location establishment. The CO should send the letters by certified mail, return receipt requested.

6C05 COUNSEL OR OTHER REPRESENTATION

A contractor or complainant may designate an attorney or other representative as his or her contact person with OFCCP prior to or during a complaint investigation. Such designation shall be at the initiation of the contractor or complainant.

a. *Written Designation.* The designation of a representative must be in writing by the contractor or complainant to an OFCCP District or Regional Director. The complainant or senior official of the contractor, respectively, must sign the letter. If the field office receives notification of the designation in another form other than in writing, the CO should contact the requester (contractor or complainant) and advise them of the necessary letter. The correspondence should provide the name, address and telephone number of the representative. In addition, the correspondence should clearly describe the extent of the representative's authority, specifically:

- if all contacts, including routine contacts to make appointments or to clarify submitted data or other information, should go through the representative;
- if the representative has the authority to negotiate settlements for the contractor or complainant; and
- if the CO should mail correspondence to the representative only, or if he or she should mail copies to the contractor or complainant as well.

The CO should send to highest ranking management official a courtesy copy of all substantive documents that this Manual requires to be mailed.

b. *Duration of Designation.* Unless the contractor or complainant indicated otherwise in the written designation letter, the designation shall only be for the duration of the complaint investigation and any applicable enforcement period.

6C06 TIMELY COMPLETION OF INVESTIGATION

The field office must complete the investigation within 60 calendar days after the regional office has sent the complaint. The field office must take all necessary steps to complete the investigation within the 60 calendar days of the investigating office's receipt. The Regional Director may grant an extension of this period if the field office shows good cause. The granted extension can be for no more than 120 calendar days for completion of the complaint investigation and no more than 60 calendar days for conciliation efforts. Examples of good cause include but are not limited to complex legal issues, unavailability of witnesses, untimely responses from contractor or the number of complainants.

6C07 OFCCP CASE MANAGEMENT SYSTEM

The CMS tracks and monitors the processing of complaints that victims have filed with OFCCP. COs have specific responsibilities for entering data and information into the automated system. These responsibilities begin with the receipt of the assigned complaint by the regional office and end when the CO closes the complaint file. The COs can find specific instructions in the CMS Manual.

6D PROVIDING THE CONTRACTOR A COPY OF THE COMPLAINT

COs will provide a copy of the complaint to the contractor upon completing perfection of the complaint. The regional office should complete perfection within 10 calendar days of receipt of the complaint. The CO should send a copy of the complaint along with notice of receipt of the complaint to the contractor, except in extenuating circumstances as discussed in 6D01 below.[235]

---

[235] See Section 6D01 for further discussion and L-7.

As provided below, when necessary and appropriate, OFCCP may redact specific information from the complaint.

6D00 REVIEW OF COMPLAINT BEFORE RELEASE

a. *Copy of Complaint.* The CO will normally provide the contractor with a full copy of the complaint except to the extent it contains the following types of information. The CO will delete the following information so that the remaining text reads as smoothly as possible.

- The name and other information that would easily identify someone other than the complainant who might suffer retaliation, be construed as an informer, or suffer embarrassment or other unwarranted invasion of privacy.
- Obscene, inflammatory or libelous language.
- Names and allegations against more than one company. The CO should delete the name and allegations against company #1, from the complaint copy provided to company #2, and vice versa.
- Identifying characteristics of individuals in a third party complaint (e.g., description of unique characteristics, unique job title or position) if the individual has not signed the complaint or authorized release of his or her identity.

b. *Summary of Complaint.* If the necessary deletions are extensive, the CO may prepare a complaint summary to forward to the contractor. If the CO uses a summary, the CO may obtain a redrafted complaint to submit to the contractor prior to the onsite investigation.

6D01 RELEASING COPY OF THE COMPLAINT

a. *General.* The CO may send correspondence related to the complaint via certified mail, return receipt requested, facsimile or e-mail. If by facsimile or e-mail transmission, the CO should take steps to ensure confidentiality. The CO should maintain documentation that certifies the correspondence was received.

b. *Notice to Contractor.* Upon receiving the assigned complaint from the regional office, the CO must send a copy of the complaint to the contractor.[236]

c. *Confirmation to the Complainant.* When the CO transmits the complaint to the contractor, the CO must also send written notice of the transmittal to the complainant.[237]

6E TYPES OF COMPLAINT ALLEGATIONS

---

[236] See Letter L-7 – Letter to Contractor.
[237] See Letter L-8 – Letter to Complainant.

This section generally discusses the types of complaint allegations that OFCCP may receive and the investigative approach to take. The CO must first determine the investigative framework (e.g., data to obtain, interviews to conduct, records to review, analyses to perform) to use in addressing the complaint allegations in order to develop the investigative plan, which is discussed in Section 6F – Investigative Plan.

6E00 APPROACH TO INVESTIGATING COMPLAINT ALLEGATIONS

In conducting a complaint investigation, the CO is a neutral fact finder. A complaint is essentially a statement of allegation(s) of discrimination or other violations. The CO conducts an investigation to determine if there is sufficient pertinent evidence to support that a violation occurred or not, in light of the allegation(s) in the complaint. In preparing for and conducting the investigation, the CO must exercise objectivity and thoroughness. The CO must conduct each investigation in an atmosphere of open mindedness and fairness to both parties. The CO should display professional conduct at all times.

a. *Relationship to Compliance Evaluations*. The CO may complete a complaint investigation with or without a compliance evaluation. If upon evaluating the complaint allegations, or at any time during the investigation of the complaint, the CO obtains information that class, systemic or other issues may be more appropriately addressed by conducting a compliance evaluation (full review, focused review or compliance check), the CO should discuss this issue with his or her supervisor, and obtain national office review and approval prior to expanding the investigation into a compliance evaluatiuon.

b. *Investigative Priority*. The CO should act expeditiously on any complaint that alleges immediate and irreparable harm. For example, a complaint alleging the threat of termination in retaliation for filing a complaint with OFCCP (or for assisting in an OFCCP compliance evaluation, complaint investigation or enforcement action) requires immediate action.

6E01 INITIAL STEPS

Initial steps needed to proceed with the investigation involve determining whether the complainant provided sufficient information to support the allegations. A complaint should provide sufficient information to describe the alleged acts of discrimination and provide factual assertions that, if proven to be true, would constitute discrimination or a violation of the regulations. When reviewing the complaint allegations, a CO may need to discuss the allegations with the complainant to ensure they have sufficient information to understand the complaint allegations.

a. *Initial Interview with the Complainant*. The information on the complaint form is not always sufficient to determine the basis for the allegation(s) of discrimination. Whether the need for clarification is apparent or not, the CO should contact each complainant before going onsite to establish a mutually agreeable time and place to conduct an interview. The CO should conduct the interview in person unless compelling circumstances preclude doing so. In these instances, the CO may conduct the interview by telephone. If the complainant resides outside the area covered by the field office, the CO and his or her supervisor should coordinate with the regional office where the complainant is located. If no personal interview takes place at anytime during the investigation, the CO should record this fact and the reason for it.

The CO should prepare an interview plan containing specific questions tailored to obtain more detailed information regarding the allegations and identification of sources of evidence necessary to support or refute the complainant's allegations. Examples of the types of information to consider are:

- Name(s) of contractor official(s) who participated in the alleged discrimination, and those who were decision makers involved in the alleged adverse action;
- Name(s) of employee(s) who may have witnessed the alleged act(s) of discrimination;
- Detailed circumstances surrounding the act(s) (e.g., dates, locations, description of actions taken or failure to take action when needed, possible witnesses);
- Description of the contractor's personnel policies and practices related to the employment action at issue;
- Explanation of why the complainant believes that the act(s) was discriminatory;
- Explanation from the contractor to the complainant for any action taken by the contractor;
- Documentation related to the allegation(s) of discrimination, such as personnel policies, job advertisements, job descriptions, written disciplinary warnings, performance appraisals, etc.; and
- Data and documents necessary to conduct appropriate comparative or statistical analyses.

b. *Assessing the Complaint Allegations.* The CO's initial steps should include a preliminary assessment of the complaint allegation(s) to determine the validity of the complaint (e.g., is the complainant protected, was there opportunity for the discrimination to have occurred, was the contractor aware of the complainant's protected status, was there an adverse action). Because each complaint is based on a unique set of factual circumstances, the CO should gain an understanding of the nature of each allegation and why the complainant(s) believes that discrimination occurred. By first assessing the allegation(s) and identifying the areas for further investigation, the CO will be able to develop an investigative plan tailored to the particular allegation(s) and circumstances described in the complaint.

6E02 INVESTIGATIVE FRAMEWORK

a. *Initial Assessment.* When the regional office transmits a complaint to a CO for investigation, it will include all attachments and a transmittal letter. The regional office letter acknowledging the complaint and the complaint form will indicate under which program(s) the complainant filed (i.e., EO 11246, Section 503 and/or Section 4212) and the basis for the complaint (race, color, religion, sex, national origin, disability or status as a protected veteran).[238] The CO will need to assess the specific allegation(s) accepted by OFCCP for investigation to determine the framework appropriate for investigating and resolving each allegation. This may require different approaches for each allegation.

b. *Multiple Allegations.* If there are multiple allegations, the CO will need to determine which framework is appropriate to use in investigating, analyzing and resolving each specific allegation. The CO should develop the investigative plan to reflect each specific allegation and the approach to investigating and resolving each.

6E03 PATTERN OR PRACTICE ALLEGATIONS

Under the three nondiscrimination laws OFCCP enforces, a complaint may raise allegations of a pattern or practice of employment discrimination. The complaint may state these allegations in terms of disparate treatment or disparate impact. COs should note that the allegation may warrant examination using both the disparate treatment and the disparate impact frameworks. These legal theories are generally discussed below.

a. *Disparate Treatment.* Disparate treatment discrimination occurs when a contractor treats an individual or group differently because of its race, color, religion, sex, national origin, disability or status as a protected veteran. Intent to discriminate is a necessary element in this type of employment discrimination. Disparate treatment complaints may include allegations of different treatment with regard to employment actions such as hiring, terminations, promotions, compensation, application of selection criteria, family and pregnancy leave issues or the denial of equal benefits and opportunities, or possibly both.

b. *Disparate Impact:* Disparate impact occurs when a facially neutral policy or procedure, including selection procedures, has an adverse impact and it is not justified by business necessity and its relationship to the job. For example, a complainant may allege that leave policy negatively impacts people with disabilities or caregivers, or both, because of their gender.

Pattern and practice discrimination is based on the notion that an employer routinely engages in discrimnination or that discrimination is just of part of how the employer conducts his business. The discrimination, therefore, is systemic and affects groups or classes of individuals. In short, pattern and practice discrimination requires proof of systemic discrimination in the workforce that goes beyond isolated individual incidents.

6E04 HARASSMENT: HOSTILE ENVIRONMENT

Harassment on the basis of race, color, religion, sex, national origin, disability or veteran status may take a variety of forms including offensive remarks about an individual, harassing or derogatory speech or actions that are not directed at a specific individual, and other such forms of negative (or different) treatment on one or more of the prohibited bases. Harassment is illegal

[238] If the complaint alleges noncompliance with Executive Order 13496, the CO should follow the procedures described in Directive Number 290, June 15, 2010.

when it is so frequent or severe that it creates a hostile or offensive work environment or when it results in an adverse employment decision (such as termination or transfer of the victim of harassment). The harasser may be the victim's supervisor, a supervisor in another area, a co-worker or a third party (such as a client or customer).

6E05 RETALIATION AND INTERFERENCE

OFCCP applies the same concepts, standards and analyses as EEOC when assessing possible retaliation under EO 11246, Section 503 and Section 4212. However, it is important to note that while the laws OFCCP and EEOC enforce all prohibit retaliation, OFCCP's regulations provide broader protection against interference with an individual's use of his or her protections under the laws OFCCP enforces. Retaliation includes adverse employment actions such as termination, demotion or failure to hire, that a contractor might take because a person has filed a discrimination complaint, opposed an act of discrimination, or participated in any way in an activity related to the administration or enforcement of any OFCCP enforced laws. The complainant may be an applicant, employee, former employee or person closely associated with an individual who filed a discrimination complaint, opposed an act of discrimination or participated in a protected activity.

A complaint for investigation may contain an allegation that retaliation or interference occurred, or the allegation may arise during the course of an investigation. If a complainant makes an allegation of retaliation in addition to another allegation of discrimination, a finding that the underlying discrimination did not occur will not defeat the allegation of retaliation. The CO must investigate any allegation of retaliation or interference and make an independent finding as to whether sufficient evidence supports it.

6E06 ALLEGATIONS SPECIFIC TO EO 11246

EO 11246 prohibits employment discrimination on the basis of race, color, religion, sex or national origin. The regional office assigns EO 11246 complaints involving class or systemic issues to a field office for investigation. Complaints may include allegations of a pattern or practice of discrimination (disparate treatment or disparate impact); harassment or hostile environment allegations; or denial of reasonable accommodation on the basis of religion. EO 11246 complaints may also raise allegations of employment discrimination based on one or more of these reasons: race, color, religion, sex or national origin. The regional office will generally refer individual complaints alleging employment discrimination in violation of EO 11246, as amended, to EEOC pursuant to the EEOC and OFCCP Memorandum of Understanding.

6E07 ALLEGATIONS SPECIFIC TO DISABILITY COMPLAINTS

Section 503 prohibits employment discrimination on the basis of disability. The regional office will assign disability complaints to a field office for investigation. Complaints may include a variety of allegations that require determination of the legal and analytical approaches to be used in conducting the complaint investigation. Allegations may raise issues of pattern or practice discrimination (disparate treatment or disparate impact allegations); harassment or hostile environment; denial of reasonable accommodation on the basis of disability, including accessibility issues; the use of medical inquiries, examinations and mental and physical job qualification standards; or issues regarding pregnancy disability leave. In examining complaint allegations filed by a protected veteran, the CO should also determine if the complaint raises issues under Section 503 and Section 4212. Complainants filing under Section 503 or Section 4212 based on disability may also allege any violation of the law or its implementing regulation unrelated to discrimination.[239]

If in evaluating the complaint allegations the CO determines that the allegation is in regard to human immunodeficiency virus (HIV) or acquired immune deficiency syndrome (AIDS), the CO will identify the issue in the CMS for tracking purposes. The CO will also bring the issue to the attention of his or her supervisor for discussion regarding possible approaches to investigating and resolving the complaint.

41 CFR Part 60-742 of the regulations delineates procedures for complaints of employment discrimination based on disability filed against contractors when the complaints fall within the jurisdiction of both Section 503 and the ADA. These disability complaints are "dual filed" under both Section 503 and the ADA.[240]

a. *Not Making Reasonable Accommodation.* An issue unique to disability complaints relates to the provision of reasonable accommodation on the basis of disability. A reasonable accommodation can include changes in the work environment or in the way things are usually done to help a qualified individual with a disability or disabled veteran apply for a job, perform the duties of a job or enjoy the benefits and privileges of employment. Reasonable accommodation may include a variety of modifications including things such as making the workplace accessible for individuals with mobility impairments, and providing a reader or interpreter for someone who is blind or hearing impaired. The law requires that the contractor provide requested reasonable accommodations to a qualified employee or job applicant with a known disability, unless doing so would cause the contractor undue hardship.

b. *Other Denial of Reasonable Accommodation Allegations.* A complainant may also allege that the establishment is not physically accessible. If requested as a reasonable accommodation, contractors are responsible under Title I of the ADA for making their facilities accessible to and useable by qualified applicants and employees with disabilities, unless this would cause undue hardship. Reasonable accommodation may also include ensuring applicants with disabilities have equal opportunities either by making the online application system accessible to them or providing them an accommodation in the application process that ensures their application will be considered in the same timely fashion as applications made through the online system. (See subsection 2F04 – Additional Requirements.)

c. *Undue Hardship Defense.* Undue hardship is a defense used by a contractor to explain why it did not provide a specific reasonable accommodation. The contractor must prove that

[239] See subsection 6E08 – Allegations Specific to Section 4212 (Non-Disability) Complaints.
[240] 41 CFR 60-742.5 - Processing of Complaints Filed with OFCCP.

providing the accommodation would have caused significant difficulty or expense for the contractor.

d. *Medical Inquiries and Examinations.* Section 503 and Section 4212 generally prohibit employers from asking applicants disability-related questions (i.e., questions that are likely to elicit information about a disability) and from conducting medical examinations of applicants before making a conditional job offer. After the contractor makes a conditional job offer, but before commencing work, the contractor may ask disability-related questions and require medical examinations, regardless of whether they are related to the job, as long as the contractor does this for all entering employees. Once the employee has commenced working, such inquiries must be job-related and consistent with business necessity.

e. *Confidentiality Issues.* A complainant may allege that the contractor breached confidentiality of medical records. Whenever a contractor inquires into an applicant's or employee's physical or mental condition or conducts a medical examination, the contractor should keep all resulting information in a separate, confidential file. The contractor may make the file available to supervisors and managers, first aid and safety personnel, and government officials investigating compliance issues.

f. *Mental and Physical Job Qualification Standards.* Contractors subject to Section 503 or Section 4212 may not use qualification standards, tests or other selection criteria that exclude a disabled veteran, individual with a disability or class or individuals with disabilities from an employment opportunity, unless the selection criteria is job-related and consistent with business necessity. A selection criterion that concerns only the performance of a marginal function is not consistent with business necessity, and the contractor may not exclude an individual with a disability simply because a disability prevents him or her from performing a marginal function. A selection criterion that is consistent with business necessity may not be used to exclude an individual on the basis of disability if the individual could satisfy the criterion with the provision of a reasonable accommodation.[241]

g. *Relationship or Association with an Individual with a Disability.* A complaint may allege that the contractor discriminated against a qualified applicant or employee because of the known disability of an individual with whom the applicant or employee has a relationship or association. The complainant making such an allegation need not have a disability or allege that the contractor regarded him or her as having a disability. Rather, the complainant need only allege that he or she was denied an equal employment opportunity or benefit because of his or her relationship with one or more persons who have a disability. Most often, the individual with whom the complainant has a relationship will be a family member, such as a child, spouse or parent, but the law applies equally to business, social and other types of relationships.

---

[241] 41 CFR 60-300.21(g) and 60-741.21(g). In addition to this nondiscrimination requirement, which applies to all types of selection criteria, contractors subject to the affirmative action requirements of Section 503 or Section 4212 have an obligation to periodically evaluate the impact of any mental and physical job qualification(s) to determine if their use tends to screen out qualified individuals with disabilities or disabled veterans. See 41 CFR 60-300.44(c) and 60-741.44(c).

6E08 ALLEGATIONS SPECIFIC TO SECTION 4212 (NON-DISABILITY) COMPLAINTS

In reviewing a complaint filed under Section 4212 and in discussing it with the complainant, the CO should clearly distinguish whether the complainant believes the alleged discriminatory treatment was based on his or her status as a covered veteran, or based on a disabling condition attributable to his or her veteran status. Complainants filing under Section 4212 may also allege any violation of the law or its implementing regulations unrelated to discrimination. This will help the CO determine the analytical framework for the investigation. If the allegation is based on the complainant's status as a disabled veteran, the CO should follow the procedures for a disability complaint.[242]

Complaints alleging discrimination on the basis of status as a protected veteran may also include veteran-related issues that OFCCP is unable to address. When perfecting the complaint, the regional office will refer these allegations to the appropriate enforcement office. If the complainant raises these allegations at a later point in the process, the CO may refer the complaint allegation to the appropriate office or work in coordination with the other enforcement office, as appropriate.[243] For example, a complainant may indicate that he or she has a reemployment issue that falls under the Uniformed Services Employment and Reemployment Rights Act (USERRA), which is administered by the U.S. Department of Labor's Veterans' Employment and Training Service (VETS).

a. *Veteran Status.* Section 4212 prohibits employment discrimination on the basis of one's status as a protected veteran. The regulations specify the specific protected categories of veterans. The complaint may contain allegations of disparate treatment or disparate impact, or both; and/or harassment, including a hostile work environment.

b. *Job Listing Requirement.* A technical requirement unique to Section 4212 is the job listing requirement. Under Section 4212, contractors must list employment openings with the appropriate employment service delivery system where the openings occur. Contractors should list all employment openings with the exception of those for executive and top management positions, positions filled internally and those lasting three days or less.

6E09 TECHNICAL AND RECORDKEEPING REQUIREMENTS

Some complaints may also contain allegations that the contractor has not met technical and recordkeeping requirements (e.g., the complainant may allege that the contractor has violated EO 11246, EO 13496 or both by failing to post required notices), or in conducting a complaint investigation the CO may find that technical and/or recordkeeping violations exist. If so, the CO should conduct appropriate inspections and examine records to discuss these concerns with the

[242] See subsection 6E07 – Allegations Specific to Disability Complaints.

[243] See MOU between OFCCP and VETS, dated May 20, 1997, that addresses the agencies' coordinated efforts in serving veterans.

contractor. If the contractor does not correct these violations, the CO should prepare a Conciliation Agreement to address these violations.[244]

6E10 NOVEL ISSUES

Novel issues are those that are unfamiliar, unique or fall outside the norm. COs may encounter novel issues in the course of complaint investigations, as well as compliance evaluations.[245] When reviewing complaint allegations, the CO should identify whether the complaint raises any novel issues (e.g., associational claims of discrimination, third party claims involving allegations of sexual harassment, retaliation or dual-race discrimination). In these instances, the CO should discuss the identified novel issues with his or her supervisor before proceeding.

6F INVESTIGATIVE PLAN

Once the CO identifies the analytical framework needed to investigate the complainant's allegations,[246] the CO must develop the investigative plan. The investigative plan will serve as a checklist or "road map" for the investigation. While the plan may not identify every step along the way, the plan should contain the major actions to take. The plan should incorporate the investigative framework for each allegation; list the data to obtain, and identify the interviews to conduct (and specific questions to ask). The investigative plan should reflect the logistics for the onsite investigation such as the OFCCP staff members who will participate in the onsite review and the dates for the onsite review.

6F00 DEVELOPMENT OF THE INVESTIGATIVE PLAN

a. *Contents of the Plan.* The Plan should include a complete list of the allegations in the complaint and a summary list of all interviewees, data and information needs. Specific to each allegation, the elements the CO should include in the Plan are as follows:

   - Statement of the allegation and the nature of the allegation (e.g., pattern or practice, different treatment in promotional opportunity, denial of reasonable accommodation, harassment);
   - Interview of the complainant regarding the specifics of the allegation(s);
   - Interviews of management officials (listed by name or position) and the issues to address;
   - Interviews of non-management individuals (listed by name or position) and the issues to address;
   - Interviews of witnesses the complainant has identified and the issues to address;

---

[244] See Chapters 1 and 2 for discussions on technical and recordkeeping requirements.
[245] See subsection 1A07 – Novel Issues.
[246] See subsections 6E02 through 6E10.

- Specific records and materials to review and analyze;
- Analyses to conduct;
- Onsite visit (agreed upon date); and
- Contact with third parties, when appropriate.

6F01 DOCUMENTARY EVIDENCE AND RECORDS

In the initial stage of the complaint investigation, the CO should take steps to gather information about the contractor's complaint and compliance evaluation history.

a. *Historical Documentation.* The CO should query the EIS to determine if there have been any prior compliance or complaint investigations of the contractor establishment. The CO will need to obtain and review copies of any investigative reports, closure letters, Conciliation Agreements or other documentation generated as a result of such complaint investigation.

   The CO should also contact and make a written request to the EEOC and other Fair Employment Practice (FEP) agencies (e.g., Division of Human Rights, Department of Justice, State Department of Labor, VETS) inquiring whether there are any complaints against the contractor. If obtained, this CO should include this information in the case file and incorporate it, as appropriate, in the investigative plan.

   If the complainant indicates that he or she has filed an EEO grievance or complaint with the contractor or union, the CO should obtain a copy of the grievance or complaint from the complainant. Upon making a data request of the contractor, the CO should request any documentation related to the grievance/complaint, complaint investigation and, if applicable, contractor findings and remedy.

   If the CO finds that the EEOC is conducting an ongoing investigation, the CO should obtain adequate information to determine whether the EEOC has exercised jurisdiction over all of the allegations over which OFCCP would also have jurisdiction and is proceeding with an investigation of the same. Upon verifying this information, the CO should discuss this with his or her supervisor.

b. *Policies and Practices.* The CO should obtain copies of all documents that explain any policy or practice bearing on the allegations in the complaint. If a practice at issue is in writing or the written material is not current, the CO should request that the contractor provide a written statement of facts or conditions currently in effect or identify a manager or supervisor who can discuss the practice.

c. *Relevance.* The CO should obtain copies of any written materials that are relevant to the complaint. The nature of the complaint allegations will determine the nature of which documents the CO needs to obtain.

For example, in a complaint alleging discriminatory discharge on the basis of disability, which the contractor states was due to poor performance, the CO would obtain documents such as the following: copies of policies and procedures for performance evaluations and terminations; a copy of the complainant's personnel file, including his or her performance evaluations; and copies of other similarly situated employees' files and performance evaluations, in order to conduct a comparative analysis. A similarly situated employee could be a non-disabled individual who received a poor performance rating and was, or was not, subject to discharge.

6G ONSITE INVESTIGATIONS

Before going onsite, the CO should ensure that he or she has fully reviewed the complaint and the contractor's compliance history and developed an Investigative Plan. The CO should provide written notice of the onsite investigation to the contractor. During the onsite investigation, the CO and other OFCCP staff members should follow the investigative plan. However, the CO should make appropriate changes to the investigative plan and implement these changes if he or she learns new information during the investigation indicating that other issues may exist. For example, a complainant may raise an allegation of retaliation during the course of the investigation that was not in the original complaint. If the CO has any concerns about making changes to the investigative plan or approach, the CO should discuss these concerns with his or her supervisor.

6G00 NOTIFYING THE CONTRACTOR OF THE ONSITE INVESTIGATION

When the investigative plan is complete, the CO should make an arrangement with the contractor for the onsite visit. Generally, the onsite investigation should at a minimum consist of a lead CO and another CO to assist in fact finding. The CO should telephone the contractor and speak with the individual who will represent the contractor during the onsite visit. The CO should advise the representative that:

- An entrance conference with the facility's senior officer or designee will take place in order for the CO to outline the investigative process, to explain what will be done onsite, and to estimate how many days the onsite investigation may take;
- Identified records should be available for review and should be as specific as possible; and
- Management employees, by name and position or title, requested to be available for interviews.

The CO should establish a mutually agreeable date for beginning the visit. A letter confirming the onsite investigation date or dates must be sent.[247]

[247] See Letter L-10 – Confirmation of Onsite Investigation.

6G01 ONSITE INVESTIGATION

a. *General.* The CO must conduct the onsite investigation in a manner that conveys the objectivity and fact finding intent of the CO. The focus of the CO's activity must be on the complainant's allegations and any contractor actions that gave rise to them. The interviews and review of records should provide information clearly related to the issues raised in the complaint. The CO will make note of any other compliance concerns that he or she observes or is aware of. (See further discussion below.)

   For each onsite investigation, the CO will use the appropriate framework to address the allegation(s) by gathering data and information and by conducting interviews. The Investigative Plan should reflect the data to obtain and the interviews to conduct. The CO should follow this "road map" to conduct the onsite investigation.

b. *Entrance Conference.* The entrance conference with the facility's senior official or designee sets the stage for the entire investigation. It is important for the CO – as a neutral fact finder – to be well organized and nonjudgmental. The CO should discuss: the investigative process (including what will actually occur onsite), an estimate of the length of the visit and a mutually agreeable date and time for an exit conference. Since the CO previously provided the contractor with a copy of the complaint and informed the contractor of the relevant law(s), there may be no need for the CO to repeat that information. However, the CO should be prepared to respond to any questions regarding the complaint allegations and should ensure that the contractor understands the allegations.

   The CO should inform the contractor that EO 11246, Section 503 and Section 4212 implementing regulations prohibit interference and intimidation, including threats, coercion, harassment and discrimination of any individual in the exercise of his or her rights protected under OFCCP enforced laws. Such protected rights include filing a complaint; assisting or participating in an investigation, compliance evaluation, hearing or any other activity related to the administration of the EO 11246, Section 503 and Section 4212 or other EEO laws; opposing any act or practice that violates any of these EEO laws; or exercising any other right afforded them by these laws.

c. *Facility Inspection.* If appropriate, the CO should conduct an inspection of the contractor's establishment during the early stages of the onsite investigation. By inspecting the establishment/facility, the CO will be able to observe the layout of the facility, what work employees may perform in the location, whether there may have been possible witnesses to an event, whether there are physical accessibility issues or whether there is any display of graffiti, inappropriate materials, etc. The CO should note, and possibly diagram, any physical setting/location identified in the complaint. The CO should also note other observations, as appropriate. For example, in investigating a class complaint alleging discrimination on the basis of sex, the CO should note the presence or absence of women in the work area or job positions at issue. When appropriate, the CO may photograph the location he or she is inspecting. If the contractor objects to the CO taking photographs, the CO should discuss the matter with his or her supervisor.

d. *Required Notices and Postings (EO 11246 and EO 13496).* During the onsite investigation of a complaint, the CO also has the opportunity to verify that the contractor is in compliance with required notices and postings. EO 11246 requires that the contractor conspicuously display the *Equal Opportunity is the Law* poster that notifies applicants and employees that federal law protects applicants and employees against discrimination. EO 13496 requires that the contractor post notice of employee rights under the National Labor Relations Act (NLRA). The NLRA guarantees employees the right to organize and bargain collectively with their employer. The CO should inspect such areas as break rooms, personnel offices, common areas and employee bulletin boards for the required postings.

e. *Prohibition against Retaliation*: In conducting a complaint investigation, the CO should inform contractor officials, employees and applicants, as well as other people who may be a part of the investigation that the law prohibits the contractor from retaliating because of their involvement in the process. Retaliation is a form of discrimination in which a contractor takes an adverse action, harasses, intimidates, threatens or coerces an individual because he or she filed a complaint of discrimination; opposed any act made unlawful under the laws enforced by OFCCP; or participated in an investigation, compliance evaluation, hearing or any other activity related to the administration or enforcement of any OFCCP enforced laws.[248]

6G02 DATA GATHERING

a. *General.* The nature of the specific allegation(s) to be investigated will determine the data and information the CO should gather. Certain data will be common to most investigations, such as applicable personnel policies, collective bargaining agreement, data regarding the employment practice in question, the personnel files of the complainant and comparators, etc. The CO's Investigative Plan should identify what information he or she will need to address each allegation. However, the CO may identify additional information, documentation or records to obtain. Provided below, by type of allegation, are general guidelines for data gathering.

b. *Pattern or Practice*

   1. *Disparate Treatment.* The CO will gather data regarding the specific employment action (e.g., use of a selection procedure), or the loss of benefit or opportunity at issue, in order to identify similarly situated individuals (applicants, candidates or employees) to the complainant(s) and whether the comparative group received more favorable treatment. The type of data needed will depend on the specific allegation. If a complainant indicates that there is an EEO grievance or complaint on file, the CO should request these records. Additionally, the CO should request copies of any grievances others have filed that raise similar issues. The CO will need other data and information including copies of any applicable policies and procedures.

      Data related to employment actions may include: applicant flow, hiring, termination, promotion, compensation data, etc. In examining selection procedures, the CO may also

[248] See 41 CFR 60-1.32, 60-250.69, 60-300.69 and 60-741.69.

need to analyze data that reflects the application of specific selection criteria (e.g., a structured interview). In addition to hiring or promotion data (who was hired or promoted and who was not), the CO should also include data such as whether the selection procedure is pass/fail or a score is used (cut-off score or weighted), and the results of the selection procedure (i.e., who advanced from the interview and who did not.)

2. *Disparate Impact*: The CO should examine employment data (e.g., applicant flow, hiring, termination, promotion, compensation data) as appropriate to the allegation. Additionally, the CO should obtain and review any policies applicable to the action in question (e.g., written policies regarding eligibility for promotion or increases in compensation). The CO will examine data regarding the specific employment action or use of selection procedure to identify individuals (applicants, candidates or employees) who are similarly situated to the complainant(s). The CO may also need to analyze data that reflects the application of a specific selection procedure. For example if the complaint alleges that a pencil and paper test has as a disparate impact as a selection criterion, the data needed may include not only hiring or promotion data such as who was hired or promoted and who was not, but it may also include data and information relevant to whether the contractor validated the selection procedure and how, and a description of how the selection procedure was applied to applicants and employees, as appropriate. A copy of the validation study should also be included.

c. *Harassment: Hostile Environment*. The CO should gather copies of relevant policies and procedures and make observations of environmental conditions (e.g., if the location of an incident is identified, observe the location and determine whether there may have been possible witnesses to the incident). The CO should request copies of any internal grievance or complaint(s) on file regarding the alleged harassment or other incidents of alleged harassment, and any documentation indicating how the contractor responded to any incidents. If it is alleged that the contractor took action against the complainant, the CO should also review the complainant's personnel records and other pertinent documents.

d. *Retaliation and Interference*. The CO should gather data and information regarding the activity that the complainant alleges was the cause for the retaliation. Because a retaliatory action can include any number of actions, including harassment, the CO will need to identify the policies and procedures at issue and obtain these for review. The CO may also need data to conduct a comparative analysis if the complainant alleges that the retaliatory act was an adverse employment action (e.g., terminated, demoted, not hired) or the contractor treated the complainant differently than other individuals.

e. *Allegations Specific to EO 11246*. Under EO 11246, a complaint may contain allegations of harassment, retaliation, or a pattern or practice of discrimination. The CO should gather data accordingly. If a complaint raises an allegation of denial of accommodation on the basis of religion, the CO should ask the contractor whether and how it made accommodation to the religious observances and practices of its employees and obtain any relevant policies and records. If the contractor denied an accommodation, the CO should ask why. If the contractor reports that no one requested an accommodation, the CO should review procedures available for evaluating such requests. The CO should review employee files and be alert for any pattern of discipline or terminations based on refusal to work on certain days for religious observances. Allegations of national origin discrimination may sometimes be closely linked to discrimination on the basis of religion. The CO should examine the factual situation to determine whether it gives rise to both forms of discrimination.

f. *Allegations Specific to Disability Complaints.* Under Section 503, a complaint may contain allegations of a pattern or practice of discrimination, harassment or retaliation (see above). The CO should gather data accordingly.

1. *Not Making Reasonable Accommodation.* If the contractor denies the allegation that it did not make a required reasonable accommodation, the CO should gain a clear understanding of the job or position in question, the requested accommodation, whether the complainant can perform the job with accommodation and the contractor's response to the request for accommodation. The CO should obtain a written job description; information regarding the processing of requests for reasonable accommodation; the specific request of the complainant; other similar requests for accommodation; information or documentation regarding the complainant's disability and the requested accommodation(s); and information to confirm whether the contractor provided the requested reasonable accommodation or an alternative accommodation in a timely and appropriate manner.

2. *Other Allegations of Not Making Reasonable Accommodation.* Depending on the nature of the complaint (e.g., the establishment is not physically accessible), the CO should gather information and make observations that may prove or disprove the allegation. This may mean physical inspection of a facility or feature of the facility (e.g., inspecting whether a testing or application kiosk is accessible to a person in a wheelchair).

3. *Undue Hardship Defense.* When a contractor defends itself by claiming it did not provide a specific reasonable accommodation because of undue hardship, the contractor must prove that to do so would have caused significant difficulty or expense. The CO should obtain information to determine whether a contractor's assertion that an accommodation would impose an undue hardship is valid, and whether it was valid at the time the contractor denied the accommodation.

4. *Medical Inquiries and Examinations.* The CO should determine whether the contractor makes such inquiries during the application and selection process and whether the contractor administers medical examinations. If so, the CO should obtain data for applicants who were screened out during these stages. The CO may then need to examine individual records and to conduct comparisons between successful and unsuccessful applicants to determine whether and how the contractor may have used the information, and whether any applied criterion is job-related and consistent with business necessity.

5. *Confidentiality Issues.* The CO should examine the contractor's policy and practices regarding confidential records. The CO may need to review records and inspect the location of the records to determine if there was a breach of confidentiality.

6. *Qualification Standards, Tests and Other Selection Criteria.* The CO should determine whether the application of a qualification standard, test, or other selection criterion excluded the complainant from an employment opportunity on the basis of his or her disability. If so, the CO should gather information to determine whether the challenged selection criterion is job-related and consistent with business necessity. The CO should obtain a written job description, an explanation from the contractor, and any supporting documentation, as to how the criterion relates to the job, and factual information about how the job is actually performed. If the criterion relates to health or safety, the CO should gather information to determine whether the criterion is necessary to avoid the existence or creation of a direct threat, or is required by federal law or regulations. Should the CO determine that the criterion is consistent with business necessity, the CO should obtain information to assess whether the complainant could satisfy the selection criterion with the provision of a reasonable accommodation.

7. *Relationship or Association with an Individual with a Disability.* The data and information gathered will vary depending upon the specific nature of the allegation. For example, if the complaint alleges that the contractor denied the complainant equal access to the contractor's health insurance plan, the CO should obtain copies of the contractor's policies and procedures related to health insurance, records related to the complainant's application for insurance, and records related to the processing of that application. If the complaint alleges that the contractor did not hire or promote the complainant because of his or her association with a person with a disability, the CO would gather information and data related to the selection process, the other applicants for the job at issue (including the applicant selected), and the reasons for the non-selection of the complainant.

g. *Allegations Specific to Veterans (Non-Disability) Complaints.* Under Section 4212, a complaint may contain allegations of a pattern or practice of discrimination, harassment or retaliation (see above). The CO should gather data accordingly.

1. *Veteran Status.* As required by regulation, the complainant must provide documentation proving his or her status as a protected veteran. If the complaint raises class issues, the CO should obtain documentation to prove that affected class members are protected veterans.

2. *Job Listing Requirement.* If a complaint alleges a violation of the job listing requirement, the CO should request job listings from the contractor and contact the employment office (employment service delivery system) that the contractor used and request confirmation that the contractor listed its employment openings with that office. The CO should obtain from the employment office a listing of the job orders that the contractor placed by job title and date. The CO should then compare this list with a list of jobs the contractor has filled through new hire, identify any such jobs not listed with the employmenet office, and determine whether they should have been listed.

h. *Technical and Recordkeeping Requirements.* The CO should conduct appropriate inspections and examine records to determine whether technical and/or recordkeeping violations exist.[249]

6G03 CONDUCTING INTERVIEWS

a. *General.* This section reflects current OFCCP policies regarding the mechanics of the interview process, but it does not teach COs how to interview witnesses. Throughout the investigation, including interviewing, the CO must maintain a high degree of objectivity and professionalism.

b. *Informing the Interviewee.* At the outset of an interview, the CO should tell each individual that after the interview, the CO will show him or her a statement containing his or her answers to the questions and will ask him or her to sign the statement. The CO should inform each interviewee that knowingly providing false or inaccurate information is unlawful and explain that the following phrase will be in the interview notes where CO will ask the interviewee to sign: "I have read the above and it is true." Additionally, in each instance when a CO speaks with non-management individuals (informal or formal) the CO should inform the individual that the interview will be kept confidential to the extent possible and that it is against the law for the contractor to take any retaliatory action or to intimidate him or her for participating in the interview.

c. *Interview Notes.* The CO should start with a list of questions or an interview outline he or she developed prior to the onsite visit. This list, with the interviewee's responses, comprises the "interview notes." The CO should add notes to document follow-up questions and answers that arise as the interview progresses. The CO should enter the following phrase above the space where the interviewee will sign: "I have read the above and it is true." At the conclusion of the interview, the CO should review the questions and answers and confirm that direct quotes are accurate or that a paraphrase conveys the intended meaning. The CO will expeditiously type (electronic record) handwritten notes from the interview to provide the interviewee with a hard copy to sign as soon as possible. The CO should obtain a personal mailing address and a telephone number from the interviewee in case the CO needs to contact the interviewee later or needs to mail a hard copy of the interview to the interviewee (for signature). In any instance, if the interviewee indicates that the notes need corrections, the CO will incorporate the corrections and send a hard copy of the interview to the interviewee to sign. The CO should maintain records of the original (electronic record) and the corrected interview in the case file. If an interviewee refuses to sign the notes, the CO should record this along with the reason(s) for refusal to sign.

d. *Management and Supervisory Officials and Witnesses.* "Management" or "supervisory" employees refer to bona fide executive employees. When these employees interview, they may be speaking not only for themselves, but also for the contractor. On the other hand, a management employee who is filing a complaint about his or her own employment is not speaking on behalf of the contractor. Contractor representatives, including attorneys, may be present at interviews of management and supervisory employees when such employees are

---

[249] See Chapter 2 Desk Audit, Section 2I: Technical Requirements.

speaking in their official capacity. In conducting such interviews in the presence of a contractor representative, the CO should explain that the presence of the representative means that the contractor acknowledges that the interviewee speaks on its behalf and that his or her statements regarding policies and actions may be fairly treated as those of the contractor. The CO should state in the interview notes the fact that he or she gave this explanation. The CO should make sure that the contractor representative does not try to speak for, influence or correct the responses of the interviewees.

e. *Contractor's Presence at Interviews.* When the CO conducts onsite interviews with non-management personnel, the contractor does not have the right to have a representative present. When the CO conducts interviews with management personnel, the contractor may have an attorney or other representative present. The exception to this is when the manager is the complainant or a member of a potential affected class speaking about his or her personal experience, rather than speaking on behalf of the management. It is the policy of OFCCP to conduct private interviews with contractor employees who are not management or supervisory employees. This helps to ensure that such employees are free from any possible intimidation or retaliation. If a contractor objects to the CO's attempt to privately interview employees on its premises, the CO should conduct the interviews away from the contractor's facility.

f. *Employee Representative Present at Interviews.* An employee may request that a representative accompany them in the interview (e.g., a union representative or legal counsel). Generally, this is acceptable. The CO should note the person's name and title on the interview documentation. Initially, the CO should discuss this with the interviewee privately to determine whether there may be a conflict of interest or whether the contractor is coercing the interviewee to have the person present. If the representative attends the interview, the interviewee may have has waived confidentiality. The CO should note this discussion with the interviewee in the interview statement. The CO is advised to contact his or her regional solicitor if additional guidance is needed on whether confidentiality was waived under these circumstances.

g. *CO is Unable to Conduct Interview.* If the CO is unable to conduct an interview, he or she should add a memorandum to the file explaining who was supposed to be interviewed, and why the interview did not occur. For example, the complainant may identify a potential witness to the alleged harassment, but the potential witness indicates to the CO that he or she was, in fact, not a witness to the alleged conduct and does not want to submit to an interview.

6G04 INTERVIEW QUESTIONS

a. *General.* In order to gain an understanding of the issues, the CO should prepare open ended questions to ask interviewees (e.g., ask interviewee to explain and describe their observations and experiences related to the issues). When appropriate, the CO should also ask direct and follow up questions. The investigative plan should include a structure (e.g., a list of interview questions or an interview outline) for the interviews the CO will conduct with contractor officials, the complainant and witnesses. The CO should develop interview questions that will elicit responses to explain the factual circumstances surrounding the allegation (e.g., who was involved and who witnessed the actions; what actions were taken;

where did the events occur; how decisions were reached; and why were specific actions taken). The CO should develop interview questions to ensure that he or she identifies and obtains all relevant documentation.

The CO should confirm and verify information obtained in interviews. For example, the CO may interview two witnesses and each witness provides a similar description of an incident that occurred in the break room; however, a supervisor provides a different description of the incident. One of the interviewee's statements indicated that some employees were clocking out at the time of the incident. Employees enter the break room to clock out. The CO should review sign out forms for the day and time in question in order to identify other possible witnesses. The CO should then interview these other possible witnesses and review any documentation that may provide confirmation or not.

The following sections provide additional guidance for developing interview questions specific to the type of allegation the CO is investigating.

b. *Pattern or Practice:*

1. *Disparate Treatment.* The CO should ask interview questions designed to determine established policies and procedures and any deviations that may have occurred in the application of the policies and procedures. In addition, the interview questions should seek to identify people who were similarly situated to the complainant but may have been treated differently. Interview questions should also cover the criteria used at each selection stage and the people who applied them at each stage.

2. *Disparate Impact.* If the complaint alleges that a specific policy or practice has a disparate impact, the CO should develop questions for appropriate contractor officials to gain an understanding of the development and application of the policy or practice in question. The CO should develop the interview questions to ensure that the CO identifies and obtains all relevant documentation.

c. *Harassment: Hostile Environment.* The CO should develop questions to assist in understanding the specifics of the alleged incident(s); applicable policies and all relevant documentation; other similar incidents; possible witnesses to the alleged discriminatory action(s); contractor response to alleged harassment, etc.

For example: The complainant alleged that a drawing, including a derogatory depiction and remark, making fun of a physically impaired person was posted on a wall in the break room. The complainant observed the drawing during his lunch break. The CO should ask the complainant to identify possible witnesses to interview but should also make a random selection of other employees to interview who may have had the opportunity to observe the drawing. The CO should develop questions for possible witnesses and contractor staff members to gather information confirming or disaffirming whether the drawing was posted; whether the poster contributed to a hostile environment; and, if so, whether the contractor took immediate and appropriate action to remedy the identified harm and to prevent future harassment.

COs should note that in conducting interviews and recording the information obtained during an investigation of an allegation of harassment they should fully and accurately document any harassing or derogatory remarks, statements or actions. This is necessary to ensure that the CO can make a determination whether the words or actions were severe enough to constitute harassment. The CO must not rephrase the interviewee's statements or make use of euphemisms. It is also important to note that witnesses may provide statements that are in direct conflict with each other. When the statements are given confidentially, it is important to make sufficient efforts to confirm and verify testimony whenever possible, while maintaining confidentiality.

d. *Retaliation and Interference.* The CO should develop questions to determine whether the complainant participated in a protected activity or opposed prohibited activity; whether the complainant was subjected to adverse action or treatment; whether there is a connection between the protected activity and the adverse action or treatment (e.g., close proximity in time or other evidence such as the complainant was treated differently than others in a similar situation);. The CO should examine contractor assertions for credibility. If the contractor makes an assertion that there is a legitimate, nondiscriminatory reason for any adverse action, the CO should examine the action accordingly.

   For example: The CO finds evidence supporting that the complainant participated in a protected activity (e.g., filed an EEO complaint), and the complainant was subjected to adverse action (e.g., demotion) shortly after the complainant's supervisor received notice of the complaint. The contractor asserts that the complainant was demoted because of poor performance and not because of having filed the complaint. For this example, the CO should review any pertinent policy regarding demotions, review the complainant's personnel record to determine whether the complainant's work performance was rated poorly and whether the complainant received any required notice that he or she would be subject to demotion. The CO should also examine other employees' personnel files to determine if similarly situated employees were treated in the same or similar manner. The CO should interview the supervisor who took the adverse action, interview other contractor officials regarding policy governing demotions and applicable procedures, and interview witnesses, as appropriate.

e. *Allegations Specific to EO 11246.* Under EO 11246, a complaint may contain allegations of harassment, retaliation, or a pattern or practice of discrimination. These are addressed above. An allegation unique to EO 11246 is the denial of a request for a reasonable accommodation on the basis of religion. In this instance, the CO should interview employees and applicants to determine whether requests were made for accommodations and how the contractor responded. Witnesses may identify other employees or former employees that the CO will also want to interview. The CO should develop questions that address the following: policy and procedures that apply to requests for reasonable accommodation; how the contractor documents requests; whether the contractor denied requests and the reasons for denial; whether the contractor considered an alternative accommodation, etc.

f. *Allegations Specific to Disability Complaints.* Under Section 503, a complaint may contain allegations of harassment, retaliation, or a pattern or practice of discrimination. These are addressed above.

1. *Not Making Reasonable Accommodation.* COs should develop interview questions regarding the functions of the job or position in question, the requested accommodation, whether the complainant can perform the job with accommodation and the contractor's response to the request for accommodation. The CO should interview the complainant as to the complainant's disability, work limitations and the accommodation(s) requested. The CO should interview contractor officials as to whether the contractor provided the requested reasonable accommodation or an alternative accommodation. The CO should also question whether the contractor responded to other similar requests for accommodation. The CO may also need to interview medical personnel regarding the condition at issue and the potential accommodation.

2. *Other Potential Allegations of Not Making Reasonable Accommodation.* If the complaint alleges that the establishment is not physically accessible or the online application system is inaccessible, the CO should conduct interviews of employees and/or applicants who may need accommodation. The CO should also interview contractor officials regarding the policies and procedures for addressing accommodation requests in this regard.

3. *Undue Hardship Defense.* The CO should obtain information to determine whether there is support for a contractor's assertion that an accommodation would impose an undue hardship on the contractor. In examining the contractor's assertion, the CO should look at such factors as:

   - business necessity, and
   - financial cost and expenses.[250]

4. *Medical Inquiries and Examinations.* The CO should interview contractor officials to determine applicable policies and procedures, including how and when the contractor makes and records medical inquiries. The CO should also question how and when the provider conducts medical examinations and how the contractor uses the information obtained from the examination. The CO should interview the providers of any medical examinations to verify instructions the contractors gave to them and identify how they reported results.

5. *Confidentiality Issues.* The CO should examine the contractor's policy and practices regarding records that are to be kept confidential. Interviews may be necessary to determine whether the contractor breached confidentiality.

6. *Qualification Standards, Tests and Other Selection Criteria.* Contractors subject to Section 503 or Section 4212 may not use qualification standards, tests or other selection criteria that exclude a disabled veteran, individual with a disability or class or individuals with disabilities from an employment opportunity, unless the selection criteria is job-related and consistent with business necessity. A selection criterion that concerns only the performance of a marginal function is not consistent with business necessity, and the

---

[250] A complete list of the five factors is in the agency's regulations at 41 CFR 60-741.3(w).

contractor may not exclude an individual with a disability simply because a disability prevents him or her from performing a marginal function. A selection criterion that is consistent with business necessity may not be used to exclude an individual on the basis of disability if the individual could satisfy the criterion with the provision of a reasonable accommodation.[251]

7. *Relationship or Association with an Individual with a Disability.* The CO should interview the complainant to determine that he or she has a relationship or association with an individual with a disability, and the reason(s) for his or her belief that contractor discriminated against him or her because of that relationship or association. The CO should also obtain an explanation from the contractor regarding the reason for the employment action or decision that is the subject of the complaint and information regarding any relevant policies or practices. If the contractor denies knowledge of the complainant's relationship with an individual with a disability, the CO should examine the credibility of the statements made and seek possible witnesses who could confirm of disaffirm whether the contractor knew of the complainant's relationship.

g. *Allegations Specific to Veterans (Non-Disability) Complaints*: Under Section 4212, a complaint may contain allegations of harassment, retaliation, or a pattern or practice of discrimination. These are addressed above.

The job listing requirement is unique to Section 4212 and state employment services have special responsibilities regarding covered veterans.[252] The local offices usually have a representative who deals primarily with veterans' matters. The CO should request any pertinent information regarding both the complainant and the contractor from the local employment service veterans' representative. Additionally, each regional office has a VETS office. The CO should contact the VETS office, in accordance with regional procedures, to obtain any information that may be pertinent to the complaint. For example, the complainant may have contacted the VETS office prior to filing the complaint; as a consequence, the VETS office may have useful information based on its contact with the complainant and possibly the contractor as well.

h. *Technical and Recordkeeping Requirements.* The CO should conduct interviews of contractor officials responsible for meeting the technical obligations and for creating and maintaining records. Interview questions should seek to determine who is responsible for meeting these obligations, whether there are policies applicable to the obligation, and whether there were deviations from the policy. If the contractor did not comply with an obligation, the CO should question responsible parties to determine why the contractor did not meet the obligation.

---

[251] 41 CFR 60-300.21(g) and 60-741.21(g). In addition to this nondiscrimination requirement, which applies to all types of selection criteria, contractors subject to the affirmative action requirements of Section 503 or Section 4212 have an obligation to periodically evaluate the impact of any mental and physical job qualification(s) to determine if their use tends to screen out qualified individuals with disabilities or disabled veterans. See 41 CFR 60-300.44(c) and 60-741.44(c).

[252] 41 CFR 60-250.44 and 41 CFR 60-300.44.

6G05 REVIEW OF RECORDS

The CO should review the records to address the allegations raised in the complaint. Section 6G02 addresses the types of data and records that the CO should obtain. The nature of the allegations and the applicable legal theories will determine the types of analyses the CO should conduct using the data obtained during the onsite visit.

6G06 EXIT CONFERENCE

Upon completing the onsite investigation, the CO should conduct an exit conference with the facility's senior official or designee (preferably the same person who was at the entrance conference). At this meeting, the CO should present a summary of any observed violations and should document any rebuttal arguments made by the contractor. The CO should emphasize that the findings are preliminary and that OFCCP will not draw final conclusions until the CO can complete analyses of all the data, and can affirm or refute each allegation. The CO should inform the contractor of the approximate length of time it will take to complete the offsite analysis, prepare the investigative report, and issue the Notification of Results of Investigation. The CO should also remind the contractor that the law prohibits retaliation and interference. COs should also inform contractors that the exit interview is not necessarily the end of the fact-finding and that more information may be requested, if necessary.

6H CONDUCTING ANALYSES AND THE INVESTIGATIVE REPORT

The CO must write an investigative report in all instances in which the CO has conducted an onsite investigation. See Appendix A-10 – Investigative Report for the format of this report. In writing this report, the CO should not express personal opinions and should not include matters unrelated to the issues of the complaint. Upon completing the investigation, the CO will analyze all data and information that explains, describes or clarifies the incident or the application of the policy, procedure or practice at issue. The CO will analyze all comparative and statistical data using the appropriate analytical framework for addressing the allegation. The results of the analyses and a description of any direct, circumstantial and anecdotal evidence either refuting or supporting the allegations will be included in the investigative report. The CO will make factual findings and cite the support for the findings with regard to each allegation. The CO will also make a determination of whether there is sufficient evidence to support that discrimination occurred. The investigative report should also include a discussion of the contractor's defenses and the COs assessment of the merits of those defenses.

6I USE OF A NOTIFICATION OF RESULTS OF INVESTIGATION

The CO prepares a Notification of Results of Investigation (NORI) to report the results of OFCCP's investigation of the complaint allegations. If the investigation does not result in a finding of discrimination, OFCCP issues a no-violation NORI. For complaints that are considered dual filed under Section 503/ADA and EO 11246/Title VII, the CO will issue a Notice of Right-to-Sue, also referred to as Notice, along with the no-violation NORI. Each Notice issued will also include the document entitled, Information Related to Filing Suit under

Title VII and the ADA.[253] If at any time the CO is informed of a resolution of the complaint satisfactory to the complainant, and the CO did not identify compliance issues, the NORI will not be prepared. In dual filed cases under Section 503/ADA and EO11246/Title VII, if OFCCP issues a violation NORI, it will not issue a Notice of Right-to-Sue.

6I00 SIGNATURES AND PROCEDURES

The CO should prepare the NORI for the signature of the Regional Director or his or her designee. After being signed, the original NORI will remain in the case file. The CO will send copies of the NORI to the complainant and the contractor with a letter of transmittal, sent certified mail, return receipt requested. The CO will provide copies of the NORI to the regional office. The CO should annotate the chronology log to reflect the transmission and as appropriate the receipt of the document.

6I01 NOTICE TO LABOR UNION VIOLATION

When the remedy for a finding of a violation would require a change in or otherwise affect a collective bargaining agreement (CBA) between the contractor and a union or require the award of retroactive seniority where seniority is governed by a CBA, the union will be notified of the particular violation, and will be invited to participate in its conciliation.[254]

6J RESOLUTION OF THE COMPLAINT

6J00 SETTLEMENT BEFORE COMPLETION OF INVESTIGATION

a. *Initiating Settlement.* The CO should be prepared to discuss settlement at any stage of the investigation as long as there is sufficient evidence to support that there is a violation, and the settlement will provide a just resolution of the violations. Before engaging in conciliation discussions, the CO should advise the contractor that there is no prejudice to the position of the contractor for participating in conciliation sessions prior to completion of the investigation, or for not participating in the discussions; and the contractor should not construe the government's participation in conciliation sessions as a waiver of the government's right to proceed to a formal NORI if the conciliation sessions are unsuccessful. The CO should provide his or her supervisor with all relevant information to assist in determining whether it is appropriate to enter conciliation discussions.

b. *Complainant Notification of Resolution.* If at any time prior to the completion of an investigation the CO receives notification that the contractor and complainant – the only alleged victim – have resolved the complaint to the complainant's satisfaction and the CO has not received any data or information indicating unresolved compliance concerns, the OFCCP may close the case. The CO should confirm that the contractor and complainant have resolved all of the complaint allegations and that no one has forced or coerced the

---

[253] See Appendix A-11 – Information Related to Filing Suit under Title VII and Title I of the ADA.
[254] See Chapter 8 – Resolution of Noncompliance.

complainant into stating that the complaint is resolved.[255]

6J01 PRIOR TO ISSUING A NO VIOLATION NORI

a. *Contact with the Complainant.* If the complaint investigation results in a proposed finding of "no violation," the CO must contact the complainant prior to the issuance of a NORI. The CO will inform the complainant of the no violation finding, the factual findings, the types of records reviewed, and whether all of the witnesses the complainant and OFCCP identified were interviewed. The discussion regarding witnesses and witness statements should be in general terms without identifying specific witnesses or their statements. This contact will give the complainant an opportunity, prior to the completion of the investigation, to introduce new or previously unconsidered evidence. This contact may be in person or by telephone, but the CO must document when and how he or she made the contact. The documentation must also identify the issues discussed, the complainant's response and any additional investigation the CO conducted as a result of this contact. If needed, the compliance officer may give the complainant 10 business days to provide additional material before issuing the NORI.

b. *Request for Release of Documents.* The CO must not release to any party any documents provided by any other party, the internal investigative report or interview transcripts. Based on Exemption 7A of the Freedom of Information Act (FOIA) (5 U.S.C. Section 552), OFCCP does not release records from an open investigation other than those provided by the requesting party itself.

6J02 CLOSURE OF COMPLAINT WITH NO VIOLATION NORI

a. *Complaint Not Dual Filed under ADA and/or Title VII.* If a complaint involves only EO 11246, Section 503 and/or Section 4212 allegations that are not dual filed under the ADA and/or Title VII, and there is no violation finding, the CO may release the NORI upon completion of the investigation.[256]

b. *Complaints Dual Filed Under Section 503/ADA and EO 11246/Title VII.* If a complaint is dual filed under Section 503 and the ADA or under EO 11246 and Title VII, and there is no violation finding, the CO may release the NORI upon completion of the investigation. The Notice of Right-to-Sue will accompany the notification.[257]

6J03 CLOSURE OF COMPLAINT AND ISSUANCE OF "NOTICE OF RIGHT-TO-SUE" UPON REQUEST

a. *Notice Upon Request.* If a complainant requests a Notice of Right-to-Sue in writing before

[255] See Letters L-11 – Letter to the Contractor Confirming Complaint Resolution; and L-12 – Letter to the Complainant Confirming Complaint Resolution.

[256] See Letter L-13 – Notification: No Violation NORI.

[257] See Letter L-14 – Notification – No Violation NORI, Notice of Right to Sue under Title I of the ADA or Title VII of the Civil Rights Act of 1964 and Appendix A-11 – Information Related to Filing Suit under Title VII and Title I of the ADA.

180 calendar days have passed and the Regional Director (or designee) can foresee that the investigation will extend beyond the 180th day, the Regional Director (or designee) will issue the Notice within 10 calendar days to the complainant. The Regional Director (or designee) should send copies to the complainant's attorney (if any), the contractor and the appropriate EEOC field office. If a complaint investigation remains open after 180 calendar days from the complaint filing date, the same procedure applies. The Regional Director (or designee) should send copies to the complainant's attorney (if any), the contractor and the appropriate EEOC field office.[258]

Consistent with Title VII and the ADA procedures set forth at 29 CFR 1601.28, issuance of a Notice of Right-to-Sue upon request immediately terminates further OFCCP processing of the Title VII/ADA component of the complaint unless it is determined at that time or at a later time that it would effectuate the purposes of Title VII/ADA to further process the Title VII/ADA component of the complaint. Upon issuance of the Notice, the Regional Director (or designee) can continue the complaint investigation or close the complaint without issuing a finding, noting his or her decision on the Notice.

6J04 NOTICE ISSUED UPON ADMINISTRATIVE CLOSURE

OFCCP must administratively close the complaint investigation for several reasons, including:

- Lack of jurisdiction;
- Complainant did not file timely;
- Complainant failed to provide requested necessary information, failed to appear or refused to be available for necessary interviews or conferences, or otherwise refused to cooperate to the extent that OFCCP is unable to complete its investigation of the complaint; or
- CO cannot locate or complainant failed to respond to notification sent to last known address within reasonable timeframe (60 calendar days).

With dual filed complaints that are administratively closed, the Regional Director or designee will issue the Notice of Right-to-Sue to the complainant and send copies of the Notice to the contractor and the appropriate EEOC field office when the:

- Complainant failed to provide requested necessary information, failed to appear or refused to be available for necessary interviews or conferences, or otherwise refused to cooperate to the extent that OFCCP is unable to complete its investigation of the complaint; or

---

[258] See Letter L-15 Notice of Right-to-Sue under Title I of the ADA or Title VII (Issued on Request); and Appendix A-11 – Information Related to Filing Suit under Title VII and Title I of the ADA.

- CO cannot locate or complainant failed to respond to notification sent to last known address within reasonable timeframe (60 calendar days).

There are several helpful references that supplement this section: Letter L-16 Notice of Right-to-Sue under Title I of the ADA or Title VII Dismissal; and Appendix A-11 - Information Related to Filing Suit under Title VII and Title I of the ADA.

6J05 SETTLEMENT AFTER COMPLETION OF INVESTIGATION

The NORI invites the contractor to resolve the complaint through conciliation by informal means. The CO should telephone the contractor within five business days of its receipt of the NORI to arrange the conciliation meeting.[259]

a. *Conciliation Meeting.* The conciliation meeting is the method by which OFCCP attempts to obtain voluntary compliance. The complainant is not a party to the conciliation. However, the CO should keep the complainant informed of the progress of any discussions and meetings, in order to gather further input and to discuss proposed settlements.

b. *Reasonable Settlement.* If the field office believes it has arrived at a reasonable settlement, which the complainant accepts, the contractor will acknowledge its responsibility to fulfill the settlement by signing a CA.[260]

   If the complainant will not accept what the field office considers to be a reasonable settlement, the field office may cease its efforts on behalf of the complainant, but must nevertheless obtain from the contractor correction of any policies or practices which caused the discrimination. The steps in accomplishing this are as follows:

   1. Request that the contractor submit in writing, a full statement of its agreed upon settlement to be maintained in the case file;

   2. Notify the complainant, in writing, of the full details of the settlement and request a written reply accepting or rejecting the settlement; and

   3. If the field office considers the offered settlement to be reasonable, and the complainant persists in refusing to accept it, the office will cease its efforts on behalf of the complainant and close the case file. The office will obtain from the contractor a Conciliation Agreement resolving all discriminatory policies and practices.[261]

c. *Seeking Punitive Damages as EEOC's Agent.* In accordance with 41 CFR Part 60-742 and the MOU with the EEOC, OFCCP will act as EEOC's agent for obtaining relief for all aggrieved people covered by a dual filed Section 503/ADA complaint or an EO 11246/Title VII complaint, respectively. The field office will attempt conciliation to obtain relief for victims who have suffered pecuniary losses and intangible injuries. The Regional Director

[259] See Letter L-17 – Notification: Violation Notification of Results of Investigation.
[260] See Chapter 8 – Resolution of Noncompliance.
[261] See Chapter 8 – Resolution of Noncompliance.

shall be involved in the conciliation process for cases involving potential compensatory and punitive damages. When potential punitive damages are involved, the Regional Director must consult with the Regional Solicitor and the Director of Program Operations.

6K ENFORCEMENT

If any matter raised in the NORI violation cannot be resolved through conciliation with the contractor, OFCCP should recommend it for enforcement.[262]

[262] See Chapter 8 – Resolution of Noncompliance.

CHAPTER 7
EMPLOYMENT DISCRIMINATION REMEDIES

7A INTRODUCTION

This chapter contains methods for designing remedies for employment discrimination. It does not address the investigative steps of a compliance review. The process to follow in investigating potential discrimination is set out in Chapter 2 of this Manual and the Standard Compliance Evaluation Report (SCER) that is appended to this Manual.

7A00 APPLICABILITY

This chapter is applicable to designing employment discrimination remedies under Executive Order 11246, as amended; Section 503 of the Rehabilitation Act of 1973, as amended (29 U.S.C. 793); and the Vietnam Era Veterans Readjustment Assistance Act of 1974, as amended (38 U.S.C. 4212).

7A01 RELATIONSHIP TO SCER

During the investigative phase of the compliance review, the CO completes the SCER Part C – Problems Identified. Once the CO completes the investigation and has analyzed all the information, the CO determines in consultation with his or her supervisor whether there are findings of discrimination that require a CA. Then the CO completes the SCER Part F – Summary of Findings.

7A02 PROCESS

When the CO concludes that there was employment discrimination, and when the contractor's response is insufficient or is pretextual, the CO in consultation with his or her supervisor will offer to conciliate a settlement with the contractor. Prior to this offer, the CO will design a remedy to present during the settlement meeting. Management will review OFCCP's proposed remedy prior to presentation to the contractor. If the contractor and CO in coordination with his or her supervisor cannot reach a settlement, OFCCP may recommend enforcement.

7A03 APPLICABLE LAW

CO's must design employment discrimination remedies in a manner consistent with Title VII principles. Remedies for disability discrimination or discrimination against disabled veterans will be consistent with Americans with Disabilities Act principles.

7B TIMELINESS AND CONTINUING VIOLATION

As a general rule, one seeking to remedy a discriminatory act must assert his or her rights within the periods established by the statute or other laws establishing the rights. Under OFCCP procedures, for an act of discrimination discovered during a compliance review to be a violation of Executive Order 11246, Section 503 or Section 4212, it must have taken place within two years prior to the initiation of the compliance evaluation (Figure F-2 Scheduling Letter), unless the violation is part of a continuing violation. Complaints filed under EO 11246 are timely if the complainant filed it within 180 calendar days of the alleged discriminatory act, except for good cause shown, in which case the Director may waive the filing deadline (41 CFR 60-1.21). Complaints filed under Section 4212 and Section 503 are timely if the complainant filed it within 300 calendar days of the alleged discriminatory act, except for good cause shown, in which case the Director may waive the filing deadline.[263]

7B00 CONTINUING VIOLATION

The courts developed the continuing violation concept to address the fact that some employment practices are not discrete incidents, beginning and ending at particular points in time. For example, a policy or practice of paying lower wages to women than to men for the same or similar work is discriminatory, and the contractor repeats the violation each time the contractor pays the women. When evaluating such violations, the courts will consider the entire time period during which the violations occurred or the time period since the effective date of the law, whichever is later. For example, a continuing violation which is grounded in racial discrimination is actionable from the date the continuing practice began or the effective date of EO 11246 (September, 1965), whichever is later. This is provided, of course, that the other requirements of coverage are met.

In compensation cases, contractors will be in violation of Executive Order 11246 any time they pay wages, benefits, or other compensation that result in whole or in part from application of any discriminatory decision or practice.

a. *Application of Continuing Violation Theory*. OFCCP applies the continuing violation theory in compliance reviews and complaint investigations. The theory is applicable to the following situations:

   1. *Series of Individual Discriminatory Acts*. A continuing violation may occur when the discrimination involves a series of closely related acts. The acts must be sufficiently related to form a pattern of discrimination. The last of these acts must have occurred within the two-year period preceding the initiation of the compliance review (Scheduling Letter) or, in the instance of a complaint investigation, within the 180-day period or 300-day period from the filing date of the complaint.

   2. *Maintenance of a Discriminatory Policy or System*. A continuing violation may occur when a contractor maintains a discriminatory policy or practice into the two-year, 180-day period or 300-day period. The violation may focus on one particular employment practice, such as promotions or compensation, or it may deal with discrimination in a

---

[263] 41 CFR 60-250.61, 41 CFR 60-300.61, 41 CFR 60-741.61.

series of areas including initial placement, promotions, transfers and salary. It is not necessary under this theory for OFCCP to show that a discrete act representing the alleged discriminatory policy occurred during the two-year period, 180-day period or 300-day period. It is sufficient to show that the policy or system continued into the period, and that if there had been a personnel action, the policy or system would have been applied in the allegedly discriminatory manner.

b. *Remedies Under a Continuing Violation*. Once the CO establishes that there is a continuing violation by showing a series of related acts, one of which occurred within the liability period or a continuing employment policy that extended into the liability period, then the contractor must remedy all acts that are part of the continuing violation since the effective date of the law under which relief is sought or from the start of the violation, whichever is later. This is so whether they occurred within or outside of the two-year or 180-day period.

7C REMEDIES

Remedy represents a separate and distinct phase of the investigation. While the CO should be thinking about remedy throughout the investigation and trying to obtain the information necessary to determine the appropriate remedy, the CO should reserve conclusions about the final definition of remedy until he or she has sufficient information to make a finding that there has been discrimination. This normally does not occur until after the CO presents the contractor with the preliminary findings, the contractor submits its response and the CO determines that the contractor's response does not adequately explain the alleged discrimination. The issues of the remedy phase of an investigation are very different from the issues of the violation phase. After establishing discrimination, the CO should begin identifying specific remedies. The remedy must address how to:

- Make the discrimination victims whole;
- Stop the violation; and
- Prevent the violation from recurring.

The remedy for a discrimination finding is in the CA. See Chapter 8 of this Manual for a discussion of the specific elements of a CA.

7C00 DESIGNING THE REMEDY

There is much more flexibility in designing remedies than there is in proving discrimination. The CO frequently develops remedies through negotiation and compromise. There are, however, general guidelines for designing remedies. The CO should always seek a complete remedy. A complete remedy will correct the causes of the discrimination and make the victims of discrimination whole.

7C01 CORRECTIVE REMEDIES

Part of a complete remedy is the corrective remedy. Corrective remedies stop the violation and protect against its recurrence. For example, to correct hiring discrimination caused by treating applicants differently during a subjective interview, corrective remedies could include stopping the use of the discriminatory interviews, substituting legitimate objective criteria (i.e., objective criteria with no unjustified adverse impact) and establishing a monitoring system to ensure that the contractor applies the criteria in a nondiscriminatory fashion.

If an unvalidated or invalid test has an adverse impact then corrective action would include eliminating the use of the test, continued use of the test in a manner that eliminates its adverse impact (e.g., changing the cut-off score) or validating the test in compliance with the *Uniform Guidelines on Employee Selection Procedures* (UGESP), thereby demonstrating its job-relatedness.

7C02 MAKE-WHOLE RELIEF

a. *General Principles.* Make-whole relief means simply that the contractor restores the victim of discrimination to the position, both economically and in terms of status that he or she would have occupied had the discrimination not occurred. This usually involves placing the person in his or her rightful place. This means placing the person in the job the person would have occupied with the seniority he or she would have had if not for the discrimination. For example, if the contractor discriminated against women in hiring for an entry-level maintenance position, make-whole relief would include placing a certain number of class members into entry-level maintenance positions as they become available. If the discrimination resulted in termination from employment, the affected class members should be reinstated to their prior positions. In addition to rightful placement, make-whole relief includes all economic benefits the victim would have received had the discrimination not occurred. This would normally include things such as back pay with interest, retirement contributions, vacation credits, sick leave credits, payment for medical expenses that would have been paid by the employer's medical plan, missed training and any other employment benefits denied to the victim.

b. *Case Law Precedent.* In construing what constitutes make-whole relief, OFCCP follows Title VII principles.

7C03 FRONT PAY

Front pay is appropriate whenever the contractor cannot place the victim immediately into his or her rightful place. Front pay is the difference between the victim's current pay and the pay associated with his or her rightful place. There are a number of circumstances that can prevent immediate achievement of rightful place, including the absence of a vacancy, training required before beginning in the position, etc. When front pay is appropriate, the victim must start receiving the earnings associated with his or her rightful place from the date of settlement until the contractor places him or her in the position at issue or his or her position pay is equal to the rate it should be in his or her rightful place.

7C04 RETROACTIVE SENIORITY

a. *Seniority as an Element of Make-Whole Relief.* Seniority is often a critical component of relief. Without seniority an individual who the contractor hires or promotes as a remedy for past discrimination may not have protection against layoff or demotion. If the contractor had hired or promoted him or her at the time the discriminatory act occurred, he or she would have had additional years of seniority and would be less vulnerable to layoff as a result. Therefore, requiring hiring or promotion as a remedy without also requiring an adjustment of seniority does not really make the victim whole. Similarly, in many situations, employers award promotions in whole or in part based upon the bidder's seniority. Merely placing a victim in the workforce without the seniority to which he or she is entitled will delay his or her attainment of his or her rightful place. Victims must receive all relevant seniority, such as job seniority where relevant in addition to plant seniority.

b. *Competitive and Noncompetitive Seniority.* There are two types of seniority: competitive and non-competitive seniority. Competitive seniority may include seniority for the purposes of shift preference, vacation schedules, promotions, job bidding, layoffs, raises or training. When retroactive competitive seniority is fashioned as a form of relief, the employees who were not victims could effectively lose out in bidding for jobs or be in greater danger of layoff, etc., to those who received retroactive seniority. On the other hand, there are some types of noncompetitive seniority matters (e.g., accrued leave, retirement computation) that when remedied for individual victims, do not create the same concerns as remedying for competitive seniority issues.

c. *Nonunion Seniority.* Some nonunion contractors operate under a system in which seniority is used in both the competitive and noncompetitive context. In other words, even without a union contract, promotions and layoffs, etc., are decided on the basis of seniority. In these situations, the victim is clearly entitled to obtain retroactive competitive seniority.

d. *Union Involvement.* When part of the remedy includes retroactive seniority, and a union agreement governs seniority, it is important to involve the union in the conciliation discussions on seniority. Although OFCCP generally does not have jurisdiction over unions, if the union consents to retroactive seniority in the CA, the agreement will be enforceable. If the union is not involved in the conciliation efforts or does not consent, the seniority relief may not be enforceable. If the union refuses to participate in the conciliation process or agree to seniority relief, the CO and his or her supervisor in coordination with their regional office should consult their local Office of the Solicitor.

e. *Procedures When Union is Involved.*

    1. *Union Participates and Consents.* OFCCP will invite the union to participate in conciliation of a violation that requires a retroactive seniority remedy. The CO will make every effort to involve the union in the conciliation process and get its consent to the award of retroactive seniority. While OFCCP usually cannot compel the union to participate, if the union does participate voluntarily and agrees to the seniority remedy, then OFCCP can enforce the remedy. If the CO invites the union to participate in the conciliation of seniority issues, its role is limited to those issues. The union should not be involved in other remedy areas (e.g., in determining back pay, changing the selection process).

2. *Union Refuses to Participate or Consent.* If the union declines to participate in conciliation or otherwise does not consent to an award of retroactive seniority, OFCCP may not be able to enforce any retroactive seniority relief. OFCCP should seek to lay the groundwork to defend its insistence upon seniority relief. In other words, OFCCP should not agree to the usual boilerplate language that says that the contractor does not admit to violating one or more of EO 11246, Section 503 or Section 4212. Instead, the CA should recite the factual bases for OFCCP's findings of violation. Under these circumstances (a) the nonadmissions clause is not included in the CA, and (b) paragraph 1 of the General Provisions of the CA will note that the union was invited to participate, but declined to do so or to otherwise consent to an award of retroactive seniority, as applicable. (See Chapter 8.)

3. *Contractor Refuses to Sign.* If a contractor refuses to sign a CA for any reason, including the fact that the CA does not contain the nonadmission language, OFCCP should inform the contractor that this failure to conciliate will result in referral for enforcement.[264]

f. *Other Methods for Addressing Retroactive Seniority*

1. *Bifurcation.* One method to avoid union objection is to bifurcate the competitive and noncompetitive seniority issues. Since the union most likely will not object to the award of noncompetitive seniority, this may be a viable option for resolution.

2. *Cash Buy-Outs.* To address competitive seniority issues, some contractors propose a cash buy-out of employee seniority rights. In other words, the contractor offers a lump sum payment to each identified victim of discrimination in exchange for a waiver of his or her entitlement to competitive seniority. Seniority buy-outs are technically possible, but the CO must carefully craft and review such proposals' fairness; many may not be acceptable. The CO in coordination with his or her supervisor must forward offers of seniority buy-outs to the National Office, DPO, for review and approval.

g. *Novel Issue.* OFCCP has determined that a contractor's refusal to provide retroactive seniority relief where it is appropriate, to be a novel issue. If a case presents this novel issue, the CO, in coordination with his or her supervisor must contact DPO in the National Office.

7C05 OTHER REMEDIES AFFECTING A UNION AGREEMENT

The CO should use the procedures described in Section 7C04 immediately above for other remedies (besides retroactive seniority) that require a change in or otherwise affect a union agreement.

7C06 BACK PAY

a. *Back Pay Required.* Back pay is normally part of any make-whole remedy. The U.S. Supreme Court stated in *Albemarle Paper Co.* v. *Moody*, 422 U.S. 405, (1975), that "...given

[264] See Chapter 8 – Resolution of Noncompliance.

a finding of unlawful discrimination, back pay should be denied only for reasons which, if applied generally, would not frustrate the central statutory purposes of eradicating discrimination throughout the economy and making persons whole for injuries suffered through past discrimination." Given this stringent standard, it would be rare for the victim not to receive back pay.

b. *Elements of Back Pay*. Back pay should reflect total earnings lost by the victim due to the discriminatory employment action, practice or procedure. Many elements of compensation, in addition to salary or wages, are normally part of a back pay award (e.g., overtime, premium pay and shift differentials, incentive pay, raises, bonuses, lost sales commissions, cost-of-living increases, tips, medical and life insurance, fringe benefits, pensions, stock options, and awards).

c. *Benefits*. For the benefits portion of the back pay, the CO should gather information about when the benefits became effective (e.g., what is the waiting period) and the monetary value of the benefits. Benefits can be calculated as a monetary figure (e.g., employer paid premiums, plus employer contributions to a retirement account amount to X per year) or as a percentage of wages or salary (e.g., 20 percent of the total compensation package).

d. *Deductions and Offsets*.

    1. *Interim Earnings*. If a victim earned money from employment elsewhere during the interim (i.e., substituting for employment with the contractor), this amount is deductible from total back pay. Not all financial compensation received by the victim during the back pay period, however, constitutes "interim earnings." For example, if an employee had both earnings from a full-time job and a part-time job and could have continued in the part-time job even absent the discrimination, the earnings from the part-time job are not deemed interim earnings and are not subtracted from back pay. Additionally, unemployment and workers compensation payments do not constitute interim earnings.

    2. *Mitigation*. Mitigation refers to the duty of the victim to use reasonable diligence in seeking alternative employment during the back pay period. Contractors may seek to reduce back pay awards by the amount the victim could have earned with reasonable diligence, less expenses reasonably incurred in looking for alternative employment (e.g., cost to prepare a resume, gas and parking fees incurred when going for an interview). Reasonable diligence does not mean that the person had to be successful in obtaining other employment, only that he or she must make a reasonable effort. The victim only needs to accept employment that is substantially equivalent to or the same as that sought or held with the employer. The victim does not need to relocate to accept alternative employment.

    3. *Burden of Proof*. The contractor bears the burden of proving the amount of interim earnings or the failure of the victim to take reasonable steps to mitigate back pay loss.

e. *Periods of Unavailability*. Back pay awards do not include periods when the victim would not have been employed even without discrimination (e.g., during periods of incarceration).

f. *Interest on Back Pay*.

1. *Purpose and Rate of Interest.* The purpose of payment of interest on back pay awards is to compensate the victim(s) for the loss of the use of his or her money. OFCCP's regulations require the contractor to calculate interest on back pay at the same percentage rate as the Internal Revenue Service's underpayment formula. Interest on back pay must be compounded quarterly in EO 11246, Section 4212 and Section 503 cases. (See 41 CFR 60-1.26(a)(2), 41 CFR 60-250.65(a)(1); 41 CFR 60-300.65(a)(1) and 41 CFR 60-741.65(a)(1).)

2. *Rate Adjustments.* The IRS may adjust its rate quarterly. The interest rates applicable to various periods may be issued in OFCCP directives but they are also available on the Internal Revenue Service Web site at www.irs.gov. The IRS site should be the primary source for this information.

g. *Withholding of Taxes.* Contractors may withhold all applicable federal, state and local income taxes; FICA (social security); and FUTA (unemployment insurance) taxes from employment discrimination settlement payments. The contractor's payments of back pay, front pay and lump sum payments made in place of lost fringe benefits are "wages" subject to such tax withholding. The contractor must supply the victim(s) with a Form W-2 showing the wage component of the settlement and the amount of taxes withheld. Note, however:

1. *FICA.* FICA requires an employer as well as an employee contribution. The employer should not pay its FICA obligation out of a settlement; the employer share must be paid on top of the negotiated back pay.

2. *FUTA.* In almost all states, FUTA (unemployment insurance) taxes are an expense paid only by the employer (i.e., there is no matching employee contribution). Therefore, the employer should not take an offset or deduction for FUTA when computing back pay awards unless the particular state where the affected party was or would have been employed required employers to withhold FUTA taxes from employees' wages or salaries during the time period for which the employer is calculating a back pay award.

3. *Interest.* Interest included in a settlement, if separately stated, is not subject to either FICA or FUTA. While interest is taxable as income to the recipient, just as interest on a bank savings account would be taxable, it is not subject to withholding by the employer. The contractor, however, must supply the victims with the Form 1099 stating the interest component of the settlement.

4. *Benefits.* Since employer contributions to most fringe benefits, such as the employer paid portion of health insurance premiums or pension funds, are not taxable (whether retroactive or not), they are not subject to withholding.

7C07 TIME LIMITS FOR RELIEF

a. *Two Year Limit.* The victim can obtain back pay for a period beginning two years prior to the date the Scheduling Letter was sent to contractor via return receipt mail, or two years before the victim filed the complaint. If the discriminatory acts took place less than two years before the Scheduling Letter was sent or the filing of the complaint, back pay is due from the date of violation forward. Back pay continues from these events until a CA or other voluntary correction stops the discriminatory actions, or until the contractor makes a bona fide offer of the position denied. Total back pay can, therefore, be for more than two years.

b. *Bona Fide Offer.* Under appropriate circumstances, the rejection of a bona fide offer of the position previously denied by the contractor terminates the further accrual of back pay liability. However, interest continues to accrue until settlement on the back pay losses prior to the bona fide offer. A bona fide offer does not require the claimant to waive any rights or remedies to which he or she is entitled. For example, the parties may disagree on whether retroactive seniority is appropriate, but as long as the contractor offers to place the claimant in the same job (including shift and location) that the contractor had without requiring that the claimant waive any right to seniority, the offer is bona fide. Under these circumstances, the parties can agree to litigate or arbitrate the seniority issue at a later date. If the victim accepts the offer, back pay is still due up to acceptance, and front pay continues to accrue for losses suffered as a result of missed promotional opportunities or increased risk of layoff. If the victim rejects a bona fide offer, he or she is not disqualified from receiving back pay; back pay merely cuts off at the date of the offer.

c. *Continuing Violation.* If the CO finds a continuing violation,[265] the contractor should provide remedies, except for back pay, for the entire period of the violation but not earlier than the effective date of EO 11246, Section 503 or Section 4212, as appropriate. Victims affected by a continuing violation can recover back pay for the effects of the violation that occur within the period beginning two years prior to the scheduling notice even when the specific act affecting them occurred outside the two year period. The effective dates of the laws administered by OFCCP are:

- Executive Order 11246 – October 24, 1965
- Executive Order 11375 (adds sex as a prohibited factor) – October 14, 1968
- Section 503 of the Rehabilitation Act – September 26, 1973
- Vietnam Era Veterans' Readjustment Assistance Act (Section 4212) – December 3, 1974

7C08 CALCULATION OF INDIVIDUAL BACK PAY AWARDS

In some cases it may be feasible to calculate individual back pay awards. When it is not, the formula relief method will be used as described in section 7C11. When individual relief is feasible, the CO determines the amount of back pay the contractor will award to victims by calculating, as accurately as possible; the pay the victims would have received if not for the discrimination. The most common way to reconstruct pay is to identify members of the favored group for comparison with affected members of the nonfavored group (or an individual without a disability in a Section 503 case). Proper comparators are those who were hired, promoted, etc., at about the same time the victims of the discrimination should have been hired, promoted, etc.

---

[265] See subsection 7B00.

The CO then traces comparators' pay history. In promotion and compensation cases, the difference between the pay received by the victims and that by the comparators within the appropriate time frame constitutes the back pay due the victims. For hiring cases, the difference between the pay received by the comparators and that by the victims if they exercised reasonable diligence to find alternative employment within the appropriate time frame constitutes back pay due the victims. If there are gaps in the comparators' employment during the back pay period (e.g., the comparators quit, had a lengthy illness), the CO should make a reasonable estimate of the amount of wages the comparators would have made without the break in service.

7C09 REMEDIES IN A PATTERN OR PRACTICE CASE

There are two models used to remedy pattern or practice problems:

- Victim-specific or individual remedies; and
- Formula relief.

The initial step in fashioning pattern or practice relief is to determine which remedy model to use. The models are different approaches to relief. The CO should not interchange the elements of the two approaches when providing relief (i.e., if adopting a victim-specific approach, the total amount of back pay is not based on a formula and if adopting a formula, potential victims are not excluded from the class because they have not been shown to be actual victims). OFCCP makes the decision about which model to apply.

7C10 VICTIM-SPECIFIC REMEDIES

a. *Approach.* The victim-specific model, which provides make-whole relief for identified victims of the discrimination, is used infrequently. Individualized relief should be sought when it is feasible to identify individual victims and to calculate their losses.

b. *Remedy Phases.* There are two stages to the remedy phase: (1) identifying the specific class members entitled to relief; and (2) determining the exact remedy to which each victim is entitled.

c. *Identifying Victims.* The first step in the process is to identify potential victims of the discriminatory policy or practice. In other words, the CO must define the group or class of individuals for whom he or she is seeking relief. These could include for example: all blacks who failed an unvalidated pass-fail test; all Hispanics who were eligible for supervisory positions, but were not promoted; or all women who were denied reinstatement following maternity leave. At the liability phase, the CO will most likely have defined this class on the basis of the violations identified. In other words, once the CO has established the time period of the violation and the nature of the violation, and the minorities or women or both who were adversely affected are set forth, the minorities or women or both who are presumptively entitled to a remedy are for all intents and purposes defined. In defining the group at this point, the CO should refer only to what he or she has determined to be the minimum objective qualifications the contractor actually imposed.

The CO should not evaluate comparative ("relative") qualifications at this stage. At this stage the "class" consists of all who met the minimum objective qualifications.

d. *Computing Lost Earnings*. The CO should gather information to compute the individual's specific losses depending on whether it is a failure to hire, wrongful termination, failure to promote, or discriminatory compensation. This information will include, but is not limited to, wages for position, interim raises, promotion potential (i.e., the earnings associated with all of the promotions the person would have received had they not been discriminated against in the first place), overtime and shift differential, and any other additions to wages or salary such as bonuses or benefits. The CO should also gather information supporting appropriate non-monetary relief that may include such relief aspriority promotions, training, counseling, and EEO counseling for supervisors.

e. *Contractor's Response.*

1. *Contractor's Burden*. The CO must inform the contractor of the names of the class members for whom the CO is seeking relief and the amount of back pay and other forms of make-whole relief necessary to fully remedy the class. All members of the class are presumed to be victims of discrimination and, thus, each member is entitled to relief unless the contractor shows that he or she is not. To show that an individual is not a victim, the employer must prove that there is a nondiscriminatory explanation for its treatment of the individual. This is a heavy burden. Once the CO has established that a class member was an actual victim of discrimination, the contractor may produce evidence about the amount of make-whole relief to which the victim is entitled.

2. *Level of Proof Required*. Proof means more than just suggesting or offering some evidence of a nondiscriminatory reason. It means the contractor must convincingly demonstrate that it is most probable that the nondiscriminatory reason was the only reason for its less favorable treatment of the alleged victim.

3. *Common Contractor Responses*. Some reasons which contractors commonly advance as nondiscriminatory include:

- The individuals in question were not qualified under standards actually applied. (These may or may not be the same as stated standards.)
- The contractor selected a better qualified candidate.
- There was no vacancy within the time period that the application was active.
- There is something in the candidate's background that caused rejection (e.g., a poor work record).

f. *Evaluation of Contractor's Response*. Once the CO has given the contractor the opportunity to prove that each identified victim is not entitled to relief, the CO must weigh the proof. The contractor must convincingly demonstrate that a given person would have been treated in exactly the same manner even in the absence of discrimination. Each person the contractor cannot eliminate from the class by this method is considered to be an actual, identified victim of the discrimination and entitled to full relief.

g. *Identification of Vacancies*. If the CO is proceeding on a victim specific basis, he or she should consider all vacancies or job opportunities denied to the victims (not merely some portion of them). In other words, once the CO has established a pattern of discrimination with regard to a particular type of employment action, the CO presumes each relevant employment decision the contractor made during the actionable period to have been discriminatory.

h. *Shortfall*. Some contractors have argued that COs should limit their consideration of the denied opportunities to those vacancies that constituted a "shortfall." When a contractor talks about shortfall vacancies, it refers to the difference between the number of opportunities that were actually awarded to minorities and women, versus the number of opportunities which one would have expected them to get based on their percentage in the relevant pool. For example, suppose a contractor has filled 100 vacancies. The applicant pool for those vacancies consisted of 100 whites and 100 blacks. However, the employer hired only 10 blacks and 90 whites. The CO has now found a violation and informs the contractor that the class for whom relief is being sought consists of the 90 black rejected applicants. The contractor might contend that, if it had hired 50 blacks, OFCCP would have found no violation. Therefore, under the shortfall vacancy argument, OFCCP may only seek instatement for 40 of the 90 rejected applicants – the difference between the 10 the contractor actually hired and the 50 it would have been expected to hire absent discrimination. Under the victim-specific model, OFCCP rejects this argument (it is also rejected when using the formula-relief model). Once discrimination has been established, all 90 of the rejected black applicants are presumed to be entitled to instatement.

i. *Individual Remedies*. The CO must then determine make-whole relief for each individual who has not been eliminated from the class by the contractor's proof that he or she was not the victim of discrimination. The CO should tailor the precise remedy to the situation of each victim. The CO should be sure to consider all the different types of harm that the victim has suffered. For example, the passage of time since the violation may mean that victims are less interested in reinstatement or hiring because they have built new careers. On the other hand, if very little time has passed since the violation occurred, and monetary damages are small, reinstatement or preferential hiring may be the most important remedy.

7C11 PREFERRED METHOD FOR DETERMINING RELIEF: FORMULA RELIEF

a. *When Used*. The CO must seek individualized relief whenever it is feasible to identify individual victims of discrimination and to calculate their losses. However, the CO should pursue formula relief wherever it is impossible or impractical to determine individual relief; that is, when the number of actual victims of discrimination is so large that case-by-case determinations would be unduly burdensome, or when reconstruction of the employment decision the contractor would have made absent discrimination involves mere speculation (such as when there are no lines of progression). Sometimes the CO knows the identity of the victims, but it is so difficult to trace their losses that the CO can only estimate them.

Perhaps the most common situation when the CO may wish to resort to a formula to determine relief is when the number of class members exceeds the number of vacancies.

b. *Definition.* Formula relief is a mechanism by which the CO determines the compensation for the loss suffered by a particular class and then divides the financial compensation (usually, though not necessarily, pro rata) among all the members of that class. Under a formula it is possible that some individuals will receive less than their total losses and some will receive more. This is the consequence of approximating losses in a situation where it is unrealistic to precisely compute individual losses.

c. *Measuring Losses.* Once the CO has decided to go forward with formula relief rather than victim-specific relief, he or she can begin the next step of the remedy phase. This includes an attempt to measure the loss which the class has suffered.

  1. *Shortfall Method.* If the CO selected the formula method because the number of class members exceeds the total number of opportunities, a "shortfall vacancies" approach may be considered for computing the amount of back pay for the class. For example, assume a situation where there are 50 black and 50 white applicants, all of whom possess the required qualifications, seeking 20 jobs. Nineteen whites were hired. The difference between the actual number of blacks hired (1) and the expected number of black hires (10) represents the shortfall (9). Shortfall vacancies do not limit the number of individuals entitled to relief. Instead, the contractor distributes the amount of money attributable to those vacancies to the whole class. In this example, the CO would compute the earnings attributable to the nine shortfall positions for the entire period, and distribute these to the 49 qualified black applicants who the contractor had not selected. Shortfall vacancies do not represent a cap on OFCCP's entitlement to relief. They are a compromise figure utilized as part of an approximation of class wide loss.

  2. *Averaging Method.* Not all formulas require the CO to look at shortfalls. There are other reasons to use a formula other than the fact that there are more victims than vacancies. For example, suppose there is a case in which the major claim is that the contractor placed the hired men and women into sex segregated departments. In such a situation, the CO may want to compare the average salary earned by men with a given level of seniority, to the average salary earned by women with the same seniority. The difference in average salary defines the measure of back pay to be awarded to each woman in that seniority group. The formula devised should be designed to address the particular violation found.

  3. *Computing Earnings.* Because the formula approach represents a compromise, it is extremely important to account fully for all the earnings attributable to a particular vacancy in computing losses such as: interest, interim raises, promotion potential (i.e., the earnings associated with all of the promotions the persons would have received had they not been discriminated against in the first place), overtime and shift differential, and any other additions to wages or salary such as bonuses or benefits. Generally, the CO should use averages. For example, the overtime calculation in a hiring case should reflect the average overtime that people hired into the job during the review period worked. Similarly, the CO should base promotions on average time to promotions.

4. *Distribution of Remedy*. When using the formula approach, the agreed upon remedy is shared by all members of the class. The CO divides the amount of money that represents the group's lost wages among the members of the class either on a pro rata basis or some other equitable basis. The CO may decide on a method of distribution based upon the facts of the case. For example, if the CO identified an incumbent class that was denied promotions or assigned to lower paying jobs, the contractor controlled their interim earnings. In that situation, a distribution based upon the number of months in the employer's workforce might be most appropriate. With a rejected applicant class, the CO might decide that a simple per capita distribution makes more sense.

5. *Nonmonetary Relief*. In addition to monetary relief for class members, the CO should also consider requiring nonmonetary remedies such as: preferential hiring or promotion goals, red circling, special training programs and EEO counseling for supervisors. With formula relief, it is difficult to provide reinstatement or retroactive promotion because, by using the formula, no individual is tied to any particular opportunity. However, the CO may create a preferential hiring or promotion list consisting of the members of the class and from which the contractor must make all selections to fill vacancies until the number of class members hired is equal to the shortfall. The contractor must hire class members before non-class members.

7C12 NOTIFICATION TO CLASS MEMBERS

The CA or other settlement document must guarantee that all class members are aware of their rights under the agreement and specify the procedures through which those rights will be protected, including counseling when appropriate. Normally, the contractor must notify all class members of their rights. That notice must include the terms and conditions under which the contractor is tendering an employment offer, including the specific amount of back pay, the retroactive seniority, as well as all other appropriate benefits.

7C13 LIABILITY OF A SUCCESSOR EMPLOYER

a. In determining whether a successor employer is liable for the discriminatory acts of its predecessor, OFCCP follows Title VII case law. The federal courts have held that such liability must be judged on a case-by-case basis considering the "MacMillan" factors (*EEOC v. MacMillan Bloedel Containers, Inc.*, 503 F.2d 1086 (6th Cir. 1974)).

b. The CO should direct requests for a determination of successor liability to DPO in the National Office. The request should include the contractor's responses, with supporting documentation, to the "MacMillan" factors described in Appendix A-13.

CHAPTER 8
RESOLUTION OF NONCOMPLIANCE

8A INTRODUCTION

This chapter outlines the procedures and documents OFCCP uses to resolve violations COs find during compliance evaluations and complaint investigations. These procedures and documents cover both affirmative action and discrimination violations and apply to all three OFCCP programs: Executive Order 11246, as amended; Section 503 of the Rehabilitation Act of 1973, as amended, 29 U.S.C. 793; and the Vietnam Era Veterans' Readjustment Assistance Act of 1974, as amended, 38 U.S.C. 4212.

8A00 APPLICABILITY

COs should consult this chapter whenever they find noncompliance. Unless otherwise specified, the guidelines in this chapter apply to both supply and service and construction contractors.

8A01 REMEDIES

If a CO identifies violations during a compliance evaluation or complaint investigation, the CO must secure remedies or sanctions, or both, to bring the contractor into compliance. COs design remedies for three reasons: to correct the violation, to prevent recurrence of the violation, and to make the victims whole. For a complete discussion of remedies and sanctions, see Chapter 7 of this Manual. Distinctions between remedies and sanctions are discussed below.

a. Remedy. Remedies are legally required actions to eliminate the effects of discrimination that include, for example, back pay or reinstatement. Remedies may also be taken or imposed to rectify noncompliance with affirmative action standards. Remember, remedies are corrective, not punitive, and are established in a Conciliation Agreement (CA).

b. Sanctions. In contrast to remedies, sanctions may be appropriate when a contractor fails to agree to acceptable remedies or fails to implement acceptable remedies for noncompliance. Examples of sanctions may include termination of a contract or debarment. Sanctions may also be appropriate, when a violation is egregious or repetitive, or both. Sanctions can only be imposed after an opportunity for a hearing.[266]

8A02 PREPARATION OF DOCUMENTS

COs are responsible for preparing all the documents in this chapter for their compliance evaluations or complaint investigations. To initiate the resolution process, a CO must review the findings and the bases for each of the findings with his or her immediate supervisor. The CO then submits the recommendation and draft documents to the supervisor for review and forwarding, through the appropriate channels, to the appropriate signatory official. All

[266] 41 CFR 60-1.26(b), 41 CFR 60-250.66, 41 CFR 60-300.66, 41 CFR 60-741.66.

documents require a signature by the appropriate OFCCP official.[267] Most notices discussed in this chapter require a CO to send the contractor a courtesy copy by e-mail or facsimile and by certified mail, return receipt requested.

8A03 COMPUTATION OF TIME

When computing the contractor's response date, the CO should begin counting from the day after the date on the return receipt requested form. If the response is received on a Saturday, Sunday or federal holiday, the actual date of receipt would be the next business day. If a CO does not receive a return receipt within 5 calendar days of mailing, the CO should contact the contractor to confirm the date of receipt and count the days from that date.

8A04 ORGANIZATION OF THIS CHAPTER

This chapter contains thirteen sections, Sections A through M. Section A provides basic terms that may be useful and Section B is the first substantive section in this chapter. Section B is an overview of the application of Show Cause Notices (SCNs) at various steps in compliance evaluations and complaint investigations, and the documents used to notify contractors and issue an SCN. Section B also reviews the notices used when a CO finds a violation during a compliance evaluation such as a Predetermination Notice (PDN) and a Notice of Violation (NOV). The Manual reviews documents used during compliance investigations, such as a Notice of Results of Investigation (NORI) and a Notification of Right-to-Sue, in this section. Among the other documents reviewed here are CAs, documents needed during the monitoring of CAs, and the notice to labor unions when a CA affects a Collective Bargaining Agreement (CBA).

Section C specifically focuses on the notice to unions, while Section D is dedicated to a full discussion of SCNs. Other section topics are listed below.

- Section E: Predetermination Notices
- Section F: Notice of Violations
- Section G: Conciliation
- Section H: Conciliation Agreements
- Section I: Post Conciliation Agreement Actions
- Section J: The 15-Day Notice
- Section K: Enforcement Recommendations
- Section L: Pre and Post Referral Issues Resulting in Enforcement Proceedings
- Section M: Types of Enforcment Proceedings

---

[267] See the "Signature Authority" section for each document for the official designated authority to sign specific documents. Information on signature authority for CAs is also in subsection 8H03.

8B OVERVIEW OF RESOLUTION AND ENFORCEMENT PROCEDURES AND DOCUMENTS

This section contains flow charts showing the normal sequence of documents COs use in compliance evaluations and complaint investigations. There is a chart for each of the following topics:

- Use of a SCN at Desk Audit (Supply & Service Compliance Evaluations);
- Use of documents in the Onsite and Offsite Phases of Compliance Evaluations (Supply & Service, and Construction);
- Use of documents in Complaint Investigations; and
- Use of documents in Monitoring Conciliation Agreements (CAs).

The text accompanying these charts references the sections of this Manual where there are detailed discussions of the particular types of violations and of the relevant notices or resolution documents. This includes the location of the sample letters, notices or documents.

8B00 GENERAL USE OF A SHOW CAUSE NOTICE

As used in this section, the term SCN includes, as appropriate, an Amended Show Cause Notice (ASCN). An ASCN is used when a CO issues an SCN to the contractor and later finds additional unresolved violations, or finds that some but not all violations were cited in error. The ASCN identifies all the unresolved or current violations.[268]

Also be aware that if a contractor properly asserts in response to an SCN or ASCN that the CO erroneously issued the notice, the CO must send a letter to the contractor or its representative rescinding the SCN or ASCN.[269]

8B01 USE OF A SHOW CAUSE NOTICE AT THE DESK AUDIT (Supply & Service Compliance Evaluations)

COs must recommend issuance of an SCN, as described in Section 8D, at the desk audit stage if the contractor:

- fails to submit an AAP as required by one or more of the following authorities: EO 11246, Section 503, or Section 4212;[270]
- fails to submit an acceptable AAP as required by one or more of the following authorities: EO 11246, Section 503, or Section 4212;[271]

[268] See subsection 8D04 – When to Use an Amended Show Cause Notice.

[269] See subsection 8D08 – Rescission of a Show Cause Notice.

[270] See Section 1C – Receipt of AAPs and Support Data, subsection 8D01 – When a Show Cause Notice is Required, and Letter L-18 – Show Cause Notice: Failure to Submit EO 11246, Section 503 or Section 4212 AAPs.

- fails to submit employment activity data or other information requested in the Scheduling Letter;[272] or

- fails to submit acceptable employment activity data and then fails to correct it.[273]

The SCN allows the contractor 30 calendar days from receiving the notice to resolve the violation. Specific actions will be taken by the CO, as described below, depending on whether the contractor resolves the violations.

- *Contractor Does Not Resolve Violation.* If the violation is not resolved within the 30-day show cause period, or during a reasonable extension, the CO should recommend enforcement. Enforcement is discussed in detail in Section 8K, Enforcement Recommendation.

- *Contractor Resolves Violation.* If the contractor resolves the violations within the 30-day show cause period by, for example, submitting a reasonable EO 11246, Section 503 or Section 4212 AAP, the review continues with a review of the AAP or moves to the onsite phase. Upon completion of the review, the CO must state the desk audit violation, along with any other violation the CO identified onsite and offsite, and agreed upon a remedy in a CA.[274]

---

[271] See subsections 8D01– When a Show Cause Notice is Required, Section 1F – Review of AAPs for Acceptability, and Letters L-19 – Show Cause Notice: Failure to Submit an Acceptable EO 11246, Section 503 or Section 4212, and L-19a – Sample Enclosure to Letter L-19.

[272] See Section 1C – Receipt of AAPs and Support Data for Desk Audit, subsection 8D01 – When a Show Cause Notice is Required, and Letter L-20 – Show Cause Notice: Failure to Submit Employment Activity and/or Compensation Data for Desk Audit.

[273] See Section 1G – Review of Executive Order Support Data for Acceptability, Section 1H – Review of Section 503 and Section 4212 Support Data for Acceptability, subsection 8D01 – When a Show Cause Notice is Required, and Letter L-21– Show Cause Notice: Failure to Submit Corrected Employment Activity and/or Compensation Data for Desk Audit.

[274] See subsection 8D07(b) – Contractor Response: Resolution in CA.

USE OF SHOW CAUSE NOTICE AT DESK AUDIT

(Supply and Service Compliance Evaluation)

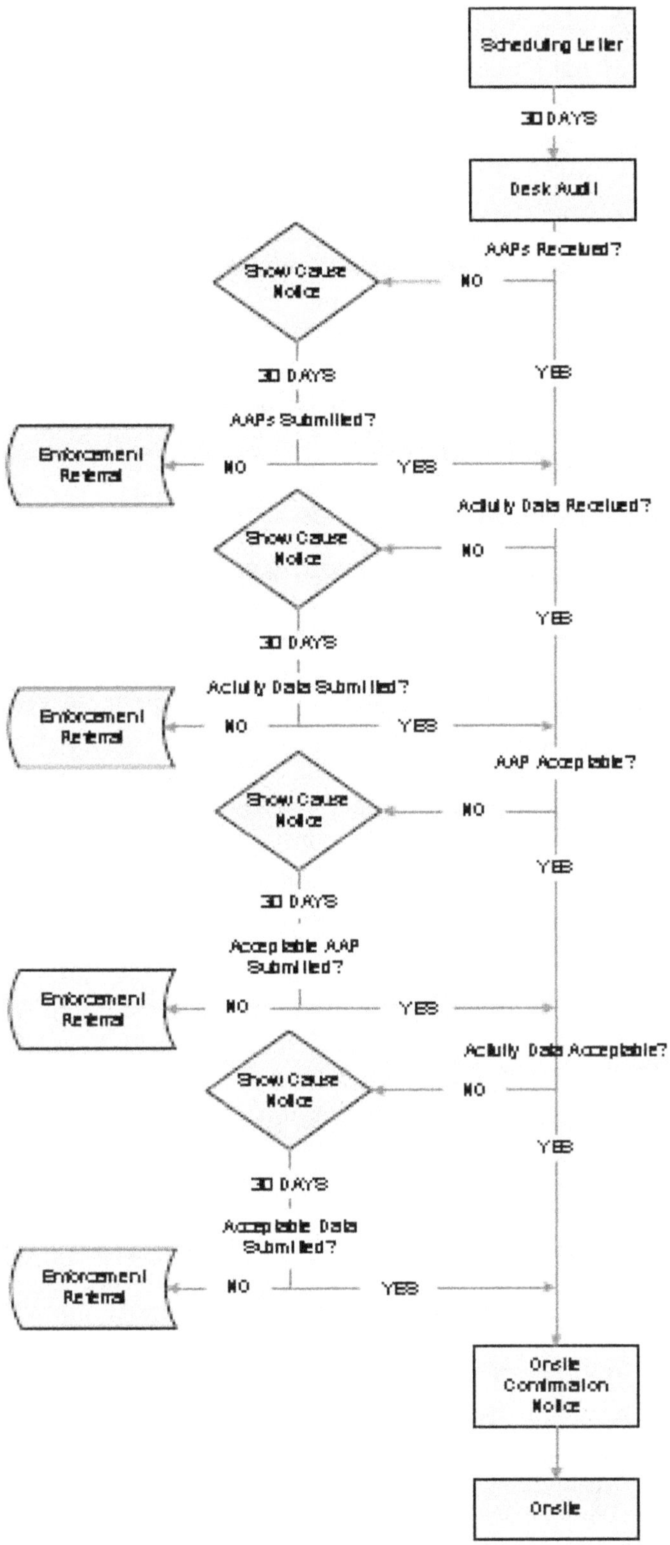

8B02 DOCUMENTS USED IN THE ONSITE AND OFFSITE PHASES OF COMPLIANCE EVALUATIONS (Supply & Service and Construction)

Based on the nature of the issue or violation in the onsite and offsite phases, in both Supply & Service and construction evaluations, COs will use different forms or documents. Below is a review of the use of SCNs, PDNs, NOVs and notices to labor unions in various situations.

a. *Denial of Access.* If a contractor denies access to its premises, records or other information necessary to conduct an onsite or offsite review, the CO must issue an SCN or proceed directly to an enforcement recommendation.[275]

b. *Interference with OFCCP.* If a contractor's representative harasses or intimidates a representative of OFCCP during the course of an onsite or offsite review or unreasonably interferes with the review process, the CO must issue an SCN or proceed directly to an enforcement recommendation.[276]

c. *Finding of a Violation.* If the CO identifies a violation under any of OFCCP's three laws during an onsite or offsite review, the type of notice the CO must issue depends on the nature of the violations.

   - *Pattern or practice employment discrimination violation.* If the CO identifies a pattern or practice of employment discrimination the following notices may be appropriate:

     - *Predetermination Notice.* A CO may issue a PDN to the contractor that describes the pattern or practice issue as well as any other violations found and offers the contractor the opportunity to respond.[277] A PDN is not required; OFCCP may proceed directly to an NOV incorporating the pattern or practice finding.

     - *Notice of Violation.* If the contractor does not adequately respond to the preliminary pattern or practice finding, or where OFCCP chooses to proceed without first issuing a PDN, a CO issues an NOV.[278] This notice incorporates both the pattern or practice finding and any other violation and invites the contractor to participate in the conciliation process.

   - *Nonpattern or nonpractice employment discrimination violation.* If all violations a CO identifies are nonpattern or nonpractice, such as those involving individual instances of discrimination or affirmative action, the CO typically does not use a PDN. Rather, the CO gives the contractor an initial written notice of the findings in an NOV.

---

[275] See subsection 8D01– When a Show Cause Notice is Required.
[276] See subsection 8D02 – When a Show Cause Notice is Not Required.
[277] See Section 8E – Predetermination Notice; Letter L-27– Predetermination Notice.
[278] See Section 8F – Notice of Violation; Letter L-28 – Notice of Violation.

d. *Notice to Labor Union.* If a proposed remedy for a violation included in an NOV requires a change in or otherwise affects a provision of a CBA between the contractor and a labor union, or requires the award of retroactive seniority where the CBA governs, the CO must notify the union of the violation and invite the union to participate in the conciliation.[279]

e. *Unresolved Violation.* If, after issuing an NOV, reasonable conciliation efforts to resolve all violations fail, the CO issues an SCN for unresolved violations.[280] The SCN allows the contractor 30 calendar days from receipt of the notice to resolve the violations.

- *Contractor Does Not Resolve Violation.* If the contractor does not resolve the violations within the 30-day show cause period, or with a reasonable extension, the CO must recommend enforcement.

- *Contractor Resolves Violation.* A CA must include resolution of any material violations of any of OFCCP's three programs.[281] When a contractor executes a CA, the CO uses the Notice of Review Completion – Major Deficiencies Resolved in a CA letter. If the CO issues an SCN, the CO uses Letter L-32, Closure Letter for Substantive Violations (with a Rescission of a Show Cause Notice). If the CO does not issue a SCN, the CO uses Letter L-33, Closure Letter for Substantive Violations (no Show Cause Notice issued).

---

[279] See Section 8C – Notice to Labor Union.

[280] See subsection 8D01– When a Show Cause Notice is Required, Letter L-22 – Show Cause Notice: Unresolved Violations, and Letter L-22a – Sample Enclosure to Letter L-22.

[281] See Section 8H – Conciliation Agreements.

ONSITE/OFFSITE COMPLIANCE EVALUATIONS

(Supply and Service and Construction)

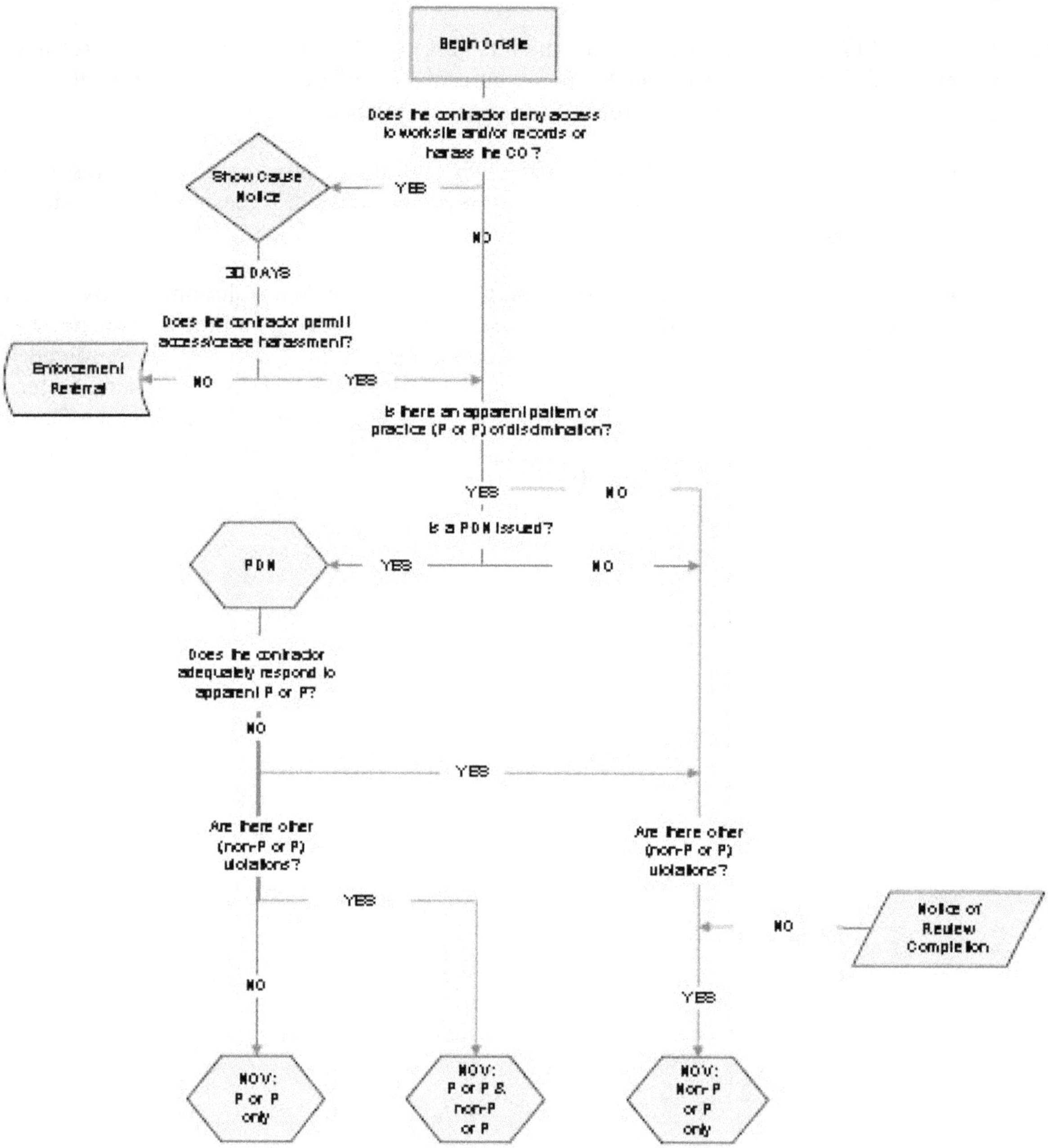

ONSITE/OFFSITE COMPLIANCE EVALUATIONS

(Supply and Service and Construction)
(continued)

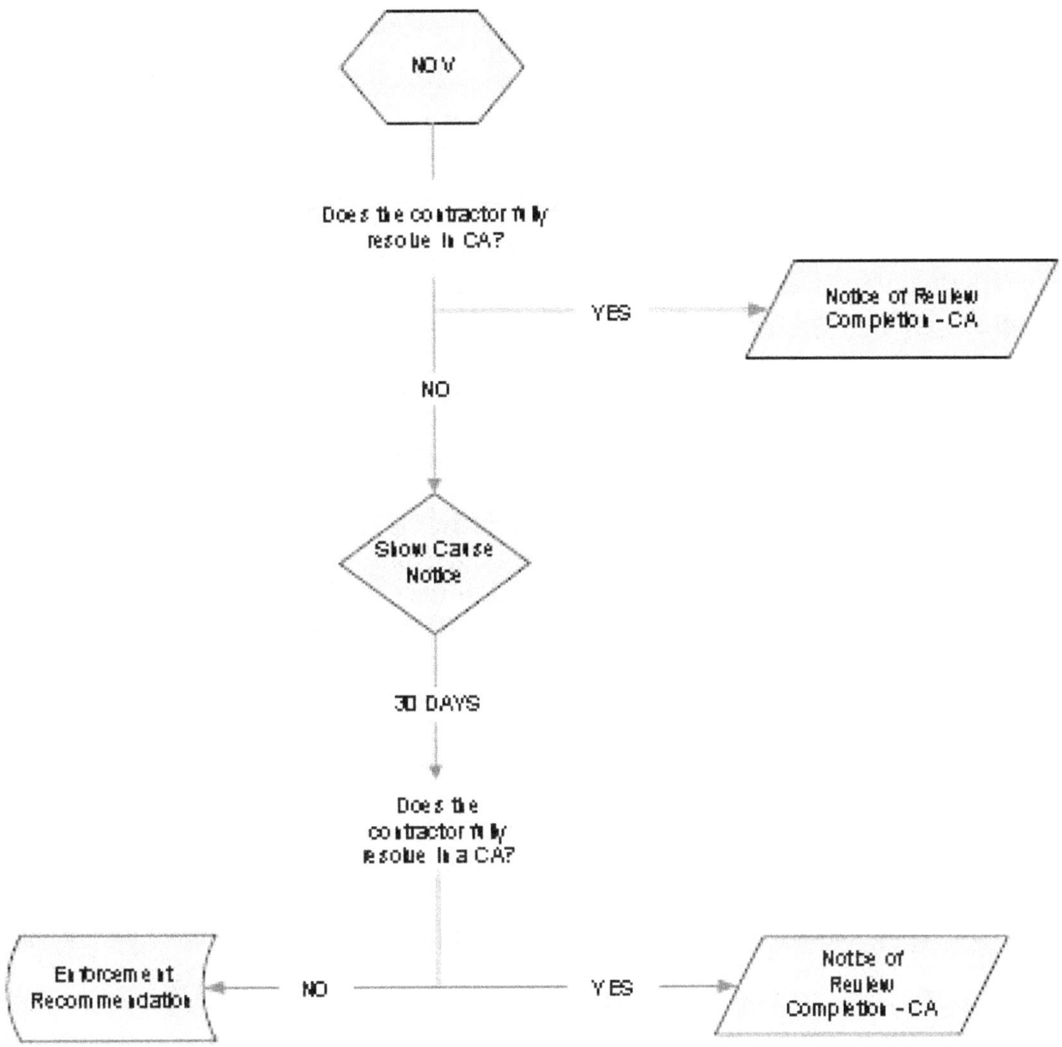

8B03 DOCUMENTS USED IN COMPLAINT INVESTIGATIONS

Based on the nature of the issue or violation in a complaint investigation, COs will use different forms or documents. Below is a review of the use of SCNs, NORIs, Notification of Right-to-Sue and notices to labor unions in various situations.

a. *Denial of Access.* If a contractor denies access to its premises, records or other information necessary to conduct an investigation of a complaint, OFCCP may issue an SCN or proceed directly to an enforcement recommendation.[282]

b. *Interference with OFCCP.* If a contractor's representative intimidates or harasses a representative of OFCCP during the course of a complaint investigation or unreasonably interferes with the investigation, a CO may issue an SCN or proceed directly to an enforcement recommendation.

c. *Transmittal of Investigation Findings.* COs transmit the findings of a complaint investigation to the complainant and the contractor through the NORI. The contractor and complainant are issued a NORI-Violation if a complaint investigation results in a finding of a violation and the complaint is not resolved.[283] In this notice, OFCCP offers to meet with the contractor to attempt to resolve the violations through conciliation. If the CO finds "no violation," he or she issues the contractor and complainant a NORI-No Violation.[284]

d. *Notification of Right-to-Sue.* If a complaint is dual filed under Section 503 of the Rehabilitation Act, as amended, and the Americans with Disabilities Act, as amended; or under EO 11246, as amended, and Title VII of the Civil Rights Act of 1964, as amended, and there is no violation finding, the Notice of Right-to-Sue accompanies the notification of closure.[285] In addition, if a complainant requests a Notice of Right-to-Sue in writing before 180 calendar days passes and the Regional Director (or designee) can foresee that the investigation will extend beyond the 180th day, the Regional Director (or designee) will issue the notice within 10 calendar days to the complainant.[286]

e. *Notice to Labor Union.* If make-whole relief for the complainant requires a change in or otherwise affects a provision of a CBA between the contractor and a labor union, COs notify the union of the violation and invite the union to participate in the conciliation.[287] An example of make-whole relief that might require a change in the CBA is an award of retroactive seniority.

f. *Conciliation Agreement.* This binding agreement is the result of negotiations between the CO and contractor to resolve findings of noncompliance.

---

[282] See subsection 8D01 and 8D02.

[283] See Letter L-17– Notification of Results of Investigation: Notification of Violation.

[284] See Letters L-13 – Notification of Results of Investigation: Notification of No Violation, and Letter L-14 – Notification of Results of Investigation and Notice of Right-to-Sue Under Title 1 of the ADA or Title VII of the Civil Rights Act of 1964.

[285] See subsection 6J02 – Closure of Complaint with No Violation.

[286] See subsection 6J03 – Closure of Complaint and Issuance of "Notice of Right-to-Sue."

[287] See Section 8C – Notice to Labor Union.

- *Conciliation Successful.* The contractor must resolve any finding of violation in a complaint investigation, whether individual or class, under any of the three OFCCP programs in a CA.

- *Conciliation Unsuccessful.* If after reasonable time and effort OFCCP and the contractor cannot agree to the resolution of the identified violation, the CO must issue a SCN. If the contractor and OFCCP do not reach a settlement within the 30 calendar day show cause period, or reasonable extensions thereof, the CO must recommend enforcement.[288]

---

[288] See Section 8K – Enforcement Recommendations.

COMPLAINT INVESTIGATION
(EO 11246 & Section 503)

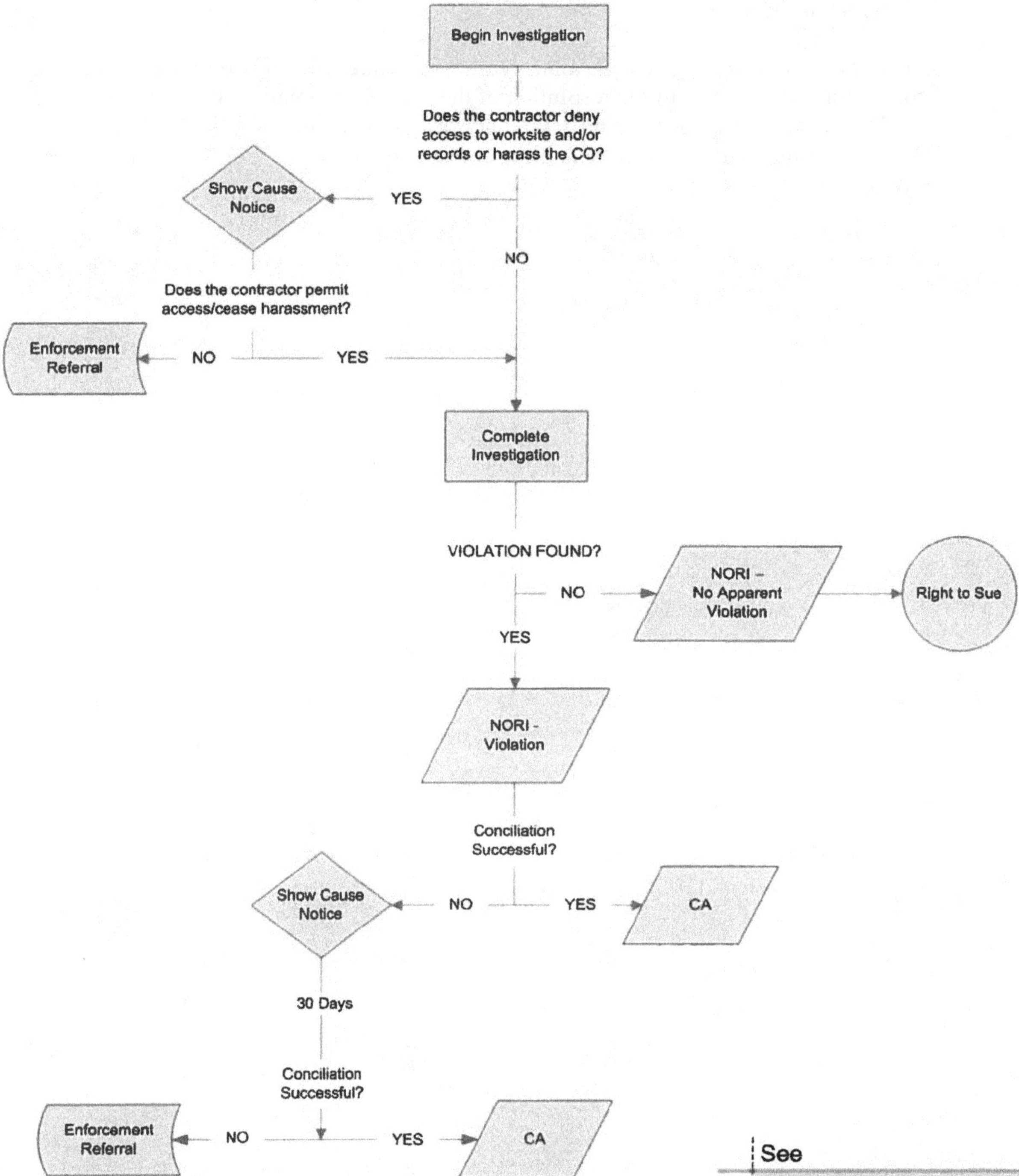

See
Chapter 7: Complaints
Section J: Resolution of the Complaint

COMPLAINT INVESTIGATION

(Section 4212)

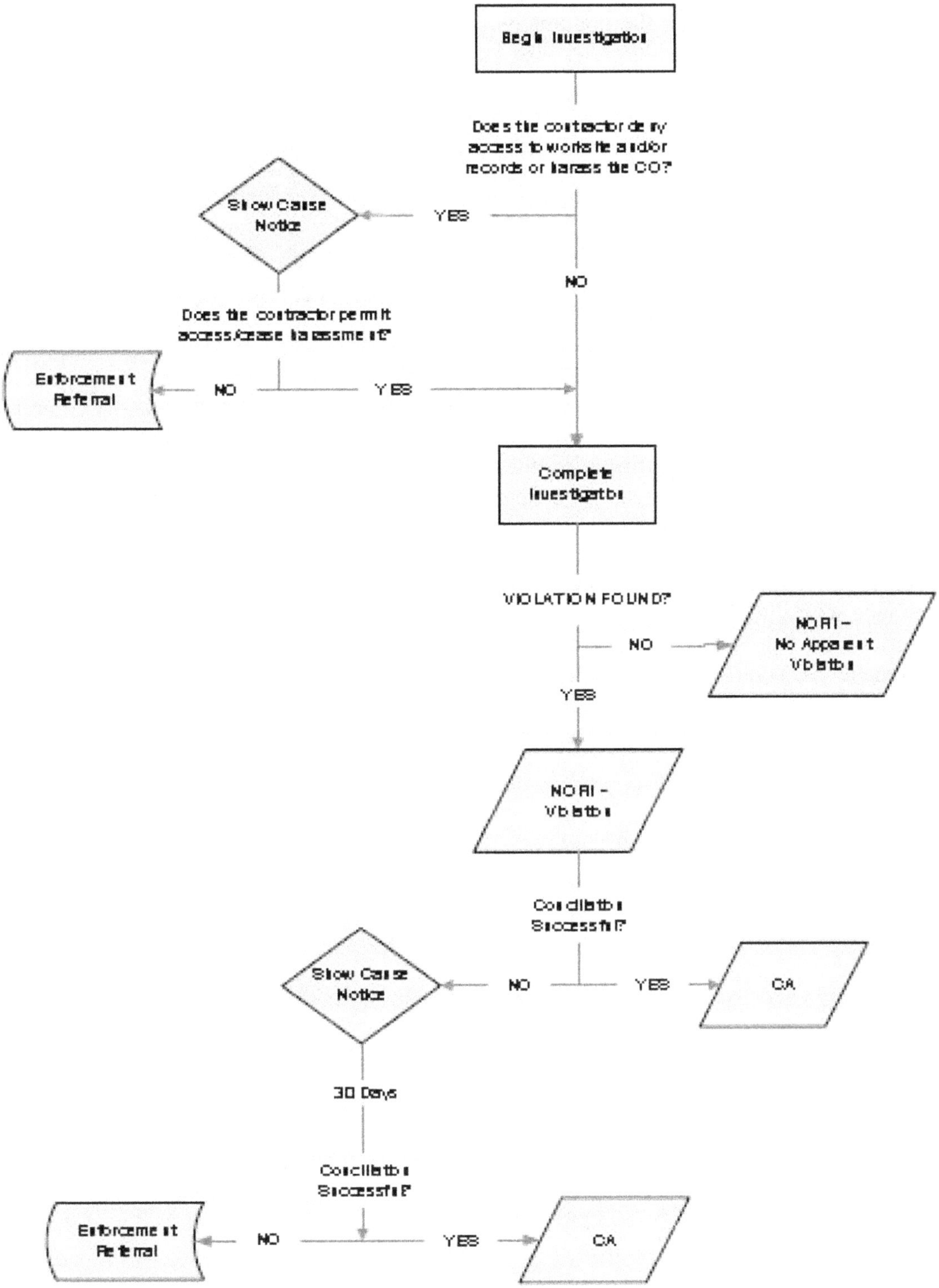

8B04 DOCUMENTS USED IN MONITORING CONCILIATION AGREEMENTS

Once executed, a CA is monitored by the CO and the contractor submits progress reports for review. This subsection reviews the documents involved in monitoring a CA such as a 15-Day Notice.

a. *Contractor Does Not Submit a Progress Report.* If a contractor fails to submit a progress report due under a CA or if the CO's review of such a report shows a violation of the CA, the contractor has violated or breached the CA. The following actions are taken:

   - *No Irreparable Injury.* In a no irreparable harm case, the CO issues the contractor a 15-Day Notice. The Notice provides 15 calendar days for the contractor to respond. The notice states the violations and summarizes the supporting evidence. The CO sends the notice by e-mail or facsimile and certified mail, return receipt requested.[289]

   - *Irreparable Injury.* When the CO alleges irreparable injury as a result of a CA violation, the CO does not issue a 15-Day Notice. Rather, OFCCP verbally informs the contractor of OFCCP's intent to proceed immediately to enforcement. This verbal notice is then followed by a written confirmation the CO sends by e-mail or facsimile and certified mail, return receipt requested. The Regional Director gives verbal notification. Prior to giving verbal notification, the Regional Director will obtain appropriate approval.[290]

b. *Enforcement Recommendation.* If the contractor does not demonstrate in writing that it is in compliance with the CA or if contractor does not resolve the breach within the 15 calendar day period, or reasonable extensions thereof, the CO must recommend the matter for enforcement. In such a situation, there is no need for the CO to issue an SCN. Also, in enforcement proceedings alleging a breach of CA, the agency seeks enforcement of the terms of the CA and is not required to present proof of the original violations that led to the CA.

---

[289] See subsection 8J01– Procedure Where No Irreparable Injury Exists.

[290] See subsection 8J02 – Procedure Where Irreparable Injury Exists.

CONCILIATION AGREEMENT (CA) MONITORING

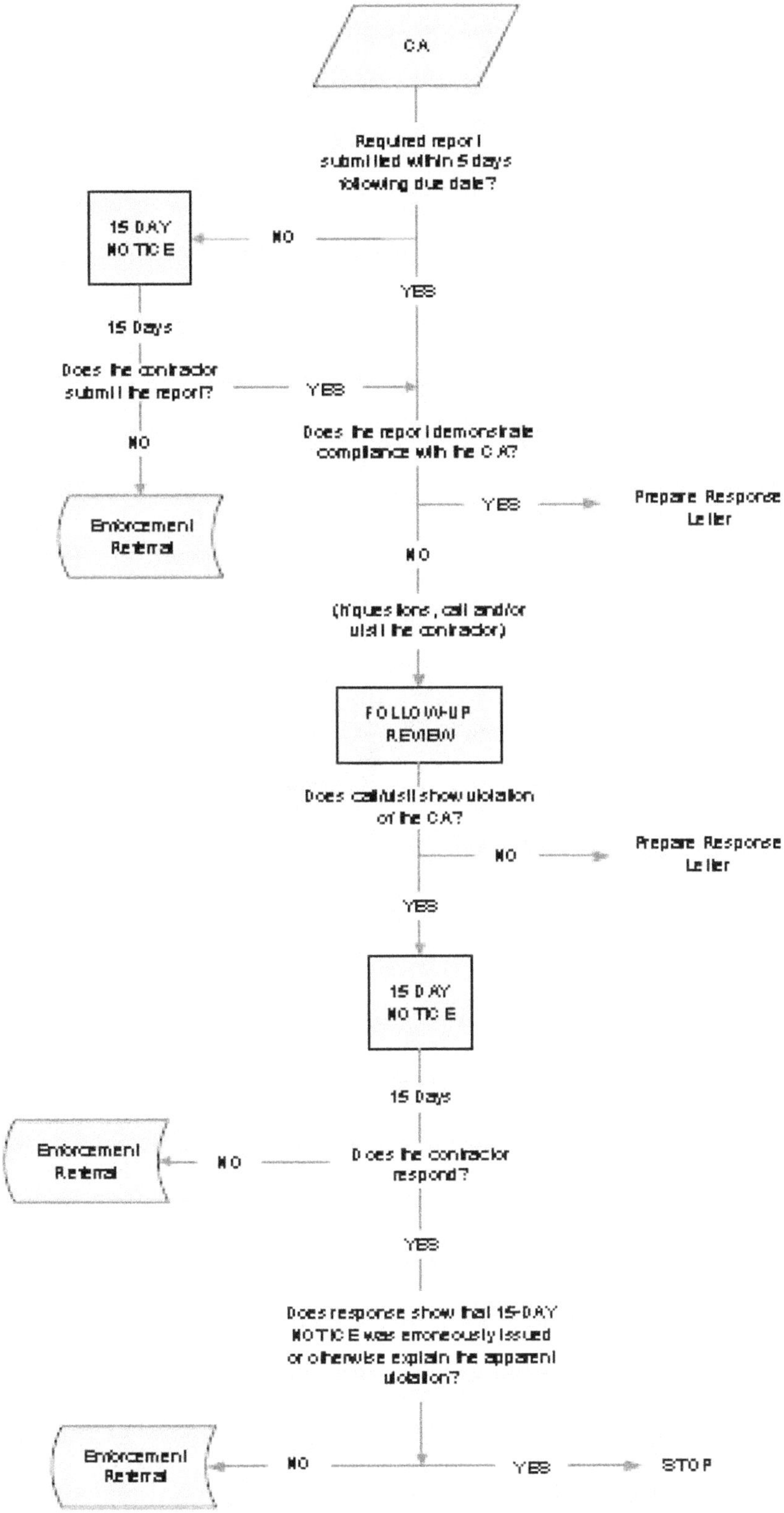

8C NOTICE TO THE LABOR UNION OF A PROPOSED REMEDY

This section reviews when a notice to the labor union of a remedy that affects a CBA is required and the timing for COs providing that notice. It also provides COs information and tools related to the:

- content of the notice,
- addressees for the notice,
- signatory on the notice, and
- union responses to the notice.

The first subsection reviews the use of a notice to the union.

8C00 WHEN TO USE A NOTICE TO THE LABOR UNION

Notice to a labor union is required when a CO proposes a remedy that affects the CBA. When a CO proposes a remedy for a violation that is identified in the course of a compliance evaluation or complaint investigation that requires a change in or otherwise affects a CBA between the contractor and a labor union, they must notify the union in writing of the violation and invite the union to participate in the conciliation process. A remedy affecting a CBA is one requiring the modification, deletion or exception to an existing provision, or the addition of a new provision. The following are examples of some remedies that may impact the terms of a current CBA:

- retroactive seniority;
- temporary suspension of promotion or transfer provisions, or both; or
- institution of or modification to a job posting process that applies to a workforce, job group or position covered by the CBA.

The CO sends this notice to the union at the same time he or she sends the NOV to the contractor in a compliance evaluation. The CO sends the notice to the union at the same time he or she sends the NORI to the contractor in a complaint investigation.

8C01 CONTENTS OF THE LABOR UNION NOTICE

If the proposed remedy affects a CBA, a CO's written notice to the union will:

- state the violation;
- describe the portions of the proposed remedy which may affect the CBA; and
- invite the union to participate in negotiation of the portion(s) of the proposed remedy that may impact the CBA.

8C02 WHO RECEIVES THE LABOR UNION NOTICE

The CO sends the notice to the president of the applicable union local by e-mail or facsimile and by certified mail, return receipt requested; a copy of the notice is also sent to the contractor.

8C03 SIGNATURE AUTHORITY

The Regional Director, or his or her designee, has signature authority for the notice to the union.

8C04 UNION'S RESPONSE TO THE NOTICE

Subsections 7C04 and 7C05 provide further background and guidance on union involvement in the conciliation process.[291] Although Subsection 7C04 deals specifically with retroactive seniority as a remedy affecting a CBA, the description of procedures there are equally applicable to other remedies affecting a CBA. Below are the two typical union responses in the conciliation context:

a. *Union Participation in Conciliation.* If the union agrees to participate in conciliation, then it may participate on issues affecting the CBA. If conciliation is successful, the CO should ask the president of the union local to sign the CA.[292]

b. *Union Refuses to Participate or Refuses to Sign CA.* If the union refuses to participate in conciliation, or participates but will not agree to the proposed relief affecting the CBA by signing the CA, the CO will not include the non-admissions clause in the CA. The non-admissions clause is in paragraph 3 of standard CA text, as described in subsection 8H0l. Under such circumstances, the CO shall amend paragraph 1 of the standard CA text to reference that the union was invited to participate and its refusal to participate or to sign.[293]

8D SHOW CAUSE NOTICE

A SCN is a letter issued to the contractor ordering it to show cause why enforcement proceedings should not be instituted. The SCN requires the contractor to come into compliance within 30 calendar days or the CO will recommend the commencement of enforcement proceedings.

8D00 PROGRAM APPLICABILITY

SCNs pertain to violations of EO 11246,[294] Section 503,[295] and Section 4212.[296]

---

[291] COs may also find it helpful to consult their regional SOL on these issues.
[292] See subsection 8H03 – Signature Authority.
[293] See subsection 8H0l – Contents of a Conciliation Agreement.
[294] See 41 CFR 60-1.28, 60-2.2(c) and 60-4.8.
[295] See 41 CFR 60-741.64.
[296] See 41 CFR 250.64 and 300.64.

8D01 WHEN A SHOW CAUSE NOTICE IS REQUIRED

As a general rule, COs must issue an SCN whenever a contractor violates EO 11246, Section 503, Section 4212 or their implementing regulations in order to proceed with an enforcement action. In certain circumstances, OFCCP may proceed directly to enforcement without issuing an SCN. This is discussed later in subsection 8D02, When a Show Cause Notice is Not Required.

COs issue SCNs in all cases after conciliation fails; however, SCNs can be issued to a supply and service contractor at the Desk Audit stage. COs issue an SCN at the Desk Audit stage when the contractor fails to provide the records, information or data requested in the scheduling letter. For example, a CO must issue an SCN when a contractor:

- fails to submit an AAP required by one or more of the authorities enforced by OFCCP: EO 11246, Section 503 or Section 4212;[297]
- fails to submit an AAP that substantially complies with regulatory requirements under one or more of the authorities enforced by OFCCP: EO 11246, Section 503 or Section 4212;[298]
- fails to submit employment activity or compensation data, or both;[299] or
- fails to submit corrected data after providing employment activity data or compensation data, or both, that are incomplete or inaccurate.[300]

COs also issue an SCN when a contractor refuses to provide access to its premises for an onsite review.[301]

8D02 WHEN A SHOW CAUSE NOTICE IS NOT REQUIRED

OFCCP may proceed directly to an enforcement recommendation without issuing an SCN in certain situations such as when a contractor intimidates or harasses an OFCCP agent or unreasonably interferes with a complaint investigation or compliance review. If the CO believes that the circumstances warrant moving directly to an enforcement recommendation without issuing an SCN, his or her District Director must seek the approval of the Regional Director.

A CO is not required to issue an SCN when a contractor violates a CA. Under such circumstances, OFCCP shall issue a 15-Day Notice.[302]

---

[297] See Section 1C – Receipt of AAPs and Support Data, and Letter L-18– Show Cause Notice: Failure to Submit EO11246, Section 503 or Section 4212 AAPs.
[298] See Section 1F – Review of AAPs for Acceptability, Letter L-19 – Show Cause Notice: Failure to Submit EO11246, Section 503 or Section 4212 AAPs That Satisfy Regulatory Requirements, and Letter L-19a – Sample Enclosure to Letter L-19.
[299] See Subsection 2C02 and Letter L-20 – Show Cause Notice: Failure to Submit Employment Activity and/or Compensation Data for Desk Audit.
[300] See Subsections 2G0l and Letter L-21 – Show Cause Notice: Failure to Submit Corrected Employment Activity and/or Compensation Data.
[301] See Letter L-25 – Show Cause Notice: Denial of Access.
[302] See Section 8J –The 15-Day Notice.

8D03 CONTENTS OF A SHOW CAUSE NOTICE

An SCN, including an ASCN, may have two parts, the notice and an enclosure; each is described below.

a. *Notice.* The Notice itself, which states the consequences under the regulations, of not coming into compliance.

b. *Enclosure.* An enclosure states the violation and the required remedies. The statement of the violation should include appropriate regulatory citations. COs are reminded that if a particular violation is not specifically named in the regulations, it is sufficient to clearly describe the violation and cite, as applicable. This approach also applies to the nondiscrimination and affirmative action provisions of the appropriate EEO clauses. The appropriate format of an SCN will depend on the particular situation. Subsection 8D01, which lists violations for which COs should issue an SCN, includes references to the letters that provide the format for each type of violation.

8D04 WHEN TO USE AN AMENDED SHOW CAUSE NOTICE

When a CO issues an SCN and subsequently identifies additional violations, the CO must issue an ASCN incorporating all violations, including the original ones. The CO may issue more than one ASCN. For example:

- *Supply and Service Contractors.* If a CO issues an SCN at desk audit for failure to submit an EO 11246 AAP, and the contractor then submits an unreasonable EO 11246 AAP, the CO may issue an ASCN citing both the initial failure to submit and the subsequent unreasonable submission. If the contractor then submits a reasonable EO 11246 AAP, but the CO identifies additional violations during the onsite review, the CO may issue a second ASCN citing all violations to date.[303]

Just as an ASCN includes all violations, including those the CO cited in the original SCN, the CO uses a single CA to resolve all violations regardless of when in the review the CO identified a particular violation.

A sample ASCN is given in Letter L-24. An ASCN is sent to the same people as an SCN, has the same signature authority as the original SCN unless the Regional Director delegates otherwise; and follows the same procedures concerning contractor responses.[304]

8D05 WHO RECEIVES A SHOW CAUSE NOTICE OR AMENDED SHOW CAUSE NOTICE

[303] The second ASCN is issued after issuing, as applicable, a Predetermination Notice or a Notice of Violation or both. Additional information on this is in Sections 8E and 8F.

[304] See subsections 8D05, 8D06, and 8D07.

COs address the SCN, including an ASCN, to the top official at the establishment of the corporation unless the establishment and corporate office are the same. A copy of the SCN is sent to the CEO. If the contractor submits a written request that the CO provide a copy of the review or investigation correspondence to an outside representative such as an outside counsel or consultant, the CO will also send a copy to the designated representative.[305] When the CO provides a copy to a corporate CEO, other contractor official or a designated representative, the CO should include a "cc:" line on all copies indicating the people to whom he or she sent the Notice.

COs always send SCNs or ASCNs by e-mail or facsimile and certified mail, return receipt requested.

8D06 SIGNATURE AUTHORITY

The Regional Directors, or their designees, have signature authority for an SCN and ASCN.

8D07 CONTRACTOR'S RESPONSE

This subsection covers the period of time the contractor has to respond to an SCN and ASCN, and resolution of the violations through a CA.

a. *Period for Response.* The contractor has 30 calendar days from the date it receives the SCN or ASCN to either adequately respond to or resolve the violations the CO specified in the Notice.

b. *Resolution in CA.* Because violations generating an SCN or ASCN are usually significant, a Conciliation Agreement is used to show how the violations were resolved. This is the case unless the contractor is able to demonstrate that it is exempt from OFCCP's requirements or that OFCCP's allegations are incorrect. The contractor may, therefore, take any of the following actions in response to an SCN or ASCN:

- *Contractor Resolves the Violation.* The contractor may resolve a violation by:
    - entering into a written CA that remedies the violation, including the provision of make-whole relief for any victims of discrimination;[306]
    - demonstrating that it is exempt from OFCCP's requirements;
    - demonstrating that OFCCP's allegations are incorrect.
- *Contractor Does Not Resolve the Violation.* If the contractor does not resolve all of the violations stated in the SCN or ASCN, the CO will normally recommend the initiation of enforcement proceedings as described in Section 8K of the chapter. Under these

[305] See subsection 2B00(b).
[306] See Section 7B.

circumstances, the Regional Director must authorize any decision not to refer the contractor for enforcement and must document the reason for the decision in the case file.

8D08 RESCISSION OF A SHOW CAUSE NOTICE

This subsection reviews when a CO can rescind an SCN, the contents of the rescission, who signs the notices and who should receive notice. Each item is reviewed below.

a. *When to Use an SCN Rescission Letter.* A Show Cause Notice will not be rescinded merely because the contractor agrees to comply in the future or corrects violations. See 41 CFR 60-1.20 (b), 604.8 and *Castillo v. Usery*, 14 Fair Empl. Prac. Cas. 1240, 1247 (N.D.Cal. 1976). A CO may rescind an SCN or ASCN only if the SCN or ASCN was issued erroneously, for example:

   - the contractor demonstrates that it is exempt from OFCCP's requirements; or

   - the contractor demonstrates that each of OFCCP's allegations is incorrect.

b. *Contents.* The notice rescinding the SCN or ASCN acknowledges that the Notice was issued and the date it was issued, the authority under which it was issued, and that it was subsequently determined that the SCN or ASCN was erroneously issued and is being rescinded for one of the above reasons, or other appropriate reason. Letter L-26 provides a sample format for rescinding an SCN or ASCN.

c. *Who Receives the Rescission Letter.* COs send the letter rescinding an SCN or ASCN to the same people who received the original notice.

d. *Signature Authority.* The Regional Director, or his or her designee, signs the letter rescinding an SCN or ASCN.

8E PREDETERMINATION NOTICE

A PDN is the letter a CO may use to notify the contractor of the preliminary finding that the contractor engaged in a pattern or practice of discrimination. The PDN states the basis for the preliminary findings and offers the contractor the opportunity to respond. This Section covers when COs use a PDN, the contents of the notice, who receives the notices, and who has signature authority for issuing the notice.

8E00 USE OF A PREDETERMINATION NOTICE

COs may use the PDN in pattern or practice cases following compliance evaluations conducted under EO 11246, Section 503 and Section 4212. COs should not use the PDN ifthere are only recordkeeping or affirmative action deficiencies such as a failure to meet the standards for AAP acceptability;[307]

A PDN is not typically used where there are only individual discrimination violations.

After a CO identifies a potentially discriminatory employment pattern or practice, the CO must investigate the matter until the file contains sufficient information to establish discrimination absent an adequate explanation by the contractor. At that point, the CO may notify the contractor of the alleged discrimination through a PDN, or may proceed directly to issuing an NOV, in consultation with their supervisor.

8E01 CONTENTS OF A PREDETERMINATION NOTICE

The PDN typically has three parts: a description of the pattern or practice of discrimination, a list of other unresolved violations and an offer of an opportunity to respond to the PDN. These three parts are described in more detail below. Letter L-27, Predetermination Notice, is a sample form letter for a PDN.

a. *Description of the Discrimination.* In this, the first part of the PDN, a CO describes the discrimination, identifies the affected class, identifies the employment action giving rise to the finding of a violation and identifies the basis for the liability determination (e.g., disparate treatment in the selection of minority technicians). The PDN should also include facts and the results of analyses that support the alleged violation and recommended remedies.

b. *Other Unresolved Issues.* After describing the discrimination, a CO identifies and addresses other unresolved AAP deficiencies, for example, minor deficiencies that did not result in an "unacceptable AAP" finding. A CO also identifies and addresses recordkeeping and technical violations like the contractor's failure to post required notices.

c. *Offer the Contractor the Opportunity to Respond.* The PDN offers the contractor an opportunity to respond in writing by a specific date. In determining how much time to allow, a CO must consider the complexity of the issues, the length of the review and the amount of information the contractor has already provided during the compliance evaluation and offsite review. The time allowed, however, should not normally exceed 30 calendar days.

If after the receipt of a PDN, the contractor does not respond by the indicated date, or obtain an extension, the CO will issue an NOV.[308] The NOV will indicate that the contractor did not rebut the pattern or practice issue.

8E02 WHO RECEIVES A PREDETERMINATION NOTICE

COs address PDNs to the top official at the establishment with a copy to the CEO of the corporation unless the establishment and corporate office are the same. If the contractor submits

---

[307] See Sections 1F and 1H, and Letter L-27 – Predetermination Notice.
[308] See Section 8F.

a written request asking that the CO send a copy to an outside representative like an attorney or consultant, the CO will also send a copy to the designated representative. If the contractor requests that the CO provide the representative with the document, the CO should send a copy to the top official at the establishment and the CEO. When the CO provides copies to a corporate CEO, another contractor official or a designated representative, the CO will include a "cc:" line on all copies indicating the people to whom the Notice was sent.

COs always send a PDN by e-mail or facsimile and certified mail, return receipt requested.

8E03 SIGNATURE AUTHORITY

The Regional Director or his or her designee has signature authority for a PDN.

8E04 CONTRACTOR'S RESPONSE TO A PREDETEMINATION NOTICE

If the contractor does respond to the PDN, the CO should review the presented information. If there are issues requiring further investigation, the CO should request and analyze the additional information needed. The CO may conduct further investigation onsite or through an offsite review of records. The CO should not only consider whether the contractor's response is a nondiscriminatory explanation for the observed results, but also whether the response is pretext. A pretextual response may exist, for example, when the response is a logical explanation but it is not an accurate reflection of why the contractor behaved as it did. In evaluating the response, the CO should remember that unsupported contractor assertions, or assertions that the CO previously fully considered, are not sufficient to rebut findings of discrimination.

A contractor may respond to the PDN in one of three ways: with a full rebuttal of all the issues, with a partial rebuttal, or with an inadequate rebuttal.

a. *Contractor Adequately Rebuts.* If the contractor's response adequately rebuts all the issues the PDN raised, and there are no other remaining issues, the CO will acknowledge acceptance of the response and issue an appropriate closure document.[309]

b. *Some Issues Rebutted.* If the contractor's response adequately rebuts some, but not all of the preliminary findings raised in the PDN, the CO should issue an NOV accepting the response in those areas where it was sufficient but will address the remaining findings of violations with recommended corrective actions.

c. *All Issues Inadequately Rebutted.* If the contractor's response does not rebut any of the issues raised in the PDN, the CO should acknowledge the response, explain that it did not sufficiently rebut the preliminary finding and give an explanation, as appropriate, and incorporate the PDN's findings and recommended corrective actions into an NOV.

---

[309] See Letter L-4 – Notice of Closing: No Violation Found.

8F NOTICE OF VIOLATION

An NOV is a letter to a contractor notifying it that during a compliance evaluation a CO found violations of one or more of the authorities enforced by OFCCP; specifically, EO 11246, Section 503 or Section 4212. The NOV also notifies the contractor that it must take corrective actions to resolve the violations. The CO must include all violations requiring corrective action, including violations of technical requirements, along with the recommended corrective actions. The NOV will cite the contractor's failure to adequately justify its actions and note that OFCCP's investigation did not identify nondiscriminatory reasons to account for its findings.

8F00 WHEN TO USE A NOTICE OF VIOLATION

The NOV letter identifies the violations and describes the recommended corrective actions. COs issue an NOV when there is a pattern or practice violation, or if other violations are found.

a. *NOV for a Pattern or Practice Violation.* An NOV is issued when OFCCP determines, based on its investigation, that sufficient evidence of a pattern or practice violation exists. Where the CO has previously issued a PDN, the CO issues an NOV where the contractor does not respond to the PDN or its response does not substantially alter a CO's preliminary determination of pattern or practice employment discrimination.[310]

b. *NOV for Other Violations.* An NOV is issued when a CO identifies other violations, that are not pattern or practice issues, during the review. Examples of other violations include individual discrimination, lack of recordkeeping and lack of outreach and recruitment.

8F01 CONTENTS OF A NOTICE OF VIOLATION

NOVs, issued by COs, initiate the conciliation and resolution process. The NOV should request that the contractor contact the appropriate field office within 5 business days of receipt of the NOV. The NOV should identify the CO or other representative who the contractor should contact and provide the contact information, including telephone numbers. Letter L-28, Notice of Violation, is a sample form letter for an NOV. NOVs issued by COs for pattern or practice violations must:

1. *Restate the Problem.* Restate the problem, with any modifications resulting from the contractor's response. Include specific facts and, where applicable, the results of analyses that support the violations.

2. *Analyze the Response.* Analyze the contractor's response, giving the reasons why it does not substantially alter OFCCP's preliminary determination.

---

[310] See 8E00 – Use of a Predetermination Notice, "After a CO identifies a potentially discriminatory employment pattern or practice, the CO must investigate the matter until the file contains sufficient information to establish discrimination absent an adequate explanation by the contractor. At that point, the CO may notify the contractor of the alleged discrimination through a PDN, or may proceed directly to issuing an NOV, in consultation with their supervisor."

3. *Describe Remedy.* Describe the proposed remedy in class terms. Include scope of relief (e.g., all minorities rejected for Technician positions since (date) will be made whole by providing), the type of relief (e.g., job offers, back pay) and, when relevant, the time period involved (e.g., back pay from date of application to date of settlement).

4. *Cease Discrimination.* Specifically require termination of the identified discriminatory practice(s) if the contractor has not already terminated the practice.

5. *Require Conciliation Agreement.* Indicate that a Conciliation Agreement must incorporate the resolution of the pattern or practice violation (and any other violations included in the Notice).

COs also issue NOVs for violations other than pattern or practices violations and they must include a complete description of each nonpattern or nonpractice violation and deficiency, and a statement of the required corrective actions or remedies. The notice should state that a CA must include the resolution of the findings.

8F02 WHO RECEIVES THE NOTICE OF VIOLATION

COs address an NOV to the top official at the establishment with a copy to the CEO of the corporation, unless the establishment and corporate office are the same. If the contractor has requested in writing that the CO provide a copy of the review or investigation correspondence to an outside representative, the CO will also send a copy to the designated representative. When the CO provides copies to a corporate CEO, other contractor official, or a designated representative, the CO will include a "cc:" line on all copies indicating the people to whom the CO sent the Notice.

The CO always sends an NOV via e-mail or facsimile, and certified mail, return receipt requested.

8F03 SIGNATURE AUTHORITY

The Regional Director, or his or her designee, has signature authority for an NOV.

8F04 CONTRACTOR'S RESPONSE TO A NOTICE OF VIOLATION

If the contractor responds to the NOV, the CO should review and evaluate the response. See 8E04 above for further guidance on evaluating the contractor's response. If any unresolved violations remain, the CO will initiate conciliation.

8G CONCILIATION

Conciliation is a negotiation between a CO and a contractor to resolve findings of noncompliance. This Section provides general information on conciliation while Section H provides COs specific information on CAs.

8G00 BACKGROUND

A compliance evaluation is complete when the CO issues a closure letter to the contractor. Of course, if the CO found violations, the contractor must correct the violations before a CO can issue a closure letter. COs use the conciliation process to resolve violations with the contractor.

8G01 GENERAL

After a CO issues an NOV, he or she will attempt to reach an acceptable resolution of the violation findings through voluntary conciliation efforts with the contractor. Conciliation discussions may involve various methods of communication including the exchange of letters and e-mails, telephone conferences and in-person meetings. If these negotiations are successful, the CO will document the terms of the settlement in a formal CA. However, if in the opinion of the CO, the contractor fails to agree to a reasonable settlement, fails to do so in a timely fashion, or fails to negotiate in good faith, OFCCP may recommend the case for enforcement. In such circumstances, the CO must prepare a "recommendation to refer for enforcement" package and submit it to the Regional Office.

8H CONCILIATION AGREEMENTS

The CO uses CAs to resolve material or major substantive violations of any of OFCCP's three programs. Figure F-5, Standard Text for Conciliation Agreement, provides sample CA language.

8H00 WHEN TO USE A CONCILIATION AGREEMENT

The CO must normally use a CA whenever he or she properly issues an SCN. However, the following circumstances require resolution in a CA irrespective of whether a CO issued an SCN:

1. if a CO finds, in a compliance evaluation or complaint investigation, that the contractor discriminated, whether on an individual, or as a pattern or practice;
2. if a supply and service contractor did not submit an AAP pursuant to one or more of OFCCP's authorities; specifically, EO 11246, Section 503 or Section 4212;
3. if a supply and service contractor's employment activity data, provided based on a desk audit request, or the EO 11246 AAP that the contractor submitted do not reflect an acceptable effort;
4. if any contractor failed to demonstrate good faith effort, including situations where a supply and service contractor deviates substantially from its EO 11246, Section 503 and/or Section 4212 AAP,[311] or where a construction contractor fails to adequately

[311] See 41 CFR 60-2.2(c)(1).

document its implementation of its affirmative action obligations and refuses to remedy those violations.[312]

8H01 CONTENTS OF A CONCILIATION AGREEMENT

All CAs use the format described in this Section. It consists of a section captioned "Heading" followed by three parts:

- Part I contains General Provisions, including a Mandatory Enforcement Clause;
- Part II contains Specific Provisions such as a description of the violations and remedies involved in the particular review or investigation; and
- Part III contains Reporting requirements on the implementation of remedies specified in Part II.

CAs may be modified under certain circumstances and with certain prior approvals. Following is a discussion of when and how CAs may be modified, changes to the format of CAs, and provisions and clauses often found in CAs. Addenda A and B contain sample CA Agreements for compensation, hiring, recordkeeping, access, and other issues.

a. *Modifications to CA Format – General Provisions.*

- *Mandatory Enforcement Clause.* COs cannot modify the Mandatory Enforcement Clause in any way without the express prior approval of the Director of OFCCP.[313]
- *Nonadmissions Clause.* COs must omit this clause[314] if a remedy in Part II of the CA affects a collective bargaining agreement (CBA) and the union did not sign the CA. When this is the case, at the end of paragraph 1 of the standard CA text the CO should add, as applicable:
    - *Union Refuses to Participate in Conciliation of the CBA Issue.* On [*insert date*], Local [*insert union number*] of the [*insert name of union*] was invited to participate in conciliation of remedy items [*insert remedy numbers from the CA*] which affect the above identified union's collective bargaining agreement with [*insert name of contractor*], but on [*insert the date*] declined to do so.
    - *Union Participates But Does Not Sign the CA.* On [*insert date*] Local [*insert local number*] of the [*insert name of union*] participated in conciliation of remedy items [*insert remedy numbers from CA*] which affect the above identified union's collective bargaining agreement with [*name of contractor*], but on [*insert date*] declined to become a signatory to this Agreement.

---

[312] See Chapter 3– Construction Industry Compliance Program.
[313] See paragraph 9 of CA standard text in subsection 8H0l.
[314] See paragraph 3 of standard CA text, subsection 8H0l(e).

- *General Provisions.* Regional Directors have the authority to modify the General Provisions of a CA, other than the Mandatory Enforcement Clause, when necessary to fit the particular situation. No modification by the Regional Director can change the meaning or intent of the Mandatory Enforcement Clause. The Regional Director must obtain appropriate approval for any such modifications, except those noted in Subsection 8H0l(a), Nonadmissions Clause, before signing the CA.

b. *Modifications to CA Format – Specific Provisions and Reporting.* These two sections are intrinsically unique to the particular review or investigation and the CO should tailor the CA appropriately.

c. *No Restrictions on Publicizing.* No provision of a CA may preclude OFCCP from issuing a press release or otherwise publicizing the results of compliance actions.

d. *Standard CA Language.* The materials on the next four pages provide the standard text of a CA in the right column, and comments on that text in the left column.

Comments	Standard Text
Heading: Each CA will be headed: **If a union is a party to the CA, add its full name to the heading*	Conciliation Agreement Between the U.S. Department of Labor Office of Federal Contract Compliance Programs and [Legal Name of Contractor] [Legal Name and address of establishment covered by the Agreement]*
	PART I – *General Provisions*
Part I – General Provisions: This will be the first section of each CA.	1. This Agreement is between the Office of Federal Contract Compliance Programs (hereinafter OFCCP) and [*name and address of contractor*] (hereinafter [*abbreviation, if desired, of contractor's name*]).**
***If a union is a party to the CA, add its full name and in parentheses, if desired, an abbreviation of its name for use in the rest of the CA. If, per the note immediately below, OFCCP invited a union to be a party, but the union refused, see 8C04 for language to add to paragraph.*	2. The violations identified in this Agreement were found during a [*as applicable*, compliance evaluation or complaint investigation] of [*name of contractor*] which began on [*date*] [*add as applicable:* and they were specified in a Notice of Violation, Show Cause Notice, Amended Show Cause Notice issued (date)]. OFCCP alleges that [*name of contractor*] has violated [*as applicable*: Executive Order 11246, as amended; Section 503 of the Rehabilitation Act of 1973, as amended; and/or the Vietnam Era Veterans' Readjustment Assistance Act of 1974, as amended] and its implementing regulations at 41 CFR Chapter 60 due to the specific violations cited in Part II below.
****Paragraph 3 is called a NON-ADMISSIONS CLAUSE. Use when the contractor refuses to admit to the violations set forth in Part II of the CA UNLESS the CA requires a change in a collective bargaining*	3.*** This Agreement does not constitute an admission by [*name of contractor*] of any violation of [*as applicable:* Executive Order 11246, as amended; Section 503 of the Rehabilitation Act of 1973, as amended; and/or the Vietnam Era Veterans' Readjustment Assistance Act of 1974, as amended] and its implementing regulations.

Comments	Standard Text
agreement (CBA) between the contractor and a labor union or requires the award of retroactive seniority where seniority is governed by a CBA and the union declines to sign the CA (see Subsections 7C06 and 8C04).	
	4. The provisions of this agreement will become part of [*name of contractor*] AAP. Subject to performance by [*name of contractor*] of all promises and representations contained herein and in its AAP, all named violations in regard to the compliance of [*name of contractor*] with all OFCCP programs will be deemed resolved. However, [*name of contractor*] is advised that the commitments contained in this Agreement do not preclude future determinations of noncompliance based on a finding that the commitments are not sufficient to achieve compliance.
**For employee interviews, "normal business hours" means the hours during which the employees to be interviewed are at work (e.g., evening hours if the employees work on an evening shift).*	5. [*Name of contractor*] agrees that OFCCP may review compliance with this Agreement. As part of such review, OFCCP may require written reports, inspect the premises, interview witnesses, and examine and copy documents, as may be relevant to the matter under investigation and pertinent to [*name of contractor*]'s compliance. [*Name of contractor*] shall permit access to its premises during normal business hours* for these purposes.
	6. Nothing herein is intended to relieve [*name of contractor*] from the obligation to comply with the requirements of Executive Order 11246, as amended; Section 503 of the Rehabilitation Act of 1973, as amended; and/or the Vietnam Era Veterans' Readjustment Assistance Act of 1974, as amended, and their implementing regulations, or any other equal employment statute or executive order or its implementing regulations.

Comments	Standard Text
	7. [*Name of contractor*] agrees that there will be no retaliation of any kind against any beneficiary of this Agreement or against any person who has provided information or assistance, or who files a complaint, or who participates in any manner in any proceedings under Executive Order 11246, as amended; Section 503 of the Rehabilitation Act of 1973, as amended; and/or, the Vietnam Era Veterans' Readjustment Assistance Act of 1974, as amended.
**If a DD is signing, change Regional to District, and say ". . . unless the Regional Director or Director…. "* ** * If the CA involves back pay, the back pay should be disbursed following this 45 day period.*	8. This Agreement will be deemed to have been accepted by the Government on the date of the signature by the Regional* Director for OFCCP, unless the Director, OFCCP, indicates otherwise within 45 calendar days of the Regional* Director's signature on this Agreement.**
** * * Paragraph 9 is called the MANDATORY ENFORCEMENT CLAUSE. This clause implements 41 CFR 60-1.34, which requires OFCCP to issue a 15-Day Notice (unless irreparable injury is involved, see Subsection 8J02) when OFCCP concludes that a CA has been violated. If during the 15-day period, the contractor cannot demonstrate in writing that it did not violate the CA, OFCCP may initiate enforcement proceedings without issuing a Show Cause Notice.*	9.*** If at any time in the future, OFCCP believes that [*name of contractor*] has violated any portion of this Agreement during the term of this Agreement, [*name of contractor*] will be promptly notified of that fact in writing. This notification will include a statement of the facts and circumstances relied upon in forming that belief. In addition, the notification will provide [*name of contractor*] with 15 calendar days from receipt of the notification to respond in writing, except where OFCCP alleges that such a delay would result in irreparable injury. Enforcement proceedings for violation of this Agreement may be initiated at any time after the 15-day period has elapsed (or sooner, if irreparable injury is alleged) without issuing a Show Cause Notice. Where OFCCP believes that [*name of contractor*] has violated this Conciliation Agreement, OFCCP may seek enforcement of this Agreement itself and shall not be required to present proof of the underlying violations resolved by this Agreement. Liability for violation of this Agreement may subject [*name of contractor*] to sanctions set forth in [*as applicable*, Section 209 of the Executive Order, 41 CFR 60-250.66, 41 CFR 60-300.66 and/or 41 CFR 60-741.66] and/or other appropriate relief.

Comments	Standard Text
Part II – Specific Provisions: This will be the second part of each CA and will describe each violation and the required remedy. See Subsection 7C and 8F.	PART II – *Specific Provisions* 1. VIOLATION: REMEDY:
As applicable, describe additional violation/remedy items numbered consecutively.	2. VIOLATION: REMEDY:
	Part III – *Reporting*
Part III – Reporting. This will be the third part of each CA and will describe the content, period to be covered and due date of each report that the contractor will file. See Subsection 8HO1.	1. [*Name of contractor*] agrees to retain records pertinent to the violations cited in Part II above, and to the reports submitted in compliance with Paragraph 2, below. These records shall include data and information underlying the required reports, specifically, but not limited to all applications and personnel records. The records will be retained until the expiration of this Agreement or consistent with regulatory requirements, whichever is later. 2. [*Name of contractor*] agrees to furnish the OFCCP [*name and address of OFCCP office*] with the following reports:
As applicable, describe additional reports numbered consecutively.	[*Fill in specific information regarding the due dates and items to be submitted with each report.*] 3. This Conciliation Agreement shall remain in effect until the review and acceptance by OFCCP of [*name of contractor*]'s final progress report.

Additional Instructions for Completing the CA Template

e. *Contents of Part II - Specific Provisions.*

1. *VIOLATION*

- *Description of the Violation.* The description of the violation must be specific enough for a reader unfamiliar with the case to understand the problem. For example: "ABC's workforce analysis listed job titles by EEO-1 category rather than by department or other similar organizational unit as required by 41 CFR 60-2.11(a);" not "ABC's workforce analysis did not meet the requirements of 41 CFR 60-2.11(a)." Note that if the violation involved issues other than strictly written AAP issues, then the violation statement must provide a brief description of the circumstances giving rise to the violation. See, for example, the violation statements in Letter L-28.

- *Regulatory Citations.* Citations of the relevant portion of the regulations will support each violation. There must be a full and accurate description and citation of the regulation. However, if the regulations do not specifically name a particular violation (for example, racial harassment), it is sufficient for the CO to describe the violation clearly and to cite, as applicable, the nondiscrimination and/or affirmative action provisions of the appropriate EEO/AA clauses.

2. *REMEDY*

- *Description of the Remedy.* A specific description of the remedies the contractor and CO agreed upon will follow the listing of each violation, including dates for completion and a commitment not to repeat the violation. The CO should phrase remedies specifically enough for the contractor's implementation of the remedy to be auditable. For example:

  - "ABC's workforce analysis in future AAPs will list job titles within ABC's departments." COs should not use "ABC's workforce analysis in future AAPs will meet the requirements of 41 CFR 60-2.11(a)."

  - "ABC will list all Drafting openings with DEF and XYZ referral sources." COs should not use "ABC will make a good faith effort to recruit more minorities for Drafting jobs."

- *Corrective Actions are Linked to the Violations.* The CA should include all identified violations, including those that the contractor has already corrected. As with any other violation, the CO should include the date of correction and the contractor's commitment to not repeating the violation. For example, if a CO issued an SCN for failure to submit an EO 11246 AAP for desk audit and the contractor later submits the AAP, the CA would include: the violation, the date the CO received the AAP and the contractor's commitment to submit future AAPs within 30 calendar days of receiving the CO's request.

f. *Contents of Part III – Reporting.*

1. *REPORTING*

- *When Required.* The contractor must report all remedies that involve future commitments or obligations. The contractor does not need to report on remedies that they have already implemented when the CO prepared the CA, unless such reporting is essential to ensure that the contractor will not repeat the violation.

- *Contents of Reports.* All reporting requirements shall specify the period for the report to cover and its contents. The description of the report contents must be sufficiently detailed to ensure that the information the contractor submits will enable the CO to thoroughly review the contractor's compliance with the CA provisions.

- *Dates of Reports.* Reporting requirements must include the dates by which the contractor should submit the reports. This includes situations where the timing of the reported event is unpredictable (e.g., an offer of the "next" Technical Illustrator opening). In such cases, the contractor should report on specified dates whether any such opening has occurred and, if so, the action the contractor took.

  The specified date of the last report must be sufficiently in advance of the expiration date of the CA to permit the CO to evaluate that report, with appropriate follow-up if the evaluation raises questions about the contractor's full implementation of the CA.

- *Frequency of Reports.* Reporting should be frequent enough to enable a thorough review of the contractor's compliance with the CA provisions. However, except in unusual circumstances, the CA should not normally require reports more frequently than semi-annually.

- *Contractor Retention of Data.* For all reporting requirements, the contractor must retain records pertinent to violations that the CA resolves and to reports the contractor submitted following the CA, including the underlying data and information on which the reports are based, until the expiration date of the CA or consistent with regulatory requirements, whichever is later. For example, a contractor is required by 41 CFR 60-3.15 to retain data on components of a selection process that has adverse impact for at least two years after the elimination of that impact.

- *Monitoring.* See Section 8I for a discussion on monitoring reports the contractor submits under a CA.

8H02 TERMINATION DATE

Conciliation Agreements shall have termination dates based on the minimum time necessary for contractors to correct all violations and for OFCCP to verify such correction.

The time period in a CA should be sufficient to ensure that the contractor can accomplish all of its corrective actions. While full correction of all violations should be possible within one or two years under most CAs, some remedies may require a longer time period. For example, if the CA requires make-whole relief for discrimination and that relief includes extending job offers as openings occur, the CA termination date could be extended until the contractor has made all the job offers and has paid all the back pay or front pay, or both.

8H03 SIGNATURE AUTHORITY

The following people must sign and date a CA:

- the contractor's top establishment official, however, if the establishment is a corporate or intermediate headquarters, the CA top official's designee may sign; and any additional contractor officials that the contractor wishes;
- the union local's top official and any additional union officials the union wishes, if the union is a party to the CA;
- the CO who conducted or led the compliance evaluation or complaint investigation;
- the Assistant District Director, if applicable;
- the District Director; and
- the Regional Director, unless the authority is otherwise delegated.

a. *Delegation of Regional Director's Authority.* Regional Directors have the authority to sign all CAs. However, a Regional Director may delegate signature authority to a District Director or other designee for CAs involving only affirmative action issues, individual discrimination issues, pattern or practice discrimination claims or both in which the class does not exceed ten people and back pay does not exceed $25,000.

b. *Notice of Review Completion.* After the required signatures are obtained on the CA, the CO will issue the contractor a "Notice of Review Completion – Major Violations Resolved in a Conciliation Agreement." If the CO issued a Show Cause Notice (SCN), the CO should use sample form Letter L-32. If the CO did not issue an SCN, the CO should use Letter L-33.

8I POST CONCILIATION AGREEMENT ACTIONS

This Section reviews the actions required after all the parties properly execute a CA. The CO and contractor have continuing obligations and duties, including maintaining all evidence of the violations in the CA, and evaluating and reporting on progress. These and other responsibilities are discussed in the following subsections.

8I00 RETENTION OF EVIDENCE OF VIOLATIONS

The CO will retain all evidence regarding violations resolved in a CA in the case file so that he or she can readily retrieve it and use it if there would be enforcement proceedings. See subsection 8H0l(g)(1), Contractor Retention of Data, for the contractor's obligation to retain records pertinent to violations and to reports submitted.

8I01 EVALUATION OF PROGRESS REPORTS

COs have different responsibilities if a required progress report is not received when compared to when a report is received from the contractor.

a. *Progress Report Not Received by a CO.* If a CO does not receive a required progress report when due, the CO will contact the contractor to determine if it is en route. If it is en route, the CO allows 5 calendar days for it to arrive. If the CO does not believe it is en route or if it does not arrive within 5 calendar days, the CO will issue a 15-Day Notice for violation of the CA.[315]

b. *Progress Reports Received by a CO.* When a CO receives a progress report, the CO must evaluate the contents of the report and determine whether the report is acceptable or whether the CO needs additional information. The CO normally evaluates a progress report within 15 calendar days of receiving it from the contractor. This evaluation must include an assessment of the report's completeness as well as the analysis of the received items. If the CO needs additional information, the CO, in consultation with his or her supervisor, will determine how to best obtain the information (e.g., by phone, mail, an onsite visit or review) and will so notify the contractor. The CO records the results of the evaluation on the Progress Report Analysis and Evaluation Spreadsheet and prepares a letter, using Letter L-31, notifying the contractor of the results. The CO evaluates each report submitted under the CA on its own Progress Report Analysis and Evaluation Spreadsheet. In addition, the CO records any questions raised by the evaluation on the Summary of Progress Report Sheet.

c. *Questions Raised by a Progress Report Evaluation.* If the evaluation of a progress report raises questions about the contractor's implementation of the provisions of a CA, OFCCP may contact the contractor to obtain clarification of the report or schedule an onsite visit, or both.

   If the onsite visit is limited to the evaluation of the implementation of a CA issue, the CO will prepare a narrative report describing the results of the investigation and recommending whether the contractor is in violation of the CA. If the CO conducts a follow-up compliance evaluation, the CO will prepare a SCER (see Appendix A-1 and A-2, or A-3, as appropriate), with special emphasis on findings and recommendations on the CA implementation question. If the onsite is proposed as the result of identifying possible new violations resulting from the evaluating the implementation of the CA, the CO should contact his or her supervisor and consult with the National Office, the Division of Program Operations, before engaging in the evaluation.

---

[315] See Section 8J and Letter L-29 and L-29a.

d. *Contractor Maintenance of Records.* In response to an inquiry or during an onsite visit, the contractor must be prepared to furnish the underlying records or information on which the contractor based the report. If a CO requests copies of this data, the contractor may provide the copies, allow the CO to use its equipment to make the copies, loan the documents to the CO for offsite copying, or make other appropriate arrangements with the CO. A failure to maintain or furnish this data is a violation of the CA.[316]

e. *Notification of Results.* If, after obtaining and evaluating contractor evidence relevant to fulfillment of CA commitments, a CO concludes that the contractor did not violate the provisions of the CA, the CO will notify the contractor in writing. If the evaluation was part of a follow-up review, this Notice can be included in the applicable standard close out letter. If, however, OFCCP concludes that the contractor violated the CA, see Subsection 8I02, Violation of a Conciliation Agreement.

f. *Retention of Progress Reports and Evaluations.* The CO will retain progress reports and a copy of his or her corresponding analysis and evaluations in the case file. Copies of correspondence sent to the contractor acknowledging the report must be filed in the case file.

8I02 VIOLATION OF A CONCILIATION AGREEMENT

The violation of a CA may occur during the term of the agreement or after the expiration of the agreement.

a. *Violation During the Term of a CA.* If a CO determines that a contractor violated the provisions of a CA prior to the expiration of the CA, the procedures set out at 41 CFR 60-1.34 require the CO to send the contractor a 15-Day Notice.[317] The Regional Director or his or her designee signs the 15-Day Notice. Prior to issuing a 15-Day Notice, the CO must obtain appropriate approval.

b. *Repetition of Violation After Expiration of a CA.* If the CO finds a violation after the CA has expired, the CO should discuss the available options with SOL.

- If the CO finds that, following expiration of a CA, the contractor repeated any of the violations addressed in the CA (e.g., see Appendix A-1, Part A.I (1)(b) of the SCER on Recurrence of Past Problems), the CO should discuss the option of pursuing an enforcement action rather than a second CA.

- If the CO and SOL decide to remedy these violations, along with any new violation, through a second CA, the CA will have a minimum term of 4 years but may be longer if it is necessary to ensure full implementation of remedy or in unusual circumstances. It will also have at least one compliance evaluation before the CA expires to ensure that the contractor is fulfilling or has fulfilled its terms.

---

[316] See Subsection 8J02 – Procedure Where Irreparable Injury Exists.

[317] See Section 8J; however, where irreparable injury is involved, see specific procedures in 8J02.

8J THE 15-DAY NOTICE

This Section reviews the proper use of a 15-Day Notice, the different procedures used when irreparable injury and no such injury exist, who signs and who receives the Notice, and how contractors respond to the Notice.

8J00 WHEN TO USE A 15-DAY NOTICE

When a CO finds that the contractor violated the CA, the CO should issue a 15-Day Notice to the contractor, unless the victim alleges irreparable injury. In the case of irreparable harm, the response is as described in subsection 8J02 below.

8J01 PROCEDURES WHERE NO IRREPARABLE INJURY EXISTS

The 15-Day Notice in this instance includes a cover letter and an enclosure citing the provisions of the CA the contractor violated and the bases for the findings.[318] It will give the contractor 15 calendar days from receipt of the Notice to demonstrate, through a written presentation of facts and evidence, that it is in compliance with the provisions cited in the CA.[319]

8J02 PROCEDURE WHERE IRREPARABLE INJURY EXISTS

Irreparable injury may occur when a violation of a CA is either in progress or expected, and the contractor would not be able to readily correct it if allowed to proceed during the 15 business days response time normally allowed. For example:

- Employees are experiencing severe harassment or retaliation.
- The contractor has a CA commitment to offer a victim of discrimination a unique job (one unlikely to open again in the foreseeable future), such an opening occurs and the contractor is about to fill it with someone other than the victim.

When a victim alleges irreparable injury, the CO will not issue a 15-Day Notice. Instead, after obtaining RSOL clearance, the Regional Director shall attempt to notify the top establishment official by telephone that OFCCP intends to proceed directly to enforcement.[320]

After oral notice of breach of the CA and irreparable injury, the CO must immediately send a confirmation letter, cleared by RSOL, that cites the provisions of the CA the contractor violated, the bases for the findings, the reason for the irreparable injury allegation and OFCCP's intent to proceed directly to enforcement.

8J03 WHO RECEIVES THE 15-DAY NOTICE

The CO addresses a 15-Day Notice, and the letter of confirmation referenced in subsection 8J02, to the top official at the establishment with a copy to the CEO of the corporation, unless the

[318] See Letter L-29 and L-29a.

[319] 41 CFR 60-1.34(a), Violation of a Conciliation Agreement; 41 CFR 60-741.63, Violations of Conciliation Agreements; 41 CFR 60-250.63, Violation of Conciliation Agreements; and 41 CFR 60-300.63, Violation of Conciliation Agreements.

[320] See 41 CFR 60-1.34(a), 41 CFR 60-741.63(a)(1), 41 CFR 60-250.63(a)(1) and 41 CFR 60-300.63(a)(1).

establishment and corporate office are the same. If the contractor requested, in writing, that the CO provide a copy of the review or investigation correspondence to an outside representative such as an outside counsel or consultant, the CO will also send a copy to the designated representative. If the CO provides copies to a corporate CEO, other contractor official and/or a designated representative, the CO will include a "cc:" line on all copies indicating the people to whom the CO sent the Notice.

The CO always sends a 15-Day Notice via e-mail or facsimile, and certified mail, return receipt requested.

8J04 SIGNATURE AUTHORITY

The Regional Director has signature authority for a 15-Day Notice and may not further delegate this authority. DDs will send a proposed 15-Day Notice to the Regional Director, along with a copy of the CA that the contractor has violated and documentation pertaining to the CA provisions violated. Unless the contractor demonstrates that the CO's findings are incorrect, the CO refers the matter to RSOL for enforcement as described in Section 8K on Enforcement.

8J05 CONTRACTOR's RESPONSE TO THE 15-DAY NOTICE

The contractor has 15 calendar days from the date it receives the 15-Day Notice to respond. If the contractor does not respond within the 15-day period, or reasonable extensions thereof, the CO refers the case for enforcement.

If the contractor does respond, OFCCP will evaluate whether the response shows that the CO erroneously issued the 15-Day Notice or otherwise explains the violations. If so, the CO will either rescind the 15-Day Notice or otherwise resolve the matter with the contractor. If not, the CO will formally refer the case to SOL. SOL, with the CO's assistance, will attempt to negotiate a consent decree that includes all appropriate remedies. If the contractor is unwilling to enter into a consent decree, SOL will treat the case as a normal enforcement referral as described in Section 8L on Stopping Enforcement Proceedings.

8K ENFORCEMENT RECOMMENDATIONS

Making an enforcement recommendation means seeking approval to refer the case to SOL for either administrative or judicial enforcement. Before a case can move to enforcement certain administrative and procedural actions must occur. This chapter reviews those steps and procedures.

8K00 WHEN TO MAKE OR SEEK APPROVAL OF AN ENFORCMENT RECOMMENDATIONS

COs should make an enforcement recommendation when the contractor, with or without an SCN:

- refuses to submit required AAPs and support data under one or more of the following: EO 11246, Section 503 or Section 4212;

- refuses to provide access to its premises for an onsite review;

- refuses to provide access to necessary information; or
- harasses or intimidates a CO or agent of OFCCP (e.g., an OFCCP or SOL employee acting on behalf of the agency).

An enforcement recommendation should be made in other situations including when:

- an SCN is not resolved within 30 calendar days, or reasonable extensions thereof.
- A settlement negotiation fails to resolve violations specified in the NORI within 15 calendar days, or reasonable extensions thereof, in a complaint investigation.
- a contractor is not negotiating in good faith, and it is unlikely an agreement will be reached.
- a 15-Day Notice of violation of the CA, with no irreparable injury involved, is not resolved within 15 calendar days, or reasonable extensions thereof.
- a violation of a CA involves irreparable injury.

8K01 CONTENTS IN A COMPLIANCE EVALUATION FILE

a. *General.* A compliance evaluation case file that OFCCP submits for enforcement consists of a brief cover memorandum, a Transmittal Memorandum and the standard compliance evaluation case file. The case file must contain every document OFCCP collected and/or generated in the course of the evaluation, including all e-mails, statistical analyses including spreadsheets properly labeled and dated, mitigation data, interview statements and detailed descriptions of the employment processes or practices at issue. The case file must include a table of contents or index that identifies all of the contents and their location within the file, tabs and labels. The case file OFCCP submits to RSOL for enforcement should be an exact copy of the original case file and contain all of the documents in the original case file.[321] The file is sent to the RO for transmittal to the RSOL. If needed, the RO can create and maintain a copy of the file at this point. The original file will remain in the field office responsible for conducting the compliance evaluation.

b. *Cover Memorandum.* The cover memorandum is typically one page. It contains a brief statement of all the violations at issue, and indicates which violations were at impasse when the conciliation process terminated (e.g., jurisdiction, whether there was a violation, the amount of back pay).

c. *Transmittal Memorandum.* Appendix A-14 describes the contents of the Transmittal Memorandum. The Transmittal Memorandum must be a stand-alone document that contains all of the information supporting why SOL and DPO should ultimately approve the

[321] In addition, a copy of the enforcement memo and list of supporting documents and tabs will be sent to DPO, Branch of Enforcement and Appeals when the file is referred to RSOL.

enforcement recommendation. It should include any strengths or weaknesses the CO uncovered during the course of the investigation or review, citations to relevant supporting documentation in the case file, contractor's response to the alleged violations, OFCCP's assessment of those responses and a history of the conciliation efforts, including any offers the CO and contractor exchanged. It should not be a Memorandum that consists solely of conclusory statements or summary information, but instead be a report explaining why SOL or DPO, or both, should pursue the case for enforcement. Every fact in the Transmittal Memorandum must contain a reference to the location of the back-up information or documents in the case file that verify the fact.

8K02 CONTENTS IN A COMPLAINT INVESTIGATION

a. *General.* A complaint investigation case file that OFCCP submits for enforcement consists of a cover memorandum and the standard complaint investigation case file. The case file must include a table of contents or index identifying all of the contents and their location within the file, tabs and labels. Regional SOLs are provided an exact a copy of the original case file.

b. *Cover Memorandum.* The cover memorandum is typically one page. It must request enforcement, briefly state the program under which the victim filed the complaint, state the allegations and basis for the complaint, state the violation(s), and the results of conciliation. This includes the issues at impasse when conciliation terminated.

c. *Transmittal Memorandum.* The Transmittal Memorandum for a complaint investigation is similar in content to the Transmittal Memorandum description above.

8K03 WHO RECEIVES THE ENFORCEMENT RECOMMENDATIONS

The CO submits the enforcement recommendation and case file simultaneously to RSOL and DPO. It must contain all of the documents in the original case file including applications. The CO sends a copy of the cover memorandum and the transmittal memorandum to DPO as well as the completed SCER (compliance evaluations) or Investigative Report (complaint investigations). Upon receipt, DPO is responsible for forwarding a copy of the enforcement recommendation and supporting documents to NSOL; specifically, the Associate Solicitor, Civil Rights and Labor Management Division, Office of the Solicitor, U.S. Department of Labor, Room N-2474, 200 Constitution Ave., N.W., Washington, D.C. 20210.

If DPO uncovers deficiencies during its preliminary review of an enforcement recommendation, it rejects the enforcement referral and returns it to the appropriate Regional Office for further action or to correct the deficiencies, or both. Examples of deficiencies that may result in rejection include lack of jurisdiction, no evidence of consultation with RSOL prior to referral, and incorrect citation of a violation. DPO concurrently informs NSOL to notify the appropriate RSOL of this action. Furthermore, should RSOL or NSOL, or both, have any concerns regarding the merits of the enforcement referral, the appropriate SOL office will notify the Regional Office to discuss the issues associated with the referral. If NSOL or RSOL, or both, reject an enforcement referral, it must explain in writing the reasons for the rejection.

8K04 SIGNATURE AUTHORITY

The applicable Regional Director has signature authority for an enforcement recommendation and cannot delegate this authority further. The originating District Office will prepare the cover memorandum and transmittal memorandum, as appropriate, for the Regional Director's signature.

8L PRE AND POST REFERRAL ISSUES RESULTING IN ENFORCEMENT PROCEEDINGS

This section reviews pre and post-referrals to the SOL as ways of stopping an enforcement action.

8L00 PRE-REFERRAL TO SOL

Efforts to reach a voluntary resolution of the noncompliance should continue up until the time the CO refers the matter to SOL. Settlement negotiations, however, may not unduly delay an enforcement recommendation. For example, an enforcement recommendation is appropriate as soon as it becomes clear that the contractor is not negotiating in good faith.

8L01 POST-REFERRAL TO SOL

Once a CO refers a matter to SOL for enforcement, settlement negotiations between the contractor and the CO must end. The SOL will conduct all further negotiations with input from the CO and other agency officials. When, as a result of negotiations between SOL and the contractor, they reach an agreement, SOL may incorporate the agreed-upon remedies in a Consent Decree (CD) and file the CD simultaneously with an administrative complaint if it was not already done. An Administrative Law Judge (ALJ) must approve the terms of the CD. The ALJ's Order approving the CD is the final administrative order in the case. The contractor will send progress reports that the CD requires to the appropriate field office working with SOL to evaluate the contractor's compliance with the CD.

8M TYPES OF ENFORCEMENT PROCEEDINGS

Once a CO refers a case to SOL for enforcement, SOL determines whether the case is litigation worthy and, in the process of doing so, may seek additional information on the case from the CO. The SOL also makes a recommendation to the Director of OFCCP on whether an enforcement proceeding should be administrative or judicial.

8M00 ADMINISTRATIVE ENFORCEMENT PROCEEDINGS

SOL normally initiates administrative enforcement proceedings unless circumstances warrant referral to the Department of Justice (DOJ) for judicial proceedings. The SOL's filing of an Administrative Complaint with the Office of Administrative Law Judges (ALJ) initiates administrative enforcement proceedings. An ALJ conducts an administrative hearing on the Complaint under the procedures set forth in 41 CFR Part 60-30.

8M01 JUDICIAL ENFORCEMENT PROCEEDINGS

The SOL may refer a case to the DOJ for judicial enforcement proceedings when circumstances so warrant and the Director of OFCCP concurs. For example, SOL may need an injunction against a sole source contractor since cancellation of federal contracts may not be practical or the Director of OFCCP may request that SOL make a referral to DOJ of a case for judicial enforcement.

The SOL may make referrals to the DOJ for judicial enforcement at any stage in the enforcement process without proceeding through conciliation efforts.[322] DOJ initiates judicial enforcement proceedings when the Attorney General files a complaint on behalf of the Department of Labor in federal district court. As with any other federal court case, the losing party may appeal to the circuit court of appeals, and the losing party in the court of appeals may request review by filing a "writ of certiorari" with the U.S. Supreme Court.

[322] See 41 CFR 60-1.26(a)(2).

KEY WORDS AND PHRASES

Accessibility

The extent to which applicants and employees with disabilities can readily approach and use a contractor's facilities, amenities, and programs – including, but not limited to, work areas, employee lounge areas and online application systems.

Accommodation

See definitions of "Reasonable Accommodation" and "Religious Accommodation."

Active Case Enforcement (ACE)

The procedures for conducting Supply & Service (S&S) compliance evaluations scheduled from the Federal Contractor Scheduling System (FCSS). Directive 295, issued December 16, 2010, established the ACE procedures. These procedures replaced the Active Case Management procedures established in 2003 and later rescinded by Directive 292 in December 2010.

Active Case Management (ACM)

A tiered compliance review process whereby the compliance officer (CO) may close supply and service compliance evaluations after the desk audit if the CO does not find indicators of systemic discrimination. Process in effect until rescinded, and replaced by ACE.

Administering Agency

Any department, agency or establishment in the executive branch of the government, including any wholly owned government corporation that administers a program involving federally assisted construction contracts. See 41 CFR 60-1.3.

Administrative Complaint

A document filed by the Solicitor's Office on behalf of OFCCP with the Office of Administrative Law Judges that begins an administrative enforcement proceeding under Executive Order 11246, Section 503, and/or Section 4212.

Administrative Law Judge (ALJ)

The presiding official at an administrative enforcement proceeding under Executive Order 11246, Section 503, and/or Section 4212. See 41 CFR Part 60-30, 41 CFR 60-1.26(b), 60-250.65(b), 60-300.65(b), and 60-741.65(b).

Administrative Procedure Act

A law enacted by Congress in 1946. It establishes basic requirements to which an administrative process must conform. It includes standards for rulemaking, for certain formal adjudication and for court reviews of certain administrative actions. See 5 U.S.C. 500 *et seq*.

Adverse Impact

As defined by UGESP at 41 CFR 60-3.16B, a substantially different rate of selection in hiring, promotion, transferring, training or other employment decision which works to the disadvantage of the members of a race, sex or ethnic group identified in 41 CFR 60-3.4. See the related term "Disparate Impact."

Affected Class

A group of people sharing common traits or characteristics (e.g., the same race, gender, ethnicity), who are the victims of systemic discrimination.

Affirmative Action

Actions, policies and procedures to which a contractor commits itself that are designed to achieve equal employment opportunity. Affirmative action obligations entail thorough, systematic efforts to prevent discrimination from occurring and to detect it and eliminate it as promptly as possible. Affirmative Action obligations also require contractors to ensure equal opportunity in their recruitment and outreach efforts.

Affirmative Action Program (AAP)

A management tool designed to ensure equal employment opportunity. The requirements for an affirmative action program that satisfies Executive Order 11246, Section 503 and Section 4212, are set forth in 41 CFR Parts 60-2; 60-741, Subpart C; 60-250, Subpart C; or 60-300, Subpart C. These include requiring a contractor to annually detail the affirmative steps it has taken and will take in the future to ensure equal employment opportunity.

American Indian/Alaskan Native (not Hispanic or Latino)

As defined by OMB's *Standards for Maintaining, Collecting, and Presenting Federal Data on Race and Ethnicity,* a person with origins in any of the original peoples of North and South America (including Central America), and who maintains cultural identification through tribal affiliation or has community recognition as an American Indian or Alaskan Native.

Americans with Disabilities Act (ADA)(Title I)

Title I of the ADA (42 U.S.C. 12101, *et seq*) prohibits private employers, state and local governments, employment agencies and labor unions from discriminating against qualified individuals on the basis of disability in job application procedures, hiring, firing, advancement, compensation, job training, and other terms, conditions, and privileges of employment. The ADA covers employers with 15 or more employees, including state and local governments. The ADA's nondiscrimination standards also apply to federal sector employees under Section 501 and federal contractors under Section 503 of the Rehabilitation Act, as amended, and its implementing rules.

Amended Show Cause Notice (ASCN)

A letter from OFCCP to the contractor that is used when a CO issues an Show Cause Notice (SCN) to the contractor and later finds additional unresolved violations, or finds that some but not all violations were cited in error. The ASCN identifies all the unresolved or current violations.

Anecdotal Evidence

Oral or written narrative or data that indirectly supports a finding of discrimination. For example, data showing that the contractor has not hired an African American in the job at issue in the past three years or interview statements from affected applicants, current employees, or selecting officials that imply that discrimination occurred. Anecdotal evidence is often contrasted to statistical evidence or direct evidence. See definitions of "Statistical Evidence" and "Direct Evidence."

Anti-nepotism Policy

A policy or practice that limits the simultaneous employment of two or more members of the same family.

Applicant

The precise definition of "applicant" depends upon the contractor's recruitment and selection procedures. The concept of an applicant is that of a person who has indicated an interest in being considered for hiring, promotion, or other employment opportunities. This interest might be expressed by completing an application, or might be expressed orally, depending upon the contractor's practice. See Question and Answer 15 to the Adoption of Questions and Answers to Clarify and Provide a Common Interpretation of the Uniform Guidelines on Employee Selection Procedures.

Applicant Flow Data (Log)

A chronological compilation of applicants (including Internet applicants) for employment or promotion showing each individual, categorized by race, sex and ethnic group, who applied for each job title (or group of jobs requiring similar qualifications) during a specific period.

Apprenticeship (Contractor or Industry Specific)

A system of agreement, written or implied, that uses practical experience to train a person in a recognized trade or craft in accordance with specified standards.

Armed Forces Service Medal Veteran

Any veteran who, while serving on active duty in the U.S. military, ground, naval or air service, participated in a United States military operation for which an Armed Forces Service Medal was awarded pursuant to Executive Order 12985 (61 FR 1209). See 41 CFR 60-300.2(r).

Asian (not Hispanic or Latino)

As defined by OMB's *Standards for Maintaining, Collecting, and Presenting Federal Data on Race and Ethnicity* (1997), a person with origins in any of the original peoples of the Far East, Southeast Asia or the Indian subcontinent. This area includes, for example, Cambodia, China, India, Japan, Korea, Malaysia, Pakistan, the Philippine Islands, Thailand and Vietnam. However, under the regulations in part 60-2, the category is called "Asian/Pacific Islander" and contractors may use either Asian or Asian/Pacific Islander in developing their AAPs.

Availability

As described in 41 CFR 60-2.14, an estimate of the number of qualified minorities or women available for employment in a given job group, expressed as a percentage of all qualified people available for employment in the given job group. The purpose of the availability determination is to establish a benchmark against which the demographic composition of the contractor's incumbent workforce can be compared in order to determine whether barriers to equal employment opportunity may exist within particular job groups.

Back Pay

Lost earnings caused by a contractor's discriminatory employment practices or procedures. Lost earnings include but are not limited to: salary, wages, overtime, premium pay and shift differentials, incentive pay, raises, bonuses, lost sales commissions, cost-of-living increases, tips, medical and life insurance, fringe benefits, pensions, stock options and awards.

Bargaining Agreement

Also referred to as "collective bargaining agreement" and sometimes known as a "labor-management agreement" or "union contract." These terms refer to an agreement between an employer and a union establishing wages, hours and other terms and conditions of employment for employees in the bargaining unit represented by the union.

Basic Qualifications

For the purpose of defining an Internet applicant, "basic qualifications" mean qualifications:[323]

(i) (A) That the contractor advertises (e.g., posts on its Web site a description of the job and the qualifications involved) to potential applicants that they must possess in order to be considered for the position, or

(B) For which the contractor established criteria in advance by making and maintaining a record of such qualifications for the position prior to considering any expression of interest for that particular position if the contractor does not advertise for the position but instead uses an alternative device to find individuals for consideration (e.g., through an external resume database), and

(ii) That meet all of the following three conditions:

(A) The qualification must be noncomparative features of a job seeker. For example, three years' experience in a particular position is a noncomparative qualification; a qualification that an individual have one of the top five number of years' experience among a pool of job seekers is a comparative qualification.

(B) The qualifications must be objective; they do not depend on the contractor's subjective judgment. For example, "a Bachelor's degree in Accounting" is objective if a third-party, with the contractor's technical knowledge, would be able to evaluate whether the job seeker possesses the qualification without more information about the contractor's judgment.

(C) The qualifications must be relevant to performance of the particular position and enable the contractor to accomplish business-related goals.

Black or African American (not Hispanic or Latino)

As defined by OMB's *Standards for Maintaining, Collecting, and Presenting Federal Data on Race and Ethnicity* (1997) an individual, not of Hispanic origin, with origins in any of the black racial groups of Africa.

---

[323] See 41 CFR 60-1.3, section 4 of definition of Internet applicant.

Bona Fide Occupational Qualification (BFOQ)

A defense to the general prohibition of discrimination in employment on the basis of sex, religion or national origin that permits an employer to limit a particular job to members of one sex, religion or national origin group. Race cannot be used as a BFOQ.

The BFOQ defense is very narrow, but has been successfully used in the gender context when privacy concerns are implicated. For example, a women's prison may be able to demonstrate a female BFOQ for the hiring of a guard to perform body searches of female prisoners.

Bona Fide Seniority, Merit or Incentive System

An employer may lawfully compensate employees differently on the basis of a bona fide seniority, merit, or incentive system. A seniority system rewards employees according to the length of their employment. A merit system rewards employees for exceptional job performance. An incentive system provides compensation on the basis of the quality or quantity of production. To be a bona fide system, it must not have been adopted with discriminatory intent; it must be based on predetermined criteria; it must have been communicated to employees; and it must have been applied consistently and even-handedly to employees of both sexes.

Bumping Rights

The rights of one employee to displace another employee during a layoff, reduction-in-force or other employment action as defined in a collective bargaining or other binding agreement.

Business Necessity

A defense used by an employer when it uses an employment practice, such as a selection criterion, that is facially neutral and consistently applied, but which excludes members of one sex, race, national origin or religious group at a substantially higher rate than members of other groups (thus creating adverse impact). The employer must prove that a requirement that causes adverse impact is job-related and consistent with business necessity. Business necessity may also have to be proven when an employer uses a qualification standard that screens out an individual because of his or her disability, such as an uncorrected vision test or standard. OFCCP uses Title VII, UGESP and ADA standards, as appropriate, when evaluating a contractor's assertion of a business necessity defense.

Caregiver Discrimination

Being a working parent or another type of caregiver is not a protected characteristic under Title VII, the ADA, or the laws enforced by OFCCP. However, there are circumstances in which discrimination against caregivers may constitute unlawful disparate treatment or disparate impact based on a protected characteristic such as sex, or race. Discrimination against a caregiver due to his or her association with an individual with a disability may be a violation of Section 503.

Case Management System (CMS)

An automated system designed to track and monitor compliance evaluations or complaint investigations of establishments or functional units. Field offices have specific responsibilities to add information into this automated system. Specific instructions are found in the online Case Management System Manual.

Caucasian (not Hispanic or Latino)

Referred to as "white" by OMB in the *Standards for Maintaining, Collecting, and Presenting Federal Data on Race and Ethnicity* (1997) "White" is a person having origins in any of the original peoples of Europe, the Middle East, or North Africa.

. ***Circumstantial Evidence***

Also referred to as inferential or indirect evidence. A method of proof relying on comparative evidence or other evidence giving rise to an inference of discrimination. Circumstantial evidence typically involves an extra (inferential) step to draw a conclusion about whether discrimination has occurred. It can include statistical evidence, suspicious or ambiguous timing, statements or behavior, or any other bits and pieces of evidence that collectively support an inference of discrimination.

Civilian Labor Force

The aggregate of people classified as employed and as unemployed in accordance with the criteria established by the Bureau of the Census and the U.S. Department of Commerce. See "Employed" and "Unemployed."

Class Complaint

A complaint brought by one or more complainants on behalf of a group (consisting of two or more) who have a common claim against a federal contractor.

Coercion

The practice of forcing another party to behave in an involuntary manner (whether through action or inaction) by use of threats, intimidation or some other forms of pressure or force.

Cohort Analysis

A non-statistical comparison of the treatment of similarly situated individuals, small groups of applicants or employees.

Collateral Estoppel

A bar to relitigating an issue that has already been litigated between the same parties or certain closely related people (sometimes known as privies). Under collateral estoppel, when an issue has been contested and finally resolved in litigation involving the parties, that resolution of the issue is binding on future litigation involving the two parties (or their privies).

Collective Bargaining Agreement

See definition of "Bargaining Agreement."

Complaint

A written document filed with OFCCP by, or on behalf of, one or more employees, applicants or former employees that alleges that such individuals have been the victim of discrimination and/or retaliation that is prohibited by the laws enforced by OFCCP, or under Section 503 or VEVRAA, alleges a violation of the pertinent Act or regulations.

Compliance Check

A compliance evaluation procedure that involves a determination of whether the contractor has maintained appropriate records consistent with the regulations at 41 CFR Parts 60-1.12, 60-250.80, 60-300.80, and 60-741.80. The contractor has the option of providing the documents either onsite or offsite. 41 CFR § 60-1.20(a)(3), 60-250.60(a)(3), 60-300.60(a)(3) and 60-741.60(a)(3).

Compliance Evaluation

The investigation and review process used by OFCCP to determine if a federal contractor is complying with the nondiscriminatory and affirmative action employment obligations outlined in 41 CFR Chapter 60. A compliance evaluation consists of any one or any combination of the following investigative procedures: compliance review, offsite review of records, compliance check or focused review. See 41 CFR 60-1.20(a), 60-250.60(a), 60-300.60(a) and 60-741.60(a).

Compliance Officer (CO)

A career ladder professional position typically located in an OFCCP district or area office, but also found in some regional offices. The career ladder includes entry level, journey level and senior level positions. As one moves up the career ladder, the CO demonstrates greater responsibility and independence in his or her work, recommendations and assignments. At each level, the CO will work individually or in teams conducting compliance evaluations, complaint investigations and monitoring federal contractors. In addition, COs provide compliance assistance to community groups and federal contractors.

As used in this Manual, all references to the term CO include any OFCCP employee that is responsible for the tasks or activities described.

Compliance Review

A comprehensive analysis and evaluation of the hiring and employment practices of the contractor, including the contractor's written affirmative action program (AAP), and the results of the affirmative action efforts undertaken by the contractor. A compliance review may proceed in three stages: desk audit, onsite review and offsite analysis. See 41 CFR 60-1.20(a)(1), 60-250.60(a)(1), 60-300.60(a)(1) and 60-741.60(a)(1).

Conciliation

Efforts between OFCCP and a contractor to resolve findings of noncompliance.

Conciliation Agreement (CA)

A binding written agreement between a contractor and OFCCP that details specific contractor commitments, actions, or both to resolve the violations set forth in the agreement.

Construction Contract

Any contract for the construction, rehabilitation, alteration, conversion, extension, demolition or repair of buildings or highways, or other changes or improvements to real property, including facilities providing utility services.

Construction Site

The general physical location of any building, highway, or other change or improvement to real property which is undergoing construction, rehabilitation, alteration, conversion, extension, demolition, or repair and any temporary location or facility at which a contractor, subcontractor, or other participating party meets a demand or performs a function relating to the contract or subcontract. 41 CFR 60-1.3 (defining "Site of construction").

Construction Work

The construction, rehabilitation, alteration, conversion, extension, demolition or repair of buildings or highways, or other changes or improvements to real property, including facilities providing utility services. The term also includes the supervision, inspection and other onsite functions incidental to the actual construction. 41 CFR 60-1.3.

Constructive Discharge

The involuntary resignation of an employee as a result of an employer making the employee's working conditions so intolerable that a reasonable person would have felt compelled to resign. OFCCP will find that an employee was constructively discharged in violation of the Executive Order 11246, Section 503 or Section 4212 when it finds that: 1) a reasonable person in the employee's position would have found the working conditions so intolerable as to compel resignation; 2) the employer's conduct created the intolerable conditions and was motivated by retaliation, or based on race, color, sex, religion, national origin, disability or status as a protected veteran; and 3) the employee's involuntary resignation resulted from the intolerable working conditions.

Continuing Violation

A continuing violation may be found to exist when it is determined that multiple related actions comprise a single act of discrimination, e.g., a hostile work environment or a contractor maintains over time a discriminatory policy or system. A continuing violation exists where: 1) at least one of the actions occurred within the liability period and the other actions are related or so similar in nature as to show a pattern or practice of employment discrimination; or 2) the contractor maintains a discriminatory policy or practice into the liability period. Continuing violations may be, but do not have to be, systemic in nature.

Contract

See definition under “Government Contract” or “Subcontract” or “Federally Assisted Construction Contract” as defined below.

Contract Cancellation

The termination of a federal contract before its expiration date by order of the appropriate government authorities. Contract cancellation is one of the sanctions authorized, in appropriate cases, for violations of the EO 11246, Section 503 or Section 4212. Compare with "Debarment" and "Contract Suspension."

Contract Suspension

The temporary interruption of a federal contract by order of the appropriate government authorities. Contract suspension is one of the sanctions authorized, in appropriate cases, for violation of EO 11246, Section 503 or Section 4212. Compare with "Contract Cancellation" and "Debarment."

Contracting Agency

Any department, agency, establishment or instrumentality of the United States (under Executive Order 11246, limited to the Executive branch of the government), including any wholly owned government corporation, [that enters into a Government Contract or

Subcontract or Federally Assisted Construction Contract or Subcontract]. 41 CFR 60-1.3, 60-250.2, 60-300.2, and 60-741.2.

Contractor

"Contractor" means, unless otherwise indicated, a "prime contractor" or "subcontractor." "Prime contractor" means any person holding a contract and, for the purposes of [the enforcement provisions], any person who has held a contract subject to [EO 11246, Section 503 or Section 4212]. "Subcontractor" means any person holding a subcontract and, for the purposes of [the enforcement provisions], any person who has held a subcontract subject to [EO 11246, Section 503 or Section 4212]. The term "first-tier subcontractor" refers to a subcontractor holding a subcontract with a prime contractor. 41 CFR 60-1.3. See definitions of "Government Contract," "Subcontract," and "Federally Assisted Construction Contract."

Covered Area

With respect to a federal or federally assisted construction contractor, the geographical area, Economic Area (EA), or Standard Metropolitan Statistical Area (SMSA), as designated in the Federal Register by the Secretary of Labor, where a federal or federally assisted construction project is being performed. See 45 FR 65976, 65984, and Appendix B-80, October 3, 1980.

Criteria Identification/Criteria Verification

The process of obtaining the contractor's stated criteria for a selection decision(s) (usually through interviewing selection officials and examining any relevant contractor documents), and then determining whether the stated criteria account for or sufficiently explain the actual selection decisions (usually through reviewing applications/files of people selected and not selected).

Davis-Bacon Act

The Davis-Bacon Act, as amended, requires that each contract over $2,000 to which the United States or the District of Columbia is a party for the construction, alteration or repair of public buildings or public works shall contain a clause setting forth the minimum wages to be paid to various classes of laborers and mechanics employed under the contract. Under the provisions of the Act, contractors or their subcontractors are to pay workers employed directly upon the site of the work no less than the locally prevailing wages and fringe benefits paid on projects of a similar character. The Davis-Bacon Act directs the Secretary of Labor to determine such local prevailing wage rates.

Debarment

A declaration that a contractor ineligible for the award of future contracts. Debarment is one of the sanctions that may be imposed upon a contractor who is found to be in violation of the EO 11246, Section 503 or Section 4212.

Deficiency

Any failure to fulfill a requirement of the EO 11246, Section 503 or Section 4212, including any failure to comply with the implementing rules, regulations and orders of OFCCP. See the definition of "Violation."

Deposition

A type of pretrial discovery. (See the definition of "Discovery.) Generally, a deposition is an oral examination of a party or potential witness in the litigation, under oath, which is taken by an opposing party and accurately recorded.

Direct Evidence of Discrimination

Proof of a discriminatory reason for an employment decision that does not use inference or presumption. Direct evidence includes statements made by a decisionmaker that are related to a contested employment decision and reflect the alleged discriminatory animus or attitude. The burden of proof in Title VII discrimination cases (including mixed-motives cases) may be met through direct or circumstantial evidence, and there is no distinction between the weight and value of either type of evidence.

Director

The Director of the Office of Federal Contract Compliance Programs (OFCCP), United States Department of Labor (DOL).

Disability

1) A physical or mental impairment that substantially limits one or more of an individual's major life activities; 2) having a record of such an impairment; or 3) being regarded as having such an impairment.

Disabled Veteran

For the purpose of 41 CFR Part 60-300 a "disabled veteran" means:[324]

(a) A veteran of the U.S. military, ground, naval or air service who is entitled to compensation (or who, but for the receipt of military retirement pay, would be

[324] 41 CFR 60-300.2(n). See also 41 CFR 60-250.2(n)(1)(defining the corresponding term "special disabled veteran," a narrower term which is used in Part 60-250).

entitled to compensation) under laws administered by the Secretary of Veterans Affairs, or

(b) A person who was discharged or released from active duty because of service-connected disability.

Disadvantaged Business Enterprise (DBE)

As defined by the Small Business Administration, DBEs are for-profit small business concerns where socially and economically disadvantaged individuals own at least 51% interest and also control management and daily business operations. African Americans, Hispanics, Native Americans, Asian-Pacific and Subcontinent Asian Americans, and women are presumed to be socially and economically disadvantaged. Other individuals can also qualify as socially and economically disadvantaged on a case-by-case basis.

Discovery

The process by which the parties litigating (through their attorneys) obtain information about the case from each other before the trial begins. Tools of discovery include: depositions, written interrogatories, requests for production of documents or things, requests for physical and mental examinations, requests for admissions of fact, and request for inspection of premises (e.g., a plant tour). See "Deposition."

Discrimination

See the definitions of "Disparate Impact," "Disparate Treatment," "Harassment," and "Retaliation." Discrimination also includes failure to provide "Religious Accommodation" or "Reasonable Accommodation" for an individual with a disability.

Disparate Impact

A theory of employment discrimination that focuses on the effect of a practice or policy. Disparate impact discrimination occurs when a contractor's use of a facially neutral policy or selection procedure (e.g., a test, an interview, a degree requirement, a leave or hours policy) disqualifies members of a protected class at a substantially higher rate than others and is not justified by business necessity and job-relatedness. Intent to discriminate is not necessary in this type of employment discrimination. The disparate impact theory may be used to analyze both objective and subjective selection standards.

Disparate Treatment

A theory of employment discrimination. Disparate treatment discrimination occurs when a contractor treats an individual or group differently on the basis of a prohibited factor (race, color, religion, sex, national origin, disability, protected activity or status as a protected veteran). Intent to discriminate is a necessary element in this type of employment discrimination..

Dodge Report

The McGraw-Hill Dodge Report is a monthly list of all construction projects (federal and nonfederal). The Dodge Report is sent to the OFCCP field offices. It may be used for identifying reviews and mega construction projects.

D-U-N-S Number

An identification number assigned to a business by Dun & Bradstreet (D&B).

Economic Area (EA)

Geographic areas, as set by OMB, that have close economic ties throughout the area.

EEO Policy

A statement made by the employer/contractor to commit to the principles of equal opportunity employment.

EEO-1 Report

The *Employer Information Report EEO-1*. An annual report filed with the Joint Reporting Committee (composed of OFCCP and EEOC) by certain employers subject to the Executive Order and/or to Title VII of the Civil Rights Act of 1964, as amended. This report details the sex, race, and ethnic composition of an employer's workforce by job category. Also termed Standard Form 100.

EEO-3 Report

The *Equal Employment Opportunity Local Union Report EEO-3*, formerly the Local Union Report, collects labor force data from Referral Unions subject to Title VII of the Civil Rights Act of 1964, as amended, with 100 or more employees within 50 U.S. states and District of Columbia. The report provide information on their employment totals, employees' job category and sex and race/ethnic groups as of December 31 of the preceding year of the survey year. The EEO-3 survey is conducted biennially in every even-numbered year.

EEO-4 Report

The *Equal Employment Opportunity Local Union Report EEO-4*, formally known as the *State and Local Government Report*, collects information in odd-numbered years from

State and local governments. All States and all other political jurisdictions with 100 or more employees must file this report.

EEO-5 Report

The *Elementary-Secondary Staff Information Report EEO*-5 is a joint requirement of the EEOC and the Office for Civil Rights (OCR) of the Department of Education. It is conducted biennially, in the even numbered years, and covers all public elementary and secondary school districts with 100 or more employees in the United States.

Employed, Census definition of

In the reports the U.S. Census Bureau issues using data from the American Community Survey (ACS), the following individuals are counted as "employed:"

All civilians 16-years-old and over who were either:

(a) "at work," meaning they performed at least some work during the reference week as paid employees or in their business or profession, or on their farm, or who worked 15 hours or more as unpaid workers on a family farm or in a family business; or

(b) "with a job but not at work," meaning they did not work during the reference week but had jobs or businesses from which they were temporarily absent due to illness, bad weather, industrial dispute, vacation or other personal reasons.

Generally excluded from the category of "employed" are people whose only activity consisted of unpaid work around the house or volunteer work for religious, charitable and similar organizations, or people on layoff. Also excluded are all institutionalized people and people on active duty in the United States Armed Forces.

Employee **(using the "common law agency test")**

OFCCP generally uses the "common law agency" test for determining who is an employee under OFCCP programs, unless otherwise defined in agency regulations or reports. The "common law agency" test generally relates to whether the employer controls the means and manner of the worker's performance. This determination requires consideration of all circumstances in the relationship between the parties such as: the skill required for the job, who provides required equipment or tools, the location of the work, the duration of the relationship between the parties, the right to assign additional projects, scheduling work hours, the method of payment, the provision of employee benefits and the tax treatment of the hired party. See *Nationwide Mut. Ins. Co. v. Darden,* 503 U.S. 318, 323-24 (1992).

Employment Agency

Any person or entity that, with or without compensation, regularly works to procure employees for a contractor or to procure for individuals opportunities to work for a contractor. Also includes an agent of such a person or entity.

Employment Offer

A contractor's offer of employment to an individual, usually for a specific job.

Employer Identification Number (EIN)

A nine-digit number assigned to a company by the Internal Revenue Service for tax and other identification purposes.

Enforcement

This term typically refers to an administrative or judicial action to compel compliance with Executive Order 11246, Section 503, or Section 4212 and their implementing regulations, or performance of a conciliation agreement or consent decree.

Equal Employment Opportunity Commission (EEOC)

A federal agency responsible for enforcing federal laws that make it illegal to discriminate against a job applicant or an employee because of the person's race, color, religion, sex (including pregnancy), national origin, age (40 or older), disability, genetic information or participation in protected activity (e.g., filing a complaint of discrimination).

Equal Opportunity Clause

The contract clauses published at 41 CFR 60-1.4(a),(b), 41 CFR 60-250.5(a), 41 CFR 60-300.5(a) and 41 CFR 60-741.5(a) outline contractors' responsibilities under Executive Order 11246, Section 503 and Section 4212. By operation of [those laws], the equal opportunity clause [is] considered to be a part of every [covered] contract and subcontract…whether or not it is physically incorporated in such contract and whether or not there is a written contract between the agency and the contractor. 41 CFR 60-1.4(e); 41 CFR 250.5 (e); 41 CFR 60-300.5(e); 41 CFR 741.5 (e).

Essential Functions

The term "essential functions" is defined and discussed at 41 CFR 60-741.2(u):

(1) In general. The term essential functions means fundamental job duties of the employment position the individual with a disability holds or desires. The term essential functions does not include the marginal functions of the position.

(2) A job function may be considered essential for any of several reasons, including but not limited to the following:

(i) The function may be essential because the reason the position exists is to perform that function;

(ii) The function may be essential because of the limited number of employees available among whom the performance of that job function can be distributed; and/or

(iii) The function may be highly specialized so that the incumbent in the position is hired for his or her expertise or ability to perform the particular function.

(3) Evidence of whether a particular function is essential includes, but is not limited to:

(i) The contractor's judgment as to which functions are essential;

(ii) Written job descriptions prepared before advertising or interviewing applicants for the job;

(iii) The amount of time spent on the job performing the function;

(iv) The consequences of not requiring the incumbent to perform the function;

(v) The terms of a collective bargaining agreement;

(vi) The work experience of past incumbents in the job; and/or

(vii) The current work experience of incumbents in similar jobs.

Establishment

A facility or unit that produces goods or services, such as a factory, office, store, or mine. In most instances, the unit is a physically separate facility at a single location. In appropriate circumstances, OFCCP may consider as an establishment several facilities located at two or more sites when the facilities are in the same labor market or recruiting area. The determination as to whether it is appropriate to group facilities as a single establishment will be made by OFCCP on a case-by-case basis.

Executive Order 11246

Executive Order 11246 (30 Fed. Reg. 12319)(Sep. 24, 1965) was amended by Executive Order 11375 (32 Fed. Reg. 14303), Executive Order 12086 (43 Fed. Reg. 46501), and Executive Order 13279 (67 Fed. Reg. 77141). All references to "Executive Order 11246," "EO 11246," or the "Order" include these amendments.

Executive Order 11246 Complaint

A complaint filed on the bases of race, color, religion, sex and/or national origin with OFCCP.

Exempt Contract

Any government contract or subcontract that is not subject to some or all obligations under one or more of the laws enforced by OFCCP. Most contracts meeting specified dollar thresholds are covered, but there are a few exemptions and waiver provisions. See 41 CFR 60-1.3, 60-1.5 (coverage and exemptions under EO 11246); 41 CFR 60-250.4, 60-300.4 (coverage and waivers under Section 4212); 41 CFR 60-741.4 (coverage and waivers under Section 503).

Exempt Jobs

Jobs that are exempt from the overtime requirements of the Fair Labor Standards Act. The term is generally used to refer to managerial, professional and, as applicable, sales positions.

Expert Witness

A person such as a doctor or statistician selected by the court or a party on account of his or her knowledge or skill, to examine, estimate and ascertain pertinent information and make a report (testimony) of his or her findings and opinions.

Facially Neutral

An employment practice, policy or selection procedure is facially neutral if it does not reference a protected characteristic such as sex (including pregnancy) or race. A contractor's facially neutral policy (e.g., excluding applicants from employment based on certain criminal conduct or lack of a high school degree) may disproportionately impact some protected individuals and violate the law if not job-related and consistent with business necessity (disparate impact liability).

Family and Medical Leave Act (FMLA)

The FMLA is designed to help employees balance their work and family responsibilities by taking reasonable unpaid leave for certain family and medical reasons. It provides certain employees with up to 12 workweeks of unpaid, job-protected leave a year, and requires continuation of group health insurance coverage under the same terms and conditions as if the employee had not taken leave. The FMLA is enforced by the U.S. Department of Labor's Wage and Hour Division.

Favored Group

The group with the highest selection rate when calculating the impact ratio or level of statistical disparity or both.

Federally Assisted Construction Contract

Any agreement or modification thereof which is paid for in whole or in part with funds obtained from the government or borrowed on the credit of the government pursuant to any federal program involving a grant, contract, loan, insurance or guarantee, or undertaken pursuant to any federal program involving such grant, contract, loan, insurance or guarantee, or any application or modification thereof approved by the government for a grant, contract, loan, insurance or guarantee under which the applicant for funds itself participates in the construction work. 41 CFR 60-1.3.

Field Office

Any office outside of the National Office and its Divisions that is responsible for the tasks or activities described in the Federal Contractor Compliance Manual (FCCM or Manual).

Fifteen (15) Day Notice

See definition of "Notice of Alleged Noncompliance."

First-tier Subcontractor

A subcontractor holding a subcontract with a prime contractor.

Focused Review

An onsite review restricted to one or more components of the contractor's organization or one or more aspects of the contractor's employment practices. See 41 CFR 60-1.20(a)(4), 60-250.60(a)(4), 60-300.60(a)(4) and 60-741.60(a)(4).

Focus Job Area

A unit of an establishment's workforce (e.g., seniority unit, department, line of progression, job title) identified at the desk audit as a potential problem area for further investigation onsite. For example: a unit where minorities or women are concentrated, underrepresented or restricted from working because of their race or sex.

Formal Training

A structured program designed to develop an individual's job- related skills and abilities. Typically classroom training, as well as on-the-job training, falls into this category.

Formula Relief

A method used in systemic discrimination cases for calculating a total amount of back pay for an affected class of discrimination victims that is then divided (pro rata or otherwise) among all members of that class. *Compare to* "Individual Relief.

Fringe Benefits

Benefits that an employer provides to employees in addition to paying their wages or salary. Examples include: profit sharing, bonus plans, stock options or awards, educational stipends, leave (e.g., annual vacation days, personal days, sick leave), life and health insurance, long-term and short-term disability benefits, severance benefits, pension or other retirement benefits, and early retirement incentives. Guidance regarding sex discrimination and benefits is available at 29 CFR 1604.9.

Front Pay

Compensation for estimated future economic loss; generally calculated based on the difference between the discrimination victim's current pay (or for a rejected applicant, the pay he or she should have received) and the pay associated with his or her rightful place. Front pay runs from the time of the settlement; e.g., Conciliation Agreement or final administrative or court order, to a certain time in the future (usually when the victim attains his or her rightful place) that is set by the settlement or final order.

Functional Affirmative Action Program (FAAP)

The development and preparation of an AAP based on clearly distinct functional or business units within a corporate structure as opposed to an AAP based solely on an establishment's physical location.

Gender Based Discrimination

See definition of "Sex Discrimination."

Goals for Supply and Service Contractors, Placement

Percentage annual placement goal[s] [for an underutilized job group that is] at least equal to the availability figure[s] derived for minorities or women, as appropriate, for that job group. 41 CFR 60-2.16(c); see also 41 CFR 60-2.14, 60-2.15.

Goals for Construction Contractors, Participation

Participation goals for minorities and women expressed as a percentage of the hours worked by the contractor's aggregate workforce, by trade, in the geographic area(s) where a federal or federally assisted construction project is located. *See* 41 CFR 60-4.6.

Good-Faith Efforts

This term refers to a contractor's appropriate efforts to meet its goals by removing identified barriers, expanding employment opportunities, and producing measurable results. See 41 CFR 60–2.16(a), 60-2.17(c), and 60-4.2(d)(2).

Government

Except where otherwise indicated, the government of the United States of America.

Government Contract

Any agreement or modification thereof between any contracting agency and any person for the purchase, sale or use of personal property or nonpersonal services. The term “personal property” includes supplies, and contracts for the use of real property (such as lease arrangements), unless the contract for the use of real property itself constitutes real property (such as easements). The term “nonpersonal services” as used in this section includes, but is not limited to, the following services: utility, construction, transportation, research, insurance and fund depository.

The term "Government Contract" does not include:

(a) agreements in which the parties stand in the relationship of employer and employee, and

(b) federally assisted construction contracts.

Harassment

Harassment is unwelcome conduct that is based on a protected characteristic (race, color, religion, sex, national origin, disability, veteran status, or protected activity). Harassment can take the form of slurs, graffiti, offensive or derogatory comments, or other verbal or physical conduct. Sexual harassment may include unwelcome sexual advances, requests for sexual favors, and other conduct of a sexual nature. Harassment is illegal if it is so frequent or severe that it creates a hostile or offensive work environment or if it results in an adverse employment decision (such as the victim being fired or demoted).

Hispanic or Latino

As defined by OMB’s *Standards for Maintaining, Collecting, and Presenting Federal Data on Race and Ethnicity* (1997) , a person of Cuban, Mexican, Puerto Rican, South or Central American or other Spanish culture or origin, regardless of race.

Immediate Labor Area

The geographic area from which employees reasonably may commute to the contractor's establishment. It may include one or more contiguous cities, counties, Metropolitan Statistical Areas (MSAs) or parts thereof.

Impact Ratio Analysis (IRA)

The Impact Ratio Analysis is a method for identifying personnel activity that should be investigated further. The IRA is a comparison of the selection rates of different racial, ethnic, and gender groups within an identified applicant or candidate pool. If the selection rate for one group is less than 80% of that of the group with the highest rate, then the IRA is adverse and further investigation or analysis is needed.

Individual Relief

The assessment of make-whole relief for identified victim(s) of discrimination on an individualized basis. This method is generally used to calculate back pay in those individual or small group discrimination cases where the victims of discrimination, and the losses they incurred, can be determined with specificity. *Compare to* "Formula Relief."

Individual with a Disability

A person with a disability. See "disability."

Injunctive Relief

A court order requiring a person (including a contractor) to perform, or to refrain from performing, one or more designated acts. For example, an order obtained by OFCCP directing a contractor to cease asking specific discriminatory questions on its job application is a form of injunctive relief.

Internet Applicant, for the purposes of EO 11246

Any individual as to whom the following four criteria are satisfied:

(i) The individual submits an expression of interest in employment through the Internet or related electronic data technologies;

(ii) The contractor considers the individual for employment in a particular position;

(iii) The individual's expression of interest indicates the individual possesses the basic qualifications for the position; and,

(iv) The individual at no point in the contractor's selection process prior to receiving an offer of employment from the contractor, removes himself or herself from further consideration or otherwise indicates that he or she is no longer interested in the position. 41 CFR 60-1.3. NOTE: the Internet Applicant definition does not apply to the Section 503/VEVRAA programs or to Title VII.

Invitation to Self-Identify

An invitation by the contractor, extended to employees and applicants for employment, to identify their race, national origin, gender, disability and/or protected veteran status. All information obtained in response to such an invitation must be kept confidential in accordance with 41 CFR 60-250.42, 60-300.42 or 60-741.42.

Job Area

Any sub-unit of a workforce sector (e.g., department, job group, job title).

Job Area Acceptance Range (JAAR)

The JAAR is an analytical tool used to analyze the distribution of employees in a workforce by comparing the actual percentage of minorities and women in a job area to their percentage in the relevant segment of the contractor's workforce.

Job Categories

The tendesignated categories of the EEO-1 report: officials and managers (divided into executive/senior level and mid/first level), professionals, technicians, sales workers, office and clerical, craft workers (skilled), operatives (semi-skilled), laborers (unskilled), and service workers.

Job Description

A written statement detailing the duties of a particular job title.

Job Group

One or more group(s) of jobs having similar content, wage rates and opportunities. See 41 CFR 60-2.12.

Journey Worker

One who has completed an apprenticeship program or otherwise possesses the full skills and licenses of workers in his or her trade. Historically referred to as "journeyman."

Labor Area

Geographic area used in calculating availability. The area may vary from local to nationwide.

Layoff

The process by which workers are removed from the active payroll to the inactive payroll during, for example, a reduction-in-force (RIF).

Let, Let a Contract

The awarding of a contract to the prime contractor.

Line of Progression

A series of related jobs in a promotional sequence, generally starting with lower-paying jobs with less responsibility and progressing to higher-paying jobs with greater responsibility. Often, the lower-level jobs provide required training for movement to the higher-level jobs.

Linkage

The connection between contractors and appropriate recruitment and training sources. Linkage agreements between contractors and recruitment and training sources are a tool that may assist the contractor in meeting its affirmative action goals and obligations and are often embodied in a CA.

Major Life Activities

A key term used in the definition of "disability" in the Rehabilitation Act and the ADA. The ADA Amendments Act of 2008 expanded the definition of "major life activities" to encompass "major bodily functions." 42 U.S.C. 12102(2). Major life activities include, but are not limited to, caring for oneself, performing manual tasks, seeing, hearing, eating, sleeping, walking, standing, lifting, bending, speaking, breathing, learning, reading, concentrating, thinking, communicating, and working. A major life activity also includes the operation of a major bodily function, including but not limited to, functions of the immune system, normal cell growth, digestive, bowel, bladder, neurological, brain, respiratory, circulatory, endocrine, and reproductive functions. 42 U.S.C. 12102(2).

Make-Whole Relief

Remedy for discrimination that restore the victim of discrimination to his or her rightful place, i.e., the position, both economically and in terms of employment status that he or she would have occupied had the discrimination not taken place. Common elements of make-whole relief include an award of the position the individual was wrongfully denied, back pay with interest and retroactive seniority.

Mandatory Job Listing (MJL)

The Section 4212 affirmative action obligation of covered employers to list suitable job openings with the appropriate employment service delivery system where the opening occurs. See 41 CFR 250.5 and 41 CFR 60-300.5.

Maternity Leave

Childbirth-related absence from work by a woman that does not directly depend on her medical condition. The term includes leave for non-disability related care and nurturing following the birth of a child. Distinguish from "pregnancy disability leave," but see Manual Section 2H01.

Mega Project

A large construction project spanning more than one year, with a value of $25 million or more, and that will have a major employment and economic impact on a community.

Minorities

Minorities include men and women who are black, Hispanic, Asian or Pacific Islander, American Indian or Alaskan Native. As used in this Manual, the term may mean these groups in the aggregate or an individual group. See 41 CFR 60-4.3(a), section 1d of Equal Opportunity clause.

Minority-Owned Business Enterprise (MBE)

As defined by the Small Business Administration, MBE is a for-profit enterprise, regardless of size, physically located in the United States or its trust territories, which is owned, operated, and controlled by minority group members. Minority ownership must be 51 percent to qualify, whether the business is publicly or privately held. If publicly held, 51 percent of its stock must be held by the minority group members.

Mixed Issues

A complaint filed on one or more bases (EO 11246, Section 503 and/or Section 4212).

MOU (Memorandum of Understanding)

A written agreement between two or more entities, which often serves to memorialize the intent and purpose of the parties' working relationship.

National Origin

EO 11246 and Title VII prohibit employer actions that have the purpose or effect of discriminating against persons on the basis of protected characteristics such as national origin, which includes: actual or *perceived* birthplace, ancestry, culture, accent, or linguistic characteristics common to a specific ethnic group; marriage or association with persons of a national origin group; membership or association with specific ethnic promotion groups; attendance or participation in schools, churches, temples or mosques generally associated with a national origin group; or a surname associated with a national origin group.

Native Hawaiian/Other Pacific Islander

As defined by OMB's *Standards for Maintaining, Collecting, and Presenting Federal Data on Race and Ethnicity* (1997), a person with origins in any of the original peoples of Hawaii, Guam, Samoa or other Pacific Islands. Under the regulations at 41 CFR part 60-2, Pacific Islanders are combined with Asians. In the 1997 OMB guidance, an Asian is defined as a person having origins in any of the original peoples of the Far East, Southeast Asia, or the Indian subcontinent including, for example, Cambodia, China, India, Japan, Korea, Malaysia, Pakistan, the Philippine Islands, Thailand, and Vietnam.

New Hire

A worker added to an establishment's payroll for the first time. Compare with "Rehire."

Noncompliance

A contractor's failure to adhere to the conditions set out in the contract's equal opportunity clauses and/or the regulations implementing those clauses (41 CFR Chapter 60) and/or failure to correct violations.

Nonfavored Group

The race, ethnic, or gender group(s) with the lower selection rates as compared to the group with the highest selection rate when calculating the impact ratio and/or the level of the statistical disparity. See 41 CFR 60-3.4D.

Normal Business Hours

For purposes of access to a contractor's premises, the hours during which employees to be interviewed are at work, regardless of the time of day or night. Also used to indicate the regular business hours during which Section 503 and Section 4212 AAPs are available for inspection by employees and applicants for employment.

North American Industry Classification System (NAICS)

The North American Industry Classification System (NAICS) is the standardized system used by federal agencies in classifying business establishments for the collection, analysis and publication of statistical data related to the business economy of the U.S. NAICS was developed under the auspices of the Office of Management and Budget (OMB), and adopted in 1997 to replace the Standard Industrial Classification (SIC) system.

Notice of Alleged Noncompliance (15-Day Notice)

A letter from OFCCP informing the contractor that the agency believes the contractor has violated the terms of a Conciliation Agreement and that enforcement proceedings may be initiated unless the contractor demonstrates within 15 calendar days from its receipt of the letter that it has not violated its commitments under the Agreement.

.

Notice of Results of Investigation (NORI)

A letter from OFCCP notifying the contractor that the agency has found violations of the Executive Order, Section 503, or Section 4212 during a complaint investigation, and inviting the contractor to join the agency in resolving the complaint through conciliation.

Notice of Violation (NOV)

A letter from OFCCP notifying the contractor that the agency has found violations of the Executive Order, Section 503 and/or Section 4212 during a compliance evaluation, the remedies that are required to resolve those violations, and invites conciliation.

O*NET (Occupational Information Network)

An electronic database maintained by the Employment and Training Administration (ETA), U.S. Department of Labor, that classifies occupations in the US economy based on their duties and commonly required qualifications.

Objective Criterion

A selection criterion is objective if it is fixed and measurable, for example, the requirement of a high school degree rather than a "good education"). The central characteristic of an objective criterion is that it can be independently verified, i.e., different people measuring objective criteria will reach the same results. Compare with "Subjective Criterion."

Offsite Review of Records

An analysis and evaluation of the AAP (or any part thereof) and supporting documentation, and other documents related to the contractor's personnel policies and employment actions that may be relevant to a determination of whether the contractor has complied with the requirements of EO 11246, Section 503 and/or Section 4212. See 41 CFR § 60-1.20(a)(2), 60-250.60(a)(2), 60-300.60(a)(2) and 60-741.60(a)(2).

On-the-Job Training (OJT)

An employer sanctioned training program, usually at the employer's worksite, conducted either under close supervision or with assistance, and designed to teach and qualify an individual to perform a job or element(s) of a job.

Order

Generally, a short-hand term meaning Executive Order 11246, as amended. The term also is used in phrases dealing with decisions in litigation matters (e.g., Final Decision and Order, Court Order).

Organizational Unit

A department, division, branch, section or other organizational entity of a contractor that operates as a single unit under a common head.

Other Protected Veteran

For the purpose of 41 CFR Part 60-250, "other protected veteran" means a person who served on active duty during a war or in a campaign or expedition for which a campaign badge has been authorized, under laws administered by the Department of Defense. 41 CFR 60-250.2(q)

For the purpose of 41 CFR Part 60-300, "other protected veteran" means a veteran who served on active duty in the U.S. military, ground, naval or air service during a war or in a campaign or expedition for which a campaign badge has been authorized, under the laws administered by the Department of Defense. 41 CFR 60-300.2(p). (Veteran means a person who served in the active military, naval, or air service of the United States, and who was discharged or released therefrom under conditions other than dishonorable. 41 CFR 60-300.2(z).)

Pacific Islander (not Hispanic or Latino)

See "Native Hawaiian/Other Pacific Islander."

Parental Leave

Absence from work by a parent to care for a child.

Pattern or Practice Discrimination

Also known as "systemic discrimination," this type of discrimination involves statistical and/or other evidence that demonstrates that discrimination is standard operating procedure – the regular rather than the unusual practice. The proof of the pattern or practice supports an inference that any particular employment decision, during the period in which the discriminatory policy was in force, was made in pursuit of that policy or practice.

Perfection (of a Complaint)

Perfection is the initial process used to determine whether OFCCP has jurisdiction over a complaint filed with the agency. Perfection includes assessing whether a complaint is complete, filed within established timeframes, and the allegation(s) fall within the agency's jurisdiction (meaning that the company is a federal contractor or subcontractor and that the allegations assert a violation under the laws enforced by OFCCP). Once a complaint is perfected, it is assigned to a CO for investigation.

Person

Any natural person, corporation, partnership, unincorporated association, state or local government, and any agency, instrumentality, or subdivision of such a government. 41 CFR 60-1.3. The term also includes joint ventures under the regulations implementing VEVRAA (41 CFR 60-250.2(i), 60-300.2(i)) and Section 503 (41 CFR 60-741.2(i).

Person of Two or More Races (Not Hispanic or Latino)

As defined by the EEOC, for purposes of EEO-1 reports, as any person who identifies with more than one race category.

Personnel Practices

Practices or actions taken by management related to decisions regarding their employees (e.g., hiring, firing, layoff, promotion, transfer, demotion, compensation, salary increase, salary decrease, work assignments, benefits).

Physical & Mental Job Qualification Requirements

Physical and mental standards that an employer requires an employee or applicant to meet to qualify for the job.

Physical or Mental Impairment

Physical or mental impairment means:

(a) Any physiological disorder, condition, cosmetic disfigurement or anatomical loss affecting one or more body systems such as neurological, musculoskeletal, special sense organs, respiratory (including speech organs), cardiovascular, reproductive, digestive, genito-urinary, immune, circulatory, hemic and lymphatic, skin, and endocrine; or

(b) Any mental or psychological disorder, such as such as an intellectual disability (formerly termed "mental retardation"), organic brain syndrome, emotional or mental illness and specific learning disabilities.

29 CFR 1630.2(h); see also 41 CFR 60-741.2(o).

Placement

In this Manual, placement is often used in the context of the selection or assignment of individuals in a particular job. Also see "Goals for Supply and Service Contractors, Placement."

Pre-employment Medical Examination

A procedure or test that seeks information about an individual's physical or mental impairments or health at the pre-offer stage of employment.

Predetermination Notice (PDN)

A letter in which OFCCP notifies the contractor of its preliminary finding that the contractor has engaged in a systemic discrimination. The PDN states the basis for the preliminary findings and offers the contractor the opportunity to respond.

Pregnancy-Disability Leave

Pregnancy and childbirth-related absence from work by a woman affected by pregnancy, childbirth or related medical conditions. It includes leave prior to childbirth when medically indicated and leave to recover from pregnancy, childbirth or related medical conditions following the birth of a child.

Pregnancy Discrimination

Discrimination based on pregnancy, childbirth, or related medical conditions that constitute unlawful sex discrimination under Title VII and EO 11246. Title VII covers employers with 15 or more employees, including state and local governments. Women who are pregnant or affected by pregnancy-related conditions must be treated in the same manner as other applicants or employees with similar abilities or limitations.

Pretext

Professed reason or motive articulated as a cover for the real (discriminatory) reason or motive.

Prevailing Wage

Under the Davis-Bacon Act (defined above), 40 U.S.C. 3141 *et seq.,* the "prevailing wage" is the combination of the basic hourly rate and any fringe benefit rates listed in a Davis-Bacon wage determination. Applicable fringe benefits include medical, pension, and life insurance coverage, among others. The Secretary, through the Wage and Hour Division, determines Davis-Bacon prevailing wage rates based on the locally prevailing wages and fringe benefits for corresponding work on similar construction, alteration, or repair projects in the area. The resulting wage determination provides the minimum rates for the different job classifications (e.g., laborer, carpenter, electrician) and is included in covered contracts.

Under the Service Contract Act (SCA), 41 U.S.C. 6701 *et seq.*, for service contracts in excess of $2,500, the required minimum wage rates and fringe benefits for the various classes of service employees are those that the Wage and Hour Division has determined prevail in the locality, or are the rates (including prospective increases) contained in a predecessor contractor's collective bargaining agreement. The resulting SCA wage determination provides the minimum rates for the different job classifications (e.g. guard, clerk, janitor) and is included in covered service contracts. The fringe benefit requirements (usually "health and welfare," vacation, and holiday benefits) are separate and in addition to the hourly monetary wage requirement under the SCA. On covered service contracts equal to or less than $2,500, the federal minimum wage under section 6(a)(1) of the Fair Labor Standards Act applies rather than the wage and fringe benefits rates on the local SCA wage determination.

Prima Facie Case

A legal term that refers to a party's production of enough evidence to establish a fact or raise a presumption unless disproved or rebutted.

Problem Areas

Aspects of the contractor's employment decisions, policies or practices that appear to raise questions regarding the contractor's compliance with the Executive Order 11246, Section 503 or Section 4212.

Progression Line Charts

Written listings of a contractor's lines of progression. See definition of "Line of Progression."

Prohibited Factor

A factor prohibited by law from being used in making employment decisions. Under Executive Order 11246, as amended, the prohibited factors are race, color, religion, sex and national origin. Under Section 503, the prohibited factor is disability. Under Section 4212, various categories of veterans' status comprise the prohibited factor.

Promotable Minorities and Women

Minorities and women who are qualified and eligible for promotion based upon legitimate selection criteria.

Promotable or Transferable

In the context of developing data for availability, those employees who are currently employed in a job group or groups that serve or could serve as a source from which selections are or could be made for other job groups.

Promotion

Any personnel action resulting in, for example, movement to a position affording higher pay, greater rank, change in job title, increase in job grade or increase in pay, requiring greater skill or responsibility, or the opportunity to attain such.

Proof of Discrimination

"Proofs" of discrimination are the factual formulations that show discrimination under a particular theory exists. These formulations describe the kinds of facts needed to show a nexus between a particular adverse action or result and a particular prohibited factor. Proof requires evidence; see "Direct Evidence," "Circumstantial Evidence," "Anecdotal Evidence," and "Statistical Evidence."

Protected Group or Category

Applicants and employees protected from discrimination based on their sex, race, national origin, color, religion, disability or status as a protected veteran.

Protected Veteran

Any veteran who is covered by 41 CFR Part 60-250 or 41 CFR Part 60-300. Protected veterans include: armed forces service medal veterans, disabled veterans, other protected veterans, recently separated veterans, special disabled veterans and veterans of the Vietnam era.

Qualified Disabled Veteran

A disabled veteran who has the ability to perform the essential functions of the employment position with or without reasonable accommodation. 41 CFR 60-300.2(o).

Qualified Individual with a Disability

The term *"qualified,"* with respect to an individual with a disability, means that the individual satisfies the requisite skill, experience, education and other job-related requirements of the employment position such individual holds or desires and, with or without reasonable accommodation, can perform the essential functions of such position. See 29 CFR 1630.3 for exceptions to this definition. 29 CFR 1630.2(m); see also 41 CFR 60-741.2(t).

Race or Color, Protected Charcteristic

EO 11246 and Title VII prohibit employer actions that have the purpose or effect of discriminating against persons on the basis of protected characteristics such as race and color, which include personal characteristics associated with race such as hair texture or certain facial features; skin color and complexion; marriage to or association with a person of a certain race or color; and association with an organization or group that is generally associated with people of a certain color or race.

Reasonable Accommodation (Section 503 and Section 4212)

The term *reasonable accommodation* means:

(i) Modifications or adjustments to a job application process that enable a qualified applicant with a disability to be considered for the position such applicant desires; or

(ii) Modifications or adjustments to the work environment, or to the manner or circumstances under which the position held or desired is customarily performed, that enable a qualified individual with a disability to perform the essential functions of that position; or

(iii) Modifications or adjustments that enable the contractor's employee with a disability to enjoy equal benefits and privileges of employment as are enjoyed by the contractor's other similarly situated employees without disabilities.

41 CFR 60-741.2(v)(1); see also 29 CFR 1630.2(o)(1); 41 CFR 60-250.2(t)(1)(definition of reasonable accommodation for "special disabled veterans"); 41 CFR 60–300.2(t)(1)(definition of reasonable accommodation for "disabled veterans"). For examples of reasonable accommodations, see 41 CFR 60- 741.2(v)(2), 250.2(t)(2), and 300.2(t)(2).

Reasonable Recruitment Area

The geographical area from which the contractor usually seeks or reasonably could seek workers to fill jobs within a particular job group.

Recall

The process or action by which workers are returned to active employment from layoff.

Recently Separated Veteran

For the purpose of 41 CFR Part 60-300 (which applies to federal contractors with a government contract of $100,000 or more that was entered into or modified after December 1, 2003), "recently separated veteran" means any veteran during the three-year period beginning on the date of such veteran's discharge or release from active duty in the U.S. military, ground, naval or air service. 41 CFR 60-300.2(q).

For the purpose of 41 CFR Part 60-250 (which applies to federal contractors with a government contract of $25,000 or more that was entered into prior to December 1, 2003), "recently separated veteran" means any veteran during the one-year period beginning on the date of such veteran's discharge or release from active duty. 41 CFR 60-250.2(r).

Recruitment Source

Any person, organization or agency used to refer or provide workers for employment.

"Regarded As" Having a Disability

The ADA and Section 503 prohibit discrimination against individuals on the basis of disability. Disability is defined to include "being regarded as having" a physical or mental impairment that is not transitory (actual or expected duration of 6 months or less) and minor. See 42 USC 12102- 1(C), 3; 29 CFR 1630.2 (g) (iii); see also 29 CFR 1630.15(f). An individual is "regarded as having such an impairment" if the individual is subjected to a prohibited action because of an actual or perceived physical or mental impairment, whether or not that impairment substantially limits, or is perceived to substantially limit, a major life activity. 29 CFR 1630.2(l)(1). However, an individual must be covered under the first prong ("actual disability") or second prong ("record of disability") in order to qualify for a reasonable accommodation. See 29 CFR 1630.2(o)(4).

Regression Analysis

A statistical analysis used to evaluate the interrelated effects of independent variables (such as education, prior experience) on a dependent variable (such as hire, compensation). Regression analyses frequently are a significant element of OFCCP's proof used in systemic discrimination cases.

Rehire

To reengage a formerly employed worker after a complete break in employment status. Compare with "Recall."

Relevant Labor Area

See the definition of "Labor Area."

Religious Accommodation

A nondiscrimination obligation of a contractor to accommodate the sincerely held religious observances and practices of its current and prospective employees. Typical religious accommodations include, but are not limited to, permitting the wearing of religious head coverings and other religious dress at the workplace, swapping employee shifts or permitting time off to allow for religious observance and modifying an employee's work schedule to permit observance of the employee's Sabbath. Employers do not have to make a religious accommodation that will cause an undue hardship on the conduct of its business. See the definition of "Undue Hardship (Religious Accommodation)."

Request for Proposal (RFP)

An invitation for suppliers or service providers, often through a bidding process, to submit a proposal on a specific project.

Requisite Skills

Those minimum skills needed to perform a job satisfactorily.

Retaliation

Any adverse action against an individual because he or she filed a complaint of discrimination; opposed any act made unlawful under any of the laws enforced by OFCCP; or participated in an investigation, compliance evaluation, hearing or any other activity related to the administration or enforcement of any of the laws enforced by OFCCP.

Right of Response

The contractor's right in an enforcement proceeding to produce a legitimate, nondiscriminatory reason for its actions once OFCCP has made a prima facie showing of discrimination.

Rightful Place

The position, both economically and in terms of employment status (usually job position and seniority), that the victim of discrimination would have held if the discrimination had not occurred. See "Make-Whole Relief."

Section 503

Section 503 of the Rehabilitation Act of 1973, as amended, 29 U.S.C. 793.

Section 503 Complaint

A complaint alleging a violation of Section 503 or the implementing regulations at 41 CFR Part 60-741.

Section 4212

The Vietnam Era Veterans' Readjustment Assistance Act of 1974, as amended (38 U.S.C. 4212).

Section 4212 Complaint

A complaint alleging a violation of VEVRAA or its implementing regulations at 41 CFR Part 60-250 or 60-300.

Seniority

Length of employment as determined by the employer's policies or the applicable collective bargaining agreement. Seniority may be defined in various terms (e.g., company seniority, facility seniority, departmental seniority). Employees may have different types of seniority for different purposes, e.g., job bidding rights governed by department seniority and leave accrual rights governed by company seniority.

Sex Discrimination, Protected Characteristic

EO 11246 and Title VII prohibit employer actions that have the purpose or effect of discriminating against persons on the basis of protected characteristics such as sex, which includes, but is not limited to, pregnancy, childbirth or related medical conditions, connection with an organization or group that is generally associated with people of a certain sex and gender stereotypes.

Shortfall

The difference between the actual number of persons in the nonfavored group that were selected for the employment opportunity at issue (hires, promotions, etc.) and the number expected to have been selected in proportion to their representation in the pool of qualified candidates, absent discrimination. This concept does not generally apply to compensation discrimination cases, which revolve around wage-setting decisions, not decisions involving job opportunities.

Show Cause Notice (SCN)

A letter from OFCCP to the contractor ordering it to provide evidence demonstrating why enforcement proceedings should not be instituted. The Show Cause Notice provides that the contractor must come into compliance within 30 calendar days or OFCCP may recommend the commencement of enforcement proceedings.

Similarly Situated

The determination of which employees are similarly situated is case specific. Relevant factors in determining similarity may include tasks performed, skills, effort, level of responsibility, working conditions, job difficulty, minimum qualifications, or other objective factors. Employees are similarly situated when they are comparable on the factors relevant to the investigation even if they are not comparable on others.

Skill Inventory

A list of people, categorized by their skills, kept by a contractor to encourage maximum use of the skills of applicants or employees.

Solicitation for Subcontractors

The process a prime contractor goes through to request bidders for work on a particular project or projects.

Special Disabled Veteran

Special disabled veteran means:
i) A veteran who is entitled to compensation (or who, but for the receipt of military retirement pay, would be entitled to compensation) under laws administered by the Department of Veterans Affairs for a disability:

(A) Rated at 30 percent or more; or

(B) Rated at 10 or 20 percent in the case of a veteran who has been determined under 38 U.S.C. 3106to have a serious employment handicap; or

ii) A person who was discharged or released from active duty because of a service-connected disability. 41 CFR 60-250.2(n)(1).

Standard Deviation

As an alternative to probability values, statisticians often express the divergence between actual and expected outcomes in units called standard deviations. The larger the difference in standard deviations, the smaller the probability that the difference is due to random chance factors alone.

Standard Form 100

See the definition of "EEO-1 Report."

Standard Metropolitan Statistical Area (SMSA)

Metropolitan area as set by OMB that refers to a geographical region with a relatively high population density at its core and close economic ties throughout the area.

Statistical Evidence

Mathematical analyses of disparities in selection rates, wages or other effects of employment practices between members of one race, sex, or other group and another comparable group. Statistical evidence may be used, in appropriate circumstances, to show whether a practice or policy has a disparate impact on a particular group, and/or to determine whether a prohibited factor such as race or gender played a role in an employment decision. Statistical evidence is typically required to prove systemic discrimination.

Statistically Significant

The results of statistical analyses (statistical evidence) are "statistically significant" if the probability the results occurred by chance is so small that chance can reasonably be ruled out as the cause. When the difference between actual and expected values is greater than 1.96 standard deviations, the probability the disparity occurred by chance is less than 5%. In employment discrimination cases, courts generally consider a difference of two or more standard deviations to be "statistically significant" and allow a valid statistical inference of discrimination to be drawn.

Subcontract

Any agreement or arrangement between a contractor and any person (in which the parties do not stand in the relationship of an employer and employee):[325]

(a) for the purchase, sale or use of personal property or nonpersonal services, which in whole or in part, is necessary to the performance of any one or more government contracts; or

(b) under which any portion of the contractor's obligation under one or more government contracts is performed, undertaken, or assumed.

Subcontractor

---

[325] 41 CFR 60-1.3; see also 41 CFR 60-250.2(l); 41 CFR 60-300.2(l); 41 CFR 60-741.2(l).

Any person holding a subcontract (as defined above) and, [for enforcement purposes], any person who has held a subcontract subject to [Executive Order 11246, Section 503, or Section 4212]. 41 CFR 60-1.3; see also 41 CFR 60-250.2(m); 41 CFR 60-300.2(m); 41 CFR 60-741.2(m).

Subjective Criteria

Employment qualifications, selection standards or processes that require judgment in their application, such that different people applying such standards would not necessarily reach the same conclusion. (Whether an applicant is certified to operate a particular machine is objective; whether an applicant had "good machine-handling skills and experience" is subjective." Compare to "Objective Criteria."

Subletting a Contract

The process of dividing up a contract into smaller parts and letting the work to other contractors.

Substantially Limits
See the definition found at 26 CFR 1630.2.

Support Data

Statistical data, documentation and other materials regarding a contractor's employment policies, practices and actions used in the development, support and justification of its affirmative action program(s), or used to assess the affirmative action program's effectiveness.

Systemic Discrimination

A pattern or practice of discrimination or an identified employment practice with a disparate impact. OFCCP defines a systemic discrimination case as meeting one of two criteria: (a) the case addresses a measurable pattern of discrimination (either based on findings from a regression analysis or based on any other appropriate aggregate analysis of data) or (b) the case addresses an identified practice applicable to multiple employees that results in discrimination (such as a practice of steering employees who are members of a protected class toward lowering paying jobs at hire). There is no specific numericthreshold used to define a systemic case.

Termination of Employment

Separation of an employee from the active and inactive payroll.

Terms and Conditions of Employment

This phrase includes all aspects of the employment relationship between an employee and his or her employer including, but not limited to, hiring, compensation, fringe benefits, leave policies, job placement, work environment, work-related rules, work assignments, training and education, opportunities to serve on committees and decision-making bodies and opportunities for promotion.

Third Party Complaint

A complaint filed by an individual or individuals, on behalf of someone else, either an individual or a group of people. See 41 CFR 60- 250.61(b)(2), 60-300.61(b)(2), and 60-741.61(c)(2).

Title VII of the Civil Rights Act of 1964

This law makes it illegal to discriminate against an applicant or employee on the basis of race, color, religion, national origin or sex. The law also makes it illegal to retaliate against a person because the person complained about discrimination, filed a charge of discrimination or participated in an employment discrimination investigation or lawsuit. The law also requires that employers reasonably accommodate applicants' and employees' sincerely held religious practices, unless doing so would impose an undue hardship on the operation of the employer's business. This law is enforced by the EEOC and its principles apply to discrimination cases arising under EO 11246.

Tolling

The suspension of the running of a statute of limitations for equitable reasons. Because the Title VII 180-day limit on filing a charge with the EEOC has been held to be a statute of limitations, there have been numerous court cases discussing tolling of that limit. By comparison, the regulations for OFCCP's three programs provide for the filing of a complaint within 180 calendar days of the alleged violation unless the time for filing is extended by the Director for good cause shown. There is no similar good cause language in Title VII. The good cause authority allows the Director to waive the 180-day limit without raising questions of tolling.

Training Agency

Any person, organization or agency whose purpose is to train workers.

Transfer

Movement (usually lateral) from one position or function to another.

Underutilization

When the percentage of minorities or women employed in a particular job group is less than would be reasonable expected given their availability percentage in that particular job group. See 41 CFR 60-2.10(a)(1).

Undue Hardship (Disability)

"Undue hardship" is the only defense for failing to make reasonable accommodations to the known physical or mental limitations of an otherwise qualified individual with a disability. The employer must demonstrate that the accommodation would cause "significant difficulty or expense" in light of its particular resources and circumstances. 42 U.S.C. 12111(10). Undue hardship refers not only to financial difficulty, but also to reasonable accommodations that are unduly extensive, substantial, or disruptive, or those that would fundamentally alter the nature or operation of the business. See 41 CFR 60-250.2(u) and 60-250 Appendix A; 41 CFR 60–300.2(u) and 60-300 Appendix A ; 41 CFR 60-741.2(w) and 60-741 Appendix A. Whether an accommodation would impose an undue hardship requires a case-by-case determination. See 41 CFR 60-741.2(w) for factors to be considered.

Undue Hardship (Religious Accommodation)

An employer is required to reasonably accommodate an employee whose sincerely held religious belief, practice, or observance conflicts with a work requirement, unless providing the accommodation would create an undue hardship. The undue hardship defense to providing religious accommodation requires a showing that the proposed accommodation in a particular case poses a "more than de minimis" cost or burden. Costs to be considered include not only direct monetary costs, but also the burden on the conduct of the employer's business. For example, courts have found undue hardship where the accommodation diminishes efficiency in other jobs, infringes on other employees' job rights or benefits, impairs workplace safety, or causes co-workers to carry the accommodated employee's share of potentially hazardous or burdensome work.

Uniformly Applied

Applying employment criteria and/or processes in the same manner to all similarly situated applicants or employees.

Uniform Guidelines on Employment Selection Procedures (UGESP)

Guidelines developed by the EEOC, Department of Justice, Department of Labor and the Civil Service Commission (now the Office of Personnel Management) to provide a single set of principles that are designed to assist employers, labor organizations, employment agencies and licensing and certification boards to comply with requirements of federal law prohibiting employment practices that discriminate on grounds of race, color, religion, sex and national origin. See 41 CFR Part 60-3. Under Executive Order 11246 UGESP were promulgated as regulations with the force and effect of law.

Union Shop

A factory, business, etc., operating under a collective bargaining agreement between the employer and a labor union that requires that all employees in specific jobs are or become members of the union within a set time frame.

Validation

The demonstration of job-relatedness by showing the relationship between the selection procedure and job performance. To be validated in accordance with UGESP the validation studies must meet the technical standards set out in 41 CFR Part 60-3.

Veteran

For the purpose of 41 CFR Part 60-300, "veteran" means a person who served in the active military, naval, or air service of the United States, and who was discharged or released therefrom under conditions other than dishonorable. 41 CFR 60-300.2(z).

Veterans Benefits and Health Care Improvement Act of 2000

Signed on November 1, 2000, to add "recently separated" veterans and covers veterans separated during a one-year period beginning on the date of the veterans' discharges or releases from active duty.

Veteran of the Vietnam Era (41 CFR Part 60-250 only)

A person who:

(1) Served on active duty for a period of more than 180 days, and was discharged or released therefrom with other than a dishonorable discharge, if any part of such active duty occurred:

(i) In the Republic of Vietnam between February 28, 1961, and May 7, 1975; or

(ii) Between August 5, 1964, and May 7, 1975, in all other cases; or

(2) Was discharged or released from active duty for a service-connected disability if any part of such active duty was performed:

(i) In the Republic of Vietnam between February 28, 1961, and May 7, 1975; or

(ii) Between August 5, 1964, and May 7, 1975, in all other cases.

41 CFR 60-250.2(p).

VETS-100 and VETS-100A Reports

The VETS-100 and VETS-100A Reports are to be completed by all non-exempt federal contractors and subcontractors with contracts or subcontracts for the furnishing of supplies and services or for the use of real or personal property. VETS-100 must be completed by contractors with contracts entered into prior to December 1, 2003, for $25,000 or more, and not modified since to a contract of $100,000 or more. VETS-100A must be completed by contractors with contracts entered into or modified on or after December 1, 2003, for $100,000 or more. The Reports require that contractors report annually the numbers of various categories of veterans they employ or have newly hired by hiring location and job category.

VEVRAA

The Vietnam Era Veterans' Readjustment Assistance Act of 1974, as amended (38 U.S.C. 4212).

Victim Specific Relief

The same as "Individual Relief." The assessment of make-whole relief for identified victim(s) of discrimination on an individualized basis. This method is generally used to calculate back pay in those individual or small group discrimination cases where the victims of discrimination, and the losses they incurred, can be determined with specificity. *Compare to* "Formula Relief."

Violation

Failure to fulfill a requirement of the Executive Order 11246, Section 503 or Section 4212 or their implementing rules, regulations and orders. The terms violation and deficiency are often used interchangeably. See the definition of "Deficiency."

White

As defined by OMB's *Standards for Maintaining, Collecting, and Presenting Federal Data on Race and Ethnicity* (1997), an individual, not of Hispanic origin, with origins in any of the original peoples of Europe, North Africa or the Middle East.

Work Assignment

Something, such as a task, that is assigned. A position or post of duty to which one is assigned.

Wrongful Discharge

Generally, unlawful employment termination. The phrase "wrongful discharge" is frequently used to refer to exceptions created by the courts in some states to the employment-at-will doctrine (see above). Courts in such states differ in the circumstances in which they will allow wrongful discharge suits challenging a termination. State law on this issue is not of direct concern to OFCCP. The Executive Order 11246, Section 503, Section 4212 and implementing regulations prohibit termination based on a prohibited factor.

38 U.S.C. 4212

The affirmative action and nondiscrimination provisions of the Vietnam Era Veterans' Readjustment Assistance Act of 1974, as amended. Also referred to as "Section 4212" and "VEVRAA."

GLOSSARY OF ABBREVIATIONS

AA	Affirmative Action
AAP	Affirmative Action Program
ACE	Active Case Enforcement
ACM	Active Case Management
AD	Area Director (formerly AOD – Area Office Director)
ADA	Americans with Disabilities Act
ADAAA	ADA Amendments Act of 2008
ADD	Assistant District Director
ALJ	Administrative Law Judge
AO	Area Office, OFCCP
APA	Administrative Procedure Act
ARB	Administrative Review Board
ASCN	Amended Show Cause Notice
BFOQ	Bona Fide Occupational Qualification
BP	Back Pay
CA	Conciliation Agreement
CBA	Collective Bargaining Agreement
CBO	Community-Based Organization
CD	Consent Decree
CEO	Chief Executive Officer
CFR	Code of Federal Regulations

CMCE	Corporate Management Compliance Evaluation
CMS	Case Management System
CMSA	Consolidated Metropolitan Statistical Area
CO	Compliance Officer (formerly an Equal Opportunity Specialist or EOS)
CSAL	Corporate Scheduling Announcement Letter
D&B	Dun & Bradstreet
DBE	Disadvantaged Business Enterprise
DD	District Director
DHS	Department of Homeland Security
DO	District Office
DOJ	Department of Justice
DOL	Department of Labor
DORO	Division of Regional Operations
DPO	Division of Program Operations
DPPPD	Division of Policy, Planning and Program Development
DRD	Deputy Regional Director
DUNS	Dun and Bradstreet Universal Numbering System
EEDS	Equal Employment Data System
EEO	Equal Employment Opportunity
EEO-1	Standard Form 100 – Employer Information Report
EEOC	Equal Employment Opportunity Commission
EIN	Employer Identification Number
EO	Executive Order

EIS	Executive Information System
ETA	Employment and Training Administration
FAAP	Functional Affirmative Action Program
FCCM	Federal Contract Compliance Manual
FCSS	Federal Contractor Selection System
FEP	Fair Employment Practices Agency
FOIA	Freedom of Information Act
FPDS	Federal Procurement Data System
FR	Federal Register
GFE	Good Faith Efforts
ICE	U.S. Immigration and Customs Enforcement (formerly INS)
ILG	Industry Liaison Group
INS	Immigration and Naturalization Service (predecessor agency to ICE, above)
IRA	Impact Ratio Analysis
IRCA	Immigration Reform and Control Act of 1986
JAAR	Job Area Acceptance Range
JAN	Job Accommodation Network
JRC	Joint Reporting Committee
JVA	Jobs for Veteran Act
LOP	Line of Progression
LVER	Local Veterans' Employment Representative – See VWS
MBE	Minority Business Enterprise
MG	Minority Group

MJL	Mandatory Job Listing
MOU	Memorandum of Understanding
MSA	Metropolitan Statistical Area
MSS	Management Support Staff
NAICS	North American Industrial Classification System (replaced SIC)
NILG	National Industry Liaison Group
NO	National Office (OFCCP)
NOC	Notice of Compliance
NORI	Notice of Results of Investigation
NOV	Notice of Violation
NSOL	National Office Solicitor of Labor
ODEP	Office of Disability Employment Policy
OFCCP	Office of Federal Contract Compliance Programs
OFIS	Office of Federal Contract Compliance Information System
OJT	On-the-Job Training
PDN	Predetermination Notice
RD	Regional Director
RO	Regional Office
RSOL	Regional Solicitor of Labor
S&S	Supply and Service
SAU	Statitical Analysis Unit
SCER	Standard Compliance Evaluation Report (Supply and Service)
SCN	Show Cause Notice

SD	Standard Deviation
SEC. 503	Section 503 of the Rehabilitation Act of 1973 (29 U.S.C. 793), as amended
SES	State Employment Service
SMSA	Standard Metropolitan Statistical Area
SOL	Solicitor of Labor
SSEG	Similarly Situated Employee Group
TERO	Tribal Employment Rights Office
TITLE VI	Title VI of the Civil Rights Act of 1964, as amended
TITLE VII	Title VII of the Civil Rights Act of 1964, as amended
USC	United States Code
UGESP	Uniform Guidelines on Employee Selection Procedures
USERRA	Uniform Services Employment and Reemployment Rights Act
VES	Veterans' Employment Service
VETS	Veterans' Employment and Training Service (DOL)
VEVRAA	Vietnam Era Veterans' Readjustment Assistance Act, as amended
VPSS	Veterans Programs Services Supervisor for EDD
VWS	Veterans Workforce Specialist (formerly EDD's LVER)
WBE	Women's Business Enterprise
WEAL	Women's Equity Action League

STANDARD FORMS LIST

NUMBER	TITLE/EXPLANATION
CC-4	Complaint Form
CC-58	Complaint Report Sheet
CC-58a	Financial Payments Sheet
CC-73	Quality Audit Form for Supply and Service Review
CC-74	Quality Audit Form for Construction Review
CC-75	Quality Audit Form for Complaint Investigation
CC-104	Report of Remedies Agreed to for Identifiable Persons
CC-257	Monthly Employment Utilization Report; an optional document used by construction companies to report monthly hours worked by trade

APPENDIX A1 – A14

APPENDIX A-1: STANDARD COMPLIANCE EVALUATION REPORT (SCER) FORM

Supply and Service Standard Compliance Evaluation Report (SCER)

U.S. Department of Labor
Office of Federal Contract Compliance Programs

COMPLIANCE EVALUATION SUMMARY

1. ESTABLISHMENT/FUNCTIONAL UNIT NAME & ADDRESS CMS Control #	2. PARENT NAME & ADDRESS

3. SMSA/MSA % Female	% Minor	% Black	% Hisp.	% Asian/PI	% AmInd AlNat	4. COMPLAINTS INVESTIGATED DURING REVIEW: ☑ =Resolved # ________ ☐ # ________ ☐

5. CONTRACT COVERAGE:

AWARDING AGENCY	IF SUBCONTRACTOR, NAME OF PRIME CONTRACTOR	CONTRACT OR PURCHASE ORDER #	CONTRACT DOLLAR AMOUNT	BEGIN AND END DATES

6. COMPANY CONTACTS:		Name	Title	Phone
Establishment/ Functional Unit	CEO/Dir /Mgr			
	EEO/AA			
Corporate	CEO			
	EEO/AA			
Outside Representative				

7. BACKGROUND INFORMATION:

Type of Industry:
Specific Facility Function:

Total # Employees	**Total # Female Employees**	**% Female Employees**	**Total # Minority Employees**	**% Minority Employees**

Date Scheduling Letter Received by Contractor	**AAP Year**	**Prior Year Data Period**	**Current Year Data Period (if applicable)**	**Union**	**If unionized, % of unionized workforce**	**NAICS**
				☐ Y / N ☐	%	

CASE SUMMARY AND RECOMMENDATIONS

Provide an assessment of compliance. If there are findings of violation, list all findings (discrimination and/or technical violations) to be included in a Predetermination Notice/Notice of Violation(s). For each one, provide a brief explanation of the supporting evidence, briefly describe conciliation efforts and specify the recommended corrective action(s). If there is no finding of a violation, and a closure letter is to be issued, provide a brief description of the basis for this action. Be sure to indicate all document(s) to be issued to the contractor (e.g., Predetermination Notice, Notice of Violation, Show Cause Notice, Conciliation Agreement, or closure letter). If the length of the Case Summary exceeds a page, include additional sheets as an attachment to the SCER and note the attachment here.

Onsite: Yes ☐ No ☐ If yes, state reason ______________ (e.g., indicator; quality check; etc.).

	COMPLIANCE OFFICER	ASST. DIST. DIR	DIST. DIR./ REG. DIR.
Signature			
Date			

PART A: PREPARATION

I. PAST PROBLEMS / KNOWN COMPLAINTS OR ENFORCEMENT PROCEEDINGS

1. **Past Problems.** If there were no prior OFCCP compliance reviews or investigations of the contractor, check here and go on to item 2 below. ( )

If any problems were identified in any past OFCCP compliance review or complaint investigation of the contractor's establishment under review or other contractor establishments, indicate "Yes" or "No" as applicable for part (a) below, and list the date(s) of the review/investigation and any major problems identified. At the point in this review at which you determine whether a problem has recurred, complete part (b) below.

a. Past Problems? Yes / No Explain if yes and identify source materials.

b. Recurrence? Yes / No Explain if yes.

2. **Known Complaints or Enforcement Proceedings.** If there are no complaints filed or pending with other agencies, e.g., EEOC, WHD, or OSHA, and no new or ongoing enforcement proceedings by any of these agencies, check here and go on to the next page. ( )

If there are any such pending complaints or enforcement proceedings, for each one, list the agency involved, the basis, issue, current status and the area of the contractor's workforce it appears to concern. Add additional sheets as an attachment to the SCER, if needed. If at any point in the review you determine there is a related potential systemic problem, complete part (b) below.

a. Complaints filed.

Agency	Basis	Issue	Status	Job Group/ Department (if available)

b. Potential Discrimination? Yes / No Explain if yes.

PART A: PREPARATION
II. INITIAL REVIEW OF AAP AND SUPPORT DATA SUBMISSIONS

	INCLUDED? Indicate Y/N	ACCEPTABLE? (Text Only) Y/N	If NO, Include in PART A.III
Example- ORGANIZATIONAL PROFILE	*Y*	*N*	*See Item 0*
ORGANIZATIONAL PROFILE (Organizational Display or Workforce Analysis) 60-2.11			
JOB GROUP ANALYSIS 60-2.12			
UTILIZATION ANALYSIS			
PLACEMENT OF INCUMBENTS IN JOB GROUPS 60-2.13			
DETERMINING AVAILABILITY 60-2.14			
COMPARISON OF INCUMBENCY TO AVAILABILITY 60-2.15			
PLACEMENT GOALS 60-2.16			
ADDITIONAL REQUIRED ELEMENTS			
DESIGNATION OF RESPONSIBILITY 60-2.17(a)			
IDENTIFICATION OF PROBLEM AREAS 60-2.17(b)			
ACTION-ORIENTED PROGRAMS 60-2.17(c)			
INTERNAL AUDIT AND REPORTING SYSTEMS 60-2.17(d)			

SUPPORT DATA AND PERSONNEL ACTIVITY 60-2.17(b) and 60-3

	PRIOR YEAR	CURR YEAR (if applic)	ACCEPTABLE? Y/N	IF NO, INCLUDE IN PART A.III
REPORT ON GOALS				
APPLICANT FLOW Internet Applicant ☐				
HIRES				
PROMOTIONS (INCLUDING POOL DATA)				
TERMINATIONS (INCLUDING INCUMBENCY DATA)				
LAYOFFS/RECALLS (IF APPLICABLE)				
COMPENSATION DATA (snapshot date (X/X/XX))				

PART A: PREPARATION

II. INITIAL REVIEW OF AAP AND SUPPORT DATA SUBMISSIONS (continued)

SECTION 503 AND VEVRAA	INCLUDED Indicate Y/N	ACCEPTABLE (text only) Indicate Y/N	If NO, include in Part A. III
EEO POLICY STATEMENT 60-250.44(a); 60-300.44(a); 60-741.44(a)			
REVIEW OF PERSONNEL PROCESSES 60-250.44(b); 60-300.44(b); 60-741.44(b)			
REVIEW OF PHYSICAL AND MENTAL JOB QUALIFICATIONS 60-250.44(c); 60-300.44(c); 60-741.44(c)			
REASONABLE ACCOMMODATION 60-250.44(d); 60-300.44(d); 60-741.44(d)			
HARASSMENT PREVENTION 60-250.44(e); 60-300.44(e); 60-741.44(e)			
EXTERNAL DISSEMINATION OF EEO POLICY 60-250.44(f); 60-300.44(f); 60-741.44(f)			
INTERNAL DISSEMINATION OF EEO POLICY 60-250.44(g); 60-300.44(g); 60-741.44(g)			
AUDIT AND REPORTING SYSTEM 60-250.44(h); 60-300.44(h); 60-741.44(h)			
ESTABLISHMENT OF RESPONSIBILITY 60-250.44(i); 60-300.44(i); 60-741.44(i)			
TRAINING TO ENSURE AAP IMPLEMENTATION 60-250.44(j); 60-300.44(j); 60-741.44(j)			

PART A: PREPARATION

III. AAP AND SUPPORT DATA SUBMISSION PROBLEMS

PROBLEM AREAS: ( ) EO 11246 ( ) SECTION 503 ( ) VEVRAA

Summary of AAP Support Data Submission Problems and Actions Taken and/or Plan to Resolve (if the action is to take place during or after onsite). If investigated onsite, provide an explanation of the findings, whether the problem was resolved and what remedial action(s) was taken. (Add additional sheets as an attachment to the SCER, if needed).

☐ Continued

#	AAP AND SUPPORT DATA PROBLEMS	Onsite ☑
0	*Example:* **PROBLEM:** Contractor's Workforce Analysis (WFA) failed to reflect Lines of Progression. **ACTION TAKEN:** CO plans to provide compliance assistance to contractor on developing a WFA during onsite. **FINDINGS:** On X day, determined contractor did not understand how to include Lines of Progression in the WFA. **RESOLUTION:** On X day, CO provided contractor with compliance assistance on developing a WFA. On X date, contractor resubmitted WFA that included Lines of Progression.	☑
1	**PROBLEM:** **ACTION TAKEN:** **FINDINGS:** **RESOLUTION:**	☐
2		☐
3		☐
4		☐
5		☐
6		☐

PART A: PREPARATION

IV. EEO TREND ANALYSIS

☐ Continued

EEO TREND ANALYSIS RESULTS
1. **Trends.** Examine long-term and short-term trends of minority and female representation in: (a) the total workforce, (b) white-collar EEO categories, and (c) blue-collar EEO categories. If there are any negative trends, discuss below. If there are no negative trends, check here and go on to number 2. ( )
2. **Job Category Patterns.** Determine if there are any negative trends of minority or female representation by EEO job category. If there were negative trends, explain below. If there are no negative trends check here and go on to number 3. ( )
3. **Particular Group.** Determine if there are any substantial disparities in the trends of a particular minority group or of men or women of a particular minority group, either in the workforce as a whole or in specific job groups? If disparities exist, explain them below. If there are no negative trends check here ( ) and go on the next page.

PART B: AFFIRMATIVE ACTION

I. EVALUATION OF GOOD FAITH EFFORTS - EO 11246

Identify goal areas where goals were established but not met. For each goal area, identify the job group, describe whether goals were for minorities, females or both, prior and current year, and identify the expected goal and actual goal. If there is a difference between the expected and actual goals, provide the contractor's explanation for the difference and pertinent AAP commitments. Identify additional information that will be requested, and whether the issue needs to be investigated onsite. Provide an explanation of any findings, indicating whether the problem was resolved, or not, and what remedial action(s) was taken.

☐ Continued

#	GOAL AREA PROBLEMS	On-site ☑
0	*Example:* **GOAL AREA (PY):** Operatives (Minority). Expected #/Actual # = 20/2 **EXPLANATION/COMMITMENTS:** Very few minorities applied. **ADDITIONAL INFO:** List of recruitment sources. **FINDINGS:** On X day, CO reviewed and contacted the contractor's recruitment sources. The CO determined that the contractor failed to provide the recruitment sources with the vacancy information for this job group. **RESOLUTION:** Not resolved, see Part C.	☑
1	**GOAL AREA (PY/CY):** **EXPLANATION/COMMITMENTS:** **ADDITIONAL INFO:** **FINDINGS:** **RESOLUTION:**	☐
2		☐
3		☐
4		☐
5		☐
6		☐

PART B: AFFIRMATIVE ACTION

II. OTHER PROBLEMS FOR INVESTIGATION

Identify any other problems that require additional information and/or require an onsite review. Provide an explanation of any findings, indicating whether the problem was resolved, or not, and what remedial action(s) was taken.

☐ Continued

#	PROBLEM AREAS	On-site ☑
0	*Example:* **PROBLEM AREA:** Minority employees are concentrated in laborer positions in the receiving department, yet under-represented in operative positions in the same department. Note: The job group analysis shows that laborers are the primary feeder job for operative positions. **ADDITIONAL INFO:** Request position descriptions, job postings, and bid lists for opportunities in the operative positions. Interview laborers, operatives and selecting officials in the receiving department. **FINDINGS:** Promotion issue identified in the movement of minority employees from laborer positions to operative positions. **RESOLUTION:** See Part C.	☐
1	**PROBLEM AREA:** **ADDITIONAL INFO:** **FINDINGS:** **RESOLUTION:**	☐
2		☐
3		☐
4		☐
5		☐

PART B: AFFIRMATIVE ACTION

III. IMPLEMENTATION OF SEX DISCRIMINATION GUIDELINES, SEX DISCRMINATION PROVISIONS OF PART 60-1, AND THE GUIDELINES ON DISCRIMINATION BECAUSE OF RELIGION AND NATIONAL ORIGIN (onsite review only)

During the onsite review, verify the contractor's implementation of the sex discrimination provisions at 41 CFR Parts 60-1 and 60-20, and the Guidelines on Discrimination Because of Religion and National Origin at 41 CFR 60-50. If the contractor is in compliance, describe below how this determination was made (e.g., reference documentation and other evidence that was reviewed and describe statements made during interviews). If not, explain the problem, whether it has been resolved, and if so, how. If you identify a potential discrimination problem, include the issue in **Part C – Problems Identified.**

☐ Continued

SEX DISCRIMINATION GUIDELINES, 41 CFR PART 60-20 VIOLATION? YES / NO EXPLAIN.
Job Policies and Practices (Pregnancy) 1.a. Contractor does/does not treat leave for pregnancy and pregnancy-related conditions the same as leave for disabilities related to medical conditions. Describe the policy related to leave for pregnancy, childbirth, and related medical conditions and how it is implemented. The CO must examine whether the contractor provides job-guaranteed medical leave, including paid sick leave, for women's pregnancy, childbirth, and related medical conditions on the same terms that medical or sick leave is provided for medical conditions that are similar in their effect on employees' ability to work. 1.b. The Contractor does/does not have employment policies or practices under which insufficient or no medical or family leave is available. The CO must examine whether such policies or practices have an adverse impact on the basis of sex and if so, whether the contractor has shown that such policies or practices are job-related and consistent with business necessity.
Seniority System Seniority system does/does not discriminate based on sex. Explain.
Discriminatory Compensation Compensation is/is not related to or based on the sex of the employee. Explain.

☐ Continued

GUIDELINES ON DISCRIMINATION BECAUSE OF RELIGION OR NATIONAL ORIGIN, 41 CFR PART 60-50 VIOLATION? YES/ NO EXPLAIN.
60-50.2 <u>Equal Employment and Anti-Harassment Policies. Outreach and Positive Recruitment.</u> 1. Contractor does/does not have a policy prohibiting discrimination and harassment on the basis of religion or national origin? 2. Description of outreach efforts:
60-50.3 <u>Accommodations to Religious Observance and Practice.</u> 1. Contractor does/does not have a policy for ensuring accommodation for religious observance and practice? 2. If "Yes," how is it implemented?

PART B: AFFIRMATIVE ACTION

IV. IMPLEMENTATION OF SECTION 503 (DISABILITY) AND VEVRAA (VETERANS)

☐ Continued

REQUIREMENTS	Did the contractor comply with the following requirements? If "Yes," indicate "Y" for *In Compliance*, and explain how this was confirmed. If "No," indicate "N" for *Not In Compliance*, and explain the problem, whether it was resolved, and if resolved, indicate how. Indicate whether the problem was resolved by placing a "Y" or "N" for *Resolved*. If potential discrimination is identified, include in **Part C – Compliance Evaluation Findings.**
AAP AND SUPPORT DATA SUBMISSIONS (items listed in PART A.II above)	**IN COMPLIANCE? (Y/N)** **PROBLEM:** **RESOLVED? (Y/N)**
AVAILABILITY OF AAPS FOR INSPECTION 60-250.41, 60-300.41, 60-741.41	**IN COMPLIANCE? (Y/N)** **PROBLEM:** **RESOLVED? (Y/N)**
INVITATION TO SELF-IDENTIFY 60-250.42, 60-300.42, 60-741.42	**IN COMPLIANCE? (Y/N)** **PROBLEM:** **RESOLVED? (Y/N)**
DISABILITY-RELATED QUESTIONS AND MEDICAL EXAMINATIONS 60-250.23, 60-300.23, 60-741.23	**IN COMPLIANCE? (Y/N)** **PROBLEM:** **RESOLVED? (Y/N)**
CONFIDENTIALITY REQUIREMENT 60-250.23(d), 60-300.23(d), 60-741.23(d)	**IN COMPLIANCE? (Y/N)** **PROBLEM:** **RESOLVED? (Y/N)**

PART B: AFFIRMATIVE ACTION

V. TECHNICAL REQUIREMENTS: EO 11246, SECTION 503, VEVRAA and EO 13496

☐ Continued

REQUIREMENTS Did the contractor comply with the following requirements (Yes/No)? If "Yes," indicate how this was confirmed. If "No," explain the problem, whether it was resolved, and if resolved, indicate how. If a technical requirement is not resolved, it must be included in **Part C – Problems Identified and Part F – Summary of Findings.**
Applicable under EO 11246, Section 503, and VEVRAA.
INCLUDED EO CLAUSE IN SUBCONTRACTS AND PURCHASE ORDERS (60- 1.4, 60-250.5, 60-300.5, 60-741.5)
POSTED NOTICES OF ITS OBLIGATIONS AND EEO POSTERS IN CONSPICUOUS PLACES (60- 1.4, 60-250.5, 60-300.5, 60-741.5)
NOTIFIED PARTIES WITH WHICH IT HAS A CBA OF ITS EEO OBLIGATIONS (60- 1.4, 60-250.5, 60-300.5, 60-741.5)
(CORPORATE MANAGEMENT EVALUATION ONLY) DEVELOPED AND MAINTAINED AN AAP AT EACH ESTABLISHMENT (60-2.1)
WRITTEN POLICY(IES) PROHIBITING DISCRIMINATION AND HARASSMENT ON THE BASIS OF RACE, COLOR, RELIGION, SEX, NATIONAL ORIGIN, DISABILITY AND VETERAN STATUS (60-1; 60-1.4; 60-20.3(A); 60-50; 60-250.44; 60-300.44; and 60-741.44)

☐ Continued

Applicable under EO 11246 only.
FILED CURRENT EEO-1 REPORT (60-1.7)
INCLUDED EEO LANGUAGE IN JOB ADVERTISEMENTS (60-1.4)
Applicable under Section 503 and VEVRAA only
PROVIDED NOTICE OF THE AVAILABILITY OF REASONABLE ACCOMODATION TO ENSURE ACCESS TO ONLINE APPLICATION SYSTEM (60-250.44(d); 60-300.44(d); 60-741.44(d))
Applicable under VEVRAA only.
FILED CURRENT VETS 100A (OR VETS 100, IF APPLICABLE) (60-250.60(c), 60-300.60(c))
LISTED JOB OPENINGS WITH EMPLOYMENT SERVICE DELIVERY SYSTEM (60-250.5(a), 60-300.5(a))
Applicable under EO 13496 only.
POSTED NOTICE OF EMPLOYEE RIGHTS UNDER THE NATIONAL LABOR RELATIONS ACT (Required poster and electronic posting, if applicable) (29 CFR 471.2)
INCLUDED NOTICE OF EO 13496 OBLIGATIONS IN SUBCONTRACTS (29 CFR 471, Subpart A, app. A)

PART C: PROBLEMS IDENTIFIED

☐ Continued

Identify any problems found during the compliance evaluation. Include a discussion of the nature of the problem, relevant evidence reviewed, actions (if any) taken to resolve the problem, and whether and how the problem was resolved. Be sure to also include any findings of violation in the next section, **Part F - Summary of Findings.**

	SUMMARY OF PROBLEMS, ACTIONS TAKEN AND RESOLUTION **(Add additional sheets as an attachment to the SCER, if needed)**
	EXAMPLE: *The impact ratio analysis showed an adverse impact ratio(0 female hires) in the craft workers job group and a shortfall of 2. None of the 10 women who applied was hired; in contrast, 8 of the 20 men who applied were hired. The difference in selection rates is statistically significant to the level of 2.34 standard deviations. Action taken: Requested applicant and hire logs, applications, selection criteria, and position descriptions during the desk audit. Onsite observed the craft worker jobs, interviewed the selecting officials, craft worker supervisors, and individuals in the positions as well as the individuals hired. Offsite analyzed the hiring process, comparing the applications of those selected and not selected to the selection criteria; also interviewed applicants who were not selected. Of the 10 women who applied, all met the stated minimum criteria (see analysis worksheet A-1, attached); 6 were never contacted by the contractor for an interview and the 4 that were interviewed were asked if they had plans to start a family. Also interviewed the males who were not selected; of the 12 men who were not selected, all were interviewed, none were asked about their plans to begin a family. (Interview statements are found at tab A-3). A predetermination notice was prepared and sent to the contractor that detailed the preliminary findings of the investigation. The contractor did not rebut the preliminary findings; a Notice of Violations was issued followed recommending corrective actions and requiring resolution in a conciliation agreement that included make-whole relief for the 10 women who applied. Following negotiations, the contractor signed a conciliation agreement. Additional details are found in Part F – Summary of Findings.*
1	
2	

3	

PART D: CORPORATE MANAGEMENT EVALUATION (CMCE) NARRATIVE

<table>
<tr><td colspan="2">When conducting a CMCE, this section of the SCER must be completed in addition to the Case Summary and Recommendations (SCER pg 2). 41 CFR Section 60-2.30 is specifically applicable to CMCEs. Parts A, B, C and F of the SCER must also be completed, as appropriate to the nature and scope of the review performed. Add additional sheets as an attachment, if needed.
Note: "protected group member" as used below refers to minorities, women, protected veterans and individuals with disabilities.</td></tr>
<tr><td><u>Introduction</u>:</td><td>Describe the corporate background, structure, observations concerning corporate culture and values. Also describe any previous OFCCP reviews/complaints, or complaints filed with other agencies, that specifically address management jobs or "glass ceiling" issues.</td></tr>
<tr><td><u>Corporate AAP</u>:</td><td>What positions at lower-level establishments are rolled-up into the Corporate AAP?</td></tr>
<tr><td><u>Scope</u>:</td><td>Did the review cover only corporate headquarters or was it extended to cover one or more intermediate headquarters or lower-level establishments?</td></tr>
<tr><td><u>Focus Level and Areas</u>:</td><td>Describe the company's pay and management structure. For each protected group (women, minorities, individuals with disabilities, and protected veterans), does the representation of protected group members decline at a certain pay or grade level? Are they concentrated in certain functional areas? Are those areas staff or line management?</td></tr>
<tr><td><u>Outreach Efforts</u>:</td><td>To what extent does the company already have outreach, training and development programs designed to increase opportunities for protected group members entry into mid- and senior level corporate management positions? Describe any such programs and what results they have yielded to date.</td></tr>
</table>

Jobs Filled at and above the Focus Level:	During the review period, what jobs have been filled at the mid- and senior corporate management levels? How were they filled (hire, promotion, transfer)? Describe external and internal opportunities.
Internal Development - Specific Programs:	Does the company have development programs/opportunities in the following areas and, if so, describe them and protected group member participation in them: 1) Succession and Related Planning; 2) Performance Appraisals; 3) Visibility (Special Projects/Task Forces; Committees; Special Assistants/Executive Assistants); 4) Management Training and Executive Development Programs; and 5) Mentoring and Networking. Identify whether any of these programs/opportunities are designed for a particular group.
Total Compensation:	Describe the compensation system including any findings with regard to 1) Bonuses; 2) Stock; 3) Perquisites; 4) Award and Honor Programs.
Terminations:	Have there been any terminations among the mid- and senior level corporate management? What are the termination policies and practices? Are they evenhandedly applied?
Conclusions:	Were any problems found? What are the reason(s) for them?
Resolution:	What commitments (whether remedial or improved good faith efforts) has the corporation made to ensure that protected group members have an equal opportunity to advance to mid- and senior level corporate management positions?

PART E: COMPLIANCE CHECK CONTROL SHEET (TO BE INSERTED BY THE CO)

PART F: SUMMARY OF FINDINGS
(Provide a detailed narrative of the evaluation findings.)

APPENDIX A-2: STANDARD COMPLIANCE EVALUATION REPORT (SCER) INSTRUCTIONS

OVERALL SCER STRUCTURE

This SCER is used to document the results of a compliance evaluation, including the findings of the desk audit review of the contractor's Affirmative Action Programs (AAP). It consists of a Compliance Evaluation Summary and six parts: Part A: Preparation; Part B: Affirmative Action; Part C: Problems Identified; Part D: Corporate Management Compliance Evaluation (CMCE) Narrative; Part E: Compliance Check Control Sheet; and Part F: Summary of Findings (Internal Document).

How much of the SCER is completed during each particular desk audit or onsite review or both will depend on the type of evaluation being performed, the extent of investigation required, and the data submitted by the contractor. It is important to remember that throughout the compliance evaluation you may obtain additional data and information that must be analyzed and noted on the SCER before you make a finding.

Each part of the SCER provides space for the compliance officer (CO) to enter a narrative describing any problems identified, action(s) taken to resolve the problems, any finding(s) of violation, the evidence examined and the basis for the finding(s), and recommended corrective action.

The specific parts of the SCER are:

COMPLIANCE EVALUATION SUMMARY

Page 1. Background Information
Page 2. Case Summary and Recommendations

PART A: PREPARATION

I. Past Problems/Known Complaints or Enforcement Proceedings
II. Initial Review of AAP and Support Data Submissions
III. AAP and Support Data Submission Problems
IV. EEO Trend Analysis

PART B: AFFIRMATIVE ACTION

I. Evaluation of Good Faith Efforts – EO 11246
II. Other Problems for Investigation
III. Implementation of Sex Discrimination Provisions of Parts 60-1 and 60-20, and Guidelines on Discrimination Because of Religion and National Origin
IV. Implementation of Section 503 and VEVRAA
V. Technical Requirements: Executive Order 11246, Section 503, VEVRAA and Executive Order 13496

PART C: PROBLEMS IDENTIFIED

PART D: CMCE NARRATIVE

PART E: COMPLIANCE CHECK CONTROL SHEET (to be inserted)

PART F: SUMMARY OF FINDINGS (INTERNAL DOCUMENT)

INSTRUCTIONS

At the top of each page described below is a "continued" box that may be checked to indicate additional pages have been inserted for the section.

COMPLIANCE EVALUATION SUMMARY

PAGE 1: INTRODUCTION

Item 1 – Establishment Name, Address and CMS Control #: Enter the name and address of the establishment or functional unit being reviewed. Also enter the CMS Control number assigned to this review.

Item 2 – Parent Name and Address: If the establishment or functional unit being reviewed is part of a larger firm, enter the name and address of the parent firm.

Item 3 – SMSA/MSA: Enter the name of the Standard Metropolitan Statistical Area (SMSA) and Metropolitan Statistical Area (MSA) in which the establishment or functional unit is located or, if it is not in an SMSA and MSA, enter the name of the appropriate labor area in which it is located. Then enter the percent of the labor force within the named geographic area that is female and the percent that is minority (in the aggregate and by each minority group).

Item 4 – Complaints Investigated During Review: Enter the complaint number of each complaint (if any) you plan to investigate as part of the compliance evaluation. At the end of the evaluation, check [✓] those complaints that have been resolved. If, during the course of a compliance evaluation, a complaint arises and is investigated, that information will be noted here.

Item 5 – Contract Coverage: Enter the following items: awarding agency; prime contractor if evaluation is being conducted of a subcontractor; the contract or purchase order number; dollar amount of the contract; and beginning and ending dates (or indicate if contract is indefinite). There are spaces for at least three contracts. More may be referenced if necessary.

Item 6 – Company Contacts and Outside Representation: List the name, title and phone number of the corporate and establishment Chief Executive Officer (CEO) (or other highest ranking executive), and the corporate and establishment contact persons for Equal Employment Opportunity and Affirmative Action (EEO and AA) matters. Also list the name and phone number of the outside representative (if applicable).

Item 7 – Background Information: To the degree known, this will include, but not be limited to:

- Type of Industry. (Example: Industry- construction materials.)
- Specific facility function. (Example: manufacturing A-frames.)
- Total Number of Employees at the Establishment or covered in the Functional Unit
- Total Number and Percentage of Female Employees
- Total Number and Percentage of Minority Employees
- Date Scheduling Letter was Received by Contractor
- AAP Year
- Prior AAP Year Data Period and
- Current AAP Year Data Period (if applicable)
- Union – indicate whether the facility has a union (Y/N)
- Percent of Unionized Workforce
- NAICS

PAGE 2: CASE SUMMARY AND RECOMMENDATIONS

After the evaluation has been completed, provide a brief summary of the findings (as contained in SCER Part F: Summary of Findings), including all unresolved technical and discrimination violations, and the recommendations for corrective action. For findings of violation, briefly explain the basis (evidence and analysis) for the violation and indicate the recommended appropriate corrective action and the documents that will be prepared (e.g., Notice of Violations, and Conciliation Agreement). If there is no finding of a violation and a closure letter is to be issued, provide a brief description of the basis for this recommended action. Because the Case Summary may exceed a single page, it may be drafted separately and included as an attachment to the SCER. This will be noted on the Case Summary SCER page.

Onsite Box: The CO will indicate whether an onsite occurred and, if so, the reason for the onsite.

Signature Blocks: The CO must sign and date the report in the space provided. Upon approval of the report, the Assistant District Director and District Director must also sign and date it.

PART A: PREPARATION

I. PAST PROBLEMS/KNOWN COMPLAINTS OR ENFORCEMENT PROCEEDINGS

1. PAST PROBLEMS: Determine whether this establishment or functional unit has been subject to past compliance evaluations or OFCCP complaint investigations. If there have been no prior evaluations or complaint investigations, check the box at the top of the page and skip to item 2 (Known Complaints or Enforcement Proceedings). If major problems were identified in previous evaluations or investigations, attach a copy of the applicable closure document. In addition, complete this Part with the following information:

   a. Past Problems – Give the date of any past compliance evaluation or complaint investigation and list any major problems identified (e.g., recordkeeping, etc.).

   b. Recurrence - At whatever point in the evaluation you have evidence that a past problem has recurred, describe the problem and evidence of recurrence. If you find that it did not recur, note "no" in this space.

2. KNOWN COMPLAINTS/ENFORCEMENT PROCEEDINGS: Review responses received from other agencies on any complaints filed, or ongoing enforcement proceedings against this establishment. If there are no such pending complaints or ongoing enforcement proceedings, state this and no further entries are needed in this part. If there are such complaints or proceedings, complete this Part as follows:

   a. For each complaint or enforcement proceeding, indicate with what agency it was filed, its basis (including whether it is an individual or class complaint), issue, current status and the part of the workforce or establishment department it appears to concern (e.g., clerical, professional, entry-level blue-collar, etc.).

   b. Potential Systemic Issues – As you review the responses from the agencies, be alert for any indications of potential systemic discrimination problems that you will investigate. Note those here.

II. INITIAL REVIEW OF AAP AND SUPPORTING DATA SUBMISSIONS

Complete this section once you have received and reviewed the contractor's initial AAP and supporting data submission. Complete this section as follows:

Included: Review the Executive Order AAP and supporting data, and the Section 503 and VEVRAA AAP(s) to ensure that all required elements are present (complete). Beside each item, enter a "Y" for "yes" if it is included, or an "N" for "no" if it is missing. If an element is missing, so indicate in the last column and include in Part A.III of the SCER.

Acceptable: Beside each listed element, enter a "Y" or "N" to indicate whether it is acceptable. If any element is not acceptable, list it in Part A. III of the SCER and describe the specific problem and actions taken. "Text only" refers to the desk audit review of the AAP contents for acceptability.

Prior year (PY) and current year (CY): Review the Executive Order supporting data to ensure that PY and CY, (if applicable), data was received. Enter a "Y" or "N" to indicate whether the items were received. If the contractor is not six months or more into its current AAP year, leave the CY column blank.

III. AAP AND SUPPORTING DATA SUBMISSION PROBLEMS

At the top of the page, check whether the page concerns the Executive Order AAP and supporting data, the Section 503 and VEVRAA AAP(s), or both. The CO must provide a detailed explanation of each AAP and support data problem. Each problem area must be described separately. If the problem is not resolved at the desk audit and onsite verification of compliance is necessary, the onsite box must be checked. The AAP and Supporting Data Problems description should include:

Problem Area: Provide a brief description of the identified problem.

Action Taken: The steps that were taken to resolve the problem or the steps that will be taken (Plan to Resolve) if the action is to take place during or after an onsite review.

Findings: Indicate whether problems were identified based on an offsite analysis or whether an onsite review was conducted. Note any finding(s) and briefly describe the basis for the finding(s).

Resolution: If the problem is resolved, explain how it was resolved. If the problem is not resolved, the issue must be included in Part C of the SCER.

IV. EEO TREND ANALYSIS

The EEO Trend Analysis must be used to examine employment trends and patterns in the contractor's workforce. Specifically, the trend analysis identifies underrepresentations and concentrations of employees by EEO-1 category. Provide a narrative of the results of the EEO trend analysis as follows:

1. *Trends*

Total Workforce: Over the long – term, has the contractor's overall workforce been relatively stable or has it been expanding or contracting? If so, how substantial has the change been? Is the change primarily, or notably, in particular categories? What has the change been in the representation throughout the overall workforce?

Address the same questions as above concerning short-term total workforce trends.

White-Collar: Over the long and short term, what has the change been in the white-collar workforce? Have there been notable gains or losses in particular categories?

Blue-Collar: Over the long and short term, what have the changes been in the blue-collar workforce? Have there been notable gains or losses in particular categories?

2. *Job Category Patterns*: Are there any EEO-1 job categories in which a particular group (e.g., whites, females, Asians, etc.) has been persistently concentrated? Are there other categories in which particular groups appear to be substantially underrepresented?

3. *Particular Groups*: Identify any substantial disparity in the representation of a particular racial/ethnic group or of men or women of a particular minority group. Is any such disparity present either in the workforce as a whole or in certain job categories?

PART B: AFFIRMATIVE ACTION

I. EVALUATION OF GOOD FAITH EFFORTS – EO 11246

Identify goal areas where goals were established but not met. For each goal area that was not met include the following:

Goal Area: Identify job group; indicate whether goals were for minorities, females, or both; identify whether the goals were for the prior (PY), the current year (CY) or both; and identify the expected goal and actual goal.

Explanation and Commitments: If there is a difference between the expected and actual goals, provide the contractor's explanation for the difference and pertinent AAP commitments.

Additional Information: Note any information that will be requested. If an onsite is needed to obtain the information or to address the problem, check the onsite box.

Findings: Indicate whether problems were identified based on an offsite analysis or whether an onsite review was conducted. Note any finding(s) and briefly describe the basis for the finding(s).

Resolution: If the problem is resolved, explain how it was resolved. If the problem is not resolved, the issue must be included in Part C of the SCER.

II. OTHER PROBLEMS FOR INVESTIGATION

Indicate other problems identified as a result of the offsite analyses conducted as a part of the compliance evaluation. For each identified problem include the following:

Problem Area: Provide a brief description of the identified problem.

Additional Information: Note any information that will be requested. If an onsite is needed to obtain the information or to address the problem, check the onsite box.

Findings: Indicate whether problems were identified based on an offsite analysis or whether an onsite review was conducted. Note any finding(s) and briefly describe the basis for the finding(s).

Resolution: If the problem is resolved, explain how it was resolved. If the problem is not resolved, the issue must be included in Part C of the SCER.

III. IMPLEMENTATION OF SEX DISCRIMINATION PROVISIONS OF PARTS 60-1 and 60-20, AND GUIDELINES ON DISCRIMINATION BECAUSE OF RELIGION AND NATIONAL ORIGIN

During the onsite review verify the contractor's implementation of the Sex Discrimination Guidelines and the Guidelines on Discrimination Because of Religion and National Origin. For each of the specified elements, indicate what action was taken by the contractor and how this was evidenced (e.g., identify or summarize the documentation and interview statements that are responsive), and whether any problems exist. If problems exist, indicate how the problems were resolved. If there is a potential finding of discrimination, the information must be included in Part C.

IV. IMPLEMENTATION OF SECTION 503 AND VEVRAA

During the onsite review evaluate the contractor's efforts toward implementing the listed elements of its Section 503 and VEVRAA AAP(s), including such issues as providing an accessible online application process, disability-related questions, use of medical examinations, and confidentiality of records. For each of these elements indicate "Y" or "N" whether the contractor complied with the requirement and how this was evidenced (e.g., identify/summarize the documentation and/or interview statements that are responsive) and whether any problems exist, and if resolved, check "Y." If problems exist, and are unresolved, indicate "N" for not "Resolved." If "N" is indicated, there is a potential finding of discrimination that must be included in Part C of the SCER.

V. TECHNICAL REQUIREMENTS: EO 11246, SECTION 503 AND EO 13496

During the onsite review evaluate whether the listed technical requirements under EO 11246, Section 503 and VEVRAA, and EO 13496 have been met. For each of these elements, indicate whether the action was taken by the contractor and how this was evidenced (e.g., identify or summarize the CO's observation, review of the documentation and interview statements that are responsive), and whether any problems exist. If problems exist, indicate how the problems were resolved. If any technical requirements are not met despite attempts to resolve the problem, include the technical violation requiring corrective action in Part C.

PART C: PROBLEMS IDENTIFIED

Record all identified problems or areas of discrimination that have been resolved, or that require corrective action in order to be resolved. Include a description of the problem or discrimination identified, actions taken to resolve the problem (if any), and whether the problem was resolved. If the problem was not resolved and will require corrective action, the problem must be included in Part F – Summary of Findings.

PART D: CMCE NARRATIVE

When conducting a Corporate Management Compliance Evaluation, or CMCE, this form must be filled out in addition to completing all other parts of the SCER. Supplement the Case Summary and Recommendations (SCER page 2) with findings specific to a CMCE. For additional information regarding CMCEs, see Chapter 4 of the Federal Contract Compliance Manual.

PART E: COMPLIANCE CHECK CONTROL SHEET (to be inserted)

PART F: SUMMARY OF FINDINGS (INTERNAL DOCUMENT)

APPENDIX A-3: STANDARD COMPLIANCE EVALUATION REPORT

U.S. Department of Labor
Office of Federal Contract Compliance Programs

STANDARD COMPLIANCE EVALUATION REPORT
(CONSTRUCTION)

Contractor's Name: ______________________________

Address: ______________________ SMSA/EA _______

______________________ NAICS CODE: ________

Telephone: ______________________ Contact Person and Title: ______

Does the Contractor have a parent company: Yes ☐ No ☐

If yes, provide the name and contact information for the point of contact for the parent company:

____

____

Date of Last Review: ________________ Closing Document: ___________________

This Review Period: This Review Date: EOS Number:

I. BACKGROUND INFORMATION

1. Describe any information regarding the contractor received from EEOC, community organizations,and other groups and organizations.

2. List all the contractor's construction projects, regardless of whether they are federal, federally assisted or nonfederally related, which were under way in the covered are during the review period.

Covered Projects (If Federally Involved)

	Funding Agency	Amount (Approximate)	Date of Award

3. Summarize the contractor's workforce as reported for the review period. If goals changed during the review period, complete Section 3a.

COVERED CRAFT	YEAR GOALS		WORK HOURS							HOURS AS A <u>%</u> OF TOTAL		**MET ALL GOALS**			
			TOTAL	MINORITY					FEMALE			YES		NO	
////////////////	M	F	////////	1	2	3	4	5	//////////	M	F	M	F	M	F

1 - Total Minority
2 - Black (Not Hispanic Origin)
3 - Hispanic
4 - Amer. Ind. & Alaskan Native
5 - Asian or Pacific Islander
M - Minority
F - Female

3a. Use for utilization summary when goals changed during the review period.

COVERED CRAFT	YEAR GOALS		WORK HOURS							HOURS AS A % OF TOTAL		MET ALL GOALS			
			TOTAL	MINORITY					FEMALE			YES		NO	
///////////////	M	F	//////////	1	2	3	4	5	//////////////	M	F	M	F	M	F

1 - Total Minority
2 - Black (Not Hispanic Origin)
3 - Hispanic
4 - Amer. Ind. & Alaskan Native
5 - Asian or Pacific Islander
M - Minority
F - Female

II. REVIEW OF RECORDS

A. Utilization Verification

Select six months, or at least one-fourth of the months summarized in Section I. 3. (3a.) above, whichever is greater, and complete the following work-hour verification from the contractor's payroll.

1. Month: ___________________

			REPORTED HOURS OF UTILIZATION (if required)					ACTUAL HOURS OF UTILIZATION FROM PAYROLLS				
CRAFT	GOAL		TOTAL	MINORITY		FEMALE		TOTAL	MINORITY		FEMALE	
/////////////	M	F	//////////	#	%	#	%	/////////	#	%	#	%

2. Month ______________ Year ____________

			REPORTED HOURS OF UTILIZATION (if required)					ACTUAL HOURS OF UTILIZATION FROM PAYROLLS				
CRAFT	GOAL		TOTAL	MINORITY		FEMALE		TOTAL	MINORITY		FEMALE	
/////////////	M	F	////////////	#	%	#	%	/////////////	#	%	#	%

3. Month ______________ Year _____________

			REPORTED HOURS OF UTILIZATION (if required)					ACTUAL HOURS OF UTILIZATION FROM PAYROLLS				
CRAFT	GOAL		TOTAL	MINORITY		FEMALE		TOTAL	MINORITY		FEMALE	
/////////////	M	F	////////////	#	%	#	%	/////////////	#	%	#	%

4. Month ______________ Year _____________

			REPORTED HOURS OF UTILIZATION (if required)					ACTUAL HOURS OF UTILIZATION FROM PAYROLLS				
CRAFT	GOAL		TOTAL	MINORITY		FEMALE		TOTAL	MINORITY		FEMALE	
/////////////	M	F	//////////////	#	%	#	%	/////////////	#	%	#	%

5. Month _______________ Year ______________

			REPORTED HOURS OF UTILIZATION (if required)					ACTUAL HOURS OF UTILIZATION FROM PAYROLLS				
CRAFT	GOAL		TOTAL	MINORITY		FEMALE		TOTAL	MINORITY		FEMALE	
/////////////	M	F	////////////	#	%	#	%	/////////////	#	%	#	%

6. Month ______________ Year _____________

			REPORTED HOURS OF UTILIZATION (if required)					ACTUAL HOURS OF UTILIZATION FROM PAYROLLS				
CRAFT	GOAL		TOTAL	MINORITY		FEMALE		TOTAL	MINORITY		FEMALE	
/////////////	M	F	////////////	#	%	#	%	/////////////	#	%	#	%

B. Employee Utilization (Determine through payroll review and supervisor/employee interviews).

1. Are any of the contractor's employees members of a union?

   YES ☐ NO ☐

2. If YES, indicate by trade the name of the union and the local number.

3. Show total overtime hours worked by minorities and women by trade.

Trade	Total Hours	Minority Hours	Female Hours

4. Is overtime worked in each trade distributed equitably among all employees?

5. Is the contractor engaged in both residential and commercial construction? YES ☐ NO ☐

a. If "YES," are there wage differentials between the two types of construction? YES ☐ NO ☐

   State amounts ______________

b. Are minorities and women assigned to both types of projects?

6. Show number of hours worked on each type of project by minorities and women.

	Commercial	Residential
Minorities	______________	______________
Women	______________	______________

7. Show <u>total</u> number of hours worked on each type of project.

Commercial _________ Residential _______

8. Do the payroll records and employee interviews reflect substantially consistent utilization of minorities and women throughout the length of the review period and on ALL the contractor's work (federally involved and nonfederally involved)?

C. <u>Summary</u> (Summarize findings for Sections IIA and IIB. Indicate whether contractor is deficient.)

III. AUDIT OF AFFIRMATIVE ACTION SPECIFICATIONS

(41 CFR 60-4.3(a)7.a.-p.)

A. AUDIT OF RECRUITMENT PRACTICES (SEE 3I00)

SPECIFICATION	Explain what actions, if any, were taken to comply with the specification/obligation. Were the contractor's actions deficient? If yes, explain.
1. Has the contractor established and maintained a current list of recruitment sources that includes sources for minorities and women, and provided written notification to these recruitment sources and to community organizations when it or its unions had opportunities available, and maintained a record of the organizations' responses? (41 CFR 60-4.3(a)7.b.)	
2. Has the contractor maintained a current file of the names, addresses, telephone numbers, sex, race, ethnicity of each walk-in applicant or referral from a union, recruitment source, or community organization, and the action taken with respect to each individual? If such individual was sent to the union hiring hall for referral and was not referred back to the contractor by the union, or if referred, was not employed by the contractor, this will be documented in the file with the reason therefore, along with whatever additional actions the contractor may have taken. (41 CFR 60-4.3(a)7.c; 60-1,12(b); and 60-3.15A)	

A. AUDIT OF RECRUITMENT PRACTICES (CONT'D)

SPECIFICATION	Explain what actions taken to comply with the specification. Indicate whether activity is deficient.
3. Has the contractor provided immediate written notification to OFCCP when the union or unions with which it has collective bargaining agreements did not refer to the contractor members of minority groups or women, or when the contractor had other information that the union referral process impeded the contractor's efforts to meet its obligations? (41 CFR 60-4.3(a)7.d.)	
4. Has the contractor engaged in recruitment efforts that are inclusive of minority, women, and community organizations, and to schools with minority and women students; and engaged in recruitment efforts that reach out to minority and women recruitment and training organizations serving the contractor's recruitment area employment needs? Did the contractor, no later than one month before the date for the acceptance of applications for apprenticeship or other training by any recruitment sources, send written notification to organizations such as the above, describing the openings, screening procedures and tests to be used in the selection process? (41 CFR 60-4.3(a)7.i.)	

A. AUDIT OF RECRUITMENT PRACTICES (CONT'D)

5. Has the contractor encouraged present minority and female employees to recruit other minority persons or women, and where reasonable, did the contractor provide after-school, summer, and vacation employment to minority and female youth both onsite and in other areas of a contractor's workforce? (41 CFR 60-4.3(a)7.j.)	

B. AUDIT OF TRAINING (SEE 3I01)

SPECIFICATION	Explain actions taken to comply with the specification. Indicate whether activities are deficient.
1. Has the contractor developed on-the-job training opportunities or participated in training programs for recruiting areas that expressly include members of minority groups and women (including upgrading programs and apprenticeship and trainee programs relevant to the contractor's employment needs), especially those programs funded or approved by the Department of Labor? The contractor should have provided notice of these programs to the recruitment sources compiled under item A.1 above. (41 CFR 60-4.3(a)7.e.)	

C. AUDIT OF EEO POLICY AND IMPLEMENTATION (SEE 3I02)

SPECIFICATION	Explain what actions taken to comply with the Specification. Indicate whether activity is deficient.
1. Has the contractor disseminated its EEO policy by providing notice of the policy to unions and training programs and requesting their cooperation in assisting the contractor in meeting its EEO obligations; by including it in any policy manual and collective bargaining agreement; by publicizing it in the company newspaper, annual report, etc.; by specific review of the policy with all management personnel and with all minority and female employees at least once a year; and by posting the company's EEO policy on bulletin boards accessible to all employees at each location where construction work is performed? (41 CFR 60-4.3(a)7.f.)	
2. Has the contractor reviewed, at least annually, the company's EEO policy and affirmative action obligations under these specifications with all employees having any responsibility for hiring, assignment, layoff, termination, or other employment decisions, including specific review of these items with onsite supervisory personnel (superintendents, general forepersons, etc.) prior to the initiation of construction work on any site? A written record should have been made and maintained identifying the time and place of these meetings, persons attending, subject matter discussed, and disposition of the subject matter. (41 CFR 60-4.3(a)7.g.)	

SPECIFICATION	Explain what actions taken to comply with the specification. Indicate whether activity is deficient.
3. Has the contractor disseminated its EEO policy externally by including it in any advertising in the news media, specifically including minority and women's news media, and providing written notification to and discussing the contractor's EEO policy with other contractors and subcontractors with whom the contractor did or anticipated doing business? (41 CFR 60-4.3(a)7.h.)	
4. Has the contractor conducted, at least annually, an inventory and evaluation of at least the currently employed minorities and women for promotional opportunities, and encouraged these employees to seek or to prepare, through appropriate training, for such opportunities? (41 CFR 60-4.3(a)7.l.)	
5. Has the contractor conducted a review, at least annually, of all supervisors' adherence to and performance under the contractor's EEO policies and affirmative action obligations? (41 CFR 60-4.3(a)7.p.)	

D. AUDIT OF PERSONNEL OPERATIONS (SEE 3I03)

SPECIFICATION	Explain what actions taken to comply with the specification. Indicate whether activity is deficient.
1. Has the contractor ensured and maintained a working environment free of harassment, intimidation and coercion at all sites and in all facilities at which the contractor's employees are assigned to work? The contractor, where possible, should have assigned two or more women to each construction project. The contractor should have specifically ensured that all supervisory personnel were aware of and carried out the contractor's obligation to maintain such a working environment, which specific attention to members of minority or women's groups working at such sites or in such facilities. (41 CFR 60-4.3(a)7.a.)	
2. Has the contractor maintained all required information and validated all tests and other selection requirements where there is an obligation to do so under 41 CFR Part 60-3? (41 CFR 60-4.3(a)7.k.)	

SPECIFICATION	Explain what actions taken to comply with the specification. Indicate whether activity is deficient.
3. Has the contractor ensured that seniority practices, job classifications, work assignments and other personnel practices had no discriminatory effect, and has it continually monitored all related personnel employment activities to ensure that the EEO policy and the contractor's obligations under these specifications were being carried out? (41 CFR 60-4.3(a)7.m.)	
4. Has the contractor ensured that all facilities and company activities were nonsegregated, except for providing separate or single-user toilet and necessary changing facilities to assure privacy between the sexes? (41 CFR 60-4.3(a)7.n.)	

E. AUDIT OF CONTRACTING ACTIVITY (SEE 3I04)

SPECIFICATION	Explain activities taken to comply with the specification. Indicate whether or not activities are deficient.
1. Has the contractor documented and maintained a record of all solicitations of offers for subcontracts from small disadvantaged businesses or disadvantaged business enterprises, including circulation of solicitations to contractor associations? (41 CFR 60-4.3(a)7.o.)	

F. SEX DISCRIMINATION PROVISIONS OF THE SEX DISCRIMINATION GUIDELINES AND PART 60-1

Has the contractor complied with CFR Part 60-20, Sex Discrimination Guidelines, and Part 60-1 ?	

G. **GUIDELINES ON DISCRIMINATION BECAUSE OF RELIGION OR NATIONAL ORIGIN**

Has the contractor complied with 41 CFR Part 60-50, Guidelines on Discrimination Because of Religion of National Origin?	

H. SECTION 503/VEVRAA(Federal contractors/subcontractors)

Has the contractor complied with 41 CFR Parts 60-250, 60-300 and 60-741, affirmative action obligations of contractors and subcontractors for covered veterans and individuals with disabilities?	

IV. Physical Inspection of Contractor's Work Sites

A. List work sites visited and indicate whether they were federal, federally assisted, or nonfederally involved projects.

(1) PROJECT NAME AND LOCATION (2) FUNDING

B. Summarize results of interviews. See Section 3J in the Manual.

V. Narrative Summary

(See Instructions in Manual, Section 3Q)

VI. COMPLIANCE REVIEW SUMMARY SHEET

1. Status (Check appropriate items)

   a. In compliance with goals in all covered crafts (Check, if yes)

      ☐ Minority

      ☐ Female

   b. ☐ In compliance with all affirmative actions specifications (Check, if yes)

   c. ☐ Noncompliance

      ii. ☐ Conciliation Agreement (signed on ____________)

      iii. ☐ Show Cause Notice (has been/will be issued on ______________)

2. Date Review Completed ____________________

3. Hours to Complete Review

   Total __________ Pre-Review _________ Onsite Review _______

   Report Writing _______ Travel _______

   Conciliation _________

4. Signature (compliance officer) __________________ Date ____________________

5. Signature (module supervisor) __________________ Date ____________________

6. Signature (approving official) __________________ Date ____________________

APPENDIX A-4: INDEX FOR A SUPPLY AND SERVICE REVIEW

Remember to Index and Tab the Materials.

File 1: SCER and Data pertaining to SCER Findings: This file contains the SCER and data pertaining to the findings. This includes worksheets, interviews, contractor records, etc. pertinent to issues investigated. Include all relevant material bearing either for or against the conclusions reached. Cross reference other files, as applicable, for example collective bargaining agreement in file 3.

Right Side of Folder

- SCER
- Worksheets
- Supporting documents
- Interviews
- Etc.

Left Side of Folder

- Form CC-100
- Extension Requests and responses
- Contractor research form and supporting jurisdiction information

File 2: Case Chronology, Correspondence and Meeting Notes: This file will contain all correspondence including attachments submitted and meeting notes. This includes any such material resulting from contacts with the contractor, union, attorneys, consultants, Congress persons, and memos to file (not investigative notes). The closure document will be tabbed. Note a copy of the closure document is also placed in File 6.

Right Side: Correspondence - The latest correspondence must be on top and it must be in chronological order. As applicable, cross reference other files.

Left Side: Case Chronology Log – CC-53 (in chronological order and legible.

File 3: Employment Handbooks, Collective Bargaining Agreement and Miscellaneous: This file will contain a copy of any employee handbooks, collective bargaining agreements, fringe benefit information, leave policy booklets, and any other similar contractor documents. Any documents that do not fit the description of materials to be included in any other file will be placed here.

File 4: SOL Opinions, JRC Memoranda, and Post-SCER Update: This file will contain any Solicitor's (SOL) opinions and Joint Review Committee (JRC) memoranda associated with this review.

Also include in this file any material generated after the CO submits the review, for example: transmittal memoranda, additional conciliation efforts, etc. These materials are other than progress reports (file 5).

File 5: Progress Reports and Quality Audit:

This file will contain:

Right Side: Any progress reports submitted under a conciliation agreement or consent decree or other court order and OFCCP's evaluation of the report and the summary of the reports submitted.

Left Side: Quality Audit Form (CC-74)

File 6: Historical Review Results

This file will contain a copy of any available closure letters and documents generated by reviews of this establishment and the closure letter or document for the current review. If reports are required under the CA when the last report is evaluated a copy of the Summary of Progress Reports.

NOTE: The Historical file will be retained in the AO or DO indefinitely. If another review of this establishment is scheduled before this case file is retired, the Historical file will be pulled from the old case file and moved to the new file. If another review has not been scheduled, the Historical file will be pulled and retained in the AO or DO when the rest of the case is retired.

File 7: AAP and AAP Support Data
This file will contain the contractor's AAP (s) and AAP support data evaluated in this review (including the EEO-1 Reports).

APPENDIX A-5: INDEX FOR A CONSTRUCTION REVIEW
Remember to Index and Tab the Materials.

File 1: Construction SCER Findings: This file contains the SCER and data pertaining to the findings. This includes worksheets, interviews, contractor records, etc. pertinent to issues investigated. Include all relevant material bearing either for or against the conclusions reached. Cross reference other files, as applicable, for example collective bargaining agreement in file 3.

Right Side of Folder
- SCER
- Worksheets
- Supporting documents
- Interviews
- Etc.

Left Side of Folder
- Form CC-100
- Extension Requests and responses
- Contractor Research Form and supporting jurisdiction information

File 2: Case Chronology, Correspondence and Meeting Notes: This file will contain all correspondence including attachments submitted and meeting notes. This includes any such material resulting from contacts with the contractor, union, attorneys, consultants, Congress persons, and memos to file (not investigative notes). The closure document will be tabbed. Note a copy of the closure document is also placed in File 6.

Right Side: Correspondence - The latest correspondence Must be on top and it must be in chronological order. As applicable, cross reference other files.

Left Side: Case Chronology Log – CC-53 (in chronological order and legible.

File 3: Employment Handbooks, Collective Bargaining Agreement and Miscellaneous: This file will contain a copy of any employee handbooks, collective bargaining agreements, fringe benefit information, leave policy booklets, and any other similar contractor documents. Any documents that do not fit the description of materials to be included in any other file will be placed here.

File 4: SOL Opinions, JRC Memoranda, and Post-SCER Update: This file will contain any Solicitor's (SOL) opinions and Joint Review Committee (JRC) memoranda associated with this review.

Also include in this file any material generated after the CO submits the review, for example: transmittal memoranda, additional conciliation efforts, etc. These materials are other than progress reports (file 5).

File 5: Progress Reports and Quality Audit:

This file will contain:

Right Side: Any progress reports submitted under a conciliation agreement or consent decree or other court order and OFCCP's evaluation of the report and the summary of the reports submitted.

Left Side: Construction Quality Audit Form

File 6: Historical Review Results:

This file will contain a copy of any available closure letters and documents generated by reviews of this establishment, and the closure letter or document for the current review. If reports are required under the CA when the last report is evaluated a copy of the Summary of Progress Reports.

NOTE: The Historical file will be retained in the AO or DO indefinitely. If another review of this establishment is scheduled before this case file is retired, the Historical file will be pulled from the old case file and moved to the new file. If another review has not been scheduled, the Historical file will be pulled and retained in the AO or DO when the rest of the case is retired.

File 7: Monthly Employment Hours and Pre-Construction Conference Materials:

This file will contain the payroll hours obtained onsite and any pre-construction conference materials.

APPENDIX A-6: SPECIAL REMEDIAL CONSIDERATIONS APPLICABLE TO STOCK

(Reference Section 4I00(b))

When there is a finding of discrimination in the awarding of stock or stock options, the following considerations apply to remedy.

I. STOCK AWARDS - VESTED

When the discrimination was in the awarding of vested stock, and the vesting date has not yet occurred, the discriminatee is simply awarded the number of shares he or she would have received, absent discrimination, with the same vesting date as other stock recipients.

> Example: Absent discrimination, on June 1, 2012, the victim would have received 100 shares of stock with a vesting period of three years. The remedy would be to immediately award the victim 100 shares of stock with a vesting date of June 1, 2012.

Where the vesting date has passed, the remedy will be calculated as indicated in II below, with the vesting date considered the date the victim would have received the stock, absent discrimination.

II. STOCK AWARDS - ONE-TIME BONUS

(a) Shares of Stock:

(1) Establish the number of shares (or additional number of shares) the discriminatee would have received, absent discrimination, and the date(s) he or she would have received them.

(2) Find the dollar value of that number of shares as of the date, absent discrimination, the discriminatee would have the shares, and the current dollar value. Take the higher of the two figures, expressed as the number of current shares.

Example: Absent discrimination, the discriminatee would have received 100 additional shares of stock. On the date he or she should have received the stock, the share price was $20, for a total dollar value of $2,000.

Scenario A: The stock has gone down to $10 a share, so the 100 shares are now worth only $1,000. The discriminatee should receive $2,000 worth of stock at the current price; i.e., 200 shares of stock.

Scenario B: The stock has gone up to $30 per share, so the 100 shares are now worth $3,000. The discriminatee should receive 100 shares at the current price.

(b) Dividends:

(1) Determine the dollar amount of stock dividends (or additional stock dividends) the discriminatee would have received, absent discrimination, and add simple interest (see Appendix 7A).

<u>Example</u>: Determine the dollar amount of dividends that would have been paid on the 100 shares of stock from the date the discriminatee should have received the stock to present, and add simple interest.

III. <u>STOCK OPTIONS</u>

When the discrimination was in the awarding of stock options, remedy will include awarding the discriminatee the number of stock options he or she would have received, absent discrimination. The period of time he or she would have had to exercise those options will be calculated from the date he or she actually receives the options.

<u>Example</u>: On January 1, 2001, absent discrimination, the victim would have received an option to buy 100 shares of stock at any time over the following four years. If settlement occurred on October 1, 2001, the victim would be able to exercise an option on the 100 shares of stock up until October 1, 2005.

CO's should consult with an OFCCP labor economist, or other appropriate staff member within DPO, for specific help and guidance on stock valuation.

APPENDIX A-7: CORPORATE MANAGEMENT COMPLIANCE EVALUATION SUPPLEMENTARY NARRATIVE REPORT (Reference Section 4K)

In a corporate management compliance evaluation (CMCE), the standard report will be supplemented by a narrative addressing the following major items (see Section number(s) indicated for discussion of each item):

(a) Introduction: Corporate background, structure, observations concerning corporate culture, and values. (4B01, 4B02, 4B11, 4G01)

(b) Corporate AAP: What positions at subordinate establishments are rolled-up into the Corporate AAP? Does this meet the intent of 41 CFR 60-2.1(d) and (e)?

(c) Scope: Did the evaluation cover only corporate headquarters or was it extended to cover one or more intermediate headquarters or subordinate establishments? (4A01, 4H04(c))

(d) Focus Level and Areas: Describe the company's pay and management structure. At what pay level does the representation of protected group members decline? Are protected group members concentrated in certain functional areas? Are those areas staff or line? (4D00, 4D01)

(e) Outreach Efforts: To what extent does the company already have in place programs designed to ensure equal employment opportunity in access to mid- and senior-level management positions? Describe any such programs and what results they have yielded to date.

(f) Jobs Filled at and above the Focus Level: During the evaluation period, what jobs have been filled around the level where protected group member participation declines? How were they filled (hire, promotion, transfer)? (4H)

(1) External Hires: If there were some hires, how were candidates located? If executive search firms were used, were protected group members among those referred? Hired? If employee referrals were used, were protected group members among those referred? Hired? (4H01, 4H02, 4H03) In either case, were any efforts made to expand the candidate pool?

(2) Internal Development - General: Where jobs were filled internally, were most by promotion? By transfer? Were most of these openings filled from within corporate headquarters or by movement into corporate from subordinate establishments? (4H04)

(g) Internal Development - Specific Programs: In each of the areas below, does the company have the program and, if so, describe it and discuss conclusions with respect to protected group member participation. (4H05)

(1) Succession and Related Planning (4H04(a))

(2) Performance Appraisals (4H04(f))

(3) Visibility (4H04(g),(h),(i)):

(i) Special Projects and Task Forces
(ii) Committees
(iii) Special Assistants and Executive Assistants

(4) Management Training and Executive Development Programs (4H05)

(5) Mentoring and Networking (4H06)

(h) Total Compensation

(1) Bonuses (4I00(a)))

(2) Stock (4I00(b))

(3) Perquisites (4I00(c))

(4) Award/Honor Programs (4I01)

(i) Terminations (4J)

(j) Conclusions: What reason(s) were found for protected group members not having moved beyond their current grade/level?

(k) Resolution: What commitments (whether remedial or improved good faith efforts) has the corporation made to ensure that protected group members have an equal opportunity to advance to mid and senior- level management positions?

APPENDIX A-8: INDEX FOR A COMPLAINT FILE
Remember to Index and Tab the Materials.

File 1: Complaint and Data Submitted by Complainant: This file contains any information submitted by the complainant including the envelope. Materials include:

Right Side of Folder
- CC-4 or letter of allegations
- Complainant's witness list
- Documents provided to support the allegation
- Interview of Complainant

Left Side of Folder
- CMS forms associated with the investigation
- Extension Requests and responses

File 2: Case Chronology, Correspondence and Meeting Notes: This file will contain all correspondence (e.g. letters and e-mails), including attachments. This includes any such material resulting from contacts with the contractor, union, witnesses, consultants, etc., and memos to file (not investigative notes).

Right Side: Correspondence

The latest correspondence must be on top and it must be in chronological order. As applicable, cross reference other files.

Left Side: Case Chronology Log – CC-53 (in chronological order and legible).

File 3: Investigative Material: This file will contain all investigative material pertaining to complaint findings. Such data include:
- The investigative plan (on top)
- The investigative report (on top when complete)
- Interview (witness) statements
- Investigative notes,
- Statistical evidence
- Comparative evidence
- Anecdotal Evidence

File 4: Medical/Veterans Documentation: This file will contain any medical/veterans documentation. This includes:
- Medical release
- Medical and disabled veteran status (e.g. DD-214)
- Medical coverage information
- Diagnosis or medical description of disabling condition
- Work restrictions
- For veterans, coverage information as needed, (e.g. Armed Forces campaign badge information)

File 5: Legal: This file will contain any documents related to legal activity including:
- NORI (on top)
- Solicitor's opinions
- Joint Review Committee meeting notes and/or report
- Conciliation Agreements (on top when completed)
- Freedom of Information Act and Privacy Act determinations
- Enforcement recommendations
- Subpoenas; and
- Jurisdictional and contract coverage information (on the bottom)

File 6: Employment Handbooks, Collective Bargaining Agreement and Miscellaneous: On the right side, this file will contain copies of any employee handbooks, collective bargaining agreements, fringe benefit information, leave policy booklets, and any other similar contractor documents. Any documents that do not fit the description of materials to be included in any other file will be placed here.

Left Side:
Quality Assurance Complaint Investigation Form CC-75

File 7: Historical Review Results: This file will contain copies of any available closure letters and documents generated during previous complaint investigations of this establishment. The closure letter for the current investigation will also be included here.

APPENDIX A-9: RETALIATION AND INTERFERENCE; COMPLAINT PROCESSING OUTLINE AND CHECKLIST

OFCCP applies the same concepts, standards and analyses as EEOC when assessing possible retaliation under E.O.11246, Section 503 and VEVRAA. However, it is important to note that although the laws enforced by OFCCP and EEOC prohibit retaliation, OFCCP regulations also provide a broader protection against interference with an individual's exercise of the rights protected by the laws enforced by OFCCP.

The OFCCP implementing regulations, titled "Intimidation and Interference,"[1] state that a contractor "...shall not harass, intimidate, threaten, coerce or discriminate against any individual" because the individual has engaged in or may engage in a protected activity. This not only encompasses protection against retaliation but it also provides protection against intimidation and interference that may not give rise to a retaliation claim. As such, examine complaint allegations to determine whether Title VII principles regarding retaliation claims apply or the broader protection of OFCCP's regulations against intimidation and interference is applicable.

Additionally, there is a difference in available remedies. Compensatory and punitive damages are only available when OFCCP is acting as EEOC's agent in the processing of complaints dually filed under Title VII or the ADA.

A. RETALIATION

When processing a complaint involving an allegation of retaliation, there are three essential elements of a retaliation claim: 1) protected activity (e.g., opposition to discrimination or participation in the filing or investigation of a complaint, compliance evaluation, hearing or other activity); 2) adverse action; and 3) causal connection between the protected activity and the adverse action.

1. Protected Activity

a. Did the Complainant oppose discrimination?

- Did the Complainant explicitly or implicitly communicate to the contractor or another covered entity a belief that its activity constituted unlawful discrimination under E.O. 11246, Section 503, or VEVRAA?

- If the protest was broad or ambiguous, would the complainant's protest reasonably have been interpreted as opposition to such unlawful discrimination?

- Did someone closely associated with the Complainant oppose discrimination?

---

[1] See regulations at Part 60-1.32; 60-250.69; 60-300.69; and 60-741.69.

b. Was the manner of opposition reasonable? Was the manner of opposition so disruptive that it significantly interfered with the contractor's legitimate business concerns?

- If the manner of opposition was not reasonable, the complainant is not protected under the anti-retaliation clauses.

c. Did the Complainant have a reasonable and good faith belief that the opposed practice violated the anti-discrimination laws?

- If so, the complainant is protected against retaliation, even if s/he was mistaken about the unlawfulness of the challenged practices.

- If not, the complainant is not protected under the anti-retaliation clauses.

d. Did the Complainant participate in the statutory complaint process or did the Complainant or someone closely associated with the Complainant file a charge, or testify, assist, or participate in any manner in an investigation, proceeding, hearing, or lawsuit under the statutes enforced by the OFCCP?

- If so, the Complainant is protected against retaliation regardless of the validity or reasonableness of the original allegation of discrimination.

- The Complainant is protected against retaliation by a respondent for participating in statutory complaint proceedings even if that complaint involved a different covered entity.

2. Adverse Action

a. Did the contractor subject the Complainant to any kind of adverse treatment?

- Adverse actions undertaken after the Complainant's employment relationship with the contractor ended, such as negative job references, can be challenged.

- Although trivial annoyances are not actionable, more significant retaliatory treatment that is reasonably likely to deter protected activity is unlawful. There is no requirement that the adverse action materially affect the terms, conditions, or privileges of employment.

3. Causal Connection

a. Is there direct evidence that retaliation was a motive for the adverse action?

b. Did the company official admit that it undertook the adverse action because of the protected activity?

c. Did the company official express bias against the Complainant based on the protected activity? If so, is there evidence linking that statement of bias to the adverse action?

- Such a link would be established if, for example, the statement was made by the decision-maker at the time of the challenged action.

- If there is direct evidence that retaliation was a motive for the adverse action, a violation must be found. Evidence as to any additional legitimate motive would be relevant only to relief, under a mixed-motives analysis.

d. Is there circumstantial evidence that retaliation was the true reason for the adverse action?

e. Is there evidence raising an inference that retaliation was the cause of the adverse action?

- Such an inference is raised if the adverse action took place shortly after the protected activity and if the decision-maker was aware of the protected activity before undertaking the adverse action.

- If there was a long period of time between the protected activity and the adverse action, determine whether there is other evidence raising an inference that the cause of the adverse action was retaliation.

f. Has the contractor produced evidence of a legitimate reason for the adverse action unrelated to the protected activity?

g. Is the contractor's explanation a pretext designed to hide retaliation?

- Did the contractor treat similarly situated employees who did not engage in protected activity differently from the Complainant?

- Did the contractor subject the Complainant to heightened scrutiny after s/he engaged in protected activity?

- If, on the basis of all of the evidence, the CO is persuaded that retaliation was the true reason for the adverse action, then "cause" must be found.

B. SPECIAL REMEDIES ISSUES

a. Is it appropriate to seek temporary or preliminary relief pending final disposition of the complaint?

b. Is there a substantial likelihood that the challenged action will be found to constitute unlawful retaliation?

c. Will the retaliation cause irreparable harm to the Complainant and/or the OFCCP?

- Will the Complainant likely incur irreparable harm beyond financial hardship because of the retaliation?

- If the retaliation appears to be based on the Complainant's filing of a prior EEO complaint, will that retaliation likely cause irreparable harm to OFCCP's ability to investigate the Complainant's original complaint of discrimination?

- If there is a substantial likelihood that the challenged action will constitute retaliation and that retaliation will cause irreparable harm to the Complainant or the OFCCP, or both, contact the Regional Solicitor's office ask about pursuing temporary or preliminary relief.

d. If the complaint is dually filed under Title VII and the ADA or both also consider whether compensatory and punitive damages are available and appropriate?

- Compensatory and punitive damages are available for retaliation claims under all of the statutes enforced by the EEOC.

- Punitive damages often are appropriate in retaliation claims under any of the statutes enforced by the EEOC.

C. INTERFERENCE

OFCCP regulations prohibit interference and intimidation, including threats, coercion, harassment and discrimination of any individual in the exercise of his or her rights under the laws enforced by OFCCP. Such interference may not give rise to a retaliation claim but may hinder an individual from exercising their rights, (e.g., interference by a contractor results in an individual being too intimidated to participate in an OFCCP review or investigation). The purpose of the regulation is to proscribe activities that interfere with a person's exercise of his or her rights. To examine whether a complainant's rights have been interfered with, consider:

a. Did the contractor intimidate, coerce, harass, or discriminate against the complainant in an attempt to hinder the complainant from exercising their rights?

b. What right under the laws enforced by OFCCP was interfered with?

- Was the complainant able to exercise the right in question at a later time?

- Were other individual's rights affected by the contractor's actions?

c. What harm resulted from the right(s) being interfered with?

- Remedy for resulting harm is determined on a case-by-case basis. It may include individual remedy, changes in policy and procedures or both, providing an assurance of cooperation and protection against retaliation, etc.

d. Was the complainant subjected to an adverse employment action?

- If so, the retaliation analysis must be applied.

e. Did interference with the complainant's right also result in hindering OFCCP from fulfilling its responsibilities?

- If so, examine whether the contractor's action (or inaction) may constitute denial of access.

- If denial of access[2] has occurred, OFCCP will take the appropriate enforcement action.

[2] Denial of access is a separate and distinct violation of the regulations enforced by OFCCP. See the regulations at Part 60-1.43; 60-250.81; 60-300.81; and 60-741.81.

APPENDIX A-10: INVESTIGATIVE REPORT

(Name of complainant) v. (CMS #)

(Name of contractor)

1. **Basis**: Insert one or more as appropriate: Executive Order 11246, as amended; Section 503 of the Rehabilitation Act of 1973, as amended; Americans with Disabilities Act of 1990, as amended; or the Vietnam Era Veterans' Readjustment Assistance Act of 1974, as amended.
2. **Contractor**: Insert the company name and address, the name of contractor's representative and that individuals contact telephone number.
3. **Contract Coverage**: Insert the contract number, agency name, date of award, duration of contract period, place of performance, and attach copy of the contract.
4. **Onsite Investigation**: Insert the date or dates.

For Each Allegation:

5. **Allegation(s)**: Provide a statement of the allegation(s) under OFCCP's authority based on what the complainant alleged happened to him/her. Include the circumstances of the action as the complainant expressed them in the complaint and in the interview.
6. **Issue(s)**: Identify the alleged discriminatory action(s) which gave rise to the complaint and the applicable regulatory citations.
7. **Rebuttal**: Include the contractor's explanation of what happened and why it happened, including the circumstances of the action.
8. **Findings of Fact**:
   a. Provide a description of contractor's relevant personnel policies and practices; relevant union rules. Reference case file location of copies;
   b. Provide the results of review of documentary evidence and records. Reference case file location of copies;
   c. Summarize the relevant information obtained from interviews of contractor officials. Reference case file location of interview notes; and
   d. Summarize the relevant information obtained from interviews of other witnesses. Reference case file location of interview notes.
9. **Analysis**: Provide an explanation of how and why the findings of fact confirm or refute the allegations.
10. **Conclusion**: Insert a statement as to whether the contractor has or has not committed a violation, include a citation to the appropriate regulation.
11. **Remedy**: Use this section when a violation by the contractor is found to:
    a. Describe all the remedies the complainant should receive; and
    b. Describe the corrective actions the contractor must take regarding its policies and practices.

APPENDIX A-11: INFORMATION RELATED TO FILING SUIT UNDER TITLE VII OF THE CIVIL RIGHTS ACT AND TITLE I OF THE ADA

This information relates to filing suit in federal or state court under federal law. If you also plan to sue claiming violations of State law, please be aware that time limits and other provisions of State law may be shorter or more limited than those described below.

PRIVATE SUIT RIGHTS – Title VII of the Civil Rights Act of 1964, as amended (Title VII) or the Americans with Disabilities Act of 1990, as amended (ADA)

In order to pursue this matter further, you must file a lawsuit against the contractor(s) named in the complaint **within 90 calendar days of receipt of Notice of Right-to-Sue.** Once this 90-day period expires, your right to sue based on the complaint covered by this Notification will be lost. If you intend to consult an attorney, you should do so promptly. Give your attorney a copy of this Notification.

Your lawsuit may be filed in U.S. District Court or a State court of competent jurisdiction. (Usually, the appropriate State court is the general civil trial court.) Whether you file in federal or state court is a matter for you to decide after talking to your attorney. Filing this Notification is not enough. You must file a "complaint" that contains a short statement of the facts of your case which shows that you are entitled to relief. Your suit may include any matter alleged in the complaint or, to the extent permitted by court decisions, matters like or related to the matters alleged in the complaint. Generally, suits are brought in the State where the alleged unlawful practice occurred, but in some cases can be brought where relevant employment records are kept, where the employment would have been, or where the contractor has its main office. If you have simple questions, you usually can get answers from the Clerk of the court where you are bringing suit, but do not expect them to write your complaint or make legal strategy decisions for you.

PRIVATE SUIT RIGHTS – Equal Pay Act (EPA)

EPA suits must be filed in court within two years (three years for willful violations) of the alleged EPA underpayment; back pay due for violations that occurred **more than two years (three years for willful violations) before you file suit** may not be collectible. For example, if you were underpaid under the EPA for work performed from July 1, 2003 to December 1, 2003, you should file suit before July 1, 2005 (not December 1, 2005) in order to recover unpaid wages due for July 2003. This EPA time limit is separate from the 90-day filing period under Title VII or the ADA referred to above. Therefore, if you also plan to sue under Title VII or the ADA, in addition to suing on the EPA claim, suit should be filed within the Title VII/ADA 90-day period and within the two or three year EPA back pay recovery period.

ATTORNEY REPRESENTATION – Title VII and the ADA

If you cannot afford or have been unable to obtain a lawyer to represent you, the U.S. District Court having jurisdiction in your case may, in limited circumstances, help you to obtain a lawyer. Requests for such assistance must be made to the U.S. District Court in the form and manner it requires (you should be prepared to explain in detail your efforts to retain an attorney). Requests should be made well before the end of the 90-day period mentioned above, because such requests do not relieve you of the requirement to bring suit within 90 calendar days.

ATTORNEY REFERRAL AND ASSISTANCE – All Statutes

If you need help in finding a lawyer or if you have any questions about your legal rights, including advice on which the U.S. District Court can hear your case, you may contact an Office of Federal Contract Compliance Programs (OFCCP) representative at [*insert the name and phone number of OFCCP district or area office that investigated complaint*], who will coordinate with the Equal Employment Opportunity Commission (EEOC) to promptly obtain that information for you. If you need to inspect or obtain a copy of information in OFCCP's file, please request it promptly in writing and provide the OFCCP complaint number. If you file suit and want to review the complaint file, **please make your review request within six months of this Notice.** (Before filing suit, any request should be made within 90 calendar days of the date of the Notification of Results of Investigation.)

If you file suit, please send a copy of your Court complaint to [*insert the name and address of EEOC office to which a copy of the dually filed complaint was sent, and which was notified of issuance of Notice of Right-to-Sue*].

APPENDIX A-12: INTEREST RATES ON BACK PAY

OFCCP's policy is that interest on back pay is calculated from the first date that is covered by the back pay award at the same percentage rate as the Internal Revenue Service's underpayment formula on interest. Interest rates for back pay calculations are based on IRS calculations.

Periodically the IRS issues press releases giving updated information on updates to interest rates. To access recent press releases on this subject go to www.irs.gov. Go to "Search for..." at the upper left hand corner of the IRS home page and type "interest rates for underpayment" and click on "go." The list of the most recent press releases on changes in IRS interest rates will then be displayed.

METHOD OF CALCULATING COMPOUND INTEREST ON BACK PAY

In a compound interest calculation, the interest due on back pay (or any other debt) for a one time period is included in the money on which interest is figured for the next time period (i.e., you pay interest on your interest). In a simple interest calculation, on the other hand, the interest due on back pay (or any other debt) for a one time period is not included in the money on which interest is figured for the next time period (i.e., you do not pay interest on your interest.)

Title 41 CFR 60-1.26(a)(2) requires that interest on back pay be compounded quarterly in EO 11246 cases. Similarly, 41 CFR 60-250.65(a)(1) requires that interest on back pay be compounded quarterly in Section 4212 cases. Further, 41 CFR 60-741.65(a)(1) requires that interest on back pay be compounded quarterly in Section 503 cases. Therefore, in determining the amount of back pay due, first determine the amount of back pay due for each quarter. Then use column Q on the previous page to find the interest rate applicable to each quarter. For example, if the back pay period were December 4, 2009 through May 25, 2010 and $12,000 back pay were due, distribute back pay by quarter as follows:

Year	Quarter	Back Pay Due for Quarter	IRS Quarterly Interest Rate
2009	10/1-12/31	$2,000	2.25%
2010	1/1-3/31	$6,000	2.25%
2010	4/1-6/30	$4,000	2.00%

Quarterly compound interest is applied to the average amount of back pay due during each quarter. This average is the total amount of back pay plus interest due at the beginning of each quarter, plus half the amount of back pay due for the quarter itself, plus the interest accrued during the previous quarter.

APPENDIX A-13: "MACMILLAN" FACTORS CONCERNING SUCCESSOR EMPLOYER LIABILITY

Requests for a determination of successor liability should include responses to the factors listed below. Responses should cite the source of the information and, where the source is written material, a copy of the relevant page(s) should be attached. Information on these factors may be obtained from a number of sources including Standard and Poor's and other corporate guides, trade magazines, annual reports, collective bargaining agreements, and the business section of local newspapers.

1. Whether the Successor Company had Notice of the Charge.

   The date the alleged discriminatory act occurred, the date the complaint was filed, and the dates concerning the transfer (announcement date, effective date of merger, acquisition, etc.).

2. The Ability of the Predecessor to Provide Relief.

   Whether the predecessor continues to operate and the extent and location of its new operations, whether the predecessor maintained any of its assets (what percentage and type), whether the transfer resulted from a bankruptcy action, whether the predecessor could provide seniority, reinstatement, hiring, back pay, etc.

3. Whether there has been a Substantial Continuity of Business Operations.

   The percentage of operating assets that were transferred to the successor, the status of the predecessor's patents, trademarks and operating name, whether there are corporate officers and members of the board of directors who are common to both the predecessor and the successor, etc.

4. Whether the Successor Uses the Same Plant.

5. Whether the Successor Uses the Same or Substantially the Same Workforce.

6. Whether the Successor Uses the Same or Substantially the Same Supervisory Personnel.

7. Whether the Same Jobs Exist Under Substantially the Same Working Conditions.

   Whether the organization of the departments, sections, etc., remain substantially the same, the percentage of old jobs maintained, whether personnel practices are substantially the same, and the status of any collective bargaining agreements, etc.

8. Whether the Successor Uses the Same Machinery, Equipment, and Methods of Production.

9. Whether the Successor Produces the Same Product.

APPENDIX A-14: TRANSMITTAL MEMORANDUM FOR AN ENFORCEMENT RECOMMENDATION (Compliance Evaluations)

The memorandum transmitting a recommendation for enforcement arising from a compliance review will contain the following sections:

1. CONTRACTOR'S IDENTITY

a. State the establishment's or functional unit's full name and mailing address, including the county in which it is located, and the names and titles of primary establishment or functional unit contact persons (i.e., top establishment or functional unit official, legal representative, EEO and Affirmative Action Coordinator).

b. If the establishment or functional unit is part of a multi-establishment corporation, also state the corporate name and address, the names and titles of primary contact persons (as above), and describe the relationship between the establishment/functional unit and corporation, e.g., unincorporated division or wholly owned subsidiary. The description of this relationship is critical when the establishment/functional unit itself does not hold a federal contract.

c. Give any known information on the ownership make-up of the business and its legal address in the state in which it is incorporated. This information is often available in Industrial directories or from the Secretary of State's office (corporations).

2. CONTRACTOR'S BUSINESS

Describe the contractor's main product(s), basic structure, total employment and major types of jobs.

3. PRIOR HISTORY

Indicate whether and when the establishment or functional unit or both, were previously reviewed or subjected to an OFCCP complaint investigation. Also note the outcome of any such review or investigation. Reference any relevant legal actions against the establishment or functional unit or both (e.g., pending Title VII suit, consent decree, etc.).

4. CONTRACT COVERAGE

Describe the basis for OFCCP jurisdiction. For basic coverage requirements, under the Executive Order, see 41 CFR 60-1.5(a); under Section 503, see 41 CFR 60-741.4; and under Section 4212, see 41 CFR 250.4. If a violation asserted relates to a written AAP, for the Executive Order, see 41 CFR 60-2, for Section

503, see 41 CFR 60-741.40-.45; and for Section 4212, see 41 CFR 60-250.40-.44 and 41 CFR 60-300-.40-.44.

As used below, the term federal contracts means federal prime contracts, subcontracts and federally assisted construction contracts and subcontracts.

a. Basic Contract Information (All Cases): List here (or in an attachment if voluminous) all known fFederal contracts held by the contractor during the review period and during the period for which violations are asserted. For each such contract, give the information requested on page 2, item 5 of the Supply and Service SCER (see Appendix 2A-1) plus the goods, services, lease arrangements, etc. provided under the contract and any available information on whether there was a break or modification during the period the contract was in effect.

   If coverage is based on contracts for indefinite quantities (for example, a blanket purchase order, a rate agreement, etc.) note (1) the amounts ordered in the business year(s) of the violations; and (2) the identity and location of contracting officers and others who may be able to provide copies of invoices and other documents verifying coverage.

b. Additional Contract Information Where Actual or Potential Coverage Dispute: If coverage is or is anticipated to become an issue, state the grounds on which the contractor claims not to be covered, and any grounds you believe the contractor might assert. You will analyze the claim asserted and potential claim.

   i. Separate Entity Issue: If the contractor claims or may claim not to be covered based on the fact it is a separate entity from the company holding the federal contract, it is critical to include information on the following factors concerning that relationship:

      - common ownership;
      - common directors and/or officers;
      - de facto exercise of control;
      - personnel policies emanating from a common source; and
      - dependency of operations.

   ii. Subcontract Issue: If coverage is based on a subcontract relationship with a prime government contractor, include:

      - the identity of the prime contractor, including contracting agency and goods or services involved in the prime contract;
      - information demonstrating that the prime contractor is covered; and

- an analysis of how the subcontract meets either or both prongs of the regulatory definition of covered subcontract.

iii. SeriousJurisdictional Question: If a serious question about jurisdiction is present or anticipated, obtain a complete copy of at least one contract which establishes coverage for the review period and the violation period from the contracting agency or the contractor. SOL will not approve an enforcement recommendation without a complete hard copy of at least one federal contract. A copy of the contract must be included in the case file.

5. SUMMARY OF EVENTS

Indicate how the company was selected for review, and then list major review events, including current status. Major events include, for example, the date the AAP was received; the dates of the onsite; the dates of any Predetermination Notice, Notice of Violation, Show Cause Notice and 15-Day Notice; the period during which conciliation was attempted; and the date conciliation was terminated. In the case of a denial of access claim, OFCCP must show that the contractor was selected in accordance with a neutral plan.

6 LIST OF VIOLATIONS FOR WHICH ENFORCEMENT IS SOUGHT

List each violation for which enforcement is being sought under the sub-headings of "Affirmative Action" or "Discrimination."

7. ANALYSIS OF VIOLATIONS

For each violation for which enforcement is sought, give the following analysis, specifically referring to the case file location by file and page number of the relevant portions of documents and interviews.

Note, however, that violations may be grouped where to do so would result in a clearer and more succinct presentation of the case. For example, many affirmative action violations are interrelated and can more easily be described together, e.g., problems with job group formation usually result in problems with utilization analysis, underutilization determinations and goals.

a. Violation: State the practice that constitutes the violation and identify the sections of the regulations and/or statutes violated. In the case of a discrimination finding, state the specific minority or gender group affected, job(s) at issue, level of disparity in standard deviations, and the shortfall. Also, identify the component(s) of the selection process that caused the adverse impact.

b. Facts: Summarize factual findings. Reference the file and page location of data such as worksheets, statistical analyses, cohort analyses, salary analyses, medical evidence, and contractor documents which are the basis for each factual finding.

c. Analysis: Conduct an analysis to determine why the facts lead to a conclusion of violation. Where discrimination is the issue, analysis should be done using the appropriate theory and burden of proof.

   Review the contractor's position and any data provided in support of its position (referencing file location), giving the reasons (referencing supporting documentation) for concluding that the contractor has not adequately responded to evidence of violation and/or that its position is a pretext for discrimination. Also determine if there are other contractor positions that could be raised in the future, and the overall strengths and weaknesses of the case.

d. Remedy: Describe the proposed remedy. Indicate the basis and support for the type of remedy proposed. Describe the contractor's position on remedy if this has been discussed with the contractor.

   i. Individually-Based Back pay: If proposed remedy includes individually-based back pay, indicate the pay rate used (and if from other than payroll records, its source), the method of computation and applicable interest rates. Include or attach a summary list of back pay due with the name of each affected class member, the period covered and amount due (referencing the file location of individual computation sheets).

   ii. Formula Relief: If proposed remedy includes formula for relief, indicate the rationale for a formula approach, the basis for calculating the total amount due, including components of the calculations, and the method of allocating the total amount among class members.

e. Where the analysis described in this item 7 has already been prepared in narrative format (addressing all sub-items given here) in the SCER, if the SCER analysis is on word processing equipment, copy it to here. If the relevant SCER analysis is not on word processing equipment, you may conventionally copy and "cut and paste" here (as neatly as possible).

f. SOL, JRC, RO and NO Opinions: If applicable, reference the tabbed file location of and summarize any Solicitor's, Joint Review Committee, Regional, and National Office opinions and recommendations, and the action taken respecting them.

8. CONCILIATION

Describe the conciliation efforts undertaken. Describe significant aspects of those efforts, e.g., what was offered, by whom, rationale for rejecting, and issues at impasse. Identify dates conciliation was attempted, the participant(s) and summarize the results, referencing the file location of meeting notes, pertinent correspondence, etc.

If, however, there has already been some discussion of conciliation, with respect to particular violations in item 7 above, (e.g., the contractor's position on the violation/remedy, etc.), that discussion may be referenced here in the context of total conciliation efforts.

IMPORTANT: If conciliation sessions continue after this Transmittal Memorandum is prepared, it is critical that, at a minimum, an addendum be attached updating the status of negotiations (including any additional violations resolved (see item 10 below) and referencing the file location of pertinent meeting notes and correspondence. SOL must receive all correspondence and other documents generated during these negotiations.

9. CONCLUSIONS/RECOMMENDATIONS

Indicate the action being recommended.

10. ATTACHMENT - VIOLATIONS FORMALLY CITED BUT RESOLVED

In an Attachment to the Transmittal Memorandum, list any violations cited in one or more of the following documents that have been resolved as of the date the Transmittal Memorandum is prepared: Predetermination Notice; Notice of Violation; Show Cause; Amended Show Cause Notice; and 15-Day Notice.

Briefly describe the resolution, referencing the file location of documents that provide more information on the issue and its resolution.

CONTACT PERSONNEL

List the contacts for the contractor and OFCCP.

FIGURES 1-5

FIGURE F-1: CASE CHRONOLOGY LOG (CC-53)

CHRONOLOGY LOG			
NAME & ADDRESS OF CONTRACTOR/COMPLAINANT		CASE EVALUATION No.	
NAME OF CHIEF EXECUTIVE OFFICER & PHONE NUMBER		NAME OF EEO COORDINATOR & PHONE NUMBER	
DATE	**PERSON CONTACTED Name and Title** (*as appropriate*)	**CHRONOLOGY** SUMMARY OF DISCUSSION OR ACTION	**OFCCP STAFF Name and Title** (*as appropriate*)

FIGURE F-2: OFCCP SCHEDULING LETTER AND ITEMIZED LISTING

OMB NO. 1250-0003
Expires OMB Approved Expiration Date

VIA CERTIFIED MAIL
(NUMBER)
RETURN RECEIPT REQUESTED

(Name of contractor official)
(Title of contractor official)
(Establishment Name)
(Street Address)
(City, State, Zip Code)

Dear (Name of contractor official):

The U.S. Department of Labor, Office of Federal Contract Compliance Programs (OFCCP), selected your ________________[**Insert:** establishment, functional unit, or corporate headquarters] located at ______________________ for a _______________ [**Insert:** compliance evaluation or corporate management compliance evaluation (CMCE)]. We are conducting this ______________ [**Insert:** compliance evaluation or CMCE] under the authority of Executive Order 11246, Section 503 of the Rehabilitation Act of 1973,[328] the affirmative action provisions of the Vietnam Era Veterans' Readjustment Assistance Act of 1974[329] and their implementing regulations in 41 CFR Chapter 60.[330] In addition to determining your compliance with these authorities, we will also verify your compliance with the regulations issued by the Veterans' Employment and Training Service (VETS) requiring contractors covered under Section 4212 to file an annual report on their employment and hiring of protected veterans.[331]

A compliance evaluation is initiated as a compliance review. The compliance review may progress in three phases: a desk audit, an on-site review, and an off-site analysis. OFCCP describes the phases of a compliance review in its regulations at 41 CFR Chapter 60.[332] For the desk audit, please submit the following information:

---

[328] 29 U.S.C. § 793 (2006).
[329] 38 U.S.C. § 4212 (2006).
[330] E.O.11246, *as amended*, 3 CFR 339 12319 (1965); Section 503 of the Rehabilitation Act of 1973, *as amended,* 29 U.S.C. 793 (2006); Vietnam Era Veterans' Readjustment Assistance Act of 1974, *as amended*, 38 U.S.C. 4212 (2006).
[331] The VETS regulations require Federal contractors to submit either or both the VETS-100 and the VETS-100A Federal Contractor Report on Veterans' Employment. See 41 CFR
§ 61-300.10.
[332] 41 CFR §§ 60-1.20(a), 60-300.60(a), and 60-741.60(a).

1. a copy of your current Executive Order Affirmative Action Program (AAP) prepared in accordance with the requirements of 41 CFR § 60-1.40, and 41 CFR § 60-2.1 through § 60-2.17;

2. a copy of your current Section 503 and Section 4212 AAPs prepared in accordance with the requirements of 41 CFR § 60-741.40 through § 60-741.44 and 41 CFR § 60-300.40 through § 60-300.44, respectively; and

3. the support data specified in the enclosed Itemized Listing.

Please submit your AAPs and the support data specified in the enclosed Itemized Listing to the address listed on page one of this letter as soon as possible, but no later than 30 days from the date you receive this letter. Pursuant to 41 CFR § 60-1.12(e), failure to preserve complete and accurate records constitutes non-compliance with your obligations as a Federal contractor or subcontractor. Once the evaluation begins, you are required to maintain all personnel and employment records described in the regulations enforced by OFCCP until the final disposition of the evaluation.[333]

We encourage you to submit your information in an electronic format to reduce the amount of time it takes to complete our evaluation of your [**Insert** establishment, functional unit, or corporate headquarters]. Should you opt to email your submissions, use email address __________.

You should be aware that OFCCP may initiate enforcement proceedings if you fail to submit AAPs and support data that represent a reasonable effort to meet the requirements of the regulations in 41 CFR Chapter 60.

Rest assured that OFCCP considers the information you provide in response to this Scheduling Letter as sensitive and confidential. Therefore, any disclosures we may make will be consistent with the provisions of the Freedom of Information Act.[334]

Please contact ____________ at ______________ if you have any questions concerning the compliance evaluation.

Sincerely,

(Name of District Director)
District Director

Enclosure (1)
Itemized Listing

---

[333] 41 CFR §§ 60-1.12(a), 60-300.80(a), and 60-741.80(a).
[334] 41 CFR § 60-1.20(g); Freedom of Information Act, *as amended*, 5 U.S.C. § 552 (2009).

ITEMIZED LISTING

Executive Order 11246

1. An organizational profile prepared according to 41 CFR § 60-2.11.

2. The formation of job groups (covering all jobs) consistent with criteria given in 41 CFR § 60-2.12.

3. For each job group, a statement of the percentage of minority and female incumbents as described in 41 CFR § 60-2.13.

4. For each job group, a determination of minority and female availability that considers the factors given in 41 CFR § 60-2.14(c)(1) and (c)(2).

5. For each job group, the comparison of incumbency to availability as explained in 41 CFR § 60-2.15.

6. Placement goals for each job group in which the percentage of minorities or women employed is less than would be reasonably expected given their availability as described in 41 CFR § 60-2.16.

Section 503

7. Results of the evaluation of the effectiveness of outreach and recruitment efforts that were intended to identify and recruit qualified individuals with disabilities (IWDs) as described in 41 CFR § 60-741.44(f).

8. Documentation of all actions taken to comply with the audit and reporting system requirements described in 41 CFR § 60-741.44(h).

9. Documentation of the computations or comparisons described in 41 CFR § 60-741.44(k)for the immediately preceding AAP year and, if you are six months or more into your current AAP year when you receive this listing, provide the information for at least the first six months of the current AAP year.

10. The utilization analysis evaluating the representation of IWDs in each job group, or, if appropriate, evaluating the representation of IWDs in the workforce as a whole, as provided in 41 CFR § 60-741.45. If you are six months or more into your current AAP year on the date you receive this listing, please also submit information that reflects current year progress.

Section 4212 (VEVRAA)

11. Results of the evaluation of the effectiveness of outreach and recruitment efforts that were intended to identify and recruit qualified protected veterans as described in 41 CFR § 60-300.44(f).

12. Documentation of all actions taken to comply with the audit and reporting system requirements described in 41 CFR § 60-300.44(h).

13. Documentation of the computations or comparisons described in 41 CFR § 60-300.44(k)for the immediately preceding AAP year and, if you are six months or more into your current AAP year when you receive this listing, provide the information for at least the first six months of the current AAP year.

14. Documentation of the hiring benchmark adopted, the methodology used to establish it if using the five factors described in § 60-300.45(b)(2). If you are six months or more into your current AAP year on the date you receive this listing, please also submit information that reflects current year results.

Support Data

15. Copies of your Employer Information Report EEO-1 (Standard Form 100 Rev.) for the last three years.[335]

16. A copy of your collective bargaining agreement(s), if applicable. Include any other documents you prepared, such as policy statements, employee notices or handbooks, etc. that implement, explain, or elaborate on the provisions of the collective bargaining agreement.

17. Information on your affirmative action goals for the immediately preceding AAP year and, where applicable (see below), progress on your goals for the current AAP year.[336]

For the immediately preceding AAP year, this report must include information that reflects:

a. job group representation at the start of the AAP year, (i.e., total incumbents, total minority incumbents, and total female incumbents);

b. the percentage placement rates (% goals) established for minorities and women at the start of the AAP year; and

c. the actual number of placements (hires plus promotions) made during the AAP year into each job group with goals (i.e., total placements, total minority placements, and total female placements. For goals not attained, describe the specific good faith efforts made to achieve them.

If you are six months or more into your current AAP year on the date you receive this listing, please also submit information that reflects progress on goals established in your current AAP year, and describe your implementation of action-oriented programs designed to achieve these goals.[337]

[335] 41 CFR § 60-1.7.

[336] 41 CFR § 60-1.12(a), 41 CFR § 60-2.1(c) and 41 CFR § 60-2.16.

[337] 41 CFR § 60-1.12 and 41 CFR § 60-2.17(c).

18. Data on your employment activity (applicants, hires, promotions, and terminations) for the immediately preceding AAP year and, if you are six months or more into your current AAP year when you receive this listing, provide the information in (a) through (c) below for at least the first six months of the current AAP year. You should present this data by job group (as defined in your AAP) or by job title.[338]

a. Applicants and Hires: For each job group or job title, this analysis must consist of the total number of applicants and the total number of hires, as well as the number of African- American/Black, Asian/Pacific Islander, Hispanic, American Indian/Alaskan Native, White, and the number of female and male applicants and hires. For each job group or job title applicants for whom race and/or sex is not known, should be included in the data submitted.

However, if some of your job groups or job titles (most commonly, entry-level) are filled from the same applicant pool, you may consolidate your applicant data (but not hiring data) for those job groups or titles. For example, where applicants expressly apply for or would qualify for a broad spectrum of jobs (such as "Production," "Office," etc.) that includes several job groups, you may consolidate applicant data.

b. Promotions: For each job group or job title, provide the total number of promotions by gender and race/ethnicity.[339] Also, include a definition of "promotion" as used by your company and the basis on which they were compiled (e.g. promotions to the job group, from and/or within the job group, etc.). If it varies for different segments of your workforce, please define the term as used for each segment. If you present promotions by job title, include the department and job group from which and to which the person(s) was promoted.

c. Terminations: For each job group or job title, provide the total number of employee terminations by gender and race/ethnicity. When presenting terminations by job title, include the department and job group from which the person(s) terminated.

19. Employee level compensation data for all employees (including but not limited to full-time, part-time, contract, per diem or day labor, temporary) as of the date of the workforce analysis in your AAP. Provide gender and race/ethnicity information and hire date for each employee as well as job title, EEO-1 Category and job group in a single file.[340] Provide all requested data electronically, if maintained in an electronic format. See Note 1, below.

---

[338] 41 CFR § 60-1.12, 41 CFR § 60-2.11-12, 41 CFR § 60-2.17(b)(2)and(d)(1), and 41 CFR §§ 60-3.4 and 3.15.

[339] The term "race/ethnicity" as used throughout the Itemized Listing includes these racial and ethnic groups: African-American/Black, Asian/Pacific Islander, Hispanic, American Indian/Alaskan Native, and White.

[340] 41 CFR § 60-2.17(b)(3) and (d).

a. For all employees, compensation includes base salary and or wage rate, and hours worked in a typical workweek. Other compensation or adjustments to salary such as bonuses, incentives, commissions, merit increases, locality pay or overtime should be identified separately for each employee.

b. You may provide any additional data on factors used to determine employee compensation, such as education, past experience, duty location, performance ratings, department or function, and salary level/band/range/grade.

c. Documentation and policies related to compensation practices of the contractor should also be included in the submission, particularly those that explain the factors and reasoning used to determine compensation.

20. Copies of reasonable accommodation policies, and documentation of any accommodation requests received and their resolution, if any.

21. Your most recent assessment of your personnel processes, as required by 41 CFR § 60-300.44(b) and § 60-741.44(b), including the date the assessment was performed, any actions taken or changes made as a result of the assessment, and the date of the next scheduled assessment.

22. Your most recent assessment of physical and mental qualifications, as required by 41 CFR § 60-300.44(c)and § 60-741.44(c), including the date the assessment was performed, any actions taken or changes made as a result of the assessment, and the date of the next scheduled assessment.

NOTES

NOTE 1: If any of the requested information is computerized, you must submit it in an electronic format that is complete, readable, and useable. Please use caution when submitting large electronic files. Check with the OFCCP Compliance Officer and your system administrator to ensure adherence to administrative and system guidelines.

Note 2: According to the Paperwork Reduction Act of 1995, an agency may not conduct or sponsor, and a person is not required to respond to, a collection of information unless it displays a valid OMB control number. The valid OMB control number for this information collection is 1250-0003. We estimate that the average time required to complete this information collection is 27.9 hours per response, including the time for evaluating instructions, searching existing data sources, gathering and maintaining the data needed, and completing and evaluating the collection of information.

Send any comments concerning this burden estimate or any other aspect of this collection of information, including suggestions for reducing the burden, to the Office of Federal Contract Compliance Programs, Room C-3325, 200 Constitution Avenue, N.W., Washington, D.C. 20210.

FIGURE F-3: COMPLIANCE CHECK CONTROL SHEET

GENERAL INFORMATION **CMS Control #:**

Establishment Name:
Street Address:
City, State, Zip Code:

Corporate Name:
Street Address:
City, State, Zip Code:

Company Contacts		Name	Title	Telephone Number
Establishment	CEO			
	EEO/AA			
Corporate	CEO			
	EEO/AA			

Outside Representation	Firm	Telephone Number

Total Employees	Total Minority	Total Female

Type of Review
☐ Initial ☐ Follow-Up

Multiple Facility
☐ Yes ☐ No

Last Review Date
/ /

DATES

Scheduling Letter Mailed	Onsite	Closure Letter Issued
/ /	/ /	/ /

FINDINGS

Inspected Items	Yes	No	N/A
• Information on prior year report	☐	☐	☐
• Job advertisements including evidence of job listings with the appropriate employment service delivery system (e.g., local or State Employment Service)	☐	☐	☐
• Accommodations for individuals with disabilities	☐	☐	☐

If an item is not applicable, indicate the reason here:

RECOMMENDATION FOR CLOSURE

- If no items missing, leave blank.
- If prior year report missing (unless contractor was not covered in prior year), check under column #1.
- If job listings information missing, check under column #2.
- If accommodations information missing, check under column #3.
- If contractor refuses to grant access, check appropriate space.

	#1 **Prior Year Report**	#2 **Job Listings**	#3 **Accommodations**
Recordkeeping			

(Checking one of the above spaces will place the contractor into a pool for further evaluation.)

Failure to Grant Access (Explain)	

(Checking the space above will indicate the contractor will be selected for another compliance evaluation method.)

Technical Assistance Needed: ☐ Yes ☐ No

Additional Pertinent Information:

	Compliance Officer	**ADD**	**DD**
Signature			
Date			

FIGURE F-4: OFCCP COMPLAINT FORM

Complaint of Discrimination in Employment
Under Federal Government Contracts

U.S. Department of Labor
Office of Federal Contract
Compliance Programs

Instructions: Before completing this form, please read all instructions, including the Privacy Act statement below. Use this form to file a complaint of discrimination in employment under any of the OFCCP programs. While your response is voluntary, OFCCP relies on this information as a source for identifying potential violations of equal employment opportunity requirements in the federal contractor community. Note: Persons are not required to respond to this collection of information unless it displays a currently valid OMB control number.

OMB No: 1250-0002
Expires: 03/31/2014

Privacy Act Notice: The authority for collecting this information is Executive Order 11246, as amended, Sec. 503 of the Rehabilitation Act of 1973, as amended; the Vietnam Era Veterans' Readjustment Assistance Act of 1974 as amended, 38 U.S.C. 4212; Title VII of the Civil Rights Act of 1964, as amended; and/or Title I of the Americans with Disabilities Act of 1990, as amended (ADA). This information is used to process complaint and conduct investigations of alleged violations of the above Order or Acts. We will provide a copy of this complaint to the employer against whom it is filed and, when matters alleged are covered by Title VII and/or the ADA, to the U.S. Equal Employment Opportunity Commission (EEOC). The information collected may be verified with others who may have knowledge relevant to the complaint. It may be used in settlement negotiations with the employer or in the course of presenting evidence at a hearing, or may be disclosed to other agencies with jurisdiction over the complaint. Providing this information is voluntary; however failure to provide the information will restrict the action that the Department of Labor can take on your behalf and, for matters covered by Title VII or the ADA, may affect your right to sue under those laws.

Non-Retaliation: OFCCP regulations and Title VII and/or the ADA where applicable, require an employer to take all necessary steps to assure that there is no retaliation against any person who files a complaint or assists in its investigation. This includes any intimidation, threat, coercion or discrimination. Please notify OFCCP immediately if any alleged attempt at retaliation is made.

Prompt Filing: All complaints must be filed within a specified number of days following the latest occurrence of the alleged discrimination: Executive Order 11246 – 180 days; Rehabilitation and Veterans Acts – 300 days. Exceptions must be approved by the Director.

Name and address:	Name and address of company you allege discriminated against you:
Name ______ Address ______ City ______ State ______ Zip ______	Name ______ Address ______ City ______ State ______ Zip ______
Telephone No. ______	Telephone No. ______
Mail this form to the Department of Labor, OFCCP Regional Office:	Give the date(s) of the latest occurrence(s) of the alleged discriminatory act(s): ______ ______ ______

Step 1: Check the box next to the program you are filing under (i.e. Executive Order 11246, as amended; Section 503 of the Rehabilitation Act of 1973, as amended, or the Vietnam Era Veterans' Readjustment Assistance Act of 1974, as amended, 38 U.S.C. 4212, or retaliation)

Step 2: Under the program, check what you believe to be the basis for the discrimination against you, such as race, sex, or national origin. If you think that thee was more than one basis, more than one basis may be checked. You may also check more than one race/ethnic category.

☐ **Executive Order 11246**, as amended. This Order covers persons alleging discrimination because of race, color, religion, sex, or national origin. If this is checked, your complaint will be dual filed as a charge under Title VII of the Civil Rights Act of 1964. I believe I was (or continue to be) discriminated against because of my:

Bases:

- ☐ Race
- ☐ Color
- ☐ Religion
- ☐ Sex ☐ Female ☐ Male
- ☐ National Origin
- ☐ Other

- ☐ Hispanic or Latino
- ☐ Not Hispanic or Latino

- ☐ American Indian or Alaskan Native
- ☐ Asian
- ☐ Black or African American
- ☐ Native Hawaiian or Other Pacific Islander
- ☐ White

☐ **Section 503 of the Rehabilitation Act of 1973**, as amended. This Act covers individuals with a disability, persons with a history of physical or mental disability, and persons regarded as disabled by the employer. If this is checked, your complaint will be dual-filed as a charge under the Americans with Disabilities Act.

Basis ☐ Disability Please check if you are a veteran: ☐ Yes ☐ No

☐ **Vietnam Era Veterans' Readjustment Assistance Act of 1974**, as amended, 38 U.S.C. 4212. This Act covers special disabled veterans, veterans of the Vietnam Era, recently separated veterans, disabled veterans, Armed Forces service medal veterans, and other protected veterans.

☐ **Retaliation**: It is unlawful to harass intimidate, threaten, coerce, or discriminate against any individual because he or she has filed a complaint, participated in a discrimination proceeding or otherwise opposed discrimination under any of the federal programs above.

Form CC-4

IF YOUR COMPLAINT IS BASED ON VETERAN STATUS, CHECK ONE OR MORE OF THE FOLLOWING APPLICABLE BOX(ES).

☐ I was discharged or released from active duty on (enter date of discharge or release) ______________

☐ I am a veteran who, while serving on active duty in the Armed Forces, participated in a United States military operation for which an Armed Forces service medal was awarded pursuant to Executive Order 12985 (61 CFR 1209).

☐ I served on active duty during a war or in a campaign or expedition for which a campaign badge has been authorized.

☐ I served on active duty for a period of more than 180 days, and was discharged or released with other than a dishonorable discharge, and the active duty occurred in the Republic of Vietnam between February 28, 1961, and May 7, 1975, or between August 5, 1964, and May 7, 1975 in all other cases.

☐ I was discharged or released from active duty for a service connected disability. If you have checked this box, submit medical information resulting in discharge or release with this form. (This information is available from your Master Military Record at the National Personnel Record Center, 9700 Page Boulevard, St. Louis, MO 63132.)

I am a veteran who is entitled to compensation (or who but for the receipt of military retired pay would be entitled to compensation) under laws administered by the Secretary of Veterans Affairs. Check one of the following.

☐ Disability rating of 30% or more ☐

☐ Disability rating at 10% or 20% and have been officially determined to have a serious employment disability

☐ Disability rating, but neither a or b

Step 3: Check those actions which you believe the employer took or failed to take because of your race, color, religion, sex, national origin, disability or veteran status (more than one may be checked):

Issue(s):

☐ Hiring	☐ Promotion	☐ Job Assignment	☐ Sabbath Day Observance
☐ Termination	☐ Demotion	☐ Training and Apprenticeship	☐ Intimidation
☐ Layoff	☐ Seniority	☐ Segregated Facilities	☐ Other ______________
☐ Recall	☐ Harassment	☐ Pregnancy Leave	
☐ Wages	☐ Job Benefits	☐ Accommodation to Disability	

FOR EACH ISSUE, EXPLAIN IN YOUR STATEMENT BELOW HOW YOU WERE DISCRIMINATED AGAINST.

1. Do you know any other employees or applicants of your group who were treated in the same way (checked above) you allege you were?

   ☐ Yes ☐ No If yes, include their names in your statement below and explain how they were treated.

2. Do you know any other employees or applicants who are not of your group who were treated in the same way (checked above) you allege you were?

   ☐ Yes ☐ No If yes, include their names in your statement below and explain how they were treated.

THE COMPLAINT

Describe in detail the alleged discriminatory/retaliatory act (s).
Please include:

- Why you believe the act(s) was because of your disability, veteran status, race, color, religion, sex, or national origin, and why you believe the act(s) was retaliation;
- Dates, places, names and titles of persons involved and witnesses, if any;
- What harm, if any, was caused to you or others with whom you work as a result of the alleged discriminatory act(s);
- What explanation, if any, was offered for the act(s) by the employer; and
- Any information you may have on federal contracts held by the employer.

If this is a complaint based on disability, describe the disability, your history of disability, or why you think the employer regarded you as disabled.

(Type as much information as required into the block above)

If you have sought assistance in resolving this complaint from another source (another agency, a lawyer, internal grievance procedure, etc.) please indicate here and the name of the source, the date you sought assistance, and result, if any:

Name ______________________________ Date ____________
Result:

FRIEND OR RELATIVE:
Please notify OFCCP if you change your address or phone number. You may indicate a person who would know how to reach you if OFCCP is unable to reach you at your own address or phone.

Name ______________________________

Address ______________________________

City ________________ State ______ Zip ______

Relationship ______________________________

Telephone ______________________________

FILED ELSEWHERE? If you have filed this complaint or a similar one elsewhere, please tell us:	ARE YOU REPRESENTED? If you are represented by an attorney or other person or organization, please tell us:
Name ____________________	Name ____________________
Address ____________________	Address ____________________
City __________ State ______ Zip ______	City __________ State ______ Zip ______
Contact ____________________	Contact ____________________
Telephone ____________________	Telephone ____________________

SIGNATURE AND VERIFICATION
I declare under penalty of perjury that the information given above is true and correct to the best of my knowledge or belief. (A willful false statement is punishable by law: 18 U.S.C. 1001.) I hereby authorize the release of any medical information needed for the investigation.

______________________________ ____________________
Signature of Complainant Date

Public Burden Statement
We estimate that it will take an average of 1.28 hours to complete this complaint form, including time for reviewing instructions, searching existing data sources, gathering and maintaining the data needed, and completing and reviewing the information. If you have any comments regarding these estimates or any other aspect of this complaint form, including suggestions for reducing this burden, send them to the Office of Federal Contract Compliance Programs Policy Division (1250-0002) 200 Constitution Avenue, N.W., Room C-3325, Washington, D.C. 20210.

DO NOT SEND THE COMPLETED FORM TO THIS OFFICE

Do not write below this line

The complainant has verified this complaint in my presence. This complaint is now the basis of an investigation under Executive Order11246, as amended; Section 503 of the Rehabilitation Act of 1973, as amended; and/or the Vietnam Era Veterans' Readjustment Assistance Act of 1974, as amended (38 U.S.C. 4212).

______________ ______________ ______________ ______________
Name of Investigator Title Signature of Investigator Date

FIGURE F-5: STANDARD TEXT FOR CONCILIATION AGREEMENT

Conciliation Agreement
Between the
U.S. Department of Labor Office of Federal Contract Compliance Programs
And
[*Name of Contractor*]
[*Name and address of establishment covered by the Agreement*]

PART I: General Provisions

1. This Agreement is between the U.S. Department of Labor, Office of Federal Contract Compliance Programs (OFCCP), and [*insert name and address of contractor*].

2. The violations identified in this Agreement were found during a [*insert as appropriate*: compliance evaluation or complaint investigation] of [*insert name of contractor*] which began on [*insert date*] and were specificed in a [*insert as appropriate*: Notice of Violation; Show Cause Notice; an Amended Show Cause Notice] that was issued on [*insert date*]. OFCCP alleges that [*insert name of contractor*] has violated [*insert as appropriate*: Executive Order 11246, as amended; Section 503 of the Rehabilitation Act of 1973, as amended; the Vietnam Era Veterans' Readjustment Assistance Act of 1974, as amended (38 U.S.C. 4212)] and implementing regulations at 41 CFR Chapter 60 due to the specific violations cited in Part II below.

3. This Agreement does not constitute an admission by [*insert name of contractor*] of any violation of [*insert as appropriate*: Executive Order 11246, as amended; Section 503 of the Rehabilitation Act of 1973, as amended; the Vietnam Era Veterans' Readjustment Assistance Act of 1974, as amended, (38 U.S.C. 4212)] and the implementing regulations.

4. The provisions of this Agreement will become part of [*insert contractor's name*] AAP. Subject of the performance by [*insert name of contractor*] of all promises and representations contained herein and in its AAP, all named violations in regard to the compliance of [*insert name of contractor*] with all OFCCP programs will be deemed resolved. However, [*insert name of contractor*] is advised that the commitments contained in this Agreement do not preclude future determinations of noncompliance based on a finding that the commitments are not sufficient to achieve compliance.

5. [*Insert name of contractor*] agrees that OFCCP may review compliance with this Agreement. As part of this review, OFCCP may require written reports, inspect the premises, interview witnesses, and examine and copy documents, as may be relevant to the matter under investigation and pertinent to [*insert name of contractor*] compliance. [*Insert name of contractor]* shall permit access to its premises during normal business hours for these purposes.

6. Nothing herein is intended to relieve [*insert name of contractor*] from the obligation to comply with the requirements of Executive Order 11246, as amended, Section 503 of the Rehabilitation Act of 1973, as amended, and/or the Vietnam Era Veterans Readjustment

Assistance Act of 1974, as amended (38 U.S.C. 4212), their implementing regulations, or any other equal employment statute or executive order or its implementing regulations.

7. [*Insert name of contractor*] agrees that there will be no retaliation of any kind against any beneficiary of this Agreement or against any person who has provided information or assistance, or who files a complaint, or who participates in any manner in any proceedings under Executive Order 11246, as amended, Section 503 of the Rehabilitation Act of 1973, as amended, and/or the Vietnam Era Veterans' Readjustment Assistance Act of 1974, as amended (38 U.S.C. 4212).

8. This Agreement will be deemed to have been accepted by the Government on the date of the signature by the Regional Director for OFCCP, unless the Director for OFCCP indicates otherwise within 45 calendar days of the Regional Director's signature on this Agreement.

9. If at any time in the future, OFCCP believes that [*insert name of contractor*] has violated any portion of this Agreement during the term of this Agreement, [*insert name of contractor*] will be promptly notified of that fact in writing. This notification will include a statement of the facts and circumstances relied upon in forming that belief. In addition, the notification will provide [*insert name of contractor*] with 15 calendar days from receipt of the notification to respond in writing, except where OFCCP alleges that such a delay would result in irreparable injury.

   Enforcement proceedings for violation of this Agreement may be initiated at any time after the 15-day period has elapsed or sooner, if irreparable injury is alleged, without issuing a Show Cause Notice.

   Where OFCCP believes that [*insert name of contractor*] has violated this Conciliation Agreement, OFCCP may seek enforcement of this Agreement itself and shall not be required to present proof of the underlying violations resolved by this Agreement.

   Liability for violation of this Agreement may subject [*insert name of contractor*] to sanctions set forth in [as applicable, Section 209 of the Executive Order, 41 CFR 60-250.66, 41 CFR 60-300.66 and/or 41 CFR 60-741.66 and/or other appropriate relief.

PART II: Specific Provisions

1. VIOLATION:

   REMEDY:

2. VIOLATION:

   REMEDY:

Part III: Reporting

1. [*Insert name of contractor*] agrees to retain records pertinent to the violations cited in Part II above, and to the reports submitted in compliance with Paragraph 2, below. These records shall include data and information underlying the required reports, specifically, but not limited to all applications and personnel records. The records will be retained until the expiration of this Agreement or consistent with regulatory requirements, whichever is later.

2. [*Insert name of contractor*] agrees to furnish the OFCCP [*insert name and address of OFCCP office*] with the following reports:

   [Fill in specific information regarding the due dates and items to be submitted with each report.]

3. This Conciliation Agreement shall remain in effect until the review and acceptance by OFCCP of [*insert name of contractor*] final progress report.

PART IV: Signatures

This Conciliation Agreement is hereby executed by and between the Office of Federal Contract Compliance Programs and [*insert Contractor*], [*insert Contractor's Address*].

(Signature – Contractor's Top Establishment Official) Name Title Organization City, State DATE: ______________________	(Signature – Compliance Officer) Name Title District Office Region DATE: ______________________
(Signature – Union's Top Official, if applicable) Name Title Organization City, State DATE: ______________________	(Signature – District Director or designee) Name Title District Office Region DATE: ______________________

LETTERS L1 – L33

LETTER L-1: SAMPLE INQUIRY LETTER FOR REQUESTING COMPLAINT DATA FROM EEOC AND STATE AND LOCAL FEPS

[*Date*]

[*Name/Title*]
[*Agency or Organization Name*]
[*Street Address*]
[*City, State, Zip Code*]

Dear__________:

The U.S. Department of Labor, Office of Federal Contract Compliance Programs (OFCCP), scheduled a compliance evaluation for (*insert name of contractor*).

Our evaluation will assess the contractor's compliance with Executive Order 11246, as amended, Section 503 of the Rehabilitation Act of 1973, as amended, the Vietnam Era Veterans' Readjustment Assistance Act of 1974, as amended, 38 U.S.C. 4212, and the implementing regulations for these authorities. These legal authorities prohibit employment discrimination and require affirmative action to provide equal employment opportunity without regard to race, color, religion, national origin, sex, disability or status as a protected veteran.

Please forward any information you have concerning complaints, charges or litigation filed against this contractor. We are also seeking any other information you may have concerning its EEO attitudes, policies and practices of the contractor which you believe we should consider during the course of the compliance evaluation.

The evaluation will begin in approximately 30 calendar days, therefore, a prompt response to this inquiry is appreciated. Please contact me at (*insert phone number*) should you have any questions or require additional information.

Sincerely,

(*insert name of compliance officer*)
Compliance Officer

LETTER L-2: SAMPLE INQUIRY LETTER FOR REQUESTING JOB LISTING FROM EMPLOYMENT SERVICE

[*Date*]

[*Name/Title*]
[*Agency or Organization Name*]
[*Street Address*]
[*City, State, Zip Code*]

Re: Request for Job Listings

Dear (*insert name*):

The U.S. Department of Labor, Office of Federal Contract Compliance Programs (OFCCP), scheduled the below listed company for a compliance evaluation under Executive Order 11246, as amended, Section 503 of the Rehabilitation Act of 1973, as amended, and the Vietnam Era Veterans' Readjustment Assistance Act of 1974 (38 U.S.C. 4212), and the implementing regulations at 41 CFR Part 60.

(*insert contractor's name and mailing address*)

As a part of the compliance evaluation, OFCCP must determine whether the company named above listed its suitable job openings with its local state employment office as required and the results of those listings. In order to determine the contractor's compliance with these mandatory job listing requirements, we are requesting that you provide this office with specific job orders placed with your office for the past two years, as well as any other information related to the contractor's compliance with its job listing obligations. Please contact me at (*insert phone number*) should you have any questions or require additional information.

Thank you for your cooperation.

Sincerely,

(*insert name of compliance officer*)
Compliance Officer

LETTER L-3 SAMPLE INQUIRY LETTER FOR REQUESTING INFORMATION ON PENDING REVIEW FROM VETERANS EMPLOYMENT AND TRAINING SERVICE

[*Date*]

[*Name/Title*]
[*DOL State VETS Office*]
[*Street Address*]
[*City, State, Zip Code*]

Dear (*insert name*):

The U.S. Department of Labor, Office of Federal Contract Compliance Programs (OFCCP), is conducting a compliance review of (*insert name of contractor*).

As a federal contractor, this company assumed obligations and responsibilities under the laws enforced by OFCCP requiring contractors to take affirmative action to employ disabled veterans, Vietnam era veterans, and other protected veterans,and to list all employment openings as defined at (*insert as appropriate:* 41 CFR 60-250.5 or 41 C.F.R 60-300.5) with the appropriate local office of the state employment service system.

Please provide any information you have concerning (*insert name of contractor*) compliance with its obligations including, but not limited to, information on job listingsand complaints for the past year. Your information should be sent to me at the above address or by e-mail to (*insert e-mail address*).

If you have any questions, please contact me at (*insert phone number*). Thank you for your assistance in this matter.

Sincerely,

(*insert name of compliance officer*)
Compliance Officer

LETTER L-4: NOTICE OF CLOSING: COMPLIANCE EVALUATION (NO VIOLATIONS FOUND)

Certified Mail, Return Receipt Requested AND Electronic Mail

[Date]

[Name of CEO]
[Title of CEO]
[Establishment Name]
[Street Address]
[City, State, Zip Code]

Dear (*insert name of contractor's official*):

The U.S. Department of Labor, Office of Federal Compliance Programs (OFCCP), recently completed a compliance evaluation of your equal employment opportunity policies and practices at (*insert name and location of the establishment or functional unit reviewed*).

(*Select either Paragraph 1 or Paragraphs 2 and 3*)

Paragraph1:
During the compliance evaluation process we found no apparent violations of Executive Order 11246, as amended, Section 503 of the Rehabilitation Act of 1973, as amended (Section 503), the Vietnam Era Veterans' Readjustment Assistance Act of 1974, as amended (Section 4212) or Executive Order 13496. The Director of OFCCP or the Regional Director may modify this determination within 45 calendar days of the issuance of this letter.

OR

Paragraphs 2 and 3:
During the compliance evaluation process we identified and resolved the following violation(s): *[insert the technical violation(s) resolved during the compliance evaluation, including the appropriate regulatory citation and specific remedy]*. It is understood that this/these violation(s) will not recur.

There were no other apparent violations of Executive Order 11246, Section 503 or Section 4212. This determination may be modified by the Regional Director, or by the Director of OFCCP, within 45 calendar days of the issuance of this letter.

The OFCCP appreciates the cooperation of you and your staff during the conduct of the compliance review.

Sincerely,

(*insert name of district director*)
District Director

cc: *[insert names]*

LETTER L-5: SAMPLE LINKAGE LETTER

[*Date*]

[*Name of Resource Head or Contact*]
[*Title of Resource Head or Contact*]
[*Resource Name*]
[*Street Address*]
[*City, State, Zip Code*]

Dear (*insert name*):

(*Select either Paragraphs 1 and 3 or Paragraphs 2 and 3*)

Paragraph 1:
As we discussed on (*insert date*), the Department of Labor, Office of Federal Contract Compliance Programs (OFCCP), recommended and *(insert name and location of the establishment reviewed)* agreed to use your services to recruit applicants as part of their effort to meet their federal contractor affirmative action goals or needs as established under laws enforced by OFCCP. The specific job titles for which applicants are sought and the number of projected vacancies are listed below:

Job Title	Projected Vacancies
(job title name)	(insert #)_________
(job title name)	(insert #)_________

OR

Paragraphs 2:
During a recent compliance review the Department of Labor, Office of Federal Contract Compliance Programs (OFCCP), recommended and *(insert name and location of the establishment reviewed)* agreed to use your services to recruit applicants as part of their effort to meet their federal contractor affirmative action goals or needs as established under laws enforced by OFCCP. The specific job titles for which applicants are sought and the number of projected vacancies are listed below:

Job Title	Projected Vacancies
(job title name)	(insert #)_________
(job title name)	(insert #)_________

Paragraph 3:
The company is a covered federal contractor that engages in affirmative action to ensure equal employment opportunity for all applicants and employees regardless of race, color, religion, sex, national origin, disability or protected veteran status. All qualified applicants referred by you will be considered.

We request that you contact *(insert contact name)* with (*insert name of the establishment reviewed*) at *(insert phone number)* to discuss how you can assist with their employment needs.

Sincerely,

(*insert name of compliance officer*)
Compliance Officer

cc: *(insert name of the OFCCP regional linkage coordinator)*
(insert name of the contractor)

LETTER L-6: REQUEST FOR LITERATURE SEARCH

[Date]

Reference Librarian
U.S. Department of Labor Library
200 Constitution Avenue, N.W.
Room N-2445
Washington, D.C. 20210

Dear Reference Librarian:

I am writing to request a literature search on the below listed corporation(s) on behalf of the Department of Labor, Office of Federal Contract Compliance Programs (OFCCP):

(*insert name and address of corporate headquarters*)

This search should include at least the following publications, providing the full text of any entry found:

America's Corporate Families
Directory of Corporate Affiliations
Hoover's Handbook
International Directory of Company Histories
Moody's Industrial Manual
Reference Book of Corporate Managements
Standard and Poor's Register

Please also include a list of articles published about this corporation over the last two years, including articles appearing in the following periodicals:

Business Week
Forbes
Fortune
The Daily Labor Report
The Wall Street Journal

For each publication, please specify the title of the publication, date of publication, title of the article, and the author(s). We would appreciate receiving this material within two weeks of your receipt of this letter. Please contact (*insert name and phone number of compliance officer*) if you have any questions.

Thank you for your assistance.

Sincerely,

(*insert name of regional or district director*)
Regional Director or District Director

LETTER L-7: LETTER TO CONTRACTOR FORWARDING EO 11246, SECTION 503 OR SECTION 4212 COMPLAINT

Certified Mail, Return Receipt Requested

[*Date*]

[*Name of CEO*]
[*Title of CEO*]
[*Establishment Name*]
[*Street Address*]
[*City, State, Zip Code*]

Dear (*insert name of contractor official)*:

The U.S. Department of Labor, Office of Federal Contract Compliance Programs (OFCCP), received a complaint filed under the provisions of (*insert one or more of the appropriate legal authorities enforced by OFCCP*). A copy of the complaint is enclosed.

This office is assigned the complaint for investigation under the (*insert the name of one or more of the appropriate legal authorities enforced by OFCCP underlying the complaint*) and its implementing regulations at (*insert the appropriate CFR part and section citations for the complaint*). A copy of the applicable regulations is enclosed. The regulations enforced by OFCCP require that federal contractors and subcontractors covered by OFCCP's jurisdiction not discriminate based on race, color, religion, sex, national origin, disability or an individual's status as a protected veteran. They generally require federal contractors and subcontractors take affirmative action to employ and advance in employment individuals from these particular groups.

As required by our regulations, please retain full accurate records relevant to this complaint and ensure that there is no harassment, intimidation, coercion or discrimination against the complainant (*insert the appropriate citations*: 41 CFR 60-741.69 and 741.80-.81); 41 CFR 60-250.69 and 250.80-.81; 41 CFR 60-300.69 and 300.80-.81; 42 CFR 60-1.32 and 1.43).

This letter is a notice that a complaint was filed and neither prejudges the issues nor implies that your company violated any law. It is also a notice to retain information that will later permit an expeditious investigation and resolution of this matter.

You may wish to review and attempt to resolve this complaint internally, and if you are successful in resolving it to the satisfaction of the complainant, we will need verification from the complainant. However, OFCCP reserves the option to conduct its own investigation if, in its judgment, the circumstances warrant.

If you do not wish to make an attempt to resolve this matter, or you are unsuccessful in doing so, you may wish to send us a statement of position or evidence concerning the complaint. Any material you submit will be included in the case file, and will be considered when the complaint is investigated. Please note that during such an investigation, we may need to examine your current Affirmative Action Program required under 41 CFR (*insert appropriate citations*: 41 CFR 60-741.44; 41 CFR 60-250.44; 41 CFR 60-300.44; 41 CFR Part 60-2).

If you have any questions, you may contact (*insert name of compliance officer*) at (*insert telephone number*).

Sincerely,

(*insert name of district director*)
District Director

Enclosure: Complaint of (*insert name of complainant and CMS#*)

LETTER L-8: LETTER ACKNOWLEDGING RECEIPT OF EO 11264, SECTION 503 AND SECTION 4212 COMPLAINT

Certified Mail, Return Receipt Requested

[*Date*]

[*Name of Complainant*]
[*Address*]
[*Street Address*]
[*City, State, Zip Code*]

Re: Complaint against [*insert name of company* and CMS #)

Dear (*insert name of complainant)*:

The U.S. Department of Labor, Office of Federal Contract Compliance Programs (OFCCP), acknowledges our receipt of your complaint against the above federal contractor. Your complaint is assigned to this office for investigation. We notified the contractor of your complaint, provided the contractor a copy of the complaint, and advised the contractor of the opportunity to attempt to resolve the complaint if it wishes to do so. We also informed the contractor that our regulations require that all relevant records be retained, and that there be no harassment, intimidation, coercion or retaliation against you.

If the contractor and you are able to resolve your complaint to your satisfaction, please let us know immediately, preferably in writing. In the meanwhile, we will schedule your complaint for investigation.

Please be sure to keep us advised of any change in your address or telephone number. If you have any questions, you may contact (*insert name of compliance officer*) at (*insert telephone number*).

Sincerely,

(*insert name of district director*)
District Director

LETTER L-9: AUTHORIZATION FOR RELEASE OF MEDICAL INFORMATION

Re: Complaint against [*insert name of contractor*]
OFCCP CMS #

I hereby authorize the release to the United States Department of Labor, Office of Federal Contract Compliance Programs (OFCCP), of any medical information needed by OFCCP in its investigation of the complaint of discrimination which I filed on (*insert date*) against the above-named contractor.

PRINTED/TYPED NAME OF PATIENT

SIGNATURE OF PATIENT DATE

LETTER L-10: CONFIRMATION OF ONSITE INVESTIGATION

Certified Mail, Return Receipt Requested

[*Date*]

[*Name of Contractor Official*]
[*Title*]
[*Street Address*]
[*City, State, Zip Code*]

Re: Complaint of (*insert complainant's name and CMS #)*

Dear (*insert name of contractor official*):

This letter confirms the telephone call of (*insert date*) between Compliance Officer (*insert name*) with the U.S. Department of Labor, Office of Federal Contract Compliance Programs (OFCCP), and (*insert name of contractor official*) scheduling the investigation of the above complaint filed under (*insert one or more of these authorities*: Executive Order 11246, as amended; Section 503 of the Rehabilitation Act of 1973, as amended; or the Vietnam Era Veterans' Readjustment Assistance Act of 1974, as amended).

As agreed, the investigation is to begin on (*insert date*) at (*insert time and location*). In the telephone call mentioned above, (*insert compliance officer's name and title*) requested that certain records and individuals be available during the visit. These are listed on the attachment to this letter.

If you have any questions, please contact (*insert name of compliance officer*) at (*insert telephone number*).

Sincerely,

(*insert name of district director*)
District Director

Attachment

LETTER L-11: LETTER TO CONTRACTOR CONFIRMING COMPLAINT RESOLUTION

Certified Mail, Return Receipt Requested

[*Date*]

[*Name of Contractor Official*]
[*Title*]
[*Street Address*]
[*City, State, Zip Code*]

Re: Complaint of (*insert name of complainant and CMS #*)

Dear (*insert name of contractor official*):

On behalf of the U.S. Department of Labor, Office of Federal Contract Compliance Programs, this correspondence confirms (*insert as appropriate*: your letter **or** our telephone conversation) of (*insert date of letter or telephone call*) in which you informed us that the above complaint was resolved to the satisfaction of the complainant. We have been in contact with the complainant who acknowledges that the parties reached a satisfactory resolution of the complaint.

We appreciate your efforts in resolving this matter.

Sincerely,

(*insert name of district director*)
District Director

LETTER L-12: LETTER TO COMPLAINANT CONFIRMING COMPLAINT RESOLUTION

Certified Mail, Return Receipt Requested

[*Date*]

[*Name of Complainant*]
[*Address*]
[*Street Address*]
[*City, State, Zip Code*]

Re: Complaint against (*insert the name of company and CMS #*)

Dear (*insert name of complainant*):

On behalf of the U.S. Department of Labor, Office of Federal Contract Compliance Programs, this correspondence confirms (*insert as appropriate:* your letter **or** our telephone conversation) of (*insert date*). During the (*insert as appropriate*: in your letter **or** during the call) you stated that your complaint against the above company was resolved to your satisfaction.

If you are satisfied with the resolution of your complaint, please sign on the line indicated below and return this letter to us in the enclosed stamped envelope.

Sincerely,

(*insert name of district director*)
District Director

Enclosure: Self addressed stamped envelope

There has been a satisfactory resolution to my complaint filed against (*insert name of contractor*). I have not been forced or coerced by the contractor, or any of its agents, into making this statement.

Signature ____________________

Date ________________________

LETTER L-13: NOTIFICATION OF RESULTS OF INVESTIGATION: NOTIFICATION OF NO VIOLATION (EO 11246, Section 503, or Section 4212 Complaint (Not Dual Filed))

Certified Mail, Return Receipt Requested

[Date]

[insert Complaint No.]

COMPLAINANT
[Complainant's Name]
[Street Address]
[City, State, Zip Code]

CONTRACTOR
[Contractor Name]
[Street Address]
[City, State, Zip Code]

On (*insert date*), the U.S. Department of Labor, Office of Federal Contract Compliance Programs (OFCCP), conducted an investigation of the allegations of (*insert type of discrimination*) made in the complaint of (*insert name of complainant*) filed on (*insert date*). The investigation resulted in the following findings:

1. (*Insert name of contractor*) is a nonexempt government contractor subject to the requirements of (*insert one or more as appropriate*: Executive Order 11246, as amended; Section 503 of the Rehabilitation Act of 1973, as amended (Section 503); the Vietnam Era Veterans' Readjustment Assistance Act of 1974, or as amended (VEVRAA)).

2. (*Insert name of complainant*) is a (*insert one or more bases for alleged discrimination:* sex, race, color, national origin, individual with a disability or a veteran covered by the laws enforced by OFCCP) within the meaning of (*insert appropriate legal authority: Executive Order 11246; Section 503; VEVRAA*) and the regulations at (*insert as appropriate*: 41 CFR 60-1 to 60-50; 41 CFR 60-250; 41 CFR 60-300; 41 CFR 60-741).

3. The complainant alleges the contractor violated its obligations under the nondiscrimination and affirmative action provisions of its federal contracts by (*insert description of employment action taken by contract:* terminating, not promoting, not hiring, etc.).

4. The contractor's position is that the complainant was (*insert description of employment action: terminated, not hired, not promoted, etc.*) because (*insert description of the contractor's reasons or position*).

5. Our investigation indicates that the contractor (*insert description of findings/evidence related to contractor's employment actions*).

6. Based on the findings of this investigation, there was insufficient evidence that the contractor violated its obligations under the nondiscrimination and affirmative action provisions of (*insert one or more as appropriate*: EO 11246; Section 503; VEVRAA). This determination concludes the processing of this complaint by this office.

On behalf of the United States Department of Labor.

__________________________ ____________________

Regional Director Date

cc: *(insert name of complainant's attorney)*
(insert name of the contractor's attorney)

LETTER L-14: NOTIFICATION OF RESULTS OF INVESTIGATION AND NOTICE OF RIGHT-TO-SUE UNDER TITLE I OF THE ADA OR TITLE VII OF THE CIVIL RIGHTS ACT OF 1964: NOTIFICATION OF NO VIOLATION

Certified Mail, Return Receipt Requested

U.S. DEPARTMENT OF LABOR
OFFICE OF FEDERAL CONTRACT COMPLIANCE PROGRAMS

[Complaint No.]

[Complainant's Name] "COMPLAINANT"
[Street Address]
[City, State, Zip Code]

[Contractor's Name] "CONTRACTOR"
[Street Address]
[City, State, Zip Code]

On [*insert date*], the U.S. Department of Labor, Office of Federal Contract Compliance Programs (OFCCP), conducted an investigation of the allegation(s) of [*insert basis of complaint*] discrimination made in the complaint of [*insert name of complainant*], filed on [*insert date*] pursuant to procedures for complaints of employment discrimination filed against employers holding government contracts or subcontracts. Our investigation has resulted in the following findings:

1. [*Insert name of contractor*] is a nonexempt government contractor subject to the requirements of [*insert one or more as appropriate*: Executive Order 11246, as amended (EO 11246) and an employer of 15 or more persons subject to Title VII of the Civil Rights Act of 1964, as amended; Vietnam Era Veterans' Readjustment Assistance Act of 1974, as amended (VEVRAA); Section 503 of the Rehabilitation Act of 1973, as amended (Section 503) and an employer of 15 or more persons subject to Title I of the Americans with Disabilities Act of 1990, as amended (ADA)].

2. [*Insert name of complainant*] is a [*insert membership in one or more protected classes*: minority, woman, veteran, disabled vereran, individual with a disabled, etc.] covered or protected by [*insert one or more as appropriate*: EO 11246 and Title VII; Section 4212 or VEVRRA; Section 503 and the ADA].

3. The complainant alleges the contractor violated its obligations under the nondiscrimination and/or affirmative action provisions of its federal contracts and under the nondiscrimination provisions of [*insert as appropriate*: Title VII or the ADA] by [*insert a description of the adverse personnel action or practice of the employer: terminating, not promoting, paying less, etc.*].

4. The contractor's position is that the complainant was [*insert description of of the adverse personnel action or practice of the employer: terminated, not hired, etc.*] because [*insert a description of the contractor's position or defense*].

5. Our investigation indicates that the contractor [*insert a description of what the contractor did or did nott do*].

The Agency's investigation found insufficient evidence that the contractor violated its obligations under the nondiscrimination and affirmative action provisions of [*insert one or more as appropriate*: EO 11246, Section 4212 (VEVRAA), or Section 503], or under the nondiscrimination provisions of the [*insert one or more as appropriate*: Title VII or the ADA]. This determination concludes the processing of this complaint by OFCCP.

On behalf of the United States Department of Labor,

__________________________________ ________________

[Regional Director or Designee] [Date]

Enclosure: Information Related to Filing Suit under Title VII and the ADA
Notice of Right to Sue

cc: [*insert name of complainant's attorney*]
[*insert name of contractor's attorney*]
[*insert name of the EEOC field office contact*]

L-14 ENCLOSURE
NOTICE OF RIGHT-TO SUE UNDER TITLE I OF THE ADA OR TITLE VII OF THE CIVIL RIGHTS ACT OF 1964: NOTIFICATION OF NO VIOLATION

U.S. DEPARTMENT OF LABOR
OFFICE OF FEDERAL CONTRACT COMPLIANCE PROGRAMS

TO: [Complainant's Name and Address]

FROM: [OFCCP Office Name and Address]

[__] On behalf of a person whose identity is confidential (29 CFR 1601.7(a))

OFCCP Representative

Complaint Number:

TO THE COMPLAINANT: You may file a lawsuit against the contractor under [*insert as appropriate*: Title VII or ADA] in federal or state court. **Your lawsuit must be filed within 90 calendar days of receipt of this notice, or your right to sue will be lost.** Please see the enclosed information sheet on filing lawsuits for further information.

With the issuance of this Notice of Right-to-Sue, OFCCP is terminating its processing of your complaint.

An information copy of this Notice has been sent to the below employer as named in your complaint.

[*insert employer's name and address*]

On behalf of the United States Department of Labor,

_________________________________ _______________

[Regional Director or Designee] [Date]
[insert appropriate OFCCP office address]

Enclosures (2): Information Related to Filing Suit under Title VII and the ADA
Copy of Complaint

cc: *[insert name of complainant's attorney]*
[insert name of the contractor's attorney]
[insert name of the EEOC field office contact]

LETTER L-15: NOTICE OF RIGHT-TO-SUE UNDER TITLE I OF THE ADA OR TITLE VII OF THE CIVIL RIGHTS ACT OF 1964 (Issued Upon Request)

Certified Mail, Return Receipt Requested

U.S. DEPARTMENT OF LABOR
OFFICE OF FEDERAL CONTRACT COMPLIANCE PROGRAMS

TO: [Complainant's Name and Address]

[__] On behalf of a person whose identity is confidential (29 CFR 1601.7(a))

FROM: [OFCCP Office Name and Address]

OFCCP Representative

Complaint Number:

TO THE COMPLAINANT: This is your NOTICE OF RIGHT-TO-SUE. It is issued at your request. If you intend to file a lawsuit against the employer named in your complaint, YOU MUST DO SO WITHIN NINETY (90) CALENDAR DAYS OF YOUR RECEIPT OF THIS NOTICE. OTHERWISE, YOUR RIGHT TO SUE IS LOST.

[__] More than 180 calendar days have elapsed since you filed your complaint.

[__] Less than 180 calendar days have elapsed since you filed your complaint, but it has been determined that OFCCP will be unable to complete its processing within 180 calendar days from the date you filed your complaint. (Note: This reason is not acceptable to the courts within the District of Columbia.)

[__] With the issuance of this Notice of Right-to-Sue, OFCCP is terminating its processing of your complaint.

[__] OFCCP will continue to investigate the following allegations in your complaint which are uniquely within OFCCP jurisdiction: [*list any allegation(s), not subject to ADA or Title VII, which are still under investigation*].

An information copy of this Notice has been sent to the below employer as named in your complaint.

[*insert employer's name and address*]

For the United States Department of Labor,

Regional Director or Designee　　　　　　　　Date

Enclosures (2):　Information Related to Filing Suit under Title VII and the ADA
Copy of Complaint

cc: *[insert name of complainant's attorney]*
[insert name of contractor's attorney]
[insert name of EEOC field office contact]

LETTER L-16: NOTICE OF RIGHT-TO-SUE UNDER TITLE I OF THE ADA OR TITLE VII OF THE CIVIL RIGHTS ACT OF 1964 (Administrative Closure)

Certified Mail, Return Receipt Requested

U.S. DEPARTMENT OF LABOR
OFFICE OF FEDERAL CONTRACT COMPLIANCE PROGRAMS

TO: [Complainant's Name
and Address]

FROM: [OFCCP Office Name
and Address]

[__] On behalf of a person whose
identity is confidential
(29 CFR 1601.7(a))

OFCCP Representative

Complaint Number:

TO THE COMPLAINANT: This is your NOTICE OF RIGHT-TO-SUE under <u>[Title I of the Americans with Disabilities Act of 1990, as amended</u> <u>[Title VII of the Civil Rights Act of 1964, as amended]</u>. It is issued because OFCCP has dismissed your complaint for the following reason:

[__] You failed to provide requested necessary information, failed to appear or refused to be available for necessary interviews or conferences,or otherwise refused to cooperate to the extent that OFCCP is unable to complete its investigation of your complaint.

[__] OFCCP has made reasonable efforts to locate you and has been unable to do so. You have had at least 60 calendar days in which to respond to a notice sent to your last known address.

The issuance of this NOTICE OF RIGHT-TO-SUE concludes OFCCP processing of your complaint. If you wish to pursue your complaint further, you have the right to sue the employer named in your complaint in federal or state court. IF YOU DECIDE TO SUE, YOU MUST DO SO WITHIN <u>NINETY (90) CALENDAR DAYS</u> OF YOUR RECEIPT OF THIS NOTICE. OTHERWISE, YOUR RIGHT TO SUE IS LOST.

An information copy of this Notice has been sent to the following employer named in your complaint:

[insert employer's name and address]

For the United States Department of Labor,

______________________________	______________________
[Regional Director or Designee]	*[Date]*

Enclosures (2): Information Related to Filing Suit under Title VII and the ADA
Copy of Complaint

cc: *[insert name of complainant's attorney]*
[insert name of the contractor's attorney]
[insert name of the EEOC field office contact]

LETTER L-17: NOTIFICATION OF RESULTS OF INVESTIGATION: NOTIFICATION OF VIOLATION

Certified Mail, Return Receipt Requested

[Complaint No.]

[Complainant's Name]
[Street]
[City, State, Zip]

COMPLAINANT

[Company Name]
[Street]
[City, State, Zip]

CONTRACTOR

On *[insert date],* the U.S. Department of Labor, the Office of Federal Contract Compliance Programs (OFCCP), conducted an investigation of the allegation(s) of *[insert the type of discrimination]* discrimination made in the complaint of *[insert name of complainant]* filed on *[insert date]*. Our investigation has resulted in the following findings:

1. *[Insert name of contractor]* is a nonexempt government contractor subject to the requirements of *[insert one or more as appropriate*: Executive Order 11246, as amended (EO 11246); Section 503 of the Rehabilitation Act of 1973, as amended (Section 503); Vietnam Era Veterans' Readjustment Assistance Act of 1974, as amended (VEVRAA); Title VII of the Civil Rights Act of 1964, as amended (Title VII); Title I of the Americans with Disabilities Act of 1990, as amended (ADA)*]*.

2. *[Insert name of complainant]* is *[insert one or more as appropriate*: a minority, woman, etc.; an individual with a disability; a disabled veteran/protected veteran*]* within the meaning of [*Insert one or more as appropriate:* EO 11246; Section 503; VEVRAA; Title VII; the ADA*]* and the regulations at 41 CFR Part *[insert one or more as appropriate*: 60-1 to 60-50; 60-250 and 60-300; 60-741*]*.

3. The complainant alleges the contractor violated its obligations under the nondiscrimination and affirmative action provisions of its federal contracts by *[insert description of the actions the complaint describes that are attributed to the employer, e.g., terminating, not promoting, etc.]*.

4. The contractor's position is that the complainant was *[insert the action taken against the complainant, e.g., terminated, not hired, etc.]* because *[insert a description of the contractor's position]*.

5. Our investigation indicates *[insert all specifics details relelvant to the complainant's status and the contractor's actions]*.

6. The action(s) described in Paragraph 4 violated the contractor's obligations under the regulations as follows:

[insert a list of the sections violated and describe violation].

In accordance with the regulations implementing, *[insert as appropriate*: EO 11246 at 41 CFR 60-1.24(c)(2) and Title VII at 29 CFR 1601.24; Section 503 at 41 CFR 60-741.62 and ADA at 29 CFR 1601.24; VEVRAA at 41 CFR 60-250.62, 60-300.62 and ADA at 29 CFR 1601.24*]* the U.S. Department of Labor, OFCCP, invites *[insert name of contractor]* to resolve this matter through conciliation by informal means. A compliance officer from this office will be in contact with *[insert name of contractor]* by *[insert date]* to begin the conciliation process.

On behalf of the United States Department of Labor.

__________________________ ____________________

Regional Director or Designee Date

cc: *[insert name of the complainant's representative]*
[insert name of the contractor's representative]

LETTER L-18: SHOW CAUSE NOTICE: FAILURE TO SUBMIT AN EO 11246, SECTION 503 OR SECTION 4212 AAP(S) (Supply & Service)

Certified Mail, Return Receipt Requested AND Electronic Mail

[DATE]

[Name of Establishment CEO]
[Title of CEO]
[Establishment Name]
[Street Address]
[City, State, Zip Code]

Dear [*Name of CEO*]:

The U.S. Department of Labor, Office of Federal Contract Compliance Programs (OFCCP), by letter dated [*insert date*], requested that you submit to this office within 30 calendar days a copy of your [*insert as appropriate*: establishment's or functional unit's] Affirmative Action Programs (AAPs) and supporting documentation prepared in accordance with our regulations implementing.

- Executive Order 11246, as amended (41 CFR Part 60-2) (Executive Order)
- Section 503 of the Rehabilitation Act of 1973, as amended (41 CFR Part 60-741) (Section 503)
- The Vietnam Era Veteran's Readjustment Assistance Act of 1974, as amended (41 CFR Part 60-250 and 41 CFR Part 60-300) (Section 4212)

We have yet to receive your *[insert as appropriate*: Executive Order, Section 503 or Section 4212*]* AAP(s). Due to your organization's failure to submit the requested AAP(s) required under *[insert as appropriate*: Executive Order, Section 503, Section 4212*]*, we are issuing this Notice to Show Cause. Within 30 calendar days of receiving this Notice, you must either submit the AAP(s) and support data specified in our original request or demonstrate, in writing, why enforcement proceedings should not be initiated pursuant to [*insert as appropriate*: Sections 208 and 209 of the Executive Order, as implemented by 41 CFR 60-1.26; 41 CFR 60-741.65 (Section 503); 41 CFR 60-250.65 and 41 CFR 60-300.65 (Section 4212)*]*. A copy of our original reqest is enclosed.

The submission of the AAP(s) and support data does not preclude the identification of further violations, based either upon a finding during the desk audit or subsequent onsite review, that your AAPs do not meet the requirements of 41 CFR Part 60-2, Part 60-741 or Part 60-250 and 60-300 or that your [*insert as appropriate*: establishment or functional unit] is not in compliance with one or more of the requirements of the Executive Order, Section 503 or Section 4212 and their implementing regulations.

Should you have any questions or wish to discuss a resolution to the issues raised herein, please contact *[insert name of compliance officer]* or *[insert appropriate pronoun: his or her]* supervisor, *[insert name of supervisor]*, at *[insert telephone number]* to schedule a meeting or telephone conference.

Sincerely,

[insert name of the regional or district director]
Regional Director or District Director

Enclosure

cc: *[insert name of the corporate CEO]*
[insert name of the designated representative]

LETTER L-19: SHOW CAUSE NOTICE: FAILURE TO SUBMIT AN ACCEPTABLE EO 11246, SECTION 503 OR SECTION 4212 AAP(S) (Supply & Service)

Certified Mail, Return Receipt Requested AND Electronic Mail

[Date]

[Name of Establishment CEO]
[Title of CEO]
[Establishment Name]
[Street Address]
[City, State, Zip Code]

Dear *[Name of CEO]*:

The U.S. Department of Labor, Office of Federal Contract Compliance Programs (OFCCP), reviewed your Affirmative Action Program (AAP) and supporting documentation prepared pursuant to *[insert one or more as appropriate*: Executive Order 11246, as amended, (Executive Order); Section 503 of the Rehabilitation Act of 1973, as amended (Section 503); the Vietnam Era Veteran's Readjustment Assistance Act of 1974, as amended (Section 4212)*]* and submitted for desk audit. The results of this review indicate that your AAP does not meet the requirements of our regulations at *[insert one or more as appropriate*: 41 CFR Part 60-2; 41 CFR 60-250.40-.44; 41 CFR 60-300.40-.44; 41 CFR 60-741.40-.45*]*. Consequently, we are issuing this Notice to Show Cause why enforcement proceedings should not be initiated pursuant to *[insert one or more as appropriate*: 41 CFR 60-1.26; 41 CFR 60-741.65 (Section 503) and/or 41 CFR 60-250.65 and 60-300.65 (Section 4212)*]*.

The specific elements of your *[insert one or more as appropriate*: Executive Order, Section 503, Section 4212*]* AAP(s) which do not meet the regulatory requirements cited above are listed in the enclosure. You are required to correct these violations as indicated within 30 calendar days of your receipt of this Notice, or we shall recommend that enforcement proceedings be initiated.

Submission of a corrected *[insert one or more as appropriate*: Executive Order, Section 503, Section 4212*]* AAP(s) does not preclude the identification of further violations based on a finding during the desk audit or subsequent onsite review that your AAPs do not meet the requirements of *[insert one or more as appropriate*: 41 CFR Part 60-2, 41 CFR Parts 60-250 and 60-300, 41 CFR Part 741*]* or that your *[insert* as *appropriate*: establishment or functional unit] is not in compliance with the requirements of the Executive Order, Section 503, or Section 4212 and their implementing regulations.

Should you have any questions or wish to discuss a resolution to the issues raised herein, please contact *[insert name of compliance officer]* or *[insert appropriate pronoun*: his or her] supervisor, *[insert name of supervisor]*, at *[insert telephone number]* to schedule a meeting or telephone conference.

Sincerely,

[insert name of the regional or district director]
Regional Drector or District Director

Enclosure

cc: *[insert name of the corporate CEO]*
[insert name of designated representative]

LETTER L-19a: SAMPLE ENCLOSURE TO LETTER L-19

1. Violation: ABC Company's affirmative action program did not include an organizational profile as required by 41 CFR 60-2.10(b)(1)(i).

   Corrective Action: Develop and include in the AAP an organizational profile that depicts staffing patterns within its establishment.

2. Violation: In four of the job groups identified in ABC Company's utilization analysis as underutilized, ABC Company failed to set goals or to explain why it did not do so as required by 41 CFR 60-2.15(b). The job groups are Design Engineers (minority and women); Health Scientists (minorities); Electronic Technicians (women); and Tool and Die Makers (minorities and women).

   Corrective Action: In the job groups specified above, either establish goals at least equal to availability for minorities, women, or both as noted, or explain in the AAP why such goals can not established.

LETTER L-20: SHOW CAUSE NOTICE: FAILURE TO SUBMIT EMPLOYMENT ACTIVITY OR COMPENSATION DATA FOR DESK AUDIT (Supply & Service Executive Order Compliance Evaluations)

Certified Mail, Return Receipt Requested AND Electronic Mail

[Date]

[Name of Establishment CEO]
[Title of CEO]
[Establishment Name]
[Street Address]
[City, State, Zip Code]

Dear *[insert name of CEO]*:

The U.S. Department of Labor, Office of Federal Contract Compliance Programs (OFCCP), by letter dated *[insert date]*, requested that you submit the below listed *[insert as appropriate*: employment activity or compensation*]* data as support data for your Affirmative Action Program (AAP) prepared pursuant to Executive Order 11246, as amended (Executive Order). The data was due to this office within 30 calendar days.

[Specify the data that were not submitted for desk audit]

The submission of this data is required by 41 CFR 1.12(c)(2). Additionally, 41 CFR 60-2.17(b), (c) and (d) require that your AAP include an analysis of your employment activity to identify and correct problem areas. This obligation cannot be adequately implemented without maintenance of the referenced data.

We have not yet received the data we requested. Consequently, we are issuing this Notice to Show Cause why enforcement proceedings should not be initiated. You are required to submit the support data as specified in our original request within 30 calendar days of your receipt of this Notice, or we will recommend that enforcement proceedings be initiated pursuant to Sections 208 and 209 of the Executive Order, as implemented by 41 CFR 60-1.26. A copy of our original request is enclosed.

The submission of these support data does not preclude the identification of additional violations based upon a finding, during the desk audit or a subsequent onsite review, that your AAPs do not meet the requirements of 41 CFR Parts 60-2, 60-741 and/or 60-250 and 60-300, or that your *[insert as appropriate*: establishment or functional unit*]* is not in compliance with the requirements of the Executive Order, Section 503 of the Rehabilitation Act, as amended, or the Vietnam Era Veterans Readjustment Assistance Act, as amended, and their implementing regulations, as appropriate.

Should you have any questions or wish to discuss a resolution to the issues raised herein, please contact *[insert name of compliance officer]* or *[insert appropriate pronoun: his or her]* supervisor, *[insert name of supervisor]*, at *[insert telephone number]* to schedule a meeting or telephone conference.

Sincerely,

[insert name of the regional or district director]
Regional Director or District Director

Enclosure

cc: *[insert name of the corporate CEO]*
[insert name of the designated representative]

LETTER L-21: SHOW CAUSE NOTICE: FAILURE TO SUBMIT CORRECTED EMPLOYMENT ACTIVITY AND/OR COMPENSATION DATA (Supply & Service Executive Order Compliance Evaluations)

Certified Mail, Return Receipt Requested AND Electronic Mail

[Date]

[Name of Establishment CEO]
[Title of CEO]
[Establishment Name]
[Street Address]
[City, State, Zip Code]

Dear *[insert name of CEO]*:

On *[insert date]*, the U.S. Department of Labor, Office of Federal Contract Compliance (OFCCP), contacted you by phone to request that you resubmit certain *[insert as appropriate*: employment activity **or** compensation*]* data which we determined to be unacceptable during the desk audit of your Affirmative Action Program (AAP). The desk audit of your AAP was prepared pursuant to Executive Order 11246, as amended (Executive Order). We asked you to provide the corrected data within ten calendar days. Further, we identified the unacceptable data, stated how they are unacceptable, and specified the required correction(s).[328]

To date, we have not received the corrected *[insert as appropriate*: employment activity or compensation*]* data. Consequently, we are issuing this Notice to Show Cause why enforcement proceedings should not be initiated pursuant to 41 CFR 60-1.26. You are required to submit the corrected data, as specified above, within 30 calendar days of receiving this Notice or we will recommend initiating enforcement proceedings in accordance with 41 CFR 60-1.26.

The submission of these data does not preclude the identification of further violations based upon a finding during the desk audit, or subsequent onsite review, that your AAP(s) does not meet the requirements of 41 CFR Parts 60-2, 60-741, or 60-250 and 60-300, or that your [*insert as appropriate:* establishment **or** functional unit] is not in compliance or has failed to comply in the past with the requirements of the Executive Order, Section 503 of the Rehabilitation Act of 1973, as amended and/or the Vietnam Era Veterans' Readjustment Assistance Act of 1974, as amended, and their implementing regulations.

---

[328] For example: " . . . your data on hires and terminations are unacceptable because they are provided for the workforce as a whole, and must be resubmitted either by job group or by job title, as required by 41 CFR 60-3.4 and 3.15."

Should you have any questions or wish to discuss a resolution to the issues raised herein, please contact *[insert name of compliance officer]* or [*insert appropriate pronoun:* his or her*]* supervisor, *[insert name of supervisor]*, at *[insert telephone number]* to schedule a meeting or telephone conference.

Sincerely,

[insert name of the regional or district director]
Regional Director

cc: *[insert name of the corporate CEO]*
[insert name of the designated representative]

LETTER L-22: SHOW CAUSE NOTICE: UNRESOLVED VIOLATIONS (Compliance Evaluations)

Certified Mail, Return Receipt Requested AND Electronic Mail

[Date]

[Name of Establishment CEO]
[Title of CEO]
[Establishment Name]
[Street Address]
[City, State, Zip Code]

Dear *[insert name of CEO]*:

On *[insert date]*, the U.S. Department of Labor, Office of Federal Contract Compliance Programs (OFCCP), sent you a Notice of Violation based on the findings of our recent compliance evaluation of your *[insert as appropriate*: establishment or functional unit*]*.[329] On [insert date], OFCCP met with *[insert name of contractor representative]* to conciliate a resolution of the violations(s) listed in that Notice. Our conciliation efforts, however, failed to resolve the violation(s). Consequently, we are issuing this Notice to Show Cause, within 30 calendar days of your receipt of this Notice, why enforcement proceedings should not be initiated pursuant to *[insert one or more as appropriate*: Sections 208 and 209 of Executive Order 11246, as amended, as implemented by 41 CFR 60-1.26; Section 503 of the Rehabilitation Act of 1973, as amended, as implemented by 41 CFR 741.64; the Vietnam Era Veterans' Readjustment Assistance Act of 1974, as amended, as implemented by 41 CFR 60-250.64 and 60-300-64*]*.

A list of the violations at issue is enclosed. You are required to correct these violations as indicated within 30 calendar days of your receipt of this Notice or we shall recommend that enforcement proceedings be initiated.

Should you have any questions or wish to discuss a resolution to the issues raised herein, please contact *[insert name of compliance officer]* or *[insert appropriate pronoun: his or her]* supervisor, *[insert name of supervisor]*, at *[insert telephone number]* to schedule a meeting or telephone conference.

Sincerely,

[insert name of the regional or district director]
Regional Director or District Director

---

[329] If the contractor did not respond to the NOV, in the remainder of this paragraph substitute: "To date, you have not responded to that Notice or otherwise indicated your willingness to remedy those violations."

Enclosure

cc: *[insert name of corporate CEO]*
[insert name of designated representative]

LETTER L-22a: SAMPLE ENCLOSURE TO LETTER L-22

1. Violation: In violation of 41 CFR 60-1.4(a)(1), ABC Company discriminated against qualified African American applicants in its hiring and selection procedures for the Laborer positions from January 1, 2011 through December 31, 2011. During this period, the qualified pool of applicants for the Laborer positions consisted of 176 white applicants and 111 African American applicants. From that pool, 17 non-minority applicants and no African American applicants were hired. Comparison of the selection rates of non-minority and African American applicants showed adverse impact (0% African Americans hired) and a shortfall of six. The disparity in the selection rates is statistically significant to a level of 3.38 standard deviations. Analysis of the steps in the selection process showed adverse impact at each step in the process affecting African American applicants. Absent discrimination, six African American applicants would have been selected given their representation in the qualified applicant pool.

   Corrective Action: ABC Company must agree to revise and maintain selection policies and procedures designed to eliminate disparate impact on African American applicants, and to ensure that all African American applicants are given an equal employment opportunity in its selection process.

   ABC Company must agree to provide make-whole relief to the 111 qualified African American applicants who applied for employment from January 1, 2011 through December 31, 2011. The relief covers the Laborer position and consists of employment opportunities for six qualified African American applicants, and monetary relief (including back pay, interest, and benefits) to all African American applicants who can be located.

2. Violation: In violation of 41 CFR 60-1.4(a)(1), ABC Company discriminated against two African American female applicants who applied for promotion into Inspection jobs.

   Specifically, ABC Company was unable to provide a legitimate, nondiscriminatory reason for rejecting Sandra Jones and Barbara Rogers (African American); both applicants were better qualified under ABC Company's stated selection criteria than two similarly situated white male applicants the company selected for Inspector positions on September 23, 2011. ABC Company's reason for rejecting Ms. Jones and Ms. Rogers was pretextual and the company did not equally apply it to the two white males promoted into Inspector positions. Ms. Rogers and Ms. Rogers would have been promoted into Inspector positions on September 23, but for being disparately treated.

   Corrective Action: ABC must make bona fide offers of employment to Ms. Rogers and Ms. Jones into the next two Inspector openings, and provide all wages, seniority and employment related benefits they would have received had they not been subjected to discrimination. Such relief shall be retroactive to the date each would have been promoted absent the discrimination and shall include: (a) back pay, plus interest; (b) retroactive seniority; (c) all employment benefits; and (d) any other appropriate make-whole relief including all wages, seniority and employment related benefits they would have received had they not been subjected to discrimination. Such relief shall be retroactive to the date each would have been promoted absent the discrimination. Additionally, ABC Company will provide Ms. Rogers and Ms. Jones with front pay from the date this violation is resolved until they are promoted to Inspector positions or refuse bona fide promotion offers.

3. Violation: In violation of 41 CFR 60-2.17(c), ABC Company did not make good faith efforts to remove identified barriers, expand employment opportunities, and produce measurable results for females and minorities in underutilized job groups.

   Corrective Action: ABC Company must agree to make good faith efforts are made to remove identified barriers, expand employment opportunities, and produce measurable results for females and minorities in underutilized job groups. To accomplish this, ABC Company must agree to the following actions:

   a. ABC Company must agree to establish a working relationship (also known as linkage) with referral organizations by taking the following actions:

      - Provide regular job listings of vacancies which have not been filled internally for all underutilized job groups; and
      - Contact the referral organization within 45 calendar days of the execution of this Agreement. The purpose of the contact is to arrange for the referral of applicants, and to provide follow-up and feedback to the recruitment sources on disposition of its referrals.

   b. ABC Company must agree to maintain documentation that demonstrates its good faith efforts.

4. Violation: In violation of 41 CFR 60-1.12(a), ABC Company failed to collect and maintain personnel and employment records for the appropriate period. ABC Company failed to collect and maintain documentation of the application process and selection decisions and did not maintain all of the applications, interview notes, and other applicant records.

   Corrective Action: ABC Company must agree to collect and maintain personnel and employment records for the appropriate period including documentation of the application process and selection decisions.

5. Violation: ABC failed to list its jobs with the State Employment Service, in violation of 41 CFR 60-250.5(a)(2) through (6) and/or 60-300.5(a)(2) through (6).

Corrective Action: ABC Company will list all suitable jobs with the Metropolis State Employment Service office. Reports to OFCCP on these listings will be required.

6. Violation: In violation of 41 CFR 60-250.44(f) and 41 CFR 60-300.44(f), ABC Company failed to take appropriate outreach and positive recruitment activities for veterans of the Vietnam era, disabled veterans, and other protected veterans.

   Corrective Action: ABC Company must agree to take appropriate outreach and positive recruitment activities for veterans of the Vietnam era, disabled veterans, and other protected veterans.

   a. ABC Company must agree to establish a working relationship with referral organizations by taking the following actions:

      - Provide regular job listings of vacancies which have not been filled internally for all underutilized job groups; and
      - Contact the referral organization within 45 calendar days of the execution of this Agreement. The purpose of the contact is to arrange for the referral of applicants, and to provide follow-up and feedback to the recruitment sources on disposition of its referrals.

   b. ABC Company must agree to maintain documentation that demonstrates its good faith efforts.

LETTER L-23: SHOW CAUSE NOTICE: UNRESOLVED VIOLATIONS (Complaint Investigations)

Certified Mail, Return Receipt Requested AND Electronic Mail

[Date]

[Name of Establishment CEO]
[Title of CEO]
[Establishment Name]
[Street Address]
[City, State, Zip Code]

Dear *[insert name of CEO]*:

On *[insert date]*, the U.S. Department of Labor, Office of Federal Contract Compliance Programs (OFCCP),sent you a Notice of Violation specifying violations found during our investigation of the complaint filed by *[insert complainant's name]* against your company. On *[insert date]* we met with *[insert name of contractor representative]* to conciliate a resolution of those violations. Our conciliation efforts, however, failed to resolve the violations.

Consequently, we are issuing this Notice to Show Cause, within 30 calendar days of your receipt of this Notice, why enforcement proceedings should not be initiated pursuant to *[insert one or more as appropriate:* Sections 208 and 209 of Executive Order 11246, as amended, as implemented by 41 CFR 60-1.26; Section 503 of the Rehabilitation Act of 1973, as amended, as implemented by 41 CFR 60-741.64 (Section 503) and/or of the Vietnam Era Veterans' Readjustment Assistance Act of 1974, as amended, as implemented by 41 CFR 60-250.64 and 60-300.64 (Section 4212)*]*.

The violations at issue are listed in the enclosure. You are required to correct these violations within 30 calendar days of your receipt of this Notice or we shall recommend the initiation of enforcement proceedings.

Should you have any questions or wish to discuss a resolution to the issues raised herein, please contact *[insertname of compliance officer]* or [*insert appropriate pronoun*: his or her*]* supervisor, *[insert name of supervisor]*, at *[insert telephone number]* to schedule a meeting or telephone conference.

Sincerely,

[insert name of the regional or district director]
Regional Director or District Director

Enclosure

cc: *[insert name of corporate CEO]*
[insert name of designated representative]

LETTER L-24: AMENDED SHOW CAUSE NOTICE FOR UNRESOLVED VIOLATIONS (Compliance Evaluations)

Certified Mail, Return Receipt Requested AND Electronic Mail

[Date]

[Name of Establishment CEO]
[Title of CEO]
[Establishment Name]
[Street Address]
[City, State, Zip Code]

Dear *[insert name of CEO]*:

On *[insert date]*, the Department of Labor, Office of Federal Contract Compliance Programs (OFCCP), issued your company a Notice to Show Cause which listed specific violations of *[insert one or more as appropriate*: Executive Order 11246, as amended (Executive Order); Section 503 of the Rehabilitation Act of 1973, as amended (Section 503), the Vietnam Era Veterans' Readjustment Assistance Act of 1974, as amended (Section 4212)*]* and offered you 30 calendar days in which to show why enforcement should not be initiated.

We have completed our subsequent review of your company's equal employment opportunity policies and practices *[Insert this language if the contractor is a construction contractor*: at your construction work sites in the [*insert name of geographic*] area and identified additional violations of the *[insert one or more as appropriate*: Executive Order, Section 503, Section 4212*]*. Consequently, we are issuing this Amended Notice to Show Cause, within 30 calendar days of your receipt of this Notice, why enforcement proceedings should not be initiated pursuant to *[insert one or more as appropriate*: Sections 208 and 209 of Executive Order, as implemented by 41 CFR 60-1.26; Section 503, as implemented by 41 CFR 60-741.64 and/or Section 4212 as implemented by 41 CFR 60-250.64 and 60-300.64*]*.

The enclosure lists the most recently identified violations along with those specified in the *[insert date]* Notice to Show Cause. You are required to correct these violations as indicated within 30 calendar days of your receipt of this Notice, or we shall recommend that enforcement proceedings be initiated.

Should you have any questions or wish to discuss a resolution to the issues raised herein, please contact *[insert name of compliance officer]* or *[insert appropriate pronoun:* his or her supervisor, *[insert name of supervisor]*, at *[insert telephone number]* to schedule a meeting or telephone conference.

Sincerely,

[insert name of the regional or district director]
Regional Director or District Director

Enclosure

cc: *[insert name of corporate CEO]*
[insert name of designated representative]

LETTER L-25: SHOW CAUSE NOTICE FOR DENIAL OF ACCESS (Compliance Evaluations)

Certified Mail, Return Receipt Requested AND Electronic Mail

[Date]

[Name of Establishment CEO]
[Title of CEO]
[Establishment Name]
[Street Address]
[City, State, Zip Code]

Dear *[insert name of CEO]*:

In our letter dated [*insert date*], the U.S. Department of Labor, Office of Federal Contract Compliance Programs (OFCCP), requested that [*insert contractor or establishment name*] submit to the onsite portion of a compliance evaluation as described at [*insert one or more as appropriate:* 41 CFR 60-1.20(a)(1)(ii); 41 CFR 60-741.60; 41 CFR 60-250.60; 41 CFR 60-300.60] at its facility located at [street address, city, state]. The onsite was to begin on *[insert date]*.

On *[insert date]*, your representative *[insert name]* responded to our request by denying access to the facility. Consequently, we are issuing this Notice to Show Cause why enforcement proceedings should not be initiated pursuant to *[insert one or more as appropriate*: Sections 208 and 209 of Executive Order 11246, as amended, as implemented by 41 CFR 60-1.26 and 1.28; Section 503 of the Rehabilitation Act of 1973, as amended, as implemented by 41 CFR 60-741.64 and 741.65; the Vietnam Era Veterans' Readjustment Assistance Act of 1974, as amended, as implemented by 41 CFR 60-250.64 and 60-300.64 and 250.65 and 300.65*]*.

[Insert contractor's name] is required to allow OFCCP access to the facility so that we can conduct an onsite compliance evaluation of your facility located at *[insert location]* within 30 calendar days of your receipt of this Notice, or we shall recommend that enforcement proceedings be initiated in accordance with the above citations. In those proceedings, you will have an opportunity to request a hearing before any sanctions are imposed.

Allowing OFCCP access to the facility in order to conduct the onsite portion of the compliance evaluation does not preclude the identification of further violations, based either upon a finding during the desk audit or subsequent onsite review, that your AAPs do not meet the requirements of 41 CFR Part 60-2, Part 60-741, and Part 60-250 or that your establishment is not in compliance or has failed to comply in the past with the requirements of the Executive Order, Section 503, and 38 USC 4212 and their implementing regulations. We will not withdraw this Notice to Show Cause until all deficiencies cited in this Notice (or subsequently identified in an Amended Show Cause Notice incorporating any additional violations found during the desk audit or onsite review) have been fully and satisfactorily resolved in a written Conciliation Agreement.

We wish to avoid enforcement proceedings, if possible. Therefore, you are asked to contact *[insert name of compliance officer]* at *[insert phone number]* within five business days of receipt of this Notice, to arrange a mutually acceptable time to conciliate a resolution of this violation.

Sincerely,

[insert name of the regional or district director]
Regional Director or District Director

Enclosure

cc: *[insert name of corporate CEO]*
[insert name of designated representative]

LETTER L-26: RESCISSION OF AN ERRONEOUSLY ISSUED SHOW CAUSE NOTICE

Certified Mail, Return Receipt Requested AND electronic mail

[Date]

[Name of Establishment CEO]
[Title of CEO]
[Establishment Name]
[Street Address]
[City, State, Zip Code]

Dear (*insert name of CEO*):

On (*insert date*), the U.S. Department of Labor, Office of Federal Contract Compliance Programs, issued a (*insert as appropriate*: Notice to Show Cause **or** Amended Notice to Show Cause) to your company. Consistent with that Notice, you have 30 calendar days to show why enforcement proceedings should not be initiated pursuant to (*insert one or more as appropriate*: Sections 208 and 209 of Executive Order 11246, as amended, as implemented by 41 CFR 60-1.26 and 1.28; Section 503 of the Rehabilitation Act of 1973, as amended, as implemented by 41 CFR 60-741.64 and 60-741.65; the Vietnam Era Veterans' Readjustment Assistance Act of 1974, as amended, as implemented by 41 CFR 60-250.64 and 250.65, and 41 CFR 60-300.64 and 300.65).

After issuing the Notice, we subsequently determined that it was erroneously issued because (*insert as appropriate*: your company has demonstrated that it is exempt from our requirements **or** your company demonstrated that the allegations giving rise to the Notice are incorrect). Therefore, we are rescinding the (*insert as appropriate*: Notice to Show Cause **or** the Amended Notice to Show Cause).

Sincerely,

(*insert the name of the regional director or designee*)
Regional Director or Designee

cc: (*insert the name of the corporate CEO*)
(*insert the name of the designated representative*)

LETTER L-27: PREDETERMINATION NOTICE

Note: To be mailed by certified mail, return receipt requested.

[Date]

[Name of CEO]
[Title of CEO]
[Company Name]
[Street Address]
[City, State, Zip Code]

Re: Compliance Evaluation of *(insert name of contractor)*
OFCCP No. ___________

Dear (Mr. or Ms. ____________):

On *(insert date)*, the U.S. Department of Labor, Office of Federal Contract Compliance Programs (OFCCP), began a compliance evaluation of *(insert name of contractor)* compliance with Executive Order 11246, as amended, Section 503 of the Rehabilitation Act of 1973, as amended, and/or the Vietnam Era Veterans' Readjustment Assistance Act of 1974, as amended and their implementing regulations at 41 Code of Federal Regulations (CFR) Chapter 60. *(Insert name of contractor)*, hereinafter referred to as the "contractor," is a federal contractor pursuant to Executive Order 11246, as amended, Section 503 of the Rehabilitation Act of 1973, as amended, and/or the Vietnam Era Veterans' Readjustment Assistance Act of 1974, as amended, and their implementing regulations at 41 CFR Chapter 60.

The purpose of this Notice is to inform you of the findings which, if not adequately rebutted, will establish that discrimination occurred (or *is occurring)* at the contractor's establishment.

(Present the evidence of pattern or practice discrimination)

(If there are additional violations or deficiencies, including technical violations, present them here)

Please be advised that this is a preliminary determination based on available information. You now have the opportunity to provide additional information or documentation that you believe we should consider before a final determination is made.

We ask that you respond to this Notice within 15 calendar days from receipt of this letter. If you do not respond, we will incorporate the preliminary finding(s) made in this Notice into a final Notice of Violation (NOV). You will receive the NOV by certified mail. If you have any questions, please call Compliance Officer *(insert name of compliance officer)*,

or his or her immediate supervisor, *(insert name of District Director or Assistant District Director)* at *(insert District Office or /Regional Office phone number)*.

Sincerely,

(insert name of the District Director or Assistant District Director)
District Director

cc: *[insert name of the head of establishment]*
[insert name of the designated representative]

LETTER L-28: NOTICE OF VIOLATION

Note: to be mailed by certified mail, return receipt requested.

[Date]

[Name of CEO]
[(Title of CEO]
[Company Name]
[Street Address)
[City, State, Zip Code]

Re: Compliance Evaluation of (insert *name of contractor*)
OFCCP No. ___________

Dear Mr. or Ms. ____________:

The U.S. Department of Labor, Office of Federal Contract Compliance Programs (OFCCP), has completed a review of *(insert name of contractor)* compliance with one or more of these authorities and their implementing regulations at 41 Code of Federal Regulations (CFR) Chapter 60: Executive Order 11246, as amended; Section 503 of the Rehabilitation Act of 1973, as amended; or the Vietnam Era Veterans' Readjustment Assistance Act of 1974, as amended.

The results of this review indicate that *(insert name of contractor)* is not in compliance with one or more of the following: Executive Order 11246, as amended, Section 503 of the Rehabilitation Act of 1973, as amended, or the Vietnam Era Veterans' Readjustment Assistance Act of 1974, as amended. Consequently, we are issuing this Notice of Violation. The violation(s) and corrective action(s) needed are set forth below:

A. **VIOLATION(S):**

(List and Describe the Violations)

B. **CORRECTIVE ACTION(S):**

(List and Describe the Needed Corrective Actions)

In order to come into compliance, *(insert name of contractor)* must enter into a binding Conciliation Agreement with OFCCP that encompasses all of the corrective actions described above. It is our sincere desire to avoid enforcement proceedings. Therefore, we ask that you contact (*name of District Director or Assistant District Director*) or Compliance Officer *(insert name of compliance officer)* within five (5) business days of receiving this letter at *(insert phone number)*, to begin conciliation and resolution of the specified violations.

Sincerely,

(*insert name of the District Director*)
District Director

cc: (insert name of the head of establishment)
(insert name of the designated representative)

LETTER L-29 15-DAY NOTICE: VIOLATION OF A CONCILIATION AGREEMENT

Certified Mail, Return Receipt Requested AND Electronic Mail

[Date]

[Name of Establishment CEO]
[Title of CEO]
[Establishment Name]
[Street Address]
[City, State, Zip Code]

Dear *[insert name of CEO]*:

On *[insert date]*, the U.S. Department of Labor, Office of Federal Contract Compliance Programs (OFCCP), entered into a Conciliation Agreement (Agreement) with your company. The Agreement sets forth your company's specific commitments to remedy violations found during a *[insert as appropriate*: compliance review or complaint investigation*]*.

We completed a review of your compliance with the Agreement on *[insert date]* that indicates that your company failed to comply with commitments set forth in the Agreement. The facts and circumstances of each violation of the Agreement are set forth in the enclosure.

Accordingly, pursuant to the Agreement referenced above *[insert one or more as appropriate*: and 41 CFR 60-1.34; and 41 CFR 60-250.63 and 41 CFR 60-300.63; and 41 CFR 60-741.63*]*,[330] you have 15 calendar days from the date you received this Notice to demonstrate that you are in compliance with the specified provisions of the Agreement. You may demonstrate your compliance through written presentation of facts and evidence; however, if you fail to do so within the specified period, we will recommend the initiation of enforcement proceedings in accordance with 41 CFR [*insert as appropriate*: 60-1.26; 60-250.65; 60-300.65, or 60-741.65]. Should this matter proceed to enforcement, you will have an opportunity for a hearing before any sanctions are imposed.

Should you have any questions or wish to discuss this matter, please contact *[insert name of compliance officer]* or *[inser tname of supervisor]*, at *[insert telephone number]*.

Sincerely,

[insert name of the regional director]
Regional Director

[330] Use this citation only if a CA provision violated involves the Executive Order.

Enclosure

cc: *[insert name of the corporate CEO]*
[insert name of the designated representative]

LETTER L-29a: SAMPLE ENCLOSURE TO LETTER L-29

1. Remedy: Provide affected class members an opportunity to bid on any position in the Finishing Department, utilizing their company seniority.

   Facts and Circumstances: An examination of bid postings and interviews with Finishing Department supervisors and affected class members indicates that the employees that were discriminated against were allowed to bid only on entry-level positions in the Finishing Department. The company continues to use job seniority, instead of company seniority, when determining the successful bidders for positions above the entry-level.

2. Remedy: To "red-circle" the wages of all affected class members transferring into the Finishing Department.

   Facts and Circumstances: Examination of pay records indicates that the wages of employees that were discriminated against that transferred into the Finishing Department have not been red-circled.

LETTER L-30: RESCISSION OF THE 15-DAY NOTICE

Certified Mail, Return Receipt Requested AND Electronic Mail

[Date]

[Name of Establishment CEO]
[Title of CEO]
[Establishment Name]
[Street Address]
[City, State, Zip Code]

Dear *[Name of CEO]*:

On *[insert date]*, the U.S. Department of Labor, Office of Federal Contract Compliance Programs, issued your company a 15-Day Notice pursuant to *[insert as appropriate*: 41 CFR 60-1.34 (Executive Order); 41 CFR 60-741.63(a)(1) (Section 503); 41 CFR 60-250.63(a)(1), 41 CFR 60-300.63(a)(1) (Section 4212)*]*. We received your written reply on *[insert date]* and it stated that the allegations giving rise to the Notice were incorrect.

We examined the evidence you presented and concluded that the allegations are, in fact, incorrect. Therefore, we are rescinding the 15-Day Notice.

Sincerely,

[insert name of the regional director]
Regional Director

cc: *[insert name of corporate CEO]*
[insert name of designated representative]

LETTER L-31: PROGRESS REPORT RESPONSE LETTER

(Date)

(Name of CEO)
(Title of CEO)
(Company Name)
(Street Address)
(City, State, Zip Code)

Dear Mr. or Ms. ____________:

On *[insert date]*, the U.S. Department of Labor, Office of Federal Contract Compliance Programs (OFCCP), received your progress report pursuant to a *[insert as appropriate*: Conciliation Agreement **or** insert the name of the report causing the progress report*]* entered into by *[insert name of contractor]* on *[insert date]*.

The terms of the *[insert as appropriate:* Conciliation Agreement **or** insert the name of the appropriate report*]* require that *[insert name of contractor*] submit certain items as a part of its progress report. Your submission must include [*list items here*] and you actually provided these items [*list items actually submitted*]. This office reviewed and conducted the appropriate analyses [*insert the analysis done*] on the items you submitted.

[*insert one of the below paragraphs as appropriate*]

<u>#1: Use if it is a final progress report</u>:
This is your final progress report. However, as long as *[insert contractor name]* is a federal contractor, *[insert contractor name]* is required to comply with all regulatory provisions of Executive Order 11246, as amended, Section 503 of the Rehabilitation Act of 1973, as amended, 38 USC 4212, the Vietnam Era Veterans' Readjustment Assistance Act of 1974, as amended, and implementing regulations at 41 CFR Chapter 60.

<u>#2: Use if it is an interim progress report</u>:
This is not a final progress report; therefore, we remind you that the next progress report is due on *[insert date]*. As long as *[insert contractor name]* is a federal contractor, *[insert contractor name]* is required to comply with all regulatory provisions of Executive Order 11246, as amended, Section 503 of the Rehabilitation Act of 1973, as amended, 38 USC 4212, the Vietnam Era Veterans' Readjustment Assistance Act of 1974, as amended, and implementing regulations at 41 CFR Chapter 60.

If you have any questions, please contact *[insert name of compliance officer]*, compliance officer, at *[insert contact information]*.

Sincerely,

(insert name of the District Director or Assistant District Director)
District Director or Assistant District Director

cc: *[insert the name of the corporate CEO]*
[insert the name of the designated representative]

LETTER L-32: CLOSURE LETTER FOR SUBSTANTIVE VIOLATIONS (with a Show Cause Notice)

Certified Mail, Return Receipt Requested AND Electronic Mail

[Date]

[Name of Establishment CEO]
[Title of CEO]
[Establishment Name]
[Street Address]
[City, State, Zip Code]

Dear *[insert the name of CEO]*:

The U.S. Department of Labor, Office of Federal Contract Compliance Programs (OFCCP), recently completed a compliance evaluation of your equal employment opportunity policies and practices at *[insert as appropriate*: establishment **or** construction work sites*]* in the *[insert name of geographic area]*.

On *[insert date]*, based on violations found during the evaluation, we issued your company a *[insert one or more as appropriate*: Notice to Show Cause or Amended Notice to Show Cause*]*. Based on this notice you had 30 calendar days to show why OFCCP should not initiate enforcement proceedings pursuant to *[insert one or more as appropriate*: Sections 208 and 209(a) of Executive Order 11246, as amended; Section 503 of the Rehabilitation Act, as amended, as implemented by 41 CFR 60-741.64, or Section 4212 of the Vietnam Era Veterans' Readjustment Assistance Act, as amended, as implemented by 41 CFR 60-250.64 and 41 CFR 60-300.64*]*.

However, on *[insert date]*, representatives of your company and this office reached a Conciliation Agreement that addresses each of the violations cited in the [*insert as appropriate*: Notice to Show Cause or Amended Notice to Show Cause].
Subject to the implementation of commitments detailed in the Conciliation Agreement dated *[insert date]*, this office determined that no other apparent violations of the regulations that OFCCP enforces exist. However, the Director of OFCCP or the Regional Director may modify this determination within 45 calendar days of the signing of the Conciliation Agreement by the District Director. If OFCCP takes no action to modify the Conciliation Agreement, within the timeframe provided, the agreement is deemed approved.

This determination does not preclude a future determination of noncompliance based on a finding that the commitments in the Conciliation Agreement are insufficient to achieve compliance.

Sincerely,

[insert name of the district director]

District Director

cc: *[insert name of the corporate CEO]*
[insert name of designated representative]

LETTER L-33: CLOSURE LETTER FOR SUBSTANTIVE VIOLATIONS (No Show Cause Notice Issued)

Certified Mail, Return Receipt Requested AND Electronic Mail

[Name of Establishment CEO]
[Title of CEO]
[Establishment Name]
[Street Address]
[City, State, Zip Code]

Dear *[Name of CEO]*:

The U.S. Department of Labor, Office of Federal Contract Compliance Programs (OFCCP), recently completed a compliance evaluation of the equal employment opportunity policies and practices at your (*insert as appropriate*: establishment or construction work sites) in the (*insert name of geographic area*).

Subject to the implementation of commitments detailed in our Conciliation Agreement dated (*insert date*), this office determined that no other apparent violations of the regulations that OFCCP enforces exist. However, the Director of OFCCP or the Regional Director may modify this determination within 45 calendar days of the signing of the Conciliation Agreement by the District Director. If OFCCP takes no action to modify the Conciliation Agreement, within the timeframe provided, the agreement is deemed approved.

This determination does not preclude a future determination of noncompliance based on a finding that the commitments in the Conciliation Agreement are insufficient to achieve compliance.

Sincerely,

(*insert name of regional director*)
Regional Director

Enclosure

cc: *[insert name of the corporate CEO]*
[insert name of the designated representative]

ADDENDUM A

Model CA for Compensation

CONCILIATION AGREEMENT

Between

THE U. S. DEPARTMENT OF LABOR

OFFICE OF FEDERAL CONTRACT COMPLIANCE PROGRAMS

and

[NAME OF CONTRACTOR]

PART I. PRELIMINARY STATEMENT

The Office of Federal Contract Compliance Programs ("OFCCP") commenced a compliance evaluation of [NAME OF CONTRACTOR]'s ("CONTRACTOR") establishment located at [FACILITY ADDRESS, CITY, STATE] on [DATE] and found that [CONTRACTOR] was not in compliance with the Executive Order 11246, as amended ("E.O. 11246"), [Section 503 of the Rehabilitation Act of 1973, as amended, 29 U.S.C. § 793 ("Section 503"), and/or the Vietnam Era Veterans' Readjustment Assistance Act of 1974, as amended, 38 U.S.C. § 4212 ("VEVRAA")][1], and [its/their] implementing regulations at [41 C.F.R. Section(s) 60-1, 60-2, 60-3, 60-4, 60-250, 60-300, and/or 60-741]. OFCCP notified [CONTRACTOR] of the initial violations found and the corrective actions required in a [NOTICE OF VIOLATIONS/SHOW CAUSE NOTICE/AMENDED SHOW CAUSE NOTICE] issued on [DATE]. In the interest of resolving the violations without engaging in further legal proceedings and in exchange for the good and valuable consideration described in this document, OFCCP and [CONTRACTOR] enter this contract ("Conciliation Agreement" or "Agreement") and agree to all the terms stated below.

PART II. GENERAL TERMS AND CONDITIONS

1. In exchange for [CONTRACTOR]'s fulfillment of all obligations in Parts III and IV of the Agreement, OFCCP agrees not to institute administrative or judicial enforcement proceedings under E.O. 11246 [Section 503, and/or VEVRAA] based on the violations described in more detail in Part III below. However, OFCCP has the right to initiate legal proceedings to enforce the Agreement itself or to correct and obtain relief for the violations described in Part III if [CONTRACTOR] violates this Agreement. Nothing in this Agreement precludes OFCCP from initiating enforcement proceedings based on future compliance evaluations or complaint investigations.

[1] Instruction: If OFCCP is not making a finding of a violation of either Section 503 of the Rehabilitation Act of 1973 (Section 503") or the Vietnam Era Veterans' Readjustment Assistance Act of 1974 ("VEVRAA"), the name and citation to the statute must not be included in paragraph. However, the first time in the document that these statutes are referenced, the full name of the statute must be stated, followed by the appropriate citation and then followed by the acronym in parentheses and quotation marks, i.e. ("Section 503") and ("VEVRAA"). Thereafter, the act may be referred to by the acronym, omitting the parentheses and quotation marks.

ADDENDUM A

Model CA for Compensation

2. [CONTRACTOR] agrees that OFCCP may review its compliance with this Agreement. As part of such review, OFCCP may require written reports, inspect the premises, interview witnesses, and examine and copy documents. [CONTRACTOR] will permit access to its premises during normal business hours for these purposes and will provide OFCCP with all reports and documents requested.

3. [CONTRACTOR] understands that nothing in this Agreement relieves [CONTRACTOR] of its obligation to fully comply with the requirements of E.O. 11246, Section 503, VEVRAA, their implementing regulations, and other applicable equal employment laws.

4. [CONTRACTOR] promises not to harass, intimidate, threaten, discriminate, or otherwise retaliate against any individual because the individual: benefits from this Agreement, files a complaint or participates in any investigation or proceeding under E.O. 11246, Section 503, and/or VEVRAA, or engages in any activity listed at 41 C.F.R. § 60-1.32(a).

5. The parties understand the terms of this Agreement and enter into it voluntarily.

6. This document and its attachments contain the complete and final understanding of the parties with respect to the matters referenced herein. This Agreement contains all terms by which the parties are bound and it supersedes all prior written or oral negotiations and agreements. There will be no modifications or amendments to this Agreement unless they are in writing, signed by all parties.

7. If one or more provisions of this Agreement are rendered unlawful or unenforceable, the remaining provisions will remain in full force and effect.

8. This Agreement becomes effective on the day it is signed by the Regional Director of the _________ Region (the "Effective Date") unless the Director of OFCCP indicates otherwise within 45 calendar days of the date the Regional Director signs the Agreement.[2]

9. This Agreement will expire sixty (60) days after [CONTRACTOR] submits the final report required in Part IV-1.D, below, unless OFCCP notifies [CONTRACTOR] in writing prior to the expiration date that [CONTRACTOR] has not fulfilled all of its obligations under the Agreement, in which case, the Agreement is automatically extended until the date that OFCCP determines [CONTRACTOR] has met all of it obligations under the agreement.

10. If [CONTRACTOR] violates this Conciliation Agreement,

A. The procedures set forth at 41 C.F.R. § 60-1.34 will govern:

1) If OFCCP believes that [CONTRACTOR] violated any term of the Agreement while it was in effect, OFCCP will send [CONTRACTOR] a written notice stating the alleged violations and summarizing any supporting evidence.

---

[2] Instruction: The title of the District Director and appropriate District Office must be substituted for recordkeeping cases and other types of cases where no findings of discrimination are made by OFCCP.

2) [CONTRACTOR] will have 15 days from receipt of such notice to demonstrate in writing that it has not violated the Conciliation Agreement, unless such a delay would result in irreparable injury to the employment rights of affected employees or applicants.

3) If [CONTRACTOR] is unable to demonstrate that it has not violated the Agreement, or if OFCCP alleges irreparable injury, enforcement proceedings may be initiated immediately without issuing a show cause notice or proceeding through any other requirement.

4) OFCCP may seek enforcement of this Agreement itself and is not required to present proof of any underlying violations resolved by this Agreement.

B. [CONTRACTOR] may be subject to the sanctions set forth in [*insert as applicable:* Section 209 of the Executive Order, 41 C.F.R. § 60-741.66, 41 C.F.R. § 60-250.66, or 41 C.F.R. § 60-300.66] and/or other appropriate relief for violation of this Agreement.

11. This Agreement does not constitute an admission by [CONTRACTOR] of any violation of E.O. 11246, Section 503, VEVRAA, or other laws, nor has there been an adjudicated finding that [CONTRACTOR] violated any laws.

PART III. <u>SPECIFIC VIOLATIONS AND REMEDIES</u>

1. COMPENSATION DISCRIMINATION.

A. STATEMENT OF VIOLATION. [INSERT BRIEF SUMMARY OF THE VIOLATION INCLUDING THE SECTION(S) OF E.O. 11246 (SECTION 503 AND/OR VEVRAA) AND THE REGULATIONS VIOLATED.] [3]

- <u>STATEMENT OF VIOLATION SAMPLE</u>:

OFCCP determined that since at least [SNAPSHOT DATE], [CONTRACTOR] has discriminated against [DISFAVORED GROUP(S) (women, Hispanics…][4] in [POSITIONS/ JOB GROUPS] in compensation in violation of 41 C.F.R. 60-[1.4(a)(1), 250.5(a)(1), 300.5(a)(1), or 741.5(a)(1)].

B. OFCCP'S SPECIFIC FINDINGS. [INSERT A SUMMARY OF OFCCP'S SPECIFIC FINDINGS AT THE TIME THE CA IS NEGOTIATED.]

- <u>COMPENSATION- SAMPLE</u>:

[3] Instruction: Each statement of violation and summary of OFCCP's findings needs to be tailored to the specific facts in the case. The sample language provided below and throughout Part III may not be appropriate in all cases. You should consult with SOL if you have any questions or concerns while drafting the CA.

[4] Instruction: You must identify the specific race/or ethnicity when you have a minority class (i.e., Black or African-American, Hispanic…).

ADDENDUM A

Model CA for Compensation

OFCCP performed a multiple regression analysis which shows that since [SNAPSHOT DATE] [CONTRACTOR] has paid [CHARACTERISTIC OF DISFAVORED GROUP (race, sex, national origin…)] [POSITION]s significantly less per year than [FAVORED GROUP CHARACTERISTIC (males, whites, …)]s [INSERT DESCRIPTION OF GROUP (with the same job, in the same grade level, in similar positions, etc.)] at the same location. OFCCP's analysis demonstrates that a statistically significant disparity in compensation remained even when legitimate factors affecting pay were taken into account. The disparity was caused by________ [Identify policy or practice that led to the disparity. e.g., differences in setting of base pay; access to add-ons such as overtime, shift differentials, pay increases, incentive pay; access to opportunities affecting compensation, such as higher paying positions, job classifications, work assignments, training; policies and practices that limit the disfavored group's opportunity to earn higher pay, such as: "glass ceiling" issues, performance appraisal process, assignment to more desirable sales territories].

C. REMEDY FOR AFFECTED CLASS. [5]

1) Notice. Within [NUMBER] calendar days of the Effective Date of this Agreement, [CONTRACTOR] must notify the [DISFAVORED GROUP] [POSITION]s listed in Attachment__ of the terms of this Agreement by mailing by [METHOD OF MAILING (first class, return-receipt requested, certified…)] mail to each individual in the affected class the: Notice to Affected Class (Attachment __, "Notice"), Information Verification Form (Attachment__, "Information Form"), and a postage paid return envelope. **[*DO NOT INCLUDE A RELEASE OF CLAIMS UNLESS REQUESTED BY THE CONTRACTOR.*]** [CONTRACTOR] will notify OFCCP of all letters returned as undeliverable [ON A MONTHLY/ WEEKLY BASIS OR __DAYS AFTER THE RESPONSE DEADLINE]. In addition, within [TIME PERIOD] after expiration of the response deadline set out in the Information Form, [CONTRACTOR] will provide OFCCP with a list of the individuals in the affected class who have not yet responded to the Notice and/or have not returned a signed Information Form. OFCCP will then attempt to obtain and provide updated addresses to [CONTRACTOR] within [TIME PERIOD] of receiving the list from [CONTRACTOR]. [CONTRACTOR] agrees to mail by [METHOD OF MAILING]first class mail a second Notice, Information Form, and postage paid return envelope to all individuals for whom updated addresses were obtained within [TIME PERIOD] of receiving the updated addresses.

[5] Instruction for when there is a Union/CBA: Before starting settlement discussions (or as soon as OFCCP becomes aware that a union is in place at the establishment) OFCCP should consult with SOL to discuss the legal requirements for CAs when the Contractor's workforce is unionized. When a proposed remedy for a violation identified in the course of a compliance review or complaint investigation under any of OFCCP's three programs would require a change in or otherwise affect a Collective Bargaining Agreement (CBA), the union must be notified in writing and invited to participate in the conciliation process. However, SOL may be able to suggest remedies that would not require union notification and involvement.

ADDENDUM A

Model CA for Compensation

2) Eligibility. All members of the affected class (listed on Attachment __) who sign and return the Information Form to [CONTRACTOR] within [__ DAYS OF THE POSTMARKED DATE ON THE ENVELOPE CONTAINING THE NOTICE AND INFORMATION FORM] ("Eligible Class Members") will receive a share of the monetary settlement. If an individual receives, but does not return the Information Form to [CONTRACTOR] within [NUMBER] calendar days of the postmarked date on the envelope containing the first or second Notice and Information Form, he/she will no longer be entitled to a payment under this Agreement.

Within [TIME PERIOD] after the response deadline set out in the Information Form, [CONTRACTOR] will provide OFCCP with a list of the Eligible Class Members (individuals who returned the Information Form by the deadline). Within [NUMBER] calendar days after receiving the list, OFCCP will approve the final list of Eligible Class Members or discuss with [CONTRACTOR] any issues necessary to finalize the list, such as the inclusion or exclusion of certain individuals.

3) Monetary Settlement (Backpay). [CONTRACTOR] agrees to distribute [SETTLEMENT AMOUNT] ($____ in back pay and $______ in interest), less legal deductions required by law from back pay only (such as federal, state and/ or local taxes and the Eligible Class Members' share of FICA taxes), [TO ALL ELIGIBLE CLASS MEMBERS ON THE FINAL APPROVED LIST IN THE AMOUNTS LISTED IN ATTACHMENT__/ IN AMOUNTS BASED ON THE FORMULA CONTAINED IN ATTACHMENT__]. [CONTRACTOR] will pay the Internal Revenue Service ("IRS") the employer's share of social security withholdings and will mail each Eligible Class Member an IRS W-2 Form reporting the portion of the payment representing back pay and an IRS Form 1099 for the portion of the payment representing interest. These IRS forms will be mailed at the end of the year. [CONTRACTOR] will disburse the monetary settlement within [NUMBER] calendar days after OFCCP approves the final list of Eligible Class Members.

Within [TIME]] calendar days of [CONTRACTOR]'s receipt of a check to an Eligible Class Member returned as undeliverable, [CONTRACTOR] will notify OFCCP of this fact via e-mail sent to [NAME AND EMAIL ADDRESSES OF OFCCP CONTACTS]. OFCCP will attempt to locate the Eligible Class Member and if OFCCP obtains an alternate address, [CONTRACTOR] will re-mail the check within [NUMBER] calendar days of receiving an alternate or corrected address. Any check that remains uncashed 120 days after the initial date the check was mailed to the Eligible Class Member will be void. With respect to any uncashed funds, [CONTRACTOR] will make a second distribution to all Eligible Class Members who cashed their first check. [INSERT DETAILS INCLUDING

THE TIME PERIOD FOR SENDING THE CHECKS AND HOW THE AMOUNT WILL BE DIVIDED AMONG CLASS MEMBERS].[6]

4) Impact Analysis and Prospective Salary Adjustments. Within [NUMBER] days of the Effective Date of this Agreement, [CONTRACTOR] will conduct a regression analysis of compensation using the methodology described in Attachment __ for [POSITION(s)] using payroll data that is current as of [DATE].[7] If the analysis results in a statistically significant disparity (t-statistic) of -1.96 or more, adverse to [DISFAVORED GROUP], [CONTRACTOR] agrees to increase the salaries of [DISFAVORED GROUP] using the formula set forth in Section __ of Attachment __ within [TIME PERIOD] after conducting the analysis.[8]

D. NON-MONETARY REMEDIES. [CONTRACTOR] will ensure that all employees are afforded equal employment opportunities. [CONTRACTOR] agrees to continue or to implement the corrective actions detailed below. [BELOW ARE VARIOUS OPTIONS FOR NON-MONETARY RELIEF. CHOOSE THOSE THAT ARE APPLICABLE TO THE SPECIFIC CIRCUMSTANCES.][9]

1) Eliminate Discriminatory Compensation Practices. [CONTRACTOR] agrees to immediately cease using [IDENTIFY THE POLICY OR PRACTICE] which negatively affects the yearly compensation of [DISFAVORED GROUP] [NAME OF JOB(S)].

2) Evaluation. For the [NAME OF JOB(s)/ JOB GROUP/ GRADE LEVEL/ OR SIMILAR POSITIONS…], [CONTRACTOR] will conduct a study to evaluate whether promotion decisions, performance evaluation ratings, procedures for assigning work, the availability of training opportunities, leave policies, steering applicants into low paying jobs, and/or limiting the opportunity to transfer to better jobs have a disproportionately negative effect on the compensation of [DISFAVORED GROUP].

3) Implement Improved Policies. [CONTRACTOR] will develop and write new policies to eliminate all practices that had an adverse effect on the compensation of [DISFAVORED GROUP].

---

[6] While it is ideal for the [CONTRACTOR] to disburse *all* of the settlement money to the class, contractors often object to the cost and time required to make a second disbursement when class members will receive a very small amount of money (less than $5 each, for example). In such cases, OFCCP may agree to include a provision like the following:

> If the total amount of uncashed funds would result in a payment of less than [$__] to each Eligible Class Member who cashed the first disbursement check, [CONTRACTOR] will use those uncashed funds to provide training in equal employment opportunity to its personnel in addition to the training it is obligated to provide concerning the Revised Hiring Process described in section _____.

[7] Instruction: Work with OFCCP's Statistician to formulate the methodology to be used for the Statistical Analysis.

[8] Instruction: Work with OFCCP's Statistician to determine the formula to be used for any salary increases.

[9] Instruction: Consider requiring contractor to retain an expert consultant to design and/ or conduct required studies and develop new compensation policies.

ADDENDUM A

Model CA for Compensation

- PERFORMANCE EVALUATIONS AND RATINGS SAMPLE:

[CONTRACTOR]'s infrequent or inconsistent ratings of employees' performance had an adverse effect on the compensation of [DISFAVORED GROUP] [POSITION]. [CONTRACTOR] will write and implement a policy requiring annual performance evaluations based on standardized criteria. [CONTRACTOR] will conduct an annual performance evaluation for each employee working as a [POSITION(s)]. Each employee's direct supervisor will evaluate the employee's performance for the purpose of providing constructive feedback and guidance to the employee, and for documenting, inter alia, the extent to which the employee has achieved his/her job goals and objectives. Supervisors are expected to identify specific examples of performance behaviors to support high or low ratings. [CONTRACTOR] will provide training to supervisors explaining rating levels and how best to document and record employees' performance. Each employee must be provided an electronic or written copy of his/her completed performance evaluation form. [CONTRACTOR] must retain an electronic or written copy of each completed evaluation form for the length of time required by 41 C.F.R. § 60- 1.12.

- SETTING STARTING SALARY SAMPLE:

[CONTRACTOR] will develop and write improved guidelines for determining the starting salaries to be assigned to newly hired employees. Factors included in setting starting salary may include information regarding the employee's certifications, previous experience, and the salaries of similarly situated [CONTRACTOR] peers. Employees' pre-hire salary at his or her former employer should not be the sole factor considered because prior salary can reflect race or sex-based compensation discrimination.

- TRACKING AND EVLAUATION SAMPLE:

[CONTRACTOR] will write and implement procedures to ensure that compensation decisions are tracked and evaluated for compliance with the Revised Compensation Policy.

- DOCUMENT RETENTION SAMPLE:

[CONTRACTOR] will write and implement procedures to ensure that documents are retained in accordance with 41 C.F.R. 60-1.12(a) and Part 60-3.

4) Training. Within [NUMBER OF WEEKS OR MONTHS] of the Effective Date of this Agreement, [CONTRACTOR] must train all individuals involved in any way in determining compensation for [NAME OF JOB] positions on all new and revised policies, procedures, and programs developed under Part III-1.D of this Agreement.

ADDENDUM A

Model CA for Compensation

5) Self-monitoring/ Auditing. [CONTRACTOR] will monitor base salary as well as the administration of non-base compensation and benefits[10] and adverse employment actions such as [OVERTIME ASSIGNMENTS/PAY, MERIT AWARDS, DISCIPLINARY ACTIONS, etc.] for any indication of statistically significant disparities based on [CHARACTERISTIC OF DISFAVORED GROUP (race, gender, national origin…)] and will investigate and remedy any such inequity that may be established. [11] [AND/ OR INSERT MORE SPECIFIC SELF-AUDITING PROVISIONS LIKE THE FOLLOWING:]

- [CONTRACTOR] expressly agrees to investigate any complaint or information it receives that may indicate compensation disparities.
- CONTRACTOR] commits to self-monitor its compensation program for [POSITION(s)] on an annual basis using the methodology described in Attachment __ ("Statistical Analysis").
- [CONTRACTOR] will evaluate (1) whether the eligibility criteria for determining non-base compensation are uniformly applied without regard to race or gender and (2) whether eligible employees receive non-base compensation in nondiscriminatory amounts. In addition to the required statistical analysis and self-auditing described above, [CONTRACTOR] will conduct a statistical analysis by [GENDER, RACE…] of the non-base pay of employees in [POSITION(s)].
- If [CONTRACTOR] finds evidence that the criteria are not uniformly applied to all employees, it will create a written guidance document explaining the criteria and procedures for awarding non-base compensation and it will provide related training to all employees who make compensation decisions.
- If there is a statistically significant difference in the non-base compensation of different race or gender groups, [CONTRACTOR] agrees to adjust non-base pay to correct any disparities found.

6) Additional Corrective Actions. [INSERT RELEVANT PROVISIONS.]

For additional suggestions and model language, review the attached memo titled "Model Equitable Relief Provisions for Conciliation Agreements and Consent Decrees," which enumerates many of the equitable remedies which have proven to be highly-effective in eliminating discrimination and/or contribute to comprehensive relief.

Part IV. REPORTS REQUIRED.

---

[10] Instruction: Base salaries or wages often make up only part of the compensation package for employees. Employee compensation can also consist of commissions, stock options, bonuses, and other payments made as remuneration for employment. Even if there are no significant disparities in base salaries, the amount of non-base compensation paid to members of a protected class still could be discriminatory.

[11] Instruction: For example, a disparity in overtime allocations (and consequently pay) might be remedied through increased cross-training of employees or rotating overtime assignments through different shifts and positions.

ADDENDUM A

Model CA for Compensation

1. [CONTRACTOR] must submit the documents and reports described below to: [_____], District Director of OFCCP, [ADDRESS].

[INCLUDE REPORTS FROM THIS LIST TO THE EXTENT APPLICABLE. ADD OTHER REPORTS TO EXTENT NECESSARY BASED ON NON-MONETARY REMEDIES.]

A. Within [TIME PERIOD; typically "60 calendar days of the Effective Date of this Agreement"] [CONTRACTOR] must submit a copy of the written Revised Compensation Policy described in section ____.

B. Within [TIME PERIOD] of the Effective Date of this Agreement, [CONTRACTOR] must submit documentation that all managers, supervisors, and other personnel involved in making compensation decisions for [POSITION]s have received training on all new and revised policies, procedures, and programs developed under Part III-1.D of this Agreement. The documentation must include the dates of the training, the names and job titles of all attendees, an outline of the topics discussed during the training, and the name and job title of each person who conducted the training.

C. Within the prescribed timeframes, [CONTRACTOR] must submit all documents and information referenced in sections ____.[12]

D. [CONTRACTOR] must submit a progress report covering each six month period this Agreement is in effect. The first progress report will be due seven months after the Effective Date of this Agreement and must cover the six-month period beginning with the Effective Date. Each subsequent report must cover the successive six-month period, and must be submitted within 30 calendar days after the close of that six-month period. [CONTRACTOR] will submit the following in each progress report: [INSERT A LIST OF THE DATA AND ANALYSES REQUIRED BY THE PRECEDING PART, THESE MAY INCLUDE:]

1) Documentation of monetary payments to all Eligible Class Members as specified in section ___. The documentation must include the names of Eligible Class Members who were paid, and, for each Eligible Class Member, the number and the amount of the check and the date the check cleared the bank. [CONTRACTOR] must provide OFCCP with copies of all canceled checks upon request;

2) Within ten (10) days of completing the Statistical Analysis described in Section__ of the Agreement, [CONTRACTOR] will provide OFCCP, via email and/or overnight mail, the database, output, and statistical log from the Statistical Analysis; and/or

---

[12] Instruction: Such documents and information may include letters returned as undeliverable, a list of individuals in the affected class who have not returned a signed Information Form before the deadline, and a list of Eligible Class Members.

ADDENDUM A

Model CA for Compensation

3) [CONTRACTOR] must provide documentation describing all Salary Adjustments required by Section __ of the Agreement. The documentation must include the amount of each adjustment, the date each adjustment will be/ was made, and the [GENDER, RACE…] of each individual receiving an adjustment.

2. [CONTRACTOR] will retain all records and data pertinent to the violations resolved by this Agreement and/ or used to prepare required reports until this Agreement expires or as long as required by OFCCP's regulations, whichever date occurs later (or "whichever time period is longer").

Part V. <u>SIGNATURES</u>.

This Conciliation Agreement is hereby executed by and between the OFCCP and [CONTRACTOR].

______________________________	______________________________
[NAME of Official] [POSITION] [CONTRACTOR]	[NAME] Regional Director OFCCP
Date:______________________	Date:______________________

____

[NAME of Union Official – only if appropriate]

Date: ______________________

ADDENDUM A

Model CA for Compensation

ATTACHMENT __

NOTICE TO AFFECTED CLASS

Dear [NAME]:

[CONTRACTOR] ("CONTRACTOR") and the Department of Labor's Office of Federal Contract Compliance Programs ("OFCCP") have entered into a Conciliation Agreement ("Agreement") to remedy the violations of [EXECUTIVE ORDER 11246 ("E.O. 11246"), SECTION 503 OF THE REHABILITATION ACT ("SECTION 503"), VIETNAM VETERANS READJUSTMENT ASSISTANCE ACT ("VEVRAA")] that OFCCP found during a compliance review of [CONTRACTOR]'s [LOCATION] facility. OFCCP's analysis showed that since [SNAPSHOT DATE] [CONTRACTOR] has paid [CHARACTERISTIC OF DISFAVORED GROUP (race, sex, national origin…)] [POSITION]s significantly less per year than [FAVORED GROUP CHARACTERISTIC (males, whites…)]s with the same job at the same location. [CONTRACTOR] has not admitted to any violation of [E.O. 11246, SECTION 503, and/or VEVRAA] and there has not been any adjudicated finding that [CONTRACTOR] violated any laws. OFCCP and [CONTRACTOR] entered into the Agreement to resolve the matter without resorting to further legal proceedings.

You have been identified as one of the individuals who worked as a [POSITION]. Under the Agreement, you may be eligible to receive a payment [INSERT APPROPRIATE AMOUNT/ DESCRIPTION SUCH AS "of at least $ ______" OR "representing a pro rata share of back pay and interest"] (less deductions required by law). Under the terms of the Agreement it may take up to [NUMBER] months from the date of this letter before you receive your payment. In order to be eligible for a payment, you must complete, sign, and return enclosed Information Verification Form. This form should be mailed as soon as possible; it *must* be postmarked to the address below no later than [TIME (typically 30-60 days)] after the date this Notice was mailed out (postmarked) for you to be entitled to participate in this settlement:

(NAME)
(POSITION)
(CONTRACTOR)
(ADDRESS)

You may use the enclosed postage-paid return envelope to return the completed and signed Information Verification Form.

If you have any questions you may call [NAME] at [CONTRACTOR] at [PHONE NUMBER], or OFCCP Compliance Officer [NAME] at [PHONE NUMBER]. Your call will be returned as soon as possible.

ADDENDUM A

Model CA for Compensation

IF YOU FAIL TO COMPLETE AND RETURN THE ENCLOSED DOCUMENT(S) TO [CONTRACTOR] WITHIN __ DAYS OF THE DATE THE ENVELOPE CONTAINING THIS NOTICE WAS POSTMARKED, YOU WILL NOT BE ELIGIBLE TO RECEIVE A PAYMENT.

Sincerely,

(NAME)

Enclosures

Information Verification Form

Release of Claims Under Executive Order 11246-**[DO NOT INCLUDE A RELEASE OF CLAIMS UNLESS REQUESTED BY THE CONTRACTOR. SEE ATTACHMENT FOR A SAMPLE RELEASE.]**

ADDENDUM A

Model CA for Compensation

ATTACHMENT __

INFORMATION VERIFICATION FORM

You must complete this form in order to be eligible for the monetary payment under the terms of the Conciliation Agreement ("Agreement") between [CONTRACTOR][("CONTRACTOR")] and the Department of Labor's Office of Federal Contract Compliance Programs. Please print legibly, except for the signature.

Name: ____

Address: ____

Telephone Nos.: Home_______________Cell________________Work________________

Notify [CONTRACTOR] at the address below if your address or phone number changes within the next twelve months.

Your Social Security Number (to be used for tax purposes only): ______-________-______

For purposes of this settlement, it is necessary to verify your [GENDER and/or RACE]:

Caucasian ☐ African American ☐ Hispanic ☐ Asian ☐ Native American ☐

Male ☐ Female ☐

IF YOU FAIL TO COMPLETE AND RETURN THE ENCLOSED DOCUMENTS TO THE ADDRESS BELOW WITHIN __ DAYS OF THE DATE THE ENVELOPE CONTAINING THIS NOTICE WAS POSTMARKED, YOU WILL NOT BE ELIGIBLE TO RECEIVE A PAYMENT.

(NAME)
(ADDRESS)

I, (print name)_____________________, certify the above is true and correct.

Signature Date

ADDENDUM A

Model CA for Compensation

ATTACHMENT__

RELEASE OF CLAIMS UNDER EXECUTIVE ORDER 11246

This Release of Claims under Executive Order 11246 ("Release") is a legal document. The document states that in return for [CONTRACTOR] ("CONTRACTOR") paying you money, you agree that you will not file any lawsuit against [CONTRACTOR] for allegedly violating Executive Order 11246 in its compensation of [INSERT GENDER, RACE OF VICTIMS] [POSITIONS]. It also says that [CONTRACTOR] does not admit it violated any laws. This Release says you had sufficient time to look at the document, to talk with others about the document, including an attorney if you choose, and that no one pressured you into signing the document. Finally, it says that if you do not sign and return the document by a certain date, you will not receive any money.

In consideration of the payment of [INSERT APPROPRIATE AMOUNT/ DESCRIPTION SUCH AS "at least $ ______" OR "a pro rata share of back pay and interest"] (less deductions required by law) by [CONTRACTOR] to me, which I agree is acceptable, I _________________________________ agree to the following:

print name

I.

I hereby waive, release and forever discharge [CONTRACTOR], its predecessors, successors, related entities, parents, subsidiaries, affiliates and organizations, and its and their shareholders, directors, officers, employees, agents, successors, and assigns, of and from any and all actions, causes of action, damages, liabilities, and claims arising out of or actionable under Executive Order 11246, as amended, which I or my representatives (heirs, executors, administrators, or assigns) have or may have which relate in any way to my compensation as a [POSITION] on the basis of my [RACE, GENDER, ETC] at any time prior to the date of my signature on this Release.

II.

I understand that [CONTRACTOR] denies that it treated me unlawfully or unfairly in any way and that [CONTRACTOR] entered into a Conciliation Agreement with the U.S. Department of Labor, Office of Federal Contract Compliance Programs ("OFCCP") and agreed to make the payment described above to resolve alleged disparities in compensation and to resolve the matter without further legal proceedings in the compliance review initiated by OFCCP on [INSERT DATE]. I further agree that the payment of the aforesaid sum by [CONTRACTOR] to me is not to be construed as an admission of any liability by [CONTRACTOR].

III.

I declare that I have read this Release and that I have had a full opportunity to consider and understand its terms and to consult with my advisors and seek legal advice. I further declare that I have decided of my own free will to sign this Release.

ADDENDUM A

Model CA for Compensation

IV.

I understand that if I do not sign this Release and return it to [CONTACTOR] [ON OR BEFORE ___ (DATE)/ WITHIN __ DAYS OF THE DATE THE ENVELOPE CONTAINING THIS RELEASE WAS POSTMARKED], I will not be entitled to receive any payment (less deductions required by law) from [CONTRACTOR].

IN WITNESS WHEREOF, I have signed this document on this ________ day of ________________________, 20__.

____

Signature

ADDENDUM B

Model CA for Hiring, Recordkeeping, Access, and other issues

CONCILIATION AGREEMENT

Between

THE U. S. DEPARTMENT OF LABOR

OFFICE OF FEDERAL CONTRACT COMPLIANCE PROGRAMS

and

[NAME OF CONTRACTOR]

PART I. PRELIMINARY STATEMENT

The Office of Federal Contract Compliance Programs ("OFCCP") evaluated [NAME OF CONTRACTOR]'s ("CONTRACTOR") facility located at [FACILITY ADDRESS, CITY, STATE] and found that [CONTRACTOR] was not in compliance with the Executive Order 11246, as amended ("E.O. 11246"), [Section 503 of the Rehabilitation Act of 1973, as amended, 29 U.S.C. § 793 ("Section 503"), and/or the Vietnam Era Veterans' Readjustment Assistance Act of 1974, as amended, 38 U.S.C. § 4212 ("VEVRAA")][1], and [its/their] implementing regulations at [41 C.F.R. Section(s) 60-1, 60-2, 60-3, 60-4, 60-250, 60-300, and/or 60-741]. OFCCP notified [CONTRACTOR] of the specific violations found and the corrective actions required in a [NOTICE OF VIOLATIONS/SHOW CAUSE NOTICE/AMENDED SHOW CAUSE NOTICE] issued on [DATE]. In the interest of resolving the violations without engaging in further legal proceedings and in exchange for the good and valuable consideration described in this document, OFCCP and [CONTRACTOR] enter this contract ("Conciliation Agreement" or "Agreement") and agree to all the terms stated below.

PART II. GENERAL TERMS AND CONDITIONS

1. In exchange for [CONTRACTOR]'s fulfillment of all obligations in Parts III and IV of the Agreement, OFCCP agrees not to institute administrative or judicial enforcement proceedings under E.O. 11246 [Section 503, and/or VEVRAA] based on the violations described in more detail in Part III below. However, OFCCP has the right to initiate legal proceedings to enforce the Agreement itself or to correct and obtain relief for the violations described in Part III if [CONTRACTOR] violates this Agreement. Nothing in this Agreement precludes OFCCP from initiating enforcement proceedings based on future compliance evaluations or complaint investigations.

---

[1] Instruction: If OFCCP is not making a finding of a violation of either Section 503 of the Rehabilitation Act of 1973 (Section 503") or the Vietnam Era Veterans' Readjustment Assistance Act of 1974 ("VEVRAA"), the name and citation to the statute must not be included in paragraph. However, the first time in the document that these statutes are referenced, the full name of the statute must be stated, followed by the appropriate citation and then followed by the acronym in parentheses and quotation marks, i.e. ("Section 503") and ("VEVRAA"). Thereafter, the act may be referred to by the acronym, omitting the parentheses and quotation marks.

ADDENDUM B

Model CA for Hiring, Recordkeeping, Access, and other issues

2. [CONTRACTOR] agrees that OFCCP may review its compliance with this Agreement. As part of such review, OFCCP may require written reports, inspect the premises, interview witnesses, and examine and copy documents. [CONTRACTOR] will permit access to its premises during normal business hours for these purposes and will provide OFCCP with all reports and documents requested.

3. [CONTRACTOR] understands that nothing in this Agreement relieves [CONTRACTOR] of its obligation to fully comply with the requirements of E.O. 11246, Section 503, VEVRAA, their implementing regulations, and other applicable equal employment laws.

4. [CONTRACTOR] promises not to harass, intimidate, threaten, discriminate, or otherwise retaliate against any individual because the individual: benefits from this Agreement, files a complaint or participates in any investigation or proceeding under E.O. 11246, Section 503, and/or VEVRAA, or engages in any activity listed at 41 C.F.R. § 60-1.32(a).

5. The parties understand the terms of this Agreement and enter into it voluntarily.

6. This document and its attachments contain the complete and final understanding of the parties with respect to the matters referenced herein. This Agreement contains all terms by which the parties are bound and it supersedes all prior written or oral negotiations and agreements. There will be no modifications or amendments to this Agreement unless they are in writing, signed by all parties.

7. If one or more provisions of this Agreement are rendered unlawful or unenforceable, the remaining provisions will remain in full force and effect.

8. This Agreement becomes effective on the day it is signed by the Regional Director of the _________ Region (the "Effective Date") unless the Director of OFCCP indicates otherwise within 45 calendar days of the date the Regional Director signs the Agreement.[2]

9. This Agreement will expire sixty (60) days after [CONTRACTOR] submits the final progress report required in Part IV (D), below, unless OFCCP notifies [CONTRACTOR] in writing prior to the expiration date that [CONTRACTOR] has not fulfilled all of its obligations under the Agreement, in which case the Agreement is automatically extended until the date that OFCCP determines [CONTRACTOR] has met all of it obligations under the Agreement.

10. If [CONTRACTOR] violates this Conciliation Agreement,

A. The procedures set forth at 41 C.F.R. § 60-1.34 will govern:

1) If OFCCP believes that [CONTRACTOR] violated any term of the Agreement while it was in effect, OFCCP will send [CONTRACTOR] a written notice stating the alleged violations and summarizing any supporting evidence.

---

[2] Instruction: The title of the District Director and appropriate District Office must be substituted for recordkeeping cases and other types of cases where no findings of discrimination are made by OFCCP.

2) [CONTRACTOR] will have 15 days from receipt of such notice to demonstrate in writing that it has not violated the Conciliation Agreement, unless such a delay would result in irreparable injury to the employment rights of affected employees or applicants.

3) If [CONTRACTOR] is unable to demonstrate that it has not violated the Agreement, or if OFCCP alleges irreparable injury, enforcement proceedings may be initiated immediately without issuing a show cause notice or proceeding through any other requirement.

4) OFCCP may seek enforcement of this Agreement itself and is not required to present proof of any underlying violations resolved by this Agreement.

B. [CONTRACTOR] may be subject to the sanctions set forth in [*insert as applicable:* Section 209 of the Executive Order, 41 C.F.R. § 60-741.66, 41 C.F.R. § 60-250.66, or 41 C.F.R. § 60-300.66] and/or other appropriate relief for violation of this Agreement.

11. This Agreement does not constitute an admission by [CONTRACTOR] of any violation of E.O. 11246, Section 503, VEVRAA, or other laws, nor has there been an adjudicated finding that [CONTRACTOR] violated any laws.

PART III. SPECIFIC VIOLATIONS AND REMEDIES

1. HIRING DISCRIMINATION

A. STATEMENT OF VIOLATION. [INSERT BRIEF SUMMARY OF THE VIOLATION INCLUDING THE SECTION(S) OF E.O. 11246 (SECTION 503 AND/OR VEVRAA) AND THE REGULATIONS VIOLATED.] [3]

- HIRING DISCRIMINATION- STATEMENT OF VIOLATION SAMPLE:

OFCCP found that [CONTRACTOR] is not in compliance with the nondiscrimination requirements of the equal opportunity clause of E.O. 11246 § 202 and 41 C.F.R. § 60-1.4(a)(1). OFCCP's analysis of [CONTRACTOR]'s hiring process and selection procedures revealed that during the period of [DATE] through [DATE] ("review period") [CONTRACTOR] discriminated against [DISFAVORED GROUP(S)][4] applicants for [NAME OF JOB(S)/ POSITION(S)]. OFCCP found that there was a statistically significant disparity in the hiring of [NAME OF JOB(S)] based on [RACE, GENDER, NATIONAL ORIGIN…].

B. OFCCP'S SPECIFIC FINDINGS. [INSERT A SUMMARY OF OFCCP'S SPECIFIC FINDINGS AT THE TIME THE CA IS NEGOTIATED.]

---

[3] Instruction: Each statement of violation and summary of OFCCP's findings needs to be tailored to the specific facts in the case. The sample language provided below and throughout Part III may not be appropriate in all cases. You should consult with SOL if you have any questions or concerns while drafting the CA.

[4] Instruction: You must identify the specific race/or ethnicity when you have a minority class (i.e., Black or African-American, Hispanic…).

ADDENDUM B

Model CA for Hiring, Recordkeeping, Access, and other issues

- HIRING DISCRIMINATION- DISPARATE IMPACT SAMPLE:

OFCCP's analysis of the applicant and hiring data demonstrates that [CONTRACTOR]'s selection process had an adverse impact on the hiring of [DISFAVORED GROUP] applicants for [NAME OF JOB(S)] positions. Of [NUMBER OF DISFAVORED GROUP] applicants, [NUMBER] or [PERCENTAGE] were hired, whereas of [NUMBER OF FAVORED GROUP] applicants, [NUMBER] or [PERCENTAGE] were hired. This resulted in a hiring shortfall of [NUMBER] [DISFAVORED GROUP] and a disparity that was statistically significant at [NUMBER] standard deviations.

OFCCP found that the disparity was caused by [CONTRACTOR'S] use of [NAME OF THE SELECTION PROCEDURE]. When analyzing the results of [SELECTION PROCEDURE], OFCCP found that [DESCRIBE RESULTS OF ANALYSIS (SHORTFALLS, STATISTICALLY SIGNIFICANT DISPARITIES)]. OFCCP further found that [CONTRACTOR] had not properly validated [SELECTION PROCEDURE] in accordance with the requirements of the Uniform Guidelines on Employee Selection Procedures, 41 C.F.R. Part 60-3. Accordingly, as a result of using [SELECTION PROCEDURE], [CONTRACTOR] discriminated against [NUMBER] [DISFAVORED GROUP] applicants who applied for [POSITION] during the review period.

- HIRING DISCRIMINATION- DISPARATE TREATMENT SAMPLE:

OFCCP's statistical findings indicate hiring discrimination against [DISFAVORED GROUP]. OFCCP found additional evidence that supports its hiring discrimination claim. [INSERT A DESCRIPTION OF THE ADDITIONAL EVIDENCE OFCCP FOUND. FOR EXAMPLE, OFCCP MAY HAVE FOUND: DIRECT EVIDENCE OF DISCRIMINATORY ANIMUS, INCONSISTENCIES IN THE SELECTION PROCESS- INCLUDING APPLYING A REQUIREMENT APPLICABLE ONLY TO MEMBERS OF THE DISFAVORED GROUP, AND/OR ANECDOTAL ("ME TOO") EVIDENCE.] Accordingly, OFCCP determined that [CONTRACTOR] engaged in a pattern or practice of discrimination against [NUMBER] [DISFAVORED GROUP] applicants who applied for [POSITION] during the review period.

C. REMEDY FOR AFFECTED CLASS.[5]

---

[5] Instruction for when there is a Union/CBA: Before starting settlement discussions (or as soon as OFCCP becomes aware that a union is in place at the establishment) OFCCP should consult with SOL to discuss the legal requirements for CAs when the Contractor's workforce is unionized. When a proposed remedy for a violation identified in the course of a compliance review or complaint investigation under any of OFCCP's three programs would require a change in or otherwise affect a Collective Bargaining Agreement (CBA), the union must be notified in writing and invited to participate in the conciliation process. However, SOL may be able to suggest remedies that would not require union notification and involvement.

ADDENDUM B

Model CA for Hiring, Recordkeeping, Access, and other issues

1) Notice. Within [NUMBER] calendar days of the Effective Date of this Agreement, [CONTRACTOR] must notify the [DISFAVORED GROUP] applicants listed in Attachment__ of the terms of this Agreement by mailing by [METHOD OF MAILING (first class, return-receipt requested, certified…)] mail to each individual in the affected class the: Notice to Affected Class (Attachment __, "Notice"), Information Verification & Employment Interest Form (Attachment__, "Interest Form"), and a postage paid return envelope. **[*DO NOT INCLUDE A RELEASE OF CLAIMS UNLESS REQUESTED BY THE CONTRACTOR.*]** [CONTRACTOR] will notify OFCCP of all letters returned as undeliverable [ON A MONTHLY/ WEEKLY BASIS OR __DAYS AFTER THE RESPONSE DEADLINE]. In addition, within [TIME PERIOD] after expiration of the response deadline set out in the Interest Form, [CONTRACTOR] will provide OFCCP with a list of the individuals in the affected class who have not yet responded to the Notice and/or have not returned a signed Interest Form. OFCCP will then attempt to obtain and provide updated addresses to [CONTRACTOR] within [TIME PERIOD] of receiving the list from [CONTRACTOR]. [CONTRACTOR] agrees to mail by [METHOD OF MAILING] mail a second Notice, Interest Form, and postage paid return envelope to all individuals for whom updated addresses were obtained within [TIME PERIOD] of receiving the updated addresses.

2) Eligibility. All members of the affected class (listed on Attachment __) who sign and return the Interest Form to [CONTRACTOR] within [NUMBER] calendar days of the postmarked date on the envelope containing the first or second Notice and Interest Form ("Eligible Class Members") will receive a share of the monetary settlement and, if indicating an interest in employment, will be eligible to be considered for a job pursuant to this Agreement. If an individual receives, but does not return the Interest Form to [CONTRACTOR] within [NUMBER] calendar days of the postmarked date on the envelope containing the first or second Notice and Interest Form, he/she will no longer be entitled to a payment or consideration for a job under this Agreement.

Within [TIME PERIOD] after the response deadline set out in the Interest Form, [CONTRACTOR] will provide OFCCP with a list of the Eligible Class Members (individuals who returned the Interest Form by the deadline). Within [NUMBER] calendar days after receiving the list, OFCCP will approve the final list of Eligible Class Members or discuss with [CONTRACTOR] any issues necessary to finalize the list, such as the inclusion or exclusion of certain individuals.

All Eligible Class Members are entitled to their share of the monetary settlement regardless of whether they are interested in employment with [CONTRACTOR].

3) Monetary Settlement. [CONTRACTOR] agrees to distribute [SETTLEMENT AMOUNT] ($____ in back pay and $______ in interest), less legal deductions required by law from back pay only (such as federal, state and/ or local taxes and the Eligible Class Members' share of FICA taxes), [IN EQUAL SHARES

AMONG ALL ELIGIBLE CLASS MEMBERS ON THE FINAL APPROVED LIST OR IN THE AMOUNTS LISTED/ IN AMOUNTS BASED ON THE FORMULA CONTAINED IN ATTACHMENT__]. [CONTRACTOR] will pay the Internal Revenue Service ("IRS") the employer's share of social security withholdings and will mail each Eligible Class Member an IRS W-2 Form reporting the portion of the payment representing back pay and an IRS Form 1099 for the portion of the payment representing interest. These IRS forms will be mailed at the end of the year. [CONTRACTOR] will disburse the monetary settlement within [NUMBER] calendar days after OFCCP approves the final list of Eligible Class Members.

Within [NUMBER] calendar days of [CONTRACTOR]'s receipt of a check to an Eligible Class Member returned as undeliverable, [CONTRACTOR] will notify OFCCP of this fact via e-mail sent to [NAME AND EMAIL ADDRESSES OF OFCCP CONTACTS]. OFCCP will attempt to locate the Eligible Class Member and if OFCCP obtains an alternate address, [CONTRACTOR] will re-mail the check within [NUMBER] calendar days of receiving an alternate or corrected address. Any check that remains uncashed 120 days after the initial date the check was mailed to the Eligible Class Member will be void. With respect to any uncashed funds, [CONTRACTOR] will make a second distribution to all Eligible Class Members who cashed their first check [INSERT DETAILS INCLUDING THE TIME PERIOD FOR SENDING THE CHECKS AND HOW THE AMOUNT WILL BE DIVIDED AMONG CLASS MEMBERS].[6]

4) <u>Employment</u>. As positions become available, [CONTRACTOR] will consider qualified Eligible Class Members not currently employed by [CONTRACTOR] who express an interest in employment with [CONTRACTOR] until [SHORTFALL NUMBER] Eligible Class Members are hired as [POSITION]s or until the list of Eligible Class Members expressing an interest in employment is exhausted, whichever occurs first.[7] Eligible Class Members will be considered in the order that [CONTRACTOR] receives their Interst Forms. If [CONTRACTOR] receives more than one response on any given day, those Eligible Class Members will be considered for employment based on the date of their original application. [CONTRACTOR] must initiate its hiring of Eligible Class Members within __ days [OF THE EFFECTIVE DATE OF THIS

---

[6] While it is ideal for the Contractor to disburse *all* of the settlement money to the class, contractors often object to the cost and time required to make a second disbursement when class members will receive a very small amount of money (less than $5 each, for example). In such cases, OFCCP may agree to include a provision such as the following:

> If the total amount of uncashed funds would result in a payment of less than [$__] to each Eligible Class Member who cashed the first disbursement check, [CONTRACTOR] will use those uncashed funds to provide training in equal employment opportunity to its personnel in addition to the training it is obligated to provide concerning the Revised Hiring Process described in section _____.

[7] Instruction: Insert this sentence if you have both female and minority class members and placement issues: "[CONTRACTOR] will make its best efforts to distribute the [SHORTFALL NUMBER] hires as follows: [LIST DISTRIBUTION OF HIRES BY RACE/GENDER/ETHNICITY]."

AGREEMENT OR AFTER THE RESPONSE DEADLINE SET OUT IN THE INTEREST FORM] and must complete its hiring obligations under this section within __ [months/years] of the Effective Date of this Agreement. If [CONTRACTOR] is not able to hire [SHORTFALL NUMBER] Eligible Class Members or exhaust the list of Eligible Class Members expressing an interest in employment within __ [months/years], OFCCP may extend the term of this Agreement for up to ____ months or until [CONTRACTOR] satisfies its hiring requirement(s), whichever occurs first.

Eligible Class Members will be allowed at least two weeks to report for work after receiving a written job offer from [CONTRACTOR]. The Eligible Class Members hired into [POSITION] positions pursuant to this Agreement must be paid $[AMOUNT] per hour or the current wage rate for the [POSITION] position, whichever is higher, and must be provided with the same benefits and opportunity to earn overtime and shift differentials as other [POSITION] employees. In addition, all Eligible Class Members hired must receive retroactive seniority[8] using the date of their original application as their hire date for all purposes, including job retention, job bidding and benefits (or a payment of $___ in lieu of retroactive seniority benefits).

D. NON-MONETARY REMEDIES. [CONTRACTOR] will ensure that all applicants are afforded equal employment opportunities. [CONTRACTOR] agrees to immediately cease using the selection procedures, practices, and/or policies which negatively affected the hiring of [DISFAVORED GROUP] applicants for [NAME OF JOB(S)] positions. [CONTRACTOR] agrees to continue and/or to implement the corrective actions detailed below.

1) Revised Hiring Process

(a) Eliminate Discriminatory Selection Procedures: [CONTRACTOR] agrees to immediately cease use of the [NAME OF SELECTION PROCEDURES (INCLUDING TESTS)] until they are validated in accordance with 41 C.F.R. Part 60-3. [CONTRACTOR] agrees to comply with all OFCCP regulations concerning selection procedures, including 41 C.F.R. Part 60-3. [CONTRACTOR] will not use any selection procedure that has an adverse impact, as defined in 41 C.F.R. § 3.4D, on applicants of a particular [CHARACTERISTIC OF DISFAVORED GROUP (i.e., race, sex, national origin…)] unless it properly validates the procedure pursuant to these regulations.

(b) Review and Revisions Required: [CONTRACTOR] will revise, in writing, the practices, policies and procedures it uses to

[8] Instruction: If the workforce at the location subject to this Agreement is unionized, a demand for retroactive seniority will usually affect the terms of the Collective Bargaining Agreement (CBA). In such cases, OFCCP should consult with SOL regarding the range of options available.

ADDENDUM B

select applicants for [POSITION] positions (hereinafter "Revised Hiring Process"). Specifically, [CONTRACTOR] will:

(i) create a job description and selection process for [NAME OF JOB GROUP/ POSITION]s which describes the essential functions; the minimum qualifications including required skills and certifications; and the criteria used in each step of the hiring process, including any application screens, interviews, tests, credit checks, review of criminal history, reference checks, testing, or other selection procedure;

(ii) develop specific, job-related qualification standards for [NAME OF JOB/ POSITION]s that reflect the duties, functions, and competencies of the position to minimize the potential for [[CHARACTERISTIC OF DISFAVORED GROUP (i.e., race, sex, national origin…)] stereotyping or other unlawful discrimination;

(iii) ensure all policies and qualification standards are uniformly applied to all applicants; and

(iv) list clearly on its recruiting materials and job postings the minimum qualifications, including required skills and certifications.

(c) <u>Recordkeeping and Retention:</u> [CONTRACTOR] will write and implement procedures to ensure that applicants are tracked and decisions are documented at each step in the hiring process. [CONTRACTOR] will write and implement procedures to ensure that documents are retained in accordance with 41 C.F.R. 60-1.12(a) and Part 60-3.

(d) <u>Training:</u> Within [NUMBER OF WEEKS OR MONTHS] of the Effective Date of this Agreement, [CONTRACTOR] must train all individuals involved in any way in recruiting, selecting, or tracking applicants for [NAME OF JOB] positions on the Revised Hiring Process. The training will include instruction in: the proper implementation of the recruitment, tracking and selection procedures; neutral application of the specified qualifications and criteria that will be used at each step in the hiring process; procedures to be used to document the decisions made at each step in the hiring process; and the procedures to be used to ensure that documents are retained in accordance with 41 C.F.R. § 60-1.12(a) and Part 60-3. [CONTRACTOR] will meet with management and all individuals responsible for the selection process and review its equal employment obligations and nondiscrimination policies related to hiring. Specific attention will be directed to ensure that [DISFAVORED GROUP] applicants, who benefit from the provisions of this agreement, are not retaliated against.

(e) Monitoring: [CONTRACTOR] agrees to monitor selection rates at each step of its selection process for [NAME OF JOB GROUP/ POSITION]s. Where it is determined that a selection procedure has an adverse impact, as defined in 41 C.F.R. § 3.4D, on the hiring of applicants of a particular race or gender, [CONTRACTOR] will eliminate the procedure, choose an alternative procedure, or validate the procedure in accordance with the UGESP codified at 41 C.F.R. Part 60-3. [CONTRACTOR] agrees to maintain and make available to OFCCP records concerning the impact of the selection process for [NAME OF JOB GROUP] at the [LOCATION] facility. This includes the number of persons hired by [DISFAVORED GROUP CHARACTERISTIC], the number of applicants who applied by [DISFAVORED GROUP CHARACTERISTIC], and the selection procedures utilized. This information will be maintained until the expiration of this Agreement or as long as required by the regulations, whichever is later.

2) Other Corrective Actions [INSERT RELEVANT PROVISIONS.]

▪ *For additional suggestions and model language, review the attached memo titled "Model Equitable Relief Provisions for Conciliation Agreements and Consent Decrees," which enumerates many of the equitable remedies which have proven to be highly-effective in eliminating discrimination and/or contribute to comprehensive relief.*

2. RECORDKEEPING/ ADVERSE IMPACT ANALYSIS VIOLATIONS

A. STATEMENT OF VIOLATIONS. [CONTRACTOR] failed to collect and maintain personnel and employment records and conduct adverse impact analyses in accordance with the requirements of 41 C.F.R. § 60-1.12(a) and Part 60-3.

B. OFCCP'S SPECIFIC FINDINGS. Specifically, during the review period,

▪ [CONTRACTOR] failed to maintain copies of [NUMBER AND DESCRIPTION OF MISSING RECORDS];

▪ **AND/OR** [CONTRACTOR] failed to conduct the adverse impact analyses required by 41 C.F.R. §§ 60-3.15A and 60-3.4.

▪ **OR** [CONTRACTOR] failed to conduct adverse impact analyses for each group constituting more than 2% of the labor force or 2% of the applicable workforce in accordance with the requirements of 41 C.F.R. § 60-3.15A.

- **OR** [CONTRACTOR] conducted adverse impact analyses for the overall selection process and identified statistically significant adverse impact but failed to evaluate the *individual* components of the selection process for adverse impact in accordance with the requirements of 41 C.F.R. §§ 60-3.15A and 60-3.4

C. REMEDY. [CONTRACTOR] will ensure that its records are collected and maintained in accordance with the requirements of 41 C.F.R. § 60-1.12(a) and Part 60-3. [CONTRACTOR] will conduct adverse impact analyses on at least an annual basis for the purpose of determining whether adverse impact exists against applicants based on race, sex, or ethnic group in hiring, promotion, termination, and other personnel activities. These analyses will be done by job for each group constituting more than 2% of the labor force in the relevant labor area or 2% of the applicable workforce. If adverse impact is identified in the total selection process, [CONTRACTOR] will evaluate each individual component of the selection process for adverse impact. If adverse impact is found to exist in any of the individual components of the selection process, [CONTRACTOR] will validate each such component in accordance with the Uniform Guidelines on Employee Selection Procedures or utilize selection procedures which do not result in adverse impact.

3. ACCESS/ PRODUCTION VIOLATIONS

A. STATEMENT OF VIOLATIONS. [CONTRACTOR] denied OFCCP access to its facility for the purpose of a compliance review and/or failed to provide the following: [INSERT THE DOCUMENT/DATA/INFORMATION NOT PROVIDED AND INCLUDE CITATION TO THE APPLICABLE REGUALTION(S)].

B. OFCCP'S SPECIFIC FINDINGS. Specifically, [STATE WHEN ACCESS AND/OR THE DOCUMENT/DATA/INFORMATION WAS REQUESTED AND THE DATE AND SUBSTANCE OF THE CONTRACTOR'S RESPONSE EITHER VERBAL OR IN WRITING].

C. REMEDY. [CONTRACTOR] will furnish all information and reports required by [EXECUTIVE ORDER 11246, SECTION 503, AND/OR VEVRAA] and by the rules, regulations and orders of the Secretary of Labor, and will permit OFCCP access to its books, records, and accounts for purposes of investigation to ascertain compliance with such rules, regulations, and orders.

Part IV. <u>REPORTS REQUIRED</u>

1. [CONTRACTOR] must submit the documents and reports described below to: [_____], District Director of OFCCP, [ADDRESS].

A. Within [TIME PERIOD; typically "60 calendar days of the Effective Date of this Agreement"] [CONTRACTOR] must submit a copy of the written Revised Hiring Process described in section ____.

ADDENDUM B

Model CA for Hiring, Recordkeeping, Access, and other issues

B. Within [TIME PERIOD] of the Effective Date of this Agreement, [CONTRACTOR] must submit documentation that all managers, supervisors and other personnel involved in recruiting, selecting, or tracking applicants for [POSITION]s have been trained on the Revised Hiring Process. The documentation must include the dates of the training, the names and job titles of all attendees, an outline of the topics discussed in the training, and the name and job title of each person who conducted the training.

C. Within the prescribed timeframes, [CONTRACTOR] must submit all documents and information referenced in sections ____.[9]

D. [CONTRACTOR] must submit a progress report covering each six month period this Agreement is in effect. The first progress report will be due seven months after the Effective Date of this Agreement and must cover the six-month period beginning with the Effective Date. Each subsequent report must cover the successive six-month period, and must be submitted within 30 calendar days after the close of that six-month period. [CONTRACTOR] will submit the following in each progress report: [INSERT A LIST OF THE DATA AND ANALYSES REQUIRED BY THE PRECEDING PART, THESE MAY INCLUDE:]

1) Documentation of monetary payments to all Eligible Class Members as specified in section ___. The documentation must include the names of Eligible Class Members who were paid, and, for each Eligible Class Member, the number and the amount of the check and the date the check cleared the bank. [CONTRACTOR] must provide OFCCP with copies of all canceled checks upon request;

2) Documentation of specific hiring activity for Eligible Class Members who were hired as [POSITION]s in accordance with this Agreement, including name, date of hire, job title hired into, rate of pay and proof of retroactive seniority and benefits;

3) For Eligible Class Members who were considered for employment but were not hired, [CONTRACTOR] will provide the reason for non-placement along with all relevant documentation (e.g., documentation that the Eligible Class Member declined a job offer);

4) The total number of applicants and hires and the breakdown by race, gender and ethnic group of applicants and hires for [POSITION] positions during the reporting period, including all temporary, part time, and seasonal workers who were referred to and/or assigned to work at [CONTRACTOR] by a staffing firm or employment agency;

---

[9] Instruction: Such documents and information may include letters returned as undeliverable, a list of individuals in the affected class who have not returned a signed Interest Form before the deadline, and a list of Eligible Class Members.

Model CA for Hiring, Recordkeeping, Access, and other issues

5) For [POSITION]s, the results of [CONTRACTOR]'s analysis as to whether its total selection process has adverse impact, as defined in 41 C.F.R. § 60-3.4D, on those members of groups set forth in 41 C.F.R. § 60-3.4B (for purposes of the adverse impact analysis, the [CONTRACTOR] must not include hires made of Eligible Class Members pursuant to this Agreement in that analysis; [CONTRACTOR] must combine the data for the current report with the data from the previous report(s) to analyze at least a 12-month period);

6) For each case where the total selection process has an adverse impact, as defined in 41 C.F.R. § 60-3.4D, the results of [CONTRACTOR]'s evaluation of the individual components of the selection process for adverse impact; and/ or

7) The actions taken by [CONTRACTOR] upon determining that any component of the selection process has an adverse impact on members of groups set forth in section __ above.

2. [CONTRACTOR] will retain all records and data pertinent to the violations resolved by this Agreement and/ or used to prepare required reports until this Agreement expires or as long as required by OFCCP's regulations, whichever date occurs later (or "whichever time period is longer").

Part V. SIGNATURES

This Conciliation Agreement is hereby executed by and between the OFCCP and [CONTRACTOR].

______________________________	______________________________
[NAME of Official] [POSITION] [CONTRACTOR]	[NAME] Regional Director[10] OFCCP
Date:________________________	Date:________________________

____

[NAME of Union Official – only if appropriate]

Date: ________________________

[10] Instruction: District Directors have been delegated signatory authority for CAs not containing a finding of discrimination. As to those agreements, substitute "District Director" on the signature line.

ADDENDUM B

Model CA for Hiring, Recordkeeping, Access and other issues

ATTACHMENT __

NOTICE TO AFFECTED CLASS

Dear [NAME]:

[CONTRACTOR] ("CONTRACTOR") and the Department of Labor's Office of Federal Contract Compliance Programs ("OFCCP") have entered into a Conciliation Agreement ("Agreement") to remedy the violations of [EXECUTIVE ORDER 11246 ("E.O. 11246"), SECTION 503 OF THE REHABILITATION ACT ("SECTION 503"), VIETNAM VETERANS READJUSTMENT ASSISTANCE ACT ("VEVRAA")] that OFCCP found during a compliance review of [CONTRACTOR]'s [LOCATION] facility. [INSERT STATEMENT OF THE VIOLATION FROM PART III OF THE CA.] [***Sample*:** OFCCP's analysis of [CONTRACTOR]'s hiring process and selection procedures revealed that during the period of [DATE] through [DATE] ("review period") [CONTRACTOR] discriminated against [DISFAVORED GROUP(S)] applicants for [NAME OF JOB(S)/ POSITION(S)]. OFCCP found that there was a disparity in the hiring of [NAME OF JOB(S)] based on [RACE, GENDER, NATIONAL ORIGIN…].**]** [CONTRACTOR] has not admitted to any violation of [E.O. 11246, SECTION 503, AND/ OR VEVRAA] and there has not been any adjudicated finding that [CONTRACTOR] violated any laws. OFCCP and [CONTRACTOR] entered into the Agreement to resolve the matter without resorting to further legal proceedings. You have been identified as an individual who applied for a [POSITION] during that time period, but was not hired.

As part of this Agreement, you are eligible to receive a distribution of at least $_______ less lawful payroll deductions. Under the terms of this Agreement it may take up to [NUMBER] months from the date of this letter before you receive your distribution. In order to be eligible for a payment, you must complete, sign, and return the enclosed Information Verification and Employment Interest Form. You should complete and mail back the form as soon as possible; it *must* be postmarked to the address below no later than [TIME PERIOD (typically 30-60 days)] after the date this Notice was mailed out (postmarked)for you to be entitled to participate in this settlement:

(NAME)
(POSITION)
(CONTRACTOR)
(ADDRESS)

You may use the enclosed postage-paid return envelope to return the completed and signed Information Verification and Employment Interest Form.

In addition to the monetary distribution, [CONTRACTOR] will be making job offers for [POSITIONS] to a limited number of individuals receiving this notification. It is not certain that you will receive a job offer. If you are still interested in employment with [CONTRACTOR], please check the appropriate box on the enclosed Information Verification and Employment Interest Form. Those receiving this notice will be considered for [POSITION] positions in the order that [CONTRACTOR] receives the Information Verification and Employment Interest Form expressing an interest in employment. All individual hired pursuant to this Agreement will be provided with retroactive seniority for purposes of benefits (or $__ in lieu of retroactive seniority). If you have any questions you may call [NAME] at [CONTRACTOR] at [PHONE NUMBER], or OFCCP Compliance Officer [NAME] at [PHONE NUMBER]. Your call will be returned as soon as possible.

IF YOU FAIL TO COMPLETE AND RETURN THE ENCLOSED DOCUMENTS TO [CONTRACTOR] WITHIN __ DAYS OF THE DATE THE ENVELOPE CONTAINING THIS NOTICE WAS POSTMARKED, YOU WILL NOT BE ELIGIBLE TO RECEIVE A PAYMENT OR TO BE CONSIDERED FOR A JOB OFFER.

Sincerely,

(NAME)

Enclosures

Information Verification and Employment Interest Form

Release of Claims Under Executive Order 11246-**[DO NOT INCLUDE A RELEASE OF CLAIMS UNLESS REQUESTED BY THE CONTRACTOR. SEE ATTACHMENT 3 FOR A SAMPLE RELEASE.]**

ADDENDUM B

Model CA for Hiring, Recordkeeping, Access and other issues

ATTACHMENT __

INFORMATION VERIFICATION & EMPLOYMENT INTEREST FORM

You must complete this form in order to be eligible for the monetary payment and/or employment opportunities under the terms of the Conciliation Agreement ("Agreement") between [CONTRACTOR][("CONTRACTOR")] and the Department of Labor's Office of Federal Contract Compliance Programs. Please print legibly, except for the signature.

Name: ____

Address: ____

Telephone Nos.: Home______________Cell_______________Work_______________

Notify [CONTRACTOR] at the address below if your address or phone number changes within the next twelve months.

Your Social Security Number (to be used for tax purposes only): ______-________-______

For purposes of this settlement, it is necessary to verify your [GENDER and/or RACE]:

Caucasian ☐ African American ☐ Hispanic ☐ Asian ☐ Native American ☐

Male ☐ Female ☐

Please indicate below whether you are currently interested in employment in a [POSITION] with [CONTRACTOR]. If you complete, sign, and return this Information Verification and Employment Interest Form, you remain eligible for the monetary payment whether or not you are interested in employment at this time.

☐ Yes, I am still interested in employment with [CONTRACTOR] as a [POSITION].

☐ No, I am not currently interested in employment with [CONTRACTOR] as a [POSITION].

IF YOU FAIL TO COMPLETE AND RETURN THE ENCLOSED DOCUMENTS TO THE ADDRESS BELOW WITHIN __ DAYS OF THE DATE THE ENVELOPE CONTAINING THIS NOTICE WAS POSTMARKED, YOU WILL NOT BE ELIGIBLE TO RECEIVE A PAYMENT OR TO BE CONSIDERED FOR A JOB OFFER.

(NAME)

ADDENDUM B

Model CA for Hiring, Recordkeeping, Access and other issues
(ADDRESS)

I, ________________________________, certify the above is true and correct.

(print name)

____ _______________

Signature Date

ADDENDUM B

Model CA for Hiring, Recordkeeping, Access and other issues

ATTACHMENT __

RELEASE OF CLAIMS UNDER EXECUTIVE ORDER 11246

This Release of Claims under Executive Order 11246 ("Release") is a legal document. This document states that in return for [CONTRACTOR] ("CONTRACTOR") paying you money, you agree that you will not file any lawsuit against [CONTRACTOR] for allegedly violating Executive Order 11246 in connection with its selection procedures for applicants for [POSITIONS] positions. It also says that [CONTRACTOR] does not admit it violated any laws. This Release says you had sufficient time to look at the document, to talk with others about the document, including an attorney if you choose, and that no one pressured you into signing the document. Finally, it says that if you do not sign and return the document by a certain date, you will not receive any money.

In consideration of the payment of at least $ ______ (less deductions required by law) by [CONTRACTOR] to me, which I agree is acceptable, I ________________________________ agree to the following:
print name

I.

I hereby waive, release and forever discharge[CONTRACTOR], its predecessors, successors, related entities, parents, subsidiaries, affiliates and organizations, and its and their shareholders, directors, officers, employees, agents, successors, and assigns, of and from any and all actions, causes of action, damages, liabilities, and claims arising out of or actionable under Executive Order 11246, as amended, which I or my representatives (heirs, executors, administrators, or assigns) have or may have which relate in any way to my non-selection for employment as a [POSITION] on the basis of my [RACE, GENDER, ETC] at any time through the effective date of this Release.

II.

I understand that [CONTRACTOR] denies that it treated me unlawfully or unfairly in any way and that [CONTRACTOR] entered into a Conciliation Agreement with the U.S. Department of Labor, Office of Federal Contract Compliance Programs ("OFCCP") and agreed to make the payment described above to resolve alleged disparities in hiring and to resolve the matter without further legal proceedings in the compliance review initiated by OFCCP on [INSERT DATE]. I further agree that the payment of the aforesaid sum by [CONTRACTOR] to me is not to be construed as an admission of any liability by [CONTRACTOR].

III.

I declare that I have read this Release and that I have had a full opportunity to consider and understand its terms and to consult with my advisors and seek legal advice. I further declare that I have decided of my own free will to sign this Release.

IV.

ADDENDUM B

Model CA for Hiring, Recordkeeping, Access and other issues

I understand that if I do not sign this Release and return it to [CONTACTOR] [ON OR BEFORE ___ (DATE)/ WITHIN __ DAYS OF THE DATE THE ENVELOPE CONTAINING THIS RELEASE WAS POSTMARKED], I will not be entitled to receive any payment (less deductions required by law) from [CONTRACTOR].

IN WITNESS WHEREOF, I have signed this document on this ________ day of _________________________, 20__.

____

Signature

CHAPTER 60

OFFICE OF FEDERAL CONTRACT COMPLIANCE PROGRAMS, EQUAL EMPLOYMENT OPPORTUNITY, DEPARTMENT OF LABOR

CHAPTER 60—OFFICE OF FEDERAL CONTRACT COMPLIANCE PROGRAMS, EQUAL EMPLOYMENT OPPORTUNITY, DEPARTMENT OF LABOR

PART 60–1—OBLIGATIONS OF CONTRACTORS AND SUBCONTRACTORS

Subpart A—Preliminary Matters; Equal Opportunity Clause; Compliance Reports

Subpart B—General Enforcement; Compliance Review and Complaint Procedure

Subpart C—Ancillary Matters

AUTHORITY: Sec. 201, E.O. 11246, 30 FR 12319, 3 CFR, 1964–1965 Comp., p. 339, as amended by E.O. 11375, 32 FR 14303, 3 CFR, 1966–1970 Comp., p. 684, E.O. 12086, 43 FR 46501, 3 CFR, 1978 Comp., p. 230 and E.O. 13279, 67 FR 77141, 3 CFR, 2002 Comp., p. 258.

SOURCE: 43 FR 49240, Oct. 20, 1978, unless otherwise noted.

Subpart A—Preliminary Matters; Equal Opportunity Clause; Compliance Reports

§ 60–1.1 Purpose and application.

The purpose of the regulations in this part is to achieve the aims of parts II, III, and IV of Executive Order 11246 for the promotion and insuring of equal opportunity for all persons, without regard to race, color, religion, sex, or national origin, employed or seeking employment with Government contractors or with contractors performing under federally assisted construction contracts. The regulations in this part apply to all contracting agencies of the Government and to contractors and subcontractors who perform under Government contracts, to the extent set forth in this part. The regulations in this part also apply to all agencies of the Government administering programs involving Federal financial assistance which may include a construction contract, and to all contractors and subcontractors performing under construction contracts which are related to any such programs. The procedures set forth in the regulations in this part govern all disputes relative to a contractor's compliance with his obligations under the equal opportunity clause regardless of whether or not his contract contains a "Disputes" clause. Failure of a contractor or applicant to comply with any provision of the regulations in this part shall be grounds for the imposition of any or all of the sanctions authorized by the order. The regulations in this part do not apply to any action taken to effect compliance with respect to employment practices subject to title VI of the Civil Rights Act of 1964. The rights and remedies of the Government hereunder are not exclusive and do not affect rights and remedies provided elsewhere by law, regulation, or contract; neither do the regulations limit the exercise by the Secretary or Government agencies of powers not herein specifically set forth, but granted to them by the order.

§ 60–1.2 Administrative responsibility.

The Deputy Assistant Secretary has been delegated authority and assigned responsibility for carrying out the responsibilities assigned to the Secretary under the Executive order. All correspondence regarding the order should be directed to the Deputy Assistant Secretary, Office of Federal Contract Compliance Programs, Employment Standards Administration, U.S. Department of Labor, 200 Constitution Avenue NW., Washington, DC 20210.

[43 FR 49240, Oct. 20, 1978, as amended at 62 FR 66971, Dec. 22, 1997]

§ 60–1.3 Definitions.

Administering agency means any department, agency and establishment in the executive branch of the Government, including any wholly owned Government corporation, which administers a program involving federally assisted construction contracts.

Administrative law judge means an administrative law judge appointed as provided in 5 U.S.C. 3105 and Subpart B of Part 930 of Title 5 of the *Code of Federal Regulations* (see 37 FR 16787) and qualified to preside at hearings under 5 U.S.C. 557.

Agency means any contracting or any administering agency of the Government.

Applicant means an applicant for Federal assistance involving a construction contract, or other participant in a program involving a construction contract as determined by regulation of an administering agency. The term also includes such persons after they become recipients of such Federal assistance.

Compliance evaluation means any one or combination of actions OFCCP may take to examine a Federal contractor or subcontractor's compliance with one or more of the requirements of Executive Order 11246.

Construction work means the construction, rehabilitation, alteration, conversion, extension, demolition or repair of buildings, highways, or other changes or improvements to real property, including facilities providing utility services. The term also includes the supervision, inspection, and other onsite functions incidental to the actual construction.

Contract means any Government contract or subcontract or any federally assisted construction contract or subcontract.

Contracting agency means any department, agency, establishment, or instrumentality in the executive branch of the Government, including any wholly owned Government corporation, which enters into contracts.

Contractor means, unless otherwise indicated, a prime contractor or subcontractor.

Deputy Assistant Secretary means the Deputy Assistant Secretary for Federal Contract Compliance, United States Department of Labor, or his or her designee.

Equal opportunity clause means the contract provisions set forth in § 60–1.4 (a) or (b), as appropriate.

Federally assisted construction contract means any agreement or modification thereof between any applicant and a person for construction work which is paid for in whole or in part with funds obtained from the Government or borrowed on the credit of the Government pursuant to any Federal program involving a grant, contract, loan, insurance, or guarantee, or undertaken pursuant to any Federal program involving such grant, contract, loan, insurance, or guarantee, or any application or modification thereof approved by the Government for a grant, contract, loan, insurance, or guarantee under which the applicant itself participates in the construction work.

Government means the government of the United States of America.

Government contract means any agreement or modification thereof between any contracting agency and any person for the purchase, sale or use of personal property or nonpersonal services. The term "personal property," as used in this section, includes supplies, and contracts for the use of real property (such as lease arrangements), unless the contract for the use of real property itself constitutes real property (such as easements). The term "nonpersonal services" as used in this section includes, but is not limited to, the following services: Utilities, construction, transportation, research, insurance, and fund depository. The term *Government contract* does not include:

(1) Agreements in which the parties stand in the relationship of employer and employee; and

(2) Federally assisted construction contracts.

Internet Applicant. (1) Internet Applicant means any individual as to whom the following four criteria are satisfied:

(i) The individual submits an expression of interest in employment through the Internet or related electronic data technologies;

(ii) The contractor considers the individual for employment in a particular position;

(iii) The individual's expression of interest indicates the individual possesses the basic qualifications for the position; and,

(iv) The individual at no point in the contractor's selection process prior to receiving an offer of employment from the contractor, removes himself or herself from further consideration or otherwise indicates that he or she is no longer interested in the position.

(2) For purposes of paragraph (1)(i) of this definition, "submits an expression of interest in employment through the Internet or related electronic data technologies," includes all expressions of interest, regardless of the means or manner in which the expression of interest is made, if the contractor considers expressions of interest made through the Internet or related electronic data technologies in the recruiting or selection processes for that particular position.

(i) Example A: Contractor A posts on its web site an opening for a Mechanical Engineer position and encourages potential applicants to complete an on-line profile if they are interested in being considered for that position. The web site also advises potential applicants that they can send a hard copy resume to the HR Manager with a cover letter identifying the position for which they would like to be considered. Because Contractor A considers both Internet and traditional expressions of interest for the Mechanical Engineer position, both the individuals who completed a personal profile and those who sent a paper resume and cover letter to Contractor A meet this part of the definition of Internet Applicant for this position.

(ii) Example B: Contractor B posts on its web site an opening for the Accountant II position and encourages potential applicants to complete an on-line profile if they are interested in being considered for that position. Contractor B also receives a large number of unsolicited paper resumes in the mail each year. Contractor B scans these paper resumes into an internal resume database that also includes all the on-line profiles that individuals completed for various jobs (including possibly for the Accountant II position) throughout the year. To find potential applicants for the Accountant II position, Contractor B searches the internal resume database for individuals who have the basic qualifications for the Accountant II position. Because Contractor B considers both Internet and traditional expressions of interest for the Accountant II position, both the individuals who completed a personal profile and those who sent a paper resume and cover letter to the employer meet this part of the definition of Internet Applicant for this position.

(iii) Example C: Contractor C advertises for Mechanics in a local newspaper and instructs interested candidates to mail their resumes to the employer's address. Walk-in applications also are permitted. Contractor C considers only paper resumes and application forms for the Mechanic position, therefore no individual meets this part of the definition of an Internet Applicant for this position.

(3) For purposes of paragraph (1)(ii) of this definition, "considers the individual for employment in a particular position," means that the contractor assesses the substantive information provided in the expression of interest with respect to any qualifications involved with a particular position. A contractor may establish a protocol under which it refrains from considering expressions of interest that are not submitted in accordance with standard procedures the contractor establishes. Likewise, a contractor may establish a protocol under which it refrains from considering expressions of interest, such as unsolicited resumes, that are not submitted with respect to a particular position. If there are a large number of expressions of interest, the contractor does not "consider the individual for employment in a particular position" by using data management techniques that do not depend on assessment of qualifications, such as random sampling or absolute numerical limits, to reduce the number of expressions of interest to be considered,

provided that the sample is appropriate in terms of the pool of those submitting expressions of interest.

(4) For purposes of paragraph (1)(iii) of this definition, "basic qualifications" means qualifications—

(i)(A) That the contractor advertises (e.g., posts on its web site a description of the job and the qualifications involved) to potential applicants that they must possess in order to be considered for the position, or

(B) For which the contractor establishes criteria in advance by making and maintaining a record of such qualifications for the position prior to considering any expression of interest for that particular position if the contractor does not advertise for the position but instead uses an alternative device to find individuals for consideration (e.g., through an external resume database), and

(ii) That meet all of the following three conditions:

(A) The qualifications must be noncomparative features of a job seeker. For example, a qualification of three years' experience in a particular position is a noncomparative qualification; a qualification that an individual have one of the top five number of years' experience among a pool of job seekers is a comparative qualification.

(B) The qualifications must be objective; they do not depend on the contractor's subjective judgment. For example, "a Bachelor's degree in Accounting" is objective, while "a technical degree from a good school" is not. A basic qualification is objective if a third-party, with the contractor's technical knowledge, would be able to evaluate whether the job seeker possesses the qualification without more information about the contractor's judgment.

(C) The qualifications must be relevant to performance of the particular position and enable the contractor to accomplish business-related goals.

(5) For purposes of paragraph (1)(iv) of this definition, a contractor may conclude that an individual has removed himself or herself from further consideration, or has otherwise indicated that he or she is no longer interested in the position for which the contractor has considered the individual, based on the individual's express statement that he or she is no longer interested in the position, or on the individual's passive demonstration of disinterest shown through repeated non-responsiveness to inquiries from the contractor about interest in the position. A contractor also may determine that an individual has removed himself or herself from further consideration or otherwise indicated that he or she is no longer interested in the position for which the contractor has considered the individual based on information the individual provided in the expression of interest, such as salary requirements or preferences as to type of work or location of work, provided that the contractor has a uniformly and consistently applied policy or procedure of not considering similarly situated job seekers. If a large number of individuals meet the basic qualifications for the position, a contractor may also use data management techniques, such as random sampling or absolute numerical limits, to limit the number of individuals who must be contacted to determine their interest in the position, provided that the sample is appropriate in terms of the pool of those meeting the basic qualifications.

Minority group as used herein shall include, where appropriate, female employees and prospective female employees.

Modification means any alteration in the terms and conditions of a contract, including supplemental agreements, amendments, and extensions.

Order, Executive order, or *Executive Order 11246* means parts II, III, and IV of the Executive Order 11246 dated September 24, 1965 (30 FR 12319), any Executive order amending such order, and any other Executive order superseding such order.

Person means any natural person, corporation, partnership, unincorporated association, State or local government, and any agency, instrumentality, or subdivision of such a government.

Prime contractor means any person holding a contract and, for the purposes of Subpart B of this part, any person who has held a contract subject to the order.

Recruiting and training agency means any person who refers workers to any contractor or subcontractor or who provides for employment by any contractor or subcontractor.

Rules, regulations, and relevant orders of the Secretary of Labor used in paragraph (4) of the equal opportunity clause means rules, regulations, and relevant orders of the Secretary of Labor or his designee issued pursuant to the order.

Secretary means the Secretary of Labor, U.S. Department of Labor, or his or her designee.

Site of construction means the general physical location of any building, highway, or other change or improvement to real property which is undergoing construction, rehabilitation, alteration, conversion, extension, demolition, or repair and any temporary location or facility at which a contractor, subcontractor, or other participating party meets a demand or performs a function relating to the contract or subcontract.

Subcontract means any agreement or arrangement between a contractor and any person (in which the parties do not stand in the relationship of an employer and an employee):

(1) For the purchase, sale or use of personal property or nonpersonal services which, in whole or in part, is necessary to the performance of any one or more contracts; or

(2) Under which any portion of the contractor's obligation under any one or more contracts is performed, undertaken or assumed.

Subcontractor means any person holding a subcontract and, for the purposes of Subpart B of this part, any person who has held a subcontract subject to the order. The term "first-tier subcontractor" refers to a subcontractor holding a subcontract with a prime contractor.

United States as used herein shall include the several States, the District of Columbia, the Commonwealth of Puerto Rico, the Panama Canal Zone, and the possessions of the United States.

United States, as used herein, shall include the several States, the District of Columbia, the Virgin Islands, the Commonwealth of Puerto Rico, Guam, American Samoa, the Commonwealth of the Northern Mariana Islands, and Wake Island.

[43 FR 49240, Oct. 20, 1978, as amended at 61 FR 19988, May 3, 1996; 62 FR 44188, Aug. 19, 1997; 62 FR 66971, Dec. 22, 1997; 70 FR 58961, Oct. 7, 2005]

§ 60–1.4 Equal opportunity clause.

(a) *Government contracts.* Except as otherwise provided, each contracting agency shall include the following equal opportunity clause contained in section 202 of the order in each of its Government contracts (and modifications thereof if not included in the original contract):

During the performance of this contract, the contractor agrees as follows:

(1) The contractor will not discriminate against any employee or applicant for employment because of race, color, religion, sex, or national origin. The contractor will take affirmative action to ensure that applicants are employed, and that employees are treated during employment, without regard to their race, color, religion, sex, or national origin. Such action shall include, but not be limited to the following: Employment, upgrading, demotion, or transfer, recruitment or recruitment advertising; layoff or termination; rates of pay or other forms of compensation; and selection for training, including apprenticeship. The contractor agrees to post in conspicuous places, available to employees and applicants for employment, notices to be provided by the contracting officer setting forth the provisions of this nondiscrimination clause.

(2) The contractor will, in all solicitations or advertisements for employees placed by or on behalf of the contractor, state that all qualified applicants will receive consideration for employment without regard to race, color, religion, sex, or national origin.

(3) The contractor will send to each labor union or representative of workers with which he has a collective bargaining agreement or other contract or understanding, a notice to be provided by the agency contracting officer, advising the labor union or workers' representative of the contractor's commitments under section 202 of Executive Order 11246 of September 24, 1965, and shall post copies of the notice in conspicuous places available to employees and applicants for employment.

(4) The contractor will comply with all provisions of Executive Order 11246 of September 24, 1965, and of the rules, regulations, and relevant orders of the Secretary of Labor.

(5) The contractor will furnish all information and reports required by Executive Order 11246 of September 24, 1965, and by the rules,

regulations, and orders of the Secretary of Labor, or pursuant thereto, and will permit access to his books, records, and accounts by the contracting agency and the Secretary of Labor for purposes of investigation to ascertain compliance with such rules, regulations, and orders.

(6) In the event of the contractor's noncompliance with the nondiscrimination clauses of this contract or with any of such rules, regulations, or orders, this contract may be canceled, terminated or suspended in whole or in part and the contractor may be declared ineligible for further Government contracts in accordance with procedures authorized in Executive Order 11246 of September 24, 1965, and such other sanctions may be imposed and remedies invoked as provided in Executive Order 11246 of September 24, 1965, or by rule, regulation, or order of the Secretary of Labor, or as otherwise provided by law.

(7) the contractor will include the provisions of paragraphs (1) through (7) in every subcontract or purchase order unless exempted by rules, regulations, or orders of the Secretary of Labor issued pursuant to section 204 of Executive Order 11246 of September 24, 1965, so that such provisions will be binding upon each subcontractor or vendor. The contractor will take such action with respect to any subcontract or purchase order as may be directed by the Secretary of Labor as a means of enforcing such provisions including sanctions for noncompliance: *Provided, however*, that in the event the contractor becomes involved in, or is threatened with, litigation with a subcontractor or vendor as a result of such direction, the contractor may request the United States to enter into such litigation to protect the interests of the United States.

(b) *Federally assisted construction contracts.* (1) Except as otherwise provided, each administering agency shall require the inclusion of the following language as a condition of any grant, contract, loan, insurance, or guarantee involving federally assisted construction which is not exempt from the requirements of the equal opportunity clause:

The applicant hereby agrees that it will incorporate or cause to be incorporated into any contract for construction work, or modification thereof, as defined in the regulations of the Secretary of Labor at 41 CFR Chapter 60, which is paid for in whole or in part with funds obtained from the Federal Government or borrowed on the credit of the Federal Government pursuant to a grant, contract, loan insurance, or guarantee, or undertaken pursuant to any Federal program involving such grant, contract, loan, insurance, or guarantee, the following equal opportunity clause:

During the performance of this contract, the contractor agrees as follows:

(1) The contractor will not discriminate against any employee or applicant for employment because of race, color, religion, sex, or national origin. The contractor will take affirmative action to ensure that applicants are employed, and that employees are treated during employment without regard to their race, color, religion, sex, or national origin. such action shall include, but not be limited to the following: Employment, upgrading, demotion, or transfer; recruitment or recruitment advertising; layoff or termination; rates of pay or other forms of compensation; and selection for training, including apprenticeship. The contractor agrees to post in conspicuous places, available to employees and applicants for employment, notices to be provided setting forth the provisions of this nondiscrimination clause.

(2) The contractor will, in all solicitations or advertisements for employees placed by or on behalf of the contractor, state that all qualified applicants will receive considerations for employment without regard to race, color, religion, sex, or national origin.

(3) The contractor will send to each labor union or representative of workers with which he has a collective bargaining agreement or other contract or understanding, a notice to be provided advising the said labor union or workers' representatives of the contractor's commitments under this section, and shall post copies of the notice in conspicuous places available to employees and applicants for employment.

(4) The contrator will comply with all provisions of Executive Order 11246 of September 24, 1965, and of the rules, regulations, and relevant orders of the Secretary of Labor.

(5) The contractor will furnish all information and reports required by Executive Order 11246 of September 24, 1965, and by rules, regulations, and orders of the Secretary of Labor, or pursuant thereto, and will permit access to his books, records, and accounts by the administering agency and the Secretary of Labor for purposes of investigation to ascertain compliance with such rules, regulations, and orders.

(6) In the event of the contractor's noncompliance with the nondiscrimination clauses of this contract or with any of the said rules, regulations, or orders, this contract may be canceled, terminated, or suspended in whole or in part and the contractor may be declared ineligible for further Government contracts or federally assisted construction contracts in accordance with procedures authorized in Executive Order 11246 of September 24, 1965, and such other sanctions may be imposed and remedies invoked as provided in Executive Order 11246 of

September 24, 1965, or by rule, regulation, or order of the Secretary of Labor, or as otherwise provided by law.

(7) The contractor will include the portion of the sentence immediately preceding paragraph (1) and the provisions of paragraphs (1) through (7) in every subcontract or purchase order unless exempted by rules, regulations, or orders of the Secretary of Labor issued pursuant to section 204 of Executive Order 11246 of September 24, 1965, so that such provisions will be binding upon each subcontractor or vendor. The contractor will take such action with respect to any subcontract or purchase order as the administering agency may direct as a means of enforcing such provisions, including sanctions for noncompliance: *Provided, however,* That in the event a contractor becomes involved in, or is threatened with, litigation with a subcontractor or vendor as a result of such direction by the administering agency the contractor may request the United States to enter into such litigation to protect the interests of the United States.

The applicant further agrees that it will be bound by the above equal opportunity clause with respect to its own employment practices when it participates in federally assisted construction work: *Provided,* That if the applicant so participating is a State or local government, the above equal opportunity clause is not applicable to any agency, instrumentality or subdivision of such government which does not participate in work on or under the contract.

The applicant agrees that it will assist and cooperate actively with the administering agency and the Secretary of Labor in obtaining the compliance of contractors and subcontractors with the equal opportunity clause and the rules, regulations, and relevant orders of the Secretary of Labor, that it will furnish the administering agency and the Secretary of Labor such information as they may require for the supervision of such compliance, and that it will otherwise assist the administering agency in the discharge of the agency's primary responsibility for securing compliance.

The applicant further agrees that it will refrain from entering into any contract or contract modification subject to Executive Order 11246 of September 24, 1965, with a contractor debarred from, or who has not demonstrated eligibility for, Government contracts and federally assisted construction contracts pursuant to the Executive order and will carry out such sanctions and penalties for violation of the equal opportunity clause as may be imposed upon contractors and subcontractors by the administering agency or the Secretary of Labor pursuant to Part II, Subpart D of the Executive order. In addition, the applicant agrees that if it fails or refuses to comply with these undertakings, the administering agency may take any or all of the following actions: Cancel, terminate, or suspend in whole or in part this grant (contract, loan, insurance, guarantee); refrain from extending any further assistance to the applicant under the program with respect to which the failure or refund occurred until satisfactory assurance of future compliance has been received from such applicant; and refer the case to the Department of Justice for appropriate legal proceedings.

(c) *Subcontracts.* Each nonexempt prime contractor or subcontractor shall include the equal opportunity clause in each of its nonexempt subcontracts.

(d) *Incorporation by reference.* The equal opportunity clause may be incorporated by reference in all Government contracts and subcontracts, including Government bills of lading, transportation requests, contracts for deposit of Government funds, and contracts for issuing and paying U.S. savings bonds and notes, and such other contracts and subcontracts as the Deputy Assistant Secretary may designate.

(e) *Incorporation by operation of the order.* By operation of the order, the equal opportunity clause shall be considered to be a part of every contract and subcontract required by the order and the regulations in this part to include such a clause whether or not it is physically incorporated in such contracts and whether or not the contract between the agency and the contractor is written.

(f) *Adaptation of language.* Such necessary changes in language may be made in the equal opportunity clause as shall be appropriate to identify properly the parties and their undertakings.

[43 FR 49240, Oct. 20, 1978, as amended at 62 FR 66971, Dec. 22, 1997]

§ 60–1.5 Exemptions.

(a) *General*—(1) *Transactions of $10,000 or under.* Contracts and subcontracts not exceeding $10,000, other than Government bills of lading, and other than contracts and subcontracts with depositories of Federal funds in any amount and with financial institutions which are issuing and paying agents for U.S. savings bonds and savings notes, are exempt from the requirements of the equal opportunity clause. In determining the applicability of this exemption to any federally assisted construction contract, or subcontract thereunder, the amount of such contract or subcontract rather than the amount of the Federal financial assistance shall govern. No agency, contractor, or subcontractor shall procure supplies or services in a manner so as to avoid applicability of the equal opportunity clause: *Provided*, that where a contractor has contracts or subcontracts with the Government in any 12-month period which have an aggregate total value (or can reasonably be expected to have an aggregate total value) exceeding $10,000, the $10,000 or under exemption does not apply, and the contracts are subject to the order and the regulations issued pursuant thereto regardless of whether any single contract exceeds $10,000.

(2) *Contracts and subcontracts for indefinite quantities.* With respect to contracts and subcontracts for indefinite quantities (including, but not limited to, open end contracts, requirement-type contracts, Federal Supply Schedule contracts, "call-type" contracts, and purchase notice agreements), the equal opportunity clause shall be included unless the purchaser has reason to believe that the amount to be ordered in any year under such contract will not exceed $10,000. The applicability of the equal opportunity clause shall be determined by the purchaser at the time of award for the first year, and annually thereafter for succeeding years, if any. Notwithstanding the above, the equal opportunity clause shall be applied to such contract whenever the amount of a single order exceeds $10,000. Once the equal opportunity clause is determined to be applicable, the contract shall continue to be subject to such clause for its duration, regardless of the amounts ordered, or reasonably expected to be ordered in any year.

(3) *Work outside the United States.* Contracts and subcontracts are exempt from the requirements of the equal opportunity clause with regard to work performed outside the United States by employees who were not recruited within the United States.

(4) *Contracts with State or local governments.* The requirements of the equal opportunity clause in any contract or subcontract with a State or local government (or any agency, instrumentality or subdivision thereof) shall not be applicable to any agency, instrumentality or subdivision of such government which does not participate in work on or under the contract or subcontract. In addition, any agency, instrumentality or subdivision of such government, except for educational institutions and medical facilities, are exempt from the requirements of filing the annual compliance report provided for by § 60–1.7(a)(1) and maintaining a written affirmative action compliance program prescribed by § 60–1.40 and Part 60–2 of this chapter.

(5) *Contracts with religious entities.* Section 202 of Executive Order 11246, as amended, shall not apply to a Government contractor or subcontractor that is a religious corporation, association, educational institution, or society, with respect to the employment of individuals of a particular religion to perform work connected with the carrying on by such corporation, association, educational institution, or society of its activities. Such contractors and subcontractors are not exempted or excused from complying with the other requirements contained in this Order.

(6) *Contracts with certain educational institutions.* It shall not be a violation of the equal opportunity clause for a school, college, university, or other educational institution or institution of learning to hire and employ employees of a particular religion if such school, college, university, or other educational institution or institution of learning is, in whole or in substantial part, owned, supported, controlled, or managed by a particular religion or by a particular religious corporation, association, or society, or if the curriculum of such school, college, university, or other educational institution or institution of learning is directed toward the propagation of a particular religion. The primary thrust of this provision is directed at religiously oriented church-related colleges and universities and should be so interpreted.

(7) *Work on or near Indian reservations.* It shall not be a violation of the equal opportunity clause for a construction or nonconstruction contractor to extend a publicly announced preference in employment to Indians living on or near an Indian reservation in connection with employment opportunities on or near an Indian reservation. The use of the word "near" would include all that area where a person seeking employment could reasonably be expected to commute to and from in the course of a work day. Contractors or subcontractors extending such a preference shall not, however, discriminate among Indians on the basis of religion, sex, or tribal affiliation, and the use of such a preference shall not excuse a contractor from complying with the other requirements contained in this chapter.

(b) *Specific contracts and facilities*—(1) *Specific contracts.* The Deputy Assistant Secretary may exempt an agency or any person from requiring the inclusion of any or all of the equal opportunity clause in any specific contract or subcontract when he deems that special circumstances in the national interest so require. The Deputy Assistant Secretary may also exempt groups or categories of contracts or subcontracts of the same type where he finds it impracticable to act upon each request individually or where group exemptions will contribute to convenience in the administration of the order.

(2) *Facilities not connected with contracts.* The Deputy Assistant Secretary may exempt from the requirements of the equal opportunity clause any of a prime contractor's or subcontractor's facilities which he finds to be in all respects separate and distinct from activities of the prime contractor or subcontractor related to the performance of the contract or subcontract, provided that he also finds that such an exemption will not interfere with or impede the effectuation of the order.

(c) *National security.* Any requirement set forth in these regulations in this part shall not apply to any contract or subcontract whenever the head of an agency determines that such contract or subcontract is essential to the national security and that its award without complying with such requirement is necessary to the national security. Upon making such a determination, the head of the agency will notify the Deputy Assistant Secretary in writing within 30 days.

(d) *Withdrawal of exemption.* When any contract or subcontract is of a class exempted under this section, the Deputy Assistant Secretary may withdraw the exemption for a specific contract or subcontract or group of contracts or subcontracts when in his judgment such action is necessary or appropriate to achieve the purposes of the order. Such withdrawal shall not apply to contracts or subcontracts awarded prior to the withdrawal, except that in procurements entered into by formal advertising, or the various forms of restricted formal advertising, such withdrawal shall not apply unless the withdrawal is made more than 10 calendar days before the date set for the opening of the bids.

[43 FR 49240, Oct. 20, 1978; 43 FR 51400, Nov. 3, 1978, as amended at 62 FR 66971, Dec. 22, 1997; 68 FR 56393, Sept. 30, 2003]

§ 60–1.6 [Reserved]

§ 60–1.7 Reports and other required information.

(a) *Requirements for prime contractors and subcontractors.* (1) Each prime contractor and subcontractor shall file annually, on or before the September 30, complete and accurate reports on Standard Form 100 (EEO–1) promulgated jointly by the Office of Federal Contract Compliance Programs, the Equal Employment Opportunity Commission and Plans for Progress or such form as may hereafter be promulgated in its place if such prime contractor or subcontractor (i) is not exempt from the provisions of these regulations in accordance with § 60–1.5; (ii) has 50 or more employees; (iii) is a prime contractor or first tier subcontractor; and (iv) has a contract, subcontract or purchase order amounting to $50,000 or more or serves as a depository of Government funds in any amount, or is a financial institution which is an issuing and paying agent for U.S. savings bonds and savings notes: *Provided*, That any subcontractor below the first tier which performs construction work at the site of construction shall be required to file such a report if it meets requirements of paragraphs (a)(1) (i), (ii), and (iv) of this section.

(2) Each person required by § 60–1.7(a)(1) to submit reports shall file such a report with the contracting or administering agency within 30 days after the award to him of a contract or subcontract, unless such person has submitted such a report within 12 months preceding the date of the award. Subsequent reports shall be submitted annually in accordance with § 60–1.7(a)(1), or at such other intervals as the Deputy Assistant Secretary may require. The Deputy Assistant Secretary may extend the time for filing any report.

(3) The Deputy Assistant Secretary or the applicant, on their own motions, may require a contractor to keep employment or other records and to furnish, in the form requested, within reasonable limits, such information as the Deputy Assistant Secretary or the applicant deems necessary for the administration of the order.

(4) Failure to file timely, complete and accurate reports as required constitutes noncompliance with the prime contractor's or subcontractor's obligations under the equal opportunity clause and is ground for the imposition by the Deputy Assistant Secretary, an applicant, prime contractor or subcontractor, of any sanctions as authorized by the order and the regulations in this part.

(b) *Requirements for bidders or prospective contractors*—(1) *Certification of compliance with Part 60–2: Affirmative Action Programs.* Each agency shall require each bidder or prospective prime contractor and proposed subcontractor, where appropriate, to state in the bid or in writing at the outset of negotiations for the contract: (i) Whether it has developed and has on file at each establishment affirmative action programs pursuant to Part 60–2 of this chapter; (ii) whether it has participated in any previous contract or subcontract subject to the equal opportunity clause; (iii) whether it has filed with the Joint Reporting Committee, the Deputy Assistant Secretary or the Equal Employment Opportunity Commission all reports due under the applicable filing requirements.

(2) *Additional information.* A bidder or prospective prime contractor or proposed subcontractor shall be required to submit such information as the Deputy Assistant Secretary requests prior to the award of the contract or subcontract. When a determination has been made to award the contract or subcontract to a specific contractor, such contractor shall be required, prior to award, or after the award, or both, to furnish such other information as the applicant or the Deputy Assistant Secretary requests.

(c) *Use of reports.* Reports filed pursuant to this section shall be used only in connection with the administration of the order, the Civil Rights Act of 1964, or in furtherance of the purposes of the order and said Act.

[43 FR 49240, Oct. 20, 1978, as amended at 62 FR 66971, Dec. 22, 1997]

§ 60–1.8 Segregated facilities.

To comply with its obligations under the Order, a contractor must ensure that facilities provided for employees are provided in such a manner that segregation on the basis of race, color, religion, sex or national origin cannot result. The contractor may neither require such segregated use by written or oral policies nor tolerate such use by employee custom. The contractor's obligation extends further to ensuring that its employees are not assigned to perform their services at any location, under the contractor's control, where the facilities are segregated. This obligation extends to all contracts containing the equal opportunity clause regardless of the amount of the contract. The term "facilities," as used in this section, means waiting rooms, work areas, restaurants and other eating areas, time clocks, restrooms, wash rooms, locker rooms, and other storage or dressing areas, parking lots, drinking fountains, recreation or entertainment areas, transportation, and housing provided for employees: *Provided,* That separate or single-user restrooms and necessary dressing or sleeping areas shall be provided to assure privacy between the sexes.

[62 FR 44189, Aug. 19, 1997]

§60–1.9 Compliance by labor unions and by recruiting and training agencies.

(a) Whenever compliance with the equal opportunity clause may necessitate a revision of a collective bargaining agreement the labor union or unions which are parties to such an agreement shall be given an adequate opportunity to present their views to the Deputy Assistant Secretary.

(b) The Deputy Assistant Secretary shall use his best efforts, directly and through agencies, contractors, subcontractors, applicants, State and local officials, public and private agencies, and all other available instrumentalities, to cause any labor union, recruiting and training agency or other representative of workers who are or may be engaged in work under contracts and subcontracts to cooperate with, and to comply in the implementation of, the purposes of the order.

(c) In order to effectuate the purposes of paragraph (a) of this section, the Deputy Assistant Secretary may hold hearings, public or private, with respect to the practices and policies of any such labor union or recruiting and training agency.

(d) The Deputy Assistant Secretary may notify any Federal, State, or local agency of his conclusions and recommendations with respect to any such labor organization or recruiting and training agency which in his judgment has failed to cooperate with himself, agencies, prime contractors, subcontractors, or applicants in carrying out the purposes of the order. The Deputy Assistant Secretary also may notify the Equal Employment Opportunity Commission, the Department of Justice, or other appropriate Federal agencies whenever he has reason to believe that the practices of any such labor organization or agency violates title VII of the Civil Rights Act of 1964 or other provisions of Federal law.

[43 FR 49240, Oct. 20, 1978, as amended at 62 FR 66971, Dec. 22, 1997]

§60–1.10 Foreign government practices.

Contractors shall not discriminate on the basis of race, color, religion, sex, or national origin when hiring or making employee assignments for work to be performed in the United States or abroad. Contractors are exempted from this obligation only when hiring persons outside the United States for work to be performed outside the United States (see 41 CFR 60–1.5(a)(3)). Therefore, a contractor hiring workers in the United States for either Federal or nonfederally connected work shall be in violation of Executive Order 11246, as amended, by refusing to employ or assign any person because of race, color, religion, sex, or national origin regardless of the policies of the country where the work is to be performed or for whom the work will be performed. Should any contractor be unable to acquire a visa of entry for any employee or potential employee to a country in which or with which it is doing business, and which refusal it believes is due to the race, color, religion, sex, or national origin of the employee or potential employee, the contractor must immediately notify the Department of State and the Deputy Assistant Secretary of such refusal.

[43 FR 49240, Oct. 20, 1978, as amended at 62 FR 66971, Dec. 22, 1997]

§60–1.11 Payment or reimbursement of membership fees and other expenses to private clubs.

(a)(1) A contractor which maintains a policy or practice of paying membership fees or other expenses for employee participation in private clubs or organizations shall ensure that the policy or practice is administered without regard to the race, color, religion, sex, or national origin of employees.

(2) Payment or reimbursement by contractors of membership fees and other expenses for participation by their employees in a private club or organization which bars, restricts or limits its membership on the basis of race, color, sex, religion, or national origin constitutes a violation of Executive Order 11246 except where the contractor can provide evidence that such restrictions or limitations do not abridge the promotional opportunities, status, compensation or other terms and conditions of employment of those of its employees barred from membership because of their race, color, religion, sex, or national origin. OFCCP shall provide the contractor with the

opportunity to present evidence in defense of its actions.

(b) The contractor has the responsibility of determining whether the club or organization restricts membership on the basis of race, color, religion, sex, or national origin. The contractor may make separate determinations for different chapters of an organization, and where it does so, may limit any necessary corrective action to the particular chapters which observe discriminatory membership policies and practices.

[46 FR 3896, Jan. 16, 1981]

EFFECTIVE DATE NOTE: At 46 FR 3896, Jan. 16, 1981, § 60–1.11 was added. At 46 FR 18951, Mar. 27, 1981, the effective date was deferred until further notice.

§ 60–1.12 Record retention.

(a) *General requirements.* Any personnel or employment record made or kept by the contractor shall be preserved by the contractor for a period of not less than two years from the date of the making of the record or the personnel action involved, whichever occurs later. However, if the contractor has fewer than 150 employees or does not have a Government contract of at least $150,000, the minimum record retention period shall be one year from the date of the making of the record or the personnel action involved, whichever occurs later. Such records include, but are not necessarily limited to, records pertaining to hiring, assignment, promotion, demotion, transfer, lay off or termination, rates of pay or other terms of compensation, and selection for training or apprenticeship, and other records having to do with requests for reasonable accommodation, the results of any physical examination, job advertisements and postings, applications, resumes, and any and all expressions of interest through the Internet or related electronic data technologies as to which the contractor considered the individual for a particular position, such as on-line resumes or internal resume databases, records identifying job seekers contacted regarding their interest in a particular position (for purposes of recordkeeping with respect to internal resume databases, the contractor must maintain a record of each resume added to the database, a record of the date each resume was added to the database, the position for which each search of the database was made, and corresponding to each search, the substantive search criteria used and the date of the search; for purposes of recordkeeping with respect to external resume databases, the contractor must maintain a record of the position for which each search of the database was made, and corresponding to each search, the substantive search criteria used, the date of the search, and the resumes of job seekers who met the basic qualifications for the particular position who are considered by the contractor), regardless of whether the individual qualifies as an Internet Applicant under 41 CFR 60–1.3, tests and test results, and interview notes. The term "personnel records relevant to the complaint," for example, would include personnel or employment records relating to the complainant and to all other employees holding positions similar to that held or sought by the complainant and application forms or test papers submitted by unsuccessful applicants and by all other candidates for the same position as that for which the complainant unsuccessfully applied. Where a compliance evaluation has been initiated, all personnel and employment records described above are relevant until OFCCP makes a final disposition of the evaluation.

(b) *Affirmative action programs.* A contractor establishment required under § 60–1.40 to develop and maintain a written affirmative action program (AAP) must maintain its current AAP and documentation of good faith effort, and must preserve its AAP and documentation of good faith effort for the immediately preceding AAP year, unless it was not then covered by the AAP requirement.

(c) *Contractor identification of record.* (1) For any record the contractor maintains pursuant to this section, the contractor must be able to identify:

(i) The gender, race, and ethnicity of each employee; and

(ii) Where possible, the gender, race, and ethnicity of each applicant or Internet Applicant as defined in 41 CFR 60–1.3, whichever is applicable to the particular position.

(2) The contractor must supply this information to the Office of Federal Contract Compliance Programs upon request.

(d) *Adverse impact evaluations.* When evaluating whether a contractor has maintained information on impact and conducted an adverse impact analysis under part 60–3 with respect to Internet hiring procedures, OFCCP will require only those records relating to the analyses of the impact of employee selection procedures on Internet Applicants, as defined in 41 CFR 60–1.3, and those records relating to the analyses of the impact of employment tests that are used as employee selection procedures, without regard to whether the tests were administered to Internet Applicants, as defined in 41 CFR 60–1.3.

(e) *Failure to preserve records.* Failure to preserve complete and accurate records as required by paragraphs (a) through (c) of this section constitutes noncompliance with the contractor's obligations under the Executive Order and this part. Where the contractor has destroyed or failed to preserve records as required by this section, there may be a presumption that the information destroyed or not preserved would have been unfavorable to the contractor: Provided, That this presumption shall not apply where the contractor shows that the destruction or failure to preserve records results from the circumstances that are outside of the contractor's control.

[65 FR 68042, Nov. 13, 2000, as amended at 70 FR 58962, Oct. 7, 2005]

Subpart B—General Enforcement; Compliance Review and Complaint Procedure

§ 60–1.20 Compliance evaluations.

(a) OFCCP may conduct compliance evaluations to determine if the contractor maintains nondiscriminatory hiring and employment practices and is taking affirmative action to ensure that applicants are employed and that employees are placed, trained, upgraded, promoted, and otherwise treated during employment without regard to race, color, religion, sex, or national origin. A compliance evaluation may consist of any one or any combination of the following investigative procedures:

(1) *Compliance review.* A comprehensive analysis and evaluation of the hiring and employment practices of the contractor, the written affirmative action program, and the results of the affirmative action efforts undertaken by the contractor. A compliance review may proceed in three stages:

(i) A desk audit of the written AAP and supporting documentation to determine whether all elements required by the regulations in this part are included, whether the AAP meets agency standards of reasonableness, and whether the AAP and supporting documentation satisfy agency standards of acceptability. The desk audit is conducted at OFCCP offices, except in the case of preaward reviews. In a preaward review, the desk audit normally is conducted at the contractor's establishment.

(ii) An on-site review, conducted at the contractor's establishment to investigate unresolved problem areas identified in the AAP and supporting documentation during the desk audit, to verify that the contractor has implemented the AAP and has complied with those regulatory obligations not required to be included in the AAP, and to examine potential instances or issues of discrimination. An on-site review normally will involve an examination of the contractor's personnel and employment policies, inspection and copying of documents related to employment actions, and interviews with employees, supervisors, managers, hiring officials; and

(iii) Where necessary, an off-site analysis of information supplied by the contractor or otherwise gathered during or pursuant to the on-site review.

(2) *Off-site review of records.* An analysis and evaluation of the AAP (or any part thereof) and supporting documentation, and other documents related to the contractor's personnel policies and employment actions that may be relevant to a determination of whether the contractor has complied with the requirements of the Executive Order and regulations;

(3) *Compliance check.* A determination of whether the contractor has maintained records consistent with § 60–1.12;

at the contractor's option the documents may be provided either on-site or off-site; or

(4) *Focused review.* An on-site review restricted to one or more components of the contractor's organization or one or more aspects of the contractor's employment practices.

(b) Where deficiencies are found to exist, reasonable efforts shall be made to secure compliance through conciliation and persuasion. Before the contractor can be found to be in compliance with the order, it must make a specific commitment, in writing, to correct any such deficiencies. The commitment must include the precise action to be taken and dates for completion. The time period allotted shall be no longer than the minimum period necessary to effect such changes. Upon approval of the commitment, the contractor may be considered in compliance, on condition that the commitments are faithfully kept. The contractor shall be notified that making such commitments does not preclude future determinations of noncompliance based on a finding that the commitments are not sufficient to achieve compliance.

(c) [Reserved]

(d) *Preaward compliance evaluations.* Each agency shall include in the invitation for bids for each formally advertised nonconstruction contract or state at the outset of negotiations for each negotiated contract, that if the award, when let, should total $10 million or more, the prospective contractor and its known first-tier subcontractors with subcontracts of $10 million or more shall be subject to a compliance evaluation before the award of the contract unless OFCCP has conducted an evaluation and found them to be in compliance with the Order within the preceding 24 months. The awarding agency will notify OFCCP and request appropriate action and findings in accordance with this subsection. Within 15 days of the notice OFCCP will inform the awarding agency of its intention to conduct a preaward compliance evaluation. If OFCCP does not inform the awarding agency within that period of its intention to conduct a preaward compliance evaluation, clearance shall be presumed and the awarding agency is authorized to proceed with the award. If OFCCP informs the awarding agency of its intention to conduct a preaward compliance evaluation, OFCCP shall be allowed an additional 20 days after the date that it so informs the awarding agency to provide its conclusions. If OFCCP does not provide the awarding agency with its conclusions within that period, clearance shall be presumed and the awarding agency is authorized to proceed with the award.

(e) *Submission of Documents; Standard Affirmative Action Formats.* Each prime contractor or subcontractor with 50 or more employees and a contract of $50,000 or more is required to develop a written affirmative action program for each of its establishments (§ 60–1.40). If a contractor fails to submit an affirmative action program and supporting documents, including the workforce analysis, within 30 days of a request, the enforcement procedures specified in § 60–1.26(b) shall be applicable. Contractors may reach agreement with OFCCP on nationwide AAP formats or on frequency of updating statistics.

(f) *Confidentiality and relevancy of information.* If the contractor is concerned with the confidentiality of such information as lists of employee names, reasons for termination, or pay data, then alphabetic or numeric coding or the use of an index of pay and pay ranges, consistent with the ranges assigned to each job group, are acceptable for purposes of the compliance evaluation. The contractor must provide full access to all relevant data onsite as required by § 60–1.43. Where necessary, the compliance officer may take information made available during the on-site evaluation off-site for further analysis. An off-site analysis should be conducted where issues have arisen concerning deficiencies or an apparent violation which, in the judgment of the compliance officer, should be more thoroughly analyzed off-site before a determination of compliance is made. The contractor must provide all data determined by the compliance officer to be necessary for off-site analysis. Such data may only be coded if the contractor makes the key to the code available to the compliance officer. If the contractor believes that particular information which is to be taken off-site is not relevant to compliance with the Executive Order, the contractor may request a ruling by the OFCCP District/Area Director. The OFCCP District/Area Director shall issue a ruling within 10 days. The contractor may appeal that ruling to the OFCCP Regional Director within 10 days. The Regional Director shall issue a final ruling within 10 days. Pending a final ruling, the information in question must be made available to the compliance officer off-site, but shall be considered a part of the investigatory file and subject to the provisions of paragraph (g) of this section. The agency shall take all necessary precautions to safeguard the confidentiality of such information until a final determination is made. Such information may not be copied by OFCCP and access to the information shall be limited to the compliance officer and personnel involved in the determination of relevancy. Data determined to be not relevant to the investigation will be returned to the contractor immediately.

(g) *Public Access to Information.* OFCCP will treat information obtained in the compliance evaluation as confidential to the maximum extent the information is exempt from public disclosure under the Freedom of Information Act, 5 U.S.C. 552. It is the practice of OFCCP not to release data where the contractor is still in business, and the contractor indicates, and through the Department of Labor review process it is determined, that the data are confidential and sensitive and that the release of data would subject the contractor to commercial harm.

[43 FR 49240, Oct. 20, 1978; 43 FR 51400, Nov. 3, 1978, as amended at 62 FR 44189, Aug. 19, 1997; 70 FR 36265, June 22, 2005]

§ 60–1.21 Filing complaints.

Complaints shall be filed within 180 days of the alleged violation unless the time for filing is extended by the Deputy Assistant Secretary for good cause shown.

[43 FR 49240, Oct. 20, 1978; 43 FR 51400, Nov. 3, 1978, as amended at 62 FR 66971, Dec. 22, 1997]

§ 60–1.22 Where to file.

Complaints may be filed with the OFCCP, 200 Constitution Avenue, NW., Washington, DC 20210, or with any OFCCP regional or area office.

§ 60–1.23 Contents of complaint.

(a) The complaint shall include the name, address, and telephone number of the complainant, the name and address of the contractor or subcontractor committing the alleged discrimination, a description of the acts considered to be discriminatory, and any other pertinent information which will assist in the investigation and resolution of the complaint. The complaint shall be signed by the complainant or his/her authorized representative. Complaints alleging class-type violations which do not identify the alleged discriminatee or discriminatees will be accepted, provided the other requirements of this paragraph are met.

(b) If a complaint contains incomplete information, OFCCP shall seek the needed information from the complainant. In the event such information is not furnished to the Deputy Assistant Secretary within 60 days of the date of such request, the case may be closed.

[43 FR 49240, Oct. 20, 1978, as amended at 62 FR 66971, Dec. 22, 1997]

§ 60–1.24 Processing of matters.

(a) *Complaints.* OFCCP may refer appropriate complaints to the Equal Employment Opportunity Commission (EEOC) for processing under Title VII of the Civil Rights Act of 1964, as amended, rather than processing under E.O. 11246 and the regulations in this chapter. Upon referring complaints to the EEOC, OFCCP shall promptly notify complainant(s) and the contractor of such referral.

(b) *Complaint investigations.* In conducting complaint investigations, OFCCP shall, as a minimum, conduct a thorough evaluation of the allegations of the complaint and shall be responsible for developing a complete case record. The case record should contain the name, address, and telephone number of each person interviewed, the interview statements, copies, transcripts, or summaries (where appropriate) of pertinent documents, a reference to at least one covered contract, and a narrative report of the investigation with references to exhibits and other evidence which relate to the alleged violations.

(c)(1) [Reserved]

(2) If any complaint investigation or compliance review indicates a violation of the equal opportunity clause, the matter should be resolved by informal means whenever possible. Such informal means may include the holding of a compliance conference.

(3) Where any complaint investigation or compliance review indicates a violation of the equal opportunity clause and the matter has not been resolved by informal means, the Deputy Assistant Secretary shall proceed in accordance with § 60–1.26.

(4) When a prime contractor or subcontractor, without a hearing, shall have complied with the recommendations or orders of the Deputy Assistant Secretary and believes such recommendations or orders to be erroneous, he shall, upon filing a request therefor within ten days of such compliance, be afforded an opportunity for a hearing and review of the alleged erroneous action.

(5) For reasonable cause shown, the Deputy Assistant Secretary may reconsider or cause to be reconsidered any matter on his/her own motion or pursuant to a request.

(d) *Reports to the Deputy Assistant Secretary.* (1) With the exception of complaints which have been referred to EEOC, within 60 days from receipt of a complaint or within such additional time as may be allowed by the Deputy Assistant Secretary for good cause shown, the complaint shall be processed and the case record developed containing the following information:

(i) Name and address of the complainant;

(ii) Brief summary of findings, including a statement regarding the contractor's compliance or noncompliance with the requirements of the equal opportunity clause;

(iii) A statement of the disposition of the case, including any corrective action taken and any sanctions or penalties imposed or, whenever appropriate, the recommended corrective action and sanctions or penalties.

(2) A written report of every preaward compliance review required by this regulation or otherwise required by the Deputy Assistant Secretary, shall be developed and maintained.

(3) A written report of every other compliance review or any other matter processed involving an apparent violation of the equal opportunity clause shall be made. Such report shall contain a brief summary of the findings, including a statement of conclusions regarding the contractor's compliance or noncompliance with the requirements of the order, and a statement of the disposition of the case, including any corrective action taken or recommended and any sanctions or penalties imposed or recommended.

[43 FR 49240, Oct. 20, 1978, as amended at 62 FR 66971, Dec. 22, 1997]

§ 60–1.25 Assumption of jurisdiction by or referrals to the Deputy Assistant Secretary.

The Deputy Assistant Secretary may inquire into the status of any matter pending before an agency. Where he considers it necessary or appropriate to the achievement of the purposes of the order, he may assume jurisdiction over the matter and proceed as provided herein. Whenever the Deputy Assistant Secretary assumes jurisdiction over any matter, or an agency refers any matter he may conduct, or have conducted, such investigations, hold such hearings, make such findings, issue such recommendations and directives, order such sanctions and penalties, and take such other action as may be necessary or appropriate to achieve the purposes of the order. The Deputy Assistant Secretary shall promptly notify the agency of any corrective action to be taken or any sanctions to be taken or any sanction to be imposed by the agency. The agency shall take such action, and report the results thereof to the Deputy Assistant Secretary within the time specified.

[43 FR 49240, Oct. 20, 1978, as amended at 62 FR 66971, Dec. 22, 1997]

§ 60–1.26 Enforcement proceedings.

(a) *General.* (1) Violations of the Order, the equal opportunity clause, the regulations in this chapter, or applicable construction industry equal employment opportunity requirements, may result in the institution of administrative or judicial enforcement proceedings. Violations may be found based upon, *inter alia*, any of the following:

(i) The results of a complaint investigation;

(ii) The results of a compliance evaluation;

(iii) Analysis of an affirmative action program;

(iv) The results of an on-site review of the contractor's compliance with the Order and its implementing regulations;

(v) A contractor's refusal to submit an affirmative action program;

(vi) A contractor's refusal to allow an on-site compliance evaluation to be conducted;

(vii) A contractor's refusal to provide data for off-site review or analysis as required by the regulations in this chapter;

(viii) A contractor's refusal to establish, maintain and supply records or other information as required by the regulations in this chapter or applicable construction industry requirements;

(ix) A contractor's alteration or falsification of records and information required to be maintained by the regulations in this chapter; or

(x) Any substantial or material violation or the threat of a substantial or material violation of the contractual provisions of the Order, or of the rules or regulations in this chapter.

(2) OFCCP may seek back pay and other make whole relief for victims of discrimination identified during a complaint investigation or compliance evaluation. Such individuals need not have filed a complaint as a prerequisite to OFCCP seeking such relief on their behalf. Interest on back pay shall be calculated from the date of the loss and compounded quarterly at the percentage rate established by the Internal Revenue Service for the under-payment of taxes.

(b) *Administrative enforcement.* (1) OFCCP may refer matters to the Solicitor of Labor with a recommendation for the institution of administrative enforcement proceedings, which may be brought to enjoin violations, to seek appropriate relief, and to impose appropriate sanctions. The referral may be made when violations have not been corrected in accordance with the conciliation procedures in this chapter, or when OFCCP determines that referral for consideration of formal enforcement (rather than settlement) is appropriate. However, if a contractor refuses to submit an affirmative action program, or refuses to supply records or other requested information, or refuses to allow OFCCP access to its premises for an on-site review, and if conciliation efforts under this chapter are unsuccessful, OFCCP may immediately refer the matter to the Solicitor, notwithstanding other requirements of this chapter.

(2) Administrative enforcement proceedings shall be conducted under the control and supervision of the Solicitor of Labor and under the Rules of Practice for Administrative Proceedings to Enforce Equal Opportunity under Executive Order 11246 contained in part 60–30 of this chapter and the Rules of Evidence set out in the Rules of Practice and Procedure for Administrative Hearings Before the Office of Administrative Law Judges contained in 29 CFR part 18, subpart B: *Provided,* That a Final Administrative Order shall be issued within on year from the date of the issuance of the recommended findings, conclusions and decision of the Administrative Law Judge, or the submission of any exceptions and responses to exceptions to such decision (if any), whichever is later.

(c) *Referrals to the Department of Justice.* (1) The Deputy Assistant Secretary may refer matters to the Department of Justice with a recommendation for the institution of judicial enforcement proceedings. There are no procedural prerequisites to a referral to the Department of Justice. Such referrals may be accomplished without proceeding through the conciliation procedures in this chapter, and a referral may be made at any stage in the procedures under this chapter.

(2) Whenever a matter has been referred to the Department of Justice for consideration of judicial enforcement, the Attorney General may bring a civil action in the appropriate district court of the United States requesting a temporary restraining order, preliminary or permanent injunction (including relief against noncontractors, including labor unions, who seek to thwart the implementation of the Order and regulations), and an order for such additional sanctions or relief, including back pay, deemed necessary or appropriate to ensure the full enjoyment of the rights secured by the Order, or any of the above in this paragraph (c)(2).

(3) The Attorney General is authorized to conduct such investigation of the facts as he/she deem necessary or appropriate to carry out his/her responsibilities under the regulations in this chapter.

(4) Prior to the institution of any judicial proceedings, the Attorney General, on behalf of the Deputy Assistant Secretary, is authorized to make reasonable efforts to secure compliance with the contract provisions of the Order. The Attorney General may do so by providing the contractor and any other respondent with reasonable notice of his/her findings, his/her intent to file suit, and the actions he/she believes necessary to obtain compliance with the contract provisions of the Order without contested litigation, and by offering the contractor and any other respondent a reasonable opportunity for conference and conciliation, in an effort to obtain such compliance without contested litigation.

(5) As used in the regulations in this Part, the Attorney General shall mean the Attorney General, the Assistant Attorney General for Civil Rights, or any other person authorized by regulations or practice to act for the Attorney General with respect to the enforcement of equal employment opportunity laws, orders and regulations generally, or in a particular matter or case.

(6) The Deputy Assistant Secretary or his/her designee, and representatives of the Attorney General may consult from time to time to determine what investigations should be conducted to determine whether contractors or groups of contractors or other persons may be engaged in patterns or practices in violation of the Executive Order or these regulations, or of resistance to or interference with the full enjoyment of any of the rights secured by them, warranting judicial proceedings.

(d) *Initiation of lawsuits by the Attorney General without referral from the Deputy Assistant Secretary.* In addition to initiating lawsuits upon referral under this section, the Attorney General may, subject to approval by the Deputy Assistant Secretary, initiate independent investigations of contractors which he/she has reason to believe may be in violation of the Order or the rules and regulations issued pursuant thereto. If, upon completion of such an investigation, the Attorney General determines that the contractor has in fact violated the Order or the rules and regulations issued thereunder, he/she shall make reasonable efforts to secure compliance with the contract provisions of the Order. He/she may do so by providing the contractor and any other respondent with reasonable notice of the Department of Justice's findings, its intent to file suit, and the actions that the Attorney General believes are necessary to obtain compliance with the contract provisions of the Order without contested litigation, and by offering the contractor and any other respondent a reasonable opportunity for conference and conciliation in an effort to obtain such compliance without contested litigation. If these efforts are unsuccessful, the Attorney General may, upon approval by the Deputy Assistant Secretary, bring a civil action in the appropriate district court of the United States requesting a temporary restraining order, preliminary or permanent injunction, and an order for such additional sanctions or equitable relief, including back pay, deemed necessary or appropriate to ensure the full enjoyment of the rights secured by the Order or any of the above in this paragraph (d).

(e) To the extent applicable, this section and part 60–30 of this chapter shall govern proceedings resulting from any

Deputy Assistant Secretary's determinations under §60–2.2(b) of this chapter.

[62 FR 44190, Aug. 19, 1997, as amended at 62 FR 66971, Dec. 22, 1997]

§60–1.27 Sanctions.

(a) *General.* The sanctions described in subsections (1), (5), and (6) of section 209(a) of the Order may be exercised only by or with the approval of the Deputy Assistant Secretary. Referral of any matter arising under the Order to the Department of Justice or to the Equal Employment Opportunity Commission shall be made by the Deputy Assistant Secretary.

(b) *Debarment.* A contractor may be debarred from receiving future contracts or modifications or extensions of existing contracts, subject to reinstatement pursuant to §60–1.31, for any violation of Executive Order 11246 or the implementing rules, regulations and orders of the Secretary of Labor. Debarment may be imposed for an indefinite term or for a fixed minimum period of at least six months.

[62 FR 44191, Aug. 19, 1997]

§60–1.28 Show cause notices.

When the Deputy Assistant Secretary has reasonable cause to believe that a contractor has violated the equal opportunity clause he may issue a notice requiring the contractor to show cause, within 30 days, why monitoring, enforcement proceedings or other appropriate action to ensure compliance should not be instituted.

[43 FR 49240, Oct. 20, 1978, as amended at 62 FR 66971, Dec. 22, 1997]

§60–1.29 Preaward notices.

(a) *Preaward compliance reviews.* Upon the request of the Deputy Assistant Secretary, agencies shall not enter into contracts or approve the entry into contracts or subcontracts with any bidder, prospective prime contractor, or proposed subcontractor named by the Deputy Assistant Secretary until a preaward compliance review has been conducted and the Deputy Assistant Secretary or his designee has approved a determination that the bidder, prospective prime contractor or proposed subcontractor will be able to comply with the provisions of the equal opportunity clause.

(b) *Other special preaward procedures.* Upon the request of the Deputy Assistant Secretary, agencies shall not enter into contracts or approve the entry into subcontracts with any bidder; prospective prime contractor or proposed subcontractor specified by the Deputy Assistant Secretary until the agency has complied with the directions contained in the request.

[43 FR 49240, Oct. 20, 1978, as amended at 62 FR 66971, Dec. 22, 1997]

§60–1.30 Notification of agencies.

The Deputy Assistant Secretary shall ensure that the heads of all agencies are notified of any debarment taken against any contractor.

[62 FR 44191, Aug. 19, 1997]

§60–1.31 Reinstatement of ineligible contractors.

A contractor debarred from further contracts for an indefinite period under the Order may request reinstatement in a letter filed with the Deputy Assistant Secretary at any time after the effective date of the debarment. A contractor debarred for a fixed period may request reinstatement in a letter filed with the Deputy Assistant Secretary 30 days prior to the expiration of the fixed debarment period, or at any time thereafter. The filing of a reinstatement request 30 days before a fixed debarment period ends will not result in early reinstatement. In connection with the reinstatement proceedings, all debarred contractors shall be required to show that they have established and will carry out employment policies and practices in compliance with the Order and implementing regulations. Before reaching a decision, the Deputy Assistant Secretary may conduct a compliance evaluation of the contractor and may require the contractor to supply additional information regarding the request for reinstatement. The Deputy Assistant Secretary shall issue a written decision on the request.

[62 FR 44192, Aug. 19, 1997]

§ 60–1.32 Intimidation and interference.

(a) The contractor, subcontractor or applicant shall not harass, intimidate, threaten, coerce, or discriminate against any individual because the individual has engaged in or may engage in any of the following activities:

(1) Filing a complaint;

(2) Assisting or participating in any manner in an investigation, compliance evaluation, hearing, or any other activity related to the administration of the Order or any other Federal, state or local law requiring equal opportunity;

(3) Opposing any act or practice made unlawful by the Order or any other Federal, state or local law requiring equal opportunity; or

(4) Exercising any other right protected by the Order.

(b) The contractor, subcontractor or applicant shall ensure that all persons under its control do not engage in such harassment, intimidation, threats, coercion or discrimination. The sanctions and penalties contained in this part may be exercised by OFCCP against any contractor, subcontractor or applicant who violates this obligation.

[62 FR 44192, Aug. 19, 1997]

§ 60–1.33 Conciliation agreements.

If a compliance review, complaint investigation or other review by OFCCP or its representative indicates a material violation of the equal opportunity clause, and (1) if the contractor, subcontractor or bidder is willing to correct the violations and/or deficiencies, and (2) if OFCCP or its representative determines that settlement (rather than referral for consideration of formal enforcement) is appropriate, a written agreement shall be required. The agreement shall provide for such remedial action as may be necessary to correct the violations and/or deficiencies noted, including, where appropriate (but not necessarily limited to), remedies such as back pay and retroactive seniority.

(E.O. 11246 (30 FR 12319) as amended by E.O. 11375 and 12086)

[44 FR 77002, Dec. 28, 1979; 70 FR 36265, June 22, 2005]

§ 60–1.34 Violation of a Conciliation Agreement.

When a conciliation agreement has been violated, the following procedures are applicable:

(a) A written notice shall be sent to the contractor setting forth the violations alleged and summarizing the supporting evidence. The contractor shall have 15 days from receipt of the notice to respond, except in those cases in which such a delay would result in irreparable injury to the employment rights of affected employees or applicants.

(b) During the 15-day period the contractor may demonstrate in writing that it has not violated its commitments.

(c) If the contractor is unable to demonstrate that it has not violated its commitments, or if the complaint alleges irreparable injury, enforcement proceedings may be initiated immediately without issuing a show cause notice or proceeding through any other requirement contained in this chapter.

(d) In any proceeding involving an alleged violation of a conciliation agreement OFCCP may seek enforcement of the agreement itself and shall not be required to present proof of the underlying violations resolved by the agreement.

(E.O. 11246 (30 FR 12319) as amended by EO 11375 and 12086)

[44 FR 77002, Dec. 28, 1979, as amended at 62 FR 44192, Aug. 19, 1997; 70 FR 36265, June 22, 2005]

Subpart C—Ancillary Matters

§ 60–1.40 Affirmative action programs.

(a)(1) Each nonconstruction (supply and service) contractor must develop and maintain a written affirmative action program for each of its establishments, if it has 50 or more employees and:

(i) Has a contract of $50,000 or more; or

(ii) Has Government bills of lading which in any 12-month period, total or can reasonably be expected to total $50,000 or more; or

(iii) Serves as a depository of Government funds in any amount; or

(iv) Is a financial institution which is an issuing and paying agent for U.S. savings bonds and savings notes in any amount.

(2) Each contractor and subcontractor must require each nonconstruction subcontractor to develop and maintain a written affirmative action program for each of its establishments if it has 50 or more employees and:

(i) Has a subcontract of $50,000 or more; or

(ii) Has Government bills of lading which in any 12-month period, total or can reasonably be expected to total $50,000 or more; or

(iii) Serves as a depository of Government funds in any amount; or

(iv) Is a financial institution which is an issuing and paying agent for U.S. savings bonds and savings notes in any amount.

(b) Nonconstruction contractors should refer to Part 60–2 for specific affirmative action requirements. Construction contractors should refer to Part 60–4 for specific affirmative action requirements.

[65 FR 68042, Nov. 13, 2000]

§ 60–1.41 Solicitations or advertisements for employees.

In solicitations or advertisements for employees placed by or on behalf of a prime contractor or subcontractor, the requirements of paragraph (2) of the equal opportunity clause shall be satisfied whenever the prime contractor or subcontractor complies with any of the following:

(a) States expressly in the solicitations or advertising that all qualified applicants will receive consideration for employment without regard to race, color, religion, sex, or national origin;

(b) Uses display or other advertising, and the advertising includes an appropriate insignia prescribed by the Deputy Assistant Secretary. The use of the insignia is considered subject to the provisions of 18 U.S.C. 701;

(c) Uses a single advertisement, and the advertisement is grouped with other advertisements under a caption which clearly states that all employers in the group assure all qualified applicants equal consideration for employment without regard to race, color, religion, sex, or national origin;

(d) Uses a single advertisement in which appears in clearly distinguishable type the phrase "an equal opportunity employer."

[43 FR 49240, Oct. 20, 1978, as amended at 62 FR 66971, Dec. 22, 1997]

§ 60–1.42 Notices to be posted.

(a) Unless alternative notices are prescribed by the Deputy Assistant Secretary, the notices which contractors are required to post by paragraphs (1) and (3) of the equal opportunity clause in § 60–1.4 will contain the following language and be provided by the contracting or administering agencies:

EQUAL EMPLOYMENT OPPORTUNITY IS THE LAW—DISCRIMINATION IS PROHIBITED BY THE CIVIL RIGHTS ACT OF 1964 AND BY EXECUTIVE ORDER NO. 11246

Title VII of the Civil Rights Act of 1964—*Administered by:*

THE EQUAL EMPLOYMENT OPPORTUNITY COMMISSION

Prohibits discrimination because of Race, Color, Religion, Sex, or National Origin by Employers with 15 or more employees, by Labor Organizations, by Employment Agencies, and by Apprenticeship or Training Programs

ANY PERSON

Who believes he or she has been discriminated against

SHOULD CONTACT

THE EQUAL EMPLOYMENT OPPORTUNITY COMMISSION

1801 L Street NW., Washington, DC 20507

Executive Order No. 11246—*Administered by:*

THE OFFICE OF FEDERAL CONTRACT COMPLIANCE PROGRAMS

Prohibits discrimination because of Race, Color, Religion, Sex, or National Origin, and requires affirmative action to ensure equality of opportunity in all aspects of employment.

By all Federal Government Contractors and Subcontractors, and by Contractors Performing Work Under a Federally Assisted Construction Contract, regardless of the number of employees in either case.

ANY PERSON

Who believes he or she has been discriminated against

SHOULD CONTACT

THE OFFICE OF FEDERAL CONTRACT COMPLIANCE PROGRAMS

U.S. Department of Labor, Washington, DC 20210

(b) The requirements of paragraph (3) of the equal opportunity clause will be satisfied whenever the prime contractor or subcontractor posts copies of the notification prescribed by or pursuant to paragraph (a) of this section in conspicuous places available to employees, applicants for employment, and representatives of each labor union or other organization representing his employees with which he has a collective-bargaining agreement or other contract or understanding.

[43 FR 49240, Oct. 20, 1978, as amended at 62 FR 44192, Aug. 19, 1997; 62 FR 66971, Dec. 22, 1997]

§ 60–1.43 Access to records and site of employment.

Each contractor shall permit access during normal business hours to its premises for the purpose of conducting on-site compliance evaluations and complaint investigations. Each contractor shall permit the inspecting and copying of such books and accounts and records, including computerized records, and other material as may be relevant to the matter under investigation and pertinent to compliance with the Order, and the rules and regulations promulgated pursuant thereto by the agency, or the Deputy Assistant Secretary. Information obtained in this manner shall be used only in connection with the administration of the Order, the Civil Rights Act of 1964 (as amended), and any other law that is or may be enforced in whole or in part by OFCCP.

[62 FR 44192, Aug. 19, 1997]

§ 60–1.44 Rulings and interpretations.

Rulings under or interpretations of the order or the regulations contained in this part shall be made by the Secretary or his designee.

§ 60–1.45 Existing contracts and subcontracts.

All contracts and subcontracts in effect prior to October 24, 1965, which are not subsequently modified shall be administered in accordance with the nondiscrimination provisions of any prior applicable Executive orders. Any contract or subcontract modified on or after October 24, 1965, shall be subject to Executive Order 11246. Complaints received by and violations coming to the attention of agencies regarding contracts and subcontracts which were subject to Executive Orders 10925 and 11114 shall be processed as if they were complaints regarding violations of this order.

§ 60–1.46 Delegation of authority by the Deputy Assistant Secretary.

The Deputy Assistant Secretary is authorized to redelegate the authority given to him by the regulations in this part. The authority redelegated by the Deputy Assistant Secretary pursuant to the regulations in this part shall be exercised under his general direction and control.

[43 FR 49240, Oct. 20, 1978, as amended at 62 FR 66971, Dec. 22, 1997]

§ 60–1.47 Effective date.

The regulations contained in this part shall become effective July 1, 1968, for all contracts, the solicitations, invitations for bids, or requests for proposals which were sent by the Government or an applicant on or after said effective date, and for all negotiated contracts which have not been executed as of said effective date. Notwithstanding the foregoing, the regulations in this part shall become effective as to all contracts executed on and after the 120th day following said effective date. Subject to any prior approval of the Secretary, any agency may defer the effective date of the regulations in this part, for such period of time as the Secretary finds to be reasonably necessary. Contracts executed prior to the effective date of the regulations in this part shall be governed by the regulations promulgated by the former President's Committee on Equal Employment Opportunity which appear at 28 FR 9812, September 2, 1963, and at 28

FR 11305, October 23, 1963, the temporary regulations which appear at 30 FR 13441, October 22, 1965, and the orders at 31 FR 6881, May 10, 1966, and 32 FR 7439, May 19, 1967.

PART 60–2—AFFIRMATIVE ACTION PROGRAMS

Subpart A—General

Subpart B—Purpose and Contents of Affirmative Action Programs

Subpart C—Miscellaneous

AUTHORITY: E.O. 11246, 30 FR 12319, and E.O. 11375, 32 FR 14303, as amended by E.O. 12086, 43 FR 46501.

SOURCE: 65 FR 68042, Nov. 13, 2000, unless otherwise noted.

Subpart A—General

§60–2.1 Scope and application.

(a) *General.* The requirements of this part apply to nonconstruction (supply and service) contractors. The regulations prescribe the contents of affirmative action programs, standards and procedures for evaluating the compliance of affirmative action programs implemented pursuant to this part, and related matters.

(b) *Who must develop affirmative action programs.* (1) Each nonconstruction contractor must develop and maintain a written affirmative action program for each of its establishments if it has 50 or more employees and:

(i) Has a contract of $50,000 or more; or

(ii) Has Government bills of lading which in any 12-month period, total or can reasonably be expected to total $50,000 or more; or

(iii) Serves as a depository of Government funds in any amount; or

(iv) Is a financial institution which is an issuing and paying agent for U.S. savings bonds and savings notes in any amount.

(2) Each contractor and subcontractor must require each nonconstruction subcontractor to develop and maintain a written affirmative action program for each of its establishments if it has 50 or more employees and:

(i) Has a subcontract of $50,000 or more; or

(ii) Has Government bills of lading which in any 12-month period, total or can reasonably be expected to total $50,000 or more; or

(iii) Serves as a depository of Government funds in any amount; or

(iv) Is a financial institution which is an issuing and paying agent for U.S. savings bonds and savings notes in any amount.

(c) *When affirmative action programs must be developed.* The affirmative action programs required under paragraph (b) of this section must be developed within 120 days from the commencement of a contract and must be updated annually.

(d) *Who is included in affirmative action programs.* Contractors subject to the affirmative action program requirements must develop and maintain a written affirmative action program for each of their establishments. Each employee in the contractor's workforce must be included in an affirmative action program. Each employee must be included in the affirmative action program of the establishment at which he or she works, except that:

(1) Employees who work at establishments other than that of the manager to whom they report, must be included in the affirmative action program of their manager.

(2) Employees who work at an establishment where the contractor employs

fewer than 50 employees, may be included under any of the following three options: In an affirmative action program which covers just that establishment; in the affirmative action program which covers the location of the personnel function which supports the establishment; or, in the affirmative action program which covers the location of the official to whom they report.

(3) Employees for whom selection decisions are made at a higher level establishment within the organization must be included in the affirmative action program of the establishment where the selection decision is made.

(4) If a contractor wishes to establish an affirmative action program other than by establishment, the contractor may reach agreement with OFCCP on the development and use of affirmative action programs based on functional or business units. The Deputy Assistant Secretary, or his or her designee, must approve such agreements. Agreements allowing the use of functional or business unit affirmative action programs cannot be construed to limit or restrict how the OFCCP structures its compliance evaluations.

(e) *How to identify employees included in affirmative action programs other than where they are located.* If pursuant to paragraphs (d)(1) through (3) of this section employees are included in an affirmative action program for an establishment other than the one in which the employees are located, the organizational profile and job group analysis of the affirmative action program in which the employees are included must be annotated to identify the actual location of such employees. If the establishment at which the employees actually are located maintains an affirmative action program, the organizational profile and job group analysis of that program must be annotated to identify the program in which the employees are included.

§ 60–2.2 Agency action.

(a) Any contractor required by § 60–2.1 to develop and maintain a written affirmative action program for each of its establishments that has not complied with that section is not in full compliance with Executive Order 11246, as amended. When a contractor is required to submit its affirmative action program to OFCCP (e.g., for a compliance evaluation), the affirmative action program will be deemed to have been accepted by the Government at the time OFCCP notifies the contractor of completion of the compliance evaluation or other action, unless within 45 days thereafter the Deputy Assistant Secretary has disapproved such program.

(b) If, in determining such contractor's responsibility for an award of a contract it comes to the contracting officer's attention, through sources within his/her agency or through the OFCCP or other Government agencies, that the contractor does not have an affirmative action program at each of its establishments, or has substantially deviated from such an approved affirmative action program, or has failed to develop or implement an affirmative action program which complies with the regulations in this chapter, the contracting officer must declare the contractor/bidder nonresponsible and so notify the contractor and the Deputy Assistant Secretary, unless the contracting officer otherwise affirmatively determines that the contractor is able to comply with the equal employment obligations. Any contractor/bidder which has been declared nonresponsible in accordance with the provisions of this section may request the Deputy Assistant Secretary to determine that the responsibility of the contractor/bidder raises substantial issues of law or fact to the extent that a hearing is required. Such request must set forth the basis upon which the contractor/bidder seeks such a determination. If the Deputy Assistant Secretary, in his/her sole discretion, determines that substantial issues of law or fact exist, an administrative or judicial proceeding may be commenced in accordance with the regulations contained in § 60–1.26; or the Deputy Assistant Secretary may require the investigation or compliance evaluation be developed further or additional conciliation be conducted: Provided, That during any pre-award conferences, every effort will be made through the processes of conciliation, mediation, and persuasion to develop an acceptable affirmative action program meeting the standards and guidelines set forth in this part so that, in the performance of the contract, the contractor is able to meet its equal employment obligations in accordance with the equal opportunity clause and applicable rules, regulations, and orders: Provided further, That a contractor/bidder may not be declared nonresponsible more than twice due to past noncompliance with the equal opportunity clause at a particular establishment or facility without receiving prior notice and an opportunity for a hearing.

(c)(1) Immediately upon finding that a contractor has no affirmative action program, or has deviated substantially from an approved affirmative action program, or has failed to develop or implement an affirmative action program which complies with the requirements of the regulations in this chapter, that fact shall be recorded in the investigation file. Except as provided in §60–1.26(b)(1), whenever administrative enforcement is contemplated, the notice to the contractor shall be issued giving the contractor 30 days to show cause why enforcement proceedings under section 209(a) of Executive Order 11246, as amended, should not be instituted. The notice to show cause should contain:

(i) An itemization of the sections of the Executive Order and of the regulations with which the contractor has been found in apparent violation, and a summary of the conditions, practices, facts, or circumstances which give rise to each apparent violation;

(ii) The corrective actions necessary to achieve compliance or, as may be appropriate, the concepts and principles of an acceptable remedy and/or the corrective action results anticipated;

(iii) A request for a written response to the findings, including commitments to corrective action or the presentation of opposing facts and evidence; and

(iv) A suggested date for the conciliation conference.

(2) If the contractor fails to show good cause for its failure or fails to remedy that failure by developing and implementing an acceptable affirmative action program within 30 days, the case file shall be processed for enforcement proceedings pursuant to §60–1.26 of this chapter. If an administrative complaint is filed, the contractor shall have 20 days to request a hearing. If a request for hearing has not been received within 20 days from the filing of the administrative complaint, the matter shall proceed in accordance with part 60–30 of this chapter.

(3) During the "show cause" period of 30 days, every effort will be made through conciliation, mediation, and persuasion to resolve the deficiencies which led to the determination of nonresponsibility. If satisfactory adjustments designed to bring the contractor into compliance are not concluded, the case shall be processed for enforcement proceedings pursuant to §60–1.26 of this chapter.

(d) During the "show cause" period and formal proceedings, each contracting agency must continue to determine the contractor's responsibility in considering whether or not to award a new or additional contract.

Subpart B—Purpose and Contents of Affirmative Action Programs

§60–2.10 General purpose and contents of affirmative action programs.

(a) *Purpose.* (1) An affirmative action program is a management tool designed to ensure equal employment opportunity. A central premise underlying affirmative action is that, absent discrimination, over time a contractor's workforce, generally, will reflect the gender, racial and ethnic profile of the labor pools from which the contractor recruits and selects. Affirmative action programs contain a diagnostic component which includes a number of quantitative analyses designed to evaluate the composition of the workforce of the contractor and compare it to the composition of the relevant labor pools. Affirmative action programs also include action-oriented programs. If women and minorities are not being employed at a rate to be expected given their availability in the relevant labor pool, the contractor's affirmative action program includes specific practical steps designed to address this underutilization. Effective affirmative action programs also include internal auditing and reporting systems as a means of measuring the contractor's progress toward achieving the workforce that would be expected in the absence of discrimination.

(2) An affirmative action program also ensures equal employment opportunity by institutionalizing the contractor's commitment to equality in every aspect of the employment process. Therefore, as part of its affirmative action program, a contractor monitors and examines its employment decisions and compensation systems to evaluate the impact of those systems on women and minorities.

(3) An affirmative action program is, thus, more than a paperwork exercise. An affirmative action program includes those policies, practices, and procedures that the contractor implements to ensure that all qualified applicants and employees are receiving an equal opportunity for recruitment, selection, advancement, and every other term and privilege associated with employment. Affirmative action, ideally, is a part of the way the contractor regularly conducts its business. OFCCP has found that when an affirmative action program is approached from this perspective, as a powerful management tool, there is a positive correlation between the presence of affirmative action and the absence of discrimination.

(b) *Contents of affirmative action programs.* (1) An affirmative action program must include the following quantitative analyses:

(i) Organizational profile—§60–2.11;

(ii) Job group analysis—§60–2.12;

(iii) Placement of incumbents in job groups—§60–2.13;

(iv) Determining availability—§60–2.14;

(v) Comparing incumbency to availability—§60–2.15; and

(vi) Placement goals—§60–2.16.

(2) In addition, an affirmative action program must include the following components specified in the §60–2.17 of this part:

(i) Designation of responsibility for implementation;

(ii) Identification of problem areas;

(iii) Action-oriented programs; and

(iv) Periodic internal audits.

(c) *Documentation.* Contractors must maintain and make available to OFCCP documentation of their compliance with §§60–2.11 through 60–2.17.

§60–2.11 Organizational profile.

(a) *Purpose.* An organizational profile is a depiction of the staffing pattern within an establishment. It is one method contractors use to determine whether barriers to equal employment opportunity exist in their organizations. The profile provides an overview of the workforce at the establishment that may assist in identifying organizational units where women or minorities are underrepresented or concentrated. The contractor must use either the organizational display or the workforce analysis as its organizational profile:

(b) *Organizational display.* (1) An organizational display is a detailed graphical or tabular chart, text, spreadsheet or similar presentation of the contractor's organizational structure. The organizational display must identify each organizational unit in the establishment, and show the relationship of each organizational unit to the other organizational units in the establishment.

(2) An organizational unit is any component that is part of the contractor's corporate structure. In a more traditional organization, an organizational unit might be a department, division, section, branch, group or similar component. In a less traditional organization, an organizational unit might be a project team, job family, or similar component. The term includes an umbrella unit (such as a department) that contains a number of subordinate units, and it separately includes each of the subordinate units (such as sections or branches).

(3) For each organizational unit, the organizational display must indicate the following:

(i) The name of the unit;

(ii) The job title, gender, race, and ethnicity of the unit supervisor (if the unit has a supervisor);

(iii) The total number of male and female incumbents; and

(iv) the total number of male and female incumbents in each of the following groups: Blacks, Hispanics, Asians/Pacific Islanders, and American Indians/Alaskan Natives.

(c) *Workforce analysis*. (1) A workforce analysis is a listing of each job title as appears in applicable collective bargaining agreements or payroll records ranked from the lowest paid to the highest paid within each department or other similar organizational unit including departmental or unit supervision.

(2) If there are separate work units or lines of progression within a department, a separate list must be provided for each such work unit, or line, including unit supervisors. For lines of progression there must be indicated the order of jobs in the line through which an employee could move to the top of the line.

(3) Where there are no formal progression lines or usual promotional sequences, job titles should be listed by department, job families, or disciplines, in order of wage rates or salary ranges.

(4) For each job title, the total number of incumbents, the total number of male and female incumbents, and the total number of male and female incumbents in each of the following groups must be given: Blacks, Hispanics, Asians/Pacific Islanders, and American Indians/Alaskan Natives. The wage rate or salary range for each job title must be given. All job titles, including all managerial job titles, must be listed.

§60–2.12 Job group analysis.

(a) Purpose: A job group analysis is a method of combining job titles within the contractor's establishment. This is the first step in the contractor's comparison of the representation of minorities and women in its workforce with the estimated availability of minorities and women qualified to be employed.

(b) In the job group analysis, jobs at the establishment with similar content, wage rates, and opportunities, must be combined to form job groups. Similarity of content refers to the duties and responsibilities of the job titles which make up the job group. Similarity of opportunities refers to training, transfers, promotions, pay, mobility, and other career enhancement opportunities offered by the jobs within the job group.

(c) The job group analysis must include a list of the job titles that comprise each job group. If, pursuant to §§60–2.1(d) and (e) the job group analysis contains jobs that are located at another establishment, the job group analysis must be annotated to identify the actual location of those jobs. If the establishment at which the jobs actually are located maintains an affirmative action program, the job group analysis of that program must be annotated to identify the program in which the jobs are included.

(d) Except as provided in §60–2.1(d), all jobs located at an establishment must be reported in the job group analysis of that establishment.

(e) Smaller employers: If a contractor has a total workforce of fewer than 150 employees, the contractor may prepare a job group analysis that utilizes EEO–1 categories as job groups. EEO–1 categories refers to the nine occupational groups used in the Standard Form 100, the Employer Information EEO–1 Survey: Officials and managers, professionals, technicians, sales, office and clerical, craft workers (skilled), operatives (semiskilled), laborers (unskilled), and service workers.

§60–2.13 Placement of incumbents in job groups.

The contractor must separately state the percentage of minorities and the percentage of women it employs in each job group established pursuant to §60–2.12.

§60–2.14 Determining availability.

(a) Purpose: Availability is an estimate of the number of qualified minorities or women available for employment in a given job group, expressed as a percentage of all qualified persons available for employment in the job group. The purpose of the availability determination is to establish a benchmark against which the demographic composition of the contractor's incumbent workforce can be compared in order to determine whether barriers to equal employment opportunity may exist within particular job groups.

(b) The contractor must separately determine the availability of minorities and women for each job group.

(c) In determining availability, the contractor must consider at least the following factors:

(1) The percentage of minorities or women with requisite skills in the reasonable recruitment area. The reasonable recruitment area is defined as the geographical area from which the contractor usually seeks or reasonably could seek workers to fill the positions in question.

(2) The percentage of minorities or women among those promotable, transferable, and trainable within the contractor's organization. Trainable refers to those employees within the contractor's organization who could, with appropriate training which the contractor is reasonably able to provide, become promotable or transferable during the AAP year.

(d) The contractor must use the most current and discrete statistical information available to derive availability figures. Examples of such information include census data, data from local job service offices, and data from colleges or other training institutions.

(e) The contractor may not draw its reasonable recruitment area in such a way as to have the effect of excluding minorities or women. For each job group, the reasonable recruitment area must be identified, with a brief explanation of the rationale for selection of that recruitment area.

(f) The contractor may not define the pool of promotable, transferable, and trainable employees in such a way as to have the effect of excluding minorities or women. For each job group, the pool of promotable, transferable, and trainable employees must be identified with a brief explanation of the rationale for the selection of that pool.

(g) Where a job group is composed of job titles with different availability rates, a composite availability figure for the job group must be calculated. The contractor must separately determine the availability for each job title within the job group and must determine the proportion of job group incumbents employed in each job title. The contractor must weight the availability for each job title by the proportion of job group incumbents employed in that job group. The sum of the weighted availability estimates for all job titles in the job group must be the composite availability for the job group.

§ 60–2.15 Comparing incumbency to availability.

(a) The contractor must compare the percentage of minorities and women in each job group determined pursuant to § 60–2.13 with the availability for those job groups determined pursuant to § 60–2.14.

(b) When the percentage of minorities or women employed in a particular job group is less than would reasonably be expected given their availability percentage in that particular job group, the contractor must establish a placement goal in accordance with § 60–2.16.

§ 60–2.16 Placement goals.

(a) Purpose: Placement goals serve as objectives or targets reasonably attainable by means of applying every good faith effort to make all aspects of the entire affirmative action program work. Placement goals also are used to measure progress toward achieving equal employment opportunity.

(b) A contractor's determination under § 60–2.15 that a placement goal is required constitutes neither a finding nor an admission of discrimination.

(c) Where, pursuant to § 60–2.15, a contractor is required to establish a placement goal for a particular job group, the contractor must establish a percentage annual placement goal at least equal to the availability figure derived for women or minorities, as appropriate, for that job group.

(d) The placement goal-setting process described above contemplates that contractors will, where required, establish a single goal for all minorities. In the event of a substantial disparity in the utilization of a particular minority group or in the utilization of men or women of a particular minority group, a contractor may be required to establish separate goals for those groups.

(e) In establishing placement goals, the following principles also apply:

(1) Placement goals may not be rigid and inflexible quotas, which must be met, nor are they to be considered as either a ceiling or a floor for the employment of particular groups. Quotas are expressly forbidden.

(2) In all employment decisions, the contractor must make selections in a nondiscriminatory manner. Placement goals do not provide the contractor with a justification to extend a preference to any individual, select an individual, or adversely affect an individual's employment status, on the basis of that person's race, color, religion, sex, or national origin.

(3) Placement goals do not create set-asides for specific groups, nor are they intended to achieve proportional representation or equal results.

(4) Placement goals may not be used to supersede merit selection principles. Affirmative action programs prescribed by the regulations in this part do not require a contractor to hire a person who lacks qualifications to perform the job successfully, or hire a less qualified person in preference to a more qualified one.

(f) A contractor extending a publicly announced preference for American Indians as is authorized in 41 CFR 60–1.5(a)(6) may reflect in its placement goals the permissive employment preference for American Indians living on or near an Indian reservation.

§60–2.17 Additional required elements of affirmative action programs.

In addition to the elements required by §60–2.10 through §60–2.16, an acceptable affirmative action program must include the following:

(a) *Designation of responsibility.* The contractor must provide for the implementation of equal employment opportunity and the affirmative action program by assigning responsibility and accountability to an official of the organization. Depending upon the size of the contractor, this may be the official's sole responsibility. He or she must have the authority, resources, support of and access to top management to ensure the effective implementation of the affirmative action program.

(b) *Identification of problem areas.* The contractor must perform in-depth analyses of its total employment process to determine whether and where impediments to equal employment opportunity exist. At a minimum the contractor must evaluate:

(1) The workforce by organizational unit and job group to determine whether there are problems of minority or female utilization (*i.e.*, employment in the unit or group), or of minority or female distribution (*i.e.*, placement in the different jobs within the unit or group);

(2) Personnel activity (applicant flow, hires, terminations, promotions, and other personnel actions) to determine whether there are selection disparities;

(3) Compensation system(s) to determine whether there are gender-, race-, or ethnicity-based disparities;

(4) Selection, recruitment, referral, and other personnel procedures to determine whether they result in disparities in the employment or advancement of minorities or women; and

(5) Any other areas that might impact the success of the affirmative action program.

(c) *Action-oriented programs.* The contractor must develop and execute action-oriented programs designed to correct any problem areas identified pursuant to §60–2.17(b) and to attain established goals and objectives. In order for these action-oriented programs to be effective, the contractor must ensure that they consist of more than following the same procedures which have previously produced inadequate results. Furthermore, a contractor must demonstrate that it has made good faith efforts to remove identified barriers, expand employment opportunities, and produce measurable results.

(d) *Internal audit and reporting system.* The contractor must develop and implement an auditing system that periodically measures the effectiveness of its total affirmative action program. The actions listed below are key to a successful affirmative action program:

(1) Monitor records of all personnel activity, including referrals, placements, transfers, promotions, terminations, and compensation, at all levels to ensure the nondiscriminatory policy is carried out;

(2) Require internal reporting on a scheduled basis as to the degree to which equal employment opportunity and organizational objectives are attained;

(3) Review report results with all levels of management; and

(4) Advise top management of program effectiveness and submit recommendations to improve unsatisfactory performance.

§60–2.18 [Reserved]

Subpart C—Miscellaneous

§60–2.30 Corporate management compliance evaluations.

(a) Purpose. Corporate Management Compliance Evaluations are designed to ascertain whether individuals are encountering artificial barriers to advancement into mid-level and senior corporate management, *i.e.*, glass ceiling. During Corporate Management Compliance Evaluations, special attention is given to those components of the employment process that affect advancement into mid-and senior-level positions.

(b) If, during the course of a Corporate Management Compliance Evaluation, it comes to the attention of OFCCP that problems exist at establishments outside the corporate headquarters, OFCCP may expand the compliance evaluation beyond the headquarters establishment. At its discretion, OFCCP may direct its attention to and request relevant data for any and all areas within the corporation to ensure compliance with Executive Order 11246.

§60–2.31 Program summary.

The affirmative action program must be summarized and updated annually. The program summary must be prepared in a format which will be prescribed by the Deputy Assistant Secretary and published in the FEDERAL REGISTER as a notice before becoming effective. Contractors and subcontractors must submit the program summary to OFCCP each year on the anniversary date of the affirmative action program.

§60–2.32 Affirmative action records.

The contractor must make available to the Office of Federal Contract Compliance Programs, upon request, records maintained pursuant to §60–1.12 of this chapter and written or otherwise documented portions of AAPs maintained pursuant to §60–2.10 for such purposes as may be appropriate to the fulfillment of the agency's responsibilities under Executive Order 11246.

§60–2.33 Preemption.

To the extent that any state or local laws, regulations or ordinances, including those that grant special benefits to persons on account of sex, are in conflict with Executive Order 11246, as amended, or with the requirements of this part, they will be regarded as preempted under the Executive Order.

§60–2.34 Supersedure.

All orders, instructions, regulations, and memorandums of the Secretary of Labor, other officials of the Department of Labor and contracting agencies are hereby superseded to the extent that they are inconsistent with this Part 60–2.

§60–2.35 Compliance status.

No contractor's compliance status will be judged alone by whether it reaches its goals. The composition of the contractor's workforce (*i.e.*, the employment of minorities or women at a percentage rate below, or above, the goal level) does not, by itself, serve as a basis to impose any of the sanctions authorized by Executive Order 11246 and the regulations in this chapter. Each contractor's compliance with its affirmative action obligations will be determined by reviewing the nature and extent of the contractor's good faith affirmative action activities as required under §60–2.17, and the appropriateness of those activities to identified equal employment opportunity problems. Each contractor's compliance with its nondiscrimination obligations will be determined by analysis of statistical data and other non-statistical information which would indicate whether employees and applicants are being treated without regard to their race, color, religion, sex, or national origin.

PART 60–3—UNIFORM GUIDELINES ON EMPLOYEE SELECTION PROCEDURES (1978)

AUTHORITY: Secs. 201, 202, 203, 203(a), 205, 206(a), 301, 303(b), and 403(b) of E.O. 11246; as amended by sec. 715 of Civil Rights Act of 1964, as amended (42 U.S.C. 2000(e)–14).

SOURCE: 43 FR 38295, 38314, August 25, 1978, unless otherwise noted.

GENERAL PRINCIPLES

§60–3.1 Statement of purpose.

A. *Need for uniformity—Issuing agencies.* The Federal government's need for a uniform set of principles on the question of the use of tests and other selection procedures has long been recognized. The Equal Employment Opportunity Commission, the Civil Service Commission, the Department of Labor, and the Department of Justice jointly have adopted these uniform guidelines to meet that need, and to apply the same principles to the Federal Government as are applied to other employers.

B. *Purpose of guidelines.* These guidelines incorporate a single set of principles which are designed to assist employers, labor organizations, employment agencies, and licensing and certification boards to comply with requirements of Federal law prohibiting employment practices which discriminate on grounds of race, color, religion, sex, and national origin. They are designed to provide a framework for determining the proper use of tests and other selection procedures. These guidelines do not require a user to conduct validity studies of selection procedures where no adverse impact results. However, all users are encouraged to use selection procedures which are valid, especially users operating under merit principles.

C. *Relation to prior guidelines.* These guidelines are based upon and supersede previously issued guidelines on employee selection procedures. These guidelines have been built upon court decisions, the previously issued guidelines of the agencies, and the practical experience of the agencies, as well as the standards of the psychological profession. These guidelines are intended to be consistent with existing law.

§60–3.2 Scope.

A. *Application of guidelines.* These guidelines will be applied by the Equal Employment Opportunity Commission in the enforcement of title VII of the Civil Rights Act of 1964, as amended by the Equal Employment Opportunity Act of 1972 (hereinafter "Title VII"); by the Department of Labor, and the contract compliance agencies until the transfer of authority contemplated by the President's Reorganization Plan No. 1 of 1978, in the administration and enforcement of Executive Order 11246, as amended by Executive Order 11375 (hereinafter "Executive Order 11246");

by the Civil Service Commission and other Federal agencies subject to section 717 of Title VII; by the Civil Service Commission in exercising its responsibilities toward State and local governments under section 208(b)(1) of the Intergovernmental-Personnel Act; by the Department of Justice in exercising its responsibilities under Federal law; by the Office of Revenue Sharing of the Department of the Treasury under the State and Local Fiscal Assistance Act of 1972, as amended; and by any other Federal agency which adopts them.

B. *Employment decisions.* These guidelines apply to tests and other selection procedures which are used as a basis for any employment decision. Employment decisions include but are not limited to hiring, promotion, demotion, membership (for example, in a labor organization), referral, retention, and licensing and certification, to the extent that licensing and certification may be covered by Federal equal employment opportunity law. Other selection decisions, such as selection for training or transfer, may also be considered employment decisions if they lead to any of the decisions listed above.

C. *Selection procedures.* These guidelines apply only to selection procedures which are used as a basis for making employment decisions. For example, the use of recruiting procedures designed to attract members of a particular race, sex, or ethnic group, which were previously denied employment opportunities or which are currently underutilized, may be necessary to bring an employer into compliance with Federal law, and is frequently an essential element of any effective affirmative action program; but recruitment practices are not considered by these guidelines to be selection procedures. Similarly, these guidelines do not pertain to the question of the lawfulness of a seniority system within the meaning of section 703(h), Executive Order 11246 or other provisions of Federal law or regulation, except to the extent that such systems utilize selection procedures to determine qualifications or abilities to perform the job. Nothing in these guidelines is intended or should be interpreted as discouraging the use of a selection procedure for the purpose of determining qualifications or for the purpose of selection on the basis of relative qualifications, if the selection procedure had been validated in accord with these guidelines for each such purpose for which it is to be used.

D. *Limitations.* These guidelines apply only to persons subject to Title VII, Executive Order 11246, or other equal employment opportunity requirements of Federal law. These guidelines do not apply to responsibilities under the Age Discrimination in Employment Act of 1967, as amended, not to discriminate on the basis of age, or under sections 501, 503, and 504 of the Rehabilitation Act of 1973, not to discriminate on the basis of handicap.

E. *Indian preference not affected.* These guidelines do not restrict any obligation imposed or right granted by Federal law to users to extend a preference in employment to Indians living on or near an Indian reservation in connection with employment opportunities on or near an Indian reservation.

§ 60–3.3 Discrimination defined: Relationship between use of selection procedures and discrimination.

A. *Procedure having adverse impact constitutes discrimination unless justified.* The use of any selection procedure which has an adverse impact on the hiring, promotion, or other employment or membership opportunities of members of any race, sex, or ethnic group will be considered to be discriminatory and inconsistent with these guidelines, unless the procedure has been validated in accordance with these guidelines, or the provisions of section 6 of this part are satisfied.

B. *Consideration of suitable alternative selection procedures.* Where two or more selection procedures are available which serve the user's legitimate interest in efficient and trustworthy workmanship, and which are substantially equally valid for a given purpose, the user should use the procedure which has been demonstrated to have the lesser adverse impact. Accordingly, whenever a validity study is called for by these guidelines, the user should include, as a part of the validity study, an investigation of suitable alternative selection procedures and suitable alternative methods of using the selection procedure which have as little adverse impact as possible, to determine the appropriateness of using or validating them in accord with these guidelines. If a user has made a reasonable effort to become aware of such alternative procedures and validity has been demonstrated in accord with these guidelines, the use of the test or other selection procedure may continue until such time as it should reasonably be reviewed for currency. Whenever the user is shown an alternative selection procedure with evidence of less adverse impact and substantial evidence of validity for the same job in similar circumstances, the user should investigate it to determine the appropriateness of using or validating it in accord with these guidelines. This subsection is not intended to preclude the combination of procedures into a significantly more valid procedure, if the use of such a combination has been shown to be in compliance with the guidelines.

§ 60–3.4 Information on impact.

A. *Records concerning impact.* Each user should maintain and have available for inspection records or other information which will disclose the impact which its tests and other selection procedures have upon employment opportunities of persons by identifiable race, sex, or ethnic group as set forth in subparagraph B of this section in order to determine compliance with these guidelines. Where there are large numbers of applicants and procedures are administered frequently, such information may be retained on a sample basis, provided that the sample is appropriate in terms of the applicant population and adequate in size.

B. *Applicable race, sex, and ethnic groups for recordkeeping.* The records called for by this section are to be maintained by sex, and the following races and ethnic groups: Blacks (Negroes), American Indians (including Alaskan Natives), Asians (including Pacific Islanders), Hispanic (including persons of Mexican, Puerto Rican, Cuban, Central or South American, or other Spanish origin or culture regardless of race), whites (Caucasians) other than Hispanic, and totals. The race, sex, and ethnic classifications called for by this section are consistent with the Equal Employment Opportunity Standard Form 100, Employer Information Report EEO–1 series of reports. The user should adopt safeguards to insure that the records required by this paragraph are used for appropriate purposes such as determining adverse impact, or (where required) for developing and monitoring affirmative action programs, and that such records are not used improperly. See sections 4E and 17(4), of this part.

C. *Evaluation of selection rates. The "bottom line."* If the information called for by sections 4A and B of this section shows that the total selection process for a job has an adverse impact, the individual components of the selection process should be evaluated for adverse impact. If this information shows that the total selection process does not have an adverse impact, the Federal enforcement agencies, in the exercise of their administrative and prosecutorial discretion, in usual circumstances, will not expect a user to evaluate the individual components for adverse impact, or to validate such individual components, and will not take enforcement action based upon adverse impact of any component of that process, including the separate parts of a multipart selection procedure or any separate procedure that is used as an alternative method of selection. However, in the following circumstances the Federal enforcement agencies will expect a user to evaluate the individual components for adverse impact and may, where appropriate, take enforcement action with respect to the individual components: (1) where the selection procedure is a significant factor in the continuation of patterns of assignments of incumbent employees caused by prior discriminatory employment practices, (2) where the weight of court decisions or administrative interpretations hold that a specific procedure (such as height or weight requirements or no-arrest records) is not job related in the same or similar circumstances. In unusual circumstances, other than those listed in paragraphs (1) and (2) of this section, the Federal enforcement agencies may request a user to evaluate the individual components for adverse impact and may, where appropriate, take enforcement action with respect to the individual component.

D. *Adverse impact and the "four-fifths rule."* A selection rate for any race, sex, or ethnic group which is less than four-fifths (4/5) (or eighty percent) of the rate for the group with the highest rate will generally be regarded by the Federal enforcement agencies as evidence of adverse impact, while a greater than four-fifths rate will generally not be regarded by Federal enforcement agencies as evidence of adverse impact. Smaller differences in selection rate may nevertheless constitute adverse impact, where they are significant in both statistical and practical terms or where a user's actions have discouraged applicants disproportionately on grounds of race, sex, or ethnic group. Greater differences in selection rate may not constitute adverse impact where the differences are based on small numbers and are not statistically significant, or where special recruiting or other programs cause the pool of minority or female candidates to be atypical of the normal pool of applicants from that group. Where the user's evidence concerning the impact of a selection procedure indicates adverse impact but is based upon numbers which are too small to be reliable, evidence concerning the impact of the procedure over a longer period of time and/or evidence concerning the impact which the selection procedure had when used in the same manner in similar circumstances elsewhere may be considered in determining adverse impact. Where the user has not maintained data on adverse impact as required by the documentation section of applicable guidelines, the Federal enforcement agencies may draw an inference of adverse impact of the selection process from the failure of the user to maintain such data, if the user has an underutilization of a group in the job category, as compared to the group's representation in the relevant labor market or, in the case of jobs filled from within, the applicable work force.

E. *Consideration of user's equal employment opportunity posture.* In carrying out their obligations, the Federal enforcement agencies will consider the general posture of the user with respect to equal employment opportunity for the job or group of jobs in question. Where a user has adopted an affirmative action program, the Federal enforcement agencies will consider the provisions of that program, including the goals and timetables which the user has adopted and the progress which the user has made in carrying out that program and in meeting the goals and timetables. While such affirmative action programs may in design and execution be race, color, sex, or ethnic conscious, selection procedures under such programs should be based upon the ability or relative ability to do the work.

§ 60–3.5 General standards for validity studies.

A. *Acceptable types of validity studies.* For the purposes of satisfying these guidelines, users may rely upon criterion-related validity studies, content validity studies or construct validity studies, in accordance with the standards set forth in the technical standards of these guidelines, section 14 of this part. New strategies for showing the validity of selection procedures will be evaluated as they become accepted by the psychological profession.

B. *Criterion-related, content, and construct validity.* Evidence of the validity of a test or other selection procedure by a criterion-related validity study should consist of empirical data demonstrating that the selection procedure is predictive of or significantly correlated with important elements of job performance. See 14B of this part. Evidence of the validity of a test or other selection procedure by a content validity study should consist of data showing that the content of the selection procedure is representative of important aspects of performance on the job for which the candidates are to be evaluated. See 14C of this part. Evidence of the validity of a test or other selection procedure through a construct validity study should consist of data showing that the procedure measures the degree to which candidates have identifiable characteristics which have been determined to be important in successful performance in the job for which the candidates are to be evaluated. See section 14D of this part.

C. *Guidelines are consistent with professional standards.* The provisions of these guidelines relating to validation of selection procedures are intended to be consistent with generally accepted professional standards for evaluating standardized tests and other selection procedures, such as those described in the Standards for Educational and Psychological Tests prepared by a joint committee of the American Psychological Association, the American Educational Research Association, and the National Council on Measurement in Education (American Psychological Association, Washington, D.C., 1974) (hereinafter "A.P.A. Standards") and standard textbooks and journals in the field of personnel selection.

D. *Need for documentation of validity.* For any selection procedure which is part of a selection process which has an adverse impact and which selection procedure has an adverse impact, each user should maintain and have available such documentation as is described in section 15 of this part.

E. *Accuracy and standardization.* Validity studies should be carried out under conditions which assure insofar as possible the adequacy and accuracy of the research and the report. Selection procedures should be administered and scored under standardized conditions.

F. *Caution against selection on basis of knowledges, skills, or ability learned in brief orientation period.* In general, users should avoid making employment decisions on the basis of measures of knowledges, skills, or abilities which are normally learned in a brief orientation period, and which have an adverse impact.

G. *Method of use of selection procedures.* The evidence of both the validity and utility of a selection procedure should support the method the user chooses for operational use of the procedure, if that method of use has a greater adverse impact than another method of use. Evidence which may be sufficient to support the use of a selection procedure on a pass/fail (screening) basis may be insufficient to support the use of the same procedure on a ranking basis under these guidelines. Thus, if a user decides to use a selection procedure on a ranking basis, and that method of use has a greater adverse impact than use on an appropriate pass/fail basis (see section 5H of this section), the user should have sufficient evidence of validity and utility to support the use on a ranking basis. See sections 3B, 14B (5) and (6), and 14C (8) and (9).

H. *Cutoff scores.* Where cutoff scores are used, they should normally be set so as to be reasonable and consistent with normal expectations of acceptable proficiency within the work force. Where applicants are ranked on the basis of properly validated selection procedures and those applicants scoring below a higher cutoff score than appropriate in light of such expectations have little or no chance of being selected for employment, the higher cutoff score may be appropriate, but the degree of adverse impact should be considered.

I. *Use of selection procedures for higher level jobs.* If job progression structures are so established that employees will probably, within a reasonable period of time and in a majority of cases, progress to a higher level, it may be considered that the applicants are being evaluated for a job or jobs at the higher level. However, where job progression is not so nearly automatic, or the time span is such that higher level jobs or employees' potential may be expected to change in significant ways, it should be considered that applicants are being evaluated for a job at or near the entry level. A "reasonable period of time" will vary for different jobs and employment situations but will seldom be more than 5 years. Use of selection procedures to evaluate applicants for a higher level job would not be appropriate:

(1) If the majority of those remaining employed do not progress to the higher level job;

(2) If there is a reason to doubt that the higher level job will continue to require essentially similar skills during the progression period; or

(3) If the selection procedures measure knowledges, skills, or abilities required for advancement which would be expected to develop principally from the training or experience on the job.

J. *Interim use of selection procedures.* Users may continue the use of a selection procedure which is not at the moment fully supported by the required evidence of validity, provided: (1) The user has available substantial evidence of validity, and (2) the user has in progress, when technically feasible, a study which is designed to produce the additional evidence required by these guidelines within a reasonable time. If such a study is not technically feasible, see section 6B. If the study does not demonstrate validity, this provision of these guidelines for interim use shall not constitute a defense in any action, nor shall it relieve the user of any obligations arising under Federal law.

K. *Review of validity studies for currency.* Whenever validity has been shown in accord with these guidelines for the use of a particular selection procedure for a job or group of jobs, additional studies need not be performed until such time as the validity study is subject to review as provided in section 3B of this part. There are no absolutes in the area of determining the currency of a validity study. All circumstances concerning the study, including the validation strategy used, and changes in the relevant labor market and the job should be considered in the determination of when a validity study is outdated.

§ 60–3.6 Use of selection procedures which have not been validated.

A. *Use of alternate selection procedures to eliminate adverse impact.* A user may choose to utilize alternative selection procedures in order to eliminate adverse impact or as part of an affirmative action program. See section 13 of this part. Such alternative procedures should eliminate the adverse impact in the total selection process, should be lawful and should be as job related as possible.

B. *Where validity studies cannot or need not be performed.* There are circumstances in which a user cannot or need not utilize the validation techniques contemplated by these guidelines. In such circumstances, the user should utilize selection procedures which are as job related as possible and which will minimize or eliminate adverse impact, as set forth below.

(1) *Where informal or unscored procedures are used.* When an informal or unscored selection procedure which has an adverse impact is utilized, the user should eliminate the adverse impact, or modify the procedure to one which is a formal, scored or quantified measure or combination of measures and then validate the procedure in accord with these guidelines, or otherwise justify continued use of the procedure in accord with Federal law.

(2) *Where formal and scored procedures are used.* When a formal and scored selection procedure is used which has an adverse impact, the validation techniques contemplated by these guidelines usually should be followed if technically feasible. Where the user cannot or need not follow the validation techniques anticipated by these guidelines, the user should either modify the procedure to eliminate adverse impact or otherwise justify continued use of the procedure in accord with Federal law.

§ 60–3.7 Use of other validity studies.

A. *Validity studies not conducted by the user.* Users may, under certain circumstances, support the use of selection procedures by validity studies conducted by other users or conducted by test publishers or distributors and described in test manuals. While publishers of selection procedures have a professional obligation to provide evidence of validity which meets generally accepted professional standards (see section 5C of this part), users are cautioned that they are responsible for compliance with these guidelines. Accordingly, users seeking to obtain selection procedures from publishers and distributors should be careful to determine that, in the event the user becomes subject to the validity requirements of these guidelines, the necessary information to support validity has been determined and will be made available to the user.

B. *Use of criterion-related validity evidence from other sources.* Criterion-related validity studies conducted by one test user, or described in test manuals and the professional literature, will be considered acceptable for use by another user when the following requirements are met:

(1) *Validity evidence.* Evidence from the available studies meeting the standards of section 14B of this part clearly demonstrates that the selection procedure is valid;

(2) *Job similarity.* The incumbents in the user's job and the incumbents in the job or group of jobs on which the validity study was conducted perform substantially the same major work behaviors, as shown by appropriate job analyses both on the job or group of jobs on which the validity study was performed and on the job for which the selection procedure is to be used; and

(3) *Fairness evidence.* The studies include a study of test fairness for each race, sex, and ethnic group which constitutes a significant factor in the borrowing user's relevant labor market for the job or jobs in question. If the studies under consideration satisfy paragraphs (1) and (2) of this section but do not contain an investigation of test fairness, and it is not technically feasible for the borrowing user to conduct an internal study of test fairness, the borrowing user may utilize the study until studies conducted elsewhere meeting the requirements of these guidelines show test unfairness, or until such time as it becomes technically feasible to conduct an internal study of test fairness and the results of that study can be acted upon. Users obtaining selection procedures from publishers should consider, as one factor in the decision to purchase a particular selection procedure, the availability of evidence concerning test fairness.

C. *Validity evidence from multiunit study.* if validity evidence from a study covering more than one unit within an organization statisfies the requirements of section 14B of this part, evidence of validity specific to each unit will not be required unless there are variables which are likely to affect validity significantly.

D. *Other significant variables.* If there are variables in the other studies which are likely to affect validity significantly, the user may not rely upon such studies, but will be expected either to conduct an internal validity study or to comply with section 6 of this part.

§60-3.8 Cooperative studies.

A. *Encouragement of cooperative studies.* The agencies issuing these guidelines encourage employers, labor organizations, and employment agencies to cooperate in research, development, search for lawful alternatives, and validity studies in order to achieve procedures which are consistent with these guidelines.

B. *Standards for use of cooperative studies.* If validity evidence from a cooperative study satisfies the requirements of section 14 of this part, evidence of validity specific to each user will not be required unless there are variables in the user's situation which are likely to affect validity significantly.

§60-3.9 No assumption of validity.

A. *Unacceptable substitutes for evidence of validity.* Under no circumstances will the general reputation of a test or other selection procedures, its author or its publisher, or casual reports of it's validity be accepted in lieu of evidence of validity. Specifically ruled out are: assumptions of validity based on a procedure's name or descriptive labels; all forms of promotional literature; data bearing on the frequency of a procedure's usage; testimonial statements and credentials of sellers, users, or consultants; and other nonempirical or anecdotal accounts of selection practices or selection outcomes.

B. *Encouragement of professional supervision.* Professional supervision of selection activities is encouraged but is not a substitute for documented evidence of validity. The enforcement agencies will take into account the fact that a thorough job analysis was conducted and that careful development and use of a selection procedure in accordance with professional standards enhance the probability that the selection procedure is valid for the job.

§60-3.10 Employment agencies and employment services.

A. *Where selection procedures are devised by agency.* An employment agency, including private employment agencies and State employment agencies, which agrees to a request by an employer or labor organization to devise and utilize a selection procedure should follow the standards in these guidelines for determining adverse impact. If adverse impact exists the agency should comply with these guidelines. An employment agency is not relieved of its obligation herein because the user did not request such validation or has requested the use of some lesser standard of validation than is provided in these guidelines. The use of an employment agency does not relieve an employer or labor organization or other user of its responsibilities under Federal law to provide equal employment opportunity or its obligations as a user under these guidelines.

B. *Where selection procedures are devised elsewhere.* Where an employment agency or service is requested to administer a selection procedure which has been devised elsewhere and to make referrals pursuant to the results, the employment agency or service should maintain and have available evidence of the impact of the selection and referral procedures which it administers. If adverse impact results the agency or service should comply with these guidelines. If the agency or service seeks to comply with these guidelines by reliance upon validity studies or other data in the possession of the employer, it should obtain and have available such information.

§ 60-3.11 Disparate treatment.

The principles of disparate or unequal treatment must be distinguished from the concepts of validation. A selection procedure—even though validated against job performance in accordance with these guidelines—cannot be imposed upon members of a race, sex, or ethnic group where other employees, applicants, or members have not been subjected to that standard. Disparate treatment occurs where members of a race, sex, or ethnic group have been denied the same employment, promotion, membership, or other employment opportunities as have been available to other employees or applicants. Those employees or applicants who have been denied equal treatment, because of prior discriminatory practices or policies, must at least be afforded the same opportunities as had existed for other employees or applicants during the period of discrimination. Thus, the persons who were in the class of persons discriminated against during the period the user followed the discriminatory practices should be allowed the opportunity to qualify under less stringent selection procedures previously followed, unless the user demonstrates that the increased standards are required by business necessity. This section does not prohibit a user who has not previously followed merit standards from adopting merit standards which are in compliance with these guidelines; nor does it preclude a user who has previously used invalid or unvalidated selection procedures from developing and using procedures which are in accord with these guidelines.

§ 60-3.12 Retesting of applicants.

Users should provide a reasonable opportunity for retesting and reconsideration. Where examinations are administered periodically with public notice, such reasonable opportunity exists, unless persons who have previously been tested are precluded from retesting. The user may however take reasonable steps to preserve the security of its procedures.

§ 60-3.13 Affirmative action.

A. *Affirmative action obligations.* The use of selection procedures which have been validated pursuant to these guidelines does not relieve users of any obligations they may have to undertake affirmative action to assure equal employment opportunity. Nothing in these guidelines is intended to preclude the use of lawful selection procedures which assist in remedying the effects of prior discriminatory practices, or the achievement of affirmative action objectives.

B. *Encouragement of voluntary affirmative action programs.* These guidelines are also intended to encourage the adoption and implementation of voluntary affirmative action programs by users who have no obligation under Federal law to adopt them; but are not intended to impose any new obligations in that regard. The agencies issuing and endorsing these guidelines endorse for all private employers and reaffirm for all governmental employers the

Equal Employment Opportunity Coordinating Council's "Policy Statement on Affirmative Action Programs for State and Local Government Agencies" (41 FR 38814, September 13, 1976). That policy statement is attached hereto as appendix, section 17.

TECHNICAL STANDARDS

§ 60–3.14 Technical standards for validity studies.

The following minimum standards, as applicable, should be met in conducting a validity study. Nothing in these guidelines is intended to preclude the development and use of other professionally acceptable techniques with respect to validation of selection procedures. Where it is not technically feasible for a user to conduct a validity study, the user has the obligation otherwise to comply with these guidelines. See sections 6 and 7 of this part.

A. *Validity studies should be based on review of information about the job.* Any validity study should be based upon a review of information about the job for which the selection procedure is to be used. The review should include a job analysis except as provided in section 14B(3) of this section with respect to criterion-related validity. Any method of job analysis may be used if it provides the information required for the specific validation strategy used.

B. *Technical standards for criterion-related validity studies*—(1) *Technical feasibility.* Users choosing to validate a selection procedure by a criterion-related validity strategy should determine whether it is technically feasible (as defined in section 16) to conduct such a study in the particular employment context. The determination of the number of persons necessary to permit the conduct of a meaningful criterion-related study should be made by the user on the basis of all relevant information concerning the selection procedure, the potential sample and the employment situation. Where appropriate, jobs with substantially the same major work behaviors may be grouped together for validity studies, in order to obtain an adequate sample. These guidelines do not require a user to hire or promote persons for the purpose of making it possible to conduct a criterion-related study.

(2) *Analysis of the job.* There should be a review of job information to determine measures of work behavior(s) or performance that are relevant to the job or group of jobs in question. These measures or criteria are relevant to the extent that they represent critical or important job duties, work behaviors or work outcomes as developed from the review of job information. The possibility of bias should be considered both in selection of the criterion measures and their application. In view of the possibility of bias in subjective evaluations, supervisory rating techniques and instructions to raters should be carefully developed. All criterion measures and the methods for gathering data need to be examined for freedom from factors which would unfairly alter scores of members of any group. The relevance of criteria and their freedom from bias are of particular concern when there are significant differences in measures of job performance for different groups.

(3) *Criterion measures.* Proper safeguards should be taken to insure that scores on selection procedures do not enter into any judgments of employee adequacy that are to be used as criterion measures. Whatever criteria are used should represent important or critical work behavior(s) or work outcomes. Certain criteria may be used without a full job analysis if the user can show the importance of the criteria to the particular employment context. These criteria include but are not limited to production rate, error rate, tardiness, absenteeism, and length of service. A standardized rating of overall work performance may be used where a study of the job shows that it is an appropriate criterion. Where performance in training is used as a criterion, success in training should be properly measured and the relevance of the training should be shown either through a comparsion of the content of the training program with the critical or important work behavior(s) of the job(s), or through a demonstration of the relationship between measures of performance in training and measures of job performance. Measures of relative success in training include but

are not limited to instructor evaluations, performance samples, or tests. Criterion measures consisting of paper and pencil tests will be closely reviewed for job relevance.

(4) *Representativeness of the sample.* Whether the study is predictive or concurrent, the sample subjects should insofar as feasible be representative of the candidates normally available in the relevant labor market for the job or group of jobs in question, and should insofar as feasible include the races, sexes, and ethnic groups normally available in the relevant job market. In determining the representativeness of the sample in a concurrent validity study, the user should take into account the extent to which the specific knowledges or skills which are the primary focus of the test are those which employees learn on the job.

Where samples are combined or compared, attention should be given to see that such samples are comparable in terms of the actual job they perform, the length of time on the job where time on the job is likely to affect performance, and other relevant factors likely to affect validity differences; or that these factors are included in the design of the study and their effects identified.

(5) *Statistical relationships.* The degree of relationship between selection procedure scores and criterion measures should be examined and computed, using professionally acceptable statistical procedures. Generally, a selection procedure is considered related to the criterion, for the purposes of these guidelines, when the relationship between performance on the procedure and performance on the criterion measure is statistically significant at the 0.05 level of significance, which means that it is sufficiently high as to have a probability of no more than one (1) in twenty (20) to have occurred by chance. Absence of a statistically significant relationship between a selection procedure and job performance should not necessarily discourage other investigations of the validity of that selection procedure.

(6) *Operational use of selection procedures.* Users should evaluate each selection procedure to assure that it is appropriate for operational use, including establishment of cutoff scores or rank ordering. Generally, if other factors reman the same, the greater the magnitude of the relationship (e.g., correlation coefficent) between performance on a selection procedure and one or more criteria of performance on the job, and the greater the importance and number of aspects of job performance covered by the criteria, the more likely it is that the procedure will be appropriate for use. Reliance upon a selection procedure which is significantly related to a criterion measure, but which is based upon a study involving a large number of subjects and has a low correlation coefficient will be subject to close review if it has a large adverse impact. Sole reliance upon a single selection instrument which is related to only one of many job duties or aspects of job performance will also be subject to close review. The appropriateness of a selection procedure is best evaluated in each particular situation and there are no minimum correlation coefficients applicable to all employment situations. In determining whether a selection procedure is appropriate for operational use the following considerations should also be taken into account: The degree of adverse impact of the procedure, the availability of other selection procedures of greater or substantially equal validity.

(7) *Overstatement of validity findings.* Users should avoid reliance upon techniques which tend to overestimate validity findings as a result of capitalization on chance unless an appropriate safeguard is taken. Reliance upon a few selection procedures or criteria of successful job performance when many selection procedures or criteria of performance have been studied, or the use of optimal statistical weights for selection procedures computed in one sample, are techniques which tend to inflate validity estimates as a result of chance. Use of a large sample is one safeguard: cross-validation is another.

(8) *Fairness.* This section generally calls for studies of unfairness where technically feasible. The concept of fairness or unfairness of selection procedures is a developing concept. In addition, fairness studies generally require substantial numbers of employees in the job or group of jobs being

studied. For these reasons, the Federal enforcement agencies recognize that the obligation to conduct studies of fairness imposed by the guidelines generally will be upon users or groups of users with a large number of persons in a job class, or test developers; and that small users utilizing their own selection procedures will generally not be obligated to conduct such studies because it will be technically infeasible for them to do so.

(a) *Unfairness defined.* When members of one race, sex, or ethnic group characteristically obtain lower scores on a selection procedure than members of another group, and the differences in scores are not reflected in differences in a measure of job performance, use of the selection procedure may unfairly deny opportunities to members of the group that obtains the lower scores.

(b) *Investigation of fairness.* Where a selection procedure results in an adverse impact on a race, sex, or ethnic group identified in accordance with the classifications set forth in section 4 of this part and that group is a significant factor in the relevant labor market, the user generally should investigate the possible existence of unfairness for that group if it is technically feasible to do so. The greater the severity of the adverse impact on a group, the greater the need to investigate the possible existence of unfairness. Where the weight of evidence from other studies shows that the selection procedure predicts fairly for the group in question and for the same or similar jobs, such evidence may be relied on in connection with the selection procedure at issue.

(c) *General considerations in fairness investigations.* Users conducting a study of fairness should review the A.P.A. Standards regarding investigation of possible bias in testing. An investigation of fairness of a selection procedure depends on both evidence of validity and the manner in which the selection procedure is to be used in a particular employment context. Fairness of a selection procedure cannot necessarily be specified in advance without investigating these factors. Investigation of fairness of a selection procedure in samples where the range of scores on selection procedures or criterion measures is severely restricted for any subgroup sample (as compared to other subgroup samples) may produce misleading evidence of unfairness. That factor should accordingly be taken into account in conducting such studies and before reliance is placed on the results.

(d) *When unfairness is shown.* If unfairness is demonstrated through a showing that members of a particular group perform better or poorer on the job than their scores on the selection procedure would indicate through comparison with how members of other groups perform, the user may either revise or replace the selection instrument in accordance with these guidelines, or may continue to use the selection instrument operationally with appropriate revisions in its use to assure compatibility between the probability of successful job performance and the probability of being selected.

(e) *Technical feasibility of fairness studies.* In addition to the general conditions needed for technical feasibility for the conduct of a criterion-related study (see section 16, below) an investigation of fairness requires the following:

(1) An adequate sample of persons in each group available for the study to achieve findings of statistical significance. Guidelines do not require a user to hire or promote persons on the basis of group classifications for the purpose of making it possible to conduct a study of fairness; but the user has the obligation otherwise to comply with these guidelines.

(2) The samples for each group should be comparable in terms of the actual job they perform, length of time on the job where time on the job is likely to affect performance, and other relevant factors likely to affect validity differences; or such factors should be included in the design of the study and their effects identified.

(f) *Continued use of selection procedures when fairness studies not feasible.* If a study of fairness should otherwise be performed, but is not technically feasible, a selection procedure may be used which has otherwise met the validity standards of these guidelines, unless the technical infeasibility resulted from discriminatory employment practices which are demonstrated by facts other than past failure to conform with requirements for validation of selection procedures. However, when it becomes technically feasible for the user to perform a study of fairness and such a study is otherwise called for, the user should conduct the study of fairness.

C. *Technical standards for content validity studies*—(1) *Appropriateness of content validity studies.* Users choosing to validate a selection procedure by a content validity strategy should determine whether it is appropriate to conduct such a study in the particular employment context. A selection procedure can be supported by a content validity strategy to the extent that it is a representative sample of the content of the job. Selection procedures which purport to measure knowledges, skills, or abilities may in certain circumstances be justified by content validity, although they may not be representative samples, if the knowledge, skill, or ability measured by the selection procedure can be operationally defined as provided in paragraph 14C(4) of this section, and if that knowledge, skill, or ability is a necessary prerequisite to successful job performance.

A selection procedure based upon inferences about mental processes cannot be supported solely or primarily on the basis of content validity. Thus, a content strategy is not appropriate for demonstrating the validity of selection procedures which purport to measure traits or constructs, such as intelligence, aptitude, personality, commonsense, judgment, leadership, and spatial ability. Content validity is also not an appropriate strategy when the selection procedure involves knowledges, skills, or abilities which an employee will be expected to learn on the job.

(2) *Job analysis for content validity.* There should be a job analysis which includes an analysis of the important work behavior(s) required for successful performance and their relative importance and, if the behavior results in work product(s), an analysis of the work product(s). Any job analysis should focus on the work behavior(s) and the tasks associated with them. If work behavior(s) are not observable, the job analysis should identify and analyze those aspects of the behavior(s) that can be observed and the observed work products. The work behavior(s) selected for measurement should be critical work behavior(s) and/or important work behavior(s) constituting most of the job.

(3) *Development of selection procedures.* A selection procedure designed to measure the work behavior may be developed specifically from the job and job analysis in question, or may have been previously developed by the user, or by other users or by a test publisher.

(4) *Standards for demonstrating content validity.* To demonstrate the content validity of a selection procedure, a user should show that the behavior(s) demonstrated in the selection procedure are a representative sample of the behavior(s) of the job in question or that the selection procedure provides a representative sample of the work product of the job. In the case of a selection procedure measuring a knowledge, skill, or ability, the knowledge, skill, or ability being measured should be operationally defined. In the case of a selection procedure measuring a knowledge, the knowledge being measured should be operationally defined as that body of learned information which is used in and is a necessary prerequisite for observable aspects of work behavior of the job. In the case of skills or abilities, the skill or ability being measured should be operationally defined in terms of observable aspects of work behavior of the job. For any selection procedure measuring a knowledge, skill, or ability the user should show that (a) the selection procedure measures and is a representative sample of that knowledge, skill, or ability; and (b) that knowledge, skill, or ability is used in and is a necessary prerequisite to performance of critical or important work behavior(s). In addition, to be content valid, a selection procedure measuring a skill or ability should either closely approximate an observable work behavior, or its product should closely approximate an observable work product. If a test purports to sample a work behavior or to provide a sample of a work product, the manner and setting of the selection procedure and its level and complexity should closely approximate the work

situation. The closer the content and the context of the selection procedure are to work samples or work behaviors, the stronger is the basis for showing content validity. As the content of the selection procedure less resembles a work behavior, or the setting and manner of the administration of the selection procedure less resemble the work situation, or the result less resembles a work product, the less likely the selection procedure is to be content valid, and the greater the need for other evidence of validity.

(5) *Reliability.* The reliability of selection procedures justified on the basis of content validity should be a matter of concern to the user. Whenever it is feasible, appropriate statistical estimates should be made of the reliability of the selection procedure.

(6) *Prior training or experience.* A requirement for or evaluation of specific prior training or experience based on content validity, including a specification of level or amount of training or experience, should be justified on the basis of the relationship between the content of the training or experience and the content of the job for which the training or experience is to be required or evaluated. The critical consideration is the resemblance between the specific behaviors, products, knowledges, skills, or abilities in the experience or training and the specific behaviors, products, knowledges, skills, or abilities required on the job, whether or not there is close resemblance between the experience or training as a whole and the job as a whole.

(7) *Content validity of training success.* Where a measure of success in a training program is used as a selection procedure and the content of a training program is justified on the basis of content validity, the use should be justified on the relationship between the content of the training program and the content of the job.

(8) *Operational use.* A selection procedure which is supported on the basis of content validity may be used for a job if it represents a critical work behavior (*i.e.*, a behavior which is necessary for performance of the job) or work behaviors which constitute most of the important parts of the job.

(9) *Ranking based on content validity studies.* If a user can show, by a job analysis or otherwise, that a higher score on a content valid selection procedure is likely to result in better job performance, the results may be used to rank persons who score above minimum levels. Where a selection procedure supported solely or primarily by content validity is used to rank job candidates, the selection procedure should measure those aspects of performance which differentiate among levels of job performance.

D. *Technical standards for construct validity studies*—(1) *Appropriateness of construct validity studies.* Construct validity is a more complex strategy than either criterion-related or content validity. Construct validation is a relatively new and developing procedure in the employment field, and there is at present a lack of substantial literature extending the concept to employment practices. The user should be aware that the effort to obtain sufficient empirical support for construct validity is both an extensive and arduous effort involving a series of research studies, which include criterion related validity studies and which may include content validity studies. Users choosing to justify use of a selection procedure by this strategy should therefore take particular care to assure that the validity study meets the standards set forth below.

(2) *Job analysis for construct validity studies.* There should be a job analysis. This job analysis should show the work behavior(s) required for successful performance of the job, or the groups of jobs being studied, the critical or important work behavior(s) in the job or group of jobs being studied, and an identification of the construct(s) believed to underlie successful performance of these critical or important work behaviors in the job or jobs in question. Each construct should be named and defined, so as to distinguish it from other constructs. If a group of jobs is being studied the jobs should have in common one or more critical or important work behav- iors at a comparable level of complexity.

(3) *Relationship to the job.* A selection procedure should then be identified or

developed which measures the construct identified in accord with subparagraph (2) of this section. The user should show by empirical evidence that the selection procedure is validly related to the construct and that the construct is validly related to the performance of critical or important work behavior(s). The relationship between the construct as measured by the selection procedure and the related work behavior(s) should be supported by empirical evidence from one or more criterion-related studies involving the job or jobs in question which satisfy the provisions of paragraph 14B of this section.

(4) *Use of construct validity study without new criterion-related evidence*—(a) *Standards for use.* Until such time as professional literature provides more guidance on the use of construct validity in employment situations, the Federal agencies will accept a claim of construct validity without a criterion-related study which satisfies paragraph 14B of this section only when the selection procedure has been used elsewhere in a situation in which a criterion-related study has been conducted and the use of a criterion-related validity study in this context meets the standards for transportability of criterion-related validity studies as set forth above in section 7. However, if a study pertains to a number of jobs having common critical or important work behaviors at a comparable level of complexity, and the evidence satisfies subparagraphs 14B (2) and (3) of this section for those jobs with criterion-related validity evidence for those jobs, the selection procedure may be used for all the jobs to which the study pertains. If construct validity is to be generalized to other jobs or groups of jobs not in the group studied, the Federal enforcement agencies will expect at a minimum additional empirical research evidence meeting the standards of subparagraphs section 14B (2) and (3) of this section for the additional jobs or groups of jobs.

(b) *Determination of common work behaviors.* In determining whether two or more jobs have one or more work behavior(s) in common, the user should compare the observed work behavior(s) in each of the jobs and should compare the observed work product(s) in each of the jobs. If neither the observed work behavior(s) in each of the jobs nor the observed work product(s) in each of the jobs are the same, the Federal enforcement agencies will presume that the work behavior(s) in each job are different. If the work behaviors are not observable, then evidence of similarity of work products and any other relevant research evidence will be considered in determining whether the work behavior(s) in the two jobs are the same.

DOCUMENTATION OF IMPACT AND VALIDITY EVIDENCE

§ 60–3.15 Documentation of impact and validity evidence.

A. *Required information.* Users of selection procedures other than those users complying with section 15A(1) of this section should maintain and have available for each job information on adverse impact of the selection process for that job and, where it is determined a selection process has an adverse impact, evidence of validity as set forth below.

(1) *Simplified recordkeeping for users with less than 100 employees.* In order to minimize recordkeeping burdens on employers who employ one hundred (100) or fewer employees, and other users not required to file EEO–1, et seq., reports, such users may satisfy the requirements of this section 15 if they maintain and have available records showing, for each year:

(a) The number of persons hired, promoted, and terminated for each job, by sex, and where appropriate by race and national origin;

(b) The number of applicants for hire and promotion by sex and where appropriate by race and national origin; and

(c) The selection procedures utilized (either standardized or not standardized).

These records should be maintained for each race or national origin group (see section 4 of this part) constituting more than two percent (2%) of the labor force in the relevant labor area. However, it is not necessary to maintain records by race and/or national origin (see section 4 of this part) if one race or national origin group in the relevant labor area constitutes more than ninety-eight percent (98%) of the labor force in the area. If the user has reason to believe that a selection procedure has an adverse impact, the user should maintain any available evidence of validity for that procedure (see sections 7A and 8).

(2) *Information on impact*—(a) *Collection of information on impact.* Users of selection procedures other than those complying with section 15A(1) of this part should maintain and have available for each job records or other information showing whether the total selection process for that job has an adverse impact on any of the groups for which records are called for by section 4B of this part. Adverse impact determinations should be made at least annually for each such group which constitutes at least 2 percent of the labor force in the relevant labor area or 2 percent of the applicable workforce. Where a total selection process for a job has an adverse impact, the user should maintain and have available records or other information showing which components have an adverse impact. Where the total selection process for a job does not have an adverse impact, information need not be maintained for individual components except in circumstances set forth in subsection 15A(2)(b) of this section. If the determination of adverse impact is made using a procedure other than the "four-fifths rule," as defined in the first sentence of section 4D of this part, a justification, consistent with section 4D of this part, for the procedure used to determine adverse impact should be available.

(b) *When adverse impact has been eliminated in the total selection process.* Whenever the total selection process for a particular job has had an adverse impact, as defined in section 4 of this part, in any year, but no longer has an adverse impact, the user should maintain and have available the information on individual components of the selection process required in the preceding paragraph for the period in which there was adverse impact. In addition, the user should continue to collect such information for at least two (2) years after the adverse impact has been eliminated.

(c) *When data insufficient to determine impact.* Where there has been an insufficient number of selections to determine whether there is an adverse impact of the total selection process for a particular job, the user should continue to collect, maintain and have available the information on individual components of the selection process required in paragraph 15(A)(2)(a) of this part until the information is sufficient to determine that the overall selection process does not have an adverse impact as defined in section 4 of this part, or until the job has changed substantially.

(3) *Documentation of validity evidence*—(a) *Types of evidence.* Where a total selection process has an adverse impact (see section 4 of this part) the user should maintain and have available for each component of that process which has an adverse impact, one or more of the following types of documentation evidence:

(i) Documentation evidence showing criterion-related validity of the selection procedure (see section 15B, of this section).

(ii) Documentation evidence showing content validity of the selection procedure (see section 15C, of this section).

(iii) Documentation evidence showing construct validity of the selection procedure (see section 15D, of this section).

(iv) Documentation evidence from other studies showing validity of the selection procedure in the user's facility (see section 15E, of this section).

(v) Documentation evidence showing why a validity study cannot or need not be performed and why continued use of the procedure is consistent with Federal law.

(b) *Form of report.* This evidence should be compiled in a reasonably complete and organized manner to permit direct evaluation of the validity of the selection procedure. Previously written employer or consultant reports of validity, or reports describing validity studies completed before the issuance of these guidelines are acceptable if they are complete in regard to the documentation requirements contained in this section, or if they satisfied requirements of guidelines which were in effect when the validity study was completed. If they are not complete, the required additional documentation should be appended. If necessary information is not available the report of the validity study may still be used as documentation, but its adequacy will be evaluated in terms of compliance with the requirements of these guidelines.

(c) *Completeness.* In the event that evidence of validity is reviewed by an enforcement agency, the validation reports completed after the effective date of these guidelines are expected to contain the information set forth below. Evidence denoted by use of the word "(Essential)" is considered critical. If information denoted essential is not included, the report will be considered incomplete unless the user affirmatively demonstrates either its unavailability due to circumstances beyond the user's control or special circumstances of the user's study which make the information irrelevant. Evidence not so denoted is desirable but its absence will not be a basis for considering a report incomplete. The user should maintain and have available the information called for under the heading "Source Data" in sections 15B(11) and 15D(11). While it is a necessary part of the study, it need not be submitted with the report. All statistical results should be organized and presented in tabular or graphic form to the extent feasible.

B. *Criterion-related validity studies.* Reports of criterion-related validity for a selection procedure should include the following information:

(1) *User(s), location(s), and date(s) of study.* Dates and location(s) of the job analysis or review of job information, the date(s) and location(s) of the administration of the selection procedures and collection of criterion data, and the time between collection of data on selection procedures and criterion measures should be provided (Essential). If the study was conducted at several locations, the address of each location, including city and State, should be shown.

(2) *Problem and setting.* An explicit definition of the purpose(s) of the study and the circumstances in which the study was conducted should be provided. A description of existing selection procedures and cutoff scores, if any, should be provided.

(3) *Job analysis or review of job information.* A description of the procedure used to analyze the job or group of jobs, or to review the job information should be provided (Essential). Where a review of job information results in criteria which may be used without a full job analysis (see section 14B(3)), the basis for the selection of these criteria should be reported (Essential). Where a job analysis is required a complete description of the work behavior(s) or work outcome(s), and measures of their criticality or importance should be provided (Essential). The report should describe the basis on which the behavior(s) or outcome(s) were determined to be critical or important, such as the proportion of time spent on the respective behaviors, their level of difficulty, their frequency of performance, the consequences of error, or other appropriate factors (Essential). Where two or more jobs are grouped for a validity study, the information called for in this subsection should be provided for each of the jobs, and the justification for the grouping (see section 14B(1)) should be provided (essential).

(4) *Job titles and codes.* It is desirable to provide the user's job title(s) for the job(s) in question and the corresponding job title(s) and code(s) from U.S. Employment Service's Dictionary of Occupational Titles.

(5) *Criterion measures.* The bases for the selection of the criterion measures should be provided, together with references to the evidence considered in making the selection of criterion measures (essential). A full description of all criteria on which data were collected and means by which they were observed, recorded, evaluated, and quantified, should be provided (essential). If rating techniques are used as criterion measures, the appraisal form(s) and instructions to the rater(s) should be included as part of the validation evidence, or should be explicitly described and available (essential). All steps taken to insure that criterion

measures are free from factors which would unfairly alter the scores of members of any group should be described (essential).

(6) *Sample description.* A description of how the research sample was identified and selected should be included (essential). The race, sex, and ethnic composition of the sample, including those groups set forth in section 4A of this part, should be described (essential). This description should include the size of each subgroup (essential). A description of how the research sample compares with the relevant labor market or work force, the method by which the relevant labor market or work force was defined, and a discussion of the likely effects on validity of differences between the sample and the relevant labor market or work force, are also desirable. Descriptions of educational levels, length of service, and age are also desirable.

(7) *Description of selection procedures.* Any measure, combination of measures, or procedure studied should be completely and explicitly described or attached (essential). If commercially available selection procedures are studied, they should be described by title, form, and publisher (essential). Reports of reliability estimates and how they were established are desirable.

(8) *Techniques and results.* Methods used in analyzing data should be described (essential). Measures of central tendency (e.g., means) and measures of dispersion (e.g., standard deviations and ranges) for all selection procedures and all criteria should be reported for each race, sex, and ethnic group which constitutes a significant factor in the relevant labor market (essential). The magnitude and direction of all relationships between selection procedures and criterion measures investigated should be reported for each relevant race, sex, and ethnic group and for the total group (essential). Where groups are too small to obtain reliable evidence of the magnitude of the relationship, need not be reported separately. Statements regarding the statistical significance of results should be made (essential). Any statistical adjustments, such as for less then perfect reliability or for restriction of score range in the selection procedure or criterion should be described and explained; and uncorrected correlation coefficients should also be shown (essential). Where the statistical technique categorizes continuous data, such as biserial correlation and the phi coefficient, the categories and the bases on which they were determined should be described and explained (essential). Studies of test fairness should be included where called for by the requirements of section 14B(8) (essential). These studies should include the rationale by which a selection procedure was determined to be fair to the group(s) in question. Where test fairness or unfairness has been demonstrated on the basis of other studies, a bibliography of the relevant studies should be included (essential). If the bibliography includes unpublished studies, copies of these studies, or adequate abstracts or summaries, should be attached (essential). Where revisions have been made in a selection procedure to assure compatability between successful job performance and the probability of being selected, the studies underlying such revisions should be included (essential). All statistical results should be organized and presented by relevant race, sex, and ethnic group (essential).

(9) *Alternative procedures investigated.* The selection procedures investigated and available evidence of their impact should be identified (essential). The scope, method, and findings of the investigation, and the conclusions reached in light of the findings, should be fully described (essential).

(10) *Uses and applications.* The methods considered for use of the selection procedure (e.g., as a screening device with a cutoff score, for grouping or ranking, or combined with other procedures in a battery) and available evidence of their impact should be described (essential). This description should include the rationale for choosing the method for operational use, and the evidence of the validity and utility of the procedure as it is to be used (essential). The purpose for which the procedure is to be used (e.g., hiring, transfer, promotion) should be described (essential). If weights are assigned to different parts of the selection procedure, these weights and the validity of the

weighted composite should be reported (essential). If the selection procedure is used with a cutoff score, the user should describe the way in which normal expectations of proficiency within the work force were determined and the way in which the cutoff score was determined (essential).

(11) *Source data.* Each user should maintain records showing all pertinent information about individual sample members and raters where they are used, in studies involving the validation of selection procedures. These records should be made available upon request of a compliance agency. In the case of individual sample members these data should include scores on the selection procedure(s), scores on criterion measures, age, sex, race, or ethnic group status, and experience on the specific job on which the validation study was conducted, and may also include such things as education, training, and prior job experience, but should not include names and social security numbers. Records should be maintained which show the ratings given to each sample member by each rater.

(12) *Contact person.* The name, mailing address, and telephone number of the person who may be contacted for further information about the validity study should be provided (essential).

(13) *Accuracy and completeness.* The report should describe the steps taken to assure the accuracy and completeness of the collection, analysis, and report of data and results.

C. *Content validity studies.* Reports of content validity for a selection procedure should include the following information:

(1) *User(s), location(s) and date(s) of study.* Dates and location(s) of the job analysis should be shown (essential).

(2) *Problem and setting.* An explicit definition of the purpose(s) of the study and the circumstances in which the study was conducted should be provided. A description of existing selection procedures and cutoff scores, if any, should be provided.

(3) *Job analysis—Content of the job.* A description of the method used to analyze the job should be provided (essential). The work behavior(s), the associated tasks, and, if the behavior results in a work product, the work products should be completely described (essential). Measures of criticality and/or importance of the work behavior(s) and the method of determining these measures should be provided (essential). Where the job analysis also identified the knowledges, skills, and abilities used in work behavior(s), an operational definition for each knowledge in terms of a body of learned information and for each skill and ability in terms of observable behaviors and outcomes, and the relationship between each knowledge, skill, or ability and each work behavior, as well as the method used to determine this relationship, should be provided (essential). The work situation should be described, including the setting in which work behavior(s) are performed, and where appropriate, the manner in which knowledges, skills, or abilities are used, and the complexity and difficulty of the knowledge, skill, or ability as used in the work behavior(s).

(4) *Selection procedure and its content.* Selection procedures, including those constructed by or for the user, specific training requirements, composites of selection procedures, and any other procedure supported by content validity, should be completely and explicitly described or attached (essential). If commercially available selection procedures are used, they should be described by title, form, and publisher (essential). The behaviors measured or sampled by the selection procedure should be explicitly described (essential). Where the selection procedure purports to measure a knowledge, skill, or ability, evidence that the selection procedure measures and is a representative sample of the knowledge, skill, or ability should be provided (essential).

(5) *Relationship between the selection procedure and the job.* The evidence demonstrating that the selection procedure is a representative work sample, a representative sample of the work behavior(s), or a representative sample of a knowledge, skill, or ability as used as a part of a work behavior and necessary for that behavior should be provided (essential). The user should identify the work behavior(s) which each item or part of the selection procedure

is intended to sample or measure (essential). Where the selection procedure purports to sample a work behavior or to provide a sample of a work product, a comparison should be provided of the manner, setting, and the level of complexity of the selection procedure with those of the work situation (essential). If any steps were taken to reduce adverse impact on a race, sex, or ethnic group in the content of the procedure or in its administration, these steps should be described. Establishment of time limits, if any, and how these limits are related to the speed with which duties must be performed on the job, should be explained. Measures of central tendency (e.g., means) and measures of dispersion (e.g., standard deviations) and estimates of realibility should be reported for all selection procedures if available. Such reports should be made for relevant race, sex, and ethnic subgroups, at least on a statistically reliable sample basis.

(6) *Alternative procedures investigated.* The alternative selection procedures investigated and available evidence of their impact should be identified (essential). The scope, method, and findings of the investigation, and the conclusions reached in light of the findings, should be fully described (essential).

(7) *Uses and applications.* The methods considered for use of the selection procedure (e.g., as a screening device with a cutoff score, for grouping or ranking, or combined with other procedures in a battery) and available evidence of their impact should be described (essential). This description should include the rationale for choosing the method for operational use, and the evidence of the validity and utility of the procedure as it is to be used (essential). The purpose for which the procedure is to be used (e.g., hiring, transfer, promotion) should be described (essential). If the selection procedure is used with a cutoff score, the user should describe the way in which normal expectations of proficiency within the work force were determined and the way in which the cutoff score was determined (essential). In addition, if the selection procedure is to be used for ranking, the user should specify the evidence showing that a higher score on the selection procedure is likely to result in better job performance.

(8) *Contact person.* The name, mailing address, and telephone number of the person who may be contacted for further information about the validity study should be provided (essential).

(9) *Accuracy and completeness.* The report should describe the steps taken to assure the accuracy and completeness of the collection, analysis, and report of data and results.

D. *Construct validity studies.* Reports of construct validity for a selection procedure should include the following information:

(1) *User(s), location(s), and date(s) of study.* Date(s) and location(s) of the job analysis and the gathering of other evidence called for by these guidelines should be provided (essential).

(2) *Problem and setting.* An explicit definition of the purpose(s) of the study and the circumstances in which the study was conducted should be provided. A description of existing selection procedures and cutoff scores, if any, should be provided.

(3) *Construct definition.* A clear definition of the construct(s) which are believed to underlie successful performance of the critical or important work behavior(s) should be provided (essential). This definition should include the levels of construct performance relevant to the job(s) for which the selection procedure is to be used (essential). There should be a summary of the position of the construct in the psychological literature, or in the absence of such a position, a description of the way in which the definition and measurement of the construct was developed and the psychological theory underlying it (essential). Any quantitative data which identify or define the job constructs, such as factor analyses, should be provided (essential).

(4) *Job analysis.* A description of the method used to analyze the job should be provided (essential). A complete description of the work behavior(s) and, to the extent appropriate, work outcomes and measures of their criticality and/or importance should be provided (essential). The report should also describe the basis on which the behavior(s) or outcomes were determined to

be important, such as their level of difficulty, their frequency of performance, the consequences of error or other appropriate factors (essential). Where jobs are grouped or compared for the purposes of generalizing validity evidence, the work behavior(s) and work product(s) for each of the jobs should be described, and conclusions concerning the similarity of the jobs in terms of observable work behaviors or work products should be made (essential).

(5) *Job titles and codes.* It is desirable to provide the selection procedure user's job title(s) for the job(s) in question and the corresponding job title(s) and code(s) from the United States Employment Service's dictionary of occupational titles.

(6) *Selection procedure.* The selection procedure used as a measure of the construct should be completely and explicitly described or attached (essential). If commercially available selection procedures are used, they should be identified by title, form and publisher (essential). The research evidence of the relationship between the selection procedure and the construct, such as factor structure, should be included (essential). Measures of central tendency, variability and reliability of the selection procedure should be provided (essential). Whenever feasible, these measures should be provided separately for each relevant race, sex and ethnic group.

(7) *Relationship to job performance.* The criterion-related study(ies) and other empirical evidence of the relationship between the construct measured by the selection procedure and the related work behavior(s) for the job or jobs in question should be provided (essential). Documentation of the criterion-related study(ies) should satisfy the provisions of paragraph 15B of this section or paragraph 15E(1) of this section, except for studies conducted prior to the effective date of these guidelines (essential). Where a study pertains to a group of jobs, and, on the basis of the study, validity is asserted for a job in the group, the observed work behaviors and the observed work products for each of the jobs should be described (essential). Any other evidence used in determining whether the work behavior(s) in each of the jobs is the same should be fully described (essential).

(8) *Alternative procedures investigated.* The alternative selection procedures investigated and available evidence of their impact should be identified (essential). The scope, method, and findings of the investigation, and the conclusions reached in light of the findings should be fully described (essential).

(9) *Uses and applications.* The methods considered for use of the selection procedure (e.g., as a screening device with a cutoff score, for grouping or ranking, or combined with other procedures in a battery) and available evidence of their impact should be described (essential). This description should include the rationale for choosing the method for operational use, and the evidence of the validity and utility of the procedure as it is to be used (essential). The purpose for which the procedure is to be used (e.g., hiring, transfer, promotion) should be described (essential). If weights are assigned to different parts of the selection procedure, these weights and the validity of the weighted composite should be reported (essential). If the selection procedure is used with a cutoff score, the user should describe the way in which normal expectations of proficiency within the work force were determined and the way in which the cutoff score was determined (essential).

(10) *Accuracy and completeness.* The report should describe the steps taken to assure the accuracy and completeness of the collection, analysis, and report of data and results.

(11) *Source data.* Each user should maintain records showing all pertinent information relating to its study of construct validity.

(12) *Contact person.* The name, mailing address, and telephone number of the individual who may be contacted for further information about the validity study should be provided (essential).

E. *Evidence of validity from other studies.* When validity of a selection procedure is supported by studies not done by the user, the evidence from the original study or studies should be compiled in a manner similar to that required in the appropriate paragraph of this section 15 above. In addition, the following evidence should be supplied:

(1) *Evidence from criterion-related validity studies*—a. *Job information.* A description of the important job behavior(s) of the user's job and the basis on which the behaviors were determined to be important should be provided (essential). A full description of the basis for determining that these important work behaviors are the same as those of the job in the original study (or studies) should be provided (essential).

b. *Relevance of criteria.* A full description of the basis on which the criteria used in the original studies are determined to be relevant for the user should be provided (essential).

c. *Other variables.* The similarity of important applicant pool or sample characteristics reported in the original studies to those of the user should be described (essential). A description of the comparison between the race, sex and ethnic composition of the user's relevant labor market and the sample in the original validity studies should be provided (essential).

d. *Use of the selection procedure.* A full description should be provided showing that the use to be made of the selection procedure is consistent with the findings of the original validity studies (essential).

e. *Bibliography.* A bibliography of reports of validity of the selection procedure for the job or jobs in question should be provided (essential). Where any of the studies included an investigation of test fairness, the results of this investigation should be provided (essential). Copies of reports published in journals that are not commonly available should be described in detail or attached (essential). Where a user is relying upon unpublished studies, a reasonable effort should be made to obtain these studies. If these unpublished studies are the sole source of validity evidence they should be described in detail or attached (essential). If these studies are not available, the name and address of the source, an adequate abstract or summary of the validity study and data, and a contact person in the source organization should be provided (essential).

(2) *Evidence from content validity studies.* See sections 14C(3) and section 15C of this section.

(3) *Evidence from construct validity studies.* See sections 14D(2) and 15D of this section.

F. *Evidence of validity from cooperative studies.* Where a selection procedure has been validated through a cooperative study, evidence that the study satisfies the requirements of sections 7, 8 and 15E should be provided (essential).

G. *Selection for higher level job.* If a selection procedure is used to evaluate candidates for jobs at a higher level than those for which they will initially be employed, the validity evidence should satisfy the documentation provisions of this section 15 for the higher level job or jobs, and in addition, the user should provide: (1) a description of the job progression structure, formal or informal; (2) the data showing how many employees progress to the higher level job and the length of time needed to make this progression; and (3) an identification of any anticipated changes in the higher level job. In addition, if the test measures a knowledge, skill or ability, the user should provide evidence that the knowledge, skill or ability is required for the higher level job and the basis for the conclusion that the knowledge, skill or ability is not expected to develop from the training or experience on the job.

H. *Interim use of selection procedures.* If a selection procedure is being used on an interim basis because the procedure is not fully supported by the required evidence of validity, the user should maintain and have available (1) substantial evidence of validity for the procedure, and (2) a report showing the date on which the study to gather the additional evidence commenced, the estimated completion date of the study, and a description of the data to be collected (essential).

DEFINITIONS

§ 60–3.16 Definitions.

The following definitions shall apply throughout these guidelines:

A. *Ability.* A present competence to perform an observable behavior or a behavior which results in an observable product.

B. *Adverse impact.* A substantially different rate of selection in hiring, promotion, or other employment decision which works to the disadvantage of members of a race, sex, or ethnic group. See section 4 of these guidelines.

C. *Compliance with these guidelines.* Use of a selection procedure is in compliance with these guidelines if such use has been validated in accord with these guidelines (as defined below), or if such use does not result in adverse impact on any race, sex, or ethnic group (see section 4, of this part), or, in unusual circumstances, if use of the procedure is otherwise justified in accord with Federal law. See section 6B, of this part.

D. *Content validity.* Demonstrated by data showing that the content of a selection procedure is representative of important aspects of performance on the job. See section 5B and section 14C.

E. *Construct validity.* Demonstrated by data showing that the selection procedure measures the degree to which candidates have identifiable characteristics which have been determined to be important for successful job performance. See section 5B and section 14D.

F. *Criterion-related validity.* Demonstrated by empirical data showing that the selection procedure is predictive of or significantly correlated with important elements of work behavior. See sections 5B and 14B.

G. *Employer.* Any employer subject to the provisions of the Civil Rights Act of 1964, as amended, including State or local governments and any Federal agency subject to the provisions of section 717 of the Civil Rights Act of 1964, as amended, and any Federal contractor or subcontractor or federally assisted construction contractor or subcontactor covered by Executive Order 11246, as amended.

H. *Employment agency.* Any employment agency subject to the provisions of the Civil Rights Act of 1964, as amended.

I. *Enforcement action.* For the purposes of section 4 a proceeding by a Federal enforcement agency such as a lawsuit or an administrative proceeding leading to debarment from or withholding, suspension, or termination of Federal Government contracts or the suspension or withholding of Federal Government funds; but not a finding of reasonable cause or a conciliation process or the issuance of right to sue letters under title VII or under Executive Order 11246 where such finding, conciliation, or issuance of notice of right to sue is based upon an individual complaint.

J. *Enforcement agency.* Any agency of the executive branch of the Federal Government which adopts these guidelines for purposes of the enforcement of the equal employment opportunity laws or which has responsibility for securing compliance with them.

K. *Job analysis.* A detailed statement of work behaviors and other information relevant to the job.

L. *Job description.* A general statement of job duties and responsibilities.

M. *Knowledge.* A body of information applied directly to the performance of a function.

N. *Labor organization.* Any labor organization subject to the provisions of the Civil Rights Act of 1964, as amended, and any committee subject thereto controlling apprenticeship or other training.

O. *Observable.* Able to be seen, heard, or otherwise perceived by a person other than the person performing the action.

P. *Race, sex, or ethnic group.* Any group of persons identifiable on the grounds of race, color, religion, sex, or national origin.

Q. *Selection procedure.* Any measure, combination of measures, or procedure used as a basis for any employment decision. Selection procedures include the full range of assessment techniques from traditional paper and pencil tests, performance tests, training programs, or probationary periods and physical, educational, and work experience requirements through informal or casual interviews and unscored application forms.

R. *Selection rate.* The proportion of applicants or candidates who are hired, promoted, or otherwise selected.

S. *Should.* The term "should" as used in these guidelines is intended to connote action which is necessary to achieve compliance with the guidelines, while recognizing that there are circumstances where alternative courses of action are open to users.

T. *Skill.* A present, observable competence to perform a learned psychomoter act.

U. *Technical feasibility.* The existence of conditions permitting the conduct of meaningful criterion-related validity studies. These conditions include: (1) An adequate sample of persons available for the study to achieve findings of statistical significance; (2) having or being able to obtain a sufficient range of scores on the selection procedure and job performance measures to produce validity results which can be expected to be representative of the results if the ranges normally expected were utilized; and (3) having or being able to devise unbiased, reliable and relevant measures of job performance or other criteria of employee adequacy. See section 14B(2). With respect to investigation of possible unfairness, the same considerations are applicable to each group for which the study is made. See section 14B(8).

V. *Unfairness of selection procedure.* A condition in which members of one race, sex, or ethnic group characteristically obtain lower scores on a selection procedure than members of another group, and the differences are not reflected in differences in measures of job performance. See section 14B(7).

W. *User.* Any employer, labor organization, employment agency, or licensing or certification board, to the extent it may be covered by Federal equal employment opportunity law, which uses a selection procedure as a basis for any employment decision. Whenever an employer, labor organization, or employment agency is required by law to restrict recruitment for any occupation to those applicants who have met licensing or certification requirements, the licensing or certifying authority to the extent it may be covered by Federal equal employment opportunity law will be considered the user with respect to those licensing or certification requirements. Whenever a State employment agency or service does no more than administer or monitor a procedure as permitted by Department of Labor regulations, and does so without making referrals or taking any other action on the basis of the results, the State employment agency will not be deemed to be a user.

X. *Validated in accord with these guidelines or properly validated.* A demonstration that one or more validity study or studies meeting the standards of these guidelines has been conducted, including investigation and, where appropriate, use of suitable alternative selection procedures as contemplated by section 3B, and has produced evidence of validity sufficient to warrant use of the procedure for the intended purpose under the standards of these guidelines.

Y. *Work behavior.* An activity performed to achieve the objectives of the job. Work behaviors involve observable (physical) components and unobservable (mental) components. A work behavior consists of the performance of one or more tasks. Knowledges, skills, and abilities are not behaviors, although they may be applied in work behaviors.

APPENDIX TO PART 60–3

§ 60–3.17 Policy statement on affirmative action (see section 13B).

The Equal Employment Opportunity Coordinating Council was established by act of Congress in 1972, and charged with responsibility for developing and implementing agreements and policies designed, among other things, to eliminate conflict and inconsistency among the agencies of the Federal Government responsible for administering Federal law prohibiting discrimination on grounds of race, color, sex, religion, and national origin. This statement is issued as an initial response to the requests of a number of State and local officials for clarification of the Government's policies concerning the role of affirmative action in the overall equal employment opportunity program. While the Coordinating Council's adoption of this statement expresses only the views of the signatory agencies concerning this important subject, the principles set forth below should serve as policy guidance for other Federal agencies as well.

(1) Equal employment opportunity is the law of the land. In the public sector of our society this means that all persons, regardless of race, color, religion,

sex, or national origin shall have equal access to positions in the public service limited only by their ability to do the job. There is ample evidence in all sectors of our society that such equal access frequently has been denied to members of certain groups because of their sex, racial, or ethnic characteristics. The remedy for such past and present discrimination is twofold.

On the one hand, vigorous enforcement of the laws against discrimination is essential. But equally, and perhaps even more important are affirmative, voluntary efforts on the part of public employers to assure that positions in the public service are genuinely and equally accessible to qualified persons, without regard to their sex, racial, or ethnic characteristics. Without such efforts equal employment opportunity is no more than a wish. The importance of voluntary affirmative action on the part of employers is underscored by title VII of the Civil Rights Act of 1964, Executive Order 11246, and related laws and regulations—all of which emphasize voluntary action to achieve equal employment opportunity.

As with most management objectives, a systematic plan based on sound organizational analysis and problem identification is crucial to the accomplishment of affirmative action objectives. For this reason, the Council urges all State and local governments to develop and implement results oriented affirmative action plans which deal with the problems so identified.

The following paragraphs are intended to assist State and local governments by illustrating the kinds of analyses and activities which may be appropriate for a public employer's voluntary affirmative action plan. This statement does not address remedies imposed after a finding of unlawful discrimination.

(2) Voluntary affirmative action to assure equal employment opportunity is construction of any affirmative action plan should be an analysis of the employer's work force to determine whether precentages of sex, race, or ethnic groups in individual job classifications are substantially similar to the precentages of those groups available in the relevant job market who possess the basic job-related qualifications.

When substantial disparities are found through such analyses, each element of the overall selection process should be examined to determine which elements operate to exclude persons on the basis of sex, race, or ethnic group. Such elements include, but are not limited to, recruitment, testing, ranking certification, interview, recommendations for selection, hiring, promotion, etc. The examination of each element of the selection process should at a minimum include a determination of its validity in predicting job performance.

(3) When an employer has reason to believe that its selection procedures have the exclusionary effect described in paragraph 2 of this section, it should initiate affirmative steps to remedy the situation. Such steps, which in design and execution may be race, color, sex, or ethnic "conscious," include, but are not limited to, the following:

(a) The establishment of a long-term goal, and short-range, interim goals and timetables for the specific job classifications, all of which should take into account the availability of basically qualified persons in the relevant job market;

(b) A recruitment program designed to attract qualified members of the group in question;

(c) A systematic effort to organize work and redesign jobs in ways that provide opportunities for persons lacking "journeyman" level knowledge or skills to enter and, with appropriate training, to progress in a career field;

(d) Revamping selection instruments or procedures which have not yet been validated in order to reduce or eliminate exclusionary effects on particular groups in particular job classifications;

(e) The initiation of measures designed to assure that members of the affected group who are qualified to perform the job are included within the pool of persons from which the selecting official makes the selection;

(f) A systematic effort to provide career advancement training, both classroom and on-the-job, to employees locked into dead end jobs; and

(g) The establishment of a system for regularly monitoring the effectiveness of the particular affirmative action program, and procedures for making timely adjustments in this program where effectiveness is not demonstrated.

(4) The goal of any affirmative action plan should be achievement of genuine equal employment opportunity for all qualified persons. Selection under such plans should be based upon the ability of the applicant(s) to do the work. Such plans should not require the selection of the unqualified, or the unneeded, nor should they require the selection of persons on the basis of race, color, sex, religion, or national origin. Moreover, while the Council believes that this statement should serve to assist State and local employers, as well as Federal agencies, it recognizes that affirmative action cannot be viewed as a standardized program which must be accomplished in the same way at all times in all places.

Accordingly, the Council has not attempted to set forth here either the minimum or maximum voluntary steps that employers may take to deal with their respective situations. Rather, the Council recognizes that under applicable authorities, State and local employers have flexibility to formulate affirmative action plans that are best suited to their particular situations. In this manner, the Council believes that affirmative action programs will best serve the goal of equal employment opportunity.

Respectfully submitted,

Harold R. Tyler, Jr.,
Deputy Attorney General and Chairman of the Equal Employment Coordinating Council.

Michael H. Moskow,
Under Secretary of Labor.

Ethel Bent Walsh,
Acting Chairman, Equal Employment Opportunity Commission.

Robert E. Hampton,
Chairman, Civil Service Commission.

Arthur E. Flemming,
Chairman, Commission on Civil Rights.

Because of its equal employment opportunity responsibilities under the State and Local Government Fiscal Assistance Act of 1972 (the revenue sharing act), the Department of Treasury was invited to participate in the formulation of this policy statement; and it concurs and joins in the adoption of this policy statement.

Done this 26th day of August 1976.

Richard Albrecht,
General Counsel,
Department of the Treasury.

§ 60–3.18 Citations.

The official title of these guidelines is "Uniform Guidelines on Employee Selection Procedures (1978)". The Uniform Guidelines on Employee Selection Procedures (1978) are intended to establish a uniform Federal position in the area of prohibiting discrimination in employment practices on grounds of race, color, religion, sex, or national origin. These guidelines have been adopted by the Equal Employment Opportunity Commission, the Department of Labor, the Department of Justice, and the Civil Service Commission.

The official citation is:

"Section 60–3, Uniform Guidelines on Employee Selection Procedure (1978); 43 FR 38295 (August 25, 1978)."

The short form citation is:

"Section 60–3, U.G.E.S.P. (1978); 43 FR 38295 (August 25, 1978)."

When the guidelines are cited in connection with the activities of one of the issuing agencies, a specific citation to the regulations of that agency can be added at the end of the above citation. The specific additional citations are as follows:

Equal Employment Opportunity Commission
29 CFR Part 1607
Department of Labor
Office of Federal Contract Compliance Programs
41 CFR Part 60–3
Department of Justice
28 CFR 50.14
Civil Service Commission
5 CFR 300.103(c)

Normally when citing these guidelines, the section number immediately preceding the title of the guidelines will be from these guidelines series 1–18. If a section number from the codification for an individual agency is needed it can also be added at the end of the agency citation. For example, section 6A of these guidelines could be cited for EEOC as follows: "Section 6A, Uniform Guidelines on Employee Selection Procedures (1978); 43 FR 38295, (August 25, 1978); 29 CFR Part 1607, section 6A."

PART 60–4—CONSTRUCTION CONTRACTORS—AFFIRMATIVE ACTION REQUIREMENTS

Sec.

AUTHORITY: Secs. 201, 202, 205, 211, 301, 302, and 303 of E.O. 11246, as amended, 30 FR 12319; 32 FR 14303, as amended by E.O. 12086.

SOURCE: 43 FR 49254, Oct. 20, 1978, unless otherwise noted.

§ 60–4.1 Scope and application.

This part applies to all contractors and subcontractors which hold any Federal or federally assisted construction contract in excess of $10,000. The regulations in this part are applicable to all of a construction contractor's or subcontractor's construction employees who are engaged in on site contruction including those construction employees who work on a non-Federal or nonfederally assisted construction site. This part also establishes procedures which all Federal contracting officers and all applicants, as applicable, shall follow in soliciting for and awarding Federal or federally assisted construction contracts. Procedures also are established which administering agencies shall follow in making any grant, contract, loan, insurance, or guarantee involving federally assisted construction which is not exempt from the requirements of Executive Order 11246, as amended.

In addition, this part applies to construction work performed by construction contractors and subcontractors for Federal nonconstruction contractors and subcontractors if the construction work is necessary in whole or in part to the performance of a nonconstruction contract or subcontract.

[43 FR 49254, Oct. 20, 1978; 43 FR 51401, Nov. 3, 1978]

§ 60–4.2 Solicitations.

(a) All Federal contracting officers and all applicants shall include the notice set forth in paragraph (d) of this section and the Standard Federal Equal Employment Opportunity Construction Contract Specifications set forth in § 60–4.3 of this part in all solicitations for offers and bids on all Federal and federally assisted construction contracts or subcontracts to be performed in geographical areas designated by the Director pursuant to § 60–4.6 of the part. Administering agencies shall require the inclusion of the notice set forth in paragraph (d) of this section and the specifications set forth in § 60–4.3 of this part as a condition of any grant, contract, subcontract, loan, insurance or guarantee involving federally assisted construction covered by this Part 60–4.

(b) All nonconstruction contractors covered by Executive Order 11246 and the implementing regulations shall include the notice in paragraph (d) of this section in all construction agreements which are necessary in whole or in part to the performance of the covered nonconstruction contract.

(c) Contracting officers, applicants and nonconstruction contractors shall given written notice to the Director within 10 working days of award of a contract subject to these provisions. The notification shall include the name, address and telephone number of the contractor; employer identification number; dollar amount of the contract, estimated starting and completion dates of the contract; the contract number; and geographical area in which the contract is to be performed.

(d) The following notice shall be included in, and shall be a part of, all solicitations for offers and bids on all Federal and federally assisted construction contracts or subcontracts in excess of $10,000 to be performed in geographical areas designated by the Director pursuant to § 60–4.6 of this part (see 41 CFR 60–4.2(a)):

NOTICE OF REQUIREMENT FOR AFFIRMATIVE ACTION TO ENSURE EQUAL EMPLOYMENT OPPORTUNITY (EXECUTIVE ORDER 11246)

1. The Offeror's or Bidder's attention is called to the "Equal Opportunity Clause"

and the "Standard Federal Equal Employment Specifications" set forth herein.

2. The goals and timetables for minority and female participation, expressed in percentage terms for the Contractor's aggregate workforce in each trade on all construction work in the covered area, are as follows:

Timetables	Goals for minority participation for each trade	Goals for female participation in each trade
	Insert goals for each year.	Insert goals for each year.

These goals are applicable to all the Contractor's construction work (whether or not it is Federal or federally assisted) performed in the covered area. If the contractor performs construction work in a geographical area located outside of the covered area, it shall apply the goals established for such geographical area where the work is actually performed. With regard to this second area, the contractor also is subject to the goals for both its federally involved and nonfederally involved construction.

The Contractor's compliance with the Executive Order and the regulations in 41 CFR Part 60–4 shall be based on its implementation of the Equal Opportunity Clause, specific affirmative action obligations required by the specifications set forth in 41 CFR 60–4.3(a), and its efforts to meet the goals. The hours of minority and female employment and training must be substantially uniform throughout the length of the contract, and in each trade, and the contractor shall make a good faith effort to employ minorities and women evenly on each of its projects. The transfer of minority or female employees or trainees from Contractor to Contractor or from project to project for the sole purpose of meeting the Contractor's goals shall be a violation of the contract, the Executive Order and the regulations in 41 CFR Part 60–4. Compliance with the goals will be measured against the total work hours performed.

3. The Contractor shall provide written notification to the Director of the Office of Federal Contract Compliance Programs within 10 working days of award of any construction subcontract in excess of $10,000 at any tier for construction work under the contract resulting from this solicitation. The notification shall list the name, address and telephone number of the subcontractor; employer identification number of the subcontractor; estimated dollar amount of the subcontract; estimated starting and completion dates of the subcontract; and the geographical area in which the subcontract is to be performed.

4. As used in this Notice, and in the contract resulting from this solicitation, the "covered area" is (insert description of the geographical areas where the contract is to be performed giving the state, county and city, if any).

[43 FR 49254, Oct. 20, 1978; 43 FR 51401, Nov. 3, 1978, as amended at 45 FR 65977, Oct. 3, 1980]

§ 60–4.3 Equal opportunity clauses.

(a) The equal opportunity clause published at 41 CFR 60–1.4(a) of this chapter is required to be included in, and is part of, all nonexempt Federal contracts and subcontracts, including construction contracts and subcontracts. The equal opportunity clause published at 41 CFR 60–1.4(b) is required to be included in, and is a part of, all nonexempt federally assisted construction contracts and subcontracts. In addition to the clauses described above, all Federal contracting officers, all applicants and all nonconstruction contractors, as applicable, shall include the specifications set forth in this section in all Federal and federally assisted construction contracts in excess of $10,000 to be performed in geographical areas designated by the Director pursuant to § 60–4.6 of this part and in construction subcontracts in excess of $10,000 necessary in whole or in part to the performance of nonconstruction Federal contracts and subcontracts covered under the Executive order.

STANDARD FEDERAL EQUAL EMPLOYMENT OPPORTUNITY CONSTRUCTION CONTRACT SPECIFICATIONS (EXECUTIVE ORDER 11246)

1. As used in these specifications:

a. "Covered area" means the geographical area described in the solicitation from which this contract resulted;

b. "Director" means Director, Office of Federal Contract Compliance Programs, United States Department of Labor, or any person to whom the Director delegates authority;

c. "Employer identification number" means the Federal Social Security number used on the Employer's Quarterly Federal Tax Return, U.S. Treasury Department Form 941.

d. "Minority" includes:

(i) Black (all persons having origins in any of the Black African racial groups not of Hispanic origin);

(ii) Hispanic (all persons of Mexican, Puerto Rican, Cuban, Central or South American or other Spanish Culture or origin, regardless of race);

(iii) Asian and Pacific Islander (all persons having origins in any of the original peoples of the Far East, Southeast Asia, the Indian Subcontinent, or the Pacific Islands); and

(iv) American Indian or Alaskan Native (all persons having origins in any of the original peoples of North America and maintaining identifiable tribal affiliations through membership and participation or community identification).

2. Whenever the Contractor, or any Subcontractor at any tier, subcontracts a portion of the work involving any construction trade, it shall physically include in each subcontract in excess of $10,000 the provisions of these specifications and the Notice which contains the applicable goals for minority and female participation and which is set forth in the solicitations from which this contract resulted.

3. If the Contractor is participating (pursuant to 41 CFR 60-4.5) in a Hometown Plan approved by the U.S. Department of Labor in the covered area either individually or through an association, its affirmative action obligations on all work in the Plan area (including goals and timetables) shall be in accordance with that Plan for those trades which have unions participating in the Plan. Contractors must be able to demonstrate their participation in and compliance with the provisions of any such Hometown Plan. Each Contractor or Subcontractor participating in an approved Plan is individually required to comply with its obligations under the EEO clause, and to make a good faith effort to achieve each goal under the Plan in each trade in which it has employees. The overall good faith performance by other Contractors or Subcontractors toward a goal in an approved Plan does not excuse any covered Contractor's or Subcontractor's failure to take good faith efforts to achieve the Plan goals and timetables.

4. The Contractor shall implement the specific affirmative action standards provided in paragraphs 7 a through p of these specifications. The goals set forth in the solicitation from which this contract resulted are expressed as percentages of the total hours of employment and training of minority and female utilization the Contractor should reasonably be able to achieve in each construction trade in which it has employees in the covered area. Covered Construction contractors performing construction work in geographical areas where they do not have a Federal or federally assisted constuction contract shall apply the minority and female goals established for the geographical area where the work is being performed. Goals are published periodically in the FEDERAL REGISTER in notice form, and such notices may be obtained from any Office of Federal Contract Compliance Programs office or from Federal procurement contracting officers. The Contractor is expected to make substantially uniform progress in meeting its goals in each craft during the period specified.

5. Neither the provisions of any collective bargaining agreement, nor the failure by a union with whom the Contractor has a collective bargaining agreement, to refer either minorities or women shall excuse the Contractor's obligations under these specifications, Executive Order 11246, or the regulations promulgated pursuant thereto.

6. In order for the nonworking training hours of apprentices and trainees to be counted in meeting the goals, such apprentices and trainees must be employed by the Contractor during the training period, and the Contractor must have made a commitment to employ the apprentices and trainees at the completion of their training, subject to the availability of employment opportunities. Trainees must be trained pursuant to training programs approved by the U.S. Department of Labor.

7. The Contractor shall take specific affirmative actions to ensure equal employment opportunity. The evaluation of the Contractor's compliance with these specifications shall be based upon its effort to achieve maximum results from its actions. The Contractor shall document these efforts fully, and shall implement affirmative action steps at least as extensive as the following:

a. Ensure and maintain a working environment free of harassment, intimidation, and coercion at all sites, and in all facilities at which the Contractor's employees are assigned to work. The Contractor, where possible, will assign two or more women to each construction project. The Contractor shall specifically ensure that all foremen, superintendents, and other on-site supervisory personnel are aware of and carry out the Contractor's obligation to maintain such a working environment, with specific attention to minority or female individuals working at such sites or in such facilities.

b. Establish and maintain a current list of minority and female recruitment sources, provide written notification to minority and female recruitment sources and to community organizations when the Contractor or its unions have employment opportunities available, and maintain a record of the organizations' responses.

c. Maintain a current file of the names, addresses and telephone numbers of each minority and female off-the-street applicant and minority or female referral from a union, a recruitment source or community organization and of what action was taken with respect to each such individual. If such individual was sent to the union hiring hall for referral and was not referred back to the Contractor by the union or, if referred, not employed by the Contractor, this shall be documented in the file with the reason therefor, along with whatever additional actions the Contractor may have taken.

d. Provide immediate written notification to the Director when the union or unions with which the Contractor has a collective bargaining agreement has not referred to the Contractor a minority person or woman sent by the Contractor, or when the Contractor has other information that the union referral process has impeded the Contractor's efforts to meet its obligations.

e. Develop on-the-job training opportunities and/or participate in training programs for the area which expressly include minorities and women, including upgrading programs and apprenticeship and trainee programs relevant to the Contractor's employment needs, especially those programs funded or approved by the Department of Labor. The Contractor shall provide notice of these programs to the sources compiled under 7b above.

f. Disseminate the Contractor's EEO policy by providing notice of the policy to unions and training programs and requesting their cooperation in assisting the Contractor in meeting its EEO obligations; by including it in any policy manual and collective bargaining agreement; by publicizing it in the company newpaper, annual report, etc.; by specific review of the policy with all management personnel and with all minority and female employees at least once a year; and by posting the company EEO policy on bulletin boards accessible to all employees at each location where construction work is performed.

g. Review, at least annually, the company's EEO policy and affirmative action obligations under these specifications with all employees having any responsibility for hiring, assignment, layoff, termination or other employment decisions including specific review of these items with onsite supervisory personnel such as Superintendents, General Foremen, etc., prior to the initiation of construction work at any job site. A written record shall be made and maintained identifying the time and place of these meetings, persons attending, subject matter discussed, and disposition of the subject matter.

h. Disseminate the Contractor's EEO policy externally by including it in any advertising in the news media, specifically including minority and female news media, and providing written notification to and discussing the Contractor's EEO policy with other Contractors and Subcontractors with whom the Contractor does or anticipates doing business.

i. Direct its recruitment efforts, both oral and written, to minority, female and community organizations, to schools with minority and female students and to minority and female recruitment and training organizations serving the Contractor's recruitment area and employment needs. Not later than one month prior to the date for the acceptance of applications for apprenticeship or other training by any recruitment source, the Contractor shall send written notification to organizations such as the above, describing the openings, screening procedures, and tests to be used in the selection process.

j. Encourage present minority and female employees to recruit other minority persons and women and, where reasonable, provide after school, summer and vacation employment to minority and female youth both on the site and in other areas of a Contractor's work force.

k. Validate all tests and other selection requirements where there is an obligation to do so under 41 CFR Part 60–3.

l. Conduct, at least annually, an inventory and evaluation at least of all minority and female personnel for promotional opportunities and encourage these employees to seek or to prepare for, through appropriate training, etc., such opportunities.

m. Ensure that seniority practices, job classifications, work assignments and other personnel practices, do not have a discriminatory effect by continually monitoring all personnel and employment related activities to ensure that the EEO policy and the Contractor's obligations under these specifications are being carried out.

n. Ensure that all facilities and company activities are nonsegregated except that separate or single-user toilet and necessary changing facilities shall be provided to assure privacy between the sexes.

o. Document and maintain a record of all solicitations of offers for subcontracts from minority and female construction contractors and suppliers, including circulation of solicitations to minority and female contractor associations and other business associations.

p. Conduct a review, at least annually, of all supervisors' adherence to and performance under the Contractor's EEO policies and affirmative action obligations.

8. Contractors are encouraged to participate in voluntary associations which assist in fulfilling one or more of their affirmative action obligations (7a through p). The efforts of a contractor association, joint contractor-union, contractor-community, or other similar group of which the contractor is a member and participant, may be asserted as fulfilling any one or more of its obligations under 7a through p of these Specifications provided that the contractor actively participates in the group, makes every effort to assure that the group has a positive impact on the employment of minorities and women in the industry, ensures that the concrete benefits of the program are reflected in the Contractor's minority and female workforce participation, makes a good faith effort to meet its individual goals and timetables, and can provide access to documentation which demonstrates the effectiveness of actions taken on behalf of the Contractor. The obligation to comply, however, is the Contractor's and failure of such a group to fulfill an

obligation shall not be a defense for the Contractor's noncompliance.

9. A single goal for minorities and a separate single goal for women have been established. The Contractor, however, is required to provide equal employment opportunity and to take affirmative action for all minority groups, both male and female, and all women, both minority and non-minority. Consequently, the Contractor may be in violation of the Executive Order if a particular group is employed in a substantially disparate manner (for example, even though the Contractor has achieved its goals for women generally, the Contractor may be in violation of the Executive Order if a specific minority group of women is underutilized).

10. The Contractor shall not use the goals and timetables or affirmative action standards to discriminate against any person because of race, color, religion, sex, or national origin.

11. The Contractor shall not enter into any Subcontract with any person or firm debarred from Government contracts pursuant to Executive Order 11246.

12. The Contractor shall carry out such sanctions and penalties for violation of these specifications and of the Equal Opportunity Clause, including suspension, termination and cancellation of existing subcontracts as may be imposed or ordered pursuant to Executive Order 11246, as amended, and its implementing regulations, by the Office of Federal Contract Compliance Programs. Any Contractor who fails to carry out such sanctions and penalties shall be in violation of these specifications and Executive Order 11246, as amended.

13. The Contractor, in fulfilling its obligations under these specifications, shall implement specific affirmative action steps, at least as extensive as those standards prescribed in paragraph 7 of these specifications, so as to achieve maximum results from its efforts to ensure equal employment opportunity. If the Contractor fails to comply with the requirements of the Executive Order, the implementing regulations, or these specifications, the Director shall proceed in accordance with 41 CFR 60–4.8.

14. The Contractor shall designate a responsible official to monitor all employment related activity to ensure that the company EEO policy is being carried out, to submit reports relating to the provisions hereof as may be required by the Government and to keep records. Records shall at least include for each employee the name, address, telephone numbers, construction trade, union affiliation if any, employee identification number when assigned, social security number, race, sex, status (e.g., mechanic, apprentice trainee, helper, or laborer), dates of changes in status, hours worked per week in the indicated trade, rate of pay, and locations at which the work was performed. Records shall be maintained in an easily understandable and retrievable form; however, to the degree that existing records satisfy this requirement, contractors shall not be required to maintain separate records.

15. Nothing herein provided shall be construed as a limitation upon the application of other laws which establish different standards of compliance or upon the application of requirements for the hiring of local or other area residents (e.g., those under the Public Works Employment Act of 1977 and the Community Development Block Grant Program).

(b) The notice set forth in 41 CFR 60–4.2 and the specifications set forth in 41 CFR 60–4.3 replace the New Form for Federal Equal Employment Opportunity Bid Conditions for Federal and Federally Assisted Construction published at 41 FR 32482 and commonly known as the Model Federal EEO Bid Conditions, and the New Form shall not be used after the regulations in 41 CFR Part 60–4 become effective.

[43 FR 49254, Oct. 20, 1978; 43 FR 51401, Nov. 3, 1978, as amended at 45 FR 65978, Oct. 3, 1980]

§ 60–4.4 Affirmative action requirements.

(a) To implement the affirmative action requirements of Executive Order 11246 in the construction industry, the Office of Federal Contract Compliance Programs previously has approved affirmative action programs commonly referred to as "Hometown Plans," has promulgated affirmative action plans referred to as "Imposed Plans" and has approved "Special Bid Conditions" for high impact projects constructed in areas not covered by a Hometown or an Imposed Plan. All solicitations for construction contracts made after the effective date of the regulations in this part shall include the notice specified in § 60–4.2 of this part and the specifications in § 60–4.3 of this part in lieu of the Hometown and Imposed Plans including the Philadelphia Plan and Special Bid Conditions. Until the Director has issued an order pursuant to § 60–4.6 of this part establishing goals and timetables for minorities in the appropriate geographical areas or for a project covered by Special Bid Conditions, the goals and timetables for minorities to be inserted in the Notice required by 41 CFR 60–4.2 shall be the goals and timetables contained in the

Hometown Plan, Imposed Plan or Special Bid Conditions presently covering the respective geographical area or project involved.

(b) Signatories to a Hometown Plan (including heavy highway affirmative action plans) shall have 45 days from the effective date of the regulations in this part to submit under such a Plan (for the director's approval) goals and timetables for women and to include female representation on the Hometown Plan Administrative Committee. Such goals for female representation shall be at least as high as the goals established for female representation in the notice issued pursuant to 41 CFR 60–4.6. Failure of the signatories, within the 45-day period, to include female representation and to submit goals for women or a new plan, as appropriate, shall result in an automatic termination of the Office of Federal Contract Compliance Program's approval of the Hometown Plan. At any time the Office of Federal Contract Compliance Programs terminates or withdraws its approval of a Hometown Plan, or when the plan expires and another plan is not approved, the contractors signatory to the plan shall be covered automatically by the specifications set forth in § 60–4.3 of this part and by the goals and timetables established for that geographical area pursuant to § 60–4.6 of this part.

§ 60–4.5 Hometown plans.

(a) A contractor participating, either individually or through an association, in an approved Hometown Plan (including heavy highway affirmative action plans) shall comply with its affirmative action obligations under Executive Order 11246 by complying with its obligations under the plan: *Provided*, That each contractor or subcontractor participating in an approved plan is individually required to comply with the equal opportunity clause set forth in 41 CFR 60–1.4; to make a good faith effort to achieve the goals for each trade participating in the plan in which it has employees; and that the overall good performance by other contractors or subcontractors toward a goal in an approved plan does not excuse any covered contractor's or subcontractor's failure to take good faith efforts to achieve the plan's goals and timetables. If a contractor is not participating in an approved Hometown Plan it shall comply with the specifications set forth in § 60–4.3 of this part and with the goals and timetables for the appropriate area as listed in the notice required by 41 CFR 60–4.2 with regard to that trade. For the purposes of this part 60–4, a contractor is not participating in a Hometown Plan for a particular trade if it:

(1) Ceases to be signatory to a Hometown Plan covering that trade;

(2) Is signatory to a Hometown Plan for that trade but is not party to a collective bargaining agreement for that trade;

(3) Is signatory to a Hometown Plan for that trade but is party to a collective bargaining agreement with labor organizations which are not or cease to be signatories to the same Hometown Plan for that trade;

(4) Is signatory to a Hometown Plan for that trade but is party to a collective bargaining agreement with a labor organization for that trade but the two have not jointly executed a specific commitment to minority and female goals and timetables and incorporated the commitment in the Hometown Plan for that trade;

(5) Is participating in a Hometown Plan for that trade which is no longer acceptable to the Office of Federal Contract Compliance Programs;

(6) Is signatory to a Hometown Plan for that trade but is party to a collective bargaining agreement with a labor organization for that trade and the labor organization and the contractor have failed to make a good faith effort to comply with their obligations under the Hometown Plan for that trade.

(b) Contractors participating in Hometown Plans must be able to demonstrate their participation and document their compliance with the provision of the Hometown Plan.

[43 FR 49254, Oct. 20, 1978; 43 FR 51401, Nov. 3, 1978]

§ 60–4.6 Goals and timetables.

The Director, from time to time, shall issue goals and timetables for minority and female utilization which shall be based on appropriate workforce, demographic or other relevant data and which shall cover construction projects or construction contracts performed in specific geographical areas. The goals, which shall be applicable to each construction trade in a covered contractor's or subcontractor's entire workforce which is working in the area covered by the goals and timetables, shall be published as notices in the FEDERAL REGISTER, and shall be inserted by the contracting officers and applicants, as applicable, in the Notice required by 41 CFR 60–4.2. Covered construction contractors performing construction work in geographical areas where they do not have a Federal or federally assisted construction contract shall apply the minority and female goals established for the geographical area where the work is being performed.

[45 FR 65978, Oct. 3, 1980]

§ 60–4.7 Effect on other regulations.

The regulations in this part are in addition to the regulations contained in this chapter which apply to construction contractors and subcontractors generally. See particularly, 41 CFR 60–1.4 (a), (b), (c), (d), and (e); 60–1.5; 60–1.7; 60–1.8; 60–1.26; 60–1.29; 60–1.30; 60–1.32; 60–1.41; 60–1.42; 60–1.43; and 41 CFR Part 60–3; Part 60–20; Part 60–30; Part 60–40; and Part 60–50.

§ 60–4.8 Show cause notice.

If an investigation or compliance review reveals that a construction contractor or subcontractor has violated the Executive order, any contract clause, specifications or the regulations in this chapter and if administrative enforcement is contemplated, the Director shall issue to the contractor or subcontractor a notice to show cause which shall contain the items specified in paragraphs (i) through (iv) of 41 CFR 60–2.2(c)(1). If the contractor does not show good cause within 30 days, or in the alternative, fails to enter an acceptable conciliation agreement which includes where appropriate, make up goals and timetables, back pay, and seniority relief for affected class members, the OFCCP shall follow the procedure in 41 CFR 60–1.26(b): *Provided,* That where a conciliation agreement has been violated, no show cause notice is required prior to the initiation of enforcement proceedings.

[43 FR 49254, Oct. 20, 1978; 43 FR 51401, Nov. 3, 1978]

§ 60–4.9 Incorporation by operation of the order.

By operation of the order, the equal opportunity clause contained in § 60–1.4, the Notice of Requirement for Affirmative Action to Ensure Equal Employment Opportunity (Executive Order 11246) contained in § 60–4.2, and the Standard Federal Equal Employment Opportunity Construction Contract Specifications (Executive Order 11246) contained in § 60–4.3 shall be deemed to be a part of every solicitation or of every contract and subcontract, as appropriate, required by the order and the regulations in this chapter to include such clauses whether or not they are physically incorporated in such solicitation or contract and whether or not the contract is written.

PART 60–20—SEX DISCRIMINATION GUIDELINES

Sec.

AUTHORITY: Sec. 201, E.O. 11246, 30 FR 12319, and E.O. 11375, 32 FR 14303, as amended by E.O. 12086.

SOURCE: 43 FR 49258, Oct. 20, 1978, unless otherwise noted.

§ 60–20.1 Title and purpose.

The purpose of the provisions in this part is to set forth the interpretations and guidelines of the Office of Federal Contract Compliance Programs regarding the implementation of Executive Order 11246, as amended for the promotion and insuring of equal opportunities for all persons employed or seeking employment with Government contractors and subcontractors or with contractors and subcontractors performing under federally assisted construction contracts, without regard to sex. Experience has indicated that special problems related to the implementation of the Executive order require a definitive treatment beyond the terms of the order itself. These interpretations are to be read in connection with existing regulations, set forth in Part 60–1 of this chapter.

§ 60–20.2 Recruitment and advertisement.

(a) Employers engaged in recruiting activity must recruit employees of both sexes for all jobs unless sex is a bona fide occupation qualification.

(b) Advertisement in newspapers and other media for employment must not express a sex preference unless sex is a bona fide occupational qualification for the job. The placement of an advertisement in columns headed "Male" or "Female" will be considered an expression of a preference, limitation, specification, or discrimination based on sex.

§ 60–20.3 Job policies and practices.

(a) Written personnel policies relating to this subject area must expressly indicate that there shall be no discrimination against employees on account of sex. If the employer deals with a bargaining representative for his employees and there is a written agreement on conditions of employment, such agreement shall not be inconsistent with these guidelines.

(b) Employees of both sexes shall have an equal opportunity to any available job that he or she is qualified to perform, unless sex is a bona fide occupational qualification.

NOTE: In most Government contract work there are only limited instances where valid reasons can be expected to exist which would justify the exclusion of all men or all women from any given job.

(c) The employer must not make any distinction based upon sex in employment opportunities, wages, hours, or other conditions of employment. In the area of employer contributions for insurance, pensions, welfare programs and other similar "fringe benefits" the employer will not be considered to have violated these guidelines if his contributions are the same for men and women or if the resulting benefits are equal.

(d) Any distinction between married and unmarried persons of one sex that is not made between married and unmarried persons of the opposite sex will be considered to be a distinction made on the basis of sex. Similarly, an employer must not deny employment to women with young children unless it has the same exclusionary policies for men; or terminate an employee of one sex in a particular job classification upon reaching a certain age unless the same rule is applicable to members of the opposite sex.

(e) The employer's policies and practices must assure appropriate physical facilities to both sexes. The employer may not refuse to hire men or women, or deny men or women a particular job because there are no restroom or associated facilities, unless the employer is able to show that the construction of the facilities would be unreasonable for such reasons as excessive expense or lack of space.

(f)(1) An employer must not deny a female employee the right to any job that she is qualified to perform in reliance upon a State "protective" law. For example, such laws include those which prohibit women from performing in certain types of occupations (e.g., a bartender or a core-maker); from working at jobs requiring more than a certain number of hours; and from working at jobs that require lifting or carrying more than designated weights.

(2) Such legislation was intended to be beneficial, but, instead, has been found to result in restricting employment opportunities for men and/or women. Accordingly, it cannot be used as a basis for denying employment or for establishing sex as a bona fide occupational qualification for the job.

(g)(1) Women shall not be penalized in their conditions of employment because they require time away from work on account of childbearing. When, under the employer's leave policy the female employee would qualify for leave, then childbearing must be considered by the employer to be a justification for leave of absence for female employees for a reasonable period of time. For example, if the female employee meets the equally applied minimum length of service requirements for leave time, she must be granted a reasonable leave on account of childbearing. The conditions applicable to her leave (other than the length thereof) and to her return to employment, shall be in accordance with the employer's leave policy.

(2) If the employer has no leave policy, childbearing must be considered by the employer to be a justification for a leave of absence for a female employee for a reasonable period of time. Following childbirth, and upon signifying her intent to return within a reasonable time, such female employee shall be reinstated to her original job or to a position of like status and pay, without loss of service credits.

(h) The employer must not specify any differences for male and female employees on the basis of sex in either mandatory or optional retirement age.

(i) Nothing in these guidelines shall be interpreted to mean that differences in capabilities for job assignments do not exist among individuals and that such distinctions may not be recognized by the employer in making specific assignments. The purpose of these guidelines is to insure that such distinctions are not based upon sex.

§ 60–20.4 Seniority system.

Where they exist, seniority lines and lists must not be based solely upon sex. Where such a separation has existed, the employer must eliminate this distinction.

§ 60–20.5 Discriminatory wages.

(a) The employer's wages schedules must not be related to or based on the sex of the employees.

NOTE: The more obvious cases of discrimination exist where employees of different sexes are paid different wages on jobs which require substantially equal skill, effort and responsibility and are performed under similar working conditions.

(b) The employer may not discriminatorily restrict one sex to certain job classifications. In such a situation, the employer must take steps to make jobs available to all qualified employees in all classifications without regard to sex. (Example: An electrical manufacturing company may have a production division with three functional units: One (assembly) all female; another (wiring), all male; and a third (circuit boards), also all male. The highest wage attainable in the assembly unit is considerably less than that in the circuit board and wiring units. In such a case the employer must take steps to provide qualified female employees opportunity for placement in job openings in the other two units.)

(c) To avoid overlapping and conflicting administration the Director will consult with the Administrator of the Wage and Hour Administration before issuing an opinion on any matter covered by both the Equal Pay Act and Executive Order 11246, as amended.

§ 60–20.6 Affirmative action.

(a) The employer shall take affirmative action to recruit women to apply for those jobs where they have been previously excluded.

NOTE: This can be done by various methods. Examples include: (1) Including in itineraries of recruiting trips women's colleges where graduates with skills desired by the employer can be found, and female students of coeducational institutions and (2) designing advertisements to indicate that women will be considered equally with men for jobs.

(b) Women have not been typically found in significant numbers in management. In many companies management trainee programs are one of the ladders to management positions. Traditionally, few, if any, women have been admitted into these programs. An important element of affirmative action shall be a commitment to include women candidates in such programs.

(c) Distinctions based on sex may not be made in other training programs. Both sexes should have equal access to all training programs and affirmative action programs should require a demonstration by the employer that such access has been provided.

PART 60–30—RULES OF PRACTICE FOR ADMINISTRATIVE PROCEEDINGS TO ENFORCE EQUAL OPPORTUNITY UNDER EXECUTIVE ORDER 11246

GENERAL PROVISIONS

Sec.

AUTHORITY: Executive Order 11246, as amended, 30 FR 12319, 32 FR 14303, as amended by E.O. 12086; 29 U.S.C. 793, as amended, and 38 U.S.C. 4212, as amended.

SOURCE: 43 FR 49259, Oct. 20, 1978, unless otherwise noted.

GENERAL PROVISIONS

§60-30.1 Applicability of rules.

This part provides the rules of practice for all administrative proceedings, instituted by the OFCCP including but not limited to proceedings instituted against construction contractors or subcontractors, which relate to the enforcement of equal opportunity under Executive Order 11246, as amended. In the absence of a specific provision, procedures shall be in accordance with the Federal Rules of Civil Procedure.

§60-30.2 Waiver, modification.

Upon notice to all parties, the Administrative Law Judge may, with respect to matters pending before him modify or waive any rule herein upon a determination that no party will be prejudiced and that the ends of justice will be served thereby.

[43 FR 49259, Oct. 20, 1978; 43 FR 51401, Nov. 3, 1978]

§60-30.3 Computation of time.

In computing any period of time under these rules or in an order issued hereunder, the time begins with the day following the act, event, or default, and includes the last day of the period, unless it is a Saturday, Sunday, or legal holiday observed by the Federal Government in which event it includes the next business day.

§60-30.4 Form, filing, service of pleadings and papers.

(a) *Form.* The original of all pleadings and papers in a proceeding conducted under the regulations in this part shall be filed with the Administrative Law Judge assigned to the case or with the Chief Administrative Law Judge if the case has not been assigned. Every pleading and paper filed in the proceeding shall contain a caption setting forth the name of the agency instituting the proceeding, the title of the action, the case file number assigned by the Administrative Law Judge, and a designation of the pleading or paper (e.g., complaint, motion to dismiss, etc.). The pleading or papers shall be signed and shall contain the address and telephone number of the person representing the party or the person on whose behalf the pleading or paper was filed. Unless otherwise ordered for good cause by the Administrative Law Judge regarding specific papers and pleadings in a specific case, all such papers and pleadings are public documents.

(b) *Service.* Service upon any party shall be made by the party filing the pleading or document by delivering a copy or mailing a copy to the party's last known address. When a party is represented by an attorney, the service shall by upon the attorney.

(c) *Proof of service.* A certificate of the person serving the pleading or other document by personal delivery or by mailing, setting forth the manner of services shall be proof of the service.

PREHEARING PROCEDURES

§ 60–30.5 Administrative complaint.

(a) *Filing.* The Solicitor of Labor, Associate Solicitor for Labor Relations and Civil Rights Regional Solicitors and Regional Attorney upon referral from the Office of Federal Contract Compliance Programs, are authorized to institute enforcement proceedings by filing a complaint and serving the complaint upon the contractor which shall be designated as the defendant. The Department of Labor, OFCCP, as shall be designated on plaintiff.

(b) *Contents.* The complaint shall contain a concise jurisdictional statement, and a clear and concise statement sufficient to put the defendant on notice of the acts or practices it is alleged to have committed in violation of the order, the regulations, or its contractual obligations. The complaint shall also contain a prayer regarding the relief being sought, a statement of whatever sanctions the Government will seek to impose and the name and address of the attorney who will represent the Government.

(c) *Amendment.* The complaint may be amended once as a matter of course before an answer is filed, and the defendant may amend its answer once as a matter of course not later than 10 days after the filing of the original answer. Other amendments of the complaint or of the answer to the complaint shall be made only by leave of the Administrative Law Judge or by written consent of the adverse party; and leave shall be freely given where justice so requires. An amended complaint shall be answered within 14 days of its service, or within the time for filing an answer to the original complaint, whichever period is longer. An amended answer shall be responded to within 14 days of its service.

(E.O. 11246 as amended; sec. 503 of Rehabilitation Act of 1973 as amended.)

[43 FR 49259, Oct. 20, 1978, as amended at 44 FR 49691, Aug. 24, 1979; 63 FR 59642, Nov. 4, 1998]

§ 60–30.6 Answer.

(a) *Filing and service.* Within 20 days after the service of the complaint, the defendant shall file an answer with the Chief Administrative Law Judge if the case has not been assigned to an Administrative Law Judge. The answer shall be signed by the defendant or its attorney, and served on the Government in accordance with § 60–30.4(b).

(b) *Contents; failure to file.* The answer shall (1) contain a statement of the facts which constitute the grounds of defense, and shall specifically admit, explain, or deny, each of the allegations of the complaint unless the defendant is without knowledge, in which case the answer shall so state; or (2) state that the defendant admits all the allegations of the complaint. The answer may contain a waiver of hearing; and if not, a separate paragraph in the answer shall request a hearing. The answer shall contain the name and address of the defendant, or of the attorney representing the defendant. Failure to file an answer or to plead specifically to any allegation of the complaint shall constitute an admission of such allegation.

(c) *Procedure, upon admission of facts.* The admission, in the answer or by failure to file an answer, of all the material allegations of fact contained in the complaint shall constitute a waiver of hearing. Upon such admission, the Administrative Law Judge, without further hearing, may prepare his decision in which he shall adopt as his proposed findings of fact the material facts alleged in the complaint. The parties shall be given an opportunity to file exceptions to his decision and to file briefs in support of the exceptions.

§60–30.7 Notice of prehearing conference.

The Administrative Law Judge shall respond to defendant's request for a hearing within 15 days and shall serve a notice of prehearing conference on the parties. The notice shall contain the time and place of the conference.

§60–30.8 Motions; disposition of motions.

(a) *Motions.* Motions shall state the relief sought, the authority relied upon and the facts alleged, and shall be filed with the Administrative Law Judge. If made before or after the hearing itself, the motions shall be in writing. If made at the hearing, motions may be stated orally; but the Administrative Law Judge may require that they be reduced to writing and filed and served on all parties in the same manner as a formal motion. Unless otherwise ordered by the Administrative Law Judge, written motions shall be accompanied by a supporting memorandum. Within 10 days after a written motion is served, or such other time period as may be fixed, any party may file a response to a motion.

(b) *Disposition of motions.* The Administrative Law Judge may not grant a written motion prior to expiration of the time for filing responses thereto, except upon consent of the parties or following a hearing, but may overrule or deny such motion without awaiting response: *Provided,* That prehearing conferences, hearings, and decisions need not be delayed pending disposition of motions.

§60–30.9 Interrogatories, and admissions as to facts and documents.

(a) *Interrogatories.* Not later than 25 days prior to the date of the hearing, except for good cause shown, or not later than 14 days prior to such earlier date as the Administrative Law Judge may order, any party may serve upon an opposing party written interrogatories. Each interrogatory shall be answered separately and fully in writing under oath, unless objected to. Answers are to be signed by the person making them and objections by the attorney or by whoever is representing the party. Answers and objections shall be filed and served within 25 days of service of the interrogatory.

(b) *Admissions.* Not later than 14 days prior to the date of the hearing, except for good cause shown, or not later than 14 days prior to such earlier date as the Administrative Law Judge may order, any party may serve upon an opposing party a written request for the admission of the genuineness and authenticity of any relevant documents described in and exhibited with the request, or for the admission of the truth of any relevant matters of fact stated in the request. Each of the matters as to which an admission is requested shall be deemed admitted, unless within 25 days after service, the party to whom the request is directed serves upon the requesting party a sworn statement either (1) denying specifically the matter as to which an admission is requested, or (2) setting forth in detail the reasons why he cannot truthfully either admit or deny such matters.

(c) *Objections or failures to respond.* The party submitting the interrogatory or request may move for an order with respect to any objection or other failure to respond.

§60–30.10 Production of documents and things and entry upon land for inspection and other purposes.

(a) After commencement of the action, any party may serve on any other party a request to produce and/or permit the party, or someone acting on his behalf, to inspect and copy any unprivileged documents, phonorecords, and other compilations, including computer tapes and printouts which contain or may lead to relevant information and which are in the possession, custody, or control of the party upon whom the request is served. If necessary, translation of data compilations shall be done by the party furnishing the information.

(b) After commencement of the action, any party may serve on any other party a request to permit entry upon designated property which may be relevant to the issues in the proceeding and, which is in the possession or control of the party upon whom the request is served for the purpose of inspection, measuring, surveying or photographing, testing, or sampling the property or any designated object or area.

(c) Each request shall set forth with reasonable particularity the items to be inspected and shall specify a reasonable time and place for making the inspection and performing the related acts.

(d) The party upon whom the request is served shall respond within 25 days after the service of the request. The response shall state, with respect to each item, that inspection and related activities will be permitted as requested, unless there are objections, in which case the reasons for each objection shall be stated. The party submitting the request may move for an order with respect to any objection or to other failure to respond.

§ 60–30.11 Depositions upon oral examination.

(a) *Depositions; notice of examination.* After commencement of the action, any party may take the testimony of any person, including a party, having personal or expert knowledge of the matters in issue, by deposition upon oral examination. A party desiring to take a deposition shall give reasonable notice in writing to every other party to the proceeding, and may use an administrative subpoena. The notice shall state the time and place for taking the deposition and the name and address of each person to be examined, if known, and, if the name is not known, a general description sufficient to identify him or the particular class or group to which he belongs. The notice shall also set forth the categories of documents the witness is to bring with him to the deposition, if any. A copy of the notice shall be furnished to the person to be examined unless his name is unknown.

(b) *Production of witnesses; obligation of parties; objections.* It shall be the obligation of each party to produce for examination any person, along with such documents as may be requested, at the time and place, and on the date, set forth in the notice, if that party has control over such person. Each party shall be deemed to have control over its officers, agents, employees, and members. Unless the parties agree otherwise, depositions shall be held within the county in which the witness resides or works. The party or prospective witness may file with the Administrative Law Judge an objection within 5 days after notice of production of such witness is served, stating with particularity the reasons why the party cannot or ought not to produce a requested witness. The party serving the notice may move for an order with respect to such objection or failure to produce a witness. All errors or irregularities in compliance with the provisions of this section shall be deemed waived unless a motion to suppress the deposition or some part thereof is made with reasonable promptness after such defect is or, with due diligence, might have been ascertained.

(c) *Before whom taken; scope of examination; failure to answer.* Depositions may be taken before any officer authorized to administer oaths by the laws of the United States or of the place where the deposition is held. At the time and place specified in the notice, each party shall be permitted to examine and cross-examine the witness under oath upon any matter which is relevant to the subject matter of the proceeding, or which is reasonably calculated to lead to the production of relevant and otherwise admissible evidence. All objections to questions, except as to the form thereof, and all objections to evidence are reserved until the hearing. A refusal or failure on the part of any person under the control of a party to answer a question shall operate to create a presumption that the answer, if given, would be unfavorable to the controlling party, unless the question is subsequently ruled improper by the Administrative Law Judge or the Administrative Law Judge rules that there was valid justification for the witness' failure or refusal to answer the question: *Provided,* That the examining party shall note on the record during the deposition the question which the deponent has failed, or refused to answer, and state his intention to invoke the presumption if no answer is forthcoming.

(d) *Subscription; certification; filing.* The testimony shall be reduced to typewriting, either by the officer taking the deposition or under his direction, and shall be submitted to the witness for examination and signing. If the deposition is not signed by the witness because he is ill, dead, cannot be found, or refuses to sign it, such fact shall be noted in the certificate of the officer and the deposition may then be used as fully as though signed. The officer shall immediately deliver the original copy of the transcript, together with his certificate, in person or by mail to the Administrative Law Judge. Copies of the transcript and certificate shall be furnished to all persons desiring them, upon payment of reasonable charges, unless distribution is restricted by order of the Administrative Law Judge for good cause shown.

(e) *Rulings on admissibility; use of deposition.* Subject to the provisions of this section, objection may be made at the hearing to receiving in evidence any deposition or part thereof for any reason which would require the exclusion of the evidence if the witness were then present and testifying. Any part or all of a deposition, so far as admissible in the discretion of the Administrative Law Judge, may be used against any party who was present or represented at the taking of the deposition or who had reasonable notice, in accordance with the following provisions:

(1) Any deposition may be used by any party for the purpose of contradicting or impeaching the testimony of the deponent as a witness.

(2) The deposition of a party or of any one who at the time of taking the deposition was an officer, director, or managing agent, or was designated to testify on behalf of a public or private corporation, partnership, association, or governmental agency which is a party may be used by the adverse party for any purpose.

(3) The deposition of a witness, whether or not a party, may be used by any party for any purpose if the administrative law judge finds: (i) That the witness is dead; or (ii) that the witness is unable to attend or testify because of age, illness, infirmity, or imprisonment; or (iii) that the party offering the deposition has been unable to procure the attendance of the witness by subpoena; or (iv) upon application and notice, that such exceptional circumstances exist as to make it desirable to allow the deposition to be used.

(4) If only part of a deposition is introduced in evidence by a party, any party may introduce any other parts by way of rebuttal and otherwise.

(f) *Stipulations.* If the parties so stipulate in writing, depositions may be taken before any person at any time or place, upon any notice and in any manner, and when so taken may be used like other depositions.

[43 FR 49259, Oct. 20, 1978; 43 FR 51401, Nov. 3, 1978]

§ 60–30.12 Prehearing conferences.

(a) Upon his own motion or the motion of the parties, the Administrative Law Judge may direct the parties or their counsel to meet with him for a conference to consider:

(1) Simplification of the issues;

(2) Necessity or desirability of amendments to pleadings for purposes of clarification, simplification, or limitation;

(3) Stipulations, admissions of fact and of contents and authenticity of documents;

(4) Limitation of number of witnesses;

(5) Scheduling dates for the exchange of witness lists and of proposed exhibits;

(6) Such other matters as may tend to expedite the disposition of the proceedings.

(b) The record shall show the matters disposed of by order and by agreement in such pretrial conferences. The subsequent course of the proceeding shall be controlled by such action.

§ 60–30.13 Consent findings and order.

(a) *General.* At any time after the issuance of a complaint and prior to or during the reception of evidence in any proceeding, the parties may jointly move to defer the receipt of any evidence for a reasonable time to permit negotiation of an agreement containing consent findings and an order disposing of the whole or any part of the proceeding. The allowance of such deferment and the duration thereof shall be in the discretion of the Administrative Law Judge after consideration of the nature of the proceeding, the requirments of the public interest, the representations of the parties, and the probability of an agreement being reached which will result in a just disposition of the issues involved.

(b) *Content.* Any agreement containing consent findings and an order disposing of a proceeding shall also provide:

(1) That the order shall have the same force and effect as an order made after full hearing;

(2) That the entire record on which any order may be based shall consist solely of the complaint and the agreement;

(3) That any further procedural steps are waived; and

(4) That any right to challenge or contest the validity of the findings and order entered into in accordance with the agreement is waived.

(c) *Submission.* On or before the expiration of the time granted for negotiations, the parties or their counsel may:

(1) Submit the proposed agreement to the Administrative Law Judge for his consideration;

(2) Inform the Administrative Law Judge that agreement cannot be reached.

(d) *Disposition.* In the event an agreement containing consent findings and an order is submitted within the time allowed, the Administrative Law Judge, within 30 days, shall accept such agreement by issuing his decision based upon the agreed findings, and his decision shall consititute the final Administrative order.

[43 FR 49259, Oct. 20, 1978; 43 FR 51401, Nov. 3, 1978]

HEARINGS AND RELATED MATTERS

§ 60–30.14 Designation of Administrative Law Judges.

Hearings shall be held before an Administrative Law Judge of the Department of Labor who shall be designated by the Chief Administrative Law Judge of the Department of Labor. After commencement of the proceeding but prior to the designation of an Administrative Law Judge, pleadings and papers shall be filed with the Chief Administrative Law Judge.

[43 FR 49259, Oct. 20, 1978; 43 FR 51401, Nov. 3, 1978]

§ 60–30.15 Authority and responsibilities of Administrative Law Judges.

The Administrative Law Judge shall propose findings and conclusions to the Secretary on the basis of the record. In order to do so, he shall have the duty to conduct a fair hearing, to take all necesssary action to avoid delay, and to maintain order. He shall have all powers necessary to those ends, including, but not limited to, the power to:

(a) Hold conferences to settle, simplify, or fix the issues in a proceeding, or to consider other matters that may aid in the expeditious disposition of the proceeding by consent of the parties or upon his own motion;

(b) Require parties to state their position with respect to the various issues in the proceeding;

(c) Require parties to produce for examination those relevant witnesses and documents under their control; and require parties to answer interrogatories and requests for admissions in full;

(d) Administer oaths;

(e) Rule on motions, and other procedural items or matters pending before him;

(f) Regulate the course of the hearing and conduct of participants therein;

(g) Examine and cross-examine witnesses, and introduce into the record documentary or other evidence;

(h) Receive, rule on, exclude, or limit evidence and limit lines of questioning or testimony which are irrelevant, immaterial, or unduly repetitious;

(i) Fix time limits for submission of written documents in matters before him and extend any time limits established by this part upon a determination that no party will be prejudiced and that the ends of justice will be served thereby;

(j) Impose appropriate sanctions against any party or person failing to obey an order under these rules which may include:

(1) Refusing to allow the disobedient party to support or oppose designated claims or defenses, or prohibiting it from introducing designated matters in evidence;

(2) Excluding all testimony of an unresponsive or evasive witness, or determining that the answer of such witness, if given, would be unfavorable to the party having control over him; and

(3) Expelling any party or person from further participation in the hearing;

(k) Take official notice of any material fact not appearing in evidence in the record, which is among the traditional matters of judicial notice;

(l) Recommend whether the respondent is in current violation of the order, regulations, or its contractual obligations, as well as the nature of the relief necessary to insure the full enjoyment of the rights secured by the order;

(m) Issue subpoenas; and

(n) Take any action authorized by these rules.

[43 FR 49259, Oct. 20, 1978; 43 FR 51401, Nov. 3, 1978]

§ 60–30.16 Appearances.

(a) *Representation.* The parties or other persons or organizations participating pursuant to this part 60–30 have the right to be represented by counsel.

(b) *Failure to appear.* In the event that a party appears at the hearing and no party appears for the opposing side, the party who is present shall have an election to present his evidence in whole or such portion thereof sufficient to make a prima facie case before the Administrative Law Judge. Failure to appear at the hearing shall not be deemed to be a waiver of the right to be served with a copy of the Administrative Law Judge's recommended decision and to file exceptions to it.

§ 60–30.17 Appearance of witnesses.

(a) A party wishing to procure the appearance at the hearing of any person having personal or expert knowledge of the matters in issue shall serve on the prospective witness a notice, which may be accomplished by an administrative subpoena, setting forth the time, date, and place at which he is to appear for the purpose of giving testimony. The notice shall also set forth the categories of documents the witness is to bring with him to the hearing, if any. A copy of the notice shall be filed with the Administrative Law Judge and additional copies shall be served upon the opposing parties.

(b) It shall be the obligation of each party to produce for examination any person, along with such documents as may be requested, at the time and place, and on the date, set forth in the notice, if that party has control over such person. Each party shall be deemed to have control over its officers, agents, employees, and members. Due regard shall be given to the convenience of witnesses in scheduling their testimony so that they will be detained no longer than reasonably necessary.

(c) The party or prospective witness may file an objection within 5 days after notice of production of such witness is served stating with particularity the reasons why the party cannot produce a requested witness. The party serving the notice may move for an order with respect to such objection or failure to produce a witness.

[43 FR 49259, Oct. 20, 1978; 43 FR 51401, Nov. 3, 1978]

§ 60–30.18 Rules of evidence.

In any hearing, decision, or administrative review conducted pursuant to this part, all evidentiary matters shall be governed by Office of Administrative Law Judges' Rules of evidence at 29 CFR part 18, subpart B, *Provided however,* That the provision at 29 CFR 18.1104 which delays the effective date of the rule with respect to certain investigations does not apply.

[55 FR 19069, May 8, 1990]

§ 60–30.19 Objections; exceptions; offer of proof.

(a) *Objections.* If a party objects to the admission or rejection of any evidence or to the limitation of the scope of any examination or cross-examination or the failure to limit such scope, he shall state briefly the grounds for such objection. Rulings on all objections shall appear in the record. Only objections made on the record may be relied upon subsequently in the proceedings.

(b) *Exceptions.* Formal exception to an adverse ruling is not required. Rulings by the Administrative Law Judge shall not be appealed prior to the transfer of the case to the Secretary, but shall be considered by the Secretary upon filing exceptions to the Administrative Law Judge's recommendations and conclusions.

(c) *Offer of proof.* An offer of proof made in connection with an objection taken to any ruling excluding proffered oral testimony shall consist of a statement of the substance of the evidence which counsel contends would be adduced by such testimony; and, if the excluded evidence consists of evidence in written form or consists of reference to documents, a copy of such evidence shall be marked for identification and shall accompany the record as the offer of proof.

[43 FR 49259, Oct. 20, 1978; 43 FR 51401, Nov. 3, 1978]

§ 60-30.20 Ex parte communications.

The Administrative Law Judge shall not consult any person, or party, on any fact in issue unless upon notice and opportunity for all parties to participate. No employee or agent of the Federal Government engaged in the investigation and prosecution of this case shall participate or advise in the rendering of the recommended or final decision in the case, except as witness or counsel in the proceeding.

§ 60-30.21 Oral argument.

Any party shall be entitled upon request to a reasonable period between the close of evidence and termination of the hearing for oral argument. Oral arguments shall be included in the official transcript of the hearing.

§ 60-30.22 Official transcript.

The official transcripts of testimony taken, together with any exhibits, briefs, or memorandums of law, shall be filed with the Administrative Law Judge. Transcripts of testimony may be obtained from the official reporter by the parties and the public as provided in section 11(a) of the Federal Advisory Committee Act (86 Stat. 770). Upon notice to all parties, the Administrative Law Judge may authorize such corrections to the transcript as are necessary to reflect accurately the testimony.

§ 60-30.23 Summary judgment.

(a) *For the Government.* At any time after the expiration of 20 days from the commencement of the action, or after service of a motion for summary judgment by the respondent, the Government may move with or without supporting affidavits for a summary judgment upon all claims or any part.

(b) *For defendant.* The defendant may, at any time after commencement of the action, move with or without supporting affidavits for summary judgment in its favor as to all claims or any part.

(c) *Other parties.* Any other party to a formal proceeding under this part may support or oppose motions for summary judgment made by the Government or respondent, in accordance with this section, but may not move for a summary judgment in his own behalf.

(d) *Statement of uncontested facts.* All motions for summary judgment shall be accompanied by a "Statement of Uncontested Facts" in which the moving party sets forth all alleged uncontested material facts which shall provide the basis for its motion. At least 5 days prior to the time fixed for hearing on the motion, any party contending that any material fact regarding the matter covered by the motion is in dispute, shall file a "Statement of Disputed Facts." Failure to file a "Statement of Disputed Facts" shall be deemed as an admission to the "Statement of Uncontested Facts."

(e) *Motion and proceedings.* The motion shall be served upon all parties at least 15 days before the time fixed for the hearing on the motion. The adverse party or parties may serve opposing affidavits prior to the day of hearing. The judgment sought shall be rendered forthwith if the complaint and answer, depositions, and admissions on file, together with the affidavits, if any, show that there is no genuine issue as to any material fact and that the moving party is entitled to a judgment as a matter of law. Summary judgment rendered for or against the Government or the respondent shall constitute the findings and recommendations on the issues involved. Hearings on motions made under this section shall be scheduled by the Administrative Law Judge.

(f) *Case not fully adjudicated on motion.* If on motion under this section judgment is not rendered upon the whole case or for all the relief asked and a final hearing is necessary, the Administrative Law Judge at the hearing of the motion, by examining the notice and answer and the evidence before him and by interrogating counsel, shall, if practicable, ascertain what material facts exist without substantial controversy and what material facts are actually and in good faith controverted. He shall thereupon make an order specifying the facts that appear without substantial controversy, including the extent to which relief is not in controversy, and directing such further proceedings as are just. At the hearing on the merits, the facts so specified shall be deemed established, and the final hearing shall be conducted accordingly.

[43 FR 49259, Oct. 20, 1978; 43 FR 51401, Nov. 3, 1978]

§ 60–30.24 Participation by interested persons.

(a)(1) To the extent that proceedings hereunder involve employment of persons covered by a collective bargaining agreement, and compliance may necessitate a revision of such agreement, any labor organization which is a signatory to the agreement shall have the right to participate as a party.

(2) Other persons or organizations shall have the right to participate as parties if the final Administrative order could adversely affect them or the class they represent, and such participation may contribute materially to the proper disposition of the proceedings.

(3) Any person or organization wishing to participate as a party under this section shall file with the Administrative Law Judge and serve on all parties a petition within 25 days after the commencement of the action or at such other time as ordered by the Administrative Law Judge, so long as it does not disrupt the proceeding. Such petition shall concisely state: (i) Petitioner's interest in the proceedings; (ii) who will appear for petitioner; (iii) the issues on which petitioner wishes to participate; and (iv) whether petitioner intends to present witnesses.

(4) The Administrative Law Judge shall determine whether each petitioner has the requisite interest in the proceedings and shall permit or deny participation accordingly. Where petitions to participate as parties are made by individuals or groups with common interest, the Administrative Law Judge may request all such petitioners to designate a single representative to represent all such petitioners: *Provided,* That the representative of a labor organization qualifying to participate under paragraph (a)(1) of the section must be permitted to participate in the proceedings. The Administrative Law Judge shall give each petitioner written notice of the decision on his petition; and if the petition is denied, he shall briefly state the grounds for denial and shall then treat the petition as a request for participation as amicus curiae. The Administrative Law Judge shall give written notice to each party of each petition granted.

(b)(1) Any other interested person or organization wishing to participate as amicus curiae shall file a petition before the commencement of the final hearing with the Administrative Law Judge. Such petition shall concisely state: (i) The petitioner's interest in the hearing; (ii) who will represent the petitioner; and (iii) the issues on which petitioner intends to present argument. The Administrative Law Judge may grant the petition if he finds that the petitioner has a legitimate interest in the proceedings, and that such participation may contribute materially to the proper disposition of the issues. An amicus curiae is not a party but may participate as provided in this section.

(2) An amicus curiae may present a brief oral statement at the hearing at the point in the proceeding specified by the Administrative Law Judge. He may submit a written statement of position to the Administrative Law Judge prior to the beginning of a hearing and shall serve a copy on each party. He may also submit a brief or written statement at such time as the parties submit briefs and exceptions, and he shall serve a copy on each party.

[43 FR 49259, Oct. 20, 1978; 43 FR 51401, Nov. 3, 1978]

POST-HEARING PROCEDURES

§ 60–30.25 Proposed findings of fact and conclusions of law.

Within 20 days after receipt of the transcript of the testimony, each party and amicus may file a brief. Such briefs shall be served simultaneously on all parties and amici, and a certificate of service shall be furnished to the Administrative Law Judge. Requests for additional time in which to file a brief shall be made in writing, and copies shall be served simultaneously on the other parties. Requests for extensions shall be received not later than 3 days before the date such briefs are due. No reply brief may be filed except by special permission of the Administrative Law Judge.

§ 60–30.26 Record for recommended decision.

The transcript of testimony, exhibits, and all papers, documents, and requests filed in the proceedings, including briefs, but excepting the correspondence section of the docket, shall constitute the record for decision.

§ 60–30.27 Recommended decision.

Within a reasonable time after the filing of briefs, the Administrative Law Judge shall recommend findings, conclusions, and a decision. These recommendations shall be certified, together with the record for recommended decision, to the Administrative Review Board, United States Department of Labor, for a final Administrative order. The recommended findings, conclusions, and decision shall be served on all parties and amici to the proceeding.

[61 FR 19988, May 3, 1996]

§ 60–30.28 Exceptions to recommended decisions.

Within 14 days after receipt of the recommended findings, conclusions, and decision, any party may submit exceptions to said recommendation. These exceptions may be responded to by other parties within 14 days of their receipt by said parties. All exceptions and responses shall be filed with the Administrative Review Board, United States Department of Labor. Service of such briefs or exceptions and responses shall be made simultaneously on all parties to the proceeding. Requests to the Administrative Review Board, United States Department of Labor, for additional time in which to file exceptions and responses shall be in writing and copies shall be served simultaneously on other parties. Requests for extensions must be received no later than 3 days before the exceptions are due.

[61 FR 19988, May 3, 1996]

§ 60–30.29 Record.

After expiration of the time for filing briefs and exceptions, the Administrative Review Board, United States Department of Labor, shall make a final decision, which shall be the final Administrative order, on the basis of the record. The record shall consist of the record for recommended decision, the rulings and recommended decision of the Administrative Law Judge and the exceptions and briefs filed subsequent to the Administrative Law Judge's decision.

[61 FR 19988, May 3, 1996]

§ 60–30.30 Final Administrative Order.

After expiration of the time for filing, the Administrative Review Board, United States Department of Labor, shall make a final Administrative order which shall be served on all parties. If the Administrative Review Board, United States Department of Labor, concludes that the defendant has violated the Executive Order, the equal opportunity clause, or the regulations, an Administrative order shall be issued enjoining the violations, and requiring the contractor to provide whatever remedies are appropriate, and imposing whatever sanctions are appropriate, or any of the above. In any event, failure to comply with the Administrative order shall result in the immediate cancellation, termination and suspension of the respondent's contracts and/or debarment of the respondent from further contracts.

[61 FR 19988, May 3, 1996]

EXPEDITED HEARING PROCEDURES

AUTHORITY: Sections 60–30.31 to 60–30.37 issued under E.O. 11246 (30 FR 12319) as amended by E.O. 11375 and 12086.

SOURCE: Sections 60–30.31 through 60–30.37 appear at 44 FR 77003, Dec. 28, 1979, unless otherwise noted.

§ 60–30.31 Expedited hearings—when appropriate.

Expedited Hearings may be used, *inter alia*, when a contractor or subcontractor has violated a conciliation agreement; has not adopted and implemented an acceptable affirmative action program; has refused to give access to or to supply records or other information as required by the equal opportunity clause; or has refused to allow an on-site compliance review to be conducted.

§ 60–30.32 Administrative complaint and answer.

(a) Expedited hearings shall be commenced by filing an administrative complaint in accordance with 41 CFR 60–30.5. The complaint shall state that the hearing is subject to these expedited hearing procedures.

(b) The answer shall be filed in accordance with 41 CFR 60–30.6 (a) and (b).

(c) Failure to request a hearing within the 20 days provided by 41 CFR 60–30.6(a) shall constitute a waiver of hearing, and all the material allegations of fact contained in the complaint shall be deemed to be admitted. If a hearing is not requested or is waived, within 25 days of the complaint's filing, the Administrative Law Judge shall adopt as findings of fact the material facts alleged in the complaint, and shall order the appropriate sanctions and/or penalties sought in the complaint. The Administrative Law Judge's findings and order shall constitute a final Administrative order, unless the Office of the Solicitor, U.S. Department of Labor, files exceptions to the findings and order within 10 days of receipt thereof. If the Office of the Solicitor, U.S. Department of Labor, files exceptions, the matter shall proceed in accordance with § 60–30.36 of this part.

(d) If a request for a hearing is received within 20 days as provided by 41 CFR 60–30.6(a), the hearing shall be convened within 45 days of receipt of the request and shall be completed within 15 days thereafter, unless more hearing time is required.

§ 60–30.33 Discovery.

(a) Any party may serve requests for admissions in accordance with § 60–30.9 (b) and (c).

(b) Witness lists and hearing exhibits will be exchanged at least 10 days in advance of the hearing.

(c) For good cause shown, and upon motion made in accordance with § 60–30.8, the Administrative Law Judge may allow the taking of depositions. Other discovery will not be permitted.

§ 60–30.34 Conduct of hearing.

(a) At the hearing, the Government shall be given an opportunity to demonstrate the basis for the request for sanctions and/or remedies, and the contractor shall be given an opportunity to show that the violation complained of did not occur and/or that good cause or good faith efforts excuse the alleged violations. Both parties shall be allowed to present evidence and argument and to cross-examine witnesses.

(b) The hearing shall be informal in nature, and the Administrative Law Judge shall not be bound by formal rules of evidence.

§ 60–30.35 Recommended decision after hearing.

Within 15 days after the hearing is concluded, the Administrative Law Judge shall recommend findings, conclusions, and a decision. The Administrative Law Judge may permit the parties to file written post-hearing briefs within this time period, but the Administrative Law Judge's recommendations shall not be delayed pending receipt of such briefs. These recommendations shall be certified, together with the record, to the Administrative Review Board, United States Department of Labor, for a final Administrative order. The recommended decision shall be served on all parties and amici to the proceeding.

[61 FR 19989, May 3, 1996]

§ 60–30.36 Exceptions to recommendations.

Within 10 days after receipt of the recommended findings, conclusions and decision, any party may submit exceptions to said recommendations. Exceptions may be responded to by other parties within 7 days after receipt by said parties of the exceptions. All exceptions and responses shall be filed with the Administrative Review Board, United States Department of Labor. Briefs or exceptions and responses shall be served simultaneously on all parties to the proceeding.

[61 FR 19989, May 3, 1996]

§ 60–30.37 Final Administrative order.

After expiration of the time for filing exceptions, the Administrative Review Board, United States Department of Labor, shall issue a final Administrative order which shall be served on all parties. Unless the Administrative Review Board, United States Department of Labor, issues a final Administrative order within 30 days after the expiration of the time for filing exceptions, the Administrative Law Judge's recommended decision shall become a final Administrative order which shall become effective on the 31st day after expiration of the time for filing exceptions. Except as to specific time periods required in this subsection, 41 CFR 60–30.30 shall be applicable to this subsection.

[61 FR 19989, May 3, 1996]

PART 60–40—EXAMINATION AND COPYING OF OFCCP DOCUMENTS

Subpart A—General

Subpart B—Procedures for Disclosure

AUTHORITY: E.O. 11246, as amended by E.O. 11375, and as amended by E.O. 12086; 5 U.S.C. 552.

SOURCE: 43 FR 49264, Oct. 20, 1978, unless otherwise noted.

Subpart A—General

§ 60–40.1 Purpose and scope.

This part contains the general rules of the OFCCP providing for public access to information from records of the OFCCP or its various compliance agencies. These regulations implement 5 U.S.C. 552, the Freedom of Information Act and supplement the policy and regulations of the Department of Labor, 29 CFR Part 70. It is the policy of the OFCCP to disclose information to the public and to cooperate with other public agencies as well as private parties seeking to eliminate discrimination in employment. This part sets forth generally the categories of records accessible to the public, the types of records subject to prohibitions or restrictions on disclosure, and the places at which and the procedures whereby members of the public may obtain access to and inspect and copy information from records in the custody of the OFCCP.

[43 FR 49264, Oct. 20, 1978; 43 FR 51401, Nov. 3, 1978]

§ 60–40.2 Information available on request.

(a) Upon the request of any person for identifiable records obtained or generated pursuant to Executive Order 11246 (as amended) such records shall be made available for inspection and copying, notwithstanding the applicability of the exemption from mandatory disclosure set forth in 5 U.S.C. 552 subsection (b), if it is determined that the requested inspection or copying furthers the public interest and does not impede any of the functions of the OFCCP, except in the case of records disclosure of which is prohibited by law.

(b) Consistent with the above, all contract compliance documents within the custody of the OFCCP shall be disclosed upon request unless specifically prohibited by law or as limited elsewhere herein. The types of documents which if in the custody of the OFCCP must be disclosed include, but are not limited to, the following:

(1) Affirmative action plans, whether or not reviewed and finally accepted by the OFCCP except as limited in 41 CFR 60–40.3(a)(1).

(2) Imposed plans and hometown plans, pending or approved.

(3) Text of final conciliation agreements.

(4) Validation studies of tests or other preemployment selection methods.

(5) Dates and times of scheduled compliance reviews.

§ 60–40.3 Information exempt from compulsory disclosure and which may be withheld.

(a) The following documents or parts thereof are exempt from mandatory disclosure by the OFCCP, and should be withheld if it is determined that the requested inspection or copying does not further the public interest and might impede the discharge of any of the functions of the OFCCP.

(1) Those portions of affirmative action plans such as goals and timetables which would be confidential commercial or financial information because they indicate, and only to the extent that they indicate, that a contractor plans major shifts or changes in his personnel requirements and he has not made this information available to the public. A determination to withhold this type of information should be made only after receiving verification and a satisfactory explanation from the contractor that the information should be withheld.

(2) Those portions of affirmative action plans which constitute information on staffing patterns and pay scales but only to the extent that their release would injure the business or financial position of the contractor, would constitute a release of confidential financial information of an employee or would constitute an unwarranted invasion of the privacy of an employee.

(3) The names of individual complainants.

(4) The assignments to particular contractors of named compliance officers if such disclosure would subject the named compliance officers to undue harassment or would affect the efficient enforcement of the Executive order.

(5) Compliance investigation files including the standard compliance review report and related documents, during the course of the review to which they pertain or while enforcement action against the contractor is in progress or contemplated within a reasonable time. Therefore, these reports and related files shall not be disclosed only to the extent that information contained therein constitutes trade secrets and confidential commercial or financial information, interagency or intra-agency memoranda or letters which would not be available by law to a private party in litigation with the agency, personnel and medical files and similar files the disclosure of which would constitute a clearly unwarranted invasion of personal privacy, data which would be exempt from mandatory disclosure pursuant to the "informants privilege" or such information the disclosure of which is prohibited by statute.

(6) Copies of preemployment selection tests used by contractors.

(b) Other records may be withheld consistent with the Freedom of Information Act on a case-by-case basis, with the prior approval of the Director, OFCCP.

§ 60–40.4 Information disclosure of which is prohibited by law.

The Standard Form 100 (EEO–1) which is submitted by contractors to the OFCCP or a Joint Reporting Committee servicing both the OFCCP and the EEOC shall be disclosed pending further instructions from the Director. The statutory prohibition on disclosure set forth in section 709(e) of the Civil Rights Act of 1964 is limited by the terms of that section to information obtained pursuant to the authority of title VII of that Act and its disclosure by employees of the EEOC.

Subpart B—Procedures for Disclosure

§ 60–40.5 Applicability of procedures.

Requests for the inspection and copying of information from records in the custody of the OFCCP which are identifiable and available under the provisions of Subpart A of this part shall be made and acted upon as provided in the following sections of this subpart. Officers and employees of the OFCCP are authorized by the Director to continue to furnish to the public, informally and without compliance with these procedures, information and copies from its records which prior to the enactment of the Freedom of Information Act (5 U.S.C. 552) were customarily furnished in the regular performance of their duties.

[43 FR 49264, Oct. 20, 1978; 43 FR 51401, Nov. 3, 1978]

§ 60–40.6 To whom to direct requests.

A request for contract compliance records or information shall be directed to the National OFCCP or appropriate OFCCP Regional or Area Office. If the person making the request does not know in which office the record is located, he may direct his request to the Director, Office of Federal Contract Compliance Programs, Department of Labor, 200 Constitution Avenue NW., Washington, DC 20210, for appropriate handling.

§ 60–40.7 Partial disclosure.

If a requested record contains some materials which are protected from disclosure and other materials which are not so protected, identifying details or protected matters shall be deleted wherever analysis indicates that such deletions are feasible. Whenever such deletions are made, the remainder of the records may be disclosed.

§ 60–40.8 Facilities and procedures for disclosure.

(a) [Reserved]

(b) Procedures relating to the avaliability of records shall be governed by the Department of Labor regulations, 29 CFR 70.35 to 70.64.

PART 60–50—GUIDELINES ON DISCRIMINATION BECAUSE OF RELIGION OR NATIONAL ORIGIN

Sec.

AUTHORITY: Sec. 201, E.O. 11246, 30 FR 12319, and E.O. 11375, 32 FR 14303, as amended by E.O. 12086.

SOURCE: 43 FR 49265, Oct. 20, 1978, unless otherwise amended.

§ 60–50.1 Purpose and scope.

(a) The purpose of the provisions in this part is to set forth the interpretations and guidelines of the Office of Federal Contract Compliance Programs regarding the implementation of Executive Order 11246, as amended, for promoting and insuring equal employment opportunities for all persons employed or seeking employment with Government contractors and subcontractors or with contractors and subcontractors performing under federally assisted construction contracts, without regard to religion or national origin.

(b) Members of various religious and ethnic groups, primarily but not exclusively of Eastern, Middle, and Southern European ancestry, such as Jews, Catholics, Italians, Greeks, and Slavic groups, continue to be excluded from executive, middle-management, and other job levels because of discrimination based upon their religion and/or national origin. These guidelines are intended to remedy such unfair treatment.

(c) These guidelines are also intended to clarify the obligations of employers with respect to accommodating to the religious observances and practices of employees and prospective employees.

(d) The employment problems of blacks, Spanish-surnamed Americans, orientals, and American Indians are treated under Part 60–2 of this chapter and under other regulations and procedures implementing the requirements of Executive Order 11246, as amended. Accordingly, the remedial provisions of § 60–50.2(b) shall not be applicable to the employment problems of these groups.

(e) Nothing contained in this Part 60–50 is intended to supersede or otherwise limit the exemption set forth in § 60–1.5(a)(5) of this chapter for contracts with certain educational institutions.

§ 60–50.2 Equal employment policy.

(a) *General requirements.* Under the equal opportunity clause contained in section 202 of Executive Order 11246, as amended, employers are prohibited from discriminating against employees or applicants for employment because of religion or national origin, and must take affirmative action to insure that applicants are employed, and that employees are treated during employment, without regard to their religion or national origin. Such action includes, but is not limited to the following: Employment, upgrading, demotion, or transfer: Recruitment or recruitment advertising; layoff or termination; rates of pay or other forms of compensation; and selection for training, including apprenticeship.

(b) *Outreach and positive recruitment.* Employers shall review their employment practices to determine whether members of the various religious and/or ethnic groups are receiving fair consideration for job opportunities. Special attention shall be directed toward executive and middle-management levels, where employment problems relating to religion and national origin are most likely to occur. Based upon the findings of such reviews, employers shall undertake appropriate outreach and positive recruitment activities, such as those listed below, in order to remedy existing deficiencies. It is not contemplated that employers necessarily will undertake all of the listed activities. The scope of the employer's efforts shall depend upon all the circumstances, including the nature and extent of the employer's deficiencies and the employer's size and resources.

(1) Internal communication of the employer's obligation to provide equal employment opportunity without regard to religion or national origin in such a manner as to foster understanding, acceptance, and support among the employer's executive, management, supervisory, and all other employees and to encourage such persons to take the necessary action to aid the employer in meeting this obligation.

(2) Development of reasonable internal procedures to insure that the employer's obligation to provide equal employment opportunity without regard to religion or national origin is being fully implemented.

(3) Periodically informing all employees of the employer's commitment to equal employment opportunity for all persons, without regard to religion or national origin.

(4) Enlisting the assistance and support of all recruitment sources (including employment agencies, college placement directors, and business associates) for the employer's commitment to provide equal employment opportunity without regard to religion or national origin.

(5) Reviewing employment records to determine the availability of promotable and transferable members of various religious and ethnic groups.

(6) Establishment of meaningful contacts with religious and ethnic organizations and leaders for such purposes as advice, education, technical assistance, and referral of potential employees.

(7) Engaging in significant recruitment activities at educational institutions with substantial enrollments of students from various religious and ethnic groups.

(8) Use of the religious and ethnic media for institutional and employment advertising.

§ 60–50.3 Accommodations to religious observance and practice.

An employer must accommodate to the religious observances and practices of an employee or prospective employee unless the employer demonstrates that it is unable to reasonably accommodate to an employee's or prospective employee's religious observance or practice without undue hardship on the conduct of the employer's business. As part of this obligation, an employer must make reasonable accommodations to the religious observances and practices of an employee or prospective employee who regularly observes Friday evening and Saturday, or some other day of the week, as his Sabbath and/or who observes certain religious holidays during the year and who is conscientiously opposed to performing work or engaging in similar activity on such days, when such accommodations can be made without undue hardship on the conduct of the employer's business. In determining the extent of an employer's obligations under this section, at least the following factors shall be considered: (a) Business necessity, (b) financial costs and expenses, and (c) resulting personnel problems.

§ 60–50.4 Enforcement.

The provisions of this part are subject to the general enforcement, compliance review, and complaint procedures set forth in Subpart B of Part 60–1 of this chapter.

§ 60–50.5 Nondiscrimination.

The provisions of this part are not intended and shall not be used to discriminate against any qualified employee or applicant for employment because of race, color, religion, sex, or national origin.

PART 60–250—AFFIRMATIVE ACTION AND NONDISCRIMINATION OBLIGATIONS OF CONTRACTORS AND SUBCONTRACTORS REGARDING SPECIAL DISABLED VETERANS, VETERANS OF THE VIETNAM ERA, RECENTLY SEPARATED VETERANS, AND OTHER PROTECTED VETERANS

Subpart A—Preliminary Matters, Equal Opportunity Clause

Sec.

Subpart B—Discrimination Prohibited

Subpart C—Affirmative Action Program

Subpart D—General Enforcement and Complaint Procedures

Subpart E—Ancillary Matters

AUTHORITY: 29 U.S.C. 793; 38 U.S.C. 4211 (2001) (amended 2002); 38 U.S.C. 4212 (2001) (amended 2002) and 4212; E.O. 11758 (3 CFR, 1971–1975 Comp., p. 841).

SOURCE: 70 FR 72151, Dec. 1, 2005, unless otherwise noted.

Subpart A—Preliminary Matters, Equal Opportunity Clause

§ 60–250.1 Purpose, applicability and construction.

(a) *Purpose.* The purpose of the regulations in this part is to set forth the standards for compliance with the Vietnam Era Veterans' Readjustment Assistance Act of 1974, as amended (38 U.S.C. 4212, or VEVRAA), which requires Government contractors and subcontractors to take affirmative action to employ and advance in employment qualified special disabled veterans, veterans of the Vietnam era, recently separated veterans, and other protected veterans.

(b) *Applicability.* This part applies to any Government contract or subcontract of $25,000 or more entered into before December 1, 2003, for the purchase, sale or use of personal property or nonpersonal services (including construction), except that the regulations in 41 CFR part 60–300, and not this part, apply to such a contract or subcontract that is modified on or after December 1, 2003 and the contract or subcontract as modified is in the amount of $100,000 or more: *Provided,* That subpart C of this part applies only as described in §60–250.40(a). Compliance by the contractor with the provisions of this part will not necessarily determine its compliance with other statutes, and compliance with other statutes will not necessarily determine its compliance with this part.

(c) *Construction*—(1) *In general.* The Interpretive Guidance on Title I of the Americans with Disabilities Act (ADA) (42 U.S.C. 12101, *et seq.*) set out as an appendix to 29 CFR part 1630 issued pursuant to Title I may be relied upon for guidance in interpreting the parallel provisions of this part.

(2) *Relationship to other laws.* This part does not invalidate or limit the remedies, rights, and procedures under any Federal law or the law of any state or political subdivision that provides greater or equal protection for the rights of special disabled veterans, veterans of the Vietnam era, recently separated veterans, or other protected veterans as compared to the protection afforded by this part. It may be a defense to a charge of violation of this part that a challenged action is required or necessitated by another Federal law or regulation, or that another Federal law or regulation prohibits an action (including the provision of a particular reasonable accommodation) that would otherwise be required by this part.

[70 FR 72151, Dec. 1, 2005, as amended at 73 FR 18715, Apr. 7, 2008]

§60–250.2 Definitions.

For the purpose of this part:

(a) *Act* means the Vietnam Era Veterans' Readjustment Assistance Act of 1974, as amended, 38 U.S.C. 4212 (2001).

(b) *Equal opportunity clause* means the contract provisions set forth in §60–250.5, "Equal opportunity clause."

(c) *Secretary* means the Secretary of Labor, United States Department of Labor, or his or her designee.

(d) *Deputy Assistant Secretary* means the Deputy Assistant Secretary for Federal Contract Compliance of the United States Department of Labor, or his or her designee.

(e) *Government* means the Government of the United States of America.

(f) *United States,* as used in this part, shall include the several States, the District of Columbia, the Virgin Islands, the Commonwealth of Puerto Rico, Guam, American Samoa, the Commonwealth of the Northern Mariana Islands, and Wake Island.

(g) *Recruiting and training agency* means any person who refers workers to any contractor, or who provides or supervises apprenticeship or training for employment by any contractor.

(h) *Contract* means any Government contract or subcontract.

(i) *Government contract* means any agreement or modification thereof between any contracting agency and any person for the purchase, sale or use of personal property or nonpersonal services (including construction). The term "*Government contract*" does not include agreements in which the parties stand in the relationship of employer and employee, and federally assisted contracts.

(1) *Modification* means any alteration in the terms and conditions of a contract, including supplemental agreements, amendments and extensions.

(2) *Contracting agency* means any department, agency, establishment or instrumentality of the United States, including any wholly owned Government corporation, which enters into contracts.

(3) *Person,* as used in this paragraph (i) and paragraph (l) of this section, means any natural person, corporation, partnership or joint venture, unincorporated association, state or local government, and any agency, instrumentality, or subdivision of such a government.

(4) *Nonpersonal services,* as used in this paragraph (i) and paragraph (l) of this section, includes, but is not limited to, the following: Utility, construction, transportation, research, insurance, and fund depository.

(5) *Construction*, as used in this paragraph (i) and paragraph (l) of this section, means the construction, rehabilitation, alteration, conversion, extension, demolition, or repair of buildings, highways, or other changes or improvements to real property, including facilities providing utility services. The term also includes the supervision, inspection, and other on-site functions incidental to the actual construction.

(6) *Personal property*, as used in this paragraph (i) and paragraph (l) of this section, includes supplies and contracts for the use of real property (such as lease arrangements), unless the contract for the use of real property itself constitutes real property (such as easements).

(j) *Contractor* means, unless otherwise indicated, a prime contractor or subcontractor holding a contract of $25,000 or more.

(k) *Prime contractor* means any person holding a contract of $25,000 or more, and, for the purposes of subpart D of this part, "General Enforcement and Complaint Procedures," includes any person who has held a contract subject to the Act.

(l) *Subcontract* means any agreement or arrangement between a contractor and any person (in which the parties do not stand in the relationship of an employer and an employee):

(1) For the purchase, sale or use of personal property or nonpersonal services (including construction) which, in whole or in part, is necessary to the performance of any one or more contracts; or

(2) Under which any portion of the contractor's obligation under any one or more contracts is performed, undertaken, or assumed.

(m) *Subcontractor* means any person holding a subcontract of $25,000 or more and, for the purposes of subpart D of this part, "General Enforcement and Complaint Procedures," any person who has held a subcontract subject to the Act.

(n)(1) *Special disabled veteran* means:

(i) A veteran who is entitled to compensation (or who but for the receipt of military retired pay would be entitled to compensation) under laws administered by the Department of Veterans Affairs for a disability:

(A) Rated at 30 percent or more; or

(B) Rated at 10 or 20 percent in the case of a veteran who has been determined under 38 U.S.C. 3106 to have a serious employment handicap; or

(ii) A person who was discharged or released from active duty because of a service-connected disability.

(2) *Serious employment handicap*, as used in paragraph (n)(1) of this section, means a significant impairment of a veteran's ability to prepare for, obtain, or retain employment consistent with such veteran's abilities, aptitudes and interests.

(o) *Qualified special disabled veteran* means a special disabled veteran who satisfies the requisite skill, experience, education and other job-related requirements of the employment position such veteran holds or desires, and who, with or without reasonable accommodation, can perform the essential functions of such position.

(p) *Veteran of the Vietnam era* means a person who:

(1) Served on active duty for a period of more than 180 days, and was discharged or released therefrom with other than a dishonorable discharge, if any part of such active duty occurred:

(i) In the Republic of Vietnam between February 28, 1961, and May 7, 1975; or

(ii) Between August 5, 1964, and May 7, 1975, in all other cases; or

(2) Was discharged or released from active duty for a service-connected disability if any part of such active duty was performed:

(i) In the Republic of Vietnam between February 28, 1961, and May 7, 1975; or

(ii) Between August 5, 1964, and May 7, 1975, in all other cases.

(q) *Other protected veteran* means a person who served on active duty during a war or in a campaign or expedition for which a campaign badge has been authorized, under laws administered by the Department of Defense.

(r) *Recently separated veteran* means any veteran during the one-year period beginning on the date of such veteran's discharge or release from active duty.

(s) *Essential functions*—(1) *In general.* The term *essential functions* means fundamental job duties of the employment position the special disabled veteran holds or desires. The term *essential functions* does not include the marginal functions of the position.

(2) A job function may be considered essential for any of several reasons, including but not limited to the following:

(i) The function may be essential because the reason the position exists is to perform that function;

(ii) The function may be essential because of the limited number of employees available among whom the performance of that job function can be distributed; and/or

(iii) The function may be highly specialized so that the incumbent in the position is hired for his or her expertise or ability to perform the particular function.

(3) Evidence of whether a particular function is essential includes, but is not limited to:

(i) The contractor's judgment as to which functions are essential;

(ii) Written job descriptions prepared before advertising or interviewing applicants for the job;

(iii) The amount of time spent on the job performing the function;

(iv) The consequences of not requiring the incumbent to perform the function;

(v) The terms of a collective bargaining agreement;

(vi) The work experience of past incumbents in the job; and/or

(vii) The current work experience of incumbents in similar jobs.

(t) *Reasonable accommodation*—(1) The term *reasonable accommodation* means:

(i) Modifications or adjustments to a job application process that enable a qualified applicant who is a special disabled veteran to be considered for the position such applicant desires;[1]

(ii) Modifications or adjustments to the work environment, or to the manner or circumstances under which the position held or desired is customarily performed, that enable a qualified special disabled veteran to perform the essential functions of that position; or

(iii) Modifications or adjustments that enable the contractor's employee who is a special disabled veteran to enjoy equal benefits and privileges of employment as are enjoyed by the contractor's other similarly situated employees who are not special disabled veterans.

(2) *Reasonable accommodation* may include but is not limited to:

(i) Making existing facilities used by employees readily accessible to and usable by special disabled veterans; and

(ii) Job restructuring; part-time or modified work schedules; reassignment to a vacant position; acquisition or modifications of equipment or devices; appropriate adjustment or modifications of examinations, training materials, or policies; the provision of qualified readers or interpreters; and other similar accommodations for special disabled veterans.

(3) To determine the appropriate reasonable accommodation it may be necessary for the contractor to initiate an informal, interactive process with the qualified special disabled veteran in need of the accommodation.[2] This process should identify the precise limitations resulting from the disability and potential reasonable accommodations that could overcome those limitations. (Appendix A of this part provides guidance on a contractor's duty to provide reasonable accommodation.)

(u) *Undue hardship*—(1) *In general. Undue hardship* means, with respect to the provision of an accommodation,

[1] A contractor's duty to provide a reasonable accommodation with respect to applicants who are special disabled veterans is not limited to those who ultimately demonstrate that they are qualified to perform the job in issue. Special disabled veteran applicants must be provided a reasonable accommodation with respect to the application process if they are qualified with respect to that process (e.g., if they present themselves at the correct location and time to fill out an application).

[2] Contractors must engage in such an interactive process with a special disabled veteran, whether or not a reasonable accommodation ultimately is identified that will make the person a qualified individual. Contractors must engage in the interactive process because, until they have done so, they may be unable to determine whether a reasonable accommodation exists that will result in the person being qualified.

significant difficulty or expense incurred by the contractor, when considered in light of the factors set forth in paragraph (u)(2) of this section.

(2) *Factors to be considered.* In determining whether an accommodation would impose an undue hardship on the contractor, factors to be considered include:

(i) The nature and net cost of the accommodation needed, taking into consideration the availability of tax credits and deductions, and/or outside funding;

(ii) The overall financial resources of the facility or facilities involved in the provision of the reasonable accommodation, the number of persons employed at such facility, and the effect on expenses and resources;

(iii) The overall financial resources of the contractor, the overall size of the business of the contractor with respect to the number of its employees, and the number, type and location of its facilities;

(iv) The type of operation or operations of the contractor, including the composition, structure and functions of the work force of such contractor, and the geographic separateness and administrative or fiscal relationship of the facility or facilities in question to the contractor; and

(v) The impact of the accommodation upon the operation of the facility, including the impact on the ability of other employees to perform their duties and the impact on the facility's ability to conduct business.

(v) *Qualification standards* means the personal and professional attributes including the skill, experience, education, physical, medical, safety and other requirements established by the contractor as requirements which an individual must meet in order to be eligible for the position held or desired.

(w) *Direct threat* means a significant risk of substantial harm to the health or safety of the individual or others that cannot be eliminated or reduced by reasonable accommodation. The determination that a special disabled veteran poses a *direct threat* shall be based on an individualized assessment of the individual's present ability to perform safely the essential functions of the job. This assessment shall be based on a reasonable medical judgment that relies on the most current medical knowledge and/or on the best available objective evidence. In determining whether an individual would pose a direct threat, the factors to be considered include:

(1) The duration of the risk;

(2) The nature and severity of the potential harm;

(3) The likelihood that the potential harm will occur; and

(4) The imminence of the potential harm.

(x) *Compliance evaluation* means any one or combination of actions OFCCP may take to examine a Federal contractor's or subcontractor's compliance with one or more of the requirements of the Vietnam Era Veterans' Readjustment Assistance Act.

[70 FR 72151, Dec. 1, 2005; 71 FR 6214, Feb. 7, 2006]

§ 60–250.3 [Reserved]

§ 60–250.4 Coverage and waivers.

(a) *General*—(1) *Contracts and subcontracts of $25,000 or more.* Contracts and subcontracts of $25,000 or more, are covered by this part. No contracting agency or contractor shall procure supplies or services in less than usual quantities to avoid the applicability of the equal opportunity clause.

(2) *Contracts for indefinite quantities.* With respect to indefinite delivery-type contracts (including, but not limited to, open end contracts, requirement-type contracts, Federal Supply Schedule contracts, "call-type" contracts, and purchase notice agreements), the equal opportunity clause shall be included unless the contracting agency has reason to believe that the amount to be ordered in any year under such contract will be less than $25,000. The applicability of the equal opportunity clause shall be determined at the time of award for the first year, and annually thereafter for succeeding years, if any. Notwithstanding the above, the equal opportunity clause shall be applied to such contract whenever the amount of a single order is $25,000 or more. Once the equal opportunity clause is determined to be applicable, the contract shall continue to be subject to such clause

for its duration, regardless of the amounts ordered, or reasonably expected to be ordered in any year.

(3) *Employment activities within the United States.* This part applies only to employment activities within the United States and not to employment activities abroad. The term "employment activities within the United States" includes actual employment within the United States, and decisions of the contractor made within the United States pertaining to the contractor's applicants and employees who are within the United States, regarding employment opportunities abroad (such as recruiting and hiring within the United States for employment abroad, or transfer of persons employed in the United States to contractor establishments abroad).

(4) *Contracts with state or local governments.* The requirements of the equal opportunity clause in any contract or subcontract with a state or local government (or any agency, instrumentality or subdivision thereof) shall not be applicable to any agency, instrumentality or subdivision of such government which does not participate in work on or under the contract or subcontract.

(b) *Waivers*—(1) *Specific contracts and classes of contracts.* The Deputy Assistant Secretary may waive the application to any contract of the equal opportunity clause in whole or part when he or she deems that special circumstances in the national interest so require. The Deputy Assistant Secretary may also grant such waivers to groups or categories of contracts: Where it is in the national interest; where it is found impracticable to act upon each request individually; and where such waiver will substantially contribute to convenience in administration of the Act. When a waiver has been granted for any class of contracts, the Deputy Assistant Secretary may withdraw the waiver for a specific contract or group of contracts to be awarded, when in his or her judgment such action is necessary or appropriate to achieve the purposes of the Act. The withdrawal shall not apply to contracts awarded prior to the withdrawal, except that in procurements entered into by formal advertising, or the various forms of restricted formal advertising, such withdrawal shall not apply unless the withdrawal is made more than 10 calendar days before the date set for the opening of the bids.

(2) *National security.* Any requirement set forth in the regulations of this part shall not apply to any contract whenever the head of the contracting agency determines that such contract is essential to the national security and that its award without complying with such requirements is necessary to the national security. Upon making such a determination, the head of the contracting agency will notify the Deputy Assistant Secretary in writing within 30 days.

(3) *Facilities not connected with contracts.* The Deputy Assistant Secretary may waive the requirements of the equal opportunity clause with respect to any of a contractor's facilities which he or she finds to be in all respects separate and distinct from activities of the contractor related to the performance of the contract, provided that he or she also finds that such a waiver will not interfere with or impede the effectuation of the Act. Such waivers shall be considered only upon the request of the contractor.

§ 60–250.5 Equal opportunity clause.

(a) *Government contracts.* Each contracting agency and each contractor shall include the following equal opportunity clause in each of its covered Government contracts or subcontracts (and modifications, renewals, or extensions thereof if not included in the original contract):

Equal Opportunity for Special Disabled Veterans, Veterans of the Vietnam Era, Recently Separated Veterans, and Other Protected Veterans.

1. The contractor will not discriminate against any employee or applicant for employment because he or she is a special disabled veteran, veteran of the Vietnam era, recently separated veteran, or other protected veteran in regard to any position for which the employee or applicant for employment is qualified. The contractor agrees to take affirmative action to employ, advance in employment and otherwise treat qualified individuals without discrimination based on their status as a special disabled veteran, veteran of the Vietnam era, recently separated veteran, or other protected veteran in

all employment practices, including the following:

i. Recruitment, advertising, and job application procedures;

ii. Hiring, upgrading, promotion, award of tenure, demotion, transfer, layoff, termination, right of return from layoff and rehiring;

iii. Rates of pay or any other form of compensation and changes in compensation;

iv. Job assignments, job classifications, organizational structures, position descriptions, lines of progression, and seniority lists;

v. Leaves of absence, sick leave, or any other leave;

vi. Fringe benefits available by virtue of employment, whether or not administered by the contractor;

vii. Selection and financial support for training, including apprenticeship, and on-the-job training under 38 U.S.C 3687, professional meetings, conferences, and other related activities, and selection for leaves of absence to pursue training;

viii. Activities sponsored by the contractor including social or recreational programs; and

ix. Any other term, condition, or privilege of employment.

2. The contractor agrees to immediately list all employment openings which exist at the time of the execution of this contract and those which occur during the performance of this contract, including those not generated by this contract and including those occurring at an establishment of the contractor other than the one wherein the contract is being performed, but excluding those of independently operated corporate affiliates, at an appropriate local employment service office of the state employment security agency wherein the opening occurs. Further, listing employment openings with the state workforce agency job bank where the opening occurs or with the local employment service delivery system where the opening occurs will satisfy the requirement to list jobs with the appropriate employment service office.

3. Listing of employment openings with the local employment service office pursuant to this clause shall be made at least concurrently with the use of any other recruitment source or effort and shall involve the normal obligations which attach to the placing of a *bona fide* job order, including the acceptance of referrals of veterans and nonveterans. The listing of employment openings does not require the hiring of any particular job applicants or from any particular group of job applicants, and nothing herein is intended to relieve the contractor from any requirements in Executive orders or regulations regarding nondiscrimination in employment.

4. Whenever the contractor becomes contractually bound to the listing provisions in paragraphs 2 and 3 of this clause, it shall advise the state employment security agency in each state where it has establishments of the name and location of each hiring location in the state: *Provided*, That this requirement shall not apply to state and local governmental contractors. As long as the contractor is contractually bound to these provisions and has so advised the state agency, there is no need to advise the state agency of subsequent contracts. The contractor may advise the state agency when it is no longer bound by this contract clause.

5. The provisions of paragraphs 2 and 3 of this clause do not apply to the listing of employment openings which occur and are filled outside of the 50 states, the District of Columbia, the Commonwealth of Puerto Rico, Guam, and the Virgin Islands.

6. As used in this clause: i. *All employment openings* includes all positions except executive and top management, those positions that will be filled from within the contractor's organization, and positions lasting three days or less. This term includes full-time employment, temporary employment of more than three days' duration, and part-time employment.

ii. *Executive and top management* means any employee: (a) Whose primary duty consists of the management of the enterprise in which he or she is employed or of a customarily recognized department or subdivision thereof; and (b) who customarily and regularly directs the work of two or more other employees therein; and (c) who has the authority to hire or fire other employees or whose suggestions and recommendations as to the hiring or firing and as to the advancement and promotion or any other change of status of other employees will be given particular weight; and (d) who customarily and regularly exercises discretionary powers; and (e) who does not devote more than 20 percent, or, in the case of an employee of a retail or service establishment who does not devote as much as 40 percent, of his or her hours of work in the work week to activities which are not directly and closely related to the performance of the work described in (a) through (d) of this paragraph 6. ii.; *Provided*, that (e) of this paragraph 6.ii. shall not apply in the case of an employee who is in sole charge of an independent establishment or a physically separated branch establishment, or who owns at least a 20-percent interest in the enterprise in which he or she is employed.

iii. *Positions that will be filled from within the contractor's organization* means employment openings for which no consideration will be given to persons outside the contractor's organization (including any affiliates, subsidiaries, and parent companies) and includes any openings which the contractor proposes to fill from regularly established "recall" lists. The exception does not apply to a particular opening once an employer decides to consider applicants outside of his or her own organization.

7. The contractor agrees to comply with the rules, regulations, and relevant orders of the Secretary of Labor issued pursuant to the Act.

8. In the event of the contractor's noncompliance with the requirements of this clause, actions for noncompliance may be taken in accordance with the rules, regulations, and relevant orders of the Secretary of Labor issued pursuant to the Act.

9. The contractor agrees to post in conspicuous places, available to employees and applicants for employment, notices in a form to be prescribed by the Deputy Assistant Secretary for Federal Contract Compliance, provided by or through the contracting officer. Such notices shall state the rights of applicants and employees as well as the contractor's obligation under the law to take affirmative action to employ and advance in employment qualified employees and applicants who are special disabled veterans, veterans of the Vietnam era, recently separated veterans, or other protected veterans. The contractor must ensure that applicants or employees who are special disabled veterans are informed of the contents of the notice (e.g., the contractor may have the notice read to a visually disabled individual, or may lower the posted notice so that it might be read by a person in a wheelchair).

10. The contractor will notify each labor organization or representative of workers with which it has a collective bargaining agreement or other contract understanding, that the contractor is bound by the terms of the Vietnam Era Veterans' Readjustment Assistance Act of 1974, as amended, and is committed to take affirmative action to employ and advance in employment qualified special disabled veterans, veterans of the Vietnam era, recently separated veterans, and other protected veterans.

11. The contractor will include the provisions of this clause in every subcontract or purchase order of $25,000 or more, unless exempted by the rules, regulations, or orders of the Secretary issued pursuant to the Vietnam Era Veterans' Readjustment Assistance Act of 1974, as amended, so that such provisions will be binding upon each subcontractor or vendor. The contractor will take such action with respect to any subcontract or purchase order as the Deputy Assistant Secretary for Federal Contract Compliance may direct to enforce such provisions, including action for noncompliance.

[End of Clause]

(b) *Subcontracts.* Each contractor shall include the equal opportunity clause in each of its subcontracts subject to this part.

(c) *Adaption of language.* Such necessary changes in language may be made to the equal opportunity clause as shall be appropriate to identify properly the parties and their undertakings.

(d) *Inclusion of the equal opportunity clause in the contract.* It is not necessary that the equal opportunity clause be quoted verbatim in the contract. The clause may be made a part of the contract by citation to 41 CFR 60–250.5(a).

(e) *Incorporation by operation of the Act.* By operation of the Act, the equal opportunity clause shall be considered to be a part of every contract and subcontract required by the Act and the regulations in this part to include such a clause, whether or not it is physically incorporated in such contract and whether or not there is a written contract between the agency and the contractor.

(f) *Duties of contracting agencies.* Each contracting agency shall cooperate with the Deputy Assistant Secretary and the Secretary in the performance of their responsibilities under the Act. Such cooperation shall include insuring that the equal opportunity clause is included in all covered Government contracts and that contractors are fully informed of their obligations under the Act and this part, providing the Deputy Assistant Secretary with any information which comes to the agency's attention that a contractor is not in compliance with the Act or this part, responding to requests for information from the Deputy Assistant Secretary, and taking such actions for noncompliance as are set forth in § 60–250.66 as may be ordered by the Secretary or the Deputy Assistant Secretary.

[70 FR 72151, Dec. 1, 2005, as amended at 73 FR 18715, Apr. 7, 2008]

Subpart B—Discrimination Prohibited

§ 60–250.20 Covered employment activities.

The prohibition against discrimination in this part applies to the following employment activities:

(a) Recruitment, advertising, and job application procedures;

(b) Hiring, upgrading, promotion, award of tenure, demotion, transfer, layoff, termination, right of return from layoff, and rehiring;

(c) Rates of pay or any other form of compensation and changes in compensation;

(d) Job assignments, job classifications, organizational structures, position descriptions, lines of progression, and seniority lists;

(e) Leaves of absence, sick leave, or any other leave;

(f) Fringe benefits available by virtue of employment, whether or not administered by the contractor;

(g) Selection and financial support for training, including apprenticeships, professional meetings, conferences and other related activities, and selection for leaves of absence to pursue training;

(h) Activities sponsored by the contractor including social and recreational programs; and

(i) Any other term, condition, or privilege of employment.

§ 60–250.21 Prohibitions.

The term "discrimination" includes, but is not limited to, the acts described in this section and § 60–250.23.

(a) *Disparate treatment.* It is unlawful for the contractor to deny an employment opportunity or benefit or otherwise to discriminate against a qualified individual because of that individual's status as a special disabled veteran, veteran of the Vietnam era, recently separated veteran, or other protected veteran.

(b) *Limiting, segregating and classifying.* Unless otherwise permitted by this part, it is unlawful for the contractor to limit, segregate, or classify a job applicant or employee in a way that adversely affects his or her employment opportunities or status on the basis of that individual's status as a special disabled veteran, veteran of the Vietnam era, recently separated veteran, or other protected veteran. For example, the contractor may not segregate qualified special disabled veterans, veterans of the Vietnam era, recently separated veterans, or other protected veterans into separate work areas or into separate lines of advancement.

(c) *Contractual or other arrangements*—(1) *In general.* It is unlawful for the contractor to participate in a contractual or other arrangement or relationship that has the effect of subjecting the contractor's own qualified applicant or employee who is a special disabled veteran, veteran of the Vietnam era, recently separated veteran, or other protected veteran to the discrimination prohibited by this part.

(2) *Contractual or other arrangement defined.* The phrase "contractual or other arrangement or relationship" includes, but is not limited to, a relationship with: an employment or referral agency; a labor organization, including a collective bargaining agreement; an organization providing fringe benefits to an employee of the contractor; or an organization providing training and apprenticeship programs.

(3) *Application.* This paragraph (c) applies to the contractor, with respect to its own applicants or employees, whether the contractor offered the contract or initiated the relationship, or whether the contractor accepted the contract or acceded to the relationship. The contractor is not liable for the actions of the other party or parties to the contract which only affect that other party's employees or applicants.

(d) *Standards, criteria or methods of administration.* It is unlawful for the contractor to use standards, criteria, or methods of administration, that are not job-related and consistent with business necessity, and that:

(1) Have the effect of discriminating on the basis of status as a special disabled veteran, veteran of the Vietnam era, recently separated veteran, or other protected veteran; or

(2) Perpetuate the discrimination of others who are subject to common administrative control.

(e) *Relationship or association with a special disabled veteran, veteran of the Vietnam era, recently separated veteran, or other protected veteran.* It is unlawful for the contractor to exclude or deny equal jobs or benefits to, or otherwise discriminate against, a qualified individual because of the known special disabled veteran, Vietnam era veteran, recently separated veteran, or other protected veteran status of an individual with whom the qualified individual is known to have a family, business, social or other relationship or association.

(f) *Not making reasonable accommodation.* (1) It is unlawful for the contractor to fail to make reasonable accommodation to the known physical or mental limitations of an otherwise qualified applicant or employee who is a special disabled veteran, unless such contractor can demonstrate that the accommodation would impose an undue hardship on the operation of its business.

(2) It is unlawful for the contractor to deny employment opportunities to an otherwise qualified job applicant or employee who is a special disabled veteran based on the need of such contractor to make reasonable accommodation to such an individual's physical or mental impairments.

(3) A qualified special disabled veteran is not required to accept an accommodation, aid, service, opportunity or benefit which such qualified individual chooses not to accept. However, if such individual rejects a reasonable accommodation, aid, service, opportunity or benefit that is necessary to enable the individual to perform the essential functions of the position held or desired, and cannot, as a result of that rejection, perform the essential functions of the position, the individual will not be considered a qualified special disabled veteran.

(g) *Qualification standards, tests and other selection criteria*

(1) *In general.* It is unlawful for the contractor to use qualification standards, employment tests or other selection criteria that screen out or tend to screen out individuals on the basis of their status as special disabled veterans, veterans of the Vietnam era, recently separated veterans, or other protected veterans, unless the standard, test or other selection criterion, as used by the contractor, is shown to be job-related for the position in question and is consistent with business necessity. Selection criteria that concern an essential function may not be used to exclude a special disabled veteran if that individual could satisfy the criteria with provision of a reasonable accommodation. Selection criteria that exclude or tend to exclude individuals on the basis of their status as special disabled veterans, veterans of the Vietnam era, recently separated veterans, or other protected veterans but concern only marginal functions of the job would not be consistent with business necessity. The contractor may not refuse to hire an applicant who is a special disabled veteran because the applicant's disability prevents him or her from performing marginal functions. When considering a special disabled veteran, veteran of the Vietnam era, recently separated veteran, or other protected veteran for an employment opportunity, the contractor may not rely on portions of such veteran's military record, including his or her discharge papers, which are not relevant to the qualification requirements of the opportunity in issue.

(2) The Uniform Guidelines on Employee Selection Procedures, 41 CFR part 60–3, do not apply to 38 U.S.C. 4212 and are similarly inapplicable to this part.

(h) *Administration of tests.* It is unlawful for the contractor to fail to select and administer tests concerning employment in the most effective manner to ensure that, when a test is administered to a job applicant or employee who is a special disabled veteran with a disability that impairs sensory, manual, or speaking skills, the test results accurately reflect the skills, aptitude, or whatever other factor of the applicant or employee that the test purports to measure, rather than reflecting the impaired sensory, manual, or speaking skills of such employee or applicant, except where such skills are the factors that the test purports to measure.

(i) *Compensation.* In offering employment or promotions to special disabled veterans, veterans of the Vietnam era, recently separated veterans, or other protected veterans, it is unlawful for the contractor to reduce the amount of compensation offered because of any income based upon a disability-related and/or military-service-related pension or other disability-related and/or military-service-related benefit the applicant or employee receives from another source.

§ 60–250.22 Direct threat defense.

The contractor may use as a qualification standard the requirement that an individual be able to perform the essential functions of the position held or desired without posing a direct threat to the health or safety of the individual or others in the workplace. (See § 60–250.2(w) defining *direct threat.*)

§ 60–250.23 Medical examinations and inquiries.

(a) *Prohibited medical examinations or inquiries.* Except as stated in paragraphs (b) and (c) of this section, it is unlawful for the contractor to require a medical examination of an applicant or employee or to make inquiries as to whether an applicant or employee is a special disabled veteran or as to the nature or severity of such a veteran's disability.

(b) *Permitted medical examinations and inquiries.* (1) *Acceptable pre-employment inquiry.* The contractor may make pre-employment inquiries into the ability of an applicant to perform job-related functions, and/or may ask an applicant to describe or to demonstrate how, with or without reasonable accommodation, the applicant will be able to perform job-related functions.

(2) *Employment entrance examination.* The contractor may require a medical examination (and/or inquiry) after making an offer of employment to a job applicant and before the applicant begins his or her employment duties, and may condition an offer of employment on the results of such examination (and/or inquiry), if all entering employees in the same job category are subjected to such an examination (and/or inquiry) regardless of their status as a special disabled veteran.

(3) *Examination of employees.* The contractor may require a medical examination (and/or inquiry) of an employee that is job-related and consistent with business necessity. The contractor may make inquiries into the ability of an employee to perform job-related functions.

(4) *Other acceptable examinations and inquiries.* The contractor may conduct voluntary medical examinations and activities, including voluntary medical histories, which are part of an employee health program available to employees at the work site.

(5) Medical examinations conducted in accordance with paragraphs (b)(2) and (b)(4) of this section do not have to be job-related and consistent with business necessity. However, if certain criteria are used to screen out an applicant or applicants or an employee or employees who are special disabled veterans as a result of such examinations or inquiries, the contractor must demonstrate that the exclusionary criteria are job-related and consistent with business necessity, and that performance of the essential job functions cannot be accomplished with reasonable accommodations as required in this part.

(c) *Invitation to self-identify.* The contractor shall invite applicants to self-identify as being covered by the Act, as specified in § 60–250.42.

(d) *Confidentiality and use of medical information.* (1) Information obtained under this section regarding the medical condition or history of any applicant or employee shall be collected and maintained on separate forms and in separate medical files and treated as a confidential medical record, except that:

(i) Supervisors and managers may be informed regarding necessary restrictions on the work or duties of the applicant or employee and necessary accommodations;

(ii) First aid and safety personnel may be informed, when appropriate, if the disability might require emergency treatment; and

(iii) Government officials engaged in enforcing the laws administered by OFCCP, including this part, or enforcing the Americans with Disabilities Act, shall be provided relevant information on request.

(2) Information obtained under this section regarding the medical condition or history of any applicant or employee shall not be used for any purpose inconsistent with this part.

§ 60–250.24 Drugs and alcohol.

(a) *Specific activities permitted.* The contractor:

(1) May prohibit the illegal use of drugs and the use of alcohol at the workplace by all employees;

(2) May require that employees not be under the influence of alcohol or be engaging in the illegal use of drugs at the workplace;

(3) May require that all employees behave in conformance with the requirements established under the Drug-Free Workplace Act of 1988 (41 U.S.C. 701 *et seq.*);

(4) May hold an employee who engages in the illegal use of drugs or who is an alcoholic to the same qualification standards for employment or job performance and behavior to which the contractor holds its other employees, even if any unsatisfactory performance or behavior is related to the employee's drug use or alcoholism;

(5) May require that its employees employed in an industry subject to such regulations comply with the standards established in the regulations (if any) of the Departments of Defense and Transportation, and of the Nuclear Regulatory Commission, and other Federal agencies regarding alcohol and the illegal use of drugs; and

(6) May require that employees employed in sensitive positions comply with the regulations (if any) of the Departments of Defense and Transportation, and of the Nuclear Regulatory Commission, and other Federal agencies that apply to employment in sensitive positions subject to such regulations.

(b) *Drug testing*—(1) *General policy*. For purposes of this part, a test to determine the illegal use of drugs is not considered a medical examination. Thus, the administration of such drug tests by the contractor to its job applicants or employees is not a violation of § 60–250.23. Nothing in this part shall be construed to encourage, prohibit, or authorize the contractor to conduct drug tests of job applicants or employees to determine the illegal use of drugs or to make employment decisions based on such test results.

(2) *Transportation employees*. Nothing in this part shall be construed to encourage, prohibit, or authorize the otherwise lawful exercise by contractors subject to the jurisdiction of the Department of Transportation of authority to test employees in, and applicants for, positions involving safety-sensitive duties for the illegal use of drugs or for on-duty impairment by alcohol; and remove from safety-sensitive positions persons who test positive for illegal use of drugs or on-duty impairment by alcohol pursuant to paragraph (b)(1) of this section.

(3) Any information regarding the medical condition or history of any employee or applicant obtained from a test to determine the illegal use of drugs, except information regarding the illegal use of drugs, is subject to the requirements of §§ 60–250.23(b)(5) and (c).

§ 60–250.25 Health insurance, life insurance and other benefit plans.

(a) An insurer, hospital, or medical service company, health maintenance organization, or any agent or entity that administers benefit plans, or similar organizations may underwrite risks, classify risks, or administer such risks that are based on or not inconsistent with state law.

(b) The contractor may establish, sponsor, observe or administer the terms of a bona fide benefit plan that are based on underwriting risks, classifying risks, or administering such risks that are based on or not inconsistent with state law.

(c) The contractor may establish, sponsor, observe, or administer the terms of a bona fide benefit plan that is not subject to state laws that regulate insurance.

(d) The contractor may not deny a qualified special disabled veteran equal access to insurance or subject a qualified special disabled veteran to different terms or conditions of insurance based on disability alone, if the disability does not pose increased risks.

(e) The activities described in paragraphs (a), (b) and (c) of this section are permitted unless these activities are used as a subterfuge to evade the purposes of this part.

Subpart C—Affirmative Action Program

§ 60–250.40 Applicability of the affirmative action program requirement.

(a) The requirements of this subpart apply to every Government contractor that has 50 or more employees and a contract of $50,000 or more.

(b) Contractors described in paragraph (a) of this section shall, within 120 days of the commencement of a contract, prepare and maintain an affirmative action program at each establishment. The affirmative action program shall set forth the contractor's policies and procedures in accordance with this part. This program may be integrated into or kept separate from other affirmative action programs.

(c) The affirmative action program shall be reviewed and updated annually.

(d) The contractor shall submit the affirmative action program within 30 days of a request from OFCCP, unless the request provides for a different time. The contractor also shall make the affirmative action program promptly available on-site upon OFCCP's request.

§ 60–250.41 Availability of affirmative action program.

The full affirmative action program shall be available to any employee or applicant for employment for inspection upon request. The location and hours during which the program may be obtained shall be posted at each establishment.

§ 60–250.42 Invitation to self-identify.

(a) *Special disabled veterans.* The contractor shall invite applicants to inform the contractor whether the applicant believes that he or she is a special disabled veteran who may be covered by the Act and wishes to benefit under the affirmative action program. Such invitation shall be extended after making an offer of employment to a job applicant and before the applicant begins his or her employment duties, except that the contractor may invite special disabled veterans to self-identify prior to making a job offer when:

(1) The invitation is made when the contractor actually is undertaking affirmative action for special disabled veterans at the pre-offer stage; or

(2) The invitation is made pursuant to a Federal, State or local law requiring affirmative action for special disabled veterans.

(b) *Veterans of the Vietnam era, recently separated veterans and other protected veterans.* The contractor shall invite applicants to inform the contractor whether the applicant believes that he or she is a veteran of the Vietnam era, recently separated veteran or other protected veteran who may be covered by the Act and wishes to benefit under the affirmative action program. Such invitation may be made at any time before the applicant begins his or her employment duties.

(c) The invitations referenced in paragraphs (a) and (b) of this section shall state that a request to benefit under the affirmative action program may be made immediately and/or at any time in the future. The invitations also shall summarize the relevant portions of the Act and the contractor's affirmative action program. Furthermore, the invitations shall state that the information is being requested on a voluntary basis, that it will be kept confidential, that refusal to provide it will not subject the applicant to any adverse treatment, and that it will not be used in a manner inconsistent with the Act. (An acceptable form for such an invitation is set forth in Appendix B of this part. Because a contractor usually may not seek advice from a special disabled veteran regarding placement and accommodation until after a job offer has been extended, the invitation set forth in Appendix B of this part contains instructions regarding modifications to be made if it is used at the pre-offer stage.)

(d) If an applicant so identifies himself or herself as a special disabled veteran, the contractor should also seek the advice of the applicant regarding proper placement and appropriate accommodation, after a job offer has been extended. The contractor also may make such inquiries to the extent they are consistent with the Americans with Disabilities Act of 1990 (ADA), 42 U.S.C. 12101, (e.g., in the context of asking applicants to describe or demonstrate how they would perform the job). The contractor shall maintain a separate file in accordance with § 60–250.23(d) on persons who have self-identified as special disabled veterans.

(e) The contractor shall keep all information on self identification confidential. The contractor shall provide the information to OFCCP upon request. This information may be used only in accordance with this part.

(f) Nothing in this section shall relieve the contractor of its obligation to take affirmative action with respect to those applicants or employees who are known to the contractor to be special disabled veterans, veterans of the Vietnam era, recently separated veterans, or other protected veterans.

(g) Nothing in this section shall relieve the contractor from liability for discrimination under the Act.

§ 60–250.43 Affirmative action policy.

Under the affirmative action obligations imposed by the Act contractors shall not discriminate because of status as a special disabled veteran, veteran of the Vietnam era, recently separated veteran, or other protected veteran and shall take affirmative action to employ and advance in employment qualified special disabled veterans, veterans of the Vietnam era, recently separated veterans, and other protected veterans at all levels of employment, including the executive level. Such action shall apply to all employment activities set forth in § 60–250.20.

§ 60–250.44 Required contents of affirmative action programs.

Acceptable affirmative action programs shall contain, but not necessarily be limited to, the following ingredients:

(a) *Policy statement.* The contractor shall include an equal opportunity policy statement in its affirmative action program, and shall post the policy statement on company bulletin boards. The contractor must ensure that applicants and employees who are special disabled veterans are informed of the contents of the policy statement (for example, the contractor may have the statement read to a visually disabled individual, or may lower the posted notice so that it may be read by a person in a wheelchair). The policy statement should indicate the chief executive officer's attitude on the subject matter, provide for an audit and reporting system (see paragraph (h) of this section) and assign overall responsibility for the implementation of affirmative action activities required under this part (see paragraph (i) of this section). Additionally, the policy should state, among other things, that the contractor will: Recruit, hire, train and promote persons in all job titles, and ensure that all other personnel actions are administered, without regard to special disabled veteran, Vietnam era veteran, recently separated veteran, or other protected veteran status; and ensure that all employment decisions are based only on valid job requirements. The policy shall state that employees and applicants shall not be subjected to harassment, intimidation, threats, coercion or discrimination because they have engaged in or may engage in any of the following activities:

(1) Filing a complaint;

(2) Assisting or participating in an investigation, compliance evaluation, hearing, or any other activity related to the administration of the affirmative action provisions of the Vietnam Era Veterans' Readjustment Assistance Act of 1974, as amended (VEVRAA) or any other Federal, state or local law requiring equal opportunity for special disabled veterans, veterans of the Vietnam era, recently separated veterans, or other protected veterans;

(3) Opposing any act or practice made unlawful by VEVRAA or its implementing regulations in this part or any other Federal, state or local law requiring equal opportunity for special disabled veterans, veterans of the Vietnam era, recently separated veterans, or other protected veterans; or

(4) Exercising any other right protected by VEVRAA or its implementing regulations in this part.

(b) *Review of personnel processes.* The contractor shall ensure that its personnel processes provide for careful, thorough, and systematic consideration of the job qualifications of applicants and employees who are known special disabled veterans, veterans of the Vietnam era, recently separated veterans, or other protected veterans for job vacancies filled either by hiring or promotion, and for all training opportunities offered or available. The contractor shall ensure that when a special disabled veteran, veteran of the

Vietnam era, recently separated veteran, or other protected veteran is considered for employment opportunities, the contractor relies only on that portion of the individual's military record, including his or her discharge papers, that is relevant to the requirements of the opportunity in issue. The contractor shall ensure that its personnel processes do not stereotype special disabled veterans, veterans of the Vietnam era, recently separated veterans, and other protected veterans in a manner which limits their access to all jobs for which they are qualified. The contractor shall periodically review such processes and make any necessary modifications to ensure that these obligations are carried out. A description of the review and any necessary modifications to personnel processes or development of new processes shall be included in any affirmative action programs required under this part. The contractor must design procedures that facilitate a review of the implementation of this requirement by the contractor and the Government. (Appendix C of this part is an example of an appropriate set of procedures. The procedures in Appendix C of this part are not required and contractors may develop other procedures appropriate to their circumstances.)

(c) *Physical and mental qualifications.* (1) The contractor shall provide in its affirmative action program, and shall adhere to, a schedule for the periodic review of all physical and mental job qualification standards to ensure that, to the extent qualification standards tend to screen out qualified special disabled veterans, they are job-related for the position in question and are consistent with business necessity.

(2) Whenever the contractor applies physical or mental qualification standards in the selection of applicants or employees for employment or other change in employment status such as promotion, demotion or training, to the extent that qualification standards tend to screen out qualified special disabled veterans, the standards shall be related to the specific job or jobs for which the individual is being considered and consistent with business necessity. The contractor shall have the burden to demonstrate that it has complied with the requirements of this paragraph (c)(2).

(3) The contractor may use as a defense to an allegation of a violation of paragraph (c)(2) of this section that an individual poses a direct threat to the health or safety of the individual or others in the workplace. (See § 60–250.2(w) defining direct threat.)

(d) *Reasonable accommodation to physical and mental limitations.* As is provided in § 60–250.21(f), as a matter of nondiscrimination the contractor must make reasonable accommodation to the known physical or mental limitations of an otherwise qualified special disabled veteran unless it can demonstrate that the accommodation would impose an undue hardship on the operation of its business. As a matter of affirmative action, if an employee who is known to be a special disabled veteran is having significant difficulty performing his or her job and it is reasonable to conclude that the performance problem may be related to the known disability, the contractor shall confidentially notify the employee of the performance problem and inquire whether the problem is related to the employee's disability; if the employee responds affirmatively, the contractor shall confidentially inquire whether the employee is in need of a reasonable accommodation.

(e) *Harassment.* The contractor must develop and implement procedures to ensure that its employees are not harassed because of their status as a special disabled veteran, veteran of the Vietnam era, recently separated veteran, or other protected veteran.

(f) *External dissemination of policy, outreach and positive recruitment.* The contractor shall undertake appropriate outreach and positive recruitment activities such as those listed in paragraphs (f)(1) through (f)(8) of this section that are reasonably designed to effectively recruit qualified special disabled veterans, veterans of the Vietnam era, recently separated veterans, and other protected veterans. It is not contemplated that the contractor will necessarily undertake all the activities listed in paragraphs (f)(1) through (f)(8) of this section or that its activities will be limited to those listed. The scope of the contractor's efforts shall depend upon all the circumstances, including the contractor's size and resources and the extent to which existing employment practices are adequate.

(1) The contractor should enlist the assistance and support of the following persons and organizations in recruiting, and developing on-the-job training opportunities for, qualified special disabled veterans, veterans of the Vietnam era, recently separated veterans, and other protected veterans, to fulfill its commitment to provide meaningful employment opportunities to such veterans:

(i) The Local Veterans' Employment Representative or his or her designee in the local employment service office nearest the contractor's establishment;

(ii) The Department of Veterans Affairs Regional Office nearest the contractor's establishment;

(iii) The veterans' counselors and coordinators ("Vet-Reps") on college campuses;

(iv) The service officers of the national veterans' groups active in the area of the contractor's establishment; and

(v) Local veterans' groups and veterans' service centers near the contractor's establishment.

(2) Formal briefing sessions should be held, preferably on company premises, with representatives from recruiting sources. Plant tours, clear and concise explanations of current and future job openings, position descriptions, worker specifications, explanations of the company's selection process, and recruiting literature should be an integral part of the briefing. Formal arrangements should be made for referral of applicants, follow up with sources, and feedback on disposition of applicants.

(3) The contractor's recruitment efforts at all educational institutions should incorporate special efforts to reach students who are special disabled veterans, veterans of the Vietnam era, recently separated veterans, or other protected veterans. An effort should be made to participate in work-study programs with Department of Veterans Affairs rehabilitation facilities which specialize in training or educating disabled veterans.

(4) The contractor should establish meaningful contacts with appropriate veterans' service organizations which serve special disabled veterans, veterans of the Vietnam era, recently separated veterans, or other protected veterans for such purposes as advice, technical assistance, and referral of potential employees. Technical assistance from the resources described in this paragraph may consist of advice on proper placement, recruitment, training and accommodations contractors may undertake, but no such resource providing technical assistance shall have authority to approve or disapprove the acceptability of affirmative action programs.

(5) Special disabled veterans, veterans of the Vietnam era, recently separated veterans, and other protected veterans should be made available for participation in career days, youth motivation programs, and related activities in their communities.

(6) The contractor should send written notification of company policy to all subcontractors, vendors and suppliers, requesting appropriate action on their part.

(7) The contractor should take positive steps to attract qualified special disabled veterans, veterans of the Vietnam era, recently separated veterans, and other protected veterans not currently in the work force who have requisite skills and can be recruited through affirmative action measures. These persons may be located through the local chapters of organizations of and for Vietnam era veterans, veterans with disabilities, recently separated veterans, and other protected veterans.

(8) The contractor, in making hiring decisions, should consider applicants who are known special disabled veterans, veterans of the Vietnam era, recently separated veterans, or other protected veterans for all available positions for which they may be qualified when the position(s) applied for is unavailable.

(g) *Internal dissemination of policy.* (1) A strong outreach program will be ineffective without adequate internal support from supervisory and management personnel and other employees. In order to assure greater employee cooperation and participation in the contractor's efforts, the contractor shall develop internal procedures such as those listed in paragraph (g)(2) of this section for communication of its obligation to engage in affirmative action efforts to employ and advance in employment qualified special disabled veterans, veterans of the Vietnam era, recently separated veterans, and other protected veterans. It is not contemplated that the contractor will necessarily undertake all the activities listed in paragraph (g)(2) of this section or that its activities will be limited to those listed. These procedures shall be designed to foster understanding, acceptance and support among the contractor's executive, management, supervisory and other employees and to encourage such persons to take the necessary actions to aid the contractor in meeting this obligation. The scope of the contractor's efforts shall depend upon all the circumstances, including the contractor's size and resources and the extent to which existing practices are adequate.

(2) The contractor should implement and disseminate this policy internally as follows:

(i) Include it in the contractor's policy manual;

(ii) Inform all employees and prospective employees of its commitment to engage in affirmative action to increase employment opportunities for qualified special disabled veterans, veterans of the Vietnam era, recently separated veterans, and other protected veterans. The contractor should periodically schedule special meetings with all employees to discuss policy and explain individual employee responsibilities;

(iii) Publicize it in the company newspaper, magazine, annual report and other media;

(iv) Conduct special meetings with executive, management, and supervisory personnel to explain the intent of the policy and individual responsibility for effective implementation, making clear the chief executive officer's attitude;

(v) Discuss the policy thoroughly in both employee orientation and management training programs;

(vi) Meet with union officials and/or employee representatives to inform them of the contractor's policy, and request their cooperation;

(vii) Include articles on accomplishments of special disabled veterans, veterans of the Vietnam era, recently separated veterans, and other protected veterans in company publications; and

(viii) When employees are featured in employee handbooks or similar publications for employees, include special disabled veterans.

(h) *Audit and reporting system.* (1) The contractor shall design and implement an audit and reporting system that will:

(i) Measure the effectiveness of the contractor's affirmative action program;

(ii) Indicate any need for remedial action;

(iii) Determine the degree to which the contractor's objectives have been attained;

(iv) Determine whether known special disabled veterans, veterans of the Vietnam era, recently separated veterans, and other protected veterans have had the opportunity to participate in all company sponsored educational, training, recreational and social activities; and

(v) Measure the contractor's compliance with the affirmative action program's specific obligations.

(2) Where the affirmative action program is found to be deficient, the contractor shall undertake necessary action to bring the program into compliance.

(i) *Responsibility for implementation.* An official of the contractor shall be assigned responsibility for implementation of the contractor's affirmative action activities under this part. His or her identity should appear on all internal and external communications regarding the company's affirmative action program. This official shall be given necessary top management support and staff to manage the implementation of this program.

(j) *Training.* All personnel involved in the recruitment, screening, selection, promotion, disciplinary, and related processes shall be trained to ensure that the commitments in the contractor's affirmative action program are implemented.

Subpart D—General Enforcement and Complaint Procedures

§60–250.60 Compliance evaluations.

(a) OFCCP may conduct compliance evaluations to determine if the contractor is taking affirmative action to employ, advance in employment and otherwise treat qualified individuals without discrimination based on their status as a special disabled veteran, veteran of the Vietnam era, recently separated veteran, or other protected veteran in all employment practices. A compliance evaluation may consist of any one or any combination of the following investigative procedures:

(1) *Compliance review.* A comprehensive analysis and evaluation of the hiring and employment practices of the contractor, the written affirmative action program, and the results of the affirmative action efforts undertaken by the contractor. A compliance review may proceed in three stages:

(i) A desk audit of the written affirmative action program and supporting documentation to determine whether all elements required by the regulations in this part are included, whether the affirmative action program meets agency standards of reasonableness, and whether the affirmative action program and supporting documentation satisfy agency standards of acceptability. The desk audit is conducted at OFCCP offices;

(ii) An on-site review, conducted at the contractor's establishment to investigate unresolved problem areas identified in the affirmative action program and supporting documentation during the desk audit, to verify that the contractor has implemented the affirmative action program and has complied with those regulatory obligations not required to be included in the affirmative action program, and to examine potential instances or issues of discrimination. An on-site review normally will involve an examination of the contractor's personnel and employment policies, inspection and copying of documents related to employment actions, and interviews with employees, supervisors, managers, hiring officials; and

(iii) Where necessary, an off-site analysis of information supplied by the contractor or otherwise gathered during or pursuant to the on-site review;

(2) *Off-site review of records.* An analysis and evaluation of the affirmative action program (or any part thereof) and supporting documentation, and other documents related to the contractor's personnel policies and employment actions that may be relevant to a determination of whether the contractor has complied with the requirements of the Executive Order and regulations;

(3) *Compliance check.* A determination of whether the contractor has maintained records consistent with §60–250.80; at the contractor's option the documents may be provided either onsite or off-site; or

(4) *Focused review.* An on-site review restricted to one or more components of the contractor's organization or one or more aspects of the contractor's employment practices.

(b) Where deficiencies are found to exist, reasonable efforts shall be made to secure compliance through conciliation and persuasion pursuant to §60–250.62.

(c) *VETS–100 Report.* During a compliance evaluation, OFCCP may verify whether the contractor has complied with its obligation, pursuant to 41 CFR part 61–250, to file its annual Veterans' Employment Report (VETS–100 Report) with the Veterans' Employment and Training Service (VETS). If the contractor has not filed its report, OFCCP will request a copy from the contractor. If the contractor fails to provide a copy of the report to OFCCP, OFCCP will notify VETS.

§60–250.61 Complaint procedures.

(a) *Place and time of filing.* Any applicant for employment with a contractor or any employee of a contractor may, personally, or by an authorized representative, file a written complaint alleging a violation of the Act or the regulations in this part. The complaint may allege individual or class-wide violation(s). Such complaint must be filed within 300 days of the date of the alleged violation, unless the time for filing is extended by OFCCP for good cause shown. Complaints may be submitted to the OFCCP, 200 Constitution Avenue, NW., Washington, DC 20210, or to any OFCCP regional, district, or area office. Complaints may also be submitted to the Veterans' Employment and Training Service of the Department of Labor directly, or through the Local Veterans' Employment Representative (LVER) or his or her designee at the local employment service office. Such parties will assist veterans in preparing complaints, promptly refer such complaints to OFCCP, and maintain a record of all complaints which they receive and forward. OFCCP shall inform the party forwarding the complaint of the progress and results of its complaint investigation. The state employment security agency shall cooperate with the Deputy Assistant Secretary in the investigation of any complaint.

(b) *Contents of complaints*—(1) *In general*. A complaint must be signed by the complainant or his or her authorized representative and must contain the following information:

(i) Name and address (including telephone number) of the complainant;

(ii) Name and address of the contractor who committed the alleged violation;

(iii) Documentation showing that the individual is a special disabled veteran, veteran of the Vietnam era, recently separated veteran, or other protected veteran. Such documentation must include a copy of the veteran's form DD–214, and, where applicable, a copy of the veteran's Benefits Award Letter, or similar Department of Veterans Affairs certification, updated within one year prior to the date the complaint is filed, indicating the veteran's level (by percentage) of disability, and whether the veteran has been determined by the Department of Veterans Affairs to have a serious employment handicap under 38 U.S.C. 3106;

(iv) A description of the act or acts considered to be a violation, including the pertinent dates (in the case of an alleged continuing violation, the earliest and most recent date that the alleged violation occurred should be stated); and

(v) Other pertinent information available which will assist in the investigation and resolution of the complaint, including the name of any known Federal agency with which the employer has contracted.

(2) *Third party complaints*. A complaint filed by an authorized representative need not identify by name the person on whose behalf it is filed. The person filing the complaint, however, shall provide OFCCP with the name, address and telephone number of the person on whose behalf it is made, and the other information specified in paragraph (b)(1) of this section. OFCCP shall verify the authorization of such a complaint by the person on whose behalf the complaint is made. Any such person may request that OFCCP keep his or her identity confidential, and OFCCP will protect the individual's confidentiality wherever that is possible given the facts and circumstances in the complaint.

(c) *Incomplete information*. Where a complaint contains incomplete information, OFCCP shall seek the needed information from the complainant. If the information is not furnished to OFCCP within 60 days of the date of such request, the case may be closed.

(d) *Investigations*. The Department of Labor shall institute a prompt investigation of each complaint.

(e) *Resolution of matters*. (1) If the complaint investigation finds no violation of the Act or this part, or if the Deputy Assistant Secretary decides not to refer the matter to the Solicitor of Labor for enforcement proceedings against the contractor pursuant to § 60–250.65(a)(1), the complainant and contractor shall be so notified. The Deputy Assistant Secretary, on his or her own initiative, may reconsider his or her determination or the determination of any of his or her designated officers who have authority to issue Notifications of Results of Investigation.

(2) The Deputy Assistant Secretary will review all determinations of no violation that involve complaints that are not also cognizable under Title I of the Americans with Disabilities Act.

(3) In cases where the Deputy Assistant Secretary decides to reconsider the

determination of a Notification of Results of Investigation, the Deputy Assistant Secretary shall provide prompt notification of his or her intent to reconsider, which is effective upon issuance, and his or her final determination after reconsideration, to the person claiming to be aggrieved, the person making the complaint on behalf of such person, if any, and the contractor.

(4) If the investigation finds a violation of the Act or this part, OFCCP shall invite the contractor to participate in conciliation discussions pursuant to § 60–250.62.

§ 60–250.62 Conciliation agreements.

If a compliance evaluation, complaint investigation or other review by OFCCP finds a material violation of the Act or this part, and if the contractor is willing to correct the violations and/or deficiencies, and if OFCCP determines that settlement on that basis (rather than referral for consideration of formal enforcement) is appropriate, a written conciliation agreement shall be required. The agreement shall provide for such remedial action as may be necessary to correct the violations and/or deficiencies noted, including, where appropriate (but not necessarily limited to) such make whole remedies as back pay and retroactive seniority. The agreement shall also specify the time period for completion of the remedial action; the period shall be no longer than the minimum period necessary to complete the action.

§ 60–250.63 Violation of conciliation agreements.

(a) When OFCCP believes that a conciliation agreement has been violated, the following procedures are applicable:

(1) A written notice shall be sent to the contractor setting forth the violation alleged and summarizing the supporting evidence. The contractor shall have 15 days from receipt of the notice to respond, except in those cases in which OFCCP asserts that such a delay would result in irreparable injury to the employment rights of affected employees or applicants.

(2) During the 15-day period the contractor may demonstrate in writing that it has not violated its commitments.

(b) In those cases in which OFCCP asserts that a delay would result in irreparable injury to the employment rights of affected employees or applicants, enforcement proceedings may be initiated immediately without proceeding through any other requirement contained in this chapter.

(c) In any proceedings involving an alleged violation of a conciliation agreement OFCCP may seek enforcement of the agreement itself and shall not be required to present proof of the underlying violations resolved by the agreement.

§ 60–250.64 Show cause notices.

When the Deputy Assistant Secretary has reasonable cause to believe that the contractor has violated the Act or this part, he or she may issue a notice requiring the contractor to show cause, within 30 days, why monitoring, enforcement proceedings or other appropriate action to ensure compliance should not be instituted. The issuance of such a notice is not a prerequisite to instituting enforcement proceedings (see § 60–250.65).

§ 60–250.65 Enforcement proceedings.

(a) *General.* (1) If a compliance evaluation, complaint investigation or other review by OFCCP finds a violation of the Act or this part, and the violation has not been corrected in accordance with the conciliation procedures in this part, or OFCCP determines that referral for consideration of formal enforcement (rather than settlement) is appropriate, OFCCP may refer the matter to the Solicitor of Labor with a recommendation for the institution of enforcement proceedings to enjoin the violations, to seek appropriate relief, and to impose appropriate sanctions, or any of the above in this sentence. OFCCP may seek back pay and other make whole relief for aggrieved individuals identified during a complaint investigation or compliance evaluation. Such individuals need not have filed a complaint as a prerequisite to OFCCP seeking such relief on their behalf. Interest on back pay shall be calculated from the date of the loss and compounded quarterly at the percentage rate established by the Internal Revenue Service for the underpayment of taxes.

(2) In addition to the administrative proceedings set forth in this section, the Deputy Assistant Secretary may, within the limitations of applicable law, seek appropriate judicial action to enforce the contractual provisions set forth in § 60–250.5, including appropriate injunctive relief.

(b) *Hearing practice and procedure.* (1) In administrative enforcement proceedings the contractor shall be provided an opportunity for a formal hearing. All hearings conducted under the Act and this part shall be governed by the Rules of Practice for Administrative Proceedings to Enforce Equal Opportunity Under Executive Order 11246 contained in 41 CFR part 60–30 and the Rules of Evidence set out in the Rules of Practice and Procedure for Administrative Hearings Before the Office of Administrative Law Judges contained in 29 CFR part 18, subpart B: Provided, That a final administrative order shall be issued within one year from the date of the issuance of the recommended findings, conclusions and decision of the Administrative Law Judge, or the submission of exceptions and responses to exceptions to such decision (if any), whichever is later.

(2) Complaints may be filed by the Solicitor, the Associate Solicitor for Civil Rights, Regional Solicitors and Associate Regional Solicitors.

(3) For the purposes of hearings pursuant to this part, references in 41 CFR part 60–30 to "Executive Order 11246" shall mean the Vietnam Era Veterans' Readjustment Assistance Act of 1974, as amended (38 U.S.C. 4212 (2001)); to "equal opportunity clause" shall mean the equal opportunity clause published at § 60–250.5; and to "regulations" shall mean the regulations contained in this part.

§ 60–250.66 Sanctions and penalties.

(a) *Withholding progress payments.* With the prior approval of the Deputy Assistant Secretary, so much of the accrued payment due on the contract or any other contract between the Government contractor and the Federal Government may be withheld as necessary to correct any violations of the provisions of the Act or this part.

(b) *Termination.* A contract may be canceled or terminated, in whole or in part, for failure to comply with the provisions of the Act or this part.

(c) *Debarment.* A contractor may be debarred from receiving future contracts for failure to comply with the provisions of the Act or this part subject to reinstatement pursuant to § 60–250.68. Debarment may be imposed for an indefinite period, or may be imposed for a fixed period of not less than six months but no more than three years.

(d) *Hearing opportunity.* An opportunity for a formal hearing shall be afforded to a contractor before the imposition of any sanction or penalty.

§ 60–250.67 Notification of agencies.

The Deputy Assistant Secretary shall ensure that the heads of all agencies are notified of any debarments taken against any contractor.

§ 60–250.68 Reinstatement of ineligible contractors.

(a) *Application for reinstatement.* A contractor debarred from further contracts for an indefinite period under the Act may request reinstatement in a letter filed with the Deputy Assistant Secretary at any time after the effective date of the debarment; a contractor debarred for a fixed period may make such a request following the expiration of six months from the effective date of the debarment. In connection with the reinstatement proceedings, all debarred contractors shall be required to show that they have established and will carry out employment policies and practices in compliance with the Act and this part. Additionally, in determining whether reinstatement is appropriate for a contractor debarred for a fixed period, the Deputy Assistant Secretary also shall consider, among other factors, the severity of the violation which resulted in the debarment, the contractor's attitude towards compliance, the contractor's past compliance history, and whether the contractor's reinstatement would impede the effective enforcement of the Act or this part. Before reaching a decision, the Deputy

Assistant Secretary may conduct a compliance evaluation of the contractor and may require the contractor to supply additional information regarding the request for reinstatement. The Deputy Assistant Secretary shall issue a written decision on the request.

(b) *Petition for review.* Within 30 days of its receipt of a decision denying a request for reinstatement, the contractor may file a petition for review of the decision with the Secretary. The petition shall set forth the grounds for the contractor's objections to the Deputy Assistant Secretary's decision. The petition shall be served on the Deputy Assistant Secretary and the Associate Solicitor for Civil Rights and shall include the decision as an appendix. The Deputy Assistant Secretary may file a response within 14 days to the petition. The Secretary shall issue the final agency decision denying or granting the request for reinstatement. Before reaching a final decision, the Secretary may issue such additional orders respecting procedure as he or she finds appropriate in the circumstances, including an order referring the matter to the Office of Administrative Law Judges for an evidentiary hearing where there is a material factual dispute that cannot be resolved on the record before the Secretary.

§ 60–250.69 Intimidation and interference.

(a) The contractor shall not harass, intimidate, threaten, coerce, or discriminate against, any individual because the individual has engaged in or may engage in any of the following activities:

(1) Filing a complaint;

(2) Assisting or participating in any manner in an investigation, compliance evaluation, hearing, or any other activity related to the administration of the Act or any other Federal, state or local law requiring equal opportunity for special disabled veterans, veterans of the Vietnam era, recently separated veterans, or other protected veterans;

(3) Opposing any act or practice made unlawful by the Act or this part or any other Federal, state or local law requiring equal opportunity for special disabled veterans, veterans of the Vietnam era, recently separated veterans, or other protected veterans, or

(4) Exercising any other right protected by the Act or this part.

(b) The contractor shall ensure that all persons under its control do not engage in such harassment, intimidation, threats, coercion or discrimination. The sanctions and penalties contained in this part may be exercised by the Deputy Assistant Secretary against any contractor who violates this obligation.

§ 60–250.70 Disputed matters related to compliance with the Act.

The procedures set forth in the regulations in this part govern all disputes relative to the contractor's compliance with the Act and this part. Any disputes relating to issues other than compliance, including contract costs arising out of the contractor's efforts to comply, shall be determined by the disputes clause of the contract.

Subpart E—Ancillary Matters

§ 60–250.80 Recordkeeping

(a) *General requirements.* Any personnel or employment record made or kept by the contractor shall be preserved by the contractor for a period of two years from the date of the making of the record or the personnel action involved, whichever occurs later. However, if the contractor has fewer than 150 employees or does not have a Government contract of at least $150,000, the minimum record retention period shall be one year from the date of the making of the record or the personnel action involved, whichever occurs later. Such records include, but are not necessarily limited to, records relating to requests for reasonable accommodation; the results of any physical examination; job advertisements and postings; applications and resumes; tests and test results; interview notes; and other records having to do with hiring, assignment, promotion, demotion, transfer, lay-off or termination, rates of pay or other terms of compensation, and selection for training or apprenticeship. In the case of involuntary termination of an employee, the personnel records of the individual terminated shall be kept for a period of two years from the date of the termination, except that contractors that have fewer than 150 employees or that do not have a Government contract of at least $150,000 shall keep such records for a period of one year from the date of the termination. Where the contractor has received notice that a complaint of discrimination has been filed, that a compliance evaluation has been initiated, or that an enforcement action has been commenced, the contractor shall preserve all personnel records relevant to the complaint, compliance evaluation or action until final disposition of the complaint, compliance evaluation or action. The term *personnel records relevant to the complaint, compliance evaluation or action* would include, for example, personnel or employment records relating to the aggrieved person and to all other employees holding positions similar to that held or sought by the aggrieved person, and application forms or test papers completed by an unsuccessful applicant and by all other candidates for the same position as that for which the aggrieved person applied and was rejected.

(b) *Failure to preserve records.* Failure to preserve complete and accurate records as required by paragraph (a) of this section constitutes noncompliance with the contractor's obligations under the Act and this part. Where the contractor has destroyed or failed to preserve records as required by this section, there may be a presumption that the information destroyed or not preserved would have been unfavorable to the contractor: *Provided,* That this presumption shall not apply where the contractor shows that the destruction or failure to preserve records results from circumstances that are outside of the contractor's control.

§ 60–250.81 Access to records.

Each contractor shall permit access during normal business hours to its places of business for the purpose of conducting on-site compliance evaluations and complaint investigations and inspecting and copying such books and accounts and records, including computerized records, and other material as may be relevant to the matter under investigation and pertinent to compliance with the Act or this part. Information obtained in this manner shall be used only in connection with the administration of the Act and in furtherance of the purposes of the Act.

§ 60–250.82 Labor organizations and recruiting and training agencies.

(a) Whenever performance in accordance with the equal opportunity clause or any matter contained in the regulations in this part may necessitate a revision of a collective bargaining agreement, the labor organizations which are parties to such agreement shall be given an adequate opportunity to present their views to OFCCP.

(b) OFCCP shall use its best efforts, directly or through contractors, subcontractors, local officials, the Department of Veterans Affairs, vocational rehabilitation facilities, and all other available instrumentalities, to cause any labor organization, recruiting and training agency or other representative of workers who are employed by a contractor to cooperate with, and to assist in, the implementation of the purposes of the Act.

§ 60–250.83 Rulings and interpretations.

Rulings under or interpretations of the Act and this part shall be made by the Deputy Assistant Secretary.

§ 60–250.84 Responsibilities of local employment service offices.

(a) Local employment service offices shall refer qualified special disabled veterans, veterans of the Vietnam era, recently separated veterans, and other protected veterans to fill employment openings listed by contractors with such local offices pursuant to the mandatory listing requirements of the equal opportunity clause, and shall give priority to special disabled veterans, veterans of the Vietnam era, recently separated veterans, and other protected veterans in making such referrals.

(b) Local employment service offices shall contact employers to solicit the job orders described in paragraph (a) of this section. The state employment security agency shall provide OFCCP upon request information pertinent to whether the contractor is in compliance with the mandatory listing requirements of the equal opportunity clause.

Appendix A to Part 60–250—Guidelines on a Contractor's Duty To Provide Reasonable Accommodation

The guidelines in this appendix are in large part derived from, and are consistent with, the discussion regarding the duty to provide reasonable accommodation contained in the Interpretive Guidance on Title I of the Americans with Disabilities Act (ADA) set out as an appendix to the regulations issued by the Equal Employment Opportunity Commission (EEOC) implementing the ADA (29 CFR part 1630). Although the following discussion is intended to provide an independent "free-standing" source of guidance with respect to the duty to provide reasonable accommodation under this part, to the extent that the EEOC appendix provides additional guidance which is consistent with the following discussion, it may be relied upon for purposes of this part as well. See §60–250.1(c). Contractors are obligated to provide reasonable accommodation and to take affirmative action. Reasonable accommodation under VEVRAA, like reasonable accommodation required under section 503 and the ADA, is a part of the nondiscrimination obligation. *See* EEOC appendix cited in this paragraph. Affirmative action is unique to VEVRAA and section 503, and includes actions above and beyond those required as a matter of nondiscrimination. An example of this is the requirement discussed in paragraph 2 of this appendix that a contractor *shall* make an inquiry of a special disabled veteran who is having significant difficulty performing his or her job.

1. A contractor is required to make reasonable accommodations to the known physical or mental limitations of an "otherwise qualified" special disabled veteran, unless the contractor can demonstrate that the accommodation would impose an undue hardship on the operation of its business. As stated in §60–250.2(o), a special disabled veteran is qualified if he or she satisfies all the skill, experience, education and other job-related selection criteria, and can perform the essential functions of the position with or without reasonable accommodation. A contractor is required to make a reasonable accommodation with respect to its application process if the special disabled veteran is qualified with respect to that process. One is "otherwise qualified" if he or she is qualified for a job, except that, because of a disability, he or she needs a reasonable accommodation to be able to perform the job's essential functions.

2. Although the contractor would not be expected to accommodate disabilities of which it is unaware, the contractor has an affirmative obligation to provide a reasonable accommodation for applicants and employees who are known to be special disabled veterans. As stated in §60–250.42 (see also Appendix B of this part), the contractor is required to invite applicants who have been provided an offer of employment, before they are placed on the contractor's payroll, to indicate whether they are covered by the Act and wish to benefit under the contractor's affirmative action program. That section further provides that the contractor should seek the advice of special disabled veterans who "self-identify" in this way as to proper placement and appropriate accommodation. Moreover, §60–250.44(d) provides that if an employee who is a known special disabled veteran is having significant difficulty performing his or her job and it is reasonable to conclude that the performance problem may be related to the disability, the contractor is required to confidentially inquire whether the problem is disability related and if the employee is in need of a reasonable accommodation.

3. An accommodation is any change in the work environment or in the way things are customarily done that enables a special disabled veteran to enjoy equal employment opportunities. Equal employment opportunity means an opportunity to attain the same level of performance, or to enjoy the same level of benefits and privileges of employment, as are available to the average similarly situated employee without a disability. Thus, for example, an accommodation made to assist an employee who is a special disabled veteran in the performance of his or her job must be adequate to enable the individual to perform the essential functions of the position. The accommodation, however, does not have to be the "best" accommodation possible, so long as it is sufficient to meet the job-related needs of the individual being accommodated. There are three areas in which reasonable accommodations may be necessary: (1) Accommodations in the application process; (2) accommodations that enable employees who are special disabled veterans to perform the essential functions of the position held or desired; and (3) accommodations that enable employees who are special disabled veterans to enjoy equal benefits and privileges of employment as are enjoyed by employees without disabilities.

4. The term "undue hardship" refers to any accommodation that would be unduly costly, extensive, substantial, or disruptive, or that would fundamentally alter the nature or operation of the contractor's business. The contractor's claim that the cost of a particular accommodation will impose an undue hardship requires a determination of which financial resources should be considered—

those of the contractor in its entirety or only those of the facility that will be required to provide the accommodation. This inquiry requires an analysis of the financial relationship between the contractor and the facility in order to determine what resources will be available to the facility in providing the accommodation. If the contractor can show that the cost of the accommodation would impose an undue hardship, it would still be required to provide the accommodation if the funding is available from another source, e.g., the Department of Veterans Affairs or a state vocational rehabilitation agency, or if Federal, state or local tax deductions or tax credits are available to offset the cost of the accommodation. In the absence of such funding, the special disabled veteran should be given the option of providing the accommodation or of paying that portion of the cost which constitutes the undue hardship on the operation of the business.

5. Section 60–250.2(t) lists a number of examples of the most common types of accommodations that the contractor may be required to provide. There are any number of specific accommodations that may be appropriate for particular situations. The discussion in this appendix is not intended to provide an exhaustive list of required accommodations (as no such list would be feasible); rather, it is intended to provide general guidance regarding the nature of the obligation. The decision as to whether a reasonable accommodation is appropriate must be made on a case-by-case basis. The contractor generally should consult with the special disabled veteran in deciding on the appropriate accommodation; frequently, the individual will know exactly what accommodation he or she will need to perform successfully in a particular job, and may suggest an accommodation which is simpler and less expensive than the accommodation the contractor might have devised. Other resources to consult include the appropriate state vocational rehabilitation services agency, the Equal Employment Opportunity Commission (1–800–669–4000 (voice), 1–800–669–6820 (TTY)), the Job Accommodation Network (JAN) operated by the Office of Disability Employment Policy in the U.S. Department of Labor (1–800-JAN–7234 or 1–800–232–9675), private disability organizations (including those that serve veterans), and other employers.

6. With respect to accommodations that can permit an employee who is a special disabled veteran to perform essential functions successfully, a reasonable accommodation may require the contractor to, for instance, modify or acquire equipment. For the visually-impaired such accommodations may include providing adaptive hardware and software for computers, electronic visual aids, braille devices, talking calculators, magnifiers, audio recordings and braille or large-print materials. For persons with hearing impairments, reasonable accommodations may include providing telephone handset amplifiers, telephones compatible with hearing aids and telecommunications devices for the deaf (TDDs). For persons with limited physical dexterity, the obligation may require the provision of goose neck telephone headsets, mechanical page turners and raised or lowered furniture.

7. Other reasonable accommodations of this type may include providing personal assistants such as a reader, interpreter or travel attendant, permitting the use of accrued paid leave or providing additional unpaid leave for necessary treatment. The contractor may also be required to make existing facilities readily accessible to and usable by special disabled veterans—including areas used by employees for purposes other than the performance of essential job functions such as restrooms, break rooms, cafeterias, lounges, auditoriums, libraries, parking lots and credit unions. This type of accommodation will enable employees to enjoy equal benefits and privileges of employment as are enjoyed by employees who do not have disabilities.

8. Another of the potential accommodations listed in §60–250.2(t) is job restructuring. This may involve reallocating or redistributing those nonessential, marginal job functions which a qualified special disabled veteran cannot perform to another position. Accordingly, if a clerical employee who is a special disabled veteran is occasionally required to lift heavy boxes containing files, but cannot do so because of a disability, this task may be reassigned to another employee. The contractor, however, is not required to reallocate essential functions, *i.e.*, those functions that the individual who holds the job would have to perform, with or without reasonable accommodation, in order to be considered qualified for the position. For instance, the contractor which has a security guard position which requires the incumbent to inspect identity cards would not have to provide a blind special disabled veteran with an assistant to perform that duty; in such a case, the assistant would be performing an essential function of the job for the special disabled veteran. Job restructuring may also involve allowing part-time or modified work schedules. For instance, flexible or adjusted work schedules could benefit special disabled veterans who cannot work a standard schedule because of the need to obtain medical treatment, or special disabled veterans with mobility impairments who depend on a public transportation system that is not accessible during the hours of a standard schedule.

9. Reasonable accommodation may also include reassignment to a vacant position. In general, reassignment should be considered only when accommodation within the special

disabled veteran's current position would pose an undue hardship. Reassignment is not required for applicants. However, in making hiring decisions, contractors are encouraged to consider applicants who are known special disabled veterans for all available positions for which they may be qualified when the position(s) applied for is unavailable. Reassignment may not be used to limit, segregate, or otherwise discriminate against employees who are special disabled veterans by forcing reassignments to undesirable positions or to designated offices or facilities. Employers should reassign the individual to an equivalent position in terms of pay, status, etc., if the individual is qualified, and if the position is vacant within a reasonable amount of time. A "reasonable amount of time" should be determined in light of the totality of the circumstances.

10. The contractor may reassign an individual to a lower graded position if there are no accommodations that would enable the employee to remain in the current position and there are no vacant equivalent positions for which the individual is qualified with or without reasonable accommodation. The contractor may maintain the reassigned special disabled veteran at the salary of the higher graded position, and must do so if it maintains the salary of reassigned employees who are not special disabled veterans. It should also be noted that the contractor is not required to promote a special disabled veteran as an accommodation.

11. With respect to the application process, appropriate accommodations may include the following: (1) Providing information regarding job vacancies in a form accessible to special disabled veterans who are vision or hearing impaired, e.g., by making an announcement available in braille, in large print, or on audio tape, or by responding to job inquiries via TDDs; (2) providing readers, interpreters and other similar assistance during the application, testing and interview process; (3) appropriately adjusting or modifying employment-related examinations, e.g., extending regular time deadlines, allowing a special disabled veteran who is blind or has a learning disorder such as dyslexia to provide oral answers for a written test, and permitting an applicant, regardless of the nature of his or her ability, to demonstrate skills through alternative techniques and utilization of adapted tools, aids and devices; and (4) ensuring a special disabled veteran with a mobility impairment full access to testing locations such that the applicant's test scores accurately reflect the applicant's skills or aptitude rather than the applicant's mobility impairment.

Appendix B to Part 60–250—Sample Invitation To Self-Identify

NOTE: When the invitation to self-identify is being extended to special disabled veterans prior to an offer of employment, as is permitted in limited circumstances under §§ 60–250.42(a)(1) and (2), paragraph 7(ii) of this appendix, relating to identification of reasonable accommodations, should be omitted. This will avoid a conflict with the EEOC's ADA Guidance, which in most cases precludes asking a job applicant (prior to a job offer being made) about potential reasonable accommodations.

[Sample Invitation To Self-Identify]

1. This employer is a Government contractor subject to the Vietnam Era Veterans' Readjustment Assistance Act of 1974, as amended, which requires Government contractors to take affirmative action to employ and advance in employment qualified special disabled veterans, veterans of the Vietnam era, recently separated veterans, and other protected veterans.

2. [The following text should be used when extending an invitation to veterans of the Vietnam era, recently separated veterans, and other protected veterans only.] If you are a veteran of the Vietnam era, recently separated veteran, or other protected veteran, we would like to include you under our affirmative action program. If you would like to be included under the affirmative action program, please tell us. The term "veteran of the Vietnam era" refers to a person who served on active duty for a period of more than 180 days, and was discharged or released therefrom with other than a dishonorable discharge, if any part of such active duty occurred in the Republic of Vietnam between February 28, 1961, and May 7, 1975 or between August 5, 1964, and May 7, 1975, in all other cases. The term also refers to a person who was discharged or released from active duty for a service-connected disability if any part of such active duty was performed in the Republic of Vietnam between February 28, 1961, and May 7, 1975, or between August 5, 1964, and May 7, 1975, in all other cases. The term "recently separated veteran" refers to any veteran during the one-year period beginning on the date of such veteran's discharge or release from active duty. The term "other protected veteran" refers to a person who served on active duty during a war or in a campaign or expedition for which a campaign badge has been authorized, under laws administered by the Department of Defense.

[The following text should be used when extending an invitation to special disabled veterans only.] If you are a special disabled veteran, we would like to include you in our affirmative action program. If you would like to be included under the affirmative action program, please tell us. This information will assist us in placing you in an appropriate position and in making accommodations for your disability. The term "special disabled veteran" refers to a veteran who is entitled to compensation (or who, but for the receipt of military retired pay, would be entitled to compensation) under laws administered by the Department of Veterans Affairs for a disability rated at 30 percent or more, or rated at 10 or 20 percent in the case of a veteran who has been determined by the Department of Veterans Affairs to have a serious employment handicap. The term also refers to a person who was discharged or released from active duty because of a service-connected disability.

[The following text should be used when extending an invitation to veterans of the Vietnam era, special disabled veterans, recently separated veterans, and other protected veterans. If you are a veteran of the Vietnam era, a special disabled veteran, a recently separated veteran, or other protected veteran, we would like to include you under our affirmative action program. If you would like to be included under the affirmative action program, please tell us. [The contractor should include here the definitions of "veteran of the Vietnam era," "special disabled veteran," "recently separated veteran" and "other protected veteran" found in the two preceding paragraphs.]

3. You may inform us of your desire to benefit under the program at this time and/or at any time in the future.

4. Submission of this information is voluntary and refusal to provide it will not subject you to any adverse treatment. The information provided will be used only in ways that are not inconsistent with the Vietnam Era Veterans' Readjustment Assistance Act of 1974, as amended.

5. The information you submit will be kept confidential, except that (i) supervisors and managers may be informed regarding restrictions on the work or duties of special disabled veterans, and regarding necessary accommodations; (ii) first aid and safety personnel may be informed, when and to the extent appropriate, if you have a condition that might require emergency treatment; and (iii) Government officials engaged in enforcing laws administered by OFCCP, or enforcing the Americans with Disabilities Act, may be informed.

6. [The contractor should here insert a brief provision summarizing the relevant portion of its affirmative action program.]

7. [The following text should be used only when extending an invitation to special disabled veterans, either by themselves or in combination with veterans of the Vietnam era, recently separated veterans, and other protected veterans. Paragraph 7(ii) should be omitted when the invitation to self-identify is being extended prior to an offer of employment.] If you are a special disabled veteran it would assist us if you tell us about (i) any special methods, skills, and procedures which qualify you for positions that you might not otherwise be able to do because of your disability so that you will be considered for any positions of that kind, and (ii) the accommodations which we could make which would enable you to perform the job properly and safely, including special equipment, changes in the physical layout of the job, elimination of certain duties relating to the job, provision of personal assistance services or other accommodations. This information will assist us in placing you in an appropriate position and in making accommodations for your disability.

APPENDIX C TO PART 60–250—REVIEW OF PERSONNEL PROCESSES

The following is a set of procedures which contractors may use to meet the requirements of § 60–250.44(b):

1. The application or personnel form of each known applicant who is a special disabled veteran, veteran of the Vietnam era, recently separated veteran, or other protected veteran should be annotated to identify each vacancy for which the applicant was considered, and the form should be quickly retrievable for review by the Department of Labor and the contractor's personnel officials for use in investigations and internal compliance activities.

2. The personnel or application records of each known special disabled veteran, veteran of the Vietnam era, recently separated veteran, or other protected veteran should include (i) the identification of each promotion for which the covered veteran was considered, and (ii) the identification of each training program for which the covered veteran was considered.

3. In each case where an employee or applicant who is a special disabled veteran, veteran of the Vietnam era, recently separated veteran, or other protected veteran is rejected for employment, promotion, or training, the contractor should prepare a statement of the reason as well as a description of the accommodations considered (for a rejected special disabled veteran). The statement of the reason for rejection (if the reason is medically related), and the description of the accommodations considered, should be treated as confidential medical records in accordance with § 60–250.23(d). These materials should be available to the applicant or employee concerned upon request.

4. Where applicants or employees are selected for hire, promotion, or training and the contractor undertakes any accommodation which makes it possible for him or her to place a special disabled veteran on the

job, the contractor should make a record containing a description of the accommodation. The record should be treated as a confidential medical record in accordance with § 60–250.23(d).

PART 60–300—AFFIRMATIVE ACTION AND NONDISCRIMINATION OBLIGATIONS OF CONTRACTORS AND SUBCONTRACTORS REGARDING DISABLED VETERANS, RECENTLY SEPARATED VETERANS, OTHER PROTECTED VETERANS, AND ARMED FORCES SERVICE MEDAL VETERANS

AUTHORITY: 29 U.S.C. 793; 38 U.S.C. 4211 and 4212; E.O. 11758 (3 CFR, 1971–1975 Comp., p. 841).

SOURCE: 72 FR 44401, Aug. 8, 2007, unless otherwise noted.

Subpart A—Preliminary Matters, Equal Opportunity Clause

§ 60–300.1 Purpose, applicability and construction.

(a) *Purpose.* The purpose of the regulations in this part is to set forth the standards for compliance with the Vietnam Era Veterans' Readjustment Assistance Act of 1974, as amended (38 U.S.C. 4212, or VEVRAA), which requires Government contractors and subcontractors to take affirmative action to employ and advance in employment qualified covered veterans. Disabled veterans, recently separated veterans, other protected veterans, and Armed Forces service medal veterans are covered veterans under VEVRAA.

(b) *Applicability.* This part applies to any Government contract or subcontract of $100,000 or more, entered into or modified on or after December 1, 2003, for the purchase, sale or use of personal property or nonpersonal services (including construction): *Provided,* that subpart C of this part applies only as described in § 60–300.40(a). Compliance by the contractor with the provisions of this part will not necessarily determine its compliance with other statutes, and compliance with other statutes will not necessarily determine its compliance with this part. Any contractor or subcontractor whose only contract(s) for the purchase, sale or use of personal property and nonpersonal services (including construction) was entered into before December 1, 2003 (and not modified as described above) must follow part 60–250. Any contractor or subcontractor who has contracts for the purchase, sale or use of personal property and nonpersonal services (including construction) that were entered into before December 1, 2003 (and not modified as described above), and contracts that were entered into on or after December 1, 2003, must follow both parts 60–250 and 60–300.

(c) *Construction*—(1) *In general.* The Interpretive Guidance on Title I of the Americans with Disabilities Act (ADA) (42 U.S.C. 12101, *et seq.*) set out as an appendix to 29 CFR part 1630 issued pursuant to Title I may be relied upon for guidance in interpreting the parallel provisions of this part.

(2) *Relationship to other laws.* This part does not invalidate or limit the remedies, rights, and procedures under any Federal law or the law of any state or political subdivision that provides greater or equal protection for the rights of disabled veterans, recently separated veterans, other protected veterans, or Armed Forces service medal veterans as compared to the protection afforded by this part. It may be a defense to a charge of violation of this part that a challenged action is required or necessitated by another Federal law or regulation, or that another Federal law or regulation prohibits an action (including the provision of a particular reasonable accommodation) that would otherwise be required by this part.

§60–300.2 Definitions.

For the purpose of this part:

(a) *Act* means the Vietnam Era Veterans' Readjustment Assistance Act of 1974, as amended, 38 U.S.C. 4212.

(b) *Equal opportunity clause* means the contract provisions set forth in §60–300.5, "Equal opportunity clause."

(c) *Secretary* means the Secretary of Labor, United States Department of Labor, or his or her designee.

(d) *Deputy Assistant Secretary* means the Deputy Assistant Secretary for Federal Contract Compliance of the United States Department of Labor, or his or her designee.

(e) *Government* means the Government of the United States of America.

(f) *United States*, as used in this part, shall include the several States, the District of Columbia, the Virgin Islands, the Commonwealth of Puerto Rico, Guam, American Samoa, the Commonwealth of the Northern Mariana Islands, and Wake Island.

(g) *Recruiting and training agency* means any person who refers workers to any contractor, or who provides or supervises apprenticeship or training for employment by any contractor.

(h) *Contract* means any Government contract or subcontract.

(i) *Government contract* means any agreement or modification thereof between any contracting agency and any person for the purchase, sale or use of personal property or nonpersonal services (including construction). The term *Government contract* does not include agreements in which the parties stand in the relationship of employer and employee, and federally assisted contracts.

(1) *Modification* means any alteration in the terms and conditions of a contract, including supplemental agreements, amendments and extensions.

(2) *Contracting agency* means any department, agency, establishment or instrumentality of the United States, including any wholly owned Government corporation, which enters into contracts.

(3) *Person*, as used in this paragraph (i) and paragraph (l) of this section, means any natural person, corporation, partnership or joint venture, unincorporated association, state or local government, and any agency, instrumentality, or subdivision of such a government.

(4) *Nonpersonal services*, as used in this paragraph (i) and paragraph (l) of this section, includes, but is not limited to, the following: Utility, construction, transportation, research, insurance, and fund depository.

(5) *Construction*, as used in this paragraph (i) and paragraph (l) of this section, means the construction, rehabilitation, alteration, conversion, extension, demolition, or repair of buildings, highways, or other changes or improvements to real property, including facilities providing utility services. The

term also includes the supervision, inspection, and other on-site functions incidental to the actual construction.

(6) *Personal property,* as used in this paragraph (i) and paragraph (l) of this section, includes supplies and contracts for the use of real property (such as lease arrangements), unless the contract for the use of real property itself constitutes real property (such as easements).

(j) *Contractor* means, unless otherwise indicated, a prime contractor or subcontractor holding a contract of $100,000 or more.

(k) *Prime contractor* means any person holding a contract of $100,000 or more, and, for the purposes of subpart D of this part, "General Enforcement and Complaint Procedures," includes any person who has held a contract subject to the Act.

(l) *Subcontract* means any agreement or arrangement between a contractor and any person (in which the parties do not stand in the relationship of an employer and an employee):

(1) For the purchase, sale or use of personal property or nonpersonal services (including construction) which, in whole or in part, is necessary to the performance of any one or more contracts; or

(2) Under which any portion of the contractor's obligation under any one or more contracts is performed, undertaken, or assumed.

(m) *Subcontractor* means any person holding a subcontract of $100,000 or more and, for the purposes of subpart D of this part, "General Enforcement and Complaint Procedures," any person who has held a subcontract subject to the Act.

(n) *Disabled veteran* means:

(1) A veteran of the U.S. military, ground, naval or air service who is entitled to compensation (or who but for the receipt of military retired pay would be entitled to compensation) under laws administered by the Secretary of Veterans Affairs, or

(2) A person who was discharged or released from active duty because of a service-connected disability.

(o) *Qualified disabled veteran* means a disabled veteran who has the ability to perform the essential functions of the employment position with or without reasonable accommodation.

(p) *Other protected veteran* means a veteran who served on active duty in the U.S. military, ground, naval or air service during a war or in a campaign or expedition for which a campaign badge has been authorized, under the laws administered by the Department of Defense.

(q) *Recently separated veteran* means any veteran during the three-year period beginning on the date of such veteran's discharge or release from active duty in the U.S. military, ground, naval or air service.

(r) *Armed Forces service medal veteran* means any veteran who, while serving on active duty in the U.S. military, ground, naval or air service, participated in a United States military operation for which an Armed Forces service medal was awarded pursuant to Executive Order 12985 (61 FR 1209).

(s) *Essential functions*—(1) *In general.* The term *essential functions* means fundamental job duties of the employment position the disabled veteran holds or desires. The term *essential functions* does not include the marginal functions of the position.

(2) A job function may be considered essential for any of several reasons, including, but not limited to, the following:

(i) The function may be essential because the reason the position exists is to perform that function;

(ii) The function may be essential because of the limited number of employees available among whom the performance of that job function can be distributed; and/or

(iii) The function may be highly specialized so that the incumbent in the position is hired for his or her expertise or ability to perform the particular function.

(3) Evidence of whether a particular function is essential includes, but is not limited to:

(i) The contractor's judgment as to which functions are essential;

(ii) Written job descriptions prepared before advertising or interviewing applicants for the job;

(iii) The amount of time spent on the job performing the function;

(iv) The consequences of not requiring the incumbent to perform the function;

(v) The terms of a collective bargaining agreement;

(vi) The work experience of past incumbents in the job; and/or

(vii) The current work experience of incumbents in similar jobs.

(t) *Reasonable accommodation*—(1) The term *reasonable accommodation* means:

(i) Modifications or adjustments to a job application process that enable a qualified applicant who is a disabled veteran to be considered for the position such applicant desires;[1] or

(ii) Modifications or adjustments to the work environment, or to the manner or circumstances under which the position held or desired is customarily performed, that enable a qualified disabled veteran to perform the essential functions of that position; or

(iii) Modifications or adjustments that enable the contractor's employee who is a disabled veteran to enjoy equal benefits and privileges of employment as are enjoyed by the contractor's other similarly situated employees who are not disabled veterans.

(2) Reasonable accommodation may include but is not limited to:

(i) Making existing facilities used by employees readily accessible to and usable by disabled veterans; and

(ii) Job restructuring; part-time or modified work schedules; reassignment to a vacant position; acquisition or modifications of equipment or devices; appropriate adjustment or modifications of examinations, training materials, or policies; the provision of qualified readers or interpreters; and other similar accommodations for disabled veterans.

(3) To determine the appropriate reasonable accommodation it may be necessary for the contractor to initiate an informal, interactive process with the qualified disabled veteran in need of the accommodation.[2] This process should identify the precise limitations resulting from the disability and potential reasonable accommodations that could overcome those limitations. (Appendix A of this part provides guidance on a contractor's duty to provide reasonable accommodation.)

(u) *Undue hardship*—(1) *In general. Undue hardship* means, with respect to the provision of an accommodation, significant difficulty or expense incurred by the contractor, when considered in light of the factors set forth in paragraph (u)(2) of this section.

(2) *Factors to be considered.* In determining whether an accommodation would impose an undue hardship on the contractor, factors to be considered include:

(i) The nature and net cost of the accommodation needed, taking into consideration the availability of tax credits and deductions, and/or outside funding;

(ii) The overall financial resources of the facility or facilities involved in the provision of the reasonable accommodation, the number of persons employed at such facility, and the effect on expenses and resources;

(iii) The overall financial resources of the contractor, the overall size of the business of the contractor with respect to the number of its employees, and the number, type and location of its facilities;

(iv) The type of operation or operations of the contractor, including the composition, structure and functions of the work force of such contractor, and the geographic separateness and administrative or fiscal relationship of the facility or facilities in question to the contractor; and

[1] A contractor's duty to provide a reasonable accommodation with respect to applicants who are disabled veterans is not limited to those who ultimately demonstrate that they are qualified to perform the job in issue. Disabled veteran applicants must be provided a reasonable accommodation with respect to the application process if they are qualified with respect to that process (e.g., if they present themselves at the correct location and time to fill out an application).

[2] Contractors must engage in such an interactive process with a disabled veteran, whether or not a reasonable accommodation ultimately is identified that will make the person a qualified individual. Contractors must engage in the interactive process because, until they have done so, they may be unable to determine whether a reasonable accommodation exists that will result in the person being qualified.

(v) The impact of the accommodation upon the operation of the facility, including the impact on the ability of other employees to perform their duties and the impact on the facility's ability to conduct business.

(v) *Qualification standards* means the personal and professional attributes including the skill, experience, education, physical, medical, safety and other requirements established by the contractor as requirements which an individual must meet in order to be eligible for the position held or desired.

(w) *Direct threat* means a significant risk of substantial harm to the health or safety of the individual or others that cannot be eliminated or reduced by reasonable accommodation. The determination that a disabled veteran poses a *direct threat* shall be based on an individualized assessment of the individual's present ability to perform safely the essential functions of the job. This assessment shall be based on a reasonable medical judgment that relies on the most current medical knowledge and/or on the best available objective evidence. In determining whether an individual would pose a direct threat, the factors to be considered include:

(1) The duration of the risk;

(2) The nature and severity of the potential harm;

(3) The likelihood that the potential harm will occur; and

(4) The imminence of the potential harm.

(x) *Compliance evaluation* means any one or combination of actions OFCCP may take to examine a Federal contractor's or subcontractor's compliance with one or more of the requirements of the Vietnam Era Veterans' Readjustment Assistance Act.

(y) *Employment service delivery system* means a service delivery system at which or through which labor exchange services, including employment, training, and placement services, are offered in accordance with the Wagner-Peyser Act.

(z) *Veteran* means a person who served in the active military, naval, or air service of the United States, and who was discharged or released therefrom under conditions other than dishonorable.

§60–300.3 [Reserved]

§60–300.4 Coverage and waivers.

(a) *General*—(1) *Contracts and subcontracts of $100,000 or more.* Contracts and subcontracts of $100,000 or more are covered by this part. No contracting agency or contractor shall procure supplies or services in less than usual quantities to avoid the applicability of the equal opportunity clause.

(2) *Contracts for indefinite quantities.* With respect to indefinite delivery-type contracts (including, but not limited to, open end contracts, requirement-type contracts, Federal Supply Schedule contracts, "call-type" contracts, and purchase notice agreements), the equal opportunity clause shall be included unless the contracting agency has reason to believe that the amount to be ordered in any year under such contract will be less than $100,000. The applicability of the equal opportunity clause shall be determined at the time of award for the first year, and annually thereafter for succeeding years, if any. Notwithstanding the above, the equal opportunity clause shall be applied to such contract whenever the amount of a single order is $100,000 or more. Once the equal opportunity clause is determined to be applicable, the contract shall continue to be subject to such clause for its duration, regardless of the amounts ordered, or reasonably expected to be ordered in any year.

(3) *Employment activities within the United States.* This part applies only to employment activities within the United States and not to employment activities abroad. The term "employment activities within the United States" includes actual employment within the United States, and decisions of the contractor made within the United States pertaining to the contractor's applicants and employees who are within the United States, regarding employment opportunities abroad (such as recruiting and hiring within the United States for employment abroad, or transfer of persons employed in the United States to contractor establishments abroad).

(4) *Contracts with state or local governments.* The requirements of the equal

opportunity clause in any contract or subcontract with a state or local government (or any agency, instrumentality or subdivision thereof) shall not be applicable to any agency, instrumentality or subdivision of such government which does not participate in work on or under the contract or subcontract.

(b) *Waivers*—(1) *Specific contracts and classes of contracts*. The Deputy Assistant Secretary may waive the application to any contract of the equal opportunity clause in whole or part when he or she deems that special circumstances in the national interest so require. The Deputy Assistant Secretary may also grant such waivers to groups or categories of contracts: where it is in the national interest; where it is found impracticable to act upon each request individually; and where such waiver will substantially contribute to convenience in administration of the Act. When a waiver has been granted for any class of contracts, the Deputy Assistant Secretary may withdraw the waiver for a specific contract or group of contracts to be awarded, when in his or her judgment such action is necessary or appropriate to achieve the purposes of the Act. The withdrawal shall not apply to contracts awarded prior to the withdrawal, except that in procurements entered into by formal advertising, or the various forms of restricted formal advertising, such withdrawal shall not apply unless the withdrawal is made more than 10 calendar days before the date set for the opening of the bids.

(2) *National security*. Any requirement set forth in the regulations of this part shall not apply to any contract whenever the head of the contracting agency determines that such contract is essential to the national security and that its award without complying with such requirements is necessary to the national security. Upon making such a determination, the head of the contracting agency will notify the Deputy Assistant Secretary in writing within 30 days.

(3) *Facilities not connected with contracts*. The Deputy Assistant Secretary may waive the requirements of the equal opportunity clause with respect to any of a contractor's facilities which he or she finds to be in all respects separate and distinct from activities of the contractor related to the performance of the contract, provided that he or she also finds that such a waiver will not interfere with or impede the effectuation of the Act. Such waivers shall be considered only upon the request of the contractor.

§ 60–300.5 Equal opportunity clause.

(a) *Government contracts*. Each contracting agency and each contractor shall include the following equal opportunity clause in each of its covered Government contracts or subcontracts (and modifications, renewals, or extensions thereof if not included in the original contract):

EQUAL OPPORTUNITY FOR DISABLED VETERANS, RECENTLY SEPARATED VETERANS, OTHER PROTECTED VETERANS, AND ARMED FORCES SERVICE MEDAL VETERANS

1. The contractor will not discriminate against any employee or applicant for employment because he or she is a disabled veteran, recently separated veteran, other protected veteran, or Armed Forces service medal veteran in regard to any position for which the employee or applicant for employment is qualified. The contractor agrees to take affirmative action to employ, advance in employment and otherwise treat qualified individuals without discrimination based on their status as a disabled veteran, recently separated veteran, other protected veteran, or Armed Forces service medal veteran in all employment practices, including the following:

i. Recruitment, advertising, and job application procedures;

ii. Hiring, upgrading, promotion, award of tenure, demotion, transfer, layoff, termination, right of return from layoff and rehiring;

iii. Rates of pay or any other form of compensation and changes in compensation;

iv. Job assignments, job classifications, organizational structures, position descriptions, lines of progression, and seniority lists;

v. Leaves of absence, sick leave, or any other leave;

vi. Fringe benefits available by virtue of employment, whether or not administered by the contractor;

vii. Selection and financial support for training, including apprenticeship, and on-the-job training under 38 U.S.C. 3687, professional meetings, conferences, and other related activities, and selection for leaves of absence to pursue training;

viii. Activities sponsored by the contractor including social or recreational programs; and

ix. Any other term, condition, or privilege of employment.

2. The contractor agrees to immediately list all employment openings which exist at the time of the execution of this contract and those which occur during the performance of this contract, including those not generated by this contract and including those occurring at an establishment of the contractor other than the one where the contract is being performed, but excluding those of independently operated corporate affiliates, with the appropriate employment service delivery system where the opening occurs. Listing employment openings with the state workforce agency job bank or with the local employment service delivery system where the opening occurs will satisfy the requirement to list jobs with the appropriate employment service delivery system.

3. Listing of employment openings with the appropriate employment service delivery system pursuant to this clause shall be made at least concurrently with the use of any other recruitment source or effort and shall involve the normal obligations which attach to the placing of a *bona fide* job order, including the acceptance of referrals of veterans and nonveterans. The listing of employment openings does not require the hiring of any particular job applicants or from any particular group of job applicants, and nothing herein is intended to relieve the contractor from any requirements in Executive orders or regulations regarding nondiscrimination in employment.

4. Whenever a contractor, other than a state or local governmental contractor, becomes contractually bound to the listing provisions in paragraphs 2 and 3 of this clause, it shall advise the state workforce agency in each state where it has establishments of the name and location of each hiring location in the state. As long as the contractor is contractually bound to these provisions and has so advised the state agency, there is no need to advise the state agency of subsequent contracts. The contractor may advise the state agency when it is no longer bound by this contract clause.

5. The provisions of paragraphs 2 and 3 of this clause do not apply to the listing of employment openings which occur and are filled outside of the 50 states, the District of Columbia, the Commonwealth of Puerto Rico, Guam, the Virgin Islands, American Samoa, the Commonwealth of the Northern Mariana Islands, Wake Island, and the Trust Territories of the Pacific Islands.

6. As used in this clause: i. *All employment openings* includes all positions except executive and senior management, those positions that will be filled from within the contractor's organization, and positions lasting three days or less. This term includes full-time employment, temporary employment of more than three days' duration, and part-time employment.

ii. *Executive and senior management* means: (1) Any employee (a) compensated on a salary basis at a rate of not less than $455 per week (or $380 per week, if employed in American Samoa by employers other than the Federal Government), exclusive of board, lodging or other facilities; (b) whose primary duty is management of the enterprise in which the employee is employed or of a customarily recognized department or subdivision thereof; (c) who customarily and regularly directs the work of two or more other employees; and (d) who has the authority to hire or fire other employees or whose suggestions and recommendations as to the hiring, firing, advancement, promotion or any other change of status of other employees are given particular weight; or (2) any employee who owns at least a bona fide 20-percent equity interest in the enterprise in which the employee is employed, regardless of whether the business is a corporate or other type of organization, and who is actively engaged in its management.

iii. *Positions that will be filled from within the contractor's organization* means employment openings for which no consideration will be given to persons outside the contractor's organization (including any affiliates, subsidiaries, and parent companies) and includes any openings which the contractor proposes to fill from regularly established "recall" lists. The exception does not apply to a particular opening once an employer decides to consider applicants outside of his or her own organization.

7. The contractor agrees to comply with the rules, regulations, and relevant orders of the Secretary of Labor issued pursuant to the Act.

8. In the event of the contractor's noncompliance with the requirements of this clause, actions for noncompliance may be taken in accordance with the rules, regulations, and relevant orders of the Secretary of Labor issued pursuant to the Act.

9. The contractor agrees to post in conspicuous places, available to employees and applicants for employment, notices in a form to be prescribed by the Deputy Assistant Secretary for Federal Contract Compliance, provided by or through the contracting officer. Such notices shall state the rights of applicants and employees as well as the contractor's obligation under the law to take affirmative action to employ and advance in employment qualified employees and applicants who are disabled veterans, recently separated veterans, other protected veterans, or Armed Forces service medal veterans. The contractor must ensure that applicants or employees who are disabled veterans are informed of the contents of the notice (e.g., the

contractor may have the notice read to a visually disabled individual, or may lower the posted notice so that it might be read by a person in a wheelchair).

10. The contractor will notify each labor organization or representative of workers with which it has a collective bargaining agreement or other contract understanding, that the contractor is bound by the terms of the Vietnam Era Veterans' Readjustment Assistance Act of 1974, as amended, and is committed to take affirmative action to employ and advance in employment qualified disabled veterans, recently separated veterans, other protected veterans, and Armed Forces service medal veterans.

11. The contractor will include the provisions of this clause in every subcontract or purchase order of $100,000 or more, unless exempted by the rules, regulations, or orders of the Secretary issued pursuant to the Vietnam Era Veterans' Readjustment Assistance Act of 1974, as amended, so that such provisions will be binding upon each subcontractor or vendor. The contractor will take such action with respect to any subcontract or purchase order as the Deputy Assistant Secretary for Federal Contract Compliance may direct to enforce such provisions, including action for noncompliance.

[End of Clause]

(b) *Subcontracts.* Each contractor shall include the equal opportunity clause in each of its subcontracts subject to this part.

(c) *Adaption of language.* Such necessary changes in language may be made to the equal opportunity clause as shall be appropriate to identify properly the parties and their undertakings.

(d) *Inclusion of the equal opportunity clause in the contract.* It is not necessary that the equal opportunity clause be quoted verbatim in the contract. The clause may be made a part of the contract by citation to 41 CFR 60–300.5(a).

(e) *Incorporation by operation of the Act.* By operation of the Act, the equal opportunity clause shall be considered to be a part of every contract and subcontract required by the Act and the regulations in this part to include such a clause, whether or not it is physically incorporated in such contract and whether or not there is a written contract between the agency and the contractor.

(f) *Duties of contracting agencies.* Each contracting agency shall cooperate with the Deputy Assistant Secretary and the Secretary in the performance of their responsibilities under the Act. Such cooperation shall include insuring that the equal opportunity clause is included in all covered Government contracts and that contractors are fully informed of their obligations under the Act and this part, providing the Deputy Assistant Secretary with any information which comes to the agency's attention that a contractor is not in compliance with the Act or this part, responding to requests for information from the Deputy Assistant Secretary, and taking such actions for noncompliance as are set forth in § 60–300.66 as may be ordered by the Secretary or the Deputy Assistant Secretary.

Subpart B—Discrimination Prohibited

§ 60–300.20 Covered employment activities.

The prohibition against discrimination in this part applies to the following employment activities:

(a) Recruitment, advertising, and job application procedures;

(b) Hiring, upgrading, promotion, award of tenure, demotion, transfer, layoff, termination, right of return from layoff, and rehiring;

(c) Rates of pay or any other form of compensation and changes in compensation;

(d) Job assignments, job classifications, organizational structures, position descriptions, lines of progression, and seniority lists;

(e) Leaves of absence, sick leave, or any other leave;

(f) Fringe benefits available by virtue of employment, whether or not administered by the contractor;

(g) Selection and financial support for training, including, apprenticeships, professional meetings, conferences and other related activities, and selection for leaves of absence to pursue training;

(h) Activities sponsored by the contractor including social and recreational programs; and

(i) Any other term, condition, or privilege of employment.

§ 60–300.21 Prohibitions.

The term *discrimination* includes, but is not limited to, the acts described in this section and § 60–300.23.

(a) *Disparate treatment.* It is unlawful for the contractor to deny an employment opportunity or benefit or otherwise to discriminate against a qualified individual because of that individual's status as a disabled veteran, recently separated veteran, other protected veteran, or Armed Forces service medal veteran.

(b) *Limiting, segregating and classifying.* Unless otherwise permitted by this part, it is unlawful for the contractor to limit, segregate, or classify a job applicant or employee in a way that adversely affects his or her employment opportunities or status on the basis of that individual's status as a disabled veteran, recently separated veteran, other protected veteran, or Armed Forces service medal veteran. For example, the contractor may not segregate qualified disabled veterans, recently separated veterans, other protected veterans, or Armed Forces service medal veterans into separate work areas or into separate lines of advancement.

(c) *Contractual or other arrangements*—(1) *In general.* It is unlawful for the contractor to participate in a contractual or other arrangement or relationship that has the effect of subjecting the contractor's own qualified applicant or employee who is a disabled veteran, recently separated veteran, other protected veteran, or Armed Forces service medal veteran to the discrimination prohibited by this part.

(2) *Contractual or other arrangement defined.* The phrase "contractual or other arrangement or relationship" includes, but is not limited to, a relationship with: an employment or referral agency; a labor organization, including a collective bargaining agreement; an organization providing fringe benefits to an employee of the contractor; or an organization providing training and apprenticeship programs.

(3) *Application.* This paragraph (c) applies to the contractor, with respect to its own applicants or employees, whether the contractor offered the contract or initiated the relationship, or whether the contractor accepted the contract or acceded to the relationship. The contractor is not liable for the actions of the other party or parties to the contract which only affect that other party's employees or applicants.

(d) *Standards, criteria or methods of administration.* It is unlawful for the contractor to use standards, criteria, or methods of administration, that are not job-related and consistent with business necessity, and that:

(1) Have the effect of discriminating on the basis of status as a disabled veteran, recently separated veteran, other protected veteran, or Armed Forces service medal veteran; or

(2) Perpetuate the discrimination of others who are subject to common administrative control.

(e) *Relationship or association with a disabled veteran, recently separated veteran, other protected veteran, or Armed Forces service medal veteran.* It is unlawful for the contractor to exclude or deny equal jobs or benefits to, or otherwise discriminate against, a qualified individual because of the known disabled veteran, recently separated veteran, other protected veteran, or Armed Forces service medal veteran status of an individual with whom the qualified individual is known to have a family, business, social or other relationship or association.

(f) *Not making reasonable accommodation.* (1) It is unlawful for the contractor to fail to make reasonable accommodation to the known physical or mental limitations of an otherwise qualified applicant or employee who is a disabled veteran, unless such contractor can demonstrate that the accommodation would impose an undue hardship on the operation of its business.

(2) It is unlawful for the contractor to deny employment opportunities to an otherwise qualified job applicant or employee who is a disabled veteran based on the need of such contractor to make reasonable accommodation to such an individual's physical or mental impairments.

(3) A qualified disabled veteran is not required to accept an accommodation, aid, service, opportunity or benefit which such qualified individual chooses

not to accept. However, if such individual rejects a reasonable accommodation, aid, service, opportunity or benefit that is necessary to enable the individual to perform the essential functions of the position held or desired, and cannot, as a result of that rejection, perform the essential functions of the position, the individual will not be considered a qualified disabled veteran.

(g) *Qualification standards, tests and other selection criteria*—(1) *In general.* It is unlawful for the contractor to use qualification standards, employment tests or other selection criteria that screen out or tend to screen out individuals on the basis of their status as disabled veterans, recently separated veterans, other protected veterans, or Armed Forces service medal veterans unless the standard, test or other selection criterion, as used by the contractor, is shown to be job-related for the position in question and is consistent with business necessity. Selection criteria that concern an essential function may not be used to exclude a disabled veteran if that individual could satisfy the criteria with provision of a reasonable accommodation. Selection criteria that exclude or tend to exclude individuals on the basis of their status as disabled veterans, recently separated veterans, other protected veterans, or Armed Forces service medal veterans but concern only marginal functions of the job would not be consistent with business necessity. The contractor may not refuse to hire an applicant who is a disabled veteran because the applicant's disability prevents him or her from performing marginal functions. When considering a disabled veteran, recently separated veteran, other protected veteran, or Armed Forces service medal veteran for an employment opportunity, the contractor may not rely on portions of such veteran's military record, including his or her discharge papers, which are not relevant to the qualification requirements of the opportunity in issue.

(2) The Uniform Guidelines on Employee Selection Procedures, 41 CFR part 60–3, do not apply to 38 U.S.C. 4212 and are similarly inapplicable to this part.

(h) *Administration of tests.* It is unlawful for the contractor to fail to select and administer tests concerning employment in the most effective manner to ensure that, when a test is administered to a job applicant or employee who is a disabled veteran with a disability that impairs sensory, manual, or speaking skills, the test results accurately reflect the skills, aptitude, or whatever other factor of the applicant or employee that the test purports to measure, rather than reflecting the impaired sensory, manual, or speaking skills of such employee or applicant, except where such skills are the factors that the test purports to measure.

(i) *Compensation.* In offering employment or promotions to disabled veterans, recently separated veterans, other protected veterans, or Armed Forces service medal veterans, it is unlawful for the contractor to reduce the amount of compensation offered because of any income based upon a disability-related and/or military-service-related pension or other disability-related and/or military-service-related benefit the applicant or employee receives from another source.

§ 60–300.22 Direct threat defense.

The contractor may use as a qualification standard the requirement that an individual be able to perform the essential functions of the position held or desired without posing a direct threat to the health or safety of the individual or others in the workplace. (See § 60–300.2(w) defining *direct threat.*)

§ 60–300.23 Medical examinations and inquiries.

(a) *Prohibited medical examinations or inquiries.* Except as stated in paragraphs (b) and (c) of this section, it is unlawful for the contractor to require a medical examination of an applicant or employee or to make inquiries as to whether an applicant or employee is a disabled veteran or as to the nature or severity of such a veteran's disability.

(b) *Permitted medical examinations and inquiries*—(1) *Acceptable pre-employment inquiry.* The contractor may make pre-employment inquiries into the ability of an applicant to perform job-related functions, and/or may ask an applicant to describe or to demonstrate how, with or without reasonable accommodation, the applicant will be able to perform job-related functions.

(2) *Employment entrance examination.* The contractor may require a medical examination (and/or inquiry) after making an offer of employment to a job applicant and before the applicant begins his or her employment duties, and may condition an offer of employment on the results of such examination (and/or inquiry), if all entering employees in the same job category are subjected to such an examination (and/or inquiry) regardless of their status as a disabled veteran.

(3) *Examination of employees.* The contractor may require a medical examination (and/or inquiry) of an employee that is job-related and consistent with business necessity. The contractor may make inquiries into the ability of an employee to perform job-related functions.

(4) *Other acceptable examinations and inquiries.* The contractor may conduct voluntary medical examinations and activities, including voluntary medical histories, which are part of an employee health program available to employees at the work site.

(5) Medical examinations conducted in accordance with paragraphs (b)(2) and (b)(4) of this section do not have to be job-related and consistent with business necessity. However, if certain criteria are used to screen out an applicant or applicants or an employee or employees who are disabled veterans as a result of such examinations or inquiries, the contractor must demonstrate that the exclusionary criteria are job-related and consistent with business necessity, and that performance of the essential job functions cannot be accomplished with reasonable accommodations as required in this part.

(c) *Invitation to self-identify.* The contractor shall invite applicants to self-identify as being covered by the Act, as specified in § 60–300.42.

(d) *Confidentiality and use of medical information.* (1) Information obtained under this section regarding the medical condition or history of any applicant or employee shall be collected and maintained on separate forms and in separate medical files and treated as a confidential medical record, except that:

(i) Supervisors and managers may be informed regarding necessary restrictions on the work or duties of the applicant or employee and necessary accommodations;

(ii) First aid and safety personnel may be informed, when appropriate, if the disability might require emergency treatment; and

(iii) Government officials engaged in enforcing the laws administered by OFCCP, including this part, or enforcing the Americans with Disabilities Act, shall be provided relevant information on request.

(2) Information obtained under this section regarding the medical condition or history of any applicant or employee shall not be used for any purpose inconsistent with this part.

§ 60–300.24 Drugs and alcohol.

(a) *Specific activities permitted.* The contractor:

(1) May prohibit the illegal use of drugs and the use of alcohol at the workplace by all employees;

(2) May require that employees not be under the influence of alcohol or be engaging in the illegal use of drugs at the workplace;

(3) May require that all employees behave in conformance with the requirements established under the Drug-Free Workplace Act of 1988 (41 U.S.C. 701 *et seq.*);

(4) May hold an employee who engages in the illegal use of drugs or who is an alcoholic to the same qualification standards for employment or job performance and behavior to which the contractor holds its other employees, even if any unsatisfactory performance or behavior is related to the employee's drug use or alcoholism;

(5) May require that its employees employed in an industry subject to such regulations comply with the standards established in the regulations (if any) of the Departments of Defense and Transportation, and of the Nuclear Regulatory Commission, and other Federal agencies regarding alcohol and the illegal use of drugs; and

(6) May require that employees employed in sensitive positions comply

with the regulations (if any) of the Departments of Defense and Transportation, and of the Nuclear Regulatory Commission, and other Federal agencies that apply to employment in sensitive positions subject to such regulations.

(b) *Drug testing*—(1) *General policy.* For purposes of this part, a test to determine the illegal use of drugs is not considered a medical examination. Thus, the administration of such drug tests by the contractor to its job applicants or employees is not a violation of § 60–300.23. Nothing in this part shall be construed to encourage, prohibit, or authorize the contractor to conduct drug tests of job applicants or employees to determine the illegal use of drugs or to make employment decisions based on such test results.

(2) *Transportation employees.* Nothing in this part shall be construed to encourage, prohibit, or authorize the otherwise lawful exercise by contractors subject to the jurisdiction of the Department of Transportation of authority to test employees in, and applicants for, positions involving safety-sensitive duties for the illegal use of drugs or for on-duty impairment by alcohol; and remove from safety-sensitive positions persons who test positive for illegal use of drugs or on-duty impairment by alcohol pursuant to paragraph (b)(1) of this section.

(3) Any information regarding the medical condition or history of any employee or applicant obtained from a test to determine the illegal use of drugs, except information regarding the illegal use of drugs, is subject to the requirements of §§ 60–300.23(b)(5) and 60–300.23(d)(2).

§ 60–300.25 Health insurance, life insurance and other benefit plans.

(a) An insurer, hospital, or medical service company, health maintenance organization, or any agent or entity that administers benefit plans, or similar organizations may underwrite risks, classify risks, or administer such risks that are based on or not inconsistent with state law.

(b) The contractor may establish, sponsor, observe or administer the terms of a bona fide benefit plan that are based on underwriting risks, classifying risks, or administering such risks that are based on or not inconsistent with state law.

(c) The contractor may establish, sponsor, observe, or administer the terms of a bona fide benefit plan that is not subject to state laws that regulate insurance.

(d) The contractor may not deny a qualified disabled veteran equal access to insurance or subject a qualified disabled veteran to different terms or conditions of insurance based on disability alone, if the disability does not pose increased risks.

(e) The activities described in paragraphs (a), (b) and (c) of this section are permitted unless these activities are used as a subterfuge to evade the purposes of this part.

Subpart C—Affirmative Action Program

§ 60–300.40 Applicability of the affirmative action program requirement.

(a) The requirements of this subpart apply to every Government contractor that has 50 or more employees and a contract of $100,000 or more.

(b) Contractors described in paragraph (a) of this section shall, within 120 days of the commencement of a contract, prepare and maintain an affirmative action program at each establishment. The affirmative action program shall set forth the contractor's policies and procedures in accordance with this part. This program may be integrated into or kept separate from other affirmative action programs.

(c) The affirmative action program shall be reviewed and updated annually.

(d) The contractor shall submit the affirmative action program within 30 days of a request from OFCCP, unless the request provides for a different time. The contractor also shall make the affirmative action program promptly available on-site upon OFCCP's request.

§ 60–300.41 Availability of affirmative action program.

The full affirmative action program shall be available to any employee or applicant for employment for inspection upon request. The location and hours during which the program may be obtained shall be posted at each establishment.

§ 60–300.42 Invitation to self-identify.

(a) *Disabled veterans.* The contractor shall invite applicants to inform the contractor whether the applicant believes that he or she is a disabled veteran who may be covered by the Act and wishes to benefit under the affirmative action program. Such invitation shall be extended after making an offer of employment to a job applicant and before the applicant begins his or her employment duties, except that the contractor may invite disabled veterans to self-identify prior to making a job offer when:

(1) The invitation is made when the contractor actually is undertaking affirmative action for disabled veterans at the pre-offer stage; or

(2) The invitation is made pursuant to a Federal, state or local law requiring affirmative action for disabled veterans.

(b) *Recently separated veterans, other protected veterans, and Armed Forces service medal veterans.* The contractor shall invite applicants to inform the contractor whether the applicant believes that he or she is a recently separated veteran, other protected veteran, or Armed Forces service medal veteran who may be covered by the Act and wishes to benefit under the affirmative action program. Such invitation may be made at any time before the applicant begins his or her employment duties.

(c) The invitations referenced in paragraphs (a) and (b) of this section shall state that a request to benefit under the affirmative action program may be made immediately and/or at any time in the future. The invitations also shall summarize the relevant portions of the Act and the contractor's affirmative action program. Furthermore, the invitations shall state that the information is being requested on a voluntary basis, that it will be kept confidential, that refusal to provide it will not subject the applicant to any adverse treatment, and that it will not be used in a manner inconsistent with the Act. (An acceptable form for such an invitation is set forth in Appendix B of this part. Because a contractor usually may not seek advice from a disabled veteran regarding placement and accommodation until after a job offer has been extended, the invitation set forth in Appendix B of this part contains instructions regarding modifications to be made if it is used at the pre-offer stage.)

(d) If an applicant so identifies himself or herself as a disabled veteran, the contractor should also seek the advice of the applicant regarding proper placement and appropriate accommodation, after a job offer has been extended. The contractor also may make such inquiries to the extent they are consistent with the Americans with Disabilities Act of 1990 (ADA), 42 U.S.C. 12101, (e.g., in the context of asking applicants to describe or demonstrate how they would perform the job). The contractor shall maintain a separate file in accordance with § 60–300.23(d) on persons who have self-identified as disabled veterans.

(e) The contractor shall keep all information on self identification confidential. The contractor shall provide the information to OFCCP upon request. This information may be used only in accordance with this part.

(f) Nothing in this section shall relieve the contractor of its obligation to take affirmative action with respect to those applicants or employees who are known to the contractor to be disabled veterans, recently separated veterans, other protected veterans, or Armed Forces service medal veterans.

(g) Nothing in this section shall relieve the contractor from liability for discrimination under the Act.

§ 60–300.43 Affirmative action policy.

Under the affirmative action obligations imposed by the Act contractors shall not discriminate because of status as a disabled veteran, recently separated veteran, other protected veteran, or Armed Forces service medal veteran and shall take affirmative action to employ and advance in employment qualified disabled veterans, recently separated veterans, other protected veterans, and Armed Forces service medal veterans at all levels of employment, including the executive level. Such action shall apply to all employment activities set forth in § 60–300.20.

§ 60–300.44 Required contents of affirmative action programs.

Acceptable affirmative action programs shall contain, but not necessarily be limited to, the following ingredients:

(a) *Policy statement.* The contractor shall include an equal opportunity policy statement in its affirmative action program, and shall post the policy statement on company bulletin boards. The contractor must ensure that applicants and employees who are disabled veterans are informed of the contents of the policy statement (for example, the contractor may have the statement read to a visually disabled individual, or may lower the posted notice so that it may be read by a person in a wheelchair). The policy statement should indicate the chief executive officer's attitude on the subject matter, provide for an audit and reporting system (see paragraph (h) of this section) and assign overall responsibility for the implementation of affirmative action activities required under this part (see paragraph (i) of this section). Additionally, the policy should state, among other things, that the contractor will: recruit, hire, train and promote persons in all job titles, and ensure that all other personnel actions are administered, without regard to disabled veteran, recently separated veteran, other protected veteran, or Armed Forces service medal veteran status; and ensure that all employment decisions are based only on valid job requirements. The policy shall state that employees and applicants shall not be subjected to harassment, intimidation, threats, coercion or discrimination because they have engaged in or may engage in any of the following activities:

(1) Filing a complaint;

(2) Assisting or participating in an investigation, compliance evaluation, hearing, or any other activity related to the administration of the affirmative action provisions of the Vietnam Era Veterans' Readjustment Assistance Act of 1974, as amended (VEVRAA) or any other Federal, state or local law requiring equal opportunity for disabled veterans, recently separated veterans, other protected veterans, or Armed Forces service medal veterans;

(3) Opposing any act or practice made unlawful by VEVRAA or its implementing regulations in this part or any other Federal, state or local law requiring equal opportunity for disabled veterans, recently separated veterans, other protected veterans, or Armed Forces service medal veterans; or

(4) Exercising any other right protected by VEVRAA or its implementing regulations in this part.

(b) *Review of personnel processes.* The contractor shall ensure that its personnel processes provide for careful, thorough, and systematic consideration of the job qualifications of applicants and employees who are known disabled veterans, recently separated veterans, other protected veterans, or Armed Forces service medal veterans for job vacancies filled either by hiring or promotion, and for all training opportunities offered or available. The contractor shall ensure that when a disabled veteran, recently separated veteran, other protected veteran, or Armed Forces service medal veteran is considered for employment opportunities, the contractor relies only on that portion of the individual's military record, including his or her discharge papers, that is relevant to the requirements of the opportunity in issue. The contractor shall ensure that its personnel processes do not stereotype disabled veterans, recently separated veterans, other protected veterans, and Armed Forces service medal veterans in a manner which limits their access to all jobs for which they are qualified. The contractor shall periodically review such processes and make any necessary modifications to ensure that these obligations are carried out. A description of the review and any necessary modifications to personnel processes or development of new processes shall be included in any affirmative action programs required under this part. The contractor must design procedures that facilitate a review of the implementation of this requirement by the contractor and the Government. (Appendix C of this part is an example of an appropriate set of procedures. The procedures in Appendix C of this part are not required and contractors may develop other procedures appropriate to their circumstances.)

(c) *Physical and mental qualifications.* (1) The contractor shall provide in its affirmative action program, and shall adhere to, a schedule for the periodic review of all physical and mental job qualification standards to ensure that, to the extent qualification standards tend to screen out qualified disabled veterans, they are job-related for the position in question and are consistent with business necessity.

(2) Whenever the contractor applies physical or mental qualification standards in the selection of applicants or employees for employment or other change in employment status such as promotion, demotion or training, to the extent that qualification standards tend to screen out qualified disabled veterans, the standards shall be related to the specific job or jobs for which the individual is being considered and consistent with business necessity. The contractor shall have the burden to demonstrate that it has complied with the requirements of this paragraph (c)(2).

(3) The contractor may use as a defense to an allegation of a violation of paragraph (c)(2) of this section that an individual poses a direct threat to the health or safety of the individual or others in the workplace. (See § 60–300.2(w) defining direct threat.)

(d) *Reasonable accommodation to physical and mental limitations.* As is provided in § 60–300.21(f), as a matter of nondiscrimination the contractor must make reasonable accommodation to the known physical or mental limitations of an otherwise qualified disabled veteran unless it can demonstrate that the accommodation would impose an undue hardship on the operation of its business. As a matter of affirmative action, if an employee who is known to be a disabled veteran is having significant difficulty performing his or her job and it is reasonable to conclude that the performance problem may be related to the known disability, the contractor shall confidentially notify the employee of the performance problem and inquire whether the problem is related to the employee's disability; if the employee responds affirmatively, the contractor shall confidentially inquire whether the employee is in need of a reasonable accommodation.

(e) *Harassment.* The contractor must develop and implement procedures to ensure that its employees are not harassed because of their status as a disabled veteran, recently separated veteran, other protected veteran, or Armed Forces service medal veteran.

(f) *External dissemination of policy, outreach and positive recruitment.* The contractor shall undertake appropriate outreach and positive recruitment activities such as those listed in paragraphs (f)(1) through (f)(8) of this section that are reasonably designed to effectively recruit qualified disabled veterans, recently separated veterans, other protected veterans, and Armed Forces service medal veterans. It is not contemplated that the contractor will necessarily undertake all the activities listed in paragraphs (f)(1) through (f)(8) of this section or that its activities will be limited to those listed. The scope of the contractor's efforts shall depend upon all the circumstances, including the contractor's size and resources and the extent to which existing employment practices are adequate.

(1) The contractor should enlist the assistance and support of the following persons and organizations in recruiting, and developing on-the-job training opportunities for, qualified disabled veterans, recently separated veterans, other protected veterans, and Armed Forces service medal veterans, to fulfill its commitment to provide meaningful employment opportunities to such veterans:

(i) The Local Veterans' Employment Representative in the local employment service office nearest the contractor's establishment;

(ii) The Department of Veterans Affairs Regional Office nearest the contractor's establishment;

(iii) The veterans' counselors and coordinators ("Vet-Reps") on college campuses;

(iv) The service officers of the national veterans' groups active in the area of the contractor's establishment; and

(v) Local veterans' groups and veterans' service centers near the contractor's establishment.

(2) Formal briefing sessions should be held, preferably on company premises, with representatives from recruiting sources. Plant tours, clear and concise explanations of current and future job openings, position descriptions, worker specifications, explanations of the company's selection process, and recruiting literature should be an integral part of the briefing. Formal arrangements should be made for referral of applicants, follow up with sources, and feedback on disposition of applicants.

(3) The contractor's recruitment efforts at all educational institutions should incorporate special efforts to reach students who are disabled veterans, recently separated veterans, other protected veterans, or Armed Forces service medal veterans. An effort should be made to participate in work-study programs with Department of Veterans Affairs rehabilitation facilities which specialize in training or educating disabled veterans.

(4) The contractor should establish meaningful contacts with appropriate veterans' service organizations which serve disabled veterans, recently separated veterans, other protected veterans, or Armed Forces service medal veterans for such purposes as advice, technical assistance, and referral of potential employees. Technical assistance from the resources described in this paragraph may consist of advice on proper placement, recruitment, training and accommodations contractors may undertake, but no such resource providing technical assistance shall have authority to approve or disapprove the acceptability of affirmative action programs.

(5) Disabled veterans, recently separated veterans, other protected veterans, or Armed Forces service medal veterans should be made available for participation in career days, youth motivation programs, and related activities in their communities.

(6) The contractor should send written notification of company policy to all subcontractors, vendors and suppliers, requesting appropriate action on their part.

(7) The contractor should take positive steps to attract qualified disabled veterans, recently separated veterans, other protected veterans, and Armed Forces service medal veterans not currently in the work force who have requisite skills and can be recruited through affirmative action measures. These persons may be located through the local chapters of organizations of and for disabled veterans, recently separated veterans, other protected veterans, and Armed Forces service medal veterans.

(8) The contractor, in making hiring decisions, should consider applicants who are known disabled veterans, recently separated veterans, other protected veterans, or Armed Forces service medal veterans for all available positions for which they may be qualified when the position(s) applied for is unavailable.

(g) *Internal dissemination of policy.* (1) A strong outreach program will be ineffective without adequate internal support from supervisory and management personnel and other employees. In order to assure greater employee cooperation and participation in the contractor's efforts, the contractor shall develop internal procedures such as those listed in paragraph (g)(2) of this section for communication of its obligation to engage in affirmative action efforts to employ and advance in employment qualified disabled veterans, recently separated veterans, other protected veterans, and Armed Forces service medal veterans. It is not contemplated that the contractor will necessarily undertake all the activities listed in paragraph (g)(2) of this section or that its activities will be limited to those listed. These procedures shall be designed to foster understanding, acceptance and support among the contractor's executive, management, supervisory and other employees and to encourage such persons to take the necessary actions to aid the contractor in meeting this obligation. The scope of the contractor's efforts shall depend upon all the circumstances, including the contractor's size and resources and the extent to which existing practices are adequate.

(2) The contractor should implement and disseminate this policy internally as follows:

(i) Include it in the contractor's policy manual;

(ii) Inform all employees and prospective employees of its commitment to engage in affirmative action to increase employment opportunities for qualified disabled veterans, recently separated veterans, other protected veterans, and Armed Forces service medal veterans. The contractor should periodically schedule special meetings with all employees to discuss policy and explain individual employee responsibilities;

(iii) Publicize it in the company newspaper, magazine, annual report and other media;

(iv) Conduct special meetings with executive, management, and supervisory personnel to explain the intent of the policy and individual responsibility for effective implementation, making clear the chief executive officer's attitude;

(v) Discuss the policy thoroughly in both employee orientation and management training programs;

(vi) Meet with union officials and/or employee representatives to inform them of the contractor's policy, and request their cooperation;

(vii) Include articles on accomplishments of disabled veterans, recently separated veterans, other protected veterans, and Armed Forces service medal veterans in company publications; and

(viii) When employees are featured in employee handbooks or similar publications for employees, include disabled veterans.

(h) *Audit and reporting system.* (1) The contractor shall design and implement an audit and reporting system that will:

(i) Measure the effectiveness of the contractor's affirmative action program;

(ii) Indicate any need for remedial action;

(iii) Determine the degree to which the contractor's objectives have been attained;

(iv) Determine whether known disabled veterans, recently separated veterans, other protected veterans, and Armed Forces service medal veterans have had the opportunity to participate in all company sponsored educational, training, recreational and social activities; and

(v) Measure the contractor's compliance with the affirmative action program's specific obligations.

(2) Where the affirmative action program is found to be deficient, the contractor shall undertake necessary action to bring the program into compliance.

(i) *Responsibility for implementation.* An official of the contractor shall be assigned responsibility for implementation of the contractor's affirmative action activities under this part. His or her identity should appear on all internal and external communications regarding the company's affirmative action program. This official shall be given necessary senior management support and staff to manage the implementation of this program.

(j) *Training.* All personnel involved in the recruitment, screening, selection, promotion, disciplinary, and related processes shall be trained to ensure that the commitments in the contractor's affirmative action program are implemented.

Subpart D—General Enforcement and Complaint Procedures

§ 60–300.60 Compliance evaluations.

(a) OFCCP may conduct compliance evaluations to determine if the contractor is taking affirmative action to employ, advance in employment and otherwise treat qualified individuals without discrimination based on their status as a disabled veteran, recently separated veteran, other protected veteran, or Armed Forces service medal veteran in all employment practices. A compliance evaluation may consist of any one or any combination of the following investigative procedures:

(1) *Compliance review.* A comprehensive analysis and evaluation of the hiring and employment practices of the contractor, the written affirmative action program, and the results of the affirmative action efforts undertaken by the contractor. A compliance review may proceed in three stages:

(i) A desk audit of the written affirmative action program and supporting documentation to determine whether all elements required by the regulations in this part are included, whether the affirmative action program meets agency standards of reasonableness, and whether the affirmative action program and supporting documentation satisfy agency standards of acceptability. The desk audit is conducted at OFCCP offices;

(ii) An on-site review, conducted at the contractor's establishment to investigate unresolved problem areas identified in the affirmative action program and supporting documentation during the desk audit, to verify that the contractor has implemented the affirmative action program and has complied with those regulatory obligations not required to be included in the affirmative action program, and to examine potential instances or issues of discrimination. An on-site review normally will involve an examination of the contractor's personnel and employment policies, inspection and copying of documents related to employment actions, and interviews with employees, supervisors, managers, hiring officials; and

(iii) Where necessary, an off-site analysis of information supplied by the contractor or otherwise gathered during or pursuant to the on-site review;

(2) *Off-site review of records.* An analysis and evaluation of the affirmative action program (or any part thereof) and supporting documentation, and other documents related to the contractor's personnel policies and employment actions that may be relevant to a determination of whether the contractor has complied with the requirements of the Executive Order and regulations;

(3) *Compliance check.* A determination of whether the contractor has maintained records consistent with § 60–300.80; at the contractor's option the documents may be provided either onsite or off-site; or

(4) *Focused review.* An on-site review restricted to one or more components of the contractor's organization or one or more aspects of the contractor's employment practices.

(b) Where deficiencies are found to exist, reasonable efforts shall be made to secure compliance through conciliation and persuasion pursuant to § 60–300.62.

(c) *Reporting requirements.* During a compliance evaluation, OFCCP may verify whether the contractor has complied with applicable reporting requirements required under regulations promulgated by the Veterans' Employment and Training Service (VETS). If the contractor has not complied with any such reporting requirement, OFCCP will notify VETS.

§ 60–300.61 Complaint procedures.

(a) *Place and time of filing.* Any applicant for employment with a contractor or any employee of a contractor may, personally, or by an authorized representative, file a written complaint alleging a violation of the Act or the regulations in this part. The complaint may allege individual or class-wide violation(s). Such complaint must be filed within 300 days of the date of the alleged violation, unless the time for filing is extended by OFCCP for good cause shown. Complaints may be submitted to the OFCCP, 200 Constitution Avenue, NW., Washington, DC 20210, or to any OFCCP regional, district, or area office. Complaints may also be submitted to the Veterans' Employment and Training Service of the Department of Labor directly, or through the Local Veterans' Employment Representative (LVER) at the local employment service office. Such parties will assist veterans in preparing complaints, promptly refer such complaints to OFCCP, and maintain a record of all complaints which they receive and forward. OFCCP shall inform the party forwarding the complaint of the progress and results of its complaint investigation. The state workforce agency shall cooperate with the Deputy Assistant Secretary in the investigation of any complaint.

(b) *Contents of complaints*—(1) *In general.* A complaint must be signed by the complainant or his or her authorized representative and must contain the following information:

(i) Name and address (including telephone number) of the complainant;

(ii) Name and address of the contractor who committed the alleged violation;

(iii) Documentation showing that the individual is a disabled veteran, recently separated veteran, other protected veteran, or Armed Forces service medal veteran. Such documentation must include a copy of the veteran's form DD–214, and, where applicable, a copy of the veteran's Benefits Award Letter, or similar Department of Veterans Affairs certification, updated within one year prior to the date the complaint is filed;

(iv) A description of the act or acts considered to be a violation, including the pertinent dates (in the case of an alleged continuing violation, the earliest and most recent date that the alleged violation occurred should be stated); and

(v) Other pertinent information available which will assist in the investigation and resolution of the complaint, including the name of any known Federal agency with which the employer has contracted.

(2) *Third party complaints.* A complaint filed by an authorized representative need not identify by name the person on whose behalf it is filed. The person filing the complaint, however, shall provide OFCCP with the name, address and telephone number of the person on whose behalf it is made, and the other information specified in paragraph (b)(1) of this section. OFCCP shall verify the authorization of such a complaint by the person on whose behalf the complaint is made. Any such person may request that OFCCP keep his or her identity confidential, and OFCCP will protect the individual's confidentiality wherever that is possible given the facts and circumstances in the complaint.

(c) *Incomplete information.* Where a complaint contains incomplete information, OFCCP shall seek the needed information from the complainant. If the information is not furnished to OFCCP within 60 days of the date of such request, the case may be closed.

(d) *Investigations.* The Department of Labor shall institute a prompt investigation of each complaint.

(e) *Resolution of matters.* (1) If the complaint investigation finds no violation of the Act or this part, or if the Deputy Assistant Secretary decides not to refer the matter to the Solicitor of Labor for enforcement proceedings against the contractor pursuant to § 60–300.65(a)(1), the complainant and contractor shall be so notified. The Deputy Assistant Secretary, on his or her own initiative, may reconsider his or her determination or the determination of any of his or her designated officers who have authority to issue Notifications of Results of Investigation.

(2) The Deputy Assistant Secretary will review all determinations of no violation that involve complaints that are not also cognizable under Title I of the Americans with Disabilities Act.

(3) In cases where the Deputy Assistant Secretary decides to reconsider the determination of a Notification of Results of Investigation, the Deputy Assistant Secretary shall provide prompt notification of his or her intent to reconsider, which is effective upon issuance, and his or her final determination after reconsideration, to the person claiming to be aggrieved, the person making the complaint on behalf of such person, if any, and the contractor.

(4) If the investigation finds a violation of the Act or this part, OFCCP shall invite the contractor to participate in conciliation discussions pursuant to § 60–300.62.

§ 60–300.62 Conciliation agreements.

If a compliance evaluation, complaint investigation or other review by OFCCP finds a material violation of the Act or this part, and if the contractor is willing to correct the violations and/or deficiencies, and if OFCCP determines that settlement on that basis (rather than referral for consideration of formal enforcement) is appropriate, a written conciliation agreement shall be required. The agreement shall provide for such remedial action as may be necessary to correct the violations and/or deficiencies noted, including, where appropriate (but not necessarily limited to) such make whole remedies as back pay and retroactive seniority. The agreement shall also specify the time period for completion of the remedial action; the period shall be no longer than the minimum period necessary to complete the action.

§ 60–300.63 Violation of conciliation agreements.

(a) When OFCCP believes that a conciliation agreement has been violated, the following procedures are applicable:

(1) A written notice shall be sent to the contractor setting forth the violation alleged and summarizing the supporting evidence. The contractor shall have 15 days from receipt of the notice to respond, except in those cases in which OFCCP asserts that such a delay would result in irreparable injury to the employment rights of affected employees or applicants.

(2) During the 15-day period the contractor may demonstrate in writing that it has not violated its commitments.

(b) In those cases in which OFCCP asserts that a delay would result in irreparable injury to the employment rights of affected employees or applicants, enforcement proceedings may be initiated immediately without proceeding through any other requirement contained in this chapter.

(c) In any proceedings involving an alleged violation of a conciliation agreement OFCCP may seek enforcement of the agreement itself and shall not be required to present proof of the underlying violations resolved by the agreement.

§ 60–300.64 Show cause notices.

When the Deputy Assistant Secretary has reasonable cause to believe that the contractor has violated the Act or this part, he or she may issue a notice requiring the contractor to show cause, within 30 days, why monitoring, enforcement proceedings or other appropriate action to ensure compliance should not be instituted. The issuance of such a notice is not a prerequisite to instituting enforcement proceedings (see § 60–300.65).

§ 60–300.65 Enforcement proceedings.

(a) *General.* (1) If a compliance evaluation, complaint investigation or other review by OFCCP finds a violation of the Act or this part, and the violation has not been corrected in accordance with the conciliation procedures in this part, or OFCCP determines that referral for consideration of formal enforcement (rather than settlement) is appropriate, OFCCP may refer the matter to the Solicitor of Labor with a recommendation for the institution of enforcement proceedings to enjoin the violations, to seek appropriate relief, and to impose appropriate sanctions, or any of the above in this sentence. OFCCP may seek back pay and other make whole relief for aggrieved individuals identified during a complaint investigation or compliance evaluation. Such individuals need not have filed a complaint as a prerequisite to OFCCP seeking such relief on their behalf. Interest on back pay shall be calculated from the date of the loss and compounded quarterly at the percentage rate established by the Internal Revenue Service for the underpayment of taxes.

(2) In addition to the administrative proceedings set forth in this section, the Deputy Assistant Secretary may, within the limitations of applicable law, seek appropriate judicial action to enforce the contractual provisions set forth in § 60–300.5, including appropriate injunctive relief.

(b) *Hearing practice and procedure.* (1) In administrative enforcement proceedings the contractor shall be provided an opportunity for a formal hearing. All hearings conducted under the Act and this part shall be governed by the Rules of Practice for Administrative Proceedings to Enforce Equal Opportunity Under Executive Order 11246 contained in 41 CFR part 60–30 and the Rules of Evidence set out in the Rules of Practice and Procedure for Administrative Hearings Before the Office of Administrative Law Judges contained in 29 CFR part 18, subpart B: *Provided,* That a final administrative order shall be issued within one year from the date of the issuance of the recommended findings, conclusions and decision of the Administrative Law Judge, or the submission of exceptions and responses to exceptions to such decision (if any), whichever is later.

(2) Complaints may be filed by the Solicitor, the Associate Solicitor for Civil Rights and Labor-Management,

Regional Solicitors, and Associate Regional Solicitors.

(3) For the purposes of hearings pursuant to this part, references in 41 CFR part 60–30 to "Executive Order 11246" shall mean the Vietnam Era Veterans' Readjustment Assistance Act of 1974, as amended; to "equal opportunity clause" shall mean the equal opportunity clause published at §60–300.5; and to "regulations" shall mean the regulations contained in this part.

§60–300.66 Sanctions and penalties.

(a) *Withholding progress payments.* With the prior approval of the Deputy Assistant Secretary, so much of the accrued payment due on the contract or any other contract between the Government contractor and the Federal Government may be withheld as necessary to correct any violations of the provisions of the Act or this part.

(b) *Termination.* A contract may be canceled or terminated, in whole or in part, for failure to comply with the provisions of the Act or this part.

(c) *Debarment.* A contractor may be debarred from receiving future contracts for failure to comply with the provisions of the Act or this part subject to reinstatement pursuant to §60–300.68. Debarment may be imposed for an indefinite period, or may be imposed for a fixed period of not less than six months but no more than three years.

(d) *Hearing opportunity.* An opportunity for a formal hearing shall be afforded to a contractor before the imposition of any sanction or penalty.

§60–300.67 Notification of agencies.

The Deputy Assistant Secretary shall ensure that the heads of all agencies are notified of any debarments taken against any contractor.

§60–300.68 Reinstatement of ineligible contractors.

(a) *Application for reinstatement.* A contractor debarred from further contracts for an indefinite period under the Act may request reinstatement in a letter filed with the Deputy Assistant Secretary at any time after the effective date of the debarment; a contractor debarred for a fixed period may make such a request following the expiration of six months from the effective date of the debarment. In connection with the reinstatement proceedings, all debarred contractors shall be required to show that they have established and will carry out employment policies and practices in compliance with the Act and this part. Additionally, in determining whether reinstatement is appropriate for a contractor debarred for a fixed period, the Deputy Assistant Secretary also shall consider, among other factors, the severity of the violation which resulted in the debarment, the contractor's attitude towards compliance, the contractor's past compliance history, and whether the contractor's reinstatement would impede the effective enforcement of the Act or this part. Before reaching a decision, the Deputy Assistant Secretary may conduct a compliance evaluation of the contractor and may require the contractor to supply additional information regarding the request for reinstatement. The Deputy Assistant Secretary shall issue a written decision on the request.

(b) *Petition for review.* Within 30 days of its receipt of a decision denying a request for reinstatement, the contractor may file a petition for review of the decision with the Secretary. The petition shall set forth the grounds for the contractor's objections to the Deputy Assistant Secretary's decision. The petition shall be served on the Deputy Assistant Secretary and the Associate Solicitor for Civil Rights and Labor-Management and shall include the decision as an appendix. The Deputy Assistant Secretary may file a response within 14 days to the petition. The Secretary shall issue the final agency decision denying or granting the request for reinstatement. Before reaching a final decision, the Secretary may issue such additional orders respecting procedure as he or she finds appropriate in the circumstances, including an order referring the matter to the Office of Administrative Law Judges for an evidentiary hearing where there is a material factual dispute that cannot be resolved on the record before the Secretary.

§ 60–300.69 Intimidation and interference.

(a) The contractor shall not harass, intimidate, threaten, coerce, or discriminate against any individual because the individual has engaged in or may engage in any of the following activities:

(1) Filing a complaint;

(2) Assisting or participating in any manner in an investigation, compliance evaluation, hearing, or any other activity related to the administration of the Act or any other Federal, state or local law requiring equal opportunity for disabled veterans, recently separated veterans, other protected veterans, or Armed Forces service medal veterans;

(3) Opposing any act or practice made unlawful by the Act or this part or any other Federal, state or local law requiring equal opportunity for disabled veterans, recently separated veterans, other protected veterans, or Armed Forces service medal veterans, or

(4) Exercising any other right protected by the Act or this part.

(b) The contractor shall ensure that all persons under its control do not engage in such harassment, intimidation, threats, coercion or discrimination. The sanctions and penalties contained in this part may be exercised by the Deputy Assistant Secretary against any contractor who violates this obligation.

§ 60–300.70 Disputed matters related to compliance with the Act.

The procedures set forth in the regulations in this part govern all disputes relative to the contractor's compliance with the Act and this part. Any disputes relating to issues other than compliance, including contract costs arising out of the contractor's efforts to comply, shall be determined by the disputes clause of the contract.

Subpart E—Ancillary Matters

§ 60–300.80 Recordkeeping.

(a) *General requirements.* Any personnel or employment record made or kept by the contractor shall be preserved by the contractor for a period of two years from the date of the making of the record or the personnel action involved, whichever occurs later. However, if the contractor has fewer than 150 employees or does not have a Government contract of at least $150,000, the minimum record retention period shall be one year from the date of the making of the record or the personnel action involved, whichever occurs later. Such records include, but are not necessarily limited to, records relating to requests for reasonable accommodation; the results of any physical examination; job advertisements and postings; applications and resumes; tests and test results; interview notes; and other records having to do with hiring, assignment, promotion, demotion, transfer, lay-off or termination, rates of pay or other terms of compensation, and selection for training or apprenticeship. In the case of involuntary termination of an employee, the personnel records of the individual terminated shall be kept for a period of two years from the date of the termination, except that contractors that have fewer than 150 employees or that do not have a Government contract of at least $150,000 shall keep such records for a period of one year from the date of the termination. Where the contractor has received notice that a complaint of discrimination has been filed, that a compliance evaluation has been initiated, or that an enforcement action has been commenced, the contractor shall preserve all personnel records relevant to the complaint, compliance evaluation or action until final disposition of the complaint, compliance evaluation or action. The term *personnel records relevant to the complaint, compliance evaluation or action* would include, for example, personnel or employment records relating to the aggrieved person and to all other employees holding positions similar to that held or sought by the aggrieved person, and application forms or test papers completed by an unsuccessful applicant and by all other candidates for the same position as that for which the aggrieved person applied and was rejected.

(b) *Failure to preserve records.* Failure to preserve complete and accurate records as required by paragraph (a) of this section constitutes noncompliance with the contractor's obligations under the Act and this part. Where the contractor has destroyed or failed to preserve records as required by this section, there may be a presumption that the information destroyed or not preserved would have been unfavorable to the contractor: *Provided*, That this presumption shall not apply where the contractor shows that the destruction or failure to preserve records results from circumstances that are outside of the contractor's control.

(c) The requirements of this section shall apply only to records made or kept on or after the date that the Office of Management and Budget has cleared the requirements.

§ 60–300.81 Access to records.

Each contractor shall permit access during normal business hours to its places of business for the purpose of conducting on-site compliance evaluations and complaint investigations and inspecting and copying such books and accounts and records, including computerized records, and other material as may be relevant to the matter under investigation and pertinent to compliance with the Act or this part. Information obtained in this manner shall be used only in connection with the administration of the Act and in furtherance of the purposes of the Act.

§ 60–300.82 Labor organizations and recruiting and training agencies.

(a) Whenever performance in accordance with the equal opportunity clause or any matter contained in the regulations in this part may necessitate a revision of a collective bargaining agreement, the labor organizations which are parties to such agreement shall be given an adequate opportunity to present their views to OFCCP.

(b) OFCCP shall use its best efforts, directly or through contractors, subcontractors, local officials, the Department of Veterans Affairs, vocational rehabilitation facilities, and all other available instrumentalities, to cause any labor organization, recruiting and training agency or other representative of workers who are employed by a contractor to cooperate with, and to assist in, the implementation of the purposes of the Act.

§ 60–300.83 Rulings and interpretations.

Rulings under or interpretations of the Act and this part shall be made by the Deputy Assistant Secretary.

§ 60–300.84 Responsibilities of appropriate employment service delivery system.

By statute, appropriate employment service delivery systems are required to refer qualified disabled veterans, recently separated veterans, other protected veterans, and Armed Forces service medal veterans to fill employment openings listed by contractors with such appropriate employment delivery systems pursuant to the mandatory job listing requirements of the equal opportunity clause and are required to give priority to disabled veterans, recently separated veterans, other protected veterans, and Armed Forces service medal veterans in making such referrals. The employment service delivery systems shall provide OFCCP, upon request, information pertinent to whether the contractor is in compliance with the mandatory job listing requirements of the equal opportunity clause.

APPENDIX A TO PART 60–300—GUIDELINES ON A CONTRACTOR'S DUTY TO PROVIDE REASONABLE ACCOMMODATION

The guidelines in this appendix are in large part derived from, and are consistent with, the discussion regarding the duty to provide reasonable accommodation contained in the Interpretive Guidance on Title I of the Americans with Disabilities Act (ADA) set out as an appendix to the regulations issued by the Equal Employment Opportunity Commission (EEOC) implementing the ADA (29 CFR part 1630). Although the following discussion is intended to provide an independent "free-standing" source of guidance with respect to the duty to provide reasonable accommodation under this part, to the extent that the EEOC appendix provides additional guidance which is consistent with the following discussion, it may be relied upon for purposes of this part as well. *See* § 60–300.1(c). Contractors are obligated to provide reasonable accommodation and to take affirmative action. Reasonable accommodation under VEVRAA, like reasonable accommodation required under Section 503 and the

ADA, is a part of the nondiscrimination obligation. *See* EEOC appendix cited in this paragraph. Affirmative action is unique to VEVRAA and Section 503, and includes actions above and beyond those required as a matter of nondiscrimination. An example of this is the requirement discussed in paragraph 2 of this appendix that a contractor shall make an inquiry of a disabled veteran who is having significant difficulty performing his or her job.

1. A contractor is required to make reasonable accommodations to the known physical or mental limitations of an "otherwise qualified" disabled veteran, unless the contractor can demonstrate that the accommodation would impose an undue hardship on the operation of its business. As stated in §60–300.2(o), a disabled veteran is qualified if he or she has the ability to perform the essential functions of the position with or without reasonable accommodation. A contractor is required to make a reasonable accommodation with respect to its application process if the disabled veteran is qualified with respect to that process. One is "otherwise qualified" if he or she is qualified for a job, except that, because of a disability, he or she needs a reasonable accommodation to be able to perform the job's essential functions.

2. Although the contractor would not be expected to accommodate disabilities of which it is unaware, the contractor has an affirmative obligation to provide a reasonable accommodation for applicants and employees who are known to be disabled veterans. As stated in §60–300.42(a) (see also Appendix B of this part), the contractor is required to invite applicants who have been provided an offer of employment, before they are placed on the contractor's payroll, to indicate whether they are a disabled veteran who may be covered by the Act and wish to benefit under the contractor's affirmative action program. Section 60–300.42(d) further provides that the contractor should seek the advice of disabled veterans who "self-identify" in this way as to proper placement and appropriate accommodation. Moreover, §60–300.44(d) provides that if an employee who is a known disabled veteran is having significant difficulty performing his or her job and it is reasonable to conclude that the performance problem may be related to the disability, the contractor is required to confidentially inquire whether the problem is disability related and if the employee is in need of a reasonable accommodation.

3. An accommodation is any change in the work environment or in the way things are customarily done that enables a disabled veteran to enjoy equal employment opportunities. Equal employment opportunity means an opportunity to attain the same level of performance, or to enjoy the same level of benefits and privileges of employment, as are available to the average similarly situated employee without a disability. Thus, for example, an accommodation made to assist an employee who is a disabled veteran in the performance of his or her job must be adequate to enable the individual to perform the essential functions of the position. The accommodation, however, does not have to be the "best" accommodation possible, so long as it is sufficient to meet the job-related needs of the individual being accommodated. There are three areas in which reasonable accommodations may be necessary: (1) Accommodations in the application process; (2) accommodations that enable employees who are disabled veterans to perform the essential functions of the position held or desired; and (3) accommodations that enable employees who are disabled veterans to enjoy equal benefits and privileges of employment as are enjoyed by employees without disabilities.

4. The term "undue hardship" refers to any accommodation that would be unduly costly, extensive, substantial, or disruptive, or that would fundamentally alter the nature or operation of the contractor's business. The contractor's claim that the cost of a particular accommodation will impose an undue hardship requires a determination of which financial resources should be considered—those of the contractor in its entirety or only those of the facility that will be required to provide the accommodation. This inquiry requires an analysis of the financial relationship between the contractor and the facility in order to determine what resources will be available to the facility in providing the accommodation. If the contractor can show that the cost of the accommodation would impose an undue hardship, it would still be required to provide the accommodation if the funding is available from another source, e.g., the Department of Veterans Affairs or a state vocational rehabilitation agency, or if Federal, state or local tax deductions or tax credits are available to offset the cost of the accommodation. In the absence of such funding, the disabled veteran should be given the option of providing the accommodation or of paying that portion of the cost which constitutes the undue hardship on the operation of the business.

5. Section 60–300.2(t) lists a number of examples of the most common types of accommodations that the contractor may be required to provide. There are any number of specific accommodations that may be appropriate for particular situations. The discussion in this appendix is not intended to provide an exhaustive list of required accommodations (as no such list would be feasible); rather, it is intended to provide general guidance regarding the nature of the obligation. The decision as to whether a reasonable accommodation is appropriate must be made

on a case-by-case basis. The contractor generally should consult with the disabled veteran in deciding on the appropriate accommodation; frequently, the individual will know exactly what accommodation he or she will need to perform successfully in a particular job, and may suggest an accommodation which is simpler and less expensive than the accommodation the contractor might have devised. Other resources to consult include the appropriate state vocational rehabilitation services agency, the Equal Employment Opportunity Commission (1–800–669–4000 (voice), 1–800–669–6820 (TTY)), the Job Accommodation Network (JAN) operated by the Office of Disability Employment Policy in the U.S. Department of Labor (1–800–526–7234 or 1–800–232–9675), private disability organizations (including those that serve veterans), and other employers.

6. With respect to accommodations that can permit an employee who is a disabled veteran to perform essential functions successfully, a reasonable accommodation may require the contractor to, for instance, modify or acquire equipment. For the visually-impaired such accommodations may include providing adaptive hardware and software for computers, electronic visual aids, braille devices, talking calculators, magnifiers, audio recordings and braille or large-print materials. For persons with hearing impairments, reasonable accommodations may include providing telephone handset amplifiers, telephones compatible with hearing aids and telecommunications devices for the deaf (TDDs). For persons with limited physical dexterity, the obligation may require the provision of goose neck telephone headsets, mechanical page turners and raised or lowered furniture.

7. Other reasonable accommodations of this type may include providing personal assistants such as a reader, interpreter or travel attendant, permitting the use of accrued paid leave or providing additional unpaid leave for necessary treatment. The contractor may also be required to make existing facilities readily accessible to and usable by disabled veterans—including areas used by employees for purposes other than the performance of essential job functions such as restrooms, break rooms, cafeterias, lounges, auditoriums, libraries, parking lots and credit unions. This type of accommodation will enable employees to enjoy equal benefits and privileges of employment as are enjoyed by employees who do not have disabilities.

8. Another of the potential accommodations listed in §60–300.2(t) is job restructuring. This may involve reallocating or redistributing those nonessential, marginal job functions which a qualified disabled veteran cannot perform to another position. Accordingly, if a clerical employee who is a disabled veteran is occasionally required to lift heavy boxes containing files, but cannot do so because of a disability, this task may be reassigned to another employee. The contractor, however, is not required to reallocate essential functions, *i.e.*, those functions that the individual who holds the job would have to perform, with or without reasonable accommodation, in order to be considered qualified for the position. For instance, the contractor which has a security guard position which requires the incumbent to inspect identity cards would not have to provide a blind disabled veteran with an assistant to perform that duty; in such a case, the assistant would be performing an essential function of the job for the disabled veteran. Job restructuring may also involve allowing part-time or modified work schedules. For instance, flexible or adjusted work schedules could benefit disabled veterans who cannot work a standard schedule because of the need to obtain medical treatment, or disabled veterans with mobility impairments who depend on a public transportation system that is not accessible during the hours of a standard schedule.

9. Reasonable accommodation may also include reassignment to a vacant position. In general, reassignment should be considered only when accommodation within the disabled veteran's current position would pose an undue hardship. Reassignment is not required for applicants. However, in making hiring decisions, contractors are encouraged to consider applicants who are known disabled veterans for all available positions for which they may be qualified when the position(s) applied for is unavailable. Reassignment may not be used to limit, segregate, or otherwise discriminate against employees who are disabled veterans by forcing reassignments to undesirable positions or to designated offices or facilities. Employers should reassign the individual to an equivalent position in terms of pay, status, etc., if the individual is qualified, and if the position is vacant within a reasonable amount of time. A "reasonable amount of time" should be determined in light of the totality of the circumstances.

10. The contractor may reassign an individual to a lower graded position if there are no accommodations that would enable the employee to remain in the current position and there are no vacant equivalent positions for which the individual is qualified with or without reasonable accommodation. The contractor may maintain the reassigned disabled veteran at the salary of the higher graded position, and must do so if it maintains the salary of reassigned employees who are not disabled veterans. It should also be noted that the contractor is not required to promote a disabled veteran as an accommodation.

11. With respect to the application process, appropriate accommodations may include

the following: (1) Providing information regarding job vacancies in a form accessible to disabled veterans who are vision or hearing impaired, e.g., by making an announcement available in braille, in large print, or on audio tape, or by responding to job inquiries via TDDs; (2) providing readers, interpreters and other similar assistance during the application, testing and interview process; (3) appropriately adjusting or modifying employment-related examinations, e.g., extending regular time deadlines, allowing a disabled veteran who is blind or has a learning disorder such as dyslexia to provide oral answers for a written test, and permitting an applicant, regardless of the nature of his or her ability, to demonstrate skills through alternative techniques and utilization of adapted tools, aids and devices; and (4) ensuring a disabled veteran with a mobility impairment full access to testing locations such that the applicant's test scores accurately reflect the applicant's skills or aptitude rather than the applicant's mobility impairment.

APPENDIX B TO PART 60–300—SAMPLE INVITATION TO SELF-IDENTIFY

NOTE: When the invitation to self-identify is being extended to disabled veterans prior to an offer of employment, as is permitted in limited circumstances under §§ 60–300.42(a)(1) and (2), paragraph 7(ii) of this appendix, relating to identification of reasonable accommodations, should be omitted. This will avoid a conflict with the EEOC's ADA Guidance, which in most cases precludes asking a job applicant (prior to a job offer being made) about potential reasonable accommodations.

[Sample Invitation to Self-Identify]

1. This employer is a Government contractor subject to the Vietnam Era Veterans' Readjustment Assistance Act of 1974, as amended, which requires Government contractors to take affirmative action to employ and advance in employment qualified disabled veterans, recently separated veterans, other protected veterans, and Armed Forces service medal veterans.

2. [THE FOLLOWING TEXT SHOULD BE USED WHEN EXTENDING AN INVITATION TO RECENTLY SEPARATED VETERANS, OTHER PROTECTED VETERANS, AND ARMED FORCES SERVICE MEDAL VETERANS ONLY.] If you are a recently separated veteran, other protected veteran, or Armed Forces service medal veteran, we would like to include you under our affirmative action program. If you would like to be included under the affirmative action program, please tell us. The term "recently separated veteran" refers to any veteran during the three-year period beginning on the date of such veteran's discharge or release from active duty. The term "other protected veteran" refers to a person who served on active duty during a war or in a campaign or expedition for which a campaign badge has been authorized, under laws administered by the Department of Defense. The term "Armed Forces service medal veteran" refers to a person who, while serving on active duty in the Armed Forces, participated in a United States military operation for which an Armed Forces service medal was awarded pursuant to Executive Order 12985 (62 FR 1209).

[THE FOLLOWING TEXT SHOULD BE USED WHEN EXTENDING AN INVITATION TO DISABLED VETERANS ONLY.] If you are a disabled veteran, we would like to include you in our affirmative action program. If you would like to be included under the affirmative action program, please tell us. This information will assist us in placing you in an appropriate position and in making accommodations for your disability. The term "disabled veteran" refers to a veteran who is entitled to compensation (or who but for the receipt of military retired pay would be entitled to compensation) under laws administered by the Secretary, or was discharged or released from active duty because of a service-connected disability.

[THE FOLLOWING TEXT SHOULD BE USED WHEN EXTENDING AN INVITATION TO DISABLED VETERANS AS WELL AS RECENTLY SEPARATED VETERANS, OTHER PROTECTED VETERANS, AND ARMED FORCES SERVICE MEDAL VETERANS.] If you are a disabled veteran, recently separated veteran, other protected veteran, or Armed Forces service medal veteran, we would like to include you under our affirmative action program. If you would like to be included under the affirmative action program, please tell us. [The contractor should include here the definitions of "disabled veteran," "recently separated veteran," "other protected veteran," and "Armed Forces service medal veteran" found in the two preceding paragraphs.]

3. You may inform us of your desire to benefit under the program at this time and/or at any time in the future.

4. Submission of this information is voluntary and refusal to provide it will not subject you to any adverse treatment. The information provided will be used only in ways that are not inconsistent with the Vietnam Era Veterans' Readjustment Assistance Act of 1974, as amended.

5. The information you submit will be kept confidential, except that (i) supervisors and managers may be informed regarding restrictions on the work or duties of disabled veterans, and regarding necessary accommodations; (ii) first aid and safety personnel may

be informed, when and to the extent appropriate, if you have a condition that might require emergency treatment; and (iii) Government officials engaged in enforcing laws administered by OFCCP, or enforcing the Americans with Disabilities Act, may be informed.

6. [The contractor should here insert a brief provision summarizing the relevant portion of its affirmative action program.]

7. [THE FOLLOWING TEXT SHOULD BE USED ONLY WHEN EXTENDING AN INVITATION TO DISABLED VETERANS, EITHER BY THEMSELVES OR IN COMBINATION WITH RECENTLY SEPARATED VETERANS, OTHER PROTECTED VETERANS, AND ARMED FORCES SERVICE MEDAL VETERANS. PARAGRAPH 7(II) SHOULD BE OMITTED WHEN THE INVITATION TO SELF-IDENTIFY IS BEING EXTENDED PRIOR TO AN OFFER OF EMPLOYMENT.] If you are a disabled veteran it would assist us if you tell us about (i) any special methods, skills, and procedures which qualify you for positions that you might not otherwise be able to do because of your disability so that you will be considered for any positions of that kind, and (ii) the accommodations which we could make which would enable you to perform the job properly and safely, including special equipment, changes in the physical layout of the job, elimination of certain duties relating to the job, provision of personal assistance services or other accommodations. This information will assist us in placing you in an appropriate position and in making accommodations for your disability.

APPENDIX C TO PART 60–300—REVIEW OF PERSONNEL PROCESSES

The following is a set of procedures which contractors may use to meet the requirements of §60–300.44(b):

1. The application or personnel form of each known applicant who is a disabled veteran, recently separated veteran, other protected veteran, or Armed Forces service medal veteran should be annotated to identify each vacancy for which the applicant was considered, and the form should be quickly retrievable for review by the Department of Labor and the contractor's personnel officials for use in investigations and internal compliance activities.

2. The personnel or application records of each known disabled veteran, recently separated veteran, other protected veteran, or Armed Forces service medal veteran should include (i) the identification of each promotion for which the covered veteran was considered, and (ii) the identification of each training program for which the covered veteran was considered.

3. In each case where an employee or applicant who is a disabled veteran, recently separated veteran, other protected veteran, or Armed Forces service medal veteran is rejected for employment, promotion, or training, the contractor should prepare a statement of the reason as well as a description of the accommodations considered (for a rejected disabled veteran). The statement of the reason for rejection (if the reason is medically related), and the description of the accommodations considered, should be treated as confidential medical records in accordance with §60–300.23(d). These materials should be available to the applicant or employee concerned upon request.

4. Where applicants or employees are selected for hire, promotion, or training and the contractor undertakes any accommodation which makes it possible for him or her to place a disabled veteran on the job, the contractor should make a record containing a description of the accommodation. The record should be treated as a confidential medical record in accordance with §60–300.23(d).

PART 60–741—AFFIRMATIVE ACTION AND NONDISCRIMINATION OBLIGATIONS OF CONTRACTORS AND SUBCONTRACTORS REGARDING INDIVIDUALS WITH DISABILITIES

Subpart A—Preliminary Matters, Equal Opportunity Clause

Subpart B—Discrimination Prohibited

Subpart C—Affirmative Action Program

Subpart D—General Enforcement and Complaint Procedures

Subpart E—Ancillary Matters

AUTHORITY: 29 U.S.C. 706 and 793; and E.O. 11758 (3 CFR, 1971–1975 Comp., p. 841).

SOURCE: 61 FR 19350, May 1, 1996, unless otherwise noted.

Subpart A—Preliminary Matters, Equal Opportunity Clause

§ 60–741.1 Purpose, applicability, and construction.

(a) *Purpose.* The purpose of this part is to set forth the standards for compliance with section 503 of the Rehabilitation Act of 1973, as amended (29 U.S.C. 793), which requires Government contractors and subcontractors to take affirmative action to employ and advance in employment qualified individuals with disabilities.

(b) *Applicability.* This part applies to all Government contracts and subcontracts in excess of $10,000 for the purchase, sale or use of personal property or nonpersonal services (including construction): *Provided,* That subpart C of this part applies only as described in § 60–741.40(a). Compliance by the contractor with the provisions of this part will not necessarily determine its compliance with other statutes, and compliance with other statutes will not necessarily determine its compliance with this part: *Provided,* That compliance shall also satisfy the employment provisions of the Department of Labor's regulations implementing section 504 of the Rehabilitation Act of 1973 (see 29 CFR 32.2(b)) when the contractor is also subject to those requirements.

(c) *Construction*—(1) *In general.* Except as otherwise provided in this part, this part does not apply a lesser standard than the standards applied under title I of the Americans with Disabilities Act of 1990 (42 U.S.C. 12101 *et seq.*), or the regulations issued by the Equal Employment Opportunity Commission pursuant to that title (29 CFR part 1630). The Interpretive Guidance on Title I of the Americans with Disabilities Act set out as an appendix to 29 CFR part 1630 issued pursuant to that title may be relied upon for guidance in interpreting the parallel provisions of this part.

(2) *Relationship to other laws.* This part does not invalidate or limit the remedies, rights, and procedures under any Federal law or the law of any State or political subdivision that provides greater or equal protection for the rights of individuals with disabilities as compared to the protection afforded by this part. It may be a defense to a charge of violation of this part that a challenged action is required or necessitated by another Federal law or regulation, or that another Federal law or regulation prohibits an action (including the provision of a particular reasonable accommodation) that would otherwise be required by this part.

§ 60–741.2 Definitions.

(a) *Act* means the Rehabilitation Act of 1973, Pub. L. 93–112 (29 U.S.C 706 and 793), as amended by sec. 111, Pub. L. 93–516; sec. 103(d)(2)(B), Pub. L. 99–506; sec. 9, Pub. L. 100–259; sec. 512, Pub. L. 101–336 ; and secs. 102 and 505, Pub. L. 102–569.

(b) *Equal opportunity clause* means the contract provisions set forth in § 60–741.5, "Equal opportunity clause."

(c) *Secretary* means the Secretary of Labor, United States Department of Labor, or his or her designee.

(d) *Deputy Assistant Secretary* means the Deputy Assistant Secretary for Federal Contract Compliance of the United States Department of Labor, or his or her designee.

(e) *Government* means the Government of the United States of America.

(f) *United States*, as used herein, shall include the several States, the District of Columbia, the Virgin Islands, the Commonwealth of Puerto Rico, Guam, American Samoa, the Commonwealth of the Northern Mariana Islands, and Wake Island.

(g) *Recruiting and training agency* means any person who refers workers to any contractor, or who provides or supervises apprenticeship or training for employment by any contractor.

(h) *Contract* means any Government contract or subcontract.

(i) *Government contract* means any agreement or modification thereof between any contracting agency and any person for the purchase, sale or use of personal property or nonpersonal services (including construction). The term *Government contract* does not include agreements in which the parties stand in the relationship of employer and employee, and federally assisted contracts.

(1) *Modification* means any alteration in the terms and conditions of a contract, including supplemental agreements, amendments and extensions.

(2) *Contracting agency* means any department, agency, establishment or instrumentality of the United States, including any wholly owned Government corporation, which enters into contracts.

(3) *Person*, as used in paragraphs (i) and (l) of this section, means any natural person, corporation, partnership or joint venture, unincorporated association, State or local government, and any agency, instrumentality, or subdivision of such a government.

(4) *Nonpersonal services*, as used in paragraphs (i) and (l) of this section, includes, but is not limited to, the following: Utility, construction, transportation, research, insurance, and fund depository.

(5) *Construction*, as used in paragraphs (i) and (l) of this section, means the construction, rehabilitation, alteration, conversion, extension, demolition, or repair of buildings, highways, or other changes or improvements to real property, including facilities providing utility services. The term also includes the supervision, inspection, and other on-site functions incidental to the actual construction.

(6) *Personal property*, as used in paragraphs (i) and (l) of this section, includes supplies and contracts for the use of real property (such as lease arrangements), unless the contract for the use of real property itself constitutes real property (such as easements).

(j) *Contractor* means, unless otherwise indicated, a prime contractor or subcontractor holding a contract in excess of $10,000.

(k) *Prime contractor* means any person holding a contract in excess of $10,000, and, for the purposes of subpart D of this part, "General Enforcement and Complaint Procedures," includes any person who has held a contract subject to the act.

(l) *Subcontract* means any agreement or arrangement between a contractor and any person (in which the parties do not stand in the relationship of an employer and an employee):

(1) For the purchase, sale or use of personal property or nonpersonal services (including construction) which, in whole or in part, is necessary to the performance of any one or more contracts; or

(2) Under which any portion of the contractor's obligation under any one or more contracts is performed, undertaken, or assumed.

(m) *Subcontractor* means any person holding a subcontract in excess of $10,000 and, for the purposes of subpart D of this part, "General Enforcement and Complaint Procedures," any person who has held a subcontract subject to the act.

(n)(1) *Individual with a disability* means any person who:

(i) Has a physical or mental impairment which substantially limits one or more of such person's major life activities;

(ii) Has a record of such an impairment; or

(iii) Is regarded as having such an impairment.

(2) See § 60–741.3 for exceptions to the definition in paragraph (n)(1) of this section.

(o) *Physical or mental impairment* means:

(1) Any physiological disorder, or condition, cosmetic disfigurement, or anatomical loss affecting one or more of the following body systems: neurological, musculoskeletal, special sense organs, respiratory (including speech organs), cardiovascular, reproductive, digestive, genito-urinary, hemic and lymphatic, skin, and endocrine; or

(2) Any mental or psychological disorder, such as mental retardation, organic brain syndrome, emotional or mental illness, and specific learning disabilities.

(p) *Major life activities* means functions such as caring for oneself, performing manual tasks, walking, seeing, hearing, speaking, breathing, learning, and working.

(q) *Substantially limits*—(1) The term *substantially limits* means:

(i) Unable to perform a major life activity that the average person in the general population can perform; [1] or

(ii) Significantly restricted as to the condition, manner or duration under which an individual can perform a particular major life activity as compared to the condition, manner, or duration under which the average person in the general population can perform that same major life activity.

(2) The following factors should be considered in determining whether an individual is substantially limited in a major life activity:

(i) The nature and severity of the impairment;

(ii) The duration or expected duration of the impairment; and

(iii) The permanent or long term impact, or the expected permanent or long term impact of or resulting from the impairment.

(3) With respect to the major life activity of working—

(i) The term *substantially limits* means significantly restricted in the ability to perform either a class of jobs or a broad range of jobs in various classes as compared to the average person having comparable training, skills, and abilities. The inability to perform a single, particular job does not constitute a substantial limitation in the major life activity of working.

(ii) In addition to the factors listed in paragraph (q)(2) of this section, the following factors may be considered in determining whether an individual is substantially limited in the major life activity of working:

(A) The geographic area to which the individual has reasonable access;

(B) The job from which the individual has been disqualified because of an impairment, and the number and types of jobs utilizing similar training, knowledge, skills or abilities, within that geographic area, from which the individual is also disqualified because of the impairment (class of jobs); and/or

(C) The job from which the individual has been disqualified because of an impairment, and the number and types of other jobs not utilizing similar training, knowledge, skills or abilities, within that geographic area, from which the individual is also disqualified because of the impairment (broad range of jobs in various classes).

(r) *Has a record of such impairment* means has a history of, or has been misclassified as having, a mental or physical impairment that substantially limits one or more major life activities.

(s) *Is regarded as having such an impairment* means:

(1) Has a physical or mental impairment that does not substantially limit major life activities but is treated by the contractor as constituting such limitation;

(2) Has a physical or mental impairment that substantially limits major

[1] People have a range of abilities with regard to many major life activities such as walking, lifting, and bending, and a range of such abilities may be considered average. Thus, the term "average" person in the general population does not indicate a need to determine a precise average ability, but rather reflects that a range of abilities may be considered average.

life activities only as a result of the attitudes of others toward such impairment; or

(3) Has none of the impairments defined in paragraph (o)(1) or (2) of this section, but is treated by the contractor as having a substantially limiting impairment.

(t) *Qualified individual with a disability* means an individual with a disability who satisfies the requisite skill, experience, education and other job-related requirements of the employment position such individual holds or desires, and who, with or without reasonable accommodation, can perform the essential functions of such position. (See §60–741.3 for exceptions to this definition.)

(u) *Essential functions*—(1) *In general.* The term *essential functions* means fundamental job duties of the employment position the individual with a disability holds or desires. The term *essential functions* does not include the marginal functions of the position.

(2) A job function may be considered essential for any of several reasons, including but not limited to the following:

(i) The function may be essential because the reason the position exists is to perform that function;

(ii) The function may be essential because of the limited number of employees available among whom the performance of that job function can be distributed; and/or

(iii) The function may be highly specialized so that the incumbent in the position is hired for his or her expertise or ability to perform the particular function.

(3) Evidence of whether a particular function is essential includes, but is not limited to:

(i) The contractor's judgment as to which functions are essential;

(ii) Written job descriptions prepared before advertising or interviewing applicants for the job;

(iii) The amount of time spent on the job performing the function;

(iv) The consequences of not requiring the incumbent to perform the function;

(v) The terms of a collective bargaining agreement;

(vi) The work experience of past incumbents in the job; and/or

(vii) The current work experience of incumbents in similar jobs.

(v) *Reasonable accommodation*—(1) The term *reasonable accommodation* means:

(i) Modifications or adjustments to a job application process that enable a qualified applicant with a disability to be considered for the position such applicant desires;[2] or

(ii) Modifications or adjustments to the work environment, or to the manner or circumstances under which the position held or desired is customarily performed, that enable a qualified individual with a disability to perform the essential functions of that position; or

(iii) Modifications or adjustments that enable the contractor's employee with a disability to enjoy equal benefits and privileges of employment as are enjoyed by the contractor's other similarly situated employees without disabilities.

(2) *Reasonable accommodation* may include but is not limited to:

(i) Making existing facilities used by employees readily accessible to and usable by individuals with disabilities; and

(ii) Job restructuring; part-time or modified work schedules; reassignment to a vacant position; acquisition or modifications of equipment or devices; appropriate adjustment or modifications of examinations, training materials, or policies; the provision of qualified readers or interpreters; and other similar accommodations for individuals with disabilities.

(3) To determine the appropriate reasonable accommodation it may be necessary for the contractor to initiate an informal, interactive process with the qualified individual with a disability in

[2] A contractor's duty to provide a reasonable accommodation with respect to applicants with disabilities is not limited to those who ultimately demonstrate that they are qualified to perform the job in issue. Applicants with disabilities must be provided a reasonable accommodation with respect to the application process if they are qualified with respect to that process (e.g., if they present themselves at the correct location and time to fill out an application).

need of the accommodation.[3] This process should identify the precise limitations resulting from the disability and potential reasonable accommodations that could overcome those limitations. (Appendix A of this part provides guidance on a contractor's duty to provide reasonable accommodation.)

(w) *Undue hardship*—(1) *In general. Undue hardship* means, with respect to the provision of an accommodation, significant difficulty or expense incurred by the contractor, when considered in light of the factors set forth in paragraph (w)(2) of this section.

(2) *Factors to be considered.* In determining whether an accommodation would impose an undue hardship on the contractor, factors to be considered include:

(i) The nature and net cost of the accommodation needed, taking into consideration the availability of tax credits and deductions, and/or outside funding;

(ii) The overall financial resources of the facility or facilities involved in the provision of the reasonable accommodation, the number of persons employed at such facility, and the effect on expenses and resources;

(iii) The overall financial resources of the contractor, the overall size of the business of the contractor with respect to the number of its employees, and the number, type and location of its facilities;

(iv) The type of operation or operations of the contractor, including the composition, structure and functions of the work force of such contractor, and the geographic separateness and administrative or fiscal relationship of the facility or facilities in question to the contractor; and

(v) The impact of the accommodation upon the operation of the facility, including the impact on the ability of other employees to perform their duties and the impact on the facility's ability to conduct business.

(x) *Qualification standards* means the personal and professional attributes including the skill, experience, education, physical, medical, safety and other requirements established by the contractor as requirements which an individual must meet in order to be eligible for the position held or desired.

(y) *Direct threat* means a significant risk of substantial harm to the health or safety of the individual or others that cannot be eliminated or reduced by reasonable accommodation. The determination that an individual with a disability poses a "direct threat" shall be based on an individualized assessment of the individual's present ability to perform safely the essential functions of the job. This assessment shall be based on a reasonable medical judgment that relies on the most current medical knowledge and/or on the best available objective evidence. In determining whether an individual would pose a direct threat, the factors to be considered include:

(1) The duration of the risk;

(2) The nature and severity of the potential harm;

(3) The likelihood that the potential harm will occur; and

(4) The imminence of the potential harm.

(z) *Compliance evaluation* means any one or combination of actions OFCCP may take to examine a Federal contractor's or subcontractor's compliance with one or more of the requirements of Section 503 of the Rehabilitation Act of 1973.

[61 FR 19350, May 1, 1996, as amended at 70 FR 36265, June 22, 2005]

§ 60–741.3 Exceptions to the definitions of "individual with a disability" and "qualified individual with a disability."

(a) *Current illegal use of drugs*—(1) *In general.* The terms *individual with a disability* and *qualified individual with a disability* do not include individuals currently engaging in the illegal use of drugs, when the contractor acts on the basis of such use.

[3] Contractors must engage in such an interactive process with an individual with disabilities whether or not a reasonable accommodation ultimately is identified. Contractors must engage in the interactive process because, until they have done so, they may be unable to determine whether a reasonable accommodation exists that will result in the person being qualified.

(2) *"Drug" defined.* The term *drug* means a controlled substance, as defined in schedules I through V of section 202 of the Controlled Substances Act (21 U.S.C. 812).

(3) *"Illegal use of drugs" defined.* The term *illegal use of drugs* means the use of drugs, the possession or distribution of which is unlawful under the Controlled Substances Act, as updated pursuant to that act. Such term does not include the use of a drug taken under supervision by a licensed health care professional, or other uses authorized by the Controlled Substances Act or other provisions of Federal law.

(4) *Construction.* (i) Nothing in paragraph (a)(1) of this section shall be construed to exclude as an "individual with a disability" or as a "qualified individual with a disability" an individual who:

(A) Has successfully completed a supervised drug rehabilitation program and is no longer engaging in the illegal use of drugs, or has otherwise been rehabilitated successfully and is no longer engaging in the illegal use of drugs;

(B) Is participating in a supervised rehabilitation program and is no longer engaging in such use; or

(C) Is erroneously regarded as engaging in such use, but is not engaging in such use.

(ii) In order to be protected by section 503 and this part, an individual described in paragraph (a)(4)(i) of this section must satisfy the requirements of the definition of *qualified individual with a disability*.

(5) *Drug testing.* It shall not be a violation of this part for the contractor to adopt or administer reasonable policies or procedures, including but not limited to drug testing, designed to ensure that an individual described in paragraphs (a)(4)(i)(A) and (B) of this section is no longer engaging in the illegal use of drugs. (See § 60–741.24(b)(1).)

(b) *Alcoholics*—(1) *In general.* The terms *individual with a disability* and *qualified individual with a disability* do not include an individual who is an alcoholic whose current use of alcohol prevents such individual from performing the essential functions of the employment position such individual holds or desires or whose employment, by reason of such current alcohol abuse, would constitute a direct threat to property or to the health or safety of the individual or others.

(2) *Duty to provide reasonable accommodation.* Nothing in paragraph (b)(1) of this section shall relieve the contractor of its obligation to provide a reasonable accommodation for an individual described in paragraph (b)(1) of this section when such an accommodation will enable the individual to perform the essential functions of the employment position such individual holds or desires, or when the accommodation will eliminate or reduce the direct threat to property or the health or safety of the individual or others posed by such individual, provided that such individual satisfies the requisite skill, experience, education and other job-related requirements of such position.

(c) *Contagious disease or infection*—(1) *In general.* The terms *individual with a disability* and *qualified individual with a disability* do not include an individual who has a currently contagious disease or infection and who, by reason of such disease or infection, would constitute a direct threat to the health or safety of the individual or others or who, by reason of the currently contagious disease or infection, is unable to perform the essential functions of the employment position such individual holds or desires.

(2) *Duty to provide reasonable accommodation.* Nothing in paragraph (c)(1) of this section shall relieve the contractor of its obligation to provide a reasonable accommodation for an individual described in paragraph (c)(1) of this section when such an accommodation will enable the individual to perform the essential functions of the employment position such individual holds or desires, or when the accommodation will eliminate or reduce the direct threat to the health or safety of the individual or others posed by such individual, provided that such individual satisfies the requisite skill, experience, education and other job-related requirements of such position.

(d) *Homosexuality or bisexuality.* The term *impairment* as defined in this part does not include homosexuality or bisexuality, and therefore the term *individual with a disability* as defined in this part does not include an individual on the basis of homosexuality or bisexuality.

(e) *Other conditions.* The term *individual with a disability* does not include an individual on the basis of:

(1) Transvestism, transsexualism, pedophilia, exhibitionism, voyeurism, gender identity disorders not resulting from physical impairments, or other sexual behavior disorders;

(2) Compulsive gambling, kleptomania, or pyromania; or

(3) Psychoactive substance use disorders resulting from current illegal use of drugs.

§ 60–741.4 Coverage and waivers.

(a) *Coverage*—(1) *Contracts and subcontracts in excess of $10,000.* Contracts and subcontracts in excess of $10,000 are covered by this part. No contracting agency or contractor shall procure supplies or services in less than usual quantities to avoid the applicability of the equal opportunity clause.

(2) *Positions engaged in carrying out a contract.* (i) With respect to the contractor's employment decisions and practices occurring before October 29, 1992, this part applies only to employees who were employed in, and applicants for, positions that were engaged in carrying out a Government contract; with respect to employment decisions and practices occurring on or after October 29, 1992, this part applies to all of the contractor's positions irrespective of whether the positions are or were engaged in carrying out a Government contract. A position shall be considered to have been engaged in carrying out a contract if:

(A) The duties of the position included work that fulfilled a contractual obligation, or work that was necessary to, or that facilitated, performance of the contract or a provision of the contract; or

(B) The cost or a portion of the cost of the position was allowable as a cost of the contract under the principles set forth in the Federal Acquisition Regulation at 48 CFR Ch. 1, part 31: *Provided,* That a position shall not be considered to have been covered by this part by virtue of this provision if the cost of the position was not allocable in whole or in part as a direct cost to any Government contract, and only a de minimis (less than 2%) portion of the cost of the position was allocable as an indirect cost to Government contracts, considered as a group.

(ii) *Application.* Where a contractor or a division or establishment of a contractor was devoted exclusively to Government contract work, all positions within the contractor, division, or establishment shall be considered to have been covered by this part. (Appendix D of this part provides guidance on positions engaged in carrying out a contract.)

(3) *Contracts and subcontracts for indefinite quantities.* With respect to indefinite delivery-type contracts and subcontracts (including, but not limited to, open end contracts, requirement-type contracts, Federal Supply Schedule contracts, "call-type" contracts, and purchase notice agreements), the equal opportunity clause shall be included unless the contracting agency has reason to believe that the amount to be ordered in any year under such contract will not be in excess of $10,000. The applicability of the equal opportunity clause shall be determined at the time of award for the first year, and annually thereafter for succeeding years, if any. Notwithstanding the above, the equal opportunity clause shall be applied to such contract whenever the amount of a single order exceeds $10,000. Once the equal opportunity clause is determined to be applicable, the contract shall continue to be subject to such clause for its duration, regardless of the amounts ordered, or reasonably expected to be ordered in any year.

(4) *Employment activities within the United States.* This part applies only to employment activities within the United States and not to employment activities abroad. The term *employment activities within the United States* includes actual employment within the United States, and decisions of the contractor made within the United States, pertaining to the contractor's applicants and employees who are within the United States, regarding employment opportunities abroad (such as recruiting and hiring within the United States for employment abroad, or

transfer of persons employed in the United States to contractor establishments abroad).

(5) *Contracts with State or local governments.* The requirements of the equal opportunity clause in any contract or subcontract with a State or local government (or any agency, instrumentality or subdivision thereof) shall not be applicable to any agency, instrumentality or subdivision of such government which does not participate in work on or under the contract or subcontract.

(b) *Waivers*—(1) *Specific contracts and classes of contracts.* The Deputy Assistant Secretary may waive the application to any contract of the equal opportunity clause in whole or part when he or she deems that special circumstances in the national interest so require. The Deputy Assistant Secretary may also grant such waivers to groups or categories of contracts: where it is in the national interest; where it is found impracticable to act upon each request individually; and where such waiver will substantially contribute to convenience in administration of the act. When a waiver has been granted for any class of contracts, the Deputy Assistant Secretary may withdraw the waiver for a specific contract or group of contracts to be awarded, when in his or her judgment such action is necessary or appropriate to achieve the purposes of the act. The withdrawal shall not apply to contracts awarded prior to the withdrawal, except that in procurements entered into by formal advertising, or the various forms of restricted formal advertising, such withdrawal shall not apply unless the withdrawal is made more than 10 calendar days before the date set for the opening of the bids.

(2) *National security.* Any requirement set forth in the regulations of this part shall not apply to any contract whenever the head of the contracting agency determines that such contract is essential to the national security and that its award without complying with such requirements is necessary to the national security. Upon making such a determination, the head of the contracting agency will notify the Deputy Assistant Secretary in writing within 30 days.

(3) *Facilities not connected with contracts.* (i) Upon the written request of the contractor, the Deputy Assistant Secretary may waive the requirements of the equal opportunity clause with respect to any of a contractor's facilities if the Deputy Assistant Secretary finds that the contractor has demonstrated that:

(A) The facility is in all respects separate and distinct from activities of the contractor related to the performance of a contract; and

(B) Such a waiver will not interfere with or impede the effectuation of the act.

(ii) The Deputy Assistant Secretary's findings as to whether the facility is separate and distinct in all respects from activities of the contractor related to the performance of a contract shall include consideration of the following factors:

(A) Whether any work at the facility directly or indirectly supports or contributes to the satisfaction of the work performed on a Government contract;

(B) The extent to which the facility benefits, directly or indirectly, from a Government contract;

(C) Whether any costs associated with operating the facility are charged to a Government contract;

(D) Whether working at the facility is a prerequisite for advancement in job responsibility or pay, and the extent to which employees at facilities connected to a Government contract are recruited for positions at the facility;

(E) Whether employees or applicants for employment at the facility may perform work related to a Government contract at another facility, and the extent to which employees at the facility are interchangeable with employees at facilities connected to a Government contract; and

(F) Such other factors that the Deputy Assistant Secretary deems are necessary or appropriate for considering whether the facility is in all respects separate and distinct from the activities of the contractor related to the performance of a contract.

(iii) The Deputy Assistant Secretary's findings as to whether granting a waiver will interfere with or impede the effectuation of the act shall include consideration of the following factors:

(A) Whether the waiver will be used as a subterfuge to circumvent the contractor's obligations under the act;

(B) The contractor's compliance with the act or any other Federal, State or local law requiring equal opportunity for disabled persons;

(C) The impact of granting the waiver on OFCCP enforcement efforts; and

(D) Such other factors that the Deputy Assistant Secretary deems are necessary or appropriate for considering whether the granting of the waiver would interfere with or impede the effectuation of the act.

(iv) A contractor granted a waiver under paragraph (b)(3) of this section shall:

(A) Promptly inform the Deputy Assistant Secretary of any changed circumstances not reflected in the contractor's waiver request; and

(B) Permit the Deputy Assistant Secretary access during normal business hours to the contractor's places of business for the purpose of investigating whether the facility granted a waiver meets the standards and requirements of paragraph (b)(3) of this section, and for inspecting and copying such books and accounts and records, including computerized records, and other material as may be relevant to the matter under investigation.

(v)(A) A waiver granted under paragraph (b)(3) of this section shall terminate on one of the following dates, whichever is earliest:

(*1*) Two years after the date the waiver was granted.

(*2*) When the facility performs any work that directly supports or contributes to the satisfaction of the work performed on a Government contract.

(*3*) When the Deputy Assistant Secretary determines, based on information provided by the contractor under this section or upon any other relevant information, that the facility does not meet the requirements of paragraph (b)(3) of this section.

(B) When a waiver terminates in accordance with paragraph (b)(3)(v)(A) of this section the contractor shall ensure that the facility complies with this part on the date of termination, except that compliance with §§ 60–741.40 through 60–741.45, if applicable, must be attained within 120 days of such termination.

(vi) False or fraudulent statements or representations made by a contractor under paragraph (b)(3) of this section are prohibited and may subject the contractor to sanctions and penalties under this part and criminal prosecution under 18 U.S.C. 1001.

[61 FR 19350, May 1, 1996, as amended at 65 FR 45179, July 20, 2000]

§ 60–741.5 Equal opportunity clause.

(a) *Government contracts.* Each contracting agency and each contractor shall include the following equal opportunity clause in each of its covered Government contracts or subcontracts (and modifications, renewals, or extensions thereof if not included in the original contract):

EQUAL OPPORTUNITY FOR WORKERS WITH DISABILITIES

1. The contractor will not discriminate against any employee or applicant for employment because of physical or mental disability in regard to any position for which the employee or applicant for employment is qualified. The contractor agrees to take affirmative action to employ, advance in employment and otherwise treat qualified individuals with disabilities without discrimination based on their physical or mental disability in all employment practices, including the following:

i. Recruitment, advertising, and job application procedures;

ii. Hiring, upgrading, promotion, award of tenure, demotion, transfer, layoff, termination, right of return from layoff and rehiring;

iii. Rates of pay or any other form of compensation and changes in compensation;

iv. Job assignments, job classifications, organizational structures, position descriptions, lines of progression, and seniority lists;

v. Leaves of absence, sick leave, or any other leave;

vi. Fringe benefits available by virtue of employment, whether or not administered by the contractor;

vii. Selection and financial support for training, including apprenticeship, professional meetings, conferences, and other related activities, and selection for leaves of absence to pursue training;

viii. Activities sponsored by the contractor including social or recreational programs; and

ix. Any other term, condition, or privilege of employment.

2. The contractor agrees to comply with the rules, regulations, and relevant orders of the Secretary of Labor issued pursuant to the act.

3. In the event of the contractor's noncompliance with the requirements of this clause, actions for noncompliance may be taken in accordance with the rules, regulations, and relevant orders of the Secretary of Labor issued pursuant to the act.

4. The contractor agrees to post in conspicuous places, available to employees and applicants for employment, notices in a form to be prescribed by the Deputy Assistant Secretary for Federal Contract Compliance Programs, provided by or through the contracting officer. Such notices shall state the rights of applicants and employees as well as the contractor's obligation under the law to take affirmative action to employ and advance in employment qualified employees and applicants with disabilities. The contractor must ensure that applicants and employees with disabilities are informed of the contents of the notice (e.g., the contractor may have the notice read to a visually disabled individual, or may lower the posted notice so that it might be read by a person in a wheelchair).

5. The contractor will notify each labor organization or representative of workers with which it has a collective bargaining agreement or other contract understanding, that the contractor is bound by the terms of section 503 of the Rehabilitation Act of 1973, as amended, and is committed to take affirmative action to employ and advance in employment individuals with physical or mental disabilities.

6. The contractor will include the provisions of this clause in every subcontract or purchase order in excess of $10,000, unless exempted by the rules, regulations, or orders of the Secretary issued pursuant to section 503 of the act, as amended, so that such provisions will be binding upon each subcontractor or vendor. The contractor will take such action with respect to any subcontract or purchase order as the Deputy Assistant Secretary for Federal Contract Compliance Programs may direct to enforce such provisions, including action for noncompliance.

[End of Clause]

(b) *Subcontracts.* Each contractor shall include the equal opportunity clause in each of its subcontracts subject to this part.

(c) *Adaption of language.* Such necessary changes in language may be made to the equal opportunity clause as shall be appropriate to identify properly the parties and their undertakings.

(d) *Inclusion of the equal opportunity clause in the contract.* It is not necessary that the equal opportunity clause be quoted verbatim in the contract. The clause may be made a part of the contract by citation to 41 CFR 60–741.5(a).

(e) *Incorporation by operation of the act.* By operation of the act, the equal opportunity clause shall be considered to be a part of every contract and subcontract required by the act and the regulations in this part to include such a clause, whether or not it is physically incorporated in such contract and whether or not there is a written contract between the agency and the contractor.

(f) *Duties of contracting agencies.* Each contracting agency shall cooperate with the Deputy Assistant Secretary and the Secretary in the performance of their responsibilities under the act. Such cooperation shall include insuring that the equal opportunity clause is included in all covered Government contracts and that contractors are fully informed of their obligations under the act and this part, providing the Deputy Assistant Secretary with any information which comes to the agency's attention that a contractor is not in compliance with the act or this part, responding to requests for information from the Deputy Assistant Secretary, and taking such actions for noncompliance as are set forth in § 60–741.66 as may be ordered by the Secretary or the Deputy Assistant Secretary.

Subpart B—Discrimination Prohibited

§ 60–741.20 Covered employment activities.

The prohibition against discrimination in this part applies to the following employment activities:

(a) Recruitment, advertising, and job application procedures;

(b) Hiring, upgrading, promotion, award of tenure, demotion, transfer, layoff, termination, right of return from layoff, and rehiring;

(c) Rates of pay or any other form of compensation and changes in compensation;

(d) Job assignments, job classifications, organizational structures, position descriptions, lines of progression, and seniority lists;

(e) Leaves of absence, sick leave, or any other leave;

(f) Fringe benefits available by virtue of employment, whether or not administered by the contractor;

(g) Selection and financial support for training, including apprenticeships, professional meetings, conferences and other related activities, and selection for leaves of absence to pursue training;

(h) Activities sponsored by the contractor including social and recreational programs; and

(i) Any other term, condition, or privilege of employment.

§ 60–741.21 Prohibitions.

The term *discrimination* includes, but is not limited to, the acts described in this section and § 60–741.23.

(a) *Disparate treatment.* It is unlawful for the contractor to deny an employment opportunity or benefit or otherwise to discriminate against a qualified individual with a disability because of that individual's disability.

(b) *Limiting, segregating and classifying.* Unless otherwise permitted by this part, it is unlawful for the contractor to limit, segregate, or classify a job applicant or employee in a way that adversely affects his or her employment opportunities or status on the basis of disability. For example, the contractor may not segregate qualified employees with disabilities into separate work areas or into separate lines of advancement.

(c) *Contractual or other arrangements*—(1) *In general.* It is unlawful for the contractor to participate in a contractual or other arrangement or relationship that has the effect of subjecting the contractor's own qualified applicant or employee with a disability to the discrimination prohibited by this part.

(2) *Contractual or other arrangement defined.* The phrase *contractual or other arrangement or relationship* includes, but is not limited to, a relationship with: an employment or referral agency; a labor organization, including a collective bargaining agreement; an organization providing fringe benefits to an employee of the contractor; or an organization providing training and apprenticeship programs.

(3) *Application.* This paragraph (c) applies to the contractor, with respect to its own applicants or employees, whether the contractor offered the contract or initiated the relationship, or whether the contractor accepted the contract or acceded to the relationship. The contractor is not liable for the actions of the other party or parties to the contract which only affect that other party's employees or applicants.

(d) *Standards, criteria or methods of administration.* It is unlawful for the contractor to use standards, criteria, or methods of administration, that are not job-related and consistent with business necessity, and that:

(1) Have the effect of discriminating on the basis of disability; or

(2) Perpetuate the discrimination of others who are subject to common administrative control.

(e) *Relationship or association with an individual with a disability.* It is unlawful for the contractor to exclude or deny equal jobs or benefits to, or otherwise discriminate against, a qualified individual because of the known disability of an individual with whom the qualified individual is known to have a family, business, social or other relationship or association.

(f) *Not making reasonable accommodation.* (1) It is unlawful for the contractor to fail to make reasonable accommodation to the known physical or mental limitations of an otherwise qualified applicant or employee with a disability, unless such contractor can demonstrate that the accommodation would impose an undue hardship on the operation of its business.

(2) It is unlawful for the contractor to deny employment opportunities to an otherwise qualified job applicant or employee with a disability based on the need of such contractor to make reasonable accommodation to such an individual's physical or mental impairments.

(3) A qualified individual with a disability is not required to accept an accommodation, aid, service, opportunity

or benefit which such qualified individual chooses not to accept. However, if such individual rejects a reasonable accommodation, aid, service, opportunity or benefit that is necessary to enable the individual to perform the essential functions of the position held or desired, and cannot, as a result of that rejection, perform the essential functions of the position, the individual will not be considered a qualified individual with a disability.

(g) *Qualification standards, tests and other selection criteria*—(1) *In general.* It is unlawful for the contractor to use qualification standards, employment tests or other selection criteria that screen out or tend to screen out an individual with a disability or a class of individuals with disabilities, on the basis of disability, unless the standard, test or other selection criterion, as used by the contractor, is shown to be job-related for the position in question and is consistent with business necessity. Selection criteria that concern an essential function may not be used to exclude an individual with a disability if that individual could satisfy the criteria with provision of a reasonable accommodation. Selection criteria that exclude or tend to exclude an individual with a disability or a class of individuals with disabilities because of disability but concern only marginal functions of the job would not be consistent with business necessity. The contractor may not refuse to hire an applicant with a disability because the applicant's disability prevents him or her from performing marginal functions.

(2) The Uniform Guidelines on Employee Selection Procedures, 41 CFR part 60–3, do not apply to the Rehabilitation Act and are similarly inapplicable to this part.

(h) *Administration of tests.* It is unlawful for the contractor to fail to select and administer tests concerning employment in the most effective manner to ensure that, when a test is administered to a job applicant or employee who has a disability that impairs sensory, manual, or speaking skills, the test results accurately reflect the skills, aptitude, or whatever other factor of the applicant or employee that the test purports to measure, rather than reflecting the impaired sensory, manual, or speaking skills of such employee or applicant, except where such skills are the factors that the test purports to measure.

(i) *Compensation.* In offering employment or promotions to individuals with disabilities, it is unlawful for the contractor to reduce the amount of compensation offered because of any income based upon a disability-related pension or other disability-related benefit the applicant or employee receives from another source.

§ 60–741.22 Direct threat defense.

The contractor may use as a qualification standard the requirement that an individual be able to perform the essential functions of the position held or desired without posing a direct threat to the health or safety of the individual or others in the workplace. (See § 60–741.2(y) defining *direct threat*.)

§ 60–741.23 Medical examinations and inquiries.

(a) *Prohibited medical examinations or inquiries.* Except as stated in paragraphs (b) and (c) of this section, it is unlawful for the contractor to require a medical examination of an applicant or employee or to make inquiries as to whether an applicant or employee is an individual with a disability or as to the nature or severity of such disability.

(b) *Permitted medical examinations and inquiries*—(1) *Acceptable pre-employment inquiry.* The contractor may make pre-employment inquiries into the ability of an applicant to perform job-related functions, and/or may ask an applicant to describe or to demonstrate how, with or without reasonable accommodation, the applicant will be able to perform job-related functions.

(2) *Employment entrance examination.* The contractor may require a medical examination (and/or inquiry) after making an offer of employment to a job applicant and before the applicant begins his or her employment duties, and may condition an offer of employment on the results of such examination (and/or inquiry), if all entering employees in the same job category are subjected to such an examination (and/or inquiry) regardless of disability.

(3) *Examination of employees.* The contractor may require a medical examination (and/or inquiry) of an employee that is job-related and consistent with business necessity. The contractor may make inquiries into the ability of an employee to perform job-related functions.

(4) *Other acceptable examinations and inquiries.* The contractor may conduct voluntary medical examinations and activities, including voluntary medical histories, which are part of an employee health program available to employees at the work site.

(5) Medical examinations conducted in accordance with paragraphs (b)(2) and (b)(4) of this section do not have to be job-related and consistent with business necessity. However, if certain criteria are used to screen out an applicant or applicants or an employee or employees with disabilities as a result of such examinations or inquiries, the contractor must demonstrate that the exclusionary criteria are job-related and consistent with business necessity, and that performance of the essential job functions cannot be accomplished with reasonable accommodations as required in this part.

(c) *Invitation to self-identify.* The contractor shall invite the applicant to self-identify as an individual with a disability as specified in § 60–741.42.

(d) *Confidentiality and use of medical information.* (1) Information obtained under this section regarding the medical condition or history of any applicant or employee shall be collected and maintained on separate forms and in separate medical files and treated as a confidential medical record, except that:

(i) Supervisors and managers may be informed regarding necessary restrictions on the work or duties of the applicant or employee and necessary accommodations;

(ii) First aid and safety personnel may be informed, when appropriate, if the disability might require emergency treatment; and

(iii) Government officials engaged in enforcing the laws administered by OFCCP, including this part, or enforcing the Americans with Disabilities Act, shall be provided relevant information on request.

(2) Information obtained under this section regarding the medical condition or history of any applicant or employee shall not be used for any purpose inconsistent with this part.

§ 60–741.24 Drugs and alcohol.

(a) *Specific activities permitted.* The contractor:

(1) May prohibit the illegal use of drugs and the use of alcohol at the workplace by all employees;

(2) May require that employees not be under the influence of alcohol or be engaging in the illegal use of drugs at the workplace;

(3) May require that all employees behave in conformance with the requirements established under the Drug-Free Workplace Act of 1988 (41 U.S.C. 701 *et seq.*);

(4) May hold an employee who engages in the illegal use of drugs or who is an alcoholic to the same qualification standards for employment or job performance and behavior to which the contractor holds its other employees, even if any unsatisfactory performance or behavior is related to the employee's drug use or alcoholism;

(5) May require that its employees employed in an industry subject to such regulations comply with the standards established in the regulations (if any) of the Departments of Defense and Transportation, and of the Nuclear Regulatory Commission, and other Federal agencies regarding alcohol and the illegal use of drugs; and

(6) May require that employees employed in sensitive positions comply with the regulations (if any) of the Departments of Defense and Transportation, and of the Nuclear Regulatory Commission, and other Federal agencies that apply to employment in sensitive positions subject to such regulations.

(b) *Drug testing*—(1) *General policy.* For purposes of this part, a test to determine the illegal use of drugs is not considered a medical examination. Thus, the administration of such drug tests by the contractor to its job applicants or employees is not a violation of § 60–741.23. Nothing in this part shall be construed to encourage, prohibit, or authorize the contractor to conduct drug tests of job applicants or employees to determine the illegal use of drugs or to make employment decisions based on such test results.

(2) *Transportation employees.* Nothing in this part shall be construed to encourage, prohibit, or authorize the otherwise lawful exercise by contractors subject to the jurisdiction of the Department of Transportation of authority to test employees in, and applicants for, positions involving safety-sensitive duties for the illegal use of drugs or for on-duty impairment by alcohol; and remove from safety-sensitive positions persons who test positive for illegal use of drugs or on-duty impairment by alcohol pursuant to paragraph (b)(1) of this section.

(3) Any information regarding the medical condition or history of any employee or applicant obtained from a test to determine the illegal use of drugs, except information regarding the illegal use of drugs, is subject to the requirements of §§ 60–741.23(b)(5) and (c).

§ 60–741.25 Health insurance, life insurance and other benefit plans.

(a) An insurer, hospital, or medical service company, health maintenance organization, or any agent or entity that administers benefit plans, or similar organizations may underwrite risks, classify risks, or administer such risks that are based on or not inconsistent with State law.

(b) The contractor may establish, sponsor, observe or administer the terms of a bona fide benefit plan that are based on underwriting risks, classifying risks, or administering such risks that are based on or not inconsistent with State law.

(c) The contractor may establish, sponsor, observe, or administer the terms of a bona fide benefit plan that is not subject to State laws that regulate insurance.

(d) The contractor may not deny a qualified individual with a disability equal access to insurance or subject a qualified individual with a disability to different terms or conditions of insurance based on disability alone, if the disability does not pose increased risks.

(e) The activities described in paragraphs (a), (b) and (c) of this section are permitted unless these activities are used as a subterfuge to evade the purposes of this part.

Subpart C—Affirmative Action Program

§ 60–741.40 Applicability of the affirmative action program requirement.

(a) The requirements of this subpart apply to every Government contractor that has 50 or more employees and a contract of $50,000 or more.

(b) Contractors described in paragraph (a) of this section shall, within 120 days of the commencement of a contract, prepare and maintain an affirmative action program at each establishment. The affirmative action program shall set forth the contractor's policies and procedures in accordance with this part. This program may be integrated into or kept separate from other affirmative action programs.

(c) The affirmative action program shall be reviewed and updated annually.

(d) The contractor shall submit the affirmative action program within 30 days of a request from OFCCP, unless the request provides for a different time. The contractor also shall make the affirmative action program promptly available on-site upon OFCCP's request.

§ 60–741.41 Availability of affirmative action program.

The full affirmative action program shall be available to any employee or applicant for employment for inspection upon request. The location and hours during which the program may be obtained shall be posted at each establishment.

§ 60–741.42 Invitation to self-identify.

(a) The contractor shall, after making an offer of employment to a job applicant and before the applicant begins his or her employment duties, invite the applicant to inform the contractor whether the applicant believes that he or she may be covered by the act and wishes to benefit under the affirmative action program. The contractor may invite self-identification prior to making a job offer only when:

(1) The invitation is made when the contractor actually is undertaking affirmative action for individuals with disabilities at the pre-offer stage; or

(2) The invitation is made pursuant to a Federal, state or local law requiring affirmative action for individuals with disabilities.

(b) The invitation referenced in paragraph (a) of this section shall state that a request to benefit under the affirmative action program may be made immediately and/or at any time in the future. The invitation also shall summarize the relevant portions of the act and the contractor's affirmative action program. Furthermore, the invitation shall state that the information is being requested on a voluntary basis, that it will be kept confidential, that refusal to provide it will not subject the applicant to any adverse treatment, and that it will not be used in a manner inconsistent with the act. If an applicant so identifies himself or herself, the contractor should also seek the advice of the applicant regarding proper placement and appropriate accommodation, after a job offer has been extended. The contractor also may make such inquiries to the extent they are consistent with the ADA (e.g., in the context of asking applicants to describe or demonstrate how they would perform the job). The contractor shall maintain a separate file on persons who have self-identified and provide that file to OFCCP upon request. This information may be used only in accordance with this part. (An acceptable form for such an invitation is set forth in Appendix B of this part. Because a contractor usually may not seek advice from an applicant regarding placement and accommodation until after a job offer has been extended, the invitation set forth in Appendix B of this part contains instructions regarding modifications to be made if it is used at the pre-offer stage.)

(c) Nothing in this section shall relieve the contractor of its obligation to take affirmative action with respect to those applicants or employees of whose disability the contractor has knowledge.

(d) Nothing in this section shall relieve the contractor from liability for discrimination under the act.

§ 60–741.43 Affirmative action policy.

Under the affirmative action obligations imposed by the act contractors shall not discriminate because of physical or mental disability and shall take affirmative action to employ and advance in employment qualified individuals with disabilities at all levels of employment, including the executive level. Such action shall apply to all employment activities set forth in § 60–741.20.

§ 60–741.44 Required contents of affirmative action programs.

Acceptable affirmative action programs shall contain, but not necessarily be limited to, the following ingredients:

(a) *Policy statement*. The contractor shall include an equal opportunity policy statement in its affirmative action program, and shall post the policy statement on company bulletin boards. The contractor must ensure that applicants and employees with disabilities are informed of the contents of the policy statement (for example, the contractor may have the statement read to a visually disabled individual, or may lower the posted notice so that it may be read by a person in a wheelchair). The policy statement should indicate the chief executive officer's attitude on the subject matter, provide for an audit and reporting system (see paragraph (h) of this section) and assign overall responsibility for the implementation of affirmative action activities required under this part (see paragraph (i) of this section). Additionally, the policy should state, among other things, that the contractor will: recruit, hire, train and promote persons in all job titles, and ensure that all other personnel actions are administered, without regard to disability; and ensure that all employment decisions are based only on valid job requirements. The policy shall state that employees and applicants shall not be subjected to harassment, intimidation, threats, coercion or discrimination because they have engaged in or may engage in any of the following activities:

(1) Filing a complaint;

(2) Assisting or participating in an investigation, compliance evaluation, hearing, or any other activity related to the administration of Section 503 of the Rehabilitation Act of 1973, as amended (Section 503) or any other Federal, State or local law requiring equal opportunity for disabled persons;

(3) Opposing any act or practice made unlawful by section 503 or its implementing regulations in this part or any other Federal, State or local law requiring equal opportunity for disabled persons; or

(4) Exercising any other right protected by section 503 or its implementing regulations in this part.

(b) *Review of personnel processes.* The contractor shall ensure that its personnel processes provide for careful, thorough, and systematic consideration of the job qualifications of applicants and employees with known disabilities for job vacancies filled either by hiring or promotion, and for all training opportunities offered or available. The contractor shall ensure that its personnel processes do not stereotype disabled persons in a manner which limits their access to all jobs for which they are qualified. The contractor shall periodically review such processes and make any necessary modifications to ensure that these obligations are carried out. A description of the review and any necessary modifications to personnel processes or development of new processes shall be included in any affirmative action programs required under this part. The contractor must design procedures that facilitate a review of the implementation of this requirement by the contractor and the Government. (Appendix C of this part is an example of an appropriate set of procedures. The procedures in Appendix C of this part are not required and contractors may develop other procedures appropriate to their circumstances.)

(c) *Physical and mental qualifications.* (1) The contractor shall provide in its affirmative action program, and shall adhere to, a schedule for the periodic review of all physical and mental job qualification standards to ensure that, to the extent qualification standards tend to screen out qualified individuals with disabilities, they are job-related for the position in question and are consistent with business necessity.

(2) Whenever the contractor applies physical or mental qualification standards in the selection of applicants or employees for employment or other change in employment status such as promotion, demotion or training, to the extent that qualification standards tend to screen out qualified individuals with disabilities, the standards shall be related to the specific job or jobs for which the individual is being considered and consistent with business necessity. The contractor shall have the burden to demonstrate that it has complied with the requirements of paragraph (c)(2) of this section.

(3) The contractor may use as a defense to an allegation of a violation of paragraph (c)(2) of this section that an individual poses a direct threat to the health or safety of the individual or others in the workplace. (See § 60–741.2(y) defining *direct threat.*)

(d) *Reasonable accommodation to physical and mental limitations.* The contractor shall make reasonable accommodation to the known physical or mental limitations of an otherwise qualified individual with a disability unless it can demonstrate that the accommodation would impose an undue hardship on the operation of its business. If an employee with a known disability is having significant difficulty performing his or her job and it is reasonable to conclude that the performance problem may be related to the known disability, the contractor shall confidentially notify the employee of the performance problem and inquire whether the problem is related to the employee's disability; if the employee responds affirmatively, the contractor shall confidentially inquire whether the employee is in need of a reasonable accommodation.

(e) *Harassment.* The contractor must develop and implement procedures to ensure that its employees with disabilities are not harassed because of disability.

(f) *External dissemination of policy, outreach and positive recruitment.* The contractor shall undertake appropriate outreach and positive recruitment activities such as those listed in paragraphs (f)(1) through (7) of this section that are reasonably designed to effectively recruit qualified individuals with disabilities. It is not contemplated that the contractor will necessarily undertake all the activities listed in paragraphs (f)(1) through (7) of this section or that its activities will be limited to those listed. The scope of the contractor's efforts shall depend upon all the circumstances, including the contractor's size and resources and the extent to which existing employment practices are adequate.

(1) The contractor should enlist the assistance and support of recruiting sources (including State employment security agencies, State vocational rehabilitation agencies or facilities, sheltered workshops, college placement officers, State education agencies, labor organizations and organizations of or for individuals with disabilities) for the contractor's commitment to provide meaningful employment opportunities to qualified individuals with disabilities. Formal briefing sessions should be held, preferably on company premises, with representatives from recruiting sources. Plant tours, clear and concise explanations of current and future job openings, position descriptions, worker specifications, explanations of the company's selection process, and recruiting literature should be an integral part of the briefing. Formal arrangements should be made for referral of applicants, follow up with sources, and feedback on disposition of applicants.

(2) The contractor's recruitment efforts at all schools should incorporate special efforts to reach students with disabilities. The contractor should engage in recruitment activities at educational institutions which participate in training of individuals with disabilities, such as schools for the blind, deaf, or learning disabled. An effort should be made to participate in work-study programs with rehabilitation facilities and schools which specialize in training or educating individuals with disabilities.

(3) The contractor should establish meaningful contacts with appropriate social service agencies, organizations of and for individuals with disabilities, and vocational rehabilitation agencies or facilities, for such purposes as advice, technical assistance and referral of potential employees. Technical assistance from the resources described in this paragraph may consist of advice on proper placement, recruitment, training and accommodations contractors may undertake, but no such resource providing technical assistance shall have authority to approve or disapprove the acceptability of affirmative action programs.

(4) The contractor should include individuals with disabilities when employees are pictured in consumer, promotional or help wanted advertising. Individuals with disabilities should be made available for participation in career days, youth motivation programs, and related activities in their communities.

(5) The contractor should send written notification of company policy to all subcontractors, vendors and suppliers, requesting appropriate action on their part.

(6) The contractor should take positive steps to attract qualified individuals with disabilities not currently in the work force who have requisite skills and can be recruited through affirmative action measures. These persons may be located through the local chapters of organizations of and for individuals with disabilities.

(7) The contractor, in making hiring decisions, should consider applicants with known disabilities for all available positions for which they may be qualified when the position(s) applied for is unavailable.

(g) *Internal dissemination of policy.* (1) A strong outreach program will be ineffective without adequate internal support from supervisory and management personnel and other employees, who may have had limited contact with individuals with disabilities in the past. In order to assure greater employee cooperation and participation in the contractor's efforts, the contractor shall develop internal procedures such as those listed in paragraph (g)(2) of this section for communication of its obligation to engage in affirmative action efforts to employ and advance in employment qualified individuals with disabilities. It is not contemplated that the contractor will necessarily undertake all the activities listed in paragraph (g)(2) of this section or that its activities will be limited to those listed. These procedures shall be designed to foster understanding, acceptance and support among the contractor's executive, management, supervisory and other employees and to encourage such persons to take the necessary actions to aid the contractor in meeting this obligation. The scope of the contractor's efforts shall depend upon all the circumstances, including the contractor's size and resources and the extent to which existing practices are adequate.

(2) The contractor should implement and disseminate this policy internally as follows:

(i) Include it in the contractor's policy manual.

(ii) Periodically inform all employees and prospective employees of its commitment to engage in affirmative action to increase employment opportunities for qualified individuals with disabilities. The contractor should schedule special meetings with all employees to discuss policy and explain individual employee responsibilities.

(iii) Publicize it in the company newspaper, magazine, annual report and other media.

(iv) Conduct special meetings with executive, management, and supervisory personnel to explain the intent of the policy and individual responsibility for effective implementation, making clear the chief executive officer's attitude.

(v) Discuss the policy thoroughly in both employee orientation and management training programs.

(vi) Meet with union officials and/or employee representatives to inform them of the contractor's policy, and request their cooperation.

(vii) Include articles on accomplishments of disabled workers in company publications.

(viii) When employees are featured in employee handbooks or similar publications for employees, include individuals with disabilities.

(h) *Audit and reporting system.* (1) The contractor shall design and implement an audit and reporting system that will:

(i) Measure the effectiveness of the contractor's affirmative action program.

(ii) Indicate any need for remedial action.

(iii) Determine the degree to which the contractor's objectives have been attained.

(iv) Determine whether individuals with known disabilities have had the opportunity to participate in all company sponsored educational, training, recreational and social activities.

(v) Measure the contractor's compliance with the affirmative action program's specific obligations.

(2) Where the affirmative action program is found to be deficient, the contractor shall undertake necessary action to bring the program into compliance.

(i) *Responsibility for implementation.* An official of the contractor shall be assigned responsibility for implementation of the contractor's affirmative action activities under this part. His or her identity should appear on all internal and external communications regarding the company's affirmative action program. This official shall be given necessary top management support and staff to manage the implementation of this program.

(j) *Training.* All personnel involved in the recruitment, screening, selection, promotion, disciplinary, and related processes shall be trained to ensure that the commitments in the contractor's affirmative action program are implemented.

[61 FR 19350, May 1, 1996, as amended at 70 FR 36265, June 22, 2005]

§ 60–741.45 Sheltered workshops.

Contracts with sheltered workshops do not constitute affirmative action in lieu of employment and advancement of qualified disabled individuals in the contractor's own work force. Contracts with sheltered workshops may be included within an affirmative action program if the sheltered workshop trains employees for the contractor and the contractor is obligated to hire trainees at full compensation when such trainees become "qualified individuals with disabilities."

Subpart D—General Enforcement and Complaint Procedures

§ 60–741.60 Compliance evaluations.

(a) OFCCP may conduct compliance evaluations to determine if the contractor maintains nondiscriminatory hiring and employment practices and is taking affirmative action to ensure that applicants are employed and that employees are placed, trained, upgraded, promoted, and otherwise treated in accordance with this part during employment. A compliance evaluation may consist of any one or any combination of the following investigative procedures:

(1) *Compliance review.* A comprehensive analysis and evaluation of the hiring and employment practices of the contractor, the written affirmative action program, and the results of the affirmative action efforts undertaken by the contractor. A compliance review may proceed in three stages:

(i) A desk audit of the written affirmative action program and supporting documentation to determine whether all elements required by the regulations in this part are included, whether the affirmative action program meets agency standards of reasonableness, and whether the affirmative action program and supporting documentation satisfy agency standards of acceptability. The desk audit is conducted at OFCCP offices;

(ii) An on-site review, conducted at the contractor's establishment to investigate unresolved problem areas identified in the affirmative action program and supporting documentation during the desk audit, to verify that the contractor has implemented the affirmative action program and has complied with those regulatory obligations not required to be included in the affirmative action program, and to examine potential instances or issues of discrimination. An on-site review normally will involve an examination of the contractor's personnel and employment policies, inspection and copying of documents related to employment actions, and interviews with employees, supervisors, managers, hiring officials; and

(iii) Where necessary, an off-site analysis of information supplied by the contractor or otherwise gathered during or pursuant to the on-site review;

(2) *Off-site review of records.* An analysis and evaluation of the affirmative action program (or any part thereof) and supporting documentation, and other documents related to the contractor's personnel policies and employment actions that may be relevant to a determination of whether the contractor has complied with the requirements of Section 503 of the Rehabilitation Act of 1973 and regulations;

(3) *Compliance check.* A determination of whether the contractor has maintained records consistent with § 60–741.80; at the contractor's option the documents may be provided either onsite or off-site; or

(4) *Focused review.* An on-site review restricted to one or more components of the contractor's organization or one or more aspects of the contractor's employment practices.

(b) Where deficiencies are found to exist, reasonable efforts shall be made to secure compliance through conciliation and persuasion pursuant to § 60–741.62.

[61 FR 19350, May 1, 1996, as amended at 70 FR 36265, June 22, 2005]

§ 60–741.61 Complaint procedures.

(a) *Coordination with other agencies.* Pursuant to section 107(b) of the Americans with Disabilities Act of 1990 (ADA), OFCCP and the Equal Employment Opportunity Commission have promulgated regulations setting forth procedures governing the processing of complaints falling within the overlapping jurisdiction of both the act and title I of the ADA to ensure that such complaints are dealt with in a manner that avoids duplication of effort and prevents the imposition of inconsistent or conflicting standards. Complaints filed under this part will be processed in accordance with those regulations, which are found at 41 CFR part 60–742, and with this part.

(b) *Place and time of filing.* Any applicant for employment with a contractor or any employee of a contractor may, personally or by an authorized representative, file a written complaint with the Deputy Assistant Secretary alleging a violation of the act or the regulations in this part. The complaint may allege individual or class-wide violation(s). Complaints may be submitted to the OFCCP, 200 Constitution Avenue, N.W., Washington, D.C. 20210, or to any OFCCP regional, district, or area office. Such complaint must be filed within 300 days of the date of the alleged violation, unless the time for filing is extended by OFCCP for good cause shown.

(c) *Contents of complaints*—(1) *In general.* A complaint must be signed by the complainant or his or her authorized representative and must contain the following information:

(i) Name and address (including telephone number) of the complainant;

(ii) Name and address of the contractor who committed the alleged violation;

(iii) The facts showing that the individual is disabled or has a history of a disability or was regarded by the contractor as having a disability;

(iv) A description of the act or acts considered to be a violation, including the pertinent dates (in the case of an alleged continuing violation, the earliest and most recent date that the alleged violation occurred should be stated); and

(v) Other pertinent information available which will assist in the investigation and resolution of the complaint, including the name of any known Federal agency with which the employer has contracted.

(2) *Third party complaints.* A complaint filed by an authorized representative need not identify by name the person on whose behalf it is filed. The person filing the complaint, however, shall provide OFCCP with the name, address and telephone number of the person on whose behalf it is made, and the other information specified in paragraph (c)(1) of this section. OFCCP shall verify the authorization of such a complaint by the person on whose behalf the complaint is made. Any such person may request that OFCCP keep his or her identity confidential, and OFCCP will protect the individual's confidentiality wherever that is possible given the facts and circumstances in the complaint.

(d) *Incomplete information.* Where a complaint contains incomplete information, OFCCP shall seek the needed information from the complainant. If the information is not furnished to OFCCP within 60 days of the date of such request, the case may be closed.

(e) *Investigations.* The Department of Labor shall institute a prompt investigation of each complaint.

(f) *Resolution of matters.* (1) If the complaint investigation finds no violation of the act or this part, or if the Deputy Assistant Secretary decides not to refer the matter to the Solicitor of Labor for enforcement proceedings against the contractor pursuant to §60–741.65(a)(1), the complainant and contractor shall be so notified. The Deputy Assistant Secretary, on his or her own initiative, may reconsider his or her determination or the determination of any of his or her designated officers who have authority to issue Notifications of Results of Investigation.

(2) The Deputy Assistant Secretary will review all determinations of no violation that involve complaints that are not also cognizable under title I of the Americans with Disabilities Act.

(3) In cases where the Deputy Assistant Secretary decides to reconsider the determination of a Notification of Results of Investigation, the Deputy Assistant Secretary shall provide prompt notification of his or her intent to reconsider, which is effective upon issuance, and his or her final determination after reconsideration, to the person claiming to be aggrieved, the person making the complaint on behalf of such person, if any, and the contractor.

(4) If the investigation finds a violation of the act or this part, OFCCP shall invite the contractor to participate in conciliation discussions pursuant to §60–741.62.

§60–741.62 Conciliation agreements.

If a compliance evaluation, complaint investigation or other review by OFCCP finds a material violation of the Act or this part, and if the contractor is willing to correct the violations and/or deficiencies, and if OFCCP determines that settlement on that basis (rather than referral for consideration of formal enforcement) is appropriate, a written conciliation agreement will be required. The agreement shall provide for such remedial action as may be necessary to correct the violations and/or deficiencies noted, including, where appropriate (but not necessarily limited to) such make whole remedies as back pay and retroactive seniority. The agreement shall also specify the time period for completion of the remedial action; the period shall be no longer than the minimum period necessary to complete the action.

[61 FR 19350, May 1, 1996, as amended at 70 FR 36266, June 22, 2005]

§ 60–741.63 Violations of Cconciliation Agreements.

(a) When OFCCP believes that a conciliation agreement has been violated, the following procedures are applicable:

(1) A written notice shall be sent to the contractor setting forth the violation alleged and summarizing the supporting evidence. The contractor shall have 15 days from receipt of the notice to respond, except in those cases in which OFCCP asserts that such a delay would result in irreparable injury to the employment rights of affected employees or applicants.

(2) During the 15-day period the contractor may demonstrate in writing that it has not violated its commitments.

(b) In those cases in which OFCCP asserts that a delay would result in irreparable injury to the employment rights of affected employees or applicants, enforcement proceedings may be initiated immediately without proceeding through any other requirement contained in this chapter.

(c) In any proceedings involving an alleged violation of a conciliation agreement OFCCP may seek enforcement of the agreement itself and shall not be required to present proof of the underlying violations resolved by the agreement.

[61 FR 19350, May 1, 1996, as amended at 70 FR 36266, June 22, 2005]

§ 60–741.64 Show cause notices.

When the Deputy Assistant Secretary has reasonable cause to believe that the contractor has violated the act or this part, he or she may issue a notice requiring the contractor to show cause, within 30 days, why monitoring, enforcement proceedings or other appropriate action to ensure compliance should not be instituted. The issuance of such a notice is not a prerequisite to instituting enforcement proceedings (see § 60–741.65).

§ 60–741.65 Enforcement proceedings.

(a) *General.* (1) If a compliance evaluation, complaint investigation or other review by OFCCP finds a violation of the act or this part, and the violation has not been corrected in accordance with the conciliation procedures in this part, or OFCCP determines that referral for consideration of formal enforcement (rather than settlement) is appropriate, OFCCP may refer the matter to the Solicitor of Labor with a recommendation for the institution of enforcement proceedings to enjoin the violations, to seek appropriate relief, to impose appropriate sanctions, or any combination of these outcomes. OFCCP may seek back pay and other make whole relief for aggrieved individuals identified during a complaint investigation or compliance review. Such individuals need not have filed a complaint as a prerequisite to OFCCP seeking such relief on their behalf. Interest on back pay shall be calculated from the date of the loss and compounded quarterly at the percentage rate established by the Internal Revenue Service for the underpayment of taxes.

(2) In addition to the administrative proceedings set forth in this section, the Deputy Assistant Secretary may, within the limitations of applicable law, seek appropriate judicial action to enforce the contractual provisions set forth in § 60–741.5, including appropriate injunctive relief.

(b) *Hearing practice and procedure.* (1) In administrative enforcement proceedings the contractor shall be provided an opportunity for a formal hearing. All hearings conducted under the act and this part shall be governed by the Rules of Practice for Administrative Proceedings to Enforce Equal Opportunity Under Executive Order 11246 contained in 41 CFR part 60–30 and the Rules of Evidence set out in the Rules of Practice and Procedure for Administrative Hearings Before the Office of

Administrative Law Judges contained in 29 CFR part 18, subpart B: *Provided*, That a final administrative order shall be issued within one year from the date of the issuance of the recommended findings, conclusions and decision of the Administrative Law Judge, or the submission of any exceptions and responses to exceptions to such decision (if any), whichever is later.

(2) Complaints may be filed by the Solicitor, the Associate Solicitor for Civil Rights, Regional Solicitors and Associate Regional Solicitors.

(3) For the purposes of hearings pursuant to this part, references in 41 CFR part 60–30 to "Executive Order 11246" shall mean section 503 of the Rehabilitation Act of 1973, as amended; to "equal opportunity clause" shall mean the equal opportunity clause published at 41 CFR 60–741.5; and to "regulations" shall mean the regulations contained in this part.

[61 FR 19350, May 1, 1996, as amended at 70 FR 36266, June 22, 2005]

§ 60–741.66 Sanctions and penalties.

(a) *Withholding progress payments*. With the prior approval of the Deputy Assistant Secretary so much of the accrued payment due on the contract or any other contract between the Government contractor and the Federal Government may be withheld as necessary to correct any violations of the provisions of the act or this part.

(b) *Termination*. A contract may be canceled or terminated, in whole or in part, for failure to comply with the provisions of the act or this part.

(c) *Debarment*. A contractor may be debarred from receiving future contracts for failure to comply with the provisions of the act or this part subject to reinstatement pursuant to § 60–741.68. Debarment may be imposed for an indefinite period, or may be imposed for a fixed period of not less than six months but no more than three years.

(d) *Hearing opportunity*. An opportunity for a formal hearing shall be afforded to a contractor before the imposition of any sanction or penalty.

§ 60–741.67 Notification of agencies.

The Deputy Assistant Secretary shall ensure that the heads of all agencies are notified of any debarments taken against any contractor.

§ 60–741.68 Reinstatement of ineligible contractors.

(a) *Application for reinstatement*. A contractor debarred from further contracts for an indefinite period under the act may request reinstatement in a letter filed with the Deputy Assistant Secretary at any time after the effective date of the debarment; a contractor debarred for a fixed period may make such a request following the expiration of six months from the effective date of the debarment. In connection with the reinstatement proceedings, all debarred contractors shall be required to show that they have established and will carry out employment policies and practices in compliance with the act and this part. Additionally, in determining whether reinstatement is appropriate for a contractor debarred for a fixed period, the Deputy Assistant Secretary also shall consider, among other factors, the severity of the violation which resulted in the debarment, the contractor's attitude towards compliance, the contractor's past compliance history, and whether the contractor's reinstatement would impede the effective enforcement of the act or this part. Before reaching a decision, the Deputy Assistant Secretary may conduct a compliance evaluation of the contractor and may require the contractor to supply additional information regarding the request for reinstatement.

(b) *Petition for review*. Within 30 days of its receipt of a decision denying a request for reinstatement, the contractor may file a petition for review of the decision with the Secretary. The petition shall set forth the grounds for the contractor's objections to the Deputy Assistant Secretary's decision. The petition shall be served on the Deputy Assistant Secretary and the Associate Solicitor for Civil Rights and shall include the decision as an appendix. The Deputy Assistant Secretary may file a response within 14 days to the petition. The Secretary shall issue the final agency decision denying or granting the request for reinstatement. Before reaching a final decision, the Secretary may issue such additional orders respecting procedure as he or she finds appropriate in the circumstances, including an order referring the matter to the Office of Administrative Law Judges for an evidentiary hearing where there is a material factual dispute that cannot be resolved on the record before the Secretary.

[61 FR 19350, May 1, 1996, as amended at 70 FR 36266, June 22, 2005]

§60–741.69 Intimidation and interference.

(a) The contractor shall not harass, intimidate, threaten, coerce, or discriminate against, any individual because the individual has engaged in or may engage in any of the following activities:

(1) Filing a complaint;

(2) Assisting or participating in any manner in an investigation, compliance evaluation, hearing, or any other activity related to the administration of the act or any other Federal, State or local law requiring equal opportunity for disabled persons;

(3) Opposing any act or practice made unlawful by the act or this part or any other Federal, State or local law requiring equal opportunity for disabled persons; or

(4) Exercising any other right protected by the act or this part.

(b) The contractor shall ensure that all persons under its control do not engage in such harassment, intimidation, threats, coercion or discrimination. The sanctions and penalties contained in this part may be exercised by the Deputy Assistant Secretary against any contractor who violates this obligation.

[61 FR 19350, May 1, 1996, as amended at 70 FR 36266, June 22, 2005]

§60–741.70 Disputed matters related to compliance with the act.

The procedures set forth in the regulations in this part govern all disputes relative to the contractor's compliance with the act and this part. Any disputes relating to issues other than compliance, including contract costs arising out of the contractor's efforts to comply, shall be determined by the disputes clause of the contract.

Subpart E—Ancillary Matters

§60–741.80 Recordkeeping.

(a) *General requirements.* Any personnel or employment record made or kept by the contractor shall be preserved by the contractor for a period of two years from the date of the making of the record or the personnel action involved, whichever occurs later. However, if the contractor has fewer than 150 employees or does not have a Government contract of at least $150,000, the minimum record retention period shall be one year from the date of the making of the record or the personnel action involved, whichever occurs later. Such records include, but are not necessarily limited to, records relating to requests for reasonable accommodation; the results of any physical examination; job advertisements and postings; applications and resumes; tests and test results; interview notes; and other records having to do with hiring, assignment, promotion, demotion, transfer, lay-off or termination, rates of pay or other terms of compensation, and selection for training or apprenticeship. In the case of involuntary termination of an employee, the personnel records of the individual terminated shall be kept for a period of two years from the date of the termination, except that contractors that have fewer than 150 employees or that do not have a Government contract of at least $150,000 shall keep such records for a period of one year from the date of the termination. Where the contractor has received notice that a complaint of discrimination has been filed, that a compliance evaluation has been initiated, or that an enforcement action has been commenced, the contractor must preserve all personnel records relevant to the complaint, compliance evaluation or action until final disposition of the complaint, compliance evaluation or action. The term "personnel records relevant to the complaint, compliance evaluation or action" will include, for example, personnel or employment records relating to the aggrieved person and to all other employees holding positions similar to that held or sought by the aggrieved person and application forms or test papers completed by an unsuccessful applicant and by all other candidates for the same position as that for which the aggrieved person applied and was rejected.

(b) *Failure to preserve records.* Failure to preserve complete and accurate records as required by paragraph (a) of this section constitutes noncompliance with the contractor's obligations under the act and this part. Where the contractor has destroyed or failed to preserve records as required by this section, there may be a presumption that the information destroyed or not preserved would have been unfavorable to the contractor: *Provided,* That this presumption shall not apply where the contractor shows that the destruction or failure to preserve records results from circumstances that are outside of the contractor's control.

(c) The requirements of this section shall apply only to records made or kept on or after August 29, 1996.

[61 FR 19350, May 1, 1996, as amended at 70 FR 36266, June 22, 2005]

§ 60–741.81 Access to records.

Each contractor must permit access during normal business hours to its places of business for the purpose of conducting on-site compliance evaluations and complaint investigations and inspecting and copying such books and accounts and records, including computerized records, and other material as may be relevant to the matter under investigation and pertinent to compliance with the act or this part. Information obtained in this manner shall be used only in connection with the administration of the act, the administration of the Americans with Disabilities Act of 1990 (ADA) and in furtherance of the purposes of the act and the ADA.

[61 FR 19350, May 1, 1996, as amended at 70 FR 36266, June 22, 2005]

§ 60–741.82 Labor organizations and recruiting and training agencies.

(a) Whenever performance in accordance with the equal opportunity clause or any matter contained in the regulations in this part may necessitate a revision of a collective bargaining agreement, the labor organizations which are parties to such agreement shall be given an adequate opportunity to present their views to OFCCP.

(b) OFCCP shall use its best efforts, directly or through contractors, subcontractors, local officials, vocational rehabilitation facilities, and all other available instrumentalities, to cause any labor organization, recruiting and training agency or other representative of workers who are employed by a contractor to cooperate with, and to assist in, the implementation of the purposes of the act.

§ 60–741.83 Rulings and interpretations.

Rulings under or interpretations of the act and this part shall be made by the Deputy Assistant Secretary.

§ 60–741.84 Effective date.

This part shall become effective August 29, 1996, and shall not apply retroactively. Contractors presently holding Government contracts shall update their affirmative action programs as required to comply with this part by December 27, 1996.

APPENDIX A TO PART 60–741—GUIDELINES ON A CONTRACTOR'S DUTY TO PROVIDE REASONABLE ACCOMMODATION

The guidelines in this appendix are in large part derived from, and are consistent with, the discussion regarding the duty to provide reasonable accommodation contained in the Interpretive Guidance on Title I of the Americans with Disabilities Act (ADA) set out as an appendix to the regulations issued by the Equal Employment Opportunity Commission (EEOC) implementing the ADA (29 CFR part 1630). Although the following discussion is intended to provide an independent "free-standing" source of guidance with respect to the duty to provide reasonable accommodation under this part, to the extent that the EEOC appendix provides additional guidance which is consistent with the following discussion, it may be relied upon for purposes of this part as well. See § 60–741.1(c). Contractors are obligated to provide reasonable accommodation and to take affirmative action. Reasonable accommodation under section 503, like reasonable accommodation required under the ADA, is a part of the nondiscrimination obligation. *See* EEOC appendix cited in this paragraph. Affirmative action is unique to section 503, and includes actions above and beyond those required as a matter of nondiscrimination. An example of this is the requirement discussed in paragraph 2 of this appendix that a contractor *shall* make an inquiry of an employee with a known disability who is having significant difficulty performing his or her job.

1. A contractor is required to make reasonable accommodations to the known physical or mental limitations of an "otherwise qualified" individual with a disability, unless the contractor can demonstrate that the accommodation would impose an undue hardship on the operation of its business. As stated in §60–741.2(t), an individual with a disability is qualified if he or she satisfies all the skill, experience, education and other job-related selection criteria, and can perform the essential functions of the position with or without reasonable accommodation. A contractor is required to make a reasonable accommodation with respect to its application process if the individual with a disability is qualified with respect to that process. One is "otherwise qualified" if he or she is qualified for a job, except that, because of a disability, he or she needs a reasonable accommodation to be able to perform the job's essential functions.

2. Although the contractor would not be expected to accommodate disabilities of which it is unaware, the contractor has an affirmative obligation to provide a reasonable accommodation for applicants and employees of whose disability the contractor has actual knowledge. As stated in §60–741.42 (see also Appendix B of this part), the contractor is required to invite applicants who have been provided an offer of employment, before they begin their employment duties, to indicate whether they may have a disability and wish to benefit under the contractor's affirmative action program. That section further provides that the contractor should seek the advice of individuals who "self-identify" in this way as to proper placement and appropriate accommodation. Moreover, §60–741.44(d) provides that if an employee with a known disability is having significant difficulty performing his or her job and it is reasonable to conclude that the performance problem may be related to the disability, the contractor is required to confidentially inquire whether the problem is disability related and if the employee is in need of a reasonable accommodation.

3. An accommodation is any change in the work environment or in the way things are customarily done that enables an individual with a disability to enjoy equal employment opportunities. Equal employment opportunity means an opportunity to attain the same level of performance, or to enjoy the same level of benefits and privileges of employment as are available to the average similarly situated employee without a disability. Thus, for example, an accommodation made to assist an employee with a disability in the performance of his or her job must be adequate to enable the individual to perform the essential functions of the position. The accommodation, however, does not have to be the "best" accommodation possible, so long as it is sufficient to meet the job-related needs of the individual being accommodated. There are three areas in which reasonable accommodations may be necessary: (1) Accommodations in the application process; (2) accommodations that enable employees with disabilities to perform the essential functions of the position held or desired; and (3) accommodations that enable employees with disabilities to enjoy equal benefits and privileges of employment as are enjoyed by employees without disabilities.

4. The term "undue hardship" refers to any accommodation that would be unduly costly, extensive, substantial, or disruptive, or that would fundamentally alter the nature or operation of the contractor's business. The contractor's claim that the cost of a particular accommodation will impose an undue hardship requires a determination of which financial resources should be considered—those of the contractor in its entirety or only those of the facility that will be required to provide the accommodation. This inquiry requires an analysis of the financial relationship between the contractor and the facility in order to determine what resources will be available to the facility in providing the accommodation. If the contractor can show that the cost of the accommodation would impose an undue hardship, it would still be required to provide the accommodation if the funding is available from another source, e.g., a State vocational rehabilitation agency, or if Federal, State or local tax deductions or tax credits are available to offset the cost of the accommodation. In the absence of such funding, the individual with a disability should be given the option of providing the accommodation or of paying that portion of the cost which constitutes the undue hardship on the operation of the business.

5. Section 60–741.2(v) lists a number of examples of the most common types of accommodations that the contractor may be required to provide. There are any number of specific accommodations that may be appropriate for particular situations. The discussion in this appendix is not intended to provide an exhaustive list of required accommodations (as no such list would be feasible); rather, it is intended to provide general guidance regarding the nature of the obligation. The decision as to whether a reasonable accommodation is appropriate must be made on a case-by-case basis. The contractor generally should consult with the individual with a disability in deciding on the appropriate accommodation; frequently, the individual will know exactly what accommodation he or she will need to perform successfully in a particular job, and may suggest an

accommodation which is simpler and less expensive than the accommodation the contractor might have devised. Other resources to consult include the appropriate State vocational rehabilitation services agency, the Equal Employment Opportunity Commission (1–800–669–EEOC (voice), 1–800–800–3302 (TDD)), the Job Accommodation Network (JAN) operated by the President's Committee on Employment of People with Disabilities (1–800–JAN–7234), private disability organizations, and other employers.

6. With respect to accommodations that can permit an employee with a disability to perform essential functions successfully, a reasonable accommodation may require the contractor to, for instance, modify or acquire equipment. For the visually-impaired such accommodations may include providing adaptive hardware and software for computers, electronic visual aids, braille devices, talking calculators, magnifiers, audio recordings and brailled or large print materials. For persons with hearing impairments, reasonable accommodations may include providing telephone handset amplifiers, telephones compatible with hearing aids and telecommunications devices for the deaf (TDDs). For persons with limited physical dexterity, the obligation may require the provision of goose neck telephone headsets, mechanical page turners and raised or lowered furniture.

7. Other reasonable accommodations of this type may include providing personal assistants such as a reader, interpreter or travel attendant, permitting the use of accrued paid leave or providing additional unpaid leave for necessary treatment. The contractor may also be required to make existing facilities readily accessible to and usable by individuals with a disability—including areas used by employees for purposes other than the performance of essential job functions such as restrooms, break rooms, cafeterias, lounges, auditoriums, libraries, parking lots and credit unions. This type of accommodation will enable employees to enjoy equal benefits and privileges of employment as are enjoyed by employees who do not have disabilities.

8. Another of the potential accommodations listed in §60–741.2(v) is job restructuring. This may involve reallocating or redistributing those nonessential, marginal job functions which a qualified individual with a disability cannot perform to another position. Accordingly, if a clerical employee is occasionally required to lift heavy boxes containing files, but cannot do so because of a disability, this task may be reassigned to another employee. The contractor, however, is not required to reallocate essential functions, *i.e.*, those functions that the individual who holds the job would have to perform, with or without reasonable accommodation, in order to be considered qualified for the position. For instance, the contractor which has a security guard position which requires the incumbent to inspect identity cards would not have to provide a blind individual with an assistant to perform that duty; in such a case, the assistant would be performing an essential function of the job for the individual with a disability. Job restructuring may also involve allowing part-time or modified work schedules. For instance, flexible or adjusted work schedules could benefit persons who cannot work a standard schedule because of the need to obtain medical treatment, or persons with mobility impairments who depend on a public transportation system that is not accessible during the hours of a standard schedule.

9. Reasonable accommodation may also include reassignment to a vacant position. In general, reassignment should be considered only when accommodation within the individual's current position would pose an undue hardship. Reassignment is not required for applicants. However, in making hiring decisions, contractors are encouraged to consider known applicants with disabilities for all available positions for which they may be qualified when the position(s) applied for is unavailable. Reassignment may not be used to limit, segregate, or otherwise discriminate against employees with disabilities by forcing reassignments to undesirable positions or to designated offices or facilities. Employers should reassign the individual to an equivalent position in terms of pay, status, etc., if the individual is qualified, and if the position is vacant within a reasonable amount of time. A "reasonable amount of time" should be determined in light of the totality of the circumstances.

10. The contractor may reassign an individual to a lower graded position if there are no accommodations that would enable the employee to remain in the current position and there are no vacant equivalent positions for which the individual is qualified with or without reasonable accommodation. The contractor may maintain the reassigned individual with a disability at the salary of the higher graded position, and must do so if it maintains the salary of reassigned employees who are not disabled. It should also be noted that the contractor is not required to promote an individual with a disability as an accommodation.

11. With respect to the application process, appropriate accommodations may include the following: (1) providing information regarding job vacancies in a form accessible to the vision or hearing impaired, e.g., by making an announcement available in braille, in large print, or on audio tape, or by responding to job inquiries via TDDs; (2) providing readers, interpreters and other similar assistance during the application, testing and

interview process; (3) appropriately adjusting or modifying employment-related examinations, e.g., extending regular time deadlines, allowing a blind person or one with a learning disorder such as dyslexia to provide oral answers for a written test, and permitting an applicant, regardless of the nature of his or her disability, to demonstrate skills through alternative techniques and utilization of adapted tools, aids and devices; and (4) ensuring an applicant with a mobility impairment full access to testing locations such that the applicant's test scores accurately reflect the applicant's skills or aptitude rather than the applicant's mobility impairment.

APPENDIX B TO PART 60–741—SAMPLE INVITATION TO SELF-IDENTIFY

NOTE: When the invitation to self-identify is being extended prior to an offer of employment, as is permitted in limited circumstances under §60–741.42(a), paragraph 2(ii) of this appendix, relating to identification of reasonable accommodations, should be omitted. This will avoid a conflict with the EEOC's ADA Guidance, which in most cases precludes asking a job applicant (prior to a job offer being made) about potential reasonable accommodations.

[Sample Invitation to Self-Identify]

1. This employer is a Government contractor subject to section 503 of the Rehabilitation Act of 1973, as amended, which requires Government contractors to take affirmative action to employ and advance in employment qualified individuals with disabilities. If you have a disability and would like to be considered under the affirmative action program, please tell us. You may inform us of your desire to benefit under the program at this time and/or at any time in the future. This information will assist us in placing you in an appropriate position and in making accommodations for your disability. [The contractor should here insert a brief provision summarizing the relevant portion of its affirmative action program.] Submission of this information is voluntary and refusal to provide it will not subject you to any adverse treatment. Information you submit about your disability will be kept confidential, except that (i) supervisors and managers may be informed regarding restrictions on the work or duties of individuals with disabilities, and regarding necessary accommodations; (ii) first aid and safety personnel may be informed, when and to the extent appropriate, if the condition might require emergency treatment; and (iii) Government officials engaged in enforcing laws administered by OFCCP or the Americans with Disabilities Act, may be informed. The information provided will be used only in ways that are not inconsistent with section 503 of the Rehabilitation Act.

2. If you are an individual with a disability, we would like to include you under the affirmative action program. It would assist us if you tell us about (i) any special methods, skills, and procedures which qualify you for positions that you might not otherwise be able to do because of your disability so that you will be considered for any positions of that kind, and (ii) the accommodations which we could make which would enable you to perform the job properly and safely, including special equipment, changes in the physical layout of the job, elimination of certain duties relating to the job, provision of personal assistance services or other accommodations.

APPENDIX C TO PART 60–741—REVIEW OF PERSONNEL PROCESSES

The following is a set of procedures which contractors may use to meet the requirements of §60–741.44(b):

1. The application or personnel form of each known applicant with a disability should be annotated to identify each vacancy for which the applicant was considered, and the form should be quickly retrievable for review by the Department of Labor and the contractor's personnel officials for use in investigations and internal compliance activities.

2. The personnel or application records of each known individual with a disability should include (i) the identification of each promotion for which the employee with a disability was considered, and (ii) the identification of each training program for which the individual with a disability was considered.

3. In each case where an employee or applicant who is an individual with a disability is rejected for employment, promotion, or training, the contractor should prepare a statement of the reason as well as a description of the accommodations considered. The statement of the reason for rejection (if the reason is medically related), and the description of the accommodations considered, should be treated as confidential medical records in accordance with §60–741.23(d). These materials should be available to the applicant or employee concerned upon request.

4. Where applicants or employees are selected for hire, promotion, or training and the contractor undertakes any accommodation which makes it possible for him or her to place an individual with a disability on the job, the contractor should make a record containing a description of the accommodation. The record should be treated as a confidential medical record in accordance with §60–741.23(d).

[61 FR 19350, May 1, 1996, as amended at 63 FR 59659, Nov. 4, 1998]

APPENDIX D TO PART 60–741—GUIDELINES REGARDING POSITIONS ENGAGED IN CARRYING OUT A CONTRACT

As stated in §60–741.4(a)(2), with respect to the contractor's employment decisions and practices occurring before October 29, 1992, this part 60–741 applies only to employees who were employed in, and applicants for, positions that were engaged in carrying out a Government contract.[1] The regulatory definition has two prongs. Under §60–741.4(a)(2)(i)(A) ("prong A"), positions are deemed to have been engaged in carrying out a Government contract if their duties included work that fulfilled a contractual obligation, or work that was necessary to, or that facilitated, performance of the contract or a provision of the contract. Alternatively, under §60–741.4(a)(2)(i)(B) ("prong B"), positions are deemed to have been engaged in carrying out a Government contract if, pursuant to principles set forth in the Federal Acquisition Regulation (FAR) at 48 CFR Ch. 1, part 31, the cost of the positions or a portion of their cost was allocable to a contract as a direct cost, or 2 percent or more of the cost was allocable as an indirect cost to Government contracts considered as a group. This appendix provides guidance as to the application of prong A of the definition.

1. The regulatory definition includes positions whose duties involved work that fulfilled a contractual obligation. Such work includes work producing the goods or providing the services that were the object of the contract and also work that fulfilled ancillary contract obligations. For example, if a contract required the contractor to keep certain cost records or to meet certain quality control standards, employees who were engaged in such functions were fulfilling a contractual obligation.

2. Positions are also included if their duties included work that was necessary to or that facilitated performance of the contract. The inclusion of work of this character is intended to reflect the practical reality that performance of a contract generally requires the cooperation of a variety of individuals engaged in auxiliary and related functions beyond direct production of the goods or provision of the services that are the object of the contract.

3. To give one example, a contract for production and sale of goods to the Government commonly requires the work not only of the production employees assembling the goods, but also of those engaged in functions such as repairing the machinery used in producing the goods; maintaining the plant and facilities; assuring quality control and security; storing the goods after production; delivering them to the Government; hiring, paying, and providing personnel services for the employees engaged in contract-related work; keeping financial and accounting records; performing related office and clerical tasks; and supervising or managing the employees engaged in such tasks. This list is not intended to be exhaustive, but only to illustrate that a variety of functions may commonly be involved in carrying out a contract.

4. Whether a particular position was engaged in carrying out a contract depends on the facts as to the nature of the duties that were actually performed and their relationship to contract performance. A position is included if its duties included work that furthered or contributed to the performance of the contract. The work need not have been essential or indispensable to performance of the contract. It is sufficient that it was useful or that it benefitted or contributed to carrying out the contract.

5. Nor is it material that the work was not required by an express contract term. For example, a contract to provide transportation services may not have explicitly incorporated terms requiring maintenance and repair of the means of transportation to keep them in safe operating condition. Such work, however, was implicitly necessary to carry out the contract.

6. It is irrelevant that the contractor could have performed the contract some other way, without making use of a particular function or particular employees, if the way the contractor chose to carry out the contract does in fact make use of them. For example, if a contractor employed three quality control inspectors, or used three quality control processes, to monitor the manufacture of goods for sale to the Government, all three were involved in carrying out the contract, notwithstanding any claim that two would have been sufficient. If a contractor manufactured goods at its plant in St. Louis for delivery in Chicago, employees who transported the goods were carrying out the contract, regardless whether the contractor

[1] Prior to October 29, 1992, section 503 applied only insofar as the contractor was "employing persons to carry out" a Government contract. On that date, the act was amended to apply to all of a covered contractor's work force, irrespective of whether particular positions are engaged in carrying out a Government contract. Accordingly, the guidance contained in this appendix will be relied on by OFCCP in monitoring and enforcing compliance with section 503 only with respect to the contractor's employment decisions and practices occurring before October 29, 1992. (Moreover, prior to that date, section 503 covered only contractors holding a contract "in excess of $2500"; this figure was amended on October 29, 1992 to "in excess of $10,000." Consequently, this appendix makes reference to the $2500 threshold level.)

could have made the goods locally at its plant in Chicago. If a contractor employed security guards or watchmen to protect its plant producing goods for the Government from vandalism or theft of equipment, because in its business judgment it was prudent to do so, employees who were engaged in those tasks were contributing to performance of the contract and were covered.

7. If a position's regular duties included work that contributed to the performance of the contract, and the contract met the act's dollar threshold for coverage, it is irrelevant that such work was only a portion of the position's total duties or that it took only a small amount of time. For example, a Government agency may have contracted to lease a photocopying machine under terms that obligated the leasing company to provide repair and maintenance service. The technician assigned to provide such service was "carrying out the contract" regardless whether he or she provided similar service for numerous private customers and spent only a small fraction of his or her time working on the agency's machine. Similarly, individuals who worked on an assembly line manufacturing automobiles, a portion of which were sold under contract to the Government, while the bulk were sold commercially, were covered. That 95% of the vehicles they produced were sold elsewhere does not negate the fact that the individuals were carrying out the contract to make vehicles for the Government.

8. A group of employees may also have performed duties that simultaneously contributed to performance of both Government and non-Government contracts. In this situation, if the contract exceeded $2500 and the duties of the position in fact contributed to carrying out the contract, the position was covered. For example, the Government may have contracted with airline carriers to provide transportation to Federal employees performing official duties. The contract was performed through the work of employees including the flight crew, the ground maintenance crew, the baggage handlers, the ticketing agents, the airport and gate staff, and other corporate personnel. Federal employees probably typically formed only a small percentage of an airline's passengers. Nonetheless, the pilots who flew the planes and the other staff were carrying out the terms of the contract.

9. These principles are illustrated by the final decision of the Department in *OFCCP* v. *Monongahela Railroad Co.*, 85–OFC–2 (Administrative Law Judge Recommended Decision, April 2, 1986), *aff'd*, (Deputy Under Secretary for Employment Standards, March 11, 1987). *Monongahela* involved the interpretation of the term "necessary" in the context of the definition of the term "subcontract" under this part 60–741. "Subcontract" is defined in relevant part as any agreement for the furnishing of supplies or services "which in whole or in part is necessary to the performance of any one or more [Government] contracts." The decision held that a railroad company's transport of coal that was used by a power company to generate electricity was "necessary" to the performance of the power company's obligation to supply the Government with power and that the railroad company was therefore a covered "subcontractor". The decision reached this result even though numerous other carriers also transported coal to the power company, the coal that the carrier delivered was used to generate electricity for the Government and for nongovernmental customers alike, and the power company sold only a small fraction (less than 1%) of its output to the Government. That is, the decision found that the crucial factor is whether the activity contributes to the performance of a Government contract, regardless of whether the contractor could have performed the contract some other way, and regardless of whether the activity contributes as well, and predominantly, to carrying out non-Government contracts.

10. Although the act broadly reached all positions that contributed to or facilitated the performance of the Government contract, its coverage was not limitless. First, positions were covered only if they bore an appropriate relationship to a covered contract. The contract must have been for the purchase, sale, or use of personal property or nonpersonal services, must have been for an amount in excess of $2500, and must not have been otherwise exempt.

11. Second, the breadth of coverage depended to a large extent on how the contractor chose to organize its work force to perform its contract obligations. A contractor who segregated contract from noncontract work necessarily employed fewer persons to carry out its contracts than one who did not. To continue the example given above, if a plant with several assembly lines produced automobiles, some of which were shipped to the Government and others sold commercially, the application of section 503 would have been limited if the Government contract automobiles were made on only one of the assembly lines. In that case, employees who were on the other lines, which never produced automobiles for the Government, were outside the act. If, however, the contractor did not segregate the contract from noncontract production, the employees on each of the lines were covered.

12. Third, while the relationship between the work of a position and the performance of the contract need not have been direct, the relationship must have been real and not hypothetical. For example, a firm may have done substantial business with both the Government and private customers. Individuals who were employed to plan and design new

facilities that were intended for use with non-Government work would not be deemed to have been covered merely because of the possibility that at some point in the future the facilities would be used to carry out Government contracts. Again, a firm may have been partly unionized and partly non-unionized. Assume the Government contract was performed exclusively in the non-union part of the work force. An individual who was assigned to represent management in dealing with the union would not have been covered simply because the arrangements he or she made with the union might subsequently influence the personnel practices followed for the nonunion employees as well.

13. Coverage depended on the regular or assigned duties and responsibilities of the position. A person that held a position did not go in and out of coverage as she performed first contract and then noncontract work if, throughout the period, one of the duties of the position was to perform contract-related work as the need or occasion arose. For example, the photocopy machine technician who was assigned responsibility to repair machines leased to the Government and to private firms was covered throughout the contract term, including the period before he or she first repaired the Government's machine. Discrimination against the employee was not permissible simply because the discrimination was effected on a day when the technician was servicing a private firm. Likewise, workers who were on an assembly line whose products were shipped at times to the Government and at times to private customers were covered, as were employees of the airline carrier whose duties included at times helping to transport Federal employees pursuant to a contract.

14. On the other hand, a person whose duties were permanently changed may have gained or lost coverage as a result. For example, an engineer who had been working on developing weapons under a contract with the military, and who accordingly was covered, may have been transferred to work on development of civilian aircraft for private customers. If the new position did not include any contract-related duties, the individual lost protection under the act at the time of the transfer.

15. It is the position's regular or assigned duties that were controlling. If a portion, however small, of a position's regular duties was necessary to or facilitated carrying out a Government contract, the position was covered. On the other hand, the isolated and unanticipated performance, outside the position's regular duties, of a contract-related task will not result in a finding of coverage. For example, suppose another employee of the photocopy machine company, whose regular duties were in no way contract-related, was unexpectedly needed to substitute for the technician who repaired the machine leased to the Government. Assuming substitution in such situations was not one of the employee's regular or foreseeable duties, his or her isolated performance of the task on a particular occasion would not result in a finding of coverage. In some cases, there will be a formal written position description that will serve as evidence of the position's actual duties and responsibilities. In other cases, there may not be a written position description, or the position description may be inaccurate or incomplete. In all cases, however, it should be possible to identify the position's actual duties, and to make a determination of coverage on that basis.

16. The fact that a position is deemed not to have been engaged in carrying out a Government contract does not affect the individual's rights under the Americans with Disabilities Act of 1990.

PART 60–742—PROCEDURES FOR COMPLAINTS/CHARGES OF EMPLOYMENT DISCRIMINATION BASED ON DISABILITY FILED AGAINST EMPLOYERS HOLDING GOVERNMENT CONTRACTS OR SUBCONTRACTS

Sec.

AUTHORITY: 42 U.S.C. 12117(b).

SOURCE: 57 FR 2962, 2965, Jan. 24, 1992, unless otherwise noted.

§60–742.1 Purpose and application.

The purpose of this part is to implement procedures for processing and resolving complaints/charges of employment discrimination filed against employers holding government contracts or subcontracts, where the complaints/charges fall within the jurisdiction of both section 503 of the Rehabilitation Act of 1973 (hereinafter "Section 503") and the Americans with Disabilities Act of 1990 (hereinafter "ADA"). The promulgation of this part is required pursuant to section 107(b) of the ADA. Nothing in this part should be deemed to affect the Department of Labor's (hereinafter "DOL") Office of Federal Contract Compliance Programs' (hereinafter "OFCCP") conduct of compliance reviews of government contractors and subcontractors under section 503. Nothing in this part is intended to create rights in any person.

§ 60–742.2 Exchange of information.

(a) EEOC and OFCCP shall share any information relating to the employment policies and practices of employers holding government contracts or subcontracts that may assist each office in carrying out its responsibilities. Such information shall include, but not necessarily be limited to, affirmative action programs, annual employment reports, complaints, charges, investigative files, and compliance review reports and files.

(b) All requests by third parties for disclosure of the information described in paragraph (a) of this section shall be coordinated with the agency which initially compiled or collected the information.

(c) Paragraph (b) of this section is not applicable to requests for data in EEOC files made by any state or local agency designated as a "FEP agency" with which EEOC has a charge resolution contract and a work-sharing agreement containing the confidentiality requirements of sections 706(b) and 709(e) of title VII of the Civil Rights Act of 1964 (42 U.S.C. 2000e *et seq.*). However, such an agency shall not disclose any of the information, initially compiled by OFCCP, to the public without express written approval by the Director of OFCCP.

§ 60–742.3 Confidentiality.

When the Department of Labor receives information obtained by EEOC, the Department of Labor shall observe the confidentiality requirements of sections 706(b) and 709(e) of title VII of the Civil Rights Act of 1964, as incorporated by section 107(a) of the ADA, as would EEOC, except in cases where DOL receives the same information from a source independent of EEOC. Questions concerning confidentiality shall be directed to the Associate Legal Counsel for Legal Services, Office of Legal Counsel of EEOC.

§ 60–742.4 Standards for investigations, hearings, determinations and other proceedings.

In any OFCCP investigation, hearing, determination or other proceeding involving a complaint/charge that is dual filed under both section 503 and the ADA, OFCCP will utilize legal standards consistent with those applied under the ADA in determining whether an employer has engaged in an unlawful employment practice. EEOC and OFCCP will coordinate the arrangement of any necessary training regarding the substantive or procedural provisions of the ADA, and of EEOC's implementing regulations (29 CFR part 1630 and 29 CFR part 1601).

§ 60–742.5 Processing of complaints filed with OFCCP.

(a) Complaints of employment discrimination filed with OFCCP will be considered charges, simultaneously dual filed, under the ADA whenever the complaints also fall within the jurisdiction of the ADA. OFCCP will act as EEOC's agent for the sole purposes of receiving, investigating and processing the ADA charge component of a section 503 complaint dual filed under the ADA, except as otherwise set forth in paragraph (e) of this section.

(b) Within ten days of receipt of a complaint of employment discrimination under section 503 (charge under the ADA), OFCCP shall notify the contractor/respondent that it has received a complaint of employment discrimination under section 503 (charge under the ADA). This notification shall state the date, place and circumstances of the alleged unlawful employment practice.

(c) Pursuant to work-sharing agreements between EEOC and state and local agencies designated as FEP agencies, the deferral period for section 503 complaints/ADA charges dual filed with OFCCP will be waived.

(d) OFCCP shall transfer promptly to EEOC a complaint of employment discrimination over which it does not have jurisdiction but over which EEOC may have jurisdiction. At the same time, OFCCP shall notify the complainant and the contractor/respondent of the transfer, the reason for the transfer, the location of the EEOC office to which the complaint was transferred and that the date OFCCP received the complaint will be deemed the date it was received by EEOC.

(e) OFCCP shall investigate and process as set forth in this section all section 503 complaints/ADA charges dual filed with OFCCP, except as specifically provided in this paragraph. Section 503 complaints/ADA charges raising Priority List issues, those which also include allegations of discrimination of an individual nature on the basis of race, color, religion, sex, or national origin, and those which also include an allegation of discrimination on the basis of age will be referred in their entirety by OFCCP to EEOC for investigation, processing and final resolution, provided that such complaints/charges do not include allegations of violation of affirmative action requirements under section 503. In such a situation, OFCCP will bifurcate the complaints/charges and refer to EEOC the Priority List issues or allegations of discrimination on the basis of race, color, religion, sex, national origin, or age. OFCCP shall normally retain, investigate, process and resolve all allegations of discrimination, over which it has jurisdiction, of a systemic or class nature on the basis of race, color, religion, sex, or national origin that it receives. However, in appropriate cases the EEOC may request that it be referred such allegations so as to avoid duplication of effort and assure effective law enforcement.

(1) *No cause section 503 complaints/ADA charges.* If the OFCCP investigation of the section 503 complaint/ADA charge results in a finding of no violation under section 503 (no cause under the ADA), OFCCP will issue a determination of no violation/no cause under both section 503 and the ADA, and issue a right-to-sue letter under the ADA, closing the complaint/charge.

(2) *Cause section 503 complaints/ADA charges*—(i) *Successful conciliation.* If the OFCCP investigation of the section 503 complaint/ADA charge results in a finding of violation under section 503 (cause under the ADA), OFCCP will issue a finding of violation/cause under both section 503 and ADA. OFCCP shall attempt conciliation to obtain appropriate full relief for the complainant (charging party), consistent with EEOC's standards for remedies. If conciliation is successful and the contractor/respondent agrees to provide full relief, the section 503 complaint/ADA charge will be closed and the conciliation agreement will state that the complainant (charging party) agrees to waive the right to pursue the subject issues further under section 503 and/or the ADA.

(ii) *Unsuccessful conciliation.* All section 503 complaints/ADA charges not successfully conciliated will be considered for OFCCP administrative litigation under section 503, consistent with OFCCP's usual procedures. (See 41 CFR part 60–741, subpart B.) If OFCCP pursues administrative litigation under section 503, OFCCP will close the complaint/charge at the conclusion of the litigation process (including the imposition of appropriate sanctions), unless the complaint/charge is dismissed on procedural grounds or because of a lack of jurisdiction, or the contractor/respondent fails to comply with an order to provide make whole relief. In these three cases, OFCCP will refer the matter to EEOC for any action it deems appropriate. If EEOC declines to pursue further action, it will issue a notice of right-to-sue. If OFCCP does not pursue administrative enforcement, it will close the section 503 component of the complaint/charge and refer the ADA charge component to EEOC for litigation review under the ADA. If EEOC declines to litigate, EEOC will close the ADA charge and issue a notice of right-to-sue.

(f) Consistent with the ADA procedures set forth at 29 CFR 1601.28, OFCCP shall promptly issue upon request a notice of right-to-sue after 180 days from the date the complaint/charge was filed. Issuance of a notice of right-to-sue shall terminate further OFCCP processing of any complaint/charge unless it is determined at that time or at a later time that it would effectuate the purposes of section 503 and/or the ADA to further process the complaint/charge.

(g) If an individual who has already filed a section 503 complaint with OFCCP subsequently attempts to file or files an ADA charge with EEOC covering the same facts and issues, EEOC will decline to accept the charge (or, alternatively, dismiss a charge that has been filed) on the grounds that such charge has already been filed under the ADA, simultaneous with the filing of the earlier section 503 complaint, and will be processed by OFCCP in accordance with the provisions of this section.

§ 60–742.6 Processing of charges filed with EEOC.

(a) *ADA cause charges falling within the jurisdiction of section 503 that the Commission has declined to litigate.* ADA cause charges that also fall within the jurisdiction of section 503 and that the Commission has declined to litigate will be referred to OFCCP for review of the file and any administrative action deemed appropriate under section 503. Such charges will be considered to be complaints, simultaneously dual filed under section 503, solely for the purposes of OFCCP review and administrative action described in this paragraph.

(b) *ADA charges which also include allegations of failure to comply with section 503 affirmative action requirements.* ADA charges filed with EEOC, in which both allegations of discrimination under the ADA and violation of affirmative action requirements under section 503 are made, will be referred in their entirety to OFCCP for processing and resolution under section 503 and the ADA, unless the charges also include allegations of discrimination on the basis of race, color, religion, sex, national origin or age, or include allegations involving Priority List issues, or the charges are otherwise deemed of particular importance to EEOC's enforcement of the ADA. In such situations, EEOC will bifurcate the charges and retain the ADA component of the charges (and when applicable, the allegations pertaining to discrimination on the basis of race, color, religion, sex, national origin or age), referring the section 503 affirmative action component of the charges to OFCCP for processing and resolution under section 503. ADA charges which raise both discrimination issues under the ADA and section 503 affirmative action issues will be considered complaints, simultaneously dual filed under section 503, solely for the purposes of referral to OFCCP for processing, as described in this paragraph.

(c) EEOC shall transfer promptly to OFCCP a charge of disability-related employment discrimination over which it does not have jurisdiction, but over which OFCCP may have jurisdiction. At the same time, EEOC shall notify the charging party and the contractor/respondent of the transfer, the reason for the transfer, the location of the OFCCP office to which the charge was transferred and that the date EEOC received the charge will be deemed the date it was received by OFCCP.

(d) Except as otherwise stated in paragraphs (a) and (b) of this section, individuals alleging violations of laws enforced by DOL and over which EEOC has no jurisdiction will be referred to DOL to file a complaint.

(e) If an individual who has already filed an ADA charge with EEOC subsequently attempts to file or files a section 503 complaint with OFCCP covering the same facts and issues, OFCCP will accept the complaint, but will adopt as a disposition of the complaint EEOC's resolution of the ADA charge (including EEOC's termination of proceedings upon its issuance of a notice of right-to-sue).

§ 60–742.7 Review of this part.

This part shall be reviewed by the Chairman of the EEOC and the Director of OFCCP periodically, and as appropriate, to determine whether changes to the part are necessary or desirable, and whether the part should remain in effect.

§ 60–742.8 Definitions.

As used in this part, the term:

ADA refers to title I of the Americans with Disabilities Act of 1990 (42 U.S.C. 12101 *et seq.*).

Affirmative action requirements refers to affirmative action requirements required by DOL pursuant to section 503 of the Rehabilitation Act of 1973, that go beyond the nondiscrimination requirements imposed by the ADA.

Chairman of the EEOC refers to the Chairman of the U.S. Equal Employment Opportunity Commission, or his or her designee.

Complaint/Charge means a section 503 complaint/ADA charge. The terms are used interchangeably.

Director of the Office of Federal Contract Compliance Programs refers to that individual or his or her designee.

DOL means the U.S. Department of Labor, and where appropriate, any of its headquarters or regional offices.

EEOC means the U.S. Equal Employment Opportunity Commission, and where appropriate, any of its headquarters, district, area, local, or field offices.

Government means the government of the United States of America.

Priority List refers to a document listing a limited number of controversial topics under the ADA on which there is not yet definitive guidance setting forth EEOC's position. The Priority List will be jointly developed and periodically reviewed by EEOC and DOL. Any policy documents involving Priority List issues will be coordinated between DOL and EEOC pursuant to Executive Order 12067 (3 CFR, 1978 Comp., p. 206) prior to final approval by EEOC.

OFCCP means the Office of Federal Contract Compliance Programs, and where appropriate, any of its regional or district offices.

Section 503 refers to section 503 of the Rehabilitation Act of 1973 (29 U.S.C. 793).

Section 503 complaint/ADA charge refers to a complaint that has been filed with OFCCP under section 503 of the Rehabilitation Act, and has been deemed to be simultaneously dual filed with EEOC under the ADA.

PART 60–999—OMB CONTROL NUMBERS FOR OFCCP INFORMATION COLLECTION REQUIREMENTS

AUTHORITY: 44 U.S.C. Ch. 35.

SOURCE: 61 FR 43467, Aug. 23, 1996, unless otherwise noted.

§ 60–999.1 Purpose.

This part displays control numbers assigned to information collection requirements of the Office of Federal Contract Compliance Programs by the Office of Management and Budget (OMB) under the Paperwork Reduction Act (PRA), 44 U.S.C. Ch. 35. This part fulfills the PRA requirement that agencies display a current control number for each agency information collection requirement approved by OMB (44 U.S.C. 3507).

§ 60–999.2 Display.

41 CFR Part where the information collection requirement is located	Current OMB control No.
Part 60–1	1215–0072, 1215–0131, 1215–0163.
Part 60–2	1215–0072.
Part 60–3	3046–0017.
Part 60–4	1215–0163.
Part 60–20	1215–0072, 1215–0163.
Part 60–30	1215–0072, 1215–0163.
Part 60–40	1215–0072, 1215–0163.
Part 60–50	1215–0072, 1215–0163.
Part 60–250	1215–0072, 1215–0131, 1215–0163.
Part 60–741	1215–0072, 1215–0131, 1215–0163.

[62 FR 66971, Dec. 22, 1997]

Executive Order 13665

Non-Retaliation for Disclosure of Compensation Information

April 8, 2014

Executive Order 13665—Non-Retaliation for Disclosure of Compensation Information

April 8, 2014

By the authority vested in me as President by the Constitution and the laws of the United States of America, including the Federal Property and Administrative Services Act, 40 U.S.C. 101 *et seq*., and in order to take further steps to promote economy and efficiency in Federal Government procurement, it is hereby ordered as follows:

Section 1. Policy. This order is designed to promote economy and efficiency in Federal Government procurement. It is the policy of the executive branch to enforce vigorously the civil rights laws of the United States, including those laws that prohibit discriminatory practices with respect to compensation. Federal contractors that employ such practices are subject to enforcement action, increasing the risk of disruption, delay, and increased expense in Federal contracting. Compensation discrimination also can lead to labor disputes that are burdensome and costly.

When employees are prohibited from inquiring about, disclosing, or discussing their compensation with fellow workers, compensation discrimination is much more difficult to discover and remediate, and more likely to persist. Such prohibitions (either express or tacit) also restrict the amount of information available to participants in the Federal contracting labor pool, which tends to diminish market efficiency and decrease the likelihood that the most qualified and productive workers are hired at the market efficient price. Ensuring that employees of Federal contractors may discuss their compensation without fear of adverse action will enhance the ability of Federal contractors and their employees to detect and remediate unlawful discriminatory practices, which will contribute to a more efficient market in Federal contracting.

Sec. 2. Amending Executive Order 11246. Section 202 of Executive Order 11246 of September 24, 1965, as amended, is hereby further amended as follows:

(a) Paragraphs (3) through (7) are redesignated as paragraphs (4) through (8).

(b) A new paragraph (3) is added to read as follows:

"The contractor will not discharge or in any other manner discriminate against any employee or applicant for employment because such employee or applicant has inquired about, discussed, or disclosed the compensation of the employee or applicant or another employee or applicant. This provision shall not apply to instances in which an employee who has access to the compensation information of other employees or applicants as a part of such employee's essential job functions discloses the compensation of such other employees or applicants to individuals who do not otherwise have access to such information, unless such disclosure is in response to a formal complaint or charge, in furtherance of an investigation, proceeding, hearing, or action, including an investigation conducted by the employer, or is consistent with the contractor's legal duty to furnish information."

Sec. 3. Regulations. Within 160 days of the date of this order, the Secretary of Labor shall propose regulations to implement the requirements of this order.

Sec. 4. Severability. If any provision of this order, or the application of such provision or amendment to any person or circumstance, is held to be invalid, the remainder of this order and the application of the provisions of such to any person or circumstances shall not be affected thereby.

Sec. 5. General Provisions. (a) Nothing in this order shall be construed to limit the rights of an employee or applicant for employment provided under any provision of law. It also shall not be construed to prevent a Federal contractor covered by this order from pursuing a defense, as long as the defense is not based on a rule, policy, practice, agreement, or other instrument that prohibits employees or applicants from discussing or disclosing their compensation or the compensation of other employees or applicants, subject to paragraph (3) of section 202 of Executive Order 11246, as added by this order.

(b) Nothing in this order shall be construed to impair or otherwise affect:

(i) the authority granted by law to a department, agency, or the head thereof; or

(ii) the functions of the Director of the Office of Management and Budget relating to budgetary, administrative, or legislative proposals.

(c) This order shall be implemented consistent with applicable law and subject to the availability of appropriations.

(d) This order is not intended to, and does not, create any right or benefit, substantive or procedural, enforceable at law or in equity by any party against the United States, its departments, agencies, or entities, its officers, employees, or agents, or any other person.

Sec. 6. Effective Date. This order shall become effective immediately, and shall apply to contracts entered into on or after the effective date of rules promulgated by the Department of Labor under section 3 of this order.

BARACK OBAMA

The White House,
April 8, 2014.

[Filed with the Office of the Federal Register, 11:15 a.m., April 10, 2014]

NOTE: This Executive order was published in the *Federal Register* on April 11.

Categories: Executive Orders : Compensation information, nonretaliation for disclosure.

Subjects: Government organization and employees : Federal Government contracting policies, reform.

DCPD Number: DCPD201400250.

41 CFR Part 60–1

Government Contractors, Prohibitions Against Pay Secrecy Policies and Actions; Final Rule

FEDERAL REGISTER

Vol. 80 Friday,

No. 176 September 11, 2015

Part III

Department of Labor

Office of Federal Contract Compliance Programs

41 CFR Part 60–1

Government Contractors, Prohibitions Against Pay Secrecy Policies and Actions; Final Rule

DEPARTMENT OF LABOR

Office of Federal Contract Compliance Programs

41 CFR Part 60–1

RIN 1250–AA06

Government Contractors, Prohibitions Against Pay Secrecy Policies and Actions

AGENCY: Office of Federal Contract Compliance Programs (OFCCP), Labor.

ACTION: Final rule.

SUMMARY: The Office of Federal Contract Compliance Programs (OFCCP) publishes this final rule to implement Executive Order 13665 (also referred to as "the Order," *infra*) issued on April 8, 2014 to prohibit Federal contractors from discriminating against, in any manner, employees and job applicants who inquire about, discuss, or disclose their own compensation or the compensation of other employees or applicants. Executive Order 13665 amends Executive Order 11246, which prohibits employment discrimination because of race, color, religion, sex, sexual orientation, gender identity, or national origin, by revising the mandatory equal opportunity clauses that are included in Federal contracts and subcontracts, and federally assisted construction contracts, and creating contractor defenses. This final rule defines key terms used in Executive Order 13665 and adopts other key provisions in the notice of proposed rulemaking (NPRM). The final rule also adds a section to the implementing regulations for Executive Order 11246. This section not only describes potential defenses for contractors but also requires contractors to notify employees and job applicants of the nondiscrimination protection created by section 2(b) of Executive Order 13665 using existing methods of communicating to applicants and employees.

The implementing regulations for Executive Order 11246 set forth the basic equal employment opportunity requirements that apply to Federal contractors and subcontractors.

DATES: *Effective Date:* These regulations are effective January 11, 2016.

FOR FURTHER INFORMATION CONTACT: Debra A. Carr, Director, Division of Policy and Program Development, Office of Federal Contract Compliance Programs, 200 Constitution Avenue NW., Room C–3325, Washington, DC 20210. Telephone: (202) 693–0104 (voice) or (202) 693–1337 (TTY). Copies of this rule in alternative formats may be obtained by calling (202) 693–0104 (voice) or (202) 693–1337 (TTY). The rule also is available on the Regulations.gov Web site at *http://www.regulations.gov* or on the OFCCP Web site at *http://www.dol.gov/ofccp.*

SUPPLEMENTARY INFORMATION:

Executive Summary

The Office of Federal Contract Compliance Programs (OFCCP) is a civil rights and worker protection agency. OFCCP enforces an Executive Order and two laws that prohibit employment discrimination and require affirmative action by companies doing business with the Federal Government.[1] Specifically, Federal contractors must not discriminate because of race, color, religion, sex, sexual orientation, gender identity, national origin, disability, or status as a protected veteran. They must also engage in affirmative action and provide equal employment opportunity without regard to race, color, religion, sex, sexual orientation, gender identity, national origin, disability, or status as a protected veteran. OFCCP evaluates the employment practices of nearly 4,000 Federal contractors and subcontractors[2] annually, and investigates individual complaints. OFCCP also engages in outreach to employees of Federal contractors to educate them about their rights, and provides technical assistance to contractors on their nondiscrimination and affirmative action obligations.

These compliance evaluations and complaint investigations determine contractor compliance with VEVRAA, which prohibits employment discrimination against certain protected veterans. OFCCP also determines compliance with Section 503, which prohibits employment discrimination against qualified individuals with disabilities. Finally, OFCCP assesses compliance with Executive Order 11246, as amended, which prohibits employment discrimination because of race, color, religion, sex, sexual orientation, gender identity, or national origin. Compensation discrimination is one form of discrimination prohibited by Executive Order 11246.

On April 8, 2014, President Obama issued Executive Order 13665, entitled "Non-Retaliation for Disclosure of Compensation Information," amending section 202 of Executive Order 11246 to prohibit Federal contractors from discharging or discriminating in any way against employees or applicants who inquire about, discuss, or disclose their own compensation or the compensation of another employee or applicant.[3] This final rule adopts key provisions in the NPRM[4] to promulgate new regulations implementing Executive Order 13665, which apply to covered federal contracts and federally assisted construction contracts. The provisions of this final rule and Executive Order 11246, as amended by Executive Order 13665, apply to covered contracts entered into or modified on or after the rule's effective date. Modified contracts are contracts with any alteration in their terms and conditions, including supplemental agreements, amendments, and extensions. See 41 CFR 60–1.3 Definitions (definition of "Government contract").

Despite the existence of laws protecting workers from gender-based compensation discrimination for more than five decades, a pay gap between men and women persists today. Among the possible contributing factors to the enduring pay gap is the prevalence of workplace prohibitions on discussing compensation.

A comparison of average annual wage data from 2013 reveals that women make 78 cents for every dollar that men make.[5] Data on average weekly wages from the Bureau of Labor Statistics (BLS) for the same year shows a similar gap, with women making 82 cents for every dollar that men make.[6] The wage

[1] Executive Order 11246, Sept. 24, 1965, 30 FR 12319, 12935, 3 CFR, 1964–1965, Comp., p. 339, as amended; Section 503 of the Rehabilitation Act of 1973, as amended, 29 U.S.C. 793, (Section 503); and the Vietnam Era Veterans' Readjustment Assistance Act of 1974, as amended, 38 U.S.C. 4212 (VEVRAA).

[2] References to "contractors" throughout the Final Rule are intended to include both contractors and subcontractors unless stated to the contrary.

[3] Executive Order 13665, Non-Retaliation for Disclosure of Compensation Information, 79 FR 20749 (April 11, 2014).

[4] Government Contractors, Prohibitions Against Pay Secrecy Policies and Actions, 79 FR 55712 (Sept. 17, 2014).

[5] U.S. Bureau of the Census, Income and Poverty in the United States: 2013 (Sept. 2014), *available at https://www.census.gov/library/publications/2014/demo/p60-249.html* (last accessed Feb.10, 2015). Calculation of the pay gap using average weekly wages has the advantage of accounting for differences in hours worked, which is not captured in calculations using annual wage data. However, calculations using weekly wage data do not account for forms of compensation other than those paid as weekly wages, unlike annual wage calculations. While neither method is perfect, analyses that account for factors like occupation and qualifications further support the existence of a significant gender-based pay disparity.

[6] Bureau of Labor Statistics, U.S. Department of Labor, Highlights of Women's Earnings (Dec. 2014) (averaging annual data collected from the Current Population Survey, Median Weekly Earnings of Full-Time Wage and Salary Workers), *available at http://www.bls.gov/opub/reports/cps/highlights-of-womens-earnings-in-2013.pdf* (last accessed Feb.10, 2015).

gap is wider for some women of color when compared to non-Hispanic white men. On average in 2014, BLS median weekly earnings data shows that African-American women earn 68 cents and Latina women earn 61 cents, and Asian women earn 94 cents for every dollar earned by a non-Hispanic white man.[7] Census data shows similar disparities, with African-American women making 64 cents, Latina women making 56 cents, and Asian women making 86 cents per dollar earned by a non-Hispanic white man.[8] Research has found that many factors contribute to the wage gap, including discrimination and occupational differences.

The impact of the wage gap remains a significant problem, especially for the working poor. While the gap may not be larger for poor women when compared to more affluent women, the economic impact of the disparity is greater for poor women who are already in financial jeopardy. U.S. Census data show that more than 15.2 million family households in the United States are headed by women.[9] Nearly 31 percent of these families, or nearly 4,700,000 family households, have incomes that fall below the poverty level.[10] Eliminating the wage gap could go a long way toward closing the overall income gap and reducing the poverty rate for working women. A 2014 report by Maria Shriver and the Center for American Progress found that a third of all American women are living at or near a space called "the brink of poverty." [11] According to the report, this equals to 42 million women plus the 28 million children who depend on them.

Generally, it is true that men and women tend to work in different industries and occupations. Women are much more likely than men to be clustered in a limited number of occupations, with slightly less than half or 44 percent of all working women employed in the 20 most common occupations for women. These occupations include secretaries and administrative assistants, registered nurses, and school teachers.[12] Only about 35 percent of men are employed in the 20 most common occupations for male workers, including truck drivers, managers, and supervisors.[13] According to some studies, these differences in occupations result in occupational segregation that significantly contributes to the wage gap. Occupational segregation contributes to the suppression of earnings for women as research shows that women-dominated industries pay lower wages than male-dominated industries requiring similar skill levels,[14] and the effect is more pronounced in jobs requiring higher levels of education.[15] Women are more likely to be concentrated in low-wage work, and they make up the majority of minimum-wage workers in the United States.

Although some of the wage gap is due to occupational segregation, that does not mean that the wage difference can be overcome by women making different career or work choices. In part, the gap is due to factors such as sex discrimination, including gender stereotyping.[16] By age 65, the typical woman will have lost $420,000 over her working lifetime because of the earnings gap. This is based on median annual earnings for full-time, year-round workers at age 25 and above in 2013 and assumes that the woman works every year between ages 25 and 65.[17]

In every racial group, women earn less than their male counterparts, according to U.S. Census Bureau data analyzed by the Institute for Women's Policy Research (IWPR).[18] In addition to demonstrating a wage gap between men and women, the research also reveals a wage gap amongst various racial groups. Moreover, at the beginning of 2015, median weekly earnings for African-American men working at full-time jobs totaled $680 per week, only 76 percent of the median for white men ($897), according to BLS data, and the median weekly earnings for African-American women equaled $611 per week, only 68 percent of the median for white men.[19]

---

[7] Bureau of Labor Statistics, U.S. Department of Labor, Current Population Survey, Median usual weekly earnings of full-time wage and salary workers by selected characteristics, annual averages, *available at http://www.bls.gov/news.release/wkyeng.t07.htm* (last accessed Feb.10, 2015).

[8] U.S. Census, Current Population Survey, 2012 Person Income, "Table PINC–10: Wage and Salary Workers—People 15 Years Old and Over, by Total Wage and Salary Income in 2012, Work Experience in 2012, Race, Hispanic Origin, and Sex," (comparing median wage for people working 50 or more weeks), *available at https://www.census.gov/hhes/www/cpstables/032013/perinc/pinc10_000.htm* (last accessed Feb.10, 2015).

[9] U.S. Census Bureau, American Community, "Survey 1-Year Estimates 2013, Table DP02: Selected Social Characteristics in the United States," *available at http://factfinder.census.gov/faces/tableservices/jsf/pages/productview.xhtml?src=bkmk* (last accessed Aug. 4, 2015). The calculation uses family households headed by females living in a household with family and no husband. A family household includes a householder, one or more people living in the same household who are related to the householder, and anyone else living in the same household.

[10] U.S. Census Bureau, American Community Survey, "1-Year Estimates 2013, Geographies: United States, Table DP03: Selected Economic Characteristics," *available at http://factfinder.census.gov/faces/tableservices/jsf/pages/productview.xhtml?pid=ACS_13_1YR_DP03&prodType=table* (last accessed Aug. 4, 2015). To determine whether a household falls below the poverty level, the U.S. Census Bureau considers the income of the householder, size of family, number of related children, and, for 1- and 2-person families, age of householder. The poverty threshold in 2013 was $18,769 for a single householder and two children under 18.

[11] Maria Shriver, "The Shriver Report A Women's Nation Pushes Back from the Brink," Executive Summary (Jan. 2014). The "brink" is defined in the report as less than 200 percent of the federal poverty line, or about $47,000 per year for a family of four.

[12] Sarah Jane Glynn, Center for American Progress, "Explaining the Gender Wage Gap," (May 2014), *available at https://www.americanprogress.org/issues/economy/report/2014/05/19/90039/explaining-the-gender-wage-gap/* (last accessed Aug. 3, 2015). *See also* Jane Farrell and Sarah Jane Glynn, "What Causes the Gender Wage Gap?," (Apr. 10, 2013). This report concluded that more than 40 percent of the gender wage gap is "unexplained," meaning that there is no obvious measureable reason for a difference in pay. This leaves us with possible explanations that range from overt sexism to unintentional gender-based discrimination to reluctance among women to negotiate for higher pay.

[13] Sarah Jane Glynn, Center for American Progress, "Explaining the Gender Wage Gap," (May 2014), *available at https://www.americanprogress.org/issues/economy/report/2014/05/19/90039/explaining-the-gender-wage-gap/* (last accessed Aug. 3, 2015).

[14] Sarah Jane Glynn, Center for American Progress, "Explaining the Gender Wage Gap," (May 2014), available at *https://www.americanprogress.org/issues/economy/report/2014/05/19/90039/explaining-the-gender-wage-gap/* (last accessed Aug. 3, 2015). *See also* National Women's Law Center, "The 10 Largest Jobs Paying Under $10.10/Hour Are Majority Women" (Apr. 2013), *available at http://www.nwlc.org/sites/default/files/pdfs/womendominatedminwageoccupations.pdf.*

[15] Sarah Jane Glynn, Center for American Progress, "Explaining the Gender Wage Gap," (May 2014), *available at https://www.americanprogress.org/issues/economy/report/2014/05/19/90039/explaining-the-gender-wage-gap/* (last accessed Aug. 3, 2015).

[16] Shelley J. Correll, Stephan Benard, and In Paik, "Getting a Job: Is There a Motherhood Penalty?" American Journal of Sociology, (Mar. 2007): 1297–1339, *available at http://gender.stanford.edu/sites/default/files/motherhoodpenalty_0.pdf.* This study found that, when comparing equally qualified women job candidates, women who were mothers were recommended for significantly lower starting salaries, perceived as less competent, and less likely to be recommended for hire than non-mothers.

[17] Calculation is based on U.S. Census Table P–24: Historical Income Tables: People. *See* Alex Wall, "Why It's Time for Equal Pay," *available at https://www.whitehouse.gov/blog/2015/04/15/tens-thousands-people-have-shared-why-its-time-equal-pay* (last accessed Aug. 21, 2015).

[18] *Id.* at 2. This study shows that Hispanic men and women, grouped together, had the smallest within-group gap yet earned the least when compared to the other major racial and ethnic groups including white, Asian American, and African-American. Asian Americans earned the most as a group yet had the largest within-group gap.

[19] Bureau of Labor Statistics, U.S. Department of Labor, "Current Population Survey, Median usual weekly earnings of full-time wage and salary workers by selected characteristics, annual averages," *available at http://www.bls.gov/news.release/wkyeng.t07.htm* (last accessed Feb.12, 2015).

A study based on the hiring pattern of male and female workers in the state of New Jersey found that employers offered African-Americans lower wages, compared to their white counterparts, when re-entering the job market after periods of unemployment.[20] The study showed that the pay gap between these two groups is typically 30 percent.[21] Controlling for various factors such as skills and previous earnings, the study found that up to a third of this pay gap could be attributed to racial discrimination in the labor market.[22] Similarly, a study based on National Longitudinal Survey data found that the pay gap between African-Americans and whites continues to exist, even after controlling for abilities and schooling choices.[23]

Many of the studies analyzing pay disparities for Hispanic populations focus on differences in education and age as compared to white workers.[24] However, even after analyzing the effect of these factors, these studies showed that these factors do not account for the entire pay gap for Hispanics.[25]

Potentially nondiscriminatory factors can explain some of the gender wage differences, but accounting for them does not account for the full pay gap.[26] Additionally, women earn less even within occupations. In a recent study of newly trained doctors, after considering the effects of specialty, practice setting, work hours and other factors, the gender pay gap was nearly $17,000 in 2008.[27] Catalyst, a nonprofit research organization, reviewed 2011 government data showing a gender pay gap for women lawyers,[28] and that data confirms that the gap exists for a range of professional and technical occupations.[29] In fact, according to a study by IWPR that used 2011 information from BLS, women frequently earn less than men within the same occupations.[30] Despite differences in the types of jobs women and men typically perform, women earn less than men in male dominated occupations such as managers, software developers and CEO's and even in those jobs commonly filled by women such as teachers, nurses and receptionists.[31]

These statistics provide an overview of the full societal impact of the pay gap, which will not be fully addressed by this rule. For example, such general information about pay differentials among men and women includes pay differentials that may not be attributed to discrimination. In addition, these statistics include all employers and all employees in the U.S., whereas this final rule applies only to Federal contractors and their employees. Therefore, the potential impact of this rule in reducing the pay gap would be much smaller than the impact of eliminating the pay gap among all working men and women.

Whether communicated through a written employment policy or through informal means, restrictions on revealing compensation can conceal compensation disparities that exist among employees. Although very little research has been conducted about pay secrecy policies and their effects, a recent survey by IWPR provides some insight into the prevalence of workplace rules against discussing compensation. The survey found that 51 percent of female respondents and 47 percent of male respondents reported that the discussion of wage and salary information is either discouraged or prohibited and/or could lead to punishment.[32] Further, the IWPR study found that institutional barriers to discussing compensation were much more common among private employers than among public employers.[33] Sixty-two percent (62 percent) of women and 60 percent of men working for private employers reported that discussion of wage and salary information is discouraged or prohibited, compared to only 18 percent of women and 11 percent of men working in the public sector.[34]

In a different survey of private sector employers, 49 percent of the employers surveyed admitted having a specific policy regarding pay secrecy or confidentiality issues,[35] and most managers agreed with the use of pay secrecy policies.[36] This survey also found that only 1 in 14 employers

---

[20] Roland G. Fryer Jr. et al., *Racial Disparities in Job Finding and Offered Wages* (2013), at 27, *available at, http://scholar.harvard.edu/files/fryer/files/racial_disparities_in_job_finding_and_offered_wages.pdf* (last accessed April 29, 2014).

[21] *Id.* at 29.

[22] *Id.*

[23] Sergio Urzua, "Racial Labor Market Gaps: The Role of Abilities and Schooling Choices," 43.4 *J. Hum. Resources*, 919, 919–971.

[24] Richard Fry & B. Lindsay Lowell, "The Wage Structure of Latino-Origin Groups across Generations," 45 *Indus. Relations* 2 (2006); Abelardo Rodriguez and Stephen Devadoss, "Wage Gap between White Non-Latinos and Latinos by Nativity and Gender in the Pacific Northwest," U.S.A., 4 *Journal of Management and Sustainability* 1 (2014).

[25] *Id.*

[26] U.S. Department of Commerce Economics and Statistics Administration and the Office of Management and Budget, "Women in America: Indicators of Social and Economic Well-Being," (March 2011), *available at http://www.whitehouse.gov/sites/default/files/rss_viewer/Women_in_America.pdf* (last accessed March 7, 2015). This report found that while earnings for women and men typically increase with higher levels of education, male-female pay gap persists at all levels of education for full-time workers (35 or more hours per week), according to 2009 BLS wage data. *See, e.g.,* June Elliot O'Neill, "The Gender Gap in Wages, Circa 2000," *American Economic Review* (May 2003). Even so, after controlling for differences in skills and job characteristics, women still earn less than men. Council of Economic Advisers, "Explaining Trends in the Gender Wage Gap," (June 1998), *http://clinton4.nara.gov/WH/EOP/CEA/html/gendergap.html* (last accessed March 6, 2015). Ultimately, the research literature still finds an unexplained gap exists even after accounting for potential explanations, and finds that the narrowing of the pay gap for women has slowed since the 1980's. Joyce P. Jacobsen, *The Economics of Gender* 44 (2007); Francine D. Blau and Lawrence M. Kahn, "The U.S. Gender Pay Gap in the 1990s: Slowing Convergence," 60 *Industrial and Labor Relations Review* 45 (2006).

[27] Anthony T. LoSasso, et al., "The $16,819 Pay Gap For Newly Trained Physicians: The Unexplained Trend of Men Earning More Than Women," 30 *Health Affairs* 193 (2011) *available at http://content.healthaffairs.org/content/30/2/193.abstract* (last accessed Feb.13, 2015).

[28] Catalyst, "Catalyst Quick Take: Women in Law in Canada and the U.S.," (2015) *http://www.catalyst.org/knowledge/women-law-us* (last accessed Feb.13, 2015).

[29] Bureau of Labor Statistics, "Median weekly earnings of full-time wage and salary workers by detailed occupation and sex," 2014, *available at http://www.bls.gov/cps/cpsaat39.pdf* (last accessed Feb.13, 2015).

[30] Ariane Hegewisch, Claudia Williams, Vanessa Harbin, "The Gender Wage Gap by Occupation," (2012), *available at http://www.iwpr.org/publications/pubs/the-gender-wage-gap-by-occupation-1/* (last accessed Feb.13, 2015).

[31] *Id.*

[32] Institute for Women's Policy Research, "Quick Figures: Pay Secrecy and Wage Discrimination," IWPR #Q016, January 2014, *available at http://www.iwpr.org/publications/pubs/pay-secrecy-and-wage-discrimination-1* (last checked Feb.13, 2015).

[33] *Id. See also* Rafael Gely and Leonard Bierman, "Love, Sex and Politics? Sure. Salary? No Way': Workplace Social Norms and the Law," 25 Berkeley J. Emp. & Lab. L. 167, 171 (2004) (arguing that pay-secrecy policies are the prevalent workplace norm); *cf.* Matthew A. Edwards, "The Law and Social Norms of Pay Secrecy," 26 Berkeley J. Emp. & Lab. L. 41 (2005) (rebutting Gely and Bierman's conclusions about the prevalence and causes of pay secrecy).

[34] Institute for Women's Policy Research, "Quick Figures: Pay Secrecy and Wage Discrimination," IWPR #Q016, January 2014, *available at http://www.iwpr.org/publications/pubs/pay-secrecy-and-wage-discrimination-1* (last accessed Feb.13, 2015).

[35] Rafael Gely and Leonard Bierman, "Pay Secrecy/Confidentiality Rules and The National Labor Relations Act," (citing HRnext, "More Employers Ducking Pay Confidentiality Issue: HRnext Survey Shows Many View it As Hot Potato," *http://www2.hrnext.conVabout/pr/pay-survey.cfm* (Apr. 4, 2001)), 6 U. Pa. Journal of Labor and Employment Law 125 (2003), *available at http://scholarship.law.upenn.edu/cgi/viewcontent.cgi?article=1162&context=jbl* (last accessed March 6, 2015).

[36] *Id.* at 122–123,125 (citing Charles M. Futrell and Omer C. Jenkins, "Pay Secrecy Versus Pay Disclosure for Salesmen: A Longitudinal Study," 15 *J. Marketing Res.* 214 (1978) ("Most sales managers contend that peer pay information should not be disclosed to their salesmen."); and Mary Williams Walsh, "Workers Challenge Employer Policies on Pay Confidentiality," *New York Times*, July 28, 2000, *available at http://www.nytimes.com/library/financial/O72800discuss-pay.html* (discussing wrongful termination actions brought by employees who violated employer wage confidentiality policies).

actively adopted "pay openness" policies.[37]

Prohibitions on discussing pay prevent employees from knowing whether they are underpaid in comparison to their peers. Underpaid employees, who may be paid less because of their gender or race, will remain unaware of the disparity if compensation remains hidden. Thus, they are precluded from exercising their rights through OFCCP's complaint procedures. OFCCP enforces the prohibition against compensation discrimination by investigating class complaints of compensation discrimination and conducting compliance evaluations under Executive Order 11246.[38] If a contractor's employees are unaware of how their compensation compares to that of employees with similar jobs because the risk of punitive action inhibits discussions about compensation, employees will not have the information they need to assert their rights. An unwarranted difference in rates of pay, or other forms of compensation, that is based on a protected status like sex or race will likely continue and potentially grow more severe over time. Simply allowing employees to discuss compensation may help bring illegal compensation practices to light and allow employees to obtain appropriate legal redress.

Policies prohibiting employee conversations about compensation can also serve as a significant barrier to Federal enforcement of the laws against compensation discrimination. OFCCP primarily enforces prohibitions in Executive Order 11246 against pay and other forms of compensation discrimination by conducting compliance evaluations of Federal contractors.[39] While OFCCP typically develops statistical analyses to establish systemic compensation discrimination, interviewing managers, human resources professionals, and employees potentially impacted by discriminatory compensation is also an invaluable way for the agency to determine whether compensation discrimination in violation of Executive Order 11246 has occurred and to support its statistical findings. Therefore, the accuracy of OFCCP's investigative findings depends in part on the willingness of a contractor's employees to speak openly with OFCCP investigators about a contractor's compensation practices. If a contractor has a policy or practice of punishing or discouraging employees from discussing their pay, the employees may be fearful and less forthcoming during interviews with OFCCP staff. Prohibiting discrimination against workers who discuss, inquire about, or disclose compensation will help dispel an atmosphere of secrecy around the topic of compensation and promote the agency's ability to uncover illegal compensation discrimination.

The experience of Lilly Ledbetter demonstrates how pay secrecy enables illegal compensation discrimination. For Ledbetter, her employer's insistence on pay secrecy likely cost her the ability to seek justice for the compensation discrimination she suffered throughout her career. Ledbetter was employed at the Gadsden, Alabama plant of Goodyear Tire and Rubber Company. While there, she filed a charge with the EEOC alleging that she was paid a discriminatorily low salary as an area manager because of her sex in violation of Title VII of the Civil Rights Act of 1964.[40] Ledbetter discovered how much her male co-workers were earning years after she began working at the plant and only after she found an anonymous note in her mailbox disclosing her pay and the pay of three males who were doing the same job. In an interview, she said that her employer told her, "You do not discuss wages with anyone in this factory."[41] The Supreme Court, in 2007, issued its ruling in *Ledbetter* v. *Goodyear Tire & Rubber Co.* holding that Ledbetter's claim was untimely.[42] The Court held that Ledbetter was required to have filed her claim within 180 days of when Goodyear initially made its discriminatory pay decision, regardless of whether Ledbetter's paycheck continued to reflect the discriminatory pay policy and regardless of when she discovered that Goodyear was discriminating against her. Congress addressed the timing issues in the Lilly Ledbetter Fair Pay Act of 2009,[43] which states that each discriminatory paycheck is a separate violation and resets the 180-day limitations period. It remains necessary, however, to end pay secrecy policies so that workers can more easily discover if they are victims of discriminatory pay policies.

Pay secrecy policies interfere with the Federal Government's interest in efficiency in procurement. Economy and efficiency in Federal procurement require that contractors compensate employees under merit-based practices, without any barriers to success. As set out in Executive Order 13665, the Federal contractors with pay secrecy practices are subject to enforcement actions and, as a result, may face a higher risk of disruption, delay and expense associated with contract performance. Allowing discussions of pay by employees of these contractors will contribute to minimizing these risks. This final rule eliminates some of the barriers created by pay secrecy policies and helps ensure that Federal contractors compensate employees based on merit.

In addition to disruptions and delays, Federal contractors with pay secrecy policies may also experience a decrease in worker productivity. Workers, due to a lack of compensation information, may experience a reduction in performance motivation and are likely to perceive their employer as unfair or untrustworthy. Both reduce work productivity.[44] For example, one study has shown that workers without access to compensation information are less satisfied and less productive.[45] The precise reasons for this drop in productivity have not been investigated; however, a number of theories can be drawn from the empirical evidence gathered in this field. Two such theories on the loss of productivity are that employees are unable to link their performance or their worth to the organization, and that employer secrecy policies foster distrust of management.

The first of these theories is based on the idea that because of pay secrecy

[37] *Id.* at 125 (citing HRnext Survey).

[38] Pursuant to a Memorandum of Understanding between OFCCP and the Equal Employment Opportunity Commission (EEOC), OFCCP generally refers individual discrimination complaints subject to both Executive Order 11246 and Title VII of the Civil Rights Act of 1964 to the EEOC for investigation, but keeps systemic discrimination complaints, 76 FR 71029 (Nov. 16, 2011).

[39] OFCCP reviews approximately 4,000 Federal contractors annually. These contractors are scheduled for compliance evaluations based on various sources of information, including federal procurement databases, Employer Information Reports (EEO–1 reports), Dun & Bradstreet (D&B) data, U.S. Census data, and statistical thresholds such as industry type and employee counts of federal contractor establishments. The scheduling process is "neutral" rather than "random" because it is based on a methodology that includes specific criteria. OFCCP does not target specific contractors.

[40] White House National Pay Task Force, "Fifty Years After the Equal Pay Act: Assessing the Past, Taking Stock of the Future," June 2013, *available at http://www.whitehouse.gov/sites/default/files/equalpay/equal_pay_task_force_progress_report_june_2013_new.pdf*, citing TAP Talks with Lilly Ledbetter. The American Prospect, April 23, 2008, *http://www.prospect.org/cs/articles?article=tap_talks_with_lilly_ledbetter* (last accessed Feb.13, 2015).

[41] *Id.* at 22.

[42] *Ledbetter* v. *Goodyear Tire & Rubber Co.*, 550 U.S. 618 (2007).

[43] Public Law 111–2, 123 Stat. 5 (Jan. 29, 2009).

[44] Adrienne Colella, Ramona L. Paetzold, Asghar Zardkoohi, and Michael J. Wesson, "Exposing Pay Secrecy," 32 Acad. of Management Rev. 55, 58 (2007).

[45] Peter Bamberger and Elena Belogolovsky, "The Impact of Pay Secrecy on Individual Task Performance," 63 Personnel Psychol. 965, 967 (2010).

policies, some workers do not know whether their own wages are reflective of job performance. This information gap makes it more difficult for workers to make informed choices about their own compensation and creates unnecessary barriers to enforcing laws against compensation discrimination. Information asymmetries provide an advantage and market power to the party with more information. When workers have access to more information about colleagues' compensation, salaries may be likely to be more closely linked to productivity on the job and compensation may be much less likely to be influenced by factors unrelated to job performance such as sex and race. As a result, workers with the ability to inquire about, discuss, and disclose compensation information may make informed decisions about their careers. These workers may become aware of their current value to the organization, but also of their potential value, based on information they receive about the salaries of longer tenured employees or employees in higher wage positions.

This phenomenon has a unique consequence in labor markets where those involved in the transaction are people who, unlike machines, are likely to be affected by the information in terms of motivation and effort. In companies with pay secrecy policies, negative influences on productivity may stem from workers overestimating the lower limits of pay for others in similar positions leading to an inaccurate compression of the pay range, and causing a perception that increased work will not result in a corresponding reward.[46] Workers with knowledge of compensation information are given accurate aspirational goals because they are aware of the salaries of the best-compensated employees, and can make rational decisions about the cost of increased effort at work in relation to the benefit of increased compensation resulting from success in the job.[47]

The second theory is that worker distrust of corporate management may be another potential cause of the lag in productivity for workers subject to pay secrecy policies. Restrictions on sharing compensation information may create a sense that the company has something to hide with respect to compensating employees. Feelings of institutional unfairness may have a negative impact on workers' productivity.[48]

Eliminating pay secrecy policies may have benefits beyond improving the productivity of Federal contractors and their employees. Generally, employers seek to provide opportunities for employees to advance within the corporate hierarchy because these employees will work harder to achieve goals and secure advancement. The result of this may be not only higher productivity and better quality, but also lower turnover, retention of organizational knowledge, and lower training and onboarding expenses.[49] Employers, including Federal contractors, may encounter more difficulty achieving these benefits if they have pay secrecy policies. Another benefit of eliminating these policies is that younger employees and jobseekers view employers without these policies more favorably. A report found that younger employees value openness in general and are more suspicious of companies instituting pay secrecy rules.[50]

Under the final rule, contractors could also realize a reduction in the cost and burden associated with investigating baseless claims of compensation discrimination. Workers with knowledge of compensation relative to other employees can make more accurate determinations about the presence or absence of discriminatory practices.[51] When workers' suspicions of discriminatory practices are discredited by information about other employees' compensation, the company avoids the costs and time associated with defending against discrimination lawsuits filed by employees.

Transparency about compensation also allows companies and their employees to identify and resolve unwarranted disparities in compensation prior to the employee filing a formal complaint or pursuing litigation. This additional openness about compensation could decrease discrimination complaints and investigations, saving both the contractor and the government time and money. Moreover, the employees may receive a faster remedy through internal resolution than would be possible through a complaint process or subsequent litigation.

The preceding paragraphs present several reasons why the final rule could yield productivity benefits or cost savings for covered Federal contractors. However, OFCCP notes that, in addition to these benefits, and in order to achieve its goal of ensuring employees receive fair wages, this final rule is expected to result in increased wage payments to employees. This may be the result of employees using the information that they receive about the compensation paid to others to pursue increased wage payments. Employers may either voluntarily increase wages or be required to do so through actions taken by employees. These higher wage payments may, in some instances, result in net costs to covered contractors.

I. Statement of Legal Authority

Issued in 1965, and amended several times in the intervening years, Executive Order 11246 has two purposes. First, it prohibits covered Federal contractors and subcontractors from discriminating against employees and applicants because of race, color, religion, sex, sexual orientation, gender identity, or national origin.[52] Second, it requires covered Federal contractors and subcontractors to take affirmative action to ensure that they provide equal opportunity in all aspects of employment. The nondiscrimination and affirmative action obligations of Federal contractors and subcontractors cover all aspects of employment, including rates of pay and other compensation.

The requirements in Executive Order 11246 generally apply to any business or organization that (1) holds a single Federal contract, subcontract, or federally assisted construction contract in excess of $10,000; (2) has Federal contracts or subcontracts that combined total in excess of $10,000 in any 12-month period; or (3) holds Government bills of lading, serves as a depository of Federal funds, or is an issuing and paying agency for U.S. savings bonds and notes in any amount.

Pursuant to Executive Order 11246, receiving a Federal contract comes with a number of responsibilities. Section

---

[46] *Id.* at 969.

[47] Lauren Weber and Rachel Emma Silverman, "Workers Share Their Salary Secrets," *Wall St. J.* (April 16, 2013), *available at http://online.wsj.com/news/articles/SB10001424127887324345804578426744168583824?mg=reno64-wsj&url=http%3A%2F%2Fonline.wsj.com%2Farticle%2FSB10001424127887324345804578426744168583824.html* (last accessed Feb.13, 2015).

[48] *See* Bamberger and Belogolovsky *supra* note 44.

[49] Heather Boushey and Sarah Jane Glynn, "There Are Significant Business Costs to Replacing Employees," Center for American Progress, Nov. 16, 2012, *available at https://www.americanprogress.org/issues/labor/report/2012/11/16/44464/there-are-significant-business-costs-to-replacing-employees/* (last accessed Feb.13, 2015).

[50] *Id.*

[51] *See* Weber and Silverman *supra* note 46.

[52] OFCCP generally interprets Executive Order 11246 consistently with Title VII principles. To the extent that this rule uses terms or concepts borrowed from Title VII or other EEO statutes, however, their usage here is limited to claims brought pursuant to Executive Order 13665 and this final rule. OFCCP's interpretation of Executive Order 13665 does not in any way limit the enforcement of Title VII or other EEO statutes.

202 of Executive Order 11246 requires every contractor to agree to comply with all provisions of Executive Order 11246 and the rules, regulations, and relevant orders of the Secretary of Labor. A contractor in violation of the Executive Order 11246 may have its contracts canceled, terminated, or suspended or may be subject to debarment after the opportunity for a hearing.[53]

II. Major Proposed Revisions in the Final Rule

The final rule protects employees' inquiries, discussions, and disclosures of their own pay and benefits, and similar employee activities related to the pay and benefits of others, if they obtained that information through ordinary means such as conversations with co-workers. What the Order, and in turn this final rule, does not protect is the disclosure of others' pay information that an employee obtained as part of the employee's essential job functions. So, for example, if the employee making the disclosure to others had access to the information as a part of carrying out the essential job functions of the position of payroll administrator or benefits administrator, the contractor may be justified in taking adverse action based on that disclosure. This is because the employee, as payroll or benefits administrator, had access to the information as an essential part of the job and shared that information with others who do not otherwise have access to such information, which could undermine a contractor's ability to maintain necessary confidentiality concerning compensation. The nondiscrimination provision of the final rule may not protect this employee. The final rule specifically allows a contractor to take adverse action when an employee, with access to compensation information as part of an essential job function, discloses that information to others and the disclosure does not fall into one of the exemptions. The exemptions are disclosures made in response to a formal complaint or charge, in furtherance of an investigation, proceeding, hearing or action, including an investigation by the contractor, or disclosures consistent with the contractor's legal duty to furnish the information.

Nothing in the final rule prohibits contractors from proactively promoting what they view as good about their pay policies and practices. As a best practice, contractors are encouraged to remove barriers to employees knowing that the contractor's pay and benefit practices are competitive with other companies within the same industry, and to promote their company's practices regarding advancement opportunities, merit increases in pay, and other factors that affect their employees' pay. The more a contractor's employees know about where they stand in terms of their pay within the company, the more the employees should feel that they have a stake in the company and its financial success.

The final rule applies to all Federal contractors with contracts entered into or modified on or after the effective date of the rule that exceed $10,000 in value. The major provisions in the final rule:

- Revise the equal opportunity clause that is currently included in qualifying Federal Government contracts, federally assisted construction contracts, subcontracts, and purchase orders. The revised clause includes a provision prohibiting contractors from discharging, or in any manner discriminating against, any employee or applicant for employment because the employee or applicant inquired about, discussed, or disclosed the compensation of the employee or applicant or another employee or applicant.
- Define "compensation" in a manner consistent with the definition used by OFCCP in other existing guidance. Compensation is defined for these purposes as any payments made to, or on behalf of, an employee or offered to an applicant as remuneration for employment, including but not limited to salary, wages, overtime pay, shift differentials, bonuses, commissions, vacation and holiday pay, allowances, insurance and other benefits, stock options and awards, profit sharing, and retirement.
- Define "compensation information" as the amount and type of compensation provided to employees or offered to applicants, including but not limited to the desire of the contractor to attract and retain a particular employee for the value they are perceived to add to the contractor's profit or productivity; the availability of employees with like skills in the marketplace; market research about the worth of similar jobs in the relevant marketplace; job analysis, descriptions, and evaluations; salary and pay structures; salary surveys; labor union agreements; and contractor decisions, statements, and policies related to setting or altering employee compensation.
- Define "essential job function" to provide clarity about the positions covered by minimizing the degree of subjectivity involved in the determination. A job function may be considered essential if: (1) The access to compensation information is necessary in order to perform that function or other routinely assigned business task; or (2) the function or duties of the position include protecting and maintaining the privacy of employee personnel records, including compensation information.
- Establish a *General defenses* provision and an *Essential job functions defense* provision. Both provide contractor defenses to alleged violations of the nondiscrimination obligation for employees who inquired about, disclosed or discussed compensation. The nature of the defenses differs, however. The essential job functions defense, per the text of the Order, is a complete defense, such that if an employee discloses compensation information accessed or received through performance of an essential job function, *unless* the disclosure falls into one or more exemptions, the protections of the Order shall not apply and a contractor is allowed to take adverse action on those grounds. Contractors may also pursue a general defense if the discipline it imposes is for violation of a consistently and uniformly applied rule, policy, practice, agreement, or other instrument that does not prohibit, or tend to prohibit, employees or applicants from discussing or disclosing their compensation or the compensation of other employees or applicants. Given the difference in structure and function of this defense, this rule clarifies that it is not a complete defense, but rather is to be employed within the analytical framework discussed herein.
- Require contractors to disseminate a nondiscrimination provision, as prescribed by the Director of OFCCP and made available on the OFCCP Web site. Contractors must disseminate the provision to employees and applicants using their existing employee manuals or handbooks, and either electronically or by posting the prescribed provision in conspicuous places available to employees and job applicants.

III. Cost and Benefits

This is not economically significant under section 3(f) of Executive Order 12866, though it is a "significant regulatory action." The total cost of the final rule is $42,726,188.

[53] E.O. 11246, sec. 209(5); 41 CFR 60–1.27.

TABLE 1—TOTAL ESTIMATED COST SUMMARY

	Hours	Costs	Total cost per company
First Year Costs	1,045,000	$42,726,188	$85
Recurring Costs	0	0	0

The final rule provisions primarily require contractors to refrain from discriminatory activity, and notify employees, job applicants, and subcontractors of the nondiscrimination obligation using existing or common methods of communication. Notice to subcontractors is provided by amending the existing equal opportunity clause that contractors are currently required to include in their subcontracts and purchase orders. Contractors are not required to develop and deliver new staff or management training on the new nondiscrimination obligation in the final rule; however, providing such training is considered a best practice. The final rule also includes a defenses provision that allow contractors to pursue a defense to a claim of discrimination under certain circumstances.

At an estimated cost of $85 per company, the final rule should result in benefits to workers who have historically experienced pay discrimination, and also transfers between groups of employees and from contractors, employers, or taxpayers to workers. The provisions in the final rule should help to ensure that fear of discrimination does not inhibit the employees of Federal contractors from sharing information with one another about their compensation. The final rule's provisions, as discussed earlier in the preamble, also promote economy and efficiency in Federal Government procurement, potentially contribute to the economic security of working women and their families, and support enforcement of nondiscrimination and equal employment opportunity protections.

Overview of the Final Rule

Prior to issuing an NPRM, OFCCP conducted listening sessions with individuals from the contractor community, civil rights groups, and other interested parties to understand their perspectives on the scope and intent of Executive Order 13665 amending Executive Order 11246. After reviewing all of the comments on the NPRM, OFCCP's final rule incorporates many of the provisions in the NPRM. However, in order to clarify and focus the scope of one or more provisions in the final rule, while not increasing the estimated burden, the final rule revises some of the NPRM's provisions.

OFCCP received 6,524 comments on the NPRM, of which 6,443 were the result of organized efforts using form letters generally in support of the NPRM. The remaining group of 81 unique or non-form letter comments represented diverse perspectives including one contractor, three law firms, four contractor associations, 13 civil rights organizations, four employee associations and unions, and 56 individuals. The commenters raised a range of issues, including concerns about the definitions of "compensation," "compensation information," and "essential job functions." A few commenters urged OFCCP to make the definition of "compensation" consistent with existing OFCCP Directive 2013–03, *Procedures for Reviewing Contractor Compensation Systems and Practices.* The final rule adopts this definition.

Another commenter was concerned that the proposed definition of "compensation information" would include information covered by the attorney-client privilege or the attorney work product doctrine. As discussed in the section-by-section analysis, the final rule modifies the definition of compensation information. It provides more specificity as to the type of information covered but the final rule does not adopt other suggested changes related to concerns about attorney-client privilege or the attorney work product doctrine. The information that OFCCP could request would not involve legal opinions or advice, but would include factual data that informed the contractor's compensation decisions. The information sought is not significantly different in nature from what OFCCP could request during a compliance evaluation or complaint investigation.

A definition for "essential job functions" that was proposed in the NPRM was based on the approach used in the Americans with Disabilities Act (ADA), as amended, and OFCCP's regulations implementing Section 503. The "essential job function" analysis and evidence in these instances relate to issues of reasonable accommodation and qualification. However, in the context of Executive Order 13665, the purpose or goal of the "essential job functions" analysis is different. Most of the commenters stated that the definition proposed in the NPRM for "essential job functions" is too broad. They proposed narrowing it to employees whose jobs are to maintain and protect the privacy of employee personnel records, and minimizing the amount of subjectivity available to contractors when determining what constitutes essential job functions. Others commented that the proposed definition of essential job functions was too narrow. Some commenters believed that the definition of essential job functions is inconsistent with the National Labor Relations Act (NLRA), and that the proposals in the NPRM are unnecessary because the NLRA covers pay secrecy issues under the right to discuss "terms and conditions of employment." The final rule rejects the ADA, as amended, definition of essential job functions as proposed in the NPRM. The final rule also rejects the comparison made by some commenters with the NLRA. Instead, the final rule identifies two types or categories of essential job functions to minimize subjectivity and provide specificity for the types of job functions that would be covered as essential.

Some commenters sought to expand the defenses provisions in the NPRM to allow contactors to take action when employees or applicants access information without the contractor's authorization, or violate contractor policies or other limitations created pursuant to applicable laws protecting private or confidential information. The final rule does not expand the defenses to include these recommendations, nor does it limit the ability of contractors to take disciplinary actions for violations of security policies and applicable privacy laws.

A significant number of commenters raised issues about the legal framework that would apply to analyzing an alleged violation. Commenters were concerned that the NPRM proposed prohibiting "discrimination" for conduct that is more appropriately considered "retaliation." The commenters noted that the proposed prohibition is not based on the employees' or applicants' membership in one of the protected categories under

Title VII. Similarly, several commenters wrote that it is unclear whether a violation would be analyzed under the "motivating factor" standard or "but for" standard under Title VII—the "but for" standard being applicable to retaliation claims while "motivating factor" applies to discrimination claims. Other commenters viewed the NPRM's prohibition as a nondiscrimination provision and asserted that the motivating factor standard would be appropriate. One commenter requested that OFCCP expressly state that it could use all Title VII discrimination remedies once a violation is established, including declaratory and injunctive relief, and attorneys' fees and costs. This final rule, as discussed in the section-by-section analysis, clarifies that adverse action taken by a contractor against an employee or applicant that violates the provisions of Executive Order 13665 and these regulations is appropriately viewed as discrimination and analyzed as such under that legal framework.

Other commenters proposed that OFCCP require contractors to take additional measures to disseminate the equal opportunity clause such as requiring mandatory training to ensure that managers and employees understand the proposed protections. The commenters considered this training especially necessary where a contractor has longstanding pay secrecy policies or a culture of secrecy surrounding pay disclosures. One commenter would require training for departmental leadership responsible for handling compensation-related matters. Several commenters opposed mandatory training but encouraged it as a best practice, including one noting that training is no guarantee of effectiveness and that compliance is best achieved through clear guidance to contractors. Another commenter believed that training on the proposed new protections described in the NPRM could result in confusion, and encourage frivolous claims because employees are already aware that compensation discrimination is unlawful. The minority of the comments included one that proposed eliminating the equal opportunity clause altogether and focusing on collecting data. The final rule declines to require mandatory staff and management training.

There were also comments associated with the cost and burden of the proposed rule, and the authority of OFCCP to undertake this rulemaking. Other comments on the NPRM addressed access to technical assistance and training, alternatives to the proposals in the NPRM, and the absence of a provision obligating the government to intervene and pay costs and attorneys' fees should a prime contractor terminate a subcontractor under a government mandate. OFCCP carefully considered all comments in the development of this final rule.

Section-By-Section Analysis

41 CFR Part 60–1—Obligations of Contractors and Subcontractors

SUBPART A—Preliminary Matters; Equal Opportunity Clause; Compliance Reports

Section 60–1.3 Definitions

The proposed rule provided definitions for three terms used in Executive Order 13665. The NPRM defined the term "compensation" to include payments made to an employee, or on behalf of an employee, or offered to an applicant as remuneration for employment, including but not limited to salary, wages, overtime pay, shift differentials, bonuses, commissions, vacation and holiday pay, allowances, insurance and other benefits, stock options and awards, profit sharing, and retirement. This definition of "compensation" aligns with the definition OFCCP uses in the context of compensation discrimination investigations. OFCCP received three comments regarding the definition of "compensation." One commenter generally supported the proposed definition. Another commenter supported the definition, but suggested expanding it to include "sick time" and "paid leave." The third commenter stated that the definition of "compensation" in the NPRM differed from the definition of that term in OFCCP's Directive 2013–03, and further suggested that both the final rule and the Directive contain the same definition.

After consideration, OFCCP does not believe it would be appropriate to include "sick time" and "paid leave" expressly in the definition of compensation. The NPRM's definition of "compensation" includes a general list of compensation types, but was not meant to be exhaustive. As a matter of consistency OFCCP will use the definition as stated in the NPRM, which aligns with the definition used in the context of its compensation discrimination investigations. OFCCP also notes the comment regarding the differing definitions in Directive 2013–03 and the NPRM, which advocates for making them consistent. However, OFCCP's guidance and regulations have historically included salary, wages, overtime pay, shift differentials, bonuses, commissions, vacation and holiday pay, allowances, insurance and other benefits, stock options, profit sharing and retirement. Though the definition of compensation in Directive 2013–03 and the final rule are not identical, Directive 2013–03 should be interpreted in a manner consistent with the final rule.

The proposed definition in the NPRM for the term "compensation information" is consistent with the approach described in OFCCP's existing compensation guidance.[54] The definition covers information related to any aspect of compensation, including but not limited to information about the amount and type of compensation as well as decisions, statements, or actions related to setting or altering employees' compensation. OFCCP intended the proposed definition of "compensation information" to be broad enough to encompass any information directly related to employee compensation, as well as the process or steps that led to a decision to award a particular type or amount of compensation. OFCCP received one comment on the definition of "compensation information." The commenter was critical of the proposed definition, stating that it was "vaguely defined and may be deemed broad enough to encompass information related to compensation that is subject to the attorney-client privilege." OFCCP does not believe that the definition of "compensation information" would interfere with the operation of the attorney-client privilege. The attorney-client privilege only protects disclosure of communication; it does not protect the disclosure of the factual bases underlying the communication between a client and his or her attorney. Therefore, the privilege generally would not cover "compensation information" data. However, in reviewing the proposed definition, the final rule slightly modifies the definition so that it would mean the amount and type of compensation provided to employees or offered to applicants, including, but not limited to, factual information about the desire of the contractor to attract and retain a particular employee for the value they are perceived to add to the contractor's profit or productivity; the availability of employees with like skills in the marketplace; market research about the worth of similar jobs in the relevant marketplace; job analysis, descriptions, and evaluations; salary and pay structures; salary surveys; labor union agreements; and contractor

[54] Directive 2013–03, Procedures for Reviewing Contractor Compensation Systems and Practices, Feb. 28, 2013.

decisions, statements and policies related to setting or altering employee compensation. This modification in the final rule, by way of including several examples, provides contractors with additional guidance.

Lastly, the NPRM also proposed a definition for the term "essential job functions." OFCCP had proposed to use the ADA, as amended, definition of essential job functions. Under that definition, a job function may be considered essential for any of several reasons, including: (1) The function may be essential because the reason the position exists is to perform that function; (2) the function may be essential because of the limited number of employees available among whom the performance of that job function can be distributed; and/or (3) the function may be highly specialized so that the incumbent in the position is hired for his or her expertise or ability to perform the particular function.

OFCCP received a number of comments, some indicating that the ADA, as amended, definition was too narrow, and others indicating that it was too broad or needed further specificity. In response to these comments, the final rule modifies the proposal in the NPRM by eliminating the use of the ADA, as amended, definition of essential job functions in favor of identifying two categories or types of essential job functions. In the final rule, a job function may be considered an essential job function if: (1) The access to compensation information is necessary in order to perform that function or another routinely assigned business task; or (2) the function or duties of the position include protecting and maintaining the privacy of employee personnel records, including compensation information.

Generally, those commenters who favored broadening the definition of "essential job functions," and therefore the exception to the rule's protections, suggested that OFCCP adopt a definition that relies more on whether employees required access to confidential compensation information in the performance of their job duties, rather than on whether the employee's position description related to handling compensation information. One commenter noted that the complexity of large enterprises made it unrealistic that such employers could effectively operate through only selected employees whose "fundamental" job duties involved access to pay information or whose job exists only to perform those functions or who have specialized expertise or ability somehow related to pay information. Another commenter suggested that the test for what constitutes an essential job function should rely on whether access to compensation information was granted as necessary to the performance of a legitimate, assigned business task. Another commenter suggested that the definition of "essential job functions" should include all employees who have authorized access to an employer's compensation information, whether or not that access falls within the employee's primary job responsibilities.

OFCCP agrees with many of these comments and has determined that a definition of "essential job functions" that is driven by the employee's position description, rather than the assigned tasks, could create confusion among employers in determining which employees are covered by the definition. Instead, the revised definition makes clear that employees performing job functions or routinely assigned tasks that require them to have access to confidential compensation information will be covered. Additionally, job functions that require protecting or maintaining the privacy of employee personnel records will be covered by the revised definition.

Some commenters identified specific occupations that they thought should be covered by the definition, such as IT employees and program staffers who prepare bids for government contracts that regularly require access to compensation information, even if the position was not created for the purpose of handling compensation data. The determination of whether any particular employee received compensation information in the course of their "essential job functions" will be determined on a case-by-case basis by OFCCP. OFCCP agrees, however, that a position where the functions of that position require access to compensation information, or protecting and maintaining the privacy of employee personnel records, should generally fall within the definition of "essential job functions."

Some commenters, on the other hand, were concerned that the exception could be construed too broadly, such that groups of employees with access to compensation information, such as human resource employees, could be denied protection under the regulations. Many of these commenters suggested that the employer's ability to assert "essential job functions" as an affirmative defense must be limited to only a very narrow subset of employees whose job is to maintain and protect the privacy of employee personnel records. One commenter also suggested that the definition should focus on whether employees used compensation information as part of their essential job functions, rather than whether they have access to such information.

The revised definition includes "protecting and maintaining the privacy of employee personnel records" as one category of "essential job functions." However, it also includes functions and routinely assigned business tasks for which accessing compensation information is necessary to their performance. This definition provides adequate protection to employers in preserving the confidentiality of compensation and personnel data but limits the scope of the exception to those positions that require access to the information to perform their job functions and tasks. Furthermore, as discussed below, the application of the "essential job functions" defense is narrowed by the fact that even employees in positions covered by the definition are protected if they discuss compensation information that they obtained from a source outside of their essential job functions, or if they discuss information relating to their own possible claim of compensation discrimination, or if they discuss compensation information of others accessed within their essential job functions so long as the discussion takes place internally with a management official of the contractor or while using the contractor's internal complaint process.

Some of the commenters favoring a narrow interpretation also wanted the definition of "essential job functions" to rely less on subjective factors. They suggested that an employer's judgment should not be given conclusive weight on the question of what constitutes an essential job function. The revised definition replaces the more subjective factors under the ADA, as amended, definition with two categories that more clearly identify which classes of job functions should be deemed essential for purposes of these regulations. As noted in paragraph 3 of the regulatory definition, this definition of "essential job functions" is limited to the discrimination claims governed by Executive Order 13665 and its implementing regulations, and does not apply to claims brought pursuant to other EEO laws.

Section 60–1.4 Equal Opportunity Clause

As proposed in the NPRM, the final rule revises the equal opportunity clause in § 60–1.4(a) and § 60–1.4(b) to include the new nondiscrimination provision. Section 60–1.4 requires contracting agencies to include this equal opportunity clause in government contracts and modifications to government contracts if the clause was not included in the original contract. By accepting Federal contracts, contractors accept the discrimination and affirmative action requirements contained in the equal opportunity clause and agree to include the requirements contained in the clause in their subcontracts and purchase orders unless exempted by law, regulations, or order of the Secretary of the U.S. Department of Labor.

The final rule revises § 60–1.4(a) by inserting a new paragraph 3 into the equal opportunity clause and by renumbering the subsequent paragraphs in the clause. The text of the new paragraph in § 60–1.4(a) is identical to the text in section 2(b) of Executive Order 13665. Under the terms of this new provision, it is unlawful for contractors to discharge or discriminate in any other manner against any employee or job applicant because such employee or applicant has inquired about, discussed, or disclosed the compensation of the employee or applicant or another employee or applicant. This provision does not apply when an employee with access to the compensation information of other employees or job applicants as a part of such employee's essential job functions discloses the compensation of such other employees or applicants to individuals who do not otherwise have access to such information, unless such disclosure is in response to a formal complaint or charge, in support of an investigation, proceeding, hearing, or action, including an investigation conducted by the employer, or is consistent with the contractor's legal duty to furnish information.

Under the equal opportunity clause in § 60–1.4(b), administering agencies involved in federally assisted construction through grants, loans, insurance, or guarantee must include text in their contracts for construction work informing the funding applicant that the equal opportunity clause must be incorporated into the contracts and contract modifications if they are funded in whole or in part by Federal money. This section further provides the exact language for the equal opportunity clause. As with § 60–1.4(a), by accepting funding the contractor agrees to assume the nondiscrimination and affirmative action obligations of Executive Order 11246, including incorporating the equal opportunity clause into their subcontracts and purchase orders unless exempted by law, regulations, or order of the Secretary of the U.S. Department of Labor. The final rule revises § 60–1.4(b) by inserting a new paragraph 3 into the equal opportunity clause, and renumbering the subsequent paragraphs in the clause. The text of the new paragraph is identical to the text in section 2(b) of Executive Order 13665.

OFCCP made changes to § 60–1.4 with the intent to eliminate the secrecy and fear surrounding a discussion or disclosure of compensation information. When employees lack access to compensation information it is more difficult for them to make informed choices about their own compensation, and it creates unnecessary barriers to filing complaints with civil rights agencies such as OFCCP. Secrecy may also have a detrimental impact on business productivity, employee morale and retention, and could drive increased cost related to human resources management as discussed earlier in the preamble to the final rule.[55] Studies have shown that these pay secrecy policies are common among contractors and foster negative consequences for some employees and applicants for employment.[56] The final rule does not require employees to share information about compensation with other employees.

OFCCP received three comments on the proposed revisions to § 60–1.4. One commenter suggested that OFCCP eliminate the proposed equal opportunity clause provisions and focus instead on establishing "thorough but undemanding reporting requirements" to detect compensation discrimination. With respect to that comment, OFCCP proposed an NPRM on August 8, 2014, entitled "Government Contractors, Requirement To Report Summary Data on Employee Compensation." [57] OFCCP will address any changes to compensation reporting requirements through this separate rulemaking. Further, eliminating the proposed equal opportunity clause provisions would be contrary to the express requirements of Executive Order 13665. OFCCP, therefore, adopts the revised equal opportunity clause provisions into the final rule.

Another commenter suggested that the final rule modify the equal opportunity clause by adding language from Sections 7 and 8 of the National Labor Relations Act (NLRA).[58] Although the language may not be identical to the NLRA, the revised equal opportunity clause language includes language detailing employees' right to engage in wage discussions and employers' nondiscrimination obligations related to this right. Consequently, OFCCP believes that inclusion of the suggested NLRA language is unnecessary. Furthermore, the language inserted into the equal opportunity clause mirrors language contained in the Order giving OFCCP the authority and responsibility to ensure Federal contractors do not discriminate against any employee or job applicant because such employee or applicant has inquired about, discussed, or disclosed the compensation of the employee or applicant or another employee or applicant.

The other comment regarding revisions to § 60–1.4 asserted that it is not necessary for OFCCP to alter the heading for § 60–1.4(d) from "Incorporation of the equal opportunity clause by reference" to "Inclusion of the equal opportunity clause by reference;" or to alter the first sentence of § 60–1.4(d) by deleting "incorporated by reference" and inserting "included by reference." OFCCP does not agree that this change is unnecessary and will change the current regulatory language of the heading and first sentence of § 60–1.4(d). Making the change to "inclusion" is consistent with the

[55] Cappelli, Peter, and Kevin Chauvin, "An Interplant Test of the Efficiency Wage Hypothesis," *Quarterly Journal of Economics*, 106, 769–787, *available at http://dx.doi.org/10.2307/2937926(1991)*; Reich, Michael, Dube, Arindrajit, and Naidu, Suresh, "Economics of Citywide Minimum Wages," Institute for Industrial Relations, University of California, Berkeley Policy Brief (2005); Cowherd, D.M. and Levine, D.I., "Product Quality and Pay Equity Between Lower-level Employees and Top Management: An Investigation of Distributive Justice Theory," *Administrative Science Quarterly* 37: 302–320 (1992).

[56] *See* Bamberger and Belogolovsky *supra* note 44; Adrienne Colella, Ramona L. Paetzold, Asghar Zardkoohi and Michael J. Wesson, "*Exposing Pay Secrecy*," 32 *Acad. of Management Rev.* 55, 58 (2007).

[57] *Government Contractors, Requirement To Report Summary Data on Employee Compensation*, 79 FR 46562 (Aug. 8, 2014). This notice of proposed rulemaking (NPRM) would amend the regulation by adding a requirement that certain Federal contractors and subcontractors supplement their Employer Information Report (EEO–1 Report) with summary information on compensation paid to employees, as contained in the Form W–2 Wage and Tax Statement (W–2) forms, by sex, race, ethnicity, and specified job categories, as well as other relevant data points such as hours worked, and the number of employees.

[58] Section 7 of the NLRA examines the right of employees to "self-organization, to form, join, or assist labor organizations, to bargain collectively through representatives of their own choosing, and to engage in other concerted activities" for the purpose of collective bargaining or other "mutual aid or protection." Section 8 of the NLRA describes unfair employer and labor organization practices that interfere with the rights granted employees in section 7. *See* 29 U.S.C. 157–158 (1935). OFCCP recognizes that the National Labor Relations Board (NLRB) interprets Section 7 to protect employees and applicants from discrimination based on discussion or disclosure of their own compensation or the compensation of other employees or applicants. *Paraxel International LLC*, 356 NLRB No. 82, slip op. at 3 (2011).

language used in other recent OFCCP rulemakings, including regulations for section 503 of the Rehabilitation Act of 1973, as amended. As proposed in the NPRM, the final rule removes the outdated reference to the "Deputy Assistant Secretary" in § 60–1.4(d), and replaces it with the "Director of OFCCP."

SUBPART B—General Enforcement; Compliance Review and Complaint Procedure

Section 60–1.35 Contractor Obligations and Defenses to Violation of the Nondiscrimination Requirement for Compensation Disclosures

As proposed in the NPRM, § 60–1.35 becomes a new section to part 60–1 in this final rule, to implement the requirements of section 2(b), as well as the contractor defenses set forth in the Executive Order.

Analytical Framework

In the NPRM, OFCCP stated that it viewed Executive Order 13665 "as establishing a new prohibition against discrimination against any employee or applicant" and announced its intent to use the burdens and standards of proof applicable to Title VII discrimination claims—including the use of a motivating factor framework for analyzing causation. OFCCP provided three broad reasons for adopting this approach in the NPRM: (1) the equal opportunity clause paragraph set out in section 2(b) of Executive Order 13665 is framed in terms of discrimination; (2) the prohibitions set forth in Executive Order 13665 diverged from the traditional Title VII retaliation framework, to which the different "but-for" standard of review applies; and (3) the application of the motivating factor framework would maintain consistency with the review of similar claims under the National Labor Relations Act (NLRA), which also utilizes the motivating factor approach.

OFCCP received seven comments on the proposed analytical framework. Five of these comments, largely from organizations representing employers, opposed the proposal, and urged instead that OFCCP adopt a "but-for" causation standard, citing the recent *Univ. of Texas Southwestern Med. Ctr.* v. *Nassar* Supreme Court case.[59] Two commenters, both civil rights advocacy organizations, strongly supported the proposed motivating factor framework and urged its inclusion in the Final Rule. As discussed below, OFCCP adopts the framework as proposed in the NPRM with some further clarification. A discussion of the various issues raised in the comments follows.

The most frequent comments on the proposed analytical framework concerned the applicability of the *Nassar* decision to Executive Order 13665. In *Nassar,* the Court analyzed the retaliation statute under Title VII, codified at 42 U.S.C. 2000e–3, which prohibits adverse employment action against an employee for opposing a practice made unlawful by Title VII, or for filing a charge, testifying, or otherwise participating in an investigation, proceeding, or hearing under Title VII.[60] The Court held that but-for causation, rather than a motivating factor review, applied to retaliation claims under Title VII.[61]

The comments from the organizations representing employers all stated that the holding in *Nassar* dictated the analytical framework that must be utilized under Executive Order 13665, as the protections under the Order are akin to Title VII retaliation claims as opposed to Title VII discrimination claims for which the motivating factor analysis is reserved. Some of these commenters also pointed to the text of the Order—such as the lack of specific "motivating factor" language—to buttress their conclusions. Comments from civil rights advocacy groups disagreed. These commenters stated that pay secrecy policies are inextricably intertwined with compensation discrimination. They further asserted that because the adverse action in the pay secrecy context often occurs before an employee engages in activity that would be protected under Title VII, the protections in the Order are fundamentally different in kind from anti-retaliation protections under Title VII.

Historically, OFCCP has followed Title VII principles in cases brought under Executive Order 11246.[62] While that approach continues, we agree with the commenters echoing our position in the NPRM that the protection afforded by Executive Order 13665 "diverges from the traditional Title VII retaliation framework" at issue in *Nassar.* Title VII retaliation claims require, as an initial matter, that the plaintiff oppose an unlawful employment practice, file a charge of discrimination, or participate in an "investigation, proceeding, or hearing" related to Title VII claims. 42 U.S.C. 2000e–3. Executive Order 13665 is different, as it protects *any* compensation inquiries, discussions, or disclosures and requires neither opposition to an alleged violation of the underlying law nor participation in an investigation, proceeding, hearing, or litigation asserting rights protected by the underlying law.[63] A benign question from co-worker to co-worker about the annual bonus she received or an employee's inadvertent disclosure of a difference in pay between herself and a colleague are conceivable predicates for a claim under the Order.

This difference in scope underpinned OFCCP's position in the NPRM that the Order is "framed in terms of discrimination" and that its protections are uniquely directed toward "protecting workers from pay discrimination itself," thus supporting a discrimination analysis. While two of the commenters took issue with this latter statement, asserting that Title VII's retaliation statute serves the same purpose, we believe there is an important difference—the Order's protections are geared not only to safeguard the integrity of existing pay discrimination laws, but to also allow workers to *discover discrimination* that would otherwise be hidden. This purpose is explicitly referenced multiple times in the text of Executive Order 13665.[64] This also dovetails with OFCCP's existing regulations, as the Order's protection of open communication regarding compensation is interrelated with contractors' existing and ongoing affirmative action obligations to evaluate and report on their compensation systems for the existence of potentially discriminatory disparities. *See* 41 CFR 60–2.17(b)(3).

While OFCCP recognizes the lack of specific "motivating factor" language in the Order and the other textual arguments raised by commenters,[65] the policy language embedded in the Order, the differences between the Order's protections and current case law

[59] 133 S.Ct. 978 (2013).

[60] *Id.*

[61] *Id.*

[62] *See OFCCP* v. *Greenwood Mills, Inc.,* No. 00–044, 2002 WL 31932547, at *4 (Admin. Rev. Bd. Dec. 20, 2002).

[63] E.O. 13665, sec. 2(b).

[64] *Id.* at sec. 1 ("When employees are prohibited from inquiring about, disclosing, or discussing their compensation with fellow workers, compensation discrimination is much more difficult to discover and remediate, and more likely to persist. . . . Ensuring that employees of Federal contractors may discuss their compensation without fear of adverse action will enhance the ability of Federal contractors and their employees to detect and remediate unlawful discriminatory practices. . . .").

[65] While the title of the Order uses the term "non-retaliation," this is not dispositive and must be read in the context of the rest of the Order. *See Lawson* v. *FMR, LLC,* 134 S. Ct. 1158, 1169 (2014) ("[H]eadings and titles can do no more than indicate the provisions in a most general manner," and they are "not meant to take the place of the detailed provisions of the text.") (citing *Trainmen* v. *Baltimore & Ohio R. Co.,* 331 U.S. 519, 67 S. Ct. 1387, 91 L. Ed. 1646 (1947)).

interpretations of the Title VII retaliation provision, and related affirmative action and nondiscrimination obligations under the existing regulations provide important text and context for determining the appropriate analytical framework to employ. Accordingly, OFCCP does not believe that *Nassar* dictates that a "but-for" analytical framework must be used to analyze pay secrecy claims under Executive Order 13665.

The NPRM also included the motivating factor framework in part because of the overlap in legal protections offered by the Order and the National Labor Relations Act, which also uses a motivating factor analysis. Two commenters took issue with this rationale. One stated simply that the NLRA was "not applicable" to claims under the Order, while another asserted that there are differences in the scope and remedial schemes of the NLRA and the Order that necessitated differing analytical frameworks.

Regarding the first of these commenters, OFCCP respectfully disagrees that the NLRA is simply "not applicable" to the discussion of how claims under Executive Order 13665 should be analyzed. As we stated in the NPRM, there is a close relationship in the type of activity each law protects. Section 7 of the NLRA guarantees the right to engage in "concerted activities for the purpose of . . . mutual aid or protection," 29 U.S.C. 157, and the National Labor Relations Board has long held that this includes the right "to ascertain what wages are paid by their employer, as wages are . . . probably the most critical element in employment."[66] This makes the NLRA the federal law that most closely mirrors the types of pay secrecy policies that the Order addresses. Given that millions of workers, employed by thousands of employers, will be affected by pay secrecy policies under both the NLRA and the Order, reference to the NLRA in an attempt to provide, to the extent possible, a uniform framework of analysis and reduce confusion over the appropriate legal standard is appropriate.

The second commenter raised two broad issues. First, it stated that the analytical framework under the NLRA was different from that proposed under the Executive Order 13665, in that under the NLRA an employer can escape all liability if it can establish that it would have taken the adverse action against the employee in any event. As stated in the NPRM, the reasoning behind the proposed motivating factor framework was "consistency with Title VII *and* NLRA principles." 79 FR 55720 (emphasis added). The initial motivating factor analysis under both laws is essentially the same: the complainant must demonstrate that discrimination was a motivating factor in the employer's action, and then the employer has a defense provided that it demonstrates that it would have taken the same action even in the absence of protected conduct. Were OFCCP to abandon a motivating factor framework, the analyses under the Order and the NLRA would then be out of alignment despite the existence of substantially identical claims under each.

The NLRA and Title VII then diverge in the remedial structure following a successful articulation of the defense: under the NLRA, the employer can escape all liability, whereas under Title VII, the court may still grant injunctive and declaratory relief, as well as attorneys' fees. While the final rule follows Title VII rather than NLRA principles in this regard, the enforcement mechanisms in the Order significantly lessen the distinction with the NLRA in two ways. First, the Order does not permit OFCCP to recover attorneys' fees and costs, thus, as with the NLRA, monetary remedies are not available if an employer establishes a defense in a case proceeding under the motivating factor framework. Second, the inclusion of a specific, complete "essential job functions" defense in the Order, discussed elsewhere in the preamble, provides a mechanism for contractors to avoid liability in certain circumstances consistent with the NLRA.

The commenter also noted that the interpretation of the Order in the NPRM covers more people and more types of activity than does the NLRA and that this will lead to an "exponential increase" in claims, and that applying a motivating factor analysis will further result in an increase in the number of frivolous claims, thus raising costs for the contractor community. As to any potential increase in claims, it is true that one specific purpose of the Order is to expand protections against pay secrecy policies to individuals and types of activities beyond that protected by the NLRA; otherwise, there would be no need for the Order. As discussed at length in the NPRM and in the preamble here, pay discrimination, as well as the existence of pay secrecy policies, remains widespread despite the protections in the NLRA. To the extent there is an increase in meritorious claims, this would indicate the Order's success at addressing these widespread problems. As to the assertion that there would be an untenable increase in the number of frivolous claims solely because of the availability of a motivating factor framework, we respectfully disagree. Significantly, there is no private right of action under Executive Orders 11246 or 13665; OFCCP is responsible for investigating complaints filed and bringing enforcement actions, which it has discretion to do only if there is a violation and it has attempted to resolve such violations through informal means. *See* 41 CFR 60–1.24. Simply put, OFCCP will not pursue frivolous claims, which substantially addresses the concerns raised by the commenter.

For the foregoing reasons, OFCCP concludes that the motivating factor framework is a permissible approach for claims brought under the Executive Order 13665. However, the fact that it is *a* permissible approach should not be interpreted to say that it is *the only* approach OFCCP may use to prove discrimination. For instance, numerous circuit courts examining Title VII discrimination claims since the Civil Rights Act of 1991, which codified the motivating factor framework, have held that, despite the availability of the motivating factor analysis, plaintiffs may also proceed under the more traditional burden shifting framework first set forth in *McDonnell Douglas Corp.* v. *Green,* 411 U.S. 792 (1973).[67] Under this approach, often referred to as the "determinative factor" approach, the plaintiff must first make a *prima facie* showing of discrimination, which includes evidence that he or she is a member of a protected class and was subjected to an adverse action. The employer then has the opportunity to articulate a legitimate nondiscriminatory reason for the adverse employment action it has taken, which the plaintiff must then demonstrate was a pretext for discrimination in order to succeed. Which approach OFCCP uses will be heavily influenced by the facts of the case as they are developed in its investigation and in discovery. In true "mixed motive" cases—where, for instance, the employer can show that it fired an employee in part for taking excessive breaks, but where there is also evidence that the employer fired the employee in part for discussing compensation—the motivating factor approach would be appropriate. Conversely, where the evidence appears

[66] *Parexel International LLC*, 356 NLRB No. 82, slip op. at 3 (2011).

[67] See, *e.g., Makky* v. *Chertoff*, 541 F.3d 205, 213–15 (3d Cir. 2008); *Fogg* v. *Gonzales*, 492 F.3d 447, 451 (D.C. Cir. 2007); *McGinest* v. *GTE Serv. Corp.*, 360 F.3d 1103, 1122 (9th Cir. 2004).

clear that there was only a single motive—where, for instance, the employer claims that it fired an employee for taking excessive breaks but the evidence shows that this is demonstrably false or otherwise unworthy of credence—OFCCP may opt to proceed under the more traditional pretext approach. OFCCP may also opt to prove its case via both frameworks, arguing, for instance, that discrimination was the determinative factor in an employer's adverse action but, in the alternative, that it was at least a motivating factor. The Supreme Court and multiple circuit courts have recognized this approach as consistent with the way in which many Title VII cases are litigated.[68] In sum, while the motivating factor analytical framework is permissible under this Final Rule, OFCCP may use other approaches, based on the evidence available in a particular case, to demonstrate that unlawful discrimination occurred.

Consistency and Compatibility With NLRA

A number of comments concerned the compatibility or consistency of the Order with the NLRA beyond those comments addressed in the analytical framework section above. Some commenters noted that the NLRA already provides some protection for disclosure of compensation information and, therefore, believe this rule is unnecessary. As an initial matter, the Order plainly requires OFCCP to draft implementing regulations. *See* E.O. 13665, sec. 3. Further, as discussed at length in the NPRM and above in this final rule, pay secrecy policies continue to be prevalent despite the existence of the NLRA, preventing workers from discovering and remedying potential discrimination. Finally, also discussed above, the scope of the Order is broader, covering a broader range of workers, including supervisors, and a broader scope of protected activity than that covered under the NLRA.

One commenter took issue with this last point, stating that the Department has not presented sufficient data to justify coverage of supervisors. Another commenter noted, conversely, that coverage of supervisors is important specifically because they are not covered by the NLRA.

We decline the recommendation to limit coverage of the Order solely to employees who are not supervisors. Neither the Order nor any of the comments provide a basis for doing so. The plain text of the Order extends protections to "*any* employee or applicant for employment," providing no language in any way limiting the scope of workers who should be covered by the rule.[69] Significantly, as discussed in the proposed rule, one of the catalysts for the signing of the Order is the case of *Ledbetter* v. *Goodyear Tire & Rubber Co.*[70] That case concerned a supervisor who discovered that her wages were less than that of male supervisors and who was warned by company management not to disclose or otherwise discuss this information. Ms. Ledbetter's experience, by no means unique, exemplifies the fact that pay secrecy policies and pay discrimination negatively affect workers on all rungs of the company ladder, and demonstrates the necessity for the broad protections in this rule. We also note that the NLRA concerns the rights of employees to organize and bargain and, therefore, excludes supervisors from its protections for reasons unrelated to this rule. This rule concerns a different policy purpose, that is, the promotion of pay transparency to ensure equitable pay for all of a contractor's employees. Therefore, it is appropriate that this rule covers a wider class of employees.

One commenter raised an issue about having the opportunity to comment on coordination it believes is necessary between the Department and the NLRB in terms of having a consistent standard and a consistent class of covered employees for pay transparency cases. Because sufficient notice about the standard to be applied as well as the covered class was provided during this comment period, there was sufficient opportunity for input on these issues. The Department enforces statutes with overlapping jurisdiction with other agencies and coordinates when necessary. There is no justification for not covering all employees who are covered generally by the protections provided under Executive Order 11246.

Contractor Defenses

As was proposed in the NPRM, and as was established in Executive Order 13665, the final rule contains contractor defenses to alleged violations. First, the contractor may pursue a defense if its adverse action against an employee or applicant is not based on a rule, policy, practice, agreement or other instrument that prohibits employees and applicants from disclosing compensation. Second, the protections of the Order do not apply, and thus a contractor is allowed to take adverse action against an employee or applicant, if the employee discloses compensation information accessed or received based on performing an essential job function unless the disclosure falls into one or more exemptions.

The structure and function of these defenses are notably different from each other in the text of Executive Order 13665 and, accordingly, are so under these regulations. The "essential job functions" defense is set forth in the same paragraph as the prohibition on discrimination, and states that the prohibition "shall not apply" in instances in which employees disclose compensation data that they have access to as part of their essential job functions.[71] This prohibition, and the defense, are incorporated into the text of Executive Order 11246, as amended.[72] The second type of defense is phrased quite differently. It is not listed alongside the complete "essential job functions" defense in the text of the Order, nor is it incorporated into the amended Executive Order 11246; rather, it is listed separately in a "General Provisions" section.[73] Further, it is described as a defense that the Order does not prohibit a contractor from pursuing, rather than one that completely excises the application of the Executive Order.[74] We believe these differences are intentional and important, and frame how the defenses are to be employed in actions brought under the Order. A discussion of the function of these defenses, and a response to the comments we received, follows.

Section 60–1.35(a) General Defenses

The NPRM proposed to include a general contractor defense to an alleged violation of paragraph (3) of the equal opportunity clauses listed in § 60–1.4(a) and (b) under which a contractor's actions would not be deemed to be discrimination if the contractor could show that it disciplined the employee for violation of a consistently and uniformly applied rule, policy, practice, agreement, or other instrument that does not prohibit, or tend to prohibit,

[68] *Price Waterhouse* v. *Hopkins*, 490 U.S. 228, 247 n.12 (1989) (plurality op.) ("Nothing in this opinion should be taken to suggest that a case must be correctly labeled as either a "pretext" case or a "mixed-motives" case from the beginning . . . indeed, we expect that plaintiffs often will allege, in the alternative, that their cases are both. Discovery often will be necessary before the plaintiff can know whether both legitimate and illegitimate considerations played a part in the decision against her."); *see also Ponce* v. *Billington*, 679 F.3d 840, 845 (D.C. Cir. 2012) (citing *Price Waterhouse, and noting that* "a plaintiff may ultimately decide to proceed under both theories of liability."); *Rapold* v. *Baxter Int'l*, 718 F.3d 602, 611–12 (7th Cir. 2013) (citing *Price Waterhouse*).

[69] E.O. 13665, sec. 2.

[70] 550 U.S. 618 (2007).

[71] E.O. 13665, sec. 2.

[72] E.O. 11246, sec. 202(3).

[73] E.O. 13665, sec. 5(a).

[74] *Id.*

employees or applicants from discussing or disclosing their compensation or the compensation of other employees or applicants. OFCCP invited comments on how to harmonize contractors' enforcement of legitimate workplace rules with the rights of applicants and employees to discuss, disclose, or inquire about compensation.

OFCCP received several comments on this proposed defense. Some commenters were concerned that the defense was so broad that it could be used as pretext for discrimination and that it allowed for excessive employer subjectivity. These commenters explained that the example cited in the NPRM, where a contractor disciplines an employee for standing on her desk and repeatedly shouting out her pay in violation of a workplace rule prohibiting disruptive behavior, illustrated that contractors could apply such workplace rules in a subjective and discriminatory manner because contractors could define "disruptive" to include all conversations about compensation. These commenters suggested that OFCCP should provide specific definitions and examples of legitimate workplace rules. One commenter also suggested that OFCCP should identify sources that employers could draw from when citing a legitimate workplace rule, such as employee handbooks or collective bargaining agreements.

One other commenter suggested that OFCCP delete "and uniformly" from the phrase "by proving that the contractor disciplined the employee for violation of a consistently and uniformly applied rule . . ." because "uniformly" was superfluous and because contractors should not be required to apply a rule "uniformly" in situations when circumstances warrant a different approach.

OFCCP believes that the defense, as proposed in the NPRM, adequately prevents contractors from using a legitimate workplace rule as a way to avoid liability in the event that it discriminated against an employee or applicant for discussing compensation. The defense requires the contractor to show that it applied a legitimate workplace rule to the employee or applicant in a consistent and uniform manner. If the contractor cannot demonstrate a track record of consistent and uniform application of the workplace rule, then the contractor will not be able to successfully use this defense. Although a contractor need not discipline all employees in an identical way under the workplace rule, it must show that it did not discipline the employee or applicant in question more severely under the rule because of the employee's or applicant's protected activity.

In response to the concern that contractors could use workplace rules, such as those that prohibit disruptive employee behavior, to target discussions of compensation, OFCCP notes that contractors may only rely on workplace rules that do not prohibit, or tend to prohibit, employees or applicants from discussing or disclosing their compensation or the compensation of other employees or applicants. A rule that treated all discussions of pay as "disruptive" would violate these regulations.

OFCCP declines to articulate specific workplace rules that contractors may assert pursuant to this defense. There are many legitimate workplace rules that contractors may be entitled to enforce; OFCCP cannot predict the content or the source of any particular rule that a contractor may rely upon in asserting this defense. Regardless of the type of workplace rule relied upon, however, every contractor must show that the identified workplace rule does not prohibit, or tend to prohibit, employees or applicants from discussing their compensation and that any such rule has been consistently and uniformly applied. For example, if a contractor disciplined an employee or applicant, who was also discussing pay, pursuant to an allegedly legitimate workplace rule, but, for example, had never promulgated or enforced that rule before, the contractor may not be able to show that the workplace rule qualified as a legitimate workplace rule under this defense.

Finally, OFCCP will retain the word "uniformly" in the final rule. OFCCP recognizes that different circumstances may warrant different forms of discipline under the same workplace rule; the fact that an employee or applicant was also discussing compensation, however, should not justify applying the workplace rule in a non-uniform manner. For example, it may be a consistent application for a contractor to suspend all employees who exceed their allotted break time by an hour, even if the contractor only provides a verbal warning to employees who exceed their allotted break time one time by five minutes. For the contractor to act in a uniform manner, it should apply the same corrective action—here, a verbal warning—to employees who exceed their allotted break time once by five minutes, including any employees who may have been discussing compensation. As mentioned above, an employee's or applicant's protected activity should not affect the severity of the discipline they receive pursuant to a workplace rule. Requiring that contractors uniformly apply workplace rules to similarly situated employees, regardless of their protected activity, prevents contractors from using the rule as a way to avoid liability for discrimination. Therefore, OFCCP believes that the use of the word "uniformly" is not superfluous and will remain in the final rule.

Two commenters proposed adding more specific defenses to the regulation. One commenter suggested that OFCCP add a defense for contractors who limit discussion or disclosure of compensation information pursuant to laws enacted to protect private and/or confidential information. Another commenter recommended that the rule include a specific defense against hacking, such that if an employee obtained salary information through unauthorized access, then the employer should be able to discipline the employee for doing so.

As previously mentioned, the final rule does not expand the defenses to include these recommendations; however, it does not limit the ability of contractors to take disciplinary actions for violations of security policies and applicable privacy laws. Furthermore, as noted in the preamble to the proposed rule, the general defense provision is intended to permit employers to have personnel policies that are uniformly applied to maintain discipline in the workplace and to protect their business. We note generally that a policy that would have the effect of broadly prohibiting employee communication about compensation would be unlawful under this rule. However, a company policy that is narrowly tailored to prohibit disclosure of specific proprietary business information or trade secrets, or that is otherwise designed to be consistent with federal or state privacy laws, if violated, could fall within the general defenses already set forth in the rule. Similarly, if a contractor consistently and uniformly applies a rule prohibiting employees from accessing information without authorization, then this too could potentially fall within the general defense provision. Whether a company policy concerning confidentiality or unauthorized access would be deemed unlawful would be a highly fact-specific inquiry. However, because the general defense set forth could potentially be invoked for these purposes, OFCCP declines to adopt the recommendations to include these specific defenses.

Accordingly, OFCCP declines to make the suggested changes and adopts the defense requirements outlined in the

NPRM into the final rule. OFCCP is, however, rewording the defense to make clear that relying on a workplace rule will not serve as a complete defense, but rather is subject to the analytical framework as discussed above. Consistent with Title VII principles, and the language of Executive Order 13665, a contractor cannot escape all liability within the "motivating factor" framework if the agency can show that discrimination motivated the contractor, even in part, to discipline an employee or applicant. The focus of the Executive Order is on "[e]nsuring that employees of Federal contractors may discuss their compensation without fear of adverse action" so that contractors and their employees can "detect and remediate unlawful discriminatory practices." E.O. 13665, sec. 1. This policy will not be truly effectuated until all forms of discriminatory actions, even if they are combined with some lawful motivations, are rooted out of the workplace. To the extent that a desire to perpetuate unlawful pay secrecy policies motivated a contractor's actions, OFCCP will seek to enjoin such practices in the future. A contractor may, however, limit the scope of an adverse remedial order if it can show that it would have taken the same action against the employee or applicant in the absence of any discriminatory motive.[75]

Section 60–1.35(b) Essential Job Functions

As proposed in the NPRM, § 1.35(b) contains a second contractor defense to a claim of discrimination under these regulations. Pursuant to this defense, a contractor will not violate these regulations if it takes adverse action against an employee, who has access to the compensation information of other employees or applicants as part of his or her essential job functions, for disclosing the compensation of other employees or applicants, unless the disclosure occurs in certain limited circumstances. These limited circumstances include disclosures in response to a formal complaint or charge, in furtherance of an investigation, proceeding, hearing or action, including an investigation conducted by the contractors, or consistent with the contractor's legal duty to provide information. A formal complaint or charge would include, for example, written and oral complaints submitted by the employee, or someone on behalf of the employee, to the contractor's human resources or other appropriate office or official, and to a Federal, state or local government entity, including courts and administrative boards and councils. Under § 1.35(b), the employee would typically be making the disclosure within, related to, or pursuant to some sort of official action, process, policy, or procedure if the conduct is to be protected from adverse action by the contractor.

As discussed above, OFCCP has revised the definition of "essential job functions" to identify two specific categories of job functions: (1) the access to compensation information is necessary in order to perform that function or other routinely assigned business task; or (2) the function or duties of the position include protecting and maintaining the privacy of employee personnel records, including compensation information. Many of the comments that OFCCP received on this topic related to the definition of "essential job functions" and have been previously addressed. To reiterate, some commenters felt that the definition of essential job functions, and therefore the accompanying defense, should be broadened, while others felt it should be narrowed.

As stated in the NPRM, this defense acknowledges that an employee who has access to compensation information of others within an organization as part of his or her essential job functions has a duty to protect such information from disclosure. The revised definition of "essential job functions" reflects these concerns, while also limiting an employer's subjectivity in deciding what functions constitute essential job functions. As was stated in the NPRM, however, if an employee discloses or discusses the compensation of other applicants or employees based on information that the employee receives through means other than essential job functions access, the defense would not apply. Similarly, the defense would not apply where such an employee pursues her own possible compensation discrimination claim or raises possible disparities involving the compensation of other employees to a management official with the contractor or while using the contractor's internal complaint process. This balance protects employers' confidential information, but does not inhibit those workers with access to such information from pursuing their own claims of compensation discrimination or raising possible disparities to the contractor's own management to consider and address if necessary to comply with the law. Without this distinction, employees with essential job functions access, who primarily work in human resources departments and who are predominantly women,[76] would receive less protection than other employees who learn of possible compensation disparities in a similar manner.

As with any defense, OFCCP will evaluate the availability of a defense under section 1.35(b) based on the specific facts and circumstances of each case. As discussed above, this defense may serve as a complete bar to liability under these regulations. The "motivating factor" framework will not limit the application of the essential job functions defense because releasing compensation information obtained during the course of an employee's essential job functions is not protected by Executive Order 13665 or this final rule. The policy underlying Executive Order 13665 recognizes that contractors are entitled to prohibit some of their employees from releasing sensitive and confidential information relating to compensation; accordingly, such prohibitions will not give rise to impermissible "motivating factors" under these regulations, and therefore will not implicate the remedial structure under the "motivating factor" framework.

Section 60–1.35(c) Dissemination of nondiscrimination provision

The NPRM proposed to require that Federal contractors incorporate the nondiscrimination provision described in section 2(b) of Executive Order 13665 into existing employee manuals or handbooks, and disseminate the nondiscrimination provision to employees and job applicants. The NPRM proposed that the Director of OFCCP would prescribe the language in the nondiscrimination provision, and that OFCCP would make the language available on the OFCCP Web site. The NPRM stated that contractors would disseminate the provision either electronically or by posting a copy of the provision in conspicuous places available to employees and job applicants. The NPRM did not require or recommend in-person or face-to-face communication of the provision, however, the proposed rule stated that contractors might use this method if they typically communicate information

[75] As discussed *supra*, if the facts of the case dictate that proceeding under the *McDonnell Douglas* determinative factor model is appropriate in a given case, the contractor could use its workplace rule as its asserted legitimate nondiscriminatory reason, which OFCCP would then have the opportunity to demonstrate was a pretext for discrimination.

[76] As was mentioned in the NPRM, in 2013 at least 71.9 percent of human resources professionals in three occupational categories were women. For further discussion, please refer to the NPRM at 79 FR 55721 (September 17, 2014).

to all employees or applicants in this manner.

OFCCP received six comments on this proposed requirement. One commenter encouraged OFCCP to create a new "pay transparency" poster and add a requirement for contractors to post it in the workplace. Two commenters recommended that OFCCP revise the current "EEO is the Law" poster to include language describing the prohibition against discrimination based on compensation inquiries, discussions, or disclosures, instead of requiring publication of the prescribed nondiscrimination provision in employee manuals and handbooks. Another commenter challenged the use of prescribed language by the OFCCP's Director. The commenter stated that contractors would be best suited to develop language that articulates both employee and employer rights and obligations.

OFCCP believes that contractors can accomplish the goal of providing notice of the nondiscrimination provision to applicants and employees through existing structures, such as handbooks and manuals. Moreover, OFCCP is mindful of the additional burden that a new posting requirement would impose on contractors, as explained in the below Regulatory Procedures section of this preamble. OFCCP also considered the suggestion that individual contractors develop the language they would use to describe the nondiscrimination provision in their employee handbooks and manuals. However, OFCCP believes that uniformity of such language is necessary to ensure consistency and clarity in the information provided to applicants and employees. Of course, nothing in this rule limits contractors' ability to provide additional information to their employees about employer and employee rights and obligations. Further, OFCCP seeks to lessen the costs and burden associated with dissemination of the nondiscrimination provision by prescribing the language to describe it. Accordingly, OFCCP declines to make the suggested changes and adopts the dissemination requirements proposed in the NPRM into the final rule.

OFCCP agrees with the suggested inclusion of language describing the prohibition against discrimination based on compensation inquiries, discussions, or disclosures on the "EEO is the Law" poster that contractors are currently required to post. OFCCP will take necessary steps toward producing a poster with this new language. However, posting the "EEO is the Law" poster will not eliminate the obligation to publish the prescribed nondiscrimination provisions in employee manuals and handbooks.

In the proposed rule, OFCCP sought comments on the feasibility of a proposition that would require contractors with existing manager trainings or meetings to include in them a review of the prohibition on discrimination based on an employee or applicant inquiring about, discussing, or disclosing compensation information. The training requirement, as proposed, would have applied only to contractors that provide manager trainings or meetings; OFCCP would have encouraged other contractors to adopt such training as a best practice for minimizing the likelihood of workplace discrimination. OFCCP received five comments in support and three comments in opposition of this proposed requirement.

Generally, commenters supporting the training proposal asserted that requiring manager training should be required for all contractors. Such a requirement would ensure effective implementation of the new provision, particularly for those contractors with longstanding polices that prohibit wage discussions. Some of these commenters asserted further that contractors with existing training could incorporate required new training into already existing training sessions, as proposed. One commenter suggested extending the training requirement to require contractors to provide employees with individual notice at staff meetings, performance reviews, and other channels.

However, commenters in opposition to the training requirement generally asserted that the proposed training provision would not guarantee effectiveness, would create confusion, would involve significant expense, and would be unnecessary given that contractors are likely already subject to similar Federal and state provisions. One commenter specifically asserted that requiring training for some contractors while only encouraging it for other contractors would create confusion amongst the regulated community with regard to what is required for compliance. Another commenter stated that contractors would achieve increased compliance with the new nondiscrimination provision through clearer guidance from OFCCP as opposed to mandated contractor training. Yet another commenter opposed the requirement because the expense for contractors to update existing training programs would be significant. Such an update would require several levels of internal company review, in addition to costs to re-deploy training modules. Rather than impose a training requirement on some contractors, some of the comments in opposition suggested that OFCCP only encourage providing this training as a best practice for all contractors.

After consideration of the foregoing comments, the final rule does not require any contractors to modify their existing trainings or meetings to include a review of the prohibition on discriminating based on an employee or applicant inquiring about, discussing, or disclosing compensation information. In making this determination, OFCCP considered the added burden to contractors resulting from them modifying their training materials, as well as the potential for contractors to become confused about which of them would be covered by the training requirement. Although this final rule does not require training, OFCCP encourages all contractors to incorporate personnel training on this new nondiscrimination provision as a best practice.

Alternatives or Additions to Proposed Regulations

In the NPRM, OFCCP requested comments from small contractors on possible alternatives that would minimize the impact of the proposed rule while still accomplishing its goals. Specifically, OFCCP invited interested persons to submit comments on NPRM estimates, including the number of small entities affected by the Order's prohibition on Federal contractors discriminating against employees and job applicants, the compliance cost estimates, and whether alternatives exist that would reduce burden on small entities while still remaining consistent with the objectives of Executive Order 13665.

OFCCP received two comments proposing alternative approaches. The commenters suggested that the final rule require Federal contractors to create and maintain publicly available employee pay scales, similar to the pay scales maintained for Federal employees. The commenters' proposal is beyond the scope of Executive Order 13665 and, even if within its scope, such an alternative would be more burdensome than what was proposed in the NPRM. OFCCP further finds that the proposed requirement to disseminate the nondiscrimination provision is the least burdensome means of fostering discussion among employees about pay and allowing for openness among employees to discuss compensation practices.

Regulatory Procedures

Executive Order 12866 (Regulatory Planning and Review) and Executive Order 13563 (Improving Regulation and Regulatory Review)

OFCCP is issuing this final rule in conformity with Executive Orders 13563 and 12866, which directs agencies to assess all costs and benefits of available regulatory alternatives and, if regulation is necessary, to select regulatory approaches that maximize net benefits (including potential economic, environmental, public health and safety effects, distributive impacts, and equity). Executive Order 13563 recognizes that some benefits are difficult to quantify and provides that, where appropriate and permitted by law, agencies may consider and discuss qualitatively values that are difficult or impossible to quantify, including equity, human dignity, fairness, and distributive impacts.

Under Executive Order 12866, OFCCP must determine whether a regulatory action is significant and therefore subject to the requirements of the Executive Order and to review by OMB.[77] Section 3(f) of Executive Order 12866 defines a "significant regulatory action" as an action that is likely to result in a rule that: (1) has an annual effect of $100 million or more, or adversely affects in a material way a sector of the economy, productivity, competition, jobs, the environment, public health or safety, or State, local, or tribal governments or communities (also referred to as economically significant); (2) creates serious inconsistency or otherwise interferes with an action taken or planned by another agency; (3) materially alters the budgetary impacts of entitlement grants, user fees, or loan programs, or the rights and obligations of recipients thereof; or (4) raises novel legal or policy issues arising out of legal mandates, the Presidents priorities, or the principles set forth in Executive Order 12866.[78]

This rule has been designated a "significant regulatory action" although not economically significant under section 3(f) of Executive Order 12866. The rule is not economically significant because it will not have an annual effect on the economy of $100 million or more. Accordingly, the rule has been reviewed by the Office of Management and Budget.

The Need for the Regulation

On April 8, 2014, President Barack Obama signed Executive Order 13665, Non-Retaliation for Disclosure of Compensation Information. 79 FR 20749 (April 11, 2014). This Executive Order prohibits Federal contractors from discharging or discriminating in any other way against employees or applicants who inquire about, discuss, or disclose their own compensation or the compensation of another employee or applicant. Executive Order 13665 necessitates the regulatory changes in this rule to ensure that employees of Federal contractors and subcontractors are able to discuss their compensation without fear of adverse action. Federal contractors also need the regulatory changes to enhance their ability to detect and remediate unlawful discriminatory practices. OFCCP designed the rule to contribute to a more efficient market in Federal contracting, and to ensure that the most qualified and productive workers receive fair wages. The existence of pay secrecy practices means some workers can be fired for even disclosing their compensation or asking their co-workers how much they earn. Even employers who do not specifically restrict employee communications about compensation take great care to guard individual compensation information. This final rule benefits OFCCP's enforcement by incorporating into the equal opportunity clauses the prohibition against pay secrecy policies, specifically that an employer cannot discriminate against an employee or applicant who has inquired about, discussed, or disclosed compensation information.[79] By including the provision in the equal opportunity clauses OFCCP clearly defines such actions as discriminatory and enhances its ability to take action when it finds pay secrecy policies or practices during compliance evaluations and investigations.

Currently, OFCCP lacks sufficient, reliable data to assess the gender- or race-based pay gap experienced by employees of Federal contractors or subcontractors, including how much of the potential pay gap is attributable to pay discrimination instead of nondiscriminatory factors, and how many contractors are violating the pay discrimination laws OFCCP enforces. Pay secrecy ranks among one of the most prevalent employer policies and practices that makes discrimination more difficult to discover and remediate.[80] OFCCP's work led to the determination that there is a substantial need for regulatory action.

U.S. Census data show that more than 15.2 million family households in the United States are headed by women.[81] Nearly 31 percent of these families, or nearly 4,700,000 family households, have incomes that fall below the poverty level.[82] These and other data provide general information about the potential impact of eliminating pay differentials among men and women, including pay differentials not attributed to discrimination, on the poverty rate of women and their families.[83] The data on earnings and the pay gap includes all

[77] 58 FR 51735.

[78] *Id.*

[79] The final rule includes an exception for employees (*e.g.*, payroll personnel) who have access to the compensation information of other employees or applicants as a part of such employee's essential job functions. In certain instances, employers may take adverse action against these employees for making compensation disclosures.

[80] National Equal Pay Task Force, *"Fifty Years After the Equal Pay Act,"* (June 2013), *available at http://www.whitehouse.gov/sites/default/files/equalpay/equal_pay_task_force_progress_report_june_2013_new.pdf (last accessed Mar.8, 2015).*

[81] U.S. Census Bureau, American Community Survey "1-Year Estimates 2013, Table DP02: Selected Social Characteristics in the United States," *available at http://factfinder.census.gov/faces/tableservices/jsf/pages/productview.xhtml?src=bkmk* (last accessed Aug. 4, 2015). The calculation uses family households headed by females living in a household with family and no husband. A family household includes a householder, one or more people living in the same household who are related to the householder, and anyone else living in the same household.

[82] U.S. Census Bureau, American Community Survey, "1-Year Estimates 2013, Geographies: United States, Table DP03: Selected Economic Characteristics," *available at http://factfinder.census.gov/faces/tableservices/jsf/pages/productview.xhtml?pid=ACS_13_1YR_DP03&prodType=table* (last accessed Aug. 4, 2015). To determine whether a household falls below the poverty level, the U.S. Census Bureau considers the income of the householder, size of family, number of related children, and, for 1- and 2-person families, age of householder. The poverty threshold in 2013 was $18,769 for a single householder and two children under 18.

[83] National Women's Law Center, "Closing the Wage Gap is Crucial for Women of Color and Their Families," (Nov. 2013), *available at http://www.nwlc.org/sites/default/files/pdfs/2013.11.13_closing_the_wage_gap_is_crucial_for_woc_and_their_families.pdf* (last accessed Aug. 20, 2015). Unequal wages exacerbate poverty rates for many women of color and their families, even among lower-wage earners. The wage gap also makes it difficult to women of color to move upward into the middle class; National Women's Law Center, "Insecure and Unequal: Poverty and Income Among Women and Families, 2000–2012," (Sept. 26, 2013), *available at http://www.nwlc.org/resource/insecure-unequal-poverty-among-women-and-families-2000-2012.* Compares poverty rates for adults 18 and older for women and men, for white, non-Hispanics, Asians and Native Americans. Only Native American women have higher poverty rates than Hispanic and African-American women; Lauren Howard, "Wage Disparity Still a Concern?," *available at http://www.state.tn.us/sos/ecw/Wage%20Disparity%20Article.pdf citing* the Institute for Women's Policy Research, "Still a Man's Labor Market: The Long-Term Earnings Gap." Vulnerability resulting from the damaging effects of lifelong pay inequity is evident in the 20 percent poverty rate shared by senior citizen women who are widowed or divorced or have never married.

employers and all employees in the U.S., whereas this rule would apply to only a subset of such employers and employees. Therefore, the potential impact of this rule would be much smaller than the impact of eliminating pay differentials among all working men and women.

Discrimination, occupational segregation, and other factors contribute to creating and maintaining a gap in earnings and keeping a significant percentage of women in poverty. It is worth noting, however, that some research has established that women earn less than men regardless of the field or occupation.[84] According to some studies, differences in occupations result in occupational segregation which contributes to the wage gap [85] and the effect is more pronounced in jobs requiring higher levels of education.[86] The gender pay gap may also affect the economy as a whole as it exists for both women and men of color when compared to white, non-Hispanic men. At the beginning of 2015, median weekly earnings for African-American men working at full-time jobs totaled $680 per week, only 76 percent of the median for white men ($897).[87] According to BLS data, the median weekly earnings for African-American women equaled $611 per week, only 68 percent of the median for white men.

[84] Ariane Hegewisch et al., "Separate and Not Equal? Gender Segregation in the Labor Market and the Gender Wage Gap," Briefing Paper IWPR #C377, Institute for Women's Policy Research (2010).

[85] Ariane Hegewisch and Heidi Hartmann, Ph.D., *Occupational Segregation and the Gender Wage Gap: A Job Half Done*, (Jan. 2014), sponsored by the U.S. Department of Labor Women's Bureau, *available at http://www.iwpr.org/publications/pubs/occupational-segregation-and-the-gender-wage-gap-a-job-half-done* (last accessed Aug. 20, 2015); U.S. Department of Labor, Women's Bureau, "The Economic Status of Women of Color: A Snapshot," *available at http://www.dol.gov/wb/media/reports/WB_WomenColorFactSheet.pdf* (last accessed Aug. 20, 2015. Ongoing occupational segregation is a persistent contributor to the wage gap for all women, but particularly so for Black and Hispanic women. *See also* National Women's Law Center, "The 10 Largest Jobs Paying Under $10.10/Hour Are Majority Women" (Apr. 2013), *available at http://www.nwlc.org/sites/default/files/pdfs/womendominatedminwageoccupations.pdf* (last accessed Aug. 4, 2015).

[86] Sarah Jane Glynn, Center for American Progress, "Explaining the Gender Wage Gap," (May 2014), available at *https://www.americanprogress.org/issues/economy/report/2014/05/19/90039/explaining-the-gender-wage-gap/* (last accessed Aug. 3, 2015).

[87] Bureau of Labor Statistics, U.S. Department of Labor, "Current Population Survey, Median usual weekly earnings of full-time wage and salary workers by selected characteristics, annual averages," *available at http://www.bls.gov/news.release/wkyeng.t07.htm* (last accessed Feb.12. 2015).

Discussion of Impacts

In this section, OFCCP presents a summary of the costs associated with the requirements in the final rule at §§ 60–1.3, 60–1.4 and 60–1.35. The estimated labor cost to contractors is based on Bureau of Labor Statistics data in the publication "Employer Costs for Employee Compensation" issued in December 2013, which lists total compensation for management, professional, and related occupations as $51.58 per hour and for administrative support as $24.23 per hour. Unless specified otherwise, OFCCP estimates that 25 percent of the time burden for complying with this rule will be spent by persons in management, professional and related occupations and 75 percent will be spent by persons in administrative support occupations.

There are approximately 500,000 contractor companies or firms registered in the General Service Administration's System for Award Management (SAM). Therefore, OFCCP estimates that 500,000 contractor companies or firms may be affected by the final rule.[88] This may be an overestimate because SAM captures firms that do not meet OFCCP's jurisdictional dollar threshold. OFCCP's jurisdiction covers active contracts with a value in excess of $10,000.

Cost of Regulatory Familiarization

OFCCP acknowledges that 5 CFR 1320.3(b)(1)(i) requires agencies to include in the burden analysis for new information collection requirements the estimated time it takes for contractors to review and understand the instructions for compliance. In order to minimize the burden, OFCCP will publish compliance assistance materials including, but not limited to, fact sheets and "Frequently Asked Questions." OFCCP will also host webinars for the contractor community that will describe the new requirements and conduct listening sessions to identify any specific challenges contractors believe they face, or may face, when complying with the requirements.

[88] Legacy CCR Extracts Public ("FOIA") Data Package, May 2014, *available at https://www.sam.gov/portal/public/SAM/* (last accessed February 12, 2015). There is at least one reason to believe the SAM data yield an underestimate of the number of entities affected by this rule and other reasons to believe the data yield an overestimate. SAM does not necessarily include all subcontractors, thus potentially leading to an underestimate, but this limitation of the data is offset somewhat because of the overlap among contractors and subcontractors; a firm may be a subcontractor on some activities but have a contract on others and thus be included in the SAM data. The SAM data may produce an overestimate of the entities affected by this rule because the data set includes: inactive contractors, contracts below this proposed rule's $10,000 threshold, and recipients of Federal grants and Federal financial assistance.

OFCCP believes that Federal contractors' human resources or personnel managers will be responsible for understanding or becoming familiar with the new requirements. OFCCP estimates that it will take one hour for a management professional at each contractor company to either read the compliance assistance materials provided by OFCCP or participate in an OFCCP webinar to learn more about the new requirements. One commenter asserted that one hour was an underestimation of the time needed for familiarization. The commenter asserted that multiple individuals at each contractor company would be required to become familiar with the requirements. OFCCP acknowledges that the precise amount of time each company will take to engage in certain activities will be difficult to estimate. However, the estimate used does take into account the fact that many contractors are smaller and may not have the same staff or human resources capabilities. Therefore, OFCCP retains its original estimate that it will take 60 minutes for regulatory familiarization. The estimated cost of this burden is assumed to be entirely at the Management, Professional, and Related Occupations level. Consequently, the estimated time burden for rule familiarization is 500,000 hours (500,000 contractor companies × 1 hour = 500,000 hours). The estimated cost is $25,790,000 (500,000 hours × $51.58/hour = $25,790,000).

Cost of New Provisions

The final rule prohibits discrimination based on employees and applicants inquiring about, discussing, or disclosing their compensation or the compensation of others unless the employee has access to compensation information of other employees or applicants as a part of such employee's essential job functions. The prohibition against discrimination would apply to all Federal contractors and subcontractors and federally assisted construction contractors and subcontractors with contracts or subcontracts in excess of $10,000. The new requirements are located at §§ 60–1.3, 60–1.4 and 60–1.35.

The final rule amends § 60–1.3 to include definitions for compensation, compensation information, and essential job functions as it relates to employees who have access to compensation information. Some commenters indicated that OFCCP should be required to assess additional burden because of the compensation definition. The commenter asserted that the definition would require contractors to change their analysis of employment processes. Another commenter suggested that OFCCP assess the burden for additional data requests that are made during compliance evaluations. OFCCP declines to adopt either of these two positions. The final rule does not change the requirement to conduct an in-depth analysis of employment practices. Contractors are required by existing regulations to analyze their personnel activity data annually, including compensation, to determine whether and where impediments to equal employment opportunity exist. The final rule establishes a definition of compensation, but does not change the existing regulatory requirement at 41 CFR 60–2.17(b)(3). OFCCP's guidance and regulations have historically included salary, wages, overtime pay, shift differentials, bonuses, commissions, vacation and holiday pay, allowances, insurance and other benefits, stock options, profit sharing and retirement.[89] Thus, OFCCP found no need to change the assessed burden for this requirement. The provision of a definition for compensation does not increase the costs of compliance with this rule. In response to the comment related to requests made during compliance evaluations, the addition of a definition of compensation does not change the manner by which OFCCP conducts its compliance evaluations, nor does it require the compliance officers to collect more data. The Federal Contract Compliance Manual and OFCCP's Directive 2013–03 instruct compliance officers to analyze all aspects of pay. Thus, the requests for additional data are not a new cost or burden to contractors.

In § 60–1.4(a)(3), the final rule mandates that each contracting agency incorporate the prohibition into the equal opportunity clause of Federal contracts and contract modifications, if the provision was not included in the original contract. More specifically, existing § 60–1.4(a)(3) provisions on notices sent to each labor union or representative of workers would be placed in § 60–1.4(a)(4); existing § 60–1.4(a)(4) would be placed in § 60–1.4(a)(5); existing § 60–1.4(a)(5) would be placed in § 60–1.4(a)(6); existing § 60–1.4(a)(6) would be placed in § 60–1.4(a)(7); and existing § 60–1.4(a)(7) would be placed in new § 60–1.4(a)(8). The equal opportunity clause may be incorporated by reference into Federal contracts and subcontracts.

In § 60–1.4(b)(3), the final rule mandates that each administering agency incorporate the prohibition into the equal opportunity clause of a grant, contract, loan, insurance, or guarantee involving federally assisted construction that is not exempted from the equal opportunity clause. More specifically, existing § 60–1.4(b)(3) provisions on notices sent to each labor union or representative of workers would be placed in § 60–1.4(b)(4); existing § 60–1.4(b)(4) would be placed in § 60–1.4(b)(5); existing § 60–1.4(b)(5) would be placed in § 60–1.4(b)(6); existing § 60–1.4(b)(6) would be placed in § 60–1.4(b)(7); and existing § 60–1.4(b)(7) would be placed in new § 60–1.4(b)(8). The equal opportunity clause may be incorporated by reference into federally assisted contracts and subcontracts.

To comply with this requirement, contractors may incorporate the equal opportunity clause into their nonexempt subcontracts either in its entirety or by including it by reference. While some contractors may need to locate the revised equal opportunity clause and incorporate it into existing contract templates, other contractors that include the clause by reference will make no change to existing subcontract language. One commenter asserted that it would take at least ten hours to comply with the new requirement. The commenter asserted that it would involve attorneys, procurement, logistics, and vendor services. However, the commenter did not provide any specificity that would explain or support this estimate. OFCCP disagrees with this assessment as the activity simply involves finding the new clause, provided by either OFCCP or the procurement officer, and incorporating that new wording into a contract template. OFCCP's estimate takes into account the fact that many contractors are smaller and may not have staffing or departments devoted to procurement, logistics, or vendor services. Therefore, OFCCP retains its original estimate that contractors will spend approximately 15 minutes modifying existing contract templates to ensure the additional language is included. The estimated time burden for this provision is 125,000 hours (500,000 contractors × 0.25 hours = 125,000 hours). The estimated cost of this provision is $3,883,438 ((125,000 hours × 0.25 × $51.58) + (125,000 × 0.75 × $24.23) = $3,883,438).

The final rule adds § 60–1.35(a) and (b) discussing contractor defenses to an allegation of violation of § 60–1.4(a)(3) and (b)(3). The text of paragraph (a) incorporates the text in section 5(a) of Executive Order 13665. The text of paragraph (b) is drawn from the text in section 2(b) of the same Executive Order. There is no burden associated with the inclusion of these new paragraphs.

Section 60–1.35(c) of the final rule requires contractors to disseminate the nondiscrimination provision by incorporating it into existing employee manuals or handbooks, and disseminating it to employees and to job applicants. This dissemination can be executed electronically or by posting a copy of the provision in conspicuous places available to employees and applicants for employment. In person or face-to-face communication of the provision is not required or recommended, however, contractors may use this method if they typically communicate information to all employees or applicants in this manner. In order to reduce the burden to contractors associated with disseminating the provision, the final rule requires contractors to adopt the nondiscrimination language provided by OFCCP into contractors' existing employee manuals or handbooks and otherwise make it available to employees and applicants. One commenter indicated that disseminating the policy to employees and applicants would take considerably more time as it would not only be necessary to incorporate the provision into handbooks and post the policy, but it would also require additional personnel to communicate and approve the changes to handbooks and postings. The provisions of this rule apply to all Federal contractors and subcontractors, thus when estimating the cost, it is necessary to factor in that many Federal contractors are small and do not have the same staff or human resources capabilities. Thus, OFCCP retains its original calculation, as it is more reflective of the range of Federal contractors and their respective practices. A second commenter indicated that contractors should be allowed to develop their own statements for incorporation into handbooks. OFCCP disagrees with both of these commenters. By providing the required language, OFCCP significantly reduces the burden of this requirement. The statement as written in the regulations must be included verbatim into existing handbooks. Allowing contractors to develop their own statements would be more burdensome for contractors, requiring additional resources for the development and review of the statement. Moreover, using a uniform statement eliminates confusion about

[89] Federal Contract Compliance Manual Chapter 2, Section 2L03 and Chapter 3, section 3H03 (Oct. 2014).

the appropriateness of the statement, and minimizes possible confusion by employees and applicants about the nature and purpose of the statement. Thus, OFCCP has selected the least burdensome alternative.

Section 60–1.35(c)(i) requires contractors to include the nondiscrimination provision in existing employee manuals or handbooks. OFCCP assumes that most contractors (98 percent) maintain these documents electronically.[90] For those contractors that maintain the documents electronically, we are not requiring contractors to physically reproduce their manuals to include the provision if they do not maintain hardcopies of manuals and handbooks. However, for those contractors that do not maintain their handbooks electronically, OFCCP believes those contractors (2 percent) will prepare and print a single errata sheet to update their hardcopy manual. OFCCP estimates it will take 20 minutes for contractors to locate, review, and reproduce the provision as provided by OFCCP and 15 minutes to incorporate it into existing employee manuals or handbooks; the total time required is 35 minutes (or 0.58 hours) to comply with this provision. Therefore, OFCCP estimates the time burden of this provision is 290,000 hours (500,000 contractor companies × 0.58 hours = 290,000 hours). The estimated cost of this provision is $9,009,575 ((290,000 hours × 0.25 × $51.58) + (290,000 hours × 0.75 × $24.23)).[91] OFCCP believes that this estimation may overstate the burden as it assumes that all 500,000 contractors have a handbook including contractors with fewer than 10 employees. The smaller contractors, those with 10 or fewer employers, represent 58 percent of the contractors in the SAM database and are the less likely to have formal employee handbooks.

Section 60–1.35(c)(ii) requires contractors to disseminate the nondiscrimination provision to employees and to job applicants. This dissemination can be executed by electronic posting or by posting a copy of the provision in conspicuous places available to employees and applicants for employment. OFCCP believes that 99 percent of contractors will post the information electronically while 1 percent will post the provision on employee bulletin boards. OFCCP's estimate is that it will take 15 minutes (or 0.25 hours) for contractors posting the provision electronically to prepare and post the provision. Additionally, OFCCP estimates it will take 75 minutes (or 1.25 hours) for contractors posting the provision manually to prepare the provision and post it in conspicuous places available to employees and applicants for employment. Therefore, OFCCP estimates that the time burden of this provision is 130,000 hours ((500,000 contractor companies × 99% × 0.25 hours) + (500,000 contractor companies × 1% × 1.25 hours) = 130,000 hours). The estimated cost of this provision is $4,038,775 ((123,750 hours × 0.25 × $51.58 + 123,750 hours × 0.75 × $24.23) + (6,250 hours × 0.25 × $51.58) + (6,250 hours × 0.75 × $24.23)).[92]

Contractors are required to maintain documentation of other notices; the regulations implementing Executive Order 11246, VEVRAA and Section 503 currently require recordkeeping related to personnel and employment activity. *See* 41 CFR 60–1.12; 60–4.3(a)(7); 60–300.80; 60–741.80. Consequently, there is no new time burden or cost for retaining copies of the notices to employees.

OFCCP estimates that the combined time burden for becoming familiar with and complying with the final rule is 1,045,000 hours (500,000 hours + 125,000 hours + 290,000 hours + 130,000 hours = 1,045,000 hours).

Operations and Maintenance Costs

In addition to the time burden calculated above, OFCCP estimates that contractors will incur operations and maintenance costs, mostly in the form of materials.

Section 60–1.35(c)(i)

OFCCP estimates that 1 percent of contractors (5,000 contractor companies) will incorporate the nondiscrimination provision into their existing hardcopy handbook or manual. OFCCP estimates that these 5,000 contractor companies will incorporate into an existing handbook or manual a single one-page errata sheet that includes the nondiscrimination provision. OFCCP estimates the one-time operations and maintenance cost of this provision is $400 (500,000 contractors × 1% × 1 page × $0.08 = $400).

Section 60–1.35(c)(ii)

OFCCP estimates that 1 percent of contractors will inform employees by posting the provision on existing employee bulletin boards. OFCCP assumes that on average these contractors will post the policy on 10 bulletin boards. Therefore OFCCP estimates the operations and maintenance cost of this provision is $4,000 (500,000 contractor companies × 1% × 10 pages × $0.08 = $4,000).

The estimated total first year cost of the final rule is $42,726,188 or $85 per contractor company. Below, in Table 1, is a summary of the burden hours and costs; Table 2 shows the total cost summary for the first year and recurring years.

TABLE 1—CONTRACTOR REQUIREMENTS

Estimated First-Year Burden Hours and Costs		
Section	Burden hours	Costs
Regulatory Familiarization	500,000	$25,790,000
60–1.3 Definitions	0	0
60–1.4(a) and (b) Contracting agencies amend the equal opportunity clause	125,000	3,883,438
60–1.4(d) Change "Deputy Assistant Secretary" to "Director of OFCCP"	0	0
60–1.35(c)(i) Incorporation into manuals or handbooks	290,000	9,009,575
60–1.35(c)(ii) Making the provision available to employees and applicants via electronic posting or manually posting a copy	130,000	4,038,775

[90] This is based on the Equal Employment Opportunity Commission representation that 98 percent of the employers submitting the EEO–1 report file their submissions electronically through a Web based online filing system. *See* Supporting Statement for Recordkeeping and Reporting Requirements for Employer Information Report (EEO–1), p. 1, OMB Control 3046–0007 Employer Information Report (EEO–1), *available at http://www.reginfo.gov/public/do/PRAViewDocument?ref_nbr=201412-3046-001* (last accessed May 5, 2015).

[91] OFCCP assumes that administrative support will identify the appropriate clause, and insert it into the handbook (75 percent) with management oversight (25 percent).

[92] OFCCP assumes that administrative support will copy and paste the clause into a notice and either post or send it electronically (75 percent) with management oversight (25 percent).

TABLE 1—CONTRACTOR REQUIREMENTS—Continued

Estimated First-Year Burden Hours and Costs		
Section	Burden hours	Costs
Total First-Year Burden Hours and Costs	1,045,000	42,721,788
Estimated Recurring Burden Hours and Costs		
Section	Burden hours	Costs
60–1.35(a) and (b) Defenses	0	0
Total Annual Recurring Burden Hours and Costs	0	0
Total Operations and Maintenance Costs	0	4,400
Total Burden Hours and Cost of the Final Rule	1,045,000	$42,726,188

TABLE 2—TOTAL COST SUMMARY

	Hours	Costs	Per contractor company
First Year Hours/Costs	1,045,000	$42,726,188	$85
Annual Recurring Hours/Cost	0	0	0

Summary of Benefits and Transfers

Executive Order 13563 recognizes that some rules have benefits that are difficult to quantify or monetize but are, nevertheless, important and states that agencies may consider such benefits. This rule, to the extent that it is effective, has equity and fairness benefits, which are explicitly recognized in Executive Order 13563. Enabling the employees and applicants of Federal contractors to discuss their compensation without fear of adverse action can contribute to reducing pay discrimination and ensuring that qualified and productive employees receive fair compensation. OFCCP designed the final rule to achieve these benefits by:

- Supporting more effective enforcement of the prohibition against compensation discrimination.
- Providing better remedies to workers victimized by compensation discrimination.
- Increasing employees' and applicants' understanding of the value of their skills in the labor market.
- Enhancing the ability of Federal contractors and their employees to detect and remediate unlawful discriminatory practices.

Social Benefits of Improved Nondiscrimination Enforcement

Social science research suggests antidiscrimination law can have broad social benefits, not only to those workers who are explicitly able to mobilize their rights and obtain redress, but also to the workforce and the economy as a whole. In general, discrimination is incompatible with an efficient labor market. Discrimination interferes with the ability of workers to find jobs that match their skills and abilities and to obtain wages consistent with a well-functioning marketplace.[93] Discrimination may reflect market failure, where collusion or other anti-discriminatory practices allow majority group members to shift the costs of discrimination to minority group members.[94]

For this reason, effective nondiscrimination enforcement can promote economic efficiency and growth. For example, a number of scholars have documented the benefits of the civil rights movement and the adoption of Title VII of the Civil Rights Act of 1964 on the economic prospects of workers and the larger economy.[95] One recent study estimated that improved workforce participation by women and minorities, including through adoption of civil rights laws and changing social norms, accounts for 15–20 percent of aggregate wage growth between 1960 and 2008.[96] On a smaller scale, the benefits of this rule have the potential to make an economic impact by providing employees of Federal contractors with a tool that allows them to identify potential compensation discrimination that undermines their financial security.

Regulatory Flexibility Act and Executive Order 13272 (Consideration of Small Entities)

The Regulatory Flexibility Act of 1980 (RFA) 5 U.S.C. 601 *et seq.*, as amended requires agencies to prepare regulatory flexibility analyses and make them available for public comment, when proposing regulations that will have a significant economic impact on a substantial number of small entities. *See* 5 U.S.C. 603. If the rule is not expected to have a significant economic impact on a substantial number of small entities the RFA allows an agency to certify such, in lieu of preparing an analysis. *See* 5 U.S.C. 605. As explained in the initial Regulatory Flexibility Act and Executive Order 13272 section of the proposed rule, OFCCP did not expect the proposed rule to have a significant economic impact on a substantial number of small entities. 79 FR 55712 (September 17, 2014). However in the interest of transparency and to provide

[93] Shelley J. Lundberg and Richard Starz, "Private Discrimination and Social Intervention in Competitive Labor Markets," 73 *American Economic Review* 340 (1983); Dennis J. Aigner and Glen G. Cain, "Statistical Theories of Discrimination in Labor Markets," 30 *Industrial and Labor Relations Review*, 175 (1977).

[94] Kenneth J. Arrow, "What Has Economics to Say about Racial Discrimination?," 12 *The Journal of Economic Perspectives* 91 (1998).

[95] J. Hoult Verkerke, "Free to Search," 105 Harvard Law Review 2080 (1992); James J. Heckman and Brook S. Payner, "Determining the Impact of Federal Anti-Discrimination Policy on the Economic Status of Blacks: A Study of South Carolina," 79 *American Economic Review* 138 (1989).

[96] Hsieh, C., Hurst, E. Jones, C. I., Klenow, P. J. "The Allocation of Talent and U.S. Economic Growth," *NBER Working Paper* (2013).

an opportunity for public comment, OFCCP prepared an initial regulatory flexibility analysis rather than certifying that the proposed rule was not expected to have a significant economic impact on a substantial number of small entities. In the NPRM, OFCCP specifically requested comments on the initial regulatory flexibility analysis, including the number of small entities affected by the Executive Order's prohibition on Federal contractors from discriminating against employees and job applicants, the compliance cost estimates, and whether alternatives exist that will reduce burden on small entities while still remaining consistent with the objective of Executive Order 13665. *See* 79 FR 55726 (September 17, 2014). While OFCCP received eleven comments that addressed the costs and burdens of the proposed rule, none commented on the initial regulatory flexibility analysis. Thus, as explained below, OFCCP is adopting the proposed rule's economic analysis for purposes of the final rule.

In the NPRM, OFCCP estimated the impact on small entities that are covered contractors of complying with the requirements contained in this final rule, OFCCP certifies that this rule will not have a significant economic impact on a substantial number of small entities. In making this certification, OFCCP determined that all small entities subject to Executive Order 11246 would be required to comply with all of the provisions of the final rule and that the compliance cost would be approximately $85 per contractor. Such compliance requirements are more fully described above in other portions of this preamble. The following section analyzes the cost of complying with Executive Order 13665.

In estimating the annual economic impact of this rule on the economy, OFCCP determined the compliance cost of the rule and whether the costs would be significant for a substantial number of small contractor firms (*i.e.* small business firms that enter into contracts with the Federal Government). If the estimated compliance costs for affected small contractor firms are less than 3 percent of small contractor firms' revenues, OFCCP considered it appropriate to conclude that this rule will not have a significant economic impact on the small contractor firms covered by Executive Order 13665. OFCCP has chosen 3 percent as the significance criteria; however, using this benchmark as an indicator of significant impact may overstate the significance of such an impact, since the costs associated with prohibiting discrimination against employees and job applicants who inquire about or discuss their own compensation or the compensation of other employees or applicants are expected to be mitigated to some degree by the benefits of the rule. The benefits, which may include improved employee productivity and decreased employee turnover, are discussed more fully in the preamble of this final rule.

The data sources used in the analysis of small business impact are the Small Business Administration's (SBA) Table of Small Business Size Standards,[97] the Current Population Survey (CPS), and the U.S. Census Bureau's Statistics of U.S. Businesses (SUSB).[98] Since Federal contractors are not limited to specific industries, OFCCP assessed the impact of the proposed rule across the 19 industrial classifications.[99] Because data limitations do not allow OFCCP to determine which of the small firms within these industries are Federal contractors, OFCCP assumes that these small firms are not significantly different from the small Federal contractors that will be directly affected by the rule.

OFCCP used the following steps to estimate the cost of the proposed rule per small contractor firm as measured by a percentage of the total annual receipts. First, OFCCP used Census SUSB data that disaggregates industry information by firm size in order to perform a robust analysis of the impact on small contractor firms. OFCCP applied the SBA small business size standards to the SUSB data to determine the number of small firms in the affected industries. Then OFCCP used receipts data from the SUSB to calculate the cost per firm as a percent of total receipts by dividing the estimated annual cost per firm by the average annual receipts per firm. This methodology was applied to each of the industries and the results by industry are presented in Tables 3–21 below.

In sum, the increased cost of compliance resulting from the proposed rule is *de minimis* relative to revenue at small contractor firms no matter their size. All of the industries had an annual cost per firm as a percent of receipts of 3 percent or less. For instance, the manufacturing industry cost is estimated to range from 0.00 percent for firms that have average annual receipts of approximately $985 million to 0.02 percent for firms that have average annual receipts of under $500,000. Management of companies and enterprises is the industry with the highest relative costs, with a range of 0.00 percent for firms that have average annual receipts of approximately $2 million to 0.36 percent for firms that have average annual receipts of under $24,000. Therefore, OFCCP determined that in no instance was the effect of the proposed rule greater than 3 percent of total receipts.

OFCCP then determined the number of small contractor firms actually affected by the proposed rule. This information is not readily available. The best source for the number of small contractor firms that are affected by this proposed rule is GSA's System for Award Management (SAM). OFCCP used SAM data to estimate the number of affected small contractor firms since SAM data allow us to directly estimate the number of small contractor firms. Federal contractor status cannot be discerned from the SBA firm size data. It can only be used to estimate the number of small firms, not the number of small contractor firms. OFCCP used the SBA data to estimate the impact of the proposed regulation on a "typical" or "average" small firm in each of the 19 industries. OFCCP then assumed that a typical small firm is similar to a small contractor firm. Thus, based on its analysis, OFCCP believes that this rule will not have a significant economic effect on a substantial number of small businesses.

Based on the most current SAM data available, if OFCCP defines small as fewer than 500 employees, then there are 328,552 small contractor firms. If OFCCP defines small as firms with less than $35.5 million in revenues, then there are 315,902 small contractor firms. Thus, OFCCP established the range from 315,902 to 328,552 as the total number of small contractor firms. Of course, not all of these contractor firms will be impacted by the proposed rule; only those contractor firms that have policies

[97] U.S. Small Business Administration, Office of Advocacy, "Firm Size Data, Statistics of U.S. Businesses, Business Dynamics Statistics, Business Employment Dynamics, and Nonemployer Statistics," *available at http://www.sba.gov/advocacy/849/12162#susb* (last accessed June 9, 2014).

[98] U.S. Census Bureau, Statistics of U.S. Businesses, "Latest SUSB Annual Data," *available at http://www.census.gov/econ/susb/* (last accessed June 9, 2014).

[99] Agriculture, Forestry, Fishing, and Hunting Industry (North American Industry Classification System (NAICS) 11, Mining NAICS 21, Utilities NAICS 22, Construction NAICS 23, Manufacturing, NAICS 31–33, Wholesale Trade NAICS 42, Retail Trade NAICS 44–45, Transportation and Warehousing NAICS 48–49, Information NAICS 51, Finance and Insurance NAICS 52, Real Estate and Rental and Leasing NAICS 53, Professional, Scientific, and Technical Services NAICS 54, Management of Companies and Enterprises NAICS 55, Administrative and Support and Waste Management and Remediation Services NAICS 56, Educational Services NAICS 61, Healthcare and Social Assistance NAICS 62, Arts, Entertainment, and Recreation NAICS 71, Accommodation and Food Services NAICS 72, Other Services NAICS 81.

that prohibit employees and job applicants from inquiring about, discussing or disclosing their own compensation or the compensation of other employees or job applicants. Thus, this range is an overestimate of the number of firms affected by the proposed rule because some of those small contractor firms do not have such a policy or practice. As the proposed regulation applies to contractors covered by Executive Order 11246, OFCCP estimates that the range of small firms impacted ranges from 315,902 to 328,552 or all covered Federal contractor companies.

OFCCP has closely reviewed the economic analysis it utilized in the proposed rule and carefully considered all the comments received. Based on its review and consideration, OFCCP has concluded that the method used to conduct the economic analysis in the proposed rule reasonably estimated the annual effect of the rule, based on the data sources available to OFCCP. OFCCP is accordingly adopting the proposed rule's economic analysis for purposes of the final rule.

TABLE 3—COST PER SMALL FIRM IN THE AGRICULTURE, FORESTRY, FISHING, AND HUNTING INDUSTRY, THE SBA SMALL BUSINESS SIZE STANDARD FOR THIS INDUSTRY IS $0.75 MILLION–$27.5 MILLION

Agriculture, forestry, fishing, and hunting industry							
	Number of firms	Total number of employees	Average number of employees per firm [1]	Annual cost per firm [2]	Annual receipts	Average receipts per firm [3]	Annual cost per firm as percent of receipts [4] (percent)
Firms with sales/receipts/revenue below $100,000	5,086	N/A	N/A	$85	$247,056,000	$48,576	0.17
Firms with sales/receipts/revenue of $100,000 to $499,999	8,939	21,523	2.4	85	2,231,355,000	249,620	0.03
Firms with sales/receipts/revenue of $500,000 to $999,999	3,670	19,631	5.3	85	2,620,344,000	713,990	0.01
Firms with sales/receipts/revenue of $1,000,000 to $2,499,999	3,230	30,944	9.6	85	4,975,078,000	1,540,272	0.01
Firms with sales/receipts/revenue of $2,500,000 to $4,999,999	1,117	20,049	17.9	85	3,811,000,000	3,411,817	0.00
Firms with sales/receipts/revenue of $5,000,000 to $7,499,999	289	8,997	31.1	85	1,730,128,000	5,986,602	0.00
Firms with sales/receipts/revenue of $7,500,000 to $9,999,999	165	7,588	46.0	85	1,340,763,000	8,125,836	0.00
Firms with sales/receipts/revenue of $10,000,000 to $14,999,999	112	6,130	54.7	85	1,288,588,000	11,505,250	0.00
Firms with sales/receipts/revenue of $15,000,000 to $19,999,999	55	4,042	73.5	85	874,841,00	15,906,200	0.00
Firms with sales/receipts/revenue of $20,000,000 to $24,999,999	44	5,325	121.0	85	858,761,000	19,517,295	0.00
Firms with sales/receipts/revenue of $25,000,000 to $29,999,999	26	2,800	107.7	85	595,387,000	22,899,500	0.00

N/A = not available, not disclosed

[1] In the case of agriculture, forestry, fishing, and hunting firms with receipts of $100,000 to $499,999, the average number of employees per firm (2.4) was derived by dividing the total number of employees (21,523) by the number of firms (8,939).

[2] The annual cost per firm ($85) accounts for regulatory familarization, including the policy in existing handbooks, including it in existing manager meetings, and informing employees of the prohibition.

[3] In the case of agriculture, forestry, fishing, and hunting firms with receipts of $100,000 to $499,999, the average receipts per firm ($249,620) was derived by dividing the total annual receipts ($2,231,355,000) by the number of firms (8,939).

[4] In the case of agriculture, forestry, fishing and hunting firms with receipts of $100,000 to $499,999, the annual cost per firms as a percent of receipts (0.03 percent) was derived by dividing the annual cost per firm ($119) by the average receipts per firm ($249,620).

TABLE 4—COST PER SMALL FIRM IN THE MINING INDUSTRY THE SBA SMALL BUSINESS SIZE STANDARD FOR THIS INDUSTRY IS 500 EMPLOYEES

Mining industry							
	Number of firms	Total number of employees	Average number of employees per firm [1]	Annual cost per firm [2]	Annual receipts	Average receipts per firm [3]	Annual cost per firm as percent of receipts [4] (percent)
Firms with 0–4 employees	11,223	17,874	1.6	$85	$6,809,517,000	$606,747	0.01
Firms with 5–9 employees	3,186	21,314	6.7	85	6,304,810,000	1,978,911	0.00
Firms with 10–19 employees	2,451	33,344	13.6	85	9,092,457,000	3,709,693	0.00
Firms with 20–99 employees	2,775	107,447	38.7	85	32,035,288,000	11,544,248	0.00
Firms with 100–499 employees	690	102,299	148.3	85	38,463,690,000	55,744,478	0.00

[1] In the case of mining firms with 0–4 employees, the average number of employees per firm (1.6) was derived by dividing the total number of employees (17,874) by the number of firms (11,223).

[2] The annual cost per firm ($85) accounts for regulatory familarization, including the policy in existing handbooks, including it in existing manager meetings, and informing employees of the prohibition.

[3] In the case of mining firms with 0 4 employees, the average receipts per firm ($606,747) was derived by dividing the total annual receipts ($6,809,517,000) by the number of firms (11,223).

[4] In the case of mining firms with 0 4 employees, the annual cost per firm as a percent of receipts (0.01 percent) was derived by dividing the annual cost per firm ($119) by the average receipts per firms ($606,747).

TABLE 5—COST PER SMALL FIRM IN THE UTILITIES INDUSTRY THE SBA SMALL BUSINESS SIZE STANDARD FOR THIS INDUSTRY IS 250–1,000 EMPLOYEES

Utilities industry							
	Number of firms	Total number of employees	Average number of employees per firm	Annual cost per firm	Annual receipts	Average receipts per firm	Annual cost per firm as percent of receipts (percent)
Firms with 0–4 employees	3,212	6,181	1.9	$85	$7,238,519,000	$2,253,586	0.00
Firms with 5–9 employees	1,020	6,546	6.4	85	4,373,888,000	4,288,125	0.00
Firms with 10–19 employees	513	6,722	13.1	85	5,657,251,000	11,027,780	0.00
Firms with 20–99 employees	870	38,602	44.4	85	27,513,924,000	31,625,200	0.00
Firms with 100–499 employees	309	52,294	169.2	85	53,091,123,000	171,815,932	0.00
Firms with 500+ employees [1]	199	512,412	2,574.9	85	475,894,489,000	2,391,429,593	0.00

[1] The small business size for several subsectors within the utilities industry is 750 or 1,000 employees; however, data are not disaggregated for firms with more than 500 employees.

TABLE 6—COST PER SMALL FIRM IN THE CONSTRUCTION INDUSTRY THE SBA SMALL BUSINESS SIZE STANDARD FOR THIS INDUSTRY IS $15 MILLION–$36.5 MILLION.

Construction industry							
	Number of firms	Total number of employees	Average number of employees per firm	Annual cost per firm	Annual receipts	Average receipts per firm	Annual cost per firm as percent of receipts (percent)
Firms with sales/receipts/revenue below $100,000	151,986	N/A	N/A	$85	$7,636,718,000	$50,246	0.17
Firms with sales/receipts/revenue of $100,000 to $499,999	316,475	776,806	2.5	85	81,110,428,000	256,293	0.03

TABLE 6—COST PER SMALL FIRM IN THE CONSTRUCTION INDUSTRY THE SBA SMALL BUSINESS SIZE STANDARD FOR THIS INDUSTRY IS $15 MILLION–$36.5 MILLION.—Continued

	Construction industry						
	Number of firms	Total number of employees	Average number of employees per firm	Annual cost per firm	Annual receipts	Average receipts per firm	Annual cost per firm as percent of receipts (percent)
Firms with sales/receipts/revenue of $500,000 to $999,999	124,214	642,823	5.2	85	88,028,843,000	708,687	0.01
Firms with sales/receipts/revenue of $1,000,000 to $2,499,999	110,546	1,049,670	9.5	85	173,054,634,000	1,565,454	0.01
Firms with sales/receipts/revenue of $2,500,000 to $4,999,999	47,962	864,701	18.0	85	167,758,626,000	3,497,740	0.00
Firms with sales/receipts/revenue of $5,000,000 to $7,499,999	16,992	492,370	29.0	85	102,502,053,000	6,032,371	0.00
Firms with sales/receipts/revenue of $7,500,000 to $9,999,999	7,801	308,512	39.5	85	66,977,650,000	8,585,777	0.00
Firms with sales/receipts/revenue of $10,000,000 to $14,999,999	8,259	427,159	51.7	85	99,174,146,000	12,008,009	0.00
Firms with sales/receipts/revenue of $15,000,000 to $19,999,999	4,354	289,441	66.5	85	73,881,089,000	16,968,555	0.00
Firms with sales/receipts/revenue of $20,000,000 to $24,999,999	2,611	209,081	80.1	85	56,928,754,000	21,803,429	0.00
Firms with sales/receipts/revenue of $25,000,000 to $29,999,999	1,621	150,754	93.0	85	43,119,720,000	26,600,691	0.00
Firms with sales/receipts/revenue of $30,000,000 to $34,999,999	1,171	121,928	104.1	85	36,848,837,000	31,467,837	0.00
Firms with sales/receipts/revenue of $35,000,000 to $39,999,999	831	94,903	114.2	85	30,307,198,000	36,470,756	0.00

N/A = not available, not disclosed

TABLE 7—COST PER SMALL FIRM IN THE MANUFACTURING INDUSTRY THE SBA SMALL BUSINESS SIZE STANDARD FOR THIS INDUSTRY IS 500–1,500 EMPLOYEES

	Manufacturing industry						
	Number of firms	Total number of employees	Average number of employees per firm	Annual cost per firm	Annual receipts	Average receipts per firm	Annual cost per firm as percent of receipts (percent)
Firms with 0–4 employees	114,635	213,123	1.9	$85	$46,236,636,000	$403,338	0.02
Firms with 5–9 employees	53,500	358,110	6.7	85	53,036,608,000	991,338	0.01
Firms with 10–19 employees	44,939	612,113	13.6	85	97,897,887,000	2,178,462	0.00

TABLE 7—COST PER SMALL FIRM IN THE MANUFACTURING INDUSTRY THE SBA SMALL BUSINESS SIZE STANDARD FOR THIS INDUSTRY IS 500–1,500 EMPLOYEES—Continued

Manufacturing industry							
	Number of firms	Total number of employees	Average number of employees per firm	Annual cost per firm	Annual receipts	Average receipts per firm	Annual cost per firm as percent of receipts (percent)
Firms with 20–99 employees	55,603	2,288,585	41.2	85	440,739,564,000	7,926,543	0.00
Firms with 100–199 employees	13,945	2,445,779	175.4	85	634,737,830,000	45,517,234	0.00
Firms with 500+ employees [1]	4,079	7,402,462	1,814.8	85	4,019,587,050,000	985,434,432	0.00

[1] The small business size standard for many subsectors within the manufacturing industry is 750, 1,000, or 1,500 employees; however, data are not disaggregated for firms with more than 500 employees.

TABLE 8—COST PER SMALL FIRM IN THE WHOLESALE TRADE INDUSTRY THE SBA SMALL BUSINESS SIZE STANDARD FOR THIS INDUSTRY IS 100 EMPLOYEES

Wholesale trade industry							
	Number of firms	Total number of employees	Average number of employees per firm	Annual cost per firm	Annual receipts	Average receipts per firm	Annual cost per firm as percent of receipts (percent)
Firms with 0–4 employees	190,153	325,412	1.7	$85	$297,267,502,000	$1,563,307	0.01
Firms with 5–9 employees	57,366	377,841	6.6	85	249,842,292,000	4,355,233	0.00
Firms with 10–19 employees	39,354	525,216	13.3	85	325,243,478,000	8,264,560	0.00
Firms with 20–99 employees	36,783	1,365,914	37.1	85	899,443,843,000	24,452,705	0.00

TABLE 9—COST PER SMALL FIRM IN THE RETAIL TRADE INDUSTRY THE SBA SMALL BUSINESS SIZE STANDARD FOR THIS INDUSTRY IS $7.5 MILLION–$38.5 MILLION

Retail trade industry							
	Number of firms	Total number of employees	Average number of employees per firm	Annual cost per firm	Annual receipts	Average receipts per firm	Annual cost per firm as percent of receipts (percent)
Firms with sales/receipts/revenue below $100,000	98,659	N/A	N/A	$85	$5,008,702,000	$50,768	0.17
Firms with sales/receipts/revenue of $100,000 to $499,999	251,705	727,585	2.9	85	67,380,242,000	267,695	0.03
Firms with sales/receipts/revenue of $500,000 to $999,999	122,575	634,006	5.2	85	87,491,736,000	713,781	0.01
Firms with sales/receipts/revenue of $1,000,000 to $2,499,999	120,985	1,019,672	8.4	85	190,373,341,000	1,573,528	0.01
Firms with sales/receipts/revenue of $2,500,000 to $4,999,999	55,634	774,581	13.9	85	193,186,239,000	3,472,449	0.00
Firms with sales/receipts/revenue of $5,000,000 to $7,499,999	19,594	418,263	21.3	85	117,223,823,000	5,982,639	0.00

TABLE 9—COST PER SMALL FIRM IN THE RETAIL TRADE INDUSTRY THE SBA SMALL BUSINESS SIZE STANDARD FOR THIS INDUSTRY IS $7.5 MILLION–$38.5 MILLION—Continued

Retail trade industry							
	Number of firms	Total number of employees	Average number of employees per firm	Annual cost per firm	Annual receipts	Average receipts per firm	Annual cost per firm as percent of receipts (percent)
Firms with sales/ receipts/revenue of $7,500,000 to $9,999,999	9,582	272,697	28.5	85	80,790,141,000	8,431,449	0.00
Firms with sales/ receipts/revenue of $10,000,000 to $14,999,999	9,824	366,889	37.3	85	115,236,313,000	11,730,081	0.00
Firms with sales/ receipts/revenue of $15,000,000 to $19,999,999	5,310	256,826	48.4	85	86,999,536,000	16,384,093	0.00
Firms with sales/ receipts/revenue of $20,000,000 to $24,999,999	3,498	201,289	57.5	85	72,964,681,000	20,858,971	0.00
Firms with sales/ receipts/revenue of $25,000,000 to $29,999,999	2,438	167,596	68.7	85	61,987,531,000	25,425,566	0.00
Firms with sales/ receipts/revenue of $30,000,000 to $34,999,999	1,835	144,987	79.0	85	55,162,317,000	30,061,208	0.00
Firms with sales/ receipts/revenue of $35,000,000 to $39,999,999	1,491	122,188	82.0	85	50,711,404,000	34,011,673	0.00

N/A = not available, not disclosed.

TABLE 10—COST PER SMALL FIRM IN THE TRANSPORTATION AND WAREHOUSING INDUSTRY THE SBA SMALL BUSINESS SIZE STANDARD FOR THIS INDUSTRY IS $7.5 MILLION–$38.5 MILLION

Transportation and warehousing industry							
	Number of firms	Total number of employees	Average number of employees per firm	Annual cost per firm	Annual receipts	Average receipts per firm	Annual cost per firm as percent of receipts (percent)
Firms with sales/ receipts/revenue below $100,000	40,510	N/A	N/A	$85	$1,939,749,000	$47,883	0.18
Firms with sales/ receipts/revenue of $100,000 to $499,999	67,987	181,924	2.7	85	16,284,066,000	239,517	0.04
Firms with sales/ receipts/revenue of $500,000 to $999,999	22,377	151,091	6.7	85	15,756,895,000	704,156	0.01
Firms with sales/ receipts/revenue of $1,000,000 to $2,499,999	20,915	271,012	13.0	85	32,305,484,000	1,544,608	0.01
Firms with sales/ receipts/revenue of $2,500,000 to $4,999,999	9,183	223,156	24.3	85	31,359,227,000	3,414,922	0.00
Firms with sales/ receipts/revenue of $5,000,000 to $7,499,999	3,550	136,436	38.4	85	20,463,648,000	5,764,408	0.00

TABLE 10—COST PER SMALL FIRM IN THE TRANSPORTATION AND WAREHOUSING INDUSTRY THE SBA SMALL BUSINESS SIZE STANDARD FOR THIS INDUSTRY IS $7.5 MILLION–$38.5 MILLION—Continued

	Transportation and warehousing industry						
	Number of firms	Total number of employees	Average number of employees per firm	Annual cost per firm	Annual receipts	Average receipts per firm	Annual cost per firm as percent of receipts (percent)
Firms with sales/ receipts/revenue of $7,500,000 to $9,999,999	1,800	91,408	50.8	85	14,261,554,000	7,923,086	0.00
Firms with sales/ receipts/revenue of $10,000,000 to $14,999,999	1,840	123,966	67.4	85	19,933,921,000	10,833,653	0.00
Firms with sales/ receipts/revenue of $15,000,000 to $19,999,999	988	85,367	86.4	85	14,057,603,000	14,228,343	0.00
Firms with sales/ receipts/revenue of $20,000,000 to $24,999,999	621	68,836	110.8	85	11,060,118,000	17,810,174	0.00
Firms with sales/ receipts/revenue of $25,000,000 to $29,999,999	429	51,989	121.2	85	8,257,805,000	19,248,963	0.00
Firms with sales/ receipts/revenue of $30,000,000 to $34,999,999	311	45,274	145.6	85	7,184,425,000	23,101,045	0.00
Firms with sales/ receipts/revenue of $35,000,000 to $39,999,999	235	32,922	140.1	85	5,902,588,000	25,117,396	0.00

N/A = not available, not disclosed.

TABLE 11—COST PER SMALL FIRM IN THE INFORMATION INDUSTRY THE SBA SMALL BUSINESS SIZE STANDARD FOR THIS INDUSTRY IS $7.5 MILLION–$38.5 MILLION

	Information industry						
	Number of firms	Total number of employees	Average number of employees per firm	Annual cost per firm	Annual receipts	Average receipts per firm	Annual cost per firm as percent of receipts (percent)
Firms with sales/ receipts/revenue below $100,000	15,960	N/A	N/A	$85	$767,642,000	$48,098	0.18
Firms with sales/ receipts/revenue of $100,000 to $499,999	27,678	80,336	2.9	85	6,876,130,000	248,433	0.03
Firms with sales/ receipts/revenue of $500,000 to $999,999	10,311	67,954	6.6	85	7,260,927,000	704,192	0.01
Firms with sales/ receipts/revenue of $1,000,000 to $2,499,999	9,808	120,499	12.3	85	15,248,992,000	1,554,750	0.01
Firms with sales/ receipts/revenue of $2,500,000 to $4,999,999	4,508	100,331	22.3	85	15,472,313,000	3,432,190	0.00
Firms with sales/ receipts/revenue of $5,000,000 to $7,499,999	1,837	65,601	35.7	85	10,856,893,000	5,910,121	0.00

TABLE 11—COST PER SMALL FIRM IN THE INFORMATION INDUSTRY THE SBA SMALL BUSINESS SIZE STANDARD FOR THIS INDUSTRY IS $7.5 MILLION–$38.5 MILLION—Continued

	Information industry						
	Number of firms	Total number of employees	Average number of employees per firm	Annual cost per firm	Annual receipts	Average receipts per firm	Annual cost per firm as percent of receipts (percent)
Firms with sales/receipts/revenue of $7,500,000 to $9,999,999	1,018	46,846	46.0	85	8,447,070,000	8,297,711	0.00
Firms with sales/receipts/revenue of $10,000,000 to $14,999,999	1,092	68,058	62.3	85	12,300,328,000	11,264,037	0.00
Firms with sales/receipts/revenue of $15,000,000 to $19,999,999	601	49,812	82.9	85	9,293,544,000	15,463,468	0.00
Firms with sales/receipts/revenue of $20,000,000 to $24,999,999	389	37,522	96.5	85	7,616,666,000	19,580,118	0.00
Firms with sales/receipts/revenue of $25,000,000 to $29,999,999	270	30,523	113.0	85	6,512,265,000	24,119,500	0.00
Firms with sales/receipts/revenue of $30,000,000 to $34,999,999	175	25,649	146.6	85	4,971,718,000	28,409,817	0.00
Firms with sales/receipts/revenue of $35,000,000 to $39,999,999	136	21,553	158.5	85	4,082,897,000	30,021,301	0.00

N/A = not available, not disclosed.

TABLE 12—COST PER SMALL FIRM IN THE FINANCE AND INSURANCE INDUSTRY THE SBA SMALL BUSINESS SIZE STANDARD FOR THIS INDUSTRY IS $7.5 MILLION–$38.5 MILLION

	Finance and insurance industry						
	Number of firms	Total number of employees	Average number of employees per firm	Annual cost per firm	Annual receipts	Average receipts per firm	Annual cost per firm as percent of receipts (percent)
Firms with sales/receipts/revenue below $100,000	61,548	N/A	N/A	$85	$2,931,522,000	$47,630	0.18
Firms with sales/receipts/revenue of $100,000 to $499,999	118,169	308,539	2.6	85	29,379,598,000	248,624	0.03
Firms with sales/receipts/revenue of $500,000 to $999,999	33,703	177,822	5.3	85	23,302,679,000	691,413	0.01
Firms with sales/receipts/revenue of $1,000,000 to $2,499,999	23,023	222,822	9.7	85	35,135,972,000	1,526,125	0.01
Firms with sales/receipts/revenue of $2,500,000 to $4,999,999	9,728	185,783	19.1	85	33,574,070,000	3,451,282	0.00
Firms with sales/receipts/revenue of $5,000,000 to $7,499,999	4,108	118,100	28.7	85	24,483,200,000	5,959,883	0.00

TABLE 12—COST PER SMALL FIRM IN THE FINANCE AND INSURANCE INDUSTRY THE SBA SMALL BUSINESS SIZE STANDARD FOR THIS INDUSTRY IS $7.5 MILLION–$38.5 MILLION—Continued

	Finance and insurance industry						
	Number of firms	Total number of employees	Average number of employees per firm	Annual cost per firm	Annual receipts	Average receipts per firm	Annual cost per firm as percent of receipts (percent)
Firms with sales/ receipts/revenue of $7,500,000 to $9,999,999	2,405	90,442	37.6	85	20,088,983,000	8,353,007	0.00
Firms with sales/ receipts/revenue of $10,000,000 to $14,999,999	2,820	148,252	52.6	85	33,267,079,000	11,796,837	0.00
Firms with sales/ receipts/revenue of $15,000,000 to $19,999,999	1,564	106,896	68.3	85	25,663,650,000	16,408,983	0.00
Firms with sales/ receipts/revenue of $20,000,000 to $24,999,999	1,028	87,611	85.2	85	21,843,640,000	21,248,677	0.00
Firms with sales/ receipts/revenue of $25,000,000 to $29,999,999	685	65,621	95.8	85	17,478,694,000	25,516,342	0.00
Firms with sales/ receipts/revenue of $30,000,000 to $34,999,999	515	58,841	113.6	85	15,619,023,000	30,328,200	0.00
Firms with sales/ receipts/revenue of $35,000,000 to $39,999,999	418	51,263	122.6	85	14,150,222,000	33,852,206	0.00

N/A = not available, not disclosed.

TABLE 13—COST PER SMALL FIRM IN THE REAL ESTATE AND RENTAL AND LEASING INDUSTRY THE SBA SMALL BUSINESS SIZE STANDARD FOR THIS INDUSTRY IS $7.5 MILLION–$38.5 MILLION

	Real estate and rental and leasing industry						
	Number of firms	Total number of employees	Average number of employees per firm	Annual cost per firm	Annual receipts	Average receipts per firm	Annual cost per firm as percent of receipts (percent)
Firms with sales/ receipts/revenue below $100,000	86,219	N/A	N/A	$85	$4,165,673,000	$48,315	0.18
Firms with sales/ receipts/revenue of $100,000 to $499,999	124,930	299,041	2.4	85	30,501,166,000	244,146	0.03
Firms with sales/ receipts/revenue of $500,000 to $999,999	39,747	191,958	4.8	85	27,836,936,000	700,353	0.01
Firms with sales/ receipts/revenue of $1,000,000 to $2,499,999	29,717	269,366	9.1	85	45,164,417,000	1,519,818	0.01
Firms with sales/ receipts/revenue of $2,500,000 to $4,999,999	10,013	181,600	18.1	85	33,652,743,000	3,360,905	0.00
Firms with sales/ receipts/revenue of $5,000,000 to $7,499,999	3,288	95,418	29.0	85	18,788,566,000	5,714,284	0.00

TABLE 13—COST PER SMALL FIRM IN THE REAL ESTATE AND RENTAL AND LEASING INDUSTRY THE SBA SMALL BUSINESS SIZE STANDARD FOR THIS INDUSTRY IS $7.5 MILLION–$38.5 MILLION—Continued

Real estate and rental and leasing industry							
	Number of firms	Total number of employees	Average number of employees per firm	Annual cost per firm	Annual receipts	Average receipts per firm	Annual cost per firm as percent of receipts (percent)
Firms with sales/ receipts/revenue of $7,500,000 to $9,999,999	1,553	62,482	40.2	85	12,221,244,000	7,869,442	0.00
Firms with sales/ receipts/revenue of $10,000,000 to $14,999,999	1,518	81,675	53.8	85	16,329,830,000	10,757,464	0.00
Firms with sales/ receipts/revenue of $15,000,000 to $19,999,999	771	48,442	62.8	85	11,037,708,000	14,316,093	0.00
Firms with sales/ receipts/revenue of $20,000,000 to $24,999,999	464	36,318	78.3	85	8,012,159,000	17,267,584	0.00
Firms with sales/ receipts/revenue of $25,000,000 to $29,999,999	365	32,555	89.2	85	7,621,190,000	20,879,973	0.00
Firms with sales/ receipts/revenue of $30,000,000 to $34,999,999	228	25,638	112.4	85	5,610,499,000	24,607,452	0.00
Firms with sales/ receipts/revenue of $35,000,000 to $39,999,999	161	17,743	110.2	85	4,144,542,000	25,742,497	0.00

N/A = not available, not disclosed.

TABLE 14—COST PER SMALL FIRM IN THE PROFESSIONAL, SCIENTIFIC, AND TECHNICAL SERVICES INDUSTRY THE SBA SMALL BUSINESS SIZE STANDARD FOR THIS INDUSTRY IS $7.5 MILLION–$38.5 MILLION

Professional, scientific and technical services industry							
	Number of firms	Total number of employees	Average number of employees per firm	Annual cost per firm	Annual receipts	Average receipts per firm	Annual cost per firm as percent of receipts (percent)
Firms with sales/ receipts/revenue below $100,000	207,967	N/A	N/A	$85	$9,968,674,000	$47,934	0.18
Firms with sales/ receipts/revenue of $100,000 to $499,999	339,834	814,116	2.4	85	82,241,004,000	242,003	0.04
Firms with sales/ receipts/revenue of $500,000 to $999,999	102,144	584,473	5.7	85	71,850,790,000	703,426	0.01
Firms with sales/ receipts/revenue of $1,000,000 to $2,499,999	78,520	870,369	11.1	85	120,442,007,000	1,533,902	0.01
Firms with sales/ receipts/revenue of $2,500,000 to $4,999,999	28,337	631,182	22.3	85	97,339,397,000	3,435,064	0.00
Firms with sales/ receipts/revenue of $5,000,000 to $7,499,999	9,714	355,210	36.6	85	57,721,674,000	5,942,112	0.00

TABLE 14—COST PER SMALL FIRM IN THE PROFESSIONAL, SCIENTIFIC, AND TECHNICAL SERVICES INDUSTRY THE SBA SMALL BUSINESS SIZE STANDARD FOR THIS INDUSTRY IS $7.5 MILLION–$38.5 MILLION—Continued

	Professional, scientific and technical services industry						
	Number of firms	Total number of employees	Average number of employees per firm	Annual cost per firm	Annual receipts	Average receipts per firm	Annual cost per firm as percent of receipts (percent)
Firms with sales/receipts/revenue of $7,500,000 to $9,999,999	4,863	245,206	50.4	85	40,592,738,000	8,347,263	0.00
Firms with sales/receipts/revenue of $10,000,000 to $14,999,999	4,658	313,530	67.3	85	53,578,044,000	11,502,371	0.00
Firms with sales/receipts/revenue of $15,000,000 to $19,999,999	2,338	211,940	90.7	85	36,728,134,000	15,709,210	0.00
Firms with sales/receipts/revenue of $20,000,000 to $24,999,999	1,381	147,737	107.0	85	27,448,191,000	19,875,591	0.00
Firms with sales/receipts/revenue of $25,000,000 to $29,999,999	954	122,039	127.9	85	22,622,723,000	23,713,546	0.00
Firms with sales/receipts/revenue of $30,000,000 to $34,999,999	603	91,258	151.3	85	15,961,413,000	26,470,005	0.00
Firms with sales/receipts/revenue of $35,000,000 to $39,999,999	511	83,414	163.2	85	15,941,272,000	31,196,227	0.00

N/A = not available, not disclosed.

TABLE 15—COST PER SMALL FIRM IN THE MANAGEMENT OF COMPANIES AND ENTERPRISES INDUSTRY THE SBA SMALL BUSINESS SIZE STANDARD FOR THIS INDUSTRY IS $20.5 MILLION

	Management of companies and enterprises industry						
	Number of firms	Total number of employees	Average number of employees per firm	Annual cost per firm	Annual receipts	Average receipts per firm	Annual cost per firm as percent of receipts (percent)
Firms with sales/receipts/revenue below $100,000	1,895	11,318	6.0	$85	$44,606,000	$23,539	0.36
Firms with sales/receipts/revenue of $100,000 to $499,999	1,387	4,529	3.3	85	293,971,000	211,947	0.04
Firms with sales/receipts/revenue of $500,000 to $999,999	964	5,082	5.3	85	373,917,000	387,881	0.02
Firms with sales/receipts/revenue of $1,000,000 to $2,499,999	2,039	18,829	9.2	85	1,087,692,000	533,444	0.02
Firms with sales/receipts/revenue of $2,500,000 to $4,999,999	2,242	26,723	11.9	85	1,698,014,000	757,366	0.01
Firms with sales/receipts/revenue of $5,000,000 to $7,499,999	1,717	28,312	16.5	85	1,855,703,000	1,080,782	0.01

TABLE 15—COST PER SMALL FIRM IN THE MANAGEMENT OF COMPANIES AND ENTERPRISES INDUSTRY THE SBA SMALL BUSINESS SIZE STANDARD FOR THIS INDUSTRY IS $20.5 MILLION—Continued

	Management of companies and enterprises industry						
	Number of firms	Total number of employees	Average number of employees per firm	Annual cost per firm	Annual receipts	Average receipts per firm	Annual cost per firm as percent of receipts (percent)
Firms with sales/ receipts/revenue of $7,500,000 to $9,999,999	1,258	22,469	17.9	85	1,711,464,000	1,360,464	0.01
Firms with sales/ receipts/revenue of $10,000,000 to $14,999,999	1,942	41,651	21.4	85	3,120,558,000	1,606,878	0.01
Firms with sales/ receipts/revenue of $15,000,000 to $19,999,999	1,423	34,363	24.1	85	2,997,064,000	2,106,159	0.00
Firms with sales/ receipts/revenue of $20,000,000 to $24,999,999	1,075	30,583	28.4	85	2,508,188,000	2,333,198	0.00

TABLE 16—COST PER SMALL FIRM IN THE ADMINISTRATIVE AND SUPPORT AND WASTE MANAGEMENT AND REMEDIATION SERVICES INDUSTRY THE SBA SMALL BUSINESS SIZE STANDARD FOR THIS INDUSTRY IS $5.5 MILLION–$38.5 MILLION

	Administrative and support, waste management and remediation services industry						
	Number of firms	Total number of employees	Average number of employees per firm	Annual cost per firm	Annual receipts	Average receipts per firm	Annual cost per firm as percent of receipts (percent)
Firms with sales/ receipts/revenue below $100,000	99,021	139,832	1.4	$85	$4,500,981,00	$45,455	0.19
Firms with sales/ receipts/revenue of $100,000 to $499,999	129,948	513,457	4.0	85	31,661,803,000	243,650	0.03
Firms with sales/ receipts/revenue of $500,000 to $999,999	40,405	409,563	10.1	85	28,444,220,000	703,978	0.01
Firms with sales/ receipts/revenue of $1,000,000 to $2,499,999	31,127	725,649	23.3	85	47,963,623,000	1,540,901	0.01
Firms with sales/ receipts/revenue of $2,500,000 to $4,999,999	12,294	678,340	55.2	85	42,093,718,000	3,423,924	0.00
Firms with sales/ receipts/revenue of $5,000,000 to $7,499,999	4,589	434,622	94.7	85	26,428,877,000	5,759,180	0.00
Firms with sales/ receipts/revenue of $7,500,000 to $9,999,999	2,411	311,321	129.1	85	19,304,673,000	8,006,915	0.00
Firms with sales/ receipts/revenue of $10,000,000 to $14,999,999	2,309	424,912	184.0	85	24,412,659,000	10,572,828	0.00
Firms with sales/ receipts/revenue of $15,000,000 to $19,999,999	1,266	292,501	231.0	85	17,408,483,000	13,750,776	0.00

TABLE 16—COST PER SMALL FIRM IN THE ADMINISTRATIVE AND SUPPORT AND WASTE MANAGEMENT AND REMEDIATION SERVICES INDUSTRY THE SBA SMALL BUSINESS SIZE STANDARD FOR THIS INDUSTRY IS $5.5 MILLION–$38.5 MILLION—Continued

Administrative and support, waste management and remediation services industry							
	Number of firms	Total number of employees	Average number of employees per firm	Annual cost per firm	Annual receipts	Average receipts per firm	Annual cost per firm as percent of receipts (percent)
Firms with sales/receipts/revenue of $20,000,000 to $24,999,999	724	208,939	288.6	85	12,542,375,000	17,323,722	0.00
Firms with sales/receipts/revenue of $25,000,000 to $29,999,999	528	174,359	330.2	85	10,341,768,000	19,586,682	0.00
Firms with sales/receipts/revenue of $30,000,000 to $34,999,999	402	173,953	432.7	85	9,015,658,000	22,427,010	0.00
Firms with sales/receipts/revenue of $35,000,000 to $39,999,999	267	122,013	457.0	85	6,382,657,000	23,905,082	0.00

TABLE 17—COST PER SMALL FIRM IN THE EDUCATIONAL SERVICES INDUSTRY THE SBA SMALL BUSINESS SIZE STANDARD FOR THIS INDUSTRY IS $7.5 MILLION–$38.5 MILLION

Educational services industry							
	Number of firms	Total number of employees	Average number of employees per firm	Annual cost per firm	Annual receipts	Average receipts per firm	Annual cost per firm as percent of receipts (percent)
Firms with sales/receipts/revenue below $100,000	21,831	50,906	2.3	$85	$1,003,931,000	$45,986	0.18
Firms with sales/receipts/revenue of $100,000 to $499,999	27,938	158,913	5.7	85	6,788,475,000	242,984	0.03
Firms with sales/receipts/revenue of $500,000 to $999,999	8,504	112,142	13.2	85	5,984,604,000	703,740	0.01
Firms with sales/receipts/revenue of $1,000,000 to $2,499,999	8,465	213,786	25.3	85	13,376,338,000	1,580,194	0.01
Firms with sales/receipts/revenue of $2,500,000 to $4,999,999	4,302	209,778	48.8	85	14,792,101,000	3,438,424	0.00
Firms with sales/receipts/revenue of $5,000,000 to $7,499,999	1,588	117,648	74.1	85	9,314,307,000	5,865,433	0.00
Firms with sales/receipts/revenue of $7,500,000 to $9,999,999	888	83,741	94.3	85	7,129,969,000	8,029,244	0.00
Firms with sales/receipts/revenue of $10,000,000 to $14,999,999	1,003	127,781	127.4	85	11,306,008,000	11,272,191	0.00
Firms with sales/receipts/revenue of $15,000,000 to $19,999,999	461	79,059	171.5	85	6,983,007,000	15,147,521	0.00

TABLE 17—COST PER SMALL FIRM IN THE EDUCATIONAL SERVICES INDUSTRY THE SBA SMALL BUSINESS SIZE STANDARD FOR THIS INDUSTRY IS $7.5 MILLION–$38.5 MILLION—Continued

	Educational services industry						
	Number of firms	Total number of employees	Average number of employees per firm	Annual cost per firm	Annual receipts	Average receipts per firm	Annual cost per firm as percent of receipts (percent)
Firms with sales/receipts/revenue of $20,000,000 to $24,999,999	355	73,045	205.8	85	6,992,060,000	19,695,944	0.00
Firms with sales/receipts/revenue of $25,000,000 to $29,999,999	268	70,191	261.9	85	6,343,422,000	23,669,485	0.00
Firms with sales/receipts/revenue of $30,000,000 to $34,999,999	172	60,202	350.0	85	5,119,182,000	29,762,686	0.00
Firms with sales/receipts/revenue of $35,000,000 to $39,999,999	138	55,753	404.0	85	4,536,897,000	32,876,065	0.00

TABLE 18—COST PER SMALL FIRM IN THE HEALTH CARE AND SOCIAL ASSISTANCE INDUSTRY THE SBA SMALL BUSINESS SIZE STANDARD FOR THIS INDUSTRY IS $7.5 MILLION–$38.5 MILLION

	Health care and social assistance industry						
	Number of firms	Total number of employees	Average number of employees per firm	Annual cost per firm	Annual receipts	Average receipts per firm	Annual cost per firm as percent of receipts (percent)
Firms with sales/receipts/revenue below $100,000	107,112	162,265	1.5	$85	$5,064,756,000	$47,285	0.18
Firms with sales/receipts/revenue of $100,000 to $499,999	242,566	1,027,234	4.2	85	66,168,531,000	272,786	0.03
Firms with sales/receipts/revenue of $500,000 to $999,999	125,095	1,054,985	8.4	85	88,227,442,000	705,284	0.01
Firms with sales/receipts/revenue of $1,000,000 to $2,499,999	84,361	1,466,391	17.4	85	126,989,626,000	1,505,312	0.01
Firms with sales/receipts/revenue of $2,500,000 to $4,999,999	26,466	1,107,445	41.8	85	91,034,690,000	3,439,685	0.00
Firms with sales/receipts/revenue of $5,000,000 to $7,499,999	9,453	712,840	75.4	85	56,541,818,000	5,981,362	0.00
Firms with sales/receipts/revenue of $7,500,000 to $9,999,999	4,867	501,258	103.0	85	41,063,966,000	8,437,223	0.00
Firms with sales/receipts/revenue of $10,000,000 to $14,999,999	5,198	760,603	146.3	85	61,116,459,000	11,757,687	0.00
Firms with sales/receipts/revenue of $15,000,000 to $19,999,999	2,468	497,184	201.5	85	40,851,963,000	16,552,659	0.00

TABLE 18—COST PER SMALL FIRM IN THE HEALTH CARE AND SOCIAL ASSISTANCE INDUSTRY THE SBA SMALL BUSINESS SIZE STANDARD FOR THIS INDUSTRY IS $7.5 MILLION–$38.5 MILLION—Continued

Health care and social assistance industry							
	Number of firms	Total number of employees	Average number of employees per firm	Annual cost per firm	Annual receipts	Average receipts per firm	Annual cost per firm as percent of receipts (percent)
Firms with sales/ receipts/revenue of $20,000,000 to $24,999,999	1,374	347,358	252.8	85	29,140,498,000	21,208,514	0.00
Firms with sales/ receipts/revenue of $25,000,000 to $29,999,999	978	284,827	291.2	85	25,026,728,000	25,589,701	0.00
Firms with sales/ receipts/revenue of $30,000,000 to $34,999,999	665	230,360	346.4	85	20,167,268,000	30,326,719	0.00
Firms with sales/ receipts/revenue of $35,000,000 to $39,999,999	485	185,982	383.5	85	16,744,181,000	34,524,085	0.00

TABLE 19—COST PER SMALL FIRM IN THE ARTS, ENTERTAINMENT, AND RECREATION INDUSTRY THE SBA SMALL BUSINESS SIZE STANDARD FOR THIS INDUSTRY IS $7.5 MILLION–$38.5 MILLION

Arts, entertainment, and recreation industry							
	Number of firms	Total number of employees	Average number of employees per firm	Annual cost per firm	Annual receipts	Average receipts per firm	Annual cost per firm as percent of receipts (percent)
Firms with sales/ receipts/revenue below $100,000	33,186	53,994	1.6	$85	$1,569,733,000	$47,301	0.18
Firms with sales/ receipts/revenue of $100,000 to $499,999	46,210	199,647	4.3	85	11,295,277,000	244,434	0.03
Firms with sales/ receipts/revenue of $500,000 to $999,999	15,493	162,642	10.5	85	10,894,947,000	703,217	0.01
Firms with sales/ receipts/revenue of $1,000,000 to $2,499,999	12,148	259,480	21.4	85	18,531,141,000	1,525,448	0.01
Firms with sales/ receipts/revenue of $2,500,000 to $4,999,999	4,674	209,762	44.9	85	16,040,448,000	3,431,846	0.00
Firms with sales/ receipts/revenue of $5,000,000 to $7,499,999	1,718	120,586	70.2	85	9,983,571,000	5,811,159	0.00
Firms with sales/ receipts/revenue of $7,500,000 to $9,999,999	806	74,628	92.6	85	6,466,756,000	8,023,270	0.00
Firms with sales/ receipts/revenue of $10,000,000 to $14,999,999	660	77,131	116.9	85	7,102,423,000	10,761,247	0.00
Firms with sales/ receipts/revenue of $15,000,000 to $19,999,999	344	49,061	142.6	85	4,965,644,000	14,435,012	0.00

TABLE 19—COST PER SMALL FIRM IN THE ARTS, ENTERTAINMENT, AND RECREATION INDUSTRY THE SBA SMALL BUSINESS SIZE STANDARD FOR THIS INDUSTRY IS $7.5 MILLION–$38.5 MILLION—Continued

	Arts, entertainment, and recreation industry						
	Number of firms	Total number of employees	Average number of employees per firm	Annual cost per firm	Annual receipts	Average receipts per firm	Annual cost per firm as percent of receipts (percent)
Firms with sales/receipts/revenue of $20,000,000 to $24,999,999	224	40,309	180.0	85	4,136,002,000	18,464,295	0.00
Firms with sales/receipts/revenue of $25,000,000 to $29,999,999	155	33,220	214.3	85	3,428,904,000	22,121,961	0.00
Firms with sales/receipts/revenue of $30,000,000 to $34,999,999	115	28,855	250.9	85	2,873,044,000	24,982,991	0.00
Firms with sales/receipts/revenue of $35,000,000 to $39,999,999	84	25,163	299.6	85	2,569,574,000	30,590,167	0.00

TABLE 20—COST PER SMALL FIRM IN THE ACCOMMODATION AND FOOD SERVICES INDUSTRY THE SBA SMALL BUSINESS SIZE STANDARD FOR THIS INDUSTRY IS $7.5 MILLION–$38.5 MILLION

	Accommodation and food services industry						
	Number of firms	Total number of employees	Average number of employees per firm	Annual cost per firm	Annual receipts	Average receipts per firm	Annual cost per firm as percent of receipts (percent)
Firms with sales/receipts/revenue below $100,000	99,592	207,093	2.1	$85	$4,845,922,000	$48,658	0.17
Firms with sales/receipts/revenue of $100,000 to $499,999	216,446	1,349,187	6.2	85	55,536,558,000	256,584	0.03
Firms with sales/receipts/revenue of $500,000 to $999,999	79,875	1,260,097	15.8	85	55,913,962,000	700,018	0.01
Firms with sales/receipts/revenue of $1,000,000 to $2,499,999	56,476	1,777,649	31.5	85	84,117,236,000	1,489,433	0.01
Firms with sales/receipts/revenue of $2,500,000 to $4,999,999	14,095	896,373	63.6	85	46,231,300,000	3,279,979	0.00
Firms with sales/receipts/revenue of $5,000,000 to $7,499,999	3,720	403,866	108.6	85	21,249,810,000	5,712,315	0.00
Firms with sales/receipts/revenue of $7,500,000 to $9,999,999	1,621	244,772	151.0	85	12,835,230,000	7,918,094	0.00
Firms with sales/receipts/revenue of $10,000,000 to $14,999,999	1,628	340,741	209.3	85	17,984,834,000	11,047,195	0.00
Firms with sales/receipts/revenue of $15,000,000 to $19,999,999	859	252,279	293.7	85	13,054,878,000	15,197,763	0.00

TABLE 20—COST PER SMALL FIRM IN THE ACCOMMODATION AND FOOD SERVICES INDUSTRY THE SBA SMALL BUSINESS SIZE STANDARD FOR THIS INDUSTRY IS $7.5 MILLION–$38.5 MILLION—Continued

Accommodation and food services industry							
	Number of firms	Total number of employees	Average number of employees per firm	Annual cost per firm	Annual receipts	Average receipts per firm	Annual cost per firm as percent of receipts (percent)
Firms with sales/receipts/revenue of $20,000,000 to $24,999,999	446	170,201	381.6	85	8,420,579,000	18,880,222	0.00
Firms with sales/receipts/revenue of $25,000,000 to $29,999,999	363	153,594	423.1	85	7,987,110,000	22,003,058	0.00
Firms with sales/receipts/revenue of $30,000,000 to $34,999,999	241	115,452	479.1	85	6,405,041,000	26,576,934	0.00
Firms with sales/receipts/revenue of $35,000,000 to $39,999,999	170	90,301	531.2	85	4,832,335,000	28,425,500	0.00

TABLE 21—COST PER SMALL FIRM IN THE OTHER SERVICES (EXCEPT PUBLIC ADMINISTRATION) INDUSTRY THE SBA SMALL BUSINESS SIZE STANDARD FOR THIS INDUSTRY IS $5.5 MILLION–$38.5 MILLION

Other services industry							
	Number of firms	Total number of employees	Average number of employees per firm	Annual cost per firm	Annual receipts	Average receipts per firm	Annual cost per firm as percent of receipts (percent)
Firms with sales receipts/revenue below $100,000	195,234	322,002	1.6	$85	$9,308,948,000	$47,681	0.18
Firms with sales receipts/revenue of $100,000 to $499,999	307,613	1,225,144	4.0	85	75,113,021,000	244,180	0.03
Firms with sales receipts/revenue of $500,000 to $999,999	87,833	756,786	8.6	85	61,131,552,000	695,998	0.01
Firms with sales receipts/revenue of $1,000,000 to $2,499,999	55,883	926,035	16.6	85	4,065,314,000	1,504,309	0.01
Firms with sales receipts/revenue of $2,500,000 to $4,999,999	16,522	531,104	32.1	85	55,620,907,000	3,366,475	0.00
Firms with sales receipts/revenue of $5,000,000 to $7,499,999	4,967	252,838	50.9	85	28,838,406,000	5,806,001	0.00
Firms with sales receipts/revenue of $7,500,000 to $9,999,999	2,326	151,376	65.1	85	18,502,407,000	7,954,603	0.00
Firms with sales receipts/revenue of $10,000,000 to $14,999,999	2,114	173,393	82.0	85	23,140,184,000	10,946,161	0.00
Firms with sales receipts/revenue of $15,000,000 to $19,999,999	1,005	104,997	104.5	85	14,696,909,000	14,623,790	0.00

TABLE 21—COST PER SMALL FIRM IN THE OTHER SERVICES (EXCEPT PUBLIC ADMINISTRATION) INDUSTRY THE SBA SMALL BUSINESS SIZE STANDARD FOR THIS INDUSTRY IS $5.5 MILLION–$38.5 MILLION—Continued

	Other services industry						
	Number of firms	Total number of employees	Average number of employees per firm	Annual cost per firm	Annual receipts	Average receipts per firm	Annual cost per firm as percent of receipts (percent)
Firms with sales receipts/revenue of $20,000,000 to $24,999,999	620	73,209	118.1	85	11,076,548,400	17,865,400	0.00
Firms with sales receipts/revenue of $25,000,000 to $29,999,999	405	50,974	125.9	85	8,159,095,000	20,145,914	0.00
Firms with sales receipts/revenue of $30,000,000 to $34,999,999	274	42,041	153.4	85	6,643,223,000	24,245,339	0.00
Firms with sales receipts/revenue of $35,000,000 to $39,999,999	227	37,259	164.1	85	5,392,740,000	23,756,564	0.00

Paperwork Reduction Act

The Paperwork Reduction Act of 1995 (PRA), 44 U.S.C. 3501 *et seq.*, and its attendant regulations, 5 CFR part 1320, requires that OFCCP consider the impact of paperwork and other information collection burdens imposed on the public. Under the PRA an agency may not collect or sponsor the collection of information, nor may impose an information collection requirement unless it displays a currently valid Office of Management and Budget (OMB) control number. *See* 5 CFR 1320.8(b)(3)(vi). The OMB has assigned control number 1250–0008 to the third party disclosure of the equal opportunity clause provisions to subcontractors. The OMB has assigned control numbers 1250–0001 and 1250–0003 to the general recordkeeping provisions of the laws administered by OFCCP. In accordance with the PRA, OFCCP solicited public comments on the proposed changes to the information collection proposed in the NPRM, as discussed below. *See* 79 FR 55712 (September 17, 2014). OFCCP also submitted a contemporaneous request for OMB review of the proposed information collection in accordance with 44 U.S.C. 3507(d). On December 5, 2014, the OMB issued a notice that instructed the agency to resubmit the information collection request upon promulgation of the final rule and after consideration of public comments received.

Compliance Date

Affected parties do not have to comply with the new information collection requirements under § 60–1.35 until the Department publishes a Notice in the **Federal Register** stating that OMB has approved the information collections under the Paperwork Reduction Act of 1995 (PRA), 44 U.S.C. 3501 *et seq.*, or until this rule otherwise takes effect, whichever is later.

Circumstances Necessitating Collection

Executive Order 13665 amends the equal opportunity clause provided in Executive Order 11246 by adding the prohibition that Federal contractors may not discriminate against employees and job applicants who inquire about, discuss or disclose their own compensation or the compensation of other employees or applicants. Federal contractors are required to amend the equal opportunity clauses incorporated into their subcontracts, and notify job applicants and employees of the requirement. Executive Order 13665 became effective at signing and applies to contracts entered into on or after the effective date of this final rule.

The final rule contains several provisions that could be considered "collections of information" as defined by the PRA: The amendment to the equal opportunity clause incorporated into contracts and subcontracts, and the notification given to employees and job applicants.

Proposed § 60–1.35(c)(i) and (ii) required the incorporation of the new provision verbatim into existing handbooks and manuals, and the dissemination of a notification to employees and applications. The disclosure of information originally supplied by the Federal government to the recipient for the purpose of disclosure is not included within the PRA's definition of "collection of information." *See* 5 CFR 1320.3(c)(2). OFCCP determined that proposed § 60–1.35(c)(i) and (ii) did not meet the PRA's definition of "collection of information" and therefore these provisions are not subject to the PRA's requirements. However, OFCCP determined that the proposed changes to § 60–1.4 could be considered information collections, therefore an information collection request (ICR) was submitted to OMB for PRA authorization.

Information and Technology

Each contractor determines its own methods for developing and maintaining information, including creating electronic templates. Contractors may meet the requirements of this rule using paper or electronic means.

Public Comments

OFCCP sought public comments regarding the potential burdens imposed by information collections contained in the NPRM which reflected burden related to the amendment to the equal opportunity clause incorporated into contracts and subcontracts.

OFCCP received 11 comments regarding costs and burdens from employer groups, women's groups, employers and individuals. Of the 11 comments, one stated that the new rule should not incur any significant cost as the language will be prescribed by OFCCP and that the rule eliminates a policy of taking adverse action against employees.

Some of the commenters indicated that the rule was unduly burdensome or unnecessary because it had no clear effect on addressing the pay gap. Some of these commenters indicated that the pay gap could be explained by other nondiscriminatory explanations. OFCCP disagrees that the rule is unnecessary and unduly burdensome. OFCCP worked with several other Federal agencies on the National Equal Pay Task Force to identify the persistent challenges to equal pay enforcement and to develop an action plan for implementing recommendations to resolve those challenges. OFCCP also consulted a number of sources in order to assess the need for the rule. For instance, OFCCP reviewed national statistics on earnings by gender produced by BLS and the U.S. Census Bureau. Those statistics show persistent pay gaps for female and minority workers. These well-documented earnings differences based on race and sex have not been fully explained by nondiscriminatory factors including differences in worker qualifications such as education and experience, occupational differences, work schedules or other similar factors. Thus, some of the remaining unexplained portion of the pay gap may be attributable to discrimination. In addition, prohibiting pay secrecy policies will enhance the ability of Federal contractors and their employees to detect and remediate unlawful discriminatory practices. Thus, the rule improves the efficacy of Executive Order 11246 and the efficiency of the market in Federal contracting. In order to reduce the burden of implementing Executive Order 13665, OFCCP allows contractors to incorporate the equal opportunity clause by reference into its subcontracts. In addition, OFCCP is providing specific language for incorporation into handbooks and the notice for applicants and employees. Thus, OFCCP has proposed the most efficient manner to implement the amendments.

Other commenters asserted that OFCCP underestimated the burdens created by the new rule. In this area, one commenter proposed alternative calculations related to the implementation of the rule. In considering the alternative calculations of burden, OFCCP took into consideration that although the commenter represents a segment of the contractor universe, it is not reflective of the entire SAM contractor universe. OFCCP expects the costs to vary by contractor. While some contractors may incur more costs, others will likely incur less. Thus, the estimates of burden reflect an average estimate for all covered contractors in the SAM contractor universe. Therefore, OFCCP has retained its calculation of the burden as proposed in the NPRM. Another commenter indicated that OFCCP did not include burdens associated with the definition of compensation and the impact that the definition proposed in the NPRM may have on Federal contractors. The commenter indicated that OFCCP should take the burden that the compensation definition "will impose on annual evaluations under contractors' identification of problem areas section of their affirmative action programs." OFCCP disagrees with this commenter's assertion. Contractors are required to perform an in-depth analysis of its total employment process to determine whether and where impediments to equal employment opportunity exist. *See* 41 CFR 60–2.17(b). The evaluation includes an analysis of each contractor's compensation system. OFCCP's guidance and regulations have historically included salary, wages, overtime pay, shift differentials, bonuses, commissions, vacation and holiday pay, allowances, insurance and other benefits, stock options, profit sharing and retirement.[100] Thus, OFCCP did not assess additional burden as this obligation has not changed. Another commenter asserted that OFCCP did not assess the additional burden associated with data requests received during compliance evaluations. The collection of information during an investigation or the conduct of a civil action is an exception within the PRA's definition of collection of information. *See* 5 CFR 1320.4(a)(2).

One commenter suggested that OFCCP allow contractors discretion regarding the wording of the notice for incorporation in the handbook and posting. In order to reduce burden, OFCCP provides the wording for the notification. As the majority of comments received related to burden were opposed to increasing burden, OFCCP declines to increase burden and instead will provide the exact wording for the notice and language to incorporate into existing employee handbooks.

OFCCP has resubmitted the revised information collection (1250–0008) to OMB for approval, and OFCCP intends to publish a notice announcing OMB's decision regarding this information collection request. A copy of the information collection request can be obtained by contacting OFCCP as shown in the **FOR FURTHER INFORMATION CONTACT** section of this preamble.

Comments to the OMB should be directed to: Office of Information and Regulatory Affairs, Attention OMB Desk Officer for the Office of Federal Contract Compliance, Office of Management and Budget, Room 10235, Washington, DC 20503; Telephone: 202–395–7316 (these are not toll-free numbers). Comments can be submitted to OMB by email at *OIRA_submission@omb.eop.gov*. The OMB will consider all written comments it receives within 30 days of publication of this final rule. The OMB and the Department are particularly interested in comments that:

- Evaluate whether the proposed collections of information are necessary for the proper performance of the functions of the agency, including whether the information will have practical utility;
- Evaluate the accuracy of the agency's estimate of the burden of the proposed collection of information, including the validity of the methodology and assumptions used;
- Enhance the quality, utility, and clarity of the information to be collected; and
- Minimize the burden of the collection of information on those who are to respond, including through the use of appropriate automated, electronic, mechanical, or other technological collection techniques or other forms of IT (*e.g.*, permitting electronic submission of responses).

Number of Respondents

All nonexempt Federal contractors with contracts, subcontracts, federally assisted construction contracts or subcontracts in excess of $10,000 are required to comply with this final rule. There are approximately 500,000 contractor firms registered in the General Service Administration's SAM. Therefore, OFCCP estimates there are 500,000 contractor firms.

Summary of Paperwork Burdens

The estimated total annual burden for complying with the new regulatory requirement is listed in Table 22, below. The burden is calculated as an annual burden based on a three-year approval of this information collection request. OFCCP believes that in the first year of implementation contractors will modify their equal opportunity clauses. Additionally, OFCCP estimates that in subsequent years 1 percent of the contractors will be required to modify

[100] Federal Contract Compliance Manual, Chapter 2, Section 2L03 and Chapter 3, section 3H03 (Oct. 2014).

their equal opportunity clauses, as they will be new contractors.

TABLE 22—ESTIMATED ANNUAL BURDEN FOR CONTRACTOR COMPANIES

New requirement	Estimated annual burden hours	Monetization
§ 60–1.4	42,500	$ 1,320,369
Total Cost	42,500	$1,320,369

These paperwork burden estimates are summarized as follows:

Type of Review: New collection.

Agency: Office of Federal Contract Compliance Programs, Department of Labor.

Title: Prohibitions Against Pay Secrecy Policies and Actions.

OMB ICR Reference Number: 1250–0008.

Affected Public: Business or other for-profit; individuals.

Estimated Number of Annual Responses: 500,000.

Frequency of Response: On occasion.

Estimated Total Annual Burden Hours: 42,500.

Estimated Total Annual PRA Costs: $0.

Small Business Regulatory Enforcement Fairness Act of 1996

This rule is not a major rule as defined by section 804 of the Small Business Regulatory Enforcement Fairness Act of 1996. This rule will not result in an annual effect on the economy of $100 million or more; a major increase in costs or prices; or significant adverse effects on competition, employment, investment, productivity, innovation, or on the ability of the United States-based companies to compete with foreign-based companies in domestic and export markets.

Unfunded Mandates Reform Act of 1995

For purposes of the Unfunded Mandates Reform Act of 1995, 2 U.S.C. 1532, this rule does not include any Federal mandate that may result in excess of $100 million in expenditures by state, local, and tribal governments in the aggregate or by the private sector.

Executive Order 13132 (Federalism)

OFCCP has reviewed this rule in accordance with Executive Order 13132 regarding federalism, and has determined that it does not have "federalism implications." This rule will not "have substantial direct effects on the States, on the relationship between the national government and the States, or on the distribution of power and responsibilities among the various levels of government."

Executive Order 13175 (Consultation and Coordination With Indian Tribal Governments)

This rule does not have tribal implications under Executive Order 13175 that requires a tribal summary impact statement. The rule does not have substantial direct effects on one or more Indian tribes, on the relationship between the Federal Government and Indian tribes or on the distribution of power and responsibilities between the Federal Government and Indian tribes.

Effects on Families

The undersigned hereby certifies that the rule would not adversely affect the well-being of families, as discussed under section 654 of the Treasury and General Government Appropriations Act, 1999.

Executive Order 13045 (Protection of Children)

This rule would have no environmental health risk or safety risk that may disproportionately affect children.

Environmental Impact Assessment

A review of this rule in accordance with the requirements of the National Environmental Policy Act of 1969 (NEPA), 42 U.S.C. 4321 *et seq.;* the regulations of the Council on Environmental Quality, 40 CFR part 1500 *et seq.;* and DOL NEPA procedures, 29 CFR part 11, indicates the rule would not have a significant impact on the quality of the human environment. There is, thus, no corresponding environmental assessment or an environmental impact statement.

Executive Order 13211 (Energy Supply)

This rule is not subject to Executive Order 13211. It will not have a significant adverse effect on the supply, distribution, or use of energy.

Executive Order 12630 (Constitutionally Protected Property Rights)

This rule is not subject to Executive Order 12630 because it does not involve implementation of a policy that has takings implications or that could impose limitations on private property use.

Executive Order 12988 (Civil Justice Reform Analysis)

This rule was drafted and reviewed in accordance with Executive Order 12988 and will not unduly burden the Federal court system. The rule was: (1) reviewed to eliminate drafting errors and ambiguities; (2) written to minimize litigation; and (3) written to provide a clear legal standard for affected conduct and to promote burden reduction.

List of Subjects in 41 CFR Part 60–1

Civil rights, Employment, Equal employment opportunity, Government contracts, Government procurement, Investigations, Labor, Reporting and recordkeeping requirements.

Patricia A. Shiu,

Director, Office of Federal Contract Compliance Programs.

Accordingly, part 60–1 of title 41 of the Code of Federal Regulations is amended as follows:

PART 60–1—OBLIGATIONS OF CONTRACTORS AND SUBCONTRACTORS

■ 1. The authority citation for part 60–1 continues to read as follows:

Authority: Sec. 201, E.O. 11246, 30 FR 12319, 3 CFR, 1964–1965 Comp., p. 339, as amended by E.O. 11375, 32 FR 14303, 3 CFR, 1966–1970 Comp., p. 684, E.O. 12086, 43 FR 46501, 1978 Comp., p. 230 and E.O. 13279, 67 FR 77141, 3 CFR, 2002 Comp., p. 258, E.O. 13665, 79 FR 20749 and E.O. 13672, 79 FR 42971.

■ 2. Section 60–1.3 is amended by adding definitions in alphabetical order for "Compensation," "Compensation information," and "Essential job functions" to read as follows:

§ 60–1.3 Definitions.

* * * * *

Compensation means any payments made to, or on behalf of, an employee or offered to an applicant as remuneration for employment, including but not limited to salary, wages, overtime pay, shift differentials, bonuses, commissions, vacation and holiday pay, allowances, insurance and other benefits, stock options and awards, profit sharing, and retirement.

Compensation information means the amount and type of compensation provided to employees or offered to applicants, including, but not limited to, the desire of the contractor to attract and retain a particular employee for the value the employee is perceived to add to the contractor's profit or productivity; the availability of employees with like skills in the marketplace; market research about the worth of similar jobs in the relevant marketplace; job analysis, descriptions, and evaluations; salary and pay structures; salary surveys; labor union agreements; and contractor decisions, statements and policies related to setting or altering employee compensation.

* * * * *

Essential job functions—(1) *In general.* The term *essential job functions* means the fundamental job duties of the employment position an individual holds.

(2) A job function may be considered essential if:

(i) The access to compensation information is necessary in order to perform that function or another routinely assigned business task; or

(ii) The function or duties of the position include protecting and maintaining the privacy of employee personnel records, including compensation information.

(3) The application or interpretation of the "essential job functions" definition in this part is limited to the discrimination claims governed by Executive Order 13665 and its implementing regulations.

* * * * *

■ 3. Section 60–1.4 is revised to read as follows:

§ 60–1.4 Equal opportunity clause.

(a) *Government contracts.* Except as otherwise provided, each contracting agency shall include the following equal opportunity clause contained in section 202 of the order in each of its Government contracts (and modifications thereof if not included in the original contract):

During the performance of this contract, the contractor agrees as follows:

(1) The contractor will not discriminate against any employee or applicant for employment because of race, color, religion, sex, sexual orientation, gender identity, or national origin. The contractor will take affirmative action to ensure that applicants are employed, and that employees are treated during employment, without regard to their race, color, religion, sex, sexual orientation, gender identity, or national origin. Such action shall include, but not be limited to the following: Employment, upgrading, demotion, or transfer, recruitment or recruitment advertising; layoff or termination; rates of pay or other forms of compensation; and selection for training, including apprenticeship. The contractor agrees to post in conspicuous places, available to employees and applicants for employment, notices to be provided by the contracting officer setting forth the provisions of this nondiscrimination clause.

(2) The contractor will, in all solicitations or advertisements for employees placed by or on behalf of the contractor, state that all qualified applicants will receive consideration for employment without regard to race, color, religion, sex, sexual orientation, gender identity, or national origin.

(3) The contractor will not discharge or in any other manner discriminate against any employee or applicant for employment because such employee or applicant has inquired about, discussed, or disclosed the compensation of the employee or applicant or another employee or applicant. This provision shall not apply to instances in which an employee who has access to the compensation information of other employees or applicants as a part of such employee's essential job functions discloses the compensation of such other employees or applicants to individuals who do not otherwise have access to such information, unless such disclosure is in response to a formal complaint or charge, in furtherance of an investigation, proceeding, hearing, or action, including an investigation conducted by the employer, or is consistent with the contractor's legal duty to furnish information.

(4) The contractor will send to each labor union or representative of workers with which it has a collective bargaining agreement or other contract or understanding, a notice to be provided by the agency contracting officer, advising the labor union or workers' representative of the contractor's commitments under section 202 of Executive Order 11246 of September 24, 1965, and shall post copies of the notice in conspicuous places available to employees and applicants for employment.

(5) The contractor will comply with all provisions of Executive Order 11246 of September 24, 1965, and of the rules, regulations, and relevant orders of the Secretary of Labor.

(6) The contractor will furnish all information and reports required by Executive Order 11246 of September 24, 1965, and by the rules, regulations, and orders of the Secretary of Labor, or pursuant thereto, and will permit access to his books, records, and accounts by the contracting agency and the Secretary of Labor for purposes of investigation to ascertain compliance with such rules, regulations, and orders.

(7) In the event of the contractor's non-compliance with the nondiscrimination clauses of this contract or with any of such rules, regulations, or orders, this contract may be canceled, terminated or suspended in whole or in part and the contractor may be declared ineligible for further Government contracts in accordance with procedures authorized in Executive Order 11246 of September 24, 1965, and such other sanctions may be imposed and remedies invoked as provided in Executive Order 11246 of September 24, 1965, or by rule, regulation, or order of the Secretary of Labor, or as otherwise provided by law.

(8) The contractor will include the provisions of paragraphs (1) through (8) in every subcontract or purchase order unless exempted by rules, regulations, or orders of the Secretary of Labor issued pursuant to section 204 of Executive Order 11246 of September 24, 1965, so that such provisions will be binding upon each subcontractor or vendor. The contractor will take such action with respect to any subcontract or purchase order as may be directed by the Secretary of Labor as a means of enforcing such provisions including sanctions for noncompliance: *Provided,* however, that in the event the contractor becomes involved in, or is threatened with, litigation with a subcontractor or vendor as a result of such direction, the contractor may request the United States to enter into such litigation to protect the interests of the United States.

(b) *Federally assisted construction contracts.* (1) Except as otherwise provided, each administering agency shall require the inclusion of the following language as a condition of any grant, contract, loan, insurance, or guarantee involving federally assisted construction which is not exempt from the requirements of the equal opportunity clause:

The applicant hereby agrees that it will incorporate or cause to be incorporated into any contract for construction work, or modification thereof, as defined in the regulations of the Secretary of Labor at 41 CFR Chapter 60, which is paid for in whole or in part with funds obtained from the Federal Government or borrowed on the credit of the Federal Government pursuant to a grant, contract, loan, insurance, or guarantee, or undertaken pursuant to any Federal program involving such grant, contract, loan, insurance, or guarantee, the following equal opportunity clause:

During the performance of this contract, the contractor agrees as follows:

(1) The contractor will not discriminate against any employee or applicant for employment because of race, color, religion, sex, sexual orientation, gender identity, or national origin. The contractor will take affirmative action to ensure that applicants are employed, and that employees are treated during employment without regard to their

race, color, religion, sex, sexual orientation, gender identity, or national origin. Such action shall include, but not be limited to the following:

Employment, upgrading, demotion, or transfer; recruitment or recruitment advertising; layoff or termination; rates of pay or other forms of compensation; and selection for training, including apprenticeship. The contractor agrees to post in conspicuous places, available to employees and applicants for employment, notices to be provided setting forth the provisions of this nondiscrimination clause.

(2) The contractor will, in all solicitations or advertisements for employees placed by or on behalf of the contractor, state that all qualified applicants will receive consideration for employment without regard to race, color, religion, sex, sexual orientation, gender identity, or national origin.

(3) The contractor will not discharge or in any other manner discriminate against any employee or applicant for employment because such employee or applicant has inquired about, discussed, or disclosed the compensation of the employee or applicant or another employee or applicant. This provision shall not apply to instances in which an employee who has access to the compensation information of other employees or applicants as a part of such employee's essential job functions discloses the compensation of such other employees or applicants to individuals who do not otherwise have access to such information, unless such disclosure is in response to a formal complaint or charge, in furtherance of an investigation, proceeding, hearing, or action, including an investigation conducted by the employer, or is consistent with the contractor's legal duty to furnish information.

(4) The contractor will send to each labor union or representative of workers with which he has a collective bargaining agreement or other contract or understanding, a notice to be provided advising the said labor union or workers' representatives of the contractor's commitments under this section, and shall post copies of the notice in conspicuous places available to employees and applicants for employment.

(5) The contractor will comply with all provisions of Executive Order 11246 of September 24, 1965, and of the rules, regulations, and relevant orders of the Secretary of Labor.

(6) The contractor will furnish all information and reports required by Executive Order 11246 of September 24, 1965, and by rules, regulations, and orders of the Secretary of Labor, or pursuant thereto, and will permit access to his books, records, and accounts by the administering agency and the Secretary of Labor for purposes of investigation to ascertain compliance with such rules, regulations, and orders.

(7) In the event of the contractor's noncompliance with the nondiscrimination clauses of this contract or with any of the said rules, regulations, or orders, this contract may be canceled, terminated, or suspended in whole or in part and the contractor may be declared ineligible for further Government contracts or federally assisted construction contracts in accordance with procedures authorized in Executive Order 11246 of September 24, 1965, and such other sanctions may be imposed and remedies invoked as provided in Executive Order 11246 of September 24, 1965, or by rule, regulation, or order of the Secretary of Labor, or as otherwise provided by law.

(8) The contractor will include the portion of the sentence immediately preceding paragraph (1) and the provisions of paragraphs (1) through (8) in every subcontract or purchase order unless exempted by rules, regulations, or orders of the Secretary of Labor issued pursuant to section 204 of Executive Order 11246 of September 24, 1965, so that such provisions will be binding upon each subcontractor or vendor. The contractor will take such action with respect to any subcontract or purchase order as the administering agency may direct as a means of enforcing such provisions, including sanctions for noncompliance:

Provided, however, that in the event a contractor becomes involved in, or is threatened with, litigation with a subcontractor or vendor as a result of such direction by the administering agency, the contractor may request the United States to enter into such litigation to protect the interests of the United States.

The applicant further agrees that it will be bound by the above equal opportunity clause with respect to its own employment practices when it participates in federally assisted construction work: *Provided,* That if the applicant so participating is a State or local government, the above equal opportunity clause is not applicable to any agency, instrumentality or subdivision of such government which does not participate in work on or under the contract.

The applicant agrees that it will assist and cooperate actively with the administering agency and the Secretary of Labor in obtaining the compliance of contractors and subcontractors with the equal opportunity clause and the rules, regulations, and relevant orders of the Secretary of Labor, that it will furnish the administering agency and the Secretary of Labor such information as they may require for the supervision of such compliance, and that it will otherwise assist the administering agency in the discharge of the agency's primary responsibility for securing compliance.

The applicant further agrees that it will refrain from entering into any contract or contract modification subject to Executive Order 11246 of September 24, 1965, with a contractor debarred from, or who has not demonstrated eligibility for, Government contracts and federally assisted construction contracts pursuant to the Executive Order and will carry out such sanctions and penalties for violation of the equal opportunity clause as may be imposed upon contractors and subcontractors by the administering agency or the Secretary of Labor pursuant to Part II, Subpart D of the Executive Order. In addition, the applicant agrees that if it fails or refuses to comply with these undertakings, the administering agency may take any or all of the following actions: Cancel, terminate, or suspend in whole or in part this grant (contract, loan, insurance, guarantee); refrain from extending any further assistance to the applicant under the program with respect to which the failure or refund occurred until satisfactory assurance of future compliance has been received from such applicant; and refer the case to the Department of Justice for appropriate legal proceedings.

(2) [Reserved]

(c) *Subcontracts.* Each nonexempt prime contractor or subcontractor shall include the equal opportunity clause in each of its nonexempt subcontracts.

(d) *Inclusion of the equal opportunity clause by reference.* The equal opportunity clause may be included by reference in all Government contracts and subcontracts, including Government bills of lading, transportation requests, contracts for deposit of Government funds, and contracts for issuing and paying U.S. savings bonds and notes, and such other contracts and subcontracts as the Director of OFCCP may designate.

(e) *Incorporation by operation of the order.* By operation of the order, the equal opportunity clause shall be considered to be a part of every contract and subcontract required by the order and the regulations in this part to include such a clause whether or not it is physically incorporated in such contracts and whether or not the contract between the agency and the contractor is written.

(f) *Adaptation of language.* Such necessary changes in language may be made in the equal opportunity clause as shall be appropriate to identify properly the parties and their undertakings.

■ 4. Section 60–1.35 is added to read as follows:

§ 60–1.35 Contractor obligations and defenses to violation of the nondiscrimination requirement for compensation disclosures.

(a) *General defenses.* A contractor may pursue a defense to an alleged violation of paragraph (3) of the equal opportunity clauses listed in § 60–1.4(a) and (b) as long as the defense is not based on a rule, policy, practice, agreement, or other instrument that prohibits employees or applicants from discussing or disclosing their compensation or the compensation of other employees or applicants, subject to paragraph (3) of the equal opportunity clause. Contractors may pursue this defense by demonstrating, for example, that it disciplined the employee for violation of a consistently and uniformly applied company policy, and that this policy does not prohibit, or tend to prohibit, employees or applicants from discussing or disclosing their compensation or the compensation of other employees or applicants.

(b) *Essential job functions defense.* Actions taken by a contractor which adversely affect an employee will not be deemed to be discriminatory if the employee has access to the compensation information of other employees or applicants as part of such employee's essential job functions and disclosed the compensation of such other employees or applicants to individuals who do not otherwise have access to such information, and the disclosure was not in response to a formal complaint or charge, in furtherance of an investigation, proceeding, hearing, or action, including an investigation conducted by the contractor, or is consistent with the contractor's legal duty to furnish information.

(c) *Dissemination of nondiscrimination provision.* The contractor or subcontractor shall disseminate the nondiscrimination provision, using the language as prescribed by the Director of OFCCP, to employees and applicants:

(1) The nondiscrimination provision shall be incorporated into existing employee manuals or handbooks; and

(2) The nondiscrimination provision shall be disseminated to employees and applicants. Dissemination of the provision shall be executed by electronic posting or by posting a copy of the provision in conspicuous places available to employees and applicants for employment.

[FR Doc. 2015–22547 Filed 9–10–15; 8:45 am]

BILLING CODE 4510–CM–P

Section 503 of the Rehabilitation Act of 1973, as amended

Office of Federal Contract Compliance Programs (OFCCP)

Section 503 of the Rehabilitation Act of 1973, as amended

29 USC Sec. 793
United States Code
Title 29
Chapter 16
Subchapter V
§ 793. Employment under Federal contracts

a. **Amount of contracts or subcontracts; provision for employment and advancement of qualified individuals with disabilities; regulations**
   Any contract in excess of $10,000 entered into by any Federal department or agency for the procurement of personal property and nonpersonal services (including construction) for the United States shall contain a provision requiring that the party contracting with the United States shall take affirmative action to employ and advance in employment qualified individuals with disabilities. The provision of this section shall apply to any subcontract in excess of $10,000 entered into by a prime contractor in carrying out any contract for the procurement of personal property and nonpersonal services (including construction) for the United States. The President shall implement the provisions of this section by promulgating regulations within ninety days after September 26, 1973.
b. **Administrative enforcement; complaints; investigations; departmental action**
   If any individual with a disability believes any contractor has failed or refused to comply with the provisions of a contract with the United States, relating to employment of individuals with disabilities, such individual may file a complaint with the Department of Labor. The Department shall promptly investigate such complaint and shall take such action thereon as the facts and circumstances warrant, consistent with the terms of such contract and the laws and regulations applicable thereto.
c. **Waiver by President; national interest special circumstances for waiver of particular agreements; waiver by Secretary of Labor of affirmative action requirements**
   1. The requirements of this secton may be waived, in whole or in part, by the President with respect to a particular contract or subcontract, in accordance with guidelines set forth in regulations which the President shall prescribe, when the President determines that special circumstances in the national interest so require and states in writing the reasons for such determination.
   2. a) The Secretary of Labor may waive the requirements of the affirmative action clause required by regulations promulgated under subsection (a) of this section with respect to any of a prime contractor's or subcontractor's facilities that are found to be in all respects separate and distinct from activities of the prime contractor or subcontractor related to the performance of the contract or subcontract, if the Secretary of Labor also finds that such a waiver will not interfere with or impede the effectuation of this chapter.
      b) Such waivers shall be considered only upon the request of the contractor or subcontractor. The Secretary of Labor shall promulgate regulations that set forth the standards used for granting such a waiver.
d. **Standards used in determining violation of section**
   The standards used to determine whether this section has been violated in a complaint alleging nonaffirmative action employment discrimination under this section shall be the standards applied under title I of the Americans with Disabilities Act of 1990 (42 U.S.C. 12111 et seq.) and the provisions of sections 501 through 504, and 510, of the Americans with Disabilities Act of 1990 (42 U.S.C. 12201-12204 and 12210), as such sections relate to employment.
e. **Avoidance of duplicative efforts and inconsistencies**
   The Secretary shall develop procedures to ensure that administrative complaint filed under this section and under the Americans with Disabilities Act of 1990 (42 U.S.C 12101 et seq.) are dealt with in a manner that avoids duplication of effort and precents imposition of inconsistent or conflicting standards for the same requirements under this section and the Americans with Disabilities Act of 1990.

41 CFR Part 60–741

Affirmative Action and Nondiscrimination Obligations of Contractors and Subcontractors Regarding Individuals With Disabilities;

Final Rule

FEDERAL REGISTER

Vol. 78 Tuesday,
No. 185 September 24, 2013

Part III

Department of Labor

Office of Federal Contract Compliance Programs

41 CFR Part 60–741

Affirmative Action and Nondiscrimination Obligations of Contractors and Subcontractors Regarding Individuals With Disabilities; Final Rule

DEPARTMENT OF LABOR

Office of Federal Contract Compliance Programs

41 CFR Part 60–741

RIN 1250–AA02

Affirmative Action and Nondiscrimination Obligations of Contractors and Subcontractors Regarding Individuals With Disabilities

AGENCY: Office of Federal Contract Compliance Programs, Labor.

ACTION: Final rule.

SUMMARY: The Office of Federal Contract Compliance Programs (OFCCP) is publishing revisions to the current regulations implementing the non-discrimination and affirmative action regulations of section 503 of the Rehabilitation Act of 1973, as amended. Section 503 prohibits discrimination by covered Federal contractors and subcontractors against individuals on the basis of disability, and requires affirmative action on behalf of qualified individuals with disabilities.

The final rule adopts several key revisions proposed in the notice of proposed rulemaking. The final rule strengthens the affirmative action provisions by, among other things, requiring data collection pertaining to applicants and hires with disabilities, and establishing a utilization goal for individuals with disabilities to assist in measuring the effectiveness of the contractor's affirmative action efforts. However, some of the NPRM's proposals, particularly with regard to the creation and maintenance of certain records and the conduct of certain affirmative action obligations, have been eliminated or made more flexible in order to reduce the compliance burden on contractors. To implement changes necessitated by the passage of the ADA Amendments Act (ADAAA) of 2008, the final rule also adopts revisions to the definitions and to the nondiscrimination provisions of the implementing regulations. The specific revisions made, and the rationale for making them, are set forth in the Section-by-Section Analysis below.

DATES: *Effective Date:* These regulations are effective March 24, 2014.

FOR FURTHER INFORMATION CONTACT: Debra A. Carr, Director, Division of Policy, Planning and Program Development, Office of Federal Contract Compliance Programs, at 200 Constitution Avenue NW., Room C–3325, Washington, DC 20210, or call (202) 693–0104 (voice) or (202) 693–1337 (TTY). Copies of this rule in alternative formats may be obtained by calling (202) 693–0103 (voice) or (202) 693–1337 (TTY). The alternative formats available are large print and electronic file on computer disk. The rule also is available on the Internet on the Regulations.gov Web site at *http://www.regulations.gov* or on the OFCCP Web site at *http://www.dol.gov/ofccp.*

SUPPLEMENTARY INFORMATION:

Executive Summary

The Office of Federal Contract Compliance Programs (OFCCP) is a civil rights, worker protection agency which enforces one Executive Order and two laws that prohibit employment discrimination and require affirmative action by companies doing business with the Federal Government.[1] Specifically, Federal contractors must engage in affirmative action and provide equal employment opportunity without regard to race, color, religion, sex, national origin, disability, or status as a protected veteran. Executive Order 11246, as amended, prohibits employment discrimination on the basis of race, religion, color, national origin, and sex. The Vietnam Era Veterans' Readjustment Assistance Act of 1974 (VEVRAA), as amended, prohibits employment discrimination against certain protected veterans. Section 503 of the Rehabilitation Act of 1973 (section 503), as amended, prohibits employment discrimination against individuals with disabilities.

OFCCP evaluates the employment practices of over 4,000 Federal contractors and subcontractors annually and investigates individual complaints. OFCCP also engages in outreach to employees of Federal contractors to educate them about their rights, and provides technical assistance to contractors on their nondiscrimination and affirmative action obligations. We estimate that our jurisdiction covers approximately 200,000 Federal contractor establishments, and more than 45,000 parent companies.[2]

Employment discrimination and underutilization of qualified workers, such as individuals with disabilities and veterans, contribute to broader societal problems such as income inequality and poverty. The median household income for "householders" with a disability, aged 18 to 64, was $25,420 compared with a median income of $59,411 for households with a householder who did not report a disability.[3] Controlling for age and race we find that workers with a disability, on average, earn less than private sector workers without a disability. The mean hourly wage of those with a disability is $17.62 (with a median of $13.73) compared to $21.67 (median $16.99) for those without a disability.[4] Controlling for age and race, male workers with a disability earn 23 percent less than males without a disability. The disability gap for females is 20 percent.[5] While 28.8 percent of individuals, ages 18 to 64, with a disability were in poverty in 2011, the data show that 12.5 percent of those individuals without a disability were in poverty.[6]

Based on our analysis of the American Community Survey (ACS) 2008–2010 Public Use Microdata (PUMS), and controlling for age and race we found that:[7]

- Males with disability had a 7.2 percentage point higher unemployment rate than males without a disability.
- Females with disability had a 6.5 percentage point higher unemployment rate than females without a disability.

[1] Executive Order 11246, as amended; Section 503 of the Rehabilitation Act of 1973, as amended, (section 503), and the Vietnam Era Veterans' Readjustment Assistance Act of 1974, as amended, 38 U.S.C. 4212 (VEVRAA).

[2] This establishment estimate is based on a review of FY 2009 EEO–1 contractor establishment data and other contractor databases, including the Federal Procurement Data System (FPDS). Based on EEO–1 data, we determined that the ratio of parent companies to the number of establishments is approximately four establishments per parent company.

[3] *Income, Poverty and Health Insurance Coverage in the United States: 2011,* Current Population Reports, issued September 2012, *http://www.census.gov/prod/2012pubs/p60-243.pdf* (last accessed July 8, 2013), p. 10. A "householder" is the person (or one of the people) in whose name the home is owned or rented and the person to whom the relationship of other household members is recorded. Typically, it is the head of a household. Only one person per household is designated the "householder."

[4] OFCCP ran wage regressions using the natural log of effective hourly wages calculated as real income divided by usual hours per week and weeks per year. The weeks per year variable is categorical so the midpoint of each category was used as a proxy for the number of weeks worked. Explanatory variables include age and race. The sample was restricted to individuals aged 18 to 64 employed in the private sector. Individuals currently in the armed forces were not included in the sample. All OFCCP models used ACS 2008–2010 Public Use Microdata (PUMS).

[5] Id.

[6] *Income, Poverty and Health Insurance Coverage in the United States: 2011,* Current Population Reports, issued September 2012, *http://www.census.gov/prod/2012pubs/p60-243.pdf* (last accessed July 8, 2013)

[7] OFCCP ran wage regressions using the natural log of effective hourly wages calculated as real income divided by usual hours per week and weeks per year. The weeks per year variable is categorical so the midpoint of each category was used as a proxy for the number of weeks worked. Explanatory variables include age and race. The sample was limited to individuals aged 18 to 64 employed in the private sector. All OFCCP models used ACS 2008–2010 Public Use Microdata (PUMS).

• Females with a disability had a 29.2 percentage point higher probability of not being in the labor force than females without a disability.

A 2009 report found that "having a disability is associated with lower earnings due to decreased ability to work, prejudice, and other factors." [8] There are a number of hypotheses concerning disparities in labor force participation, employment rates, and wages. While knowledge of opportunities, differences in access and attainment of training and education, and underutilization of individuals with disabilities likely contribute to these disparities, the culture of the typical workplace and discrimination are also factors in some employment settings. However, there is little empirical data upon which to base targeted interventions. Data collection remains a critical need.

The final rule is intended to provide contractors with the tools needed to evaluate their own compliance and proactively identify and correct any deficiencies in their employment practices. Because the existing regulations implementing section 503 do not provide contractors with adequate tools to assess whether they are complying with their nondiscrimination and affirmative action obligations to recruit and employ qualified individuals with disabilities, the revisions of the final rule will assist contractors in averting potentially expensive violation findings by OFCCP.

I. Statement of Legal Authority

Enacted in 1973, the purpose of section 503 of the Rehabilitation Act, as amended, is twofold. First, section 503 prohibits employment discrimination on the basis of disability by Federal Government contractors and subcontractors. Second, it requires each covered Federal Government contractor and subcontractor to take affirmative action to employ and advance in employment qualified individuals with disabilities.

The nondiscrimination and general affirmative action requirements of section 503 apply to all Government contractors with contracts or subcontracts in excess of $10,000 for the purchase, sale, or use of personal property or nonpersonal services (including construction). *See* 41 CFR 60–741.4. The requirement to prepare and maintain an affirmative action program, the specific obligations of which are described at 41 CFR 60–741.44, apply to those contractors that have a contract or subcontract of $50,000 or more and 50 or more employees.

In the section 503 context, receipt of a Federal contract comes with a number of responsibilities, including compliance with the section 503 nondiscrimination and anti-retaliation provisions, meaningful and effective efforts to recruit and employ individuals with disabilities, creation and enforcement of personnel policies that support the contractor's affirmative action efforts, maintenance of accurate records on its affirmative action efforts, and OFCCP access to these records upon request. Failure to abide by these responsibilities may result in various sanctions, including withholding of progress payments, termination of contracts, and debarment from receiving future contracts.

II. Major Provisions

The following major provisions in the Final Rule would:

• Establish, for the first time, a 7 percent workforce utilization goal for individuals with disabilities. This goal is not a quota or a ceiling that limits or restricts the employment of individuals with disabilities. Instead, the goal is a management tool that informs decision-making and provides real accountability. Failing to meet the disability utilization goal, alone, is not a violation of the regulation and it will not lead to a fine, penalty, or sanction. OFCCP is mindful that smaller contractors may find it more difficult to attain the goal in each of their job groups. Therefore, the final rule permits contractors with a total workforce of 100 or fewer employees to apply the 7 percent goal to their entire workforce, rather than to each job group.

• Require contractors to invite applicants to voluntarily self-identify as an individual with a disability at the pre-offer stage of the hiring process, in addition to the existing requirement that contractors invite applicants to voluntarily self-identify after receiving a job offer. The purpose of this data collection is to provide contractors with useful information about the extent to which their outreach and recruitment efforts are effectively reaching people with disabilities.

• Require contractors to invite incumbent employees to voluntarily self-identify on a regular basis. The status of employees may change and a regular invitation to self-identify provides employees a way to self-identify for the first time, or to change their previously reported status. Providing a regular invitation should contribute to increased self-identification rates. Improving data collection is important to assessing employment practices.

• Require contractors to maintain several quantitative measurements and comparisons for the number of individuals with disabilities who apply for jobs and the number of individuals with disabilities they hire in order to create greater accountability for employment decisions and practices. Having this data will enable contractors and OFCCP to evaluate the effectiveness of contractors' outreach and recruitment efforts, and examine hiring and selection processes related to individuals with disabilities.

• Require prime contractors to include specific, mandated language in their subcontracts in order to provide knowledge and increase compliance by alerting subcontractors to their responsibilities as Federal contractors.

• Implement changes necessitated by the passage of the ADA Amendments Act (ADAAA) of 2008 by revising the definition of "disability" and certain nondiscrimination provisions of the implementing regulations.

III. Cost and Benefits

This is an economically significant and major rule. Individuals with disabilities make up 4.83 percent of the employed.[9] The section 503 rule establishes a utilization goal for employing individuals with disabilities of 7 percent. To meet the goal, OFCCP estimates that Federal contractors would hire an additional 594,580 individuals with disabilities. There are tangible and intangible benefits from investing in the recruitment and hiring of individuals with disabilities. Among them are employer tax credits, access to a broader talent pool, an expanded pool of job applicants, access to new markets by developing a workforce that mirrors the general customer base, lower turnover based on increased employee loyalty, and lower training costs resulting from lower staff turnover.[10] According to the U.S. Business Leadership Network (USBLN), "corporate CEOs understand that it's cost effective to recruit and retain the best talent regardless of

[8] *Changing Demographic Trends that Affect the Workplace and Implications for People with Disabilities*, Executive Summary (Nov. 30, 2009), p. 4. "Studies agree that disability incidence is related to income and earnings. A number of intertwined relationships, however, make it somewhat difficult to sort out cause and effect."

[9] U.S. Census Bureau, 2011 American Community Survey. There are a variety of sources for this estimate. The Current Population Survey estimates a lower rate, 3.5 percent, and the Survey of Income and Program Participation estimates 9.4 percent.

[10] Job Accommodation Network, "Workplace Accommodations: Low Cost, High Impact," Sept. 1, 2012. *Accommodation and Compliance Series*, *http://askjan.org/media/lowcosthighimpact.html* (last accessed Aug. 9, 2013).

disability."[11] Broad public policy considerations also exist related to the decreased demand for and cost of social services as more people move into jobs and pay taxes.

These projected hires, some of whom will require reasonable accommodation, will not add significant costs for the employers. The requirement to provide reasonable accommodation exists under the ADA, and now exists under the ADA Amendments Act for employers. This is not a new obligation created by this rule. According to a study conducted by the Job Accommodation Network (JAN), of the employers who gave the researchers cost information related to accommodations they had provided, 57 percent said the accommodations needed by employees cost absolutely nothing.[12] For 43 percent of employers, the typical one-time expenditure by employers to provide a reasonable accommodation was $500. Finally, 2 percent reported that accommodations required a combination of one-time and annual costs.

In projecting the overall increase in Federal contractor employment of protected veterans under the VEVRAA rule and individuals with disabilities under the section 503 rule, there is likely to be an interaction between the two categories. Some of the newly hired individuals with disabilities will likely be protected veterans. There are 5.78 million people 18 years or older in the labor force with a disability, 822,000, or 14.21 percent, of whom are veterans.[13]

To meet the section 503 rule's utilization goal of 7 percent, Federal contractors would have to hire an additional 594,580 individuals with disabilities. Assuming that the number of disabled veterans hired will be proportional to their share of the disabled labor force, then we estimate that 84,490 of the newly hired individuals with disabilities will also be protected veterans.[14] Subtracting 84,490 protected veterans from the target of 205,500 leaves 121,010 non-disabled veterans needed to meet the hiring goal. Viewed independently, Federal contractors under VEVRAA would employ an additional 205,500 protected veterans and under section 503 employ an additional 594,580 individuals with disabilities. In the aggregate, we anticipate the overall number of hires across both rules will be closer to 715,590. We adjust the reasonable accommodation cost estimates based on the aforementioned assumptions. The total cost of providing reasonable accommodation to employees with disabilities who are not protected veterans is $114,770,291 in the year the target is met and $48,524,879 in recurring costs. The requirement to provide reasonable accommodation, however, existed under the ADA, and now exists under the ADAAA for employers. This is not a new obligation created by this rule. Nonetheless, the estimated cost of providing reasonable accommodations is included in this rule.

Employers often think providing a reasonable accommodation is more costly than it actually is. Sometimes an accommodation may be something as simple as allowing someone to have their instructions tape recorded, or allowing someone to wear ear phones so they are not distracted by noise around them, or allowing someone an empty office as space when they have difficulty with concentration or attention span. Employers must provide effective accommodations but are not expected to create an undue hardship for themselves by doing so. Individuals seeking reasonable accommodation beyond what is effective have the option of paying the difference between the cost of the more expensive accommodation and the cost of what the employer will pay for the effective reasonable accommodation.

	Final rule low[15]	Final rule high
Total Cost	$349,510,926	$659,877,833
Cost Per Company	7,550	9,716
Cost Per Establishment	2,040	2,626
Cost Per New Hire	588	1,110

[15] The high cost estimates in this chart are based on a contractor establishment count of 251.300 and 67,919 companies while the low estimates are based on 171,275 establishments and 46,291 companies.

Present value costs over ten years for the final rule range from $1.84 billion to $3.91 billion using a 3 percent discount rate. If we use a 7 percent discount rate then the present value costs range from $1.53 billion to $3.25 billion. Annualizing these costs yields a cost range of $215 million to $459 million at the 3 percent discount rate and $218 million to $463 million using a 7 percent discount rate.

	7% Discount rate	3% Discount rate
Benefits	Not Quantified.	Not Quantified
Costs	$1.53 billion to $3.25 billion.	$1.84 billion to $3.91 billion

Introduction

Strengthening the implementing regulations of section 503, whose stated purpose "requires Government contractors and subcontractors to take affirmative action to employ and advance in employment qualified individuals with disabilities," is an important means by which the Government can contribute to reducing the employment disparity between those with and without disabilities. The objective of these regulations is to ensure that employers doing business with the Federal Government do not discriminate and that they take affirmative action to recruit, hire, promote and retain individuals with disabilities. More specifically, the final

[11] USBLN Disability at Work, and U.S. Chamber of Commerce, "Leading Practices on Disability Inclusion," *http://www.usbln.org/pdf-docs/Leading_Practices_on_Disability_Inclusion.pdf* (last accessed Aug. 9, 2013). The USBLN and Chamber report shares best practices from larger corporations for hiring and providing reasonable accommodations.

[12] Job Accommodation Network, "Workplace Accommodations: Low Cost, High Impact," Sept. 1, 2012. *Accommodation and Compliance Series, http://askjan.org/media/lowcosthighimpact.html* (last accessed Aug. 9, 2013), p.3; "Fast Facts: Reasonable Accommodations & The Americans with Disabilities Act," U.S. Chamber of Commerce & the Virginia Commonwealth University, Rehabilitation Research and Training Center on Workplace Supports, *http://www.worksupport.com/Topics/downloads/rrtcfactsheet2.pdf.*

[13] Calculation based on unpublished table, *Employment status of persons 18 years and over by veteran status, period of service, sex, race, Hispanic or Latino ethnicity, and disability status, Annual Average 2012 (Source: Current Population Survey).*

[14] Because of data limitations, OFCCP is using the share of veterans as a proxy for "protected" veterans. For more information on the difference between protected and unprotected veterans, please visit, *http://www.dol.gov/ofccp/regs/compliance/factsheets/vetrights.htm#Q2*

rule has the potential to reduce the employment gap in a number of ways. It adds and strengthens affirmative action requirements designed to improve outreach and recruitment of qualified individual with disabilities; establishes an aspirational goal for the employment of qualified individuals with disabilities that will allow contractors to measure and improve (where appropriate) the effectiveness of those affirmative efforts; provides for greater accountability regarding employment of individuals with disabilities through collection of several quantitative measures; and provides stronger dissemination of contractor obligations to subcontractors and unions. These measures, taken together, are designed to bring more qualified individuals with disabilities into the Federal contractor workforce and provide them with an equal opportunity to advance in employment.

OFCCP published a Notice of Proposed Rulemaking (NPRM) in the **Federal Register** on December 9, 2011 (76 FR 77056), seeking comment on a number of proposals that would strengthen the regulations implementing section 503. The NRPM was published for a 60-day public comment period. The NPRM proposed specific actions that contractors and subcontractors must satisfy to meet their section 503 obligations, including increased data collection obligations, and the establishment of a utilization goal for individuals with disabilities. After receiving several requests to extend the public comment period, OFCCP published a subsequent notice in the **Federal Register** on February 10, 2012 (77 FR 7108), extending the public comment period an additional 14 days.

OFCCP received more than 400 comments on the NPRM. Commenters represented diverse perspectives including: 185 individuals; 105 contractors; 41groups representing contractors; 48 disability and veterans' rights advocacy groups; and 11 governmental entities. The commenters raised a broad range of issues, including concerns with the cost and burden associated with the proposed rule, the extended recordkeeping requirements, the proposed utilization goal, and the new categories of data collection and analyses. OFCCP carefully considered all comments in the development of this final rule.

Pursuant to Executive Order (EO) 13563, the final rule was developed through a process that involved public participation. Indeed, prior to issuing an NPRM, OFCCP had previously issued an Advanced Notice of Proposed Rulemaking (ANPRM), 75 FR 43116 (July 23, 2010), requesting public comment regarding potential ways to strengthen the section 503 affirmative action regulations. During 2010 and 2011, OFCCP also conducted multiple town hall meetings, webinars, and listening sessions with individuals from the contractor community, state employment services, disability organizations, and other interested parties to understand the features of the section 503 regulations that work well, those that can be improved, and possible new requirements that could help to effectuate the overall objective of increasing employment opportunities for individuals with disabilities with Federal contractors.

Compliance With the Final Rule

Although this final rule becomes effective 180 days after publication, full compliance with the requirements of this final rule by current contractors will be phased in as follows. Current contractors subject to subpart C of the existing 41 CFR part 60–741 regulations that have written affirmative action programs (AAP) prepared pursuant to those regulations in place on the effective date of this final rule may maintain that AAP for the duration of their AAP year. Such contractors are required to update their affirmative action programs to come into compliance with the requirements of subpart C of this final rule at the start of their next standard 12-month AAP review and updating cycle. OFCCP will verify compliance with the requirements of this final rule when a contractor is selected for a compliance evaluation pursuant to § 60–741.60 or subject to a complaint investigation pursuant to § 60–741.61.

Overview of the Final Rule

The final rule incorporates several of the changes proposed in the NPRM. However, in order to focus the scope of the final rule more closely on key issues, and in an effort to reduce the burden of compliance on contractors, the final rule also revises or declines to adopt some of the NPRM's proposals.

The final rule strengthens the affirmative action provisions for Federal contractors in a number of ways. The rule addresses the increased use of technology in the workplace by allowing for the electronic posting of employee rights and contractor obligations, and by codifying contractors' reasonable accommodation obligation to ensure that any use of electronic job application systems do not result in the denial of equal employment opportunity to individuals with disabilities. Further, the regulations establish a utilization goal, and increase data collection pertaining to applicants and hires, including modifying and standardizing the requirement to invite applicants and existing employees to self-identify as individuals with a disability. These revisions will help contractors better evaluate their outreach and recruitment efforts, and to modify them as needed, toward the end of increasing employment opportunities for individuals with disabilities by Federal contractors and subcontractors. Additionally, as proposed in the NPRM, changes necessitated by the passage of the ADA Amendments Act (ADAAA) of 2008, Public Law110–325, and the subsequent amendment by the Equal Employment Opportunity Commission (EEOC) of their implementing regulations at 29 CFR part 1630 have been made to the rule's definitions and nondiscrimination provisions.

OFCCP revised or eliminated a number of provisions from the NPRM in response to the comments that were received, particularly with regard to the cost and burden of the rule, recordkeeping requirements, data collection and analyses, and the goal. These changes are discussed in full in the Section-by-Section Analysis. However, a summary of the most significant provisions is below.

OFCCP received approximately 130 comments concerning the burdens and costs of the proposed rule from contractor groups, contractors, individuals and government entities. Many of these commenters stated that OFCCP's estimates of costs and hours were too low. A few commenters also suggested that OFCCP's contractor universe was too small. In response to these concerns, OFCCP modified the burden and cost estimates for the final rule. These changes provide a more accurate estimation of the burden and costs associated with the final rule. As discussed in the NPRM, the overall contractor universe of 171,275 contractor and subcontractor establishments was derived from the Fiscal Year 2009 Employer Information Report EEO–1 (EEO–1), the Federal Procurement Data System-Next Generation (FPDS–NG) report data on contractor establishments, and other pertinent information. OFCCP notes that there were comments on the contractor universe recommending an establishment count of 285,390 using the Veterans Employment Training Services (VETS) annual report. While OFCCP declines to exclusively rely on the VETS report number, we present an estimated high end for the range of the cost of the rule based on a contractor establishment number of 251,300. This number is based on 2010 VETS data from their pending Information Collection Request.[16] As discussed in more detail below, OFCCP also made key changes to the recordkeeping requirements to minimize the burden on contractors.

The NPRM proposed that contractors maintain data pursuant to §§ 60–741.44(f)(4) (linkage agreements and other outreach and recruiting efforts) and 60–741.44(k) (collection of applicant and hire data) for five years. More than 50 commenters opposed these provisions. Several of the commenters were particularly concerned about the burden associated with the five-year requirement. In response, OFCCP has reduced the proposed five-year recordkeeping requirement to three years in the final rule. Further, in light of the comments we received, the final rule does not incorporate the proposal in § 60–741.44(k) of the NPRM to maintain data related to referrals from State agencies and other organizations. Commenters expressed concern with this requirement, indicating that State agencies either cannot provide data or provide data inconsistently across the states. In reviewing the practical utility of the referral data in light of the burden that it would create on contractors, OFCCP has eliminated the requirement to collect and analyze referral data. Eliminating the referral data requirement and reducing the length of recordkeeping minimizes the burden on contractors, while still requiring contractors to keep adequate records to aid and inform their outreach and recruitment efforts.

The NPRM also proposed to require many of the affirmative action efforts that are only suggested in § 60–741.44 of the existing rule. Among these were proposals requiring contractors to: review personnel processes on an annual basis (§ 60–741.44(b)); review physical and mental qualification standards on an annual basis (§ 60–741(c)); establish linkage agreements with three disability-related agencies or organizations to increase connections between contractors and individuals with disabilities seeking employment (§ 60–741.44(f)); take certain specified actions to internally disseminate its affirmative action policy (§ 60–741.44(g)); and train personnel on specific topics related to the employment of individuals with disabilities (§ 60–741.44(j)). After consideration of the comments and taking into account the expected utility of these provisions in light of the burden that contractors would incur to comply with the proposals, OFCCP decided not to incorporate the majority of these proposals into the final rule, and instead retains the language in the existing rule. These NPRM proposals, for the most part, would have required certain specific actions contractors must take to fulfill their already existing, general affirmative action obligations. These general affirmative action obligations—reviewing personnel processes and qualification standards on a periodic basis, undertaking appropriate outreach and positive recruitment activities, developing internal procedures to disseminate affirmative action policies, and training its employees on these policies—remain in the final rule. By eliminating the specific provisions but maintaining the general affirmative action obligations, the final rule provides the contractor flexibility and lesser burden, while still requiring the maintenance and implementation of a robust affirmative action program.

The final rule adopts, but modifies, the proposed establishment of a national utilization goal for individuals with disabilities. The NPRM proposed to establish a single utilization goal of 7 percent per job group. OFCCP also requested public comment on several issues, including the possible establishment of a sub-goal for specific targeted disabilities, the availability of alternative data sources, and a range of potential goal values between 4 percent and 10 percent and the justification for their use. As discussed in more detail in the preamble to § 60–741.45, below, OFCCP received approximately 250 comments on the proposed goal. Disability and veterans' organizations, as well as many individuals, supported the establishment of a goal, while most contractors and employer associations were generally opposed. Most commenters who opposed the proposed goal asserted that any goal would be arbitrary and ineffective because of deficiencies in source data regarding the availability of qualified individuals with disabilities. In addition, some commenters stated their belief that the goals were illegal quotas and would adversely impact other protected groups. Supporters of the goal argued that the establishment of a goal was long overdue, given the long history of employment discrimination against individuals with disabilities, and the extremely low participation rate of people with disabilities in the labor force. The final rule retains the 7 percent per job group national utilization goal, but declines to adopt a sub-goal at this time. In response to commenters, the final rule clarifies that the failure to meet the goal, in and of itself, is not a violation of this part, and what contractors must do when the goal is not met. More specifically, the final rule identifies steps for the contractor to take to ascertain whether there are impediments to equal employment opportunity and, if impediments are found, to correct any identified problems. If no impediments are identified, then no corrective action is required. The goal is not a rigid and inflexible quota which must be met, nor is it to be considered either a ceiling or a floor for the employment of particular groups. Quotas are expressly forbidden.

The NPRM proposed substantial changes to the requirement that contractors invite applicants to self-identify as individuals with disabilities by adding to the existing post-offer invitation requirement both a pre-offer invitation requirement and an annual survey of all employees. It also detailed proposed mandatory language for these invitations. As discussed in detail in the Section-by-Section Analysis, OFCCP received more than 130 comments on this provision from a broad range of perspectives. The final rule adopts the NPRM requirement to invite self-identification from applicants both before and after a job offer has been made. Instead of adopting the proposal for annual self-identification, the final rule adopts an every five year invitation for employees to self-identify with an interim reminder to employees of their ability to change their status. In response to the comments, OFCCP will simplify the language of the invitations and consolidate them into a single form for contractors to use when inviting self-identification. When finalized, the form will be available on the OFCCP Web site.

The NPRM proposed to require that contractors develop and implement written procedures for processing requests for reasonable accommodation and prescribed specific mandatory elements that the procedures must contain. This proposal prompted strong support and strong criticism from commenters. After consideration of the comments, OFCCP decided not to require the development of written reasonable accommodation procedures and eliminated proposed § 60–741.45. Instead, the final rule notes that using written reasonable accommodation procedures is a best practice that may assist contractors in meeting their

[16] OMB Control Number 1293–0005, Federal Contractor Veterans' Employment Report, VETS–100/VETS–100A, *http://www.reginfo.gov/public/do/PRAViewDocument?ref_nbr=201104-1293-003* (last accessed Aug. 13, 2013).

reasonable accommodation obligations. The final rule states that contractors are not required to use such procedures and will not be found in violation of this part for not using such procedures. However, for the benefit of contractors that choose to adopt this best practice, the final rule also contains a new Appendix B that provides guidance for contractors on establishing written reasonable accommodation procedures.

The final rule presents a significant revision of the section 503 regulations. The detailed Section-by-Section Analysis below identifies and discusses all of the final changes in each section. For ease of reference, part 60–741 will be republished in its entirety in the final rule.

Section-By-Section Analysis

41 CFR Part 60–741

Subpart A—Preliminary Matters, Equal Opportunity Clause

Section 60–741.1 Purpose, Applicability, and Construction

Section 60–741.1 of the current rule sets forth the scope of section 503 and the purpose of its implementing regulations. The NPRM proposed three minor changes to this section. Specifically, it proposed to add language to paragraph (a) referencing contractors' nondiscrimination obligation; to modify the citation to the "Americans with Disabilities Act of 1990" (ADA) in paragraph (c) to reflect that statute's amendments by the ADA Amendments Act of 2008; and to add a new paragraph (c)(2) (and renumber existing paragraph (c)(2) as (c)(3)) to reflect the ADAAA's affirmation, in section 6(a)(1), that nothing in the statute "alters the standards for determining eligibility for benefits" under State worker's compensation laws or under State and Federal disability benefit programs. We received no comments on these proposed changes. Accordingly, OFCCP adopts the proposed revisions in the final rule without alteration.

Section 60–741.2 Definitions

The NPRM incorporated the vast majority of existing definitions contained in § 60–741.2 without change. However, OFCCP proposed several changes to the substance and structure of this section. With regard to structure, OFCCP proposed to reorder the definitions so that they are primarily in alphabetical order, rather than in order by subject matter.

With regard to substantive changes, the NPRM proposed several revisions relating to the definition of "disability" and its component parts resulting from the passage of the ADAAA, which became effective on January 1, 2009, and which amends both the ADA and Section 503. These include revisions to the definitions of "disability" (paragraph (g)), "major life activities" (paragraph (m)), "mitigating measures" (paragraph (n)), "regarded as having such an impairment" (paragraph (v)), and "substantially limits" (paragraph (z)). It is OFCCP's intention that these terms will have the same meaning as set forth in the ADAAA, and as implemented by the EEOC in its revised regulations published at 76 FR 16978 (March 25, 2011). In addition to revisions related to the definition of "disability," the NPRM also proposed to replace the term "Deputy Assistant Secretary" with the term "Director," and added a definition of "linkage agreement." OFCCP received 18 comments on the proposed changes to § 60–741.2 from a variety of entities including individuals, contractors, and associations.

• *Definitions related to "Disability"*

Commenters generally commended OFCCP for its efforts to bring consistency to the definitions used in section 503 and those in the ADAAA, noting, for example, that the "contractor community and individuals with disabilities are well-served by a consistent and uniform approach." A few commenters asserted that the new definition of "disability" was overly broad and that, as a result, these commenters were concerned that "a majority of individuals in the labor force may consider themselves as disabled."

In amending the ADA, Congress made clear its intent to ensure a "broad scope of protection" for "disability," and to ensure that this broad scope is not unduly "narrowed" by administrative or court rulings. See ADAAA at section 2. OFCCP's revised definitions incorporate the ADAAA's requirements, which, as previously noted, apply equally to section 503. We therefore adopt the NPRM's revised definitions related to "disability" into the final rule.

• *Definition of "Director"*

We received no comments on the new definition of "Director," and it is adopted into the final rule as proposed.

• *Definition of "Linkage Agreement"*

We received no comments on the proposed definition of "linkage agreement." However, as the final rule eliminates the requirement for contractors to enter into linkage agreements, there is no need for the regulation to contain a definition for it, and thus it is eliminated from the final rule. *See* discussion of § 60–741.44(f) below.

• *Additional Definitions*

Several commenters representing the contractor community requested that OFCCP add formal definitions for "applicant" and for "Internet applicant," as those terms are defined in the Executive Order 11246 (EO 11246) implementing regulations at 41 CFR part 60–1. While OFCCP does not formally adopt the definition of "Internet applicant" into the section 503 regulations, OFCCP is harmonizing the requirements of the section 503 regulations and the Internet Applicant Rule. OFCCP provides further guidance on this issue in the preamble discussion related to § 60–741.42.

Section 60–741.3 Exceptions to the Definitions of "Disability" and "Qualified Individual"

The NPRM proposed to modify this section by changing the terms "individual with a disability" and "qualified individual with a disability" in the section title, as well as throughout the section, to "disability" and "qualified individual," respectively, in accordance with the ADAAA. No comments were received regarding these non-substantive changes, and OFCCP therefore adopts them in the final rule.

Section 60–741.4 Coverage and Waivers

The proposed rule removed the text of paragraph (a)(2) as the "contract work only" exception applied to "employment decisions and practices occurring before October 29, 1992" and has now expired. Accordingly, the NPRM also renumbered paragraphs (3), (4), and (5) as paragraphs (2), (3), and (4). No comments were received on this proposed revision and OFCCP adopts it into the final rule.

Section 60–741.5 Equal Opportunity Clause

The NPRM proposed several changes to the content of the Equal Opportunity (EO) Clause found in § 60–741.5, and to the manner in which the EO Clause is included in Federal contracts. We received a total of 23 comments on these proposals. The proposals, the comments to these proposals, and the revisions made to the final rule are discussed in turn below.

• *EO Clause Paragraph 1—Statement Requiring that Contractors Not Discriminate on the Basis of Disability*

In paragraph 1 of the EO clause, the NPRM proposed to modify the phrase "to employ, advance in employment and otherwise treat qualified individuals with disabilities without discrimination based on their physical or mental disability" to read "to employ and advance in employment individuals with disabilities, and to treat qualified individuals without discrimination on the basis of their physical or mental disability . . . ." This formulation more closely mirrors the language and intent of the ADAAA. Only two comments were received regarding this change. One requested that we also delete the word "because" from the first sentence of paragraph 1 for consistency with the ADAAA, while the other asked that we add the word "qualified" before the phrase "individuals with disabilities." OFCCP does not believe that the first sentence of paragraph 1 is inconsistent with the ADAAA and declines to make this change. OFCCP also declines to add the word "qualified" as requested. The phrase "qualified individuals with disabilities" is used in the ADAAA solely in the context of the entitlement to reasonable accommodation, which is not the subject of the revised sentence. Thus, it would not be consistent with the ADAAA to use that phrasing in this sentence. The NPRM's changes to paragraph 1 of the NPRM are adopted and set forth in the final rule as proposed.

• *EO Clause Paragraph 4—Electronic Notice Posting and Accessible Formats*

In paragraph 4, we proposed two revisions. First, the proposed regulation revised the parenthetical at the end of the third sentence of this paragraph to replace the outdated suggestion of reading the notice to a visually impaired individual as an accommodation with the suggestion to provide the notice in Braille, large print, or other alternative formats, so that the individual with a disability may read the notice him/herself. The proposed regulation also addressed the electronic posting of notices by contractors to satisfy the contractors' posting obligation in the context of telecommuting, work arrangements that do not include a physical office setting, and the use of electronic or Internet-based application systems. It proposed that the contractor be able to satisfy its posting obligation through electronic means for employees who telework, provided that the contractor provides computers to its employees or otherwise has actual knowledge that employees can access the notice. To clarify, "actual knowledge" does not mean actual knowledge that the employee accessed the notice, but rather actual knowledge that the notice was posted or disseminated in such a way that would be accessible to the employee. The NPRM further proposed that contractors that use an electronic application process be required to use an electronic posting, and be required to conspicuously store the electronic notice with, or as part of, the electronic application.

OFCCP received two comments regarding paragraph 4 of the EO Clause. One commenter expressed uncertainty as to what point in the hiring process a contractor is required to provide an alternative version of the notice. A contractor must provide an alternate version of the notice to an applicant with a disability at the same point in the process that it would provide the notice to applicants without disabilities, and upon request. The second commenter recommended that the EO Clause require that electronic notices be available in an accessible format. Paragraph 4 of the EO Clause clearly states that "The contractor must ensure that applicants or employees with disabilities are provided the notice in a form that is accessible and understandable to the individual applicant or employee." Contractors are thus already expected to provide the notice in accessible format, if needed.

In the final rule, OFCCP has adopted the proposed changes to paragraph 4 of the EO Clause. We have also added a clarification stating that a contractor is able to satisfy its posting obligation by electronic means for employees who do not work at a physical location of the contractor, provided that the contractor provides computers or access to computers that can access the electronically posted notices. This clarifies that electronic posting is appropriate not only for employees who telework, but also for those who share work space—and contractor provided computers– at a remote work center.

• *EO Clause Paragraph 7—Contractor Solicitations and Advertisements*

The proposed rule added a new paragraph 7 to the EO clause that would require the contractor to state and thereby affirm in solicitations and advertisements that it is an equal employment opportunity employer of individuals with disabilities. A comparable clause already exists in the equal opportunity clause of Executive Order 11246 regulations. *See* 41 CFR 60–1.4(a)(2).

OFCCP received three comments objecting to this proposal. These commenters asserted that this requirement would be too burdensome since newspapers and other publications charge for each word of a solicitation and that the word "solicitation" was undefined and thus open to broad interpretation.

The word "solicitation" is also used, along with the word "advertisements," in the Executive Order regulations. It has been broadly construed for many years to refer to any job listing, announcement, or advertisement, and would have the same meaning in the section 503 regulations. With regard to the assertion of burdensomeness, as noted in the NPRM, contractors are already required under Executive Order 11246 to state in advertisements and solicitations that "all qualified applicants will receive consideration for employment without regard to race, color, religion, sex, or national origin." *See* 41 CFR 60–1.4(a)(2). The requirement set forth in paragraph 7 of the NPRM would require adding the single word "disability" to the language that contractors are already required to use in advertisements. This is a very minor change involving nominal time and expense to contractors that will affirm to jobseekers and the public the fact that individuals with disabilities are entitled to non-discrimination and affirmative action in the workplaces of Federal contractors. Accordingly, the language in paragraph 7 of the NPRM is adopted into the final rule as proposed.

• *Inclusion of EO Clause in Federal Contracts (proposed 60–741.5(d)*

Finally, the NPRM proposed requiring that the entire EO Clause be included verbatim in Federal contracts. This proposed change was to ensure that the contractor, and particularly any subcontractor, who often relies on the prime contractor to inform it of its nondiscrimination and affirmative action obligations, reads and understands the language in this clause. OFCCP received nineteen comments, all opposing the verbatim inclusion of the EO Clause in contracts. The commenters primarily asserted that this requirement would be too burdensome, as the length of the contract would increase significantly to perhaps double or even triple its original length in some instances.

In light of the comments and upon further consideration of the issue, the final rule does not require express inclusion of the entire EO Clause into Federal contracts. In addition to the burden concerns set forth by commenters, there is concern that the length of the EO Clause will dissuade, rather than promote, contractors and subcontractors from reading and taking note of their non-discrimination and affirmative action obligations. This is contrary to the intent behind the proposal in the NPRM.

However, the requirement in the existing regulations does little to notify contractors and subcontractors of the nature of their obligations to employ and advance in employment qualified individuals with disabilities, which was a primary objective of the NPRM proposal. Accordingly, in order to draw greater attention to the contractors' obligations under section 503 without the burden of including the entire section 503 EO Clause, the final rule revises paragraph (d) of this section to require the following text, set in bold text, in each contract, following the reference to the section 503 regulations: "This contractor and subcontractor shall abide by the requirements of 41 CFR 60–741.5(a). This regulation prohibits discrimination against qualified individuals on the basis of disability, and requires affirmative action by covered prime contractors and subcontractors to employ and advance in employment qualified individuals with disabilities."

Subpart B—Discrimination Prohibited

Section 60–741.21 Prohibitions

This section of the rule describes types of conduct that would violate the non-discrimination requirements of section 503. The NPRM renumbered the section's paragraphs, captioning the introductory sentence as (a), and renumbering existing paragraphs (a) through (i) as paragraphs (1) through (9). The NPRM also proposed several substantive changes, most of which are necessitated by the ADAAA. A new paragraph (iv) was added to paragraph (a)(6) regarding reasonable accommodation (§ 60–741.21(f) of the existing regulations) to clarify that a contractor is "not required" to provide reasonable accommodation to individuals who "satisfy only the 'regarded as having such an impairment' prong of the definition of disability." A new paragraph (ii) was added to paragraph (a)(7) regarding qualification standards (§ 60–741.21(g) of the existing regulations) to incorporate the ADAAA's specific prohibition on the use of qualification standards, employment tests, or other selection criteria that are "based on an individual's uncorrected vision" unless the standard, test, or other selection criteria, as used by the contractor, "is shown to be job-related for the position in question and consistent with business necessity." We also proposed adding a sentence to paragraph (a)(9) regarding compensation (§ 60–741.21(i) of the existing regulations) to clarify that it would be impermissible for a contractor to reduce the compensation provided to an individual with a disability because of the "actual or anticipated cost of a reasonable accommodation the individual needs or may request." Lastly, the NPRM added a new subsection (b) to incorporate the ADAAA's prohibition on claims of discrimination because of an individual's lack of disability.

OFCCP received no comments regarding any of these proposed changes. We did, however, receive one comment suggesting we add "disparate work assignments" as an example of a method by which an employer may discriminate against an employee with a disability. While we agree with the point, we note that the nondiscrimination requirement of the rule already broadly encompasses "any other term, condition, or privilege of employment," including work assignments, as well as every other aspect of employment. *See* § 60–741.20(i). We therefore decline to make this suggested change, as discrimination in work assignments is already prohibited by the section 503 regulations. Accordingly, OFCCP adopts the revisions proposed in the NPRM into the final rule, except that proposed paragraph (a)(6)(iv) is renumbered paragraph (a)(6)(v) in the final rule.

In addition, the final rule adds two new paragraphs to paragraph (a)(6). The NPRM proposed, in section § 60–741.44(d), that as a matter of affirmative action, the contractor "must ensure" that its online job application systems are "compatible with" assistive technology used by individuals with disabilities. In response to concerns raised by commenters, OFCCP decided not to include this provision in the final rule and to instead codify its publicly stated position that the nondiscrimination obligation to make reasonable accommodation includes contractors' use of electronic or online job application systems and requires that contractors ensure equal access to job opportunities. Although we are not including the proposed provision in the final rule, OFCCP notes in paragraph (a)(6)(iii) that it is a best practice for contractors to make their online systems accessible and compatible with assistive technologies used by individuals with disabilities. *See* the preamble to § 60–741.44(d), below, for a discussion of the comments. The codification of this position, first stated publicly in Directive 281, *Federal Contractor's Online Application Selection System* (July 10, 2008), on line at *http://www.dol.gov/ofccp/regs/compliance/directives/dir281.htm,* is in paragraph (a)(6)(iii) of the final rule.

Paragraph (a)(6)(vi) of § 60–741.21of the final rule is also new. The NPRM proposed a new § 60–741.45 requiring contractors to develop and implement written procedures for processing requests for reasonable accommodation, and providing minimum elements that contractors' reasonable accommodation procedures must address. After further consideration of the burden associated with this provision, OFCCP has decided not to incorporate this obligation in the final rule. *See* the preamble to § 60–741.45, below, for a discussion of the comments regarding this section. Instead, in new paragraph (vi) to paragraph (a)(6) of § 60–741.21, the final rule notes that using written reasonable accommodation procedures is a best practice that may assist contractors in meeting their reasonable accommodation obligations. This paragraph states that contractors are not required to use such procedures and will not be found in violation of this part for not using such procedures. However, for the benefit of contractors that choose to adopt this best practice, the final rule also contains a new Appendix B that provides guidance for contractors on establishing written reasonable accommodation procedures.

Section 60–741.23 Medical Examinations and Inquiries

The proposed rule modified paragraph (b)(4) to clarify that voluntary medical examinations and activities need not be job-related and consistent with business necessity, and revised paragraph (b)(5) to eliminate the existing paragraph's reference to (b)(4). We received no comments on these proposed changes and adopt them into the final rule as proposed.

Section 60–741.25 Health Insurance, Life Insurance and Other Benefit Plans

The proposed rule revised paragraph (d) by changing the current rule's two references to "qualified individual with a disability" to "individual with a disability," as the ability to perform essential functions, inherent in the definition of "qualified individual," is not relevant to insurance considerations. We received no comments on this proposed change and adopt it into the final rule as proposed.

Subpart C—Affirmative Action Program

Section 60–741.40 General Purpose and Applicability of the Affirmative Action Program Requirement

The proposed rule proposed changes to the structure of this section by adding a statement of purpose in new paragraph (a), reordering and recaptioning existing paragraphs (a), (b), (c), and (d), and revising the language of existing paragraph (c), renumbered as paragraph (b)(3) in the final rule, to require that the affirmative action program be reviewed and updated annually "by the official designated by the contractor pursuant to § 60–741.44(i)."

• *Paragraph (a): General Purpose*

Proposed paragraph (a) stated that an affirmative action program is a management tool designed to ensure equal employment opportunity and foster employment opportunities for individuals with disabilities. The proposed paragraph also noted that an affirmative action program "is more than a paperwork exercise," and "includes measurable objectives, quantitative analyses, and internal auditing and reporting systems that measure the contractor's progress toward achieving equal employment opportunity for individuals with disabilities."

A total of 22 comments were received from disability, veteran and employer associations, and from several individual employers about paragraph (a). Eighteen of the 22 comments expressed support for proposed paragraph (a) as "helpful," and asserted that the proposal would bring the section 503 regulations in line with the regulations implementing the affirmative action obligations of EO 11246 on behalf of minorities and women. These commenters also asserted that paragraph (a) would be strengthened by the addition of language that the AAP is designed to "effectuate" and measure the contractor's progress toward achieving equal employment opportunity for individuals with disabilities. In contrast, three comments from employers and an employer association expressed general opposition to the proposed paragraph. One commenter asserted the transportation industry should be exempt. Another commenter stated that the proposed changes to the regulations would impose financial burdens on small and medium sized businesses.

OFCCP agrees with the majority of commenters that proposed paragraph (a) accurately describes the general purpose of contractors' affirmative action program obligations and is consistent with the implementing regulations of EO 11246. We believe it is important to clearly articulate OFCCP's expectation that contractors' affirmative action programs will result in progress toward effectuating equal employment opportunity objectives for individuals with disabilities. With respect to the comment requesting an exemption for the transportation industry, we note that such a request must be made to the Director as provided in § 60–741.4(b) of the regulations and cannot be sought through a public comment on the NPRM. OFCCP therefore declines to grant the requested waiver. Consequently, proposed paragraph (a) is adopted without change.

• *Paragraph (b): Applicability of the affirmative action program*

No comments were received regarding the addition to proposed new paragraph (b)(3), previously paragraph (c), indicating that the affirmative action program shall be reviewed and updated annually "by the official designated by the contractor pursuant to § 60–741.44(i)." Proposed paragraph (b) is adopted without change.

No comments were received regarding the reordering of § 60–741.40, and these changes are, likewise, adopted without change.

Section 60–741.41 Availability of Affirmative Action Program

The proposed regulation proposed requiring that, in instances where the contractor has employees who "telework" or otherwise do not work at the contractor's physical establishment, the contractor shall inform these employees about the availability of the affirmative action program by means other than a posting at its establishment. This proposal in many respects mirrored the electronic notice requirements set forth in paragraph 4 of the EO Clause at § 60–741.5 of the rule.

A few commenters from the contractor community asserted that the NPRM's inclusion in the AAP of the data required to be collected and analyzed by proposed § 60–741.44(k) could result in the AAP including sensitive, trade secret, or proprietary information. These commenters expressed concern that this information would be available, under proposed § 60–741.41 to any applicant or employee.

In response to these comments, OFCCP revises the language for the final rule to state that "[t]he full affirmative action program, *absent the data metrics required by § 60–741.44(k)*, shall be made available to any employee or applicant . . . " (revisions emphasized). This balances the interest in confidentiality of the contractor and its employees with the need for transparency regarding the contractor's affirmative action efforts. In addition, as part of the effort to focus the final rule on those elements that are of critical importance to OFCCP, while reducing the burden on contactors where possible, the final rule does not incorporate the NPRM proposals regarding informing off-site individuals about the availability of the contractor's affirmative action program. Rather, the final rule retains the language in the existing § 60–741.41 in that regard.

Section 60–741.42 Invitation to Self-Identify

The NPRM proposed five significant revisions to this section of the regulation: (1) Requiring the contractor to invite all applicants to self-identify as having a disability prior to an offer of employment, using the language and manner prescribed by the Director (paragraph (a)); (2) retaining but modifying the post-offer self-identification invitation requirement in the existing regulation (paragraph (b)); (3) requiring contractors to annually, and anonymously, survey their employees, using the language and manner prescribed by the Director (paragraph (c)); (4) emphasizing that the contractor is prohibited from compelling or coercing individuals to self-identify (paragraph (d)); and (5) requiring contractors to keep all information regarding self-identification as an individual with a disability confidential, and maintained in a data analysis file in accordance with § 60–741.23 of this part. The NPRM also proposed eliminating the sample invitation to self-identify in Appendix B of the existing rule, and invited public comment on potential language for the text of the mandated invitation to self-identify for contractors to use.

OFCCP received 136 comments on this section from a broad array of perspectives, including contractors, law firms, government agencies and individuals, as well as from organizations representing individuals with disabilities, veterans, and contractors. By and large, individuals with disabilities, and disability advocacy organizations were supportive of the three-step approach to voluntary self-identification of disability proposed in the NPRM, while contractors and contractor organizations opposed the proposed approach.

Commenters opposed to the proposed self-identification rubric raised various concerns, including: (1) That the pre-offer invitation to self-identify allegedly conflicts with the Americans with Disabilities Act (ADA); (2) the potential interplay between the pre-offer data collection requirement and the Internet Applicant Rule set forth in regulations for Executive Order 11246; (3) the possibility of inaccurate self-reporting and underreporting; (4) the potential for contractors to be exposed to discrimination claims as a result of having knowledge about the existence of a disability; and (5) cost and burden issues. Additionally, some of those who favored the proposed self-identification approach joined those opposed in questioning the wording and readability of the proposed invitation to self-identify included in the NPRM preamble. The proposals, the comments regarding these proposals, and the revisions made in the final rule are discussed in turn below (with the exception of some specific comments on burden, which are addressed in the Regulatory Procedures section of the final rule).

• *Paragraph (a): Pre-offer invitation to self-identify*

Paragraph (a) of the NPRM proposed requiring the contractor to invite all applicants to voluntarily self-identify as individuals with disabilities whenever the applicant applies for or is considered for employment. As discussed in the NPRM, the primary reason for proposing a pre-offer invitation to voluntarily self-identify is to collect important data pertaining to the participation of individuals with disabilities in the contractor's applicant pools and workforces. This data would enable the contractor and OFCCP to better monitor and evaluate the contractor's hiring and selection practices with respect to individuals with disabilities. Furthermore, data related to the pre-offer stage of the employment process would be particularly helpful, as it would provide the contractor and OFCCP with valuable information regarding the number of individuals with disabilities who apply for jobs with contractors. In turn, this data would assist OFCCP and the contractor in assessing the effectiveness of the contractor's recruitment efforts over time, and in refining and improving the contractor's recruitment strategies, where necessary.

There was support for this provision, among individuals with disabilities and disability advocacy organizations. One commenter stated that a study conducted by the Cornell University ILR School and the American Association of People with Disabilities had found that applicants are most likely to self-identify as having a disability during the recruitment process. On the other hand, several other commenters expressed concern about this paragraph. Most prominently, commenters were concerned that requiring contractors to invite applicants to reveal whether they have a disability pre-offer could expose contractors to an increased risk of liability under the ADA, and that pre-offer self-identification conflicted with that statute's general ban on pre-offer inquiries about disability and guidance issued by EEOC and OFCCP.

OFCCP believes that concerns regarding the possibility of a conflict with the ADA or related guidance are based on an incorrect reading of the ADA and its regulations. As discussed in the NPRM, the ADA and section 503 regulations specifically permit the contractor to conduct a pre-offer inquiry about disability if it is "made pursuant to a Federal, state or local law requiring affirmative action for individuals with disabilities," such as section 503. Furthermore, EEOC has clearly stated that "collecting information and inviting individuals to identify themselves as individuals with disabilities as required to satisfy the affirmative action requirements of section 503 of the Rehabilitation Act is not restricted" by the ADA or EEOC's implementing regulations. *See* 29 CFR 1630.13, 1630.14 and its Appendix; 41 CFR 60–741.42. EEOC has reiterated this exception to the prohibition on pre-offer inquiries about disability in sub-regulatory technical assistance guidance.[17] For example, EEOC's Title I Technical Assistance Manual, online at *www.askjan.org/LINKS/ADAtam1.html*, states:

> 5.5(c) *Exception for Federal Contractors Covered by Section 503 of the Rehabilitation Act and Other Federal Programs Requiring Identification of Disability.* Federal contractors and subcontractors who are covered by the affirmative action requirements of Section 503 of the Rehabilitation Act may invite individuals with disabilities to identify themselves on a job application form or by other pre-employment inquiry, to satisfy the affirmative action requirements of Section 503 of the Rehabilitation Act. Employers who request such information must observe Section 503 requirements regarding the manner in which such information is requested and used, and the procedures for maintaining such information as a separate, confidential record, apart from regular personnel records.

The ADA, thus, clearly allows the type of pre-offer self-identification invitation proposed in the NPRM.

Some commenters were also concerned that obtaining information about the disability status of an applicant could potentially expose contractors to claims of discrimination by disappointed job seekers. These commenters stated that obtaining information that an applicant has a disability would give them "knowledge" of the existence of a disability—a necessary component to any disparate treatment discrimination claim—and that the pre-offer invitation requirement eliminates an important protection for contractors.

OFCCP acknowledges that knowledge of the existence of a disability, like knowledge of a person's race, ethnicity, or gender, which are regularly self-reported and collected by contractors, is a component of an intentional discrimination claim. However, to find intentional discrimination it must be *proven* not only that the contractor knew that a person had a disability (or was of a particular race, ethnicity, or gender), but that the contractor treated the person less favorably because of his or her disability (or race, ethnicity, or gender). We note, moreover, that contractors have long had knowledge of the disabilities of applicants who have visible disabilities, such as blindness, deafness, or paraplegia, but that OFCCP has had no means of knowing of their presence in the applicant pool or their experience in the application and selection process. Requiring contractors to invite pre-offer self-identification will help fill this void. Lastly, OFCCP points out that, generally, self-identification information will be obtained by, and reside with, Human Resources (HR) offices and will not be provided to interviewing, testing, or hiring officials, as it is confidential information that must be kept separate from regular personnel records. This will help ensure that these officials do not, in fact, have knowledge of which applicants have chosen to self-identify as having a disability.

Several commenters were concerned that self-identification would be unreliable in truly measuring the number of individuals with disabilities in the applicant pool, as many applicants will not self-identify or will do so incorrectly. Indeed the same study cited above showed that at best, only about 50 percent of those with disabilities were likely to respond. Commenters also asked OFCCP to clarify whether contractors would be allowed to identify an individual as having a disability who does not self-identify. These commenters expressed concern that not permitting contractors to identify applicants with known or obvious disabilities who do not self-identify as having a disability, would only increase the degree of underreporting, make it more difficult for contractors to meet the NPRM's proposed utilization goal, and possibly result in erroneous findings that the goal has not been met.

OFCCP concedes that there likely will be significant underreporting, especially at the beginning, meaning that self-reported data regarding disability will not give a full picture of the applicant

[17] To assuage any remaining doubt on this matter, OFCCP obtained a letter from EEOC's Office of Legal Counsel in advance of the publication of this rule affirming that the pre-offer invitation to self-identify as an individual with a disability required by this final rule is permissible under the ADA and its implementing regulations. This letter will be posted on the OFCCP Web site.

pool. We disagree, though, that this is alone sufficient reason to eliminate the pre-offer invitation. While not perfect, the data that will result from the pre-offer invitation requirement will provide the contractor and OFCCP with important data that does not now exist pertaining to the participation of individuals with disabilities in the contractor's applicant pools. The hope is that this will allow the contractor and OFCCP to better identify, monitor, and evaluate the contractor's hiring and selection practices with respect to individuals with disabilities. We also believe that the response rate to the invitation to self-identify will increase over time, as people become accustomed to the invitation and workplaces become more welcoming to individuals with disabilities.

With regard to the question of contractors identifying individuals with disabilities who do not self-identify, we note that contractors subject to Executive Order 11246 have long been permitted to identify the race, gender, and ethnicity of applicants who do not voluntarily self-identify, but may not guess or speculate when so doing. *See Frequently Asked Questions for the Employer,* online at *http://www.dol.gov/ofccp/regs/compliance/faqs/emprfaqs.htm#Q10.* OFCCP believes that a comparable interpretation of the section 503 voluntary self-identification provisions is appropriate. The final rule requires contractors to maintain several quantitative measurements regarding individuals with disabilities who have applied or been hired for jobs (§ 60–741.44(k)). Contractors are also required to annually assess their utilization of individuals with disabilities in each job group against a national utilization goal, and to take specific steps to ascertain the existence of, and correct, any impediments to equal employment opportunity if the goal is not met (§ 60–741.45). In light of these requirements and the overall objective of measuring progress toward equal employment opportunity for people with disabilities, it is important that the reporting of disability demographic information be as accurate as possible. OFCCP therefore believes that it is appropriate to allow contractors to identify an individual as having a disability for the purposes of §§ 60–741.44(k) and 60–741.45, if the individual does not voluntarily self-identify when: (1) The disability is obvious (e.g., someone is blind or missing a limb) or (2) the disability is known to the contractor (e.g., an individual says that he or she has a disability or requests reasonable accommodation for a disability).

OFCCP believes that this approach strikes the appropriate balance between the privacy concerns of those with disabilities and the need for reporting information to be as accurate as possible. Pursuant to the final rule, disability demographic information must be kept confidential and maintained in a data analysis file. Such information may not be included in an individual's personnel file. Contractors are also reminded that they may not guess or speculate when identifying an individual as having a disability. Nor may they assume that an individual has a disability because he or she "looks sickly" or behaves in an unusual way.

Another concern raised by several commenters is that the requirement to collect and maintain self-identification data from applicants does not comport with the Internet Applicant Rule found in the regulations to Executive Order 11246. *See* 41 CFR 60–1.3, 1.12. These commenters recommended that OFCCP add a definition of "applicant" and "Internet applicant" to this final rule and ensure that wherever in the regulations the term "applicant" is used, the term "Internet applicant" applies as well. OFCCP did not propose to add a definition of "applicant" or "Internet applicant" in its NPRM. Therefore, the final rule does not do so. However, the discussion that follows provides guidance about how contractors may invite Internet applicants to self-identify as an individual with a disability under section 503 in a manner consistent with demographic collection requirements under the Executive Order Internet Applicant Rule. Under this final rule, contractors will be able to invite applicants to self-identify as an individual with a disability at the same time the contractor solicits demographic data on applicants under the Executive Order 112146 Internet Applicant Rule. For Internet applicants this generally will be after the contractor has determined the individual has been screened for basic qualifications and meets other requirements for being an Internet applicant.

Therefore, this rule does not require contractors to change their existing systems for screening Internet applicants so long as those systems comply with existing law.

By way of background, OFCCP's longstanding definition of "applicant" is contained in agency subregulatory guidance. See the Uniform Guidelines on Employee Selection Procedures (UGESP), Question and Answer 15, 44 FR 11996 (March 2, 1979).[18] According to that guidance, in general, an applicant is a person who has indicated an interest in being considered for hiring, promotion, or other employment opportunities, either in writing (by completing an application form or submitting a resume) or orally, depending upon the contractor's practice. The Internet Applicant Rule came into effect in February 2006, and pertains to recordkeeping by contractors on Internet-based hiring processes and the solicitation of race, gender, and ethnicity data, in conjunction with their recordkeeping obligations under the Executive Order implementing regulation at § 60–1.12. Under § 60–1.12, contractors' recordkeeping obligations include maintaining expressions of interest through the Internet that the contractor considered for a particular position, as well as applications and resumes. Contractors also are required to maintain, where possible, data about the race, sex, and ethnicity of applicants and Internet Applicants, as appropriate. The term Internet Applicant is defined in § 60–1.3 and generally means an individual who: (1) Submitted an expression of interest in employment through the Internet; (2) is considered by the contractor for employment in a particular position; (3) possessed the basic qualifications for the position; and (4) did not remove himself or herself from consideration.

OFCCP has taken into account contractors' concerns about inviting self-identification for applications submitted electronically, particularly for those contractors who create resume databases which they mine for applicants when they have a job opening. In recognition of these concerns, and consistent with EO 13563's focus on simplifying and harmonizing requirements, OFCCP will permit contractors to invite applicants to self-identify as an individual with a disability at the same time as contractors collects the demographic data for applicants required under Executive Order 11246.

The Internet Applicant rule under EO 11246 generally allows contractors to do a "first cut" and screen out individuals whom they believe do not meet the

[18] Question and Answer 15 reads: "Q. What is meant by the terms "applicant" and "candidate" as they are used in the Uniform Guidelines? A: The precise definition of the term "applicant" depends upon the user's recruitment and selection procedures. The concept of an applicant is that of a person who has indicated an interest in being considered for hiring, promotion, or other employment opportunities. This interest might be expressed by completing an application form, or might be expressed orally, depending upon the employer's practice."

basic qualifications of the position—without capturing or retaining any demographic documentation on these individuals. There is the concern, however, that in doing this "first cut" contractors may be engaging in discrimination (e.g., if they are incorrectly applying their basic qualifications, or the basic qualifications have an adverse impact on a protected group and are not job-related and consistent with business necessity), and by not keeping the demographic information on the individuals they screened out they are eliminating evidence to prove that discrimination may be occurring. This concern is even greater in the section 503 context because these Executive Order "first cuts" are not designed to take into account the possibility that someone with a disability might be able to meet the qualification standard or perform the essential functions of the job with the provision of a reasonable accommodation.

Under existing law, it is unlawful under section 503 to use qualification standards, including at the "basic qualifications" screen stage, that screen out or tend to screen out an individual with a disability or a class of individuals with disabilities unless the standard is shown to be job-related for the position in question and consistent with business necessity. Selection criteria that concern an essential function may not be used to exclude an individual with a disability if that individual could satisfy the criteria with a reasonable accommodation. *See* § 60–741.21(a)(7). These requirements, therefore, apply when contractors design and implement their "basic qualifications" screens. In addition, after the initial screening for "basic qualifications," contractors must also ensure that they are complying with their duty to evaluate all applicants for jobs based on the applicant's ability to perform the essential functions of the job with or without reasonable accommodation.

OFCCP will treat the recordkeeping provisions of section 503 at § 60–741.80 in the same manner as the recordkeeping requirements under Executive Order 11246 at 41 CFR 60–1.12 as applied to Internet applicants. These recordkeeping requirements are not new and will impose no additional burden on contractors. The record retention requirements exist independently of whether and when individuals are invited to self identify under section 503.

The section 503 recordkeeping provisions require contractors to retain personnel or employment records made or kept by the contractor for one or two years depending on the size of the contractor and contract. Those records include the records contractors are required to maintain under 41 CFR 60–1.12. Section 60–1.12 requires contractors to maintain all expressions of interest through the Internet or related technologies considered by the contractor for a particular position, such as on-line resumes or internal resume databases, and records identifying job seekers contacted regarding their interest in a particular position. For purposes of recordkeeping with respect to internal resume databases, the contractor also must maintain a record of each resume added to the database, a record of the date each resume was added to the database, the position for which each search of the database was made, and corresponding to each search, the substantive search criteria used and the date of the search. For purposes of recordkeeping with respect to external databases the contractor must maintain a record of the position for which each search of the database was made, and corresponding to each search, the substantive criteria used, the date of the search, and the resumes of job seekers who met the basic qualifications for the particular position who are considered by the contractor. As with records retained under EO 11246 regulations, these records are to be maintained regardless of whether the job seeker is an Internet applicant.

If a contractor has a practice of welcoming unsolicited resumes regardless of current job openings, OFCCP will permit the contractor to invite self-identification only of those considered for employment, consistent with requirements under Executive Order 11246 and its regulations at 41 CFR 60–1.3 and 60–1.12. The obligation to invite self-identification is triggered by considering the job seeker for employment, not by including the resume in the resume database. For example, if a contractor has an internal resume database with 1,000 resumes and is looking for applicants to fill a job as an engineer in Omaha, the contractor could limit the pool of resumes under review by applying a "basic qualifications" screen that identifies those who have a masters degree in electrical engineering, at least three years of experience as an electrical engineer, and further limit the review to resumes submitted within the last three months. If that search produced a pool of 30 job seekers, the contractor might narrow the pool further by asking the 30 job seekers if they are interested in being considered for the job. If 10 job seekers indicate interest in being considered, they would be applicants and the contractor would invite the 10 job seekers to self-identify. In contrast, if a contractor has a practice of not accepting unsolicited resumes, job seekers who submit an unsolicited resume are not applicants. Accordingly, the contractor would have no obligation to invite them to self-identify as an individual with a disability.

It is also possible that potential and qualified job applicants with disabilities may not apply for jobs posted on contractors' online application systems because, for example, they are not aware that selection criteria concerning essential functions may not be used to exclude them if they can satisfy the criteria with a reasonable accommodation. Contractors seeking to fill jobs should seek to attract the best possible pool of applicants; this includes applicants with disabilities who could perform the job with or without reasonable accommodations. OFCCP notes that a best practice for ensuring a diverse, qualified pool of applicants for contractors using online application systems is posting a notice on their human resources Web page or online application portal that notifies job applicants that may need a reasonable accommodation to perform the functions of a job that they are entitled to one under the ADAAA. This best practice encourages qualified individuals with disabilities to pursue job vacancies, and provides contractors with access to a wide range of skills and talents.

In providing this guidance as to application of the self-identification requirement under section 503, contractors should be able to operate as they have been using their existing systems and processes because this rule does not change how contractors handle Internet applicants. This should allow contractors to avoid creating separate data collection and storage systems as many contractors feared. For those contractors that need further help determining which individuals must be given a pre-offer self-identification inquiry, OFCCP is available to provide technical guidance.

- *Paragraph (a)(1): Requirement that the contractor invite self-identification using the language and manner prescribed by the Director*

Paragraph (a)(1) of the NPRM proposed requiring contractors to invite applicants to self-identify using language prescribed by the Director and provided a sample of what that language might look like for public comment. Several commenters responded, the majority of which expressed support for the proposed text, but suggested that modifications be made to it.

Commenters asserted that the proposed language was too long, wordy and complex. Many of these commenters offered suggestions to simplify the language, thereby increasing the likelihood that the invitation would be read, understood and responded to. Commenters also suggested that we state that self-identifying is "voluntary" before, rather than after, individuals are asked to identify their disability status. OFCCP agrees with these criticisms and is developing a form that will address them. When finalized, the form will be available on the OFCCP Web site.

Some commenters opposed the use of uniform language for the self-identification invitation, arguing that uniform language will not allow contractors flexibility to modify the self-identification language as necessary based on geographic location. They recommended that we provide a framework with suggested language and allow contractors the flexibility to design invitations they believed would maximize response rates. Other commenters expressed a willingness to use self-identification language prescribed by OFCCP, but only if the EEOC has approved the inquiry. As noted in the NPRM, OFCCP believes that the use of uniform language is needed to ensure consistency in all self-identification invitations, and to reassure individuals with disabilities that the self-identification request is routine and executed pursuant to obligations created by OFCCP. Standardized language will also minimize any burden to contractors associated with this responsibility, and will facilitate contractor compliance. With respect to the concern about EEOC approval, pursuant to the rulemaking process, both the NPRM and this final rule were coordinated with EEOC, among other agencies, prior to their publication. EEOC will be asked for input in the process that Secretary uses to finalize the form.

Finally, few commenters commented on the portion of the text inviting applicants to request any needed accommodation in the application process. Those who did suggested that we either separate language concerning reasonable accommodation from the invitation, or include clarification that applicants are not being asked to disclose accommodations they need to perform the job they are seeking. We will address this issue when finalizing the language of the form.

• *Paragraph (b): Post-Offer Invitation to Self-identify*

Paragraph (b) of the NPRM proposed modifying, but retaining, the current rule's requirement that contractors invite individuals, after an offer of employment is extended, but before the applicant begins work, to voluntarily self-identify as an individual with a disability. As explained in the NPRM, we proposed to retain this requirement, in addition to the new pre-offer invitation requirement, so that individuals with hidden disabilities who fear potential discrimination if their disability is revealed prior to receiving a job offer will, nevertheless, have the opportunity to provide this valuable data. We received no comments on this paragraph. Accordingly, the language in the NPRM is adopted as proposed.

• *Paragraph (c): Annual Employee Survey*

Paragraph (c) proposed requiring that, on an annual basis, contractors invite all of their employees to voluntarily and anonymously self-identify as having a disability using the language and manner prescribed by the Director.

We received several comments that addressed whether the annual employee survey should be anonymous. Some of these commenters generally supported an anonymous survey. These commenters asserted that having the survey be anonymous would permit contractors to collect the data necessary to evaluate the effectiveness of their affirmative action efforts while ensuring that applicants and employees with disabilities are protected from discrimination. Others contended that an anonymous survey would be critical to increasing the likelihood that individuals would choose to self-identify.

Several other commenters opposed the anonymity requirement, arguing that it would impede the ability of contractors to comply with the NPRM's proposed requirements for collecting and analyzing data regarding individuals with disabilities. These commenters pointed out that contractors would be unable to comply with the goal requirement of proposed § 60–741.46 to determine their utilization of individuals with disabilities by job group from anonymous self-identification forms. Such assessments would require an individual's name and other identifying information. Moreover, without identifying information, it would not be possible for contractors to know whether any of the employees who self-identified had self-identified previously, leading to the possibility of double counting employees with disabilities.

OFCCP agrees that identifying information is needed in order for contractors to assess their utilization of individuals with disabilities by job group. We have, accordingly, revised paragraph (c) to remove the word "anonymous." However, as noted previously, disability demographic information must be kept strictly confidential, apart from regular personnel files. We have also recaptioned paragraph (c) as "Employees" and removed the word "survey." This clarifies that contractors are to provide employees with the same invitation to voluntarily self-identify as an individual with a disability that is provided to applicants, and do not need to canvass their employees in some other fashion.

Divergent views were also expressed by commenters regarding the proposal to invite employees to voluntarily self-identify on an annual basis. Commenters supporting the annual requirement contended that it would provide an opportunity for employees who have become disabled since employment, or who were hesitant to self-identify during the hiring process, to be counted for affirmative action purposes. They also asserted that an annual employee survey would provide contractors with current information and enable them to measure the impact of changes in their hiring and employment practices.

Commenters opposed to the annual survey requirement contended that it would be superfluous in light of the requirement in the existing regulations for contractors to advise employees of their right to self-identify at any time. They also argued that it is redundant to require contractors to survey all employees annually in addition to the pre- and post-offer invitations to self-identify. These commenters argued that a single solicitation of applicants post-offer would be more appropriate, and would provide an opportunity for interactive discussions about reasonable accommodation. Other commenters opposed to the annual survey asserted that the inclusion of individuals who become disabled after becoming employed would not help contractors in analyzing and improving recruiting and outreach efforts. These commenters also contended the annual survey would deter employees from participating in the interactive reasonable accommodation process, and make employees suspicious of management's persistence in asking them to identify their disability status, making them less likely to self-identify.

Finally, some commenters opposed to the annual employee survey proposed alternative ways to achieve the desired result. For example, one commenter recommended that we allow the contractor to post the invitation to self-identify in a conspicuous location and allow employees to self-identify at any time, rather than once per year, and require the contractor to record the data annually. Another proposal was to reduce the frequency of the survey to every two or three years instead of annually, or to make the annual survey optional, rather than mandatory.

As stated in the NPRM, because baseline data regarding the number of individuals with disabilities in the contractor's workforce is not available, it is important to provide all employees with an initial opportunity to self-identify. It is also important that contractors continue to have the most accurate data possible in order to be able to conduct meaningful self-assessments of their employment practices and recruitment efforts. This is especially important in the disability context because the status of employees may change over time and the snapshot of the makeup of the contractor's workforce may become outdated for planning and self-assessment purposes. In light of both the importance of employee data and the concerns raised by commenters, the final rule revises the requirement to invite employee self-identification as follows: The contractor is to invite employee self-identification during the first year it becomes subject to the requirements of this section, and at five year intervals, thereafter. At least once during the years between each invitation, the contractor must remind their employees that they may voluntarily update their disability status at any time.

• *Paragraph (d): Prohibits contractor from compelling or coercing individuals to self-identify*

Proposed paragraph (d) emphasized that the contractor is prohibited from compelling or coercing individuals to self-identify. While a majority of commenters supported this proposal, a few commenters opposed it. Commenters opposing this paragraph argued that the adoption of any utilization goal should be predicated upon mandatory self-identification for applicants and employees to eliminate inaccurate reporting.

The language of the NPRM is adopted into the final rule as proposed. OFCCP notes that self-identification for affirmative action purposes has always been voluntary under section 503, and is, likewise, voluntary with regard to race, gender, and ethnicity under Executive Order 11246, which OFCCP also enforces. While the final rule adds a goal requirement to section 503 for the first time, we find this an insufficient reason to mandate self-identification by applicants and employees. Executive Order 11246 has long had a goal requirement, but has never mandated self-reporting by applicants or employees. Moreover, such a mandate would be virtually unenforceable as many disabilities are hidden and would not be known to the contractor. In addition, as previously discussed, OFCCP will permit contractors to identify as individuals with disabilities applicants and employees with known or obvious disabilities who decline to voluntarily self-identify. Permitting such identification by contractors for affirmative action purposes, we believe, adequately addresses the concerns of commenters seeking a mandatory self-identification requirement. OFCCP, therefore, adopts paragraph (d) into the final rule as proposed.

• *Paragraph (e): Requirement that information concerning disability be kept confidential*

Proposed paragraph (e) emphasized that all information regarding self-identification as an individual with a disability shall be kept confidential and maintained in a data analysis file in accordance with § 60–741.23 of this part.

Some commenters offered recommendations to modify paragraph (e). Commenters suggested that a clear definition of what constitutes a "data analysis file" be provided and include clarification regarding who may have access to the information in such a file. It was also suggested that OFCCP expand the language of paragraph (e) to state that self-identification information should not be placed in an individual's personnel file. Still others suggested that self-identification information should be kept in the confidential medical file required by the ADA and the Genetic Information Nondiscrimination Act (GINA), and the implementing regulations for those statutes. OFCCP believes that paragraph (e) is sufficiently descriptive to instruct contractors to maintain self-identification information in a single confidential file maintained solely for the purpose of conducting data analysis required by section 503 and this part, and that a definition of "data analysis file" is not necessary. As section 503 already prohibits the maintenance of disability-related information in personnel files, there is no need to so state in this paragraph. *See* 41 CFR 60–741.23(d). Lastly, OFCCP rejects the suggestion that contractors be permitted to maintain self-identification information in employees' individual confidential medical files. This would impede contractors' ability to use the data for the collective analysis for which the data are collected, and to provide the self-identification information to OFCCP when requested to do so.

Section 60–741.44 Required Contents of Affirmative Action Programs

The proposed rule contained significant revisions to several paragraphs of this section. These proposals, the comments to these proposals, and the revisions made to the final rule are discussed below.

A total of 133 comments addressed the required contents of a section 503 affirmative action program (AAP). Commenters included disability, employer, veterans and other groups and associations, contractors, law firms, government offices, and individuals.

• *Paragraph (a): Affirmative action policy statement*

Proposed § 60–741.44(a) requires contractors to state their equal employment opportunity policy in the company's AAP. The NPRM proposed revising the second sentence of the existing paragraph to clarify the contractor's duty to provide notice of employee rights and contractor obligations in a manner that is accessible and understandable to persons with disabilities. It also proposed revising the parenthetical at the end of the sentence, replacing the outdated suggestion of "hav[ing] the notice read to a visually disabled individual" as an accommodation with the suggestion to provide Braille, large print, or other versions of the notice that allow persons with disabilities to read the notice themselves. The NPRM also proposed revising paragraph (a) to require the contractor's chief executive officer to clearly articulate his or her support for the company's AAP in the policy statement.

OFCCP received sixteen comments on these proposed revisions, most of which supported the changes. Commenters noted that the requirement for contractors to provide accommodations such as large print, Braille and other means to enable individuals with visual impairments to read for themselves brings the regulation in line with current practice under the ADA and Rehabilitation Act.

An employer association questioned the feasibility of obtaining the required notice in Braille. This comment also stated that the proposed requirement would impose an insurmountable burden because providing notices that are understandable to an individual with a disability requires identification, understanding, and anticipation of the varying types and degrees of learning disabilities that individuals may possess.

OFCCP declines to revise § 60–741.44(a) with regard to the provision of alternative formats that are accessible and understandable to persons with disabilities. The proposed wording indicates that the listed alternative formats are simply examples of reasonable accommodation that may be needed by particular individuals; there may be other ways to comply with this requirement, depending on the specific circumstances. With regard to the concern that there may be varying types and degrees of learning disabilities requiring accommodation, OFCCP notes that paragraph (a) is consistent with the existing section 503 reasonable accommodation obligation that requires contractors to accommodate the specific limitations of their applicants and employees with disabilities, unless to do so would impose an undue hardship on its operations. *See* 41 CFR 60–741.21(f).

OFCCP, however, agrees with commenters' suggestion to revise the language of paragraph (a) to clarify the level of company leadership that must demonstrate their support for the company's AAP. The purpose of this paragraph is to ensure that the statement of policy communicates to employees that support for the AAP goes to the very top of the contractor's organization. For contractors with foreign-based parent companies, it is appropriate to require the company leadership that is based in the United States to express that support. Therefore, § 60–741.44(a) of the final rule is revised to state "[t]he policy statement shall indicate the top United States executive's (such as the Chief Executive Officer or the President of the United States Division of a foreign company) support for the contractor's affirmative action program . . ."

• *Paragraph (b): Review of personnel processes*

The NPRM proposed three changes to this paragraph. First, it required that the contractor review its personnel processes on at least an annual basis, rather than "periodically," to ensure that its obligations are being met.

Second, proposed paragraph (b) mandated certain specific steps (based on existing Appendix C) that the contractor must take, at a minimum, in the review of its personnel processes, including: (1) Identifying the vacancies and training programs for which protected applicants and employees were considered; (2) providing a statement of reasons explaining the circumstances for rejecting individuals with disabilities for vacancies and training programs and a description of considered accommodations; and (3) describing the nature and type of accommodations for individuals with disabilities who were selected for hire, promotion, or training programs.

Third, the NPRM proposed to require that the contractor "ensure that its use of information and communication technology is accessible to applicants and employees with disabilities." A footnote citing resources related to technological accessibility, such as the Web Content Accessibility Guidelines (WCAG 2.0) and the regulations implementing the accessibility requirements for Federal agencies prescribed in section 508 of the Rehabilitation Act was also included.

OFCCP received 56 comments regarding these proposals. Some supported an annual review of personnel processes, while other commenters suggested a less frequent review, occurring every three or five years, would be sufficient. Several comments asserted that significant burden and costs would result from the proposed requirement, much greater than that calculated by OFCCP in the NPRM's Regulatory Procedures section. The comments also asserted that promotion and training opportunities, unlike hiring, are not as readily distinguishable for individual candidates. Such opportunities may be available to all employees, take a number of different forms, and may be noncompetitive. These commenters further objected to the requirement to create and maintain a statement of reasons for every instance in which an individual with a disability is denied a position or training as tantamount to requiring a drafted legal defense before any claims were brought, and warned that it could serve to "drive underground" the real reason for rejection. Lastly, the comments raised confidentiality concerns and cited difficulties the proposed requirement would create in terms of recordkeeping and access to human resource information systems currently used by contractors. The comments asserted that it would therefore be unreasonable to make the proposed procedures mandatory.

Based on the comments submitted, and questions about the efficacy of these requirements toward the end of increasing employment opportunities for individuals with disabilities, OFCCP does not adopt the proposal as drafted in the NPRM. Instead, the final rule retains the language in existing § 60–741.44(b) that contractors shall review their personnel processes "periodically," but eliminates existing Appendix C. However, in so doing, OFCCP reiterates that existing paragraph (b) contains several requirements—including ensuring that its personnel processes are careful, thorough, and systematic; ensuring that these processes do not stereotype individuals with disabilities; and designing procedures that facilitate a review of the implementation of these requirements—that continue to apply to contractors. OFCCP will vigorously enforce these requirements.

With respect to the proposed technological accessibility requirement, some disability advocacy groups supported the proposed requirement. However, other commenters asserted that this requirement was too vague, and asked for clarification as to what they would have to do to comply and how OFCCP intended to enforce it. These commenters also asserted that there is not a single, accepted standard of "accessibility," that technology is constantly changing, and that it could be tremendously expensive and time-consuming for contractors to have to ensure on an annual basis that all of its information and communication technology are fully accessible and technologically up-to-date.

In response to these comments OFCCP has revised and clarified paragraph (b) in the final rule. It requires that the "contractor shall ensure" that applicants and employees with disabilities have "equal access to its personnel processes, including those implemented through information and communication technologies." The final rule requires, further, that contractors must provide "necessary reasonable accommodation to ensure applicants and employees with disabilities receive equal employment opportunity in the operation of personnel processes." Contractors are also "encouraged" to make their information and communication systems accessible, even in the absence of a specific accommodation request. To assist contractors in making their systems accessible, the final rule retains the footnote highlighting the Web Content Accessibility Guidelines (WCAG 2.0) and the regulations implementing the Federal sector accessibility requirements of section 508 of the Rehabilitation Act as examples of readily available accessibility resources.

• *Paragraph (c): Physical and mental qualifications*

The NPRM proposed three substantive revisions to this paragraph. First, it required that all physical and mental job qualification standards must be reviewed and updated, as necessary, on an annual, as opposed to a "periodic," basis. Second, paragraph (c)(1) of the NPRM required the contractor to document its annual review of physical and mental job qualification standards. Third, paragraph (c)(3) of the NPRM required the contractor to timely document those instances in which it believes that an individual would constitute a "direct threat" as understood under the ADA and defined in these regulations, and to maintain this document as set forth in the recordkeeping requirements in § 60–741.80.

OFCCP received 37 comments addressing the proposal to require annual reviews of physical and mental job qualification standards. Comments from disability and other associations, as well as a few law firms, supported the annual review requirement. Some of these commenters stated that all qualifications that needlessly screen out people with disabilities should be reviewed including such qualifications as having a driver's license. Contrasting comments from contractors, employer associations, and other law firms stated that the requirement to review physical and mental qualifications of all jobs with openings during the AAP period would be burdensome because of the number of job openings, variety of jobs, time, staff and needed changes to HR systems. Several comments suggested less burdensome approaches. Most of these comments suggested reviewing the qualifications only when it is a new position or a significant change in the job occurs. Other commenters suggested that reviews occur on a three or five year basis.

With regard to the second proposed change in paragraph (c)(1) requiring that the contractor document its job qualification standard reviews, commenters questioned what evidence will be necessary to demonstrate that a review has been completed, including whether a job analysis and validation are needed. One of these comments noted that the proposed regulation lacks clarity as to how job-relatedness is evidenced and asserted that the ADA practice of examining "essential functions" of a job should be sufficient.

Finally, the third proposed change requires the contractor to timely document those instances in which it believes that an individual would constitute a "direct threat." Comments on this proposal were limited. One comment asserted that this proposed requirement would be burdensome and other comments expressed concern that contractors may become overzealous in documenting incidents involving persons with disabilities. In contrast, another commenter stated that documentation should be subject to disclosure to the individual.

We note at the outset that the existing regulation clearly prohibits the contractor from using a job qualification standard that screens out or tends to screen out an individual or class of individuals on the basis of disability unless the standard is job-related and consistent with business necessity. *See* 41 CFR 60–741.21(g), 60–741.44(c)(2). This is a primary reason that the existing regulations require the contractor to periodically review its physical and mental job qualification standards. To the extent that contractors are not currently conducting these reviews at all, they are already in violation of the existing regulations.

With this in mind, and taking into account commenters' concerns about the burden associated with the proposal, the final rule does not adopt the proposal as drafted in the NPRM. Instead, the final rule retains the language in existing § 60–741.44(c), requiring that contractors adhere to a schedule for the "periodic review of all physical and mental job qualification standards," and providing that contractors have the burden to demonstrate that qualification standards that tend to screen out qualified individuals with disabilities are job-related and consistent with business necessity. The burden analysis in the Regulatory Procedures section of the final rule has been amended accordingly.

• *Paragraph (d): Reasonable accommodation to physical and mental limitations.*

The NPRM proposed a single revision to this provision of the regulations. The proposed change required the contractor to ensure that its electronic or online job application systems are compatible with assistive technology commonly used by individuals with disabilities, such as screen reading and speech recognition software.

Thirteen comments were received on this proposed change. One of these comments asserted that OFCCP should require adoption of a universal design approach or of a regulatory scheme such as section 508. Commenters who opposed the requirement spoke to the potential burden the requirement would impose. One comment submitted by an employer association asserted that OFCCP's proposed change is premature and pointed out that the Department of Justice and the Access Board are currently examining requiring Web site and technology accessibility and the availability of processes or technology to facilitate such access.

OFCCP has revised and clarified this requirement in the final rule, and determined that, as revised, this obligation is more appropriately addressed in § 60–741.21(a)(6)(iii) as part of the fundamental, nondiscrimination reasonable accommodation obligation of all contractors subject to section 503. This revised provision makes clear that the reasonable accommodation obligation extends to contractors' "use of electronic or online application systems." A contractor using such a system must provide necessary reasonable accommodation to "ensure" that qualified individuals with disabilities who are unable to fully utilize the system are provided "equal opportunity to apply and be considered for all jobs."

• *Paragraph (f): Outreach and recruitment efforts*

Existing paragraph (f) requires contractors to engage in outreach and recruitment of individuals with disabilities and suggests a number of outreach and recruitment efforts that the contractor could undertake to comply with this obligation. The NPRM proposed several changes to this paragraph: proposed paragraph (f)(1)(i) required that contractors promptly list all of their employment opportunities, with limited exceptions, with the nearest Employment One-Stop Career Center; paragraph (f)(1)(ii) required that the contractor enter into three linkage agreements with various entities to serve as sources of potential applicants with disabilities; paragraph (f)(2) included a list of additional suggested outreach and recruitment efforts that contractors could take; paragraph (f)(3) proposed a new requirement that the contractor conduct an annual self-assessment of their outreach and recruitment efforts; and paragraph (f)(4) clarified the contractor's recordkeeping obligations with regard to these outreach and recruitment efforts.

Overall, OFCCP received 112 comments on the proposed changes to § 60–741.44(f). While a number of commenters praised OFCCP's efforts to strengthen Federal contractors' recruitment and outreach efforts, the majority of the comments expressed concerns about the proposed requirements. Commenters raised a variety of issues, including concerns about the burden associated with the proposed mandatory requirements, technical questions regarding the drafting of the proposed rule language, and the utility of some of the recommended provisions. We address the proposals in each subparagraph, and the comments to these proposals, in turn below.

Commenters voiced several concerns with the (f)(1)(i) proposed requirement that contractors promptly list all of their employment opportunities with the nearest Employment One-Stop Career Center. Commenters stated that the requirement to provide information about each job vacancy in the manner and format required by the appropriate One-Stop would be extremely burdensome because the One-Stops have a wide variety of different manners of submission and required formats. Some commenters suggested that OFCCP should establish a uniform format and manner for job listings or reestablish the national "job bank" that previously existed under VEVRAA.

As stated above, paragraph (f)(1)(ii) required contractors to enter into three linkage agreements with three different entities: Specifically, the proposal required linkage agreements with (1) the State Vocational Rehabilitation Agency nearest the contractor's establishment or a local organization listed in the Social Security Administration's Ticket to Work Employment Network Directory; (2) at least one of several other listed organizations and agencies for purposes of recruitment and developing training opportunities; and (3) an organization listed in the Employer Resources section of the National Resource Directory (NRD), an online collaboration among the Departments of Labor, Defense, and Veterans Affairs. Commenters expressed concern about the administrative and financial burden related to the linkage agreement requirement. Several commenters also opined that requiring contractors to have three linkage agreements per establishment could result in a Federal contractor with multiple establishments having to enter into hundreds of linkage agreements. Commenters also questioned the capacity of some of the organizations mentioned in the proposed rule to enter into a significant number of linkage agreements with contractors. Additionally, we received comments from contractors that were already party to linkage agreements with various groups. These commenters asked whether they would need to enter into three additional linkage agreements, or if their existing agreements could be used to satisfy the requirement. Some commenters stated that contractors should be allowed the flexibility to develop relationships with potential resource organizations that may better meet their needs but that were not among those listed in the NPRM. Finally, many commenters suggested adding other specific recruitment sources to those listed in the NPRM or on the NRD, such as State developmental disability, and mental health agencies. These commenters also suggested that the NPRM's reference to career offices of educational institutions and private recruitment sources be revised to specify that these be offices and recruitment sources that "specialize in the placement of individuals with disabilities."

In light of these comments, and in order to reduce the burden on contractors, the final rule does not incorporate the proposal to mandate contractors' listing of employment opportunities with the One Stop Career Centers. Additionally, the final rule does not incorporate the proposal to require contractors to enter into linkage agreements. Rather, the final rule retains the existing language of § 60–741.44(f)(1)(i) which requires the contractor to undertake "appropriate outreach and positive recruitment activities," and provides a number of suggested resources, in paragraph (f)(2)(i), that contractors may utilize to carry out this general outreach and recruitment obligation. The final rule also includes, as suggested resources, the Employment One-Stop Career Centers (One-Stops) and American Job Centers, State mental health agencies, and State developmental disability agencies. Additionally, language was added to the recommended resources of "placement or career offices of educational institutions" and "private recruitment sources, such as professional organizations or employment placement services" to clarify that these should be resources "that specialize in the placement of individuals with disabilities."

The final rule's approach requires contractors to engage in outreach and recruitment efforts, but allows each individual contractor the flexibility to choose the specific resources they believe will be most helpful in identifying and attracting protected individuals with disabilities, given their particular needs and circumstances. It will also enhance contractors' capability to switch between and among different resources in order to find and maintain the resource "mix" that is most effective.

Lastly with regard to paragraph (f)(1), several commenters argued that OFCCP underestimated the burden hours associated with complying with the proposed paragraph (f)(1)(iii) (paragraph (f)(1)(ii) in the final rule), which requires the contractor to send written notification of company policy related to its affirmative action efforts to all subcontractors, including subcontracting vendors and suppliers. OFCCP retains this requirement as proposed, as we believe it is crucial to effective implementation and enforcement of the regulations that subcontractors are aware of their section 503 affirmative action obligations. A discussion of commenters' concerns regarding the burden of compliance with this requirement is found in the Regulatory Procedures section of this final rule.

OFCCP received several comments regarding proposed paragraph (f)(2), which set forth additional suggested outreach efforts that contractors could engage in to increase the effectiveness of its recruitment efforts. These comments centered on paragraph (f)(2)(vi), which stated that contractors, in making hiring decisions, "shall" consider applicants who are known individuals with disabilities for all available positions for which they may be qualified when the position(s) applied for is unavailable. Commenters indicated that despite paragraph (f)(2)'s language that it contains "suggested outreach efforts," the word "shall" suggested that the contents of paragraph (f)(2)(vi) were mandatory. The use of "shall" in this paragraph was an inadvertent error in the NPRM. The content of proposed paragraph (f)(2) appears in paragraph (f)(2)(ii) of the final rule. The content of proposed (f)(2)(vi) appears in paragraph (f)(2)(ii)(F) of the final rule, revised to state that contractors "should consider applicants..." We also note that this suggested activity is intended to be a limited one. Contractors who choose to consider individuals with disabilities for jobs other than those for which they applied may exercise discretion to limit this consideration based on geography, the qualifications of the applicant, and other factors. Contractors may also exercise discretion with respect to the time period for which they will consider applicants for other positions. This provision is intended to be flexible and is not required of contractors.

Paragraph (f)(3) of the NPRM proposed to require the contractor, on an annual basis, to review the outreach and recruitment efforts it has undertaken over the previous twelve months and evaluate their effectiveness in identifying and recruiting individuals with disabilities, and document its review. Some commenters supported the proposed requirement, some suggested less frequent review, and others opposed this proposed requirement. Several commenters expressed concern about the utility of the suggested metrics for analyzing external outreach and recruitment efforts. One commenter stated that if the only standard used for assessing outreach and recruitment is the number of individuals with disabilities who are hired, the proposed rule would effectively become a quota system for hiring individuals with disabilities. Another commenter questioned whether overall hiring statistics would provide much useful information about the effectiveness of specific outreach efforts. Commenters also expressed concerns about the requirement to analyze hiring data for the current year as well as the previous two years. Commenters argued that the most recent year is the most relevant year in measuring effectiveness of affirmative action efforts. Finally, commenters also questioned OFCCP's calculation of the cost of compliance with this provision.

OFCCP declines to make changes to the proposed paragraph (f)(3). The purpose of the mandated self-assessment is to ensure that the contractor thinks critically about its recruitment and outreach efforts, and modifies its efforts as needed to ensure that its obligations are being met. OFCCP disagrees that the number of individuals with disabilities who are hired is the "only" standard for analyzing the effectiveness of outreach efforts. The proposed rule made clear that the number of individuals with disabilities who are hired is to be a primary factor considered, given section 503's stated purpose to "employ and advance in employment" individuals with disabilities, but is not the only metric for contractors to use for analyzing the effectiveness of external outreach and recruitment efforts. Rather, as stated in the NPRM, the regulation requires the contractor to consider all the metrics required by § 60–741.44(k) (which includes both applicant and hiring data), and also clearly allows the contractor to consider any other criteria, including factors that are unique to a particular contractor, in determining the effectiveness of its outreach, so long as the criteria are reasonable and documented by the contractor so that OFCCP compliance officers can understand the rationale behind the contractor's self-assessment and the conclusions reached. OFCCP believes that this self-assessment is crucial to the contractor's section 503 affirmative action obligations, and that the final rule provides the contractor a significant amount of flexibility in meeting this requirement.

With regard to the lengthened timeframe of applicant and hire data that the contractor must consider when evaluating its outreach efforts, OFCCP notes that in response to comments, it has reduced this time period from 5 years to 3 years. As explained in the NPRM, the purpose of requiring consideration of additional data for the self-assessment is to provide more complete information with which a contractor can assess the effectiveness of its outreach and recruitment efforts over time. In short, the additional information will enable the contractor and OFCCP to more accurately review outreach and recruitment efforts to ensure that the affirmative action obligations of paragraph (f) are satisfied. Accordingly, we retain paragraph (f)(3) in the final rule as proposed in the NPRM. The comments regarding the burden imposed by this provision, including a revised calculation of its cost, can be found in the Regulatory Procedures section of this final rule.

The final rule makes one minor change to the second to last sentence in paragraph (f)(3). As explained in the preamble to the NPRM, OFCCP proposed that the contractor's conclusion as to the effectiveness of its outreach efforts "shall be reasonable as determined by OFCCP in light of these regulations." The final rule replaces the word "shall" with "must," which more clearly describes the requirement.

• *Paragraph (g): Internal dissemination of affirmative action policy*

Paragraph (g) of the existing rule requires contractors to develop internal procedures to communicate to employees their obligation to engage in affirmative action efforts to employ and advance in employment qualified individuals with disabilities. The NPRM proposed requiring the contractor to undertake many specific actions that are only suggested in the existing rule, including incorporating the affirmative action policy in company policy manuals, discussing the affirmative action policy during management training programs to ensure they are informed about the contractor's obligations, and if the contractor is a party to a collective bargaining agreement, meeting with union officials and employee representatives to inform them of the policy and ask for their cooperation. OFCCP received nine comments regarding § 60–741.44(g), including comments from a disability association, employer associations, contractors, and a law firm.

Several of these comments supported the proposed requirement, while others sought some clarification, and still others indicated that the requirement imposed an unnecessary burden.

Some commenters requested alternative options to including the affirmative action policy in the contractor's policy manual pursuant to the proposed 60–741.44(g)(2)(i). One commenter suggested instead, for example, that contractors be permitted to post the policy on the company's intranet where similar human resources and EEO pronouncements are found. One comment requested that OFCCP clarify how contractors could post their policy in the absence of having a policy manual.

The final rule adopts the proposed language in § 60–741.44(g)(1) without change. This paragraph sets out the general requirement that contractors internally disseminate their affirmative action policy and explains the reasons for the requirement. It clearly states that the procedures for internally disseminating affirmative action policies "shall be designed to foster understanding, acceptance and support among the contractor's executive, management, supervisory and other employees and to encourage such persons to take the necessary actions to aid the contractor in meeting this obligation."

The remainder of paragraph (g) is streamlined and revised in the final rule to ease the burden on contractors, while ensuring that contractors must communicate their affirmative action obligations and policies internally. Two of the three actions the NPRM proposed in paragraph (g)(2) are maintained as requirements in paragraph (g)(2) of the final rule: (1) including the policy in the contractor's policy manual; and (2) informing union officials of the policy and requesting their cooperation, if the contractor is party to a collective bargaining agreement. However, these requirements are modified slightly, based on the comments received. The first has been modified to allow contractors to include the affirmative action policy either in the contractor's policy manual, or to "otherwise make the policy available to employees." We believe that most companies generally have some form of document that provides guidance on human resources policies and procedures—either a policy manual, employee handbook, or similar document—that is available to employees that is an appropriate place to put the policy. OFCCP believes including the affirmative action policy in these documents will enhance the visibility of the contractor's commitment to individuals with disabilities. However, the final rule also allows contractors the flexibility to make the policy available to its employees through other means. This could include posting the policy on a company intranet, but this will only fulfill the requirement if all employees have access to this intranet. The second requirement, regarding informing union officials, is modified for consistency and clarity to reflect the requirement in § 60–741.5(a)(5) that the contractor "notify" union officials of its policy.

The remaining elements that were required in the NPRM or suggested in the existing rule now appear in paragraph (g)(3) of the final rule as actions that the contractor is "encouraged" to take. The recordkeeping provision that was in proposed paragraph (g)(3) is eliminated in the final rule. We note, however, that to the extent any activities undertaken pursuant to paragraph (g) involve the creation of records, they are subject to the general recordkeeping requirement of § 60–741.80 and contractors will be required to maintain such documents as specified by § 60–741.80.

• *Paragraph (h): Audit and reporting system for affirmative action program*

Paragraph (h) of the existing rule outlines the contractor's responsibility to design and implement an audit and reporting system for the company's AAP. It also requires, in paragraph (h)(2), that contractors undertake necessary action to bring deficient programs into compliance. The NPRM proposed a new requirement that contractors document the actions taken to comply with paragraph (h). The NPRM also proposed that contractors maintain the records of their documentation subject to the recordkeeping requirements of § 60–741.80. OFCCP received nine comments on this provision. Of these, seven asserted that the proposed recordkeeping requirement would be burdensome and require the development of new processes, while two supported this requirement recognizing the need for and benefits of self-audits.

This section is adopted into the final rule as proposed. The section requires the contractor to measure the effectiveness of its affirmative action program, indicate any need for remedial action, determine the degree to which the contractor's objectives have been attained, determine whether individuals with disabilities have had the opportunity to participate in all company professional and social activities, and measure the contractor's compliance with the affirmative action program's specific obligations. OFCCP believes that the proper conduct of the analysis required in paragraph (h) will necessitate the creation of documentation. Paragraph (h)(1)(vi) makes this expectation clear by requiring that the contractor document the actions it takes to comply with self-audit requirements of paragraph (h)(i). Contractors are further required to maintain this documentation in accordance with the recordkeeping requirements of § 60–741.80. OFCCP believes that this requirement will allow for a more effective assessment, by contractors and by OFCCP, of whether the contractor is meeting its affirmative action obligations, including whether deficiencies have been identified and corrected.

• *Paragraph (i): Responsibility for implementation*

The NPRM proposed to modify existing paragraph (i) to require that the identity of the official responsible for a contractor's affirmative action activities appear on all internal and external communications regarding the contractor's affirmative action program. Upon further review, OFCCP does not believe that the benefit of this suggested change outweighs the potential burden that it would place on contractors. Accordingly, the final rule restores the text of the existing regulation, which states that the identity of the official responsible for a contractor's affirmative action activities "should" appear in all communications about the contractor's affirmative action program.

• *Paragraph (j): Training*

Paragraph (j) of the existing regulation requires that the contractor train "[a]ll personnel involved in the recruitment, screening, selection, promotion, disciplinary and related processes . . . to ensure that the commitments in the contractor's affirmative action program are implemented." The NPRM proposed revising this paragraph to specify topics required to be included in this training, including: the business and societal benefits of employing individuals with disabilities; appropriate sensitivity toward recruits, applicants, and employees with disabilities; and the legal responsibilities of the contractor and its agents regarding individuals with disabilities, including the obligation to provide reasonable accommodation to qualified individuals with disabilities. The NPRM also proposed requiring the contractor to record which of its personnel receive this training, when they receive it, and the person(s) who administered the training, and to maintain these records, along with all written or electronic training materials used, pursuant to the recordkeeping requirements of § 60–741.80.

OFCCP received 15 comments from disability and employer associations, contractors, and a law firm. Approximately half of the comments supported the proposed requirements, while the others opposed it. These latter comments raised concerns regarding the burden that training requirements place on contractors and the manner in which OFCCP calculated it. One comment noted specific concerns about what constitutes "sensitivity" training. Several commenters suggested that OFCCP develop a model training for contractors to use, instead of the contractor having to create additional training to what it currently provides.

In light of these concerns, and balancing the utility of the proposal against the burden that it would create for contractors, the final rule does not incorporate the NPRM proposal requiring specific training topics and the maintenance of all training materials pursuant to § 60–741.80. Instead, the final rule retains the existing rule's general requirement that "[a]ll personnel involved in the recruitment, screening, selection, promotion, disciplinary, and related processes" must be trained to ensure that the contractor's affirmative action commitments are implemented. However, we note that documents created by the contractor in connection with activities undertaken pursuant to paragraph (j) are subject to the general recordkeeping requirement of § 60–741.80.

• *Paragraph (k): Data Collection Analysis*

The proposed regulation added paragraph (k) to the rule, proposing to require that the contractor document and update annually the following information: (1) For referral data, the number of referrals of individuals with disabilities received from entities with which the contractor has a linkage agreement and the number of referrals of individuals with disabilities received from employment service delivery systems; (2) for applicant data, the total number of applicants for employment, the number of applicants who are known individuals with disabilities, and the "applicant ratio" of known individuals with disabilities who are applicants to total applicants; (3) for hiring data, the total number of job openings, the number of jobs filled, the number of known individuals with disabilities hired, and the "hiring ratio" of known individuals with disabilities to total hires; and (4) the total number of job openings, the number of jobs that are filled, and the "job fill ratio" of job openings to job openings filled.

The NPRM stated that OFCCP is also considering adding a reporting requirement, and invited public comment on this option. Under this proposal, contractors would be required to provide OFCCP with a report containing the measurements and computations required by proposed paragraph (k), including the percentage of applicants, new hires, and total workforce for each EEO–1 category. The report would be provided to OFCCP on an annual basis, regardless of whether the contractor has been selected for a compliance evaluation.

As stated in the NPRM, the impetus behind this new section is that no structured data regarding the number of individuals with disabilities who are referred for or apply for jobs with Federal contractors is currently maintained. This absence of data makes it nearly impossible for the contractor and OFCCP to perform even rudimentary evaluations of the availability of individuals with disabilities in the workforce, or to make any sort of objective, data-based assessments of how effective contractor outreach and recruitment efforts have been in attracting individuals with disabilities as candidates. Maintaining this information will provide meaningful data to assist the contractor in evaluating and tailoring its recruitment and outreach efforts.

OFCCP received a total of 80 comments from disability, contractor and other associations, law firms, government offices, contractors, and individuals. Disability and other associations, and some contractors and individuals that commented supported the required data collection and the objectives behind it. The contractor community, by and large, opposed the proposal on varying grounds, including: concerns regarding the integrity of the data to be collected (particularly data on referrals); assertions that some of the data conflicts with the Internet Applicant Rule in the Executive Order regulations; and assertions that collecting, analyzing, and maintaining the data would be unduly burdensome. Several commenters from the construction and transportation industries asserted that they should be exempt from the requirement due to the unique nature of their respective industries. Finally, a number of commenters sought clarification of some of the processes set forth in paragraph (k). These issues are addressed below.

Several comments articulated data integrity concerns regarding the data to be used in calculating the referral ratio. Commenters characterized the state employment service delivery systems as "self-service," leaving source identification to the job candidates, thus making referral data unreliable and not meaningful. Examples were provided indicating that individuals frequently apply directly online with a company and may fail to identify that he or she was referred, and that he or she is an individual with a disability. These commenters also expressed concern that referral data may include referrals of individuals that are not qualified for the position(s) at issue. OFCCP believes that the points raised regarding the practical utility of the referral data have merit. Accordingly, OFCCP has eliminated from the final rule the requirement, in proposed paragraphs (k)(1) and (k)(2), for contractors to collect, maintain, and analyze information on the number of referrals it receives.

Many of these comments also asserted data integrity concerns regarding the requirement to document and maintain applicant and hiring ratios, including that applicant data appears to be dependent upon self-identification, which is not reliable. These issues were previously addressed in the discussion of the requirement to invite applicants to self-identify as individuals with disabilities in § 60–741.42(a). In short, demographic data based on self-identification is not perfect, but it is nonetheless valuable and the best data that is available.

Another concern asserted by commenters is that the proposed data collection and analysis is not "aligned" with the availability analysis conducted when examining employment activities for females and minorities. However, as discussed in the preamble to the goal requirement in § 60–741.45, below, it is not feasible to have the data collection for section 503 exactly mirror that of the Executive Order 11246 regulations.

Commenters also questioned the purpose of the job opening/job filled ratio. Upon reconsideration, OFCCP agrees that it is not necessary for contractors to calculate the job fill ratio and has deleted from the final rule the requirement, in proposed paragraph (k)(5), for contractors to calculate and maintain the ratio of jobs filled to job openings. OFCCP has also eliminated the requirement to calculate an applicant ratio in proposed paragraph (k)(7), and the requirement to calculate a hiring ratio in proposed paragraph (k)(10). Thus, the final rule requires that contractors need only collect and maintain the raw data regarding the number of applicants with disabilities, the total number of job openings and jobs filled, the total number of applicants, the number of applicants with disabilities hired, and the total number of applicants hired.

Several commenters also objected to the collection of data about the disability status of applicants because it differs from the recordkeeping requirements related to Internet applicants under the Executive Order 11246 implementing regulations at 41 CFR 60–1.12. In recognition of these concerns, and as explained in the preamble discussion of § 60–741.42(a), in an effort to harmonize requirements across the various regulations OFCCP enforces, OFCCP will permit contractors to invite applicants to self-identify as an individual with a disability at the same time as the contractor collects the demographic data for applicants required under the Executive Order. OFCCP will also treat the recordkeeping provisions of section 503 at 41 CFR 60–741.80 in the same manner as the recordkeeping requirements under the Executive Order at 41 CFR 60–1.12 as applied to Internet applicants. With regard to burden calculation issues, many commenters, including employer associations, contractors, and individuals, indicated that OFCCP had not correctly calculated the burden of this section. Specific cost information was provided by several commenters. A revised burden calculation is included in the Regulatory Procedures section of this final rule. We highlight a few points here, however, because it appears that the contractor community may misunderstand portions of the obligation they are expected to undertake. First, as stated above, the referral data metrics have been eliminated, which reduces the burden. We have also eliminated the calculation of the job fill, applicant, and hiring ratios. Second, job-specific hiring data is already collected and maintained by contractors pursuant to the Executive Order 11246 program. Moreover, hiring metrics are also maintained and calculated by Federal contractors subject to VEVRAA pursuant to their existing obligation, under 41 CFR part 61–300, to file the VETS–100A form. Therefore, that portion of paragraph (k) requiring contractors to document the total number of job openings and total number of hires does not create any additional burden. The only "new" items are those pertaining to the self-identification applicant data. However, the burden for collecting and maintaining the applicant data is already partially calculated under § 60–741.42(a).

Also pertaining to burden, commenters for the construction and transportation industries asserted that they should be exempted from this section of the proposed regulation because of the unique nature of the industries. Traditionally, construction and transportation contractors who meet the basic coverage thresholds (contract amount and number of employees) of section 503 have not been exempted from any of its provisions. Accordingly, we decline to exempt construction and transportation contractors.

The majority of commenters also cited burden concerns with the proposed requirement to maintain the paragraph (k) computations for a period of five (5) years. As set forth in the discussions of § 60–741.44(f)(4) and § 60–741.80 herein, the final rule reduces the document retention requirement to three (3) years, and revises the language of paragraph (k) to reflect this change.

A few of the comments also raised clarification questions we would like to address, including: (1) Whether the intent of the analyses is to measure change from year to year; (2) whether the ratios should be run by job group, job title, or establishment; and (3) how compliance determinations will be made. As to the first question, measuring change from year to year, and looking at two previous years of data, is a central intent of the analyses, as that can aid the contractor in seeing trends that may be associated with certain of its outreach and recruitment efforts over time. However, as previously discussed with regard to the self-assessment required in paragraph (f)(3) of this section, contractors are also free to use any other reasonable criteria in addition to the applicant and hiring data they feel is relevant to evaluate the effectiveness of its efforts. As to the second question, the ratios in paragraph (k) will be calculated by establishment, and not by job groups or titles within a given establishment, unless OFCCP has approved the contractor's development and use of a functional affirmative action program (FAAP) pursuant to 41 CFR 60–2.1(d)(4).

With regard to the third question, compliance determinations for paragraph (k) will be made based simply on whether the contractor has completely and accurately documented and maintained the eight listed metrics in the final rule. OFCCP Compliance Officers will not be using the applicant and hiring data to conduct underutilization or impact ratio analyses, as is the case under Executive Order 11246, and enforcement actions will not be brought solely on the basis of statistical disparities between individuals with, and without, disabilities in this data. Rather, Compliance Officers will look to see whether the contractor has fulfilled its various obligations under § 60–741.44, including its obligation, pursuant to § 60–741.44(f)(3), to critically analyze and assess the effectiveness of its recruitment efforts, using the data in paragraph (k) and any other reasonable criteria the contractor believes is relevant, and has pursued different or additional recruitment efforts if the contractor concludes that its efforts were not effective.

On the topic of OFCCP's invitation for public comments regarding the possible addition of a new annual reporting requirement, we received 20 comments. The majority of these comments asserted that the proposed requirement would impose an unnecessary additional burden. Several commenters stated that OFCCP did not provide any support or justification for proposing the requirement. A few of these commenters indicated that such a report would serve no other purpose than to assist OFCCP in the scheduling of compliance reviews. A few commenters supported the proposed reporting requirement, asserting that the data is needed to better ensure equal employment opportunities for individuals with disabilities. After weighing the practical utility of this potential reporting requirement against its anticipated burden OFCCP has determined that the imposition of this new reporting requirement is not warranted at this time. Accordingly, this proposal is not adopted into the final rule.

Section 60–741.45 Reasonable Accommodation Procedures

The NPRM proposed a new provision at § 60–741.45 requiring contractors to develop and implement written procedures for processing requests for reasonable accommodation. The proposal identified specific elements that the contractor's reasonable accommodation procedures, at a minimum, would be required to address. These included: (1) contact information for the official responsible for implementation of the procedures; (2) to whom a request for reasonable accommodation may be made; (3) a statement that requests for reasonable accommodation may be made orally or in writing by an applicant, employee, or third party on his or her behalf; (4) written confirmation of receipt of a reasonable accommodation request; (5) a timeframe for the processing of reasonable accommodation requests; (6) a description of the contractor's reasonable accommodation process and circumstances under which the contractor may request medical documentation to support a reasonable accommodation request; and (7) provision of a written explanation by the contractor for any denials of reasonable accommodation.

OFCCP received 80 comments on this proposal from disability associations, employer associations, contractors, and law firms. The disability associations were strongly supportive of the proposed requirement. They asserted that it would foster contractor understanding of their reasonable accommodation obligation, encourage individuals who need reasonable accommodation to come forward and make a request, and promote efficiency in the processing of reasonable accommodation requests. Many of these commenters also recommended that the scope of the proposed requirement be expanded to encompass all Federal contractors subject to section 503 by relocating the requirement from the "affirmative action" subpart of the regulations (Subpart C) to the "nondiscrimination" subpart of the regulations (Subpart B).

In contrast, the majority of the contractor community objected to the new requirement for a variety of reasons. Many stated their belief that a mandated, "formal" process was unnecessary since most employers were already accustomed to making reasonable accommodations as required by the ADA. Some characterized the proposal as a "one size fits all" approach that would impede the ability of contractors to individually address reasonable accommodation requests, and to grant requests for accommodation informally (e.g., leave time for doctor visits or a modified work schedule to attend therapy sessions). Finally, commenters asserted that the requirement to develop written reasonable accommodation procedures, to provide written confirmation of reasonable accommodation requests, and to provide written explanations of any denials of reasonable accommodation was unduly burdensome.

Upon further consideration of the burden associated with this provision, OFCCP has decided not to incorporate this proposal into the final rule. OFCCP, however, notes in new paragraph (d)(2) to § 60–741.44 of the final rule, that the use of written reasonable accommodation procedures is a best practice that may assist contractors in meeting their reasonable accommodation obligations. The paragraph makes clear that contractors are not required to have or use such procedures, and that not having such procedures is not violation of this part. OFCCP has also added a new Appendix B entitled *Developing Reasonable Accommodation Procedures* providing specific guidance that contractors may use should they choose to adopt this best practice.

Although OFCCP is not incorporating the written reasonable accommodation procedures requirement into the final rule, we wish to note our disagreement with those commenters who assert that written procedures would prevent contractors from individually addressing reasonable accommodation requests. Rather, we believe that having such procedures would serve to reinforce the obligation to individually address each person's request for reasonable accommodation. Moreover, in OFCCP's view, written reasonable accommodation procedures would not hamper a contractor's ability to informally grant accommodation requests, such as leave for visits to the doctor or a modified work schedule to attend therapy sessions. If a contractor has flexible leave or scheduling policies, having written reasonable accommodation procedures would not interfere with the granting of requests for leave or modified work schedules by employees with disabilities simply because the request is made to accommodate a disability.

Section 60–741.46 Utilization Goals

Section 60–741.46 of the NPRM (renumbered as § 60–741.45 in the final rule) proposed a single, national 7 percent utilization goal for individuals with disabilities for each job group in a contractor's workforce. It proposed that covered contractors annually evaluate the representation of individuals with disabilities in each job group in the contractor's workforce against the 7 percent utilization goal. If the percentage of employees with disabilities in one or more job groups is less than the 7 percent utilization goal, the NPRM proposed that the contractor develop and execute action-oriented programs designed to correct any identified barriers to equal employment opportunity for qualified individuals with disabilities. Although it proposed a 7 percent goal, the NPRM invited the public to comment on a range of goal values between 4 percent and 10 percent. In addition, the NPRM alerted the public that OFCCP was considering an option of a sub-goal of 2 percent for individuals with certain particularly severe disabilities as part of the overall 7 percent goal, and invited public comment on this sub-goal option. Specifically, OFCCP requested comment on the concept of a sub-goal, as well as the disabilities to be included in the sub-goal.

OFCCP received 250 comments on this section from a broad range of perspectives, including contractors, law firms, government agencies, organizations representing individuals with disabilities and those representing contractors, as well as from individuals. The comments represented divergent views on the institution of a single, national utilization goal. In general, the disability community and those representing their interests were strongly in support of this new requirement. For these commenters, affirmative action efforts under section 503 have been largely meaningless without, among other things, measurable goals for the employment of people with disabilities. By and large, these commenters urged OFCCP to increase the utilization goal from 7 percent to 10 percent and to adopt a sub-goal of 5 percent for individuals with severe disabilities. In contrast, commenters from the contractor community and those representing their interests were largely opposed to this provision and to the sub-goal option for various reasons, including: (1) OFCCP lacks authority to mandate the 7 percent goal; (2) the utilization goal is equivalent to a quota; (3) use of ACS data is arbitrary and ineffective; and (4) the goal approach is unworkable as proposed. The proposed utilization goal, comments to the proposal, and the subsequent revisions made in the final rule are discussed in turn below. Comments related to the burden estimates associated with this section are addressed in the Regulatory Procedures section of the final rule.

• *Paragraph (a): Establishment of a single, national utilization goal*

Paragraph (a) of the NPRM proposed to establish for the first time a single, national utilization goal of 7 percent for employment of individuals with disabilities for each job group within a contractor's workforce.[19] As explained in the NPRM, the current section 503 regulatory framework requires affirmative action but lacks a goal. This has been the case since the initial publication of the section 503 regulations in the 1970s, but the intervening years have seen little improvement in the unemployment and workforce participation rates of individuals with disabilities. OFCCP determined that affirmative action process requirements, without a quantifiable means of assessing whether progress toward equal employment opportunity is occurring, are insufficient. We therefore concluded that the establishment of a utilization goal would create more accountability within the contractor's organization and provide a much-needed tool to help ensure that progress toward equal employment opportunity is achieved.

• *Methodology for Setting the Utilization Goal*

As explained in the NPRM, the utilization goal established in this section is derived primarily from the disability data collected as part of the American Community Survey. The American Community Survey (ACS) was designed to replace the census "long form" of the decennial census, last sent out to U.S. households in 2000, to gather information regarding the demographic, socioeconomic and housing characteristics of the nation. Whereas the Census Bureau now only administers a very short survey for the decennial census, a more detailed view of the social and demographic characteristics of the population is provided by the ACS, which collects data from a sample of 3 million residents on a continuing basis.[20]

The ACS was first launched in 2005, after a decade of testing and development by the Census Bureau. Refinement of the questions designed to characterize disability status has been continuous, with the current set of disability-related questions incorporated into the ACS in 2008. Taken together, the six dichotomous ("yes" or "no") disability-related questions[21] comprise a function-based definition of "disability," used in the ACS and by most of the other major surveys administered by the Federal Statistical System.

The definition of disability used by the ACS, however, is clearly not as broad as that of the Rehabilitation Act and the ADA. For example, since the ACS questions do not say that one should respond without considering mitigating measures (*e.g.*, medication or aids), some individuals with disabilities that are well-controlled by medication (*e.g.*, depression or epilepsy) or in

[19] OFCCP received several comments seeking clarification of the difference between a utilization goal and a placement goal. A placement or hiring goal relates to the percentage of new hires from a particular group, such as individuals with disabilities. In contrast, a utilization goal relates to the percentage of a contractor's workforce represented by a particular group, in this instance, individuals with disabilities.

[20] A national sample of approximately 3 million addresses nationwide receives the ACS each year, with a portion of this total receiving the survey each month. For more information on the American Community Service visit the Census Bureau's ACS Web page at *www.census.gov/acs*.

[21] The six questions are: Is this person deaf or does he/she have serious difficulty hearing? Is this person blind or does he/she have serious difficulty seeing even when wearing glasses? Because of a physical, mental, or emotional condition, does this person have serious difficulty concentrating, remembering, or making decisions? Does this person have serious difficulty walking or climbing stairs? Does this person have difficulty dressing or bathing? Because of a physical, mental, or emotional condition, does this person have difficulty doing errands alone such as visiting a doctor's office or shopping? 2009 American Community Survey, Questions 17–19.

remission might respond to the ACS that he or she does not have a disability. Likewise, since the ACS questions do not include major bodily functions, an individual who has a disability that substantially limits a major bodily function, but does not limit a major life activity as originally defined in the ADA, might respond that he or she does not have a disability on the ACS. Despite its limitations, the ACS is the best source of nationwide disability data available today, and, thus, an appropriate starting place for developing a utilization goal.

In developing the utilization goal, OFCCP considered two general approaches. The first approach OFCCP considered aimed to mirror precisely the goals framework for minorities and women that is used by supply and service (non-construction) contractors subject to Executive Order (EO) 11246. Such an approach would have required individual contractor establishments to set their own goals for each of their job groups [22] based on the percentage of individuals with disabilities available in the particular recruitment area from which the contractor sought to fill the jobs in the job group. Where there are fewer than expected incumbent employees with disabilities in a job group given their availability percentage, a contractor would be required to establish a goal for the specific job group that is at least equal to the availability percentage in the job group's recruitment area. *See* 41 CFR 60–2.12—60–2.16 for a more detailed description of the EO 11246 goals provisions for supply and service contractors.

After careful consideration of the available data and consultation with the U.S. Census Bureau regarding the level of geographic aggregation at which the disability data could be analyzed, OFCCP became convinced that replicating the supply and service goals framework would not be the most effective approach for the establishment of goals for individuals with disabilities. Supply and service contractors establishing goals for minorities and women typically use the Special EEO Tabulation of census data to assist them. The results of the 2000 decennial census can be tabulated for 472 occupation categories and thousands of geographic areas. However, because the ACS disability data is based on sampling, and because the percentage of that sample who identify as having a disability is considerably smaller than the percentage that provide race and gender information, it cannot be broken down into as many job titles, or as many geographic areas as the data for race and gender. That is, the confidence intervals on such estimates are large and the estimates are not statistically significant when broken down to the degree of detail required by the supply and service goals framework. Contractors therefore would not be able to use the job groups established under Executive Order 11246 to establish goals for individuals with disabilities, and would often be unable to utilize the geographic recruitment areas established under the Executive Order when determining the availability of individuals with disabilities (as queried in the ACS).[23] In addition, the Executive Order supply and service goals framework does not include consideration of discouraged workers in computing availability, a factor particularly important in the context of disability, as discussed below.

In light of the difficulties replicating the supply and service goals approach in the context of disability, OFCCP considered other options. OFCCP concluded that the establishment of a single, national goal [24] for all jobs in all geographic areas is a more viable approach to the establishment of a goal for individuals with disabilities. This approach allows for the continued use of the contractor's Executive Order 11246 job groups, and requires that those job groups be used to measure the representation of individuals with disabilities in the contractor's workforce, except in cases of contractors with fewer than 100 employees, where contractors will have the option to apply the goal to their workforce as a whole. The goal established in this section is based on the 2009 ACS disability data for the "civilian labor force" and the "civilian population," [25] first averaged by EEO–1 job category, and then averaged across EEO–1 category totals. Specifically, we used the mean across these EEO–1 groups to estimate that 5.7 percent of the civilian labor force has a disability as defined by the ACS.[26] However, OFCCP acknowledges that this number does not encompass all individuals with disabilities as defined under the broader definition in section 503 and the ADAAA. Therefore, 5.7 percent is an insufficient figure to use as an affirmative action goal for individuals with disabilities under section 503.

Even if the 5.7 percent represented a complete availability figure for all individuals with disabilities as defined under section 503, such an availability figure does not take into account discouraged workers, or the effects of historical discrimination against individuals with disabilities that has suppressed the representation of such individuals in the workforce. Discouraged workers are those individuals who are not now seeking

---

[22] Job groups usually contain one to three jobs each. However, contractors with fewer than 150 employees may use the broader EEO–1 job categories in place of smaller job groups.

[23] On November 29, 2012, the Census Bureau released the new 2006–2010 EEO Tabulation (EEO Tab) to the public. The new EEO Tab replaces the 2000 Special EEO Tabulation. It is based on five years of demographic data from the ACS, rather than on a decennial census, tabulates data for 488 occupations including several occupations not previously included in the 2000 Special EEO Tabulation, and includes data by citizenship status. The EEO Tab is online at *http://www.census.gov/people/eeotabulation/*.

On March 14, 2013, the Census Bureau launched the first of its kind 2008–2010 Disability Employment Tabulation (Disability Tab) containing statistical information regarding the employment status, earnings, race, ethnicity and occupations of individuals with disabilities. The Disability Tab, online at *http://www.census.gov/people/disabilityemptab/data*, was sponsored by the U.S. Department of Labor and, in contrast to the EEO Tab, is intended to be a research resource rather than an enforcement tool. Although the Disability Tab includes data for each occupation in the EEO Tab, important differences between the tabs make the Disability Tab impractical for contractors to use to set individual placement goals for each of their Executive Order job groups. These differences include: (1) the Disability Tab uses three years of ACS data rather than the five years used in the EEO Tab; (2) the geographical designations of "county sets" and "places" (cities) are used in the EEO Tab but not in the Disability Tab; (3) the geographical designation of public use microareas (PUMAs) are used in the Disability Tab but not in the EEO Tab; and (4) the citizen-only tables in the Disability Tab contain occupation-specific data solely at the national level. In light of these differences, were we to require the establishment of individual disability placement goals using the Disability Tab many contractors would be forced to identify and utilize recruitment areas for this purpose different from those they currently use when establishing individual Executive Order goals. The creation of such a "parallel" process for the establishment of disability goals would be far more burdensome for contractors than the single, national utilization goal process established in this final rule.

[24] Disability rates by State for the civilian labor force has a mean of 6.32, median of 6.20, and standard deviation of 1.29. There are only two states, Alaska (9.0%) and Oklahoma (9.5%) that are outside the 95% confidence interval of this otherwise almost uniform distribution. This general uniformity is consistent with the use of a single national goal. See Table 15 in *Affirmative Action for People with Disabilities—Volume I: Data Sources and Models*, Economic Systems, Inc. (April 30, 2010) at 55.

[25] The civilian labor force is the sum of people who are employed and those who are unemployed and looking for work. The civilian population is the civilian labor force plus civilians who are not in the labor force, excluding those in institutions.

[26] Similarly, the Disability Tab found that between 2008 and 2010 individuals with disabilities were 6% of the civilian labor force. See Census Bureau press release, *Workers with a Disability Less Likely to be Employed, More Likely to Hold Jobs with Lower Earnings, Census Bureau Reports*, (March 14, 2013) available online at *http://www.census.gov/newsroom/releases/archives/american_community_survey_acs/cb13-47.html*.

employment, but who might do so in the absence of discrimination or other employment barriers. There are undoubtedly some individuals with disabilities who, for a variety of reasons, would not seek employment even in the absence of employment barriers. However, given the acute disparity in the workforce participation rates of those with and without disabilities, it is reasonable to assume that at least a portion of that gap is due to a lack of equal employment opportunity.

To estimate the size of the discouraged worker effect, we compared the percent of the civilian population with a disability (per the ACS definition) who identified as having an occupation to the percent of the civilian labor force with a disability who identified as having an occupation. Though not currently seeking employment, it is reasonable to believe that those in the civilian population who identify as having an occupation, but who are currently not in the labor force, remain interested in working should job opportunities become available. Using the 2009 ACS EEO–1 category data, the result of this comparison is 1.7 percent.[27]

Adding this figure to the 5.7 percent availability figure above, resulted in 7.4 percent.[28] The national utilization goal prescribed in this section is derived from this total, rounded to 7 percent to avoid implying a false level of precision.

• *Comments on paragraph (a)*

Many of the comments received on the proposed utilization goal addressed OFCCP's methodology for arriving at the 7 percent availability estimate, including the use of a discouraged worker estimate within the 7 percent figure. In general, commenters in favor of the proposed single, national utilization goal accepted the methodology used by OFCCP to derive the goal but urged OFCCP to increase the goal from 7 percent to 10 percent given that the ACS data upon which the goal is based is only partially representative of those covered by section 503. As confirmation that the 7 percent figure is too low, these commenters referred to the Final Regulatory Impact Analysis for the EEOC regulations implementing the ADA Amendments Act which estimated that somewhere between 20 percent and 64 percent of individuals covered by the ADA as amended participate in the labor force. Given this estimate, the commenters stated that OFCCP ought to aim higher than 7 percent. Within OFCCP's suggested range of between 4 percent and 10 percent, these commenters urged the goal be set at 10 percent.

With regard to OFCCP's use of the discouraged worker effect, commenters in favor of the proposal noted that discouraged workers are those who have not looked for work not because they lack the desire to work, but rather because they believe that no work is available for them. The goal requirement should reflect the assumption that new outreach and recruiting efforts will have some effect in correcting the notion among discouraged workers that no jobs are available for individuals with disabilities. A number of these commenters also noted that the 1.7 percent estimate used by OFCCP is likely under-inclusive since the value was derived from the ACS data.

OFCCP declines to adopt a 10 percent goal at this time. We recognize that 7 percent is an imprecise estimate based on a data set that is more narrow than the universe of individuals with disabilities protected under section 503. However, as explained above, this figure is derived from the best available source of workforce disability data that presently exists. In contrast, the 10 percent figure urged by many of the commenters is based solely on the general notion that 7 percent is too low, in light of the differing definitions of "disability" in the ACS and the ADA, and the EEOC's general estimate that somewhere between 20 percent and 64 percent of individuals covered by the ADA participate in the labor force. The commenters, however, did not suggest an alternative data base from which OFCCP could derive an appropriate utilization goal. Nor does the EEOC estimate, which juxtaposes the workforce participation rate of individuals with disabilities with the overall workforce participation rate for all adults (with and without a disability) age 16 and older, provide sufficiently specific information on which OFCCP could rationally base a utilization goal for individuals with disabilities. Indeed, EEOC did not use this estimate for such a purpose. See 76 FR 16978, 16991 (March 25, 2011). Having said that, as indicated in the final rule at § 60–741.45(c), OFCCP will periodically review and update the utilization goal as data becomes more refined.

A substantial number of commenters from the contractor community objected to the proposed 7 percent utilization goal on the grounds that it is arbitrary. They argued that the 7 percent figure is based on ACS data that is based on a definition of "disability" that is narrower than the term used under section 503. Without consistent definitions, they argue, the results are meaningless for establishing a goal for utilization of individuals with disabilities. Furthermore, the figure fails to take into account variations in occupational requirements, geography, industry, and nature of disabilities. Many commenters asserted that there is no statistical evidence to support the idea that the population of those with disabilities is distributed equally across all geographic areas. Additionally, one commenter noted that across the board goals are unrealistic because certain job groups will have inherent limitations. The commenter noted that there are some jobs for which some individuals with certain disabilities will never qualify. For instance, a person who is blind, deaf, or paralyzed would not be granted a commercial pilot's license by the Federal Aviation Administration. Given these variations, even the best intentioned contractor may have significant challenges meeting the utilization goal across all job groups.

Still other commenters were opposed to applying a national goal to each job group because the goal as proposed represents an aggregate availability for individuals with disabilities across EEO category totals. Applying a number that represents the average availability across all categories to individual job groups would, thus, be inappropriate. Many of these commenters argued that OFCCP should delay imposing a utilization goal requirement until such time that data is available to enable goal setting in a manner similar to what is done under the EO 11246 supply and service affirmative action program.

Finally, several commenters expressed concern about OFCCP's discouraged worker estimate. These commenters questioned the accuracy of the estimate and posited that many of those discouraged are not actually interested in employment at all. They state that the most obvious explanation for an individual's departure from the workforce is the disability itself. One commenter also objected to OFCCP inclusion in the goal of a 1.7 percent figure to account for individuals with disabilities who have become discouraged workers and for the effects of historical discrimination. This commenter stated that the Bureau of Labor Statistics reports discouraged workers with disabilities account for only 0.1 percent of the workforce.

[27] This number was derived from an updated 2009 version of Table 24 in *Affirmative Action for People with Disabilities—Volume I: Data Sources and Models*, Economic Systems, Inc. (April 30, 2010) at 64. The original table uses ACS data from 2008.

[28] As it is derived from ACS data, the 1.7% is also a limited number that does not fully encompass all individuals with disabilities as defined in section 503 and the ADA.

OFCCP recognizes that the 7 percent figure is less precise than the geographically specific availability information that contractors are familiar with under the Executive Order 11246 program, and that for some jobs in some locations availability of qualified individuals may be less than 7 percent. Furthermore, we recognize that the ACS data is based on a definition of disability that is narrower than that used under section 503. We disagree, however, that this is sufficient reason to eliminate the utilization goal. While not perfect, the goal will provide a yardstick against which contractors will be able to measure the effectiveness of their equal employment opportunity efforts. It is our belief that the goal will enable contractors to think critically about their employment practices, including their outreach, recruitment, and retention efforts, and help them to assess whether and where any barriers to equal employment opportunity for individuals with disabilities remain. If barriers are identified, then the contractor can move to take corrective action. Because the goal is intended solely as a tool, the final rule clearly states that a failure to meet the goal will not, in and of itself, result in a violation of section 503 or a finding of discrimination. The goal is not a rigid and inflexible quota which must be met, nor is it to be considered either a ceiling or a floor for the employment of particular groups. OFCCP will look at the totality of the contractor's affirmative action efforts to determine whether it is in compliance with its affirmative action obligations under this section. As discussed below, if the contractor has complied with the requirements of this part and no impediments to equal employment opportunity exist, then the fact that the contractor does not meet the goal will not result in a violation.

With regard to commenter concerns regarding the use of the discouraged worker effect, more than twenty years after the passage of the ADA and nearly forty years after the passage of the Rehabilitation Act, there continues to be a substantial discrepancy between the workforce participation and unemployment rates of working age [29] individuals with and without disabilities. According to the U.S. Department of Labor's Bureau of Labor Statistics (BLS), just 20.9 percent of working age individuals with certain functional disabilities were in the labor force in 2011, compared with 69.7 percent of working age individuals without such disabilities. This same data also indicates that the unemployment rate for those with these disabilities was 15.0 percent, compared with an 8.7 percent unemployment rate for those without a disability. This acute disparity in the workforce participation and unemployment rates of working age individuals with disabilities persists, despite the many technological advances that now make it possible for a broad array of jobs to be successfully performed by individuals with severe disabilities. OFCCP therefore believes that at least a portion of this gap is due to discrimination and sought to take this gap into account in the establishment of the goal by including in its calculation a discouraged worker figure. OFCCP acknowledges that the 1.7 percent figure we included in the goal is different from the 0.1 percent BLS figure cited by a commenter. However, the BLS figure represents the number of discouraged workers with disabilities among the universe of discouraged workers, whereas the 1.7% figure we used approximates the number of discouraged disabled workers among the universe of individuals with disabilities.

In addition to the concerns about the methodology used to derive the goal, several commenters asserted that OFCCP lacked authority to mandate a 7 percent utilization goal. These commenters noted that section 503 requires affirmative action for *qualified* individuals with disabilities; they assert that there is no duty to take affirmative action with regard to a general category of "individuals with disabilities." Because section 503 requires affirmative action only for qualified individuals with disabilities, these commenters argue that a 7 percent utilization goal is impermissible unless the availability data revealed that underutilization of qualified individuals with disabilities exists for each job group in every geographic area.

It appears from these comments that the NPRM did not make explicit enough that the utilization goal requirement is for the utilization of qualified individuals with disabilities. OFCCP did not intend, nor do we believe that the proposed rule would have required, that a contractor employ and advance in employment individuals with disabilities who are not qualified for the position in question. Nevertheless, to address this confusion, we have revised paragraph (a) of the utilization goal requirement in the final rule by inserting the word "qualified" before the term "individuals with disabilities" to clarify that the 7 percent utilization goal is for the employment of qualified individuals with disabilities.

OFCCP also received a number of comments objecting to the proposed utilization goal set forth in paragraph (a) on the grounds that job group specific utilization goals are fundamentally unworkable as proposed. Commenters argued that anonymous self-identification will impede a contractor's ability to analyze utilization of individuals with disabilities and furthermore that such goals will ultimately belie any assurance of confidentiality as the identities of disabled persons would become evident as soon as the AAP data were produced to show the representation of individuals with disabilities in each job group. Moreover, commenters expressed concern that a utilization goal will be difficult to attain because many applicants and employees will be unwilling to disclose their disability, particularly hidden disabilities. Still others expressed concern that pre-offer self-identification will render companies vulnerable to lawsuits for wrongfully failing to hire an individual with a disability.

OFCCP disagrees that job group specific utilization goals are unworkable. First, with regard to the concerns that anonymous self-identification will hinder the contractor's ability to perform a utilization analysis by job group, OFCCP concurs that identifying information is in fact needed in order for contractors to assess their utilization of individuals by job group. We have, therefore, revised § 60–741.42, the provision related to self-identification, by removing the anonymity requirement. Second, as explained above in the preamble for § 60–741.42, Invitation to Self-Identify, OFCCP concedes the possibility that self-reported data regarding disability will not be entirely accurate. While not perfect, the data that will result from the invitation to self-identify will provide the contractor and OFCCP with important data that do not now exist pertaining to the participation of individuals with disabilities in the contractor's applicant pools and labor force. This will allow the contractor and OFCCP to better identify and monitor the contractor's hiring and selection practices with respect to individuals with disabilities. Finally, regarding the concern that pre-offer self-identification will render contractors vulnerable to lawsuits for wrongfully failing to hire an individual with a disability, OFCCP is not persuaded. While knowledge of the existence of a disability is a component of an intentional discrimination claim, the contractor must not only have

[29] The working age population consists of people between the ages of 16 and 64, excluding those in the military and people who are in institutions.

known of the person's disability, but must also have treated the person less favorably because of his/her disability. We note that contractors have long had knowledge of a person's race and gender. Having knowledge of a person's disability should be no different. In addition, we note that contractors have long had knowledge of the disabilities of applicants who have visible disabilities, such as blindness, deafness, or paraplegia, but that OFCCP has had no means of knowing of their presence in the applicant pool or their experience in the application process. Requiring contractors to invite pre-offer self-identification will help fill this void.

Finally, several commenters requested that OFCCP create an exemption from the goal requirement for industries with physically demanding jobs, namely the construction industry, and for safety-sensitive positions, including flight crewmembers, flight attendants, flight instructors, aircraft dispatchers, aircraft maintenance and preventive maintenance workers, ground security coordinators, aviation security screeners, and air traffic controllers. Another commenter requested that AbilityOne contractors be exempt from the goal requirement because they are already operating under high standards. This commenter stated that the AbilityOne program requires that at least 75 percent of the direct labor in a participating nonprofit agency be performed by people who are blind or have other significant disabilities.

OFCCP declines to adopt exemptions from the goal requirement in the final rule. Requests to exempt contractors from meeting the utilization goal for safety sensitive positions or for physically demanding jobs are fundamentally based on the flawed notion that individuals with disabilities as a group are incapable of working in these jobs. OFCCP does not support this belief and will not construct an avenue to permit contractors to avoid hiring individuals with disabilities for certain jobs. OFCCP acknowledges that some individuals with certain disabilities may not be able to perform some jobs, but does not believe exemptions are necessary for two reasons. First, neither section 503 nor this part require a contractor to hire an individual who cannot perform the essential functions of the job, or who poses a direct threat to the health or safety of the individual or others. Second, the goal is not a quota and failure to meet the goal will not, in and of itself, result in any violation or enforcement action. With regard to the request to exempt AbilityOne contractors from the goal requirement, we likewise do not believe that a regulatory exemption is warranted. The final rule applies, not just to "direct labor," but to the entirety of a covered contractor's workforce, and to the entirety of covered subcontractors' workforces, as well. In short, the goal requirement is a management tool from which all contractors can benefit.

• *Comments on sub-goal option*

As noted above, in the NPRM OFCCP indicated that it was considering the option of including within the 7 percent goal for individuals with disabilities a sub-goal of 2 percent for individuals with certain particularly severe disabilities and invited public comment on the sub-goal concept, as well as on which disabilities should be included within the sub-goal. OFCCP specifically sought comments addressing (1) the data or research available that informs the design of an appropriate sub-goal, including which severe disabilities should be covered by the sub-goal and the appropriate sub goal target; (2) how a sub-goal furthers the overall objective of increasing employment opportunities for individuals with severe disabilities; and (3) the data or research available on the need for a sub-goal for specific disabilities.

OFCCP received 126 comments on this sub-goal option. Many commenters from the disability community favored such an approach but urged OFCCP to increase the sub-goal from 2 percent to 5 percent. These commenters stated that any serious effort to measure the effectiveness of one's affirmative action efforts must look not only at the overall group of individuals with disabilities but also at those within that group who have had the greatest barriers to employment and are most in need of affirmative action. Having only an overall goal for the extremely broad group of people with disabilities would permit contractors to employ individuals with less stigmatized disabilities, and would do little to ensure that those individuals with the greatest history of exclusion from the workforce would benefit from affirmative action. These commenters urged OFCCP to increase the sub-goal to 5 percent, because they believe that the group of individuals who would likely be captured by a sub-goal would be greater than 2 percent of the labor force.

In response to OFCCP's request as to which disabilities to include in the sub-goal, a substantial number of commenters from the disability community emphasized the need to fashion a sub-goal that captures individuals "with the lowest employment rates and greatest barriers to employment." These commenters urged OFCCP to not rely on the "targeted disabilities" list the Federal government uses to monitor its internal hiring as the source of its sub-goal, but should instead develop its own, more expansive list of "targeted disabilities." Commenters proffered several approaches, discussed below, that OFCCP could use to create a section 503 sub-goal.

One approach would entail OFCCP working with experts from various universities to identify those categories of disabilities that have caused people to face the greatest employment barriers. OFCCP would then create a "targeted disabilities" list comprised of the identified disabilities. While several if not all of the conditions currently on the Federal government's list would be on this list, commenters anticipated that this new "targeted disabilities" list would also include conditions not on the current list, such as autism spectrum disorders and Down syndrome, among others.

A second approach recommended by these commenters was to base a sub-goal on the statutory definition of "significant disability," at 29 U.S.C. 705(21)(A), that is used for determining selection for vocational rehabilitation services. This definition not only specifies a list of covered conditions, but also requires an assessment of whether each individual's condition is "a severe physical or mental impairment which seriously limits one or more functional capacities (such as mobility, communication, self-care, self-direction, interpersonal skills, work tolerance, work skills) in terms of an employment outcome." There are 26 conditions on the covered conditions list, some of which are very specific, such as amputation, paraplegia, quadriplegia, blindness, and deafness. Other listed conditions, though, encompass broad categories of impairments that can vary widely in their nature and severity, such as arthritis, head injury, burn injury, heart disease, musculo-skeletal disorders, and neurological disorders.

A third approach commenters identified was for OFCCP to analyze a variety of data sources, including ACS, the Survey on Income and Program Participation (SIPP), the Current Population Survey (CPS), CDC data, and other data, to identify which individuals with disabilities experience the greatest employment barriers. OFCCP would then design a sub-goal focused on the disabilities associated with these individuals.

Many of the commenters opposed to the utilization goal requirement also opposed a sub-goal option. The reasons for their opposition were similar to those already expressed in opposition to the 7 percent utilization goal. Many asserted that the 2 percent figure was arbitrary and that it would be incongruous to hold contractors to a standard that the Federal government itself has proven unable to meet. The comments received also stated that there would be many industries for which those with severe disabilities would be unable to work. One commenter highlighted that the sub-goal for individuals with severe disabilities is inconsistent with the Federal Aviation Administration's regulatory scheme regarding medical certification of persons employed in certain safety sensitive positions, and that if a safety exception is not recognized, then OFCCP should establish a lesser goal, because the availability of applicants with severe disabilities qualified for safety sensitive positions would necessarily be fewer. One advocacy organization for individuals with disabilities stated that a sub-goal was not necessary, because it would require a more detailed inquiry regarding the specific nature of an individual's disability by contractors, which would cause discomfort among people with disabilities. A sub-goal also disregards the fact that often the severity of the disability, not just the type of disability, significantly impacts an individual's employment opportunities.

OFCCP declines to adopt a sub-goal option at this time. Although the comments presented a variety of general approaches to designing a sub-goal, none provided a clear methodology or data source for the identification of a sub-goal target. Nor did they provide for the identification of a clear, practicable list of specific conditions that a sub-goal should encompass. We also note that the approach regarding the use of the vocational rehabilitation definition of "significant disability" as the basis of a sub-goal would require the application of a definition of "disability" that is different from that in section 503. Moreover, it would, in many instances require contractors to ask for detailed disability-related information, beyond the mere existence of a specific condition, so that the contractor could determine whether an individual has a "severe" physical or mental impairment that is encompassed by the sub-goal. This does not mean that contractors may not, on their own, establish appropriate mechanisms and goals to affirmatively seek to encourage the employment of individuals with significant or severe disabilities. However, these regulations do not include such requirements.

• *Paragraph (b): Purpose*

Proposed § 60–741.46(b) stated that the purpose of the utilization goal is to establish a benchmark against which the contractor must measure the representation of individuals within each job group in its workforce. Proposed § 60–741.46(b) also stated that the utilization goal serves as an equal employment opportunity objective that should be attainable by complying with all aspects of the affirmative action requirements of this part.

Many commenters opposed to the proposed utilization goal stated that the goal was equivalent to an inflexible "quota" because a contractor who fails to achieve the 7 percent utilization goal would be required to take specific measures to address the disparity. According to these commenters, there is nothing aspirational about this requirement and, unlike the Executive Order 11246 regulations implementing the affirmative action requirements for supply and service contractors, the NPRM implementing section 503 failed to state specifically that the utilization goal is not a rigid, inflexible quota nor does it state that quotas are expressly forbidden. Other commenters stated that any required objective or goal that imposes a penalty if not met is a quota. Still another intimated that the utilization goal as proposed would fail to survive a constitutional challenge because such a requirement would be subject to the highest level of judicial scrutiny.

The proposed utilization goal is not an inflexible quota and should not be perceived as one. The goal is intended to serve as a management tool to help contractors measure their progress toward achieving equal employment opportunity for individuals with disabilities and to assess whether barriers to equal employment opportunity remain. OFCCP recognizes that a failure to meet the 7 percent utilization goal does not necessarily mean that the contractor is discriminating against individuals with disabilities. It is for this reason that the NPRM stated in proposed § 60–741.46(f) that a contractor's determination that it has not attained the utilization goal in one or more job groups does not constitute either a finding or admission of discrimination in violation of this part. Nevertheless, in light of the comments, OFCCP has revised the regulatory language to clarify that a failure to meet the utilization goal triggers an assessment of whether there is a barrier to equal employment opportunity, and if so, what the barrier is. Specifically, new paragraph (e) in the final rule states that when the goal has not been met in one or more job groups the contractor must "determine whether and where impediments to equal employment opportunity exist." This determination is to be based on reviews of the contractor's personnel processes and affirmative action efforts that the contractor is already required to perform. Only if a problem or barrier to equal employment opportunity is identified, must the contractor then develop and execute an action-oriented program to address the problem.

With regard to the comment that the proposed utilization goal would fail to survive a constitutional challenge because such a requirement would be subject to the highest level of judicial scrutiny, we again note that the utilization goal established herein is not a quota and does not require disability-based decision making. Rather, the goal is a tool to measure the effectiveness of the Federal contractor's employment practices as they relate to equal employment opportunity for qualified individuals with disabilities. A failure to meet the goal does not result in any violation; it triggers a critical review by the Federal contractor of its employment practices. Furthermore, even if a court were to determine that the framework set forth herein required disability-based decision making, strict scrutiny review is not applied to decisions based on disability. Instead, classifications based on disability are subject to "rational basis review," and are legally permissible so long as the governmental action—in this case, the setting of a 7 percent utilization goal—is rationally related to a legitimate governmental interest. *See, e.g., Contractors Ass'n of E. Pa., Inc.* v. *City of Phila.*, 6 F.3d 990 (3rd Cir. 1993) (applying rational basis review of a city ordinance that established goals for the participation of disability-owned businesses in city contracts); *City of Cleburne, Tex.* v. *Cleburne Living Center,* 473 U.S. 432, 442–45 (1985). OFCCP believes that establishing a utilization goal of 7 percent for individuals with disabilities is clearly related to the legitimate governmental interest of increasing outreach to and employment opportunities for individuals with disabilities—a segment of the population that suffers from staggering levels of unemployment and a significant history of discrimination.

• *Paragraph (c): Periodic review of the goal*

Proposed paragraph (c) stated that the Director of OFCCP will periodically review and update the 7 percent utilization goal requirement as appropriate. One commenter expressed concern that in light of the Federal government's current fiscal situation, future budget constraints would likely impede OFCCP from ever revising the proposed goal. OFCCP, like many other Federal agencies, has experienced fluctuations in its funding throughout its more than 40 years of continuous operation. We have no reason to anticipate, however, that such fluctuations would impede our ability to periodically review and update the goal, as appropriate, as provided in the final rule.

• *Paragraph (d): Utilization analysis*

Proposed paragraph (d) set forth the purpose of a utilization analysis and required that covered contractors annually evaluate the representation of individuals with disabilities in each job group in the contractor's workforce that the contractor uses for utilization analyses under Executive Order 11246 and compare the rate of representation for each group against the 7 percent utilization goal. For purposes of clarity and in response to numerous commenters' concern that the goal is really a quota, OFCCP has revised proposed paragraph (d)(1), which set forth the purpose of a utilization analysis, by deleting the sentence that states: "If individuals with disabilities are employed in a job group at a rate less than the utilization goal, the contractor must take specific measures to address this disparity." Paragraph (d)(1) is intended to state the purpose of the utilization analysis. This deleted sentence was unrelated to the purpose. Moreover, as explained earlier in the preamble, failure to meet the goal does not automatically trigger the execution of action-oriented programs. For this reason, we found the sentence misleading.

OFCCP received a number of alternatives to the proposed utilization goal, somewhat related to the utilization analysis. Several commenters requested that if the agency were to move forward with the goal requirement, the goal should apply to the entire corporation across all establishments rather than to each job group. One commenter suggested that two goals be implemented—one for supply and service contractors and another for construction contractors. Another recommended that the goal apply by AAP location or organizational unit. Still another suggested that OFCCP remove a set figure and allow each contractor to establish a reasonable utilization goal for its establishments taking into account specific factors involved at each particular workplace. Finally, at least one commenter requested that a range of 4 percent to 10 percent be adopted to allow contractors the flexibility to account for variations in geography, occupational requirements, and nature of disabilities.

OFCCP declines to adopt these proposed alternatives. As explained in the NPRM, we did consider permitting contractors to compare the individuals with disabilities in its workforce as a whole to the proposed 7 percent goal. We decided against adopting this approach on a broad scale because of its potential for masking discrimination and segregation. For example, a contractor that has segregated all of its employees with disabilities into one or two low-paying jobs might be able to conceal this discrimination and satisfy this 7 percent goal if only a single whole-workforce comparison were required by this section.

However, we are mindful that certain small contractors may find it more difficult than other contractors to attain the goal if compelled to apply it to each of their job groups, simply because of their small size. In recognition of this fact, the final rule is revised, with the addition of paragraph (d)(2)(i), to create an exception that permits contractors with a total workforce of 100 or fewer employees to apply the 7 percent goal to their entire workforce as a whole, rather than to each job group. This will ensure that the burden on these small companies is minimized, while still providing them with a yardstick by which to measure the effectiveness of their efforts to recruit and hire individuals with disabilities. These contractors are reminded, though, that while they are permitted to measure their utilization of individuals with disabilities in their workforce as a whole, they may not attain the goal by engaging in the unlawful segregation of employees with disabilities.[30]

OFCCP declines to adopt the other approaches proposed by contractors because they would all result in greater burden on contractors than the approach we have chosen. None of the alternative proposals would allow contractors to use their existing EO 11246 job groups, and all would require contractors to identify organizational units for the purpose of establishing or effectuating a goal, and to explain the factors they applied in making their determinations. A number of commenters expressed concern that contractors may be able to use their relationship with sheltered workshops to circumvent the goal requirement. Some of these commenters fear that contractors will be able to count toward their goal the employees of a sheltered workshop subcontractor. Some fear that contractors will be able to meet their goal by establishing their own sheltered workshop, or by counting toward the goal those individuals being trained for future employment at a sheltered workshop. Still others asked that OFCCP ban sheltered workshops and prohibit contractors from using them at all.

Sheltered workshops are segregated facilities that exclusively or primarily employ persons with disabilities. Many sheltered workshops are authorized to pay special minimum wages under an exemption in section 14(c) of the Fair Labor Standards Act (FLSA), 29 U.S.C. 214(c), after receiving a certificate from the U.S. Department of Labor's Wage and Hour Division. The certificate allows the payment of special minimum wages to certain workers with disabilities for work being performed. The Department's Wage and Hour Division has jurisdiction over the administration of the FLSA, including the provisions of section 14(c). OFCCP thus has no authority to ban sheltered workshops or prohibit contractors from using them. However, § 60–741.45 of the existing section 503 regulations (renumbered section 60–741.47 in the final rule) addresses the relationship between sheltered workshops and contractors' affirmative action obligations. Specifically, this section provides that "[c]ontracts with sheltered workshops do not constitute affirmative action in lieu of employment and advancement of qualified disabled individuals" in the contractor's workforce. Merely providing a subcontract to a sheltered workshop is, therefore, not a form of affirmative action. Section 60–741.45 further provides that a contract with a sheltered workshop may only be considered to be affirmative action "if the sheltered workshop trains employees for the contractor and the contractor is obligated to hire trainees at full compensation" when they become qualified for the job(s) for which they are being trained. Only after these trainees become employees of the contractor and are receiving full compensation comparable to what other similarly situated employees who did not participate in a sheltered workshop are earning, may they be counted toward the contractor's goal. Contractors may not discriminate in compensation based on disability, which would include discriminating against an

[30] The exception created in paragraph (d)(2)(i) of this section is in addition to the existing exception under Executive Order 11246 that permits contractors with a total workforce of fewer than 150 employees to use the nine broad EEO–1 occupational categories as their job groups. *See* 41 CFR 60–2.12(e).

individual based on his or her past participation in a sheltered workshop.

Commenters also need not be concerned that contractors could circumvent the goal by means of a subcontractor relationship with a sheltered workshop or by establishing their own sheltered workshop. First, we note that contractors may only include in their AAPs and count toward their goal their own applicants and employees. Applicants and employees of subcontractors, whether or not that subcontractor is a sheltered workshop, may not be included in the contractor's AAP or counted toward the contractor's goal. Second, to comply with the goal requirement, contractors must apply the goal to each of its job groups, not to its workforce as a whole. Consequently, even if a contractor established its own sheltered workshop inside the company, that would only satisfy the contractor's goal with respect to the specific job(s) performed by the sheltered workshop in the specific contractor facility where the sheltered workshop is located.

• *Paragraph (e): Action-oriented programs*

Proposed paragraph (e) directed that the contractor develop and execute action-oriented programs designed to correct any identified problem areas when underutilization is identified. The proposed rule stated that examples of such programs may include alternative or additional efforts from among those outreach efforts listed in §§ 60–741.44(f)(1) and 60–741.44(f)(2) and/or any other appropriate actions.

Many commenters opposed to the proposed utilization goal objected in part because proposed paragraph (e) required the development and execution of action-oriented programs when the percentage of individuals with disabilities in one or more job groups fell below the 7 percent utilization goal, regardless of the reason the goal was not met. These commenters argued that proposed paragraph (e) imposed a penalty and therefore, the goal acted more like a quota.

As explained earlier, the goal is not a quota. Nevertheless, it appears that many misunderstood the framework for the goal requirement. To allay these concerns, OFCCP has revised paragraph (e), renumbered it as paragraph (f), and inserted a new paragraph (e) into the final rule that clarifies that a failure to meet the utilization goal requires that the contractor make an assessment as to whether any impediments to equal employment opportunity exist. This assessment is to be based on reviews the contractor is already required to undertake as part of its annual review of its affirmative action program. These include reviews of its personnel processes (§ 60–741.44(b)) and its external outreach and recruitment efforts (§ 60–741.44(f)), and the results of its affirmative action program audit (§ 60–741.44(h)) and any other areas that might affect the success of the affirmative action program. Paragraph (e) is, thus, captioned "Identification of problem areas." Proposed paragraph (e), entitled "Action-oriented programs" (paragraph (f) in the final rule) has been revised to direct the contractor to undertake action-oriented programs only when problem areas have been identified. Paragraph (f) also clarifies that action-oriented programs need not be limited to engaging in additional outreach and recruitment efforts. Rather, such programs may also include the modification of personnel processes to ensure equal employment opportunity for individuals with disabilities and/or other actions designed to correct the identified problem areas, such as improving retention of employees with disabilities.

• *Paragraph (f): Failure to meet the goal does not constitute discrimination*

Proposed paragraph (f) clarified that a contractor's determination that it has not attained the utilization goal in one or more job groups does not in and of itself constitute either a finding or admission of discrimination in violation of this part. OFCCP received no comments regarding this provision. We have adopted this provision, as proposed, in the final rule, renumbered as paragraph (g). Failure to meet the goal would not be a violation of this part and would not lead to a fine, penalty or sanction.

As previously noted, if a contractor does not meet the goal, the contractor must take steps to determine whether and where impediments to equal opportunity exist. When making this determination the contractor must assess its personnel processes, the effectiveness of its outreach and recruitment efforts, the results of its affirmative action program audits, and any other areas that might affect the success of the affirmative action program. If the contractor reasonably determines there are no impediments, no further action is necessary. If, as a result of its review, the contractor identifies problem areas, then it must develop and execute action-oriented programs designed to correct the problems, as required by paragraph (f). The contractor may choose the programs to institute. The programs do not need to result in achieving the goal, so long as they are designed to remove obstacles to doing so.

So, for example, if a contractor does not meet the goal, but has developed and implemented an affirmative action program, including conducting outreach and positive recruitment of individuals with disabilities and has evaluated whether barriers to equal opportunity exist and, if they do, implemented action-oriented programs to correct and remove them, the contractor would not be found to be in violation of this part simply because it did not meet the goal.

On the other hand, if, for example, a contractor meets the goal, but fails to develop an AAP, the contractor could be cited for failure to develop an AAP. Goal achievement does not guarantee compliance with section 503 or this part, just as failure to meet the goal does not result in a violation of section 503 or this part.

• *Paragraph (g): Utilization goal is not a quota or a ceiling*

Proposed paragraph (g) stated that the goal proposed in this section must not be used as a quota or ceiling that limits or restricts the employment of individuals with disabilities. This paragraph is adopted, as proposed, in the final rule, renumbered as paragraph (h).

Section 60–741.47 Voluntary Affirmative Action Programs for Employees With Disabilities

The proposed rule added a new section encouraging contractors to voluntarily develop and implement programs that provide priority consideration to individuals with disabilities in recruitment or hiring. The proposal provided examples of priority consideration programs, and required contractors who elect to implement such a program to include in their AAP a description of the program and an annual report describing activities taken pursuant to the program and their outcomes. In addition, the proposal cautioned that a priority consideration program cannot be used to segregate or restrict the employment opportunities of individuals with disabilities.

We received 28 comments concerning this section, primarily from employer groups, but also from disability groups, law firms, and others. The employer groups overwhelmingly opposed this section, asserting that priority consideration amounted to a quota or preferential treatment for persons with disabilities and contradicted equal employment opportunity principles. Contractors, they stated, should only hire the best qualified person for a job. Commenters opposed to this new provision asserted, further, that it would foster discrimination against other protected groups and generate increased employment discrimination litigation. A few commenters questioned how this section would be implemented; for example, how a contractor would establish a point system. Some commenters requested clarification on the definition of priority consideration.

Those commenters in favor of this section, mostly disability groups, stated that this section would assist in the employment of persons with disabilities and would not result in unlawful discrimination of any kind. They asserted, further, that this section does not violate section 503 or the ADA.

After consideration of the comments, OFCCP adopts the proposed provision into the final rule with modifications to address concerns raised by contractors. First several contractors were concerned that the provision would require contractors to provide priority consideration to individuals with disabilities, including addition "points" in the hiring process, that would amount to a quota. This is not OFCCP's intention. By way of background, several contractors in the past have asked OFCCP informally whether it would be permissible to establish a job training or employment program for individuals with specific disabilities, such as traumatic brain injury or developmental disabilities. It has been OFCCP's longstanding policy that such programs are permissible though not required. To address this concern we have clarified the section to refer to voluntary affirmative action programs for employees with disabilities, rather than as providing priority consideration in employment. In addition, we have removed the example of a program assigning a weighted value or additional "points" to job applicants who self-identify as having a disability. We reiterate that proposed § 60–741.47 (§ 60–741.46 in the final rule) creates no new obligations or responsibilities with which contractors must comply. Rather, it simply highlights the availability to contractors of an important affirmative action tool, and, provides a non-exhaustive list of examples of voluntary affirmative action programs for employees with disabilities that contractors are permitted to voluntarily develop and implement. A number of private companies have successfully used various types of voluntary affirmative action programs to increase training and employment opportunities for individuals with disabilities, and OFCCP desires to be clear that other companies also may consider their use. However, contractors who do not adopt such programs are not penalized in any way by OFCCP for that decision. OFCCP believes these modifications will allay concerns that this provision amounts to a quota or requires preferential treatment.

We disagree with the suggestion that this provision would foster discrimination against other groups and generate increased litigation. As we noted in the NPRM, the ADA Amendments Act explicitly states that neither the ADA nor the Rehabilitation Act provides "the basis for a claim . . . that [an] individual was subject to discrimination because of the individual's lack of disability." ADAAA at sec. 6(a)(1)(g). We note, too, that having a disability is a characteristic that cuts across race, gender and ethnicity lines, and that affirmative efforts to increase employment opportunities for individuals with disabilities will, therefore, not impede affirmative efforts to include women and minorities. We have added a new paragraph (d) to make clear that this section should not be used to foster discrimination against other groups by stating that this section shall not relieve a contractor from liability for discrimination under any of the laws enforced by OFCCP.

Section 60–741.48 Sheltered workshops

We proposed to make a single technical change to this existing regulation. Specifically, the NPRM proposed to replace the phrase "qualified disabled individuals" in the first sentence with "qualified individuals with disabilities" to be consistent with the terminology used elsewhere in this part. We received no comments on this change and it is adopted into the final rule as proposed, but the section is renumbered as § 60–741.47. Several commenters expressed concern about the interaction of this existing provision with the new utilization goal requirement in § 60–741.45 of the final rule (originally proposed as § 60–741.46). Those comments are addressed in the preamble to § 60–741.46, above.

Subpart D—General Enforcement and Complaint Procedures

Section 60–741.60 Compliance Evaluations

The proposed rule set forth several changes to the process the contractor and OFCCP will follow in conducting compliance evaluations. We received 28 comments concerning this section, including comments focusing on contractor burden, which are addressed in the Regulatory Procedures section of this preamble. These proposals, the comments to these proposals, and the revisions made to the final rule are discussed in turn below.

- *Paragraph (a)*

The NPRM modified the wording of paragraph (a) to more clearly state the section 503 obligation of the contractor to employ, "advance in employment and otherwise treat qualified individuals without discrimination on the basis of disability in all employment practices." We received no comments to this paragraph and adopt the language into the final rule as proposed.

- *Paragraph (a)(1): Compliance review*

The NPRM proposed adding a sentence to paragraph (a)(1)(i) regarding the temporal scope of desk audits performed by OFCCP, stating that OFCCP "may extend the temporal scope of the desk audit beyond that set forth in the scheduling letter if OFCCP deems it necessary to carry out its investigation of potential violations of this part." Most of the comments concerned this paragraph. Many of these commenters, primarily contractors, employer groups, and law firms, objected to this proposed change and asked that it be withdrawn. These commenters asserted that the language of the proposed rule could result in "perpetual" audits of contractors, was contrary to a recent Administrative Law Judge (ALJ) decision in the case *OFCCP* v. *Frito-Lay*, Case No. 2010–OFC–00002, Recommended Decision and Order (ALJ July 23, 2010), and would lead to an increased burden for contractors.

As stated in the NPRM, the purpose of this proposal was to clarify that OFCCP may need to examine information after the date of the scheduling letter during the desk audit in order to determine, for instance, if violations are continuing or have been remedied. While the existing section 503 provision addresses the authority of the agency to conduct desk audits, it does not expressly state the temporal scope of these audits. It has been OFCCP's longstanding position that the agency has authority to obtain information pertinent to the review for periods after the date of the letter scheduling the review, including during the desk audit. However, in 2010 an ALJ disagreed in a recommended decision in the *Frito-Lay* case, in part because the parallel Executive Order 11246 desk audit regulation at issue in the case does not address the temporal scope of a desk audit. *OFCCP* v. *Frito-Lay, Inc.*, Case No. 2010–OFC–00002, ALJ Recommended Decision and Order (July 23, 2010). On May 8, 2012, the Department's Administrative Review Board (ARB) reversed this recommended decision, concluding that a desk audit authorized by the regulation permitted OFCCP to request additional information relating to periods after the scheduling letter. The ARB concluded that the regulation does not have an inflexible temporal limitation. *OFCCP* v. *Frito-Lay, Inc.*, Case No. 2010–OFC–00002, ARB Final Administrative Order (May 8, 2012). OFCCP views the *Frito-Lay* decision as equally applicable to desk audits concluded under its section 503 authority as to those conducted under its Executive Order 11246 authority. Nevertheless, the final rule makes the clarification explicit in the text of the regulation. OFCCP notes that paragraph (a)(1) also authorizes OFCCP to request during the desk audit additional information pertinent to the review after reviewing the initial submission. *See United Space Alliance* v. *Solis,* 824 F.Supp.2d 68, 81–82 (D.D.C. 2011) (holding that agency's interpretation of its desk audit regulation to authorize additional information requests when necessary was entitled to deference).

Finally, commenters' concerns that this revision will lead to "never-ending" audits are unfounded. As stated above, the clarifying language set forth in the final rule does not change OFCCP's longstanding policy, or contractors' obligations, regarding the temporal scope of the desk audit. Further, because the clarification does not represent a change, concerns about increases in burden are similarly unfounded.

• *Paragraphs (a)(3) and (a)(4): Compliance check and focused reviews*

The NPRM revised paragraph (a)(3) to permit OFCCP to review documents pursuant to a compliance check either on-site or off-site, at OFCCP's option. Similarly, paragraph (a)(4) was revised to allow OFCCP to conduct focused reviews, at its discretion, either on-site or off-site. Many employer groups objected to this change, citing confidentiality concerns over the transfer, management, and maintenance of employment and medical records. Some commenters requested safeguards to protect these records, asked for additional guidance concerning confidentiality of medical records, or asked that these records not be subject to the Freedom of Information Act.

We received similar comments concerning the confidentiality of records with regard to § 60–741.81, Access to records, and we address those comments in more detail in the preamble to that section. Briefly, we note that the section 503 regulations have long required contractors to provide relevant medical and related records to OFCCP officials during a compliance evaluation or complaint investigation "upon request." § 60–741.23(d)(1)(iii). This regulation contains no requirement that OFCCP must request such records "on-site." We also note that there is significant precedent for OFCCP obtaining contractor records off-site, as the scheduling letter has long required that contractors scheduled for a compliance evaluation send their AAPs and supporting documentation to OFCCP. The final rule adopts the changes to these paragraphs as proposed.

• *Paragraph (c): Pre-award compliance evaluations*

Finally, the proposed rule added a new paragraph (c) to this section detailing a new procedure for pre-award compliance evaluations under section 503, much like the procedure that currently exists in the Executive Order regulations. *See* 41 CFR 60–1.20(d). A few employer groups objected to the change, asserting that the new paragraph was too prescriptive and questioned how the procedure would work in practice.

These concerns are misplaced. The pre-award compliance evaluation is a long-standing requirement under the Executive Order. This addition simply brings the section 503 regulations in line with the Executive Order regulations and assures that the pre-award compliance evaluation process will also encompass compliance with section 503. OFCCP adopts this new provision into the final rule as proposed.

Section 60–741.62 Conciliation Agreements

The proposed rule renumbered the existing rule as paragraph (a), and added a new paragraph (b) permitting the establishment of benchmarks in conciliation agreements as one possible form of remedial action. As we stated in the NPRM, benchmarks may be established for outreach, recruitment, hiring, or other employment activities of the contractor, as appropriate, and will provide a quantifiable method for measuring the contractor's progress toward correcting identified violations or deficiencies.

We received five comments from employer groups concerning new paragraph (b). None favored the new provision. Some of these commenters asserted that remedial benchmarks for hiring are unnecessary, would be similar to a quota, and recommended that the paragraph be eliminated from the final rule. Others requested that we further define "benchmark," or clarify that a benchmark must be linked to a finding of discrimination.

The use of remedial benchmarks is not a new OFCCP policy or practice. Remedial benchmarks have long been included in conciliation agreements, when appropriate, to resolve violations under the Executive Order. New paragraph (b) simply clarifies that remedial benchmarks may also be used, when appropriate, to remedy violations of section 503. Lastly, we note that § 60–741.62(a) provides that conciliation agreements may be used when "OFCCP finds a material violation of the act or this part." We, therefore, do not believe that further clarification regarding when a benchmark may be used is warranted. Nor do we believe that additional definition of the term "benchmark," which the American Heritage Dictionary of the English Language defines "a standard by which something can be measured or judged," is necessary. Accordingly, paragraph (b) is adopted into the final rule as proposed.

Section 60–741.68 Reinstatement of Ineligible Contractors

The proposed rule added a sentence at the end of paragraph (a) to clarify that the Director shall issue a written decision on a contractor's request for reinstatement. No comments were received regarding this change, and OFCCP adopts it into the final rule as proposed.

Subpart E—Ancillary Matters

Section 60–741.80 Recordkeeping

This section describes the recordkeeping requirements that apply to the contractor under section 503, and the consequences for the failure to preserve records in accordance with these requirements. The NRPM modified this provision to incorporate the five (5) year records retention timeframe required under proposed § 60–741.44(f)(4) (linkage agreements and other outreach and recruiting efforts), and proposed § 60–741.44(k) (collection of referral, applicant and hire data).

While comments regarding the proposed recordkeeping requirements under § 60–741.44(f)(4) and § 60–741.44(k) are addressed in the discussions of those provisions, a total of 25 comments were received specific to § 60–741.80. Commenters included disability, employer, veterans and other associations, contractors, law firms, government offices and individuals. Generally, the disability and veterans associations favored the longer record retention period, while other commenters argued that this was overly burdensome, inconsistent with OFCCP's other recordkeeping requirements, and confusing.

As previously noted in this preamble, in response to comments regarding the burden associated with maintaining records for five years, the final rule reduces the recordkeeping requirements for §§ 60–741.44(f)(4) and 60–741.44(k) to three years. To reduce any potential for confusion, the final rule includes a new paragraph (b) in § 60–741.80 specifying in one place those records that have the three-year requirement, and renumbering paragraph (b) of the existing rule as paragraph (c). OFCCP feels strongly that extending the recordkeeping requirements for these particular provisions, which are primarily related to recruitment and outreach, will enable contractors to better determine the effectiveness of their recruitment and outreach activities over time. As noted in the NPRM, the absence of data makes it nearly impossible for contractors and OFCCP to perform even rudimentary evaluations of the availability of individuals with disabilities in the workforce, or to make any quantitative assessments of how effective contractor outreach and recruitment efforts have been in attracting candidates with disabilities. These records will give contractors historical data that can be used for analyzing their compliance efforts.

Paragraph (d) of the existing rule provides that the "requirements of this section shall apply only to records made or kept on or after August 19, 1996," the effective date of a previous amendment to the section 503 implementing regulations. The final rule deletes this paragraph, as it is now obsolete.

Section 60–741.81 Access to records

This section describes a contractor's obligations to permit OFCCP to access its records during compliance evaluations and complaint investigations. The NPRM proposed two changes to the current regulation. First, it added a sentence requiring the contractor to provide off-site access to materials if requested by OFCCP investigators or officials as part of a compliance evaluation or complaint investigation. Second, it required that the contractor specify to OFCCP all formats (including specific electronic formats) in which its records are available, and produce records to OFCCP in the formats selected by OFCCP.

Sixteen comments were received from contractors, employer associations and law firms regarding this proposal. Most of the commenters requested that OFCCP eliminate the proposed changes. A few commenters objected specifically to the requirement to provide records in the format(s) OFCCP selects, and almost all expressed concern that allowing OFCCP access to records off-site raised potential confidentiality risks.

The final rule retains the proposed requirement that contractors provide OFCCP off-site access to materials upon request. As an initial matter, we note that access to company records off-site is not a novel approach, as Executive Order 11246 contains no limitation on the location of access to records for a scheduled compliance evaluation, and indeed specifically references off-site access. The final rule's general access regulation conforms to those principles. Moreover, in light of contractors' increased use of readily portable electronic records in multiple locations, this change will provide OFCCP with greater flexibility during evaluations and investigations, promoting increased efficiency.

However, OFCCP modified § 60–741.81 of the final rule in response to concerns regarding record confidentiality. Section 60–741.81 now includes the following language: "OFCCP will treat records provided by the contractor to OFCCP under this section as confidential to the maximum extent the information is exempt from public disclosure under the Freedom of Information Act, 5 U.S.C. 552." It is the practice of OFCCP not to release data where the contractor is still in business, and the contractor indicates, and through the Department of Labor review process it is determined, that the data are confidential and sensitive and that release of the data would subject the contractor to commercial harm. This language affirms OFCCP's commitment to ensure confidentiality to the fullest extent allowed by law. Further, all OFCCP Compliance Officers receive training on the importance of keeping records confidential during compliance evaluations and complaint investigations. OFCCP will continue to stress this policy to ensure that contractor records are kept secure by the agency at all times.

The final rule also clarifies the provision regarding OFCCP's ability to request records in specific formats. The final rule states that: "[t]he contractor must provide records and other information in any of the formats in which they are maintained, as selected by OFCCP." This language makes clear that the provision will not require contractors to invest time or resources creating records in a specific format, or creating a documented "list" of the formats in which they have documents available. Rather, contractors merely need to inform OFCCP of the formats in which they maintain their records and other information, and allow OFCCP to select the format(s) in which the records or other information will be provided. This provision should result in more efficient OFCCP evaluations and investigations.

Appendix A to Part 60–741—Guidelines on a Contractor's Duty To Provide Reasonable Accommodation

The proposed rule included several changes to Appendix A to reflect updated terminology and revisions made elsewhere in the regulations. Specifically, we: (1) Proposed changing the term "otherwise qualified" to "qualified," in paragraph 1, to conform more closely to the terminology used in the ADA, as amended, and this part; (2) added a reference to the proposed new requirement, in proposed § 60–741.45, that contractors develop written reasonable accommodation procedures; (3) proposed revising paragraph 2 to reflect the new requirement, in § 60–741.42, that contractors invite applicants to self-identify as an individual with a disability at the pre-offer stage; (4) noted that the invitation to self-identify also invites individuals with disabilities to request any reasonable accommodation that they might need; (5) proposed requiring, in paragraph 4, that, in the event that a needed reasonable accommodation constitutes an undue hardship for the contractor, the individual with a disability be given the option of providing the accommodation or paying the portion of the cost that constitutes the undue hardship for the contractor; (6) proposed revising paragraph 5 to require the contractor to seek the advice of the individual with a disability when providing reasonable accommodation; (7) proposed changing the reference to "§ 60–741.2(v)" in paragraphs 5 and 8 of the appendix to "§ 60–741.2(t)" to reflect the revised alphabetical structure of the rule's definitions; and (8) updated the reference to various information resources, and replaced the term "TDD" with "TTY" to reflect current technology.

Just one commenter addressed the proposed revisions to Appendix A. This commenter recommended that we add a network of State vocational rehabilitation agencies to the examples of reasonable accommodation resources referenced in paragraph 5. OFCCP declines to add this reference as State vocational rehabilitation services agencies are already listed as a reasonable accommodation resource for contractors. OFCCP, therefore, adopts the proposed changes into the final rule with the following modifications: (1) The reference to the proposed requirement to establish written reasonable accommodation procedures is deleted, consistent with the elimination of proposed § 60–741.45; (2) the third sentence of paragraph 2 is revised to reflect the use of a single voluntary self-identification form for the pre-offer and post-offer invitations to self-identify as an individual with a disability; and (3) the reference to the definition of "reasonable accommodation" is renumbered § 60–741.2(s).

Regulatory Procedures

Executive Order 13563 and Executive Order 12866

Executive Order 13563 directs agencies to propose or adopt a regulation only upon a reasoned determination that its benefits justify its costs; tailor the regulation to impose the least burden on society, consistent with obtaining the regulatory objectives; and, in choosing among alternative regulatory approaches, select those approaches that maximize net benefits. Executive Order 13563 recognizes that some benefits are difficult to quantify and provides that, where appropriate and permitted by law, agencies may consider and discuss qualitatively values that are difficult or impossible to quantify, including equity, human dignity, fairness, and distributive impacts.

This rule is economically significant as it will have an annual effect on the economy of $100 million or more. EO 12866 sec. 3 at (f). In this section, we present a summary of the costs and benefits associated with the revisions to part 60–741. OFCCP estimates that first-year costs in the rule to be in the range of $349,510,926 to $659,877,833. This includes (1) One-time costs; (2) recurring costs; (3) capital start-up costs; and (4) operations and maintenance costs.[31] The recurring costs in years contractors do not invite all employees to voluntarily self-identify as an individual with a disability will range from $162,371,816 to $395,258,387. The recurring costs in the years that contractors do invite all employees to voluntarily self-identify as an individual with a disability will range from $242,345,778 to $480,476,442.

A. *Introduction*

The final regulatory impact analysis is substantially different from the preliminary regulatory impact analysis presented in the section 503 NPRM based on comments received during the public and interagency comment period. First, the final rule has been scaled down significantly so that it focuses on requirements essential to creating accountability, and supporting the ability of contractors to conduct meaningful self-assessments using more data. This rule also minimizes the costs to contractors while not sacrificing the agency's ability to conduct effective compliance evaluations. A detailed discussion of the proposals in the NPRM that OFCCP did not adopt in the final rule is included in the Discussion of Impacts section below. Second, OFCCP increased the number of contractor establishments affected by the rule to take into account some of the public comments at the NPRM phases of the rulemaking. Third, the analysis acknowledges that some establishments and/or companies may incur higher costs under the final rule and illustrates a range of costs to implement several provisions. The analysis considers, when appropriate, costs that may be incurred by contractors' headquarters versus establishments, and differences between contractors with automated human resources and systems and those with manual systems.

1. Eliminated Several Proposals in the NPRM

While all the proposals in the NPRM had value, after assessing the comments received on the NPRM published on December 9, 2011, we made several changes in the final rule. OFCCP reconsidered whether the cost of several proposals in the NPRM could be justified by their potential benefits, and whether alternative methods or approaches could achieve comparable or acceptable benefits for less cost or burden. We retain in the final rule those provisions proposed in the NPRM that create greater contractor accountability through enhanced data collection and recordkeeping. Therefore, as an example, the final rule does not require each contractor to establish three "linkage" agreements with various disability service organizations to facilitate disability recruitment.

Other examples of how the final rule takes a tailored approach include, but are not limited to, eliminating the proposal that contractors reproduce the entire equal opportunity clause in all contracts and subcontracts; the proposal that contractor staff training must cover a list of specific training items; the proposal to mandate the adoption of written reasonable accommodation procedures; the proposal to mandate annual reviews of personnel policies; and the proposal to mandate that contractors identify the official responsible for the affirmative action program on all communications are also eliminated in the final rule.

2. Increased the Contractor Establishment Count

OFCCP received comments on the estimated number of contractor establishments, including a recommendation to accept a count of 285,390 using the Veterans Employment Training Services (VETS) annual report. While OFCCP declines to exclusively rely on the VETS report, we present an estimated high end for the range of the cost of the rule based on a contractor establishment number of 251,300. This number is based on 2010 VETS data from their pending Information Collection Request.[32]

All costs and hours in the burden analysis of this final rule are calculated using these revised numbers for Federal contractor establishments. Federally-assisted construction contractors are not subject to these regulations and, therefore, are not included in this total. *See* § 60–741.2(i) for the definition of "Government contract."

3. Revised and Increased Burden Estimates

OFCCP received approximately 130 comments on the burden imposed by the section 503 NPRM from individuals, disability associations, companies and industry groups. A few commenters stated that the benefits of the proposed rule outweigh the costs. The majority of comments on the burden of the proposed rule expressed different views. Commenters noted that OFCCP dramatically underestimated the burden associated with the rule. Several commenters provided their own burden estimates, though often with little discussion or explanation of their methodology, that they asserted more accurately reflected the impact that the proposed provisions would have on contractors. The estimates provided by commenters were significantly higher than those used in the NPRM and resulted in total costs that far exceeded the NPRM's estimate. Commenters also expressed concern that the proposals in the NPRM seeking to require contractors to collect data and engage in other personnel activities would change their business functions and would not lead to jobs for individuals with disabilities. Commenters especially emphasized the costs of modifying their existing human

[31] These costs include both establishment and contractor company level costs.

[32] OMB Control Number 1293–0005, Federal Contractor Veterans' Employment Report, VETS—100/VETS–100A, *http://www.reginfo.gov/public/do/PRAViewDocument?ref_nbr=201104-1293-003* (last accessed Aug. 13, 2013).

resources information systems in order to collect new categories of data on individuals with disabilities.

OFCCP acknowledges that it is challenging to estimate the precise amount of time each establishment or headquarters, as appropriate, will take to engage in certain activities. However, in response to public comments, the final regulatory impact analysis attempts to account for the fact that smaller contractors may not have the same human resources capabilities as larger contractors. OFCCP does so by providing low and high range estimates for certain requirements. This approach is taken to distinguish between contractors with automated application and human resources information systems represented at the low end of the range in terms of burden, and contractors with manual systems represented at the high end of the range. The distinction is applied, for example, when estimating burden related to meeting the data collection requirements of the final rule. The high end of the range estimate is based on the assumption that smaller contractors with 50–100 employees may still use manual application or human resources processes. These contractors would likely expend more time conducting the kind of data collection and analysis required under the final rule. The range also factors in varying estimates for the number of applicants who would fill out the invitation to self-identify.

In addition, as mentioned earlier, OFCCP presents burden estimates based on two different contractor establishment numbers in order to reflect the range of opinions about the size of the universe of contractors affected by this rule.

Elsewhere in this issue of the **Federal Register**, OFCCP is publishing a final rule amending the VEVRAA implementing regulations at 41 CFR part 60–300. Many of the revisions contained in this section 503 final rule mirror revisions contained in the VEVRAA final rule. In consideration of the fact that contractors will, thus, already be required to perform certain activities, OFCCP eliminated the burden in this analysis for provisions that mirror requirements in part 60–300. OFCCP also decreased the burden for one-time or capital and start-up costs that are substantially similar to those that are already required under the VEVRAA final rule.

B. The Need for the Regulation

Employment discrimination and underutilization of qualified workers, such as individuals with disabilities and veterans, contribute to broader societal problems such as income inequality and poverty. The median household income for "householders" with a disability, aged 18 to 64, was $25,420 compared with a median income of $59,411 for households with a householder who did not report a disability.[33] Controlling for age and race we find that workers with a disability, on average, earn less than private sector workers without a disability. The mean hourly wage of those with a disability is $17.62 (with a median of $13.73) compared to $21.67 (median $16.99) for those without a disability.[34] Controlling for age and race, male workers with a disability earn 23 percent less than males without a disability. The disability gap for females is 20 percent.[35] While 28.8 percent of individuals, ages 18 to 64, with a disability were in poverty in 2011, the data show that 12.5 percent of those individuals without a disability were in poverty.[36]

Based on our analysis of the American Community Survey (ACS) 2008–2010 Public Use Microdata (PUMS), and controlling for age and race we found that:[37]

- Males with disability had a 7.2 percentage point higher unemployment rate than males without a disability.
- Females with disability had a 6.5 percentage point higher unemployment rate than females without a disability.
- Females with a disability had a 29.2 percentage point higher probability of not being in the labor force than females without a disability.

A 2009 report found that "having a disability is associated with lower earnings due to decreased ability to work, prejudice, and other factors."[38] There are a number of hypotheses concerning disparities in labor force participation, employment rates, and wages. While knowledge of opportunities, differences in access and attainment of training and education, and underutilization of individuals with disabilities likely contribute to these disparities, the culture of the typical workplace and discrimination are also factors in some employment settings. However, there is little empirical data upon which to base targeted interventions. Data collection remains a critical need.

The final rule is intended to provide contractors with the tools needed to evaluate their own compliance and proactively identify and correct any deficiencies in their employment practices. Because the existing regulations implementing section 503 do not provide contractors with adequate tools to assess whether they are complying with their nondiscrimination and affirmative action obligations to recruit and employ qualified individuals with disabilities, the revisions of the final rule will assist contractors in averting potentially expensive violation findings by OFCCP.

C. Discussion of Impacts

In this section, OFCCP presents a summary of the costs associated with the revisions to part 60–741. The estimated cost to contractors is based on Bureau of Labor Statistics data in the publication "Employer Costs for Employee Compensation" (September 2011), which lists total compensation for management, professional, and related occupations as $50.11 per hour and administrative support as $23.72 per hour. OFCCP estimates that 52 percent of the burden hours will be management, professional, and related occupations and 48 percent will be administrative support.

[33] *Income, Poverty and Health Insurance Coverage in the United States: 2011*, Current Population Reports, issued September 2012, *http://www.census.gov/prod/2012pubs/p60-243.pdf* (last accessed July 8, 2013), p. 10. A "householder" is the person (or one of the people) in whose name the home is owned or rented and the person to whom the relationship of other household members is recorded. Typically, it is the head of a household. Only one person per household is designated the "householder."

[34] OFCCP ran wage regressions using the natural log of effective hourly wages calculated as real income divided by usual hours per week and weeks per year. The weeks per year variable is categorical so the midpoint of each category was used as a proxy for the number of weeks worked. Explanatory variables include age and race. The sample was restricted to individuals aged 18 to 64 employed in the private sector. Individuals currently in the armed forces were not included in the sample. All OFCCP models used ACS 2008–2010 Public Use Microdata (PUMS).

[35] Id.

[36] *Income, Poverty and Health Insurance Coverage in the United States: 2011*, Current Population Reports, issued September 2012, *http://www.census.gov/prod/2012pubs/p60-243.pdf* (last accessed July 8, 2013).

[37] OFCCP ran wage regressions using the natural log of effective hourly wages calculated as real income divided by usual hours per week and weeks per year. The weeks per year variable is categorical so the midpoint of each category was used as a proxy for the number of weeks worked. Explanatory variables include age and race. The sample was limited to individuals aged 18 to 64 employed in the private sector. All OFCCP models used ACS 2008–2010 Public Use Microdata (PUMS).

[38] *Changing Demographic Trends that Affect the Workplace and Implications for People with Disabilities*, Executive Summary (Nov. 30, 2009), p. 4. "Studies agree that disability incidence is related to income and earnings. A number of intertwined relationships, however, make it somewhat difficult to sort out cause and effect."

TABLE 1—CONTRACTOR NEW REQUIREMENTS—171,275 ESTABLISHMENTS

Burden	Low cost	High cost
One-Time Burden		
EO Clause, Parag 10 (Include "Disability" EEO Statement)	$320,660.14	$320,660.14
741.5(d) (Modify EO Clause)	1,603,263.00	1,603,263.00
741.42 (Modify Application Systems)	2,101,102.72	2,583,328.54
Total	4,025,025.86	4,507,251.68
Recurring Burden		
741.42 (Invitation to Self-Identify)	9,619,542.08	9,619,542.08
741.42 (Invitation to Self-Identify Employee Burden)	68,751,157.00	68,751,157.00
741.42 (Recordkeeping)	1,603,263.25	1,603,263.25
741.44(f) (Review Outreach and Recruitment)	3,174,438.00	3,174,438.00
741.44(f)(4) (Outreach and Recruitment Recordkeeping)	1,068,842.17	1,068,842.17
741.44(h) (AAP Audit Recordkeeping)	1,068,842.17	1,068,842.17
741.44(k) (Data Collection and Analysis)	3,740,925.75	6,840,549.94
741.45 (Utilization Analysis)	6,413,015.00	8,978,223.00
741.45 (Utilization Analysis Recordkeeping)	1,068,842.00	1,068,842.00
Total	96,508,867.42	102,173,699.61
Capital and Start-up	28,312,120.00	39,086,481.00
Rule Familiarization	8,582,590.25	34,330,361.00
Operations and Maintenance	616,590.00	1,356,498.00
Reasonable Accommodations	114,770,291.00	114,770.291.00
Total	252,815,484.53	296,224,582.29

TABLE 2—CONTRACTOR NEW REQUIREMENTS—251,300 ESTABLISHMENTS

Provision	Low cost	High cost
One-Time Burden		
EO Clause, Parag 10 (Include "Disability" EEO Statement)	$470,468.00	$470,468.00
741.5(d) (Modify EO Clause)	784,115.00	784,115.00
741.42 (Modify Application Systems)	3,102,510.41	3,814,616.30
Total	4,357,093.41	5,069,199.30
Recurring Burden		
741.42 (Invitation to Self-Identify)	14,114,063.00	14,114,063.00
741.42 (Invitation to Self-Identify Employee Burden)	68,751,667.00	68,751,667.00
741.42 (Recordkeeping)	2,352,344.00	2,352,344.00
741.44(f) (Review Outreach and Recruitment)	4,704,687.82	4,704,687.82
741.44(f)(4) (Outreach and Recruitment Recordkeeping)	1,568,229.27	1,568,229.27
741.44(h) (AAP Audit Recordkeeping)	1,568,229.27	1,568,229.27
741.44(k) (Data Collection and Analysis)	5,488,802.46	10,036,667.35
741.45 (Utilization Analysis)	9,409,375.64	13,173,125.90
741.45 (Utilization Analysis Recordkeeping)	1,568,229.27	1,568,229.27
Total	109,525,627.73	117,837,242.88
Capital and Start-up	41,555,091.78	57,716,207.82
Rule Familiarization	12,592,643.00	50,370,572.00
Operations and Maintenance	904,680.00	1,990,296.00
Reasonable Accommodation	114,770,291.00	114,770,291.00
Costs to Companies	283,705,426.92	347,753,809.00

TABLE 3—COMPLETING PRE-OFFER SELF-IDENTIFICATION

Provision	171,275 establishments		251,300 establishments	
	Low cost	High cost	Low cost	High cost
741.42(a)	$96,695,442.00	$212,729,213.00	$141,874,556.25	$312,124,023.75

1. Regulatory Familiarization

Several commenters noted that the proposed rule did not quantify the burden of reading and understanding the section 503 revisions on contractors. OFCCP acknowledges that 5 CFR 1320.3(b)(1)(i) requires agencies to include in the burden analysis for new information collection requirements the estimated time it takes for contractors to review and understand the instructions for compliance. In order to minimize the burden, OFCCP will publish compliance assistance materials including, but not limited to, factsheets and "Frequently Asked Questions." OFCCP will also host webinars for the contractor community that will describe the key provisions in the final rule, and conduct listening session to identify any specific challenges contractors believe they face, or may face, when complying with the requirements of the final rule.

OFCCP estimates it will take, at a minimum, 1 hour to have a management professional at each establishment either read compliance assistance materials provided by OFCCP or participate in an OFCCP webinar to learn about the new requirements of the final rule. OFCCP believes that this is a reasonable estimate since there are substantially fewer new requirements in the final rule than proposed in the NPRM, and contractors already have at least one person that is responsible for overseeing their compliance with OFCCP's regulations. The estimated cost of this burden is based on data from the Bureau of Labor Statistics in the publication "Employer Costs for Employee Compensation" (September 2011), which lists total compensation for a management professional at $50.11. Therefore, the estimated burden for rule familiarization is 171,275 hours (171,275 contractor establishments × 1 hour = 171,275 hours). We calculate the total estimated minimum costs as $8,582,590 (171,275 hours × $50.11/hour = $8,582,590) or $50 per establishment.

Commenters suggested that reviewing the requirements of the final rule would take up to 6 hours. OFCCP declines to adopt this calculation since it is based on reviewing the proposed rule which included a significant number of additional requirements that are not in the final rule. Therefore, OFCCP estimates the maximum for reviewing the rule would be 4 hours for a total of 685,100 (171,275 contractor establishments × 4 hour = 685,100 hours). We calculate the total maximum estimated start-up costs as $34,330,361 (685,100 × $50.11/hour = $34,330,361) or $200 per establishment.

Assuming there are 251,300 establishments impacted by the final rule, the estimated minimum burden for rule familiarization would be 251,300 hours (251,300 contractor establishments × 1 hour = 251,300 hours). The total estimated minimum costs would be $12,592,643 (251,300 hours × $50.11/hour = $12,592,643) or $50 per establishment. OFCCP estimates the maximum for reviewing the rule would be 4 hours for a total of 1,005,200 hours (251,300 contractor establishments × 4 hour = 1,005,200 hours). The total maximum estimated maximum costs would be $50,370,572 (1,005,200 hours × $50.11/hour = $50,370,572) or $200 per establishment.

2. Section 60–741.5 Equal Opportunity Clause (EO Clause)

EO Clause, Paragraph 4

Paragraph 4 of the final rule clarifies the contractor's duty to provide notices of employee rights and contractor obligations in a manner that is accessible and understandable to persons with disabilities. The final rule revises the parenthetical at the end of the sentence by replacing the outdated suggestion of "hav[ing] the notice read to a visually disabled person" as an accommodation with the suggestion to provide Braille, large print, or other versions that allow persons with disabilities to read the notices themselves. The NPRM estimated that it would take contractors ten (10) minutes to receive an accommodation request and maintain records of compliance.

Upon further consideration, OFCCP determines that there are no new costs related to this provision. The nondiscrimination requirements of section 503 currently require contractors to provide reasonable accommodation. *See* 41 CFR 60–741.21(f). This modification simply updates the example of a possible accommodation that contractors may provide to a visually impaired person, and does not impose any new obligation on contractors.

Paragraph 4 of the final rule also allows contractors to post notices regarding employee rights and their equal employment opportunity obligations electronically if the contractor has actual knowledge that employees will have access to them. OFCCP estimates no additional burden for contractors that opt to post relevant notices electronically. This provision simply provides contractors with another, more expedient, means to meet its existing obligations.

Paragraph 4 of the final rule requires contractors to electronically post a notice of job applicants' rights if the contractor utilizes an electronic application. The existing regulations require contractors to post notices regarding employee rights and equal employment opportunity obligations in conspicuous places for employees and applicants. *See* 41 CFR 60–741.5(a)(4). The final rule clarifies how contractors can meet this existing obligation for on-line applicants. Therefore, there is no new burden for this provision.

EO Clause, Paragraph 7

Under existing Federal requirements, including EO 11246, contractors are required to state in solicitations and advertisements that the company is an equal opportunity employer. *See* 41 CFR 60–1.4(a)(2). The NPRM proposed adding a new paragraph 7 to the EO Clause that would require the contractor to also state in solicitations and advertisements that it is an equal opportunity employer of individuals with disabilities. The NPRM estimated that it would take contractors five (5) minutes to comply with this provision. A few commenters noted that this would increase the costs of solicitations and advertisements since some newspapers and other publications charge for each word of a solicitation.

The final rule incorporates the requirement for contractors to state in all solicitations and advertisements that the company is an equal opportunity employer of individuals with disabilities. OFCCP acknowledges that some contractors may experience an increased cost in light of this requirement. However, there is no indication based on the comments that OFCCP received on this issue that this would be a significant problem for a substantial number of contractors. In fact, the cost of many advertisements and solicitations are based on size (i.e., quarter-page, half-page, full-page) or by listing, rather than the number of words in the text. Moreover, the cost of an advertisement will also depend on the publication's circulation and location. The number of words in the text actually appears be a lesser factor when determining cost. After some research, OFCCP determined that the average cost per word nationally is between 10 and 20 cents for a classified advertisement. Therefore, the cost would not be greatly impacted by adding individuals with disabilities to the affirmative action statement in advertisements.

Information from OFCCP field staff indicates that many contractors already include "disabilities" in their equal employment opportunity statement for solicitations. Therefore, based on field experience evaluating contractor practices, OFCCP estimates that approximately 40 percent of contractor establishments, or 68,510, currently comply with this requirement. OFCCP estimates that the remaining 102,765 contractor establishments will have a one-time burden of 5 minutes for amending their existing standard equal employment opportunity statement to include "individuals with disabilities" or similar language. Therefore, the total burden for this provision is 8,564 hours (102,765 contractor establishments × 5 minutes/60 = 8,564 hours). The cost for this provision is approximately $320,660.

Assuming there are 251,300 contractor establishments impacted by the final rule, the burden for this provision would be 12,565 hours (150,780 contractor establishments × 5 minutes/60 = 12,565 hours). The total cost of the provision would be $470,469.

Section 60–741.5(d)

The NPRM proposed requiring the entire EO Clause be included verbatim in Federal contracts. The NPRM estimated that it would take contractors 5 minutes to download and incorporate the required text in contract templates. OFCCP received nineteen comments regarding the proposed provision. Commenters primarily asserted that the proposed requirement would be too burdensome, since the length of contracts would increase significantly, and requested that incorporation by reference be retained. In response to these comments, the final rule permits incorporation of the EO Clause by reference with the addition of some additional language that OFCCP has provided in the regulatory text summarizing VEVRAA's purpose. OFCCP estimates that contractors will spend approximately 15 minutes modifying existing contract templates to ensure the additional language is included. The burden for this provision is 42,819 hours (171,275 contractor establishments × 5 minutes/60 = 42,819 hours). The cost for this provision is $1,603,263.

Assuming there are 251,300 contractor establishments impacted by the final rule, the burden for this provision would be 20,942 hours (251,300 contractor establishments × 5 minutes/60 = 20,942 hours). The cost for this provision would be $784,115.

3. Section 60–741.41 Availability of the Affirmative Action Program

The NRPM proposed requiring contractors to inform off-site employees of the availability of the affirmative action program for review. The burden for this provision was accounted for in the Paperwork Reduction Act Analysis of the VEVRAA NPRM. The final rule does not incorporate this proposal. Instead, the final rule retains the language in the existing § 60–741.41, but notes that the data metrics required by § 60–741.44(k) are not required to be made available to the contractor's employees or applicants. Therefore, no new burden is created.

4. Section 60–741.42 Invitation to Self-Identify

The NPRM proposed several significant revisions to this section, including requiring the contractor to invite all applicants to self-identify as an individual with a disability prior to an offer of employment and adding a new requirement for contractors to annually invite all employees to self-identify as an individual with a disability, among other things. The NPRM estimated that it would take 5 minutes for the contractor to download and save the text prescribed by OFCCP for the invitation to self-identify into a separate document that it can store electronically, include it in electronic applications, or print out to include in a hard copy application package, as needed. The NPRM further estimated that it would take contractors 5 minutes to download and save the prescribed text for the annual survey to invite employees to self-identify as an individual with a disability. Finally, the NPRM estimated that it would take contractors 1 minute to maintain the self-identification forms.

Several commenters expressed concern about the burden associated with the pre-offer invitation to self-identify. Commenters stated that OFCCP's estimate of 5 minutes was unreasonable. Commenters asserted that the pre-offer invitation to self-identify would require substantial modifications to contractors' application systems. Human resources personnel would also have to expend time and resources gathering and filing the documents. Commenters further asserted that the administrative costs would greatly outweigh the benefits of the pre-offer self-identification. At least two commenters stated that the pre-offer self-identification should not present a significant burden since contractors currently invite individuals to self-identify their race, gender, and status as a protected veteran.

The final rule adopts the voluntary, pre-offer self-identification invitation requirement. *See* 41 CFR 60–741.42 (a). However, in order to ease the burden on contractors, OFCCP is creating a single, one-page form entitled "Voluntary Self-Identification of Disability." This standard form will be used for the pre-offer, post-offer, and the invitation to self-identify; it will be made available on the OFCCP Web site. This should decrease the administrative time that contractors will need to spend putting policies and procedures in place to comply with this requirement.

OFCCP modified its approach to this calculation to specifically distinguish between contractors with web-based or automated systems and those relying on manual or paper-based systems. Larger contractors, those with more than 100 employees are more likely to have web-based systems. OFCCP estimates that 72 percent of contractor companies utilize Web-based application systems.[39] Working at the corporate level, contractors will take 1.5 hours to review and retrieve existing sample invitations to self-identify, adopt the sample "as is" or make revisions to their existing form, save the invitation to self-identify and incorporate the document in the contractor's application form. This burden estimate should be considered in conjunction with the start-up costs associated with this rule. OFCCP allotted 18 hours in the section 503 final rule to modify human resources information systems or establish a process to comply with the rules' new data collection requirements. This is in addition to costs specified for incorporating the invitation to self-identify in the application process. Taken together, contractors will have over 21 hours to modify their existing application process. The burden for these contractors would be 49,676 hours (33,117 contractor companies × 1.5 hours = 49,676 hours). The remaining contractors would simply have to incorporate the invitation to self-identify in paper applications. OFCCP estimates this will take approximately 30 minutes. The burden for these contractors would be 6,440 hours (12,879 × 30 minutes/60 = 6,440 hours). The minimum cost for this provision is approximately $2,101,103. If all contractors used a web-based application the one-time burden of preparing the form and making the IT changes for this provision is 68,994 hours (45,996 contractor companies × 90 minutes/60 = 68,994 hours). The maximum cost for this provision is $2,583,328.

Assuming there are 251,300 contractor establishments, or 67,919 contractor companies,[40] in OFCCP's

[39] This estimate is based on the assumption that 72 percent of regulated contractor companies have greater than 100 employees and will likely use a web-based application system.

[40] OFCCP utilized the same ratio (approximately 3.7) of parent companies to number of

jurisdiction, contractors working at the corporate level, will take 1.5 hours to review and retrieve existing sample invitations to self-identify, adopt the sample "as is" or make revisions to their existing form, save the invitation to self-identify and incorporate the document in the contractor's application form. The burden for these contractors would be 73,352 hours (48,901 contractor companies × 1.5 hours = 73,352 hours). The remaining contractors would simply have to incorporate the invitation to self-identify in paper applications. OFCCP estimates this will take approximately 30 minutes. The burden for these contractors would be 9,509 hours (19,017 contractor companies × 30 minutes/60 = 9,509 hours). The minimum cost for this provision would be approximately $3,102,510.

If all contractors used a web-based application the one-time burden of preparing the form and making the IT changes for this provision is 101,879 hours (67,919 contractor companies × 90 minutes/60 = 101,879 hours). The maximum cost for this provision would be approximately $3,814,616.

Applicants for available positions with covered Federal contractors will have a minimal burden complying with section 60–741.42(a) in the course of completing their application for employment with the contractor. Section 60–741.42(a), on pre-offer self-identification, requires contractors to invite all applicants to self-identify whether or not they are an individual with a disability. OFCCP estimates that there will be a minimum of 15 applicants per job vacancy for on average 15 vacancies per year. OFCCP further estimates that it will take applicants approximately 5 minutes to complete the form. The burden for this provision is 3,211,406 hours (171,275 contractor establishments × 15 listings × 15 applicants × 5 minutes/60 = 3,211,406 hours). The minimum costs for this provision is $96,695,442. OFCCP estimates that there will be a maximum of approximately 33 applicants per job vacancy for on average 15 vacancies per year per establishment. OFCCP further estimates that it will take applicants approximately 5 minutes to fill out the self-identification form. The burden for this provision is 7,065,093 hours (171,275 contractor establishments × 15 listings × 33 applicants × 5 minutes/60 = 7,065,093 hours). The maximum costs for this provision would be $212,729,213.

Assuming that 251,300 establishments are impacted by the final rule, the minimum burden for this provision would be 4,711,875 hours (251,300 contractor establishments × 15 listings × 15 applicants × 5 minutes/60 = 4,711,875 hours). The minimum costs for this provision would be $141,874,556. OFCCP estimates that there will be a maximum of approximately 33 applicants per job vacancy for on average 15 vacancies per year per establishment. OFCCP further estimates that it will take applicants approximately 5 minutes to fill out the self-identification form. The burden under this scenario would be 10,366,125 hours (251,300 contractor establishments × 15 listings × 15 applicants × 5 minutes/60 = 10,366,125 hours). The costs would be $312,124,024.

Commenters also expressed concern about the proposed requirement to anonymously survey all employees to provide an opportunity to voluntarily self-identify as an individual with a disability. Commenters were particularly concerned about the administrative costs related to this provision. A few commenters suggested that complying with this requirement would cost thousands of dollars. These commenters emphasized the costs related to conducting the survey, securely maintaining the data, or consulting with an outside entity to administer the survey. Several commenters noted that the information would lack any value because it would be highly unreliable.

The final rule, at § 60–741.42(c), requires contractors to invite each of their employees to self-identify as an individual with a disability during the first year it becomes subject to the requirements of this section, and at five year intervals, thereafter. At least once during the years between each invitation, contractors must remind their employees that they may voluntarily update their disability status at any time. As noted earlier, the invitation to self-identify is a critical component to allowing contractors, and subsequently OFCCP, to collect valuable, targeted data on the number of individuals with disabilities in the contractors' workforce. Furthermore, inviting self-identification on a periodic basis will enable contractors to capture employees who may become disabled after their hire date or may feel more comfortable self-identifying once he or she has been employed for some time. Contractors will incur the costs of the invitation essentially every other year.

In light of the various comments raised regarding the burden associated with this requirement, the final rule revises the burden estimate for this provision. The contractors' employees will be asked to self-identify utilizing the same "Voluntary Self-Identification of Disability" form provided by OFCCP to be used at the pre-offer and post-offer invitation. Therefore, the time needed by employees to review and complete the form for the voluntary self-identification should be nominal. The form will be simple, written plainly, and will provide employees the option of selecting between one of two identification options.

The employee invitation to self-identify does not require creating an entirely new database or methodology for capturing employee data. Nor does this requirement necessitate procuring an outside consultant to administer this invitation. Rather, OFCCP envisions that this process will require a dedicated period of time during which contractors will enable existing employees to voluntarily self-identify as an individual with a disability using the same "Voluntary Self-Identification of Disability" form mentioned previously. Contractors can also track the data in the same manner that they use for other required invitations to self-identify.

However, OFCCP acknowledges that this process may take longer than the 5 minutes estimated by the NPRM. The final rule estimates that it will take contractors 1.5 hours to conduct the invitation to self-identify. This includes the time needed to develop communications regarding the invitation, distribute communications, and collect and track self-identification forms. OFCCP believes this process will become much more streamlined over time and will likely require significantly less than 1.5 hours in subsequent years. The estimated burden for this provision is 256,913 hours (171,275 contractor establishments × 90 minutes/60 = 256,913 hours). The approximate cost of this provision is $9,619,542.

Assuming there are 251,300 establishments impacted by the final rule, the burden for this provision would be 376,950 hours (251,300 contractor establishments × 5 minutes/60 = 376,950 hours). The total cost of the provision would be $14,114,063.

Contractor employees will have to spend some time reviewing and/or completing the survey. There are approximately 27,400,000 Federal contractor employees. OFCCP estimates that employees will take 5 minutes to complete the self-identification form. The burden for this provision is 2,283,333 hours (27,400,000 employees

establishments from the EEO–1 data to determine that among the universe of 251,300 establishments there are approximately 67,919 Federal contractor companies

× 5 minutes/60 = 2,283,333 hours). Utilizing Bureau of Labor Statistics data in the publication "Employer Costs for Employee Compensation" (September 2011), which lists an average total compensation for all civilian workers as $30.11 per hour, the cost of this provision would be $68,751,157.

OFCCP further estimates that it will take contractors 15 minutes to maintain self-identification forms. This time includes either manually storing the forms in a filing cabinet or saving them to an electronic database. The burden for this provision is 42,819 hours (171,275 contractor establishments × 15 minutes/60 = 42,819 hours). The approximate cost of this provision is $1,603,263.

Assuming there are 251,300 establishments impacted by the final rule, the burden for this provision would be 62,825 hours (251,300 contractor establishments × 15 minutes/60 = 62,825 hours). The cost for this provision would be $2,352,344.

5. Section 60–741.44 Required Contents of the Affirmative Action Program

Paragraph (a): Affirmative Action Policy Statement

Section 60–741.44(a) of the final rule clarifies the contractor's duty to make the equal opportunity policy statement accessible to all employees. The final rule revises the parenthetical at the end of the sentence by replacing the outdated suggestion of "hav[ing] the notice read to a visually disabled person" as an accommodation with the suggestion to provide Braille, large print, or other versions that allow persons with disabilities to read the notices themselves. It also requires the policy statement to indicate the top United States executive, such as the Chief Executive Officer (CEO) or the President of the United States Division of a foreign company, who supports the contractor's affirmative action program. The NPRM estimated that it would take contractors 10 minutes to receive requests for accommodation, provide the document in an alternative format, and maintain records of compliance. Some commenters expressed concern that contractors would have a significant burden making the affirmative action policy available in multiple formats to accommodate various disabilities.

Upon further consideration, OFCCP determines that there is no additional cost for this provision in the final rule. The nondiscrimination requirements of OFCCP's existing regulations require contractors to provide reasonable accommodation. *See* 41 CFR 60–741.21(f)(1). This modification simply updates the example of a possible accommodation that contractors may provide to a visually impaired person, and does not impose a new obligation on contractors. Similarly, no burden is associated with providing more specificity to the existing requirement that the contractor indicate the CEO's "attitude on the subject matter."

Paragraph (b): Review of Personnel Processes

Section 60–741.44(b) currently requires contractors to periodically review personnel processes to ensure that they do not screen out individuals with disabilities. The NPRM proposed requiring contractors to conduct this review annually and mandated specific steps contractors must take during the review, including: (1) Identifying the vacancies and training programs for which protected applicants and employees were considered; (2) providing a statement of reasons explaining the circumstances for rejecting individuals with disabilities for vacancies and training programs and a description of considered accommodations; and (3) describing the nature and type of accommodations for individuals with disabilities who were selected for hire, promotion, or training programs. The NPRM did not assign burden for identifying vacancies and training programs since these provisions mirrored proposed requirements in OFCCP's VEVRAA NPRM, 76 FR 23358 (April 26, 2011). The NPRM estimated that it would take contractors 30 minutes to provide a statement explaining the reasons for rejecting individuals with disabilities for vacancies and training programs. Finally, the NPRM estimated that it would take 30 minutes for contractors to describe accommodations for individuals with disabilities who were selected for hire, promotion, or training programs.

Several commenters noted that proposed § 60–741.44(b) would create a significant burden and costs on contractors. Commenters asserted that the proposed provision would require contractors to create documents related to thousands of employment transactions per year. Commenters also asserted that OFCCP's estimate of 30 minutes to develop these records was too low. Several commenters provided their own estimates that were significantly higher than those proposed by OFCCP. In response to these concerns, OFCCP does not adopt the proposal as drafted in the NPRM, and the final rule retains the existing language in § 60–741.44(b). Therefore, there is no new burden associated with this provision.

The NPRM also proposed requiring contractors to ensure that its use of information and communication technology is accessible to applicants and employees with disabilities. Some commenters objected to this provision, stating that it would be costly and time-consuming for contractors to ensure that all of its information and communication technology was fully accessible and up-to-date. The final rule clarifies the language in this section by stating that contractors must ensure that applicants and employees with disabilities have "equal access to its personnel processes, including those implemented through information and communication technologies." Further, contractors must provide "necessary reasonable accommodation to ensure applicants and employees with disabilities receive equal employment opportunity in the operation of personnel processes." Since contractors already have a duty to provide reasonable accommodations for individuals with disabilities, there is no new burden for this provision. *See* 41 CFR 60–741.21(f).

Paragraph (c): Physical and Mental Qualifications

The NPRM proposed requiring contractors to annually review all physical and mental job qualification standards and for contractors to document their annual review. The NPRM also proposed requiring the contractor to document those instances in which it believes that an individual would constitute a "direct threat" as understood under the ADA, as defined in these regulations, and to maintain the written statement as set forth in the recordkeeping requirement in § 60–741.80. The NPRM did not assign burden for the proposed provision since it mirrored requirements in section 60–300.44(c) of the VEVRAA proposed rule, 76 FR 23358 at 23417. Several commenters expressed concern with this provision. Commenters noted that annual review of all job qualifications and standards could cost some contractors thousands of dollars, especially larger contractors that may have thousands of job titles. Commenters recommended that OFCCP consider requiring the review less frequently. In order to minimize the burden, the final rule retains the existing language in 41 CFR 60–741.44 requiring periodic review of physical and mental job qualifications to ensure they do not screen out individuals with disabilities. Therefore, there is no new burden for this provision.

Paragraph (d): Reasonable Accommodation to Physical and Mental Limitations

The NPRM proposed requiring contractors to ensure that its electronic or online job application systems are compatible with assistive technology commonly used by individuals with disabilities, such as screen reading and speech recognition software. OFCCP determined that this requirement is more appropriately addressed in § 60–741.21(a)(6)(iii) as a part of the fundamental reasonable accommodations obligations of contractors. The existing regulations make clear that it is "unlawful for [a] contractor to fail to make reasonable accommodation to the known physical or mental limitations of an otherwise qualified applicant or employee." 41 CFR 60–741.21(f). Further, the existing definition of "reasonable accommodation" includes "[m]odification or adjustments to a job application process that enable a qualified applicant with a disability to be considered for the position such applicant desires." 41 CFR 60–741.2(v)(1)(i). Since Federal contractors have a duty to ensure that individuals with disabilities who require assistive technology are able to use their job application process, the proposed language does not create any new burden on contractors. The proposal simply clarifies how contractors can meet their existing obligations. Therefore, there is no new burden for this provision.

Paragraph (f): Outreach and Recruitment Efforts

The NPRM proposed several revisions to § 60–741.44(f). The NPRM proposed requiring contractors to list all of their employment opportunities, with limited exceptions, with the nearest Employment One-Stop Career Center. The NPRM did not estimate any burden for this provision since it mirrored an existing VEVRAA requirement. The proposed paragraph (f)(1)(ii) required contractors to enter into three linkage agreements with various entities to help recruit applicants with disabilities. The NPRM estimated that it would take contractors on average 3.2 hours to enter into these linkage agreements. The proposed paragraph (f)(1)(iv) required contractors to notify subcontractors, vendors, and suppliers of the company's affirmative action policies. The NPRM estimated that it would take contractors 5 minutes to revise notices created under a similar proposed requirement in the VEVRAA NPRM to include references to the company's nondiscrimination and affirmative action policies for individuals with disabilities. The proposed paragraph (f)(3) required contractors to conduct self-assessments of their outreach and recruitment efforts. The NPRM estimated that it would take contractors 30 minutes to conduct an assessment of outreach and recruitment in conjunction with correlating assessments under EO 11246 and VEVRAA. Finally, the proposed paragraph (f)(4) clarified the contractor's recordkeeping obligations with regard to these outreach and recruitment efforts.

Several commenters expressed concern regarding the potential burden of the proposed revisions to § 60–741.44(f). Commenters noted that submitting job listings to Employment One-Stop Career Centers in the manner and format required by the center would require a significant expenditure of time. Commenters further noted that it would take much longer than OFCCP estimated to develop meaningful relationships with recruitment entities through linkage agreements. Further, some larger contractors with multiple establishments could be required to enter into hundreds of different linkage agreements. Commenters stated that a less burdensome approach would be for OFCCP to create a job bank that would enable Federal contractors to centrally post all of their job listings to promote recruitment of individuals with disabilities. Other commenters objected to the burden created by the five-year recordkeeping requirements. In response to these concerns, the final rule eliminates the proposed requirements to list all job opportunities with the nearest Employment One-Stop Career Center and enter into linkage agreements. The final rule retains the existing language of § 60–741.44(f), which requires that the contractor undertake "appropriate outreach and positive recruitment activities," and provides a number of suggested resources that contractors may utilize to carry out this general recruitment obligations. Therefore, there is no new burden for these provisions.

The final rule adopts the requirement for contractors to send written notification to subcontractors, vendors, and suppliers of the company's affirmative action policy. Section 60–300.44(f)(1)(ii) of the VEVRAA final rule also requires contractors to send written notification of the company policy related to its affirmative action efforts to all subcontractors, including subcontracting vendors and suppliers. OFCCP therefore expects that contractors will send a single, combined notice, informing subcontractors, vendors and suppliers of their VEVRAA and section 503 policies. Accordingly, OFCCP determined that there is no additional burden for this provision.

Paragraph (f)(3) of the NPRM required contractors to annually review their outreach and recruitment efforts to determine whether they were effective and document its review. Several commenters stated that this requirement would be unduly burdensome and would result in little benefit to contractors' affirmative action efforts. Commenters also stated that OFCCP's estimate of the time required for the review was too low. Commenters offered their own estimates that were significantly higher than that proposed by OFCCP.

Section 60–741.44(f)(3) of the final rule adopts this requirement as proposed. OFCCP expects that contractors will conduct this assessment in conjunction with the correlating assessments required under EO 11246 and VEVRAA. Further, OFCCP believes that if a contractor has been complying with its recruitment, outreach, data collection, and recordkeeping responsibilities throughout the affirmative action program year, as well as its general obligation under § 60–741.40(c) to review and update its affirmative action program on an annual basis (which includes its outreach and recruitment efforts, *see* § 60–741.44(f)), it will take an average of 30 additional minutes for the contractor to conduct the specific effectiveness assessment of its outreach and recruitment efforts, which would include a simple comparison of the annual raw data on applicants and hires that contractors collect pursuant to § 60–741.44(k) to previous years' data, as well as their hiring benchmark, and determining in light of these numbers and any other relevant circumstances whether adjustments in their outreach efforts is necessary. OFCCP estimates that 1 percent of contractors are first-time contractors during an abbreviated affirmative action program year and will be unable to complete the review. The recurring burden for this provision is 84,781 hours (169,562 contractor establishments × 30 minutes/60 = 84,781 hours). The estimated cost for this provision is $3,174,438.

Assuming that 251,300 establishments would be impacted by the final rule, the burden for this provision would be 124,394 hours (248,787 contractor establishments × 30 minutes/60 = 124,394 hours). The cost for this provision would be $4,657,641.

Section 60–741.44(f)(4) of the final rule requires contractors to document all the outreach and recruitment activities they undertake to comply with § 60–741.44(f) and retain these documents for a period of 3 years. Under the existing regulations, contractors are required to establish meaningful outreach and recruitment contacts. Consequently, contractors' outreach and recruitment should already be the subject of some documentation. This documentation may take several forms. It may include, for example, the numbers and types of outreach and recruitment events, the targeted groups or types of participants for each event, the dates or timeframes, location of the events, and who conducted and participated in the outreach and recruitment on behalf of the contractor.

OFCCP estimates that it will take contractors 10 minutes to maintain the outreach and recruitment documentation that would typically be generated as a result of their obligations pursuant to other provisions in the regulations. This does not include any additional time to make the software configuration needed to tell the contractor's computer system to store data for an additional year, as this burden was previously accounted for in the VEVRAA final rule's burden analysis of § 60–300.80(b). Therefore, the recurring burden for this provision is 28,546 hours (171,275 contractor establishments × 10 minutes/60 = 28,546 hours). The approximate cost for this provision is $1,068,842. Assuming there are 251,300 contractor establishments impacted by the final rule, the burden for this provision would be 41,833 hours (251,300 contractor establishments × 10 minutes/ 60 = 41,833 hours). The cost for this provision would be $1,568,229.

Paragraph (g): Internal Dissemination of Affirmative Action Policy

The NPRM proposed requiring the contractor to take several specific actions to disseminate its affirmative action policy, including incorporating the affirmative action policy in company policy manuals, informing all applicants and employees of the contractor's affirmative action obligations, and conducting meetings with management and company leadership to ensure they are informed about the contractor's obligations. The NPRM also proposed requiring contractors to hold meetings with employees at least once a year to discuss the section 503 affirmative action policy. The NPRM estimated that contractors would have a one-time burden of 20 minutes to develop the employee orientation presentation on the company's affirmative action requirements and an additional burden of 5 minutes to conduct the presentation. The NPRM further estimated that it would take contractors 30 minutes to disseminate the equal employment policy to any entity that the contractor has a collective bargaining agreement with and 5 minutes to maintain records of compliance with § 60–741.44(g).

OFCCP received several comments asserting that the agency underestimated the amount of time it would take to comply with the provision. One commenter provided its own estimates from an internal survey of companies that estimated compliance times ranging from 5 to 20 hours. The commenter further asserted that OFCCP failed to consider the number of meetings required or coordination with the internal communications and web services to disseminate the policy. Finally, commenters stated that OFCCP underestimated the costs of this provision by failing to account for the cost of staff time to attend the meetings. In response to these concerns, the final rule does not incorporate the requirement to have contractors conduct meetings with management and all other employees at least once a year to discuss the section 503 affirmative action policy.

The final rule adopts the requirement to include the affirmative action policy in the contractor's policy manual or otherwise make it available to its employees. The existing regulations currently require contractors to develop some internal procedure to communicate to employees its affirmative action obligation to employ and advance in employment individuals with disabilities. *See* 41 CFR 60–741.44(g)(1). The final rule simply clarifies that one of the means by which contractors can do that is by including this in the policy manual. The final rule also gives contractors the flexibility to disseminate the policy by another means, which can include the method they are currently using to comply with the law. Therefore, there is no new burden related to this provision.

The remaining elements that were required in the NPRM and/or were suggested in the existing rule remain in paragraph (g)(3) of the final rule as actions that the contractor is suggested to take, with the exception of the recordkeeping provision, which has been eliminated.

Section 60–741.44(h) Audit and Reporting System

Section 60–741.44(h)(1)(vi) of the final rule requires contractors to document the actions taken to comply with the obligations of paragraphs (h)(1)(i) through (v) of this section, and retain these documents as employment records subject to the recordkeeping requirements of § 60–741.80. Seven commenters stated that the proposed requirement would impose a burden and require new processes for tracking and recordkeeping.

This section is adopted in the final rule as proposed. Under the existing rule, most contractors should document and maintain their analysis of the affirmative action program as a normal part of their review and assessment process. Compliance officers report that, on request, they review or are provided a range of documents related to the analysis including, for example, reports, summaries and data. In many regards, this provision merely acknowledges and formalizes a current contractor practice. OFCCP estimates that it will take contractors 10 minutes to document the actions taken to comply with § 60–741.44(h) and retain those documents. The recurring burden for this provision is 28,546 hours (171,275 contractor establishments × 10 minutes = 856,375/ 60 = 28,546 hours). The estimated cost of this provision is $1,068,842. Assuming there are 251,300 establishments impacted by the final rule, the burden for this provision would be 41,833 hours (251,300 contractor establishments × 10 minutes/ 60 = 41,833 hours). The cost for this provision would be $1,568,229.

Paragraph (i): Responsibility for Implementation

The NPRM proposed requiring contractors to identify the official responsible for affirmative action activities on all internal and external communications regarding the contractor's affirmative action program. In the current regulation, this disclosure is only suggested. Upon further review, OFCCP does not believe that the benefit of this suggested change outweighs the potential burden that it would place on contractors. Accordingly, the language in the existing regulation that contractors should, but are not required to, take this step is retained. Therefore, there is no new burden for this provision.

Paragraph (j): Training

Section 60–741.44(j) of the existing regulation requires training for all personnel involved in recruitment, hiring and promotion decisions to ensure that the contractor's affirmative action program is implemented. The NPRM proposed revising this paragraph to outline specific topics that must be covered in the training. The NPRM also proposed requiring contractors to make specific records and maintain these records, along with all written or electronic training materials used. Since this provision mirrored a similar proposed requirement in the VEVRAA NPRM, the section 503 NPRM estimated that it would take contractors 40 minutes to develop the section 503 aspects of the training and 20 minutes to present it.

Several commenters raised concerns regarding the burden that the training requirements would place on contractors. Commenters noted it would take hours to create their own training modules to adequately cover all of the information required by the proposed rule. Commenters suggested that OFCCP provide a training module to alleviate the burden of this provision to contractors. Commenters further noted that OFCCP did not adequately assess the cost of the provision since the NPRM did not include the cost of staff time to participate in the trainings.

In consideration of these comments, the final rule does not incorporate the portion of the proposed rule listing specific training items that must be covered by contractors or the specific recordkeeping requirement. Accordingly, no new burden is created by this provision in the final rule.

Paragraph (k): Data Collection Analysis

The NPRM proposed requiring contractors to make several quantitative measurements and comparisons regarding referrals, applicants and hires with disabilities and job fill ratios. The NPRM estimated that it would take contractors 1 hour to conduct the required data analysis.

Several commenters expressed concern about the burden associated with this proposal. Commenters were particularly concerned about the requirement to track and analyze referral data since applicants often do not indicate whether they were referred by a state employment service delivery system on their applications. Commenters further asserted that the newly required data collection and analysis would require expensive modifications to existing HRIS. Some commenters noted that the requirement would place a substantial burden on small businesses or contractors that do not have sophisticated electronic databases. One commenter noted that some contractors would be required to manually search paper records and compile data using pencil and paper. Commenters that were opposed to this requirement further noted that the results of the analysis would be questionable in light of the concerns regarding reliability of self-identification data.

The final rule adopts the requirement to collect and maintain data regarding applicants and hires with disabilities. The final rule eliminates the requirement for contractors to collect, maintain and analyze referral data on individuals with disabilities. The final rule also does not require contractors to calculate applicant, hiring, and job fill ratios in this provision. This eliminates many of the concerns commenters raised regarding this paragraph, and also serves to significantly decrease the burden on contractors. OFCCP also included a substantial initial capital or start-up cost estimate for contractors to put systems in place to efficiently track the data.

OFCCP disagrees with the assertion that a significant number of establishments would have to complete this analysis using paper and pencil. Feedback received from public comments regarding the concerns over costs for modifying human resources information systems further indicate that most contractors will have the capability to conduct the required calculations electronically. There are spreadsheet databases that are commonly used by businesses and have the capability to complete the kind of analysis required by § 60–741.44(k) in a manner of minutes. Contractors using this basic kind of tracking database may need to spend some time entering data by hand. However, the amount of time spent should be minimal, as this section only requires the calculation of a few workforce-wide comparisons regarding applicants and hires with disabilities.

Further, OFCCP clarifies the only "new" items in this section are those pertaining to the self-identification applicant and hiring data. The burden for collecting and maintaining the applicant data is already partially calculated under § 60–741.42(a); the burden associated with this section is largely just totaling the raw data on applicants.

OFCCP estimates that it will, at a minimum, take contractors 25 minutes to tabulate the applicant data using an electronic database that is integrated with the contractors' human resources information database where the data is typically stored. In addition, we estimate that an additional 10 minutes is required to electronically or otherwise store the records (e.g., the report or other written documentation generated by the calculations that explain the methodology, the data used, and the findings and conclusions; the data used to conduct the calculations for subsequent validation of the results; and other material used by the contractor for the calculations). The recurring burden for this provision is 99,910 hours (171,275 contractor establishments × 35 minutes/60 = 99,910 hours). The minimum cost for this provision is approximately $3,740,926.

However, some commenters noted that companies may have to calculate this information manually. Commenters stated that these calculations could take more than 6 hours. OFCCP declines to adopt the 6 hour estimate for manual calculations in large part because the estimate and the requirements of this section are significantly scaled back from the proposed rule, as the final rule does not require contractors to tabulate referral data. Accordingly, starting with the 6 hour estimate and scaling it back given the reduced burden of the final rule, OFCCP estimates that establishments without web-based application systems would take approximately 3 hours to tabulate the information required by this section. The burden for these establishments would be 102,765 hours (34,255 contractor establishments × 3 hours= 102,765 hours). The remaining establishments would incur the 35 minute burden, for a total of 79,928 hours (137,020 establishments × 35 minutes/60 = 79,928 hours). The maximum cost for this provision is approximately $6,840,550.

Assuming there are 251,300 contractor establishments impacted by the final rule, OFCCP estimates that it will, at a minimum, take contractors 25 minutes to tabulate the applicant data using an electronic database and an additional 10 minutes to electronically or otherwise store the records (e.g., the report or other written documentation generated by the calculations that explain the methodology, the data used, and the findings and conclusions; the data used to conduct the calculations for subsequent validation of the results; and other material used by the contractor for the calculations). The recurring burden for this provision would be 146,592 hours (251,300 contractor establishments × 35 minutes/60 = 146,592 hours). The minimum cost for this provision would be approximately $5,488,802.

The NPRM also proposed requiring contractors to maintain that data for 5 years. In response to the comments, the final rule reduces the record retention requirement for § 60–741.44(k) to 3 years. No new software needs are anticipated, however, a software switch or configuration may be required to tell the system to retain the records for the additional 1 year (or an additional 2 years in the case of a smaller contract or contractor). According to an IT professional, this is a simple configuration and should take about 15 minutes to execute. No new burden is added because the change required by the recordkeeping provisions of §§ 60–741.44(f)(4) of this final rule and 60–300.(80)(b) of the VEVRAA final rule include this IT change.

OFCCP also solicited comments regarding adding a reporting requirement that would contain the measurements and computations required by proposed paragraph (k), and including the percentage of applicants, new hires, and total workforce for each EEO–1 category. The majority of comments on this proposal asserted that the requirement would impose an unnecessary burden. Several commenters stated that OFCCP did not provide any support or justification for proposing the requirement. As noted in the Section-by-Section analysis, OFCCP weighed the utility of this reporting requirement and found that it may create unnecessary burden. Therefore, the final rule does not adopt the proposed reporting requirement.

6. Section 60–741.45 Utilization Goal

The NPRM proposed a new § 60–741.46 that would establish a single, national utilization goal for individual with disabilities. The proposed § 60–741.46 also outlined steps contractors must take to determine whether they have met the utilization goal and develop and execute "action–oriented programs" to correct any identified problems related to attaining the goal. Finally, the NPRM sought comment on whether there should be a sub-goal for individuals with targeted disabilities. The NPRM estimated that it would take 5 minutes of recordkeeping time per contractor to document the goal. The NPRM further estimated that it would take contractors 1 hour in the first year to determine whether the company has met the goal.

Several commenters stated that establishing a utilization goal for individuals with disabilities would be extremely burdensome. Commenters noted that the proposed provision would require a substantial amount of staff time to research and collect the data for the utilization analysis. One commenter noted that the utilization goal would be particularly onerous for larger contractors as the requirement could result in creating thousands of new goals. The burden would be doubled if contractors had to establish a sub-goal.

The final rule adopts the proposed utilization goal of 7 percent, now § 60–741.45 of the final rule. As noted in the preamble, the long-term, employment disparities between individuals with and without a disability necessitate a quantifiable means by which to assess whether contractors are achieving equal employment opportunity. Further, OFCCP received significant support for the goal from commenters. The disability community and those representing their interests, in particular, were strongly in support of this new requirement. For these commenters, affirmative action efforts under section 503 have been largely meaningless without, among other things, measurable goals for the employment of people with disabilities.

OFCCP disagrees with the assertion that this provision would require contractors to create thousands of new goals. The final rule establishes one goal that applies to all contractors and all different job groups. Section 60–741.45 creates no obligation for contractors to independently create goals specific to their organization or any particular job group. Contractors will use the standard 7 percent goal when conducting their utilization analysis.

Individuals with disabilities make up 4.83 percent of the employed.[41] The section 503 rule establishes a utilization goal for employing individuals with disabilities of 7 percent. To meet the goal, OFCCP estimates that Federal contractors would hire an additional 594,580 individuals with disabilities. This amounts to an additional 2.37 employees per establishment or 8.75 employees per company.[42] Some of these new hires may require a reasonable accommodation. According to research conducted by the Job Accommodation Network (JAN), employers in the study reported that 57 percent of accommodations cost absolutely nothing. For the remaining 43 percent, the typical cost of providing a reasonable accommodation was approximately $500.[43] Few employers, about 4 percent, reported incurring ongoing annual costs associated with providing accommodations. We estimate, in light of this information, that 219,338 disabled non-protected veterans may need accommodations with a total cost of $114,770,291 in the year the target is met and $48,524,879 in recurring costs.

A few commenters stated that one hour is not a sufficient amount of time to conduct the required utilization analysis. OFCCP also disagrees with this assertion. As noted earlier, supply and service contractors are already required to conduct a utilization analysis. *See* 41 CFR 60–2.15(a). These contractors should have some mechanisms in place to conduct this analysis efficiently. Furthermore, OFCCP has estimated a substantial amount of initial capital and start-up costs for contractors to put procedures in place for the annual analysis to be conducted efficiently. OFCCP also increased the estimate of the amount of time necessary to conduct the self-identification process, which will inform the utilization analysis. Therefore, the final rule estimates that, at a minimum, contractors will take 1 hour to conduct the utilization analysis. The burden for this provision is 171,275 hours (171,275 contractor establishments × 1 hour = 171,275 hours). The minimum costs for this provision is $6,413,015.

However, some commenters noted that companies may have to calculate this information manually. Utilizing data from the EEO–1 regarding the number of establishments with fewer than 100 employees, OFCCP estimates that 20 percent of establishments may have to conduct the analysis manually. These establishments would take approximately 3 hours to tabulate the information required by this section. The burden for these establishments would be 102,765 hours (34,255 contractor establishments × 3 hours= 102,765). The remaining establishments would incur the 1 hour burden, for a total of 137,020 hours (137,020 contractor establishments × 1 hour = 137,020 hours). The maximum cost for this provision is approximately $8,978,223.

Assuming there are 251,300 contractor establishments impacted by the final rule and they all utilized some form of electronic system to conduct the analysis, the burden for this provision would be 251,300 hours (251,300 contractor establishments × 1 hour = 251,300 hours). The cost for this

[41] U.S. Census Bureau, 2011 American Community Survey. There are a variety of sources for this estimate. The Current Population Survey estimates a lower rate, 3.5 percent, and the Survey of Income and Program Participation estimates 9.4 percent.

[42] This assumes that there are 251,300 contractor establishments and 67,919 companies. Under an alternative scenario of 171,275 establishments and 46,291 companies, the additional number of disabled hires per establishment and company is 3.52 and 13.02, respectively.

[43] Job Accommodation Network, "Workplace Accommodations: Low Cost, High Impact," Sept. 1, 2012. *Accommodation and Compliance Series*, *http://askjan.org/media/lowcosthighimpact.html* (last accessed Aug. 9, 2013).

provision would be $9,409,376. OFCCP estimates that 20 percent of these establishments may have to conduct the analysis manually. These establishments would take approximately 3 hours to tabulate the information required by this section. The burden would be 150,780 hours (50,260 contractor establishments × 3 hours= 150,780 hours). The remaining establishments would incur the 1 hour burden, for a total of 201,040 hours (201,040 establishments × 1 hour = 201,040 hours). The maximum cost for this provision would be approximately $13,173,126.

OFCCP further estimates that it will take contractors an additional 10 minutes to maintain records of the utilization analysis. This simply requires filing away any records created while conducting the analysis. The recordkeeping burden is 28,546 hours (171,275 contractor establishments × 10 minutes/60 = 28,546 hours). The total cost for this provision is $1,068,836.

Assuming there are 251,300 establishments impacted by the final rule, the burden for this provision would be 41,833 hours (251,300 contractor establishments × 10 minutes/ 60 = 41,833 hours). The cost for this provision would be $1,568,229. Section 60–741.45(e) requires contractors to make an assessment of whether any impediments to equal employment opportunity for individuals with disabilities exist. This assessment can be based on reviews currently required under §§ 60–741.44(b) (review of personnel processes), 60–741.44(f) (review of outreach and recruitment efforts), and 60–741.44(h) (audit of the affirmative action program). A new paragraph (f) entitled "Action-oriented programs" requires contractors to develop action-oriented programs when problem areas have been identified by the utilization analysis. These action-oriented programs may include the modification of personnel processes, alternative or additional outreach and recruitment efforts, and/or other actions designed to correct the identified problem areas and attain the established goal. The existing regulations require contractors to measure the effectiveness of the affirmative action program and correct any identified deficiencies. *See* 41 CFR 60–741.44(h). Therefore, there is no new burden created by paragraphs (f) or (e).

7. Section 60–741.60 Compliance evaluations

Section 60–741.60 of the final rule allows OFCCP to request that contractors make documents available on or off-site during a compliance evaluation and establishes new procedures for pre-award compliance evaluations under section 503. Since contractors are currently required to make documents available to OFCCP during a compliance evaluation, there is no additional cost for allowing OFCCP off-site access to documents. This provision simply affords OFCCP the opportunity to conduct reviews of relevant materials at any appropriate location. The newly created pre-award compliance evaluation requires no action by the contractor and only places a burden on the Federal contracting agency and OFCCP.

8. Section 60–741.80 Recordkeeping

The NPRM proposed requiring contractors to maintain records created pursuant to the proposed §§ 60–741.44(f)(4) and 60–741.44(k) for five years. Commenters stated this requirement was overly burdensome as contractors would be required to maintain a substantial amount of new records either physically or electronically for a longer period of time than required by the existing regulations.

Section 60–741.80 of the final rule requires contractors to maintain data pursuant to §§ 60–741.741(f)(4) (outreach and recruiting efforts) and 60–741.44(k) (applicant and hire data) for 3 years. OFCCP disagrees with the assertion that this requirement would create a need to secure substantial electronic or physical storage space to keep these records. For example, compliance with § 60–741.44(f)(4) can include material evidence that the contractor has attended recruiting events or other similar activities. Since contractors no longer need to maintain referral records, the recordkeeping burden of § 60–741.44(k) requirement is substantially reduced. The primary record contractors would have to maintain is the self-identification forms that the data analysis is based on. As such, there should be no need to secure substantial new storage space beyond what the contractor already maintains in its normal course of business to maintain these forms. There is no additional burden assessed here because it is included in the estimates for §§ 60–741.44(f)(4) and 60–741.44(k). In those sections, we determined that no new software needs are anticipated, however, a software switch or configuration may be required to instruct the system to retain the records for the additional 1 year (or an additional 2 years in the case of a smaller contract or contractor).

9. Section 60–741.81 Access to records

Section 60–741.81 of the final rule requires contractors to specify all available records formats and allow OFCCP to select preferred record formats from those identified by the contractor during a compliance evaluation. Upon request, the contractor must provide OFCCP information about all format(s), including specific electronic formats, in which the contractor maintains its records and other information.

A few commenters objected to the requirement to provide records in formats OFCCP selects. The final rule clarifies this provision to make clear that contractors will not be required to invest time or resources creating records in a specific format, or creating a documented "list" of the formats in which they have documents available. Rather, contractors merely need to inform OFCCP of the formats in which they maintain records and other information, and allow OFCCP to select the format(s) in which the records or other information will be provided.

10. Appendix A, Guidelines on a Contractor's Duty To Provide Reasonable Accommodation

Appendix A includes several changes that reflect updated terminology and revisions made elsewhere in the regulations. These revisions create no new costs for contractors, therefore, there is no burden for Appendix A.

11. Appendix B—Developing Reasonable Accommodation Procedures

The NPRM proposed a new provision at § 60–741.45 that would require contractors to establish formal, written reasonable accommodation procedures. The proposed provision required including various elements in the reasonable accommodation procedures; disseminating the procedures to all employees; informing applicants of the reasonable accommodation procedures; training for all managers on the procedures; and documenting specific information regarding reasonable accommodation requests. The NPRM estimated the following related to this provision: 30 minutes to develop the reasonable accommodation procedures; 5 minutes for first-time contractors to designate a responsible official for implementing the procedures; 15 minutes to disseminate the procedures to employees; 2 hours to develop the training on the procedures; and an additional 5 minutes to maintain records of compliance with the provision.

Several commenters stated that the proposed § 60–741.45 was an overly burdensome requirement. Commenters expressed particular concern about the burden of providing written confirmation of reasonable accommodation requests and explanations of any denials of reasonable accommodation. Some commenters noted that the burden of this requirement would be enormous, such that it was difficult to even quantify how much time it would take to comply with this provision.

Upon further review, OFCCP does not believe that the benefit of this suggested change outweighs the potential burden that it would place on contractors. Therefore, the final rule creates a new Appendix B entitled *Developing Reasonable Accommodation Procedures* that provides specific guidance and sets forth recommended elements similar to those proposed in the NPRM that contractors may use when voluntarily establishing written reasonable accommodation procedures. The final rule also adds a new paragraph (vi) to § 60–741.21(a)(6) that acknowledges that the development and use of written reasonable accommodation procedures is a best practice. However, it does not require that contractors develop such procedures. Therefore, no new burden is assessed for this provision.

12. Initial Capital or Start-Up Costs

Human Resources Information Systems Modifications

Several commenters noted that the new data collection requirements in the proposed rule would require modifications to existing HRIS. In order to estimate the start-up costs for the final rule, OFCCP considered what would be required to modify existing HRIS to track the number of applicants and hires that self-identify as an individual with a disability. Because contractors must already maintain information on their employees by race/ethnicity and sex, contractors should have some mechanism in place to track the newly required information. Further, the VEVRAA final rule requires contractors to make similar revisions to their HRIS to accommodate the new VEVRAA data collection requirements. OFCCP reasonably anticipates that contractors will make the HRIS changes necessitated by this final rule in conjunction with the analogous changes needed to comply with the VEVRAA final rule, resulting in increased efficiency and reduced burden.

The minimum costs for modifying HRIS is based on the estimate that 72 percent of contractors utilize this kind of electronic system.[44] Based on information from IT professionals, OFCCP estimates it would take each contractor company on average 18 hours to make the needed systems modifications to track applicant and hiring information for individuals with disabilities. This includes IT and administrative professionals to make the changes. The estimated costs for these modifications are based on data from the Bureau of Labor Statistics in the publication "Employer Costs for Employee Compensation" (September 2011), which lists total compensation for a professional of $47.21 per hour. Therefore, the minimum estimated burden for the capital and start-up costs is 599,706 hours (33,317 contractor companies × 18 hours = 599,706 hours). We calculate the total minimum estimated start-up costs as $28,312,120 (599,706 × $47.21/hour = $28,312,120) or $849 per establishment. Assuming all contractor companies utilize HRIS, the maximum estimated burden for modifying the systems is 827,928 hours (45,996 contractor companies × 18 hours = 827,928 hours). We calculate the total costs as $39,086,480 (827,928 hours × $47.21/hour = $39,086,480).

Assuming there are 251,300 contractor establishments in OFCCP's jurisdiction, or 67,919 companies, the minimum estimated burden for the capital and start-up costs would be 880,218 hours (48,901 contractor companies × 20 hours = 880,218 hours). The total minimum estimated start-up costs would be $41,555,092 (978,020 hours × $47.21/hour = $41,555,092) or $849 per parent company. Assuming all contractor companies utilize HRIS, the maximum burden would be 1,222,542 hours (67,919 contractor companies × 18 hours = 1,222,542 hours). We calculate the total maximum estimated start-up costs as $57,716,208 (1,358,380 hours × $47.21/hour = $57,716,208) or $849 per parent company.

Operations and Maintenance Costs

OFCCP estimates that the contractor will have some operations and maintenance costs in addition to the burden calculated above.

Section 60–741.42 Invitation to Self Identify

OFCCP estimates that the contractor will have some operations and maintenance cost associated with the invitations to self-identify. The contractor must invite all applicants to self-identify at both the pre-offer and post-offer stage of the employment process. Given the increasingly widespread use of electronic applications, any contractor that uses such applications to invite self-identification would not incur copy costs. However, to account for contractors who may still choose to use paper applications, we are including printing and/or copying costs. The final rule reduces the numbers of forms to one to make the self-identification process less paperwork intensive and to reduce costs. We also estimate an average copying cost of $.08 per page. Assuming contractors using a paper-based application system, used 15 applications for an average of 15 listings per establishment, the minimum estimated total cost to contractors will be $616,590 (34,255 contractor establishments × 225 copies × $.08 = $616,590). Assuming contractors using a paper-based application system, used 33 applications for an average of 15 listings per establishment, the maximum estimated cost to contractors will be $1,356,498 (34,255 contractor establishments × 30 × $.08 = $1,356,498).

Assuming that 50,260 of 251,300 contractor establishments with a paper-based application system, used 15 applications for an average of 15 listings per establishment, the minimum estimated total cost to contractors will be $904,680 (50,260 contractor establishments × 225 copies × $.08 = $904,680). Assuming contractors using a paper-based application system, used 33 applications for an average of 15 listings per establishment, the maximum estimated cost to contractors will be $1,990,296 (50,260 contractor establishments × 495 copies × $.08 = $1,990,296).

D. Summary of Benefits

As a result of this Final Rule, it is estimated that 594,580 individuals with disabilities could be hired in the first year alone.[45] There are tangible and intangible benefits from investing in the recruitment and hiring of individuals with disabilities. Among them are employer tax credits, access to a broader talent pool, an expanded pool of job applicants, access to new markets by developing a workforce that mirrors the general customer base, lower turnover

[44] Utilizing EEO–1 data, OFCCP estimates that 72 percent of regulated contractor companies have greater than 100 employees and will likely use an electronic human resources system.

[45] Individuals with disabilities make up 4.83 percent of the employed. The estimate is based on calculating the number of hires needed to reach the 7% goal in the first year, the estimated number of employees working for covered Federal contractors, and the number of contractor establishments covered by OFCCP jurisdiction. To reach the goal, 594,580 additional individuals with disabilities would be hired. This number also assumes that contractors will not exceed the goal.

based on increased employee loyalty, and lower training costs resulting from lower staff turnover.[46] According to the U.S. Business Leadership Network (USBLN), "corporate CEOs understand that it's cost effective to recruit and retain the best talent regardless of disability."[47] Broad public policy considerations also exist related to the decreased demand for and cost of social services as more people move into jobs and pay taxes.

E. Conclusion

OFCCP concludes in the final regulatory impact analysis that the costs of the final rule will range and likely exceed $100 million annually. The variations in costs depend on the number of establishments impacted by the final rule. Costs will also vary by company depending on their existing infrastructure. We estimate that the lower end costs would be $349,510,926 assuming that there are approximately 171,275 contractor establishments impacted by the final rule. The lower end estimate also relies on the assumption that many of these establishments have some form of electronic application and human resources information systems that would make complying with the rules requirements more efficient. The higher end estimate of $659,877,833 assumes that there are 251,300 establishments impacted by the final rule. The higher end further assumes that a portion of those contractors, primarily smaller ones with fewer employees, would have to expend more personnel time complying with the rules requirements. The recurring costs in years contractors do not invite all employees to identify as an individual with a disability will range from $162,371,816 to $395,258,387. The recurring costs in year contractors do invite all employees to identify as an individual with a disability will range from $242,345,778 to $480,476,442. Therefore, the rule will have a significant economic impact. However, OFCCP believes that the final rule will have extensive benefits for individuals with disabilities who are prospective and current employees of Federal contractors and Federal subcontractors. As such, OFCCP concludes that the benefits of the rule justify the costs.

Regulatory Flexibility Act and Executive Order 13272 (Consideration of Small Entities)

The Regulatory Flexibility Act of 1980 (RFA), 5 U.S.C. 601 *et seq.*, requires agencies promulgating rules to consider the impact they are likely to have on small entities. More specifically, the RFA requires agencies to "review rules to assess and take appropriate account of the potential impact on small businesses, small governmental jurisdictions, and small organizations." If a rule is expected to have a "significant economic impact on a substantial number of small entities," the agency must prepare an initial regulatory flexibility analysis (IRFA). If, however, a rule is not expected to have a significant economic impact on a substantial number of small entities, the agency may so certify, and need not perform an IRFA.

Based on the analysis below, in which OFCCP has estimated the impact on small entities that are covered contractors of complying with the requirements contained in this rule, OFCCP certifies that this rule will not have a significant economic impact on a substantial number of small entities.

In making this certification, OFCCP first determined the approximate number of small regulated entities that would be subject to the rule. OFCCP's review of the FY 2009 EEO–1 data revealed that the final rule directly impacts 20,490 Federal contractors with between 50 and 500 employees.[48] OFCCP analyzed the number of small entities impacted by the rule as compared to the agency's entire universe of regulated entities of approximately 45,996 Federal contractors.[49] OFCCP estimates that approximately 44 percent of the total number of Federal contractors, or 20,490, are small entities with between 50 and 500 employees. OFCCP further refined the analysis to compare the impacted small entities to just the universe of 21,541 small entities in OFCCP's jurisdiction. Under this scenario, approximately 95 percent of small entities would be impacted by the requirements of the rule. Utilizing these comparisons, the final rule may have an impact on a substantial number of small entities.

OFCCP has determined, though, that the impact on entities affected by the final rule would not be significant. In order to further inform our analysis of the economic impact of this rule on small entities, we considered the cost impact of the rule on 2 sizes of entities. We estimated the compliance costs of the final rule on Federal contractors with 50 to 100 employees and 100 to 500 employees. Contractors with less than 50 employees would not be subject to the new requirements affirmative action requirements in subpart C of the rule. OFCCP's analysis of the impact on small entities compared the estimated cost of compliance with the final rule for small entities to the estimated annual receipts of these entities as provided by the SBA. If the estimated compliance costs are less than 1 percent of the estimated revenues, OFCCP considers it appropriate to conclude that there is no significant economic impact.[50]

Contractors With 50–100 Employees

We estimate the first-year cost of this rule to a contractor with 50 to 100 employees to be approximately $3,318. The first-year cost of the rule is the year with the highest compliance cost as the contractor is incurring the start-up costs of the rule. This primarily includes the time contractors will expend reviewing the new requirements of the rule and costs for reasonable accommodations for approximately five newly hired individuals with disabilities.[51]

In order to estimate the cost of this rule on an entity with 50 to 100 employees, we are applying the same

[46] Job Accommodation Network, "Workplace Accommodations: Low Cost, High Impact," Sept. 1, 2012. *Accommodation and Compliance Series, http://askjan.org/media/lowcosthighimpact.html* (last accessed Aug. 9, 2013).

[47] USBLN Disability at Work, and U.S. Chamber of Commerce, "Leading Practices on Disability Inclusion," *http://www.usbln.org/pdf-docs/Leading_Practices_on_Disability_Inclusion.pdf* (last accessed Aug. 9, 2013). The USBLN and Chamber report shares best practices from larger corporations for hiring and providing reasonable accommodations.

[48] The Small Business Administration (SBA) Office of Advocacy reports that there are 27.4 million small entities in the United States. Since Federal contracts are not limited to specific industries, OFCCP assessed the impact of this final rule on small entities overall. If OFCCP used this approach, the final rule will impact less than .07% of non-employer firms and .34% of employer firms nationwide.

[49] The EEO–1data base separately identifies contractor entities (companies) and the facilities that comprise them. The FPDS –NG data base, by contrast, identifies contractor facilities, but does not identify the larger entities of which they are a part. OFCCP utilized the ratio (approximately 3.7) of parent companies to number of establishments from the EEO–1 data to determine that among the universe of 171,275 contractor establishments there are approximately 45,996 Federal contractor companies.

[50] Id. at 18 (impact could be significant if the costs of compliance with the rule "exceeds 1% of the gross revenues of the entities in a particular sector.")

[51] Individuals with disabilities make up 4.83 percent of the employed. The utilization goal under the final rule is 7 percent. To close the gap, federal contractors would need to hire an additional 594,580 disabled people. This amounts to an additional 2.37 employees per establishment or 8.75 employees per company. Some of these new hires may require reasonable accommodation. According to research conducted by the Job Accommodation Network (JAN), employers in the study reported that a high percentage (57%) of accommodations cost absolutely nothing. For the remaining 43%, the typical cost of providing a reasonable accommodation was approximately $500.

type of compliance cost structure previously described in the above cost analysis. However, for this small contractor, we assume they would have a manual application process and not require costly human resources information systems changes. We further assume these contractors would expend: 3 hours manually conducting the data analysis required by the new 41 CFR 60–741.44(k); 3 hours conducting the utilization analysis; 4 hours having a manager review the new requirements of the rule; and incur approximately $40 in copying costs in order to print out the newly required pre-offer invitation to self-identify for applicants. This also includes a cost of approximately $2,500 for providing reasonable accommodation to at least five newly hired individuals with disabilities.[52]

Utilizing data from the SBA Office of Advocacy regarding average receipts for firms, OFCCP determined that entities with 50 to 100 employees average receipts of approximately $14,079,844 per year.[53] The $3,318 costs of compliance with the final rule in the first year would be approximately .02 percent of the average value of receipts for these entities. Therefore, there is not a significant economic impact on contractors with 50 to 100 employees.

Contractors With 100–500 Employees

We estimate the first-year cost of this rule to contractors with 100 to 500 employees to be approximately $5,197. The first-year cost is the year with the highest compliance cost as the contractor is incurring the start-up costs of the rule. The start-up for contractors with 100 to 500 employees primarily includes modifying any existing web-based application and human resources information systems to include the pre-offer invitation to self-identify, becoming familiar with the new requirements of the rule, and costs for reasonable accommodations for approximately five newly hired individuals with disabilities.

In order to estimate the cost of this rule on contractors with 100 to 500 employees, we are applying the same type of compliance cost structure previously described in the above cost analysis. However, for this small contractor, we assume they may incur more costs analyzing data, establishing benchmarks, and modifying human resources information systems. Specifically, we assume these contractors would expend: 3 hours manually conducting the data analysis required by the new 41 CFR 60–741.44(k); 3 hours conducting the utilization analysis; 4 hours having a manager review the new requirements of the rule; and incur approximately $40 in copying costs in order to print out the newly required pre-offer invitation to self-identify for applicants. We further assume these contractors will spend approximately $850 modifying their human resources information systems to accommodate the new pre-offer invitation to self-identify. This also includes a cost of approximately $2,500 for providing reasonable accommodation to at least five newly hired individuals with disabilities.

Utilizing data from the SBA Office of Advocacy regarding average receipts for firms, OFCCP determined that entities with 100 to 500 employees average receipts of approximately $43,547,170 per year.[54] The $5,197 costs of compliance with the final rule in the first year would be approximately .01 percent of the average value of receipts for these entities. Therefore, there is not a significant economic impact on contractors with 50 to 500 employees.

Notwithstanding our determination that there is not a significant impact as a result of this rule, OFCCP considered and implemented a number of alternatives in the final rule as compared to what was proposed in the NPRM. As noted in the preamble, the final rule provides an exception that permits contractors with a total workforce of 100 or fewer employees to compare the individuals with disabilities in their entire workforce to the 7 percent goal. Further, the final rule does not adopt the following proposals: Review personnel processes on an annual basis (§ 60–741.44(b)); review physical and mental qualification standards on an annual basis (§ 60–741(c)); establish linkage agreements with three disability-related agencies or organizations to increase connections between contractors and individuals with disabilities seeking employment (§ 60–741.44(f)); take certain specified actions to internally disseminate its affirmative action policy (§ 60–741.44(g)); and train personnel on specific topics related to the employment of individuals with disabilities (§ 60–741.44(j)). After consideration of the comments and taking into account the expected utility of these provisions in light of the burden that contractors would incur to comply with the proposals, OFCCP decided not to incorporate the majority of these proposals into the final rule, and instead retains the language in the existing rule. These changes will substantially decrease the burden on small entities.

The significant benefits to individuals with disabilities, as well as to contractors, are discussed extensively in the Section-by-Section Analysis of the final rule and in the discussion of the final rule's conformity with Executive Order 12866. Although the primary objective of the final rule is to strengthen the affirmative action requirements of section 503 to employ and advance in employment individuals with disabilities, the rule will benefit both individuals with disabilities and contractors. As modified, the final rule provides contractors mechanisms for collecting data on applicants and employees with disabilities and promotes accountability by requiring contractors to review the effectiveness of their affirmative action efforts. The benefits of proactive recruitment particularly will accrue to individuals with disabilities who may face significant barriers in obtaining employment. The revisions will also promote access to a well-trained, job-ready employment pool for contractors.

Paperwork Reduction Act

Effective Date: This final rule is effective March 24, 2014.

Compliance Dates: Affected parties do not have to comply with the new information collection requirements in §§ 60–741.5(a), paragraph 7; 60–741.42; 60–741.44(f)(4); 60–741.44(k); 60–741.45; and 60–741.80(a) (requirement to maintain records under §§ 60–741.44(f)(4) and 60–741.44(k)) until the

[52] To close the current gap that exists between the target rate of employment for disabled individuals and the actual rate, firms would need to hire an additional 594,580 disabled individuals. This amounts to an additional 2.37 employees per establishment or 8.75 employees per company. This assumes 251,300 establishments and 67,919 companies. Under an alternative scenario of 171,275 establishments and 46,291 companies, the additional number of disabled hires per establishment and company is 3.52 and 13.02, respectively. According to research conducted by the Job Accommodation Network (JAN), employers in the study reported that a high percentage (57%) of accommodations cost absolutely nothing. For the remaining 43%, the typical cost of providing a reasonable accommodation was approximately $500.

[53] In order to calculate this figure, OFCCP averaged the total receipts of firms with 50 to 99 employees provided by the SBA, Office of Advocacy. See Firm Size Data, *available at www.sba.gov/advo/research/data.html#us.* Since the data was issued in 2007, OFCCP utilized a compound 2007–2008 Consumer Price Index inflation rate equaling 6.8% (1.0285 × 1.0385) to calculate the 2009 average receipts of $14,079,844 per year.

[54] In order to calculate this figure, OFCCP averaged the total receipts of firms with 100 to 499 employees provided by the SBA, Office of Advocacy. See Firm Size Data, available at *www.sba.gov/advo/research/data.html#us.* Since the data was issued in 2007, OFCCP utilized a compound 2007–2008 Consumer Price Index inflation rate equaling 6.8% (1.0285 x 1.0385) to calculate the 2009 average receipts of $43,547,170 per year.

Department publishes a Notice in the Federal Register stating that the Office of Management and Budget (OMB) has approved these information collection requirements under the Paperwork Reduction Act of 1995 (PRA), or until this rule otherwise takes effect, whichever date is later.

The Department notes that no person is required to respond to a collection of information request unless the collection of information has a valid OMB Control Number. The new collections of information contained in this rulemaking have been submitted for review to OMB, in accordance with the PRA, under Control Number 1250–0004. That review is ongoing; consequently, the Control Number has not been activated. OFCCP will publish a Notice in the Federal Register announcing the results of OMB's review and the date the information collection requirements will take effect.

The information collection requirements in this final rule relate to the information required to be maintained by contractors regarding their nondiscrimination and affirmative action obligations concerning individuals with disabilities and disclosures workers may make to their employers.

Sections 60–741.40 through 60–741.44 contain currently approved collections of information. Section 60–741.40 requires contractors with 50 or more employees and contracts of $50,000 or more to develop an affirmative action program for individuals with disabilities. An affirmative action program is a written program in which contractors annually outline the steps the contractor will take and has already taken to ensure equal employment opportunity for individuals with disabilities. Section 60–741.41 describes a contractor's responsibility to make the affirmative action program available to all employees. Section 60–741.42 outlines the contractor's responsibilities and the process through which applicants are invited to self-identify as an individual with a disability.

Section 60–741.44 outlines the required contents of the affirmative action program. Contractors must develop and include an equal opportunity policy statement in the program. Contractors must also periodically review their personnel processes to ensure that individuals with disabilities are provided equal opportunity and that the contractor is engaged in outreach to recruitment sources. Further, contractors must develop procedures for disseminating the policy internally and externally and establish an audit and reporting system to measure the effectiveness of the affirmative action program.

The currently approved collections of information for these sections are OMB Control Number 1250–0004 (VEVRAA). Information collection package 1250–0004 covers the nondiscrimination and affirmative action requirements of VEVRAA and its implementing regulations. The VEVRAA information collection package estimates that first-time contractors will take 18 hours to develop and document a joint section 503/VEVRAA written affirmative action program. It estimates that existing contractors take 7.5 hours to document and maintain material evidence of annually updating the affirmative action program. These estimates are based on previously approved information collection requests that quantified the estimated time to develop and maintain a joint section 503/VEVRAA written affirmative action program.

A. Number of Respondents

OFCCP estimates that 171,275 Federal contractor establishments will be impacted by the final rule. However, OFCCP received comments on the estimated number of contractor establishments, including recommending an establishment count of 285,390 using the Veterans Employment Training Services (VETS) annual report. While OFCCP declines to exclusively rely on the VETS report number, we present an estimated high end for the range of the cost of the rule based on a contractor establishment number of 251,300. This number is based on 2010 VETS data from their pending information collection request.[55]

For the purposes of this information collection request, OFCCP averaged the 171,275 and 251,300 contractor establishment figures to come up with a total of 211,287 establishments that will have to respond to the information collection requirements. All costs and hours in the burden analysis of this final rule are calculated using this adjusted number of federal contractor establishments. Further, the burden for several information collection requirements in the final rule are presented in ranges. These estimates are also averaged for this information collection request.

[55] OMB Control Number 1293–0005, Federal Contractor Veterans' Employment Report, VETS–100/VETS–100A, *http://www.reginfo.gov/public/do/PRAViewDocument?ref_nbr=201104-1293-003* (last accessed Aug. 13, 2013).

B. Information Collections

OFCCP's new information collection request under Control Number 1250–0005 for section 503 includes the burden hours and costs for the new information collection requirements outlined in the final rule. The burden for several information collection requirements in the final rule are presented in ranges. These estimates are averaged for the purposes of this information collection request.

New Standard Form—Voluntary Self-Identification of Disability

This information collection package requests approval of a new standard form entitled "Voluntary Self-Identification of Disability." Pursuant to § 60–741.42, contractors will use this standard form to invite applicants, hires and employees, to identify as an individual with a disability pre-offer, post-offer, and through an invitation to all employees.

Section 60–741.42(a) requires contractors to extend a pre-offer invitation to self-identify as an "individual with a disability." OFCCP estimates that contractors working at the company level will take 1.5 hours to review and retrieve existing sample invitations to self-identify, adopt the sample "as is" or make revisions to their existing form, save the invitation to self-identify and incorporate the document in the contractor's application form.[56] The burden for this provision is 85,656 hours (57,104 contractor companies × 1.5 hours = 85,656 hours).

Applicants for available positions with covered Federal contractors will have a minimal burden complying with § 60–741.42(a) in the course of completing their application for employment with the contractor. Section 60–741.42(a), on pre-offer self-identification, requires contractors to invite all applicants to self-identify whether or not they are a protected veteran. OFCCP estimates that there will be an average of 24 applicants per job vacancy for on average 15 vacancies per year. OFCCP further estimates that it will take applicants approximately 5 minutes to complete the form. The burden for this provision is 6,388,610 hours (211,287 contractor establishments × 15 listings × 24 applicants × 5 minutes/60 = 6,388,610 hours). This is a third-party disclosure.

OFCCP estimates that it will take contractors 1.5 hours to conduct the

[56] OFCCP utilized the same ratio (approximately 3.7) of parent companies to number of establishments from the EEO–1 data to determine that among the universe of 251,300 establishments there are approximately 57,104 Federal contractor companies.

invitation to self-identify survey. This includes the time needed to set up procedures to conduct the invitation, distribute communications, and collect and track self-identification forms. OFCCP believes this process will become much more streamlined over time and will likely require significantly less than 1.5 hours in subsequent years. The estimated burden for this provision is 316,931 hours (211,287 contractor establishments × 90 minutes/60 = 316,930 hours).

Contractor employees will have to spend some time reviewing and/or completing the survey. There are approximately 27,400,000 Federal contractor employees. OFCCP estimates that employees will take 5 minutes to complete the self-identification form. The burden for this provision is 2,283,333 hours (27,400,000 employees × 5 minutes/60 = 2,283,333 hours). Utilizing Bureau of Labor Statistics data in the publication "Employer Costs for Employee Compensation" (September 2011), which lists an average total compensation for all civilian workers as $30.11 per hour, the cost of this provision would be $68,751,157.

OFCCP further estimates that it will take contractors 15 minutes to maintain self-identification forms. This time includes either manually storing the forms in a filing cabinet or saving them to an electronic database. The burden for this provision is 52,822 hours (211,287 contractor establishments × 15 minutes/60 = 52,822 hours).

Section 60–741.44 Required Contents of the Affirmative Action Program

OMB Control Number 1250–0004 contains the burden estimates for documenting and maintaining material evidence of annually updating a joint section 503 and VEVRAA affirmative action program. Therefore, there is no additional burden for this provision in this information collection request. OFCCP separately identified below, in § 60–741.44, provisions that are not included in burden estimates currently approved by 1250–0004.

• *Section 60–741.44(f) External Dissemination of Policy, Outreach and Positive Recruitment*

Section 60–741.44(f)(1)(ii) requires contractors to send written notification of the company's affirmative action program policies to subcontractors, vendors, and suppliers. Section 60–300.44(f)(1)(ii) of the VEVRAA final rule also requires contractors to send written notification of the company policy related to its affirmative action efforts to all subcontractors, including subcontracting vendors and suppliers. OFCCP therefore expects that contractors will send a single, combined notice, informing subcontractors, vendors and suppliers of their VEVRAA and section 503 policies. Accordingly, OFCCP estimates that there is no additional burden for this provision.

Section 60–741.44(f)(4) requires a contractor to document all activities it undertakes to comply with the obligations of this paragraph, and retain these documents for a period of 3 years. OFCCP estimates that it will take contractors 10 minutes to maintain the outreach and recruitment documentation that would typically be generated as a result of their obligations pursuant to other provisions in the regulations. This does not include any additional time to make the software configuration needed to tell the contractor's computer system to store data for an additional year, as this burden was previously accounted for in the VEVRAA final rule's burden analysis of § 60–300.80(b). Therefore, the recurring burden for this provision is 35,215 hours (211,287 contractor establishments × 10 minutes/60 = 35,215 hours).

• *Section 60–741.44(h) Audit and Reporting System*

Section 60–741.44(h)(1)(vi) requires contractors to document the actions taken to meet the requirements of 60–741.44(h), as mandated in the current regulations. OFCCP estimates that it will take contractors 10 minutes to document compliance with this existing provision. Documentation may include, as an example, the standard operating procedure of the system including roles and responsibilities, and audit and reporting timeframes and lifecycles. Because contractors are currently required to have an audit and reporting system, it is expected that some documentation of the process and operation of the system audit already exists. The annual recordkeeping burden of this provision is 35,215 (211,287 contractor establishments × 10 minutes = 856,375/60 = 35,215 hours).

• *Section 60–741.44(k) Data Collection and Analysis*

Section 60–741.44(k) requires contractors to collect and analyze certain categories of data. Based on feedback received from public comments expressing concerns about the costs of modifying human resources information systems, OFCCP believes that most contractors will have the capability to conduct the required calculations electronically. However, some companies may have to calculate this information manually. Therefore, OFCCP estimates that the average time to conduct the analysis and maintain the relevant documentation would be 1 hour 25 minutes. Relevant documentation could include the report or other written documentation generated by the calculations that explain the methodology, the data used, and the findings and conclusions; the data used to conduct the calculations for subsequent validation of the results; and other material used by the contractor for the calculations. The recurring burden for this provision is 299,233 hours (251,300 contractor establishments × 85 minutes/60 = 299,233 hours).

No new software needs are anticipated for compliance with § 60–741.44(k), however, a software switch or configuration may be required to tell the system to retain the records for the additional 1or 2 years, as appropriate. The estimated time needed for making this switch is included with the burden estimate for § 60–71.44(f)(4).

Section 60–741.45 Utilization Goal

Section 60–741.45 of the final rule requires contractors to conduct a utilization analysis to evaluate the representation of individuals with disabilities in each job group within the contractor's workforce with the utilization goal established in paragraph (a) of this section. OFCCP estimates that contractors will take 1 hour to conduct the utilization analysis. The burden for this provision is 211,287 hours (211,287 contractor establishments × 1 hour = 211,287 hours).

OFCCP further estimates that it will take contractors an additional 10 minutes to maintain records of the utilization analysis. The recordkeeping burden is 35,215 hours (211,287 contractor establishments × 10 minutes/60 = 35,215 hours).

Section 60–741.81 Access to Records

Section 60–741.81 of the final rule requires contractors who are the subject of a compliance evaluation or complaint investigation to specify all available record formats and allow OFCCP to select preferred record formats from those identified by the contractor during a compliance evaluation. Pursuant to the regulations implementing the PRA at 5 CFR 1320.4(a)(2), this information collection is excluded from the PRA requirements because it is related to an "administrative action, investigation, or audit involving an agency against specific individuals or entities."

C. Summary of Costs

The estimated cost to contractors is based on Bureau of Labor Statistics data in the publication "Employer Costs for

Employee Compensation" (September 2011), which lists total compensation for management, professional, and related occupations as $50.11 per hour and administrative support as $23.72 per hour. OFCCP estimates that 52 percent of the burden hours will be management, professional, and related occupations and 48 percent will be administrative support.

TABLE 1—TOTAL BURDEN FOR §§ 60–741.42; 60–741.44; AND 60–741.45

Recordkeeping Burden Hours	633,861
Reporting Burden Hours	0
Third Party Disclosure Burden Hours	9,077,352
Total Burden Hours	9,711,213

TABLE 2—SUMMARY OF BURDEN HOURS AND COSTS FOR CONTRACTORS

PRA burden	Burden hours	Total
741.42 (Survey)	316,931	$11,866,765.33
741.42 (Survey Employee Burden)	2,283,333	68,751,166.67
741.42 (Modifying Application System)	85,656	2,342,234.35
741.42 (Recordkeeping)	52,822	1,977,794.22
741.44(f)(4) (Recordkeeping Outreach Activities)	52,822	1,977,794.22
741.44(h) (Recordkeeping Affirmative Action Program Audit)	35,215	1,318,529.48
741.44(k) (Data Collection and Analysis)	299,323	11,207,500.59
741.45 (Utilization Analysis)	211,287	7,911,176.88
741.45 (Utilization Analysis Recordkeeping)	35,215	1,318,529.48
Total	3,372,603	108,671,491.22

TABLE 3—SUMMARY OF NON-CONTRACTOR BURDEN HOURS AND COSTS

Existing requirement	Burden hours	Burden costs
Section 60–741.42 (Self-Identification)	6,338,610	$190,855,547

The total estimated cost for applicants to fill out the self-identification form is based on Bureau of Labor Statistics data in the publication "Employer Costs for Employee Compensation" (September 2011), which lists an average total compensation for all civilian workers as $30.11.

D. Initial Capital or Start-Up Costs

Human Resources Information Systems

OFCCP estimates on average it will take each contractor, working at the company level, on average 18 hours to have a professional make the needed systems modifications to track applicant and hiring information for individuals with disabilities. This includes IT and administrative professionals to make any necessary changes. The estimated costs for these modifications are based on data from the Bureau of Labor Statistics in the publication "Employer Costs for Employee Compensation" (September 2011), which lists total compensation for a professional of $47.21 per hour. The cost for these modifications is $48,525,837 (57,104 contractor companies × $47.21 = $48,525,837).

5 CFR 1320.3(b)(1)(i)—Reviewing Instructions

Several commenters noted that the proposed rule did not quantify the burden of reading and understanding the section 503 revisions on contractors. OFCCP acknowledges that 5 CFR 1320.3(b)(1)(i) requires agencies to include in the burden analysis for new information collection requirements the estimated time it takes for contractors to review and understand the instructions for compliance. In order to minimize the burden, OFCCP will publish several compliance assistance materials including factsheets and "Frequently Asked Questions." OFCCP will also host webinars for the contractor community that will describe the key provisions in the final rule.

OFCCP estimates it will take, on average, 2.5 hours to have a management professional at each establishment either read compliance assistance materials provided by OFCCP or participate in an OFCCP webinar to learn about the new requirements of the final rule. The estimated cost of this burden is based on data from the Bureau of Labor Statistics in the publication "Employer Costs for Employee Compensation" (September 2011), which lists total compensation for a management professional at $50.11. Therefore, the estimated burden for the capital and start-up costs is 528,217 hours (211,287 contractor establishments × 2.5 hours = 528,217 hours). We calculate the total estimated cost for rule familiarization as $26,468,979 (528,217 hours × $50.11/hour = $26,468,979).

Operations and Maintenance Costs

OFCCP estimates that the contractor will have some operations and maintenance costs in addition to the burden calculated above.

Section 60–741.42 Invitation to Self Identify

OFCCP estimates that the contractor will have some operations and maintenance cost associated with the invitations to self-identify. The contractor must invite all applicants to self-identify at both the pre-offer and post-offer stage of the employment process. Given the increasingly widespread use of electronic applications, any contractor that uses such applications would not incur copy costs. However, to account for contractors who may still choose to use paper applications, we are including printing and/or copying costs. Therefore, we estimate a single one page form for both the pre- and post-offer invitation. Assuming contractors using a paper-based application system, used 24 applications for an average of 15 listings per establishment, the minimum estimated total cost to contractors will be $1,217,002 (42,257 establishments × 360 copies × $.08 = $1,217,002).

These paperwork burden estimates are summarized as follows:

Type of Review: New collection.

Agency: Office of Federal Contract Compliance Programs, Department of Labor.

Title: Section 503 of the Rehabilitation Act of 1973, as amended

OMB ICR Reference Number: 1250–0005

Affected Public: Business or other for-profit; individuals.

Estimated Number of Annual Responses: 9,711,213.

Frequency of Response: On occasion.

Estimated Total Annual Burden Hours:

Estimated Total Initial and Other Costs: $375,738,856.

The estimated $375,738,856 is the total of the PRA costs resulting from the new requirements of this final rule.

Small Business Regulatory Enforcement Fairness Act of 1996

This rule is a major rule as defined by Section 804 of the Small Business Regulatory Enforcement Fairness Act of 1996. This rule will result in an annual effect on the economy of $100 million or more; a major increase in costs or prices; or significant adverse effects on competition, employment, investment, productivity, innovation, or on the ability of the United States-based companies to compete with foreign-based companies in domestic and export markets.

Unfunded Mandates Reform Act of 1995

For purposes of the Unfunded Mandates Reform Act of 1995, 2 U.S.C. 1532, this final rule includes a Federal mandate that may result in excess of $100 million in expenditures in the private sector in any one year. Accordingly, in compliance with 2 U.S.C. 1532, OFCCP provides the following written statement. All references to other sections of this final rule are incorporated by reference pursuant to 2 U.S.C. 1532(c).

(1) The final rule is authorized by the section 503 of the Rehabilitation Act.

(2) A qualitative and quantitative assessment of the anticipated costs and benefits of this final rule, including the costs and benefits to the private sector, are set forth in the Regulatory Procedures section of the final rule (specifically the sections describing Executive Orders 12866 and 13563, the Regulatory Flexibility Act, and the Paperwork Reduction Act) and the Section-by-Section Analysis in the preamble to the final rule. OFCCP anticipates no effect of the final rule on health, safety, and the natural environment not otherwise discussed in the sections set forth above.

(3) Estimates of future compliance costs are set forth in the Regulatory Procedures section of the final rule (specifically the sections describing Executive Orders 12866 and 13563, the Regulatory Flexibility Act, and the Paperwork Reduction Act). OFCCP anticipates none of the disproportionate budgetary effects of the final rule set forth in 2 U.S.C. 1532(a)(3)(B).

(4) To the extent feasible and relevant, OFCCP has estimated the effect of the final rule on the national economy in the Regulatory Procedures section of the final rule (specifically the sections describing Executive Orders 12866 and 13563, the Regulatory Flexibility Act, and the Paperwork Reduction Act).

(5) The provisions of 2 U.S.C. 1532(a)(5) do not apply to this final rule.

Finally, OFCCP identified, considered, and implemented a reasonable number of regulatory alternatives that were the least burdensome alternative. In those cases where OFCCP did not select the least burdensome alternative, it has provided an explanation of the reasons these suggestions were not adopted in the corresponding section of the Section-by-Section Analysis in the preamble to the final rule and/or the Regulatory Procedures section of the final rule (specifically the sections describing Executive Orders 12866 and 13563, the Regulatory Flexibility Act, and the Paperwork Reduction Act).

Executive Order 13132 (Federalism)

OFCCP has reviewed this final rule in accordance with Executive Order 13132 regarding federalism, and has determined that it does not have "federalism implications." This rule will not "have substantial direct effects on the States, on the relationship between the national government and the States, or on the distribution of power and responsibilities among the various levels of government."

Executive Order 13175 (Consultation and Coordination With Indian Tribal Governments)

This final rule does not have tribal implications under Executive Order 13175 that requires a tribal summary impact statement. The final rule does not have substantial direct effects on one or more Indian tribes, on the relationship between the Federal government and Indian tribes or on the distribution of power and responsibilities between the Federal government and Indian tribes.

Effects on Families

The undersigned hereby certifies that the final rule would not adversely affect the well-being of families, as discussed under section 654 of the Treasury and General Government Appropriations Act, 1999.

Executive Order 13045 (Protection of Children)

This final rule would have no environmental health risk or safety risk that may disproportionately affect children.

Environmental Impact Assessment

A review of this final rule in accordance with the requirements of the National Environmental Policy Act of 1969 (NEPA), 42 U.S.C. 4321 *et seq.;* the regulations of the Council on Environmental Quality, 40 CFR part 1500 *et seq.;* and DOL NEPA procedures, 29 CFR part 11, indicates the final rule would not have a significant impact on the quality of the human environment. There is, thus, no corresponding environmental assessment or an environmental impact statement.

Executive Order 13211 (Energy Supply)

This final rule is not subject to Executive Order 13211. It will not have a significant adverse effect on the supply, distribution, or use of energy.

Executive Order 12630 (Constitutionally Protected Property Rights)

This final rule is not subject to Executive Order 12630 because it does not involve implementation of a policy that has takings implications or that could impose limitations on private property use.

Executive Order 12988 (Civil Justice Reform Analysis)

This final rule was drafted and reviewed in accordance with Executive Order 12988 and will not unduly burden the Federal court system. The final rule was: (1) Reviewed to eliminate drafting errors and ambiguities; (2) written to minimize litigation; and (3) written to provide a clear legal standard for affected conduct and to promote burden reduction.

List of Subjects in 41 CFR Part 60–741

Administrative practice and procedure, Civil rights, Employment, Equal employment opportunity, Government contracts, Government procurement, Individuals with disabilities, Investigations, and Reporting and recordkeeping requirements.

Patricia A. Shiu

Director, Office of Federal Contract Compliance Programs.

Accordingly, under authority of 29 U.S.C. 793, Title 41 of the Code of

Federal Regulations, Chapter 60, part 60–741 is revised to read as follows:

PART 60–741—AFFIRMATIVE ACTION AND NONDISCRIMINATION OBLIGATIONS OF FEDERAL CONTRACTORS AND SUBCONTRACTORS REGARDING INDIVIDUALS WITH DISABILITIES

Subpart A—Preliminary Matters, Equal Opportunity Clause

Sec.

Subpart B—Discrimination Prohibited

Subpart C—Affirmative Action Program

Subpart D—General Enforcement and Complaint Procedures

Subpart E—Ancillary Matters

Authority: 29 U.S.C. 705 and 793; E.O. 11758 (3 CFR, 1971–1975 Comp., p. 841).

Subpart A—Preliminary Matters, Equal Opportunity Clause

§ 60–741.1 Purpose, applicability, and construction.

(a) *Purpose.* The purpose of this part is to set forth the standards for compliance with section 503 of the Rehabilitation Act of 1973, as amended (29 U.S.C. 793), which prohibits discrimination against individuals with disabilities and requires Government contractors and subcontractors to take affirmative action to employ and advance in employment qualified individuals with disabilities.

(b) *Applicability.* This part applies to all Government contracts and subcontracts in excess of $10,000 for the purchase, sale or use of personal property or nonpersonal services (including construction): *Provided,* That subpart C of this part applies only as described in § 60–741.40(a). Compliance by the contractor with the provisions of this part will not necessarily determine its compliance with other statutes, and compliance with other statutes will not necessarily determine its compliance with this part: *Provided,* That compliance shall also satisfy the employment provisions of the Department of Labor's regulations implementing section 504 of the Rehabilitation Act of 1973 (see 29 CFR 32.2(b)) when the contractor is also subject to those requirements.

(c) *Construction*—(1) *In general.* Except as otherwise provided in this part, this part does not apply a lesser standard than the standards applied under title I of the Americans with Disabilities Act (ADA) of 1990, as amended, (42 U.S.C. 12101 *et seq.*) or the regulations issued by the Equal Employment Opportunity Commission pursuant to that title (29 CFR part 1630). The Interpretive Guidance on Title I of the Americans with Disabilities Act set out as an appendix to 29 CFR part 1630 issued pursuant to that title may be relied upon for guidance in interpreting the parallel non-discrimination provisions of this part.

(2) *Benefits under State worker's compensation laws.* Nothing in this part alters the standards for determining eligibility for benefits under State worker's compensation laws or under State and Federal disability benefit programs.

(3) *Relationship to other laws.* This part does not invalidate or limit the remedies, rights, and procedures under any Federal law or the law of any State or political subdivision that provides greater or equal protection for the rights of individuals with disabilities as compared to the protection afforded by this part. It may be a defense to a charge of violation of this part that a challenged action is required or necessitated by another Federal law or regulation, or that another Federal law or regulation prohibits an action (including the provision of a particular reasonable accommodation) that would otherwise be required by this part.

§ 60–741.2 Definitions.

For the purpose of this part:

(a) *Act* means the Rehabilitation Act of 1973, as amended, 29 U.S.C. 706 and 793.

(b) *Compliance evaluation* means any one or combination of actions OFCCP may take to examine a Federal contractor's or subcontractor's compliance with one or more of the requirements of section 503 of the Rehabilitation Act of 1973.

(c) *Contract* means any Government contract or subcontract.

(d) *Contractor* means, unless otherwise indicated, a prime contractor or subcontractor holding a contract in excess of $10,000.

(e) *Direct threat* means a significant risk of substantial harm to the health or safety of the individual or others that cannot be eliminated or reduced by reasonable accommodation. The determination that an individual with a disability poses a direct threat shall be based on an individualized assessment of the individual's present ability to perform safely the essential functions of the job. This assessment shall be based on a reasonable medical judgment that relies on the most current medical knowledge and/or on the best available objective evidence. In determining whether an individual would pose a direct threat, the factors to be considered include:

(1) The duration of the risk;

(2) The nature and severity of the potential harm;

(3) The likelihood that the potential harm will occur; and

(4) The imminence of the potential harm.

(f) *Director* means the Director, Office of Federal Contract Compliance Programs of the United States Department of Labor, or his or her designee.

(g) *Disability*—(1) The term disability means, with respect to an individual:

(i) A physical or mental impairment that substantially limits one or more major life activities of such individual;

(ii) A record of such an impairment; or

(iii) Being regarded as having such an impairment (as defined in paragraph (v) of this section).

(2) As used in this part, the definition of "disability" must be construed in favor of broad coverage of individuals, to the maximum extent permitted by law. The question of whether an individual meets the definition under this part should not demand extensive analysis.

(3) An impairment that substantially limits one major life activity need not limit other major life activities in order to be considered a disability.

(4) An impairment that is episodic or in remission is a disability if it would substantially limit a major life activity when active.

(5) See paragraphs (m), (o), (t), (v), and (z) of this section, respectively, for definitions of "major life activities," "physical or mental impairment," "record of such an impairment," "regarded as having such an impairment," and "substantially limits."

(6) See § 60–741.3 for exceptions to the definition of "disability."

(h) *Equal opportunity clause* means the contract provisions set forth in § 60–741.5, "Equal opportunity clause."

(i) *Essential functions*—(1) *In general.* The term *essential functions* means fundamental job duties of the employment position the individual with a disability holds or desires. The term *essential functions* does not include the marginal functions of the position.

(2) A job function may be considered essential for any of several reasons, including but not limited to the following:

(i) The function may be essential because the reason the position exists is to perform that function;

(ii) The function may be essential because of the limited number of employees available among whom the performance of that job function can be distributed; and/or

(iii) The function may be highly specialized so that the incumbent in the position is hired for his or her expertise or ability to perform the particular function.

(3) Evidence of whether a particular function is essential includes, but is not limited to:

(i) The contractor's judgment as to which functions are essential;

(ii) Written job descriptions prepared before advertising or interviewing applicants for the job;

(iii) The amount of time spent on the job performing the function;

(iv) The consequences of not requiring the incumbent to perform the function;

(v) The terms of a collective bargaining agreement;

(vi) The work experience of past incumbents in the job; and/or

(vii) The current work experience of incumbents in similar jobs.

(j) *Government* means the Government of the United States of America.

(k) *Government contract* means any agreement or modification thereof between any contracting agency and any person for the purchase, sale or use of personal property or nonpersonal services (including construction). The term *Government contract* does not include agreements in which the parties stand in the relationship of employer and employee, and federally assisted contracts.

(1) *Construction,* as used in paragraphs (k) and (x)(1) of this section, means the construction, rehabilitation, alteration, conversion, extension, demolition, or repair of buildings, highways, or other changes or improvements to real property, including facilities providing utility services. The term also includes the supervision, inspection, and other on-site functions incidental to the actual construction.

(2) *Contracting agency* means any department, agency, establishment, or instrumentality of the United States, including any wholly owned Government corporation, which enters into contracts.

(3) *Modification* means any alteration in the terms and conditions of a contract, including supplemental agreements, amendments, and extensions.

(4) *Nonpersonal services,* as used in paragraphs (k) and (x)(1) of this section, includes, but is not limited to, the following: utility, construction, transportation, research, insurance, and fund depository.

(5) *Person,* as used in paragraphs (k), (p), (u), (x), and (y) of this section, means any natural person, corporation, partnership or joint venture, unincorporated association, State or local government, and any agency, instrumentality, or subdivision of such a government.

(6) *Personal property,* as used in paragraphs (k) and (x)(1) of this section, includes supplies and contracts for the use of real property (such as lease arrangements), unless the contract for the use of real property itself constitutes real property (such as easements).

(l) *Individual with a disability*—See definition of "disability" in paragraph (g) of this section.

(m) *Major life activities* —(1) *In general.* Major life activities include, but are not limited to, caring for oneself, performing manual tasks, seeing, hearing, eating, sleeping, walking, standing, sitting, reaching, lifting, bending, speaking, breathing, learning, reading, concentrating, thinking, communicating, interacting with others, and working.

(2) *Major bodily functions.* For purposes of paragraph (m)(1) of this section, a major life activity also includes the operation of a major bodily function, including, but not limited to, functions of the immune system, special sense organs and skin, normal cell growth, digestive, genitourinary, bowel, bladder, neurological, brain, respiratory, circulatory, cardiovascular, endocrine, hemic, lymphatic, musculoskeletal, and reproductive functions. The operation of a major bodily function includes the operation of an individual organ within a body system.

(3) In determining other examples of major life activities, the term "major" shall not be interpreted strictly to create a demanding standard for disability. Whether an activity is a "major life activity" is not determined by reference to whether it is of "central importance to daily life."

(n) *Mitigating measures*—(1) *In general.* The term mitigating measures includes, but is not limited to:

(i) Medication, medical supplies, equipment, or appliances, low-vision devices (which do not include ordinary eyeglasses or contact lenses), prosthetics including limbs and devices, hearing aids and cochlear implants or other implantable hearing devices, mobility devices, or oxygen therapy equipment and supplies;

(ii) Use of assistive technology;

(iii) Reasonable accommodations or "auxiliary aids or services" (as defined by 42 U.S.C. 12103(1));

(iv) Learned behavioral or adaptive neurological modifications; or

(v) Psychotherapy, behavioral therapy, or physical therapy.

(2) *Ordinary eyeglasses or contact lenses.* The term *ordinary eyeglasses or contact lenses* means lenses that are intended to fully correct visual acuity or to eliminate refractive error.

(3) *Low-vision devices.* The term *low-vision devices* means devices that magnify, enhance, or otherwise augment a visual image, but not including ordinary eyeglasses or contact lenses.

(4) *Auxiliary aids and services.* The term *auxiliary aids and services* includes—

(i) Qualified interpreters or other effective methods of making aurally delivered materials available to individuals with hearing impairments;

(ii) Qualified readers, taped texts, or other effective methods of making visually delivered materials available to individuals with visual impairments;

(iii) Acquisition or modification of equipment or devices; and

(iv) Other similar services and actions.

(o) *Physical or mental impairment* means:

(1) Any physiological disorder, or condition, cosmetic disfigurement, or anatomical loss affecting one or more body systems such as neurological, musculoskeletal, special sense organs, respiratory (including speech organs), cardiovascular, reproductive, digestive, genitourinary, immune, circulatory, hemic, lymphatic, skin, and endocrine; or

(2) Any mental or psychological disorder, such as an intellectual disability (formerly termed mental retardation), organic brain syndrome, emotional or mental illness, and specific learning disabilities.

(p) *Prime contractor* means any person holding a contract in excess of $10,000, and, for the purposes of subpart D of this part, "General Enforcement and Complaint Procedures," includes any person who has held a contract subject to the act.

(q) *Qualification standards* means the personal and professional attributes including the skill, experience, education, physical, medical, safety, and other requirements established by the contractor as requirements which an individual must meet in order to be eligible for the position held or desired.

(r) *Qualified individual* means an individual who satisfies the requisite skill, experience, education, and other job-related requirements of the employment position such individual holds or desires, and who, with or without reasonable accommodation, can perform the essential functions of such position. See § 60–741.3 for exceptions to this definition.

(s) *Reasonable accommodation*—(1) *In general.* The term *reasonable accommodation* means modifications or adjustments:

(i) To a job application process that enable a qualified applicant with a disability to be considered for the position such applicant desires; [1] or

(ii) To the work environment, or to the manner or circumstances under which the position held or desired is customarily performed, that enable a qualified individual with a disability to perform the essential functions of that position; or

(iii) That enable the contractor's employee with a disability to enjoy equal benefits and privileges of employment as are enjoyed by the contractor's other similarly situated employees without disabilities.

(2) *Reasonable accommodation* may include but is not limited to:

(i) Making existing facilities used by employees readily accessible to and usable by individuals with disabilities; and

(ii) Job restructuring; part-time or modified work schedules; reassignment to a vacant position; acquisition or modifications of equipment or devices; appropriate adjustments or modifications of examinations, training materials, or policies; the provision of qualified readers or interpreters; and other similar accommodations for individuals with disabilities.

(3) To determine the appropriate reasonable accommodation it may be necessary for the contractor to initiate an informal, interactive process with the qualified individual with a disability in need of the accommodation.[2] This process should identify the precise limitations resulting from the disability and potential reasonable accommodations that could overcome those limitations. (Appendix A of this part provides guidance on a contractor's duty to provide reasonable accommodation.)

(4) Individuals who meet the definition of "disability" solely under the "regarded as" prong of the definition of "disability" as defined in paragraph (v)(1) of this section are not entitled to receive reasonable accommodation.

(t) *Record of such impairment* means has a history of, or has been misclassified as having, a mental or physical impairment that substantially limits one or more major life activities. An individual shall be considered to have a record of a disability if the individual has a history of an impairment that substantially limited one or more major life activities when compared to most people in the general population, or was misclassified as having had such an impairment.

(u) *Recruiting and training agency* means any person who refers workers to any contractor, or who provides or supervises apprenticeship or training for employment by any contractor.

(v) *Regarded as having such an impairment*—(1) Except as provided in paragraph (v)(4) of this section, an individual is regarded as having such an impairment if the individual is subjected to an action prohibited under subpart B (Discrimination Prohibited) of these regulations because of an actual or perceived physical or mental impairment, whether or not the impairment substantially limits or is perceived to substantially limit a major life activity. Prohibited actions include but are not limited to refusal to hire, demotion, placement on involuntary leave, termination, exclusion for failure to meet a qualification standard, harassment, or denial of any other term, condition, or privilege of employment.

(2) Except as provided in paragraph (v)(4) of this section, an individual is regarded as having such an impairment any time a contractor takes a prohibited action against the individual because of an actual or perceived impairment, even if the contractor asserts, or may or does ultimately establish a defense to such action.

(3) Establishing that an individual is regarded as having such an impairment does not, by itself, establish liability for unlawful discrimination in violation of this part. Such liability is established only when an individual proves that a contractor discriminated on the basis of disability as prohibited by this part.

(4) *Impairments that are transitory and minor.* Paragraph (v)(1) of this section shall not apply to an impairment that is shown by the contractor to be transitory and minor. The contractor must demonstrate that the impairment is *both* "transitory" *and* "minor." Whether the impairment at issue is or would be "transitory and "minor" is to be determined objectively. The fact that a contractor subjectively believed the impairment was transitory and minor is not sufficient to defeat an individual's coverage under paragraph (v)(1) of this section.

(i) An impairment is transitory if it has an actual or expected duration of six months or less.

(ii) [Reserved]

(w) *Secretary* means the Secretary of Labor, United States Department of Labor, or his or her designee.

(x) *Subcontract* means any agreement or arrangement between a contractor and any person (in which the parties do

[1] A contractor's duty to provide a reasonable accommodation with respect to applicants with disabilities is not limited to those who ultimately demonstrate that they are qualified to perform the job in issue. Applicants with disabilities must be provided a reasonable accommodation with respect to the application process if they are qualified with respect to that process (e.g., if they present themselves at the correct location and time to fill out an application).

[2] Before providing a reasonable accommodation, the contractor is strongly encouraged to verify with the individual with a disability that the accommodation will effectively meet the individual's needs.

not stand in the relationship of an employer and an employee):

(1) For the purchase, sale or use of personal property or nonpersonal services (including construction) which, in whole or in part, is necessary to the performance of any one or more contracts; or

(2) Under which any portion of the contractor's obligation under any one or more contracts is performed, undertaken, or assumed.

(y) *Subcontractor* means any person holding a subcontract in excess of $10,000 and, for the purposes of subpart D of this part, "General Enforcement and Complaint Procedures," any person who has held a subcontract subject to the act.

(z) *Substantially limits*—(1) *In general.* The term "substantially limits" shall be construed broadly in favor of expansive coverage, to the maximum extent permitted by law. *Substantially limits* is not meant to be a demanding standard and should not demand extensive analysis.

(i) An impairment is substantially limiting within the meaning of this section if it substantially limits the ability of an individual to perform a major life activity as compared to most people in the general population. An impairment need not prevent, or significantly or severely restrict, the individual from performing a major life activity in order to be considered "substantially limiting." Nonetheless, not every impairment will constitute a disability within the meaning of this section.

(ii) The comparison of an individual's performance of a major life activity to the performance of the same major life activity by most people in the general population usually will not require scientific, medical, or statistical analysis. However, nothing in this section is intended to prohibit the presentation of scientific, medical, or statistical evidence to make such a comparison where appropriate.

(iii) In determining whether an individual is substantially limited in a major life activity, it may be useful in appropriate cases to consider, as compared to most people in the general population, the condition under which the individual performs the major life activity; the manner in which the individual performs the major life activity; and/or the duration of time it takes the individual to perform the major life activity, or for which the individual can perform the major life activity. This may include consideration of facts such as the difficulty, effort, or time required to perform a major life activity; pain experienced when performing a major life activity; the length of time a major life activity can be performed; and/or the way an impairment affects the operation of a major bodily function.

(2) *Non-applicability to the "regarded as" prong.* Whether an individual's impairment substantially limits a major life activity is not relevant to a determination of whether the individual is regarded as having a disability within the meaning of paragraph (g)(1)(iii) of this section.

(3) *Ameliorative effects of mitigating measures.* Except as provided in paragraph (z)(3)(i) of this section, the determination of whether an impairment substantially limits a major life activity shall be made without regard to the ameliorative effects of mitigating measures as defined in paragraph (n) of this section.

(i) The ameliorative effects of the mitigating measures of ordinary eyeglasses or contact lenses shall be considered when determining whether an impairment substantially limits a major life activity. See paragraph (n)(2) of this section for a definition of "ordinary eyeglasses or contact lenses."

(ii) *Non-ameliorative effects of mitigating measures.* The non-ameliorative effects of mitigating measures, such as negative side effects of medication or burdens associated with following a particular treatment regimen, may be considered when determining whether an individual's impairment substantially limits a major life activity.

(4) In determining whether an individual is substantially limited the focus is on how a major life activity is substantially limited, and not on the outcomes an individual can achieve. For example, someone with a learning disability may achieve a high level of academic success, but may nevertheless be substantially limited in the major life activity of learning because of the additional time or effort he or she must spend to read, write, or learn compared to most people in the general population.

(5) *Predictable assessments.* The determination of whether an impairment substantially limits a major life activity requires an individualized assessment. However, the principles set forth in this section are intended to provide for generous coverage through a framework that is predictable, consistent, and workable for all individuals and contractors with rights and responsibilities under this part. Therefore, the individualized assessment of some types of impairments will, in virtually all cases, result in a determination of coverage under paragraph (g)(1)(i) or (ii) of this section. Given their inherent nature, these types of impairments will, as a factual matter, virtually always be found to impose a substantial limitation on a major life activity. With respect to these types of impairments, the necessary individualized assessment should be particularly simple and straightforward.

(i) *Examples of predictable assessments.* Applying the principles set forth in this section it should easily be concluded that the following types of impairments will, at a minimum, substantially limit the major life activities indicated: deafness substantially limits hearing; blindness substantially limits seeing; an intellectual disability (formerly termed mental retardation) substantially limits brain function; partially or completely missing limbs or mobility impairments requiring the use of a wheelchair substantially limit musculoskeletal function; autism substantially limits brain function; cancer substantially limits normal cell growth; cerebral palsy substantially limits brain function; diabetes substantially limits endocrine function; epilepsy substantially limits neurological function; Human Immunodeficiency Virus (HIV) infection substantially limits immune function; multiple sclerosis (MS) substantially limits neurological function; muscular dystrophy substantially limits neurological function; and major depressive disorder, bipolar disorder, post-traumatic stress disorder (PTSD), obsessive compulsive disorder, and schizophrenia substantially limit brain function. The types of impairments described in this section may also substantially limit additional major life activities not explicitly listed above.

(ii) [Reserved].

(aa) *Undue hardship*—(1) *In general. Undue hardship* means, with respect to the provision of an accommodation, significant difficulty or expense incurred by the contractor, when considered in light of the factors set forth in paragraph (aa)(2) of this section.

(2) *Factors to be considered.* In determining whether an accommodation would impose an undue hardship on the contractor, factors to be considered include:

(i) The nature and net cost of the accommodation needed, taking into consideration the availability of tax credits and deductions, and/or outside funding;

(ii) The overall financial resources of the facility or facilities involved in the provision of the reasonable accommodation, the number of persons employed at such facility, and the effect on expenses and resources;

(iii) The overall financial resources of the contractor, the overall size of the business of the contractor with respect to the number of its employees, and the number, type and location of its facilities;

(iv) The type of operation or operations of the contractor, including the composition, structure and functions of the work force of such contractor, and the geographic separateness and administrative or fiscal relationship of the facility or facilities in question to the contractor; and

(v) The impact of the accommodation upon the operation of the facility, including the impact on the ability of other employees to perform their duties and the impact on the facility's ability to conduct business.

(bb) *United States,* as used herein, shall include the several States, the District of Columbia, the Virgin Islands, the Commonwealth of Puerto Rico, Guam, American Samoa, the Commonwealth of the Northern Mariana Islands, and Wake Island.

§ 60–741.3 Exceptions to the definitions of "disability" and "qualified individual."

(a) *Current illegal use of drugs*—(1) *In general.* The terms "disability" and "qualified individual" do not include individuals currently engaging in the illegal use of drugs, when the contractor acts on the basis of such use.

(2) *"Drug" defined.* The term *drug* means a controlled substance, as defined in schedules I through V of Section 202 of the Controlled Substances Act (21 U.S.C. 812).

(3) *"Illegal use of drugs" defined.* The term *illegal use of drugs* means the use of drugs, the possession or distribution of which is unlawful under the Controlled Substances Act, as updated pursuant to that act. Such term does not include the use of a drug taken under supervision by a licensed health care professional, or other uses authorized by the Controlled Substances Act or other provisions of Federal law.

(4) *Construction.* (i) Nothing in paragraph (a)(1) of this section shall be construed to exclude from the definition of *disability* or *qualified individual* an individual who:

(A) Has successfully completed a supervised drug rehabilitation program and is no longer engaging in the illegal use of drugs, or has otherwise been rehabilitated successfully and is no longer engaging in the illegal use of drugs;

(B) Is participating in a supervised rehabilitation program and is no longer engaging in such use; or

(C) Is erroneously regarded as engaging in such use, but is not engaging in such use.

(ii) In order to be protected by section 503 and this part, an individual described in paragraph (a)(4)(i) of this section must, as appropriate, satisfy the requirements of the definition of *disability* and *qualified individual.*

(5) *Drug testing.* It shall not be a violation of this part for the contractor to adopt or administer reasonable policies or procedures, including but not limited to drug testing, designed to ensure that an individual described in paragraphs (a)(4)(i)(A) and (B) of this section is no longer engaging in the illegal use of drugs. (See § 60–741.24(b)(1).)

(b) *Alcoholics*— (1) *In general.* The terms *disability* and *qualified individual* do not include an individual who is an alcoholic whose current use of alcohol prevents such individual from performing the essential functions of the employment position such individual holds or desires or whose employment, by reason of such current alcohol abuse, would constitute a direct threat to property or to the health or safety of the individual or others.

(2) *Duty to provide reasonable accommodation.* Nothing in paragraph (b)(1) of this section shall relieve the contractor of its obligation to provide a reasonable accommodation for an individual described in paragraph (b)(1) of this section when such an accommodation will enable the individual to perform the essential functions of the employment position such individual holds or desires, or when the accommodation will eliminate or reduce the direct threat to the health or safety of the individual or others posed by such individual, provided that such individual satisfies the requisite skill, experience, education, and other job-related requirements of such position.

(c) *Contagious disease or infection*— (1) *In general.* The terms *disability* and *qualified individual* do not include an individual who has a currently contagious disease or infection and who, by reason of such disease or infection, would constitute a direct threat to the health or safety of the individual or others or who, by reason of the currently contagious disease or infection, is unable to perform the essential functions of the employment position such individual holds or desires.

(2) *Duty to provide reasonable accommodation.* Nothing in paragraph (c)(1) of this section shall relieve the contractor of its obligation to provide a reasonable accommodation for an individual described in paragraph (c)(1) of this section when such an accommodation will enable the individual to perform the essential functions of the employment position such individual holds or desires, or when the accommodation will eliminate or reduce the direct threat to the health or safety of the individual or others posed by such individual, provided that such individual satisfies the requisite skill, experience, education, and other job-related requirements of such position.

(d) *Homosexuality and bisexuality.* Homosexuality and bisexuality are not impairments and so are not disabilities as defined in this part.

(e) *Other conditions.* The term *disability* does not include:

(1) Transvestism, transsexualism, pedophilia, exhibitionism, voyeurism, gender identity disorders not resulting from physical impairments, or other sexual behavior disorders;

(2) Compulsive gambling, kleptomania, or pyromania; or

(3) Psychoactive substance use disorders resulting from current illegal use of drugs.

§ 60–741.4 Coverage and waivers.

(a) *Coverage*— (1) *Contracts and subcontracts in excess of $10,000.* Contracts and subcontracts in excess of $10,000 are covered by this part. No contracting agency or contractor shall procure supplies or services in less than usual quantities to avoid the applicability of the equal opportunity clause.

(2) *Contracts and subcontracts for indefinite quantities.* With respect to indefinite delivery-type contracts and subcontracts (including, but not limited to, open end contracts, requirement-type contracts, Federal Supply Schedule contracts, "call-type" contracts, and purchase notice agreements), the equal opportunity clause shall be included unless the contracting agency has reason to believe that the amount to be ordered in any year under such contract will not be in excess of $10,000. The applicability of the equal opportunity clause shall be determined at the time of award for the first year and annually thereafter for succeeding years, if any. Notwithstanding the above, the equal opportunity clause shall be applied to such contract whenever the amount of a single order exceeds $10,000. Once the equal opportunity clause is determined to be applicable, the contract shall continue to be subject to such clause for its duration, regardless of the amounts ordered, or reasonably expected to be ordered in any year.

(3) *Employment activities within the United States.* This part applies only to employment activities within the United States and not to employment activities abroad. The term *employment activities within the United States* includes actual employment within the United States, and decisions of the contractor made within the United States, pertaining to the contractor's applicants and employees who are within the United States, regarding employment opportunities abroad (such as recruiting and hiring within the United States for employment abroad, or transfer of persons employed in the United States to contractor establishments abroad).

(4) *Contracts with State or local governments.* The requirements of the equal opportunity clause in any contract or subcontract with a State or local government (or any agency, instrumentality or subdivision thereof) shall not be applicable to any agency, instrumentality or subdivision of such government which does not participate in work on or under the contract or subcontract.

(b) *Waivers*—(1) *Specific contracts and classes of contracts.* The Director may waive the application to any contract of the equal opportunity clause in whole or part when he or she deems that special circumstances in the national interest so require. The Director may also grant such waivers to groups or categories of contracts: where it is in the national interest; where it is found impracticable to act upon each request individually; and where such waiver will substantially contribute to convenience in administration of the act. When a waiver has been granted for any class of contracts, the Director may withdraw the waiver for a specific contract or group of contracts to be awarded, when in his or her judgment such action is necessary or appropriate to achieve the purposes of the act. The withdrawal shall not apply to contracts awarded prior to the withdrawal, except that in procurements entered into by formal advertising, or the various forms of restricted formal advertising, such withdrawal shall not apply unless the withdrawal is made more than 10 calendar days before the date set for the opening of the bids.

(2) *National security.* Any requirement set forth in the regulations of this part shall not apply to any contract whenever the head of the contracting agency determines that such contract is essential to the national security and that its award without complying with such requirements is necessary to the national security. Upon making such a determination, the head of the contracting agency will notify the Director in writing within 30 days.

(3) *Facilities not connected with contracts.* (i) Upon the written request of the contractor, the Director may waive the requirements of the equal opportunity clause with respect to any of a contractor's facilities if the Director finds that the contractor has demonstrated that:

(A) The facility is in all respects separate and distinct from activities of the contractor related to the performance of a contract; and

(B) Such a waiver will not interfere with or impede the effectuation of the act.

(ii) The Director's findings as to whether the facility is separate and distinct in all respects from activities of the contractor related to the performance of a contract shall include consideration of the following factors:

(A) Whether any work at the facility directly or indirectly supports or contributes to the satisfaction of the work performed on a Government contract;

(B) The extent to which the facility benefits, directly or indirectly, from a Government contract;

(C) Whether any costs associated with operating the facility are charged to a Government contract;

(D) Whether working at the facility is a prerequisite for advancement in job responsibility or pay, and the extent to which employees at facilities connected to a Government contract are recruited for positions at the facility;

(E) Whether employees or applicants for employment at the facility may perform work related to a Government contract at another facility, and the extent to which employees at the facility are interchangeable with employees at facilities connected to a Government contract; and

(F) Such other factors that the Director deems are necessary or appropriate for considering whether the facility is in all respects separate and distinct from the activities of the contractor related to the performance of a contract.

(iii) The Director's findings as to whether granting a waiver will interfere with or impede the effectuation of the act shall include consideration of the following factors:

(A) Whether the waiver will be used as a subterfuge to circumvent the contractor's obligations under the act;

(B) The contractor's compliance with the act or any other Federal, State or local law requiring equal opportunity for disabled persons;

(C) The impact of granting the waiver on OFCCP enforcement efforts; and

(D) Such other factors that the Director deems are necessary or appropriate for considering whether the granting of the waiver would interfere with or impede the effectuation of the act.

(iv) A contractor granted a waiver under paragraph (b)(3) of this section shall:

(A) Promptly inform the Director of any changed circumstances not reflected in the contractor's waiver request; and

(B) Permit the Director access during normal business hours to the contractor's places of business for the purpose of investigating whether the facility granted a waiver meets the standards and requirements of paragraph (b)(3) of this section, and for inspecting and copying such books and accounts and records, including computerized records, and other material as may be relevant to the matter under investigation.

(v)(A) A waiver granted under paragraph (b)(3) of this section shall terminate on one of the following dates, whichever is earliest:

(*1*) Two years after the date the waiver was granted.

(*2*) When the facility performs any work that directly supports or contributes to the satisfaction of the work performed on a Government contract.

(*3*) When the Director determines, based on information provided by the contractor under this section or upon any other relevant information, that the facility does not meet the requirements of paragraph (b)(3) of this section.

(B) When a waiver terminates in accordance with paragraph (b)(3)(v)(A) of this section the contractor shall ensure that the facility complies with this part on the date of termination, except that compliance with §§ 60–741.40 through 60–741.44, if applicable, must be attained within 120 days of such termination.

(vi) False or fraudulent statements or representations made by a contractor under paragraph (b)(3) of this section are prohibited and may subject the contractor to sanctions and penalties under this part and criminal prosecution under 18 U.S.C. 1001.

§ 60–741.5 Equal opportunity clause.

(a) *Government contracts.* Each contracting agency and each contractor shall include the following equal opportunity clause in each of its covered Government contracts or subcontracts (and modifications, renewals, or extensions thereof if not included in the original contract):

Equal Opportunity for Workers With Disabilities

1. The contractor will not discriminate against any employee or applicant for employment because of physical or mental disability in regard to any position for which the employee or applicant for employment is qualified. The contractor agrees to take affirmative action to employ and advance in employment individuals with disabilities, and to treat qualified individuals without discrimination on the basis of their physical or mental disability in all employment practices, including the following:

i. Recruitment, advertising, and job application procedures;

ii. Hiring, upgrading, promotion, award of tenure, demotion, transfer, layoff, termination, right of return from layoff and rehiring;

iii. Rates of pay or any other form of compensation and changes in compensation;

iv. Job assignments, job classifications, organizational structures, position descriptions, lines of progression, and seniority lists;

v. Leaves of absence, sick leave, or any other leave;

vi. Fringe benefits available by virtue of employment, whether or not administered by the contractor;

vii. Selection and financial support for training, including apprenticeship, professional meetings, conferences, and other related activities, and selection for leaves of absence to pursue training;

viii. Activities sponsored by the contractor including social or recreational programs; and

ix. Any other term, condition, or privilege of employment.

2. The contractor agrees to comply with the rules, regulations, and relevant orders of the Secretary of Labor issued pursuant to the act.

3. In the event of the contractor's noncompliance with the requirements of this clause, actions for noncompliance may be taken in accordance with the rules, regulations, and relevant orders of the Secretary of Labor issued pursuant to the act.

4. The contractor agrees to post in conspicuous places, available to employees and applicants for employment, notices in a form to be prescribed by the Director, Office of Federal Contract Compliance Programs, provided by or through the contracting officer. Such notices shall state the rights of applicants and employees as well as the contractor's obligation under the law to take affirmative action to employ and advance in employment qualified employees and applicants with disabilities. The contractor must ensure that applicants or employees with disabilities are provided the notice in a form that is accessible and understandable to the individual applicant or employee (e.g., providing Braille or large print versions of the notice, or posting a copy of the notice at a lower height for easy viewing by a person using a wheelchair). With respect to employees who do not work at a physical location of the contractor, a contractor will satisfy its posting obligations by posting such notices in an electronic format, provided that the contractor provides computers, or access to computers, that can access the electronic posting to such employees, or the contractor has actual knowledge that such employees otherwise are able to access the electronically posted notices. Electronic notices for employees must be posted in a conspicuous location and format on the company's intranet or sent by electronic mail to employees. An electronic posting must be used by the contractor to notify job applicants of their rights if the contractor utilizes an electronic application process. Such electronic applicant notice must be conspicuously stored with, or as part of, the electronic application.

5. The contractor will notify each labor organization or representative of workers with which it has a collective bargaining agreement or other contract understanding, that the contractor is bound by the terms of section 503 of the Rehabilitation Act of 1973, as amended, and is committed to take affirmative action to employ and advance in employment, and shall not discriminate against, individuals with physical or mental disabilities.

6. The contractor will include the provisions of this clause in every subcontract or purchase order in excess of $10,000, unless exempted by the rules, regulations, or orders of the Secretary issued pursuant to section 503 of the act, as amended, so that such provisions will be binding upon each subcontractor or vendor. The contractor will take such action with respect to any subcontract or purchase order as the Director, Office of Federal Contract Compliance Programs may direct to enforce such provisions, including action for noncompliance.

7. The contractor must, in all solicitations or advertisements for employees placed by or on behalf of the contractor, state that all qualified applicants will receive consideration for employment and will not be discriminated against on the basis of disability.

[End of Clause]

(b) *Subcontracts.* Each contractor shall include the equal opportunity clause in each of its subcontracts subject to this part.

(c) *Adaption of language.* Such necessary changes in language may be made to the equal opportunity clause as shall be appropriate to identify properly the parties and their undertakings.

(d) *Inclusion of the equal opportunity clause in the contract.* It is not necessary to include the equal opportunity clause verbatim in the contract. The clause shall be made a part of the contract by citation to 41 CFR 60–741.5(a) and inclusion of the following language, in bold text, after the citation: "This contractor and subcontractor shall abide by the requirements of 41 CFR 60–741.5(a). This regulation prohibits discrimination against qualified individuals on the basis of disability, and requires affirmative action by covered prime contractors and subcontractors to employ and advance in employment qualified individuals with disabilities."

(e) *Incorporation by operation of the act.* By operation of the act, the equal opportunity clause shall be considered to be a part of every contract and subcontract required by the act and the regulations in this part to include such a clause, whether or not it is physically incorporated in such contract and whether or not there is a written contract between the agency and the contractor.

(f) *Duties of contracting agencies.* Each contracting agency shall cooperate with the Director and the Secretary in the performance of their responsibilities under the act. Such cooperation shall include insuring that the equal opportunity clause is included in all covered Government contracts and that contractors are fully informed of their obligations under the act and this part, providing the Director with any information which comes to the agency's attention that a contractor is not in compliance with the act or this part, responding to requests for information from the Director, and taking such actions for noncompliance as are set forth in § 60–741.66 as may be ordered by the Secretary or the Director.

Subpart B—Discrimination Prohibited

§ 60–741.20 Covered employment activities.

The prohibition against discrimination in this part applies to the following employment activities:

(a) Recruitment, advertising, and job application procedures;

(b) Hiring, upgrading, promotion, award of tenure, demotion, transfer, layoff, termination, right of return from layoff, and rehiring;

(c) Rates of pay or any other form of compensation and changes in compensation;

(d) Job assignments, job classifications, organizational structures, position descriptions, lines of progression, and seniority lists;

(e) Leaves of absence, sick leave, or any other leave;

(f) Fringe benefits available by virtue of employment, whether or not administered by the contractor;

(g) Selection and financial support for training, including apprenticeships, professional meetings, conferences and other related activities, and selection for leaves of absence to pursue training;

(h) Activities sponsored by the contractor including social and recreational programs; and

(i) Any other term, condition, or privilege of employment.

§ 60–741.21 Prohibitions.

(a) The term *discrimination* includes, but is not limited to, the acts described in this section and § 60–741.23.

(1) *Disparate treatment.* It is unlawful for the contractor to deny an employment opportunity or benefit or otherwise to discriminate against a qualified individual on the basis of disability.

(2) *Limiting, segregating and classifying.* Unless otherwise permitted by this part, it is unlawful for the contractor to limit, segregate, or classify a job applicant or employee in a way that adversely affects his or her employment opportunities or status on the basis of disability. For example, the contractor may not segregate employees into separate work areas or into separate lines of advancement on the basis of disability.

(3) *Contractual or other arrangements*—(i) *In general.* It is unlawful for the contractor to participate in a contractual or other arrangement or relationship that has the effect of subjecting the contractor's own qualified applicant or employee with a disability to the discrimination prohibited by this part.

(ii) *Contractual or other arrangement defined.* The phrase *contractual or other arrangement or relationship* includes, but is not limited to, a relationship with: an employment or referral agency; a labor organization, including a collective bargaining agreement; an organization providing fringe benefits to an employee of the contractor; or an organization providing training and apprenticeship programs.

(iii) *Application.* This paragraph (a)(3) applies to the contractor, with respect to its own applicants or employees, whether the contractor offered the contract or initiated the relationship, or whether the contractor accepted the contract or acceded to the relationship. The contractor is not liable for the actions of the other party or parties to the contract which only affect that other party's employees or applicants.

(4) *Standards, criteria or methods of administration.* It is unlawful for the contractor to use standards, criteria, or methods of administration, that are not job-related and consistent with business necessity, and that:

(i) Have the effect of discriminating on the basis of disability; or

(ii) Perpetuate the discrimination of others who are subject to common administrative control.

(5) *Relationship or association with an individual with a disability.* It is unlawful for the contractor to exclude or deny equal jobs or benefits to, or otherwise discriminate against, a qualified individual because of the known disability of an individual with whom the qualified individual is known to have a family, business, social, or other relationship or association.

(6) *Not making reasonable accommodation.* (i) It is unlawful for the contractor to fail to make reasonable accommodation to the known physical or mental limitations of an otherwise qualified applicant or employee with a disability as defined in §§ 60–741.2(g)(1)(i) or (ii), unless such contractor can demonstrate that the accommodation would impose an undue hardship on the operation of its business.

(ii) It is unlawful for the contractor to deny employment opportunities to an otherwise qualified job applicant or employee with a disability based on the need of such contractor to make reasonable accommodation to such an individual's physical or mental impairments.

(iii) The reasonable accommodation obligation extends to the contractor's use of electronic or online job application systems. If a contractor uses such a system, it must provide necessary reasonable accommodation to ensure that an otherwise qualified individual with a disability who is not able to fully utilize that system is nonetheless provided with equal opportunity to apply and be considered for all jobs. Though not required by this part, it is a best practice for the contractor to make its online job application system accessible and compatible with assistive technologies used by individuals with disabilities.

(iv) A qualified individual with a disability is not required to accept an accommodation, aid, service, opportunity, or benefit which such qualified individual chooses not to accept. However, if such individual rejects a reasonable accommodation, aid, service, opportunity or benefit that is necessary to enable the individual to perform the essential functions of the position held or desired, and cannot, as a result of that rejection, perform the essential functions of the position, the individual will not be considered a qualified individual with a disability.

(v) A contractor is not required to provide reasonable accommodation to an individual who satisfies only the "regarded as having such an impairment" prong of the definition of "disability," as defined in § 60-741.2(v)(1).

(vi) *Reasonable accommodation procedures.* The development and use of written procedures for processing requests for reasonable accommodation is a best practice that may assist the contractor in meeting its reasonable accommodation obligations under section 503 and this part. Such procedures help ensure that applicants and employees are informed as to how to request a reasonable accommodation and are aware of how such a request will be processed by the contractor. They also help ensure that the contractor's supervisors and managers know what to do should they receive a request for reasonable accommodation, and that all requests for accommodation are processed swiftly, within a reasonable period of time. The development and use of written reasonable accommodation procedures is not required by this part, and it is not a violation of this part for a contractor not to have or use such procedures. However, Appendix B of this part provides guidance to contractors that choose to develop and use written reasonable accommodation procedures.

(7) *Qualification standards, tests and other selection criteria*—(i) *In general.* It is unlawful for the contractor to use qualification standards, employment tests, or other selection criteria that screen out or tend to screen out an individual with a disability or a class of individuals with disabilities, on the basis of disability, unless the standard, test, or other selection criterion, as used by the contractor, is shown to be job-related for the position in question and is consistent with business necessity. Selection criteria that concern an essential function may not be used to exclude an individual with a disability if that individual could satisfy the criteria with provision of a reasonable accommodation. Selection criteria that exclude or tend to exclude an individual with a disability or a class of individuals with disabilities on the basis of disability but concern only marginal functions of the job would not be consistent with business necessity. The contractor may not refuse to hire an applicant with a disability because the applicant's disability prevents him or her from performing marginal functions.

(ii) *Qualification standards and tests related to uncorrected vision.* It is unlawful for the contractor to use qualification standards, employment tests, or other selection criteria based on an individual's uncorrected vision unless the standard, test, or other selection criteria, as used by the contractor, is shown to be job-related for the position in question and consistent with business necessity. An individual challenging a contractor's application of a qualification standard, test, or other criterion based on uncorrected vision need not be an individual with a disability, but must be adversely affected by the application of the standard, test, or other criterion.

(iii) The Uniform Guidelines on Employee Selection Procedures, 41 CFR part 60–3, do not apply to the Rehabilitation Act and are similarly inapplicable to this part.

(8) *Administration of tests.* It is unlawful for the contractor to fail to select and administer tests concerning employment in the most effective manner to ensure that, when a test is administered to a job applicant or employee who has a disability that impairs sensory, manual, or speaking skills, the test results accurately reflect the skills, aptitude, or whatever other factor of the applicant or employee that the test purports to measure, rather than reflecting the impaired sensory, manual, or speaking skills of such employee or applicant, except where such skills are the factors that the test purports to measure.

(9) *Compensation.* In offering employment or promotions to individuals with disabilities, it is unlawful for the contractor to reduce the amount of compensation offered because of any income based upon a disability-related pension or other disability-related benefit the applicant or employee receives from another source. Nor may the contractor reduce the amount of compensation offered to an individual with a disability because of the actual or anticipated cost of a reasonable accommodation the individual needs or may request.

(b) *Claims of No Disability.* Nothing in this part shall provide the basis for a claim that an individual without a disability was subject to discrimination because of the lack of disability, or because an individual with a disability was granted an accommodation that was denied to an individual without a disability.

§ 60–741.22 Direct threat defense.

The contractor may use as a qualification standard the requirement that an individual be able to perform the essential functions of the position held or desired without posing a direct threat to the health or safety of the individual or others in the workplace. (See § 60–741.2(e) defining *direct threat.*)

§ 60–741.23 Medical examinations and inquiries.

(a) *Prohibited medical examinations or inquiries.* Except as stated in paragraphs (b) and (c) of this section, it is unlawful for the contractor to require a medical examination of an applicant or employee or to make inquiries as to whether an applicant or employee is an individual with a disability or as to the nature or severity of such disability.

(b) *Permitted medical examinations and inquiries*—(1) *Acceptable pre-employment inquiry.* The contractor may make pre-employment inquiries into the ability of an applicant to perform job-related functions, and/or may ask an applicant to describe or to demonstrate how, with or without reasonable accommodation, the applicant will be able to perform job-related functions.

(2) *Employment entrance examination.* The contractor may require a medical examination (and/or inquiry) after making an offer of employment to a job applicant and before the applicant begins his or her employment duties, and may condition an offer of employment on the results of such examination (and/or inquiry), if all entering employees in the same job category are subjected to such an examination (and/or inquiry) regardless of disability.

(3) *Examination of employees.* The contractor may require a medical examination (and/or inquiry) of an employee that is job-related and consistent with business necessity. The contractor may make inquiries into the ability of an employee to perform job-related functions.

(4) *Other acceptable examinations and inquiries.* The contractor may conduct voluntary medical examinations and activities, including voluntary medical histories, which are part of an employee health program available to employees at the work site. These medical examinations and activities do not have to be job-related and consistent with business necessity.

(5) Medical examinations conducted in accordance with paragraph (b)(2) of this section do not have to be job-related and consistent with business necessity. However, if certain criteria are used to screen out an applicant or applicants or an employee or employees with disabilities as a result of such examinations or inquiries, the contractor must demonstrate that the exclusionary criteria are job-related and consistent with business necessity, and that performance of the essential job functions cannot be accomplished with reasonable accommodations as required in this part.

(c) *Invitation to self-identify.* The contractor shall invite the applicant to self-identify as an individual with a disability as specified in § 60–741.42.

(d) *Confidentiality and use of medical information.* (1) Information obtained under this section regarding the medical condition or history of any applicant or employee shall be collected and maintained on separate forms and in separate medical files and treated as a confidential medical record, except that:

(i) Supervisors and managers may be informed regarding necessary restrictions on the work or duties of the applicant or employee and necessary accommodations;

(ii) First aid and safety personnel may be informed, when appropriate, if the disability might require emergency treatment; and

(iii) Government officials engaged in enforcing the laws administered by OFCCP, including this part, or enforcing the Americans with Disabilities Act, as amended, shall be provided relevant information on request.

(2) Information obtained under this section regarding the medical condition or history of any applicant or employee shall not be used for any purpose inconsistent with this part.

§ 60–741.24 Drugs and alcohol.

(a) *Specific activities permitted.* The contractor:

(1) May prohibit the illegal use of drugs and the use of alcohol at the workplace by all employees;

(2) May require that employees not be under the influence of alcohol or be engaging in the illegal use of drugs at the workplace;

(3) May require that all employees behave in conformance with the requirements established under the Drug-Free Workplace Act of 1988 (41 U.S.C. 701 *et seq.*);

(4) May hold an employee who engages in the illegal use of drugs or who is an alcoholic to the same qualification standards for employment or job performance and behavior to which the contractor holds its other employees, even if any unsatisfactory performance or behavior is related to the employee's drug use or alcoholism;

(5) May require that its employees employed in an industry subject to such regulations comply with the standards established in the regulations (if any) of the Departments of Defense and Transportation, and of the Nuclear Regulatory Commission, and other Federal agencies regarding alcohol and the illegal use of drugs; and

(6) May require that employees employed in sensitive positions comply with the regulations (if any) of the Departments of Defense and Transportation, and of the Nuclear Regulatory Commission, and other Federal agencies that apply to employment in sensitive positions subject to such regulations.

(b) *Drug testing*—(1) *General policy.* For purposes of this part, a test to determine the illegal use of drugs is not considered a medical examination. Thus, the administration of such drug tests by the contractor to its job applicants or employees is not a violation of § 60–741.23. Nothing in this part shall be construed to encourage, prohibit, or authorize the contractor to conduct drug tests of job applicants or employees to determine the illegal use of drugs or to make employment decisions based on such test results.

(2) *Transportation employees.* Nothing in this part shall be construed to encourage, prohibit, or authorize the otherwise lawful exercise by contractors subject to the jurisdiction of the Department of Transportation of authority to test employees in, and applicants for, positions involving safety-sensitive duties for the illegal use of drugs or for on-duty impairment by alcohol; and remove from safety-sensitive positions persons who test positive for illegal use of drugs or on-duty impairment by alcohol pursuant to paragraph (b)(1) of this section.

(3) Any information regarding the medical condition or history of any employee or applicant obtained from a test to determine the illegal use of drugs, except information regarding the illegal use of drugs, is subject to the requirements of § 60–741.23(b)(5) and (c).

§ 60–741.25 Health insurance, life insurance, and other benefit plans.

(a) An insurer, hospital, or medical service company, health maintenance organization, or any agent or entity that administers benefit plans, or similar organizations may underwrite risks, classify risks, or administer such risks that are based on or not inconsistent with State law.

(b) The contractor may establish, sponsor, observe, or administer the terms of a bona fide benefit plan that are based on underwriting risks, classifying risks, or administering such risks that are based on or not inconsistent with State law.

(c) The contractor may establish, sponsor, observe, or administer the terms of a bona fide benefit plan that is not subject to State laws that regulate insurance.

(d) The contractor may not deny an individual with a disability equal access to insurance or subject an individual with a disability to different terms or conditions of insurance based on disability alone, if the disability does not pose increased risks.

(e) The activities described in paragraphs (a), (b), and (c) of this section are permitted unless these activities are used as a subterfuge to evade the purposes of this part.

Subpart C—Affirmative Action Program

§ 60–741.40 General purpose and applicability of the affirmative action program requirement.

(a) *General purpose.* An affirmative action program is a management tool designed to ensure equal employment opportunity and foster employment opportunities for individuals with disabilities. An affirmative action program institutionalizes the contractor's commitment to equality in every aspect of employment and is more than a paperwork exercise. An affirmative action program is dynamic in nature and includes measurable objectives, quantitative analyses, and internal auditing and reporting systems that measure the contractor's progress toward achieving equal employment opportunity for individuals with disabilities.

(b) *Applicability of the affirmative action program.* (1) The requirements of this subpart apply to every Government contractor that has 50 or more employees and a contract of $50,000 or more.

(2) Contractors described in paragraph (b)(1) of this section shall, within 120 days of the commencement of a contract, prepare and maintain an affirmative action program at each establishment. The affirmative action program shall set forth the contractor's policies and procedures in accordance with this part. This program may be integrated into or kept separate from other affirmative action programs.

(3) The affirmative action program shall be reviewed and updated annually by the official designated by the contractor pursuant to § 60–741.44(i).

(c) *Submission of program to OFCCP.* The contractor shall submit the affirmative action program within 30 days of a request from OFCCP, unless the request provides for a different time. The contractor also shall make the affirmative action program promptly available on-site upon OFCCP's request.

§ 60–741.41 Availability of affirmative action program.

The full affirmative action program, absent the data metrics required by § 60–741.44(k), shall be available to any employee or applicant for employment for inspection upon request. The location and hours during which the program may be obtained shall be posted at each establishment.

§ 60–741.42 Invitation to self-identify.

(a) *Pre-offer.* (1) As part of the contractor's affirmative action obligation, the contractor shall invite applicants to inform the contractor whether the applicant believes that he or she is an individual with a disability as defined in § 60–741.2(g)(1)(i) or (ii). This invitation shall be provided to each applicant when the applicant applies or is considered for employment. The invitation may be included with the application materials for a position, but must be separate from the application.

(2) The contractor shall invite an applicant to self-identify as required in paragraph (a) of this section using the language and manner prescribed by the Director and published on the OFCCP Web site.

(b) *Post-offer.* (1) At any time after the offer of employment, but before the applicant begins his or her job duties, the contractor shall invite the applicant to inform the contractor whether the applicant believes that he or she is an individual with a disability as defined in § 60–741.2(g)(1)(i) or (ii).

(2) The contractor shall invite an applicant to self-identify as required in paragraph (b) of this section using the language and manner prescribed by the Director and published on the OFCCP Web site.

(c) *Employees.* The contractor shall invite each of its employees to voluntarily inform the contractor whether the employee believes that he or she is an individual with a disability as defined in § 60–741.2(g)(1)(i) or (ii). This invitation shall be extended the first year the contractor becomes subject to the requirements of this section and at five year intervals, thereafter, using the language and manner prescribed by the Director and published on the OFCCP Web site. At least once during the intervening years between these invitations, the contractor must remind their employees that they may voluntarily update their disability status.

(d) The contractor may not compel or coerce an individual to self-identify as an individual with a disability.

(e) The contractor shall keep all information on self-identification confidential, and shall maintain it in a data analysis file (rather than in the medical files of individual employees). *See* § 60–741.23(d). The contractor shall provide self-identification information to OFCCP upon request. Self-identification information may be used only in accordance with this part.

(f) Nothing in this section shall relieve the contractor of its obligation to take affirmative action with respect to those applicants or employees of whose disability the contractor has knowledge.

(g) Nothing in this section shall relieve the contractor from liability for discrimination in violation of section 503 or this part.

§ 60–741.43 Affirmative action policy.

Under the affirmative action obligations imposed by the act, contractors shall not discriminate because of physical or mental disability and shall take affirmative action to employ and advance in employment qualified individuals with disabilities at all levels of employment, including the executive level. Such action shall apply to all employment activities set forth in § 60–741.20.

§ 60–741.44 Required contents of affirmative action programs.

Acceptable affirmative action programs shall contain, but not necessarily be limited to the following elements:

(a) *Policy statement.* The contractor shall include an equal opportunity policy statement in its affirmative action program, and shall post the policy statement on company bulletin boards. The contractor must ensure that applicants and employees with disabilities are provided the notice in a form that is accessible and understandable to the individual with a disability (e.g., providing Braille or large print versions of the notice, or posting a copy of the notice at a lower height for easy viewing by a person using a wheelchair). The policy statement shall indicate the top United States executive's (such as the Chief Executive Officer or the President of the United States Division of a foreign company) support for the contractor's affirmative action program, provide for an audit and reporting system (see paragraph (h) of this section) and assign overall responsibility for the implementation of affirmative action activities required under this part (see paragraph (i) of this section). Additionally, the policy shall state, among other things that the contractor will: recruit, hire, train, and promote persons in all job titles, and ensure that all other personnel actions are administered without regard to disability; and ensure that all employment decisions are based only on valid job requirements. The policy shall state that employees and applicants shall not be subjected to harassment, intimidation, threats, coercion, or discrimination because they have engaged in or may engage in any of the following activities:

(1) Filing a complaint;

(2) Assisting or participating in an investigation, compliance evaluation, hearing, or any other activity related to the administration of section 503 or any other Federal, State, or local law requiring equal opportunity for individuals with disabilities;

(3) Opposing any act or practice made unlawful by section 503 or its implementing regulations in this part, or any other Federal, State or local law requiring equal opportunity for individuals with disabilities; or

(4) Exercising any other right protected by section 503 or its implementing regulations in this part.

(b) *Review of personnel processes.* The contractor shall ensure that its personnel processes provide for careful, thorough, and systematic consideration of the job qualifications of applicants and employees with known disabilities for job vacancies filled either by hiring or promotion, and for all training opportunities offered or available. The contractor shall ensure that its personnel processes do not stereotype individuals with disabilities in a manner which limits their access to all jobs for which they are qualified. In addition, the contractor shall ensure that applicants and employees with disabilities have equal access to its personnel processes, including those implemented through information and communication technologies. The contractor is required to provide necessary reasonable accommodation to ensure applicants and employees with disabilities receive equal opportunity in the operation of personnel processes. The contractor is also encouraged to make its information and communication technologies accessible, even absent a specific request for reasonable accommodation.[3] The contractor shall periodically review such processes and make any necessary modifications to ensure that these obligations are carried out. A description of the review and any necessary modifications to personnel processes or development of new processes shall be included in any affirmative action programs required under this part. The contractor must design procedures that facilitate a review of the implementation of this requirement by the contractor and the Government.

(c) *Physical and mental qualifications.* (1) The contractor shall provide in its affirmative action program, and shall adhere to, a schedule for the review of all physical and mental job qualification standards to ensure that, to the extent qualification standards tend to screen out qualified individuals with disabilities, they are job-related for the position in question and are consistent with business necessity.

(2) Whenever the contractor applies physical or mental qualification standards in the selection of applicants or employees for employment or other change in employment status such as promotion, demotion or training, to the extent that qualification standards tend to screen out qualified individuals on the basis of disability, the standards shall be related to the specific job or jobs for which the individual is being considered and consistent with business necessity. The contractor shall have the burden to demonstrate that it has complied with the requirements of this paragraph (c).

(3) The contractor may use as a defense to an allegation of a violation of paragraph (c)(2) of this section that an individual poses a direct threat to the health or safety of the individual or others in the workplace. (*See* § 60–741.2(e) defining direct threat.)

(d) *Reasonable accommodation to physical and mental limitations.* (1) As is provided in § 60–741.21(a)(6), as a matter of nondiscrimination, the contractor must make reasonable accommodation to the known physical or mental limitations of an otherwise qualified individual with a disability unless it can demonstrate that the accommodation would impose an undue hardship on the operation of its business. As a matter of affirmative action, if an employee with a known disability is having significant difficulty performing his or her job and it is reasonable to conclude that the performance problem may be related to the known disability, the contractor shall confidentially notify the employee of the performance problem and inquire whether the problem is related to the employee's disability. If the employee responds affirmatively, the contractor shall confidentially inquire whether the employee is in need of a reasonable accommodation.

(2) *Reasonable accommodation procedures.* The development and use of written procedures for processing requests for reasonable accommodation is a best practice that may assist the contractor in meeting its reasonable

[3] Contractors are encouraged to make their information and communication technology accessible. There are a variety of resources that may assist contractors in assessing and ensuring the accessibility of its information and communication technology. These include the Web Content Accessibility Guidelines (WCAG 2.0) of the World Wide Web Consortium Web Accessibility Initiative, online at *www.w3.org/WAI/intro/wcag.php,* and the regulations implementing the accessibility requirements for Federal agencies prescribed in section 508 of the Rehabilitation Act. Information on section 508 may be found online at *http://www.section508.gov/index.cfm.* This Web site also provides information about various State accessibility requirements and initiatives.

accommodation obligations under section 503 and this part. Such procedures help ensure that applicants and employees are informed as to how to request a reasonable accommodation and are aware of how such a request will be processed by the contractor. They also help ensure that the contractor's supervisors and managers know what to do should they receive a request for reasonable accommodation, and that all requests for accommodation are processed swiftly, within a reasonable period of time. The development and use of written reasonable accommodation procedures is not required by this part, and it is not a violation of this part for a contractor not to have or use such procedures. However, Appendix B of this part provides guidance to contractors that choose to develop and use written reasonable accommodation procedures.

(e) *Harassment.* The contractor must develop and implement procedures to ensure that its employees are not harassed on the basis of disability.

(f) *External dissemination of policy, outreach, and positive recruitment*—(1) *Required outreach efforts.* (i) The contractor shall undertake appropriate outreach and positive recruitment activities such as those listed in paragraph (f)(2) of this section that are reasonably designed to effectively recruit qualified individuals with disabilities. It is not contemplated that the contractor will necessarily undertake all the activities listed in paragraph (f)(2) of this section or that its activities will be limited to those listed. The scope of the contractor's efforts shall depend upon all the circumstances, including the contractor's size and resources and the extent to which existing employment practices are adequate.

(ii) The contractor must send written notification of company policy related to its affirmative action efforts to all subcontractors, including subcontracting vendors and suppliers, requesting appropriate action on their part.

(2) Examples of *outreach and recruitment activities.* Below are examples of outreach and positive recruitment activities referred to in paragraph (f)(1) of this section.

(i) Enlisting the assistance and support of the following persons and organizations in recruiting, and developing on-the-job training opportunities for individuals with disabilities, in order to fulfill its commitment to provide equal employment opportunity for such individuals:

(A) The State Vocational Rehabilitation Service Agency (SVRA), State mental health agency, or State developmental disability agency in the area of the contractor's establishment;

(B) The Employment One-Stop Career Center (One-Stop) or American Job Center nearest the contractor's establishment;

(C) The Department of Veterans Affairs Regional Office nearest the contractor's establishment (*www.va.gov*);

(D) Entities funded by the Department of Labor that provide recruitment or training services for individuals with disabilities, such as the services currently provided through the Employer Assistance and Resource Network (EARN) (*www.earnworks.com*);

(E) Local Employment Network (EN) organizations (other than the contractor, if the contractor is an EN) listed in the Social Security Administration's Ticket to Work Employment Network Directory (*www.yourtickettowork.com/endir*);

(F) Local disability groups, organizations, or Centers for Independent Living (CIL) near the contractor's establishment;

(G) Placement or career offices of educational institutions that specialize in the placement of individuals with disabilities; and

(H) Private recruitment sources, such as professional organizations or employment placement services that specialize in the placement of individuals with disabilities.

(ii) The contractor should also consider taking the actions listed below to fulfill its commitment to provide equal employment opportunities to individuals with disabilities:

(A) Formal briefing sessions should be held, preferably on company premises, with representatives from recruiting sources. Contractor facility tours, clear and concise explanations of current and future job openings, position descriptions, worker specifications, explanations of the company's selection process, and recruiting literature should be an integral part of the briefing. At any such briefing sessions, the company official in charge of the contractor's affirmative action program should be in attendance when possible. Formal arrangements should be made for referral of applicants, follow up with sources, and feedback on disposition of applicants.

(B) The contractor's recruitment efforts at all educational institutions should incorporate special efforts to reach students who are individuals with disabilities.

(C) An effort should be made to participate in work-study programs for students, trainees, or interns with disabilities. Such programs may be found through outreach to State and local schools and universities, and through EARN.

(D) Individuals with disabilities should be made available for participation in career days, youth motivation programs, and related activities in their communities.

(E) The contractor should take any other positive steps it deems necessary to attract individuals with disabilities not currently in the work force who have requisite skills and can be recruited through affirmative action measures. These individuals may be located through State and local agencies supported by the U.S. Department of Education's Rehabilitation Services Administration (RSA) (*http://rsa.ed.gov/*), local Ticket-to-Work Employment Networks, or local chapters of groups or organizations that provide services for individuals with disabilities.

(F) The contractor, in making hiring decisions, should consider applicants who are known to have disabilities for all available positions for which they may be qualified when the position(s) applied for is unavailable.

(3) *Assessment of external outreach and recruitment efforts.* The contractor shall, on an annual basis, review the outreach and recruitment efforts it has taken over the previous twelve months to evaluate their effectiveness in identifying and recruiting qualified individuals with disabilities. The contractor shall document each evaluation, including at a minimum the criteria it used to evaluate the effectiveness of each effort and the contractor's conclusion as to whether each effort was effective. Among these criteria shall be the data collected pursuant to paragraph (k) of this section for the current year and the two most recent previous years. The contractor's conclusion as to the effectiveness of its outreach efforts must be reasonable as determined by OFCCP in light of these regulations. If the contractor concludes the totality of its efforts were not effective in identifying and recruiting qualified individuals with disabilities, it shall identify and implement alternative efforts listed in paragraphs (f)(1) or (f)(2) of this section in order to fulfill its obligations.

(4) *Recordkeeping obligation.* The contractor shall document all activities it undertakes to comply with the obligations of this section, and retain these documents for a period of three (3) years.

(g) *Internal dissemination of policy.* (1) A strong outreach program will be ineffective without adequate internal support from supervisory and management personnel and other employees. In order to assure greater employee cooperation and participation in the contractor's efforts, the contractor shall develop the internal procedures listed in paragraph (g)(2) of this section for communication of its obligation to engage in affirmative action efforts to employ and advance in employment qualified individuals with disabilities. It is not contemplated that the contractor's activities will be limited to those listed. These procedures shall be designed to foster understanding, acceptance and support among the contractor's executive, management, supervisory, and other employees and to encourage such persons to take the necessary actions to aid the contractor in meeting this obligation.

(2) The contractor shall implement and disseminate this policy internally as follows:

(i) Include it in the contractor's policy manual or otherwise make the policy available to employees;

(ii) If the contractor is a party to a collective bargaining agreement, it shall notify union officials and/or employee representatives of the contractor's policy and request their cooperation;

(3) The contractor is encouraged to additionally implement and disseminate this policy internally as follows:

(i) Inform all employees and prospective employees of its commitment to engage in affirmative action to increase employment opportunities for individuals with disabilities. The contractor should periodically schedule special meetings with all employees to discuss policy and explain individual employee responsibilities;

(ii) Publicize it in the company newspaper, magazine, annual report and other media;

(iii) Conduct special meetings with executive, management, and supervisory personnel to explain the intent of the policy and individual responsibility for effective implementation making clear the chief executive officer's support for the affirmative action policy;

(iv) Discuss the policy thoroughly in both employee orientation and management training programs;

(v) Include articles on accomplishments of individuals with disabilities in company publications; and

(vi) When employees are featured in employee handbooks or similar publications for employees, include individuals with disabilities.

(h) *Audit and reporting system.* (1) The contractor shall design and implement an audit and reporting system that will:

(i) Measure the effectiveness of the contractor's affirmative action program;

(ii) Indicate any need for remedial action;

(iii) Determine the degree to which the contractor's objectives have been attained;

(iv) Determine whether known individuals with disabilities have had the opportunity to participate in all company sponsored educational, training, recreational, and social activities;

(v) Measure the contractor's compliance with the affirmative action program's specific obligations; and

(vi) Document the actions taken to comply with the obligations of paragraphs (h)(1)(i) through (v) of this section, and retain these documents as employment records subject to the recordkeeping requirements of § 60–741.80.

(2) Where the affirmative action program is found to be deficient, the contractor shall undertake necessary action to bring the program into compliance.

(i) *Responsibility for implementation.* An official of the contractor shall be assigned responsibility for implementation of the contractor's affirmative action activities under this part. His or her identity should appear on all internal and external communications regarding the company's affirmative action program. This official shall be given necessary senior management support and staff to manage the implementation of this program.

(j) *Training.* All personnel involved in the recruitment, screening, selection, promotion, disciplinary, and related processes shall be trained to ensure that the commitments in the contractor's affirmative action program are implemented.

(k) *Data collection analysis.* The contractor shall document the following computations or comparisons pertaining to applicants and hires on an annual basis and maintain them for a period of three (3) years:

(1) The number of applicants who self-identified as individuals with disabilities pursuant to § 60–741.42(a), or who are otherwise known to be individuals with disabilities;

(2) The total number of job openings and total number of jobs filled;

(3) The total number of applicants for all jobs;

(4) The number of applicants with disabilities hired; and

(5) The total number of applicants hired.

§ 60–741.45 Utilization goals.

The utilization goal is not a rigid and inflexible quota which must be met, nor is it to be considered either a ceiling or a floor for the employment of particular groups. Quotas are expressly forbidden.

(a) *Goal.* OFCCP has established a utilization goal of 7 percent for employment of qualified individuals with disabilities for each job group in the contractor's workforce, or for the contractor's entire workforce as provided in paragraph (d)(2)(i) of this section.

(b) *Purpose.* The purpose of the utilization goal is to establish a benchmark against which the contractor must measure the representation of individuals within each job group in its workforce, or within the contractor's entire workforce as provided in paragraph (d)(2)(i) of this section. The utilization goal serves as an equal employment opportunity objective that should be attainable by complying with all aspects of the affirmative action requirements of this part.

(c) *Periodic review of goal.* The Director of OFCCP shall periodically review and update, as appropriate, the utilization goal established in paragraph (a) of this section.

(d) *Utilization analysis*—(1) *Purpose.* The utilization analysis is designed to evaluate the representation of individuals with disabilities in each job group within the contractor's workforce, or to evaluate the representation of individuals with disabilities in the contractor's entire workforce as provided in paragraph (d)(2)(i) of this section, with the utilization goal established in paragraph (a) of this section.

(2) *Grouping jobs for analysis.* The contractor must use the same job groups established for utilization analyses under Executive Order 11246, either in accordance with 41 CFR part 60–2, or in accordance with 41 CFR part 60–4, as appropriate, except as provided below.

(i) *Contractors with 100 or fewer employees.* If a contractor has a total workforce of 100 or fewer employees, it need not use the jobs groups established for utilization analyses under Executive Order 11246, and has the option to measure the representation of individuals with disabilities in its entire workforce with the utilization goal established in paragraph (a) of this section.

(ii) [Reserved].

(3) *Annual evaluation.* The contractor shall annually evaluate its utilization of individuals with disabilities in each job group, or in its entire workforce as provided in paragraph (d)(2)(i) of this section.

(e) *Identification of problem areas.* When the percentage of individuals with disabilities in one or more job groups, or in a contractor's entire workforce as provided in paragraph (d)(2)(i) of this section, is less than the utilization goal established in paragraph (a) of this section, the contractor must take steps to determine whether and where impediments to equal employment opportunity exist. When making this determination, the contractor must assess its personnel processes, the effectiveness of its outreach and recruitment efforts, the results of its affirmative action program audit, and any other areas that might affect the success of the affirmative action program.

(f) *Action-oriented programs.* The contractor must develop and execute action-oriented programs designed to correct any identified problems areas. These action-oriented programs may include the modification of personnel processes to ensure equal employment opportunity for individuals with disabilities, alternative or additional outreach and recruitment efforts from among those listed in § 60–741.44 (f)(1) and (f)(2), and/or other actions designed to correct the identified problem areas and attain the established goal.

(g) A contractor's determination that it has not attained the utilization goal established in paragraph (a) of this section in one or more job groups does not constitute either a finding or admission of discrimination in violation of this part.

(h) The utilization goal established in paragraph (a) of this section shall not be used as a quota or ceiling that limits or restricts the employment of individuals with disabilities.

§ 60–741.46 Voluntary affirmative action programs for employees with disabilities.

(a) The contractor is permitted to develop and implement training and employment for employees with disabilities. Examples include, developing a job training program focused on the specific needs of individuals with certain disabilities such as traumatic brain injury (TBI) or developmental disabilities and utilizing linkage agreements to recruit program trainees. Successful programs such as these have been developed by some contractors and OFCCP desires to make clear they are permissible, though not required.

(1) If a contractor elects to implement a voluntary affirmative action program for employees with disabilities, a description of the program and the policies governing the program, including the name and title of the official responsible for the program, shall be included in the contractor's written affirmative action program. An annual report describing the contractor's activities pursuant to the program and identifying the outcomes achieved should also be included in the contractor's affirmative action program.

(2) Disability-related information from the applicant and/or employee self-identification request required by § 60–741.42 may be used to identify individuals with disabilities who are eligible to benefit from a voluntary affirmative action program for employees with disabilities.

(b) The contractor shall not use such programs to segregate individuals with disabilities or to limit or restrict the employment opportunities of any individual with a disability.

(c) The contractor shall not discriminate against an individual with a disability who has participated in a voluntary affirmative action program for employees with disabilities with respect to any term, condition, or benefit of employment, including, but not limited to, employment acts such as compensation, promotion, and termination, that are listed in § 60–741.20.

(d) These voluntary training and development programs should not result in discrimination against other groups and do not relieve a contractor from liability for discrimination under this act, Executive Order 11246, or the Vietnam Era Vetrans' Readjustment Assistance Act.

§ 60–741.47 Sheltered workshops.

Contracts with sheltered workshops do not constitute affirmative action in lieu of employment and advancement of qualified individuals with disabilities in the contractor's own work force. Contracts with sheltered workshops may be included within an affirmative action program if the sheltered workshop trains employees for the contractor and the contractor is obligated to hire trainees at full compensation when such trainees become "qualified individuals with disabilities."

Subpart D—General Enforcement and Complaint Procedures

§ 60–741.60 Compliance evaluations.

(a) OFCCP may conduct compliance evaluations to determine if the contractor is taking affirmative action to employ, advance in employment, and otherwise treat qualified individuals without discrimination on the basis of disability in all employment practices. A compliance evaluation may consist of any one or any combination of the following investigative procedures:

(1) *Compliance review.* A comprehensive analysis and evaluation of the hiring and employment practices of the contractor, the written affirmative action program, and the results of the affirmative action efforts undertaken by the contractor. A compliance review may proceed in three stages:

(i) A desk audit of the written affirmative action program and supporting documentation to determine whether all elements required by the regulations in this part are included, whether the affirmative action program meets agency standards of reasonableness, and whether the affirmative action program and supporting documentation satisfy agency standards of acceptability. OFCCP may extend the temporal scope of the desk audit beyond that set forth in the scheduling letter if OFCCP deems it necessary to carry out its investigation of potential violations of this part. The desk audit is conducted at OFCCP offices;

(ii) An on-site review is conducted at the contractor's establishment to investigate unresolved problem areas identified in the affirmative action program and supporting documentation during the desk audit, to verify that the contractor has implemented the affirmative action program and has complied with those regulatory obligations not required to be included in the affirmative action program, and to examine potential instances or issues of discrimination. An on-site review normally will involve an examination of the contractor's personnel and employment policies, inspection and copying of documents related to employment actions, and interviews with employees, supervisors, managers, hiring officials; and

(iii) Where necessary, an off-site analysis of information supplied by the contractor or otherwise gathered during or pursuant to the on-site review;

(2) *Off-site review of records.* An analysis and evaluation of the affirmative action program (or any part thereof) and supporting documentation, and other documents related to the contractor's personnel policies and employment actions that may be relevant to a determination of whether the contractor has complied with the requirements of section 503 and its regulations;

(3) *Compliance check.* A determination of whether the contractor has maintained records consistent with § 60–741.80; OFCCP may request the documents be provided either on-site or off-site; or

(4) *Focused review.* A review restricted to one or more components of the contractor's organization or one or more aspects of the contractor's employment practices.

(b) Where deficiencies are found to exist, reasonable efforts shall be made to secure compliance through conciliation and persuasion pursuant to § 60–741.62.

(c) *Pre-award compliance evaluations.* Each agency will include in the invitation for bids for each formally advertised nonconstruction contract or state at the outset of negotiations for each negotiated contract, that if the award, when let, should total $10 million or more, the prospective contractor and its known first-tier subcontractors with subcontracts of $10 million or more will be subject to a compliance evaluation before the award of the contract unless OFCCP has conducted an evaluation and found them to be in compliance with section 503 within the preceding 24 months. The awarding agency will notify OFCCP and request appropriate action and findings in accordance with this subsection. Within 15 days of the notice, OFCCP will inform the awarding agency of its intention to conduct a pre-award compliance evaluation. If OFCCP does not inform the awarding agency within that period of its intention to conduct a pre-award compliance evaluation, clearance shall be presumed and the awarding agency is authorized to proceed with the award. If OFCCP informs the awarding agency of its intention to conduct a pre-award compliance evaluation, OFCCP will be allowed an additional 20 days after the date that it so informs the awarding agency to provide its conclusions. If OFCCP does not provide the awarding agency with its conclusions within that period, clearance will be presumed and the awarding agency is authorized to proceed with the award.

§ 60–741.61 Complaint procedures.

(a) *Coordination with other agencies.* Pursuant to section 107(b) of the Americans with Disabilities Act of 1990, as amended (ADA), OFCCP and the Equal Employment Opportunity Commission (EEOC) have promulgated regulations setting forth procedures governing the processing of complaints falling within the overlapping jurisdiction of both the act and title I of the ADA to ensure that such complaints are dealt with in a manner that avoids duplication of effort and prevents the imposition of inconsistent or conflicting standards. Complaints filed under this part will be processed in accordance with those regulations, which are found at 41 CFR part 60–742, and with this part.

(b) *Place and time of filing.* Any applicant for employment with a contractor or any employee of a contractor may, personally, or by an authorized representative, file a written complaint with the Director alleging a violation of the act or the regulations in this part. The complaint may allege individual or class-wide violation(s). Complaints may be submitted to the OFCCP, 200 Constitution Avenue NW., Room C–3325, Washington, DC 20210, or to any OFCCP regional, district, or area office. Such complaint must be filed within 300 days of the date of the alleged violation, unless the time for filing is extended by OFCCP for good cause shown.

(c) *Contents of complaints.* (1) *In general.* A complaint must be signed by the complainant or his or her authorized representative and must contain the following information:

(i) Name and address (including telephone number) of the complainant;

(ii) Name and address of the contractor who committed the alleged violation;

(iii) The facts showing that the individual has a disability, a record or history of a disability, or was regarded by the contractor as having a disability;

(iv) A description of the act or acts considered to be a violation, including the pertinent dates (in the case of an alleged continuing violation, the earliest and most recent date that the alleged violation occurred should be stated); and

(v) Other pertinent information available which will assist in the investigation and resolution of the complaint, including the name of any known Federal agency with which the employer has contracted.

(2) *Third party complaints.* When a written complaint is filed by an authorized representative, that complaint need not identify by name the person on whose behalf it is filed. However, the authorized representative must nonetheless provide the name, address and telephone number of the person on whose behalf the complaint is filed to OFCCP, along with the other information specified in paragraph (c)(1) of this section. OFCCP shall verify the authorization of such complaint with the person on whose behalf the complaint is filed. Any such person may request that OFCCP keep his or her identity confidential during the investigation of the complaint, and OFCCP will protect the individual's confidentiality wherever that is possible given the facts and circumstances in the complaint.

(d) *Incomplete information.* Where a complaint contains incomplete information, OFCCP shall seek the needed information from the complainant. If the information is not furnished to OFCCP within 60 days of the date of such request, the case may be closed.

(e) *Investigations.* The Department of Labor shall institute a prompt investigation of each complaint.

(f) *Resolution of matters.* (1) If the complaint investigation finds no violation of the act or this part, or if the Director decides not to refer the matter to the Solicitor of Labor for enforcement proceedings against the contractor pursuant to § 60–741.65(a)(l), the complainant and contractor shall be so notified. The Director, on his or her own initiative, may reconsider his or her determination or the determination of any of his or her designated officers who have authority to issue Notifications of Results of Investigation.

(2) The Director will review all determinations of no violation that involve complaints that are not also cognizable under title I of the Americans with Disabilities Act.

(3) In cases where the Director decides to reconsider the determination of a Notification of Results of Investigation, the Director shall provide prompt notification of his or her intent to reconsider, which is effective upon issuance, and his or her final determination after reconsideration to the person claiming to be aggrieved, the person making the complaint on behalf of such person, if any, and the contractor.

(4) If the investigation finds a violation of the act or this part, OFCCP shall invite the contractor to participate in conciliation discussions pursuant to § 60–741.62.

§ 60–741.62 Conciliation agreements.

(a) If a compliance evaluation, complaint investigation, or other review by OFCCP finds a material violation of the act or this part, and if the contractor is willing to correct the violations and/or deficiencies, and if OFCCP determines that settlement on that basis (rather than referral for consideration of formal enforcement) is appropriate, a written conciliation agreement will be required. The agreement shall provide for such remedial action as may be necessary to correct the violations and/or deficiencies noted, including, where appropriate (but not necessarily limited to) such make whole remedies as back pay and retroactive seniority. The agreement shall also specify the time period for completion of the remedial action; the period shall be no longer than the minimum period necessary to complete the action.

(b) *Remedial benchmarks.* The remedial action referenced in paragraph (a) of this section may include the establishment of benchmarks for the contractor's outreach, recruitment, hiring, or other employment activities. The purpose of such benchmarks is to create a quantifiable method by which the contractor's progress in correcting identified violations and/or deficiencies can be measured.

§ 60–741.63 Violations of conciliation agreements.

(a) When OFCCP believes that a conciliation agreement has been violated, the following procedures are applicable:

(1) A written notice shall be sent to the contractor setting forth the violation alleged and summarizing the supporting evidence. The contractor shall have 15 days from receipt of the notice to respond, except in those cases in which OFCCP asserts that such a delay would result in irreparable injury to the employment rights of affected employees or applicants.

(2) During the 15-day period the contractor may demonstrate in writing that it has not violated its commitments.

(b) In those cases in which OFCCP asserts that a delay would result in irreparable injury to the employment rights of affected employees or applicants, enforcement proceedings may be initiated immediately without proceeding through any other requirement contained in this chapter.

(c) In any proceedings involving an alleged violation of a conciliation agreement, OFCCP may seek enforcement of the agreement itself and shall not be required to present proof of the underlying violations resolved by the agreement.

§ 60–741.64 Show cause notices.

When the Director has reasonable cause to believe that the contractor has violated the act or this part, he or she may issue a notice requiring the contractor to show cause, within 30 days, why monitoring, enforcement proceedings, or other appropriate action to ensure compliance should not be instituted. The issuance of such a notice is not a prerequisite to instituting enforcement proceedings (see § 60–741.65).

§ 60–741.65 Enforcement proceedings.

(a) *General.* (1) If a compliance evaluation, complaint investigation, or other review by OFCCP finds a violation of the act or this part, and the violation has not been corrected in accordance with the conciliation procedures in this part, or OFCCP determines that referral for consideration of formal enforcement (rather than settlement) is appropriate, OFCCP may refer the matter to the Solicitor of Labor with a recommendation for the institution of enforcement proceedings to enjoin the violations, to seek appropriate relief, and to impose appropriate sanctions, or any combination of these outcomes. OFCCP may seek back pay and other make whole relief for aggrieved individuals identified during a complaint investigation or compliance review. Such individuals need not have filed a complaint as a prerequisite to OFCCP seeking such relief on their behalf. Interest on back pay shall be calculated from the date of the loss and compounded quarterly at the percentage rate established by the Internal Revenue Service (IRS) for the underpayment of taxes.

(2) In addition to the administrative proceedings set forth in this section, the Director may, within the limitations of applicable law, seek appropriate judicial action to enforce the contractual provisions set forth in § 60–741.5, including appropriate injunctive relief.

(b) *Hearing practice and procedure.* (1) In administrative enforcement proceedings the contractor shall be provided an opportunity for a formal hearing. All hearings conducted under the act and this part shall be governed by the Rules of Practice for Administrative Proceedings to Enforce Equal Opportunity Under Executive Order 11246 contained in 41 CFR part 60–30 and the Rules of Evidence set out in the Rules of Practice and Procedure for Administrative Hearings Before the Office of Administrative Law Judges contained in 29 CFR part 18, subpart B: *Provided,* That a final administrative order shall be issued within one year from the date of the issuance of the recommended findings, conclusions, and decision of the Administrative Law Judge, or the submission of any exceptions and responses to exceptions to such decision (if any) whichever is later.

(2) Complaints may be filed by the Solicitor, the Associate Solicitor for Civil Rights and Labor-Management, Regional Solicitors and Associate Regional Solicitors.

(3) For the purposes of hearings pursuant to this part, references in 41 CFR part 60–30 to "Executive Order 11246" shall mean section 503 of the Rehabilitation Act of 1973, as amended; references to "equal opportunity clause"' shall mean the equal opportunity clause published at § 60–741.5; and references to "regulations" shall mean the regulations contained in this part.

§ 60–741.66 Sanctions and penalties.

(a) *Withholding progress payments.* With the prior approval of the Director, so much of the accrued payment due on the contract or any other contract between the Government contractor and the Federal Government may be withheld as necessary to correct any violations of the provisions of the act or this part.

(b) *Termination.* A contract may be canceled or terminated, in whole or in part, for failure to comply with the provisions of the act or this part.

(c) *Debarment.* A contractor may be debarred from receiving future contracts for failure to comply with the provisions of the act or this part subject to reinstatement pursuant to § 60–741.68. Debarment may be imposed for an indefinite period, or may be imposed for a fixed period of not less than six months, but no more than three years.

(d) *Hearing opportunity.* An opportunity for a formal hearing shall be afforded to a contractor before the imposition of any sanction or penalty.

§ 60–741.67 Notification of agencies.

The Director shall ensure that the heads of all agencies are notified of any debarments taken against any contractor.

§ 60–741.68 Reinstatement of ineligible contractors.

(a) *Application for reinstatement.* A contractor debarred from further contracts for an indefinite period under the act may request reinstatement in a letter filed with the Director at any time after the effective date of the debarment; a contractor debarred for a fixed period may make such a request following the expiration of six months from the effective date of the debarment. In connection with the reinstatement proceedings, all debarred contractors shall be required to show that they have established and will carry out employment policies and practices in compliance with the act and this part. Additionally, in determining whether reinstatement is appropriate for a contractor debarred for a fixed period, the Director also shall consider, among other factors, the severity of the violation which resulted in the debarment, the contractor's attitude towards compliance, the contractor's past compliance history, and whether the contractor's reinstatement would impede the effective enforcement of the act or this part. Before reaching a decision, the Director may conduct a compliance evaluation of the contractor and may require the contractor to supply additional information regarding the request for reinstatement. The Director shall issue a written decision on the request.

(b) *Petition for review.* Within 30 days of its receipt of a decision denying a request for reinstatement, the contractor may file a petition for review of the decision with the Secretary. The petition shall set forth the grounds for the contractor's objections to the Director's decision. The petition shall be served on the Director and the Associate Solicitor for Civil Rights and Labor-Management and shall include the decision as an appendix. The Director may file a response within 14 days to the petition. The Secretary shall issue the final agency decision denying or granting the request for reinstatement. Before reaching a final decision, the Secretary may issue such additional orders respecting procedure as he or she finds appropriate in the circumstances, including an order referring the matter to the Office of Administrative Law Judges for an evidentiary hearing where there is a material factual dispute that cannot be resolved on the record before the Secretary.

§ 60–741.69 Intimidation and interference.

(a) The contractor shall not harass, intimidate, threaten, coerce, or discriminate against any individual because the individual has engaged in or may engage in any of the following activities:

(1) Filing a complaint;

(2) Assisting or participating in any manner in an investigation, compliance evaluation, hearing, or any other activity related to the administration of the act or any other Federal, State, or local law requiring equal opportunity for individuals with disabilities;

(3) Opposing any act or practice made unlawful by the act or this part or any other Federal, State, or local law requiring equal opportunity for individuals with disabilities; or

(4) Exercising any other right protected by the act or this part.

(b) The contractor shall ensure that all persons under its control do not engage in such harassment, intimidation, threats, coercion, or discrimination. The sanctions and penalties contained in this part may be exercised by the Director against any contractor who violates this obligation.

§ 60–741.70 Disputed matters related to compliance with the act.

The procedures set forth in the regulations in this part govern all disputes relative to the contractor's compliance with the act and this part. Any disputes relating to issues other than compliance, including contract costs arising out of the contractor's efforts to comply, shall be determined by the disputes clause of the contract.

Subpart E—Ancillary Matters

§ 60–741.80 Recordkeeping.

(a) *General requirements.* Except as set forth in paragraph (b) of this section, any personnel or employment record made or kept by the contractor shall be preserved by the contractor for a period of two years from the date of the making of the record or the personnel action involved, whichever occurs later. However, if the contractor has fewer than 150 employees or does not have a Government contract of at least $150,000, the minimum record retention period shall be one year from the date of the making of the record or the personnel action involved, whichever occurs later, except as set forth in paragraph (b) of this section. Such records include, but are not necessarily limited to, records relating to requests for reasonable accommodation; the results of any physical examination; job advertisements and postings; applications and resumes; tests and test results; interview notes; and other records having to do with hiring, assignment, promotion, demotion, transfer, lay-off or termination, rates of pay or other terms of compensation, and selection for training or apprenticeship. In the case of involuntary termination of an employee, the personnel records of the individual terminated shall be kept for a period of two years from the date of the termination, except that contractors that have fewer than 150 employees or that do not have a Government contract of at least $150,000 shall keep such records for a period of one year from the date of the termination. Where the contractor has received notice that a complaint of discrimination has been filed, that a compliance evaluation has been initiated, or that an enforcement action has been commenced, the contractor must preserve all personnel records relevant to the complaint, compliance evaluation, or action until final disposition of the complaint, compliance evaluation or action. The term "personnel records relevant to the complaint, compliance evaluation, or action" will include, for example, personnel or employment records relating to the aggrieved person and to all other employees holding positions similar to that held or sought by the aggrieved person and application forms or test papers completed by an unsuccessful applicant and by all other candidates for the same position as that for which the aggrieved person applied and was rejected.

(b) *Records with three-year retention requirement.* Records required by § 60–741.44(f)(4) and (k) shall be maintained by all contractors for a period of three years from the date of the making of the record.

(c) *Failure to preserve records.* Failure to preserve complete and accurate records as required by this part constitutes noncompliance with the contractor's obligations under the act and this part. Where the contractor has destroyed or failed to preserve records as required by this section, there may be a presumption that the information destroyed or not preserved would have been unfavorable to the contractor: *Provided,* That this presumption shall not apply where the contractor shows that the destruction or failure to preserve records results from circumstances that are outside of the contractor's control.

§ 60–741.81 Access to records.

Each contractor shall permit access during normal business hours to its places of business for the purpose of conducting on-site compliance evaluations and complaint investigations and inspecting and copying such books, accounts, and records, including electronic records, and any other material OFCCP deems relevant to the matter under investigation and pertinent to compliance with the act or this part. Contractors must also provide OFCCP access to these materials, including electronic records, off-site for purposes of conducting compliance evaluations and complaint investigations. Upon request, the contractor must provide OFCCP information about all format(s), including specific electronic formats, in which the contractor maintains its records and other information. The contractor must provide records and other information in any of the formats in which they are maintained, as selected by OFCCP. Information obtained in this manner shall be used only in connection with the administration of the act, the Americans with Disabilities Act of 1990, as amended (ADA), and in furtherance of the purposes of the act and the ADA. OFCCP will treat records provided by the contractor to OFCCP under this section as confidential to the maximum extent the information is exempt from public disclosure under the Freedom of Information Act, 5 U.S.C. 552.

§ 60–741.82 Labor organizations and recruiting and training agencies.

(a) Whenever performance in accordance with the equal opportunity clause or any matter contained in the regulations in this part may necessitate a revision of a collective bargaining agreement, the labor organizations which are parties to such agreement shall be given an adequate opportunity to present their views to OFCCP.

(b) OFCCP shall use its best efforts, directly or through contractors, subcontractors, local officials, vocational rehabilitation facilities, and all other available instrumentalities, to cause any labor organization, recruiting and training agency, or other representative of workers who are employed by a contractor to cooperate with, and to assist in, the implementation of the purposes of the act.

§ 60–741.83 Rulings and interpretations.

Rulings under or interpretations of the act and this part shall be made by the Director.

Appendix A to Part 60–741—Guidelines on a Contractor's Duty To Provide Reasonable Accommodation

The guidelines in this appendix are in large part derived from, and are consistent with, the discussion regarding the duty to provide reasonable accommodation contained in the Interpretive Guidance on title I of the Americans with Disabilities Act, as amended (ADA), set out as an appendix to the regulations issued by the Equal Employment Opportunity Commission (EEOC) implementing the ADA (29 CFR part 1630). Although the following discussion is intended to provide an independent "free-standing" source of guidance with respect to the duty to provide reasonable accommodation under this part, to the extent that the EEOC appendix provides additional guidance which is consistent with the following discussion, it may be relied upon for purposes of this part as well. *See* § 60–741.1(c). Contractors are obligated to provide reasonable accommodation and to take affirmative action. Reasonable accommodation under section 503, like reasonable accommodation required under the ADA, is a part of the nondiscrimination obligation. *See* EEOC appendix cited in this paragraph. Affirmative action is unique to section 503, and includes actions above and beyond those required as a matter of nondiscrimination. An example of this is the requirement discussed in paragraph 2 of this appendix that a contractor shall make an inquiry of an employee with a known disability who is having significant difficulty performing his or her job.

1. A contractor is required to make reasonable accommodations to the known physical or mental limitations of a qualified individual with a disability, unless the contractor can demonstrate that the accommodation would impose an undue hardship on the operation of its business. As stated in § 60–741.2(r), an individual with a disability is qualified if he or she satisfies all the skill, experience, education, and other job-related selection criteria, and can perform the essential functions of the position with or without reasonable accommodation. A contractor is required to make a reasonable accommodation with respect to its application process if the individual with a disability is qualified with respect to that process. One is qualified within the meaning of section 503 if he or she is qualified for a job, except that, because of a disability, he or she needs a reasonable accommodation to be able to perform the job's essential functions.

2. Although the contractor would not be expected to accommodate disabilities of which it is unaware, the contractor has an affirmative obligation to provide reasonable accommodation for applicants and employees of whose disabilities the contractor has actual knowledge. As stated in § 60–741.42, as part of the contractor's affirmative action obligation, the contractor is required to invite applicants to inform the contractor whether the applicant believes that he or she is an individual with a disability both prior to an offer of employment, and after an offer of employment but before he or she begins his/her employment duties. That invitation also informs applicants of the contractor's reasonable accommodation obligation and invites individuals with disabilities to request any accommodation they might need. Moreover, § 60–741.44(d) provides that if an employee with a known disability is having significant difficulty performing his or her job and it is reasonable to conclude that the performance problem may be related to the disability, the contractor is required to confidentially inquire whether the problem is disability related and if the employee is in need of a reasonable accommodation.

3. An accommodation is any change in the work environment or in the way things are customarily done that enables an individual with a disability to enjoy equal employment opportunities. Equal employment opportunity means an opportunity to attain the same level of performance, or to enjoy the same level of benefits and privileges of employment as are available to the average similarly situated employee without a disability. Thus, for example, an accommodation made to assist an employee with a disability in the performance of his or her job must be adequate to enable the individual to perform the essential functions of the position. The accommodation, however, does not have to be the "best" accommodation possible, so long as it is sufficient to meet the job-related needs of the individual being accommodated. There are three areas in which reasonable accommodations may be necessary: (1) Accommodations in the application process; (2) accommodations that enable employees with disabilities to perform the essential functions of the position held or desired; and (3) accommodations that enable employees with disabilities to enjoy equal benefits and privileges of employment as are enjoyed by employees without disabilities.

4. The term "undue hardship" refers to any accommodation that would be unduly costly, extensive, substantial, or disruptive, or that would fundamentally alter the nature or operation of the contractor's business. The contractor's claim that the cost of a particular accommodation will impose an undue hardship requires a determination of which financial resources should be considered—those of the contractor in its entirety or only those of the facility that will be required to provide the accommodation. This inquiry requires an analysis of the financial relationship between the contractor and the facility in order to determine what resources will be available to the facility in providing the accommodation. If the contractor can show that the cost of the accommodation would impose an undue hardship, it would still be required to provide the accommodation if the funding is available from another source (*e.g.*, a State vocational rehabilitation agency) or if Federal, State, or local tax deductions or tax credits are available to offset the cost of the accommodation. In the absence of such funding, the individual with a disability must be given the option of providing the accommodation or of paying that portion of the cost which constitutes the undue hardship on the operation of the business.

5. The definition for "reasonable accommodation" in § 60–741.2(s) lists a number of examples of the most common types of accommodations that the contractor may be required to provide. There are a number of specific accommodations that may be appropriate for particular situations. The discussion in this appendix is not intended to provide an exhaustive list of required accommodations (as no such list would be feasible); rather, it is intended to provide general guidance regarding the nature of the obligation. The decision as to whether a reasonable accommodation is appropriate must be made on a case-by-case basis. The contractor generally should consult with the individual with a disability in deciding on the appropriate accommodation; frequently, the individual will know exactly what accommodation he or she will need to perform successfully in a particular job, and may suggest an accommodation which is simpler and less expensive than the accommodation the contractor might have devised. Other resources to consult include the appropriate State vocational rehabilitation services agency, the Equal Employment Opportunity Commission (1–800–669–4000 (voice) or 1–800–669–6820 (TTY)), the Job Accommodation Network (JAN)—a service of the U.S. Department of Labor's Office of Disability Employment Policy (1–800–526–7234 (voice) or 1–877–781–9403 (TTY)), private disability organizations, and other employers.

6. With respect to accommodations that can permit an employee with a disability to perform essential functions successfully, a reasonable accommodation may require the contractor to, for instance, modify or acquire equipment. For those visually-impaired, such accommodations may include providing adaptive hardware and software for computers, electronic visual aids, Braille writers, talking calculators, magnifiers, audio recordings, and Braille or large print materials. For persons with hearing

impairments, reasonable accommodations may include providing telephone handset amplifiers, telephones compatible with hearing aids, and TTY machines. For persons with limited physical dexterity, the obligation may require the provision of telephone headsets, mechanical page turners, and raised or lowered furniture.

7. Other reasonable accommodations of this type may include providing personal assistants such as a reader, interpreter, or travel attendant, permitting the use of accrued paid leave or providing additional unpaid leave for necessary treatment. The contractor may also be required to make existing facilities readily accessible to and usable by individuals with disabilities—including areas used by employees for purposes other than the performance of essential job functions—such as restrooms, break rooms, cafeterias, lounges, auditoriums, libraries, parking lots, and credit unions. This type of accommodation will enable employees to enjoy equal benefits and privileges of employment as are enjoyed by employees who do not have disabilities.

8. Another of the potential accommodations listed in § 60–741.2(s) is job restructuring. This may involve reallocating or redistributing those nonessential, marginal job functions which a qualified individual with a disability cannot perform to another position. Accordingly, if a clerical employee is occasionally required to lift heavy boxes containing files, but cannot do so because of a disability, this task may be reassigned to another employee. The contractor, however, is not required to reallocate essential functions, *i.e.*, those functions that the individual who holds the job would have to perform, with or without reasonable accommodation, in order to be considered qualified for the position. For instance, the contractor that has a security guard position which requires the incumbent to inspect identity cards would not have to provide a blind individual with an assistant to perform that duty; in such a case, the assistant would be performing an essential function of the job for the individual with a disability. Job restructuring may also involve allowing part-time or modified work schedules. For instance, flexible or adjusted work schedules could benefit individuals with disabilities who cannot work a standard schedule because of the need to obtain medical treatment, or individuals with mobility impairments who depend on a public transportation system that is not accessible during the hours of a standard schedule.

9. Reasonable accommodation may also include reassignment to a vacant position. In general, reassignment should be considered only when accommodation within the individual's current position would pose an undue hardship. Reassignment is not required for applicants. However, in making hiring decisions, contractors are encouraged to consider known applicants with disabilities for all available positions for which they may be qualified when the position(s) applied for is unavailable. Reassignment may not be used to limit, segregate, or otherwise discriminate against employees with disabilities by forcing reassignments to undesirable positions or to designated offices or facilities. Employers should reassign the individual to an equivalent position in terms of pay, status, etc., if the individual is qualified, and if the position is vacant within a reasonable amount of time. A reasonable amount of time should be determined in light of the totality of the circumstances.

10. The contractor may reassign an individual to a lower graded position if there are no accommodations that would enable the employee to remain in the current position and there are no vacant equivalent positions for which the individual is qualified with or without reasonable accommodation. The contractor may maintain the reassigned individual with a disability at the salary of the higher graded position, and must do so if it maintains the salary of reassigned employees who are not disabled. It should also be noted that the contractor is not required to promote an individual with a disability as an accommodation.

11. With respect to the application process, appropriate accommodations may include the following: (1) Providing information regarding job vacancies in a form accessible to those with vision or hearing impairments (*e.g.*, by making an announcement available in Braille, in large print, or on audio tape, or by responding to job inquiries via TTY); (2) providing readers, interpreters and other similar assistance during the application, testing and interview process; (3) appropriately adjusting or modifying employment-related examinations (*e.g.*, extending regular time deadlines, allowing a blind person or one with a learning disorder such as dyslexia to provide oral answers for a written test, and permitting an applicant, regardless of the nature of his or her disability to demonstrate skills through alternative techniques and utilization of adapted tools, aids and devices); and (4) ensuring an applicant with a mobility impairment full access to testing locations such that the applicant's test scores accurately reflect the applicant's skills or aptitude rather than the applicant's mobility impairment.

Appendix B to Part 60–741—Developing Reasonable Accommodation Procedures

As stated in §§ 60–741.21(a)(6) and 60–741.44(d), the development and use of written procedures for processing requests for reasonable accommodation is a best practice. This Appendix provides guidance contractors may wish to use should they decide to adopt this best practice. As stated in the regulations, contractors are not required to use written reasonable accommodation procedures, and the failure to use such procedures will not result in a finding of violation.

1. *Designation of responsible official.* The contractor should designate an official to be responsible for the implementation of the reasonable accommodation procedures. The responsible official may be the same official who is responsible for the implementation of the contractor's affirmative action program. The responsible official should have the authority, resources, support, and access to top management that is needed to ensure the effective implementation of the reasonable accommodation procedures. The name, title/office, and contact information (telephone number and email address) of the responsible official should be included in the reasonable accommodation procedures, and should be updated when changes occur.

2. *Description of process.* The contractor's reasonable accommodation procedures should contain a description of the steps the contractor takes when processing a reasonable accommodation request, including the process by which the contractor renders a final determination on the accommodation request. If specific information must be provided to the contractor in order to obtain a reasonable accommodation, the description should identify this information. For example, the contractor's reasonable accommodation procedures may state that to obtain a reasonable accommodation, the contractor must be informed of the existence of a disability, the disability-related limitation(s) or workplace barrier(s) that needs to be accommodated, and, if known, the desired reasonable accommodation. The description should also indicate that, if the need for accommodation is not obvious, or if additional information is needed, the contractor may initiate an interactive process with the accommodation requester.

3. *Form of requests for reasonable accommodation.* The reasonable accommodation procedures should specify that a request for reasonable accommodation may be oral or written and should explain that there are no required "magic words" that must be used by the requester to request an accommodation. The procedures should also state that requests for reasonable accommodation may be made by an applicant, employee, or by a third party, such as a relative, job coach, or friend, on his or her behalf.

4. *Submission of reasonable accommodation requests by employees.* The reasonable accommodation procedures should identify to whom an employee (or a third party acting on his or her behalf) must submit an accommodation request. At a minimum, this should include any supervisor or management official in the employee's chain of command, and the official responsible for the implementation of the reasonable accommodation procedures.

5. *Recurring requests for a reasonable accommodation.* The reasonable accommodation procedures should provide that in instances of a recurring need for an accommodation (*e.g.*, a hearing impaired employee's need for a sign language interpreter for meetings) the requester will not be required to repeatedly submit or renew their request for accommodation each time the accommodation is needed. In the absence of a reasonable belief that the individual's recurring need for the accommodation has changed, requiring the repeated submission of a request for the accommodation could be considered harassment on the basis of disability in violation of this part.

6. *Supporting medical documentation.* The reasonable accommodation procedures

should explain the circumstances, if any, under which the contractor may request and review medical documentation in support of a request for reasonable accommodation. The procedures should explain that any request for medical documentation may not be open ended, and must be limited to documentation of the individual's disability and the functional limitations for which reasonable accommodation is sought. The procedures should also explain that the submission of medical documentation is not required when the disability for which a reasonable accommodation is sought is known or readily observable and the need for accommodation is known or obvious.

7. *Written confirmation of receipt of request.* The reasonable accommodation procedures should specify that written confirmation of the receipt of a request for reasonable accommodation will be provided to the requester, either by letter or email. The written confirmation should include the date the accommodation request was received, and be signed by the authorized decisionmaker or his or her designee.

8. *Timeframe for processing requests.* The reasonable accommodation procedures should state that requests for accommodation will be processed as expeditiously as possible. Oral requests for reasonable accommodation should be considered received on the date they are initially made, even if the contractor has a reasonable accommodation request form that has not been completed. Requests for reasonable accommodation must be processed within a reasonable period of time. What constitutes a reasonable period of time will depend upon the specific circumstances. However, in general, if supporting medical documentation is not needed, that timeframe should not be longer than 5 to 10 business days. If supporting medical documentation is needed, or if special equipment must be ordered, that timeframe should not exceed 30 calendar days, unless there are extenuating circumstances beyond the control of the contractor. The procedures should explain what constitutes extenuating circumstances. However, reasonable accommodations may need to be provided even more expeditiously for applicants. See the discussion of accommodation requests from applicants in section 10, below.

9. *Delay in responding to request.* If the contractor's processing of an accommodation request will exceed established timeframes, written notice should be provided to the requester. The notice should include the reason(s) for the delay and a projected date of response. The notice should also be dated and signed by the authorized decisionmaker or his or her designee.

10. *Reasonable accommodation requests by applicants.* The reasonable accommodation procedures should include procedures to ensure that all applicants, including those using the contractor's online or other electronic application system, are made aware of the contractor's reasonable accommodation obligation and are invited to request any reasonable accommodation needed to participate fully in the application process. All applicants should also be provided with contact information for contractor staff able to assist the applicant, or his or her representative, in making a request for accommodation. The contractor's procedures should provide that reasonable accommodation requests by or on behalf of an applicant are processed expeditiously, using timeframes tailored to the application process.

11. *Denial of reasonable accommodation.* The contractor's reasonable accommodation procedures should specify that any denial or refusal to provide a requested reasonable accommodation will be provided in writing. The written denial should include the reason for the denial and be dated and signed by the authorized decisionmaker or his or her designee. If the contractor provides an internal appeal or reconsideration process, the written denial should inform the requester about this process.

12. *Confidentiality.* The contractor's reasonable accommodation procedures should indicate that all requests for reasonable accommodation, related documentation (such as request confirmation receipts, requests for additional information, and decisions regarding accommodation requests), and any medical or disability-related information provided to the contractor will be treated as confidential medical records and maintained in a separate medical file, in accordance with section 503 and this part.

13. *Dissemination of procedures to employees.* The contractor should disseminate its written reasonable accommodation procedures to all employees. Notice of the reasonable accommodation procedures may be provided by their inclusion in an employee handbook that is disseminated to all employees and/or by email or electronic posting on a company Web page where work-related notices are ordinarily posted. Notice of the reasonable accommodation procedures should be provided to employees who work off-site in the same manner that notice of other work-related matters is ordinarily provided to these employees.

14. *Training.* The contractor should provide annual training for its supervisors and managers regarding the implementation of the reasonable accommodation procedures. Training should also be provided whenever significant changes are made to the reasonable accommodation procedures. Training regarding the reasonable accommodation procedures may be provided in conjunction with other required equal employment opportunity or affirmative action training.

[FR Doc. 2013–21228 Filed 9–23–13; 8:45 am]

BILLING CODE 4510–45–P

Vietnam Era Veterans' Readjustment Assistance Act of 1974, as amended

Office of Federal Contract Compliance Programs (OFCCP)

Vietnam Era Veterans' Readjustment Assistance Act of 1974, as amended

38 USC Sec. 4212

United States Code
Title 38
Part 3
Chapter 42

§ 4212. Veterans' employment emphasis under Federal contracts [1]

a. (1) Any contract in the amount of $100,000 or more entered into by any department or agency of the United States for the procurement of personal property and nonpersonal services (including construction) for the United States, shall contain a provision requiring that the party contracting with the United States take affirmative action to employ and advance in employment qualified covered veterans. This section applies to any subcontract in the amount of $100,000 or more entered into by a prime contractor in carrying out any such contract.
   (2) In addition to requiring affirmative action to employ such qualified covered veterans under such contracts and subcontracts and in order to promote the implementation of such requirement, the Secretary of Labor shall prescribe regulations requiring that -
   - (A) each such contractor for each such contract shall immediately list all of its employment openings with the appropriate employment service delivery system (as defined in section 4101(7) of this title), and may also list such openings with one-stop career centers under the Workforce Investment Act of 1998, other appropriate service delivery points, or America's Job Bank (or any additional or subsequent national electronic job bank established by the Department of Labor), except that the contractor may exclude openings for executive and senior management positions and positions which are to be filled from within the contractor's organization and positions lasting three days or less;
   - (B) each such employment service delivery system shall give such qualified covered veterans priority in referral to such employment openings; and
   - (C) each such employment service delivery system shall provide a list of such employment openings to States, political subdivisions of States, or any private entities or organizations under contract to carry out employment, training, and placement services under chapter 41 of this title.

   (3) In this section:
   - (A) The term "covered veteran" means any of the following veterans:
     - (i) Disabled veterans.
     - (ii) Veterans who served on active duty in the Armed Forces during a war or in a campaign or expedition for which a campaign badge has been authorized.
     - (iii) Veterans who, while serving on active duty in the Armed Forces, participated in a United States military operation for which an Armed Forces service medal was awarded pursuant to Executive Order No. 12985 (61 Fed. Reg. 1209).
     - (iv) Recently separated veterans.
   - (B) The term "qualified", with respect to an employment position, means having the ability to perform the essential functions of the position with or without reasonable accommodation for an individual with a disability.

b. If any veteran covered by the first sentence of subsection (a) believes any contractor of the United States has failed to comply or refuses to comply with the provisions of the contractor's contract relating to the employment of veterans, the veteran may file a complaint with the Secretary of Labor, who shall promptly investigate such complaint and take appropriate action in accordance with the terms of the contract and applicable laws and regulations.

c. The Secretary of Labor shall include as part of the annual report required by section 4107(c) of this title the number of complaints filed pursuant to subsection (b) of this section, the actions taken thereon and the resolutions thereof. Such report shall also include the number of contractors listing employment openings, the nature, types, and number of positions listed and the number of veterans receiving priority pursuant to subsection (a)(2)(B).

d. (1) Each contractor to whom subsection (a) applies shall, in accordance with regulations which the Secretary of Labor shall prescribe, report at least annually to the Secretary of Labor on -
    - (A) the number of employees in the workforce of such contractor, by job category and hiring location, and the number of such employees, by job category and hiring location, who are qualified covered veterans;
    - (B) the total number of new employees hired by the contractor during the period covered by the report and the number of such employees who are qualified covered veterans; and
    - (C) the maximum number and the minimum number of employees of such contractor during the period covered by the report.

   (2) The Secretary of Labor shall ensure that the administration of the reporting requirement under paragraph (1) is coordinated with respect to any requirement for the contractor to make any other report to the Secretary of Labor.
   (3) The Secretary of Labor shall establish and maintain an Internet website on which the Secretary of Labor shall publicly disclose the information reported to the Secretary of Labor by contractors under paragraph (1).

[1]The Federal Acquisition Regulatory Council adjusted the dollar threshold under VEVRAA to $150,000. This adjustment is reflected in the Federal Acquisition Regulation, at 48 CFR 1.109

41 CFR Parts 60–250 and 60–300

Affirmative Action and Nondiscrimination Obligations of Contractors and Subcontractors Regarding Special Disabled Veterans, Veterans of the Vietnam Era, Disabled Veterans, Recently Separated Veterans, Active Duty Wartime or Campaign Badge Veterans, and Armed Forces Service Medal Veterans;

Final Rule

FEDERAL REGISTER

Vol. 78 Tuesday,

No. 185 September 24, 2013

Part II

Department of Labor

Office of Federal Contract Compliance Programs

41 CFR Parts 60–250 and 60–300

Affirmative Action and Nondiscrimination Obligations of Contractors and Subcontractors Regarding Special Disabled Veterans, Veterans of the Vietnam Era, Disabled Veterans, Recently Separated Veterans, Active Duty Wartime or Campaign Badge Veterans, and Armed Forces Service Medal Veterans; Final Rule

DEPARTMENT OF LABOR

Office of Federal Contract Compliance Programs

41 CFR Parts 60–250 and 60–300

RIN 1250–AA00

Affirmative Action and Nondiscrimination Obligations of Contractors and Subcontractors Regarding Special Disabled Veterans, Veterans of the Vietnam Era, Disabled Veterans, Recently Separated Veterans, Active Duty Wartime or Campaign Badge Veterans, and Armed Forces Service Medal Veterans

AGENCY: Office of Federal Contract Compliance Programs, Labor.

ACTION: Final rule.

SUMMARY: The Office of Federal Contract Compliance Programs (OFCCP) is publishing revisions to the current implementing regulations of the Vietnam Era Veterans' Readjustment Assistance Act of 1974, as amended by the Jobs for Veterans Act of 2002, (VEVRAA). OFCCP is responsible for enforcement of VEVRAA, which prohibits employment discrimination against protected veterans by covered Federal contractors and subcontractors. VEVRAA also requires each covered Federal contractor and subcontractor to take affirmative action to employ and advance in employment these veterans.

The final rule strengthens several provisions that are intended to aid in recruitment and hiring efforts, such as clarifying the mandatory job listing requirements, requiring data collection pertaining to protected veteran applicants and hires, and establishing hiring benchmarks to assist in measuring the effectiveness of their affirmative action efforts. However, some of the proposals set forth in the NPRM, particularly with regard to the creation and maintenance of certain records and specific mandated affirmative action obligations, have been eliminated or made more flexible in order to reduce the time and cost burden on contractors. The specific revisions made, and the rationale for making them, are set forth in the Section-by-Section Analysis.

DATES: *Effective Date:* These regulations are effective March 24, 2014.

FOR FURTHER INFORMATION CONTACT: Debra A. Carr, Director, Division of Policy, Planning and Program Development, Office of Federal Contract Compliance Programs, at 200 Constitution Avenue NW., Room C–3325, Washington, DC 20210, or by calling (202) 693–0104 (voice) or (202) 693–1337 (TTY). Copies of this rule in alternative formats may be obtained by calling (202) 693–0103 (voice) or (202) 693–1337 (TTY). The alternative formats available are large print and electronic file on computer disk. The rule also is available on the Internet on the Regulations.gov Web site at *http://www.regulations.gov* or on the OFCCP Web site at *http://www.dol.gov/ofccp.*

Executive Summary

I. Purpose of the Regulatory Action

The Office of Federal Contract Compliance Programs (OFCCP) is a civil rights, worker protection agency which enforces an Executive Order and two laws that prohibit employment discrimination and require affirmative action by companies doing business with the Federal Government.[1] Specifically, Federal contractors must engage in affirmative action and provide equal employment opportunity without regard to race, color, religion, sex, national origin, disability, or status as a protected veteran. Executive Order 11246, as amended, prohibits employment discrimination on the basis of race, religion, color, national origin, and sex. Section 503 of the Rehabilitation Act of 1973, as amended, prohibits employment discrimination against individuals with disabilities. The Vietnam Era Veterans' Readjustment Assistance Act of 1974, as amended, (VEVRAA) prohibits employment discrimination against certain protected veterans. Contemporaneous with these revisions, OFCCP is also publishing revisions to the implementing regulations of Section 503 of the Rehabilitation Act of 1973 (section 503). OFCCP has historically viewed these regulations together, maintaining identity between the two regulations where possible and allowing contractors to prepare an Affirmative Action Plan that covers both laws jointly. Accordingly, the vast majority of the revisions announced here in the VEVRAA regulation are also present in the section 503 rule. The exceptions to this—mainly in the structure of the hiring benchmark/goal for the two rules, are discussed in further detail below.

The existing implementing regulations for VEVRAA are split into two separate parts: 41 CFR part 60–250 (part 60–250) and 41 CFR part 60–300 (part 60–300). Part 60–250 applies to any Government contract or subcontract of $25,000 or more entered into before December 1, 2003, while part 60–300 applies to any Government contract or subcontract of $100,000 or more entered into on or after December 1, 2003. The final rule rescinds the regulations at part 60–250, as discussed in full in the Section-by-Section Analysis below. With regard to part 60–300, however, the final rule retains many of the revisions set forth in the notice of proposed rulemaking (NPRM).

OFCCP evaluates the employment practices of over 4,000 Federal contractors and subcontractors annually, and investigates individual complaints. OFCCP also engages in outreach to employees of Federal contractors to educate them about their rights, and provides technical assistance to contractors on their nondiscrimination and affirmative action obligations. We estimate that our jurisdiction covers approximately 200,000 Federal contractor establishments, and an estimated 50,000 parent companies.[2]

Although progress has been made in the employment of veterans, the number of unemployed veterans still remains too high, and substantial disparities in unemployment and pay rates continue to persist, especially for some categories of veterans. The annual unemployment rate for post-September 2001 veterans, referred to as "Gulf War-era II veterans," is higher than the rates for all veterans and for nonveterans. BLS data on the 2012 employment situation of veterans show that about 2.6 million of the nation's veterans had served during Gulf War-era II.[3] In 2012, the unemployment rate for Gulf War-era II veterans was 9.9 percent compared to nonveterans at 7.9 percent.[4] However, the unemployment rate, in the same year, for male Gulf War-era II veterans age 18 to 24 was 20.0 percent, higher than the rate for nonveterans of the same age group (16.4 percent).[5]

OFCCP also found that, on average, wages of veterans (defined as anyone who is employed and reported serving

[1] Executive Order 11246, as amended; Section 503 of the Rehabilitation Act of 1973, as amended, (Section 503); and the Vietnam Era Veterans' Readjustment Assistance Act of 1974, as amended, 38 U.S.C. 4212 (VEVRAA.).

[2] This establishment estimate is based on a review of FY 2009 EEO–1 contractor establishment data and other contractor databases, including the Federal Procurement Data System (FPDS). Based on EEO–1 data, we determined that the ratio of parent companies to the number of establishments is approximately four establishments per parent company.

[3] U.S. Bureau of Labor Statistics, Economic News Release, "Employment Situation of Veterans Summary 2012," March 20, 2013, *http://www.bls.gov/news.release/vet.nr0.htm* (last accessed Aug. 8, 2013).

[4] *Id.*, "Table A: Employment situation of the civilian non-institutionalized population 18 years and over by veteran status, period of service, and sex, 2011–2012 annual averages."

[5] *Id.*

in the military in the past) are higher than non-veterans. However, there are different age groups represented in each era, and because earnings generally increase with age, we controlled for age and race in a regression analysis. Using America Community Survey (ACS) data and conducting a regression analysis, OFCCP found that:

• Male veterans earn 2.7 percent less than non-veterans.

• Female veterans earn 6.3 percent than non-veterans.[6]

Controlling for the era of service, rather than just whether or not the person served,

• OFCCP finds that: Male Gulf War-era II veterans earn 1.4 percent less than non-veterans.

• Male Vietnam era veterans earn 6.9 percent less than non-veterans.[7]

Though it is unclear what portion of these disparities is caused by discrimination, employment discrimination and underutilization of qualified workers, such as veterans and individuals with disabilities, contribute to broader societal problems such as income inequality and poverty.

The final rule is intended to provide contractors with the tools needed to evaluate their own compliance and proactively identify and correct any deficiencies in their employment practices. These tools include, for example, removing barriers related to job postings so both contractors can effectively post or advertise their jobs, and jobseekers can take full advantage of these job opportunities. It also includes data collection to support meaningful self-assessments of employment practices and the ability for contractors to adjust their outreach and recruitment efforts for greater effectiveness and efficiency when needed.

II. Statement of Legal Authority

Initially enacted into law in 1974 and amended several times in the intervening years, the purpose of VEVRAA is twofold. First, VEVRAA prohibits employment discrimination against specified categories of veterans by Federal Government contractors and subcontractors. The universe of protected veterans includes disabled veterans, veterans who have separated from the military within the past three years (recently separated veterans), veterans who received an Armed Forces service medal while on active duty, and veterans who served in active duty during a war or in a campaign or expedition for which a campaign badge was authorized. Second, it requires each covered Federal Government contractor and subcontractor to take affirmative action to employ and advance in employment these veterans.

The VEVRAA regulations found at 41 CFR part 60–250 generally apply to Government contracts of $25,000 or more entered into before December 1, 2003. The threshold amount for coverage is a single contract of $25,000 or more; contracts are not aggregated to reach the coverage threshold. If a Federal contractor received a Government contract of at least $50,000 prior to December 1, 2003, an affirmative action program (AAP), the specific obligations of which are detailed at 41 CFR 60–250.44, must be developed. *See* 41 CFR 60–250.40.

The VEVRAA regulations found at 41 CFR part 60–300 apply to Government contracts entered into on or after December 1, 2003. The threshold amount for VEVRAA coverage and AAP threshold coverage is a single contract of $100,000 or more, entered into on or after December 1, 2003; contracts are not aggregated to reach the coverage threshold. Federal contractors and subcontractors that meet the coverage threshold and have 50 or more employees must develop an AAP. *See* 41 CFR 60–300.40. The regulations found at 41 CFR part 60–300 also apply to modifications of otherwise covered Government contracts made on or after December 1, 2003. Consequently, a contract that was entered into before December 1, 2003, will be subject only to the part 60–300 regulations if it is modified on or after December 1, 2003, and meets the contract dollar threshold of $100,000 or more.

In the VEVRAA context, receiving a Federal contract comes with a number of responsibilities, including compliance with the VEVRAA non-discrimination and non-retaliation provisions, meaningful and effective efforts to recruit and employ veterans protected under VEVRAA, creation and enforcement of personnel policies that support the contractor's affirmative action obligations, maintenance of accurate records documenting the contractor's affirmative action efforts, and providing OFCCP access to these records upon request. Contractor compliance with these provisions is, therefore, vital to improving the employment opportunities of veterans protected by VEVRAA. And, given the unique skills and experiences that veterans have acquired as a result of their service, improving employment opportunities benefits not only the veterans and their families but also the contractor as an employer. Failure to abide by these responsibilities may result in various sanctions, including withholding progress payments, termination of contracts, and debarment from receiving future contracts. It also deprives the contractor of the opportunity to benefit from this uniquely qualified pool of applicants.

III. Major Provisions

The following major provisions in the final rule would:

• Provide contractors with a quantifiable means to measure their success in recruiting and employing veterans by requiring, for the first time, that contractors establish their own or adopt a predetermined annual hiring benchmark (currently 8 percent based on national labor force data).

• Create greater accountability for employment decisions and practices by requiring that contractors maintain several quantitative measurements and comparisons for the number of veterans who apply for jobs and the number of veterans they hire. Having this data will also assist contractors and OFCCP in measuring the effectiveness of contractors' outreach and recruitment efforts.

• Provide knowledge and support to veterans seeking jobs by improving the effectiveness of the VEVRAA requirement that contractors list their job openings with the appropriate state employment service agency. Contractor job listings must be provided in a format that the state agency can access and use to make the job listings available to job seekers.

• Provide knowledge and increasing compliance by subcontractors with their obligations by requiring prime contractors to include specific, mandated language in their subcontracts alerting subcontractors to their responsibilities as Federal contractors.

• Create flexibility for contractors when they are establishing formal relationships with organizations that provide recruiting or training services to veterans. The relationships or "linkage agreements" can be established to meet the contractors' specific needs, while assuring outreach to veterans seeking employment.

• Clarify the contractor's mandatory job listing requirements and the relationship between the contractor, its agents, and the state employment

[6] OFCCP's labor economist conducted the regression analysis. All models were run using the American Community Survey 2008–2010 Public Use Microdata (PUMS). The models that examine veterans only were also run with the ACS 2006–2010 files, but the results were largely the same, so we use the 2008–10 for all (since questions on disability were only available in 2008 and after). The analysis was run on the private sector.

[7] Females comprise an estimated 14.2% (nearly 167,000 women) in the enlisted ranks.

services that providepriority referral of protected veterans.

• Repeal outdated and obsolete regulations at 41 CFR Part 60–250 that apply to contracts entered into before December 1, 2003 and not since modified. OFCCP believes that all such contracts have either expired or been modified, and that there is, therefore, no longer a need for the Part 60–250 regulations.

IV. Costs and Benefits

This is an economically significant and major rule. Veterans make up 7.25 percent of the employed population.[8] Under the VEVRAA rule, contractors have the option of establishing their own benchmark for employing protected veterans or meeting a benchmark set by OFCCP, currently 8 percent. Assuming all contractors will choose to meet the OFCCP benchmark of 8 percent, OFCCP estimates that Federal contractors would need to hire an additional 205,500 protected veterans.[9] Dividing our estimate of this rule's first-year cost by our estimate of the number of protected veterans expected to be hired in the first year because of this rule returns a cost of approximately $863 to $2,353 per new hire.

TOTAL COST OF THE FINAL RULE (YEAR ONE) [10]

	Low	High
Total Cost of the Rule	$177,296,772	$483,560,138
Cost Per Company	3,830	7,120
Cost Per Establishment	1,035	1,924
Company Cost Per Hire	863	2,353

PROJECTED VETERAN HIRES

	Year 1	Year 2	Year 3	Year 4	Year 5
Employees of Fed Contractors (assuming steady with population)	27,400,000.00	27,610,980.00	27,823,584	28,037,826.15	28,253,717.41
Veterans	2,192,000.00	2,208,878.40	2,225,886.76	2,243,026.09	2,260,297.39
Veterans Gap	205,500.00	207,082.35	208,676.88	210,283.70	211,902.88

Present value costs over ten years for the final rule range from $1.08 billion to $3.1 billion using a 3 percent discount rate. If we use a 7 percent discount rate then the present value costs range from $899 million to $2.57 billion. Annualizing these costs yields a cost range of $127 million to $363 million at the 3 percent discount rate and $128 million to $366 million using a 7 percent discount rate.

	7% discount rate	3% discount rate
Benefits	Not Quantified	Not Quantified.
Costs	$899 million to $2.57 billion	$1.08 billion to $3.1 billion.

These projected hires, some of whom will require reasonable accommodation, will not add significant costs for the employers. According to a study conducted by the Job Accommodation Network (JAN), of the employers who gave the researchers cost information related to accommodations they had provided, 57 percent said the accommodations needed by employees cost absolutely nothing.[11] For 43 percent of employers, the typical one-time expenditure by employers to provide a reasonable accommodation was $500. Finally, 2 percent reported that accommodations required a combination of one-time and annual costs.

In projecting the overall increase in Federal contractor employment of protected veterans under the VEVRAA rule and individuals with disabilities under the section 503 rule, there is likely to be an interaction between the two categories. Some of the newly hired individuals with disabilities will likely be protected veterans. There are 5.78 million people 18 years or older in the labor force with a disability, 822,000, or 14.21 percent, of whom are veterans.[12]

To meet the section 503 rule's utilization goal of 7 percent, Federal contractors would have to hire an additional 594,580 individuals with disabilities. Assuming that the number of disabled veterans hired will be proportional to their share of the disabled labor force, then we estimate that 84,490 of the newly hired

[8] Calculation based on unpublished table, *Employment status of persons 18 years and over by veteran status, period of service, sex, race, Hispanic or Latino ethnicity, and disability status, Annual Average 2012 (Source: Current Population Survey).* (10,233/141,050) * 100 = 7.25%. The table is available on request from the Bureau of Labor Statistics at the Department of Labor. BLS does not release some tables for a variety of reasons, such as sample size or possibility of confusion. Finally, this estimate includes all veterans, not only the protected veterans.

[9] Based on data from the Bureau of Labor Statistics Quarterly Census of Employment and Wages, OFFCP estimates that approximately 27.4 million employees could be affected.

[10] The high cost estimates are based on the highest contractor establishment count of 251,300 and 67,919 companies while the low estimates are based on a contractor establishment count of 171,275 and 46,291 companies.

[11] Job Accommodation Network, "Workplace Accommodations: Low Cost, High Impact," Sept. 1, 2012. *Accommodation and Compliance Series, http://askjan.org/media/lowcosthighimpact.html* (last accessed Aug. 9, 2013), p.3; "Fast Facts: Reasonable Accommodations & The Americans with Disabilities Act," U.S. Chamber of Commerce & the Virginia Commonwealth University, Rehabilitation Research and Training Center on Workplace Supports," *http://www.worksupport.com/Topics/downloads/rrtcfactsheet2.pdf* (last accessed August 12, 2013).

[12] Calculation based on unpublished table, *Employment status of persons 18 years and over by veteran status, period of service, sex, race, Hispanic or Latino ethnicity, and disability status, Annual Average 2012* (Source: Current Population Survey).

individuals with disabilities will also be protected veterans.[13] Subtracting 84,490 protected veterans from the target of 205,500 leaves 121,010 non-disabled veterans needed to meet the hiring goal. Viewed independently, Federal contractors under VEVRAA would employ an additional 205,500 protected veterans and under section 503 employ an additional 594,580 individuals with disabilities. In the aggregate, we anticipate the overall number of hires across both rules will be closer to 715,590. We adjust the reasonable accommodation estimates based on the aforementioned assumptions. The total cost of providing reasonable accommodation to protected veterans with disabilities is $19,010,209 in the year the target is met and $8,037,516 in recurring costs.

Employers often think providing a reasonable accommodation is more costly than it actually is. Sometimes an accommodation may be something as simple as allowing someone to have their instructions tape recorded, or allowing someone to wear ear phones so they are not distracted by noise around them, or allowing someone an empty office as space when they have difficulty with concentration or attention span. Employers must provide effective accommodations but are not expected to create an undue hardship for themselves by doing so. Individuals seeking reasonable accommodation beyond what is effective have the option of paying the difference between the cost of the more expensive accommodation and the cost of what the employer will pay for an effective reasonable accommodation.

We estimate the percentage of veterans in the civilian labor force with disabilities, with service-connected disabilities, to be 12 percent.[14] For all Gulf War-era veterans it is 19 percent but for Gulf War-era II veterans it is 24 percent.[15] We have not found projections on the percentage of these populations that are likely to seek reasonable accommodation. The requirement to provide reasonable accommodations to individuals with disabilities existed under the ADA, and now exists under the ADA Amendments Act for employers. This is not a new obligation created by this rule. However, because this rule seeks to increase employment of protected veterans, and some of those veterans are expected to meet the ADA's definition of disabled and, therefore, are entitled to a reasonable accommodation, we estimate the cost of providing reasonable accommodations to those disabled protected veterans that we expect to be hired because of this rule.

There are tangible and intangible benefits to investing in the recruitment and hiring of disabled veterans. Among them are employer tax credits, access to a broader talent pool, an expanded pool of job applicants, access to new markets by developing a workforce that mirrors the general customer base, lower turnover based on increased employee loyalty, and lower training costs resulting from lower staff turnover.[16] According to the U.S. Business Leadership Network (USBLN), "corporate CEOs understand that it's cost effective to recruit and retain the best talent regardless of disability." [17] Broad public policy considerations also exist related to the decreased demand for and cost of social services as more people move into jobs and pay taxes. We were not able to quantitatively assess these broad societal benefits.

Introduction

Addressing the barriers our veterans face in returning to civilian life, particularly with regard to employment, is the focus of a number of Federal efforts. Among these efforts is the VOW to Hire Heroes Act signed into law by President Obama on November 21, 2011, which provides tax credits for businesses that hire veterans who are unemployed or have service-connected disabilities and creates a new Veteran's Retraining Assistance Program for unemployed veterans. Other Federal efforts presented during the August 2011 announcement by President Obama included a plan for the private sector to hire 100,000 veterans by the end of 2013 and creating a "career-ready military" which will "ensure that every member of the service receives the training, education, and credentials they need to transition to the civilian workforce or to pursue higher education." These efforts are now a part of the Administration's Joining Forces Initiative. Strengthening the implementing regulations of VEVRAA, whose stated purpose is "to require Government contractors to take affirmative action to employ and advance in employment qualified protected veterans," is another important means by which the government can address the issue of veterans' employment.

To that end, OFCCP published a notice of proposed rulemaking (NPRM) on April 26, 2011 in the **Federal Register** (76 FR 23358), seeking comment on a number of proposals that would strengthen the regulations implementing VEVRAA. The NRPM was published for a 60-day public comment period. The proposed regulations detailed specific actions that contractors and subcontractors must satisfy to meet their VEVRAA obligations, including increasing data collection obligations, and requiring covered Federal contractors and subcontractors to establish hiring benchmarks for protected veterans. The NPRM also proposed the rescission of 41 CFR part 60–250. After receiving several requests to extend the public comment period, OFCCP published a subsequent notice in the **Federal Register** on June 22, 2011 (76 FR 36482), extending the public comment period an additional 14 days.

OFCCP received over 100 comments on the NPRM. Commenters represented diverse perspectives including: Approximately 40 individuals; ten groups representing contractors; three disability rights advocacy groups; two veterans' associations; two unions; and two governmental entities. Commenters raised a broad range of issues, including concerns with the cost and burden associated with the proposed rule, the extended recordkeeping requirements, developing benchmarks, and the new categories of data collection and analyses. OFCCP carefully considered the comments in the development of this final rule.

Pursuant to Executive Order (EO) 13563, the final rule was developed through a process that involved public participation. In addition to the 60-day public comment period, OFCCP conducted multiple town hall meetings, webinars, and listening sessions with individuals from the contractor community, state employment services, disability organizations, veterans' service organizations and other interested parties to understand the features of VEVRAA regulations that

[13] Because of data limitations, OFCCP is using the share of veterans as a proxy for "protected" veterans. For more information on the difference between protected and unprotected veterans, please visit, *http://www.dol.gov/ofccp/regs/compliance/factsheets/vetrights.htm#Q2*.

[14] Bureau of Labor Statistics, Table 6: Employment status of veterans 18 years and over by presence of service-connected disability, reported disability rating, period of service, and sex, August 2012, not seasonally adjusted *http://www.bls.gov/news.release/vet.t06.htm* (last accessed July 9, 2013).

[15] *Id.*

[16] Job Accommodation Network, "Workplace Accommodations: Low Cost, High Impact," Sept. 1, 2012. *Accommodation and Compliance Series. http://askjan.org/media/lowcosthighimpact.html* (last accessed Aug. 9, 2013).

[17] USBLN Disability at Work, and U.S. Chamber of Commerce, "Leading Practices on Disability Inclusion," *http://www.usbln.org/pdf-docs/Leading_Practices_on_Disability_Inclusion.pdf* (last accessed Aug. 9, 2013). The USBLN and Chamber report shares best practices from larger corporations for hiring and providing reasonable accommodations.

work well, those that can be improved, and possible new requirements that could help to effectuate the overall goal of increasing the employment opportunities for qualified veterans with Federal contractors.

I. Compliance With the Final Rule

Although this final rule becomes effective 180 days after publication, full compliance with the requirements of this final rule by current contractors will be phased in as follows. Current contractors subject to subpart C of the existing 41 CFR part 60–300 regulations that have written affirmative action programs (AAP) prepared pursuant to those regulations in place on the effective date of this final rule may maintain that AAP for the duration of their AAP year. Such contractors are required to update their affirmative action programs to come into compliance with the requirements of subpart C of this final rule at the start of their next standard 12-month AAP review and updating cycle. OFCCP will verify a contractor's compliance with the requirements of this final rule if the contractor is selected for a compliance evaluation pursuant to § 60–300.60 or subject to a complaint investigation pursuant to § 60–300.61. The effective date and the approach to compliance are the same as those set forth in the section 503 Final Rule. OFCCP believes that adopting similar approaches to the effective date and to compliance makes the most sense based on the similarity of the two rules, and will help contractors make required system and process changes at one time.

II. Overview of the Final Rule

As stated above, the final rule incorporates many of the proposed changes set forth in the NPRM. However, in order to focus the scope of the final rule more closely on key issues, and in an effort to reduce the burden of compliance on contractors, the final rule also revises or eliminates some of the NPRM's proposals. This discussion highlights the major provisions of the final rule and summarizes relevant comments. The fuller discussion of the provisions of the rule is in the Section-by-Section Analysis.

The final rule strengthens the affirmative action provisions for Federal contractors in several ways. The regulations reiterate the contractor's mandatory job listing requirements and the relationship between the contractor, its agents, and the state employment services that provide priority referral of protected veterans. The mandatory job listing obligation, which is set forth in and required by the VEVRAA statute, *see* 38 U.S.C. 4212(a)(2)(A), ensures that veterans seeking the assistance of state employment service delivery systems to find employment will be able to find job listings from Federal contractors, and that the delivery systems will be able to provide priority referral of these veterans back to contractors. The final rule also addresses the increased use of technology in the workplace by allowing for the electronic posting of employee rights and contractor obligations under VEVRAA and updating the manner in which compliance evaluations are conducted. Further, the regulations enhance data collection pertaining to protected applicants and hires in order to provide contractors vital information against which they can effectively measure their recruitment efforts, and establish two mechanisms—the flexible approach set forth in the NPRM, or a more simplified, single national target—from which contractors may choose in order to establish a hiring benchmark. These revisions will help contractors better evaluate their outreach efforts and modify them as needed, toward the end of increasing employment opportunities for protected veterans by Federal contractors and subcontractors. Additionally, as proposed in the NPRM, part 60–250 of these regulations is rescinded. However, as we discuss further in the Section-by-Section Analysis, part 60–300 is revised to provide that any protected veteran as defined in the former part 60–250 regulations who is employed by or applies for a position with a part 60–250 covered contractor will still be protected under the anti-discrimination provisions of part 60–300, and will be able to file complaints with OFCCP regarding discriminatory treatment.

OFCCP revised or eliminated a number of provisions from the NPRM in response to the comments that were received, particularly as they relate to the cost and burden of the rule, recordkeeping requirements, data collection and analyses, and benchmarks. These changes are summarized below.

OFCCP received 55 comments concerning the overall burdens and costs of the proposed rule from several contractor groups and contractors, including 21 form letters. Most commenters stated that OFCCP's estimates in costs and hours were too low. Commenters also noted that OFCCP's contractor universe was too small. In response to these concerns, OFCCP modified the burden and costs estimates for the final rule. As discussed further in the Regulatory Procedures section, OFCCP also increased the overall contractor and subcontractor establishment count to 171,275 based on Fiscal Year 2009 Employer Information Report EEO–1 (EEO–1), the Federal Procurement Data System-Next Generation (FPDS–NG) report data on contractor establishments, and other information. These changes provide a more accurate depiction of the burden and cost associated with the final rule. As discussed in more detail below, OFCCP also made key changes to the recordkeeping requirements to minimize the burden on contractors.

We received comments on the estimated number of contractor establishments as well, including recommending an establishment count of 285,390 using the Veterans Employment Training Services (VETS) annual report. While OFCCP declines to exclusively rely on the VETS report number, we present an estimated high end for the range of the cost of the rule based on a contractor establishment number of 251,300. This number is based on 2010 VETS data from their pending Information Collection Request.[18]

The NPRM proposed that contractors maintain data pursuant to §§ 60–300.44(f)(4) (linkage agreements and other outreach and recruiting efforts), 60–300.44(k) (collection of referral, applicant, and hire data), and 60–300.45(c) (criteria and conclusions regarding hiring benchmarks) for five years. Twenty-three commenters opposed these provisions. Several of the commenters were particularly concerned with the burden associated with the five-year requirement. In response, OFCCP reduces the proposed five-year recordkeeping requirement to three years in the final rule. Further, in light of the comments we received, the final rule does not incorporate the proposal under paragraph 5 of the Equal Opportunity (EO) Clause and § 60–300.44(k) of the NPRM to maintain data related to referrals from employment service delivery systems. The proposal required contractors to maintain quantitative measurements and comparisons regarding those protected veterans who were referred by state employment services. Commenters were concerned with the requirement to obtain referral data, as they indicated that the state employment delivery service either cannot provide data or provides data inconsistently across the states, and that acquiring the data and

[18] OMB Control Number 1293–0005, Federal Contractor Veterans' Employment Report, VETS–100/VETS–100A, *http://www.reginfo.gov/public/do/PRAViewDocument?ref_nbr=201104-1293-003* (last accessed Aug. 13, 2013).

synthesizing it would be burdensome. In reviewing the practical utility of the referral data in light of the burden that it would create on contractors, OFCCP has eliminated the requirement to collect and analyze referral data. Eliminating the referral data requirement and reducing the length of recordkeeping for the other provisions minimizes the burden on contractors yet still requires contractors to keep adequate records to aid and inform their outreach and recruitment efforts.

The NPRM also proposed to require many of the affirmative action efforts that are only suggested in § 60–300.44 of the existing rule. Among these were proposals requiring contractors to: review personnel processes on an annual basis (§ 60–300.44(b)); establish linkage agreements with three veteran-related organizations to increase connections between contractors and veterans seeking employment (§ 60–300.44(f)); take certain specified actions to internally disseminate its affirmative action policy (§ 60–300.44(g)); and train all personnel on specific topics related to the employment of protected veterans (§ 60–300.44(j)). After consideration of the comments and taking into account the expected utility of these provisions in light of the burden that contractors would incur to comply with the proposals, OFCCP decided not to incorporate the majority of these proposals, and instead retains the language in the existing rule. The proposals in the NPRM, for the most part, required certain specific steps contractors must take to fulfill their already existing, general affirmative action obligations. These general affirmative action obligations—reviewing personnel processes on a periodic basis, undertaking appropriate outreach and positive recruitment activities, developing internal procedures to disseminate affirmative action policies, and training its employees on these policies—remain in the final rule. By eliminating the specific provisions but maintaining the general affirmative action obligations, the final rule provides the contractor flexibility and lesser burden while maintaining a robust affirmative action program.

The final rule also modifies the approach to setting benchmarks. The NPRM proposed requiring contractors to establish annual hiring benchmarks, expressed as the percentage of total hires who are protected veterans that the contractor seeks to hire in the following year. The hiring benchmarks were to be established by the contractor using existing data on veteran availability, while also allowing the contractor to take into account other factors unique to its establishment that would tend to affect the availability determination. OFCCP received a total of 38 comments on the proposed benchmarks. Twelve commenters questioned whether contractor established benchmarks would be arbitrary and ineffective because of concerns about the reliability of data on the number of protected veterans in the workforce. Commenters also sought clarity on exactly how they should develop benchmarks based on the varying sources of data available. In addition, commenters asserted that the benchmarks were quotas that would adversely impact women and minorities since demographically veterans are predominantly white males. In response to these concerns, OFCCP has revised § 60–300.45 to provide a simpler, nationwide benchmark as another option that contractors can use, in addition to the flexible approach set forth in the NPRM. Further, the final rule addresses the incorrect assumptions—*e.g.*, that goals represent a "quota" or will place contractors in jeopardy of violating the sex discrimination provisions of Executive Order 11246—that many comments in the NPRM detailed.

Finally, in response to some comments and to further reduce costs, the final rule eliminates a few other minor requirements included in the NPRM. For instance, the final rule does not include the proposed requirement in § 60–300.42(d) of the NPRM that contractors affirmatively ask disabled veterans if they require a reasonable accommodation, retaining the requirement in the existing rule that contractors must take part in an interactive process regarding accommodation and should, but are not required to, seek the advice of the applicant regarding such accommodation. This aligns the rule with the obligations set forth in the Americans with Disabilities Act. Additionally, the final rule eliminates the specific obligation to inform off-site employees about the availability of the contractor's affirmative action plan, and instead retains the existing obligation that requires the affirmative action plan to be available upon request with the location and hours of availability posted publicly. As with the other changes discussed, these revisions maintain the general obligations while reducing the burden of compliance for contractors.

The final rule presents the most substantial re-write of VEVRAA regulations since their inception. In light of these significant changes, and in response to contractors' requests to delay implementation due to these changes, the effective date of this final rule is set for 180 days after publication in the **Federal Register**. The detailed Section-by-Section Analysis below identifies and discusses all of the final changes in each section. For ease of reference, part 60–300 will be republished in its entirety in the final rule.

Section-by-Section Analysis

41 CFR Part 60–250

Rescission of Part 60–250

The NPRM proposed two alternative approaches to updating part 60–250. The first approach proposed rescinding part 60–250 in its entirety. The second approach proposed revising part 60–250 so that it mirrors the proposed changes to part 60–300. OFCCP received 16 comments on these proposals from a variety of entities including individuals, law firms, contractors, and associations representing veterans, contractors, or individuals with disabilities.

OFCCP received few comments supporting retaining part 60–250. One commenter stated that it held several contracts that are covered under parts 60–250 and 60–300. One individual commenter stated that part 60–250 should remain in place as some major contractors have contracts spanning several decades that are still in force. The commenter also expressed concern about eliminating the definition of "special disabled veteran." The commenter noted that 30 percent of disabled veterans may need additional affirmative action since it would be difficult to compete with a veteran that has no service connected disability.

OFCCP received 14 comments that either recommended rescinding part 60–250, indicated that the commenter was unaware of contractors that were subject to part 60–250, or stated that the commenter was neutral on the proposal to rescind part 60–250. Many commenters questioned whether there were any remaining active contracts that would still be covered by part 60–250. One commenter, an industry group, stated that one of its members has a continuing contract from the 1980s; however, that contract has since been modified and is no longer covered under part 60–250.

Commenters provided alternative recommendations to implementing a part 60–250 that mirrors part 60–300. An equal employment opportunity consulting firm recommended allowing contractors to combine their obligations under both parts 60–250 and 60–300 into a single AAP to eliminate unnecessary duplication. Another commenter recommended widening the scope of part 60–300 to incorporate contracts that are covered under part 60–250.

Part 60–250 is rescinded. As stated in the NPRM and echoed by many commenters, we do not believe that there are any remaining contracts for $25,000 or more entered into prior to December 1, 2003, that have not either terminated or since been modified (which, if over $100,000 in value, would fall under part 60–300's coverage). While the agency received one comment from a company that asserted that it held contracts that are subject to part 60–250, OFCCP's research revealed that the commenter is a grantee. However, out of an abundance of caution that any contracts falling under part 60–250's coverage still exist, and to ensure that all veterans that are protected by part 60–250 (and not part 60–300 as well) will be able to pursue complaints of discrimination, the final rule includes a definition of "pre-JVA veteran" in § 60–300.2, and provides that such individuals continue to be protected by the non-discrimination prohibitions in § 60–300.21 and are able to file discrimination complaints pursuant to § 60–300.61. There is further discussion of this definition in the analysis of Section 60–300.2.

41 CFR Part 60–300

Subpart A—Preliminary Matters, Equal Opportunity Clause

Section 60–300.1 Purpose, Applicability and Construction

Section 60–300.1 of the current rule sets forth the scope of VEVRAA and the purpose of its implementing regulations. The NPRM proposed deleting references throughout the regulation to the "Vietnam Era Veterans' Readjustment Assistance Act of 1974" or "VEVRAA" and replacing it in this section and throughout the regulation with "Section 4212." OFCCP proposed the change due to concerns that the continued reference to "Vietnam era veterans" leads to confusion regarding the categories of veterans that are protected under the law. There were a total of six comments on the proposed revision.

Some commenters supported referring to the regulations as "Section 4212." One commenter stated that the change would be an important and positive step to clarifying the fact that the regulations are no longer focused on issues that only concern veterans of the Vietnam era. Another commenter believed that the proposed change would eliminate confusion entirely regarding whether VEVRAA applied to only Vietnam era veterans. One commenter opposed the revision and argued that deleting the reference to "VEVRAA" would be an insult to Vietnam era veterans. Commenters also provided several recommendations for this section. One commenter suggested that if the agency is going to use the term "Section 4212," it should do so consistently. The commenter cited several examples where "Section 4212" was used inconsistently in the NPRM. Other commenters suggested that the agency utilize a name that connects "Section 4212" to the veterans who are protected, such as "Section 4212/Protected Veterans." The commenter that opposed the revision stated that OFCCP should invest resources into properly advertising the law rather than changing the name.

The final rule does not incorporate the proposal to use the term "Section 4212," and instead continues the use of the term "VEVRAA." While referring to the law as "Section 4212" had potential benefits as described in the NPRM, there was also concern that the new term "Section 4212" might invite further confusion. For instance, for those unfamiliar with the law, the term "Section 4212" does not indicate any relationship to veterans' rights on its face. Further, there was concern that some may think that "Section 4212" and "VEVRAA" were two unrelated laws. Accordingly, the final rule retains the term "VEVRAA," and in response to comments we have ensured that the term is used consistently throughout the regulation.

In addition, to address confusion among contractors and veterans regarding the scope of the various veterans' employment rights statutes, the final rule adds language to the discussion in paragraph (c)(2) of VEVRAA's "relationship to other laws." New paragraph (c)(2)(i) highlights that VEVRAA and the Uniformed Services Employment and Reemployment Rights Act (USERRA) are separate laws with distinct obligations for contractors and distinct protections for employees who have past, present or future military service, status or obligations. It clarifies that this part does not limit the contractor's obligations, responsibilities, and requirements under USERRA, including the obligation to reemploy employees returning from qualifying military service, and emphasizes that compliance with this part is not determinative of compliance with USERRA.

Section 60–300.2 Definitions

The NPRM proposed clarifying several key definitions in part 60–300. The current classifications of protected veterans under VEVRAA include: (1) Disabled veterans, (2) veterans who served on active duty in the Armed Forces during a war or in a campaign or expedition for which a campaign badge was authorized, (3) veterans who, while serving on active duty in the Armed Forces, participated in a United States military operation for which an Armed Forces service medal was awarded pursuant to Executive Order No. 12985, and (4) recently separated veterans. The regulations define "disabled veteran," "recently separated veteran," and "Armed Forces service medal veteran." The definition of "other protected veteran" in the existing regulation applies to veterans who served on active duty in the Armed Forces during a war or in a campaign or expedition for which a campaign badge has been authorized. OFCCP proposed replacing "other protected veteran" with "active duty wartime or campaign badge veteran" to eliminate confusion regarding the veterans that are protected under this category. Some have interpreted erroneously the "other protected veteran" category as a "catch-all" that includes all veterans. The proposed rule also added new definitions for "protected veteran" and "linkage agreement." OFCCP received a total of 18 comments on the proposed changes to § 60–300.2 from a variety of entities including individuals, law firms, contractors, and associations representing veterans, contractors, or disability rights.

• *Definition for "Active Duty Wartime or Campaign Badge Veteran"*

There were a total of eight comments on the proposal to change the category of veterans referred to as "other protected veteran" in the existing rule to "active duty wartime or campaign badge veteran." This category of veteran includes all those who served on active duty in the U.S. military, ground, naval, or air service either: (a) during a war; or (b) in a campaign or expedition for which a campaign badge was authorized by the Department of Defense (DOD). The proposal did not change which veterans are covered; we made the change so that the category name was more accurately descriptive of who it covered.

Most commenters supported the proposal. One commenter noted that the proposed language would more accurately reflect the language in the statute and alleviate some of the past confusion surrounding the wording. Another commenter stated that the proposed change is helpful in understanding the nature of veterans protected by this category.

A few commenters expressed concern about the proposed definition. One commenter argued that the law is quite clear on who is protected by VEVRAA and that the proposed term "active duty wartime or campaign badge veteran" does not provide any additional clarification. A human resources consulting company suggested that using "active duty" may lead to under-reporting. The company asserted that individuals may interpret this to mean that they have to be on active duty to qualify. Commenters also stated that it is unclear who qualifies as a "wartime" or "campaign badge veteran." One commenter noted that the clearest guidance on who qualifies as a "campaign badge veteran" could only be found on the United States Department of Defense and Office of Personnel Management Web sites. The commenter further stated that many contractors do not want to directly reference the information on those sites because they are related to the Federal government's veterans' preference. The commenter requested that OFCCP develop guidance specifically for contractors clearly identifying which veterans are protected under the "wartime" or "campaign badge veteran" classification.

The final rule adopts the definition "active duty wartime or campaign badge veteran" as proposed in the NPRM. OFCCP believes that this is a more accurate description, and less subject to confusion, than the general "other protected veteran" classification. OFCCP notes that the Department of Defense and the individual services of the Armed Forces (*e.g.*, Army; Navy) administer these campaign badges, and thus contractors should consult with DOD or the issuing military service if they have questions about whether a particular badge is a campaign badge that provides coverage under VEVRAA.

- *Definition for "Protected Veterans," "Pre-JVA Veterans"*

While commenters were generally supportive of the proposal to create a definition for "protected veteran," there were a few concerns regarding using the term "protected" to label the definition. One commenter argued that using the term "protected veteran" may cause further confusion since many mistakenly interpreted "other protected veteran" to mean all other veterans not protected under the other defined categories. Another commenter argued that the definition should utilize the label "protected veteran," since this is the statutory language in VEVRAA.

The final rule retains the proposed definition for "protected veteran." As this final rule eliminates the "other protected veteran" definition and replaces it with a clearer, more specific alternative, we believe that the new "protected veteran" term will not be confused with the previous "other protected veteran" term. Further, while we understand that the VEVRAA statute uses the term "protected veterans" to describe the various categories of veterans protected by VEVRAA, we use the term "protected veteran" in the regulations for consistency with other regulations administered by OFCCP. The Executive Order 11246 and section 503 regulations, as well as the VEVRAA regulations to date, have used the term "protected" to refer to the individuals and groups of individuals who have rights under the various statutes (*e.g.*, "protected classes"). Meanwhile, the term "covered" has typically referred to the contractors to whom the regulations apply (*e.g.*, "covered contractor"). Therefore, in order to maintain word usage continuity with all of OFCCP's laws, we retain the term "protected veteran" as proposed in the NPRM.

One commenter suggested that OFCCP expand the types of veterans protected under VEVRAA to include Desert Storm-era veterans, veterans that served in a war zone and veterans who utilize service dogs. The categories of "protected veterans" are not set by OFCCP, but rather are defined by the VEVRAA statute codified at 38 U.S.C. 4212(a)(3). OFCCP cannot expand the categories beyond those set forth in the statute. We note that most of the types of veterans listed above are protected by the categories of veterans set forth in the statute. Veterans that served in the Desert Storm-era or otherwise in a war zone likely will be protected under the "active duty wartime or campaign badge veteran" category of protected veteran, and possibly the "recently separated veteran" category as well. As for veterans who use service dogs, if they were discharged or released from active duty due to a service-connected disability, or are otherwise entitled to compensation for disability under laws administered by the Department of Veterans Affairs, they would already be protected under the "disabled veteran" classification.

Finally, as noted in the discussion on the rescission of part 60–250, the final rule also includes a definition for "pre-JVA veteran," which incorporates those individuals who were previously protected under part 60–250 into part 60–300. The definition is as follows:

"*Pre-JVA veteran* means an individual who is an employee of or applicant to a contractor with a contract of $25,000 or more entered into prior to December 1, 2003, and who is a special disabled veteran, veteran of the Vietnam era, pre-JVA recently separated veteran, or other protected veteran, as defined below:

(1) Special disabled veteran (also referred to in this regulation as 'Pre-JVA special disabled veteran') means:

(i) a veteran who is entitled to compensation (or who but for the receipt of military retired pay would be entitled to compensation) under laws administered by the Department of Veterans Affairs for a disability:

(A) Rated at 30 percent or more; or

(B) Rated at 10 or 20 percent in the case of a veteran who has been determined under 38 U.S.C. 3106 to have a serious employment handicap; or

(ii) A person who was discharged or released from active duty because of a service-connected disability.

(2) Veteran of the Vietnam era means a person who:

(i) Served on active duty for a period of more than 180 days, and was discharged or released there from with other than a dishonorable discharge, if any part of such active duty occurred:

(A) In the Republic of Vietnam between February 28, 1961, and May 7, 1975; or

(B) Between August 5, 1964, and May 7, 1975, in all other cases; or

(ii) Was discharged or released from active duty for a service-connected disability if any part of such active duty was performed:

(A) In the Republic of Vietnam between February 28, 1961, and May 7, 1975; or

(B) Between August 5, 1964, and May 7, 1975, in all other cases.

(3) Pre-JVA recently separated veteran means a pre-JVA veteran during the one-year period beginning on the date of the pre-JVA veteran's discharge or release from active duty.

(4) Other protected veteran means a person who served on active duty during a war or in a campaign or expedition for which a campaign badge has been authorized, under the laws administered by the Department of Defense."

As stated in the discussion of the rescission of part 60–250, references to "Pre-JVA veteran" are included in the discrimination prohibition section for the final rule (§ 60–300.21) and the complaint procedures section of the final rule (§ 60–300.61) to ensure that, if there are any individuals remaining who are protected solely by part 60–250, such individuals will be able to avail themselves of their rights and file complaints for discrimination based on their veteran status just as "protected veterans" under part 60–300 are able to do. We do not include "pre-JVA veterans" along with "protected veterans'' in the sections of the regulation pertaining to contractors' affirmative action obligations. As we have noted above, we have no evidence that there are any contracts remaining that fall solely under part 60–250's coverage, and thus requiring contractors to engage in affirmative action efforts pursuant to contracts that by all accounts no longer exist is not a good use of resources. Regardless, the protected veteran categories under part 60–300 include the vast majority of veterans who were protected under the part 60–250 categories—indeed, the part 60–300 categories are even broader with regard to recently separated veterans and disabled veterans. To the extent they do not, many of contractors' affirmative action obligations under part 60–300 would likely reach such individuals anyway (*e.g.*, a contractor's recruitment and outreach effort, which could include a linkage agreement with a local veterans service group).

• *Definition for ''Linkage Agreements''*

Commenters expressed a variety of concerns regarding the proposed definition of ''linkage agreements.'' However, as the final rule eliminates the requirement for contractors to enter into linkage agreements—see discussion of § 60–300.44(f), below—there is no need for the regulation to contain a definition for it, and thus it is eliminated from the final rule.

• *Additional Definitions*

Commenters recommended adding certain definitions to § 60–300.2 for clarification purposes. Two commenters stated that OFCCP needed to clearly define ''priority referral.'' One of the commenters, a law firm, expressed concern that contractors are specifically directed to request ''priority referrals'' and conduct analyses of ''priority referrals'' in comparison to other referrals, but the regulations do not clearly define ''priority referral.'' Another commenter requested that OFCCP define ''external job search organizations'' because the term has been broadly interpreted to encompass a broad range of organizations including online job search engines, veterans' service organizations, and other third parties that provide candidates for contractors.

OFCCP declines to include a definition of ''priority referral'' in § 60–300.2. OFCCP believes that it is clear from the statute that the term refers to individuals referred pursuant to a local employment services office's requirement to give ''veterans priority in referral'' for contractor employment listings. *See* 38 U.S.C. 4212(a)(2). Further, the requirement that the One-Stop service delivery systems provide priority referral of veterans is not administered and carried out by OFCCP, but by other agencies within the Department. The Department's Employment and Training Administration (ETA) and Veterans' Employment and Training Service (VETS) have published guidance on implementing priority of service requirements for veterans, including: the Training and Employment Guidance Letter 10–09 (accessible on ETA's Web site at *http://wdr.doleta.gov/directives/corr_doc.cfm?DOCN=2816*); Veterans' Program Letter 07–09; and Training and Employment Notice 15–10, ''A Protocol for Implementing Priority of Service for Veterans and Eligible Spouses.'' However, we note that the final rule eliminates the proposed requirement to collect and maintain data on priority referrals, which should limit any concerns raised in response to the NPRM about how to specifically categorize priority referrals.

OFCCP also disagrees with the assertion that the agency should define ''external job search organization.'' The NPRM noted in the discussion of the proposed Paragraph 4 of the EO Clause that if a ''contractor uses any outside job search companies (such as a temporary employment agency) to assist in its hiring, the contractor must provide the state employment service with the contact information for these outside job search companies.'' This context clarifies the kinds of organizations that are considered ''external job search organizations.'' OFCCP intends for ''external job search organization'' to be read as broadly as possible. ''External job search organization'' includes any entity not wholly owned and operated by the contractor that assists with its hiring.

Finally, the final rule appends additional language to the definition for ''employment service delivery system'' (ESDS). The existing rule references that the ESDS offers services in accordance with the Wagner-Peyser Act. The final rule adds some additional background and explanation of the Wagner-Peyser Act, stating that ''[t]he Wagner-Peyser Act requires that these services be provided as part of the One-Stop delivery system established by the States under Section 134 of the Workforce Investment Act of 1998.'' The Wagner-Peyser Act of 1933 established a national network of Employment Service offices that provided labor exchange services to jobseekers and employers. The Workforce Investment Act of 1998 (WIA) amended the Wagner-Peyser Act and required states and localities to integrate employment and training programs into a single public workforce system. Thus, employment services and training programs are all provided through a national network of One-Stop Career Centers established in the local workforce investment areas of the states. The description of the Employment Service's role in the public workforce system can be found at 20 CFR 652.202, and Section 7(e) of the Wagner-Peyser Act.

We also note that several commenters representing the contractor community requested that OFCCP add formal definitions for ''applicant'' and for ''Internet applicant,'' as those terms are defined in the Executive Order 11246 (EO 11246) implementing regulations at 41 CFR part 60–1. While OFCCP does not formally adopt the definition of ''Internet applicant'' into the section VEVRAA regulations, OFCCP is harmonizing the requirements of these regulations and the EO 11246 Internet Applicant Rule. OFCCP provides further guidance on this issue in the preamble discussion related to § 60–300.42.

Section 60–300.5 Equal Opportunity Clause

The NPRM proposed several changes to the content of the Equal Opportunity Clause found in § 60–300.5, and the manner in which the Clause is included in Federal contracts. These proposals, the comments to these proposals, and the revisions made to the final rule are discussed in turn below.

• *EO Clause Paragraph 2—Clarification of Mandatory Job Listing Obligations*

The NPRM proposed additional language to this paragraph clarifying that the contractor must provide job vacancy information to the appropriate employment service in the manner that the local employment service delivery system (ESDS) requires in order to include the job in their database so that they may provide priority referral of veterans. The NPRM also proposed additional language to this paragraph clarifying that, for any contractor who utilizes a privately-run job service or exchange to comply with its mandatory listing obligation, the information must be provided to the appropriate employment service in the manner that the employment service requires. OFCCP received 14 comments concerning this section from an individual, law firms, contractors, contractor groups, a veteran's group, and others. As explained below, we adopt the language proposed in the NPRM for this paragraph with one minor revision.

The majority of the comments received asserted that posting jobs in the format required by a given ESDS was burdensome, as ESDSs in varying states and localities require different submission formats and information for their job listing system. On a related note, several commenters suggested that the Department reinstitute America's Job Bank, a nationwide job listing service operated and eventually eliminated several years ago by the Employment and Training Administration. OFCCP did not develop or maintain America's Job Bank, as one law firm commenter asserted.

A bit of historical background is perhaps helpful in addressing these comments. As was discussed in the NPRM, the requirement to list jobs with the appropriate ESDS is not a purely regulatory creation, but is established in the statute itself. *See* 38 U.S.C. 4212(a)(2)(A). The statute has long required that each contractor "shall immediately list all of its employment openings with the appropriate employment service delivery system." *Id.* The JVA, in amending VEVRAA in 2002, further specified that while contractors could also list a job with America's Job Bank or any additional or subsequent national electronic job bank established by the Department of Labor, this *was not in and of itself sufficient* to satisfy the job listing requirement. *Id.* at 4212(a)(2)(A). Accordingly, reinstitution of America's Job Bank or something similar would not change the statutory requirement that contractors list their jobs with the appropriate ESDS. OFCCP is obligated to comply with the statute as written.

Thus, the mandatory job listing requirement set forth in the NPRM is not a new creation; it merely clarified that contractors list their jobs with the ESDS "in the manner and format required" by the ESDS. This, for example, could include requiring electronic transmission through a web-based form or electronic document format (such as PDF), requiring paper transmission using mail or facsimile, or requiring the contractor to provide particular types of information in its submissions. As we stated in the NPRM, this clarification stems from numerous reports received by OFCCP that contractors were occasionally providing job listing information to the ESDS in an unusable format, such that their jobs were not being listed and the ESDS could not properly carry out the priority referral of veterans, which is required by VEVRAA and its regulations. We received input during the public comment period from individuals working for or with an ESDS that corroborated these reports. If the purpose of the mandatory job listing requirement is to help veterans find work with Federal contractors, then surely Congress did not intend to permit contractors to provide information about their job openings in an unusable format, completely defeating the purpose of the requirement. Some commenters were concerned that the proposed language in the NPRM required contractors to provide information about their job openings in one specific format mandated by the ESDS. This was not the intention of the proposal. Rather, the aim of the proposal was simply to ensure that contractors provide information about their job openings with the ESDS in a format that the ESDS can use to provide priority referrals of protected veterans to contractors. If an ESDS permits the contractor to provide this information in various formats, the contractor would be free to use any one of them. To clarify this requirement, the final rule revises the proposal's language (providing the listing "in the manner or format required by the appropriate [ESDS] . . .") to require contractors to list their jobs "in *a* manner and format *permitted* by the appropriate [ESDS] which will allow that system to provide priority referral of veterans. . ."

Finally, a few commenters questioned whether the language proposed in the NPRM for the last sentence of this paragraph, which clarifies that any contractor using a privately-run job service or exchange to list its jobs is still required to have the job listed with the appropriate ESDS in a usable format, would forbid third parties from posting jobs for contractors or the use of private job boards. The language in the NPRM, now adopted into the final rule, does not prevent a contractor from utilizing a third party to list its jobs, so long as the job listing is submitted to the appropriate ESDS in any manner and format permitted by the ESDS. However, if the job is not listed by the third party with the appropriate ESDS in a permitted manner and format, the contractor will be held responsible. Similarly, the language in the NPRM, now adopted into the final rule, does not prevent a contractor from listing its jobs on any privately-run job boards it may deem worthwhile; however, it may only do so in addition to, and not instead of, the mandatory job listing requirement established by statute and set forth in the rule.

• *EO Clause Paragraph 4—Information Provided to State Employment Services*

The NPRM proposed that the contractor, when it becomes obligated to list its job openings with the appropriate state employment service, must provide additional information, including its status as a Federal contractor, the contact information for the contractor hiring official at each location in the state, and its request for priority referrals of protected veterans for job openings at all its locations within the state, and that this information must be updated annually. These requirements were added in response to feedback received from ESDSs that there is no centralized list of Federal contractors that they can consult in order to determine if a listing employer is a Federal contractor, and to ensure that these ESDSs have contact information for the listing contractor if there are any questions that need to be resolved in the job listing or priority referral process. The NPRM also required that the contractor provide the ESDS with the contact information for any outside job search companies (such as a temporary employment agency) assisting with its hiring process.

OFCCP received four comments specific to these proposed changes. One commenter stated that GSA has a list of Federal contractors and, therefore, the Federal Government should make this list available to the ESDS and not require listing companies to indicate whether or not they are a Federal contractor as defined by the VEVRAA regulations. While it is true that the GSA e-library Web site has a list of contractors, this list does not contain companies that have contracts with all agencies throughout the Federal Government, and in fact did not include certain contractors that OFCCP has investigated in recent years and for whom coverage is not disputed. Additionally, the library is not limited to those contracts entered into on or after December 1, 2003 with a value of $100,000 or more, the criteria for coverage under part 60–300 of the regulations. As such, this list is both under-inclusive and over-inclusive, and cannot be relied upon for VEVRAA enforcement purposes. In this context, and in the interest of insuring that Federal contractors are properly identified so an ESDS can fulfill its duty to give priority referral of protected veterans to contractors, we believe that requiring contractors to simply indicate "VEVRAA Federal Contractor" on its job listings facilitates the business engagement efforts of the ESDS and is not unduly burdensome for either the contractor or the ESDS (this revision does not add any additional reporting requirements for the ESDS aside from those already set forth in the VEVRAA and these regulations). Accordingly, the final rule incorporates this proposal.

Some commenters stated that posting the contact information for "the contractor official responsible for hiring at each location" would be burdensome on that person, especially if recruiting nationwide, and might be confusing, as multiple persons could be involved in hiring. Among the alternative suggestions in the comments was using "chief hiring official," "HR contact," or "senior management contact" in the place of "contractor official responsible for hiring at each location."

As stated in the NPRM, the reason for requiring this information was to ensure that the ESDS had the contact information for someone working for the contractor that could answer any questions the ESDS may have about the listing to ensure it is processed appropriately and was the proper recipient of priority referrals of veterans. In order to make this requirement less vague and to provide contractors with greater flexibility, the final rule includes a sentence providing further guidance that the "contractor official" may be a chief hiring official, a Human Resources contact, a senior management contact, or any other manager for the contractor that can verify the information set forth in the job listing. Additionally, the final rule makes a small change to the reporting schedule for the information required by this paragraph. While the NPRM required that this information be reported annually, the final rule requires that contractors provide this information at the time of its first job listing, and then update it for subsequent job listings only if any of the provided information has changed. This will ensure that the ESDS has the information it needs while potentially limiting the reporting burden on contractors.

The NPRM also required that the contractor provide the ESDS with the contact information for any outside job search companies (such as a temporary employment agency) assisting with its hiring process, and replaced the term "state workforce agency" and "state agency" throughout the regulation with the term "employment service delivery system," which was already a defined term in the regulation. We did not receive any comments specific to these proposals, and thus they are adopted in the final rule as proposed.

- *EO Clause Paragraph 5—Maintaining Referral Data*

The NPRM proposed an entirely new paragraph 5 to the EO Clause that would require contractors to collect and maintain data on the number of referrals and priority referrals they receive, in order to give the contractor and OFCCP a quantifiable measure of the availability of protected veterans and, therefore, provide part of a baseline for measuring the success of a contractor's outreach and recruitment programs. The NPRM also proposed that contractors maintain this data for five years, in order to ensure that contractors had enough historical referral data to consider when evaluating its outreach efforts (*see* § 60–300.44(f)(3)) and establishing benchmarks (*see* § 60–300.45).

OFCCP received several comments on this proposal, the majority of which stated that the data collection and five-year recordkeeping requirements were unduly burdensome. Other commenters believed that it would be difficult and perhaps impossible to obtain accurate referral data, and thus the practical utility of the data collection requirement was limited. For instance, one commenter asserted that accurate referral data would be difficult to obtain if an applicant filed directly with a contractor, and that referral data from private Web sites would not be counted as referral. Several commenters representing the contractor community also asserted that requiring contractors to collect and maintain this data was inconsistent with the Internet Applicant rule set forth in the Executive Order 11246 regulations.

OFCCP has considered these comments and believes that the points raised by commenters regarding the practical utility of the referral data, in light of the burden of collecting it, have merit. Accordingly, the final rule deletes the proposed paragraph 5 and renumbers the subsequent paragraphs in the EO Clause accordingly.

- *EO Clause Paragraph 10 (NPRM)/Paragraph 9 (Final Rule)—Providing Notice to People with Disabilities*

In paragraph 10 of the EO Clause in the NPRM, we proposed two changes. First, we updated the contractor's duty to provide notices of rights and obligations that are accessible to individuals with disabilities, replacing the outdated suggestion of "hav[ing] the notice read to a visually disabled individual" as an accommodation with the suggestion to provide Braille, large print, or other versions that allow persons with disabilities to read the notice themselves. OFCCP received one comment from a contractor asserting that there were "too many" types of notices possible for all types of disabilities. We respectfully disagree with this commenter's assertion. The context of the existing regulation and the proposed changes clearly and specifically refer to providing an alternative notice to individuals who are unable to read it due to visual impairment or visual inaccessibility (such as an individual who uses a wheelchair being unable to read the fine print of a notice posted high on a wall). The commenter did not specify any other disabilities for which contractors would need to create alternative notices, and we cannot conceive of any that would create any significant burden. Further, any burden in providing a notice in Braille is slight given the fact that they are available from the EEOC's Office of Communications and Legislative Affairs, who may be contacted at 202–663–4191 or TTY 202–663–4494. *See http://www1.eeoc.gov/eeoc/publications/.* We have amended the language slightly in the final rule to clarify that among the "other versions" of the notice there are additional technological options available to contractors that would fulfill the requirement, such as providing it electronically or on computer disc.

Second, we proposed additional language detailing that a contractor can satisfy its posting obligations through electronic means for employees who use telework arrangements or otherwise do not work at the physical location of the contractor, provided that the contractor provides computers to its employees or otherwise has actual knowledge that employees can access the notice. The addition of this language is in response to several things: the increased use of telecommuting and other work arrangements that do not include a physical office setting; internet-based application processes in which applicants never enter a contractor's physical office; and a number of complaints received by OFCCP in recent years from individuals employed by contractors without a constant physical workplace—such as airline pilots—who assert that they were unaware of their rights under VEVRAA. OFCCP received two comments on this proposal, one from a law firm and one from a contractor, raising two separate issues.

The first issue raised by one of these comments was that "actual knowledge" of an off-site employee being able to access the notice is unduly burdensome. We respectfully disagree. First, to clarify, "actual knowledge" does not mean actual knowledge that the employee accessed the notice, but rather actual knowledge that the notice was posted or disseminated in such a way that would be accessible to the employee. As set forth in the proposed language, for a contractor with employees who do not work at a physical location of the contractor, electronic notices that are posted in a conspicuous location and format on the company's intranet or sent by electronic mail to employees satisfies the posting obligations. In the example of electronic mail, "actual knowledge" could easily be documented merely by maintaining an electronic copy of the email message sent to employees—something that is done (or can be done) automatically by virtually all enterprise-based email systems. Similarly, "actual knowledge" for postings on a company intranet can be verified simply by having an employee in personnel or IT periodically check the link to the electronic posting to ensure that it works and the posting is readable. Performing these types of checks on information posted on a company intranet is a common best practice that takes seconds to complete. In light of the numerous comments and complaints OFCCP has received from protected veteran employees of Federal contractors—particularly those without a traditional physical workplace—that they were unaware of their rights or their contractor's affirmative action obligations, we believe the importance of ensuring that employees have access to statements of their rights and the contractor's obligations far outweighs the slight burden that compliance creates.

The second issue raised in the comments pertained to the requirement that, for contractors using electronic or internet-based application processes, an electronic notice of employee rights and contractor obligations must be "conspicuously stored with, or as part of, the electronic application." One commenter opined that storing the electronic notice with the application would increase the size of applicant files. The potentially small increase in the size of the electronic file does not outweigh the benefit of providing employees notice of their employment rights and protections.

Accordingly, for the reasons stated above, OFCCP has adopted the proposed changes to paragraph 10 of the EO Clause into paragraph 9 of the final rule. We have also added a clarification stating that a contractor is able to satisfy its posting obligation by electronic means for employees who do not work at a physical location of the contractor, provided that the contractor provides computers "or access to computers" that can access the electronically posted notices. This clarifies that electronic posting is appropriate not only for employees who telework, but also for those who share work space—and contractor-provided computers—at a remote work center.

• *EO Clause Paragraph 11 (NPRM)/ Paragraph 10 (Final Rule)—Providing Notice to Labor Organizations*

The NPRM proposed additional language that a contractor, in addition to its existing obligation to notify labor organizations with which it has collective bargaining agreements about its affirmative action efforts, must also notify the labor organizations about its non-discrimination obligations as well. There were no comments specific to this minor change, and thus the language in paragraph 11 of the NPRM is adopted as paragraph 10 of the final rule as proposed.

• *EO Clause Paragraph 13 (NPRM)/ Paragraph 12 (Final Rule)—Contractor Solicitations and Advertisements*

The proposed regulation added a new paragraph 13 to the EO clause which would require the contractor to state and thereby affirm in solicitations and advertisements that it is an equal employment opportunity employer of veterans protected by VEVRAA, much like it is already required to do under the Executive Order 11246 regulations.

OFCCP received one comment from a contractor group, objecting to this proposal on the grounds that advertisements would cost more due to their increased word length. However, as stated in the NPRM, contractors are already required under Executive Order 11246 to state in advertisements and solicitations that "all qualified applicants will receive consideration for employment without regard to race, color, religion, sex, or national origin." *See* 41 CFR 60–1.4(a)(2). The requirement set forth in paragraph 13 of the NPRM would require adding "protected veteran status," or an abbreviation thereof, to the language that contractors are already required to use in advertisements. This is a very minor change involving nominal time and expense to contractors that will affirm to the public a fact that many do not know—that protected veterans are entitled to non-discrimination and affirmative action in the workplace of Federal contractors. Accordingly, the language in paragraph 13 of the NPRM is adopted as paragraph 12 of the final rule as proposed.

• *Inclusion of EO Clause in Federal Contracts (proposed §§ 60–300.5(d) and (e))*

Finally, the NPRM proposed requiring that the entire equal opportunity clause be included verbatim in Federal contracts. This proposed change was to ensure that the contractor, and particularly any subcontractor, who often relies on the prime contractor to inform it of nondiscrimination and affirmative action obligations, reads and understands the language in this clause. OFCCP received four comments—from two law firms, a contractor, and a contractor group—all of whom opposed this proposed new requirement. These commenters asserted that the requirement to incorporate the EO Clause into Federal contracts was too burdensome, as the length of a contract would increase greatly in size to perhaps double or triple its original length. The commenters further opined that the increase in the length would cause contracts to be rewritten, and that the increase in paper that would accompany such a requirement was not environmentally friendly. Finally, the commenters asserted that cutting and pasting the text of the clause into the text of contracts was not a simple task, and would require time to reformat and otherwise edit the contract prior to signing it.

In light of the comments and upon further consideration of the issue, OFCCP withdraws and revises the proposal to incorporate the entire EO Clause into Federal contracts. In addition to the burden concerns set forth by commenters, there is concern that the length of the EO Clause will dissuade, rather than promote, contractors and subcontractors from reading and taking note of the non-discrimination and affirmative action obligations toward protected veterans. This is contrary to the intent behind the proposal in the NPRM.

However, the requirement in the existing regulations does little to notify contractors and subcontractors of the nature of their obligations to employ and advance in employment protected veterans, which was a primary objective of the NPRM proposal. Accordingly, in order to draw greater attention to the contractors' obligations under VEVRAA without the burden of including the entire VEVRAA EO clause, the final rule revises paragraph (d) of this section to require the following text, set in bold text, in each contract, following the reference to VEVRAA required by the FAR:

"This contractor and subcontractor shall abide by the requirements of 41 CFR 60–300.5(a). This regulation prohibits discrimination against qualified protected veterans, and requires affirmative action by covered prime contractors and subcontractors to employ and advance in employment qualified protected veterans."

This requirement would apply to all contracts entered into after the effective date of the rule.

Lastly, the final rule does not incorporate the proposed change to paragraph (e), and instead reverts to the existing language in that subsection. The NPRM proposed eliminating the last clause of the paragraph ("whether or not it is physically incorporated in such contract and whether or not there is a written contract between the agency and the contractor") to align with the proposed paragraph (d), which required incorporation of the entire EO Clause into Federal contracts. Because paragraph (d) of the final rule does not include this requirement, the final rule revises paragraph (e) accordingly back to its existing form.

Subpart B—Discrimination Prohibited

Section 60–300.21 Prohibitions

The proposed rule included clarifying language to paragraph (f)(3) of this section, qualifying that an individual who rejects a reasonable accommodation made by the contractor may still be considered a qualified disabled veteran if the individual subsequently provides or pays for a reasonable accommodation. One law firm commenter stated that the proposal to allow individuals to provide their own accommodations could lead to legal, safety, and equal treatment issues.

OFCCP opts to retain the proposed language in the final rule. First, this proposal is not "wholly inconsistent" with the ADA like the commenter suggested. Rather, it is entirely consistent with longstanding EEOC ADA reasonable accommodation policies. *See, e.g.*, EEOC's "Enforcement Guidance on Reasonable Accommodation and Undue Hardship Under the Americans with Disabilities Act," October 17, 2002 ("to the extent that a portion of the cost of an accommodation causes undue hardship, the employer should ask the individual with a disability if s/he will pay the difference.") We likewise do not believe that safety concerns warrant a change in the regulation, as the provisions on "direct threat" in this regulation and any contractors' general workplace safety policies will guard against these concerns. Nor would a contractor have to permit a disabled veteran to provide an accommodation if the contractor can show that that accommodation would significantly disrupt the workplace or otherwise impose an undue hardship on its operations.

Finally, as set forth in the discussion of the new "pre-JVA veteran" definition in § 300.2, the final rule adds "or pre-JVA veteran" after each instance of "protected veteran" in this section, and adds "or pre-JVA special disabled veteran" after each instance of "disabled veteran" in this section. This incorporates the categories of veterans protected by the now rescinded part 60–250 into this part, ensuring that pre-JVA veterans, if any still exist, are protected by the anti-discrimination provisions of this section.

Subpart C—Affirmative Action Program

Section 60–300.40 Applicability of the affirmative action program requirement

The NPRM proposed one small change to paragraph (c) of this section, specifying that a contractor's affirmative action program shall be reviewed and updated annually "by the official designated by the contractor pursuant to § 60–300.44(i)." We received no comments on this section. Accordingly, § 60–300.40 is adopted in the final rule as proposed.

Section 60–300.41 Availability of affirmative action program

The proposed regulation added a sentence requiring that, in instances where the contractor has employees who do not work at the contractor's physical establishment, the contractor shall inform these employees about the availability of the affirmative action program by means other than a posting at its establishment, in light of the increased use of telecommuting and other flexible workplace arrangements. This proposal in many respects mirrored the electronic notice requirements set forth in paragraph 10 of the EO Clause at § 60–300.5 of the rule. OFCCP received 6 comments from an individual, two law firms, two contractors and a contractor association regarding the proposed revisions to this section, discussed in turn below.

The comments from the two law firms assert that the proposed changes regarding data collection and analysis in §§ 60–300.44(f) and 60–300.44(k) change the character of the VEVRAA AAP by including potentially confidential information and should warrant excluding "data metrics" contained in the AAP when the AAP is accessible by applicants and employees. One of these comments indicated that even if data is aggregated, it may still identify an employee as a veteran violating confidentiality, *e.g.*, one hire occurs for which the position is named and the individual is identified as a disabled veteran. Another comment similarly recommended that a "soft" copy of the AAP be made available to those requesting a copy. Finally, one comment noted that the AAP should simply be made available at the convenience of the requesting applicant and/or employee, which is essentially the function of the existing rule.

In response to these comments, and as part of the effort to focus the final rule on those elements that are of critical importance to OFCCP and reduce burden on contractors where possible, the final rule does not incorporate the proposals in the NPRM regarding informing off-site individuals about the availability of the contractor's affirmative action program. Rather, the final rule retains the language in the existing § 60–300.41 in that regard. Therefore, contractors must still make available their affirmative action programs to employees and applicants for inspection upon request. We further clarify, in light of the modern workplace in which more and more workplaces house information electronically, that contractors may respond to requests by making their AAPs available electronically, so long as the requester is able to access the electronic version of the information. In response to the law firm commenters' concerns about confidentiality and the AAP's "data metrics," OFCCP revises the language for the final rule to state that "[t]he full affirmative action program, *absent the data metrics required by § 60–300.44(k)*, shall be made available to any employee or applicant . . ." (revisions emphasized). This balances the interest in confidentiality of the contractor and its employees with the need for transparency regarding the contractor's affirmative action efforts.

Section 60–300.42 Invitation to self-identify

The NPRM included three significant revisions to this section: (1) Requiring the contractor to invite all applicants to self-identify as a "protected veteran" prior to the offer of employment without disclosing the particular category of veteran; (2) in addition to the new pre-offer inquiry, requiring a post-offer self-identification process to collect more refined data regarding the specific category or categories of protected veteran to which an applicant belongs; and (3) requiring, rather than suggesting, that the contractor seek the advice of the applicant regarding accommodation. OFCCP received 28 comments on this section, 9 of which were in support of the self-identification proposals in the NPRM. For those that opposed portions of the NPRM, most comments centered on the issues of burden, the possibility of inaccurate self-reporting, alleged conflict between the pre-offer inquiry and requirement to seek accommodation advice with State and Federal laws (most notably the ADA and the ADAAA), and interplay between the pre-offer data collection requirement and the Internet Applicant Rule set forth in the regulations for Executive Order 11246. The proposals and the comments to these proposals, and the revisions made to the final rule are discussed in turn below (with the exception of some specific comments on burden, which are addressed in the Regulatory Procedures section of the final rule).

• *Paragraph (a): Pre-offer invitation to self-identify*

As discussed in the NPRM, the primary reason for proposing a pre-offer invitation to self-identify was to allow the contractor, and subsequently OFCCP, to collect valuable, targeted data on the number of protected veterans who apply for Federal contractor positions. The data would enable the contractor and OFCCP to measure the effectiveness of the contractor's recruitment and affirmative action efforts over time, and thereby identify and promote successful recruitment and affirmative efforts taken by the contractor community.

At the outset, several commenters addressed the issue of whether a pre-offer invitation to self-identify as a protected veteran was legally permissible under the Americans with Disabilities Act regulations, which limit the extent to which employers may inquire about disabilities prior to an offer of employment. The vast majority of commenters addressing the issue—including disability rights groups, veterans groups, and two commenters representing the contractor community—stated that the proposed pre-offer inquiry was legally permissible. Two commenters representing contractors on EEO matters disagreed. One stated that its clients avoid pre-offer inquiries specifically to avoid "running afoul" of the ADA. The other stated that "[w]hile the ADA provides that an applicant can ask for a reasonable accommodation during the hiring process, employers cannot otherwise ask any questions about an individual's disability."

OFCCP believes the concerns of these two commenters are based on an incorrect reading of the ADA and its regulations. As we discussed in the NPRM, the ADA and section 503 regulations specifically permit the contractor to conduct a pre-offer inquiry into disability status if it is "made pursuant to a Federal, state or local law requiring affirmative action for individuals with disabilities," such as VEVRAA. *See* 29 CFR 1630.13, 1630.14; 41 CFR 60–741.42. Further, as discussed in the NPRM, even though a pre-offer inquiry into disability status is legally permissible, the proposed pre-offer inquiry does not ask about disability status specifically; rather, it only asks that the applicant identify whether he or she is a protected veteran generally. Regardless, the "affirmative action" exception carved into the ADA clearly allows the type of pre-offer self-identification proposed in the NPRM, and thus there is no legal reason to modify it.[19]

Among those commenters agreeing that the proposed pre-offer inquiry was legally permissible, however, two commenters—a disability rights association and a contractor—stated that the inclusion of paragraphs (a)(1) and (a)(2), which describe the conditions under which pre-offer invitations of disabled veterans are legally allowed, is confusing when they are stated "additionally" to the required pre-offer invitation in paragraph (a). One of these commenters stated it was unclear whether the inclusion of these paragraphs "intended to require pre-offer invitation for all protected veterans or only for non-disabled protected veterans." Given that the new regulation requires all contractors to conduct a pre-offer inquiry that is lawful under the ADA, this guidance is now largely superfluous. Accordingly, as suggested by these commenters, this language (*i.e.*, the third sentence of paragraph (a), and subparagraphs (1) and (2)) are not included in the final rule.

The majority of those commenting upon the scope of the proposed pre-offer inquiry—requesting "protected veteran" status in the aggregate, as opposed to inviting individuals to identify as one or more of the categories of protected veteran—approved of it, but one HR consulting firm commenter stated that the pre-offer inquiry should ask individuals to denote the specific categories of veteran under which they fall, and that contractors could then aggregate the data for purposes of evaluating their outreach efforts and setting benchmarks. OFCCP declines to require contractors to collect data by protected veteran category at the pre-offer stage. We believe maintaining such refined data at this stage would be more burdensome on contractors than simply capturing whether interested job seekers are protected veterans or not, particularly given that the overall population of protected veterans is relatively small and that further division of the pool would tend to reduce the contractor's ability to engage in any meaningful data analysis. Further, as discussed in the NPRM, the contractor's obligations would be the same with respect to each category of protected veteran at the pre-offer stage, thus there is limited benefit at that stage to knowing the specific categories of protected veteran to which each individual belongs.

The majority of those commenters opposed to the proposed pre-offer inquiry expressed concerns about the accuracy of veteran self-identification data. First, several commenters from the contractor community asserted that not all protected veterans will self-identify—either due to privacy concerns, fear of reprisal, or a failure to understand that they fall within one of the four listed categories of protected veterans—which will result in an underreporting of actual protected veteran applicants. Second, the commenters asserted that some veterans that are not protected by VEVRAA may nevertheless choose to self-identify as a protected veteran due to a misunderstanding of the four categories of protected veterans, which could lead to an inaccurate over-reporting of protected veterans. While some commenters urged OFCCP to eliminate the pre-offer inquiry entirely on these grounds, others propounded suggestions for how to increase the accuracy of self-reporting. One commenter suggested that the invitation include language that the applicant must *know* he or she is a protected veteran in order to self-identify as such (rather than the model language in Appendix B, which asks applicants to self-identify if they believe they are a veteran who may be protected), in order to "minimize the possibility of self-identification error." Several other commenters requested that OFCCP provide contractors (and, in turn, applicants) with more detailed descriptions of the protected veteran categories, including, for instance, the specific campaign badges or Armed Forces service medals that qualify a veteran as an "active duty wartime or campaign badge veteran" or "Armed Forces service medal veteran," respectively.

At the outset, while OFCCP concedes the possibility that self-reporting data on veterans will not be entirely accurate, OFCCP disagrees that this is sufficient reason to eliminate the pre-offer inquiry. Contractors already collect and report data on the number of protected veteran employees and new hires on an annual basis pursuant to the VETS–100A form. While this data is subject to the same accuracy concerns, it provides the Department with a useful measure for identifying and tracking the number of protected veteran new hires and employees among the Federal contractor workforce. Similarly, while self-reported applicant data will never be perfect, it is nonetheless a useful

[19] To assuage any remaining doubt on this matter, OFCCP obtained a letter from EEOC's Office of Legal Counsel in advance of the publication of this rule affirming that a requirement to invite pre-offer self-identification of disability is permissible under the ADA and its regulations. This letter will be posted on OFCCP's Web site.

mechanism for collecting important information that currently goes completely unrecorded—the number of protected veterans who are able to connect to Federal contractors and submit an expression of interest in employment. With regard to more detailed descriptions of the protected veteran categories, we note that the campaign badges and service medals are created and administered by the Department of Defense and the individual services of the Armed Forces, and thus those with questions would be best served consulting with DOD or the issuing military service if they have questions about whether a particular badge or medal is a campaign badge or service medal that provides coverage under VEVRAA.

Another concern raised by several commenters is that the requirement to collect and maintain self-identification data from applicants does not comport with the Internet Applicant Rule found in the regulations to Executive Order 11246. *See* 41 CFR 60–1.3, 1.12. These commenters recommended that OFCCP add a definition of "applicant" and "Internet applicant" to this final rule and ensure that wherever in the regulations the term "applicant" is used, the term "Internet applicant" applies as well. OFCCP did not propose to add a definition of "applicant" or "Internet applicant" in its NPRM. Therefore, the final rule does not do so. However, the discussion that follows provides guidance about how contractors may invite Internet applicants to self-identify as a protected veteran under VEVRAA in a manner consistent with demographic collection requirements under the Executive Order Internet Applicant Rule. Under this final rule, contractors will be able to invite applicants to self-identify as a protected veteran at the same time the contractor solicits demographic data on applicants under the Executive Order 112146 Internet Applicant Rule. For Internet applicants this generally will be after the contractor has determined the individual has been screened for basic qualifications and meets other requirements for being an Internet applicant. Therefore, this final rule does not require contractors to change their existing systems for screening Internet applicants so long as those systems comply with existing law.

By way of background, OFCCP's longstanding definition of "applicant" is contained in agency subregulatory guidance. See the Uniform Guidelines on Employee Selection Procedures (UGESP), Question and Answer 15, 44 FR 11996 (March 2, 1979).[20] According to that guidance, in general, an applicant is a person who has indicated an interest in being considered for hiring, promotion, or other employment opportunities, either in writing (by completing an application form or submitting a resume) or orally, depending upon the contractors' practice. The Internet Applicant Rule came into effect in February 2006, and pertains to recordkeeping by contractors on Internet-based hiring processes and the solicitation of race, gender, and ethnicity data, in conjunction with their recordkeeping obligations under the Executive Order implementing regulation at § 60–1.12. Under § 60–1.12, contractors' recordkeeping obligations include maintaining expressions of interest through the Internet that the contractor considered for a particular position, as well as applications and resumes. Contractors also are required to maintain, where possible, data about the race, sex, and ethnicity of applicants and Internet applicants, as appropriate. The term Internet applicant is defined in § 60–1.3 and generally means an individual who: (1) Submitted an expression of interest in employment through the Internet; (2) is considered by the contractor for employment in a particular position; (3) possessed the basic qualifications for the position; and (4) did not remove himself or herself from consideration.

OFCCP has taken into account contractors' concerns about inviting self-identification for applications submitted electronically, particularly for those contractors who create resume data bases which they mine for applicants when they have a job opening. In recognition of these concerns, and consistent with EO 13563's focus on simplifying and harmonizing requirements, OFCCP will permit contractors to invite applicants to self-identify as a protected veteran at the same time as the contractor collects the demographic data for applicants required under EO 11246. The Internet Applicant Rule under EO 11246 generally allows contractors to do a "first cut" and screen out individuals whom they believe do not meet the basic qualifications of the position—without capturing or retaining any demographic documentation on these individuals. There is the concern, however, that in doing this "first cut" contractors may be engaging in discrimination (e.g., if they are incorrectly applying their basic qualifications, or the basic qualifications have an adverse impact on a protected group and are not job related and consistent with business necessity), and by not keeping the demographic information on the individuals they screened out they are eliminating evidence to prove that discrimination may be occurring. This concern is even greater with regard to disabled veterans because these Executive Order "first cuts" are not designed to take into account the possibility that someone with a disability might be able to meet the qualification standard or perform the essential functions of the job with the provision of a reasonable accommodation.

Under existing law, it is unlawful under VEVRAA to use qualification standards, including at the "basic qualifications" screen stage, that screen out or tend to screen out a disabled veteran or class of disabled veterans unless the standard is shown to be job-related for the position in question and consistent with business necessity. Selection criteria that concern an essential function may not be used to exclude a disabled veteran if that individual could satisfy the criteria with a reasonable accommodation. See § 60–300.21(g). These requirements, therefore, apply when contractors design and implement their "basic qualifications" screens. In addition, after the initial screening for "basic qualifications," contractors must also ensure that they are complying with their duty to evaluate all applicants for jobs based on the applicant's ability to perform the essential functions of the job with or without reasonable accommodation.

OFCCP will treat the recordkeeping provisions of VEVRAA at 60–300.80 in the same manner as the recordkeeping requirements under EO 11246 at 41 CFR 60–1.12 as applied to Internet applicants. These recordkeeping requirements are not new and will impose no additional burden on contractors. The record retention requirements exist independently of whether and when individuals are invited to self identify under VEVRAA.

The VEVRAA recordkeeping provisions require contractors to retain personnel or employment records made or kept by the contractor for one or two years depending on the size of the contractor and contract. These records

[20] Question and Answer 15 reads: "Q. What is meant by the terms "applicant" and "candidate" as they are used in the Uniform Guidelines? A: The precise definition of the term "applicant" depends upon the user's recruitment and selection procedures. The concept of an applicant is that of a person who has indicated an interest in being considered for hiring, promotion, or other employment opportunities. This interest might be expressed by completing an application form, or might be expressed orally, depending upon the employer's practice."

include the records contractors are required to maintain under 41 CFR 60–1.12. Section 60–1.12 requires contractors to maintain all expressions of interest through the Internet or related technologies considered by the contractor for a particular position, such as on-line resumes or internal resume databases, and records identifying job seekers contacted regarding their interest in a particular position. For purposes of recordkeeping with respect to internal resume databases, the contractor also must maintain a record of each resume added to the database, a record of the date each resume was added to the database, the position for which each search of the database was made, and corresponding to each search, the substantive search criteria used and the date of the search. For purposes of recordkeeping with respect to external databases the contractor must maintain a record of the position for which each search of the database was made, and corresponding to each search, the substantive criteria used, the date of the search, and the resumes of job seekers who met the basic qualifications for the particular position who are considered by the contractor. As with records retained under the EO 11246, these records are to be maintained regardless of whether the job seeker is an Internet applicant.

If a contractor has a practice of welcoming unsolicited resumes regardless of current job openings, OFCCP will permit the contractor to invite self-identification only of those considered for employment, consistent with requirements under EO 11246 and its regulations at 41 CFR 60–1.3 and 60–1.12. The obligation to invite self-identification is triggered by considering the job seeker for employment, not by including the resume in the resume database. For example, if a contractor has an internal resume database with 1,000 resumes and is looking for applicants to fill a job as an engineer in Omaha, the contractor could limit the pool of resumes under review by applying a "basic qualifications" screen that identifies those who have a masters degree in electrical engineering, at least three years of experience as an electrical engineer, and further limit the review to resumes submitted within the last three months. If that search produced a pool of 30 job seekers, the contractor might narrow the pool further by asking the 30 job seekers if they are interested in being considered for the job. If 10 job seekers indicate interest in being considered, they would be applicants and the contractor would invite the 10 job seekers to self-identify. In contrast, if a contractor has a practice of not accepting unsolicited resumes, job seekers who submit an unsolicited resume are not applicants. Accordingly, the contractor would have no obligation to invite them to self-identify as a protected veteran.

It is also possible that potential and qualified job applicants with disabilities may not apply for jobs posted on contractors' online application systems because, for example, they are not aware that selection criteria concerning essential functions may not be used to exclude them if they can satisfy the criteria with a reasonable accommodation. Contractors seeking to fill jobs should seek to attract the best possible pool of applicants; this includes applicants who are disabled veterans who could perform the job with or without reasonable accommodations. OFCCP notes that a best practice for ensuring a diverse, qualified pool of applicants for contractors using online application systems is posting a notice on their human resources Web page or online application portal that notifies job applicants who may need a reasonable accommodation to perform the functions of a job that they are entitled to one under the ADAAA. This best practice encourages qualified individuals with disabilities to pursue job vacancies, and provides contractors with access to a wide range of skills and talents.

In providing this guidance as to application of the self-identification requirement under VEVRAA, contractors should be able to operate as they have been using their existing systems and processes because this final rule does not change how contractors handle Internet applicants. This should allow contractors to avoid creating separate data collection and storage systems as many contractors feared. For those contractors that need further help determining which individuals must be given a pre-offer self-identification inquiry, OFCCP is available to provide technical guidance.

One commenter expressed concern regarding possible liability in connection with storing large amounts of sensitive data, such as that disclosed in an applicant's pre-offer self-identification form. However, the current regulations have long required contractors to maintain sensitive self-identification data that comes from post-offer inquiries, thus contractors should already have a mechanism in place for the proper storage of this information. While the additional pre-offer data increases the amount of data that contractors will need to maintain, this is largely a scope or resources question, not an information security issue. We have addressed the expected cost and burden of the pre-offer requirement in the revised Regulatory Procedures section of the final rule.

Finally, several commenters asserted that the new pre-offer inquiry would require significant lead time for contractors to change their current human resources information and applicant tracking systems so as to capture the pre-offer self-identification data. A revised burden analysis for these endeavors is included in the Regulatory Procedures section of the final rule. With regard to the amount of lead time necessary to incorporate the changes in this paragraph, one law firm commenter suggested that contractors be given "a substantial grace period, which we propose to be at least one to two years," so that contractors and their systems providers can get up to speed. Another law firm commenter was less specific with the time needed, but said that "90 days would not be enough time for some companies that do not have the internal resources to do it themselves." OFCCP has consulted with information systems analysts regarding an appropriate amount of preparation time, and on the basis of those discussions believes an effective date of 180 days after publication of the final rule is sufficient for contractors to incorporate Appendix B, or a substantially similar form, into their systems. Moreover, as noted in the Introduction to this preamble, contractors are permitted to update their affirmative action programs to come into compliance with the new requirements during their standard 12-month AAP review and updating cycle. If a contractor has prepared an AAP under the old regulations it may maintain that AAP for the duration of the AAP year even if that AAP year overlaps with the effective date of this final rule.

• *Paragraph (b): Post-offer invitation to self-identify*

The NPRM created a new paragraph (b) to describe the contractor's duty to invite applicants to submit post-offer self-identification regarding the specific category of protected veteran to which the applicant belongs, and retain this information. As we explained in the NPRM, this self-identification requirement will enable the contractor to capture refined data pertaining to each category of protected veteran to foster the contractor's compliance with the requirement to report such data set forth in the Veterans' Employment and Training Service (VETS) regulations at 41 CFR part 61–300. Although OFCCP received no comments specific to new paragraph (b), the paragraph is revised in the final rule to make this intent explicit. Accordingly, paragraph (b) is revised to state that, post-offer, "the contractor shall invite applicants to inform the contractor" if they belong to one or more of the categories of protected veteran "for which the contractor is required to report pursuant to 41 CFR part 61–300." This clarifies that the contractor's paragraph (b) obligation to ask applicants to identify their specific protected veteran classification(s) is contingent upon their having an obligation to report that information on the VETS–100A, or other future form, pursuant to 41 CFR part 61–300.

• *Paragraph (c): Content of invitations*

The NPRM revised paragraph (c) of this section by deleting the second sentence of the parenthetical at the end of the paragraph. This sentence described the format of and rationale behind the current Appendix B, which has been substantially amended in light of the new self-identification procedures proposed herein. We received no comments on this paragraph. Accordingly, the language in the NPRM is adopted as proposed. In addition, we revised the first sentence of paragraph (c) to say that invitations to self-identify "shall state that the contractor is a Federal contractor required to take affirmative action to employ and advance in employment protected veterans pursuant to the Act." This language replaces the statement in the existing regulation that "a request to benefit under the affirmative action program may be made immediately and/or at any time in the future." OFCCP believes that this statement could be misinterpreted to suggest that affirmative action must be "requested" by a protected veteran, thus confusing protected veterans and contractors alike.

• *Paragraph (d): Requirement that contractor seek applicant's advice regarding accommodation*

There were three proposed changes to paragraph (d). First, we revised the language to reflect the newly proposed self-identification process in which applicants will only identify themselves as disabled veterans at the post-offer self-identification stage. Second, we replaced the term "appropriate accommodation" in paragraph (d) with "reasonable accommodation," which is the more broadly used and accepted legal term. OFCCP received no comments on these two changes, and thus the language in the NPRM is adopted as proposed.

As for the third proposed change to paragraph (d), the NPRM required, rather than suggested, that the contractor seek the advice of the applicant regarding accommodation. As we explained in the NPRM, the idea was that this requirement would help to initiate a robust interactive and collaborative process between the contractor and the employee or applicant to identify effective accommodations that will facilitate a disabled veteran's ability to perform the job. OFCCP received 10 comments from various organizations on this change, all of which opposed the proposal.

Several of these commenters argued that the proposed change is inconsistent with (and, according to some commenters, in violation of) the ADA, which states that an employer may ask all individuals if they require a reasonable accommodation, not just individuals that self-identify as disabled. Specifically, several commenters cited ADA enforcement guidance from the EEOC stating that if an employer asks post-offer disability-related questions to entering employees, it must ask the same question to all entering employees in the same job group, and not a single classification of employees (such as "disabled veterans"). However, as set forth in the discussion of paragraph (a) of this section, both herein and in the NPRM, the EEOC's interpretive guidance for its ADA regulations permits inquiries into disability status if made pursuant to another Federal law or regulation. It states that "[t]he ADA does not preempt any Federal law, or any State or local law, that grants to individuals with disabilities protection greater than or equivalent to that provided by the ADA. This means that the existence of a lesser standard of protection to individuals with disabilities under the ADA will not provide a defense to failing to meet a higher standard under another law." *See* Appendix to 29 CFR part 1630. Accordingly, the proposed affirmative action obligation, in requiring contractors to inquire with disabled veterans offered employment to determine if they need a reasonable accommodation, is not inconsistent with the ADA.

However, other commenters, including a human resources association, asserted that disabled veterans should not be treated differently than disabled non-veterans with regard to reasonable accommodations, and that creating unique processes for veterans could serve to stigmatize veterans rather than help them. One commenter argued that the proposed change implies that contractors should assume that just because an individual self-identifies as a disabled veteran, they are in need of an accommodation, which may have negative and unintended consequences. Several other comments suggested that the proposed change does not take into account the administrative burden associated with ascertaining whether an individual is legally entitled to an accommodation and to research alternative sources of funding for requested accommodations when the accommodation is financially burdensome. Since the contractor is to be proactive in determining whether an individual needs an accommodation, the contractor would potentially have to conduct this research for each person that self-identifies as having a disability.

The final rule does not incorporate the proposed requirement, and instead retains the existing rule's suggestion that contractors ask disabled veteran applicants whether an accommodation is necessary. The final rule also states that the contractor should engage in an interactive process with the applicant to help identify a reasonable accommodation, which is consistent with ADA guidance. Eliminating the proposed requirement alleviates the administrative burden concerns raised by some commenters, thus reducing the burden associated with the rule, while highlighting the importance of the reasonable accommodation obligation.

Finally, the final rule makes a technical, non-substantive change by eliminating the parenthetical at the end of the second sentence which provides an example of a post-offer inquiry. OFCCP finds that this language is unnecessary and potentially confusing.

Section 60–300.43 Affirmative action policy

The NPRM proposed replacing the phrase "because of status as a" in this section to "against," in order to clarify that the nondiscrimination requirements of VEVRAA are limited to protected veterans and that reverse discrimination claims may not be brought by individuals who do not fall under one of the protected veteran categories. We received no comments on this section. Accordingly, § 60–300.43 is adopted in the final rule as proposed.

Section 60–300.44 Required contents of affirmative action programs

The proposed rule contained significant revisions to several of the paragraphs under this section. These proposals, the comments to these proposals, and the revisions made to the final rule are discussed in turn below.

• *Paragraph (a): Affirmative action policy statement*

Section 60–300.44(a) requires contractors to state their equal employment opportunity policy in the company's AAP. The NPRM proposed revising the section to clarify the contractor's duty to provide notice of employee rights and contractor obligations in a manner that is accessible and understandable to persons with disabilities. The NPRM also proposed revising paragraph (a) to require the contractor's chief executive officer to clearly articulate their support for the company's AAP in the policy statement. OFCCP received three comments on the proposed revisions from an individual, a law firm and a human resources consulting group.

There were a variety of comments on this section. One individual suggested that the policy statement include 'retain' in the following sentence "* * * the contractor will: Recruit, hire, train and promote persons in all job titles * * *" Another commenter, a law firm, recommended revising the language so that it is inclusive of contractors that have foreign parent companies by requiring the top United States based executive to attest to their support for the contractor's AAP. Finally, the human resources consulting group expressed concern that OFCCP seemed to dictate the terms of the policy statement, but did not provide a sample statement as an Appendix.

OFCCP declines to add the term "retain" to this section. The regulation currently states that the contractor's affirmative action policy must state that it will "recruit, hire, train and promote persons in all job titles, *and ensure that all other personnel actions are administered,* without regard to" protected veteran status. Given that the regulation already prohibits veteran status to be a consideration for "all other personnel actions," there is no need to delineate further specific personnel actions in the regulatory text.

OFCCP agrees with the suggestion to revise the language of this section to clarify the level of company leadership that must demonstrate their support for the company's AAP. The purpose of the proposed revision is to ensure that the statement communicates to employees that support for the AAP goes to the very top of the contractor's organization. For contractors with foreign-based parent companies, it is appropriate to require the company leadership that is based in the United States to express that support. Therefore, § 60–300.44(a) of the final rule is revised to state "[t]he policy statement shall indicate the top United States executive's (such as the Chief Executive Officer or the President of the United States Division of a foreign company) support for the contractor's affirmative action program * * *."

OFCCP declines to make any modifications to the portion of § 60–300.44(a) related to the content of the policy statement. OFCCP outlined the required content of the policy statement when the agency issued the final rule implementing VEVRAA in 2007 (72 FR 44408). The NPRM did not propose any revisions to this language. OFCCP declines to append a policy statement to the rule. OFCCP believes that providing a policy statement in the Appendix may discourage contractors from proactively developing a policy statement that reflects the company's culture and values. If contractors need additional guidance on how to develop an equal opportunity policy statement, OFCCP staff is available to provide technical assistance.

• *Paragraph (b): Review of personnel processes*

The proposed rule made two changes to this paragraph. First, it required that the contractor review its personnel processes on at least an annual basis to ensure that its obligations are being met, as opposed to "periodically." Second, the proposed paragraph (b) mandated certain specific steps (carried over from the existing Appendix C) that the contractor must take, at a minimum, in the review of its personnel processes, including: (1) Identifying the vacancies and training programs for which protected veteran applicants and employees were considered; (2) providing a statement of reasons explaining the circumstances for rejecting protected veterans for vacancies and training programs and a description of considered accommodations; and (3) describing the nature and type of accommodations for disabled veterans who were selected for hire, promotion, or training programs.

OFCCP received 13 comments from contractors, contractor associations and law firms regarding these proposals. Eleven of the 13 comments asserted that a significant burden was imposed by the proposed section, much greater than that calculated by OFCCP in the NPRM's Regulatory Procedures section. For instance, regarding compliance with item (1) above, the commenters indicated that for most contractors there are no such tracking systems in place and these will take time, staff, and money to establish. The comments also indicate that promotion and training opportunities, unlike hiring, are not as readily distinguishable for individual candidates. It is noted that these opportunities may be available to all employees, take a number of different forms, and may be noncompetitive. The comments indicate it is "unreasonable" to make this mandatory because it fails to recognize these differences and creates additional administrative and documentary burdens. These commenters further objected that the requirement to create and maintain a statement of reasons for every instance in which a protected veteran was denied a position or training activity was unreasonable and tantamount to requiring a drafted legal defense before any claims were brought, could serve to "drive underground" the real reason for the rejection, and treated protected veterans differently than protected classes under E O 11246 and section 503.

Based on the comments submitted and the questions raised about the efficacy of these requirements toward the end of increasing employment of protected veterans as compared to the burden that it creates, OFCCP does not adopt the proposal as drafted in the NPRM, and the final rule retains the existing language in § 60–300.44(b). However, in so doing, OFCCP reiterates that the existing paragraph (b) contains several requirements—including ensuring that its personnel processes are careful, thorough, and systematic, ensuring that these processes do not stereotype protected veterans, and designing some kind of procedures that facilitate a review of the implementation of these obligations—that still apply to contractors. As they do currently, contractors may coordinate the periodic review of their personnel processes for compliance with both VEVRAA and section 503.

• Paragraph (c): Physical and mental qualifications

The NPRM proposed three substantive revisions to this paragraph. First, it required that all physical and mental job qualification standards must be reviewed and updated, as necessary, on an annual, as opposed to a "periodic," basis. Second, paragraph (c)(1) of the NPRM required the contractor to document its annual review of physical and mental job qualification standards. Third, paragraph (c)(3) of the NPRM required the contractor to contemporaneously document those instances in which it believes that an individual would constitute a "direct threat" as understood under the ADA and as defined in these regulations.

As to the proposal to require annual reviews of physical and mental job qualification standards, OFCCP received 10 comments from contractors, a contractor association, employee and other associations, and law firms. Nine of the 10 comments stated that the requirement to review physical and mental qualifications of all jobs with openings during the AAP period would be burdensome because of the number of job openings, variety of jobs, time, staff and needed changes to HRIS systems. One employment benefit consultant firm commenter characterized the burden as "one of the most burdensome requirements of the proposal." Additionally, one comment noted that the assumption that a description of the job's physical and mental requirements should already be available when a job opening occurs is a false assumption.

Five comments suggested less burdensome approaches. One comment suggested continuing to follow the current regulation and conducting periodic reviews. Three comments suggested reviewing the qualifications only when a change in the job occurs. One of the three comments also noted that an initial review should occur with the start of the covered contract along with reviews when changes occur. One comment suggested doing reviews of only "jobs filled," not all job openings.

We note at the outset that the existing regulation clearly prohibits the contractor from using job qualification standards that are not job related and consistent with business necessity and have the effect of discriminating (or perpetuating discrimination) against protected veterans. *See* 41 CFR 60–300.21(d), 60–300.44(c)(2). This is a primary reason that the affirmative action provisions require reviews of physical and mental job qualification standards. To the extent that contractors are not conducting these reviews at all, they are already in violation of the existing regulations.

With this in mind, and taking into account the commenters' concerns about the burden associated with the proposal, the final rule does not adopt the proposal as drafted in the NPRM. Instead, the final rule retains the language in existing § 60–741.44(c)(1), requiring that contractors adhere to a schedule for the "periodic review of all physical and mental job qualification standards," and providing that contractors have the burden to demonstrate that qualification standards that tend to screen out qualified individuals with disabilities are job related and consistent with business necessity.

With regard to the second proposed change in paragraph (c)(1) requiring that the contractor document its job qualification standard reviews, we received four comments. All of these commenters questioned what evidence will be necessary to demonstrate that a review has been completed. One of these comments noted that the proposed regulation lacks clarity as to how job-relatedness is evidenced and asserted that the ADA practice of examining "essential functions" of a job should be sufficient. OFCCP declines to adopt this proposal into the final rule as well, and retains the existing provision. As for the comment that the "job relatedness" standard lacks clarity and should be replaced with an "essential functions" standard, we note that the "job related and consistent with business necessity" standard has been used in the existing VEVRAA regulations for several years, and is the same standard that is well-understood and applies to the section 503 regulations prohibiting discrimination on the basis of disability. We therefore decline to revise the standard in the final rule.

Finally, with regard to the third proposed change requiring the contractor to contemporaneously document those instances in which it believes that an individual would constitute a "direct threat," one comment raised the concern that the provision differed from the requirement in proposed § 300.44(b)(3) to disclose the "direct threat" determination to the affected applicant or employee. However, because proposed § 60–300.44(b)(3) was not adopted into the final rule, we decline to amend this paragraph to coordinate with it. Rather, we adopt paragraph (c)(3) as proposed in the NPRM.

- Paragraph (f): Outreach and recruitment efforts

Paragraph (f) as it existed prior to the NPRM suggested a number of outreach and recruitment efforts that the contractor could undertake in order to increase the employment opportunities for protected veterans. The NPRM proposed several changes to this paragraph: the proposed paragraph (f)(1) required that the contractor enter into three linkage agreements with veteran-related entities to serve as sources of finding potential veteran applicants; paragraph (f)(2) included a list of additional suggested outreach and recruitment efforts that contractors could take; paragraph (f)(3) proposed a new requirement that the contractor conduct self-assessments of their outreach and recruitment efforts; and paragraph (f)(4) clarified the contractor's recordkeeping obligations with regard to these outreach and recruitment efforts.

Overall, OFCCP received 34 comments on the proposed changes to § 60–300.44(f). While a few commenters praised OFCCP's efforts to strengthen Federal contractors' recruitment and outreach efforts, the majority of the comments expressed concerns about the proposed rule. Commenters raised a variety of issues including concerns about the burden associated with the proposed mandatory requirements, technical questions regarding the drafting of the proposed rule language, and the utility of some of the recommended provisions.

As stated above, paragraph (f)(1) required contractors to enter into three linkage agreements with three different veteran-related entities: specifically, the proposal required linkage agreements with (1) the Local Veterans' Employment Representative (LVER) in the local employment service office nearest the contractor's establishment; (2) one of several organizations listed in the existing regulation, with the addition of the Department of Defense Transition Assistance Program (TAP); and (3) an organization listed on the National Resource Directory (NRD), a Web site provided by the Departments of Labor, Defense, and Veterans Affairs. Commenters voiced several concerns with this proposal. Several commenters expressed concern about the administrative and financial burden related to requiring three linkage agreements. Further, a specific point made by one commenter echoed in general terms by several others was that, if the linkage agreement requirement was to be a "per establishment" requirement rather than a "per contractor" requirement, a Federal contractor with multiple establishments could end up entering into hundreds of linkage agreements. Commenters also questioned the capacity of the organizations that are outlined in the proposed rule, noting that some of the entities listed in the NRD do not exist anymore, the DOD's TAP program does not reach all service members, and that some veterans' service organizations have difficulty generally getting through to staff or returning phone calls. While two commenters stated that entering into linkage agreements with LVERs was an appropriate requirement, several others raised the concern that LVERs, of which there are fewer than 1,000 in the entire country, may not have the capacity to enter into and manage linkage agreements with all Federal contractor establishments.

In light of these comments, and in order to reduce the burden on contractors, the final rule does not incorporate the proposal requiring contractors to enter into linkage agreements. Rather, the final rule retains the existing language of § 60–300.44(f), which requires that the contractor undertake "appropriate outreach and positive recruitment activities," in paragraph (f)(1)(i) of the final rule, and then provides a number of suggested resources in paragraph (f)(2)(i) that contractors should utilize to carry out their general recruitment obligations. Paragraph (f)(2)(i) of the final rule differs from the existing rule only in that it adds two additional resources discussed in the NPRM—the Department of Defense Transition Assistance Program (TAP) and the National Resource Directory—to the list of suggested resources that contractors should consult. This will allow contractors flexibility to choose the resources they feel will be most helpful in identifying and attracting protected veteran job seekers. It will also provide contractors with greater flexibility to switch between and among different resources in order to find those that are the most effective, in light of the self-assessment obligation set forth in paragraph (f)(3) of the final rule. For those commenters who had concerns that the NRD contained resources that were out of date or did not contain additional resources that would be a good source for protected veteran job seekers, we note that the NRD is a dynamically-updated resource, and that contractors may suggest that additional veterans groups and service organizations be added to it through the "Suggest a Resource" link on the NRD's front page. On a related note, however, the reference to the specific URL address for the NRD's employment resources in the text of the regulation has been revised to refer to the NRD's home page. As one commenter noted, the URL listed in the regulation had changed since the publication of the NPRM, and may very well change again in the future, thus listing the URL address for a specific Web page in the regulation text makes little sense.

Lastly with regard to paragraph (f)(1), several commenters argued that OFCCP underestimated the burden hours associated with complying with the proposed paragraph (f)(1)(iii) (paragraph (f)(1)(ii) in the final rule), which requires the contractor to send written notification of company policy related to its affirmative action efforts to all subcontractors, including subcontracting vendors and suppliers. OFCCP retains this requirement as proposed, as we believe it is crucial to effective implementation and enforcement of the regulations that subcontractors are aware of VEVRAA's affirmative action obligations. Compliance with this requirement could be met by providing subcontractors with the affirmative action policy statement it is already required to post on company bulletin boards pursuant to § 60–300.44(a), either electronically or in paper form. A discussion responding to commenters' concerns regarding the burden of compliance with this requirement is found in the Regulatory Procedures section of this final rule.

OFCCP received relatively few comments regarding the proposed paragraph (f)(2) (paragraph (f)(2)(ii) in the final rule), which set forth additional suggested outreach efforts that contractors could engage in to increase its recruitment efforts. These comments centered on the proposed paragraph (f)(2)(vi) (which is paragraph (f)(2)(ii)(F) in the final rule), which states that "the contractor, in making hiring decisions, *shall* consider applicants who are known protected veterans for all available positions for which they may be qualified when the position(s) applied for is unavailable" (emphasis added). The commenters indicated that the word "shall" suggested that contents of that paragraph were mandatory. The use of "shall" in this paragraph was an inadvertent error in the NPRM. OFCCP intended the paragraph to state that contractors "should consider applicants * * *" and the final rule amends the NPRM in that regard. We also note that this suggested activity is intended to be a limited one. Contractors who choose to consider protected veterans for jobs other than those for which they applied may exercise discretion to limit this consideration based on geography, the qualifications of the applicant, and other factors. Contractors may also exercise discretion with respect to the time period by which they will consider applicants for other positions. This provision is intended to be flexible and is not required of contractors.

The final rule adds an additional resource to paragraph (f)(2)(ii) that contractors are suggested to use, and that is the Veterans Job Bank. The Veterans Job Bank, created by the Obama Administration and launched in November 2011 as part of the National Resource Directory Web site, is an easy-to-use tool aimed at helping veterans find job postings from companies looking to hire them. Through the Veterans Job Bank, veterans are able to search hundreds of thousands of jobs (500,000 at the time the Veterans Job Bank was launched) by location, keyword, and military occupation code (MOC). Further, the Web site provides detailed instructions for employers wishing to post their job openings with the Veterans Job Bank, so that the resource can continue to grow and become an even more effective resource for veterans seeking new job opportunities and employers seeking qualified workers.

Paragraph (f)(3) of the NPRM required the contractor, on an annual basis, to review the outreach and recruitment efforts it has undertaken over the previous twelve months and evaluate their effectiveness in identifying and recruiting qualified protected veterans, and document its review. Several commenters expressed concern about the utility of the suggested metrics for analyzing external outreach and recruitment efforts. One commenter stated that if the only standard used for assessing outreach and recruitment is the number of veterans hired, the proposed rule would effectively become a quota system for hiring protected veterans. Another commenter questioned whether overall hiring statistics would provide much useful information about the effectiveness of specific outreach efforts. Commenters also had concerns about the requirement to analyze hiring data for the current year as well as the previous two years. One commenter stated that "[e]very other analytical requirement under the affirmative action regulations, including Executive Order 11246, focuses on reviewing the past one-year recordkeeping period." Commenters argued that the most recent year is the most relevant year in measuring effectiveness of affirmative action efforts. Finally, commenters also questioned OFCCP's calculation of the cost of compliance with this provision.

OFCCP declines to make changes to the proposed paragraph (f)(3) in response to these comments. With regard to the comment suggesting that the number of veterans hired was the "only" standard for analyzing the effectiveness of outreach efforts, OFCCP respectfully disagrees. The proposed rule makes clear that the number of veterans hired should be a primary factor considered, given VEVRAA's stated purpose to "employ and advance in employment" protected veterans, but is far from the only metric used for analyzing external outreach and recruitment efforts. Rather, the proposed rule required that the contractor consider all the metrics required by § 60–300.44(k) (which includes applicant and hiring data), but also clearly allows the contractor to consider any other criteria, including "a number of factors that are unique to a particular contractor establishment," in determining the effectiveness of its outreach, so long as these criteria—whatever they are—are reasonable and documented so that OFCCP compliance officers can understand what they are. The purpose of the self-assessment is simply to ensure that the contractor thinks critically about how to evaluate and improve upon its recruitment and outreach efforts in order to maximize its connections to protected veterans seeking jobs. OFCCP strongly believes this is a worthy goal—indeed, a goal central to the very heart of VEVRAA's affirmative action obligations—and that the proposal provides the contractor a significant amount of flexibility to meet that goal.

With regard to the timeframe of applicant and hire data that a contractor must consider when evaluating its outreach efforts—the current year and two previous years—OFCCP understands that this is a longer period than that required by, for instance, the Executive Order, which looks to hiring and applicant data over the previous year. However, VEVRAA is a different law with different analytic mechanisms. As explained in the NPRM, the purpose of considering a longer history of data under VEVRAA is because it will provide more complete information through which a contractor can understand which outreach efforts it has engaged in historically have tended to correspond with increased veteran applicants and hires. Further, we do not believe that requiring contractors to look at and compare a few additional numbers, which are already calculated pursuant to § 60–300.44(k), is onerous, particularly compared to the potential benefit. Accordingly, we retain the paragraph (f)(3) in the final rule as written in the NPRM. OFCCP has conducted an amended calculation of the cost of this provision in light of the comments provided, set forth in the Regulatory Procedures section of this final rule.

The final rule makes one small change to the second to last sentence in paragraph (f)(3). As explained in the preamble to the NPRM, OFCCP proposed that the contractor's conclusion as to the effectiveness of its outreach efforts "shall be reasonable as determined by OFCCP in light of these regulations." The final rule replaces the word "shall" with "must," which more clearly describes the requirement.

Finally, several commenters expressed concern about the five-year recordkeeping requirement set forth in paragraph (f)(4). As discussed previously in this final rule and in the discussion of recordkeeping in § 60–300.80, and for the reasons stated therein, OFCCP amends this to a three-year recordkeeping requirement. While this documentation may take several forms, such documentation may include, for example, the numbers and types of outreach and recruitment events, the targeted group(s) or types of participants, when and where the events occurred, and who conducted and participated in the outreach and recruitment efforts on behalf of the contractor.

• *Paragraph (g): Internal dissemination of affirmative action policy*

This section requires contractors to develop internal procedures to communicate to employees their obligation to engage in affirmative action efforts to employ and advance in employment qualified protected veterans. The NPRM proposed requiring the contractor to undertake many specific actions that are only suggested in the existing rule, including incorporating the affirmative action policy in company policy manuals, informing all applicants and employees of the contractor's affirmative action obligations, and conducting meetings with management and company leadership to ensure they are informed about the contractor's obligations. The NPRM also proposed requiring contractors to hold meetings with employees at least once a year to discuss the company's VEVRAA affirmative action policy. OFCCP received 17 comments on § 60–300.44(g) from a variety of groups, including a disability association, an employee association, four contractor associations, four law firms, and two individuals, among others.

One commenter proposed maintaining some of the language in the current § 60–300.44(g)(1). The commenter expressed concern about the NPRM's deletion of the following sentence: "[t]he scope of the contractor's efforts shall depend upon all the circumstances, including the contractor's size and resources and the extent to which existing practices are adequate." The commenter asserted that deleting this sentence leaves the requirement without an applicable measure of compliance. The commenter recommended maintaining the language in the section and defining "adequate" to mean "being received and understood by veterans, as determined in sample interviews."

The final rule adopts the proposed language in § 60–300.44(g)(1) without change because the rule provides a measure of compliance, thus making the suggested change unnecessary. This section clearly states that the procedures for internally disseminating affirmative action policies ". . . shall be designed to foster understanding, acceptance and support among the contractor's executive, management, supervisory and other employees and to encourage such persons to take the necessary actions to aid the contractor in meeting this obligation." Further, the revisions clearly identify the actions that contractors must undertake to meet this obligation.

With regard to the remainder of paragraph (g), the existing rule has a single paragraph (g)(2) that lists eight separate actions that contractors were suggested to undertake to implement and internally disseminate their internal affirmative action policies. The NPRM proposed to mandate some of these actions and thus restructured the remainder of paragraph (g). Paragraph (g)(2) of the NPRM listed five internal dissemination efforts that would be required of all contractors: (i) Including the contractor's affirmative action policy toward veterans in the contractor's policy manual; (ii) informing all employees and prospective employees of the contractor's affirmative action obligations and having annual meetings with employees to discuss these obligations; (iii) conducting meetings with executive, managerial and supervisory personnel to ensure they understood the intent of the policy and responsibility for its implementation; (iv) discussing the policy thoroughly in employee orientation and management training programs; and (v) if the contractor is party to a collective bargaining agreement, informing union officials and/or employee representatives of the contractor's affirmative action policy and requesting the union's cooperation in implementing it. Paragraph (g)(3) of the NPRM listed additional dissemination efforts that would continue to be suggested efforts as in the existing rule, such as publicizing its affirmative action policy in company publications and including in these publications features and articles of protected veteran employees. Finally, paragraph (g)(4) of the NPRM set forth the recordkeeping obligations in connection with those actions contractors undertook.

We received many comments in response to the elements that were required in paragraph (g)(2) of the NPRM. Some commenters requested alternative options to including the affirmative action policy in the contractor's policy manual pursuant to the proposed § 60–300.44(g)(2)(i). A law firm suggested allowing for posting the policy on the company's intranet where similar human resources and EEO pronouncements are found. One comment requested that OFCCP clarify the requirement to make it optional for contractors that do not have policy manuals. Several of the comments expressed concern about the requirement in the proposed paragraph (g)(2)(ii) to hold a meeting at least once a year with employees to discuss affirmative action obligations. Commenters asserted the OFCCP miscalculated the burden associated with hosting these meetings, stating that requiring this element would incur a much higher burden. Commenters stated that OFCCP should allow contractors to disseminate the equal employment opportunity policy at regularly scheduled meetings and allow for electronic and web-based formats. Commenters also stated that it was unclear what would constitute adequate training and compliance with the newly required elements of paragraph (g)(2).

In response to the comments, and with an eye toward reducing the burden on contractors, the final rule narrows the scope of the internal dissemination efforts that will be required of contractors from that set forth in the NPRM. Two of the five elements that the NPRM proposed to require are maintained as requirements in paragraph (g)(2) of the final rule: (1) Including the policy in the contractor's policy manual; and (2) notifying (a change from "meeting with" in the NPRM, in order to facilitate compliance) union officials to inform them of the policy and request their cooperation, if the contractor is party to a collecting bargaining agreement. The first of these requirements is modified slightly from what was proposed in the NPRM based on comments received so as to allow contractors to include the affirmative action policy either in the contractor's policy manual, or to otherwise make the policy available to its employees. We believe that most companies generally have some form of document that provides guidance on human resources policies and procedures—either a policy manual, employee handbook, or similar document– that is available to employees that is an appropriate place to put the policy. OFCCP believes including the affirmative action policy in these documents will enhance the visibility of the contractor's commitment to protected veterans. However, the final rule also allows contractors the flexibility to make the policy available to its employees through other means. This could include posting the policy on a company intranet, but this will only fulfill the requirement if all employees have access to this intranet.

The remaining elements that were required in the NPRM and/or were suggested in the existing rule remain in paragraph (g)(3) of the final rule as actions that the contractor is suggested to take, with the exception of the recordkeeping provision, which has been eliminated. We note, however, that to the extent any activities undertaken pursuant to paragraph (g) involve the creation of records that are subject to the general recordkeeping requirement of § 60–300.80, contractors will still be required to maintain such documents as specified by § 60–300.80.

• *Paragraph (h): Audit and reporting system for affirmative action program*

Section 60–300.44(h) outlines the contractor's responsibility to design and implement an audit and reporting system for the company's AAP. The NPRM proposed requiring contractors to document the actions taken to comply with the section. The NPRM also proposed that contractors maintain the records of their documentation subject to the recordkeeping requirements of § 60–300.80. OFCCP received one substantive comment on the proposed revisions. The commenter, a human resources consulting group, stated that the documentation requirement would be potentially burdensome.

This section is adopted in the final rule as proposed. Many of the requirements of § 60–300.44(h) necessitate developing documentation. The section requires contractors to measure the effectiveness of its affirmative action program, indicate any need for remedial action, determine the degree to which the contractor's objectives have been attained, determine whether protected veterans have had the opportunity to participate in all company professional and social activities, and measure the contractor's compliance with the program's specific obligations. Section 60–300.44(h)(2) requires contractors to undertake necessary action to bring the program into compliance. In order to conduct this kind of analysis, many contractors will likely develop documentation. The final rule formalizes that process for all contractors and requires that the documentation be maintained in accordance with the recordkeeping requirements of § 60–300.80. OFCCP feels strongly that this requirement will allow for a more effective review of whether the contractor's affirmative action obligations in this paragraph are being met.

• *Paragraph (i): Responsibility for implementation*

The only substantive proposed change in paragraph (i) required that the identity of the officials responsible for a contractor's affirmative action activities must appear on all internal and external communications regarding the contractor's affirmative action program. In the current regulation, this disclosure is only suggested. Upon further review, OFCCP does not believe that the benefit of this suggested change outweighs the potential burden that it would place on contractors. Accordingly, the final rule does not incorporate the proposal, and the language in the existing regulation that contractors should, but are not required, to take this step is retained.

• *Paragraph (j): Training*

Paragraph (j) of the existing regulation already requires that the contractor train "[a]ll personnel involved in the recruitment, screening, selection, promotion, disciplinary and related processes . . . to ensure that the commitments in the contractor's affirmative action program are implemented." The NPRM proposed revising this paragraph to identify specific topics that must be considered in this training, including: the benefits of employing protected veterans; appropriate sensitivity toward protected veteran recruits, applicants and employees; and the legal responsibilities of the contractor and its agents regarding protected veterans generally and disabled veterans specifically, such as reasonable accommodation for qualified disabled veterans and the related rights and responsibilities of the contractor and protected veterans. The NPRM also required that the contractor record which of its personnel receive this training, when they receive it, and the person(s) who administer(s) the training, and maintain these records, along with all written or electronic training materials used.

OFCCP received 12 comments from law firms, disability and veterans associations, and contractors and contractor associations. The majority of these comments raised concern regarding the burden the training requirements places on contractors and the manner in which OFCCP calculated it. Several comments noted specific concerns about what constitutes "sensitivity" training. Two commenters suggested that OFCCP or OFCCP-approved training programs should be offered, instead of the contractor having to create additional training to what is done now.

Taking these comments into account, and balancing the utility of the proposal against the burden that it would create for contractors, the final rule does not incorporate the portion of the proposed rule listing specific training items that must be covered by contractors or the specific recordkeeping requirement. However, the final rule does retain the existing rule's general requirement that "[a]ll personnel involved in the recruitment, screening, selection, promotion, disciplinary, and related processes" must be trained to ensure that the contractor's affirmative action commitments are implemented. Further, we note that to the extent any activities undertaken pursuant to paragraph (j) involve the creation of records that are subject to the general recordkeeping requirement of § 60–300.80, contractors will still be required to maintain such documents as specified by § 60–300.80.

• *Paragraph (k): Data Collection Analysis*

The proposed regulation added paragraph (k) to the rule, requiring that the contractor document and update annually the following information: (1) For referral data, the total number of referrals, the number of priority referrals of protected veterans, and the "referral ratio" of referred protected veterans to total referrals; (2) for applicant data, the total number of applicants for employment, the number of applicants who are known protected veterans, and the "applicant ratio" of known protected veteran applicants to total applicants; (3) for hiring data, the total number of job openings, the number of jobs filled, the number of known protected veterans hired, and the "hiring ratio" of known protected veteran hires to total hires; and (4) the total number of job openings, the number of jobs that are filled, and the "job fill ratio" of job openings to job openings filled.

As stated in the NPRM, the impetus behind this new section is that no structured data regarding the number of protected veterans who are referred for or apply for jobs with Federal contractors is currently maintained. This absence of data makes it nearly impossible for the contractor and OFCCP to perform even rudimentary evaluations of the availability of protected veterans in the workforce, or to make any sort of objective, data-based assessments of how effective contractor outreach and recruitment efforts have been in attracting protected veteran candidates. Conversely, maintaining this information will provide the contractor with much more meaningful data for evaluating and tailoring its recruitment and outreach efforts.

OFCCP received a total of 52 comments from veterans' associations, a disability association, an employee association, contractor associations, medical and other associations, law firms, and contractors. The three veterans and disability associations that commented on the proposal supported the required data collection and the goal behind it. Virtually all commenters from the contractor community opposed the proposal on varying grounds, including: issues with the integrity of the data to be collected (and particularly data on referrals); assertions that some of the data conflicts with the Internet Applicant Rule in the Executive Order regulations; and assertions that collecting, analyzing, and maintaining the data would be unduly burdensome. Further, 19 commenters, all of whom were members of the construction industry, submitted form letters asserting that they should be exempted from the requirement due to the unique nature of their industry. Finally, a number of commenters sought clarification of some of the processes set forth in paragraph (k). These issues are considered in turn below.

With regard to the eleven data elements required by the proposed new section, 40 comments (total includes 19 form letters) articulated data integrity concerns regarding data to be used in calculating the referral ratio. Comments describe the state employment service delivery systems as "self-service," leaving source identification to the candidate for the job, and as such making data unreliable in terms of identifying referrals. Examples were provided indicating that veterans may apply directly online with a company and may fail to identify that he/she was referred and even that he/she is a veteran. These comments also raised the issue that the referral ratio does not account for referrals from sources other than the state employment service delivery systems and may include referrals of veterans that are not qualified for the position(s) at issue. For the reasons set forth in the discussion of the proposed paragraph 5 of the EO Clause (§ 60–300.5), OFCCP has eliminated from the final rule the requirement for contractors to collect, maintain, and analyze information on the number of referrals and the ratio of priority referrals of veterans to total referrals, *i.e.*, paragraphs (k)(1), (k)(2), and (k)(3) in the NPRM. This eliminates many of the concerns commenters had with regard to this paragraph, and also serves to decrease the burden on contractors.

However, eight of these comments also discussed the requirement to document and maintain applicant and hiring ratios. These comments reiterated data integrity issues and questions about the purpose of conducting the calculations or comparisons. One of the primary issues identified by commenters is that applicant data appears to be dependent upon self-identification which is not reliable. These issues were addressed in the discussion of the invitation to self-identify proposals in § 60–300.42(a). In short, demographic data based on self-identification will never be perfect, but it is the best data that is available.

Another identified concern is that the proposed data collection and analysis is not aligned with the availability analysis conducted when examining employment activities for females and minorities. However, as stated previously in this preamble, VEVRAA and the Executive Order are different laws with different data calculation and enforcement schemes, largely because of the differences in the Census and other data available. It is, therefore, not feasible to pattern data collection after the Executive Order regulations.

Comments also questioned the purpose of the job opening/job filled ratio. On a related point, one comment from a law firm noted that there appears to be an underlying assumption that there will be jobs that are not filled which is seldom true in the current economic environment. While it may not be a common occurrence in the current economic environment: (a) this does not mean it never happens (and if it never does, the burden on the contractor to calculate a "job fill ratio" shrinks to virtually nothing); and (b) the current economic environment will not last forever, at which point these regulations will still be in effect. The job fill ratio is a commonly recorded metric by companies and HR professionals, as it measures the effectiveness of a company's recruiting efforts. Also, in some cases, a particularly low job fill ratio could be an indicator that the company's hiring process is being conducted incorrectly. This is useful information for both the contractor and OFCCP. We have eliminated the requirement, however, that contractors document and maintain for three years the ratio of jobs filled to job openings and the ratio of protected veterans hired to all hires. The remaining data points permit OFCCP and the contractor to make those calculations; thus separate data collection is unnecessary. Several commenters also objected to the collection of data about protected veteran status of applicants because it differs from the recordkeeping requirements related to Internet Applicants under the EO 11246 implementing regulations at 41 CFR 60–1.12. We addressed this issue in the discussion of the pre-offer self-identification requirement, and incorporate by reference that discussion here, but we wish to reiterate the salient points here in response. Under § 60–1.12, contractors' recordkeeping obligations include maintaining expressions of interest through the Internet that the contractor considered for a particular position, as well as applications and resumes. Contractors also are required to maintain, where possible, data about the race, sex, and ethnicity of applicants and Internet Applicants, as applicable. The term Internet Applicant is defined at § 60–1.3. The term "applicant" is defined in OFCCP subregulatory guidance. The Internet Applicant definition is limited to OFCCP recordkeeping and data collection requirements under the Executive Order implementing regulations in § 60–1.12.

In sum, after consideration of the comments received, the final rule retains the NPRM's proposal for contractors to document and maintain applicant, hiring, and job fill ratio data, but eliminates the requirement for contractors to document and maintain referral data.

With regard to burden calculation issues, 43 of the 52 commenters, entirely from the contractor community, indicated that OFCCP had not correctly calculated the burden of this section. Specific cost information was provided by two commenters. A contractor association that combined comments from three such entities indicated that a survey conducted by the association found OFCCP's estimate of six minutes a year to collect, maintain and "in some cases" calculate the data elements should be stated more accurately as six hours. A revised burden calculation is included in the Regulatory Procedures section of this final rule, as well as the methodology behind the revised calculation, but we wish to highlight a few points here where we believe the contractor community may have misunderstood portions of the burden we proposed they undertake. First, as stated above, the referral data metrics have been eliminated, which reduces the burden. Second, the hiring metrics are already maintained and calculated by the contractor as part of its existing obligation under 41 CFR part 61–300; therefore, that portion of paragraph (k) does not create any additional burden. The only "new" items proposed were those pertaining to the self-identification applicant data and the job fill ratio.

Also pertaining to burden, 19 commenters from the construction industry asserted that they should be exempted from this section of the proposed regulation because of the unique nature of the industry, namely that it is project-based and its workers are transitory and seasonal. Traditionally, construction contractors who meet the basic coverage requirements (contract amount and number of employees) of VEVRAA have not been exempted from any of its provisions. This includes the collection of data under part 61–300 for the VETS-100A report, which tracks the numbers of new hires and overall employees who are protected veterans, data which makes up a significant portion of the requirements under paragraph (k). Accordingly, we decline to exempt construction contractors.

Commenters from the contractor community also cited burden concerns with the proposed requirement to maintain the paragraph (k) computations for a period of five (5) years. As set forth in the discussions of § 60–300.44(f)(4) and § 60–300.80 herein, the final rule reduces the document retention requirement to three (3) years, and revises the language of paragraph (k) to reflect this change.

Finally, a few of the comments raised clarification questions we would like to address, including: (1) Whether the intent of the analyses is to measure change from year to year; (2) whether the ratios should be run by job group, job title, or establishment; and (3) how compliance determinations will be made. As to the first question, as set forth in the discussion of § 60–300.44(f)(3), measuring change from year to year, and looking at two previous years of data, is a central intent of the analyses, as that can aid the contractor in seeing trends that may be associated with certain of its outreach and recruitment efforts over time. However, as discussed in that section, contractors are also free to use any other reasonable criteria in addition to the applicant and hiring data they feel is relevant to evaluate the effectiveness of their efforts. As to the second question, the ratios in paragraph (k) will be calculated by establishment, and not by job groups or titles within a given establishment. The number of protected veterans in the civilian workforce is relatively small (at least compared to the number of women or minorities nationwide), and thus we believe that running analyses by job groups or titles is unlikely to provide any meaningful analysis.

With regard to the third question, compliance determinations for paragraph (k) will be made based simply on whether the contractor has documented and maintained the five listed metrics in the final rule. OFCCP Compliance Officers will not be using the applicant and hiring data to conduct underutilization or impact ratio analyses, as is the case under the Executive Order, and enforcement actions will not be brought solely on the basis of statistical disparities between veterans and non-veterans in this data. Compliance officers will look to see whether the contractor has fulfilled its obligations under § 60–300.44(f)(3) to critically analyze and assess the effectiveness of its recruitment efforts, using the data in paragraph (k) as well as any other reasonable criteria the contractor believes is relevant, and has pursued different and/or additional recruitment efforts if the contractor concludes that its efforts were not effective.

Section 60–300.45 Benchmarks for hiring

The NPRM proposed that the contractor establish annual hiring benchmarks by using existing data on veteran availability from five different sources of information: (1) Bureau of Labor Statistics data of the average percentage of veterans in the civilian labor force in the State where the contractor is located; (2) the raw number of protected veterans who participated in the employment service delivery system (*i.e.,* One-Stop Career Centers) in the State where the contractor is located; (3) the referral, applicant, and hire data collected by the contractor pursuant to § 60–300.44(k); (4) the contractor's recent assessments of its outreach and recruitment efforts as set forth in § 60–300.44(f)(3); and (5) any other factors, including but not limited to the nature of the contractor's job openings and/or its location, which would tend to affect the availability of protected veterans. The last of these factors would allow the contractor to take into account other factors unique to its establishment that would tend to affect the availability determination. The NPRM also proposed to require contractors to document the hiring benchmark it established each year, detailing each of the factors that it considered in establishing the hiring benchmark and the relative significance of each of these factors, and required the contractor to retain this document for a period of five years.

OFCCP received a total of 38 comments on the proposed new requirement to establish annual hiring benchmarks for protected veterans. Three comments from organizations representing employee interests, including a disability association and a veterans association, stated that requiring benchmarks using available statistics was an important development, and supported the proposed regulation in general terms. The remaining comments, virtually all of which were from contractors or those representing contractors, opposed the requirement for contractor-established benchmarks as proposed. The reasons set forth for their opposition fell into five general categories: (1) A belief that the benchmarks were equivalent to "quotas"; (2) hiring benchmarks for protected veterans would adversely impact women and minorities; (3) the benchmarks as proposed were arbitrary and ineffective given that the data to be relied upon is not specific to veterans protected by VEVRAA and does not correlate to specific job groups, skills, or geographical areas; (4) the proposed five-year recordkeeping requirement conflicts with equivalent requirements in other laws administered by OFCCP; and (5) that setting benchmarks as proposed in the NPRM was unduly burdensome for contractors, and OFCCP underestimated the cost and burden of the proposal. Further, some commenters provided recommendations for how to amend the proposed benchmarks, and others submitted questions seeking clarification of aspects of OFCCP's proposal. As detailed below, the final rule contains a substantial revision, allowing contractors the option of using a benchmark based on national veteran data. This option would substantially decrease the burden on contractors.

Before addressing each of the issues raised by the commenters, providing some further context and explanation for the proposal and how OFCCP envisioned the proposed requirement would work in practice is appropriate.

The primary intent of the benchmark proposal was to provide the contractor a yardstick that could be used to measure progress in employing protected veterans. OFCCP recognized that data demonstrating the availability of protected veterans that is similar to the data used to compute availability and establish goals under the EO 11246 program does not exist. Owing to the imprecise nature of the data upon which benchmarks would be based, OFCCP did not propose additional affirmative action obligations (or OFCCP enforcement actions) if a contractor did not meet the benchmark that it set. To be sure, OFCCP would expect that as part of its annual recruitment and outreach assessment, the contractor would assess why it did not meet the benchmark and adjust its recruitment efforts for the following year based on what it has learned. However, the proposal would not have OFCCP undertake enforcement action solely on the basis of a disparity between the benchmark and the actual percentage of veterans hired.

Further highlighting the difference between the benchmark proposal and the availability and utilization calculations traditionally required under the Executive Order 11246 program, OFCCP designed the benchmark proposal to allow the contractor maximum flexibility to take into account any additional factors it thought would increase or decrease a reasonable benchmark and to weigh these factors in any reasonable manner it saw fit. For instance, the contractor might start with the average veteran population for its state, reduce this number slightly to account for the fact that this data was not limited to protected veterans, average this number with the percentage of protected veteran applicants it had received over the past three years, and increase the resulting percentage slightly in anticipation of additional recruiting efforts it knew it would be doing in the next year. Then, the contractor could adjust this number up or down depending on the overall nature of the work performed at the establishment and how that coincides with experience veterans generally have, whether the contractor knew that there was a particularly high or low number of veterans in the relevant hiring area, or any other reasonable factor. So long as the contractor adequately described and documented the factors it took into account, it would comply with the § 60–300.45 requirement.

Finally, OFCCP intended the benchmark proposal to raise awareness of the significant number of veterans who, having made enormous sacrifices defending our nation on our behalf, nevertheless continue to face considerable difficulties finding work upon their return home. These veterans are highly trained, highly skilled, disciplined, and possess considerable leadership and team-building experience—in other words, excellent candidates for employment. While recent Federal efforts have greatly helped veterans' employment prospects, the service of these veterans to our nation abroad is still too often forgotten, and the lasting contribution they can make to our private sector at home is still too often unfulfilled. The proposed hiring benchmark, therefore, is a tool to address this pressing national issue and the important role Federal contractors have in addressing it.

The purposes and intentions of the benchmark proposal made clear, we turn to the concerns raised by commenters.

Five commenters stated that the proposed benchmarks were the equivalent of a "quota." One commenter stated that the benchmark requirement would make contractors feel the need to meet the data requirements by hiring protected veterans who may not be qualified in order to meet the benchmark. Another believed the benchmarks suggested "quotas" because the availability analysis factors proposed do not factor in the approximate percentage of qualified protected veterans by occupational codes or geographical areas. Still another asserted that the proposed benchmarks were "quotas" and thus unconstitutional, as they were not "narrowly tailored" to "a compelling governmental interest."

The proposed benchmarks are not quotas and should not be conceived as quotas. The benchmark is not a rigid and inflexible quota which must be met, nor is it to be considered either a ceiling or a floor for the employment of particular groups. Quotas are expressly forbidden. We hope the discussion in the previous paragraphs clarifying that contractors have significant flexibility to set their own benchmarks, and will not be cited for violations solely for failing to meet the benchmarks they set, allay the fears of these commenters. Further, the omission of breaking down the benchmarks by occupational codes or geographical areas is merely a function of the fact that such data does not exist for protected veterans; it does not evince an intent to set rigid quotas. Finally, we note that the legal standard raised by the final commenter regarding the constitutionality of the benchmarks is incorrect. The "narrowly tailored to a compelling governmental interest" standard, otherwise known as "strict scrutiny," is applied to race-based decision making. *See Adarand Constructors, Inc.* v. *Pena,* 515 U.S. 200 (1996). The benchmarks proposed in the VEVRAA regulations are not race-based. Classifications that are based on veteran status are subject to so-called "rational basis review," and are legally permissible so long as the government action—in this case, the setting of benchmarks—is "rationally related" to a "legitimate governmental interest." *See, e.g., Sturgell* v. *Creasy,* 640 F.2d 843, 852 (6th Cir. 1981). Clearly, requiring contractors to set benchmarks for the hiring of protected veterans—particularly benchmarks that afford the contractor significant flexibility in their establishment and are not rigidly applied so as to automatically create a violation of the law if they are not met—is rationally related to the legitimate governmental interest of increasing outreach to and employment opportunities for protected veterans.

Six commenters, including individuals, contractor associations, consultants, and human resource management firms, expressed concern that requiring contractors to establish annual hiring benchmarks for protected veterans would adversely impact women and minorities, and thus impede contractors' nondiscrimination efforts under EO 11246, due to low numbers of minorities and women among protected veterans. One commenter asked for clarity on whether contractor veteran affirmative action efforts could be used as an affirmative defense if those efforts result in adverse impact against women, because a large percentage of protected veterans are men. Finally, a commenter asked whether OFCCP would still require contractors to establish annual hiring benchmarks for protected veterans if women and minorities were underutilized. OFCCP does not agree that contractor-established benchmarks will adversely affect women or minorities. As an initial matter, recent Department of Veterans Affairs (DVA) data indicate that for Gulf War-era I veterans 30.3 percent were minority; Gulf War-era II veterans 33.6 percent were minority; and Vietnam era veterans 16.4 percent were minority.[21] This compares quite closely with the 27 percent national non-white population figure calculated by recent Census data.[22] For this reason alone we do not anticipate any potential effect on minorities. Although the representation of women among veterans is lower than in the civilian labor force, as discussed in more detail below, the employment of women will not be adversely affected by VEVRAA affirmative action requirements.

The purpose of, and requirements related to, VEVRAA benchmarks do not serve to impact the hiring of women or minorities. The purpose of VEVRAA hiring benchmarks is simply to provide the contractor a quantifiable means to measure its progress towards achieving equal employment opportunity for protected veterans. The contractor's obligation under § 60–300.45 is to establish a benchmark and document that it has done so. Contractors will not be subject to an enforcement action or found to be in violation of the VEVRAA regulations for failing to meet the benchmark. Hiring preferences are not required, the rule does not state that contractors will be expected to achieve benchmarks, and the VEVRAA rule does not prescribe actions the contractor must take if the benchmark is not achieved. The benchmark simply provides the contractor a tool to measure its progress in employing protected veterans. Consequently, the VEVRAA enforcement scheme does not provide an incentive for contractors to disfavor non-protected veterans in employment. The point of the benchmark is to encourage contractors to be inclusive of protected veterans rather than to discriminate against nonveterans through preferences or quotas.

OFCCP sees no reason why a contractor's VEVRAA obligations would affect its nondiscrimination obligations under EO 11246 or Title VII. VEVRAA does not require hiring preferences or veteran quotas. Because contractors are not required to meet the VEVRAA benchmark, efforts by contractors to do so would not be a defense to a charge of employment discrimination, including adverse impact, under another law. Further, a contractor's obligations under other civil rights laws will not create a violation of VEVRAA. To avoid this problem § 60–300.1(c)(2) provides that it may be a defense to a charge of violation of VEVRAA regulations that a challenged action is required or necessitated by another Federal law or regulation, or that another Federal law or regulation prohibits an action that would be required by VEVRAA.

Finally, in response to the question about whether a contractor will need to establish a VEVRAA hiring benchmark regardless of its utilization of women and minorities, the answer is yes. The VEVRAA benchmark is to be established annually regardless of the contractor's utilization of any group of employees, including protected veterans. The hiring benchmark is simply a tool to allow contractors to measure their progress in providing equal opportunity to protected veterans.

A number of commenters objected to the proposed benchmarks on the grounds that the data upon which the contractors are required to rely generally is structurally incompatible with the contractor's workplace. For instance, one commenter asserted that it opposes hiring benchmarks because the metrics outlined in the proposal have no relationship at all to the population of qualified candidates eligible for employment. Additionally, an organization argued that just because there may be a high availability of veterans in a specific location, does not mean those same veterans are qualified for the types of jobs available in that same location. Furthermore, commenters in opposition to the proposed rule argued that the benchmark proposal is flawed because it contemplates facility-wide goals. Another organization explains that placement goals for an accounting firm will look very different than the placement goals for a manufacturing company, and the placement goals for entry-level production positions at the manufacturing company will look very different than the placement goals for management positions at the same company.

These comments are well-taken, and we submit that some of these issues are precisely why the benchmarks we proposed allowed the contractor such a significant amount of flexibility in creating them. This would allow, for instance, an accounting firm and a manufacturing firm in the same city to have different hiring benchmarks, depending on the types of positions available and the skill sets required for these positions. The decision to have the regulation require the contractor to create facility-wide benchmarks rather than goals tied to particular job codes or titles is dictated by the limited scope of the veteran data available.

A substantial number of commenters objected to the proposed benchmarks on the grounds that the specific categories of data which the contractors are required to consider are not specific to protected veterans, and otherwise do not provide clear guidance to contractors on how to arrive at an overall benchmark. With regard to the BLS data specified in paragraph (b)(1), commenters argued that relying on such data would inflate benchmarks because data collected by BLS and state employment services reflects all veterans in the civilian labor force—not just protected veterans, and that such data would be based on the entire state rather than a more narrow recruitment area. With regard to the VETS data specified in paragraph (b)(2), commenters contended that this statewide data would have limited relevance to the recruiting that occurs in most companies because contractors may recruit from a very local market for some positions and may recruit on a national basis for other positions. Additionally, commenters argued that to the extent contractors are required to rely on statewide data to inform localized hiring benchmarks, there are no assurances the statewide data is an accurate reflection of the composition of protected veterans in the subject locale. Regarding consideration of the contractor's own referral, applicant and hiring data of protected veterans in paragraph (b)(3), commenters generally questioned the reliability of the data, specifically the referral and applicant data, for reasons that have been

[21] U.S. Department of Veteran Affairs, National Center for Veterans Analysis and Statistics, "Minority Veterans 2011," May 2013, *http://www.va.gov/vetdata/docs/SpecialReports/Minority_Veterans_2011.pdf* (last accessed Aug. 15, 2013).

[22] U.S. Census Bureau, *Overview of Race and Hispanic Origin:2010*, Table 1: Population by Hispanic or Latino Origin and by Race for the United States: 2000 and 2010, Mar. 11, 2011, *http://www.census.gov/prod/cen2010/briefs/c2010br-02.pdf* (last accessed Aug. 15, 2013).

thoroughly addressed in previous sections.

In response to the comments on the proposed data considerations in paragraphs (b)(1) and (b)(2), as previously discussed, OFCCP agrees that precise and statistically meaningful availability data specifically capturing veterans protected under VEVRAA at the local level, divided by job group, would be optimal in setting specific, refined goals. However, such data does not exist. Accordingly, the proposal had contractors consider a variety of sources of data capturing large portions of the relevant population (including actual applicant flow and hiring data from the contractor's establishment), and provided contractors with the flexibility, in the proposed paragraphs (b)(4) and (b)(5), to take into account any other factors which could reasonably affect protected veteran availability. However, commenters also asserted that paragraphs (b)(4) and (b)(5) were unhelpfully vague and introduced a high degree of subjectivity into the entirety of the benchmark setting process that was uncomfortable. Multiple commenters suggested alternative methods for setting benchmarks, including a nationwide goal for hiring protected veterans. One commenter in particular, a consultant to contractors on EEO issues, proposed a mechanism by which aggregate annual VETS–100A data could be used to estimate the number of protected veterans in the civilian workforce, and by dividing this number by the total civilian workforce, arrive at a national goal for protected veterans.

OFCCP does not believe that VETS–100 data, as currently collected and reported, is an appropriate source for establishing benchmarks. However, should the VETS data collection and reporting structures change in the future, the VETS 100–A data may be a source contractors could use when establishing their own benchmarks or that is considered by OFCCP should it revise the national benchmark. First, the structure of the VETS–100 form is such that contractors do not record a total number of protected veteran employees or hires, but rather how many veterans fall within each of the four protected categories. Because a veteran may fall within multiple categories (*e.g.*, a disabled veteran who is also recently separated and earned a campaign badge for his or her service), VETS–100 data can double, triple, or even quadruple-count the number of protected veteran hires and employees. Also, VETS–100 data only reflects those protected veterans employed by Federal contractors, and not the population of protected veterans available for work. Accordingly, if a contractor's protected veteran recruitment efforts were deficient and resulted in an unreasonably small number of protected veteran hires and employees, this deficiency would therefore be incorporated into the contractor's benchmark.

However, in order to address the concerns of those commenters seeking greater clarity and objectivity in setting hiring benchmarks, the final rule contains a significant revision allowing contractors another method for establishing a hiring benchmark: simply using the national percentage of veterans in the civilian labor force, which will be published and updated annually on OFCCP's Web site, as the annual hiring benchmark. As of September 2011, the national percentage of veterans in the civilian labor force was 8.0 percent. OFCCP recognizes that this data captures all veterans, and not just veterans protected by VEVRAA, but OFCCP reiterates that the benchmark is not a quota. It serves primarily as a yardstick by which contractors can measure the effectiveness of their affirmative action efforts, and a tool for contractors to use in the evaluation of their outreach and recruitment efforts. Importantly, as with benchmarks calculated under the five-factor method set forth in the NPRM, contractors will not be cited simply for failing to meet it. For those commenters who asserted that the proposed five-factor approach to setting benchmarks was unduly burdensome, this approach will decrease the burden significantly, as set forth in the Regulatory Procedures section of this final rule.

For those contractors that would rather use the five-factor approach to setting benchmarks proposed in the NPRM, the final rule retains this as an option. This option, however, is modified slightly to eliminate the consideration of referral data, which contractors are no longer required to collect and maintain in the final rule. For those who choose this method of setting benchmarks, OFCCP will provide technical assistance to contractors upon request.

With regard to commenters' concerns about the proposed five-year recordkeeping requirement in paragraph (c) of this section, the final rule reduces this to a three-year requirement, for the reasons set forth in the discussion of § 60–300.80 below and previous sections that had a proposed five-year recordkeeping requirement discussed above.

Some commenters questioned why the term "benchmarks" was used in this section as opposed to the term "goals" which is used in the EO 11246 program. We proposed a different term to avoid confusion and to highlight the difference in how the two concepts operate. The purposes of the EO 11246 placement goals are twofold: (1) "to serve as objectives or targets reasonably attainable by means of applying every good faith effort to make all aspects of the entire affirmative action program work" and (2) "to measure progress toward achieving equal employment opportunity." 41 CFR 60–2.16(a). The benchmarks established under this regulation are intended to serve only the second of these two objectives, that is, they serve as a measure of progress and the effectiveness of a contractor's outreach and recruitment efforts. The Executive Order regulations state goals are "reasonably attainable" when sufficiently robust data exists describing the availability of women and minority workers, the groups for which goals may be established under the Executive Order program. As discussed previously in this section, however, we do not believe that the data currently available is sufficiently robust on the issue of the availability of protected veterans. Consequently, the purpose and function of goals established in the Executive Order regulations differ from benchmarks under the VEVRAA regulations. Therefore, we use different terminology to distinguish the terms clearly. To further clarify this difference, the final rule slightly revises the language in paragraph (b) of this section. The proposal defined hiring benchmarks as "the percentage of total hires that are protected veterans that the contractor will seek to hire. . . ." The final rule deletes the clause "that the contractor will seek to hire" from the text of paragraph (b) given the explanation above.

Finally, one commenter asked if the annual hiring benchmark it sets should be included in the text of the AAP or maintained on-site in the event of an OFCCP audit. It is OFCCP's position that annual hiring benchmarks should be included in both the text of the AAP and maintained on-site in the event of an OFCCP audit, for maximum transparency.

Subpart D—General Enforcement and Complaint Procedures

Section 60–300.60 Compliance evaluations

The proposed rule set forth several changes to the process the contractor and OFCCP will follow in conducting compliance evaluations. These proposals, the comments to these proposals, and the revisions made to the final rule are discussed in turn below.

• *Paragraph (a)(1): Review of personnel processes*

The NPRM added a sentence to paragraph (a)(1)(i) regarding the temporal scope of desk audits performed by OFCCP, stating that OFCCP "may extend the temporal scope of the desk audit beyond that set forth in the scheduling letter if OFCCP deems it necessary to carry out its investigation of potential violations of this part." Several commenters, including those from individuals, contractors, contractor associations, and law firms, objected to this proposed change and asked that it be withdrawn. These commenters asserted that the language of the proposed rule could result in "never-ending" audits for contractors, was contrary to a 2010 Administrative Law Judge (ALJ) decision in the case *OFCCP* v. *Frito-Lay* and would lead to an increased burden for contractors.

As stated in the NPRM, the purpose of this proposal was to clarify that OFCCP may need to examine information after the date of the scheduling letter during the desk audit in order to determine, for instance, if violations are continuing or have been remedied. While the existing VEVRAA provision addresses the authority of the agency to conduct desk audits, it does not expressly state the temporal scope of these audits. It has been OFCCP's longstanding position that the agency has authority to obtain information pertinent to the review for periods after the date of the letter scheduling the review, including during the desk audit. However, in 2010 an ALJ disagreed in a recommended decision in the *Frito-Lay* case, in part because the parallel Executive Order 11246 desk audit regulation at issue in the case does not address the temporal scope of a desk audit. *OFCCP* v. *Frito-Lay, Inc.*, Case No. 2010–OFC–00002, ALJ Recommended Decision and Order (July 23, 2010). On May 8, 2012, the Department's Administrative Review Board (ARB) reversed this recommended decision, concluding that a desk audit authorized by the regulation permitted OFCCP to request additional information relating to periods after the scheduling letter. The ARB concluded that the regulation does not have an inflexible temporal limitation. *OFCCP* v. *Frito-Lay, Inc.*, Case No. 2010–OFC–00002, ARB Final Administrative Order (May 8, 2012). OFCCP views the *Frito-Lay* decision as equally applicable to desk audits concluded under its VEVRAA authority as to those conducted under its EO 11246 authority. Nevertheless, the final rule makes the clarification explicit in the text of the regulation. OFCCP notes that paragraph (a)(1) also authorizes OFCCP to request during the desk audit additional information pertinent to the review after reviewing the initial submission. *See United Space Alliance* v. *Solis*, 824 F.Supp.2d 68, 81–82 (D.D.C. 2011) (holding that agency's interpretation of its desk audit regulation to authorize additional information requests when necessary was entitled to deference).

Finally, commenters' concerns that this revision will lead to "never-ending" audits are inapposite. As stated above, the clarifying language set forth in the final rule does not change OFCCP's longstanding policy, or contractors' obligations, regarding the temporal scope of the desk audit. Further, because the clarification does not represent a change, concerns about increases in burden are similarly unfounded.

• *Paragraph (a)(2): Off-site review of records*

The NPRM sought to correct an error in the existing regulations in this paragraph, changing the reference to the "requirements of the Executive Order" to the "requirements of Section 4212." We received no comments on this proposed change, but in light of the discussion of § 60–300.2 above, we replace the reference to "Section 4212" with "VEVRAA."

• *Paragraph (a)(3) and (a)(4): Nature of document production and scope of focused reviews*

The NPRM revised these two paragraphs to allow OFCCP to review documents pursuant to a compliance check and conduct focused reviews either on-site or off-site, at OFCCP's option. We received no comments on these specific paragraphs, and thus adopt the proposed language into the final rule as written.

• *Paragraph (d): Pre-award compliance evaluation*

Finally, the proposed rule added a new paragraph (d) to this section detailing a new procedure for pre-award compliance evaluations under VEVRAA, much like the procedure that currently exists in the Executive Order regulations (*see* 41 CFR 60–1.20(d)). We received one comment on this proposal that supported adding pre-award compliance evaluation options. Accordingly, this paragraph is adopted into the final rule as proposed.

Subpart E—Ancillary Matters

Section 60–300.80 Recordkeeping

Section 60–300.80 describes the recordkeeping requirements that apply to contractors under VEVRAA. The NPRM proposed adding a sentence at the end of paragraph (a) of this section clarifying that the newly proposed recordkeeping requirements set forth in §§ 60–300.44(f)(4) (linkage agreements and other outreach and recruiting efforts), 60–300.44(k) (collection of referral, applicant and hire data), 60–300.45(c) (criteria and conclusions regarding contractor established hiring benchmarks), and paragraph 5 of the EO Clause in § 60–300.5(a) (referral data) must be maintained for five years. OFCCP received twenty-four comments on the proposed provision from an individual, contractors, associations representing veterans or individuals with disabilities, law firms, industry groups, and human resources consulting firms. Twenty-three of the commenters opposed the new requirement, citing burden and inconsistency with existing regulations.

In response to comments regarding the burden associated with maintaining records for five years, the final rule reduces the recordkeeping requirements for §§ 60–300.44(f)(4), 60–300.44(k), and 60–300.45(c) to three years. The final rule also eliminates the recordkeeping requirements for referral data under the proposed paragraph 5 of the EO Clause and § 60–300.44(k). The comments regarding the burden associated with the proposed revisions and OFCCP's response are discussed in further detail in the Regulatory Procedures section.

Commenters also expressed the view that all of the VEVRAA recordkeeping requirements should be consistent with EO 11246, section 503, and other laws that have recordkeeping obligations. Nearly all commenters believed the difference in timeframes would lead to confusion, and ultimately non-compliance, even for the most well-intentioned contractors. One comment asserted that the proposed provision is inconsistent with State laws that require employers to destroy personal information of job seekers after two years when records contain personal information. Several comments indicated that the proposed requirement contradicts the Internet Applicant rule, which sets forth certain requirements for applications received through the internet or related electronic data technologies.

In response to these comments, the final rule includes a three-year recordkeeping requirement, rather than the proposed five-year requirement, for §§ 60–300.44(f)(4), 60–300.44(k), and 60–300.45(c). In order to clearly indicate this, the final rule includes a new paragraph (b) specifying those records that have the three-year requirement, moving paragraphs (b) and (c) in the existing rule to paragraphs (c) and (d), respectively. OFCCP feels strongly that extending the recordkeeping requirements for these particular provisions, all primarily related to recruitment and outreach, will enable contractors to better determine the effectiveness of their recruitment and outreach activities over time. As noted in the NPRM, the absence of data makes it nearly impossible for contractors and OFCCP to perform even rudimentary evaluations of the availability of protected veterans in the workforce, or to make any quantitative assessments of how effective contractor outreach and recruitment efforts have been in attracting protected veteran candidates. These records will give contactors historical data that can be used for analyzing their compliance efforts. As to conflicts with other laws, particularly the Internet Applicant Rule, as set forth in detail in the discussion of § 60–300.42(a), the final rule harmonizes its requirements with the Internet Applicant Rule in the EO 11246 regulations. With regard to the comment vaguely referencing State law conflicts, generally speaking, State laws have provisions that acknowledge Federal preemption if there is a conflict, and thus we see no reason to change the proposal on that basis.

Commenters were particularly concerned about retaining referral data for five years under paragraph 5 of the EO Clause and § 60–300.44(k). As discussed previously, the final rule eliminates the recordkeeping requirements for referral data, eliminating this concern.

Section 60–300.81 Access to records

The NPRM made two changes to the current regulation. First, it added a sentence requiring the contractor to provide off-site access to materials if requested by OFCCP investigators or officials as part of an evaluation or investigation. Second, it required that the contractor specify to OFCCP all formats (including specific electronic formats) in which its records are available, and produce records to OFCCP in the formats selected by OFCCP. OFCCP received seven comments regarding the proposed § 60–300.81. All seven comments opposed the proposed changes, citing confidentiality and burden concerns.

Commenters expressed concerns about providing records in a format requested by OFCCP. Two commenters requested clarification regarding whether OFCCP will require contractors to convert records into formats requested by the agency. Several commenters stated that contractors should have the discretion to determine the format that is most efficient for records production based on organizational resources and sensitivity of information.

The final rule clarifies the provision regarding OFCCP's ability to request records in specific formats. The final rule states that: "[t]he contractor must provide records and other information in any of the formats in which they are maintained, as selected by OFCCP." The final rule language makes clear that the provision will not require contractors to invest time or resources creating records in a specific format, or to create a documented "list" of the formats in which they have documents available. Rather, contractors merely need to inform OFCCP of the formats in which they maintain their records and other information, and allow OFCCP to select the format(s) in which the records or information will be provided. This provision should result in more efficient OFCCP investigations.

Commenters also criticized the proposal to allow OFCCP access to records off-site, particularly as it relates to the security of confidential records. One comment identified an alleged incident where an OFCCP Compliance Officer lost contractor information during a compliance evaluation. In light of this alleged security breach, the comment suggested that contractors should be permitted to determine how records are produced to OFCCP. This commenter did not provide further details of the incident, and OFCCP is unaware of any specific incident such as the one described. Another commenter noted that the language could be interpreted broadly to permit others outside of OFCCP to gain access to vendor data. Yet another comment stated that it may be difficult and time-consuming for contractors to make data accessible to OFCCP off-site.

In order to address the above-referenced concerns, commenters provided several recommendations to modify the proposed language of this section. One comment recommended that OFCCP clarify that the agency is the only entity that may be permitted access to information submitted. Another commenter recommended including language in the final regulation that states that OFCCP is committed to the confidentiality of contractor information and that confidential information related to individual employees is not subject to Freedom of Information Act requests.

The final rule retains the proposed requirement to provide OFCCP off-site access to materials by request. As an initial matter, it is worth noting that access to company records off-site is not a novel approach, as the Executive Order contains no limitation on the location of access for the compliance evaluation, and indeed specifically references off-site access. Thus, this general access regulation conforms to those principles. In light of contractors' increased use of electronic records in multiple locations, OFCCP feels that this change will provide the agency greater flexibility during evaluations and investigations. However, OFCCP modified § 60–300.81 of the final rule in response to comments regarding record confidentiality. Section 60–300.81 now includes the following language: "OFCCP will treat records provided by the contractor to OFCCP under this section as confidential to the maximum extent the information is exempt from public disclosure under the Freedom of Information Act, 5 U.S.C. 552." It is the practice of OFCCP not to release data where the contractor is still in business, and the contractor indicates, and through the Department of Labor review process it is determined, that the data are confidential and sensitive and that release of the data would subject the contractor to commercial harm. This language affirms OFCCP's commitment to ensure confidentiality to the fullest extent allowed by law. Further, all OFCCP Compliance Officers receive training on the importance of keeping records confidential during compliance evaluations and complaint investigations. OFCCP will continue to stress this policy to ensure that contractor records are kept secure by the agency at all times, and will work with contractors to respond to specific data confidentiality concerns they may have.

Appendix A to Part 60–300—Guidelines on a Contractor's Duty To Provide Reasonable Accommodation

The proposed rule included three changes to Appendix A which would mandate activities that previously were only suggested. First, in the third sentence of paragraph 2 and the fourth sentence of paragraph 5, we proposed changing the language to reflect the change to § 60–300.42(d) requiring a contractor to seek the advice of disabled veterans in providing reasonable accommodation. Second, in the last sentence of paragraph 4, the NPRM proposed requiring that disabled veterans, in the event an accommodation would constitute an undue hardship for the contractor, be given the option of providing the accommodation or paying the portion of the cost that constitutes the undue hardship for the contractor, consistent with the change to § 60–300.21(f)(3).

Finally, in the last sentence of paragraph 9, the proposed rule is changed to require that a contractor must consider the totality of the circumstances when determining what constitutes a "reasonable amount of time" in the context of available vacant positions.

Comments describing concerns with the first and second proposed changes were addressed in the discussion of §§ 60–300.42(d) and 60–300.21(f)(3), respectively. We received no comments on the third proposed change. Accordingly, Appendix A is incorporated into the final rule as proposed, with small changes to update the references to specific accommodations to reflect current technology and terminology (such as replacing the reference to "telecommunication devices for the deaf (TDD)" to the more current "text telephones (TTYs)," and including modern technology such as speech activated software, and as set forth in the discussion of paragraph 9 of the EO Clause in § 60–300.5. Consistent with the change to § 60–300.42(c), we also deleted the words "and wish to benefit under the contractor's affirmative action program" from paragraph 1.

Appendix B to Part 60–300—Sample Invitation to Self-Identify

The proposed rule amends Appendix B consistent with the proposed changes to the self-identification regulation found at § 60–300.42. The majority of comments pertaining to aspects of Appendix B were addressed in the discussion of § 60–300.42 above. Separately, three commenters stated specifically that the proposed Appendix B would be a useful tool for contractors. One commenter stated that OFCCP should make clear that a goal of a reasonable accommodation is to enable an individual with a disability "to perform the essential functions of the job," as this is the accepted legal standard, while the proposed paragraph 2 of Appendix B uses "to perform the job properly and safely." OFCCP adopts this commenter's language into the final rule. OFCCP also eliminates from paragraph 2 of the sample invitation to self-identify the option to "choose not to provide this information." This option may serve to discourage applicants from self-identifying, and is unnecessary, as applicants who wish not to reveal their protected veteran status may simply choose not to respond to the invitation. Consistent with the change to § 60–300.42(c), paragraph 3 is deleted, and paragraphs 4, 5, and 6 are renumbered, accordingly, as paragraphs 3, 4, and 5. In addition, to address confusion among veterans regarding the scope of the protections afforded by the various veterans' employment rights statutes, the final rule adds clarifying language to paragraph 1 of Appendix B. The new language explains that protected veterans with past, present or future military service, status or obligations may have additional rights under USERRA, including the right to be reemployed by an employer for whom they worked immediately prior to their military service.

Appendix C—Review of Personnel Processes

The NPRM proposed eliminating Appendix C and incorporating relevant parts of it into § 60–300.44(b). However, as stated in the discussion of § 60–300.44(b), we have eliminated the proposal in the NPRM that required specific personnel process reviews. Accordingly, the final rule reinstates Appendix C, but substitutes the updated term "protected veteran" in paragraphs 1, 2, and 3, in place of "disabled veteran, recently separated veteran, other protected veteran, or Armed Forces service medal veteran."

Regulatory Procedures

Executive Order 12866 (Regulatory Planning and Review) and Executive Order 13563 (Improving Regulation and Regulatory Review)

OFCCP is issuing this final rule in conformity with Executive Orders 13563 and 12866, which direct agencies to assess all costs and benefits of available regulatory alternatives and, if regulation is necessary, to select regulatory approaches that maximize net benefits (including potential economic, environmental, public health and safety effects, distributive impacts, and equity). Executive Order 13563 emphasizes the importance of quantifying both costs and benefits, of reducing costs, of harmonizing rules, and of promoting flexibility.

This rule is economically significant and major as it will have an annual effect on the economy of $100 million or more. EO 12866 § 3(f). OFCCP estimates that first year costs in the rule to be in the range of $177,296,772 to $483,560,138. This includes (1) One-time costs; (2) recurring costs; (3) capital start-up costs; and (4) operations and maintenance costs.[23] The range of recurring costs of the final rule in subsequent years will be approximately $120,386,058 to $347,617,359.[24] This rule was reviewed by the Office of Management and Budget.

A. Introduction

The final regulatory impact analysis is substantially different from the preliminary regulatory impact analysis presented in the VEVRAA NPRM based on comments received during the public and interagency comment period. First, the final rule has been scaled down significantly in order to minimize the costs employers would incur under the rule. Second, OFCCP modified the contractor establishment count to more accurately reflect the number of contractors that would be impacted by the rule. Third, the analysis acknowledges that some establishments and or companies may incur higher costs under the final rule and illustrates a range of costs to implement several provisions.

1. Eliminated Several Provisions in the NPRM

While all the proposals in the NPRM had value, after assessing the comments received on the NPRM published on April 26, 2011, we made several changes in the final rule. OFCCP reconsidered whether the cost of several proposals in the NPRM could be justified by their potential benefits, and whether alternative methods or approaches could achieve comparable or acceptable benefits for less cost or burden. We retain in the final rule those provisions proposed in the NPRM that create greater contractor accountability through enhanced data collection and recordkeeping. Therefore, as an example, the final rule does not require each contractor to establish three "linkage" agreements with various veteran service organizations to facilitate recruitment.

Other examples of how the final rule takes a tailored approach include, but are not limited to, eliminating the proposal that contractors reproduce the entire equal opportunity clause in all contracts and subcontracts; the proposal that contractor staff training must cover a list of specific training items; the proposal to mandate annual reviews of personnel policies; and the proposal to mandate that contractors identify the official responsible for the affirmative action program on all communications are also eliminated in the final rule.

2. Increased the Contractor Establishment Count

In light of the comments concerning the size of the Federal contractor

[23] These costs include both establishment and contractor company level costs.

[24] The recurring costs include those related to the recurring substantive provisions and the copying costs identified in the Operations and Maintenance Costs section.

establishment universe, OFCCP reexamined the original number of 108,288 contractor establishments it used in the NPRM. For the final rule, we combined Equal Employment Data System (EEDS) data with several other information sources.[25] We used FY 2009 EEDS data to determine the number of Federal contractor establishments with 50 or more employees; this resulted in a total of 87,013 Federal contractor establishments.[26] An additional 10,518 establishments were identified through a cross-check of other contractor databases for a total of 97,531 establishments. Covered Federal contractors must develop AAPs for all of their establishments, even those with fewer than 50 employees. Therefore, OFCCP added an additional 73,744 establishments, using EEO–1 and FPDS data, for an adjusted total of 171,275 Federal contractor establishments affected by the final rule. This adjustment to the methodology for calculating the number of contractors and contractor establishments results in a 58 percent increase over the earlier estimate used in the NPRM.

We received comments on the estimated number of contractor establishments as well, including recommending an establishment count of 285,390 using the VETS annual report. While OFCCP declines to exclusively rely on the VETS report number, we present an estimated high end for the range of the cost of the rule based on a contractor establishment number of 251,300 for comparison. This number is based on 2010 VETS data from their pending Information Collection Request.[27]

All costs and hours in the burden analysis of this final rule are calculated using adjusted numbers of Federal contractor establishments. Federally assisted construction contractors are not subject to these regulations and, therefore, are not included in this total. *See* section 60–300.2(n) for the definition of "Government contract."

3. Revised and Increased Burden Estimates

OFCCP received 55 comments concerning overall burden hours from several employer groups and employers, including 21 form letters. Most stated that OFCCP's overall estimate of dollars and hours was much too low. Some commenters included estimates of their own for dollar costs and burden hours. Several commenters specifically expressed concern about the potential burden on smaller contractors, including smaller construction contractors, veteran owned businesses, and service-disabled veteran owned businesses.

OFCCP acknowledges that estimating the precise amount of time each company will take to engage in certain activities will be difficult. However in response to public comments, the final regulatory impact analysis attempts to account for the fact that smaller contractors may not have the same human resources capabilities as larger contractors. Specifically, OFCCP has provided low and high range estimates for certain requirements either based on the comparison of contractor establishment numbers, assumptions about the use of automated application systems and human resources information systems,[28] and/or other factors.

B. The Need for the Regulation

Some commenters stated that OFCCP did not adhere to the requirements of Executive Order 13563 or Executive Order 12866, which require Federal agencies to identify a specific need for any regulation they promulgate. These commenters asserted that the unemployment rate for veterans was an insufficient basis for such "extensive regulations." Another commenter questioned the need for new regulations and asserted that better enforcement of the current regulations would achieve the same goals. Commenters further stated that the anticipated benefits did not outweigh the overall costs of the NPRM.

The current regulations are simply not sufficient to facilitate the process of connecting veteran job-seekers with Federal contractors seeking to hire qualified employees. The framework articulating a contractor's responsibilities with respect to affirmative action, recruitment, and placement of veterans has remained largely unchanged since the VEVRAA implementing rules were first published in 1976. Meanwhile, veterans are returning from tours of duty in Iraq, Afghanistan, and other places around the world. These veterans possess skills and personal qualities that are highly sought after in the job market. However, veterans face substantial obstacles in finding employment upon leaving the service and returning home. Addressing the barriers our veterans face upon returning to civilian life is the focus of a number of Federal efforts, including these revised VEVRAA regulations.

Although progress has been made in the employment of veterans, the number of unemployed veterans still remains too high, and substantial disparities in unemployment and pay rates continue to persist, especially for some categories of veterans. Annual unemployment rate for post-September 2001 veterans, referred to as "Gulf War-era II veterans," is higher than the rates for all veterans and for non-veterans. In 2012, according to BLS data on the employment situation of veterans for that year, about 2.6 million of the nation's veterans had served during Gulf War era II. The unemployment rate for this category of veterans was 9.9 percent compared to nonveterans at 7.9 percent.[29] In this same year, the unemployment rate for male Gulf War-era II veterans age 18 to 24 was 20.0 percent, higher than the rate for nonveterans of the same age group (16.4 percent).

OFCCP found that process and institutional barriers, and data collection issues are factors contributing to veterans being underutilized in the Federal contractor workforce. We learned much from conducting multiple town hall meetings, webinars, and listening sessions with representatives of the contractor community, state employment services, veterans' organizations and other interested parties to understand those features of the current VEVRAA regulations that work well, those that can be improved, and whether there was a need for new requirements to help effectuate the regulations' goal of increasing

[25] OFCCP determined that the VETS–100 database is not the most appropriate resource for calculating the number of federal contractors and contractor establishments. Among the concerns surrounding this data source are the use of contractor established 12-month reporting timeframes, the degree to which there is overlap or duplication in the VETS–100 and VETS–100A reports, and the absence of an employee threshold for reporting purposes.

[26] A single firm, business, or "entity" may have multiple establishments or facilities. Thus, the number of contractor establishments or facilities is significantly greater than the number of parent contractor firms or companies.

[27] OMB Control Number 1293–0005, Federal Contractor Veterans' Employment Report, VETS–100/VETS–100A, *http://www.reginfo.gov/public/do/PRAViewDocument?ref_nbr=201104-1293-003* (last accessed Aug. 13, 2013).

[28] The human resources system low range estimates assume that most contractors have automated application systems and human resources information systems to meet the data collection requirements of the final rule. The high range estimate is based on the assumption that contractors with 50–100 employees may still use manual application or human resources processes. These contractors would likely expend more time conducting the kind of data collection and analysis required under the final rule.

[29] U.S. Bureau of Labor Statistics, Economic News Release: Employment Situation of Veterans Summary, Table A: *Employment status of the civilian noninstitutional population 18 years and over by veteran status, period of service, and sex, 2011–2012 annual averages*, available online at *http://www.bls.gov/news.release/vet.nr0.htm*.

employment opportunities for qualified protected veterans with Federal contractors. We received information indicating that improvements to the regulations were needed to assist protected veterans in gaining and keeping employment. For instance, OFCCP learned that there were significant problems with contractors submitting their job listings to state agencies in usable formats—a requirement in the VEVRAA statute—which would impede the veteran's ability to learn about job openings with Federal contractors and receive priority referral to contractors with available positions. In addition, the lack of veteran applicant data hindered contractors' ability to assess the success of their outreach and recruitment efforts, and whether alternative outreach methods might attract greater numbers of protected veteran into their applicant pools.

Efforts to address veterans' unemployment must be sustained, multi-faceted, and coordinated; these regulations create an enforcement structure that supports long-term monitoring, self-assessment, data collection and accountability by employers doing business with the Federal government. The benchmark created by the regulations provides contractors with an aspirational hiring target against which they can measure the success of their efforts, and identify any impediments to hiring veterans. The regulations also provide more notice or knowledge to subcontractors by requiring prime contractors to include specific, mandated language in their subcontracts alerting subcontractors to their responsibilities as Federal contractors. This supports voluntary compliance by subcontractors and should increase job opportunities for veterans.

The regulations address concerns surrounding process and institutional challenges related to identifying available veteran job applicants. The regulations clarify the contractor's mandatory job listing requirements and the relationship between the contractor, its agents, and the state employment services that provide priority referral of protected veterans; and create flexibility for contractors when they are establishing formal relationships with organizations that provide recruiting or training services to veterans. The relationships or "linkage agreements" can be established to meet the contractors' specific needs, while assuring outreach to veterans seeking employment.

C. Discussion of Impacts

In this section, we present a summary of the costs associated with the revisions to part 60–300. The estimated cost to contractors is based on Bureau of Labor Statistics data in the publication "Employer Costs for Employee Compensation" (September 2011), which lists total compensation for management, professional, and related occupations as $50.11 per hour and administrative support as $23.72 per hour. OFCCP estimates that 52 percent of the burden hours will be management, professional, and related occupations and 48 percent will be administrative support.

TABLE 1—CONTRACTOR NEW REQUIREMENTS—171,275 ESTABLISHMENTS

Provision	Low cost	High cost
EO Clause, Parag 12	$240,495.10	$240,495.10
EO Clause, Parag 10	534,418.00	534,418.00
300.42	2,101,102.72	2,583,328.54
300.45	2,404,913.60	2,404,913.60
Total	5,280,929.38	5,763,155.20
EO Clause, Parag 4	1,736,859.16	1,736,859.16
300.44(f)(1)	4,328,771.47	4,809,761.68
300.44(f)(3)	3,174,438.00	3,174,438.00
300.44(f)(4)	1,603,263.25	1,603,263.25
300.44(h)	1,068,842.17	1,068,842.17
300.44(k)	3,740,925.75	6,840,549.94
Total	17,256,363.05	20,836,977.45
Reasonable Accommodation	19,010,209.00	19,010,209.00
Capital and Start-up	31,457,911.40	43,429,423.20
Rule Familiarization	8,582,590.25	34,330,361.00
Operations and Maintenance	616,590.00	1,356,498.00
Costs to Companies	80,601,329.83	123,123,360.60

TABLE 2—CONTRACTOR NEW REQUIREMENTS—251,300 ESTABLISHMENTS

Provision	Low cost	High cost
EO Clause, Parag 12	$352,851.59	$352,851.59
EO Clause, Parag 10	784,114.64	784,114.64
300.42	3,102,510.41	3,814,616.30
300.45	3,528,515.87	3,528,515.87
Total	7,767,992.51	8,480,098.40
EO Clause, Parag 4	2,548,372.57	2,548,372.57
300.44(f)(1)	6,351,328.56	7,057,031.73
300.44(f)(3)	4,657.640.94	4,657,640.94
300.44(f)(4)	2,352,343.91	2,352,343.91
300.44(h)	1,568,229.27	1,568,229.27

TABLE 2—CONTRACTOR NEW REQUIREMENTS—251,300 ESTABLISHMENTS—Continued

Provision	Low cost	High cost
300.44(k)	5,488,802.46	10,036,667.35
Total	23,013,764.59	28,267,332.65
Reasonable Accommodation	19,010,209.00	19,010,209.00
Capital and Start-up	46,172,324.20	64,129,119.80
Rule Familiarization	12,592,643.00	50,370,572.00
Operations and Maintenance	904,680.00	1,990,296.00
Costs to Companies	108,650,099.89	171,436,114.44

TABLE 3—COMPLETING PRE-OFFER SELF-IDENTIFICATION

Provision	171,275 Establishments		251,300 Establishments	
	Low cost	High cost	Low cost	High cost
300.42(a)	$96,695,442.00	$212,729,213.00	$141,874,556.25	$312,124,023.75

1. Section 60–300.5 Equal Opportunity Clause

The Equal Opportunity Clause (EO Clause) in the current rule, as well as the VEVRAA statute itself, requires Federal contractors to list their job openings with the state or local employment service delivery system (employment service). *See* 38 U.S.C. 4212(a)(2)(a); 41 CFR 60–300.5(a)(2). Paragraph 2 of the EO Clause in the current regulations does not expressly address the manner in which contractors provide job openings to the employment delivery service system. The NPRM proposed requiring contractors to provide information to the employment service in the manner and format that the employment delivery service system requires. The NPRM estimated that collecting, informing the employment service delivery system and recordkeeping would take 15 minutes per job listing for an average of two listings per year. Some commenters asserted that OFCCP significantly underestimated the number of annual listings or the time required to post a listing, or both.

The final rule clarifies the intent of the provision by stating that contractors need only provide job openings in a format that the employment service delivery system will accept. The clarification in the final rule does not create a new requirement; rather it explains OFCCP's longstanding position regarding the statutory requirement to list job openings. This position is explained in publically available Frequently Asked Questions (FAQs), published several years ago, addressing the various ways contractors must list job openings, the documentation contractors must maintain to demonstrate compliance, what contractors should do if they send an email and it is returned from the state as undeliverable, and how to comply with the job listing requirement by using third parties.[30] Therefore, the final rule does not assess burden for complying with existing requirements concerning listing job openings in a manner permitted by the employment service delivery system. We also do not assess burden for new language clarifying that contractors may utilize privately run third-party services or exchanges to list its jobs, in addition to listing them with the employment service delivery system.

Paragraph 4 of the EO Clause of the current rule requires contractors to provide the appropriate employment service delivery system with the name and location of each of the contractor's hiring locations. *See* 41 CFR 60–300.5(a)(4). The NPRM proposed requiring a contractor to inform the employment service delivery system that: (1) It is a Federal contractor; (2) it is requesting priority referrals of protected veterans; and (3) it is providing the contact information for the hiring official at each location in the state. The NPRM also proposed requiring contractors to provide the employment service with the contact information for each external job search organization used by the contractor. Several contractors use job search and human resources firms to fill job vacancies in the belief that using these firms saves them money, gives them greater staffing flexibility and increases their access to talent. These firms can search for, recruit and even train contractors' employees using human resource software solutions that work independently or that can be integrated into a contractor's own human resources information system. The NPRM estimated that 25 percent of the Federal contractors use job search or similar firms and that 20 minutes would be required to provide the four types of information proposed in the NPRM. The status of the employer as a Federal contractor, the need for priority referrals, the hiring official's contact information and the information identifying the contractor's external job search firm are all pieces of information that should be readily available to the contractor and any job search or human resources firm the contractor uses. Transmission of the information via email or facsimile is not complex or time consuming and can be done from a desktop computer, standalone facsimile or business multi-function printer. We received no comments on this burden estimate.

The final rule adopts proposed paragraph 4 of the EO Clause and further clarifies the unchallenged burden analysis for this provision. OFCCP estimates a total of 15 minutes to ensure that the new information required by the regulation is provided to the employment service. Because submitting job openings is already required by paragraph 2 of the EO Clause, and burden was assessed for that provision, we are only assessing additional burden for including a few lines of text to identify the contractor as a "Federal contractor, request priority referrals, and identify the contractor's official that is responsible for hiring.

[30] Office of Federal Contract Compliance Programs, Jobs for Veterans Act Frequently Asked Questions, Can a contractor satisfy the job listing requirement by sending to the appropriate employment delivery system a link to a specific job opening posted on the contractor's Web site? *http://www.dol.gov/ofccp/regs/compliance/faqs/jvafaqs.htm#Q20* (last accessed April 16, 2012).

This calculation assumes that the required information is readily available within the contractor's human resources department, or the job search or similar firm used by the contractor, or both. It is also assumed that the language is being incorporated into a job listing template and stored electronically, and that this template or similar form is easily accessible for use and revision, as needed. The minimum recurring burden estimate for this provision is 42,819 hours (171,275 contractor establishments × 15 minutes/60 = 42,819 hours). As in the NPRM, OFCCP estimates that 25 percent of contractors, or 42,819, will use outside job search organizations and incur an additional 5 minute burden to simultaneously notify the employment service of the contact information for its outside job search organizations when submitting the required job posting. The burden for this provision is 3,568 hours (42,819 contractor establishments × 5 minutes/ 60 = 3,568 hours). The minimum cost for this provision is approximately $1,736,859.[31]

Assuming there are 251,300 establishments that are impacted by the final rule, the recurring burden for updating existing mandatory job listing templates to include the required information would be 62,825 hours (251,300 contractor establishments × 15/ 60 = 62,825 hours). The burden for providing information regarding job search organizations would be 5,235 hours (251,300 contractor establishments × 25 percent × 5 minutes/60 = 5,235 hours. The cost for this provision would be $2,548,372.

Paragraph 9 of the EO Clause in the final rule clarifies that contractors have a duty to provide notices of employee rights and contractor obligations in a manner that is accessible and understandable to persons with disabilities. The final rule revises the parenthetical at the end of the sentence by replacing the outdated suggestion of "hav[ing] the notice read to a visually disabled person" as an accommodation with the suggestion to provide Braille, large print, or other versions that allow persons with disabilities to read the notices themselves. The NPRM estimated that contractors would take 10 minutes to receive this accommodation request, provide the document in an alternative format and maintain a record of its disposition of the request. Upon further consideration, OFCCP determines that there is no additional cost for this provision. We specifically note that the nondiscrimination requirements of VEVRAA currently require contractors to provide reasonable accommodation upon request. *See* 41 CFR 60–300.21(f). Therefore, this modification in the final rule simply updates the examples of possible accommodations that contractors may provide to a visually impaired person, and does not impose a new obligation on contractors.

Paragraph 9 of the final rule also allows, but does not require, contractors to post notices regarding employee rights and its equal employment opportunity obligations electronically if the contractor provides computers that can access the electronic posting to employees working remotely or has actual knowledge the employees have access to the postings. This provision simply provides contractors with another, more expedient, way to meet their existing obligations. OFCCP estimates no additional burden for contractors that opt to post relevant notices electronically.

Paragraph 9 of the final rule requires contractors to electronically post a notice of job applicants' rights if the contractor utilizes an electronic application. The existing regulations require contractors to post notices regarding employee rights and equal employment opportunity obligations in conspicuous places for employees and applicants. *See* 41 CFR 60–300.5(a)(9). The final rule clarifies how contractors can meet this existing obligation for on-line applicants. Therefore, there is no new burden for this provision.

The NPRM proposed adding a new paragraph 13 to the EO Clause that would require contractors to add to their solicitations and advertisements that they are an equal opportunity employer of veterans covered under VEVRAA. Under existing Federal requirements, including EO 11246, contractors are required to state in solicitations and advertisements that the company is an equal opportunity employer. *See* 41 CFR 60–1.4(a)(2). The final rule adopts the proposed requirement, now paragraph 12 of the EO Clause, requiring contractors to state in all solicitations and advertisements that they are equal opportunity employers of protected veterans. The NPRM estimated that it would take contractors 1 minute to comply with this provision. We received one comment from an employer group stating that ads would cost more due to their increased word length. OFCCP acknowledges that some contractors may experience an increased cost in light of this requirement. However, based on the comments that OFCCP received on this issue, there is no indication that this would be a significant problem for a substantial number of contractors. In fact, the cost of some advertisements and solicitations are based on size (i.e., quarter-page, half-page, full-page) or number of lines, and the type of listing. Moreover, the cost of an advertisement will also depend on the publication's circulation and location. The number of words in the text actually appears be a lesser factor when determining cost. After some research, OFCCP determined that the average cost per word nationally is between .10 and .20 cents for a classified advertisement. Therefore, the cost would not be greatly impacted by adding two words, "protected veterans," to the advertisement.

Information from OFCCP field staff indicates that many contractors already include "veterans" in their equal employment opportunity statement for solicitations, particularly universities and defense contractors. These entities are often seeking the particular skills and training that veterans receive while in the military. Therefore, based on field experience evaluating contractor practices, OFCCP estimates that approximately 55 percent of contractors, or 94,201, currently comply with this requirement. OFCCP estimates that the remaining 77,074 contractors will have a one-time burden of 5 minutes for amending their existing standard equal employment opportunity statement to include "protected veterans" or similar language. Though no commenter specifically objected to the 1 minute estimate of time required to incorporate the reference to veterans into an existing form or template, OFCCP determined that additional time appears justified and adjusted the time required from 1 minute to 5 minutes in the final rule to ensure that the document is revised, saved or uploaded so that it is readily available for use. Therefore, the total burden for this provision is 6,423 hours (77,074 contractor establishments × 5 minutes/60 = 6,423 hours). The total cost of this provision is approximately $240,495.

Assuming there are 251,300 establishments impacted by the final rule, the burden for this provision would be 9,424 hours (113,085 contractor establishments × 5 minutes/ 60 = 9,424 hours). The total cost of the provision would be $352,852.

Paragraph 10 of the EO Clause in the final rule, originally paragraph 11 in the

[31] All of the estimated costs to contractors is based on Bureau of Labor Statistics data in the publication "Employer Costs for Employee Compensation" (September 2011), which lists total compensation for management, professional, and related occupations as $50.11 per hour and administrative support as $23.72 per hour. OFCCP estimates that 52 percent of the burden hours will be management, professional, and related occupations and 48 percent will be administrative support.

NPRM, clarifies that the existing requirement to notify labor unions about a contractor's affirmative action efforts also includes notifying them of the contractor's nondiscrimination obligations. This provision in the NPRM is adopted as proposed. No additional burden is created by this clarification of an existing requirement.

Paragraphs 1, 3, 5–8, and 11–12 of the EO Clause in the final rule remain unchanged from the current rule. Consequently, no burden is created.

Section 41 CFR 60–300.5(d) currently allows contractors to incorporate the EO Clause into contracts by reference. Further, the EO Clause is considered part of every covered contract and subcontract even if it is not physically incorporated into the contract. *See* 41 CFR 60–300.5(e). The NPRM proposed requiring that the entire EO Clause be included verbatim in Federal contracts. The NPRM estimated that it would take 1 minute for contractors to copy and paste the clause into its contracts. We received six comments on the burden created by this paragraph, all opposing the requirement to include the entire EO Clause verbatim in contracts. The commenters stated that this requirement would be too burdensome, as the length of a contract, subcontract, or purchase order would increase greatly in size, causing contracts to be rewritten, and that the EO Clause could not, as we had suggested, be readily cut and pasted into these documents. Commenters requested retaining incorporation by reference, consistent with other statutory and equal opportunity requirements. In light of these comments, the final rule permits incorporation of the EO Clause, with the addition of some additional language that OFCCP has provided in the regulatory text summarizing VEVRAA's purpose. OFCCP estimates that contractors will spend approximately 15 minutes modifying existing contract templates to ensure the additional language is included. The burden for this provision is 14,273 hours (171,275 contractor establishments × 5 minutes/ 60 = 14,273 hours). The cost for this provision is $534,418.

Assuming there are 251,300 establishments impacted by the final rule, the burden for this provision would be 20,942 hours (251,300 contractor establishments × 5 minutes/ 60 = 20,942 hours). The cost for this provision would be $784,115.

To align with the incorporation by reference approach in 41 CFR 60–300.5(d), the final rule section 60–300.5(e) reverts back to the current language in the regulations. That language considers the EO Clause a part of the contract whether or not it is physically incorporated into a written contract and whether or not there is a written contract. No new burden is created by reverting back to the existing language.

2. Section 60–300.21 Prohibitions

The NPRM proposed clarifying that an individual who rejects a reasonable accommodation made by the contractor may still be considered a qualified disabled veteran if the individual subsequently provides or pays for a reasonable accommodation. *See* 41 CFR 300.21(f)(3). The final rule retains the proposals in the NPRM; however, no new burden is created.

3. Section 60–300.40 Applicability of the Affirmative Action Program Requirement

The final rule adopts the small change to paragraph (c) of this section. The change specifies that the official designated by the contractor pursuant to § 60–300.44(i) reviews and annually updates the contractor's affirmative action program. This change reflects the intent of the existing language. No burden is generated by this change.

4. Section 60–300.41 Availability of the Affirmative Action Program

Though changes to this section were proposed in the NPRM, OFCCP is not incorporating those proposals into the final rule. Instead, the final rule retains the language in the existing § 60–300.41, with a small adjustment to clarify that contractors do not need to include the data metrics required by § 60–300.44(k) in their AAP, due to commenters' concerns about confidentiality. This small clarification creates no new or additional burden.

5. Section 60–300.42 Invitation to Self-Identify

The current regulation requires the contractor to invite applicants who are disabled veterans, as defined in section 60–300.2, to self-identify only after making an offer of employment, subject to two exceptions. *See* 41 CFR 60–300.42(a). For all other veterans protected by part 60–300, the current regulation requires the contractor to invite the applicant to self-identify "before the applicant begins his or her employment duties." *See* 41 CFR 60–300.42(b).

The final rule retains the mandatory pre-offer invitation to self-identify as a "protected veteran" in § 60–300.42(a), but eliminates the language proposed in paragraphs (a)(1) and (a)(2) describing the conditions under which pre-offer invitations of disabled veterans are legally allowed because contractors found this language confusing. The post-offer invitation to self-identify that is in the existing rule remains in the final rule. Finally, instead of requiring contractors to seek input from applicants regarding accommodation, the final rule suggests that they should do so. The NPRM estimated that it would take contractors 1 minute to copy and paste an OFCCP sample invitation to identify into a separate form for electronic and paper applications. The NPRM also estimated burdens for veterans to fill out the self-identification form.

OFCCP received 11 comments opposing the proposed new pre-offer inquiry requirement in section 60–300.42(a). The comments generally stated that the estimated burden was too low because, even with the sample invitations OFCCP included as Appendix B to the regulation, contractors would still need to rewrite existing self-identification forms and modify or update their human resources or applicant tracking systems.

Based on feedback from commenters, OFCCP modified its approach to this calculation. OFCCP's estimate is based on the assumption that modifications to a contractor's application system would be conducted at the parent company level.[32] This estimate distinguishes between contractors with web-based or automated application systems and those relying on manual or paper-based systems. Larger contractors, those with more than 100 employees are more likely to have web-based systems. OFCCP estimates that 72 percent of contractors utilize web-based application systems.[33] Working at the corporate level, contractors will take 1.5 hours to review and retrieve existing sample invitations to self-identify, adopt the sample "as is" or make revisions to their existing form, save the invitation to self-identify and incorporate the document in the contractor's application form. This burden estimate

[32] The EEO–1 data base separately identifies contractor entities (companies) and the facilities that comprise them. The FPDS–NG data base, by contrast, identifies contractor facilities, but does not identify the larger entities of which they are a part. OFCCP utilized the ratio (approximately 3.7) of parent companies to number of establishments from the EEO–1 data to determine that among the universe of 171,275 establishments there are approximately 45,996 Federal contractor companies.

[33] Based on EEO–1 data on the number of establishments 100 or fewer employees we determined that 28% were at this level and would likely have manual systems as "smaller" establishments. Moreover, we used a 100 employee threshold as a cut-off for small employers for application of the 7% goal at the workforce or EEO–1 job category level.

should be considered in conjunction with the start-up costs associated with this rule. OFCCP allotted 20 hours in the VEVRAA final rule to modify human resources information systems or establish a process to comply with the rules' new data collection requirements. This is in addition to costs specified for incorporating the invitation to self-identify in the application process. Taken together, contractors will have over 21 hours to modify their existing application process. The burden for these contractors would be 49,676 hours (33,117 contractor companies × 1.5 hours = 49,676 hours). The remaining contractors would simply have to incorporate the invitation to self-identify in paper applications. OFCCP estimates this will take approximately 30 minutes. The burden for these contractors would be 6,440 hours (12,879 contractor companies × 30 minutes/60 = 6,440 hours). The minimum cost for this provision is approximately $2,101,103.

If all contractors used a web-based application the one-time burden of preparing the form and making the IT changes for this provision is 68,994 hours (45,996 contractor companies × 90 minutes/60 = 68,994 hours). The maximum cost for this provision is $2,583,328.

Assuming there are 251,300 establishments, or 67,919 contractor companies,[34] in OFCCP's jurisdiction, contractors working at the corporate level will take 1.5 hours to review and retrieve existing sample invitations to self-identify, adopt the sample "as is" or make revisions to their existing form, save the invitation to self-identify and incorporate the document in the contractor's application form. The burden for these contractors would be 73,352 hours (48,901 contractor companies × 1.5 hours = 73,352 hours). The remaining contractors would simply have to incorporate the invitation to self-identify in paper applications. OFCCP estimates this will take approximately 30 minutes. The burden for these contractors would be 9,509 hours (19,017 contractor companies × 30 minutes/60 = 9,509 hours). The minimum cost for this provision would be approximately $3,102,510.

If all contractors used a web-based application, the one-time burden of preparing the form and making the IT changes for this provision is 101,879 hours (67,919 contractor companies × 90 minutes/60 = 101,879 hours). The maximum cost for this provision would be approximately $3,814,616.

Applicants for available positions with covered Federal contractors will have a minimal burden complying with section 60–300.42(a) in the course of completing their application for employment with the contractor. Section 60–300.42(a), on pre-offer self-identification, requires contractors to invite all applicants to self-identify whether or not they are a protected veteran. OFCCP estimates that there will be a minimum of 15 applicants per job vacancy for on average 15 vacancies per year. OFCCP further estimates that it will take applicants approximately 5 minutes to complete the form. The burden for this provision is 3,211,406 hours (171,275 contractors × 15 listings × 15 applicants × 5 minutes/60 = 3,211,406 hours). The minimum costs for this provision is $96,695,442. OFCCP estimates that there will be a maximum of approximately 33 applicants per job vacancy for on average 15 vacancies per year per establishment. OFCCP further estimates that it will take applicants approximately 5 minutes to fill out the self-identification form. The burden for this provision is 7,065,093 hours (171,275 contractors × 15 listings × 33 applicants × 5 minutes/60 = 7,065,093 hours). The maximum costs for this provision would be $212,729,213.

Assuming there were 251,300 establishments impacted by the final rule, the minimum burden for this provision would be 4,711,875 hours (251,300 contractors × 15 listings × 15 applicants × 5 minutes/60 = 4,711,875 hours). The minimum costs for this provision would be $141,874,556. OFCCP estimates that there will be a maximum of approximately 33 applicants per job vacancy for on average 15 vacancies per year per establishment. OFCCP further estimates that it will take applicants approximately 5 minutes to fill out the self-identification form. The burden for this provision is 10,366,125 hours (251,300 contractors × 15 listings × 15 applicants × 5 minutes/60 = 10,366,125 hours). The maximum costs for this provision would be $312,124,024.

Several other changes to section 60–300.42 do not create new burdens or costs to contractors. Section 60–300.42(b) of the final rule carries forward the existing requirement that contractors invite voluntary self-identification of all applicants post-offer. Section 60–300.42(c) of the final rule revises paragraph (c) of this section by deleting the second sentence of the parenthetical at the end of the paragraph. Neither of these provisions includes a new substantive requirement.

Section 60–300.42(d) of the final rule does not incorporate the proposal in the NPRM that would have required contractors to ask disabled veterans whether any necessary reasonable accommodation is needed, and if so, engage in an "interactive process" regarding reasonable accommodation. Instead, the final rule retains the language in the existing rules which is permissive and also eliminates the parenthetical text that provides an example of when a contractor could make an inquiry about a reasonable accommodation. The text is unnecessary and likely confusing. We note that several comments suggested that the proposed change in the NPRM does not take into account the administrative burden associated with ascertaining whether an individual is legally entitled to an accommodation and to research alternative sources of funding for requested accommodations when the accommodation is financially burdensome. We are using the existing regulatory language in the final rule and, therefore, are no longer creating a new burden.

6. Section 60.300.43 Affirmative Action Policy

The final rule clarifies that the nondiscrimination requirements of VEVRAA are limited to protected veterans and that claims of reverse discrimination may not be brought by individuals who do not fall into one of the "protected veteran" categories. No burden is incurred by this clarification because the final rule merely deleted the phrase ". . . because of status as a . . ."

7. Section 60–300.44 Required Contents of the Affirmative Action Program

Section 60–300.44(a) Policy Statement

Section 60–300.44(a) of the final rule clarifies the contractor's duty to make the equal opportunity policy statement accessible to all employees. The final rule revises the parenthetical at the end of the sentence by replacing the outdated suggestion of "hav[ing] the notice read to a visually disabled person" as an accommodation with the suggestion to provide Braille, large print, or other versions that allow persons with disabilities to read the notices themselves. It also requires the policy statement to include the attitude of the top United States executive, such as the Chief Executive Officer (CEO) or the President of the United States Division of a foreign company, toward

[34] OFCCP utilized the same ratio (approximately 3.7) of parent companies to number of establishments from the EEO–1 data to determine that among the universe of 251,300 establishments there are approximately 67,919 Federal contractor companies

the contractor's affirmative action program.

The NPRM estimated that it would take contractors 10 minutes to receive the request, provide the document in an alternative format, and maintain records of compliance. OFCCP determines that there is no additional cost for this provision in the final rule. The nondiscrimination requirements of OFCCP's regulations currently require contractors to provide reasonable accommodation upon request. *See* 41 CFR 60–300.21(f). This modification simply updates the example of a possible accommodation that contractors may provide to a visually impaired person, and does not impose a new obligation on contractors. Similarly, no burden is associated with requiring that the contractor indicate the CEO's support for the affirmative action program rather than his or her "attitude on the subject matter."

Section 60–300.44(b) Review of Personnel Processes

Section 60–300.44(b) currently outlines the requirements for reviewing personnel processes to ensure that they provide for consideration of protected veteran applicants. The NPRM proposed requiring contractors to review their personnel processes on an annual basis to ensure that their obligations are being met, and mandated several steps that contractors must take as part of the review process, including: (1) Identifying the vacancies and training programs for which protected veteran applicants and employees were considered; (2) providing a statement of reasons explaining the circumstances for rejecting protected veterans for vacancies and training programs; and (3) describing the nature and type of accommodations for special disabled veterans who were selected for hire, promotion, or training programs. The NPRM estimated that it would take contractors 15 minutes per listing to identify vacancies; 15 minutes to identify training programs; 30 minutes to provide a statement of the reasons for rejecting protected veterans for vacancies and training programs; and 30 minutes per accommodation request. Commenters stated that the burden for performing this review would be significantly higher than OFCCP estimated since contractors would have to update human resources information systems to track the relevant data.

In response to the comments received, the final rule does not adopt the proposals in the NPRM but retains the existing language in 60–300.42(b) and no new burden is created.

Section 60–300.44(c) Physical and Mental Qualifications

The current rule requires contractors to "periodically" review physical and mental job qualification standards to ensure that, to the extent the qualification standards screen out qualified, disabled veterans, they are job-related for the position in question and are consistent with business necessity. *See* 41 CFR 60–300.44(c)(1). The NPRM proposed modifying this section to require the reviews annually and contractors to document the methods used to complete the review, the results of the review, and any actions taken in response to the review.

We received several comments regarding this provision expressing concern that the revision would require contractors to review every job on an annual basis whether or not changes occurred, and that OFCCP underestimated the burden. In order to minimize the burden, the final rule retains the existing language in 41 CFR 60–300.44(c)(1). Therefore, there is no new burden for this provision.

Section 60–300.44(c)(3) of the final rule requires contractors to document the specific reasons behind its belief that the "direct threat" defense applies and maintain this document as a confidential medical record. The existing regulations allow contractors to use as a defense to an allegation that a job qualification screened out a disabled veteran that the disabled veteran poses a "direct threat" to the health or safety of the individual or others in the workplace. *See* 41 CFR 60–300.22. A contractor seeking to establish such a defense would have to document its rationale in order to do so. The final rule requires that the contractor create and maintain a summary of the statement of reasons for its direct threat finding. As contractors would already normally document these instances, we assess no burden for this provision.

Section 60–300.44(f) External Dissemination of Policy, Outreach and Positive Recruitment

Section 300.44(f)(1) of the current rule suggests a number of outreach and recruitment activities that a contractor can undertake in order to increase employment opportunities for protected veterans. The NPRM proposed requiring contractors to enter into linkage agreements with three veterans' recruitment sources: (1) The Local Veterans' Employment Representative (LVERs) in the local employment service office nearest the contractor's establishment; (2) one of several other listed organizations and agencies; and (3) one of the veterans' service organizations listed in the National Resource Directory (NRD). The NPRM estimated that it would take an average of 1.5 hours to establish one new linkage agreement for contractors obtaining OFCCP Compliance Officer assistance. The NPRM further estimated that it would take contractors an average of 5.5 hours to establish a linkage agreement without such assistance.

We received 12 comments regarding the potential burden of this requirement. Commenters asserted that this requirement was more burdensome than we had projected. Commenters also asserted that the NPRM's requirement to enter into local agreements would not be practical for many establishments, especially for contractors that recruit in multiple states or nationally, and for contractors in remote locations. In addition, commenters expressed concern about how the proposed provision would impact existing linkages with organizations that may not be included among OFCCP's listed resources. Others objected to the five (5) year recordkeeping requirements.

In response to the comments, OFCCP revised the final rule in several ways. First, OFCCP eliminated the requirement to establish three linkage agreements. The final rule retains the existing language of § 60–300.44(f)(1)(i) which requires that the contractor undertake "appropriate outreach and positive recruitment activities," and then provides a number of suggested resources. No burden is created in the final rule by this provision.

Section 60–300.44(f)(1)(ii) of the final rule requires contractors to send written notification of the company's affirmative action program policies to subcontractors, vendors, and suppliers. The NPRM estimated that it would take contractors 5 minutes to prepare the notification and provide it to its subcontractors via the Internet in a group email and 1 minute to add or subtract any additions or deletions to the email group. The final rule recalculates the estimated burden of this provision. The existing regulations recommend that contractors send written notification of the company's affirmative action policies to subcontractors, vendors, and suppliers. *See* 41 CFR 60–300.44(f)(6). OFCCP's consultation with field staff indicates that approximately 10 percent of contractors, or 17,128, currently implement this recommendation so no additional burden is calculated for this population. At a minimum, OFCCP estimates that the remaining 154,147 contractors will take 15 minutes to prepare the notification and send it to subcontractors, vendors, and suppliers, and an additional 15 minutes to execute the email address changes in the company's email system. The recurring burden for preparing the notice is 38,537 hours (154,147 contractor establishments × 15 minutes/60 = 38,537 hours). Likewise, the IT burden is estimated at 38,537 hours (154,147 contractor establishments × 15 minutes/60 = 38,537 hours). The minimum cost for this provision is $4,328,771. Assuming that all 171,275 establishments incurred the combined 45 minute burden, the maximum cost of this provision is $4,809,762.

Assuming 251,300 establishments would be impacted by the final rule, OFCCP estimates that 226,170 contractors will take 45 minutes to prepare the notification and send it to subcontractors, vendors, and suppliers. The burden for this provision would be 169,628 hours (226,170 contractor establishments × 15 minutes/60 = 169,628 hours). The minimum cost for this provision would be $6,351,328. Assuming that all 251,300 establishments incurred the combined 45 minute burden, the burden would be 188,475 hours (251,300 × 45 minutes/60 = 188,475 ours). The maximum cost for the provision would be $7,057,032.

Section 60–300.44(f)(2)(ii) in the final rule sets forth additional suggested outreach efforts that contractors could engage in to increase its recruitment efforts. The final rule adds an additional resource to paragraph (f)(2)(ii) that contractors are suggested to use, and that is the Veterans Job Bank. No burden is created by this change.

Section 60–300.44(f)(2)(ii)(F) in the final rule is different than in the NPRM, reverting back to the language in the existing regulation. The NPRM stated that contractors "must consider" protected veteran applicants for jobs other than the one for which they applied. The final rule states that contractors "should consider applicants . . ." and the final rule amends the NPRM in that regard. No burden is created by this provision.

Section 60–300.44(f)(3) of the final rule requires the contractor to review the effectiveness of its outreach and recruitment efforts annually. In response to comments that OFCCP underestimated the time necessary to conduct the annual review, the final rule increases the time to comply with this provision from 20 to 30 minutes. OFCCP expects that contractors will conduct this assessment in conjunction with the correlating assessments required under EO 11246 and section 503 of the Rehabilitation Act (section 503). OFCCP believes that if a contractor has been complying with its recruitment, outreach, data collection, and recordkeeping responsibilities throughout the affirmative action program year, as well as its general obligation under § 60–300.40(c) to review and update its affirmative action program on an annual basis (which includes its outreach and recruitment efforts, *see* § 60–300.44(f)), it will take an average of 30 additional minutes for the contractor to conduct the specific effectiveness assessment of its outreach and recruitment efforts, which would include a simple comparison of the annual raw data on applicants and hires that contractors collect pursuant to § 60–300.44(k) to previous years' data, as well as their hiring benchmark, and determining in light of these numbers and any other relevant circumstances whether adjustments in their outreach efforts is necessary. OFCCP estimates that 1 percent of contractors are first-time contractors during an abbreviated affirmative action program year and will be unable to complete the review. The recurring burden for this provision is 84,781 hours (169,562 contractor establishments × 30 minutes/60 = 84,781 hours). The estimated cost for this provision is $3,174,438.

Assuming that 251,300 establishments would be impacted by the final rule, the burden for this provision would be 124,394 hours (248,787 contractor establishments × 30 minutes/60 = 124,394 hours). The cost for this provision would be $4,657,641.

Section 60–300.44(f)(4) of the final rule is a recordkeeping provision. In the final rule, this provision requires contractors to document all the outreach and recruitment activities they undertake to comply with the obligations of this paragraph, and retain these documents for a period of 3 years. Under the existing regulations, contractors are required to establish meaningful outreach and recruitment contacts. Consequently, contractors' outreach and recruitment should already be the subject of some documentation. This documentation may take several forms. It may include, for example, the numbers and types of outreach and recruitment events, the targeted groups(s) or types of participants for each event, the dates or timeframes, location of the events, and who conducted and participated in the outreach and recruitment on behalf of the contractor. OFCCP estimates that it will take contractors 15 minutes to maintain this basic outreach and recruitment documentation, much of which would typically be generated as a result of their obligations pursuant to other provisions in the regulations. This includes IT time to make the software configuration needed to tell the system to store the data for an additional year. The recurring burden for this provision is 42,819 hours (171,275 contractor establishments × 15 minutes/60 = 42,819 hours). The estimated cost for this provision is $1,603,263. Assuming there are 251,300 establishments impacted by the final rule, the burden for this provision would be 62,825 hours (251,300 contractor establishments × 15 minutes/60 = 62,825 hours). The cost for this provision would be $2,352,344.

Section 60–300.44(g) Internal Dissemination of Policy

The final rule adopts the proposed language in section 60–300.44(g)(1) without change. This section requires contractors to develop the internal procedures listed in paragraph (g)(2) of this section to communicate to employees its obligation to engage in affirmative action efforts to employ and advance in employment qualified protected veterans. No additional burden is assessed here because the existing regulations require the development of internal dissemination procedures.

The NPRM proposed, in paragraph (g)(2), making a number of currently suggested actions in this section mandatory, including incorporating the affirmative action policy in company policy manuals, informing all applicants and employees of the contractor's affirmative action obligations, and conducting meetings with management and company leadership to ensure they are informed about the contractor's obligations. The NPRM also proposed requiring contractors to hold meetings with employees at least once a year to discuss the company's affirmative action policy. The NPRM estimated that it would take contractors 15 minutes to download an OFCCP training module or 10 hours for contractors to develop their own training that communicates the company's affirmative action obligations.

We received 12 comments concerning the potential burden associated with this paragraph. Commenters asserted that the burden calculation was too low because it did not account for the cost of materials, class time and lost productivity. In order to decrease the cost of the provision, commenters suggested: (1) Allowing contractors to conduct the training during other existing meetings related to equal employment opportunity; (2) training managers only, who can then disseminate the information to their staff; or (3) specifically allowing contractors to use Internet based training to satisfy the requirement.

The final rule narrows the scope of the internal dissemination efforts that will be required of contractors from that set forth in the NPRM in section 60–300.44(g)(2)(i). Two of the five elements that the NPRM proposed to require are maintained as requirements in paragraph (g)(2) of the final rule. The two provisions require (1) including the policy in the contractor's policy manual; and (2) notifying union officials of the policy and requesting their cooperation, if the contractor is party to a collecting bargaining agreement. We assume that the majority of Federal contractors have employee manuals and other information stored and available electronically, and thus we believe no additional burden stems from this requirement. Further, the EO Clause currently requires contractors to notify unions of their affirmative action policy so there is no new burden associated with this requirement. *See* § 60–300.5, EO Clause paragraph 10 of the final rule. Section 60–300.44(g)(3) of the final rule suggests, but does not require, the elements that were proposed as requirements in the NPRM. Elements that were suggested in the existing rule remain in paragraph (g)(3) as suggestions in the final rule, with the exception of the recordkeeping provision, which has been eliminated. The provisions in the final rule are in the existing regulation so no new burden is created.

Section 60–300.44(h) Audit and Reporting System

The proposals in the NPRM for § 60–300.44(h) outline the contractor's responsibility for designing and implementing an audit and reporting system for the company's AAP. The only change proposed in the NPRM was for the contractor to document the actions taken to comply with the obligations set forth in this section and to maintain these documents subject to the requirements of § 60–300.80. This would allow both the contractor and OFCCP to evaluate the effectiveness of its audit and reporting system. The final rule adopts the proposal in the NPRM. Under the existing rule, most contractors should document and maintain their analysis of the AAPs as a normal part of their review and assessment process. Compliance officers report that, on request, they review or are provided a range of documents related to the analysis including, for example, reports, summaries and data. In many regards, this provision merely acknowledges and formalizes a current contractor practice. OFCCP estimates that it will take contractors 10 minutes to document the actions taken to comply with section 60–300.44(h) and retain those documents. The recurring burden for this provision is 28,546 hours (171,275 contractor establishments × 10 minutes/60 = 28,546 hours). The estimated cost of this provision is $1,068,842. Assuming there are 251,300 establishments impacted by the final rule, the burden for this provision would be 41,833 hours (251,300 establishments × 10 minutes/60 = 41,833 hours). The cost for this provision would be $1,568,229.

Section 60–300.44(h)(2) requires contractors to undertake action necessary for bringing the program into compliance. This is an existing provision and generates no additional burden.

Section 60–300.44(i) Responsibility for Implementation

The final rule does not incorporate the proposal in the NPRM and the language in the existing regulation that contractors should, but are not required, to take this step is retained. Therefore, no burden is created.

Section 60–300.44(j) Training

The final rule restores the existing regulatory requirements. The final rule does not incorporate the portion of the proposed rule listing specific training items that must be covered by contractors or the specific recordkeeping requirement. However, it does retain the existing rule's general requirement that "[a]ll personnel involved in the recruitment, screening, selection, promotion, disciplinary, and related processes" be trained to ensure that the contractor's affirmative action commitments are implemented. Accordingly, no new burden is created by this provision in the final rule.

Section 60–300.44(k) Data Collection and Analysis

The NPRM proposed adding a new section 60–300.44(k) that would require contractors to maintain several quantitative measurements and comparisons regarding protected veterans who have been referred by state employment services, have applied for positions with the contractor, and those that were hired by the contractor. The final rule retains the NPRM's proposal for contractors to document and maintain applicant and hire data, but eliminates from the final rule the requirement for contractors to collect, maintain, and analyze information on the number of referrals and the ratio of priority referrals of veterans to total referrals, *i.e.*, paragraphs (k)(1), (k)(2), and (k)(3) in the NPRM. The final rule also does not require contractors to calculate applicant, hiring, and job fill ratios in this provision. This eliminates many of the concerns commenters had with regard to this paragraph, and also serves to decrease the burden on contractors. The other calculations mentioned in this section are already required by other sections of part 60–300 or by EO 11246. In response to the comments, OFCCP accounts for the costs of modifying human resources information systems in the Initial Capital and Start-up Costs section, *infra*.

Based on feedback received from public comments expressing concerns about the costs of modifying human resources information systems, OFCCP believes that most contractors will have the capability to conduct the required calculations electronically. Therefore, OFCCP estimates that it will, at a minimum, take contractors 25 minutes to tabulate the applicant data using an electronic database that is integrated with the contractors' human resources information database where the data is typically stored. In addition, we estimate that an additional 10 minutes is required to electronically or otherwise store the records (e.g., the report or other written documentation generated by the calculations that explain the methodology, the data used, and the findings and conclusions; the data used to conduct the calculations for subsequent validation of the results; and other material used by the contractor for the calculations). The recurring burden for this provision is 99,910 hours (171,275 contractor establishments × 35 minutes/60 = 99,910 hours). The minimum cost for this provision is approximately $3,740,926.

However, some commenters noted that companies may have to calculate this information manually. Commenters stated that these calculations could take more than 6 hours. OFCCP declines to adopt the 6 hour estimate for manual calculations in large part because the estimate and the requirements of this section are significantly scaled back from the proposed rule, as the final rule does not require contractors to tabulate referral data or applicant and hiring ratios. Accordingly, starting with the 6 hour estimate and scaling it back given the reduced burden of the final rule, OFCCP estimates that establishments without web-based application systems would take approximately 3 hours to tabulate the information required by this section. The burden for these establishments would be 102,765 hours (34,255 contractor establishments × 3 hours = 102,765). The remaining establishments would incur the 35 minute burden, for a total of 79,928 hours (137,020 contractor establishments × 35 minutes/60 = 79,928 hours). The maximum cost for this provision would be approximately $6,840,550.

Assuming there are 251,300 establishments impacted by the final rule, OFCCP estimates that it will, at a minimum, take contractors 25 minutes to tabulate the applicant data using an electronic database and an additional 10 minutes to electronically or otherwise store the records (e.g., the report or other written documentation generated by the calculations that explain the methodology, the data used, and the findings and conclusions; the data used to conduct the calculations for subsequent validation of the results; and other material used by the contractor for the calculations). The recurring burden for this provision would be 146,592 hours (251,300 contractor establishments × 35 minutes/60 = 146,592 hours). The minimum cost for this provision would be approximately $5,488,802.

OFCCP estimates that establishments without web-based application systems would take approximately 3 hours to tabulate the information required by this section. The burden for these establishments would be 150,780 hours (50,260 contractor establishments × 3 hours = 150,780 hours). The remaining establishments would incur the 35 minute burden, for a total of 117,273 hours (201,040 contractor establishments × 35 minutes/60 = 117,723 hours). The maximum cost for this provision would be approximately $10,036,667.

The NPRM also proposed requiring contractors to maintain that data for 5 years. In response to the comments, the final rule reduces the record retention requirement for section 60–300.44(k) to 3 years. Since some of the data calculations are already required by the implementing regulations for EO 11246, the NPRM estimated that it would take contractors 6 minutes to comply with the additional requirements of this provision. We received nine comments concerning section 60–300.44(k). Generally, these commenters asserted that OFCCP's burden estimate was too low. More specifically, some commenters asserted that OFCCP did not include the costs of new software to collect the data. No new software needs are anticipated; however, a software switch or configuration may be required to tell the system to retain the records for the additional time period. According to an IT professional, this is a simple configuration and should take about 15 minutes to execute. No new burden is added because the change required by the § 60–300.44(f)(4) recordkeeping provision would include this IT change and they would benefit from the economy of scale.

8. *Section 60–300.45 Benchmarks for Hiring*

The NPRM proposed requiring contractors to establish annual hiring benchmarks, expressed as the percent of total hires who are protected veterans that the contractor seeks to hire in the following year. The NPRM proposed allowing contractors to consult a number of different data sources to develop benchmarks that reflect the contractor's unique hiring circumstances. It also required contractors to document the annual hiring benchmark and detail the factors they considered when establishing the benchmark and significance of each of the factors. The NPRM proposed requiring that contractors retain these records for five years.

The NPRM estimated a total of 1 hour per contractor establishment for compliance with this requirement. The NPRM further estimated that it would take contractors 30 minutes to maintain records of the benchmark calculation. We received 10 comments on the proposed requirement. Some commenters asserted that OFCCP significantly underestimated the burden hours and dollar costs of this provision. Commenters stated that OFCCP did not account for the number of openings per contractor per year, costs for software, and data storage. One commenter stated that the burden would be lower than for EO 11246 because OFCCP did not propose to require availability or utilization analysis.

The final rule, in consideration of the comments received, requires the contractor to establish benchmarks in one of two ways. A contractor may use the national percentage of veterans in the civilian labor force as the benchmark, or, the contractor may establish its own benchmark using the method proposed in the NPRM that fits the company's specific needs. OFCCP will provide, and periodically update on its public Web site, the national percentage of veterans in the civilian labor force.

In light of the significant revisions to this section in the final rule, we revised the burden estimate. OFCCP estimates that 90 percent of contractors, or 154,147, will use the national benchmark provided on the OFCCP Web site because it is the easiest approach. The remaining 10 percent of contractors, or 17,128, will likely opt to develop their own benchmarks using the various data sources described in the final rule. We estimate that it will take 5 minutes to access, view and print the national benchmark we will make available on the OFCCP Web site, and another 5 minutes to maintain the relevant documentation for the 90 percent of contractors that use the national average provided by OFCCP. The relevant documentation could, for example, include but is not limited to any information showing the official adoption of the national benchmark by the appropriate officials and how that was communicated to the appropriate staff. We propose creating a specific Web page to make locating the information easy for contractors; moreover, updating the information is the responsibility of OFCCP and not the contractors.

The one-time burden for using the national benchmark is 12,846 hours (154,147 contractor establishments × 5 minutes/60 = 12,846 hours). The burden for maintaining the relevant documentation is 12,846 hours (154,147 contractor establishments × 5 minutes/60 = 12,846 hours).

OFCCP further estimates that it will take the remaining 10 percent of contractors 2 hours to establish their own benchmark and 15 minutes to maintain documentation demonstrating how the benchmark was determined. We expect that this type of documentation would ordinarily be generated during the process of establishing the contractor's benchmark and obtaining its approval by the appropriate internal officials. The amount of detail included in this documentation remains in the discretion of the contractors, but OFCCP suggests that the documentation provide adequate information as to how the benchmark was developed, approved and communicated to the appropriate officials and staff. The one-time burden for these contractors is 34,256 hours (17,128 contractor establishments × 2 hours = 34,256 hours). The burden for maintaining the associated documentation is 4,282 hours (17,128 contractor establishments × 15 minutes/60 = 4,282 hours). The total cost for this provision is approximately $2,404,914.

Assuming that 251,300 establishments would be impacted by the final rule, one-time burden for using the national benchmark would be 37,695 hours (226,170 contractor establishments × 10 minutes/60 = 37,695 hours). The burden for contractors that choose to establish their own benchmarks would be 56,543 hours (25,130 contractor establishments × 2.25 hours = 34,256 hours). The total cost for this provision would be $3,528,516.

Veterans make up 7.25 percent of the employed population.[35] Under the rule, contractors have the option of establishing their own benchmark for employing protected veterans or meeting a benchmark set by OFCCP, currently 8 percent. Assuming all contractors will choose to meet the OFCCP benchmark, OFCCP estimates that Federal contractors would need to hire an additional 205,500 protected veterans.[36] This amounts to approximately one veteran per establishment or three veterans per company. According to research conducted by the Job Accommodation Network (JAN), employers in the study reported that a high percentage (57 percent) of accommodations cost absolutely nothing. For the remaining 43 percent, the typical cost of providing a reasonable accommodation was approximately $500.[37] Assuming that disabled veteran hiring will be consistent with their share of the disabled labor force that consists of individuals with disabilities, then we estimate that 36,330 veterans with disabilities may need accommodations with a total cost of $19,010,209 in the year the target is met and $8,037,516 in recurring costs. The cost of providing these reasonable accommodations is included in the cost of this rule.

9. Section 60–300.60 Compliance Evaluations

The proposed rule set forth several changes to the process the contractor and OFCCP will follow in conducting compliance evaluations. The NPRM added a sentence to paragraph 60–300.60 (a)(1)(i) regarding the temporal scope of desk audits performed by OFCCP, stating that OFCCP "may extend the temporal scope of the desk audit beyond that set forth in the scheduling letter if OFCCP deems it necessary to carry out its investigation of potential violations of this part." The final rule adopts this proposal. No burden is created by this provision, as it merely clarifies existing agency policy to ensure that it is understood and interpreted correctly.

The NPRM, in § 60–300.60(a)(2), proposed correcting an error in the existing regulations in this paragraph, changing the reference from the "requirements of the Executive Order" to the "requirements of Section 4212." The final rule adopts this proposal and replaces the reference to "Section 4212" with "VEVRAA." No burden is created by this change.

Sections 60–300.60(a)(3) and (a)(4) in the NPRM revised these two paragraphs to allow OFCCP to review documents pursuant to a compliance check and conduct focused reviews either on-site or off-site, at OFCCP's option. The proposals are adopted in the final rule but no burden is created.

The NPRM proposed adding a new paragraph (d) to § 60–300.60 detailing a new procedure for pre-award compliance evaluations under VEVRAA, much like the procedure that currently exists in the Executive Order regulations (*see* 41 CFR 60–1.20(d)). This proposal is adopted in the final rule without creation of additional burden.

10. Section 60–300.80 Recordkeeping

Section 60–300.80 describes the recordkeeping requirements that apply to contractors under VEVRAA. The final rule also eliminates the recordkeeping requirements for referral data under the proposed paragraph 5 of the EO Clause and § 60–300.44(k). Consequently, we assess no burden for these provisions.

The final rule includes a three-year recordkeeping requirement, rather than the proposed five-year requirement, for §§ 60–300.44(f)(4), 60–300.44(k), and 60–300.45(c). No new burden is assessed under this section because it is carried under the burden assessed for §§ 60–300.44(f)(4) and 60–300.44(k) and the contractors benefit from the economy of scale. In that section, we determined that no new software needs are anticipated; however, a software switch or configuration may be required to tell the system to retain the records for the additional time period.

11. Section 60–300.81 Access to Records

Section 60–300.81 of the final rule requires contractors to specify all available records formats and allow OFCCP to select preferred record formats from those identified by the contractor during a compliance evaluation. OFCCP completed 4,014 compliance evaluations in Fiscal Year 2011. We estimate fewer evaluations for Fiscal Year 2012. Upon request, the contractor must provide OFCCP information about all format(s), including specific electronic formats, in which the contractor maintains its records and other information. No burden is assessed as there are no recordkeeping or document production requirements.

Commenters criticized the proposal to allow OFCCP access to records off-site, particularly as it relates to the security of confidential records. The final rule retains the proposed requirement to provide OFCCP off-site access to materials by request. However, OFCCP modified § 60–300.81 of the final rule in response to comments regarding record confidentiality.

12. Appendix A, Guidelines on Reasonable Accommodation

We received one comment from an employer association that asserted contractors would have a burden if they were to be assessed liability and costs associated with accommodations to be determined by employees.

Although an individual's preference for a particular reasonable accommodation should be given primary consideration, a contractor is not obligated to provide an employee with the accommodation of his or her choice, as long as the accommodation the contractor provides is effective. Nor does a contractor have to provide an employee with an accommodation that would impose an undue hardship on its operations, create a "direct threat" for the employee or others, or result in a violation of another Federal law. Accordingly, no additional burden is created as asserted by the commenter.

Appendix A is incorporated into the final rule as proposed, with small changes to update the references to specific accommodations to reflect current technology and terminology (such as replacing the reference to "telecommunication devices for the deaf (TDD)" with the more current "text telephones (TTYs)," and including modern technology such as speech activated software, and as set forth in the discussion of paragraph 9 of the EO Clause in § 60–300.5). Consistent with the change to § 60–300.42(c), we also deleted the words "and wish to benefit under the contractor's affirmative action program" from paragraph 1. Because it does not contain new requirements there is no burden associated with Appendix A.

13. Initial Capital or Start-up Costs

Human Resource Information Systems

Several commenters noted that the new data collection requirements in the

[35] Calculation based on unpublished table, *Employment status of persons 18 years and over by veteran status, period of service, sex, race, Hispanic or Latino ethnicity, and disability status, Annual Average 2012* (Source: Current Population Survey). (10,233/141,050)*100=7.25%. The table is available on request from the Bureau of Labor Statistics at the Department of Labor. BLS does not release some tables for a variety of reasons, such as sample size or possibility of confusion. Finally, this estimate includes all veterans, not only the protected veterans.

[36] Based on data from the Bureau of Labor Statistics Quarterly Census of Employment and Wages, OFFCP estimates that approximately 27.4 million employees could be affected.

[37] Job Accommodation Network, "Workplace Accommodations: Low Cost, High Impact," Sept. 1, 2012. *Accommodation and Compliance Series, http://askjan.org/media/lowcosthighimpact.html* (last accessed Aug. 9, 2013).

proposed rule would require modifications to existing human resources information systems (HRIS). In order to estimate the start-up costs for the final rule, OFCCP considered what would be required to modify existing HRIS to track the number of protected veteran applicants and hires. Because contractors must already maintain information on their employees by race/ethnicity and sex, contractors should have some mechanism in place to track the newly required information.

OFCCP assumes that modifications to contractor HRIS will be done at the parent company level. The minimum cost for modifying HRIS is based on the estimate that 72 percent of contractors utilize this kind of electronic system.[38] Based on information from IT professionals, OFCCP estimates it would take each contractor company on average 20 hours to make the needed systems modifications to track applicant and hiring information for protected veterans. This includes IT and administrative professionals to make the changes. The estimated costs for these modifications are based on data from the Bureau of Labor Statistics in the publication "Employer Costs for Employee Compensation" (September 2011), which lists total compensation for a professional of $47.21 per hour. Therefore, the minimum estimated burden for the capital and start-up costs is 666,340 hours (33,317 contractor companies × 20 hours = 666,340 hours). We calculate the total minimum estimated start-up costs as $31,457,911.40 (666,340 hours × $47.21/hour = $31,457,911.40) or $944 per parent company. Assuming all contractor companies utilize HRIS, the maximum burden would be 919,920 hours (45,996 contractor companies × 20 hours = 919,920 hours). We calculate the total maximum estimated start-up costs as $43,429,423 (919,920 hours × $47.21/hour = $43,429,423) or $944 per parent company.

Assuming there are 251,300 establishments in OFCCP's jurisdiction, or 67,919 companies, the minimum estimated burden for the capital and start-up costs would be 978,020 hours (48,901 contractor companies × 20 hours = 978,020 hours). The total minimum estimated start-up costs would be $46,172,324 (978,020 hours × $47.21/hour = $46,172,324) or $944 per parent company. Assuming all contractor companies utilize HRIS, the maximum burden would be 1,358,380 hours (67,919 contractor companies × 20 hours = 1,358,380 hours). We calculate the total maximum estimated start-up costs as $64,129,120 (1,358,380 hours × $47.21/hour = $64,129,120) or $944 per parent company.

[38] Utilizing EEO–1 data, OFCCP estimates that 72 percent of regulated contractor companies have greater than 100 employees and will likely use an electronic human resources system.

5 CFR 1320.3(b)(1)(i)—Reviewing Instructions

Several commenters noted that the proposed rule did not quantify the burden of reading and understanding the VEVRAA revisions on contractors. OFCCP acknowledges that 5 CFR 1320.3(b)(1)(i) requires agencies to include in the burden analysis for new information collection requirements the estimated time it takes for contractors to review and understand the instructions for compliance. In order to minimize the burden, OFCCP will publish several compliance assistance materials including factsheets and "Frequently Asked Questions." OFCCP will also host webinars for the contractor community that will describe the key provisions in the final rule.

OFCCP estimates it will take, at a minimum, 1 hour to have a management professional at each establishment either read compliance assistance materials provided by OFCCP or participate in an OFCCP webinar to learn about the new requirements of the final rule. OFCCP believes that this is a reasonable estimate since there are substantially fewer new requirements in the final rule than proposed in the NPRM. The estimated cost of this burden is based on data from the Bureau of Labor Statistics in the publication "Employer Costs for Employee Compensation" (September 2011), which lists total compensation for a management professional at $50.11. Therefore, the estimated burden for rule familiarization is 171,275 hours (171,275 contractor establishments × 1 hour = 171,275 hours). We calculate the total estimated minimum start-up costs as $8,582,590 (171,275 hours × $50.11/hour = $8,582,590) or $50 per establishment.

Commenters suggested that reviewing the requirements of the final rule would take up to 6 hours. OFCCP declines to adopt this calculation since it is based reviewing the proposed rule which included a significant number of additional requirements that are not in the final rule. Therefore, OFCCP estimates the maximum for reviewing the rule would be 4 hours for a total of 685,100 (171,275 contractor establishments × 4 hour = 685,100 hours). We calculate the total maximum estimated start-up costs as $34,330,361 (685,100 × $50.11/hour = $34,330,361) or $200 per establishment.

Assuming there are 251,300 establishments impacted by the final rule, the estimated minimum burden for the capital and start-up costs would be 251,300 hours (251,300 contractor establishments × 1 hour = 251,300 hours). The total estimated minimum costs would be $12,592,643 (251,300 hours × $50.11/hour = $12,592,643) or $50 per establishment. OFCCP estimates the maximum for reviewing the rule would be 4 hours for a total of 1,005,200 hours (251,300 contractor establishments × 4 hour = 1,005,200 hours). The total maximum estimated maximum costs would be $50,370,572 (1,005,200 hours × $50.11/hour = $50,370,572) or $200 per establishment.

Operations and Maintenance Costs

OFCCP estimates that the contractor will have some operations and maintenance costs in addition to the burden calculated above.

60–300.42 Invitation to Self Identify

OFCCP estimates that the contractor will have some operations and maintenance costs associated with the invitations to self-identify. The contractor must invite all applicants to self-identify at both the pre-offer and post-offer stage of the employment process. Given the increasingly widespread use of electronic applications, any contractor that uses such applications to invite self-identification would not incur copy costs. However, to account for contractors who may still choose to use paper applications, we are including printing and/or copying costs. Therefore, we estimate a single one page form for both the pre- and post-offer invitation. The final rule reduced the number of forms to one instead of two to make the self-identification process less paperwork intensive and to reduce costs. We also estimate an average copying cost of $.08 per page. Assuming contractors using a paper-based application system, used 15 applications for an average of 15 listings per establishment, the minimum estimated total cost to contractors will be $616,590 (34,255 establishments × 225 copies × $.08 = $616,590). Assuming contractors using a paper-based application system, used 33 applications for an average of 15 listings per establishment, the maximum estimated cost to contractors will be $1,356,498 (34,255 establishments × 495 copies × $.08 = $1,356,498).

Assuming that 50,260 of 251,300 establishments with a paper-based application system, used 15 applications for an average of 15 listings per establishment, the minimum estimated total cost to contractors will be $904,680 (50,260 contractor establishments × 225 copies × $.08 = $904,680). Assuming contractors using a paper-based application system, used 33 applications for an average of 15 listings per establishment, the maximum estimated cost to contractors will be $1,990,296 (50,260 contractor establishments × 495 copies × $.08 = $1,990,296).

D. Summary of Benefits

OFCCP's analysis of the benefits of this proposal emphasizes the non-monetary benefits. Pursuant to Executive Order 13563, agencies "may consider (and discuss qualitatively) values that are difficult or impossible to quantify, including equity* * *" in their analysis of the costs and benefits of a proposed regulation. E.O. 13563 § 1(c).

As revised, the final rule creates a number of benefits that will further the equal employment opportunity and affirmative action objectives of VEVRAA. First, the final rule will facilitate the connection of job-seeking veterans with contractors looking to hire. The final rule clarifies the mandatory job listing requirements and requires the contractor to provide additional, regularly updated information to employment service delivery systems to ensure its job openings are listed accurately. This clarification will help to ensure that veterans can easily learn about all available jobs with Federal contractors in their state.

Second, the final rule will ensure that the contractor understands and effectively communicates its affirmative action obligations to its workforce and the other entities with which it does business. This, in turn, will facilitate a greater understanding of the purpose of the affirmative action policies among the contractor's employees and business associates and promote their active support for the contractor's affirmative action efforts.

The final rule also provides increased tools with which the contractor can assess its affirmative action efforts. Until now, the contractor had few objective criteria by which it could measure the effectiveness of its affirmative action efforts. To that end, the final rule requires the contractor to collect data that will enable the contractor and OFCCP to more accurately assess the contractor's efforts. This includes collecting data about applicants so the contractor knows how many protected veterans it is reaching. The final rule also calls for the establishment of a benchmark that can serve as a tool to help the contractor objectively evaluate its recruitment efforts and determine which ones are fruitful in attracting qualified protected veteran candidates, and which ones need to be changed.

Finally, the final rule modifies requirements regarding the manner in which OFCCP conducts its compliance reviews of contractor establishments. These changes include a greater emphasis on OFCCP review of available electronic data, greater flexibility in where reviews take place, and a new procedure for a pre-award compliance review like that currently contained in the EO 11246 regulations. These revisions will allow OFCCP to conduct contractor compliance reviews far more efficiently.

E. Conclusion

OFCCP concludes in the final regulatory impact analysis that the costs of the final rule will range and likely exceed $100 million annually. The variations in costs depend on the number of establishments impacted by the final rule and applicants who respond to the pre-offer invitation to self-identify. Costs will also vary by company depending on their existing infrastructure. We estimate that the lower end costs would be $177,296,772 assuming that there are approximately 171,275 establishments impacted by the final rule. The lower end estimate also relies on the assumption that many of these establishments have some form of electronic application and human resources information systems that would make complying with the rules requirements more efficient. The higher end estimate of $483,560,138 assumes that there are 251,300 establishments impacted by the final rule. The higher end further assumes that a portion of those contractors, primarily smaller ones with fewer employees, would have to expend more personnel time complying with the rules requirements. Therefore, the rule will have a significant economic impact. However, OFCCP believes that the final rule will have extensive benefits for veterans who are prospective and current employees of Federal contractors and Federal contractors. As such, OFCCP concludes that the benefits of the rule justify the costs.

Regulatory Flexibility Act and Executive Order 13272 (Consideration of Small Entities)

The Regulatory Flexibility Act of 1980 (RFA), 5 U.S.C. 601 *et seq.*, requires agencies promulgating rules to consider the impact they are likely to have on small entities. More specifically, the RFA requires agencies to "review rules to assess and take appropriate account of the potential impact on small businesses, small governmental jurisdictions, and small organizations." If a rule is expected to have a "significant economic impact on a substantial number of small entities," the agency must prepare an initial regulatory flexibility analysis (IRFA). If, however, a rule is not expected to have a significant economic impact on a substantial number of small entities, the agency may so certify, and need not perform an IRFA.

Based on the analysis below, in which OFCCP has estimated the impact on small entities that are covered contractors of complying with the requirements contained in this rule, OFCCP certifies that this rule will not have a significant economic impact on a substantial number of small entities.

In making this certification, OFCCP first determined the approximate number of small regulated entities that would be subject to the rule. OFCCP's review of the FY 2009 EEO–1 data revealed that the final rule directly impacts 20,490 Federal contractors with between 50 and 500 employees.[39] OFCCP also analyzed the number of small entities impacted by the rule as compared to the agency's entire universe of regulated entities of approximately 45,996 Federal contractors.[40] OFCCP estimates that approximately 44 percent of the total number of Federal contractors, or 20,490, are small entities with between 50 and 500 employees. OFCCP further refined the analysis to compare the impacted small entities to just the universe of 21,541 small entities in OFCCP's jurisdiction. Under this scenario, approximately 95 percent of small entities would be impacted by the requirements of the rule. Utilizing these comparisons, the final rule may have an impact on a substantial number of small entities.

OFCCP has determined, though, that the impact on entities affected by the

[39] The Small Business Administration (SBA) Office of Advocacy reports that there are 27.4 million small entities in the United States. Since Federal contracts are not limited to specific industries, OFCCP assessed the impact of this final rule on small entities overall. If OFCCP used this approach, the final rule will impact less than .07% of non-employer firms and .34% of employer firms nationwide.

[40] The EEO–1 data base separately identifies contractor entities (companies) and the facilities that comprise them. The FPDS–NG data base, by contrast, identifies contractor facilities, but does not identify the larger entities of which they are a part. OFCCP utilized the ratio (approximately 3.7) of parent companies to number of establishments from the EEO–1 data to determine that among the universe of 171,275 establishments there are approximately 45,996 Federal contractor companies.

final rule would not be significant. In order to further inform our analysis of the economic impact of this rule on small entities, we considered the cost impact of the rule on 2 sizes of entities. We estimated the compliance costs of the final rule on Federal contractors with 50 to 100 employees and 100 to 500 employees. Contractors with less than 50 employees will not be subject to the new affirmative action requirements in subpart C of the final rule. OFCCP's analysis of the impact on small entities compared the estimated cost of compliance with the final rule for small entities to the estimated annual receipts of these entities as provided by the SBA. If the estimated compliance costs are less than 1 percent of the estimated revenues, OFCCP considers it appropriate to conclude that there is no significant economic impact.[41]

Contractors with 50–100 Employees

We estimate the first year cost of this rule to a contractor with 50 to 100 employees to be approximately $1536. The first year cost of the rule is the year with the highest compliance cost as the contractor is incurring the start-up costs of the rule. This primarily includes the time contractors will expend reviewing the new requirements of the rule and the costs of any reasonable accommodations provided to newly hired disabled veterans.

In order to estimate the cost of this rule on an entity with 50 to 100 employees, we are applying the same type of compliance cost structure previously described in the above cost analysis. However, for this small contractor, we assume they would have a manual application process and not require costly human resources information systems changes. We further assume these contractors would expend: 3 hours manually conducting the data analysis required by the new 41 CFR 60–300.44(k); 2 hours establishing their own benchmark; 4 hours having a manager review the new requirements of the rule; and incur approximately $40 in copying costs in order to print out the newly required pre-offer invitation to self-identify for applicants. This also includes a cost of approximately $1,000 for providing reasonable accommodation to two newly hired disabled veterans.[42]

Utilizing data from the SBA Office of Advocacy regarding average receipts for firms, OFCCP determined that entities with 50 to 100 employees average receipts of approximately $14,079,844 per year.[43] The $1,536 costs of compliance with the final rule in the first year would be approximately .01 percent of the average value of receipts for these entities. Therefore, there is not a significant economic impact on contractors with 50 to 100 employees.

Contractors with 100–500 Employees

We estimate the first year cost of this rule to contractors with 100 to 500 employees to be approximately $2,518. The first year cost is the year with the highest compliance cost as the contractor is incurring the start-up costs of the rule. The start-up for contractors with 100 to 500 employees primarily includes modifying any existing web-based application and human resources information systems to include the pre-offer invitation to self-identify, becoming familiar with the new requirements of the rule, and providing reasonable accommodations to any newly hired disabled veterans.

In order to estimate the cost of this rule on contractors with 100 to 500 employees, we are applying the same type of compliance cost structure previously described in the above cost analysis. However, for this small contractor, we assume they may incur more costs analyzing data, establishing benchmarks, and modifying human resources information systems. Specifically, we assume these contractors would expend: 3 hours manually conducting the data analysis required by the new 41 CFR 60–300.44(k); 2 hours establishing their own benchmark; 4 hours having a manager review the new requirements of the rule; and incur approximately $40 in copying costs in order to print out the newly required pre-offer invitation to self-identify for applicants. We further assume these contractors will spend approximately $994 modifying their human resources information systems to accommodate the new pre-offer invitation to self-identify. OFCCP estimates that these contractors would spend approximately $1,000 providing reasonable accommodations to approximately two newly hired disabled veterans.

Utilizing data from the SBA Office of Advocacy regarding average receipts for firms, OFCCP determined that entities with 100 to 500 employees average receipts of approximately $43,547,170 per year.[44] The $2,518 costs of compliance with the final rule in the first year would be approximately .005 percent of the average value of receipts for these entities. Therefore, there is not a significant economic impact on contractors with 50 to 500 employees.

Notwithstanding our determination that there is not a significant impact as a result of this rule, OFCCP considered and implemented a number of alternatives in the final rule as compared to what was proposed in the NPRM. As noted in the preamble, the final rule no longer requires linkage agreements, increased review of personnel processes, increased review of physical and mental job qualifications, and prescribed training on the nondiscrimination and affirmative action obligations for veterans. These changes were made in large part to substantially decrease the burden on small entities.

The significant benefits to covered veterans, as well as to contractors, are discussed extensively in the Section-by-Section and Executive Order 12866 analyses of the final rule. Although the primary objective of the final rule is to strengthen the affirmative action requirements of VEVRAA to employ and advance in employment protected veterans, the rule will benefit both veterans and contractors. As modified, the final rule provides contractors mechanisms for collecting data on protected veteran applicants and employees and promotes accountability by requiring contractors to review the effectiveness of their affirmative action efforts. The benefits of proactive recruitment particularly will accrue to veterans who may face significant barriers in returning to civilian employment. The revisions will also

[41] *Id.* at 18: "The impact could be significant if the costs of compliance with the rule "exceeds 1% of the gross revenues of the entities in a particular sector."

[42] To close the current gap that exists between the target rate of employment as proposed in VEVRAA for veterans and the actual rate, firms would need to hire an additional 205,000 veterans. This amounts to approximately 1 veteran per establishment or 3 veterans per company, assuming 251,300 establishments and 67,919 companies. Moreover, 14.21% of disabled workers in the labor force are veterans. According to research conducted by the Job Accommodation Network (JAN), employers in the study reported that a high percentage (57%) of accommodations cost absolutely nothing. For the remaining 43%, the typical cost of providing a reasonable accommodation was approximately $500.

[43] In order to calculate this figure, OFCCP averaged the total receipts of firms with 50 to 99 employees provided by the SBA, Office of Advocacy. See Firm Size Data, available at *www.sba.gov/advo/research/data.html#us*. Since the data was issued in 2007, OFCCP utilized a compound 2007–2008 Consumer Price Index inflation rate equaling 6.8% (1.0285 × 1.0385) to calculate the 2009 average receipts of $14,079,844 per year.

[44] In order to calculate this figure, OFCCP averaged the total receipts of firms with 100 to 499 employees provided by the SBA, Office of Advocacy. See Firm Size Data, available at *www.sba.gov/advo/research/data.html#us*. Since the data was issued in 2007, OFCCP utilized a compound 2007–2008 Consumer Price Index inflation rate equaling 6.8% (1.0285 × 1.0385) to calculate the 2009 average receipts of $43,547,170 per year.

promote access to a well-trained, job-ready employment pool for contractors.

Paperwork Reduction Act

DATES: Effective Date: This final rule is effective ______.

Compliance Dates: Affected parties do not have to comply with the new information collection requirements in §§ 60–300.5(a)(4); 60–300.42; 60–300.44(f)(4); 60–300.44(g)(3); 60–300.44(k); 60.300.45; and 60–300.80(a) (requirement to maintain records under sections 60–300.44(f)(4), 60–300.44(k), and 60–300.45(c)) until the Department publishes a Notice in the **Federal Register** stating that the Office of Management and Budget (OMB) has approved these information collection requirements under the Paperwork Reduction Act of 1995 (PRA), or until this rule otherwise takes effect, whichever date is later.

The Department notes that no person is required to respond to a collection of information request unless the collection of information has a valid OMB Control Number. The new collections of information contained in this rulemaking have been submitted for review to OMB, in accordance with the PRA, under Control Number 1250–0004. That review is ongoing; consequently, the Control Number has not been activated. OFCCP will publish a Notice in the **Federal Register** announcing the results of OMB's review and the date the information collection requirements will take effect.

The information collection requirements in this final rule relate to the information required to be maintained by contractors regarding their nondiscrimination and affirmative action obligations concerning protected veterans and disclosures workers may make to their employers.

Sections 60–300.40 through 60–300.44 contain currently approved collections of information. Section 60–300.40 requires contractors with 50 or more employees (and contracts of $100,000 or more entered into or modified after December 1, 2003, as set forth in § 60–300.1(b)) to develop a VEVRAA affirmative action program. An affirmative action program is a written program in which contractors annually outline the steps the contractor will take and has already taken to ensure equal employment opportunity for protected veterans. Section 60–300.41 describes a contractor's responsibility to make the affirmative action program available to all employees. Section 60–300.42 outlines the contractor's responsibilities and the process through which applicants are invited to self-identify as a veteran protected under the part 60–300 regulations. Section 60–300.43 describes the breadth of the contractor's affirmative action obligation required by VEVRAA.

Section 60–300.44 outlines the required contents of the affirmative action program. Contractors must develop and include an equal opportunity policy statement in the program. Contractors must also periodically review their personnel processes to ensure that qualified, protected veterans are provided equal opportunity and that the contractor is engaged in outreach to recruitment sources. Further, contractors must develop procedures for disseminating the policy internally and externally and establish an audit and reporting system to measure the effectiveness of the affirmative action program.

The currently approved collections of information for these sections are OMB Control Numbers 1250–0001 (construction) and 1250–0003 (supply and service).[45] Information collection package 1250–0001 covers the construction aspects of OFCCP's EO 11246, VEVRAA, and section 503 programs. The construction information collection package estimates that first-time contractors will take 18 hours to develop and document a joint section 503/VEVRAA written affirmative action program. It estimates that existing contractors take 7.5 hours to document and maintain material evidence of annually updating the affirmative action program. These estimates are based on previously approved information collection requests that quantified the estimated time to develop and maintain a joint section 503/VEVRAA written affirmative action program. Information collection 1250–0003 covers the supply and service aspects of OFCCP's program. This package outlines the burden required for contractors to develop and maintain an affirmative action program for women and minorities based on the contractor's number of employees, and also references the current VEVRAA requirements. The burden for first-time contractors to develop a written affirmative action program is between 73 and 186 hours. The burden for all other contractors to maintain documentation of annually updating the affirmative action program is between 18 and 105 hours. The VEVRAA portion of these information collections will be eliminated from these control numbers once the final rule becomes effective.

Paperwork Burden Hours and Related Costs

OFCCP's new information collection request under Control Number 1250–0004 for VEVRAA includes the burden hours and costs for the existing regulations and the new information collection requirements outlined in the final rule. This presentation separately states existing requirements currently approved under other OMB Control Numbers that will now be included under the 1250–0004 Control Number.

A. Number of Respondents

In light of the comments received on the VERAA NPRM regarding the "Federal contractor establishment universe, OFCCP reexamined the original number of 108,288 contractor establishments it used in the NPRM. For the final rule and this information collection request, we combined Equal Employment Data System (EEDS) data with several other information sources.[46] We used FY 2009 EEDS data to determine the number of Federal contractor establishments with 50 or more employees; this resulted in a total of 87,013 Federal contractor establishments.[47] An additional 10,518 establishments were identified through a cross-check of other contractor databases for a total of 97,531 establishments. Covered Federal contractors must develop AAPs for all of their establishments, even those with fewer than 50 employees. Therefore, OFCCP added an additional 73,744 establishments, using EEO–1 and FPDS data, for an adjusted total of 171,275 Federal contractor establishments affected by the final rule. This adjustment to the methodology for calculating the number of contractors and contractor establishments results in a 58 percent increase over the earlier estimate used in the NPRM.

However, OFCCP received comments on the estimated number of contractor establishments as well, including recommending an establishment count of 285,390 using the Veterans

[45] OMB Control Number 1250–0001 for construction is approved through December 31, 2014. OMB Control Number 1250–0003 is currently on a month-to-month renewal and is approved through April 30, 2012.

[46] OFCCP determined that the VET–100 database is not the most appropriate resource for calculating the number of federal contractors and contractor establishments. Among the concerns surrounding this data source are the use of contractor established 12-month reporting timeframes, the degree to which there is overlap or duplication in the VETS–100 and VETS–100A reports, and the absence of an employee threshold for reporting purposes.

[47] A single firm, business, or "entity" may have multiple establishments or facilities. Thus, the number of contractor establishments or facilities is significantly greater than the number of parent contractor firms or companies.

Employment Training Services (VETS) annual report. While OFCCP declines to exclusively rely on the VETS report number, we present an estimated high end for the range of the cost of the rule based on a contractor establishment number of 251,300. This number is based on 2010 VETS data from their pending information collection request.[48]

For the purposes of this information collection request, OFCCP averaged the 171,275 and 251,300 establishment figures to come up with a total of 211,287 establishments that will have to respond to the information collection requirements. All costs and hours in the burden analysis of this final rule are calculated using this adjusted number of Federal contractor establishments. Further, the burden for several information collection requirements in the final rule is presented in ranges. These estimates are also averaged for this information collection request.

B. Information Collections

Section 60–300.5 Equal Opportunity Clause

Paragraph 2 of the Equal Opportunity Clause (EO Clause) requires contractors to list their job openings with the state or local employment service delivery system (employment service). OFCCP estimates that gathering records and providing the job listing to the employment service will take 25 minutes for approximately 15 listings per year. The burden for this third-party disclosure is 1,320,544 hours (211,287 contractor establishments × 25 minutes × 15 listings/60 = 1,320,544 hours). This is a third-party disclosure.

Paragraph 4 of the EO Clause requires contractors to provide the appropriate employment service with the name and location of each of the contractor's hiring locations, a statement of its status as a Federal contractor, the contact information for the hiring official at each location in the state, and a request for priority referrals of protected veterans. Paragraph 4 also requires contractors that use job search organizations to provide the employment service with the contact information for each job search organization. OFCCP estimates a total of 15 minutes to ensure that the information newly required by this regulation is provided to the employment service. The annual burden for this provision is 52,822 hours (211,287 contractor establishments × 15 minutes/60 = 52,822 hours). OFCCP further estimates that 25 percent of contractors, or 52,821, will use outside job search organizations and incur an additional 5-minute burden to notify the employment service of the contact information for its outside job search organizations. The annual burden for this provision is 4,402 hours (52,821 contractor establishments × 5 minutes/60 = 4,402 hours). This is a third-party disclosure.

Section 60–300.42 Invitation to Self-Identify

Section 60–300.42(a) requires contractors to extend a pre-offer invitation to self-identify as a "protected veteran." OFCCP estimates that contractors working at the company level will take 1.5 hours to review and retrieve existing sample invitations to self-identify, adopt the sample "as is" or make revisions to their existing form, save the invitation to self-identify and incorporate the document in the contractor's application form. The burden for this provision is 85,656 hours (57,104 contractor companies × 1.5 hours = 85,656 hours).

Applicants for available positions with covered Federal contractors will have a minimal burden complying with § 60–300.42(a) in the course of completing their application for employment with the contractor. Section 60–300.42(a), on pre-offer self-identification, requires contractors to invite all applicants to self-identify whether or not they are a protected veteran. OFCCP estimates that there will be an average of 24 applicants per job vacancy for on average 15 vacancies per year. OFCCP further estimates that it will take applicants approximately 5 minutes to complete the form. The burden for this provision is 6,388,610 hours (211,287 contractor establishments × 15 listings × 15 applicants × 5 minutes/60 = 6,388,610 hours). This a third-party disclosure.

Section 60–300.44 Required Contents of the Affirmative Action Program

OFCCP estimates that it takes existing contractors, or 209,174, approximately 7.5 hours to document and maintain material evidence of annually updating a joint section 503 and VEVRAA affirmative action program. The burden for this requirement is 1,568,805 hours (209,174 contractor establishments × 7.5 hours = 1,568,805 hours).

OFCCP estimates that 1 percent of all contractors, or 2,112, are new contractors that will need to initially develop a joint section 503 and VEVRAA affirmative action program. OFCCP estimates that it takes approximately 18 hours to document and maintain material evidence of developing the program. Therefore, the recordkeeping burden for this provision is 38,016 hours (2,112 contractor establishments × 18 hours = 38,016 hours).

Section 60–300.44(f) External Dissemination of Policy, Outreach and Positive Recruitment

Section 60–300.44(f)(1)(ii) of the final rule requires contractors to send written notification of the company's affirmative action program policies to subcontractors, vendors, and suppliers. The existing regulations recommend that contractors send written notification of the company's affirmative action policies to subcontractors, vendors, and suppliers. *See* 41 CFR 60–300.44(f)(6). OFCCP estimates that contractors will take 15 minutes to prepare the notification and send it to subcontractors, vendors, and suppliers, and an additional 15 minutes to execute the email address changes in the company's email system. Likewise, the burden for any information technology assistance needed to send the written communication is estimated at 15 minutes. The burden for this request is 158,465 hours (211,287 contractor establishments × 45 minutes/60 = 158,465 hours).

Section 60–300.44(f)(4) of the final rule requires contractors to document all activities it undertakes to comply with the obligations of this paragraph, and retain these documents for a period of 3 years. OFCCP estimates that it will take contractors 15 minutes to retain the required documentation. Retaining these records means storing the records generated either electronically or in hardcopy, consistent with the contractor's existing business practices for how to store records. The annual recordkeeping burden for this provision is 52,822 hours (211,287 contractor establishments × 15 minutes/60 = 52,822 hour).

Section 60–300.44(h) Audit and Reporting System

Section 60–300.44(h)(1)(vi) requires contractors to document the actions taken to meet the requirements of 60–300.44(h), as mandated in the current regulations. OFCCP estimates that it will take contractors 10 minutes to document compliance with this existing provision to create an audit and reporting system. Documentation may include, as an example, the standard operating procedure of the system including roles and responsibilities, and audit and reporting timeframes and

[48] OMB Control Number 1293–0005, Federal Contractor Veterans' Employment Report, VETS–100/VETS–100A, *http://www.reginfo.gov/public/do/PRAViewDocument?ref_nbr=201104-1293-003* (last accessed Aug. 13, 2013).

lifecycles. Because contractors are currently required to have an audit and reporting system, it is expected that some documentation of the process and operation of the system audit already exists. The annual recordkeeping burden of this provision is 35,215 hours (211,287 contractor establishments × 10 minutes/60 = 35,215 hours).

Section 60–300.44(k) Data Collection and Analysis

Section 60–300(k) of the final rule requires contractors to collect and analyze certain categories of data.

Based on feedback received from public comments expressing concerns about the costs of modifying human resources information systems, OFCCP believes that most contractors will have the capability to conduct the required calculations electronically. However, some companies may have to calculate this information manually. Therefore, OFCCP estimates that the average time to conduct the analysis and maintain the relevant documentation would be 1 hour 25 minutes. Relevant documentation could include the report or other written documentation generated by the calculations that explain the methodology, the data used, and the findings and conclusions; the data used to conduct the calculations for subsequent validation of the results; and other material used by the contractor for the calculations. The recurring burden for this provision is 299,233 hours (251,300 contractor establishments × 85 minutes/60 = 299,233 hours).

No new software needs are anticipated for compliance with section 60–300.44(k); however, a software switch or configuration may be required to tell the system to retain the records for the additional required time period. The estimated time needed for making this switch is included with the burden estimate for section 60–300.44(f)(4).

Section 60–300.45 Benchmarks for Hiring

The final rule requires the contractor to establish benchmarks in one of two ways. A contractor may use as its benchmark the national average number of veterans in the civilian labor force, which OFCCP will provide (and periodically update) on its public Web site. Or, alternatively, the contractor may establish its own individual benchmark using the five-factor method proposed in the NPRM (and retained in the final rule) to develop a benchmark that fits the company's specific needs. OFCCP estimates that it will take contractors on average 10 minutes to maintain material evidence of compliance with this provision. The burden of this provision would be 35,215 hours (211,287 establishments × 10 minutes/60 = 35,215 hours).

Section 60–300.81 Access to Records

Section 60–300.81 of the final rule requires contractors who are the subject of a compliance evaluation or complaint investigation to specify all available record formats and allow OFCCP to select preferred record formats from those identified by the contractor during a compliance evaluation. Pursuant to 5 CFR 1320.4(a)(2), this information collection is excluded from the PRA requirements because it is related to an "administrative action, investigation, or audit involving an agency against specific individuals or entities."

C. Summary of Costs

The estimated cost to contractors is based on Bureau of Labor Statistics data in the publication "Employer Costs for Employee Compensation" (September 2011), which lists total compensation for management, professional, and related occupations as $50.11 per hour and administrative support as $23.72 per hour. OFCCP estimates that 52 percent of the burden hours will be management, professional, and related occupations and 48 percent will be administrative support.

TABLE 1—TOTAL BURDEN FOR §§ 60–300.5; 60–300.42; 60–300.44; AND 60–300.45

Recordkeeping Burden Hours	2,029,395
Reporting Burden Hours	0
Third Party Disclosure Burden Hours	7,960,499
Total Burden Hours	9,989,894

TABLE 2—SUMMARY OF BURDEN HOURS AND COSTS FOR CONTRACTORS

Existing requirements	Burden hours	Total
EO Clause, Parag 2 (Mandatory Job Listing)	1,320,544	$49,444,855.52
Current Existing Contractors (Written Affirmative Action Program)	1,568,805	58,740,451.85
Current New Contractors (Written Affirmative Action Program)	38,016	1,423,425.48
Total	2,927,365	109,608,732.86
New requirements	**Burden hours**	**Burden costs**
EO Clause, Parag 4 (Mandatory Job Listing)	52,822	1,977,794.22
EO Clause, Parag 4 (Mandatory Job Listing)	4,402	164,813.84
300.42 (Invitation to Self-Identify)	85,656	2,342,234.35
300.44(f)(1) (Notice to Subcontractors, etc.)	158,465	5,933,382.66
300.44(f)(4) (Outreach and Recruitment Recordkeeping)	52,822	1,977,794.22
300.44(h) (Affirmative Action Program Audit Recordkeeping)	35,215	1,318,529.48
300.44(k) (Data Collection Analysis)	299,323	11,207,500.59
300.45 (Benchmarks Recordkeeping)	35,215	1,318,529.48
Total	3,651,284	135,849,311.71

TABLE 3—SUMMARY OF NON-CONTRACTOR BURDEN HOURS AND COSTS

Existing requirement	Burden hours	Burden costs
Section 60–300.42 (Self-Identification)	6,338,610	$190,855,547

The total estimated cost for applicants to fill out the self-identification form is based on Bureau of Labor Statistics data in the publication "Employer Costs for Employee Compensation" (September 2011), which lists an average total compensation for all civilian workers as $30.11.

D. Initial Capital or Start-up Costs

Human Resources Information Systems

OFCCP estimates on average it will take each contractor, working at the company level, on average 20 hours to have a professional make the needed systems modifications to track applicant and hiring information for protected veterans. This includes IT and administrative professionals to make any necessary changes. The estimated costs for these modifications are based on data from the Bureau of Labor Statistics in the publication "Employer Costs for Employee Compensation" (September 2011), which lists total compensation for a professional of $47.21 per hour. The cost for these modifications is $53,917,597 (57,104 contractor companies × $47.21 = $53,917,597).

5 CFR 1320.3(b)(1)(i)—Reviewing Instructions

Several commenters noted that the proposed rule did not quantify the burden of reading and understanding the VEVRAA revisions on contractors. OFCCP acknowledges that 5 CFR 1320.3(b)(1)(i) requires agencies to include in the burden analysis for new information collection requirements the estimated time it takes for contractors to review and understand the instructions for compliance. In order to minimize the burden, OFCCP will publish several compliance assistance materials including factsheets and "Frequently Asked Questions." OFCCP will also host webinars for the contractor community that will describe the key provisions in the final rule.

OFCCP estimates it will take, on average, 2.5 hours to have a management professional at each establishment either read compliance assistance materials provided by OFCCP or participate in an OFCCP webinar to learn about the new requirements of the final rule. The estimated cost of this burden is based on data from the Bureau of Labor Statistics in the publication "Employer Costs for Employee Compensation" (September 2011), which lists total compensation for a management professional at $50.11. Therefore, the estimated burden for rule familiarization is 528,217 hours (211,287 contractor establishments × 2.5 hours = 528,217 hours). We calculate the total estimated cost for rule familiarization as $26,468,979 (528,217 hours × $50.11/hour = $26,468,979).

Operations and Maintenance Costs

OFCCP estimates that the contractor will have some operations and maintenance costs in addition to the burden calculated above.

60–300.42 Invitation to Self Identify

OFCCP estimates that the contractor will have some operations and maintenance cost associated with the invitations to self-identify. The contractor must invite all applicants to self-identify at both the pre-offer and post-offer stage of the employment process. Given the increasingly widespread use of electronic applications, any contractor that uses such applications would not incur copy costs. However, to account for contractors who may still choose to use paper applications, we are including printing and/or copying costs. Therefore, we estimate a single one page form for both the pre- and post-offer invitation. Assuming contractors using a paper-based application system, used 24 applications for an average of 15 listings per establishment, the minimum estimated total cost to contractors will be $1,217,002 (42,257 establishments × 360 copies × $.08 = $1,217,002).

E. Transfer of Burden From OMB Control Numbers 1250–0001 and 1250–0003 to 1250–0004

As a result of the final rule, the information collection requirements of VEVRAA will be placed under a separate information collection package. OMB Control Numbers 1250–0001 for the agency's construction enforcement program and 1250–0003 for its supply and service program currently include the annual burden hours and related costs for the time contractors take to document the contents of the written affirmative action program under VEVRAA. When the information collection requirements in this Final Rule become effective, the Department will submit non-substantive change requests for Control Numbers 1250–0001 and 1250–0003 to reflect the fact that the VEVRAA portions of burden hours and costs are included in this separate information collection package, OMB Control Number 1250–0004.

These paperwork burden estimates are summarized as follows:

Type of Review: New collection.

Agency: Office of Federal Contract Compliance Programs, Department of Labor.

Title: Vietnam Era Veterans' Readjustment Assistance Act of 1974, as amended by the Jobs for Veterans Act of 2002, 38 U.S.C. 4212 (VEVRAA).

OMB ICR Reference Number: 1250–0004.

Affected Public: Business or other for-profit; individuals.

Estimated Number of Annual Responses: xxxx.

Frequency of Response: On occasion.

Estimated Total Annual Burden Hours: 9,989,894.

Estimated Total Initial and Other Costs: $408,308,436.

The estimated $408,308,436 is the total of the PRA costs resulting from the existing requirements of part 60–300 and the new requirements of this final rule.

Small Business Regulatory Enforcement Fairness Act of 1996

This rule is a major rule as defined by Section 804 of the Small Business Regulatory Enforcement Fairness Act of 1996. This rule may result in an annual effect on the economy of $100 million or more; a major increase in costs or prices; or significant adverse effects on competition, employment, investment, productivity, innovation, or on the ability of the United States-based companies to compete with foreign-based companies in domestic and export markets.

Unfunded Mandates Reform Act of 1995

For purposes of the Unfunded Mandates Reform Act of 1995, 2 U.S.C. 1532, this final rule includes a Federal mandate that may result in excess of $100 million in expenditures in the private sector in any one year. Accordingly, in compliance with 2 U.S.C. 1532, OFCCP provides the following written statement. All references to other sections of this final rule are incorporated by reference pursuant to 2 U.S.C. 1532(c).

(1) The final rule is authorized by the Vietnam Era Veterans' Readjustment Assistance Act, as amended, 38 U.S.C. 4212.

(2) A qualitative and quantitative assessment of the anticipated costs and benefits of this rule, including the costs and benefits to the private sector, are set forth in the Regulatory Procedures section of the final rule (specifically the sections describing Executive Orders 12866 and 13563, the Regulatory Flexibility Act, and the Paperwork Reduction Act) and the Section-by-Section Analysis in the preamble to the final rule. OFCCP anticipates no effect of the final rule on health, safety, and the natural environment not otherwise

discussed in the sections set forth above.

(3) Estimates of future compliance costs are set forth in the Regulatory Procedures section of the final rule (specifically the sections describing Executive Orders 12866 and 13563, the Regulatory Flexibility Act, and the Paperwork Reduction Act). OFCCP anticipates none of the disproportionate budgetary effects of the rule set forth in 2 U.S.C. 1532(a)(3)(B).

(4) To the extent feasible and relevant, OFCCP has estimated the effect of the rule on the national economy in the Regulatory Procedures section of the final rule (specifically the sections describing Executive Orders 12866 and 13563, the Regulatory Flexibility Act, and the Paperwork Reduction Act).

(5) The provisions of 2 U.S.C. 1532(a)(5) do not apply to this final rule.

Finally, OFCCP identified, considered, and implemented a reasonable number of regulatory alternatives that were the least burdensome alternative. In those cases where OFCCP did not select the least burdensome alternative, it has provided an explanation of the reasons these suggestions were not adopted in the corresponding section of the Section-by-Section Analysis in the preamble to the final rule and/or the Regulatory Procedures section of the final rule (specifically the sections describing Executive Orders 12866 and 13563, the Regulatory Flexibility Act, and the Paperwork Reduction Act).

Executive Order 13132 (Federalism)

OFCCP has reviewed this final rule in accordance with Executive Order 13132 regarding federalism, and has determined that it does not have "federalism implications." This rule will not "have substantial direct effects on the States, on the relationship between the national government and the States, or on the distribution of power and responsibilities among the various levels of government."

Executive Order 13175 (Consultation and Coordination With Indian Tribal Governments)

This final rule does not have tribal implications under Executive Order 13175 that requires a tribal summary impact statement. The final rule does not have substantial direct effects on one or more Indian tribes, on the relationship between the Federal government and Indian tribes or on the distribution of power and responsibilities between the Federal government and Indian tribes.

Effects on Families

The undersigned hereby certifies that the final rule would not adversely affect the well-being of families, as discussed under section 654 of the Treasury and General Government Appropriations Act, 1999.

Executive Order 13045 (Protection of Children)

This final rule would have no environmental health risk or safety risk that may disproportionately affect children.

Environmental Impact Assessment

A review of this final rule in accordance with the requirements of the National Environmental Policy Act of 1969 (NEPA), 42 U.S.C. 4321 *et seq.*; the regulations of the Council on Environmental Quality, 40 CFR 1500 et seq.; and DOL NEPA procedures, 29 CFR part 11, indicates the final rule would not have a significant impact on the quality of the human environment. There is, thus, no corresponding environmental assessment or an environmental impact statement.

Executive Order 13211 (Energy Supply)

This final rule is not subject to Executive Order 13211. It will not have a significant adverse effect on the supply, distribution, or use of energy.

Executive Order 12630 (Constitutionally Protected Property Rights)

This final rule is not subject to Executive Order 12630 because it does not involve implementation of a policy that has takings implications or that could impose limitations on private property use.

Executive Order 12988 (Civil Justice Reform Analysis)

This final rule was drafted and reviewed in accordance with Executive Order 12988 and will not unduly burden the Federal court system. The final rule was: (1) Reviewed to eliminate drafting errors and ambiguities; (2) written to minimize litigation; and (3) written to provide a clear legal standard for affected conduct and to promote burden reduction.

List of Subjects in 41 CFR Part 60–300

Administrative practice and procedure, Civil rights, Employment, Equal employment opportunity, Government contracts, Government procurement, Individuals with disabilities, Investigations, Reporting and recordkeeping requirements, and Veterans.

Patricia A. Shiu,
Director, Office of Federal Contract Compliance Programs.

Accordingly, under authority of 38 U.S.C. 4212, Title 41 of the Code of Federal Regulations, Chapter 60, is amended to read as follows:

PART 60–250 [REMOVED]

■ 1. Remove Part 60–250

■ 2. Revise Part 60–300 to read as follows:

PART 60–300—AFFIRMATIVE ACTION AND NONDISCRIMINATION OBLIGATIONS OF FEDERAL CONTRACTORS AND SUBCONTRACTORS REGARDING DISABLED VETERANS, RECENTLY SEPARATED VETERANS, ACTIVE DUTY WARTIME OR CAMPAIGN BADGE VETERANS, AND ARMED FORCES SERVICE MEDAL VETERANS

Subpart A—Preliminary Matters, Equal Opportunity Clause

Sec.

Subpart B—Discrimination Prohibited

Subpart C—Affirmative Action Program

Subpart D—General Enforcement and Complaint Procedures

Subpart E—Ancillary Matters

Authority: 29 U.S.C. 793; 38 U.S.C. 4211 and 4212; E.O. 11758 (3 CFR, 1971–1975 Comp., p. 841).

Subpart A—Preliminary Matters, Equal Opportunity Clause

§ 60–300.1 Purpose, applicability and construction.

(a) *Purpose.* The purpose of the regulations in this part is to set forth the standards for compliance with the Vietnam Era Veterans' Readjustment Assistance Act of 1974, as amended, 38 U.S.C. 4212, (VEVRAA), which prohibits discrimination against protected veterans and pre-JVA veterans as defined in this part, and requires Government contractors and subcontractors to take affirmative action to employ and advance in employment qualified protected veterans.

Disabled veterans, recently separated veterans, active duty wartime or campaign badge veterans, and Armed Forces service medal veterans are protected veterans under VEVRAA.

(b) *Applicability.* This part applies to any Government contract or subcontract of $100,000 or more, entered into or modified on or after December 1, 2003, for the purchase, sale or use of personal property or nonpersonal services (including construction): Provided, that subpart C of this part applies only as described in § 60–300.40(a); and that the non-discrimination protections in § 60–300.21 and the right to file complaints alleging discriminatory conduct set forth in § 60–300.61 also apply to "pre-JVA veterans" as defined in § 60–300.2, who are applicants or employees of a contractor with a Government contract of $25,000 or more entered into prior to December 1, 2003, and unmodified since to a contract amount of $100,000. Compliance by the contractor with the provisions of this part will not necessarily determine its compliance with other statutes, and compliance with other statutes will not necessarily determine its compliance with this part.

(c) *Construction*—(1) *In general.* The Interpretive Guidance on Title I of the Americans with Disabilities Act (ADA) (42 U.S.C. 12101, *et seq.*) set out as an appendix to 29 CFR part 1630 issued pursuant to Title I may be relied upon for guidance in interpreting the parallel provisions of this part.

(2) *Relationship to other laws.* This part does not invalidate or limit the remedies, rights, and procedures under any Federal law or the law of any state or political subdivision that provides greater or equal protection for the rights of disabled veterans, recently separated veterans, active duty wartime or campaign badge veterans, or Armed Forces service medal protected veterans as compared to the protection afforded by this part. It may be a defense to a charge of violation of this part that a challenged action is required or necessitated by another Federal law or regulation, or that another Federal law or regulation prohibits an action (including the provision of a particular reasonable accommodation) that would otherwise be required by this part.

(i) *Uniformed Services Employment and Reemployment Rights Act.* This part does not invalidate or limit the obligations, responsibilities, and requirements of the contractor pursuant to the Uniformed Services Employment and Reemployment Rights Act (USERRA) (38 U.S.C. 4301, *et seq.*). This includes the obligation under USERRA to reemploy employees of the contractor following qualifying service in the uniformed services in the position the employee would have obtained with reasonable certainty had the employee been continuously employed during the period of uniformed service. Compliance by the contractor with the provisions of this part will not necessarily determine its compliance with USERRA, and compliance with USERRA will not necessarily determine its compliance with this part.

§ 60–300.2 Definitions.

For the purpose of this part:

(a) *Act* means the Vietnam Era Veterans' Readjustment Assistance Act of 1974, as amended, 38 U.S.C. 4212, also referred to throughout this regulation as "VEVRAA."

(b) *Active duty wartime or campaign badge veteran* means a veteran who served on active duty in the U.S. military, ground, naval or air service during a war or in a campaign or expedition for which a campaign badge has been authorized, under the laws administered by the Department of Defense.

(c) *Armed Forces service medal veteran* means any veteran who, while serving on active duty in the U.S. military, ground, naval or air service, participated in a United States military operation for which an Armed Forces service medal was awarded pursuant to Executive Order 12985 (61 FR 1209).

(d) *Compliance evaluation* means any one or combination of actions OFCCP may take to examine a Federal contractor's or subcontractor's compliance with one or more of the requirements of the Act.

(e) *Contract* means any Government contract or subcontract.

(f) *Contractor* means, unless otherwise indicated, a prime contractor or subcontractor holding a contract of $100,000 or more.

(g) *Direct threat* means a significant risk of substantial harm to the health or safety of the individual or others that cannot be eliminated or reduced by reasonable accommodation. The determination that an individual poses a direct threat shall be based on an individualized assessment of the individual's present ability to perform safely the essential functions of the job. This assessment shall be based on a reasonable medical judgment that relies on the most current medical knowledge and/or on the best available objective evidence. In determining whether an individual would pose a direct threat, the factors to be considered include:

(1) The duration of the risk;

(2) The nature and severity of the potential harm;

(3) The likelihood that the potential harm will occur; and

(4) The imminence of the potential harm.

(h) *Director* means the Director, Office of Federal Contract Compliance Programs of the United States Department of Labor, or his or her designee.

(i) *Disabled veteran* means:

(1) A veteran of the U.S. military, ground, naval or air service who is entitled to compensation (or who but for the receipt of military retired pay would be entitled to compensation) under laws administered by the Secretary of Veterans Affairs, or

(2) A person who was discharged or released from active duty because of a service-connected disability.

(j) *Employment service delivery system* means a service delivery system at which or through which labor exchange services, including employment, training, and placement services, are offered in accordance with the Wagner-Peyser Act. The Wagner-Peyser Act requires that these services be provided as part of the One-Stop delivery system established by the

States under Section 134 of the Workforce Investment Act of 1998.

(k) *Equal opportunity clause* means the contract provisions set forth in § 60–300.5, "Equal opportunity clause."

(l) *Essential functions*—(1) *In general.* The term essential functions means fundamental job duties of the employment position the disabled veteran holds or is seeking. The term essential functions does not include the marginal functions of the position.

(2) A job function may be considered essential for any of several reasons, including, but not limited to, the following:

(i) The function may be essential because the reason the position exists is to perform that function;

(ii) The function may be essential because of the limited number of employees available among whom the performance of that job function can be distributed; and/or

(iii) The function may be highly specialized so that the incumbent in the position is hired for his or her expertise or ability to perform the particular function.

(3) Evidence of whether a particular function is essential includes, but is not limited to:

(i) The contractor's judgment as to which functions are essential;

(ii) Written job descriptions prepared before advertising or interviewing applicants for the job;

(iii) The amount of time spent on the job performing the function;

(iv) The consequences of not requiring the incumbent to perform the function;

(v) The terms of a collective bargaining agreement;

(vi) The work experience of past incumbents in the job; and/or

(vii) The current work experience of incumbents in similar jobs.

(m) *Government* means the Government of the United States of America.

(n) *Government contract* means any agreement or modification thereof between any contracting agency and any person for the purchase, sale or use of personal property or nonpersonal services (including construction). The term *Government contract* does not include agreements in which the parties stand in the relationship of employer and employee, and federally assisted contracts.

(1) *Construction,* as used in the definition of Government contract and subcontract of this section, means the construction, rehabilitation, alteration, conversion, extension, demolition, or repair of buildings, highways, or other changes or improvements to real property, including facilities providing utility services. The term also includes the supervision, inspection, and other on-site functions incidental to the actual construction.

(2) *Contracting agency* means any department, agency, establishment or instrumentality of the United States, including any wholly owned Government corporation, which enters into contracts.

(3) *Modification* means any alteration in the terms and conditions of a contract, including supplemental agreements, amendments and extensions.

(4) *Nonpersonal services,* as used in the definition of Government contract and subcontract of this section, includes, but is not limited to, the following: Utility, construction, transportation, research, insurance, and fund depository.

(5) *Person,* as used in the definition of Government contract and subcontract of this section, means any natural person, corporation, partnership or joint venture, unincorporated association, state or local government, and any agency, instrumentality, or subdivision of such a government.

(6) *Personal property,* as used in the definition of Government contract and subcontract of this section, includes supplies and contracts for the use of real property (such as lease arrangements), unless the contract for the use of real property itself constitutes real property (such as easements).

(o) *Pre-JVA veteran* means an individual who is an employee of or applicant to a contractor with a contract of $25,000 or more entered into prior to December 1, 2003 and unmodified since to $100,000 or more, and who is a special disabled veteran, veteran of the Vietnam era, pre-JVA recently separated veteran, or other protected veteran, as defined below:

(1) *Special disabled veteran* means:

(i) A veteran who is entitled to compensation (or who but for the receipt of military retired pay would be entitled to compensation) under laws administered by the Department of Veterans Affairs for a disability:

(A) Rated at 30 percent or more; or

(B) Rated at 10 or 20 percent in the case of a veteran who has been determined under 38 U.S.C. 3106 to have a serious employment handicap; or

(ii) A person who was discharged or released from active duty because of a service-connected disability.

(2) Veteran of the Vietnam Era means a person who:

(i) Served on active duty for a period of more than 180 days, and was discharged or released therefrom with other than a dishonorable discharge, if any part of such active duty occurred:

(A) In the Republic of Vietnam between February 28, 1961, and May 7, 1975; or

(B) Between August 5, 1964, and May 7, 1975, in all other cases; or

(ii) Was discharged or released from active duty for a service-connected disability if any part of such active duty was performed:

(A) In the Republic of Vietnam between February 28, 1961, and May 7, 1975; or

(B) Between August 5, 1964, and May 7, 1975, in all other cases.

(3) Pre-JVA recently separated veteran means a pre-JVA veteran during the one-year period beginning on the date of the pre-JVA veteran's discharge or release from active duty.

(4) Other protected veteran means a person who served on active duty during a war or in a campaign or expedition for which a campaign badge has been authorized, under the laws administered by the Department of Defense.

(p) *Prime contractor* means any person holding a contract of $100,000 or more, and, for the purposes of subpart D of this part, "General Enforcement and Complaint Procedures," includes any person who has held a contract subject to the Act.

(q) *Protected veteran* means a veteran who is protected under the non-discrimination and affirmative action provisions of the Act; specifically, a veteran who may be classified as a "disabled veteran," "recently separated veteran," "active duty wartime or campaign badge veteran," or an "Armed Forces service medal veteran," as defined by this section.

(r) *Qualification standards* means the personal and professional attributes including the skill, experience, education, physical, medical, safety and other requirements established by the contractor as requirements which an individual must meet in order to be eligible for the position held or desired.

(s) *Qualified disabled veteran* means a disabled veteran who has the ability to perform the essential functions of the employment position with or without reasonable accommodation.

(t) *Reasonable accommodation*—(1) The term *reasonable accommodation* means:

(i) Modifications or adjustments to a job application process that enable a qualified applicant who is a disabled veteran to be considered for the position such applicant desires; [1] or

[1] A contractor's duty to provide a reasonable accommodation with respect to applicants who are

(ii) Modifications or adjustments to the work environment, or to the manner or circumstances under which the position held or desired is customarily performed, that enable a qualified disabled veteran to perform the essential functions of that position; or

(iii) Modifications or adjustments that enable the contractor's employee who is a disabled veteran to enjoy equal benefits and privileges of employment as are enjoyed by the contractor's other similarly situated employees who are not disabled veterans.

(2) Reasonable accommodation may include but is not limited to:

(i) Making existing facilities used by employees readily accessible to and usable by disabled veterans; and

(ii) Job restructuring; part-time or modified work schedules; reassignment to a vacant position; acquisition or modifications of equipment or devices; appropriate adjustment or modifications of examinations, training materials, or policies; the provision of qualified readers or interpreters; and other similar accommodations for disabled veterans.

(3) To determine the appropriate reasonable accommodation it may be necessary for the contractor to initiate an informal, interactive process with the qualified disabled veteran in need of the accommodation.[2] This process should identify the precise limitations resulting from the disability and potential reasonable accommodations that could overcome those limitations. (Appendix A of this part provides guidance on a contractor's duty to provide reasonable accommodation.)

(u) *Recently separated veteran* means any veteran during the three-year period beginning on the date of such veteran's discharge or release from active duty in the U.S. military, ground, naval or air service.

(v) *Recruiting and training agency* means any person who refers workers to any contractor, or who provides or supervises apprenticeship or training for employment by any contractor.

disabled veterans is not limited to those who ultimately demonstrate that they are qualified to perform the job in issue. Disabled veteran applicants must be provided a reasonable accommodation with respect to the application process if they are qualified with respect to that process (*e.g.*, if they present themselves at the correct location and time to fill out an application).

[2] Contractors must engage in such an interactive process with a disabled veteran, whether or not a reasonable accommodation ultimately is identified that will make the person a qualified individual. Contractors must engage in the interactive process because, until they have done so, they may be unable to determine whether a reasonable accommodation exists that will result in the person being qualified.

(w) *Secretary* means the Secretary of Labor, United States Department of Labor, or his or her designee.

(x) *Subcontract* means any agreement or arrangement between a contractor and any person (in which the parties do not stand in the relationship of an employer and an employee):

(1) For the purchase, sale or use of personal property or nonpersonal services (including construction) which, in whole or in part, is necessary to the performance of any one or more contracts; or

(2) Under which any portion of the contractor's obligation under any one or more contracts is performed, undertaken, or assumed.

(y) *Subcontractor* means any person holding a subcontract of $100,000 or more and, for the purposes of subpart D of this part, "General Enforcement and Complaint Procedures," any person who has held a subcontract subject to the Act.

(z) *TAP* means the Department of Defense's Transition Assistance Program, or any successor programs thereto. The TAP was designed to smooth the transition of military personnel and family members leaving active duty via employment workshops and individualized employment assistance and training.

(aa) *Undue hardship*—(1) *In general. Undue hardship* means, with respect to the provision of an accommodation, significant difficulty or expense incurred by the contractor, when considered in light of the factors set forth in paragraph (2) of this section.

(2) *Factors to be considered.* In determining whether an accommodation would impose an undue hardship on the contractor, factors to be considered include:

(i) The nature and net cost of the accommodation needed, taking into consideration the availability of tax credits and deductions, and/or outside funding;

(ii) The overall financial resources of the facility or facilities involved in the provision of the reasonable accommodation, the number of persons employed at such facility, and the effect on expenses and resources;

(iii) The overall financial resources of the contractor, the overall size of the business of the contractor with respect to the number of its employees, and the number, type and location of its facilities;

(iv) The type of operation or operations of the contractor, including the composition, structure and functions of the work force of such contractor, and the geographic separateness and administrative or fiscal relationship of the facility or facilities in question to the contractor; and

(v) The impact of the accommodation upon the operation of the facility, including the impact on the ability of other employees to perform their duties and the impact on the facility's ability to conduct business.

(bb) *United States*, as used in this part, shall include the several States, the District of Columbia, the Virgin Islands, the Commonwealth of Puerto Rico, Guam, American Samoa, the Commonwealth of the Northern Mariana Islands, and Wake Island.

(cc) *Veteran* means a person who served in the active military, naval, or air service of the United States, and who was discharged or released therefrom under conditions other than dishonorable.

§ 60–300.3 [Reserved]

§ 60–300.4 Coverage and waivers.

(a) *General*—(1) *Contracts and subcontracts of $100,000 or more.* Contracts and subcontracts of $100,000 or more are covered by this part. No contracting agency or contractor shall procure supplies or services in less than usual quantities to avoid the applicability of the equal opportunity clause.

(2) *Contracts for indefinite quantities.* With respect to indefinite delivery-type contracts (including, but not limited to, open end contracts, requirement-type contracts, Federal Supply Schedule contracts, "call-type" contracts, and purchase notice agreements), the equal opportunity clause shall be included unless the contracting agency has reason to believe that the amount to be ordered in any year under such contract will be less than $100,000. The applicability of the equal opportunity clause shall be determined at the time of award for the first year, and annually thereafter for succeeding years, if any. Notwithstanding the above, the equal opportunity clause shall be applied to such contract whenever the amount of a single order is $100,000 or more. Once the equal opportunity clause is determined to be applicable, the contract shall continue to be subject to such clause for its duration, regardless of the amounts ordered, or reasonably expected to be ordered in any year.

(3) *Employment activities within the United States.* This part applies only to employment activities within the United States and not to employment activities abroad. The term "employment activities within the United States" includes actual employment within the United States, and decisions of the contractor made

within the United States pertaining to the contractor's applicants and employees who are within the United States, regarding employment opportunities abroad (such as recruiting and hiring within the United States for employment abroad, or transfer of persons employed in the United States to contractor establishments abroad).

(4) *Contracts with State or local governments.* The requirements of the equal opportunity clause in any contract or subcontract with a State or local government (or any agency, instrumentality or subdivision thereof) shall not be applicable to any agency, instrumentality or subdivision of such government which does not participate in work on or under the contract or subcontract.

(b) *Waivers*—(1) *Specific contracts and classes of contracts.* The Director may waive the application to any contract of the equal opportunity clause in whole or part when he or she deems that special circumstances in the national interest so require. The Director may also grant such waivers to groups or categories of contracts: Where it is in the national interest; where it is found impracticable to act upon each request individually; and where such waiver will substantially contribute to convenience in administration of the Act. When a waiver has been granted for any class of contracts, the Director may withdraw the waiver for a specific contract or group of contracts to be awarded, when in his or her judgment such action is necessary or appropriate to achieve the purposes of the Act. The withdrawal shall not apply to contracts awarded prior to the withdrawal, except that in procurements entered into by formal advertising, or the various forms of restricted formal advertising, such withdrawal shall not apply unless the withdrawal is made more than 10 calendar days before the date set for the opening of the bids.

(2) *National security.* Any requirement set forth in the regulations of this part shall not apply to any contract whenever the head of the contracting agency determines that such contract is essential to the national security and that its award without complying with such requirements is necessary to the national security. Upon making such a determination, the head of the contracting agency will notify the Director in writing within 30 days.

(3) *Facilities not connected with contracts.* The Director may waive the requirements of the equal opportunity clause with respect to any of a contractor's facilities which he or she finds to be in all respects separate and distinct from activities of the contractor related to the performance of the contract, provided that he or she also finds that such a waiver will not interfere with or impede the effectuation of the Act. Such waivers shall be considered only upon the request of the contractor.

§ 60–300.5 Equal opportunity clause.

(a) *Government contracts.* Each contracting agency and each contractor shall include the following equal opportunity clause in each of its covered Government contracts or subcontracts (and modifications, renewals, or extensions thereof if not included in the original contract):

EQUAL OPPORTUNITY FOR VEVRAA PROTECTED VETERANS [3]

1. The contractor will not discriminate against any employee or applicant for employment because he or she is a disabled veteran, recently separated veteran, active duty wartime or campaign badge veteran, or Armed Forces service medal veteran (hereinafter collectively referred to as "protected veteran(s)") in regard to any position for which the employee or applicant for employment is qualified. The contractor agrees to take affirmative action to employ, advance in employment and otherwise treat qualified individuals without discrimination based on their status as a protected veteran in all employment practices, including the following:

i. Recruitment, advertising, and job application procedures.

ii. Hiring, upgrading, promotion, award of tenure, demotion, transfer, layoff, termination, right of return from layoff and rehiring.

iii. Rates of pay or any other form of compensation and changes in compensation.

iv. Job assignments, job classifications, organizational structures, position descriptions, lines of progression, and seniority lists.

v. Leaves of absence, sick leave, or any other leave.

vi. Fringe benefits available by virtue of employment, whether or not administered by the contractor.

vii. Selection and financial support for training, including apprenticeship, and on-the-job training under 38 U.S.C. 3687, professional meetings, conferences, and other related activities, and selection for leaves of absence to pursue training.

viii. Activities sponsored by the contractor including social or recreational programs.

ix. Any other term, condition, or privilege of employment.

2. The contractor agrees to immediately list all employment openings which exist at the time of the execution of this contract and those which occur during the performance of this contract, including those not generated by this contract and including those occurring at an establishment of the contractor other than the one where the contract is being performed, but excluding those of independently operated corporate affiliates, with the appropriate employment service delivery system where the opening occurs. Listing employment openings with the state workforce agency job bank or with the local employment service delivery system where the opening occurs will satisfy the requirement to list jobs with the appropriate employment service delivery system. In order to satisfy the listing requirement described herein, contractors must provide information about the job vacancy in any manner and format permitted by the appropriate employment service delivery system which will allow that system to provide priority referral of veterans protected by VEVRAA for that job vacancy. Providing information on employment openings to a privately run job service or exchange will satisfy the contractor's listing obligation if the privately run job service or exchange provides the information to the appropriate employment service delivery system in any manner and format that the employment service delivery system permits which will allow that system to provide priority referral of protected veterans.

3. Listing of employment openings with the appropriate employment service delivery system pursuant to this clause shall be made at least concurrently with the use of any other recruitment source or effort and shall involve the normal obligations which attach to the placing of a *bona fide* job order, including the acceptance of referrals of veterans and nonveterans. The listing of employment openings does not require the hiring of any particular job applicants or from any particular group of job applicants, and nothing herein is intended to relieve the contractor from any requirements in Executive orders or regulations regarding nondiscrimination in employment.

4. Whenever a contractor, other than a state or local governmental contractor, becomes contractually bound to the listing provisions in paragraphs 2 and 3 of this clause, it shall advise the employment service delivery system in each state where it has establishments that: (a) It is a Federal contractor, so that the employment service delivery systems are able to identify them as such; and (b) it desires priority referrals from the state of protected veterans for job openings at all locations within the state. The contractor shall also provide to the employment service delivery system the name and location of each hiring location within the state and the contact information for the contractor official responsible for hiring at each location. The "contractor official" may be a chief hiring official, a Human Resources contact, a senior management contact, or any other manager for the contractor that can verify the information set forth in the job listing and receive priority referrals from employment service delivery systems. In the event that the contractor uses any external job search organizations to assist in its hiring, the contractor shall also provide to the employment service delivery system the contact information for the job search organization(s). The disclosures required by this paragraph shall be made simultaneously

[3] The definitions set forth in 41 CFR 60–300.2 apply to the terms used throughout this Clause, and they are incorporated herein by reference.

with the contractor's first job listing at each employment service delivery system location after the effective date of this final rule. Should any of the information in the disclosures change since it was last reported to the employment service delivery system location, the contractor shall provide updated information simultaneously with its next job listing. As long as the contractor is contractually bound to these provisions and has so advised the employment service delivery system, there is no need to advise the employment service delivery system of subsequent contracts. The contractor may advise the employment service delivery system when it is no longer bound by this contract clause.

5. The provisions of paragraphs 2 and 3 of this clause do not apply to the listing of employment openings which occur and are filled outside of the 50 states, the District of Columbia, the Commonwealth of Puerto Rico, Guam, the Virgin Islands, American Samoa, the Commonwealth of the Northern Mariana Islands, Wake Island, and the Trust Territories of the Pacific Islands.

6. As used in this clause: i. *All employment openings* includes all positions except executive and senior management, those positions that will be filled from within the contractor's organization, and positions lasting three days or less. This term includes full-time employment, temporary employment of more than three days' duration, and part-time employment.

ii. *Executive and senior management* means: (1) Any employee (a) compensated on a salary basis at a rate of not less than $455 per week (or $380 per week, if employed in American Samoa by employers other than the Federal Government), exclusive of board, lodging or other facilities; (b) whose primary duty is management of the enterprise in which the employee is employed or of a customarily recognized department or subdivision thereof; (c) who customarily and regularly directs the work of two or more other employees; and (d) who has the authority to hire or fire other employees or whose suggestions and recommendations as to the hiring, firing, advancement, promotion or any other change of status of other employees are given particular weight; or (2) any employee who owns at least a bona fide 20-percent equity interest in the enterprise in which the employee is employed, regardless of whether the business is a corporate or other type of organization, and who is actively engaged in its management.

iii. *Positions that will be filled from within the contractor's organization* means employment openings for which no consideration will be given to persons outside the contractor's organization (including any affiliates, subsidiaries, and parent companies) and includes any openings which the contractor proposes to fill from regularly established "recall" lists. The exception does not apply to a particular opening once an employer decides to consider applicants outside of his or her own organization.

7. The contractor agrees to comply with the rules, regulations, and relevant orders of the Secretary of Labor issued pursuant to the Act.

8. In the event of the contractor's noncompliance with the requirements of this clause, actions for noncompliance may be taken in accordance with the rules, regulations, and relevant orders of the Secretary of Labor issued pursuant to the Act.

9. The contractor agrees to post in conspicuous places, available to employees and applicants for employment, notices in a form to be prescribed by the Director, Office of Federal Contract Compliance Programs, provided by or through the contracting officer. Such notices shall state the rights of applicants and employees as well as the contractor's obligation under the law to take affirmative action to employ and advance in employment qualified employees and applicants who are protected veterans. The contractor must ensure that applicants or employees who are disabled veterans are provided the notice in a form that is accessible and understandable to the disabled veteran (e.g., providing Braille or large print versions of the notice, posting the notice for visual accessibility to persons in wheelchairs, providing the notice electronically or on computer disc, or other versions). With respect to employees who do not work at a physical location of the contractor, a contractor will satisfy its posting obligations by posting such notices in an electronic format, provided that the contractor provides computers that can access the electronic posting to such employees, or the contractor has actual knowledge that such employees otherwise are able to access the electronically posted notices. Electronic notices for employees must be posted in a conspicuous location and format on the company's intranet or sent by electronic mail to employees. An electronic posting must be used by the contractor to notify job applicants of their rights if the contractor utilizes an electronic application process. Such electronic applicant notice must be conspicuously stored with, or as part of, the electronic application.

10. The contractor will notify each labor organization or representative of workers with which it has a collective bargaining agreement or other contract understanding that the contractor is bound by the terms of VEVRAA, and is committed to take affirmative action to employ and advance in employment, and shall not discriminate against, protected veterans.

11. The contractor will include the provisions of this clause in every subcontract or purchase order of $100,000 or more, unless exempted by the rules, regulations, or orders of the Secretary issued pursuant to VEVRAA so that such provisions will be binding upon each subcontractor or vendor. The contractor will take such action with respect to any subcontract or purchase order as the Director, Office of Federal Contract Compliance Programs, may direct to enforce such provisions, including action for noncompliance.

12. The contractor must, in all solicitations or advertisements for employees placed by or on behalf of the contractor, state that all qualified applicants will receive consideration for employment without regard to their protected veteran status.

[End of Clause]

(b) *Subcontracts.* Each contractor shall include the equal opportunity clause in each of its subcontracts subject to this part.

(c) *Adaptation of language.* Such necessary changes in language may be made to the equal opportunity clause as must be appropriate to identify properly the parties and their undertakings.

(d) *Inclusion of the equal opportunity clause in the contract.* It is not necessary to include the equal opportunity clause verbatim in the contract. The clause shall be made a part of the contract by citation to 41 CFR 60–300.5(a) and inclusion of the following language, in bold text, after the citation: **"This contractor and subcontractor shall abide by the requirements of 41 CFR 60–300.5(a). This regulation prohibits discrimination against qualified protected veterans, and requires affirmative action by covered prime contractors and subcontractors to employ and advance in employment qualified protected veterans."**

(e) *Incorporation by operation of the Act.* By operation of the Act, the equal opportunity clause shall be considered to be a part of every contract and subcontract required by the Act and the regulations in this part to include such a clause, whether or not it is physically incorporated in such contract and whether or not there is a written contract between the agency and the contractor.

(f) *Duties of contracting agencies.* Each contracting agency shall cooperate with the Director and the Secretary in the performance of their responsibilities under the Act. Such cooperation shall include insuring that the equal opportunity clause is included in all covered Government contracts and that contractors are fully informed of their obligations under the Act and this part, providing the Director with any information which comes to the agency's attention that a contractor is not in compliance with the Act or this part, responding to requests for information from the Director, and taking such actions for noncompliance as are set forth in § 60–300.66 as may be ordered by the Secretary or the Director.

Subpart B—Discrimination Prohibited

§ 60–300.20 Covered employment activities.

The prohibition against discrimination in this part applies to the following employment activities:

(a) Recruitment, advertising, and job application procedures;

(b) Hiring, upgrading, promotion, award of tenure, demotion, transfer, layoff, termination, right of return from layoff, and rehiring;

(c) Rates of pay or any other form of compensation and changes in compensation;

(d) Job assignments, job classifications, organizational structures, position descriptions, lines of progression, and seniority lists;

(e) Leaves of absence, sick leave, or any other leave;

(f) Fringe benefits available by virtue of employment, whether or not administered by the contractor;

(g) Selection and financial support for training, including, apprenticeships, professional meetings, conferences and other related activities, and selection for leaves of absence to pursue training;

(h) Activities sponsored by the contractor including social and recreational programs; and

(i) Any other term, condition, or privilege of employment.

§ 60–300.21 Prohibitions.

The term discrimination includes, but is not limited to, the acts described in this section and § 60–300.23.

(a) *Disparate treatment.* It is unlawful for the contractor to deny an employment opportunity or benefit or otherwise to discriminate against a qualified individual because of that individual's status as a protected veteran or pre-JVA veteran.

(b) *Limiting, segregating and classifying.* Unless otherwise permitted by this part, it is unlawful for the contractor to limit, segregate, or classify a job applicant or employee in a way that adversely affects his or her employment opportunities or status on the basis of that individual's status as a protected veteran or pre-JVA veteran. For example, the contractor may not segregate protected veterans as a whole, or any classification of protected veterans or pre-JVA veterans, into separate work areas or into separate lines of advancement.

(c) *Contractual or other arrangements*—(1) *In general.* It is unlawful for the contractor to participate in a contractual or other arrangement or relationship that has the effect of subjecting the contractor's own qualified applicant or employee who is a protected veteran or pre-JVA veteran to the discrimination prohibited by this part.

(2) *Contractual or other arrangement defined.* The phrase "contractual or other arrangement or relationship" includes, but is not limited to, a relationship with: an employment or referral agency; a labor organization, including a collective bargaining agreement; an organization providing fringe benefits to an employee of the contractor; or an organization providing training and apprenticeship programs.

(3) *Application.* This paragraph (c) applies to the contractor, with respect to its own applicants or employees, whether the contractor offered the contract or initiated the relationship, or whether the contractor accepted the contract or acceded to the relationship. The contractor is not liable for the actions of the other party or parties to the contract which only affect that other party's employees or applicants.

(d) *Standards, criteria or methods of administration.* It is unlawful for the contractor to use standards, criteria, or methods of administration, that are not job-related and consistent with business necessity, and that:

(1) Have the effect of discriminating on the basis of status as a protected veteran or pre-JVA veteran; or

(2) Perpetuate the discrimination of others who are subject to common administrative control.

(e) *Relationship or association with a protected veteran.* It is unlawful for the contractor to exclude or deny equal jobs or benefits to, or otherwise discriminate against, a qualified individual because of the known protected veteran or pre-JVA veteran status of an individual with whom the qualified individual is known to have a family, business, social or other relationship or association.

(f) *Not making reasonable accommodation.* (1) It is unlawful for the contractor to fail to make reasonable accommodation to the known physical or mental limitations of an applicant or employee who is a qualified disabled veteran or pre-JVA special disabled veteran, unless such contractor can demonstrate that the accommodation would impose an undue hardship on the operation of its business.

(2) It is unlawful for the contractor to deny employment opportunities to an applicant or employee who is a qualified disabled veteran or pre-JVA special disabled veteran based on the need of such contractor to make reasonable accommodation to such an individual's physical or mental impairments.

(3) A qualified disabled veteran or pre-JVA special disabled veteran is not required to accept an accommodation, aid, service, opportunity or benefit which such qualified individual chooses not to accept. However, if such individual rejects a reasonable accommodation, aid, service, opportunity or benefit that is necessary to enable the individual to perform the essential functions of the position held or desired, and cannot, as a result of that rejection, perform the essential functions of the position, the individual will not be considered a qualified disabled veteran or pre-JVA special disabled veteran.

(g) *Qualification standards, tests and other selection criteria*—(1) *In general.* It is unlawful for the contractor to use qualification standards, employment tests or other selection criteria that screen out or tend to screen out individuals on the basis of their status as protected veterans or pre-JVA veterans unless the standard, test or other selection criterion, as used by the contractor, is shown to be job-related for the position in question and is consistent with business necessity. Selection criteria that concern an essential function may not be used to exclude a disabled veteran if that individual could satisfy the criteria with provision of a reasonable accommodation. Selection criteria that exclude or tend to exclude individuals on the basis of their status as protected veterans or pre-JVA veterans but concern only marginal functions of the job would not be consistent with business necessity. The contractor may not refuse to hire an applicant who is a disabled veteran or pre-JVA special disabled veteran because the applicant's disability prevents him or her from performing marginal functions. When considering a protected veteran or pre-JVA veteran for an employment opportunity, the contractor may not rely on portions of such veteran's military record, including his or her discharge papers, which are not relevant to the qualification requirements of the opportunity in issue.

(2) The Uniform Guidelines on Employee Selection Procedures, 41 CFR part 60–3, do not apply to 38 U.S.C. 4212 and are similarly inapplicable to this part.

(h) *Administration of tests.* It is unlawful for the contractor to fail to select and administer tests concerning employment in the most effective manner to ensure that, when a test is administered to a job applicant or employee who is a disabled veteran or pre-JVA special disabled veteran with a disability that impairs sensory, manual, or speaking skills, the test results accurately reflect the skills, aptitude, or whatever other factor of the applicant or employee that the test purports to measure, rather than reflecting the impaired sensory, manual, or speaking skills of such employee or applicant, except where such skills are the factors that the test purports to measure.

(i) *Compensation.* In offering employment or promotions to protected veterans or pre-JVA veterans, it is unlawful for the contractor to reduce the amount of compensation offered because of any income based upon a disability-related and/or military-service-related pension or other disability-related and/or military-service-related benefit the applicant or employee receives from another source.

§ 60–300.22 Direct threat defense.

The contractor may use as a qualification standard the requirement that an individual be able to perform the essential functions of the position held or desired without posing a direct threat to the health or safety of the individual or others in the workplace. (See § 60–300.2(g) defining *direct threat*.).

§ 60–300.23 Medical examinations and inquiries.

(a) *Prohibited medical examinations or inquiries.* Except as stated in paragraphs (b) and (c) of this section, it is unlawful for the contractor to require a medical examination of an applicant or employee or to make inquiries as to whether an applicant or employee is a disabled veteran or as to the nature or severity of such a veteran's disability.

(b) *Permitted medical examinations and inquiries*—(1) *Acceptable pre-employment inquiry.* The contractor may make pre-employment inquiries into the ability of an applicant to perform job-related functions, and/or may ask an applicant to describe or to demonstrate how, with or without reasonable accommodation, the applicant will be able to perform job-related functions.

(2) *Employment entrance examination.* The contractor may require a medical examination (and/or inquiry) after making an offer of employment to a job applicant and before the applicant begins his or her employment duties, and may condition an offer of employment on the results of such examination (and/or inquiry), if all entering employees in the same job category are subjected to such an examination (and/or inquiry) regardless of their status as a disabled veteran.

(3) *Examination of employees.* The contractor may require a medical examination (and/or inquiry) of an employee that is job-related and consistent with business necessity. The contractor may make inquiries into the ability of an employee to perform job-related functions.

(4) *Other acceptable examinations and inquiries.* The contractor may conduct voluntary medical examinations and activities, including voluntary medical histories, which are part of an employee health program available to employees at the work site.

(5) Medical examinations conducted in accordance with paragraphs (b)(2) and (b)(4) of this section do not have to be job-related and consistent with business necessity. However, if certain criteria are used to screen out an applicant or applicants or an employee or employees who are disabled veterans as a result of such examinations or inquiries, the contractor must demonstrate that the exclusionary criteria are job-related and consistent with business necessity, and that performance of the essential job functions cannot be accomplished with reasonable accommodations as required in this part.

(c) *Invitation to self-identify.* The contractor shall invite applicants to self-identify as being covered by the Act, as specified in § 60–300.42.

(d) *Confidentiality and use of medical information.* (1) Information obtained under this section regarding the medical condition or history of any applicant or employee shall be collected and maintained on separate forms and in separate medical files and treated as a confidential medical record, except that:

(i) Supervisors and managers may be informed regarding necessary restrictions on the work or duties of the applicant or employee and necessary accommodations;

(ii) First aid and safety personnel may be informed, when appropriate, if the disability might require emergency treatment; and

(iii) Government officials engaged in enforcing the laws administered by OFCCP, including this part, or enforcing the Americans with Disabilities Act, shall be provided relevant information on request.

(2) Information obtained under this section regarding the medical condition or history of any applicant or employee shall not be used for any purpose inconsistent with this part.

§ 60–300.24 Drugs and alcohol.

(a) *Specific activities permitted.* The contractor: (1) May prohibit the illegal use of drugs and the use of alcohol at the workplace by all employees;

(2) May require that employees not be under the influence of alcohol or be engaging in the illegal use of drugs at the workplace;

(3) May require that all employees behave in conformance with the requirements established under the Drug-Free Workplace Act of 1988 (41 U.S.C. 701 *et seq.*);

(4) May hold an employee who engages in the illegal use of drugs or who is an alcoholic to the same qualification standards for employment or job performance and behavior to which the contractor holds its other employees, even if any unsatisfactory performance or behavior is related to the employee's drug use or alcoholism;

(5) May require that its employees employed in an industry subject to such regulations comply with the standards established in the regulations (if any) of the Departments of Defense and Transportation, and of the Nuclear Regulatory Commission, and other Federal agencies regarding alcohol and the illegal use of drugs; and

(6) May require that employees employed in sensitive positions comply with the regulations (if any) of the Departments of Defense and Transportation, and of the Nuclear Regulatory Commission, and other Federal agencies that apply to employment in sensitive positions subject to such regulations.

(b) *Drug testing*—(1) *General policy.* For purposes of this part, a test to determine the illegal use of drugs is not considered a medical examination. Thus, the administration of such drug tests by the contractor to its job applicants or employees is not a violation of § 60–300.23. Nothing in this part shall be construed to encourage, prohibit, or authorize the contractor to conduct drug tests of job applicants or employees to determine the illegal use of drugs or to make employment decisions based on such test results.

(2) *Transportation employees.* Nothing in this part shall be construed to encourage, prohibit, or authorize the otherwise lawful exercise by contractors subject to the jurisdiction of the Department of Transportation of authority to test employees in, and applicants for, positions involving safety-sensitive duties for the illegal use of drugs or for on-duty impairment by alcohol; and remove from safety-sensitive positions persons who test positive for illegal use of drugs or on-duty impairment by alcohol pursuant to paragraph (b)(1) of this section.

(3) Any information regarding the medical condition or history of any employee or applicant obtained from a test to determine the illegal use of drugs, except information regarding the illegal use of drugs, is subject to the requirements of §§ 60–300.23(b)(5) and 60–300.23(d)(2).

§ 60–300.25 Health insurance, life insurance and other benefit plans.

(a) An insurer, hospital, or medical service company, health maintenance organization, or any agent or entity that administers benefit plans, or similar organizations may underwrite risks, classify risks, or administer such risks that are based on or not inconsistent with state law.

(b) The contractor may establish, sponsor, observe or administer the terms of a bona fide benefit plan that are based on underwriting risks, classifying risks, or administering such risks that are based on or not inconsistent with state law.

(c) The contractor may establish, sponsor, observe, or administer the terms of a bona fide benefit plan that is not subject to state laws that regulate insurance.

(d) The contractor shall not deny a qualified disabled veteran equal access to insurance or subject a qualified disabled veteran to different terms or conditions of insurance based on disability alone, if the disability does not pose increased risks.

(e) The activities described in paragraphs (a), (b) and (c) of this section are permitted unless these activities are used as a subterfuge to evade the purposes of this part.

Subpart C—Affirmative Action Program

§ 60–300.40 Applicability of the affirmative action program requirement.

(a) The requirements of this subpart apply to every Government contractor that has 50 or more employees and a contract of $100,000 or more.

(b) Contractors described in paragraph (a) of this section shall, within 120 days of the commencement of a contract, prepare and maintain an affirmative action program at each establishment. The affirmative action program shall set forth the contractor's policies and procedures in accordance with this part. This program may be integrated into or kept separate from other affirmative action programs.

(c) The affirmative action program shall be reviewed and updated annually by the official designated by the contractor pursuant to § 60–300.44(i).

(d) The contractor shall submit the affirmative action program within 30 days of a request from OFCCP, unless the request provides for a different time. The contractor also shall make the affirmative action program promptly available on-site upon OFCCP's request.

§ 60–300.41 Availability of affirmative action program.

The full affirmative action program, absent the data metrics required by § 60–300.44(k), shall be made available to any employee or applicant for employment for inspection upon request. The location and hours during which the program may be obtained shall be posted at each establishment.

§ 60–300.42 Invitation to self-identify.

(a) *Pre-offer.* The contractor shall invite applicants to inform the contractor whether the applicant believes that he or she is a protected veteran who may be covered by the Act. This invitation may be included in the application materials for the position, but in any circumstance shall be provided to applicants prior to making an offer of employment to a job applicant.

(b) *Post-offer.* In addition to the invitation in paragraph (a) of this section, the contractor shall invite applicants to inform the contractor whether the applicant believes that he or she belongs to one or more of the specific categories of protected veteran for which the contractor is required to report pursuant to 41 CFR part 61–300. Such an invitation shall be made at any time after the offer of employment but before the applicant begins his or her job duties.

(c) The invitations referenced in paragraphs (a) and (b) of this section shall state that the contractor is a Federal contractor required to take affirmative action to employ and advance in employment protected veterans pursuant to the Act. The invitations also shall summarize the relevant portions of the Act and the contractor's affirmative action program. Furthermore, the invitations shall state that the information is being requested on a voluntary basis, that it will be kept confidential, that refusal to provide it will not subject the applicant to any adverse treatment, and that it will not be used in a manner inconsistent with the act. (An acceptable form for such an invitation is set forth in Appendix B of this part.)

(d) If an applicant identifies himself or herself as a disabled veteran in the post-offer self-identification detailed in paragraph (b) of this section, the contractor should inquire of the applicant whether an accommodation is necessary, and if so, should engage with the applicant regarding reasonable accommodation. The contractor may make such inquiries to the extent they are consistent with the Americans with Disabilities Act of 1990 (ADA), 42 U.S.C. 12101, *et seq.* The contractor shall maintain a separate file in accordance with § 60–300.23(d) on persons who have self-identified as disabled veterans.

(e) The contractor shall keep all information on self-identification confidential. The contractor shall provide the information to OFCCP upon request. This information may be used only in accordance with this part.

(f) Nothing in this section relieves the contractor of its obligation to take affirmative action with respect to those applicants or employees who are known to the contractor to be protected veterans.

(g) Nothing in this section relieves the contractor from liability for discrimination under the Act.

§ 60–300.43 Affirmative action policy.

Under the affirmative action obligations imposed by the Act, contractors shall not discriminate against protected veterans, and shall take affirmative action to employ and advance in employment qualified protected veterans at all levels of employment, including the executive level. Such action shall apply to all employment activities set forth in § 60–300.20.

§ 60–300.44 Required contents of affirmative action programs.

Acceptable affirmative action programs shall contain, but not necessarily be limited to, the following elements:

(a) *Policy statement.* The contractor shall include an equal opportunity policy statement in its affirmative action program, and shall post the policy statement on company bulletin boards. The contractor must ensure that applicants and employees who are disabled veterans are provided the notice in a form that is accessible and understandable to the disabled veteran (e.g., providing Braille or large print versions of the notice, or posting the notice for visual accessibility to persons in wheelchairs). The policy statement shall indicate the top United States executive's (such as the Chief Executive Officer or the President of the United States Division of a foreign company) support for the contractor's affirmative action program, provide for an audit and reporting system (see paragraph (h) of this section) and assign overall responsibility for the implementation of affirmative action activities required under this part (see paragraph (i) of this section). Additionally, the policy shall state, among other things, that the contractor will: recruit, hire, train and promote persons in all job titles, and ensure that all other personnel actions are administered, without regard to protected veteran status; and ensure that all employment decisions are based only on valid job requirements. The policy shall state that employees and applicants shall not be subjected to harassment, intimidation, threats, coercion or discrimination because they have engaged in or may engage in any of the following activities:

(1) Filing a complaint;

(2) Assisting or participating in an investigation, compliance evaluation, hearing, or any other activity related to the administration of the affirmative action provisions of VEVRAA or any other Federal, state or local law requiring equal opportunity for protected veterans;

(3) Opposing any act or practice made unlawful by VEVRAA or its implementing regulations in this part or any other Federal, state or local law requiring equal opportunity for protected veterans; or

(4) Exercising any other right protected by VEVRAA or its implementing regulations in this part.

(b) *Review of personnel processes.* The contractor shall ensure that its personnel processes provide for careful, thorough, and systematic consideration of the job qualifications of applicants and employees who are known protected veterans for job vacancies filled either by hiring or promotion, and for all training opportunities offered or available. The contractor shall ensure that when a protected veteran is considered for employment opportunities, the contractor relies only on that portion of the individual's military record, including his or her discharge papers, relevant to the requirements of the opportunity in issue. The contractor shall ensure that its personnel processes do not stereotype protected veterans in a manner which limits their access to all jobs for which they are qualified. The contractor shall periodically review such processes and make any necessary modifications to ensure that these obligations are carried out. A description of the review and any necessary modifications to personnel processes or development of new processes shall be included in any affirmative action programs required under this part. The contractor must design procedures that facilitate a review of the implementation of this requirement by the contractor and the Government (Appendix C of this part is an example of an appropriate set of procedures. The procedures in Appendix C are not required and contractors may develop other procedures appropriate to their circumstances.)

(c) *Physical and mental qualifications.* (1) The contractor shall provide in its affirmative action program, and shall adhere to, a schedule for the periodic review of all physical and mental job qualification standards to ensure that, to the extent qualification standards tend to screen out qualified disabled veterans, they are job-related for the position in question and are consistent with business necessity. (2) Whenever the contractor applies physical or mental qualification standards in the selection of applicants or employees for employment or other change in employment status such as promotion, demotion or training, to the extent that qualification standards tend to screen out qualified disabled veterans, the standards shall be related to the specific job or jobs for which the individual is being considered and consistent with business necessity. The contractor has the burden to demonstrate that it has complied with the requirements of this paragraph (c)(2).

(3) The contractor may use as a defense to an allegation of a violation of paragraph (c)(2) of this section that an individual poses a direct threat to the health or safety of the individual or others in the workplace. (See § 60–300.2(g) defining direct threat.) (d) *Reasonable accommodation to physical and mental limitations.* As is provided in § 60–300.21(f), as a matter of nondiscrimination the contractor must make reasonable accommodation to the known physical or mental limitations of an otherwise qualified disabled veteran unless it can demonstrate that the accommodation would impose an undue hardship on the operation of its business. As a matter of affirmative action, if an employee who is known to be a disabled veteran is having significant difficulty performing his or her job and it is reasonable to conclude that the performance problem may be related to the known disability, the contractor shall confidentially notify the employee of the performance problem and inquire whether the problem is related to the employee's disability; if the employee responds affirmatively, the contractor shall confidentially inquire whether the employee is in need of a reasonable accommodation.

(e) *Harassment.* The contractor must develop and implement procedures to ensure that its employees are not harassed because of their status as a protected veteran.

(f) *External dissemination of policy, outreach and positive recruitment.*

(1) *Required outreach efforts.*

(i) The contractor shall undertake appropriate outreach and positive recruitment activities such as those listed in paragraph (f)(2) of this section that are reasonably designed to effectively recruit protected veterans. It is not contemplated that the contractor will necessarily undertake all the activities listed in paragraph (f)(2) of this section or that its activities will be limited to those listed. The scope of the contractor's efforts shall depend upon all the circumstances, including the contractor's size and resources and the extent to which existing employment practices are adequate.

(ii) The contractor must send written notification of company policy related to its affirmative action efforts to all subcontractors, including subcontracting vendors and suppliers, requesting appropriate action on their part.

(2) *Examples of outreach and recruitment activities* . Below are examples of outreach and positive recruitment activities referred to in paragraph (f)(1) of this section. This is an illustrative list, and contractors may choose from these or other activities, as appropriate to their circumstances.

(i) Enlisting the assistance and support of the following persons and organizations in recruiting, and developing on-the-job training opportunities for veterans, in order to fulfill its commitment to provide meaningful employment opportunities for such veterans:

(A) The Local Veterans' Employment Representative in the local employment service office (i.e., the One-Stop) nearest the contractor's establishment;

(B) The Department of Veterans Affairs Regional Office nearest the contractor's establishment;

(C) The veterans' counselors and coordinators ("Vet-Reps") on college campuses;

(D) The service officers of the national veterans' groups active in the area of the contractor's establishment;

(E) Local veterans' groups and veterans' service centers near the contractor's establishment;

(F) The Department of Defense Transition Assistance Program (TAP), or any subsequent program that, in whole or in part, might replace TAP; and

(G) Any organization listed in the Employer Resources section of the National Resource Directory (*http://www.nationalresourcedirectory.gov/*), or any future service that replaces or complements it.

(ii) The contractor should also consider taking the actions listed below, as appropriate, to fulfill its commitment to provide meaningful employment opportunities to protected veterans:

(A) Formal briefing sessions should be held, preferably on company premises, with representatives from recruiting sources. Contractor facility tours, clear and concise explanations of current and future job openings, position descriptions, worker specifications, explanations of the company's selection process, and recruiting literature should be an integral part of the briefing. At any such briefing sessions, the company official in charge of the contractor's affirmative action program should be in attendance when possible. Formal arrangements should be made for referral of applicants, follow up with sources, and feedback on disposition of applicants.

(B) The contractor's recruitment efforts at all educational institutions should incorporate special efforts to reach students who are protected veterans.

(C) An effort should be made to participate in work-study programs with Department of Veterans Affairs rehabilitation facilities which specialize in training or educating disabled veterans.

(D) Protected veterans should be made available for participation in career days, youth motivation programs, and related activities in their communities.

(E) The contractor should take any other positive steps it deems necessary to attract qualified protected veterans not currently in the work force who have requisite skills and can be recruited through affirmative action measures. These persons may be located through the local chapters of organizations of and for any of the classifications of protected veterans.

(F) The contractor, in making hiring decisions, should consider applicants who are known protected veterans for all available positions for which they may be qualified when the position(s) applied for is unavailable.

(G) The contractor should consider listing its job openings with the National Resource Directory's Veterans Job Bank, or any future service that replaces or complements it.

(3) *Assessment of external outreach and recruitment efforts.* The contractor shall, on an annual basis, review the outreach and recruitment efforts it has taken over the previous twelve months to evaluate their effectiveness in identifying and recruiting qualified protected veterans. The contractor shall document each evaluation, including at a minimum the criteria it used to evaluate the effectiveness of each effort and the contractor's conclusion as to whether each effort was effective. Among these criteria shall be the data collected pursuant to paragraph (k) of this section for the current year and the two most recent previous years. The contractor's conclusion as to the effectiveness of its outreach efforts must be reasonable as determined by OFCCP in light of these regulations. If the contractor concludes the totality of its efforts were not effective in identifying and recruiting qualified protected veterans, it shall identify and implement alternative efforts listed in paragraphs (f)(1) or (f)(2) of this section in order to fulfill its obligations.

(4) *Recordkeeping obligation.* The contractor shall document all activities it undertakes to comply with the obligations of this section, and retain these documents for a period of three (3) years.

(g) *Internal dissemination of policy.* (1) A strong outreach program will be ineffective without adequate internal support from supervisory and management personnel and other employees. In order to assure greater employee cooperation and participation in the contractor's efforts, the contractor shall develop the internal procedures listed in paragraph (g)(2) of this section for communication of its obligation to engage in affirmative action efforts to employ and advance in employment qualified protected veterans. It is not contemplated that the contractor's activities will be limited to those listed. These procedures shall be designed to foster understanding, acceptance and support among the contractor's executive, management, supervisory and other employees and to encourage such persons to take the necessary actions to aid the contractor in meeting this obligation.

(2) The contractor shall implement and disseminate this policy internally as follows:

(i) Include it in the contractor's policy manual or otherwise make the policy available to employees;

(ii) If the contractor is party to a collective bargaining agreement, it shall notify union officials and/or employee representatives to inform them of the contractor's policy, and request their cooperation;

(3) The contractor is encouraged to additionally implement and disseminate this policy internally as follows:

(i) Inform all employees and prospective employees of its commitment to engage in affirmative action to increase employment opportunities for protected veterans;

(ii) Publicize it in the company newspaper, magazine, annual report and other media;

(iii) Conduct special meetings with executive, management, and supervisory personnel to explain the intent of the policy and individual responsibility for effective implementation, making clear the chief executive officer's support for the affirmative action policy;

(iv) Discuss the policy thoroughly in both employee orientation and management training programs;

(v) When employees are featured in employee handbooks or similar publications for employees, include disabled veterans.

(h) *Audit and reporting system.* (1) The contractor shall design and implement an audit and reporting system that will:

(i) Measure the effectiveness of the contractor's affirmative action program;

(ii) Indicate any need for remedial action;

(iii) Determine the degree to which the contractor's objectives have been attained;

(iv) Determine whether known protected veterans have had the opportunity to participate in all company sponsored educational, training, recreational and social activities;

(v) Measure the contractor's compliance with the affirmative action program's specific obligations; and

(vi) Document the actions taken to comply with the obligations of paragraphs (i) through (v) above, and retain these documents as employment records subject to the recordkeeping requirements of § 60–300.80.

(2) Where the affirmative action program is found to be deficient, the contractor shall undertake necessary action to bring the program into compliance.

(i) *Responsibility for implementation.* An official of the contractor shall be assigned responsibility for implementation of the contractor's affirmative action activities under this part. His or her identity should appear on all internal and external communications regarding the company's affirmative action program. This official shall be given necessary senior management support and staff to manage the implementation of this program.

(j) *Training.* All personnel involved in the recruitment, screening, selection, promotion, disciplinary, and related processes shall be trained to ensure that the commitments in the contractor's affirmative action program are implemented.

(k) *Data collection analysis.* The contractor shall document the following computations or comparisons pertaining to applicants and hires on an annual basis and maintain them for a period of three (3) years:

(1) The number of applicants who self-identified as protected veterans pursuant to § 60–300.42(a), or who are otherwise known as protected veterans;

(2) The total number of job openings and total number of jobs filled;

(3) The total number of applicants for all jobs;

(4) The number of protected veteran applicants hired; and

(5) The total number of applicants hired.

§ 60–300.45 Benchmarks for hiring.

The benchmark is not a rigid and inflexible quota which must be met, nor is it to be considered either a ceiling or a floor for the employment of particular groups. Quotas are expressly forbidden.

(a) *Purpose:* The purpose of establishing benchmarks is to create a quantifiable method by which the contractor can measure its progress toward achieving equal employment opportunity for protected veterans.

(b) Hiring benchmarks shall be set by the contractor on an annual basis. Benchmarks shall be set using one of the two mechanisms described below:

(1) Establish a benchmark equaling the national percentage of veterans in the civilian labor force, which will be published and updated annually on the OFCCP Web site; or

(2) Establish a benchmark by taking into account:

(i) The average percentage of veterans in the civilian labor force in the State(s) where the contractor is located over the preceding three years, as calculated by the Bureau of Labor Statistics and published on the OFCCP Web site;

(ii) The number of veterans, over the previous four quarters, who were participants in the employment service delivery system in the State where the contractor is located, as tabulated by the Veterans' Employment and Training Service and published on the OFCCP Web site;

(iii) The applicant ratio and hiring ratio for the previous year, based on the data collected pursuant to § 60–300.44(k);

(iv) The contractor's recent assessments of the effectiveness of its external outreach and recruitment efforts, as set forth in § 60–300.44(f)(3); and

(v) Any other factors, including but not limited to the nature of the contractor's job openings and/or its location, which would tend to affect the availability of qualified protected veterans.

(c) The contractor shall document the hiring benchmark it has established each year. If the contractor sets its benchmark using the procedure in paragraph (b)(2) of this section, it shall document each of the factors that it considered in establishing the hiring benchmark and the relative significance of each of these factors. The contractor shall retain these records for a period of three (3) years.

Subpart D—General Enforcement and Complaint Procedures

§ 60–300.60 Compliance evaluations.

(a) OFCCP may conduct compliance evaluations to determine if the contractor is taking affirmative action to employ, advance in employment and otherwise treat qualified individuals without discrimination based on their status as a protected veteran in all employment practices. A compliance evaluation may consist of any one or any combination of the following investigative procedures:

(1) *Compliance review.* A comprehensive analysis and evaluation of the hiring and employment practices of the contractor, the written affirmative action program, and the results of the affirmative action efforts undertaken by the contractor. A compliance review may proceed in three stages:

(i) A desk audit of the written affirmative action program and supporting documentation to determine whether all elements required by the regulations in this part are included, whether the affirmative action program meets agency standards of reasonableness, and whether the affirmative action program and supporting documentation satisfy agency standards of acceptability. OFCCP may extend the temporal scope of the desk audit beyond that set forth in the scheduling letter if OFCCP deems it necessary to carry out its investigation of potential violations of this part. The desk audit is conducted at OFCCP offices;

(ii) An on-site review, conducted at the contractor's establishment to investigate unresolved problem areas identified in the affirmative action program and supporting documentation during the desk audit, to verify that the contractor has implemented the affirmative action program and has complied with those regulatory obligations not required to be included in the affirmative action program, and to examine potential instances or issues of discrimination. An on-site review normally will involve an examination of the contractor's personnel and employment policies, inspection and copying of documents related to employment actions, and interviews with employees, supervisors, managers, hiring officials; and

(iii) Where necessary, an off-site analysis of information supplied by the contractor or otherwise gathered during or pursuant to the on-site review;

(2) *Off-site review of records.* An analysis and evaluation of the affirmative action program (or any part thereof) and supporting documentation, and other documents related to the contractor's personnel policies and employment actions that may be relevant to a determination of whether the contractor has complied with the requirements of VEVRAA and its regulations;

(3) *Compliance check.* A determination of whether the contractor has maintained records consistent with § 60–300.80; OFCCP may request the documents be provided either on-site or off-site; or

(4) *Focused review.* A review restricted to one or more components of the contractor's organization or one or more aspects of the contractor's employment practices.

(b) Where deficiencies are found to exist, reasonable efforts shall be made to secure compliance through conciliation and persuasion pursuant to § 60–300.62.

(c) *Reporting requirements.* During a compliance evaluation, OFCCP may verify whether the contractor has complied with applicable reporting requirements required under regulations promulgated by the Veterans' Employment and Training Service (VETS). If the contractor has not complied with any such reporting requirement, OFCCP will notify VETS.

(d) *Pre-award compliance evaluations.* Each agency will include in the invitation for bids for each formally advertised nonconstruction contract or state at the outset of negotiations for each negotiated contract, that if the award, when let, should total $10 million or more, the prospective contractor and its known first-tier subcontractors with subcontracts of $10 million or more will be subject to a compliance evaluation before the award of the contract unless OFCCP has conducted an evaluation and found them to be in compliance with VEVRAA within the preceding 24 months. The awarding agency will notify OFCCP and request appropriate action and findings in accordance with this subsection. Within 15 days of the notice OFCCP will inform the awarding agency of its intention to conduct a pre-award compliance evaluation. If OFCCP does not inform the awarding agency within that period of its intention to conduct a pre-award compliance evaluation, clearance shall be presumed and the awarding agency is authorized to proceed with the award. If OFCCP informs the awarding agency of its intention to conduct a pre-award compliance evaluation, OFCCP will be allowed an additional 20 days after the date that it so informs the awarding agency to provide its conclusions. If OFCCP does not provide the awarding agency with its conclusions within that period, clearance will be presumed and the awarding agency is authorized to proceed with the award.

§ 60–300.61 Complaint procedures.

(a) *Place and time of filing.* Any applicant for employment with a contractor or any employee of a contractor may, personally, or by an authorized representative, file a written complaint alleging a violation of the Act or the regulations in this part. The complaint may allege individual or class-wide violation(s). Such complaint must be filed within 300 days of the date of the alleged violation, unless the time for filing is extended by OFCCP for good cause shown. Complaints may be submitted to OFCCP, 200 Constitution Avenue NW., Washington, DC 20210, or to any OFCCP regional, district, or area office. Complaints may also be submitted to the Veterans' Employment and Training Service of the Department of Labor directly, or through the Local Veterans' Employment Representative (LVER) at the local employment service office. Such parties will assist veterans in preparing complaints, promptly refer such complaints to OFCCP, and maintain a record of all complaints which they receive and forward. OFCCP shall inform the party forwarding the complaint of the progress and results of its complaint investigation. The state employment service delivery system shall cooperate with the Director in the investigation of any complaint.

(b) *Contents of complaints.*—(1) *In general.* A complaint must be signed by the complainant or his or her authorized representative and must contain the following information:

(i) Name and address (including telephone number) of the complainant;

(ii) Name and address of the contractor who committed the alleged violation;

(iii) Documentation showing that the individual is a protected veteran or pre-JVA veteran. Such documentation must include a copy of the veteran's form DD–214, and, where applicable, a copy of the veteran's Benefits Award Letter, or similar Department of Veterans Affairs certification, updated within one year prior to the date the complaint is filed;

(iv) A description of the act or acts considered to be a violation, including the pertinent dates (in the case of an alleged continuing violation, the earliest and most recent date that the alleged violation occurred should be stated); and

(v) Other pertinent information available which will assist in the investigation and resolution of the complaint, including the name of any known Federal agency with which the employer has contracted.

(2) *Third party complaints.* A complaint filed by an authorized representative need not identify by name the person on whose behalf it is filed. The person filing the complaint, however, shall provide OFCCP with the name, address and telephone number of the person on whose behalf it is made, and the other information specified in paragraph (b)(1) of this section. OFCCP shall verify the authorization of such a complaint by the person on whose behalf the complaint is made. Any such person may request that OFCCP keep his or her identity confidential, and OFCCP will protect the individual's confidentiality wherever that is possible given the facts and circumstances in the complaint.

(c) *Incomplete information.* Where a complaint contains incomplete information, OFCCP shall seek the needed information from the complainant. If the information is not furnished to OFCCP within 60 days of the date of such request, the case may be closed.

(d) *Investigations.* The Department of Labor shall institute a prompt investigation of each complaint.

(e) *Resolution of matters.* (1) If the complaint investigation finds no violation of the Act or this part, or if the Director decides not to refer the matter to the Solicitor of Labor for enforcement proceedings against the contractor pursuant to § 60–300.65(a)(1), the complainant and contractor shall be so notified. The Director, on his or her own initiative, may reconsider his or her determination or the determination of any of his or her designated officers who have authority to issue Notifications of Results of Investigation.

(2) The Director will review all determinations of no violation that involve complaints that are not also cognizable under Title I of the Americans with Disabilities Act.

(3) In cases where the Director decides to reconsider the determination of a Notification of Results of Investigation, the Director shall provide prompt notification of his or her intent to reconsider, which is effective upon issuance, and his or her final determination after reconsideration, to the person claiming to be aggrieved, the person making the complaint on behalf of such person, if any, and the contractor.

(4) If the investigation finds a violation of the Act or this part, OFCCP shall invite the contractor to participate in conciliation discussions pursuant to § 60–300.62.

§ 60–300.62 Conciliation agreements.

If a compliance evaluation, complaint investigation or other review by OFCCP finds a material violation of the Act or this part, and if the contractor is willing to correct the violations and/or deficiencies, and if OFCCP determines that settlement on that basis (rather than referral for consideration of formal enforcement) is appropriate, a written conciliation agreement shall be required. The agreement shall provide for such remedial action as may be necessary to correct the violations and/or deficiencies noted, including, where appropriate (but not necessarily limited to) such make whole remedies as back pay and retroactive seniority. The agreement shall also specify the time period for completion of the remedial action; the period shall be no longer than the minimum period necessary to complete the action.

§ 60–300.63 Violation of conciliation agreements.

(a) When OFCCP believes that a conciliation agreement has been violated, the following procedures are applicable:

(1) A written notice shall be sent to the contractor setting forth the violation alleged and summarizing the supporting evidence. The contractor shall have 15 days from receipt of the notice to respond, except in those cases in which OFCCP asserts that such a delay would result in irreparable injury to the employment rights of affected employees or applicants.

(2) During the 15-day period the contractor may demonstrate in writing that it has not violated its commitments.

(b) In those cases in which OFCCP asserts that a delay would result in irreparable injury to the employment rights of affected employees or applicants, enforcement proceedings may be initiated immediately without proceeding through any other requirement contained in this chapter.

(c) In any proceedings involving an alleged violation of a conciliation agreement OFCCP may seek enforcement of the agreement itself and shall not be required to present proof of the underlying violations resolved by the agreement.

§ 60–300.64 Show cause notices.

When the Director has reasonable cause to believe that the contractor has violated the Act or this part, he or she may issue a notice requiring the contractor to show cause, within 30 days, why monitoring, enforcement proceedings or other appropriate action to ensure compliance should not be instituted. The issuance of such a notice is not a prerequisite to instituting enforcement proceedings (see § 60–300.65).

§ 60–300.65 Enforcement proceedings.

(a) *General.* (1) If a compliance evaluation, complaint investigation or other review by OFCCP finds a violation of the Act or this part, and the violation has not been corrected in accordance with the conciliation procedures in this part, or OFCCP determines that referral for consideration of formal enforcement (rather than settlement) is appropriate, OFCCP may refer the matter to the Solicitor of Labor with a recommendation for the institution of enforcement proceedings to enjoin the violations, to seek appropriate relief, and to impose appropriate sanctions, or any of the above in this sentence. OFCCP may seek back pay and other make whole relief for aggrieved individuals identified during a complaint investigation or compliance evaluation. Such individuals need not have filed a complaint as a prerequisite to OFCCP seeking such relief on their behalf. Interest on back pay shall be calculated from the date of the loss and compounded quarterly at the percentage rate established by the Internal Revenue Service for the underpayment of taxes.

(2) In addition to the administrative proceedings set forth in this section, the Director may, within the limitations of applicable law, seek appropriate judicial action to enforce the contractual provisions set forth in § 60–300.5, including appropriate injunctive relief.

(b) *Hearing practice and procedure.* (1) In administrative enforcement proceedings the contractor shall be provided an opportunity for a formal hearing. All hearings conducted under the Act and this part shall be governed by the Rules of Practice for Administrative Proceedings to Enforce Equal Opportunity Under Executive Order 11246 contained in 41 CFR part 60–30 and the Rules of Evidence set out in the Rules of Practice and Procedure for Administrative Hearings Before the Office of Administrative Law Judges contained in 29 CFR part 18, subpart B: *Provided,* That a final administrative order shall be issued within one year from the date of the issuance of the recommended findings, conclusions and decision of the Administrative Law Judge, or the submission of exceptions and responses to exceptions to such decision (if any), whichever is later.

(2) Complaints may be filed by the Solicitor, the Associate Solicitor for Civil Rights and Labor-Management, Regional Solicitors, and Associate Regional Solicitors.

(3) For the purposes of hearings pursuant to this part, references in 41 CFR part 60–30 to "Executive Order 11246" shall mean the Vietnam Era Veterans' Readjustment Assistance Act of 1974, as amended; references to "equal opportunity clause" shall mean the equal opportunity clause published at § 60–300.5; and references to "regulations" shall mean the regulations contained in this part.

§ 60–300.66 Sanctions and penalties.

(a) *Withholding progress payments.* With the prior approval of the Director, so much of the accrued payment due on the contract or any other contract between the Government contractor and the Federal Government may be withheld as necessary to correct any violations of the provisions of the Act or this part.

(b) *Termination.* A contract may be canceled or terminated, in whole or in part, for failure to comply with the provisions of the Act or this part.

(c) *Debarment.* A contractor may be debarred from receiving future contracts for failure to comply with the provisions of the Act or this part subject to reinstatement pursuant to § 60–300.68. Debarment may be imposed for an indefinite period, or may be imposed for a fixed period of not less than six months but no more than three years.

(d) *Hearing opportunity.* An opportunity for a formal hearing shall be afforded to a contractor before the imposition of any sanction or penalty.

§ 60–300.67 Notification of agencies.

The Director shall ensure that the heads of all agencies are notified of any debarments taken against any contractor.

§ 60–300.68 Reinstatement of ineligible contractors.

(a) *Application for reinstatement.* A contractor debarred from further contracts for an indefinite period under the Act may request reinstatement in a letter filed with the Director at any time after the effective date of the debarment; a contractor debarred for a fixed period may make such a request following the expiration of six months from the effective date of the debarment. In connection with the reinstatement proceedings, all debarred contractors shall be required to show that they have established and will carry out employment policies and practices in compliance with the Act and this part. Additionally, in determining whether reinstatement is appropriate for a contractor debarred for a fixed period, the Director also shall consider, among other factors, the severity of the violation which resulted in the debarment, the contractor's attitude towards compliance, the contractor's past compliance history, and whether the contractor's reinstatement would impede the effective enforcement of the Act or this part. Before reaching a decision, the Director may conduct a compliance evaluation of the contractor and may require the contractor to supply additional information regarding the request for reinstatement. The Director shall issue a written decision on the request.

(b) *Petition for review.* Within 30 days of its receipt of a decision denying a request for reinstatement, the contractor may file a petition for review of the decision with the Secretary. The petition shall set forth the grounds for the contractor's objections to the Director's decision. The petition shall be served on the Director and the Associate Solicitor for Civil Rights and Labor-Management and shall include the decision as an appendix. The Director may file a response within 14 days to the petition. The Secretary shall issue the final agency decision denying or granting the request for reinstatement. Before reaching a final decision, the Secretary may issue such additional orders respecting procedure as he or she finds appropriate in the circumstances, including an order referring the matter to the Office of Administrative Law Judges for an evidentiary hearing where there is a material factual dispute that cannot be resolved on the record before the Secretary.

§ 60–300.69 Intimidation and interference.

(a) The contractor shall not harass, intimidate, threaten, coerce, or discriminate against any individual because the individual has engaged in or may engage in any of the following activities:

(1) Filing a complaint;

(2) Assisting or participating in any manner in an investigation, compliance evaluation, hearing, or any other activity related to the administration of the Act or any other Federal, state or local law requiring equal opportunity for protected veterans;

(3) Opposing any act or practice made unlawful by the Act or this part or any other Federal, state or local law requiring equal opportunity for protected veterans, or

(4) Exercising any other right protected by the Act or this part.

(b) The contractor shall ensure that all persons under its control do not engage in such harassment, intimidation, threats, coercion or discrimination. The sanctions and penalties contained in this part may be exercised by the

Director against any contractor who violates this obligation.

§ 60–300.70 Disputed matters related to compliance with the Act.

The procedures set forth in the regulations in this part govern all disputes relative to the contractor's compliance with the Act and this part. Any disputes relating to issues other than compliance, including contract costs arising out of the contractor's efforts to comply, shall be determined by the disputes clause of the contract.

Subpart E—Ancillary Matters

§ 60–300.80 Recordkeeping.

(a) *General requirements.* Except as set forth in paragraph (b) of this section, any personnel or employment record made or kept by the contractor shall be preserved by the contractor for a period of two years from the date of the making of the record or the personnel action involved, whichever occurs later. However, if the contractor has fewer than 150 employees or does not have a Government contract of at least $150,000, the minimum record retention period will be one year from the date of the making of the record or the personnel action involved, whichever occurs later, except as set forth in paragraph (b) of this section. Such records include, but are not necessarily limited to, records relating to requests for reasonable accommodation; the results of any physical examination; job advertisements and postings; applications and resumes; tests and test results; interview notes; and other records having to do with hiring, assignment, promotion, demotion, transfer, lay-off or termination, rates of pay or other terms of compensation, and selection for training or apprenticeship. In the case of involuntary termination of an employee, the personnel records of the individual terminated shall be kept for a period of two years from the date of the termination, except that contractors that have fewer than 150 employees or that do not have a Government contract of at least $150,000 shall keep such records for a period of one year from the date of the termination. Where the contractor has received notice that a complaint of discrimination has been filed, that a compliance evaluation has been initiated, or that an enforcement action has been commenced, the contractor shall preserve all personnel records relevant to the complaint, compliance evaluation or action until final disposition of the complaint, compliance evaluation or action. The term *personnel records relevant to the complaint, compliance evaluation or action* would include, for example, personnel or employment records relating to the aggrieved person and to all other employees holding positions similar to that held or sought by the aggrieved person, and application forms or test papers completed by an unsuccessful applicant and by all other candidates for the same position as that for which the aggrieved person applied and was rejected.

(b) *Records with three-year retention requirement.* Records required by §§ 60–300.44(f)(4), 60–300.44(k), and 60–300.45(c) shall be maintained by all contractors for a period of three years from the date of the making of the record.

(c) *Failure to preserve records.* Failure to preserve complete and accurate records as required by this part constitutes noncompliance with the contractor's obligations under the Act and this part. Where the contractor has destroyed or failed to preserve records as required by this section, there may be a presumption that the information destroyed or not preserved would have been unfavorable to the contractor: *Provided,* That this presumption shall not apply where the contractor shows that the destruction or failure to preserve records results from circumstances that are outside of the contractor's control.

(d) The requirements of this section shall apply only to records made or kept on or after the date that the Office of Management and Budget has cleared the requirements.

§ 60–300.81 Access to records.

Each contractor shall permit access during normal business hours to its places of business for the purpose of conducting on-site compliance evaluations and complaint investigations and inspecting and copying such books, accounts, and records, including electronic records, and any other material OFCCP deems relevant to the matter under investigation and pertinent to compliance with the Act or this part. Contractors must also provide OFCCP access to these materials, including electronic records, off-site for purposes of conducting compliance evaluations and complaint investigations. Upon request, the contractor must provide OFCCP information about all format(s), including specific electronic formats, in which the contractor maintains its records and other information. The contractor must provide records and other information in any of the formats in which they are maintained, as selected by OFCCP. Information obtained in this manner shall be used only in connection with the administration of the Act and in furtherance of the purposes of the Act. OFCCP will treat records provided by the contractor to OFCCP under this section as confidential to the maximum extent the information is exempt from public disclosure under the Freedom of Information Act, 5 U.S.C. 552.

§ 60–300.82 Labor organizations and recruiting and training agencies.

(a) Whenever performance in accordance with the equal opportunity clause or any matter contained in the regulations in this part may necessitate a revision of a collective bargaining agreement, the labor organizations which are parties to such agreement shall be given an adequate opportunity to present their views to OFCCP.

(b) OFCCP shall use its best efforts, directly or through contractors, subcontractors, local officials, the Department of Veterans Affairs, vocational rehabilitation facilities, and all other available instrumentalities, to cause any labor organization, recruiting and training agency or other representative of workers who are employed by a contractor to cooperate with, and to assist in, the implementation of the purposes of the Act.

§ 60–300.83 Rulings and interpretations.

Rulings under or interpretations of the Act and this part shall be made by the Director.

§ 60–300.84 Responsibilities of appropriate employment service delivery system.

By statute, appropriate employment service delivery systems are required to refer qualified protected veterans to fill employment openings listed by contractors with such appropriate employment delivery systems pursuant to the mandatory job listing requirements of the equal opportunity clause and are required to give priority to protected veterans in making such referrals. The employment service delivery systems shall provide OFCCP, upon request, information pertinent to whether the contractor is in compliance with the mandatory job listing requirements of the equal opportunity clause.

Appendix A to Part 60–300—Guidelines on a Contractor's Duty To Provide Reasonable Accommodation

The guidelines in this appendix are in large part derived from, and are consistent with, the discussion regarding the duty to provide reasonable accommodation contained in the Interpretive Guidance on

Title I of the Americans with Disabilities Act (ADA) set out as an appendix to the regulations issued by the Equal Employment Opportunity Commission (EEOC) implementing the ADA (29 CFR part 1630). Although the following discussion is intended to provide an independent "free-standing" source of guidance with respect to the duty to provide reasonable accommodation under this part, to the extent that the EEOC appendix provides additional guidance which is consistent with the following discussion, it may be relied upon for purposes of this part as well. *See* § 60–300.1(c). Contractors are obligated to provide reasonable accommodation and to take affirmative action. Reasonable accommodation under VEVRAA, like reasonable accommodation required under section 503 and the ADA, is a part of the nondiscrimination obligation. *See* EEOC appendix cited in this paragraph. Affirmative action is unique to VEVRAA and section 503, and includes actions above and beyond those required as a matter of nondiscrimination. An example of this is the requirement discussed in paragraph 2 of this appendix that a contractor *shall* make an inquiry of a disabled veteran who is having significant difficulty performing his or her job.

1. A contractor is required to make reasonable accommodations to the known physical or mental limitations of an "otherwise qualified" disabled veteran, unless the contractor can demonstrate that the accommodation would impose an undue hardship on the operation of its business. As stated in § 60–300.2(s), a disabled veteran is qualified if he or she has the ability to perform the essential functions of the position with or without reasonable accommodation. A contractor is required to make a reasonable accommodation with respect to its application process if the disabled veteran is qualified with respect to that process. One is "otherwise qualified" if he or she is qualified for a job, except that, because of a disability, he or she needs a reasonable accommodation to be able to perform the job's essential functions.

2. Although the contractor would not be expected to accommodate disabilities of which it is unaware, the contractor has an affirmative obligation to provide a reasonable accommodation for applicants and employees who are known to be disabled veterans. As stated in § 60–300.42(b) (see also Appendix B of this part), the contractor is required to invite applicants who have been provided an offer of employment, before they are placed on the contractor's payroll, to indicate whether they are a disabled veteran who may be protected by the Act. Section 60–300.42(d) further provides that the contractor must seek the advice of disabled veterans who "self-identify" in this way as to reasonable accommodation. Moreover, § 60–300.44(d) provides that if an employee who is a known disabled veteran is having significant difficulty performing his or her job and it is reasonable to conclude that the performance problem may be related to the disability, the contractor is required to confidentially inquire whether the problem is disability related and if the employee is in need of a reasonable accommodation.

3. An accommodation is any change in the work environment or in the way things are customarily done that enables a disabled veteran to enjoy equal employment opportunities. Equal employment opportunity means an opportunity to attain the same level of performance, or to enjoy the same level of benefits and privileges of employment, as are available to the average similarly situated employee without a disability. Thus, for example, an accommodation made to assist an employee who is a disabled veteran in the performance of his or her job must be adequate to enable the individual to perform the essential functions of the position. The accommodation, however, does not have to be the "best" accommodation possible, so long as it is sufficient to meet the job-related needs of the individual being accommodated. There are three areas in which reasonable accommodations may be necessary: (1) accommodations in the application process; (2) accommodations that enable employees who are disabled veterans to perform the essential functions of the position held or desired; and (3) accommodations that enable employees who are disabled veterans to enjoy equal benefits and privileges of employment as are enjoyed by employees without disabilities.

4. The term "undue hardship" refers to any accommodation that would be unduly costly, extensive, substantial, or disruptive, or that would fundamentally alter the nature or operation of the contractor's business. The contractor's claim that the cost of a particular accommodation will impose an undue hardship requires a determination of which financial resources should be considered—those of the contractor in its entirety or only those of the facility that will be required to provide the accommodation. This inquiry requires an analysis of the financial relationship between the contractor and the facility in order to determine what resources will be available to the facility in providing the accommodation. If the contractor can show that the cost of the accommodation would impose an undue hardship, it would still be required to provide the accommodation if the funding is available from another source, *e.g.*, the Department of Veterans Affairs or a state vocational rehabilitation agency, or if Federal, state or local tax deductions or tax credits are available to offset the cost of the accommodation. In the absence of such funding, the disabled veteran must be given the option of providing the accommodation or of paying that portion of the cost which constitutes the undue hardship on the operation of the business.

5. The definition for "reasonable accommodation" in § 60–300.2(t) lists a number of examples of the most common types of accommodations that the contractor may be required to provide. There are any number of specific accommodations that may be appropriate for particular situations. The discussion in this appendix is not intended to provide an exhaustive list of required accommodations (as no such list would be feasible); rather, it is intended to provide general guidance regarding the nature of the obligation. The decision as to whether a reasonable accommodation is appropriate must be made on a case-by-case basis. The contractor must consult with the disabled veteran in deciding on the reasonable accommodation; frequently, the individual will know exactly what accommodation he or she will need to perform successfully in a particular job, and may suggest an accommodation which is simpler and less expensive than the accommodation the contractor might have devised. Other resources to consult include the appropriate state vocational rehabilitation services agency, the Equal Employment Opportunity Commission (1–800–669–4000 (voice), 1–800–669–6820 (TTY)), the Job Accommodation Network (JAN) operated by the Office of Disability Employment Policy in the U.S. Department of Labor (1–800–526–7234 or 1–800–232–9675), private disability organizations (including those that serve veterans), and other employers.

6. With respect to accommodations that can permit an employee who is a disabled veteran to perform essential functions successfully, a reasonable accommodation may require the contractor to, for instance, modify or acquire equipment. For the visually-impaired, such accommodations may include providing adaptive hardware and software for computers, electronic visual aids, Braille devices, talking calculators, magnifiers, audio recordings and Braille or large-print materials. For persons with hearing impairments, reasonable accommodations may include providing telephone handset amplifiers, telephones compatible with hearing aids and text telephones (TTYs). For persons with limited physical dexterity, the obligation may require the provision of telephone headsets, speech activated software and raised or lowered furniture.

7. Other reasonable accommodations of this type may include providing personal assistants such as a reader, sign language interpreter or travel attendant, permitting the use of accrued paid leave or providing additional unpaid leave for necessary treatment. The contractor may also be required to make existing facilities readily accessible to and usable by disabled veterans—including areas used by employees for purposes other than the performance of essential job functions such as restrooms, break rooms, cafeterias, lounges, auditoriums, libraries, parking lots and credit unions. This type of accommodation will enable employees to enjoy equal benefits and privileges of employment as are enjoyed by employees who do not have disabilities.

8. Another of the potential accommodations listed in § 60–300.2(t) is job restructuring. This may involve reallocating or redistributing those nonessential, marginal job functions which a qualified disabled veteran cannot perform to another position. Accordingly, if a clerical employee who is a disabled veteran is occasionally required to lift heavy boxes containing files, but cannot do so because of a disability, this task may be reassigned to another employee. The contractor, however, is not required to reallocate essential functions, i.e., those functions that the individual who holds the job would have to perform, with or without

reasonable accommodation, in order to be considered qualified for the position. For instance, the contractor which has a security guard position which requires the incumbent to inspect identity cards would not have to provide a blind disabled veteran with an assistant to perform that duty; in such a case, the assistant would be performing an essential function of the job for the disabled veteran. Job restructuring may also involve allowing part-time or modified work schedules. For instance, flexible or adjusted work schedules could benefit disabled veterans who cannot work a standard schedule because of the need to obtain medical treatment, or disabled veterans with mobility impairments who depend on a public transportation system that is not accessible during the hours of a standard schedule.

9. Reasonable accommodation may also include reassignment to a vacant position. In general, reassignment should be considered only when accommodation within the disabled veteran's current position would pose an undue hardship. Reassignment is not required for applicants. However, in making hiring decisions, contractors are encouraged to consider applicants who are known disabled veterans for all available positions for which they may be qualified when the position(s) applied for is unavailable. Reassignment may not be used to limit, segregate, or otherwise discriminate against employees who are disabled veterans by forcing reassignments to undesirable positions or to designated offices or facilities. Employers should reassign the individual to an equivalent position in terms of pay, status, etc., if the individual is qualified, and if the position is vacant within a reasonable amount of time. A "reasonable amount of time" must be determined in light of the totality of the circumstances.

10. The contractor may reassign an individual to a lower graded position if there are no accommodations that would enable the employee to remain in the current position and there are no vacant equivalent positions for which the individual is qualified with or without reasonable accommodation. The contractor may maintain the reassigned disabled veteran at the salary of the higher graded position, and must do so if it maintains the salary of reassigned employees who are not disabled veterans. It should also be noted that the contractor is not required to promote a disabled veteran as an accommodation.

11. With respect to the application process, reasonable accommodations may include the following: (1) providing information regarding job vacancies in a form accessible to disabled veterans who are vision or hearing impaired, e.g., by making an announcement available in braille, in large print, or on computer disc, or by responding to job inquiries via TTYs; (2) providing readers, sign language interpreters and other similar assistance during the application, testing and interview process; (3) appropriately adjusting or modifying employment-related examinations, e.g., extending regular time deadlines, allowing a disabled veteran who is blind or has a learning disorder such as dyslexia to provide oral answers for a written test, and permitting an applicant, regardless of the nature of his or her ability, to demonstrate skills through alternative techniques and utilization of adapted tools, aids and devices; and (4) ensuring a disabled veteran with a mobility impairment full access to testing locations such that the applicant's test scores accurately reflect the applicant's skills or aptitude rather than the applicant's mobility impairment.

Appendix B to Part 60–300—Sample Invitation to Self-Identify

[Sample Invitation to Self-Identify]

1. This employer is a Government contractor subject to the Vietnam Era Veterans' Readjustment Assistance Act of 1974, as amended by the Jobs for Veterans Act of 2002, 38 U.S.C. 4212 (VEVRAA), which requires Government contractors to take affirmative action to employ and advance in employment: (1) disabled veterans; (2) recently separated veterans; (3) active duty wartime or campaign badge veterans; and (4) Armed Forces service medal veterans. These classifications are defined as follows:

- A "disabled veteran" is one of the following:
- a veteran of the U.S. military, ground, naval or air service who is entitled to compensation (or who but for the receipt of military retired pay would be entitled to compensation) under laws administered by the Secretary of Veterans Affairs; or
- a person who was discharged or released from active duty because of a service-connected disability.
- A "recently separated veteran" means any veteran during the three-year period beginning on the date of such veteran's discharge or release from active duty in the U.S. military, ground, naval, or air service.
- An "active duty wartime or campaign badge veteran" means a veteran who served on active duty in the U.S. military, ground, naval or air service during a war, or in a campaign or expedition for which a campaign badge has been authorized under the laws administered by the Department of Defense.
- An "Armed forces service medal veteran" means a veteran who, while serving on active duty in the U.S. military, ground, naval or air service, participated in a United States military operation for which an Armed Forces service medal was awarded pursuant to Executive Order 12985.

Protected veterans may have additional rights under USERRA—the Uniformed Services Employment and Reemployment Rights Act. In particular, if you were absent from employment in order to perform service in the uniformed service, you may be entitled to be reemployed by your employer in the position you would have obtained with reasonable certainty if not for the absence due to service. For more information, call the U.S. Department of Labor's Veterans Employment and Training Service (VETS), toll-free, at 1–866–4–USA–DOL.

2. [THE FOLLOWING TEXT SHOULD BE USED WHEN EXTENDING THE "PRE-OFFER" INVITATION AS REQUIRED BY 41 CFR 60–300.42(a). THE DEFINITIONS OF THE SEPARATE CLASSIFICATIONS OF PROTECTED VETERANS SET FORTH IN PARAGRAPH 1 MUST ACCOMPANY THIS SELF–IDENTIFICATION REQUEST.] If you believe you belong to any of the categories of protected veterans listed above, please indicate by checking the appropriate box below. As a Government contractor subject to VEVRAA, we request this information in order to measure the effectiveness of the outreach and positive recruitment efforts we undertake pursuant to VEVRAA.

[ ] I IDENTIFY AS ONE OR MORE OF THE CLASSIFICATIONS OF PROTECTED VETERAN LISTED ABOVE

[ ] I AM NOT A PROTECTED VETERAN

[THE FOLLOWING TEXT SHOULD BE USED IF REQUIRED TO EXTEND THE "POST–OFFER" INVITATION DESCRIBED IN 41 CFR 60–300.42(b). THE DEFINITIONS OF THE SEPARATE CLASSIFICATIONS OF PROTECTED VETERAN INCLUDED IN THE POST–OFFER INVITATION MUST ACCOMPANY THIS SELF–IDENTIFICATION REQUEST.]

As a Government contractor subject to VEVRAA, we are required to submit a report to the United States Department of Labor each year identifying the number of our employees belonging to each specified "protected veteran" category. If you believe you belong to any of the categories of protected veterans listed above, please indicate by checking the appropriate box below.

I BELONG TO THE FOLLOWING CLASSIFICATIONS OF PROTECTED VETERANS (CHOOSE ALL THAT APPLY):

[ ] DISABLED VETERAN

[ ] RECENTLY SEPARATED VETERAN

[ ] ACTIVE WARTIME OR CAMPAIGN BADGE VETERAN

[ ] ARMED FORCES SERVICE MEDAL VETERAN

[ ] I am a protected veteran, but I choose not to self-identify the classifications to which I belong.

[ ] I am NOT a protected veteran.

If you are a disabled veteran it would assist us if you tell us whether there are accommodations we could make that would enable you to perform the essential functions of the job, including special equipment, changes in the physical layout of the job, changes in the way the job is customarily performed, provision of personal assistance services or other accommodations. This information will assist us in making reasonable accommodations for your disability.

3. Submission of this information is voluntary and refusal to provide it will not subject you to any adverse treatment. The information provided will be used only in ways that are not inconsistent with the Vietnam Era Veterans' Readjustment Assistance Act of 1974, as amended.

4. The information you submit will be kept confidential, except that (i) supervisors and managers may be informed regarding restrictions on the work or duties of disabled veterans, and regarding necessary accommodations; (ii) first aid and safety personnel may be informed, when and to the

extent appropriate, if you have a condition that might require emergency treatment; and (iii) Government officials engaged in enforcing laws administered by the Office of Federal Contract Compliance Programs, or enforcing the Americans with Disabilities Act, may be informed.

5. [The contractor should here insert a brief provision summarizing the relevant portion of its affirmative action program.]

Appendix C to Part 60–300—Review of Personnel Processes

The following is a set of procedures which contractors may use to meet the requirements of § 60–300.44(b):

1. The application or personnel form of each known applicant who is a protected veteran should be annotated to identify each vacancy for which the applicant was considered, and the form should be quickly retrievable for review by the Department of Labor and the contractor's personnel officials for use in investigations and internal compliance activities.

2. The personnel or application records of each known protected veteran should include (i) the identification of each promotion for which the protected veteran was considered, and (ii) the identification of each training program for which the protected veteran was considered.

3. In each case where an employee or applicant who is a protected veteran is rejected for employment, promotion, or training, the contractor should prepare a statement of the reason as well as a description of the accommodations considered (for a rejected disabled veteran). The statement of the reason for rejection (if the reason is medically related), and the description of the accommodations considered, should be treated as confidential medical records in accordance with § 60–300.23(d). These materials should be available to the applicant or employee concerned upon request.

4. Where applicants or employees are selected for hire, promotion, or training and the contractor undertakes any accommodation which makes it possible for him or her to place a disabled veteran on the job, the contractor should make a record containing a description of the accommodation. The record should be treated as a confidential medical record in accordance with § 60–300.23(d).

[FR Doc. 2013–21227 Filed 9–23–13; 8:45 am]

BILLING CODE 4510–45–P

Judges' Deskbook:

Office of Federal Contract Compliance Programs (OFCCP)

U.S. Department of Labor

Office of Administrative Law Judges
800 K Street, NW, Suite 400-N
Washington, DC 20001-8002

(202) 693-7300
(202) 693-7365 (FAX)

May 2, 2011
Edited by: Seena Foster[1]

Judges' Deskbook:
Office of Federal Contract Compliance Programs (OFCCP)

The Office of Federal Contract Compliance Programs is charged with investigating and prosecuting alleged violations of Executive Order 11246, Section 503 of the Rehabilitation Act of 1973 (Rehabilitation Act), and Section 402 of the Vietnam Era Veterans' Readjustment Assistance Act of 1974 (Veterans' Act or VEVRAA). The purpose of Executive Order 11246 is to promote and ensure equal employment opportunity for all persons without regard to race, color, religion, sex, or national origin. It applies to those persons who are employed or seeking employment with government contractors or with contractors performing under federally assisted construction contracts. The Veterans' Act requires that government contractors take affirmative action to employ and advance qualified disabled veterans and veterans of the Vietnam Era. Finally, the Rehabilitation Act requires that government contractors take affirmative action to employ and promote qualified handicapped individuals.

Captions for these cases are: *Department of Labor, Office of Federal Contract Compliance Programs, Plaintiff v. ____________________, Defendant. See* 41 C.F.R. §§ 60-30.5 and 60-30.6. Pursuant to 41 C.F.R. § 60-30.35 the administrative law judge issues a recommended decision and "[t]he recommendations shall be certified, together with the record, to the Administrative Review Board, . . . for a final Administrative order."

---

[1] Some of the older case law was incorporated from materials developed by the Department of Labor's Solicitor's office.

[c] Discretion to investigate incomplete complaints
2. Who may file
[a] Generally
[b] Impleader and intervener
[c] Class actions permitted
3. Exhaustion of remedies
4. Service
B. Scope of investigation
1. Generally
2. Discretionary decisions by the Secretary not presumptively reviewable by federal courts
C. Time limit for filing a complaint; 180 days
1. Generally
[a] Complaint for discrimination
[b] Administrative complaint based on compliance review
2. Each claim analyzed separately
[a] Generally
[b] Continuing violations
i. Established
ii. Not established
3. Extension of time to file claim
[a] ALJ without authority to grant
[b] Director with authority to grant for good cause
i. Generally
ii. Abuse of discretion
4. Not controlled by Title VII statute of limitations
D. Laches
E. Collateral estoppel
1. Held applicable
2. Held inapplicable
F. Bankruptcy stay not apply
G. Bifurcated hearing; no jurisdiction over appeal
H. Issues of constitutionality and validity
1. ALJ without authority to determine validity of regulations
2. Language not unconstitutionally vague
I. "Working on the contract" is a jurisdictional issue and cannot be presumed
1. Generally
2. Admission by defendant; insufficient to establish
J. Included in contract by law
K. Interplay with other statutes
1. Department of Transportation jurisdiction
2. Civil Rights Act of 1964
3. Contract Disputes Act
IV. Standard of review
A. By the ALJ
B. By the ARB
1.Generally
2. Interlocutory appeal not favored

J. Sanctions for failure to comply with discovery
    1. No authority to impose attorney fees and costs
    2. Debarment
    3. Discovery requests must be decided prior to issuance of summary judgment
K. Privileges
    1. Informant's privilege
    2. Deliberative process privilege
    3. Attorney-client privilege
    4. Work-product privilege

VII. Constitutional issues
A. First Amendment
B. Fourth Amendment
    1. Generally
    2. "Consent" exception
    3. Requirements of the Fourth Amendment
        a. Violated
        b. Not violated
C. Fifth Amendment
D. Expedited hearing procedures

VIII. Government contractor
A. Federal contracts
    1. Generally
        a. Apply to all operations absent obtaining a waiver
        b. Does not apply to all operations; waiver regulations
    2. Obligation to ensure that subcontractor complies
    3. Federal government may be a purchaser or seller
    4. Waiver for independent facilities
B. Federal contract defined
    1. Established
        a. Depository of federal funds
        b. Bills of lading
        c. Contract for use of federal property and services
        d. Blanket purchase agreement
        e. Subcontractor performs "necessary" services for the federal contract
    2. Not established
        a. Lease of space in a government building
        b. Subcontractor not perform "necessary" services for
        c. Federal grant monies not constitute federal contracts
    3. Term of contract

IX. Compliance Review
A. Generally
    1. Desk audit not required to precede on-site review
    2. Follow-up "on-site review" permitted
    3. SCHEDULING LETTER, LIMITATION ON SCOPE OF REVIEW
B. Reporting requirements
C. Establishing affirmative action plans

X. The Rehabilitation Act
A. Generally

1. Types of adverse actions
2. Affirmative action requires more than obligation not to discriminate
3. Employer's knowledge of disability at time of adverse action required
4. Sovereign immunity of states

B. Qualified handicapped individual; "substantially limited in a major life activity"
   1. Burdens
      a. Generally
      b. Dual motives
      c. Worker argued not handicapped; complaint dismissed
   2. Major life activity, defined
   3. Employee regarded as a handicapped individual
   4. Ability at the time of employment decision relevant
      a. Generally
      b. Employer must reconsider decision on request if condition has changed
   5. Assessment of disability must be based on mitigated condition
      a. Myopia
      b. Radial keratomy

C. Business necessity for job requirements
   1. Defendant's burden to establish
   2. Defendant must adequately research employee's condition
      a. Defendant has right to medical records/releases
      b. Failure to gather sufficient information
   3. "Business necessity" established
   4. "Business necessity" not established
   5. Likelihood and imminence of injury
      a. Generally
      b. Defendant's burden to establish
         i. Generally
         ii. Failure to gather sufficient information
      c. Factors to be considered; individualized consideration
         i. Generally
         ii. Risk of higher premiums
      d. Circumstances at time of decision considered
      e. Complainant's actions

D. Accommodation
   1. Defendant's burden to establish undue hardship
      a. Generally
      b. Must gather information to make determination of reasonable accommodation
         i. Generally
   2. Undue hardship
      a. Established
         i. Conflict with seniority rules
      b. Not established
      c. Not at issue; worker capable of performing job without accommodation
      d. Use of transfer as accommodation
         i. Generally
         ii. Not constitute accommodation; lower pay

E. Employee has duty to mitigate damages

XI. Retaliation
    A. Protected activity, generally
    B. Burdens of persuasion and production
        1. Generally
        2. Types of protected activity
        3. Defendant's burden to put forth non-discriminatory reasons for its action
        4. Dual motives
XII. Relief
    A. Generally
    B. Back wage award
        1. Purpose
        2. May be awarded
            a. Generally
            b. Subject to mitigation
        3. Payment not tolled because of delay in adjudication
        4. Not barred by collective bargaining agreement
        5. Not offset by unemployment compensation
        6. Factors to consider in calculating back pay award
    C. Costs incurred by employee as result of adverse action
    D. Employee voluntarily leaves work; no relief
    E. Pre-judgment and post-judgment interest
    F. Compensatory damages not precluded by FECA
    G. Violation of conciliation agreement
        1. Enforcement by third-party beneficiaries
        2. Cancellation of contract
        3. Debarment
    H. Debarment
        1. Generally
        2. Conduct warranting debarment
            a. Failure to submit written affirmative action program
            b. Denial of access to premises
            c. Violation of conciliation agreement
        3. Conduct not warranting debarment automatically
    I. Sanctions
        1. Due process required
        2. Attorney misconduct
    J. Equal Access to Justice Act (EAJA) inapplicable
XIII. Types of dispositions
    A. Consent decree
        1. Generally
        2. Not subject to ARB review
        3. May be amended by the ALJ
        4. May not be blocked by intervener
        5. Factors to be considered
    B. Conciliation required under the Rehabilitation Act
        1. Generally
        2. Sufficiency of conciliation efforts
        3. Amended complaint; effect on conciliation

4. Distinction between conciliation and letter of commitment

C. Dismissal
   1. Upon compliance with consent decree
   2. Complaint is moot
   3. Settlement
   4. Factors to be considered
   5. Types of dismissal
      a. With prejudice
      b. Voluntary
   6. Dismissal versus summary judgment

D. Summary judgment

I. Statutory and regulatory authority

A. Executive Order 11246 at 30 Fed. Reg. 12319, enacted on September 28, 1965 (as amended by Executive Order 11375 at 32 Fed. Reg. 14303 and Executive Order 12086 at 43 Fed. Reg. 46501)
41 C.F.R. Parts 60-1, 60-2, 60-3, 60-4, 60-20, and 60-50.

B. Section 503 of the Rehabilitation Act of 1973 at 29 U.S.C. § 793
41 C.F.R. § 60-741

C. Section 402 of the Vietnam Era Veterans' Readjustment Assistance Act of 1974 at 38 U.S.C. § 4212
41 C.F.R. § 60-250

The rules of practice and procedure before the Office of Administrative Law Judges for the foregoing Executive Orders and enactments are found at 41 C.F.R. § 60-30. *See* 41 C.F.R. § 60-250.29 (Vietnam Act); 41 C.F.R. § 60-741.65 (Rehabilitation Act).

II. Generally

A. Purpose

The purpose of Executive Order 11246 is to provide a more efficient and effective method of redressing discrimination than was possible by other means requiring federal court litigation. ***Uniroyal, Inc. v. Marshall***, Case No. OFCCP 79-1702 (Sec'y., July 20, 1979).

The purpose of the Rehabilitation Act is essentially the same as that of Title VII of the Civil Rights Act of 1964 and Executive Order 11246; namely, the purpose is to eradicate discrimination against handicapped persons and to make victims of such discrimination whole for injustices suffered. ***OFCCP v. Black***, 482 F. Supp. 364 (D. D.C. 1979).

B. Executive Order 11246 has "force and effect of law"

In ***OFCCP v. Uniroyal, Inc.***, OFCCP 1977-1 (Sec'y., June 28, 1979), *aff'd. sub. nom.*, ***Uniroyal, Inc. v. Marshall***, 482 F. Supp. 364 (D.C. D.C. 1979), the Secretary cited to numerous decisions, including ***Regents of the University of California v. Bakke***, 98 S. Ct. 2733, 2781 n. 28 (1978) and ***United States v. New Orleans Public Service, Inc.***, 553 F.2d 459 (5th Cir. 1977), and stated that "it has been held by the courts that the Executive Order program has the force and effect of law."

III. Jurisdiction

A. The complaint

1. Where to file

[a] Generally

The regulations at 41 C.F.R. § 60-741.26(a) require that a complaint be filed "with the Director." It was further held that a signed statement accompanying the complaint demonstrating that the complainant was "regarded as having an impairment" was for the benefit of the agency and any alleged deficiencies in the statement do not constitute grounds for dismissal. ***OFCCP v. E.E. Black Ltd.***, Case No. 1977-OFCCP-7R (ALJ, Sept. 13, 1978), *aff'd*. (Ass't. Sec'y., Feb. 26, 1979).

[b] No requirement that individual complaint be filed prior to compliance review complaint

The filing of a Section 503 complaint by a worker is not a condition precedent to the filing of an administrative complaint by OFCCP. The regulations provide OFCCP with express authority to conduct compliance reviews and to follow-up such investigations by the filing of an administrative complaint. ***OFCCP v. Conagra Poultry Co.***, Case No. 1989-OFC-15 (ALJ, Feb. 5, 1990) (order denying summary judgment).

[c] Discretion to investigate incomplete complaints

OFCCP has the discretion to act or decline to act on an unsigned and, therefore, incomplete complaint. ***OFCCP v. Yellow Freight System, Inc.***, Case No. 1979-OFCCP-7 (ALJ, Aug. 26, 1988), *remanded on other grounds* (Ass't. Sec'y., Aug. 24, 1992). *See also* ***OFCCP v. Southern Pacific Transportation Co.***, Case No. 1979-OFC-10A (ALJ, Nov. 9, 1982), *remanded on other grounds*, (Ass't. Sec'y., Feb. 24, 1994) (although the regulations impose a requirement that the complaint be in writing and signed by the complainant, an informal presentation reduced to writing by the agency itself and sufficiently documented as to the identity of the discriminatee constitutes substantial compliance with the regulation).

2. Who may file

[a] Generally

The regulatory provisions at 41 C.F.R. § 60-741.15 authorize any one of several interests, such as the agency, the director, the prime contractor, or subcontractor, to precipitate an agency investigation without a discriminatee's formal complaint. However, the investigation must follow the same procedures and it carries the same potential consequences. ***OFCCP v. Southern Pacific Transportation Co.***, Case No. 1979-OFC-10A (ALJ, Nov. 9, 1982), *remanded on other grounds*, (Ass't. Sec'y., Feb. 24, 1994). It was further held that all facts and issues which come to light from the investigation of a properly filed complaint may be used against Defendant at trial.

[b] Impleader and intervener

In ***OFCCP v. Burlington Northern Railroad***, Case No. 1981-OFCCP-21 (ALJ, Feb. 8, 1984), the ALJ denied Defendant's motion to implead two unions on the ground that any retroactive seniority could not be effective without their approval. The requirement of Fed.R.Civ.P. 19, that complete relief cannot be accorded without the third party, was not established.

The ALJ issued orders which affirmed a union's right to intervene in a case between OFCCP and United Airlines under 41 C.F.R. § 60-30.24(a)(3) without "[disrupting] the proceeding." The ALJ held that Air Line Pilots Association's (ALPA) petition was untimely, but granted the petition to the extent that its counsel would be allowed to participate at the hearing by cross examining any witnesses whose testimony is related to ALPA's collective bargaining agreement with United Airlines and any remedy which could affect seniority/working conditions of ALPA pilots. ***OFCCP v. United Airlines***, Case No. 1994-OFC-1 (ALJ, Aug. 17, 1995).

[c] Class actions permitted

A class action for monetary damages is maintainable under Executive Order 11246. ***OFCCP v. Uniroyal, Inc.***, Case No. OFCCP 1977-1 (ALJ, Apr. 11, 1977), *aff'd.* (Sec'y., June 28, 1979) (citing to 41 C.F.R. § 60-2.1(b), ***United States v. Allegheny-Ludlum Industries, Inc.***, 517 F.2d 826 (5th Cir. 1975), and ***United States v. Duquesne Light Co.***, 423 F. Supp. 507 (W.D. Pa. 1976)).

3. Exhaustion of remedies

In ***NationsBank Corp. v. Herman***, 174 F.3d 424 (4th Cir.), *cert. denied*, Case No. 99-394 (1999) (Case No. 1997-OFC-16), the Fourth Circuit held that Defendant was required to exhaust administrative remedies in bringing a Fourth Amendment suit against OFCCP based on the alleged improper selection of certain facilities for compliance reviews. In support of its holding, the court cited to ***Volvo GM Heavy Truck Corp. v. Dep't. of Labor***, 118 F.3d 205 (4th Cir. 1997) and ***Thetford Properties IV L.P. v. Dep't. of Housing and Urban Dev.***, 907 F.2d 445 (4th Cir. 1990). The Fourth Circuit required exhaustion of remedies even where the suit was premised on constitutional challenges and it reasoned as follows:

> If, as NationsBank alleges and the district court suspected, the OFCCP did single out NationsBank for investigation and either has no policy governing its selection of targets for compliance review or has one but intentionally disregarded it, exhausting would serve the frequently noted purpose of allowing the agency to correct its mistakes before facing judicial review.

Id. at 430. The court determined that NationsBank was not entitled to a waiver from the requirement that it exhaust all administrative remedies on grounds that constitutional claims are unsuited for administrative exhaustion or that "OFCCP's questionable behavior, which so aroused the district court's suspicion" would justify waiver.

In ***American Airlines, Inc. v. Herman***, 176 F.3d 283 (5th Cir. 1999) (Case No. 1994-OFC-9), OFCCP alleged that American Airlines (American) failed to comply with Section 503 of the Rehabilitation Act of 1973 and its implementing regulations. These laws require that every covered government contractor not discriminate against any employee or applicant on grounds of physical or mental handicap. Under the procedural history of the case, the ALJ recommended dismissal of the complaint against American on grounds that the government conducted an unauthorized compliance review. The parties appealed to the "then-highest authority within the DOL," the Assistant Secretary who, in turn, disagreed with the ALJ's decision and remanded the case for further proceedings. Rather than permitting the case to be remanded to the ALJ, American filed for declaratory and injunctive relief in federal district court. The district court judge entered judgment in favor of American. OFCCP appealed and argued that the district court erred in denying its motion for summary judgment "based on American's failure to exhaust administrative remedies." The circuit court agreed and stated the following:

> Neither the ALJ, the Assistant Secretary, nor the Administrative Review Board has ruled on the merits of the OFCCP's claim that American discriminated in employment on the basis of disability.
>
> . . .
>
> Grants of partial summary disposition by an agency are generally considered interlocutory orders not subject to immediate review. American has not demonstrated that it will suffer irreparable injury that cannot be remedied by petitioning for review at the conclusion of the administrative proceedings.

As a result, the appellate court reversed the judgment of the district court and dismissed the complaint for lack of subject matter jurisdiction.

For an additional discussion of constitutional issues, see Chapter VII.

4. Service

In ***OFCCP v. Penzoil Exploration and Production Co.***, Case No. 1995-OFC-11 (ALJ, Apr. 17, 1995) (order pursuant to conference call), the question involved when the time for answering a complaint begins to run. Under the expedited hearing procedures of 41 C.F.R. § 60-30.31, OFCCP contended that the date mailed starts the time in which Defendant has to answer. The ALJ agreed with OFCCP that, under the Fed.R.Civ.P. 4, a complaint is served when mailed, but since this complaint was mailed first class, OFCCP was required to take additional steps, such as supplying a return envelope and postage. *See* Fed. R. Civ. P. 4(c)(2)(C)(ii). The ALJ reasoned that, if a complaint was considered served upon first class mailing, it would place a defendant in an unfair position because it could not be determined that the mail was received in a timely fashion.

B. Scope of investigation

1. Generally

In ***OFCCP v. City Public Service of San Antonio***, Case No. 1989-OFC-5 (Ass't. Sec'y., Jan.18, 1995), the Assistant Secretary held that a complaint investigation is distinct from a compliance review and the investigation is more narrow than the compliance review. The scope of a complaint investigation should be reasonably related to the violations alleged in "such complaint." However, the Assistant Secretary found that the fact that OFCCP sought to conduct an investigation which exceeded its authority is not a ground for dismissal of the complaint.

For a discussion of case law related to Fourth Amendment challenges to the scope of an investigation and other constitutional issues, see Chapter VII.

2. Discretionary decisions by the Secretary not presumptively reviewable by federal courts

In ***Greer v. Chao***, 492 F.3d 962 (8th Cir. 2007), the court held that the Secretary of Labor discharged her statutory obligations under the Vietnam Era Veterans Readjustment Assistance Act of 1974 (VEVRAA) to investigate a complaint filed by appellant Greer even though the Secretary declined to seek an enforcement action against Eaton Corporation, the employer.

Under the relevant facts of the case, Greer filed a complaint with the OFCCP alleging that Eaton had not adequately trained its employees regarding VEVRAA "and had not adhered to the affirmative obligations that the statute imposes." The court noted that OFCCP's investigation began in less than two weeks and was concluded 18 months later after an on-site visit, interviews with co-workers and managers, and review of Greer's employment file. In the end, OFCCP found no violations under the VEVRAA and declined to seek an enforcement action.

Greer sought district court review of OFCCP's actions pursuant to 5 U.S.C. § 701 *et seq.* of the Administrative Procedure Act (APA). Here, although the court noted a "stong presumption that agency action is reviewable by courts," the Eighth Circuit held that an agency's decision to seek (or not seek) an enforcement action is "not presumptively reviewable." In this vein, the court cited to 5 U.S.C. § 701(a)(2) of the APA, which provides an exception to judicial reviewability where agency action is "committed to agency discretion by law."

C. Time limit for filing a complaint; 180 days

1. Generally

[a] Complaint for discrimination

In ***OFCCP v. Southern Pacific Transportation Co.***, Case No. 1979-OFC-10A (ALJ, Nov. 9, 1982), *remanded on other grounds*, (Ass't. Sec'y., Feb. 24, 1994), it was held that the 180-day time limit for filing a complaint is for the agency's benefit and is not jurisdictional.

The Assistant Secretary held that 41 C.F.R. § 60-741.26(a), providing that a complaint under Section 503 of the Rehabilitation Act must be filed within 180 days from the date of the alleged violation, is not jurisdictional. ***OFCCP v. CSX Transportation, Inc.***, Case No. 1988-OFC-24 (Ass't. Sec'y., Oct. 13, 1994).

[b] Administrative complaint based on compliance review

The regulations implementing Section 503 of the Rehabilitation Act, which require the filing of a complaint within 180 days, refer solely to the individual complaint filed with the Director. The regulations contain no time limits for formal administrative complaints, filed by the Solicitor with the Office of Administrative Law Judges arising out of compliance reviews. ***OFCCP v. American Airlines, Inc.***, Case No. 1994-OFC-9 (Ass't. Sec'y., Apr. 26, 1996).

2. Each claim analyzed separately

[a] Generally

When the complainant alleged two distinct claims of discrimination (denial of full-time employment and denial of re-employment) the timeliness of each claim should be analyzed separately. ***OFCCP v. Yellow Freight Systems, Inc.***, Case No. 1982-OFC-2 (ALJ, Sept. 30, 1986), *remanded on other grounds* (Ass't. Sec'y., Oct. 6, 1993). The ALJ found that the complainant did not have sufficient information to make a charge of discrimination when complainant was told by Defendant's doctor that he would not be hired as a full-time employee, but complainant continued to work for Defendant. On the other hand, the complainant had sufficient information to make a charge of discrimination when the discriminatee was told by his supervisor that Defendant would no longer need his services, and this confirmed the earlier statement made by Defendant's doctor. Even if the function of particular procedural requirements of the regulations, such as the 180-day filing deadline, is to provide notice to Defendant that OFCCP has made an initial finding of discrimination and intends to act upon such finding, a procedurally deficient claim will not be barred if administrative convenience outweighs prejudicial harm to Defendant. OFCCP may waive the 180-day filing requirement upon a showing of good cause.

[b] Continuing violations

i. Established

In ***OFCCP v. CSX Transportation, Inc.***, Case No. 1988-OFC-24 (ALJ, Mar. 23, 1990) (order granting dismissal), *rev'd. and remanded on other grounds* (Ass't. Sec'y., Oct. 13, 1994), the Assistant Secretary held that a complaint alleging a violation under Section 503 is timely, if an incident of repeat violation occurred within 180 days of the filing of the complaint. Under the facts of the case, the union's letter to Defendant requesting that the complainant be reinstated and Defendant's denial constituted a refusal to re-employ him. Because this rejection occurred within 180 days of the filing of the complaint, it was timely. It was further determined that an employer should not be allowed to shield itself in perpetuity from its obligations under Section 503 by arguing that past circumstances rendered the employee disqualified. Rather, upon request, Defendant is required to reconsider its employment decision after the passage of time when the employee's handicap is subject to change over time.

ii. Not established

A complaint alleging a violation of Section 503 filed by a complainant with OFCCP is timely, if an incidence of repeat violation occurs within 180 days of the filing of the complaint. ***OFCCP v. CSX Transportation, Inc.***, Case No. 1988-OFC-24 (Ass't. Sec'y., Oct. 13, 1994). Indeed, a continuing violation may be relevant to the timeliness of a complaint, or to the issue of relief. Under the facts of the case, the ALJ held that Defendant did not commit a continuing violation by failing to pay the complainant's back wages or by failing to rehire the complainant after new medical evidence was submitted which allegedly demonstrated that complainant was capable of returning to work. Rather, the ALJ concluded that a continuing violation is where there is a prevailing scheme of alleged discrimination. Based upon the facts before him, the ALJ found that Defendant's decision to disqualify the complainant from employment as a track repairman for medical reasons was a single act and, although the complainant suffered the effects of the act, the act only occurred once.

In ***OFCCP v. Burlington Northern, Inc.***, Case No. 1980-OFCCP-6 (Ass't. Sec'y., Dec. 11, 1991), the Assistant Secretary held that Defendant's single refusal to hire did not constitute a continuing violation.

3. Extension of time to file claim

[a] ALJ without authority to grant

In ***OFCCP v. CSX Transportation, Inc.***, Case No. 1988-OFC-24 (ALJ, Mar. 23, 1990) (order granting dismissal), *rev'd. and remanded on other grounds* (Ass't. Sec'y., Oct. 13, 1994), the ALJ declined to extend the 180-day filing period for good cause shown because the regulation at 41 C.F.R. § 60-741.26 granted such authority only to the Director of OFCCP.

[b] Director with authority to grant for good cause

i. Generally

Although the complainant filed his complaint with OFCCP in April 1988, allegations of discrimination occurring before that time are not time-barred by the 180-day time period for filing complaints. The ALJ held that OFCCP's motion to amend the complaint to embrace an earlier time period constituted an extension by the OFCCP Director of the time for filing the complaint. ***OFCCP v. Jefferson County Board of Eduction***, Case No. 1990-OFC-4 (ALJ, Nov. 21, 1990) (order granting motion to amend complaint).

In ***OFCCP v. Norfolk and Western Railway Co.***, Case No. 1990-OFC-8 (ALJ, July 9, 1991), the ALJ held that OFCCP's investigation and prosecution of a complaint received 187 days after the filing deadline constituted an implicit waiver by the OFCCP Director of the

180-day limit.

In ***OFCCP v. Yellow Freight Systems, Inc.***, Case No. 1982-OFC-2 (ALJ, Sept. 30, 1986), *remanded on other grounds* (Ass't. Sec'y., Oct. 6, 1993), the ALJ held that OFCCP may not waive the 180-day filing requirement for administrative convenience, but only for good cause. Good cause is an abstract term and its meaning must be determined not only from the verbal context of the statute, but also from the context of the action and procedures involved and the type of case presented. If the Director's finding of good cause appears reasonable and does not represent an abuse of discretion, it will be upheld. Under the facts presented, the ALJ concluded that good cause was established where there was evidence that the complainant made a good faith effort to file a cause of action at the state level and sought federal relief, but was told no such relief existed.

In ***OFCCP v. Norfolk & Western Railway Co.***, Case No. 1993-OFC-4 (Ass't. Sec'y., July 20, 1995), the Assistant Secretary held that it was improper for the ALJ to grant Defendant's motion for summary judgment while OFFCP's discovery motions were pending. OFCCP was entitled to have access to information that would support its determination that Defendant's continuous refusal to reinstate the complainant for medical reasons constituted a continuing violation and was "good cause" to extend the filing date past 180 days. Because the plaintiff should also have the opportunity to make specific arguments in support of its opposition to Defendant's summary judgment motion, OFCCP had a right to discovery prior to the adjudication of the summary judgment motion.

ii. Abuse of discretion

In ***OFCCP v. Norfolk & Western Railway Co.***, Case No. 1993-OFC-4 (ALJ, Aug. 19, 1993), *remanded on other grounds,* (Ass't. Sec'y., July 20, 1995)[2], the ALJ held that the regulatory provisions at 41 C.F.R. § 60-741.26 provide that a Section 503 complaint must be filed within 180 days of the alleged violation, unless the time is extended by the OFCCP Director for good cause shown. A union grievance initiated on behalf of a Section 503 complainant does not constitute a Section 503 complaint. Because Defendant posted notices regarding employees' rights under the Rehabilitation Act, the ALJ was not persuaded by a suggestion that Complainant was unaware of his Section 503 rights and, thus, the ALJ declined to find good cause for Complainant's failure to file a timely complaint. Indeed, the ALJ concluded that the OFCCP Director accepted the untimely filing in error because: 1) the record did not support a finding of a continuing violation; 2) the complaint was filed more than two years after the alleged violation; and 3) Defendant had posted notices regarding employees' Rehabilitation Act rights.

4. Not controlled by Title VII statute of limitations

[2] The case was remanded without addressing the merits because the ALJ improperly granted summary judgment without resolving pending discovery requests.

The Title VII statute of limitations does not extend to actions brought under Executive Order 11246. There was no authority to support a finding that the Title VII statute of limitations applied to Executive Order actions. Moreover, Defendant's argument that the government's claim for back pay and seniority relief stemming from conduct which occurred more than 180 days from the date of filing the complaint was rejected. ***Dep't. of the Treasury v. Harris Trust***, Case No. 1978-OFCCP-2 (ALJ, Jan. 30, 1981). *See also* ***OFCCP v. Uniroyal, Inc.***, Case No. OFCCP 1977-1 (Sec'y., June 28, 1979).

D. Laches

Held inapplicable

In ***OFCCP v. First Federal Savings Bank of Indiana***, Case No. 1991-OFC-23 (Sec'y., Oct. 26, 1995), the Secretary adopted the ALJ's holding and reasoning on the issue of laches. Under the facts of the case, there was a ten month delay between the date OFCCP informed First Federal that the matter was being referred to the Solicitor's Office for formal enforcement and the filing of the administrative complaint. The ALJ concluded that the defense of laches requires a showing of lack of due diligence by the party against whom the defense is asserted, and prejudice to the party asserting the defense. As a general rule, actions by the government to protect the public interest are not subject to the defense. The ALJ found that the ten month delay between the final notice of referral for enforcement and filing the administrative complaint was not so lengthy as to amount to a lack of due diligence, citing ***OFCCP v. Georgia-Pacific Corp.***, Case No. 1990-OFC-25 (Sec'y., Dec. 28, 1990) (19-month delay not unreasonable). The ALJ also noted that the regulations provide no statute of limitations applicable to the filing of a complaint by OFCCP, and that First Federal failed to show that the delay prejudiced its defense.

In **OFCCP v. *East Kentucky Power Cooperative, Inc.***, Case No. 1985-OFC-7 (ALJ, Mar. 17, 1988), the ALJ concluded that the first element of laches, inexcusable delay, was met where OFCCP offered no excuse for the lapse of more than two years between the end of conciliation and the filing of an administrative complaint. However, it was determined that the second element, substantial prejudice to Defendant, was not established. The ALJ noted that Defendant was able to introduce key documents at the hearing and was able to offer testimony from crucial witnesses.

E. Collateral estoppel

1. Held applicable

In ***OFCCP v. Beverly Enterprises, Inc.***, 1999-OFC-11 (ALJ, Nov. 5, 2001), the ALJ applied collateral estoppel and adopted a finding by the National Labor Relations Board, which was affirmed on appeal, that the parent and subsidiaries of Beverly Enterprises constituted a "single employer." The case was appealed to the ARB and the parties subsequently submitted a consent decree which "resolved the outstanding issues. ***OFCCP v. Beverly Enterprises, Inc.***, ARB Case No. 02-009, 1999-OFC-11 (ARB, Apr. 30, 2002).

In ***Exxon Corp. v. U.S. Dep't. of Labor***, 2002 WL 356517 (N.D. Tex. Mar. 5, 2002) (Memorandum Opinion and Order), the court concluded that OFCCP was collaterally estopped from litigating the issue of whether a recovering alcoholic was discriminated against through the employer's policy where the employer precluded him from "safety sensitive" positions in the company. In particular, OFCCP pursued a complaint under Section 503 of the Rehabilitation Act alleging that Exxon violated the affirmative action requirements of the Act in a non-safety sensitive position. The ALJ and ARB held that the Act was violated because Mr. Strawser was "a qualified individual with a disability and . . . Exxon failed to show that the policy, as applied to Strawser, was supported by 'business necessity and safe job performance.'" The court then noted that, in a related matter styled ***EEOC v. Exxon Corp.***, Civil Action Nos. 3:95-CV-1311-H and 3:95-CV-2537-H, it adopted findings by a magistrate judge and entered judgment for Exxon "holding that the Plaintiffs were not disabled under the ADA and therefore, the policy as applied to them, did not violate the ADA. *See EEOC v. Exxon Corp.*, 124 F. Supp.2d 987, 1015 (N.D. Tex. 2000)." Because the definition of a "disabled individual" under the Americans With Disabilities Act (ADA) and the Rehabilitation Act is identical, the court held that OFCCP was collaterally estopped from pursuing its complaint under the Rehabilitation Act with regard to Strawser. In applying collateral estoppel, the court noted that the EEOC and OFCCP "are charged with the same mission and purpose in addressing claims of disability and discrimination." Moreover, the issue in both cases was whether the "Plaintiffs are individuals with disabilities." In addition, the court found that the "same judicial body is addressing both cases, both agencies are arguing that the same Exxon policy is discriminatory for the same reasons, and but burden of proof under the summary judgment standard is the same." As a result, summary judgment in favor of Exxon was granted. For a review of the underlying ALJ and ARB decisions in this case, see ***OFCCP v. Exxon Corp.***, Case No. 1992-OFC-4 (ALJ, June 15, 1993), *aff'd. in part,* (ARB, Oct. 28, 1996).

2. Held inapplicable

In ***OFCCP v. Norfolk Southern Corp.,*** 1989-OFC-31 (Ass't. Sec'y., Oct. 3, 1995), the Assistant Secretary concluded that OFFCP was not collaterally estopped from litigating a Section 503 enforcement action where the state civil rights commission issued an adverse decision in a case involving the same alleged victim of discrimination (among others) and the same employer. The Assistant Secretary found both that: (1) the state commission did not rule on the nondiscrimination/affirmative action employment policy and standards issues relating to the OFCCP action; (2) OFCCP was not a party, nor in privity with the employee or the state commission in the state proceeding; and (3) traditional collateral estoppel doctrines do not apply to Section 503 litigation. The Assistant Secretary concluded that the ALJ failed, under ***University of Tennessee v. Elliott,*** 478 U.S. 788 (1986), to first determine whether Section 503 expressly or impliedly treats judicially unreviewed state agency decisions as preclusive. *See also* ***Astoria Federal Savings and Loan Association v. Solimino,*** 501 U.S. 104 (1991). Although there is a presumption is favor of estoppel where the statute is silent on the issue, the Assistant Secretary concluded that implicit Congressional intent was to except Section 503 litigation from traditional collateral estoppel in regard to handicap discrimination decisions of state agencies acting under state laws, because Congressional policy was that Sections 503 and 504 of the Rehabilitation Act be enforced in a consistent and effective manner. *See* ***Daniels v. Barry,*** 659 F. Supp. 999 (D.D.C. 1987).

A decision by an arbitrator in favor of Defendant on the union's grievance concerning

Defendant's removal of the complainant from active duty and retention of sick benefits does not divest OFCCP of jurisdiction in this case, nor do principles of collateral estoppel or res judicata apply. ***OFCCP v. American Telephone and Telegraph Co. (AT&T)***, Case No. 1992-OFC-5 (ALJ, Apr. 23, 1995). In so holding, the ALJ stated that a labor arbitrator has only authority to resolve questions of contractual rights and his task is to "effectuate the intent of the parties." However, the arbitrator lacks general authority to invoke public laws that conflict with the bargain between the parties, such as Title VII or Section 503 of the Rehabilitation Act. Therefore, even had the arbitrator's decision not been made pursuant to a collective bargaining agreement, OFCCP could have brought an action in its role as a government agency charged with enforcement of federal anti-discrimination statutes. The principles of *res judicata* or collateral estoppel do not apply to such an action based on an arbitrator's decision. Moreover, the ALJ concluded that Defendant's argument that OFCCP lacked subject matter jurisdiction because ERISA preempts the Act was wholly without merit. *Id.* at 8.

There is no collateral estoppel or *res judicata* in a complaint filed under Executive Order 11246 based on a prior Title VII court action. The parties and issues were different in the two proceedings-the legal issues in the Title VII court action were limited to discrimination practices against black applicants or employees whereas the administrative proceeding also addressed affirmative action for Vietnam veterans and other minority groups. ***OFCCP v. First Alabama Bank of Montgomery***, Case No. 1980-OFCCP-32 (ALJ, Dec. 5, 1980), *aff'd.* (Sec'y., Mar. 16, 1981).

F. Bankruptcy stay not apply

In ***OFCCP v. Jacksonville Shipyards, Inc.***, Case No. 1989-OFC-1 (ALJ, June 10, 1997), the ALJ found that the automatic stay provisions of the Bankruptcy Code did not apply to a back pay award because the proceeding fell under the Department of Labor's regulatory authority. *See* ***Eddleman v. U.S. Dep't of Labor***, 923 F.2d 782 (10th Cir. 1991); ***In Re James H. Crockett***, 204 B.R. 705 (Bank. W.D. Tex. 1997); ***Martin v. Safety Electric Construction Co.***, 151 B.R. 637 (Bank. D. Conn. 1993).

G. Bifurcated hearing; no jurisdiction over appeal

In ***OFCCP v. Interstate Brands Corp.***, ARB Case No. 00-071, Case No. 1997-OFC-6 (ARB, Sept. 29, 2000), after a bifurcated hearing process, the ALJ issued a decision on liability while reserving the decision on damages. The ALJ advised the parties that, after the ARB's review of the liability issue, he would adjudicate the remedy. Citing to various environmental whistleblower decisions, the ARB initially noted that it disfavored interlocutory appeals and piecemeal litigation. In addition, the ARB stated that, in ***OFCCP v. The Cleveland Clinic Foundation***, Case No. 1991-OFC-20 (Sec'y., Apr. 18, 1995), the Secretary refused to consider an interlocutory appeal under Executive Oder 11246 where the ALJ bifurcated the liability and damages issues and the case involved damages owed only to two individuals. On the other hand, the ARB found that the Secretary accepted an interlocutory appeal in ***OFCCP v. Honeywell, Inc.***, Case No. 1977-OFC-3 (Sec'y., June 2, 1993) where "the case was one of the largest compliance cases ever submitted for decision and the case had been pending before a succession of Secretaries for over ten years." Upon review of the facts in ***Interstate Brands***, the ARB concluded that it would not accept an interlocutory appeal. It stated that "[w]hile we are not unsympathetic to Interstate's concerns regarding the complexity of the damages calculations and the time and cost involved in litigating the issue, these factors are inherent in all complex litigation." The ARB also rejected the argument that it must accept the appeal upon agreement of the parties; rather, the ARB concluded that its acceptance or rejection of an appeal "is not subject to agreement by the private parties."

H. Issues of constitutionality and validity

For an in-depth discussion of constitutional challenges to investigations under the anti-discrimination enactments, see Chapter VII.

1. ALJ without authority to determine validity of regulations

In ***OFCCP v. Goya De Puerto Rico, Inc.***, Case No. 1998-OFC-8 (ALJ, June 22, 1999), *aff'd.*, ARB No. 99-104 (ARB, Mar. 21, 2002), the ALJ stated that he was without authority to rule on the validity of the Executive Order or its implementing regulations. *See* ***Stouffer Foods Corp. v. Dole***, 1990 WL 58502 1 (D. S.C., Jan. 23, 1990) (citing to ***Oesterich v. Selective Service System***, 393 U.S. 233, 241-42 (concurring opinion) (1968)).

The Secretary of Labor may void regulations only through proper rule-making pursuant to the Administrative Procedure Act. ***OFCCP v. Ozark Air Lines, Inc.***, Case No. 1980-OFCCP-24 (Dep'y. Under Sec'y., June 13, 1986).

An administrative tribunal is without jurisdiction to adjudicate the validity of OFCCP regulations which implement the Rehabilitation Act. ***OFCCP v. American Airlines***, Case No. 1979-OFCCP-2 (ALJ, June 30, 1980), *aff'd.*, (Dep'y. Under Sec'y., May 2, 1985).

The ALJ and Assistant Secretary have the power to decide if an employer has violated Section 503 and the implementing regulations, but may not determine the underlying validity of the regulations. ***OFCCP v. Western Electric Co.***, Case No. 1980-OFCCP-29 (Dep'y. Under Sec'y., Apr. 24, 1985). For purposes of administrative enforcement proceedings, the validity of the waiver provisions at 20 C.F.R. § 60-741.25(a)(5) must be assumed.

2. Language not unconstitutionally vague

The definition of "handicapped individual" contained in the Act and the regulations is not unconstitutionally vague. ***E. E. Black, Ltd. v. Marshall***, 497 F. Supp. 1088, 1097-98 (D. Hi. 1980).

I. "Working on the contract" is a jurisdictional issue and cannot be presumed

1. Generally

The issue of "working-on-the-contract" is one of subject matter jurisdiction, which cannot be presumed. ***OFCCP v. Texas Industries,Inc.***, Case No. 1980-OFCCP-28 (Ass't.

Sec'y., June 21, 1996). Although neither party raised the contract issue before the ALJ or the Assistant Secretary, the Assistant Secretary is required to address the issue before the case may proceed. *See also* ***OFCCP v. Texas Utilities Generating Co.***, Case No. 1985-OFC-13 (Ass't. Sec'y., Aug. 25, 1994).

The "working-on-the-contract" issue is jurisdictional and must be specifically addressed by the ALJ prior to proceeding to the merits. ***OFCCP v. Norfolk Southern Corp.***, Case No. 1989-OFC-31 (Ass't. Sec'y., Oct. 3, 1995).

In ***OFCCP v. United Airlines, Inc.***, Case No. 1986-OFC-12 (Ass't. Sec'y., Dec. 22, 1994), the Assistant Secretary remanded the case to the ALJ for appropriate findings on the "working-on-the-contract" issue, and held that, "[a]lthough the "working-on-the-contract" jurisdictional issue was not raised or addressed below or in the pleadings filed subsequent to the [ALJ] Recommended Decision and Order, I am required to address this matter before the case can proceed."

For a discussion of whether a defendant is a government contractor, see Chapter VIII.

2. Admission by defendant; insufficient to establish "working on the contract"

Defendant's mere acknowledgment that it is a federal contractor under Section 503 of the Rehabilitation Act cannot be construed as an admission that it had federal contracts which complainants would have performed. ***OFCCP v. Yellow Freight Systems, Inc.***, Case No. 1979-OFCCP-7 (Ass't. Sec'y., Aug. 24, 1992).

J. Included in contract by law

In ***OFCCP v. First Federal Savings Bank of Indiana***, Case No. 1991-OFC-23 (Sec'y., Oct. 26, 1995), Defendant asserted that it was not covered by Executive Order 11246 because the agreements under which Defendant was an issuing agent for United States Savings Bonds and a depository for federal funds did not include the equal opportunity clause. The Secretary rejected this argument and held that the regulations establish that "[b]y operation of the [Executive] order, the equal opportunity clause shall be considered to be a part of every contract . . . required by the order and regulations . . . to include such a clause whether or not it is physically incorporated in such contracts . . .." *See* 41 C.F.R. § 60-1.4(e). *See also* ***OFCCP v. Southern Pacific Transportation***, Case No. 1979-OFC-10A (ALJ, Nov. 9, 1982), *remanded on other grounds* (Ass't. Sec'y., Feb. 24, 1994).

In ***OFCCP v. Goya De Puerto Rico, Inc.***, Case No. 1998-OFC-8 (ALJ, June 22, 1999), *aff'd.,* ARB No. 99-104 (ARB, Mar. 21, 2002), the ALJ concluded that Defendant violated the provisions of Executive Order 11246, the Vietnam Era Veterans' Readjustment Assistance Act of 1974, and Section 503 of the Rehabilitation Act of 1973 for failing to develop and maintain a written affirmative action program. Defendant operated under federal contracts to distribute food to two United States commissaries in Puerto Rico and argued that OFCCP's exclusive remedy lie under the Contract Disputes Act at 41 U.S.C. §§

601-613. Citing to the implementing regulations at 41 C.F.R. § 60-1.1, the ALJ noted that the procedures underlying the Executive Order apply "regardless of whether or not the contract contains a 'Disputes' clause."

K. Interplay with other statutes

1. Department of Transportation jurisdiction

Where an overlap of jurisdiction occurs, the agency exercising its authority cannot take actions which impinge on another Federal agency's jurisdiction. However, the fact that there is overlap of jurisdiction between Department of Transportation truck driver qualifications and Rehabilitation Act's prohibition against handicap-based discrimination does not necessarily constitute an intrusion into another agency's jurisdiction. ***OFCCP v. Yellow Freight Systems, Inc.***, Case No. 1979-OFCCP-7 (Dep'y. Under Sec'y., Apr. 8, 1987). The Deputy Under Secretary held that, requiring that OFCCP wait until the Department of Transportation has ruled on the qualifications of drivers who fail to meet carriers' additional requirements before it can institute proceedings, preempts jurisdiction of the Rehabilitation Act and deprives drivers of remedies provided through Section 503, *i.e.*, back pay, lost fringe benefits, and reinstatement, which are not available under the Motor Carrier Act. It was noted that OFCCP conceded that the Department of Transportation had authority to set minimum qualification standards for drivers and that OFCCP and the Department of Transportation have concurrent jurisdiction over job qualifications imposed by the carrier. Where drivers are qualified under Department of Transportation standards, they also meet the definition of qualified handicapped individuals under the Rehabilitation Act.

In ***OFCCP v. Texas Industries, Inc.***, 1980-OFCCP-28 (Sec'y., June 7, 1988), the Secretary stated the following with regard to DOT authority as it relates to complaints filed under the Rehabilitation Act:

> [A]fter a thorough consideration of DOT's authority over physical qualifications for drivers, it was held that exhaustion of DOT administrative remedies is not a prerequisite to a Rehabilitation Act proceeding where the handicapped employee or applicant for employment holds a valid DOT medical certificate.

2. Civil Rights Act of 1964

The Civil Rights Act of 1964 does not limit application of Executive Order 11246. The legislative history of the Act indicate that enforcement is to be separate from that of the Executive Order and that, while the purpose of Title VII is remedial and preventive, the goal of the Executive Order is to promote job opportunities irrespective of a finding of discrimination. ***In the Matter of Firestone***, Case No. 1978-OFCCP-13 (Sec'y., Dec. 8, 1978).

A federal contractor is not exempt from complying with the affirmative action requirements of Executive Order 11246 on grounds that those requirements might conflict with Title VII. The courts, and not an administrative tribunal, are the appropriate forum in which to challenge the constitutionality of the Executive Order. ***Dep't. of Treasury v. Nat'l. Bank of Commerce of San Antonio***, Case No. 1977-OFCCP-2 (Sec'y., May 3, 1978).

In ***OFCCP v. The Cleveland Clinic Foundation***, Case No. 1991-OFC-20 (ARB, July 17, 1996), the ARB adopted the ALJ's approach of paralleling the regulations implementing Executive Order 11246, which required covered contractors "to ensure that no person intimidates, threatens, coerces, or discriminates against any individual for the purpose of interfering with the filing of a complaint, furnishing information, or assisting or participating in any manner in an investigation, compliance review, hearing, or any other activity related to the administration of the order . . .", with the anti-retaliation provision at § 704(a) of Title VII of the Civil Rights Act.

3. Contract Disputes Act

In ***OFCCP v. Goya De Puerto Rico, Inc.***, Case No. 1998-OFC-8 (ALJ, June 22, 1999), *aff'd.,* ARB No. 99-104 (ARB, Mar. 21, 2002), the ALJ concluded that Defendant violated the provisions of Executive Order 11246, the Vietnam Era Veterans' Readjustment Assistance Act of 1974, and Section 503 of the Rehabilitation Act of 1973 for failing to develop and maintain a written affirmative action program. Defendant operated under federal contracts to distribute food to two United States commissaries in Puerto Rico. Defendant argued that OFCCP's exclusive remedy lie under the Contract Disputes Act at 41 U.S.C. §§ 601-613. Citing to the implementing regulations at 41 C.F.R. § 60-1.1, the ALJ noted that the procedures underlying the Executive Order apply "regardless of whether or not the contract contains a 'Disputes' clause." In addition, the ALJ noted that Section 605(a) of the Contract Disputes Act provided that it did not apply "to a claim or dispute for penalties or forfeitures prescribed by statute or regulation which another Federal agency is specifically authorized to administer, settle or determine." Consequently, it was determined that OFCCP had a right of action against Defendant which was not barred by the Contract Disputes Act.

IV. Standard of review

A. By the ALJ

The ALJ conducts a *de novo* review of the record. *See e.g.,* ***OFCCP v. Bridgeport Hosp.***, 1997-OFC-1 (ALJ, Jan. 21, 2000), *aff'd. in relevant part*, ARB Case No. 00-034 (ARB, Jan. 31, 2003); ***OFCCP v. Beverly Enterprises, Inc.***, 1999-OFC-11 (ALJ, July 22, 1999), *remanded on other grounds*, ARB Case No. 01-028 (ARB, Jan. 31, 2001).[3]

B. By the ARB

1. Generally

In ***OFCCP v. Goodyear Tire & Rubber Co.***, ARB Case No. 97-039, Case No. 1994-OFC-11 (ARB, Aug. 30, 1999), the ARB held that it "retains complete freedom of decision" as though it heard the case when reviewing an ALJ's recommended decision under Section 503 of the Rehabilitation Act. *See also* ***OFCCP v. Keebler Co.***, ARB Case No. 97-127, Case No. 1987-OFC-20 (ARB, Dec. 21, 1999) ("[o]ur review is *de novo*").

In ***OFCCP v. Yellow Freight Systems, Inc.,*** Case No. 1989-OFC-40 (Sec'y., Sept. 18, 1995) (order), OFCCP moved to strike a letter from the Chief Counsel of the Federal Highway Administration, United States Department of Transportation, which was attached to Defendant's exceptions. The Secretary denied the motion because he found that the letter contained only legal argument and, therefore, did not violate the regulation requiring that the Secretary render a decision "on the basis of the record" made before the ALJ. 41 C.F.R. §§ 60-30.29 and 60-741.29(b)(1). Similarly, the Secretary denied a motion to strike portions of the exceptions that relied on arguments made in Chief Counsel's letter on grounds that the portions of the letter which were targeted did not contain references to extra-record evidence.

In ***OFCCP v. Bank of America***, ARB Case No. 00-079, 1997-OFC-16 (ARB, Mar. 31, 2003), the ARB concluded that the ALJ erred in granting summary judgment because "genuine issues of material fact" existed. Citing to 41 C.F.R. §§ 60-30.29 and 60-30.30 as well as Secretary's Order No. 1-2002, the ARB held that it has "plenary power to determine whether summary judgment should be granted."

2. Interlocutory appeal not favored

---

[3] No case or regulation could be located wherein the standard of review was specifically stated. However, all ALJ decisions which were reviewed for this *Deskbook* contained a *de novo* review of the record. On April 30, 2002, while the case was on appeal to the ARB, the Board approved of the parties' consent decree.

In ***OFCCP v. Bank of America***, ARB Case No. 04-169, *remanding* 1997-OFC-16 (ARB, Dec. 17, 2004), the Board declined to accept Defendant's interlocutory appeal of the ALJ's *Recommended Decision and Order on Cross-Motions for Summary Judgment*. In particular, the ALJ issued partial summary judgment in favor of Plaintiff on the issue of Defendant's Fourth Amendment challenge to its selection for a compliance review. The ALJ further noted that the merits of Plaintiff's complaint had yet to be litigated. Citing to ***Plumley v. Federal Bureau of Prisons***, 1986-CAA-6 (Sec'y., Apr. 29, 1987), the Board addressed the procedure for requesting an interlocutory appeal. After noting its "strong policy against . . . piecemeal appeals," coupled with the ALJ's denial of Defendant's request that the case be certified for interlocutory review, the Board denied the interlocutory appeal and remanded the matter for adjudication on the merits of Plaintiff's complaint.

Subsequently, on January 21, 2010, the ALJ issued a *Recommended Decision and Order* finding that Defendant had intentionally and unlawfully discriminated against African-American candidates in hiring. Defendant appealed and the Board declined to accept the appeal on grounds that it was interlocutory. Notably, the Board found that the ALJ retained jurisdiction to adjudicate remedies such that the case was remanded to the ALJ for adjudication of damages. ***OFCCP v. Bank of America***, ARB Case No. 10-048, ALJ Case No. 1997-OFC-016 (ARB, Apr. 29, 2010) (a party seeking review of a non-final order must demonstrate that the order "involves a controlling question of law", there is "substantial ground for difference of opinion in resolving the issues presented by the order", and an "immediate appeal from the order may materially advance the ultimate termination of the litigation"; here, the Board found "at least nine" controlling questions of law and decline to accept the appeal).

C. By the courts

When a final agency action is challenged under the APA in district court, if the relevant statute does not provide for direct review by the court of appeals, the district court is to sit as an appellate tribunal and determine whether the agency made an error of law. If such an error has been made, the court must remand the matter to the agency for further action consistent with the corrected legal standard. ***PPG Industries, Inc. v. United States of America***, 52 F.3d 363 (D.C. Cir. 1995) (formerly Case No. 1986-OFC-9). In addition, there is nothing to restrict an agency from reopening proceedings for the admission of new evidence, after the grounds on which it relied are determined by a reviewing court to be invalid. *See also* ***Partridge v. Reich***, 141 F.3d 920 (9th Cir. 1998) (application of "arbitrary and capricious" standard; questions of law are reviewed *de novo*).

V. Evidence

A. Back wages owed

1. Burdens, generally

Complainant has the initial burden of production in establishing back pay. ***Pettway v. American Cast Iron Pipe Co.***, 494 F.2d 211 (5th Cir. 1974). Back pay is calculated by establishing what the worker's earnings and fringe benefits would have been had the discrimination not occurred. This figure should include promotions and raises. Moreover, the employment history of co-workers may be used to establish the injured worker's career path and his or her hypothetical earnings. ***E.E.O.C. v. Korn Industries, Inc.***, 662 F.2d 256 (4th Cir. 1981).

Examination of company payroll records and time cards as well as interviewing employees is an acceptable method of reconstructing back pay damages. Under these circumstances, it is not necessary to prove the precise amount of uncompensated or under-compensated wage payments to affected employees. Rather, the reconstructed records must only demonstrate wages owed for the amount and extent of work done in the job classification as a matter of reasonable inference, even though the result is approximate. Defendant bears the consequence of the imprecision because of its failure to maintain accurate records of hours worked in violation of its contractual and statutory responsibilities. ***Dep't. of the Treasury v. Harris Trust***, Case No. 1978-OFCCP-2 (ALJ, Jan. 30, 1981) (citing to ***Anderson v. Mt. Clemens Pottery Co.***, 328 U.S. 680 (1946)).

2. Utilization of a class-wide analysis to establish

In ***OFCCP v. Jacksonville Shipyards, Inc.***, Case No. 1989-OFC-1 (ALJ, June 10, 1997), the ALJ determined that a class wide approach to the measure of back pay was necessitated because the employer's hiring requirements and the qualifications of the job applicants were ambiguous. The facts of the case did not provide a clear indication of which individuals would have been hired absent discrimination. *See* ***Pettway v. American Case Iron Pipe Co.***, 494 F.2d 211, 260-61 (5th Cir. 1974). In addition to the 69 women who applied for 191 positions, 1,065 men (93.92% of the applicant pool) also applied, making it statistically impossible to say that all 69 women would have been hired. The ALJ concluded that a more likely outcome is that the number of females hired would be the same proportion as the total proportion of female applicants, *i.e.* since 6.08% of the applicants were female, 6.08% of the total hired should have been female. As it was virtually impossible to determine which of the 69 applicants would actually have been hired, a class wide approach based on the percentage of overall hires who, absent discrimination, would have been women is more equitable. This approach has been accepted and utilized by numerous courts. *See* ***Dougherty v. Barry***, 869 F.2d 605 (D.C. Cir. 1989); ***Pitre v. Western Elec. Co.***, 843 F.2d 1262 (10th Cir. 1988); ***Stewart v. General Motors Corp.***, 542 F.2d 445 (7th Cir. 1986). Consequently, it was noted that three women were actually hired which equaled 1.57% of the total number hired. As previously noted, absent discrimination, it would have been expected that 6.08% of the persons hired would be female. Therefore, the shortfall percentage was 4.51%. The back pay determination was then calculated by taking the number of total earnings by all hirees during the applicable time period and multiplying that number by the shortfall percentage. *See* ***EEOC v. Spring and Wire Forms Specialty Co.***, 790 F. Supp. 776, 780 (N.D.Ill. 1992).

3. After-acquired evidence

Defendant's contention that the complainant is not entitled to relief because of "after acquired evidence" consisting of omissions on his application is a remedial issue to be addressed on remand. ***OFCCP v. Yellow Freight System, Inc.***, Case No. 1984-OFC-17 (Ass't. Sec'y., Dec. 22, 1993).

B. The Rehabilitation Act

See also Chapter X for an in-depth discussion of case law under Section 503 of the Rehabilitation Act.

1. Burdens, generally

The shifting, tripartite burdens of proof established under Title VII apply to cases brought under Section 503 of the Rehabilitation Act. ***OFCCP v. Yellow Freight Systems, Inc.***, Case No. 1982-OFC-2 (ALJ, Sept. 30, 1986), *remanded on other grounds* (Ass't. Sec'y., Oct. 6, 1993). Specifically, to establish a *prima facie* claim, OFCCP must demonstrate that the employee is a qualified handicapped person and Defendant utilized a physical job requirement that excluded the handicapped worker from employment. Once OFCCP establishes a *prima facie* case, the burden of proof shifts to Defendant who may rebut this inference by establishing that (1) the physical requirement is job related and consistent with business necessity and safe job performance, or (2) the adverse employment decision was based on prior poor performance. If Defendant rebuts the *prima facie* case, then OFCCP must establish that Defendant's justification is based on misconceptions or is a pretext for a discriminatory motive.

In ***OFCCP v. American Commercial Barge Line Co.***, Case No. 1984-OFC-13 (Ass't. Sec'y., Apr. 15, 1992), the Assistant Secretary held that burdens of proof and production in Title VII cases apply to individual handicap discrimination cases. It was initially noted that the burden of establishing a *prima facie* case was not an onerous one and required that OFCCP merely establish that the worker was discharged under circumstances which give rise to unlawful discrimination. Once OFCCP established a *prima facie* case, Defendant had the burden of articulating some legitimate, non-discriminatory reason for the employee's discharge. Once Defendant offers a legitimate, non-discriminatory reason for the discharge, the burden of production shifts back to OFCCP to establish that the proffered reasons were pretextual, *i.e.* the true motivation for the discharge was the intent to discriminate. It is noted that OFCCP bears the ultimate burden of persuading the fact-finder that Defendant intentionally discriminated against the worker. As an example, under the facts of ***American Commercial***, Defendant met its burden of demonstrating that a manic depressive employee's termination was for a non-discriminatory reason, *i.e.*, his failure to release his psychiatric records held by the VA hospital to the employer. OFCCP failed to prove that the manic depressive employee actually and seriously re-applied for an available position after he was terminated. Thus, the fact that the contractor did not re-employ him, even after he released his medical records, did not establish that the stated reason for discharge (failure to release medical records) was a pretext for discrimination.

2. Dual motives

In ***OFCCP v. Norfolk & Western Railway Co.***, Case No. 1980-OFCCP-14 (Assoc. Dep'y. Under Sec'y., Dec. 8, 1986), it was determined that the burdens of proof to be applied in dual motive cases arising under the Rehabilitation Act are those enunciated in ***Dartey v. Zack Co. of Chicago***, Case No. 1982-ERA-2 (Sec'y., Aug. 25, 1983) (a case arising under the Energy Reorganization Act of 1974 at 42 U.S.C. § 585). In ***Dartey***, the Secretary applied the Supreme Court's analysis in ***Mt. Healthy City School District Board of Education v. Doyle***, 429 U.S. 274 (1976). The Secretary further held that the burdens of proof set forth in ***Texas Department of Community Affairs v. Burdine***, 450 U.S. 248 (1981) are not to be applied in dual or mixed motive cases. Upon application of the ***Mt. Healthy*** standards, if OFCCP proves by a preponderance of evidence that the protected conduct was a motivating factor in the company's adverse employment action, then the employer must prove by a preponderance of the evidence that it would have reached the same decision even in the absence of the protected conduct. When there is an even balance of evidence as to whether the employee was discharged for legitimate or illegitimate reasons, the burdens of proof for a mixed motive case should be applied. Under this analysis, in considering whether the employer's justification for taking the employment action was pretext, the ALJ may properly consider evidence presented as part of the *prima facie* case.

In ***OFCCP v. Yellow Freight System Inc.***, Case No. 1989-OFC-40 (ALJ, May 17, 1994), in defense of a *prima facie* case of discrimination, Defendant has the burden of producing evidence that the alleged disparate treatment was motivated by legitimate, nondiscriminatory reasons. Where both legitimate and prohibited motives constitute the basis for the adverse employment action, Defendant has the burden of proof to establish by a preponderance of the evidence that it would have reached the same decision even in the absence of the protected conduct.

C. Executive Order 11246

1. Burdens, generally

In an Executive Order 11246 class action, it is the government's burden to establish a *prima facie* case of the existence of a discriminatory system affecting a class of employees. After this discriminatory system is established, the government must demonstrate that certain employees are members of the affected class and are entitled to compensatory relief. Then, the burden shifts to the employer to provide that the individuals are not entitled to relief. ***OFCCP v. Honeywell, Inc.***, Case No. 1977-OFCCP-3 (Sec'y., Mar. 2, 1994).

Based on statistical data and testimony, the government demonstrated by a preponderance of the evidence that a few women and minorities managed to attain managerial positions or become officers, but their scarcity in comparison to the numerous comparably qualified white males who have attained such positions established the continuing effects of Defendant's employment discrimination. ***Dep't. of the Treasury v. Harris Trust***, Case No. 1978-OFCCP-2 (ALJ, Dec. 22, 1986).

In ***OFCCP v. Greenwood Mills, Inc.,*** Case No. 1989-OFC-39 (Sec'y., Nov. 20, 1995), the Secretary held that Defendant's successful hiring of females into positions in a job group about which it had received notice of an OFCCP audit "might tend to show the existence of prior discrimination and an effort to repair the harm after discovery." Slip op. at 17-18, quoting ***Rich v. Martin Marietta Corp.***, 522 F.2d 333, 346 (10th Cir. 1975) (footnote omitted). Moreover, the Secretary held that "ulterior motives" are not a prerequisite to a finding of sex discrimination. Rather, the test is whether a person was treated in a manner but for which his or her sex, the treatment would have been different.

In ***OFCCP v. The Cleveland Clinic Foundation***, Case No. 1991-OFC-20, slip op. at 7, 8 (ARB, July 17, 1996), the ARB found evidence of discriminatory intent and disparate treatment where a black employee was fired for sending a letter to the employer's Board of Governors alleging racial discrimination, but where a white employee, who repeatedly violated the employer's disciplinary procedures and work rules to an extreme degree, never received more than "verbal counseling." Other evidence of disparate treatment was found where a black employee, who lied on her application about previous applications for worker's compensation, was terminated from employment, but a white employee only received a one day suspension for making false statements.

In ***OFCCP v. Burlington Industries, Inc.***, Case No. 1990-OFC-10 (ALJ, Nov. 1, 1991), the ALJ dismissed the government's complaint under Executive Order 11246 for failure to sustain its burden of establishing disparate treatment of its minority applicants. Citing to ***McDonnell Douglas Corp. v. Green***, 411 U.S. 792 (1973), the ALJ noted that the government has the threshold burden of establishing by a preponderance of the evidence a *prima facie* case of discrimination. Under ***Texas Dep't. of Community Affairs v. Burdine***, 450 U.S. 248 (1981) and ***United Postal Service Board of Governors v. Aikens***, 460 U.S. 709 (1983), the Supreme Court clarified its holding regarding the *prima facie* burden of establishing discrimination to state that it gives rise to a presumption that the employer engaged in unlawful discrimination; "plaintiff need only show that qualified minority applicants were rejected under circumstances which give rise to an inference of unlawful discrimination." Under the facts of the case, the ALJ noted that the evidence of record demonstrated that non-minority applicants were hired when qualified minority applicants were available. The selection process "was not random" and "[n]on-minorities were accorded a limited preference." The ALJ concluded that the "hiring data together with the hiring practice, which Burlington has admitted, resulted in an affirmative hiring of non-minorities . . .." As a result, the presumption of disparate treatment of minorities was invoked and the burden shifted to Burlington to provide legitimate, non-discriminatory reasons for its hiring practices.

Upon establishing a *prima facie* case, the burden then shifts to the employer to put forth evidence that minority applicants were rejected, or non-minorities were preferred, for legitimate, non-discriminatory reasons. ***Burdine***, 450 U.S. at 254; ***Aikens***, 460 U.S. at

714. If the employer sustains this burden, then the government must demonstrate that the proffered reasons were not the true reasons underlying the employment decisions, but were merely a pretext. The government carries the burden of adducing evidence that the purported reason for the rejection of qualified minority applicants was, in fact, a pretext for unlawful discrimination. *See* ***International Brotherhood of Teamsters v. United States***, 431 U.S. 324, 362 n. 50 (1977). The ALJ emphasized that the ultimate burden of persuasion that Burlington "intentionally discriminated" against minority applicants "remains at all times with the Plaintiff." In this vein, the ALJ noted that the ***Burdine*** presumption was designed "progressively to sharpen the inquiry into the elusive factual question of intentional discrimination." *See also* ***E.E. Black Ltd. v. Marshall***, 1981 WL 265 (D. Hi. 1981).

2. Rebuttal by defendant

In ***OFCCP v. Burlington Industries, Inc.***, Case No. 1990-OFC-10 (ALJ, Nov. 1, 1991), the government established a *prima facie* case of disparate treatment of minorities. In particular, the ALJ noted that the evidence of record demonstrated that non-minority applicants were hired when qualified minority applicants were available. The selection process "was not random" and "[n]on-minorities were accorded a limited preference." The ALJ concluded that the "hiring data together with the hiring practice, which Burlington has admitted, resulted in an affirmative hiring of non-minorities . . . ." As a result, the presumption of disparate treatment of minorities was invoked and the burden shifted to Burlington to provide legitimate, non-discriminatory reasons for its hiring practices. To rebut the presumption, the ALJ held that "Burlington must come forward with evidence that minority applicants were rejected, or non-minority applicants were preferred, for legitimate, non-discriminatory reasons. Upon review of the record, the ALJ concluded that Defendant sustained this burden:

> Burlington explained that (certain) job groups . . . were concentrated with minorities, and, as such, it sought to address the concentration problem by hiring non-minorities. It further emphasizes that it forthrightly described this hiring strategy to OFCCP in its (Affirmative Action Plan), and OFCCP approved the Plan.

Slip. op. at 17. The ALJ noted that Burlington was required to consider the eight factors set forth at 41 C.F.R. § 60-2.11, but that it was entitled to calculate concentration in accordance with the "C-3 Agreement" underlying the Affirmative Action Plan. The ALJ stated the following:

> OFCCP's contention that its post-hearing brief that the JTAR formula and the JAAR formula are the same, thereby suggesting that calculations under both formulas should yield the same result, seems to ignore that fact that the C-3 agreement uses external availability for each job group, as well as the fact that the OFCCP investigator admitted at the hearing that job groups . . . were concentrated using the JTAR formula. The testimony of OFCCP witnesses at the hearing indicate that JTAR and JAAR calculations would not be expected to yield the same results.

Slip op. at 17. The ALJ also placed significant importance on the fact that Burlington disclosed its Affirmative Action Plan to OFFCP and it was approved. Moreover, he found that "[i]t is also probative that OFCCP had approved precisely the same hiring policy in years past at other Burlington facilities which experienced instances of concentration of particular job groups." Slip op. at 17, 18. In sum, the ALJ concluded that the evidence demonstrated that "Burlington attempted to reduce the minority concentration in these entry level jobs, because OFCCP viewed the minority concentration as a 'red flag' that the concentration itself may be due to discrimination." Consequently, the ALJ determined that Burlington rebutted the government's *prima facie* case.

3. Pretext

In ***OFCCP v. Burlington Industries, Inc.***, Case No. 1990-OFC-10 (ALJ, Nov. 1, 1991), the ALJ dismissed OFCCP's complaint on grounds that it could not demonstrate that Burlington's proffered reasons for its hiring practices were pre-textual. *See* ***International Brotherhood of Teamsters v. United States***, 431 U.S. 324, 362 n. 50 (1977). The ALJ noted that no present or past employee "testified that they perceived any discriminatory animus in any of the personnel decisions at the plant." Moreover, OFCCP officials did not testify that Burlington's "strategy of hiring non-minority applicants was based on anything other than the concerns expressed in the (Affirmative Action Plan) to soften the concentration of minorities in the entry level 6B and 7B jobs." The ALJ further noted that hiring non-minorities in jobs concentrated with minorities was not Burlington's idea; rather, the record contained a memorandum to the company from a Department of Defense Equal Opportunity Specialist recommending the hiring practice which the company implemented:

> Whether or not the Specialist was authorized to make the recommendation, the record shows that the hiring strategy was devised, not as a pretext by Burlington, but rather was accepted by Burlington at the insistence of the Specialist to facilitate an 'in compliance' report. The record reveals no hint of animus or pretextual motivation on Burlington's part in accepting the hiring policy here challenged. *See* ***New York Transit Authority v. Beuzer***, 440 U.S. 568, 584 (1979).

Slip. op. at 19. The ALJ further noted that Burlington revealed its Affirmative Action Plan to OFCCP and it was approved. Indeed, the ALJ stated that "[b]oth Burlington and OFCCP knew that job groups 6B and 7B at Pioneer I were concentrated (with minorities) for reasons wholly unrelated to discrimination"; yet, OFCCP was "unwilling to advise the company that it did not need to de-concentrate the job groups" to avoid prosecution. In conclusion, the ALJ stated:

> Now, this is not to suggest that an approved (Affirmative Action Plan), which contains isolated but discriminatory proposals inadvertently overlooked by OFCCP provides a defense in all cases. The hiring of non-minorities as a means of addressing minority concentration was repeatedly approved over a period of many years. The acceptance and approval was not a singular and inadvertent oversight. Nor was the hiring plan one which the contractor originated and then buried in a voluminous (Affirmative Action Plan).

As a result, the ALJ dismissed OFCCP's complaint to state that the government did not establish that the company's employment decisions were motivated by discriminatory reasons.

4. Cost of compliance not a valid defense to discrimination

The cost of compliance does not constitute a valid defense to discriminatory conduct. ***OFCCP v. Black***, Case No. 1977-OFCCP-7R (Dep'y. Sec'y., Feb. 26, 1979).

D. Use of statistical data; circumstantial evidence of discrimination

In ***Dep't. of the Treasury v. Harris Trust***, Case No. 1978-OFCCP-2 (ALJ, Dec. 22, 1986), the ALJ noted that "[s]tatistics may be used as circumstantial evidence of intentional discrimination" but they are "not irrefutable . . .." The ALJ further found that "statisticians conventionally consider statistics to be significant at two or three deviations."

In ***OFCCP v. Southern Pacific Transportation Co.***, Case No. 1979-OFC-10A (ALJ, Nov. 9, 1982), *remanded on other grounds*, (Ass't. Sec'y., Feb. 24, 1994), the ALJ held that one consideration which justifies discrimination based on mere statistical probability has been the degree of risk to human life. Where it cannot be determined whether an individual is qualified for a position, Defendant may determine the job qualifications by applying the criterion of a class characteristic if (1) the discriminatee is a member of that class, and (2) all or substantially all members of that class are immediately unable to do the job. When there is statistically a risk of massive loss of human life, then (1) the degree of risk of harm, (2) the degree of probability of defect, and (3) the immediacy of the danger may be weighed.

In ***OFCCP v. Jacksonville Shipyards, Inc.***, Case No. 1989-OFC-01 (Sec'y., May 9, 1995), the Secretary advised that statistical evidence has long been accepted as an appropriate method for establishing a violation of Title VII of the Civil Rights Act of 1964. A defendant cannot rebut statistical evidence by mere conjectures or assertions; rather, the defendant must introduce evidence establishing that missing factors can explain how the disparities in employment were a product of a legitimate, nondiscriminatory selection criterion.

Proof that a disparity between the selections of men and women for particular jobs was caused by sex discrimination need not be direct. Circumstantial evidence that the disparity, more likely than not, was a product of prohibited discrimination will suffice to prove a pattern or practice of discrimination. The circumstantial evidence may be entirely statistical in nature. Gross statistical disparities alone may be *prima facie* proof of a pattern or practice of discrimination. However, the probative weight of statistical evidence is weak if it fails to focus on the appropriate labor pool. In ***OFCCP v. Greenwood Mills, Inc.,*** Case No. 1989-OFC-39 (Sec'y., Nov. 20, 1995), OFCCP alleged that Defendant discriminated against women in entry level positions in one job group involving transportation and cleaning. The ALJ found that OFCCP's statistical evidence was based on too narrow a time frame and job grouping. The ALJ concluded that the job group in issue should have been considered together with two other job groups because all three groups drew new hires from a common pool of individuals chosen for entry level positions.

However, the Secretary held it was error for the ALJ to view all three groups together because the three job groups had different sets of qualifications and, in reality, there were different applicant pools for each group. The Secretary observed that grouping the three pools masked the statistical disparity in hiring women for the job group at issue, which was inconsistent with the regulatory framework at 41 C.F.R. §§ 60-2.1(b), 60-2.11(b), and 60-2.23 for remedying discrimination through focused analysis of job groups. While the ALJ noted that Defendant's overall female employment statistics were good, the Secretary disproved the ALJ's notation of this fact, noting that the proper focus is on individual discrimination. The Secretary cited to case law to state that an employer's apparent nondiscrimination in various jobs or employment categories does not immunize or exonerate that employer's discrimination in particular jobs or organizational units. In regard to the appropriate time period, the ALJ criticized OFCCP for not waiting until the end of the Affirmative Action Plan year to conduct its audit and found that, when the statistical period was extended to the end of the plan year, rather than the period of alleged discrimination, any *prima facie* case of discrimination was rebutted. In this vein, the ALJ noted that Defendant hired several women near the end of the plan year apparently upon realizing that it had not yet met its goal for hiring women for the subject job group.

The Secretary concluded, to the contrary, that the fact that Defendant met its female affirmative action plan goal by the end of the plan year did not prove that it did not discriminate against female applicants prior to that date. The Secretary cited to case law and held that the effect that post- complaint actions of an employer do not remedy past discrimination or rebut a *prima facie* case. Such evidence, if anything, confirms the discrimination and goes to proper remedy rather than the existence of discrimination. The Secretary also noted that, even assuming it was correct to extend the statistic period, the hiring rate for females was approximately 3.3 standard deviations below the hiring rate for males, and that a disparity of two or three standard deviations is sufficient to establish a *prima facie* case of discrimination.

In ***OFCCP v. Interstate Brands Corp.***, Case No. 1997-OFC-6 (ALJ, July 19, 2000), OFCCP alleged that Defendant violated Executive Order 11246 by discriminating against minorities for entry-level bakery positions. Initially, the ALJ noted that OFCCP must demonstrate disparate treatment based on race, color, religion, sex, or national origin. Although evidence of discriminatory intent is required, such proof may be based on circumstantial evidence, including statistical evidence. Indeed, "[a]n unlawful motive may be inferred from a disparity between class members and comparably qualified members of a minority group." Citing to ***Hazelwood School District v. United States***, 433 U.S. 299 (1977) and ***OFCCP v. Greenwood Mills, Inc.***, Case No. 1989-OFC-39 (Sec'y. Nov. 20, 1995), the ALJ noted that a *prima facie* case of discrimination "may be entirely statistical." It was noted that, in ***Hazelwood***, the Supreme Court held that "a disparity of two or three standard deviations is sufficient to establish *prima facie* case of unlawful discriminatory animus."

If a *prima facie* case exists, then the burden shifts to Defendant to demonstrate that OFCCP's statistical evidence is inadequate, *i.e.* by "attacking" the government's statistical methods or by demonstrating that the disparity arose from legitimate, non-discriminatory factors. If rebuttal is established, then the burden shifts again to OFCCP to prove that the proffered reasons were pretext. The ALJ found, based on the statistical evidence before him, that Defendant hired black applicants at a statistically significantly lower rate than non-black applicants. In particular, he noted that the standard deviation exceeded 3.8. Although Defendant proffered rebuttal, the ALJ was not persuaded by it. He stated the following with regard to Defendant's rebuttal:

> For example, IBC rejected 14 out of 102 black applicants in 1992-93 because they 'could not get references.' In all of 1990, 1991, and 1994, IBC never used this reason for rejecting any applicant. Also, during the 1992-93 period, no whites were rejected on this basis. I consider (1) the numerically disparate treatment of blacks, and (2) the unique use of the 'could not get references' reason to be significant evidence of pretext even though there is relatively little evidence specific to individual applicants that any given reason was false.
>
> In addition, during the 1992-93 period, 30 black applicants were rejected because they 'did not demonstrate interest in the position,' whereas only four whites were rejected for this reason. Prior to 1992, this reason was never used as a basis for rejection of an applicant. Again, I find that the selective and discriminatory use of the all-purpose reason for rejection is strong circumstantial evidence that it is pre-textual.

Slip op. at 30-31.

E. Carrying out a government contract; burden to establish on OFCCP

For additional discussion of government contracts, see Chapter VIII.

1. Generally

Coverage extends to employees who were employed in, and applicants for, positions that are engaged in carrying out a government contract. To establish coverage, OFCCP must demonstrate that the duties of the position included work that fulfilled, was necessary to, or facilitated a contract. In ***OFCCP v. Keebler Co.***, ARB Case No. 97-127, 1987-OFC-20 (ARB, Dec. 12, 1996), the ARB held that OFCCP had met this burden where the employee was a production attendant at one of only two Keebler facilities that produced 'Tato Skins, some which it had contracted to provide to the government. Although the products were not designated for any particular designation, and the attendants at the two locations were not separated according to who worked on goods designated to fulfill government contracts, the ARB found that OFCCP had established that the employee was covered under § 60-741.4(a)(2) because the duties of the production attendant included work on government contracts.

2. Rebuttable presumption

In ***OFCCP v. Southern Pacific Transportation Co.***, Case No. 1979-OFC-10A (ALJ, Nov. 9, 1982), *aff'd.*, (Ass't. Sec'y., Feb. 24, 1994), the ALJ held that there is a rebuttable presumption that a discriminatee was employed to carry out the federal contract as long as s/he was working at a site which was not totally segregated from the federal contract site.

F. Admissibility issues

1. Hearsay

Exclusion of a deceased physician's report

In ***Texas Eastern Transmission Corp.***, Case No. 1988-OFC-30 (ALJ, June 11, 1990), the ALJ denied OFCCP's motion to admit into evidence the medical report of a deceased physician containing his opinion regarding complainant's ability to perform the job in question on the grounds that the report constituted hearsay and did not fall within a recognized exception at Fed.R.Evid. 803. Moreover, the ALJ held that the deceased physician's report constituted an unsworn statement of a declarant who could not be subjected to cross-examination and, thus, the report lacked sufficient indicia of reliability to be considered probative. In determining that report of deceased physician should not be admitted in evidence, the ALJ interpreted the standards of admissibility set forth at 41 C.F.R. § 60-30.18 as substantially the same as the standards imposed under the Federal Rules of Evidence, even though the regulation provides that formal rules of evidence do not apply in Section 503 administrative proceedings.

2. Admissions

In ***OFCCP v. USAir, Inc.***, Case No. 1991-OFC-2 (ALJ, Feb. 24, 1993), the ALJ held that Defendant's admission that it rejected the complainant because of his handicap obviated the need for OFCCP to commence discovery to prove that Defendant knew about the handicap and considered it as part of its decision-making process. However, the ALJ further determined that the admission did not foreclose the presentation of evidence by Defendant regarding other factors which it considered in deciding to reject the complainant.

Defendant's failure to file an answer constitutes an admission of OFCCP's complaint allegations pursuant to 41 C.F.R. § 60-30.6(b). Moreover, the failure to file an answer will result in a waiver of the right to a hearing and the ALJ may properly adopt OFCCP's materials fact as alleged in the complaint pursuant to 41 C.F.R. § 60-30.6(c). On this basis, default judgment and sanctions, including debarment, may be entered. ***OFCCP v. Rampart Electric, Inc.***, Case No. 1989-OFC-14 (Sec'y., Sept. 11, 1995).

In ***OFCCP v. Owens-Illinois***, Case No. 1977-OFCCP-11 (ALJ, Nov. 21, 1980), the government was not permitted to compel disclosure of prior settlements made by Defendant based on prior sex discrimination claims. The ALJ noted that evidence of the settlements would be inadmissible and there was no indication that the settlements would lead to the discovery of admissible evidence. Further, the ALJ reasoned that if such discovery was allowed, it would discourage employers from settling employment discrimination claims, with the result that the prescribed conference, conciliation, and mediation which are prerequisites to sanctions would be greatly hindered, if not nullified.

3. Studies from other federal agencies

In ***Exxon Corp. v. U.S. Dep't. of Labor***, 2002 WL 356517 (N.D. Tex. Mar. 5, 2002) (Memorandum Opinion and Order), the court concluded that Mr. Strawser was not a "disabled individual" under the Rehabilitation Act because OFCCP was collaterally estopped from litigating the issue as EEOC had unsuccessfully litigated the same issue under the Americans With Disabilities Act before the same court in a case involving the same employer and the same allegedly discriminatory policy. However, the holdings of the ALJ and ARB may be instructive. *See* ***OFCCP v. Exxon Corp.***, Case No. 1992-OFC-4 (ALJ, June 15, 1993), *aff'd. in part,* (ARB, Oct. 28, 1996).

In ***OFCCP v. Exxon Corp.***, Case No. 1992-OFC-4 (ALJ, June 15, 1993), *aff'd. on other grounds*, (ARB, Oct. 28, 1996), the ALJ concluded that FAA studies regarding its policy of returning recovering alcoholic pilots into the work place are relevant in determining the risk of relapse of a recovering alcoholic because the FAA policy appeared to be the only industry-wide program of its kind.

4. Evidence admitted on remand; legal error committed by ALJ

In ***Cissell Mfg. Co. v. U.S. Dep't. of Labor***, 101 F.3d 1132 (6th Cir. 1996), the circuit court concluded that the agency committed a "legal error" in the adjudication of the complaint below such that it was proper to remand the case to the Department of Labor to reopen the record and allow OFCCP to present evidence that the complainant was employed to carry out a government contract.

G. Credibility determinations

In ***OFCCP v. Jacor, Inc.***, Case No. 1995-OFC-17 (Sec'y., Jan. 19, 1996)(interim order), OFCCP challenged a finding that Defendant made oral contacts with recruitment sources and argued that there was no corroborating evidence on the point. The Secretary concluded that corroborating evidence is not required for any finding in hearings convened pursuant to Executive Order 11246 and 41 C.F.R. Part 60-30. The Secretary further noted that the ALJ found the witness testimony on this matter to be highly credible.

In ***OFCCP v. Beverly Enterprises, Inc.***, ARB No. 99-112, Case No. 1999-OFC-11 (ARB, Sept. 1, 1999), the ARB held that a government official is presumed to be telling the truth when making a sworn statement. It is noted that, in a subsequent appeal to the ARB, in ***OFCCP v. Beverly Enterprises, Inc.***, ARB Case No. 02-009, 1999-OFC-11 (ARB, Apr. 30, 2002), the parties submitted a consent decree which was approved by the Board.

H. Expert opinions

1. Generally

An expert opinion may be important in drawing inferences or estimates regarding harm to an affected class as well as the amount of damages resulting from the class discrimination practices. However, an expert opinion is not required to establish discriminatory practices, where such practices are otherwise demonstrated. ***Dep't. of the Treasury v. Harris Trust***, Case No. 1978-OFCCP-2 (ALJ, Dec. 22, 1986).

2. Treating physician entitled to particular deference

In ***OFCCP* v. *Norfolk and Western Railway Co.***, Case No. 1990-OFC-1 (ALJ, June 26, 1991), a case arising under Section 503 of the Rehabilitation Act, the ALJ held that the opinion of the complainant's treating physician is entitled to particular deference. Under the facts of the case, Defendant demonstrated that employment of the complainant, who suffered from monocular vision, may pose a possibility of injury or an elevated risk of harm. However, Defendant failed to establish a reasonable probability of substantial harm in light of the opinions of the complainant's treating physician and OFCCP's other medical expert as well as the fact that the record contained evidence that the complainant performed the job duties in question and that other individuals with monocular vision safely performed the job.

VI. Discovery

A. Generally

Discovery rules are to be liberally construed in favor of the requesting party. Under the facts before him, the Secretary determined that discovery addressing past conduct may be appropriate in employment discrimination cases. Moreover, he found that the pre-hearing discovery rules are reasonable in light of the broad grant of power and detailed enforcement procedures. ***OFCCP v. Uniroyal, Inc.***, Case No. OFCCP 1977-1 (Sec'y., June 28, 1979), *aff'd. sub. nom.,* ***Uniroyal, Inc. v. Marshall***, 482 F. Supp. 364 (D.C. D.C. 1979) (the Executive Order's discovery provisions and implementing regulations are valid).

In discrimination actions, where statistical data is often of critical importance, discovery is particularly essential to the production of material evidence and, hence, should not be proscribed or unduly limited. ***OFCCP v. Owens-Illinois, Inc.***, Case No. 77-OFCCP-11 (ALJ, Nov. 21, 1980); ***Donaldson v. Pillsbury Co.***, 554 F.2d 825.832 (8th Cir. 1977); ***Burns v. Thiokol Chemical Corp.***, 483 F.2d 300, 304-305 (5th Cir. 1973).

In ***OFCCP v. Owens-Illinois, Inc.***, Case No. 1977-OFCCP-11 (ALJ, Nov. 21, 1980), the ALJ held that, in discrimination cases, discovery is not restricted to the narrow inquiry of an individual violation; rather, it is extended to obtain evidence which demonstrates patterns of discriminatory action in other aspects of employment from which a reasonable inference of discriminatory motivation may be drawn. The ALJ cited to ***Laufman v. Oakley Building and Loan Co.***, 72 F.R.D. 116, 120 (S.D. Ohio 1976) and ***Bluebell Boots, Inc. v. Equal Employment Opportunity Commission***, 418 F.2d 355, 358 (6th Cir. 1969) in support of this holding.

B. Applicability of the Federal Rules of Civil Procedure

All hearings under Section 503 of the Rehabilitation Act shall be governed by the rules of procedure at 41 C.F.R. Part 60-30. However, in the absence of a specific provision on point, the Federal Rules of Civil Procedure shall apply. ***OFCCP v. Mississippi Power Co.***, Case No. 1992-OFC-8 (ALJ, July 16, 1993), *rev'd. on other grounds* (Ass't. Sec'y., July 19, 1995).

In ***OFCCP v. American Airlines, Inc.***, Case No. 1994-OFC-9 (ALJ, Jan. 19, 1995), the ALJ held that the Federal Rules of Civil Procedure only apply in the absence of an applicable regulatory provision. The implementing regulations for actions brought under Section 503 of the Rehabilitation Act of 1973, 29 U.S.C. § 793, are found at 41 C.F.R. Chapter 60. With regard to interrogatories, he noted that 41 C.F.R. § 60-30.9 does not limit the number of interrogatories which one party may serve upon another party. Thus, the 25 interrogatory limit contained in Fed.R.Civ.P 33 did not apply. However, a test of reasonableness would be imposed.. Under the particular circumstances of the case, the ALJ declined to further expand the issues in this case and denied OFCCP's motion to compel responses to discovery requests pertaining to events that occurred subsequent to the period covered by the 1988-1989 compliance review. The ALJ held that, in his judgment, the interests of all concerned will be served by ordering Defendant to supply the requested telephone numbers and addresses for all former and current employees except those with authority to speak for the company; and, further, to supply addresses, either work addresses or home addresses, of former and current management employees with authority to bind the company for the limited purpose of allowing OFCCP to notice depositions. Finding OFCCP's subject requests overbroad and unduly burdensome and oppressive, the ALJ denied OFCCP's request to compel Defendant to respond to its interrogatories concerning Defendant's system of storing personnel information on computers. On the other hand, the ALJ granted OFCCP's request to compel Defendant to respond to a second set of interrogatories which sought "facts and documents which American relied upon in support of each of the 24 affirmative defenses raised in its Answer, as well as the individuals with knowledge of such facts." The ALJ held that, by raising affirmative defenses, Defendant has placed at issue the specific facts, documents, regulations, and statutes upon which they are based. OFCCP is entitled to sufficient information regarding these affirmative defenses to enable it to prepare for trial.

C. Discovery of testimony of government officials

In ***Beverly Enterprises, Inc. v. Herman***, Civil Action No. 99-2408 (RMU) (D. D.C. Aug. 24, 2000), a case arising under anti-discrimination laws, the district judge determined that it was within the ALJ's discretion to decline discovery of the testimony of Solicitor of Labor Henry Solano where the testimony would "only repeat information that was included with other evidence."

D. Failure to file an answer, effect of

Defendant's failure to file an answer constitutes an admission of OFCCP's complaint allegations pursuant to 41 C.F.R. § 60-30.6(b). Moreover, the failure to file an answer will result in a waiver of the right to a hearing and the ALJ may properly adopt OFCCP's material facts as alleged in the complaint pursuant to 41 C.F.R. § 60-30.6(c). On this basis, default judgment and sanctions, including debarment, may be entered. ***OFCCP v. Rampart Electric, Inc.***, Case No. 1989-OFC-14 (Sec'y., Sept. 11, 1995).

E. Failure to comply with pre-hearing exchange, effect of

In ***OFCCP v. United Parcel Service, Inc.***, Case No. 1988-OFC-7 (ALJ, Sept. 25, 1990), *stipulated dismissal* (Ass't. Sec'y., Jan. 14, 1992), the ALJ held that Defendant demonstrated good cause for failure to request a hearing and failure to file a pre-hearing exchange as ALJ ordered where counsel candidly admitted that lack of hearing request resulted from oversight or absence of memory and counsel did not receive ALJ's order regarding pre-hearing exchange. The ALJ further noted that the case was allowed to languish in the Office of Administrative Law Judges for two years before it was assigned and parties had pursued discovery such that the proceedings were not prejudiced.

In ***OFCCP v. Brown Transport Co.***, 1979-OFCCP-20 (ALJ, Apr. 20, 1980), the ALJ held that a response by Defendant that it is "without knowledge or information to admit or deny" the request for admission is an insufficient response under 41 C.F.R. § 60-30.1, unless the party states that it made a reasonable inquiry and the information is not available. Moreover, the ALJ concluded that an inadequate response to a request constitutes an admission.

In ***OFCCP v. Rowan Companies, Inc.***, Case No. 1989-OFC-41 (Sec'y., Apr. 11, 1995), the Secretary held that a party cannot respond to an interrogatory request by directing the discovering party to an undifferentiated mass of records. If the party responding to the interrogatories is the only one familiar with the organization of the information, then that party must assist the interrogating party in locating and deciphering the requested information.

In ***OFCCP v. Holly Farms Foods, Inc.***, Case No. 1991-OFC-15 (ALJ, Oct. 24, 1991), the ALJ concluded that 41 C.F.R. § 60-30.9(b), which addresses answers to admission requests, does not require less than Fed.R.Civ.P. 36(a), and thus, does not permit Defendant to simply plead lack of knowledge in response to a request for admission. Rather, a failure to admit a request for lack of sufficient knowledge must also include a statement that a reasonable inquiry has been made.

In ***OFCCP v. Crown Zellerbach Corp.***, Case No. 1987-OFC-23 (ALJ, June 6, 1989), the ALJ held that OFCCP failed to file its objections to Defendant's First Request for Production of Documents within the 25-day period allowed for responses to discovery requests under the regulations at 41 C.F.R. §§ 60-30.9 and 60-30.10. As a result, the ALJ determined that OFCCP waived any objection to producing the documents requested.

F. Compelling participation in discovery

1. Generally

In ***Uniroyal, Inc. v. Marshall***, Case No. OFCCP 1977-1 (Sec'y., June 28, 1979), *aff'd. sub. nom.*, ***Uniroyal, Inc. v. Marshall***, 482 F. Supp. 364 (D.C. D.C. 1979), the Secretary held that the ALJ has authority under 41 C.F.R. §§ 60-30.9, 30.10, 30.11, and 30.15 to compel the contracting party to participate in depositions and discovery.

In ***OFCCP v. Jefferson County Board of Education***, Case No. 1990-OFC-4 (ALJ, Nov. 16, 1990), the ALJ granted OFCCP's motion to compel Defendant to provide names, addresses, phone numbers, positions, dates of employment educational background, and previous employment for all hires for two-year period because it would be significantly more burdensome on OFCCP to search for this information in Defendant's records as Defendant has greater familiarity with its own records.

2. Failure to comply

a. Exclusion of evidence

In ***OFCCP v. Owens-Illinois***, Case No. 1977-OFCCP-11 (ALJ, Nov. 21, 1980), the ALJ held that Defendant was entitled to know how the government intended to calculate back pay for affected class members. Therefore, where the government failed to provide a complete and detailed answer to Defendant's interrogatory regarding back pay calculations, then Defendant is entitled to seek a Rule 37(b)(2)(B) order precluding the government from introducing any evidence related to back pay owed at the hearing.

b. Adverse inference

In ***OFCCP v. Beverly Enterprises, Inc.***, 1999-OFC-11 (ALJ, Nov. 5, 2001), the ALJ concluded that the subsidiaries of Beverly Enterprises are considered a "single entity" and, as a result, the subsidiaries "may be sanctioned for the actions of the parent." The ALJ based his holding on the fact that Employer failed to respond to interrogatories and document production requests which related to "whether Defendant and its subsidiaries are a single entity." Employer's failure to respond to these discovery requests resulted in the conclusion, pursuant to 29 C.F.R. § 18.6(d)(2)(i) and 41 C.F.R. § 60-30.15(j), that the "requested responses, if given, would have been adverse to the Defendant on the single entity/single employer issue." Slip op. at 3. In particular, based on adverse inferences drawn from Employer's failure to respond to discovery requests, the ALJ concluded that the parent and its subsidiaries had common ownership and the same directors and/or officers. Moreover, the parent company and its subsidiaries emanated from a common source, were dependent on each other, and the parent had *de facto* control over the subsidiaries. Slip op. at 8-9. On the most recent appeal of this case to the ARB, the parties submitted a consent decree which was approved. ***See OFCCP v. Beverly Enterprises, Inc.***, ARB Case No. 02-009, 1999-OFC-11 (ARB, Apr. 30, 2002).

G. Interrogatories

1. Limitation of number

In ***OFCCP v. American Airlines, Inc.***, Case No. 1994-OFC-9 (ALJ, Jan. 19, 1995), the ALJ held that the Federal Rules of Civil Procedure only apply in the absence of an applicable regulatory provision. The implementing regulations for actions brought under Section 503 of the Rehabilitation Act of 1973, 29 U.S.C. § 793, are found at 41 C.F.R. Chapter 60. With regard to interrogatories, he noted that 41 C.F.R. § 60-30.9 does not limit the number of interrogatories which one party may serve upon another party. Thus, the 25 interrogatory limit contained in Fed.R.Civ.P 33 did not apply. However, a test of reasonableness would be imposed.. Under the particular circumstances of the case, the ALJ declined to further expand the issues in this case and denied OFCCP's motion to compel responses to discovery requests pertaining to events that occurred subsequent to the period covered by the 1988-1989 compliance review.

The ALJ held that, in his judgment, the interests of all concerned will be served by ordering Defendant to supply the requested telephone numbers and addresses for all former and current employees except those with authority to speak for the company; and, further, to supply addresses, either work addresses or home addresses, of former and current management employees with authority to bind the company for the limited purpose of allowing OFCCP to notice depositions. Finding OFCCP's subject requests overbroad and unduly burdensome and oppressive, the ALJ denied OFCCP's request to compel Defendant to respond to its interrogatories concerning Defendant's system of storing personnel information on computers. On the other hand, the ALJ granted OFCCP's request to compel Defendant to respond to a second set of interrogatories which sought "facts and documents which American relied upon in support of each of the 24 affirmative defenses raised in its Answer, as well as the individuals with knowledge of such facts." The ALJ held that, by raising affirmative defenses, Defendant has placed at issue the specific facts, documents, regulations, and statutes upon which they are based. OFCCP is entitled to sufficient information regarding these affirmative defenses to enable it to prepare for trial.

2. Cannot be served on non-parties

In ***OFCCP v. Crown Zellerbach Corp.***, Case No. 1987-OFC-23 (ALJ, June 6, 1989), the ALJ held that, under the regulations and the Federal Rules of Civil Procedure, interrogatories may only be served on persons who are "parties" to the litigation. The regulatory definition of "party" does not expressly include those persons who were allegedly discriminated against, although their complaints may constitute the basis of any action initiated by OFCCP. As a result, the two job applicants were not considered "parties" to the action and as such, interrogatories could not be served on them. The ALJ further reasoned that OFCCP does not have sufficient "control" over the job applicants, who are the alleged discriminatees in the case, to justify an order compelling OFCCP to obtain their individual employment history details. The only connection the applicants have to OFCCP is as reporters of potential wrongful conduct by Defendant. They are outside persons with relevant knowledge of the facts at issue in the case and are equally available to both parties for questioning. If Defendant or OFCCP seek to obtain formal discovery from these two individuals, they may do so by deposition pursuant to 41 C.F.R. § 60-30.11(a).

H. Document production

1. Medical examinations, records, and releases

When an employer inquires into an employee's mental condition, the employer must preserve the confidentially of the information that it obtains in response to its inquiry. ***OFCCP v. American Commercial Barge Line***, Case No. 1984-OFC-13 (ALJ, Sept. 30, 1986), *rev'd. on other grounds* (Ass't. Sec'y., Apr. 15, 1992). The ALJ further held that the complainant's refusal to release medical records is relevant to the issue of liability, but not to the issue of relief.

In ***OFCCP v. American Commercial Barge Line Co.***, Case No. 1984-OFC-13 (Ass't. Sec'y., Apr. 15, 1992), the Assistant Secretary held that the contractor was "within its rights" in seeking more detailed medical records from a manic depressive employee to enable contractor to make an employment decision consistent with business necessity and the safe performance of the job. Indeed, the contractor's request for medical records from an employee is authorized under 41 C.F.R. § 60.741.6(c)(3). Moreover, § 60-741.6(c)(3) does not require that the contractor provide an employee a specific assurance of confidentiality before it may obtain his medical records; the regulation simply requires that contractor observe the confidentiality of these records. As a result, Defendant met its burden of demonstrating that manic depressive employee's termination was for a non-discriminatory reason, *i.e.*, his failure to release to his employer his psychiatric records held by the VA hospital.

In ***OFCCP v. Yellow Freight System, Inc.***, Case No. 1984-OFC-17 (Ass't. Sec'y.,

July 27, 1993), it was held that Defendant's determination of whether an individual's employment would pose a reasonable probability of substantial harm cannot be based merely on medical reports "except in cases of a most apparent nature." This phrase refers to situations that are very clear, evident and obvious, and not subject to serious dispute. Under the facts before him, the ALJ concluded that the complainant's back x-ray results were not a "case of a most apparent nature" upon which contractor could rely exclusively in determining whether the complainant posed a reasonable probability of substantial harm. Moreover, the Assistant Secretary discounted Defendant's physician's assertions that complainant's employment with a back impairment would pose a reasonable probability of substantial harm. The physician merely reviewed complainant's back x-rays and provided no concrete data or other information to fully justify his position. Defendant's reliance on the complainant's back x-rays in determining whether he posed a reasonable probability of substantial harm constituted a violation of Section 503 because Defendant failed to gather all relevant information and assess both the probability and severity of potential injury in a meaningful and comprehensive manner.

2. Defendant's computer tapes; not entitled to confidentiality

Where an on-site investigation of Defendant's operations indicated various deficiencies and violations which, in turn, required additional off-site analysis of Defendant's computer information, the government was entitled to the computer tapes. Defendant failed to demonstrate that the production of the requested material was unreasonable or unduly burdensome. The government was entitled to receive copies of any computer tapes which included personnel information and data pertaining to applicants, employees, or former employees of the facilities covered by the compliance review. The government, and not Defendant, must make a determination regarding the confidentiality of the requested materials. ***OFCCP v. Prudential Insurance Co.***, Case No. 1980-OFCCP-19 (Sec'y., July 27, 1980).

3. Intervener's right to discovery of settlement

In ***OFCCP v. Cambridge Wire, Inc.***, Case No. 1994-OFC- 12 (ALJ, June 1995) (procedural order), OFCCP and Defendant submitted a proposed consent decree. An intervener-union was granted party status to challenge the fairness of certain retroactive seniority provisions contained in the decree. The intervener sought to compel production by OFCCP of documents, and both OFCCP and Cambridge Wire filed oppositions. The ALJ reviewed the documents *in camera* to determine whether they were properly discoverable. The ALJ rejected OFCCP's arguments that the documents were protected from discovery pursuant to Fed. R. Evid. 408, as they related to the negotiation of a settlement of the complaint and, therefore, the documents were irrelevant in determining whether the consent decree was fair, reasonable and adequate.

The ALJ also rejected Cambridge Wire's arguments that intervener already had sufficient information from which to determine whether the consent decree was fair, reasonable and adequate, and that the documents were protected as attorney-client work product. The ALJ recognized that the scope of intervener's participation in the instant case was to challenge the fairness of the retroactive seniority provisions contained in the consent agreement with regard to its members which necessarily limited the scope of discovery to which it would be entitled. However, the ALJ noted the intervener's right to limited discovery was a corollary to its ability to raise meaningful and informed objections to the consent decree, particularly where, as here, the intervener was not included in the settlement negotiations pertaining to the retroactive seniority provisions.

4. No right to harass defendant through discovery

In ***OFCCP v. Prudential Insurance Co.***, Case No. 1980-OFCCP-19 (ALJ, June 13, 1980), the ALJ concluded that a search of records, which could have been accomplished during a prior compliance review, would not be permitted. The ALJ determined that the government must establish good cause for searching the records, such as intentional concealment of information or independent evidence not previously considered which indicated the possible existence of an affected class. To hold otherwise, the ALJ reasoned, would be unfair to contractors as new compliance staff could reopen investigations at any time they determine that the previous review was inadequate.

5. Prepared in anticipation of litigation

In ***Dep't. of the Treasury v. Harris Bank***, Case No. 1978-OFCCP-2 (Sec'y., May 17, 1983), the Secretary held that Harris Trust was not required to produce statistical studies which were prepared in anticipation of litigation. He determined that the studies would be discoverable only if they were relied upon by Harris Trust's experts testifying at the hearing.

I. Interference with investigation

In ***OFCCP v. Uniroyal***, Case No. OFCCP 1977-1 (Sec'y., June 28, 1979), the Secretary held that, as a matter of law, it was a violation of 41 C.F.R. § 60-1.32 where Defendant's counsel was present during interviews between the government and Defendants' employees. In so holding, the Secretary held that the regulatory provision could not be waived by the government.

J. Sanctions for failure to comply with discovery

1. No authority to impose attorney fees and costs

In ***OFCCP v. Mississippi Power Co.***, Case No. 1992-OFC-8 (Ass't. Sec'y., July 19, 1995), it was held that there is no provision in Department of Labor regulations governing administrative proceedings under Section 503 for an appeal of an ALJ order imposing or denying sanctions for alleged misconduct of an attorney. The only provision for review of ALJ orders in Section 503 cases permits any party to file exceptions to the recommended decision after the hearing. Neither an ALJ nor the Secretary has the authority, absent an explicit grant by statute, to impose the personal sanctions provided for in the Federal Rules of Civil Procedure, *e.g.*, requiring payment of attorneys' fees and costs or holding an individual in contempt for failure to comply with a subpoena. The ALJ had no authority to issue the sanctions order, rather, his authority to regulate discovery and the conduct of parties and their representative is limited to that provided in the regulations. The Assistant Secretary does have the authority to review an ALJ's order imposing sanctions for failure to comply with the regulations where it is material to the issues decided in a recommended decision. The Assistant Secretary may review the propriety of the sanction or take other action provided for in the regulations. The Assistant Secretary may debar a contractor for refusal to comply with the discovery regulations.

2. Debarment

Debarment may be imposed not only for violations of Executive Order 11246, but also for failure to comply with discovery procedures. ***Uniroyal, Inc. v. Marshall***, 482 F. Supp. 364 (D.C. D.C. 1979) (Case No. OFCCP 1977-1). *See also* ***OFCCP v. The Prudential Insurance Co. of America***, Case No. 1980-OFCCP-19 (Sec'y., July 27, 1980).

Debarment and other procurement-related sanctions are authorized for both substantive and procedural violations of Executive Order 11246 and its implementing regulations. ***OFCCP v. Rampart Electric, Inc.,*** Case No. 1989-OFC-14 (Sec'y., Sept. 11, 1995).

In ***Dep't. of the Treasury v. Harris Bank***, Case No. 1978-OFCCP-2 (Sec'y., May 17, 1983), the Secretary noted that the ALJ recommended that Defendant's contracts with the government be cancelled, terminated, or suspended, until it established compliance with the ALJ's inspection and discovery orders. Although the case was remanded for resolution of certain discovery matters, and the ALJ's discovery rulings were reversed, the Secretary did not dispute the ALJ's authority to sanction a recalcitrant party, including the authority to use debarment as a sanction.

3. Discovery requests must be decided prior to issuance of summary judgment

In ***OFCCP v. Norfolk & Western Railway***, Case No. 1993-OFC-04 (Sec'y., July 20, 1995), the ALJ granted Respondent's Motion for Summary Decision, while the Complainant's Motions for Discovery were unresolved. The Secretary held that the ALJ's decision to grant Respondent's Motion for Summary Decision went beyond the scope of his authority under the circumstances presented and was inappropriate. The Secretary held that the ALJ must allow OFCCP the opportunity to present all information pertinent to the case. Therefore, the Secretary held that OFCCP's Motion for Discovery must be granted before ruling on the Respondent's Motion for Summary Decision.

K. Privileges

1. Informant's privilege

In ***OFCCP v. Owens-Illinois***, Case No. 1977-OFCCP-11 (ALJ, Nov. 21, 1980), the government refused to answer certain interrogatories and document production requests by Defendant on grounds that the information was protected by informant's privilege. Citing to ***Wirtz v. Robinson & Stephens, Inc.***, 368 F.2d 114 (5th Cir. 1966), the ALJ noted that reasonable measures should be taken to preserve the anonymity of those employees who replied to inquires during the course of the compliance review. However, it was held that, under the "informant's privilege," the identity of the informant is protected, but the contents of the communication are not privileged. In this vein, the ALJ cited to ***Roviaro v. United States***, 353 U.S. 53, 60 (1957). As a result, the government was ordered to provide "sanitized" copies of the requested documents where the informant's name, address, and social security number were redacted.

In ***OFCCP v. Crown Zellerbach Corp.***, Case No. 1987-OFC-23 (ALJ, June 6, 1989), the ALJ held that the initial burden of establishing the existence of, and properly asserting, the "informer's privilege" falls on the party opposing discovery. The "informer's privilege," as the Department of Labor concedes, is a qualified privilege and the public interest in protecting the flow of information to aid law enforcement must be balanced against Defendant's need for disclosure. Under the facts presented before him, the ALJ concluded that invocation of the informer's privilege by the Department was insufficient because the government failed to provide enough information to enable the ALJ to determine the validity of the assertion. In particular, the government failed to submit affidavits confirming the existence of employees whose identities need to be protected, and failed to request an *in camera* review of any other evidence to support the applicability of the privilege.

In ***OFCCP v. Holly Farms Foods, Inc.***, Case No. 1991-OFC-15 (ALJ, Feb. 19, 1993), the ALJ concluded that the informer's privilege is, in reality, the government's privilege to withhold from disclosure the identity of persons who furnish information of law violations to officers charged with enforcement of that law. The purpose of the informer's privilege is to promote and protect the public interest in effective law enforcement, and the scope of the privilege is limited by its underlying purpose. Moreover, executive privileges must be invoked by the head of the agency or his/her delegee after actual personal consideration by that officer. As a result, the invocation of the informer's privilege by a departmental attorney, without any evidence of a proper delegation of authority from the Secretary of Labor, was defective. Although OFCCP's failure to have the Secretary of Labor invoke the informer's privilege would justify rejection of the claim of privilege, the ALJ was reluctant to disregard the important policy underlying the privilege and, therefore, ordered OFCCP to provide contractor with a more detailed description of the documents withheld on the basis of the privilege and, if contractor continued to challenge the assertions of privilege, OFCCP was required to submit the documents for *in camera* inspection. The party asserting that documents are protected by a privilege must give sufficient identification of the material withheld so that opposing counsel can determine whether the privilege ought to apply.

2. Deliberative process privilege

In ***OFCCP v. Owens-Illinois***, Case No. 1977-OFCCP-11 (ALJ, Nov. 21, 1980), the government could not refuse to produce requested documents during discovery by labeling them "official papers" or "inter-agency communications." Rather, if the requested papers contain decisional or policy-making material, the proper procedure is to identify each paper, and upon notice to the party who requested production, to submit it for *in camera* inspection and ruling. In so holding, the ALJ cited to ***Kerr v. U.S. District Court***, 426 U.S. 394, 405-6 (1976).

In ***OFCCP v. Crown Zellerbach Corp.***, Case No. 1987-OFC-23 (ALJ, June 6, 1989), the ALJ held that a claim of privilege, in contrast to a claim of relevancy, is generally narrowly construed and the initial burden of establishing the applicability of an accepted privilege falls upon the party asserting that privilege. The intra-governmental opinion privilege applies to intra-agency memoranda and documents that record the deliberative pre-decisional process leading to an agency decision. The privilege, however, must be claimed in the form of an affidavit, rather than a mere assertion in a production answer. The affidavit must either by sworn by the head of the agency which has control over the matter or by an official with delegated authority from the agency head, after actual personal consideration by that officer. With the intra-governmental opinion privilege, the agency must demonstrate the precise reasons for preserving the confidentiality of the governmental communication, and must designate and describe those documents claimed to be privileged with sufficient detail so that the validity of the privilege may be determined.

In ***OFCCP v. USAA Federal Savings Bank***, Case No. 1987-OFC-27 (ALJ, Dec. 20, 1989), the ALJ held that the deliberative process privilege applies where disclosure of pre-decisional deliberative documents would discourage open, candid communication in the decision-making process or would mislead the public about the agency's policies or the bases for maintaining them. The deliberative process privilege must be invoked after personal consideration by the head of the agency with control of the matter or by a delegate acting under specific guidelines. Because the Secretary of Labor is the final adjudicator of cases filed under both Executive Order 11246 and Section 503 of the Rehabilitation Act, s/he is not the proper official to assert the deliberative process privilege after personal consideration of the documents. The Director of OFCCP is the proper official to review deliberative material and invoke the deliberative process privilege in cases which the Secretary of Labor will decide because the Director is a political appointee with political accountability and because s/he is the highest official with detailed knowledge of the case who will not be performing judicial role in the case.

In ***OFCCP v. USAir, Inc.***, Case No. 1991-OFC-2 (ALJ, Nov. 24, 1992), *aff'd*, (ALJ,

Feb. 24, 1993), the ALJ held that memoranda prepared by the OFCCP investigator did not fall within the deliberative process privilege because they were primarily factual and did not contain deliberations involving legal strategies or enforcement approaches, or a discussion of strengths and weaknesses of the case or policy pros or cons. Moreover, the memoranda did not place selective emphasis on particular facts or assign relative weight to a conflicting or ambiguous fact situation such that there was no "intertwining of facts with a deliberative or policy making process or discussion." On the other hand, the ALJ concluded that a draft "Notification of Results of Investigation" fell within the deliberative process privilege.

3. Attorney-client privilege

In ***OFCCP v. Crown Zellerbach Corp.***, Case No. 1987-OFC-23 (ALJ, June 6, 1989), the ALJ held that, to assert the attorney-client privilege, the party must, at a minimum, establish that any such communication concerned the seeking of legal advice was (1) between a client and an attorney acting in his professional capacity, (2) that the communication was related to legal matters, and (3) the communication was made in confidence by the client with the intention that the communication would be permanently protected from disclosure by himself or by the legal advisor.

In ***OFCCP v. USAir, Inc.***, Case No. 1991-OFC-2 (ALJ, Nov. 24, 1992), *aff'd*, (ALJ, Feb. 24, 1993), the ALJ initially noted that the attorney/client privilege applies to communications intended to be confidential. The mere existence of an attorney/client relationship or even the exchange of information with an attorney is not enough to establish the applicability of the privilege. To effectively assert the attorney/client privilege, the party must, at a minimum, establish that the communication involved the seeking of legal advice, was between a client and an attorney acting in his professional capacity, was actually related to legal matters, and was made in confidence by the client with the intention that the communication would be permanently protected from disclosure. The attorney/client privilege applies to the communications themselves, not to any underlying facts or to the particular documents. Non-privileged portions of a multiple-subject document are not exempt from production. Therefore, documents which were prepared by EOS after Joint Review Committee meeting involving OFCCP personnel and their attorneys did not fall within the attorney/client privilege because no legal advice was specifically sought in the documents and none was reported to have been given. The documents were neither responsive to counsel's inquiries nor designed, formulated, or initiated by counsel. On the other hand, the ALJ concluded that a memorandum detailing a conversation between counsel and an OFCCP supervisor, which involved a candid appraisal of legal, procedural and other confidential evaluations of issues, fell within the attorney-client privilege.

In ***OFCCP v. American Airlines, Inc.***, Case No. 1994-OFC-9 (ALJ, Jan. 19, 1995), the ALJ held that, pursuant to ***Upjohn Co. v. United States***, 449 U.S. 383, 395 (1981), and ***Hickman v. Taylor***, 329 U.S. 495, 511 (1947), Defendant may invoke the attorney-client privilege for any discovery request that requires the disclosure of the substance of a confidential communication between an attorney and client. Moreover, Defendant may invoke the attorney work product privilege for any requests to produce documents that were prepared in anticipation of litigation, in contrast to documents prepared in the normal course of business. However, Defendant must identify and justify all instances in which it withholds information on the basis of these privileges. The ALJ noted that Defendant set forth general objections to the discovery of any information that would violate the Defendant's privacy or the privacy of any third party. However, in determining the extent to which privacy rights can foreclose discovery, courts generally "balance the interests." ***Farnsworth v. Proctor & Gamble***, 758 F.2d 1545, 1547 (1985). Citing to ***OFCCP v. USAir***, Case No. 1988-OFC-17 (ALJ, 1990), the ALJ concluded that "OFCCP's interest in pursuing effective and informal discovery outweighs the privacy interests of those individuals whose addresses and telephone numbers are sought." Thus, the privacy interests of third parties did not constitute an absolute privilege.

4. Work-product privilege

In ***OFCCP v. Crown Zellerbach Corp.***, Case No. 1987-OFC-23 (ALJ, June 6, 1989), the ALJ held that OFCCP made an untimely, inadequate, and ambiguous argument that the requested documents constituted work product because OFCCP's general descriptions of various documents (*e.g.*, "Letter," "Memo to File") did not provide enough information to determine the validity of its work-product claim. OFCCP submitted no affidavits, no requests for *in camera* review of the documents at issue, and no request for a protective order. Consequently, the ALJ concluded that OFCCP submitted insufficient information and argument to sustain an objection to production on the basis of work product.

VII. Constitutional issues

A. First Amendment

In ***OFCCP v. Aid Association for Lutherans,*** Case No. 1993-OFC-11 (Sec'y., Sept. 26, 1995), Defendant was a non-profit fraternal benefit society created for the purpose of benefiting and supporting Lutherans and Lutheran organizations. Defendant's various activities, such as insurance programs, a credit union, a capital management corporation, and a real estate management company, generated substantial amounts of income (e.g., $119.3 million in net income in 1992). When a mortgagee defaulted on an office building on which Defendant held the mortgage, Defendant foreclosed and assumed ownership. Among the tenants was the United States Government. Defendant entered into a lease with the GSA, followed by eleven leases and supplemental leases. Each lease contained an equal opportunity clause requiring development of written affirmative action programs for each of its establishments. OFCCP scheduled a general compliance review, and it become apparent that Defendant refused to submit affirmative action programs based on the First Amendment.

During the pendency of an enforcement action, Defendant sold the property in question. The ALJ found that requiring Defendant to submit an affirmative action program would pose a constitutionally unacceptable risk of government entanglement with religion (e.g., requiring identification of every position for which being a Lutheran is a bona fide job qualification). On review, the Secretary noted that questions of constitutionality should not be passed on unless such adjudication is unavoidable. Finding this doctrine applicable in administrative adjudication, the Secretary stated that the determination of whether a particular case calls for restraint requires close examination of the specific facts of the case to identify the danger to be avoided, the seriousness of the alleged statutory infraction, the risk of repetition, and the harm to innocent third parties. The Secretary noted the difficulty of applying statutes regulating employment to religious institutions and organizations. He also noted that there is a distinction between enforcement of anti-discrimination laws in individual cases of alleged discrimination, and application of statutes with the potential for pervasive regulation of employment practices. The Secretary concluded that "the exercise of proper restraint dictates dismissal of this matter."

The Secretary examined OFCCP's purpose in seeking enforcement -- uncovering past acts of discrimination, and preventing the occasional contractor from avoiding its contractual obligations. He noted that Defendant no longer held a government contract, and that the risk of repetitious violations by an occasional or sporadic contractor was minor and could be resolved by requiring Defendant to notify OFCCP prior to submitting any future bid for a federal government contract. The Secretary noted that this action was based on OFCCP's compliance review and not on an allegation of discrimination, and that there did not appear to be any employees or applicants who would suffer from dismissal of the matter. He found that no purpose would be served by requiring Defendant to file affirmative actions plans when it no longer hold government contracts and was no longer subject to the Acts and regulations. He found that it was too speculative to support jurisdiction based the possibility that OFCCP might uncover discriminatory employment practices in analysis of the statistics in a putative affirmative action plan.

B. Fourth Amendment

1. Generally

In ***OFCCP v. Bank of America***, ARB No. 00-079, 1997-OFC-16 (ARB, Mar. 31, 2003), the Board held that the Fourth Amendment applies to administrative searches. The ARB stated that the Supreme Court issued a seminal decision on this issue in ***Marshall v. Barlow's Inc.***, 436 U.S. 307, 311-12 (1978) holding that the Fourth Amendment's requirements apply to the search of a business by an administrative agency. The ***Marshall*** Court required a warrant for OSHA administrative searches, stating that "[a] warrant . . . would provide assurances from a neutral officer that the inspection is reasonable under the Constitution, is authorized by statute, and is pursuant to an administrative plan containing specific neutral criteria." The Court further held the "reasonableness of a warrantless search . . . will depend upon the specific enforcement needs and privacy guarantees of each statute."

The ARB noted that the Supreme Court's interpretation of Fourth Amendment requirements for administrative searches was specifically applied to investigations under Executive Order 11246 in ***United States v. Mississippi Power & Light Co.***, 638 F.2d 899 (5th Cir. Unit A 1981). The court in ***Mississippi Power*** held that ***Marshall*** did not require a warrant for administrative searches in all circumstances. Indeed, the ***Mississippi Power*** court held that Executive Order 11246 "satisfied the requirements of the Fourth Amendment because the regulatory scheme provided for resort to the courts before an inspection is conducted."

2. "Consent" exception

In ***OFCCP v. Bank of America***, ARB No. 00-079, 1997-OFC-16 (ARB, Mar. 31, 2003), the ARB noted that "[c]onsent is an exception to the requirement that searches be conducted under the authority of a warrant or its equivalent." In ***Schneckloth v. Bustamonte***, 412 U.S. 218, 219 (1973), the Court held that it was "well settled that one of the specifically established exceptions to the requirements of both a warrant and probable cause is a search that is conducted pursuant to consent." The ARB noted that "[c]onsent can be established by proof of contemporaneous consent at the time of the actual search" or with "[e]vidence of a prior agreement to permit a search for specific documents and of specific places in connection with obtaining a government benefit or contract . . .." However, the ARB noted a split in circuit court decisions where some cases held that consent to search by contract rendered the search lawful, but other cases held that consent to search by contract only authorized a reasonable search. Under the facts in ***Bank of America***, OFCCP alleged that the bank voluntarily consented to the search of its records when it did not object to the scheduling letter sent by OFCCP notifying the bank of the fact that OFCCP would be conducting a search of its records. The ARB noted the following:

> BOA urges us to find, based on the scheduling letter alone, that it could not

> have given voluntary contemporaneous consent, and that OFCCP cannot succeed as a matter of law. That would require us to determine, as BOA suggests, that the scheduling letter can only be construed as coercive or as misrepresenting OFCCP's authority. Moreover, we would have to find that the language of the letter was so coercive or so misrepresented OFCCP's actual authority with respect to the instant review, that any subsequent consent could not have been voluntary. The evidence submitted by BOA on this issue has not indisputably established that that was the case.
>
> We note that the scheduling letter preceded the actual review by more than thirty days, it is susceptible of interpretation both as to content and effect . . ., and factors other than the letter could have entered into whether voluntary contemporaneous consent was given. Also, there is no evidence that the Bank could not have inquired as to its selection, leaving aside the question of voluntary contemporaneous consent. We therefore remand the case for hearing. The Board expects that the evidence submitted on remand will fully establish the totality of the circumstances pertinent to whether consent was voluntarily given to the compliance review.

Id.

On remand, in ***OFCCP v. Bank of America, N.A.***, Case No. 1997-OFC-16 (ALJ, Aug. 11, 2004), a different ALJ issued a *Recommended Decision and Order on Cross-Motions for Summary Judgment* finding that Defendant voluntarily consented to Plaintiff's warrantless search. Citing to ***United States v. Cotnam***, 88 F.3d 487, 495 (7th Cir. 196), *cert. denied*, 519 U.S. 942 (1996), the ALJ concluded that "BOA failed to demonstrate any indicia of reluctance to cooperate with OFCCP." Specifically, the ALJ found that "BOA did not raise objections or refuse to comply, but submitted each document requested (by OFCCP in its scheduling letter), along with many other correspondences, without a single objection." In this vein, the ALJ noted that OFCCP's scheduling letter was not misleading or coercive. In addition, the ALJ noted that when:

> . . . OFCCP officials arrived at BOA's . . . facility . . . to conduct its onsite investigation, BOA did not refuse access to its facility, but BOA representatives permitted OFCCP officials to proceed with their inspection without a single objection.

Having concluded that Defendant voluntarily consented to the warrantless search, the ALJ determined that "OFCCP's actions are removed from the requirements of the Fourth Amendment" and the parties were advised that a hearing on the merits of OFCCP's compliance action would be held. *See also* ***OFCCP v. Bank of America***, 2006-OFC-3 (ALJ, May 22, 2007) (OFCCP failed to prove selection of Respondent for a compliance review based on a neutral administrative plan, but there was no Fourth Amendment violation because Respondent gave "consent" to search; OFCCP's issuance of a letter advising that enforcement proceedings could commence if Respondent failed to cooperate did "not negate the voluntariness of Defendant's consent to the desk audit").

3. Requirements of the Fourth Amendment

In ***OFCCP v. Bank of America***, 2006-OFC-3 (ALJ, May 22, 2007), the ALJ cited to ***Marshall v. Barlow's, Inc.***, 436 U.S. 307, 320-23 (1978) and set forth the following test of "reasonableness" in conducting a warrantless administrative search of a business. The proposed search is "reasonable" if it is: (1) authorized by statute; (2) properly limited in scope; and (3) initiated in a proper manner. Utilizing these criteria, the ALJ concluded that the OFCCP search in this case met the first two criteria as a matter of law. As to the third criterion, OFCCP's decision to initiate a search is proper if the decision is based on: (1) specific evidence of an existing violation; (2) reasonable legislative or administrative standards that have been met with respect to a particular contractor; or (3) showing that the search was initiated pursuant to an administrative plan containing specific, neutral criteria. With regard to the third avenue of initiating a search, the ALJ concluded that "the Fourth Amendment does not require that OFCCP implement a *random* process for contractor selection; only a *neutral* process is required." (italics in original).

a. Violated

In ***OFCCP v. City Public Service of San Antonio***, Case No. 1989-OFC-5 (Ass't. Sec'y., Jan. 18, 1995), a case arising under Section 503 of the Rehabilitation Act, the Assistant Secretary found that Defendant consented to be searched by the government in administering and enforcing the Act. In providing its consent, Defendant waived its Fourth Amendment rights, which would otherwise be protected by the warrant application process. An investigation which is conducted where Defendant has consented to the search is of the same scope as would be permissible under a warrant issued on the basis of an individual complaint; that is, one which is reasonably related to the allegations of the complaint. Therefore, the scope of the investigation is dictated by certain factors, including the detail of the allegations within the complaint and the knowledge and experience of the OFCCP investigators evaluating the nature of the violation. Absent such facts or credible allegations which could form the basis for a reasonable belief that Defendant discriminated against individuals with other handicaps, the Assistant Secretary held that expansion of the investigation beyond the specific disability (back condition) raised by the individual complaint was unreasonable.

Moreover, the defendant cannot be deemed to have consented to an expansive investigation. The Assistant Secretary stated that "the evidence of specific violation required to establish administrative probable cause [is] less than that needed to show a probability of a violation [but] must . . . show that the proposed search is based upon a reasonable belief that a violation has been committed." As a result, it was determined that OFCCP's decision to conduct an investigation covering "the past 24 months, for those applicants denied employment for [any] medical reason" was not based on an administrative plan or a regulation with explicit criteria. The Assistant Secretary held that, "without explicit criteria to guide and constrain it, such a decision violates the Fourth Amendment because it devolves almost unbridled discretion upon executive and administrative officers, particularly those in the field, as when to search and whom to search." From this, it was determined that OFCCP demonstrated probable cause to conduct an investigation covering only the treatment of the individual complainant and City Public Service of San Antonio's policy on hiring applicants with back conditions. On the other hand, the fact that OFCCP sought and litigated its right to conduct an investigation which exceeded its authority is not ground for dismissal of the complaint. Fourth Amendment standards are satisfied for a search in the absence of a formal judicial warrant "if the enforcement procedures . . . in the . . . regulations provide, in both design and practice, safeguards roughly equivalent to those contained in traditional warrants."

b. Not violated

In ***OFCCP v. Bank of America***, 2006-OFC-3 (ALJ, May 22, 2007), the ALJ concluded that, although Defendant had not been selected for an on-site review "pursuant to (a) neutral administrative plan requiring strict sequential selection," OFCCP was nevertheless entitled to conduct the on-site review because it "had a reasonable suspicion of a violation of the Executive Order." The ALJ noted the results of OFCCP's desk audit revealed "that the average salary for male employees in (certain) job groups was anywhere from 9.08% to 23.33% higher than the average salary for female employees." Moreover, the desk audit indicated "that the average salary for non-minority employees was anywhere from 5.18% to 23.15% higher than the average slary of minority employees." The ALJ concluded that the foregoing data "provide(d) OFCCP with a reasonable basis for a belief that violations of the Executive Order may be occurring, supporting the agency's request for an on-site review."

In ***OFCCP v. Bank of America, N.A.***, Case No. 1997-OFC-16 (ALJ, Aug. 25, 2000), *remanded*, ARB No. 00-079 (ARB, Mr. 31, 2003), the ALJ held that Defendant's challenge regarding the constitutionality of its selection for compliance review under Executive Order 11246 was proper and the complaint was dismissed. The ALJ noted that the Supreme Court held, in ***Donovan v. Dewey***, 452 U.S. 594, 598-99 (1981), that the Fourth Amendment's prohibition against unreasonable searches "applies to administrative searches of private commercial property." In particular, the search of commercial property by federal agents may be deemed unreasonable if it is not legally authorized or it is "unnecessary for the furtherance of federal interests." The ALJ concluded that, in the case before him, Defendant's records regarding its affirmative action policies were searched pursuant to Executive Order 11246 as amended by Executive Orders 11375 and 12806. The contract between the government and Defendant included a clause requiring that Defendant permit access to its records for purposes of investigating compliance with the Executive Orders. Citing to ***United States v. New Orleans Public Service, Inc.***, 723 F.2d 422, 426 (5th Cir. 1984), the ALJ noted that three requirements must be met before a search is justified under the Fourth Amendment: (1) the search is authorized by statute; (2) the search is properly limited in scope; and (3) the agency initiated the search in a proper manner. With regard to the third requirement, the ALJ stated that the search is reasonable if one of the following criteria is satisfied: (1) the search is based on evidence of an existing violation; (2) reasonable administrative standards for conducting the search are satisfied; or (3) the search is conducted "pursuant to an administrative plan containing specific neutral criteria." ***New Orleans***, 723 F.2d at 426. It was undisputed in ***Bank of America*** that the search was not based upon an existing violation and it was not conducted to review Defendant's compliance with the Executive Orders.

As a result, the ALJ determined that the reasonableness of the search would be dependent upon whether the search was conducted pursuant to an administrative plan containing specific neutral criteria. Upon review of the record, the ALJ found that OFCCP's *Equal Employment Data System (EEDS) Manual* set forth the neutral administrative plan to follow. However, OFFCP failed to comply with the Manual's requirements. In this vein, the ALJ noted that OFCCP's selection of Defendant was unconstitutionally arbitrary and based, in part, on the testimony which revealed a premise that banks are "notorious" for having the "worst record of affirmative action." Consequently, the ALJ concluded that OFCCP's selection process was undocumented and unexplained such that Defendant's motion for summary judgment was granted and the complaint was dismissed.

On appeal, the ARB determined that the *EEDS Manual* did not confer any rights on private parties and "OFCCP, therefore, had no obligation to BOA to utilize on EEDS procedures for selecting contractors for compliance reviews." However, the ARB remanded the case for further proceedings because "genuine issues of material fact" existed with regard to (1) what plan with criteria actually applied to selecting the Charlotte facility, (2) whether the plan actually was implemented in Charlotte's selection, and (3) whether the plan and its application met Fourth Amendment requirements."

The ARB did find that the criteria used by OFCCP to "narrow down the list" of potential facilities to be reviewed in Charlotte were not arbitrary on their face. These criteria were that the "facility must be the headquarters of a corporation on the Fortune 500 or 1,000 list; that the corporation have at least 4,000 to 5,000 employees; that the corporation must be a multi-establishment company; that the facility must not have been previously reviewed." Moreover, the "company must have been one of the top five in the region, and there must have been significant opportunities for affirmative action at the facility."

On remand, in ***OFCCP v. Bank of America, N.A.***, Case No. 1997-OFC-16 (ALJ, Aug. 11, 2004), a different ALJ issued a *Recommended Decision and Order on Cross-Motions for Summary Judgment* finding that Defendant voluntarily consented to Plaintiff's warrantless search. Citing to ***United States v. Cotnam***, 88 F.3d 487, 495 (7th Cir. 196), *cert. denied*, 519 U.S. 942 (1996), the ALJ concluded that "BOA failed to demonstrate any indicia of reluctance to cooperate with OFCCP." Specifically, the ALJ found that "BOA did not raise objections or refuse to comply, but submitted each document requested (by OFCCP in its scheduling letter), along with many other correspondences, without a single objection." In this vein, the ALJ noted that OFCCP's scheduling letter was not misleading or coercive. In addition, the ALJ noted that when:

> . . . OFCCP officials arrived at BOA's . . . facility . . . to conduct its onsite investigation, BOA did not refuse access to its facility, but BOA representatives permitted OFCCP officials to proceed with their inspection without a single objection.

Having concluded that Defendant voluntarily consented to the warrantless search, the ALJ determined that "OFCCP's actions are removed from the requirements of the Fourth Amendment" and the parties were advised that a hearing on the merits of OFCCP's compliance action would be held.

In ***OFCCP v. First Alabama Bank of Montgomery***, Case No. 1980-OFCCP-32 (Sec'y., Dec. 5, 1980), the Secretary concluded that the government's request for access to Defendant's premises during normal business hours to conduct a compliance review was not violative of Defendant's Fourth Amendment rights. The Secretary noted that the purpose of the compliance review was to ensure that the contractor was in compliance with the non-discrimination and affirmative action regulations. As a part of the government's enforcement responsibilities, the government was entitled to such access. The Secretary further noted that Defendant's objections to the search were raised after an administrative complaint was issued. In particular, Defendant did not raise the search warrant objection until after commencement of the debarment proceedings, while it had specifically consented to a search of its records earlier.

In ***OFCCP v. Beverly Enterprises, Inc.***, Case No. 1999-OFC-11 (ALJ, July 22, 1999), Defendant, a corporation which operated nursing homes for veterans, argued that OFCCP's investigation violated the Fourth Amendment because the government did not select Defendant pursuant to a neutral administrative plan. Citing to ***United States v. Mississippi Power & Light Co.***, 638 F.2d 899 (5th Cir.), *cert. denied*, 454 U.S. 892 (1981), the ALJ concluded that Defendant's Fourth Amendment rights had not been violated and stated the following:

> In the instant case, OFCCP developed a written plan for conducting CMRs (corporate management reviews). Utilizing computer tapes containing the data provided by employers filing Form EEO-1, OFCCP developed a list of all federal contractors that had 4000 total employees and were corporate headquarters. These contractors were assigned a random number and then sorted by random number within each district office. Mr. Maltbia then followed the dictates of the written plan and Beverly was thereafter recommended for a CMR.

Slip op. at 6-7. Defendant maintained that OFCCP failed to establish through witness testimony "the intricate details of the computer code used to generate" the list. The ALJ concluded that such testimony was unnecessary. Management witnesses for OFCCP credibly testified that the program code was written to reflect the neutral plan and "tests were run to ensure the instructions regarding the criteria were met . . .." The ALJ ordered that Defendant was enjoined from refusing to comply with the requirements of Executive Order 11246, Section 503 of the Rehabilitation Act of 1973, and the Vietnam Era Veterans' Readjustment Assistance Act of 1974. He further recommended that Defendant be debarred until it established compliance with the foregoing laws.

The ALJ's recommended decision was reviewed by the ARB in ***OFCCP v. Beverly Enterprises, Inc.***, ARB Case No. 99-112, Case No. 1999-OFC-11 (ARB, Sept. 1, 1999). Defendant continued to assert that it had not been selected for a compliance review pursuant to a neutral administrative plan. The ARB initially noted that the Fourth Amendment privacy interest in data compiled by commercial enterprises is diminished when the data is compiled pursuant to federal requirements. Moreover, citing to ***Donovan v. Lone Steer, Inc.***, 464 U.S. 408 (1984), the ARB stated that the reasonableness of an agency's demand for access to records is governed by much less stringent standards than an agency's demand to enter the premises. Indeed, the inspection of a commercial enterprise's data requires, under the Fourth Amendment, that the agency's selection be "the product of a neutral administrative plan that is definite and regular, clearly limited in scope." The ARB cited to ***United States v. Mississippi Power & Light***, 638 F.2d 899,

907-08 (5th Cir.), *cert. denied*, 454 U.S. 892 (1981) to hold that OFCCP's selection of a company for a compliance review must meet the requirements set forth in ***Marshall v. Barlow's, Inc.***, 436 U.S. 307 (1978):

> A warrantless inspection satisfies the Fourth Amendment if it is: (1) authorized by statute; (2) properly limited in scope; and (3) initiated in a neutral fashion. An OFCCP search, as a matter of law, meets the first two elements; that is, it is statutorily authorized and is properly limited in scope. As to the third element, OFCCP's decision to initiate a particular search is deemed reasonable if based either on: (1) specific evidence of an existing violation; or (2) a showing that the search was initiated pursuant to an administrative plan containing specific neutral criteria. An agency must show not only that its selection plan is neutral, but also that the plan is 'actually applied neutrally.' (citation omitted).

Slip op. at 6. In applying the Fourth Amendment criteria to the facts of the case, the ARB concluded that OFCCP utilized a neutral administrative plan where its witness testified that "each year he reviewed all the computer codes to ensure that the resulting program (was) consistent with the new year's requirements." Slip op. at 8. The ARB held that OFCCP is not required to "produce documentary evidence or testimony from an official with personal knowledge of every aspect of the OFFCP selection system." The ARB concluded that the Fourth Amendment did not impose such stringent requirements on the government. It was determined that the compliance review plan was neutrally applied. In light of Defendant's failure to cooperate with OFCCP's investigation, the ARB concluded that the company would have 30 days to comply with OFCCP's requests and, its failure to do so, would result in termination of federal contracts and debarment.

On appeal, in ***Beverly Enterprises, Inc. v. Herman***, Civil Action No. 99-2408 (RMU) (D. D.C. Aug. 24, 2000), the district judge entered summary judgment against Beverly Enterprises. The court concluded that the company's Fourth Amendment rights against unreasonable searches and seizures were not violated. Turning to the legal standard for asserting Fourth Amendment challenges, the court cited to ***Marshall v. Barlows***, 436 U.S. 307, 320 (1978) to state that a valid administrative search under the Fourth Amendment requires probable cause. Probable cause is established where there is specific evidence of an existing violation or where a particular company was selected for review according to "reasonable legislative or administrative standards."

Citing to ***Uniroyal, Inc. v. Marshall***, 482 F. Supp. 364, 368 (D.C. D.C. 1979), the court held that the administrative search was conducted to enforce compliance with affirmative action programs as authorized by Executive Order 11246, which has a force of law. Moreover, the court found that Beverly Enterprises did not contest that the search was properly limited in scope. The issue, as noted by the judge, was whether the search was initiated in a proper manner. The court noted that it is the government's burden to demonstrate that selection of Beverly Enterprises for a compliance review was based on specific evidence of a violation or it was selected pursuant to an administrative plan containing specific neutral criteria. Under the facts presented before him, the district judge concluded that Beverly Enterprises was properly selected for a review. Computer generated lists were used and the district judge held that "in order to prove that a company was properly selected for a compliance review from a computerized list, the employees of the agency need only attest that the target of the search was selected under the agency's normal procedures." *See* ***National Eng'g. & Contracting co. v. OSHA***, 45 F.3d 476, 480 (D.C. Cir. 1995). Therefore, the court concluded that Beverly Enterprise's Fourth Amendment rights were not violated.

On the most recent appeal of the case to the ARB, the parties submitted a consent decree which was approved. ***See OFCCP v. Beverly Enterprises, Inc.***, ARB Case No. 02-009, 1999-OFC-11 (ARB, Apr. 30, 2002). The consent decree provided, in part, Beverly Enterprises would open its headquarters and homes for review by the Department. The consent decree further provides that OFCCP may initiate a "corporate management review" at Beverly headquarters at any time after two months and that Beverly will open 10 of its nursing homes that had been scheduled for compliance actions between 1999 and 2001.

c. OFCCP's "threshold indicator test" and issues of "vindictive" prosecution

In ***United Space Alliance LLC v. Solis***, Case No. 11-00746, based on a complaint filed on April 19, 2011 with the federal district court of the District of Columbia, United Space challenges OFCCP's authority to require that the company produce detailed compensation data or risk termination of federal funding and debarment despite the fact that its "threshold indicator test" did not produce gender-based pay discrepancies. By decision in ***OFCCP v. United Space Alliance LLC***, Case No. 2011-OFC-2 (ALJ, Feb. 28, 2011), the Administrative Law Judge found that, even though a "threshold indicator test" conducted by OFCCP revealed no indicators of pay discrimination based on gender, it was within OFCCP's discretion to request additional information from United Space and conduct two additional tests—a "pattern analysis" test and a "30 and 5" test. Despite argument to the contrary, the Administrative Law Judge declined to find that OFCCP engaged in "vindictive" prosecution as United Space did not present "strong evidence of motive."

C. Fifth Amendment

In view of the size and scope of Defendant's corporation, which consisted of 258 offices in 186 locations with 7,800 employees, requiring an expenditure of $25,000 to $30,000 for establishing an affirmative action program as well as $60,000 to $70,000 for annual data gathering and reporting, is not an unreasonable burden and does not violate Defendant's Fifth Amendment rights to due process. ***Dep't. of Labor v. Coldwell Banker & Co.***, Case No. 1978-OFCCP-12 (ALJ, June 8, 1979).

In ***Beverly Enterprises, Inc. v. Herman***, Civil Action No. 99-2408 (RMU) (D. D.C. Aug. 24, 2000), Beverly Enterprises alleged that its Fifth Amendment due process rights were violated because of the government's use of the expedited hearing procedures. Citing to ***Mathews v. Eldridge***, 424 U.S. 319, 333 (1976), the court noted that Beverly Enterprises must demonstrate the following factors in support of a Fifth Amendment violation: (1) it has a constitutionally protected life, liberty, or property interest; and (2) the procedures employed deprived Beverly Enterprises of that interest without constitutionally adequate procedures. Initially, the court held that Beverly Enterprises has constitutionally protected interests such that it must be determined whether its rights were violated in the context of each of those interests. Because Beverly Enterprises was a commercial entity with federal contracts, the court concluded that the company had a "weakened expectation of privacy" in protecting its documents from an administrative inspection. The judge determined that it was within the ALJ's discretion to decline discovery of the testimony of Solicitor of Labor Henry Solano where the testimony would "only repeat information that was included with other evidence." The court determined that the expedited procedures served the government's interest in expeditious enforcement of the anti-discrimination laws. As a result, the judge concluded that Beverly Enterprise's Fifth Amendment rights were not violated.

In ***OFCCP v. First Alabama Bank of Montgomery***, Case No. 1980-OFCCP-32 (Sec'y., Dec. 5, 1980), the Secretary held that, pursuant to its administrative and investigative powers, the government's request for access to Defendant's premises, in order to inspect books, records, accounts, and affirmative action programs, did not deprive Defendant of its property without due process of law.

D. Expedited hearing procedures

In ***OFCCP v. The Boeing Co.***, Case No. 1999-OFC-14 (ALJ, Aug. 16, 1999), the ALJ issued an *Order Granting Motion to Remove from Expedited Hearing Procedures, Granting Document and Other Discovery, and Notice of Hearing*. Defendant challenged the selection of its Wichita facility for a compliance review under the Fourth Amendment to state that it was not chosen "through random selection criteria or specific complaints of discrimination" at the facility. Indeed, Defendant argued that the OFCCP investigation was "a means of exerting pressure on Boeing to settle two other pending matters." Boeing cited "a temporal nexus of approximately one to two months between the collapse of settlement negotiations and the commencement of the Wichita compliance review." In addition, Defendant asserted that OFCCP solicited interviews with Boeing employees as a pretext for an improper investigation. Contrary to OFCCP's contention that an ALJ does not have authority to remove a case from the expedited hearing procedures and permit limited document discovery under 41 C.F.R. § 60-30.33(c), the ALJ held otherwise. He noted that Boeing's rights under the Fourth Amendment required application of the modification or waiver provisions at § 60-30.2 as "no party is prejudiced" and the "ends of justice would be served."

In ***OFCCP v. University of North Carolina***, Case No. 1984- OFC-20 (Sec'y., Jan. 27, 1987), the Secretary held that, although complaint was filed under expedited hearing procedures, neither the ALJ nor the parties treated the case as though it were entitled to expedited handling. As a result, the Secretary concluded that the ALJ's Recommended Decision would be reviewed under the regular hearing procedures.

VIII. Government contractor

A. Federal contracts

For an additional discussion of the burdens involved in establishing a government contractor or "working-on-the-contract," *see* Chapters III and V.

1. Generally

[a] Apply to all operations absent obtaining a waiver

In ***OFCCP v. Beverly Enterprises, Inc.***, 1999-OFC-11 (ALJ, Nov. 5, 2001), the ALJ concluded that the subsidiaries of Beverly Enterprises are considered a "single entity" and, as a result, the subsidiaries "may be sanctioned for the actions of the parent." The ALJ based his holding on the fact that Employer failed to respond to interrogatories and document production requests which related to "whether Defendant and its subsidiaries are a single entity." Employer's failure to respond to these discovery requests resulted in the conclusion, pursuant to 29 C.F.R. § 18.6(d)(2)(i) and 41 C.F.R. § 60-30.15(j), that the "requested responses, if given, would have been adverse to the Defendant on the single entity/single employer issue." Slip op. at 3. In particular, based on adverse inferences drawn from Employer's failure to respond to discovery requests, the ALJ concluded that the parent and its subsidiaries had common ownership and the same directors and/or officers. Moreover, the parent company and its subsidiaries emanated from a common source, they were dependent on each other, and the parent had *de facto* control over the subsidiaries. Slip op. at 8-9. On appeal to the ARB, the parties submitted a consent decree which was approved by the Board. ***See OFCCP v. Beverly Enterprises, Inc.***, ARB Case No. 02-009, 1999-OFC-11 (ARB, Apr. 30, 2002).

In ***Trinity Industries, Inc. v. Herman***, 173 F.3d 527 (4th Cir. 1999) (Case No. 1997-OFC-14), the circuit court held that the affirmative action reporting requirements applied to all of Trinity's facilities despite the fact that the company argued that one of the facilities was autonomous and did not perform federal government contract work. The case arose under Section 503 of the Rehabilitation Act of 1973, Section 402 of the Vietnam Era Veterans' Readjustment Assistance Act of 1974, and Executive Order 11246. The court noted that the Executive Order requires that a contractor who employs 50 or more employees and contracts with the United States for payment of $50,000 or more must develop an affirmative action program. Moreover, the Executive Order and Rehabilitation Act provide that the Secretary of Labor "may" waive the affirmative action requirement for an independent facility of the contractor. However, the court noted that no waiver was accorded Trinity in this case as the company never filed a request for approval of a waiver with the appropriate government official. Trinity argued that the facility under investigation did not have a federal contract and the facility:

> . . . is autonomous in organization, function, and management; and . . . it makes its own decisions concerning hiring, firing, discipline, discharges,

promotions, and pay increases.

The court held that, while these facts may indeed support waiver, there was no express waiver from the Secretary of Labor in the record. The court noted that Trinity unsuccessfully argued similar issues before another circuit court in ***Trinity Industries, Inc. v. Reich***, 33 F.3d 942 (8th Cir. 1994) which "suggests that the company is well-informed of the need to obtain a waiver, and of the proper method for doing so."

In ***OFCCP v. Yellow Freight Systems, Inc.***, Case No. 1989-OFC-40 (ALJ, May, 17, 1994), OFCCP alleged that Yellow Freight discriminated against a truck driver, Mr. Wilson, in contravention of Section 503 of the Rehabilitation Act of 1973. Initially, Defendant argued that there was no evidence of record that the driver hauled freight pursuant to a federal government contract such that the Rehabilitation Act did not apply. The ALJ disagreed to state:

> To the extent that the government contracting sector of the trucking industry as a whole may tend to assign loads to drivers on a random basis, OFCCP's proof is more than sufficient . . . when, as here, it demonstrates that employees occupying jobs in the category sought by the handicapped applicant perform government contract work on a random basis. Under these circumstances, the qualified handicapped individual is as likely as any other similarly employed individual to work on a government contract job.

Slip op. at 18.

In ***OFCCP v. Burlington Industries, Inc.***, Case No. 1990-OFC-10 (ALJ, Nov. 1, 1991), the government sought cancellation of Burlington's federal contracts as well as debarment from future contracts pending Defendant's compliance with Executive Order 11246. Initially, the ALJ rejected Burlington's argument that the particular plant which was the subject of OFCCP's investigation, did not have any federal government contracts. The ALJ held that Burlington had government contracts at its other plants and that all contracts with the government contain an Executive Order 11246 non-discrimination provision which is, in turn, applicable to all of the company's operations. Because the government contracts with Burlington were valued in excess of $50,000, the employer's entire workforce was covered. As support for this holding, the ALJ cited to a decision of the Secretary of Labor in ***OFCCP v. Preister***, Case No. 1978-OFC-12 (Sec'y., Feb. 27, 1983). The ALJ held that "[i]t is not necessary for OFCCP to establish a link between a particular plant suspected of discrimination and a government contractor." Citing to ***University of North Carolina v. Dep't. of Labor***, 917 F.2d 812 (4th Cir. 1990), the ALJ concluded that "[a] contract between the corporate owner of the plant and the government is enough . . .." Slip op. at 15.

A federal contractor's affirmative action clause obligations are not limited solely to federal contract jobs, but extend to any position for any of its operations. ***E.E. Black, Ltd. v. Marshall***, 497 F. Supp. 1088 (D. Hi. 1980).

[b] Does not apply to all operations; waiver regulations are inconsistent with the Act

In ***Washington Metropolitan Area Transit Authority v. DeArment (WMATA)***, 55 Empl. Prac. Dec. 40,505 (D. D.C. 1991), the district judge held that the waiver provisions at 41 C.F.R. § 60-741.3(a)(5) are inconsistent with the statute. In particular, the court stated the following:

> All employees of the contractor are not swept in, which is basically what Labor is trying to do by their waiver provision. The Act itself says, employing persons to carry out such (federal) contract are the people who are covered and Labor's reading is far too broad.

Slip op. at 1. *See also* ***Cissell Mfg. Co. v. Dep't. of Labor***, 101 F.3d 1132 (6th Cir. 1996).

It is noted that, in ***OFCCP v. Keebler Co.***, ARB Case No. 97-127, Case No. 1987-OFC-20 (ARB, Dec. 21, 1999), the ARB noted several flaws in the district court's analysis in ***WMATA***.

2. Obligation to ensure that subcontractor complies

In ***OFCCP v. First Federal Savings Bank of Indiana***, Case No. 1991-OFC-23 (Sec'y., Oct. 26, 1995), the Secretary held that First Federal had an obligation to assure that its subcontractors complied with the requirements of Section 503 of the Rehabilitation Act, as implemented at 41 C.F.R. § 60-741.4(f). In so holding, the Secretary rejected the ALJ's conclusion that Defendant did not violate Section 503 by failing to assure that the lessor of office space to Defendant provide parking spaces for handicapped employees. The Secretary concluded that the building owner is a subcontractor because it supplies services necessary to the performance of Defendant's government contracts. 41 C.F.R. § 60-.4; ***OFCCP v. Coldwell, Banker and Co.***, Case No. 1978-OFC-12, slip op. at 7-8 (Sec'y., Aug. 14, 1987). Since the owner of the building provided handicapped parking spaces before the hearing in the case at Defendant's request, the Secretary did not reach the question of what action would have been required if the building owner had not promptly complied with Defendant's request.

3. Federal government may be a purchaser or seller

For the purposes of coverage under the Act, it does not matter whether the federal government is the purchaser or seller. ***OFCCP v. Ozark Air Lines, Inc.***, Case No. 1980-OFCCP-24 (ALJ, Dec. 7, 1982), *aff'd.* (Dep'y. Under Sec'y., June 13, 1986).

4. Waiver for independent facilities

The North Carolina statute and regulations establishing and governing the University of North Carolina (UNC) make it clear that the UNC is a single agency of which UNC-A and NCSA are only parts. It is not necessary, therefore, to make a finding of privity of contract to establish coverage. ***OFCCP v. University of North Carolina***, Case No. 1984-OFC-20 (Sec'y., Jan. 23, 1989), *aff'd.*, ***Board of Governors of the University of North Carolina v. United States Department of Labor***, 917 F. 2d 812 (4th Cir. 1990), *cert. denied*, 500 U.S. 916 (1991). In so holding, it was determined that the rationale of the Supreme Court's decision in ***Pennhurst State School and Hospital v. Halderman***, 451 U.S. 1 (1981) was not applicable to Section 503 coverage of the University of North Carolina constituent institutions, because the equal opportunity clause was presumably included in each contract required to include it and, if it was not, the clause would have been incorporated by operation of law. The exemption in 41 C.F.R. § 60-1.5(a)(4) did not cover the constituent campuses of UNC because they were not considered separate state agencies. The exemption applies only to agencies separate and distinct from the agency holding the contract. In so holding, it was noted that, under North Carolina General Statutes Chapter 116, Article 1, the University of North Carolina at Asheville and the North Carolina School of the Arts are not separate agencies and, therefore, are not entitled to the exemptions contained at 41 C.F.R. §§1 60-1.5(a)(4), 60-250.3(a)(4), and 60-741.3(a)(4).

In ***Trinity Industries, Inc. v. Herman***, 173 F.3d 527 (4th Cir. 1999) (Case No. 1997-OFC-14), the circuit court held that the affirmative action reporting requirements applied to all of Trinity's facilities despite the fact that the company argued that one of the facilities was autonomous and did not perform government contract work. The case arose under Section 503 of the Rehabilitation Act of 1973, Section 402 of the Vietnam Era Veterans' Readjustment Assistance Act of 1974, and Executive Order 11246. The court noted that the Executive Order requires that a contractor who employs 50 or more employees and contracts with the United States for payment of $50,000 or more must develop an affirmative action program. Moreover, the Executive Order and Rehabilitation Act provide that the Secretary of Labor "may" waive the affirmative action requirement for an independent facility of the contractor. However, the court noted that no waiver was accorded Trinity in this case as the company never filed a request for approval of a waiver with the appropriate government official. Trinity argued that the facility under investigation did not have a federal contract and the facility:

> . . . is autonomous in organization, function, and management; and . . . it makes its own decisions concerning hiring, firing, discipline, discharges, promotions, and pay increases.

The court held that, while these facts may indeed support waiver, there is no express waiver from the Secretary of Labor in the record. The court noted that Trinity unsuccessfully argued similar issues before another circuit court in ***Trinity Industries, Inc. v. Reich***, 33 F.3d 942 (8th Cir. 1994) which "suggests that the company is well-informed of the need to obtain a waiver, and of the proper method for doing so."

A contractor with a federal contract of over $2,500 at any facility must utilize the waiver provisions at 41 C.F.R. § 60-741.3(a)(5) in order to avoid the Act's affirmative action obligations at any of its other facilities on all work performed on contracts of over $2,500. ***OFCCP v. W.S. Hatch Trucking Co.***, Case No. 1984-OFCCP-15 (ALJ, June 5, 1986) (denial of summary judgment). Requiring a contractor to be an affirmative action employer at its government contract facility, as opposed to the non-government contract facilities, would result in disparate treatment of handicapped persons.

The regulatory provisions at 41 C.F.R. § 60-741.3(a)(5) provide that a federal contractor's facilities are covered, unless a waiver was requested and granted. Defendant did not request a waiver for its coal car shop and, therefore, it was a covered facility.

OFCCP v. Norfolk and Western Railway Co., Case No. 1988-OFC-4 (ALJ, June 28, 1989).

A federal contractor's affirmative action clause obligations are not limited solely to federal contract jobs, but extend to any position at its operations. ***E.E. Black. Ltd. v. Marshall***, 497 F. Supp. 1088 (D. Hi. 1980). Even if a particular contract has no connection with any of the contractor's federal contracts, it is a covered contract (if over $2,500), unless there is a specific waiver.

B. Federal contract defined

1. Established

[a] Depository of federal funds

In ***OFCCP v. First Federal Savings Bank of Indiana***, Case No. 1991-OFC-23 (Sec'y., Oct. 26, 1995), the Secretary rejected Defendant's argument that it was not a government contractor covered by Executive Order 11246. Defendant argued that its agreements to act as an issuing agent for United States Savings Bonds and a depository for federal funds did not constitute government contracts within the meaning of the Order and regulations. The Secretary rejected this assertion, noting that DOL regulations explicitly provide that government contract means "any agreement . . . between any contracting agency and any person for the furnishing of supplies or services and that [t]he term services . . . includes . . . fund depository." *See* 41 C.F.R. § 60-1.3. *See also* ***OFCCP v. USAA Federal Savings Bank***, Case No. 1987-OFC-27 (Sec'y., Mar. 16, 1995).

[b] Bills of lading

Bills of lading supply coverage. ***OFCCP v. Southern Pacific Transportation***, Case No. 1979-OFC-10A (ALJ, Nov.9, 1982), *remanded on other grounds* (Ass't. Sec'y., Feb. 24, 1994). A tariff constitutes only an offer until the government shipper avails itself of the terms through a bill of lading, at which time it is a contract. All the terms of the contract do not have to be spelled out in a single formal document. The value of the federal contract is the crucial matter, not how it is divided among those who enter into the federal contract. *See also* ***OFCCP v. Yellow Freight Systems, Inc.***, 1979-OFCCP-7 (Ass't. Sec'y., Aug. 24, 1992).

[c] Contract for use of federal property and services

A contract for the use of federal property and services provides coverage under the Act. ***OFCCP v. Ozark Air Lines, Inc.***, Case No. 1980-OFCCP-24 (Dep'y. Under Sec'y., June 30, 1986).

[d] Blanket purchase agreement

A blanket purchase agreement, rather than the orders placed under it, constitutes the federal contract for purposes coverage under Section 503 of the Rehabilitation Act. The blanket purchase agreement at issue, although it did not state specific prices, provided that the price for each purchase would be set at a published market rate. The annual value of orders under the blanket purchase agreement exceeded $50,000 each year since 1981 and, thus, was sufficient to establish coverage. ***OFCCP v. Bruce Church, Inc.***, Case No. 1987-OFC-7 (Sec'y., June 13, 1987).

[e] Subcontractor performs "necessary" services for the federal contract

A subcontractor is subject to the requirements of 41 C.F.R. § 60-741.2 when the type of service it provides is necessary to the contractor's performance of its agreement with the federal government, even though this specific subcontractor's service may not be necessary. ***OFCCP v. Monongahela Railroad Co.***, Case No. 1985-OFC-2 (ALJ, Apr. 2, 1986), *aff'd.* (Dep'y. Under Sec'y., Mar. 11, 1987).

Defendant, a bulk power supplier, was covered under the provisions of Section 503 because it was a corporate sibling to a government contractor and operated to supply electricity to service companies which, in turn, supplied electricity to the government. To allow a government contractor to elude coverage by maintaining a subsidiary supplier would be inconsistent with Section 503's purpose. ***OFCCP v. Texas Utilities Generating Co.***, Case No. 1985-OFC-13 (ALJ, Mar. 2, 1988), *remanded on other grounds* (Ass't. Sec'y., Aug. 25, 1994).

Defendant had an obligation to assure that its subcontractors complied with the requirements of Section 503 of the Rehabilitation Act and 41 C.F.R. § 60-741.4(f) and, by failing to make an effort to obtain handicapped parking spaces, Defendant violated that obligation. ***OFCCP v. First Federal Savings Bank of Indiana***, Case No. 1991-OFC-23 (Sec'y., Nov. 20, 1995).

In ***OFCCP v. UPMC Braddock, et al.***, 2007-OFC-1, 2, and 3 (ALJ, Jan. 16, 2008), *aff'd.*, ARB Case No. 08-048 (ARB, May 29, 2009) (on appeal with D.C. Circuit Court as *UPMC Braddock v. Solis,* D.D.C. Case No. 1:09-cv-01210), Respondent hospitals challenged OFCCP's authority to conduct a compliance review under Executive Order 11246, Section 503 of the Rehabilitation Act of 1973, and Section 402 of the Vietnam Era Veterans' Readjustment Assistance Act of 1974 on grounds that they did not have a direct, contractual relationship with the United States government.

The judge agreed that the Respondents, which were non-stock, non-profit entities each employing more than 50 people, did not have a direct contractual relationship with the United States government. However, he concluded that OFCCP did have authority to conduct a compliance review. In support of this holding, the ALJ held that Respondents, as contracting hospitals with an HMO, met the definition of subcontractors at 41 C.F.R. § 60-13:

> Arguably, fee-for-service organizations, or strictly insurance providers, are not subcontractors under *Bridgeport*, as such organizations are charged with providing reimbursement to their members for health care expenses without concern over who actually provides the health care. However, an HMO by its nature arranges and provides for the medical services through the medical

> providers such as the Defendant hospitals with which it contracts. Thus, the hospitals and other medical providers are clearly necessary for the fulfillment of UPMC's contract with OPM and are subcontractors under 41 C.F.R. § 60-1.3. The ARB decision in *Bridgeport* does not preclude a finding that Defendant hospitals are subcontractors under 41 C.F.R. § 60.13.

Id.

In affirming the ALJ's decision on appeal, the ARB held that the "equal opportunity" clauses of the Rehabilitation Act, VEVRAA, and Executive Order 11246 at 41 C.F.R. §§ 60-1.4(e), 60-250.5(e), and 60-741.5(e) are incorporated by operation of law "whether or not (the equal opportunity clause) is physically incorporated in each such contract and whether or not the contract between the agency and the contractor is written." Moreover, the ARB rejected Respondents' argument that the equal opportunity clause "applies only to prime contractors who voluntarily enter into a contract with the government"; rather, the ARB cited to the plain language of the regulations, which require that the clause is considered part of every contract *and subcontract*.

See also ***OFCCP v. Fla. Hosp. of Orlando***, Case No. 2009-OFC-2 (ALJ, Oct. 18, 2010).

[f] "Subcontractor" defined

In ***OFCCP v. UPMC Braddock***, ARB No. 08-048, Case Nos. 2007-OFC-1, 2, and 3 (ARB, May 29, 2009) (on appeal with D.C. Circuit Court as *UPMC Braddock v. Solis,* D.D.C. Case No. 1:09-cv-01210), Defendants argued that they were not "subcontractors" and, therefore, were not required to comply with equal opportunity laws set forth at 41 C.F.R. §§ 60-1.4(e), 60-250.5(e), and 60-741.5(e). In support of their position, Defendant hospitals maintained that they had HMO contracts with the University of Pittsburgh Medical Center (UPMC), which, in turn, had a contract with the Office of Personnel Management (OPM) to provide medical products and services to U.S. government employees. Notably, the contracts between UPMC and OPM expressly excluded the Defendant hospitals from the definition of "subcontractors" in the contracts. Moreover, Defendant hospitals argued that they are not subcontractors under the definitions set forth in the Federal Acquisition Regulations (FAR) at 48 C.F.R. § 1602.170-14. The ALJ and ARB agreed with Defendants on these points but held that equal opportunity laws at issue could not be invalidated by contractual arrangements between UPMC and OPM, nor was the definition of a "subcontractor" in the FAR controlling in this case. The ARB held that the ALJ "refused to apply the Part 1602 definition because he found that it conflicted with federal law." The ARB further stated:

> Recognizing that provisions in a government contract that violate to conflict with a federal statute are invalid or void, (the ALJ) reasoned that an interpretation that would exclude subcontractors like the Defendant hospitals from compliance with the three laws would be invalid as contrary to the three laws giving the Secretary of Labor authority in these matters. We agree. The Secretary has promulgated regulations implementing the Executive Order. These regulations do not exclude providers like the Defendants from the

definition of 'subcontractor.' Furthermore, these regulations have the force and effect of law. Because the FAR regulation that the Defendants ask us to apply directly contradicts the Secretary's regulations, it is invalid, and we decline to apply it.

Slip op. at 8. Turning to the definitions of "subcontract" set forth at 41 C.F.R. §§ 60-1.3, 60-741.2, and 60-250.2(l) as well as the FAR definition of "non-personal services" at 48 C.F.R. § 37.101, the ARB agreed with the ALJ that the Defendants met the definition of "subcontractors" as they provided "necessary" services for UPMC to meet its contractual obligations and, consequently, Defendants were obliged to comply with the equal opportunity laws.

See also ***OFCCP v. Fla. Hosp. of Orlando***, Case No. 2009-OFC-2 (ALJ, Oct. 18, 2010).

2. Not established

[a] Lease of space in a government building

The lease of space in a federal office building is a government contract within the meaning of 41 C.F.R. § 60-1.3. ***Dep't. of Labor v. Coldwell Banker & Co.***, Case No. 1978-OFCCP-2 (Sec'y., June 8, 1979).

[b] Subcontractor not perform "necessary" services for federal contract

In ***OFCCP v. Bridgeport Hospital***, Case No. 1997-OFC-1 (ALJ, Jan. 21, 2000), *rev'd. in part*, ARB Case No. 00-034 (ARB, Jan. 31, 2003), the sole issue before the ALJ was whether Defendant was a covered subcontractor under Executive Order 11246, Section 503 of the Rehabilitation Act, and the Vietnam Era Veterans' Readjustment Assistance Act. Citing to the definition of a subcontractor at 41 C.F.R. § 60-1.3, the ALJ entered summary judgment in favor of Defendant after concluding that Defendant was not a covered subcontractor. In particular, Defendant hospital was not covered because it did not provide services to the contractor (Blue Cross/Blue Shield), which was "necessary" to the contractor's performance of its prime contract with the federal government. The ALJ reasoned as follows:

> Bridgeport's agreement with Blue results in Bridgeport being either a Preferred or a Member hospital. In either case Blue pays a higher percentage of the cost of its members' treatment than if no agreement existed. Clearly, a consequence of the agreement between Blue and Bridgeport is less cost to Blue members, less cost to Blue and thus an overall less costly Federal Employees Health Benefits Program. Conversely, however, the lack of the reimbursement agreement would not preclude Blue from being able to offer medical benefit insurance to its federal employee members, and would not preclude Blue from paying insurance benefits to those treated at Bridgeport as the federal employees members would be reimbursed in accord with the

provisions for treatment at non-member hospitals.

DOL's argument that the Bridgeport reimbursement agreement is 'necessary' to Blue's contract with OPM apparently stems from the fact that the agreement lowers costs to Blue and its members. However, under such reasoning, any concern that does business with Blue, and whose business potentially affects Blue's costs, such as public utilities, advertising, real estate costs, space rental, etc., would be considered 'necessary.' Such an expansive interpretation of the definition of a subcontractor would read the modifier 'necessary' out of the definition as all third party contracts would be considered necessary.

Slip op. at 8-9. In support of his holding, the ALJ further noted that, pursuant to the contract between OPM and Blue Cross, providers of direct medical services, such as Defendant, were not considered subcontractors. The ARB reversed the ALJ's decision and held the following:

Unlike the ALJ, . . . we do not reach the question of whether Blue's non-existent obligation to deliver medical services to Blue enrollees did or did not constitute partial performance by Bridgeport of Blue's contract with OPM or was 'necessary to performance' of the prime contract. This is because the first premise of OFCCP's argument fails – Blue has no commitment to OPM to provide its policyholders with medical care. Therefore, questions concerning the terms 'necessary to' or 'part performance of' do not arise in this appeal.

[c] Federal grant monies not constitute federal contracts

In ***Partridge et. al. v. Reich***, 141 F.3d 920 (9th Cir. 1998), OFCCP declined to prosecute alleged acts of discrimination on grounds that it lacked jurisdiction because the employer was not a federal contractor. Specifically, employees of the Clark County Fire Department alleged discrimination in violation of the Vietnam Era Veterans' Readjustment Assistance Act of 1974 at 38 U.S.C. § 4212. It was noted that the Act applied only to procurement contracts valued at $10,000 or more. In this vein, the court found that 41 C.F.R. § 60-250.2 did not provide that federal grants were included in the definition of procurement contracts. The court cited to the Federal Grant and Cooperative Agreement Act at 31 U.S.C. §§ 6301-6305 in further support of its holding. Plaintiffs argued that the fire department and Clark County should be considered one entity in support of jurisdiction. Said differently, since Clark County received federal contracts and the fire department was part of the County, a basis for jurisdiction existed. In support of their position, Plaintiffs cited to ***Bd. of Governors of the University of North Carolina v. U.S. Dep't. of Labor***, 917 F.2d 812 (4th Cir. 1990) wherein the circuit court held that "all UNC campuses were subject to compliance laws regardless of their individual lack of contracts with the federal government." However, the court noted that the Fourth Circuit narrowly interpreted 41 C.F.R. § 60-1.5(a)(4) and relied on a state statute which specifically identified the University of North Carolina as one state agency. The ***Partridge*** court declined to read the Fourth Circuit's decision more broadly and held that Clark County's contracts with the federal government could not be imputed to the fire department so as to give rise to OFCCP jurisdiction.

3. Term of contract

In ***OFCCP v. Keebler Co.***, ARB Case No. 97-127, Case No. 1987-OFC-20 (ARB, Dec. 21, 1999), a case arising under Section 503 of the Rehabilitation Act of 1973, the ARB analyzed the contract clause at Section 503 and stated "we are able to see that a contract clause serves as a temporal limit on coverage and that Congress intended to protect all employees of federal contractors from disability discrimination during the life of the contract." Slip op. at 15.

IX. Compliance Review

A. Generally

1. Desk audit not required to precede on-site review

The three-step procedure in Part 60-60 for compliance reviews suggests that the desk audit precede the on-site review. However, the regulations do not require that the audit be completed first if good reason exists for an immediate on-site review. ***OFCCP v. Prudential Insurance Co.***, Case No. 1980-OFCCP19 (Sec'y., July 27, 1980).

2. Follow-up "on-site review" permitted

After an on-site investigation of Defendant's affirmative action plan, OFCCP concluded that Defendant discriminated against women and minorities in hiring for entry level jobs in ***OFCCP v. Georgia-Pacific Corp.***, Case No. 1990-OFC-25 (Dep'y. Sec'y., Dec. 28, 1990). The affected class totaled 24 minorities and three women. Defendant denied the existence of an affected class and, for the first time after the first on-site investigation, it put forth alleged additional reasons for not hiring 11 of the named class members, including alcoholism, obesity, and poor work history. OFCCP, therefore, sought an additional on-site investigation which was denied by Defendant on grounds that OFCCP is entitled to only one on-site investigation. The Deputy Secretary disagreed and concluded that OFCCP was entitled to a second on-site review of records where, as in this case, "particular circumstances warrant a follow-up review."

3. Scheduling letter, limitations on scope of review

In ***OFCCP v. Frito-Lay, Inc.***, Case No. 2010-OFC-2 (ALJ, July 23, 2010), the Administrative Law Judge held that OFCCP was not authorized to obtain employment records relating to hiring decisions occurring *after* the date the contractor received the "scheduling letter" initiating the compliance review. Citing to Executive Order 11246 and its implementing regulations, the Administrative Law Judge noted that Defendant complied with its obligations under the scheduling letter and he stated the following:

> . . . this compliance evaluation was to cover the period January 2006 to July 2007. As this is the matter under investigation, Frito-Lay is only required to permit access to materials that are relevant to the investigation. Far from being unambiguous, I find nothing in the regulations that would require Frito-Lay to permit OFCCP access to the 2008 and 2009 data.

The Administrative Law Judge determined that "the temporal scope of a desk audit phase of a compliance review cannot be extended beyond the date" that a scheduling letter is received by a contractor.

B. Reporting requirements

The purpose of the reporting requirements are to ensure compliance by government contractors of the affirmative action requirements of Executive Order 11246 and to ensure equal opportunity for all persons without regard to race, color, sex, religion, or national origin. ***HUD v. S.T.C. Construction Co.***, Case No. 1977-OFCCP-5 (ALJ, May 22, 1978).

C. Establishing affirmative action plans

Where Defendant had 258 offices in 186 locations world-wide, it was not required to establish separate affirmative action plans for each office. Rather, the ALJ determined that a more reasonable interpretation of the regulations was to require establishment of an affirmative action plan on a regional or national basis. ***Dep't. of Labor v. Coldwell Banker & Co.***, Case No. 1978-OFCCP-12 (ALJ, June 8, 1979).

For additional discussion of affirmative action plans, *see* Chapters X and XI.

X. The Rehabilitation Act

For a discussion of applicable jurisdictional issues, including collateral estoppel under the Rehabilitation Act, *see* Chapter III, Jurisdiction.

A. Generally

1. The Americans With Disabilities Act of 1990

The Americans With Disabilities Act of 1990, as amended by the Americans With Disabilities Amendments Act of 2008, contain useful guidance in determining whether an individual's disability substantially limits a major life activity, or whether an individual is "regarded as" having a disability. Therefore, this Desk Reference contains citations to the ADA and ADA Amendments Act.

2. Disability could cause harm to individual's health

The United States Supreme Court has held that a regulation by the Equal Employment Opportunity Commission authorizing an employer's refusal to hire a worker because the worker's disability would cause harm to his own health if hired for the job was valid. Under the facts of ***Chevron U.S.A., Inc. v. Echazabal***, 122 S. Ct. 2045 (2002), a worker's physical examination revealed that he suffered from Hepatitis C and Employer's physicians opined that the worker's condition would be aggravated by continued exposure to toxins at Employer's factory. As a result, Employer properly refused to hire the disabled worker.

3. ADA Amendments Act of 2008—Congressional disagreement with Supreme Court interpretations

In 2008, Congress amended the ADA based on its disagreement with certain Supreme Court holdings. One of the Court's decisions addressed whether a worker's carpal tunnel syndrome rendered her "substantially limited" in performing major life activities. Here, the Supreme Court held that the Court of Appeals erred in focusing on whether the condition left the worker unable to perform manual tasks associated with her job. In ***Toyota Motor Mfg. Kentucky, Inc. v. Williams***, 122 S. Ct. 681 (2002), an assembly line worker sued Employer for failing to make reasonable accommodations for her when carpal tunnel syndrome precluded her from performing her job. The Court held that, instead of focusing only on the manual tasks performed by the worker on the assembly line, it must be determined whether the worker's "impairments prevented or restricted her from performing tasks that are of central importance to most people's daily lives." To establish disability under the ADA, it is insufficient to merely submit a medical diagnosis of an impairment. The Court stated:

> In this case, repetitive work with hands and arms extended at or above shoulder levels for extended periods, the manual task on which

> the Sixth Circuit relied, is not an important part of most people's daily lives. Household chores, bathing, and brushing one's teeth, in contrast, are among the types of manual tasks of central importance to people's daily lives, so the Sixth Circuit should not have disregarded respondent's ability to do these activities.

Id. at 692-94.

Congress expressed its disagreement with this decision in the ADA Amendments Act of 2008.

First, the definition of "major life activity" was amended. The Americans With Disabilities Act Amendments of 2008 specifically broadened the scope of coverage of the 1990 Americans With Disabilities Act by revising the definition of "major life activity" as follows:

> IN GENERAL.—For purposes of paragraph (1), major life activities include, but are not limited to, caring for oneself, performing manual tasks, seeing, hearing, eating, sleeping, walking, lifting, bending, speaking, breathing, learning, reading, concentrating, thinking, communicating, and working.

MAJOR BODILY FUNCTIONS.—For purposes of paragraph (1), a major life activity also includes the operation of a major bodily function, including but not limited to, functions of the immune system, normal cell growth, digestive, bowel, bladder, neurological, brain, respiratory, circulatory, endocrine, and reproductive functions.

Moreover, the 2008 Amendments set forth mandatory "Rules of Construction Regarding the Definition of Disability" as follows:

> (A) The definition of disability in this Act shall be construed in favor of broad coverage of individuals under this Act, to the maximum extent permitted by the terms of this Act.
> (B) The term 'substantially limits' shall be interpreted consistently with the findings and purposes of the ADA Amendments Act of 2008.
> (C) An impairment that substantially limits a major life activity need not limit other major life activities in order to be considered a disability.
> (D) An impairment that is episodic or in remission is a disability if it would substantially limit a major life activity when active.
> (E)(i) The determination of whether an impairment substantially limits a major life activity shall be made without regard to the ameliorative effects of mitigating measures such as –
>> (I) medication, medical supplies equipment, or appliances, low-vision devices (which do not include ordinary eyeglasses or contact lenses), prosthetics including limbs and devices, hearing aids and cochlear implants or other implantable hearing devices, mobility devices, or oxygen therapy equipment and supplies;
>> (II) use of assistive technology;

(III) reasonable accommodations or auxiliary aids or services; or

(IV) learned behavioral or adaptive neurological modifications.

(ii) The ameliorative effects of mitigating measures of ordinary eyeglasses or contact lenses shall be considered in determining whether an impairment substantially limits a major life activity.

Finally, with the 2008 Amendments addressed the use of "Qualification Standards and Tests Related to Uncorrected Vision" and state the following:

> . . . a covered entity shall not use qualification standards, employment tests, or other selection criteria based on an individual's uncorrected vision unless the standard, test, or other selection criteria, as used by the covered entity, is shown to be job-related for the position in question and consistent with business necessity.

42 U.S.C. § 12112(c).

4. Types of adverse actions

In ***OFCCP v. Western Electric Co.***, Case No. 1980-OFCCP-29 (ALJ, Mar. 4, 1981), *rev'd. and remanded on other grounds* (Dep'y. Under Sec'y., Apr. 24, 1985), the ALJ held that a decision to refuse to hire, to layoff, to terminate, or to put a worker on disability are actions that come under the purview of Section 503 of the Rehabilitation Act.

"Constructive" discharge assumes that the employee was not formally discharged, the issue being whether he was forced to resign or whether he quit voluntarily. A finding of constructive discharge requires proving that working conditions were rendered so difficult, unpleasant, unattractive, or unsafe that a reasonable person would have felt compelled to resign, *i.e.*, that the resignation was involuntary. ***OFCCP v. Mt. Bell Telephone Co.***, Case No. 1987-OFC-25 (Ass't. Sec'y., Aug. 25, 1994).

5. Affirmative action--requires more than obligation not to discriminate

In ***OFCCP v. American Airlines, Inc.***, Case No. 1994-OFC-9 (Ass't. Sec'y., Apr. 26, 1996), the Assistant Secretary held, that as a matter of logic, the concept of "affirmative action" must include a duty not to discriminate against members of the class protected by Section 503. Nondiscrimination is the starting point-the first step required of any contractor in fulfilling its affirmative action obligation. If a contractor could freely discriminate against employees and applicants for employment on the grounds that they are disabled, and without regard to their ability to perform the job, the contractor could avoid any responsibility for affirmative action. It was noted that the term "affirmative action" is not defined in the Rehabilitation Act but, if it has any "plain meaning," the phrase must clearly prohibit discrimination. Even if the meaning of the term "affirmative action" is unclear, there can be no question that the Secretary's interpretation of it in the Section 503 regulations as prohibiting discrimination and requiring all covered contracts to include an affirmative action clause is reasonable. The Assistant Secretary held that OFCCP may enforce Section 503 through compliance reviews, since affirmative action requires significantly more than simple nondiscrimination and the regulations specify, in considerable detail, the steps required of contractors to meet that obligation. The Assistant Secretary reasoned that, because individual complaints are unlikely to raise issues beyond the narrow question of a contractor's treatment of one person, without an investigation it would be impossible to determine whether a contractor is in compliance with all of its commitments under the affirmative action clause. In addition, it was noted that the affirmative action mandate is broader than a nondiscrimination mandate--the affirmative action requirement of section 503 includes an obligation not to discriminate.

At a minimum, "affirmative action" in favor of handicapped individuals means to avoid discrimination against them. ***OFCCP v. Southern Pacific Transportation Co.***, Case No. 1979-OFC-10A (ALJ, Nov. 9, 1982), *remanded on other grounds* (Ass't. Sec'y., Feb. 24, 1994). An employer's affirmative action obligation includes notifying the discriminatee of the existence of the affirmative action obligations and plan (either directly or indirectly), and how the discriminatee may obtain additional information about that plan. A prospective employer who denies employment has a duty under this law to inform the rejected applicant of the basis for the rejection and to give information on the existence either of alternative employment with it. Moreover, the employer must advise of other possible assignments for which the individual discriminatee might be considered or how the discriminatee may obtain information about other employment opportunities with the employer.

The Rehabilitation Act requires federal contractors to take affirmative action in employing qualified handicapped individuals, including a contractual pledge of non-discrimination. ***OFCCP v. Exide Corp.***, Case No. 1984-OFC-11 (Ass't. Sec'y., Apr. 30, 1991), *vac'd. on other grounds*, **Exide Corp. v. Martin**, Civil Action No. 91-242 (E.D. Ky. 1992).

In ***Exxon Corp. v. U.S. Dep't. of Labor***, 2002 WL 356517 (N.D. Tex. Mar. 5, 2002) (Memorandum Opinion and Order), the court concluded that Mr. Strawser was not a "disabled individual" under the Rehabilitation Act because OFCCP was collaterally estopped from litigating the issue as EEOC had unsuccessfully litigated the same issue under the Americans With Disabilities Act before the same court in a case involving the same employer and the same allegedly discriminatory policy. However, the holdings of the ALJ and ARB may be instructive. *See* ***OFCCP v. Exxon Corp.***, Case No. 1992-OFC-4 (ALJ, June 15, 1993), *aff'd. in part,* (ARB, Oct. 28, 1996). Because the regulations require (1) that contractors take affirmative action to employ and advance qualified handicapped individuals, and (2) actual recruitment of handicapped individuals, it is clear that Section 503 obliges a contractor to more than non-discrimination. ***OFCCP v. Exxon Corp.***, Case No. 1992-OFC-4 (ALJ, June 15, 1993), *aff'd.*, (ARB, Oct. 28, 1996). Under the facts of the case, the ALJ found that Defendant's decision to transfer the worker to a non-safety sensitive job, based on its policy of excluding all recovering alcoholics from safety-sensitive jobs, was unlawful and violated Section 503. Because the policy did not differentiate between those employees who successfully rehabilitated themselves and those who had not, the policy ran afoul of Section 503's mandate of affirmative action and non-discrimination.

3. Employer's knowledge of disability at time of adverse action required

In ***OFCCP v. Goodyear Tire & Rubber Co.***, ARB Case No. 97-039, Case No. 1994-

OFC-11 (ARB, Aug. 30, 1999), the ARB dismissed OFCCP's complaint on grounds that Defendant did not know of the employee's disability when it discharged him. Under the facts of the case, the employee sustained a brain injury in an automobile accident, but was released to work without restrictions. While on the job, and during the 30 day probationary period, the employee worked as a tire builder. However, the training coordinator for the position noted that the employee would "wander outside of his work area" and could not remember the job instructions. The employee mentioned to management that he had been in an automobile accident, but he did not state that he had any disabilities. The employee's work was below the required production level and he was discharged. The ARB noted that a person is substantially limited in a major life activity if s/he is disqualified from employment in his or her chosen field.

Citing to ***EE. Black Ltd. v. Marshall***, 497 F. Supp. 1088 (D. Hi. 1980), the Board noted that three factors must be considered in determining whether a person is disqualified from employment: (1) the number and types of jobs from which the impaired individual is disqualified; (2) the geographical area to which the individual has reasonable access; and (3) the individual's job expectations and training. In this vein, the ARB noted that "[w]here a person is disqualified only from one particular position, but still is able to work in many, if not most, other positions in his chosen field, the employee is not substantially limited in working." Consequently, the ARB held that the employee's disqualification as a tire builder was insufficient to demonstrate that he was substantially limited in working. However, the ARB did find that, based upon a review of the employee's educational and vocational history, the employee's chosen field was manufacturing and he was substantially limited in this major life activity. In this vein, the ARB reasoned that the evidence of record revealed that the employee could perform only two out of 17 jobs at the Goodyear plant. Experts testified that the employee was disqualified from performing "assembly tasks requiring speed, manual dexterity or piecework with production standards." The ARB stated:

> In keeping with the remedial nature of the Rehabilitation Act, we decline to require a plaintiff to provide a detailed job analysis of many jobs in the employee's chosen field, as the ALJ did. Rather, we find that the testimony of Barnes and Dr. Long meets the preponderance of the evidence standard: it is more likely than not that White cannot perform, without accommodation, any assembly line and piecework manufacturing jobs requiring manual dexterity, speed, or production standards.

Although the ARB concluded that OFCCP demonstrated that the employee was limited in a major life activity due to his brain injury, the complaint was dismissed because, at the time the employee was discharged, Defendant did not know about his impairment. The ARB concluded that "[t]he regulations implementing the Rehabilitation Act are clear that an employer has a duty to accommodate only for *known* physical or mental limitations." (emphasis in original).

4. Sovereign immunity of states

In ***Reickenbacker v. Foster, et al.***, 274 F.3d 974 (5th Cir. 2001), the Fifth Circuit held that the "accommodation obligation" imposed by Title II of the Americans With Disabilities Act and Section 504 of the Rehabilitation Act "far exceeds that imposed by the

Constitution" and does not apply to states. The court concluded that it was improper for the statutes to require that public entities make "'reasonable modifications'" for handicapped persons as an abrogation of the states' sovereign immunity. Specifically, it concluded that Congress did not validly act through its Fourteenth Amendment § 5 power to abrogate state sovereign immunity. Moreover, because the issue was not raised before the district court, the Fifth Circuit declined to rule on whether the state of Louisiana "waived its sovereign immunity under the Rehabilitation Act by accepting federal monies."

B. Qualified handicapped individual; "substantially limited in a major life activity"

1. Burdens

[a] Generally

In order to establish a *prima facie* case of discrimination under Section 503, OFCCP must demonstrate that (1) an individual with a disability, (2) who was "qualified," (3) for a job covered by the Act, (4) was denied an employment opportunity or advantage, (5) on the basis of his or her disability. ***OFCCP v. Holly Farms Foods, Inc.***, Case No. 1991-OFC-15 (ALJ, Oct. 24, 1991)(order). *See also* **Exide Corp. v. Martin**, Civil Action No. 91-242 (E.D. Ky. 1992) (in order to prevail in a Section 503 case, OFCCP must establish a *prima facie* that an "otherwise qualified handicapped" person was rejected for employment under circumstances which give rise to an inference that his rejection was based solely on his mental or physical handicap; if this burden is carried, then Defendant has the burden of proving either that the complainant was not an "otherwise qualified handicapped" person or that he was rejected for reasons other than his mental or physical handicap).

In ***OFCCP v. Ford Motor Co.***, Case No. 1980-OFCCP-12 (ALJ, Oct. 4, 1985)[4], the ALJ held that proof that Defendant has medical guidelines which arbitrarily restrict epileptics to ground level work constitutes a *prima facie* case of employment discrimination. Once OFCCP establishes a *prima facie* case, Defendant has the burden of proving that the individual is not a qualified handicapped individual, or that the person's rejection from work was for reasons other than his handicap.

In ***OFCCP v. Keebler Co.***, ARB Case No. 97-127, Case No. 1987-OFC-20 (ARB, Dec. 21, 1999), a case arising under Section 503 of the Rehabilitation Act of 1973, the ARB dismissed the complaint on grounds that OFCCP failed to establish that Defendant's employee was a "qualified handicapped individual" capable of performing the job of production attendant with or without reasonable accommodation. Under the facts of the case, OFCCP alleged a violation of 41 C.F.R. § 60-741(a) based on Defendant's failure to take affirmative action on the employee's behalf and, in particular, Defendant adhered to "physical job qualification requirements which screened out DeAngelis (a production attendant) as a qualified handicapped individual but were not job related or consistent with business necessity or the safe performance of the job, and . . . by failing to make reasonable accommodation to DeAngelis' physical limitations." The ARB held that OFCCP

---

[4] The ALJ issued a supplemental recommended decision on March 20, 1987.

had the burden of production and persuasion to establish, by a preponderance of the evidence, that Keebler committed the violations alleged. The testimony of DeAngelis' co-workers and supervisors persuaded the ARB that the epileptic seizures placed her "in obviously helpless states near moving conveyor belts, in the path of a tow motor, (and) with her hand inches from 300 (degree) plus liquid glue." Slip op. at 30. In allocating the burdens of proof, the ARB stated:

> OFCCP had the burden to produce credible evidence that DeAngelis' on-the-job seizures did not impair her ability to perform her work safely with or without accommodation. If Keebler did not rebut OFCCP's showing with credible evidence that the production attendant position jeopardized DeAngelis' safety, then OFCCP would win (assuming business necessity was not an issue in play).

Slip op. at 31. Moreover, the ARB stated that, if the evidence was in equipoise, OFCCP would lose.

The issue presented to the Board was whether DeAngelis' continued work posed a "'reasonable possibility of substantial harm.'" The factors to be considered in determining this issue are: (1) duration of the risk; (2) nature and severity of the potential harm; (3) likelihood that the potential harm will occur; and (4) imminence of the potential harm. Slip op. at 32. The ARB noted that the employee never sought accommodation for her epilepsy; rather, she argued that she could perform the job of a production attendant and "her epilepsy was irrelevant to her job performance." Slip op. at 34. However, the ARB concluded that, because the employee's epileptic seizures placed her at high risk of serious harm but the employee argued that the condition was irrelevant to her work performance, Keebler did not commit a violation of the Act in firing her from the position of production attendant. Moreover, the ARB declined to find a violation based on OFCCP's argument that Defendant inadequately investigated the employee's medical and work history prior to firing her. The Board concluded that OFCCP failed to establish that DeAngelis was a qualified handicapped individual based on her own testimony that she was not handicapped.

[b] Dual motives

In order to invoke the protection of the Rehabilitation Act, OFCCP must demonstrate that the employee is a qualified handicapped individual within the meaning of 41 C.F.R. § 60-741.2. ***OFCCP v. Norfolk and Western Railway Co.***, Case No. 1990-OFC-1 (ALJ, June 26, 1991). In this vein, OFCCP has the burden of proving that worker's handicap prevents him or her from performing the demands of a particular job and that it forecloses, generally, the type of employment involved, assuming that all employers offering the job would use the same requirement or screening process.

Under the facts of ***Norfolk and Western***, OFCCP met its burden of proving that the employee's monocular condition substantially limited his ability to find work as a brakeman/conductor or similar employment. Defendant rejected the worker because of his monocular condition and it was properly assumed that all employers offering the job would reject him on that basis. However, on review of the evidence presented, the ALJ determined that legitimate and discriminatory motives were also presented for the adverse employment action. In a dual motive case, an "inference" of discrimination is not sufficient to shift the burden Defendant to demonstrate that it would have discharged the worker, even if he had not been handicapped. Rather, in a dual motive case, the burden shifts to Defendant to prove that it would have discharged the worker, even if he had not been handicapped, only after the trier of fact concludes that the contractor acted for a legitimate reason *and* because the employee was handicapped. Defendant may avoid liability only by establishing that it would have made the same decision because of legitimate management reasons.

[c] Worker argued not handicapped; complaint dismissed

In ***OFCCP v. Keebler Co.***, ARB Case No. 97-127, Case No. 1987-OFC-20 (ARB, Dec. 21, 1999), a case arising under Section 503 of the Rehabilitation Act of 1973, the ARB dismissed the complaint on grounds that OFCCP failed to establish that Defendant's employee was a "qualified handicapped individual" capable of performing the job of production attendant with or without reasonable accommodation. Under the facts of the case, OFCCP alleged a violation of 41 C.F.R. § 60-741(a) based on Defendant's failure to take affirmative action on the employee's behalf and, in particular, Defendant adhered to "physical job qualification requirements which screened out DeAngelis (a production attendant) as a qualified handicapped individual but were not job related or consistent with business necessity or the safe performance of the job, and . . . by failing to make reasonable accommodation to DeAngelis' physical limitations." The ARB concluded that OFCCP failed to establish that DeAngelis was a qualified handicapped individual based on her own testimony that she was not handicapped.

2. Major life activity, defined

Maintaining consciousness, hearing, seeing, and, for employees who lift or perform extended driving, physical strength and spinal health are major life activities necessary for employability. Moreover, when an employer discriminates based on criteria that would disqualify the individual from employment in the entire industry, this constitutes a substantial interference with a major life activity. ***OFCCP v. Southern Pacific Transportation Co.***, Case No. 1979-OFC-10A (ALJ, Nov. 9, 1982), *remanded on other grounds* (Ass't. Sec'y., Feb. 24, 1994). *See* discussion of ADA Amendments Act of 2008, *supra*.

In ***Exxon Corp. v. U.S. Dep't. of Labor***, 2002 WL 356517 (N.D. Tex. Mar. 5, 2002) (Memorandum Opinion and Order), the court concluded that Mr. Strawser was not a "disabled individual" under the Rehabilitation Act because OFCCP was collaterally estopped from litigating the issue as EEOC had unsuccessfully litigated the same issue under the Americans With Disabilities Act before the same court in a case involving the same employer and the same allegedly discriminatory policy. However, the holdings of the ALJ and ARB may be instructive. *See* ***OFCCP v. Exxon Corp.***, Case No. 1992-OFC-4 (ALJ, June 15, 1993), *aff'd. in part,* (ARB, Oct. 28, 1996). In ***OFCCP v. Exxon Corp.***, Case No. 1992-OFC-4 (ARB, Oct. 28, 1996), an impairment may affect a major life activity without significantly limiting it.

Special considerations apply where, as here, the major life activity is "working." In this context, "substantially limits" means being restricted in the ability to perform either (1) a class of jobs, or (2) a broad range of jobs in various classes. A "class of jobs" would include jobs requiring similar training, knowledge, skills and abilities. 29 C.F.R. Part 1630, App. at 403. On the other hand, citing to ***E.E. Black, Ltd. v. Marshall***, 497 F.Supp. 1088, 1101-1102 (D. Hi. 1980) (substantial limitation means more than an inability to perform one particular job but less that a general inability to work; evaluation should focus on the number and the type of jobs from which the employee is disqualified), the ARB held that an inability to perform a single job does not qualify as a substantial limitation. The Board also held that major life activities may include activities other than "working" and are those basic activities that the average person in the general population can perform with little or no difficulty, *e.g.*, caring for oneself, performing manual tasks, walking, seeing, hearing, speaking, breathing, learning, sitting, standing, lifting, reaching, thinking, reading, concentrating and interacting with others.

3. Employee *regarded as* a handicapped individual

Importantly, the ADA Amendments Act of 2008 stressed the importance of broad coverage of its provisions to prohibit discrimination against persons with disabilities. The phrase "regarded as having such an impairment" is defined under the Amendments as:

> (A) An individual meets the requirement of 'being regarded as having such an impairment' if the individual establishes that he or she has been subjected to an action prohibited under this Act because of an actual or perceived physical or mental impairment whether or not the impairment limits or is perceived to limit a major life activity.
>
> (B) Paragraph (1)(C) shall not apply to impairments that are transitory and minor. A transitory impairment is an impairment with an actual or expected duration of 6 months or less.

In ***Exxon Corp. v. U.S. Dep't. of Labor***, 2002 WL 356517 (N.D. Tex. Mar. 5, 2002) (Memorandum Opinion and Order), the court concluded that Mr. Strawser was not a "disabled individual" under the Rehabilitation Act because OFCCP was collaterally estopped from litigating the issue as EEOC had unsuccessfully litigated the same issue under the Americans With Disabilities Act before the same court in a case involving the same employer and the same allegedly discriminatory policy. However, the holdings of the ALJ and ARB may be instructive. *See* ***OFCCP v. Exxon Corp.***, Case No. 1992-OFC-4 (ALJ, June 15, 1993), *aff'd. in part,* (ARB, Oct. 28, 1996). Based on case law, legislative history, and the regulations, in ***OFCCP v. Exxon Corp.***, Case No. 1992-OFC-4 (ALJ, June 15, 1993), *aff'd.* (ARB, Oct. 28, 1996), the ALJ concluded that Complainant, a recovering alcoholic, could not be considered an "individual with handicaps" under 29 U.S.C. § 706(8)(B)(ii) because his alcoholism had not substantially limited his major life activities. Nonetheless, the ALJ concluded that Complainant was considered a handicapped individual under 29 U.S.C. § 7(6)(C) (1976), *amended by* 29 U.S.C. § 706(8)(B)((1986) because "individuals may be discriminated against merely because they are *regarded* as handicapped." Slip op. at 26 (citation omitted).

The ARB agreed that an employee may fall under subpart (iii) of the definition of individual with a disability, if s/he has an impairment that does not substantially limit a major life activity, but the impairment is *regarded as* being substantially limiting. Individuals fall into this category if they have an impairment which is substantially limiting only because of attitudes of others toward the impairment. For example, a job applicant's facial scar may be substantially limiting because the prospective employer believes it will dissuade customers. Said differently, an individual with no impairment may be regarded as having a substantially limiting handicap based on an employer's mistaken belief that an individual is physically or mentally impaired or based on genetic information relating to illness, disease or disorders. Citing to ***School Board of Nassau County v. Arline***, 480 U.S. 273, 283 (1987), the ARB noted that, by including the "regarded as" criterion, "Congress acknowledged that society's accumulated myths and fears about disability and diseases are as handicapping as are the physical limitations that flow from actual impairment."

To determine whether a person is handicapped under the statutory definition of being regarded as having such impairment depends upon perceptions of the worker at the time of the employment discrimination rather than the discriminatee's actual physical conditions and capacities. ***OFCCP v. Southern Pacific Transportation Co.***, Case No. 1979-OFC-10A (ALJ, Nov. 9, 1982), *remanded on other grounds* (Ass't. Sec'y., Feb. 24, 1994). *See also* ***E.E. Black, Ltd. v. Marshall***, 497 F. Supp. 1088 (D. Hi. 1980); ***OFCCP v. Texas Utilities Generating Co.***, Case No. 1985-OFC-13 (ALJ, Mar. 2, 1988), *remanded on other grounds* (Ass't. Sec'y., Aug. 25, 1994) (applicants were qualified individuals with disabilities where Defendant denied them employment because of its perception that they were handicapped based on back x-ray results, whether or not the impairment actually existed); ***OFCCP v. Central Power & Light Co.***, Case No. 1982-OFC-5 (ALJ, Mar. 30, 1987).

In ***OFCCP v. Louisville Gas & Electric Co.***, Case No. 1988-OFC-12 (ALJ, Jan. 29, 1990), *aff'd.*, (Ass't. Sec'y., Jan. 14, 1992), the Assistant Secretary held that, under ***Jasany v. U.S. Postal Service***, 755 F.2d 1244 (6th Cir. 1985), the burden is on Plaintiff to establish, as part of its *prima facie* case, the existence of an impairment that substantially limits a major life activity. The burden then shifts Defendant to demonstrate that challenged criteria are job related, required by business necessity, and reasonable accommodation is not possible. Under the facts of ***Louisville Gas***, the Assistant Secretary held that Plaintiff must establish that the employee with perceived lumbar lordosis was a qualified handicapped individual. It was determined that Defendant failed to gather sufficient information as required under ***Mantolete v. Bolger***, 767 F.2d 1416 (9th Cir. 1985), to make a reasoned judgment on whether the employee's perceived impairment (lumbar lordosis) prevented him from performing the essential requirements of the job without a reasonable probability of substantial harm to himself or others. Thus, Defendant failed to carry its burden and establish that employee was not a qualified handicapped individual.

4. Ability at the time of employment decision relevant

[a] Generally

Defendant is entitled to make its employment determination on the basis of the worker's condition at the time of the testing with regard to the job requirements and it is not required to delay a hiring decision on the possibility that an applicant may become qualified. ***OFCCP v. Southern Pacific Transportation Co.***, Case No. 1979-OFC-10A (ALJ, Nov. 9, 1982), *remanded on other grounds* (Ass't. Sec'y., Feb. 24, 1994).

Evidence regarding complainant's physical condition after the time he was placed on disability pension is not relevant as it did not form the basis for Defendant's action regarding the complainant. ***OFCCP v. American Telephone and Telegraph Co. (AT&T)***, Case No. 1992-OFC-5 (ALJ, Apr. 23, 1995).

[b] Employer must reconsider decision on request if condition has changed

An employer should not be allowed to shield itself in perpetuity from its obligations under Section 503 by arguing that past circumstances rendered the employee disqualified. Thus, on request, an employer is required to reconsider its employment decision after the passage of time when the employee's handicap is subject to change over time. ***OFCCP v. CSX Transportation, Inc.***, Case No. 1988-OFC-24 (Ass't. Sec'y., Oct. 13, 1994).

5. Assessment of disability must be based on mitigated condition

The 2008 Americans With Disabilities Act Amendments set forth mandatory "Rules of Construction Regarding the Definition of Disability" as follows:

> (A) The definition of disability in this Act shall be construed in favor of broad coverage of individuals under this Act, to the maximum extent permitted by the terms of this Act.
> (B) The term 'substantially limits' shall be interpreted consistently with the findings and purposes of the ADA Amendments Act of 2008.
> (C) An impairment that substantially limits a major life activity need not limit other major life activities in order to be considered a disability.
> (D) An impairment that is episodic or in remission is a disability if it would substantially limit a major life activity when active.
> (E)(i) The determination of whether an impairment substantially limits a major life activity shall be made without regard to the ameliorative effects of mitigating measures such as –
>
>> (I) medication, medical supplies equipment, or appliances, low-vision devices (which do not include ordinary eyeglasses or contact lenses), prosthetics including limbs and devices, hearing aids and cochlear implants or other implantable hearing devices, mobility devices, or oxygen therapy equipment and

supplies;
(II) use of assistive technology;
(III) reasonable accommodations or auxiliary aids or services; or
(IV) learned behavioral or adaptive neurological modifications.

(ii) The ameliorative effects of mitigating measures of ordinary eyeglasses or contact lenses shall be considered in determining whether an impairment substantially limits a major life activity.

The foregoing amendments were enacted by Congress to broaden the scope of coverage of the ADA and to expressly depart from certain U.S. Supreme Court decisions related to determining whether a person has a "disability." The following cases were issued prior to the ADA Amendments.

[a] Myopia

In ***OFCCP v. Delta Airlines, Inc.***, Case No. 1994-OFC-8 (ALJ, Mar. 20, 1996), OFCCP argued that Defendant's vision standard for flight officers violated Section 503 of the Rehabilitation Act and that the vision condition at issue in the instant case--myopia--constituted "an impairment under the Act because it is a refractive error that without correction prevents a pilot from receiving a first or second class medical certificate from the FAA to fly commercial airlines, thereby substantially limiting a myopic pilot's employability." Slip op. at 6. The ALJ recommended a finding that myopia is not an impairment under the Act because the condition is an average characteristic shared by many people. Alternatively, the ALJ found that even if myopia is an impairment, it is not disabling because it does not "substantially limit an individual's employability." Slip op. at 7-8 (citing ***Welsh v. City of Tulsa, Okl.***, 977 F.2d 1145, 1419 (10th Cir. 1992)).

The ALJ observed that, if OFCCP's position were accepted, a large percentage of Americans would be considered disabled. It was noted that the courts focus on whether eyesight could be improved or corrected when determining whether an individual is disabled. Consequently, the ALJ found that myopic pilots are only disqualified from working as pilots for the Delta Airlines or for the military. He rejected OFCCP's contention that it must be assumed that all airlines have the same requirements for their flight officers. *See* ***E.E. Black, Ltd. v. Marshall***, 497 F. Supp. 1088 (D. Haw. 1980). Thus, the ALJ found that ion 503 of the Rehabilitation Act of a commercial airline pilot for Defendant did not prove that the individual is disabled within the meaning of the Act. The ALJ also found that myopic pilots are not regarded by Defendant as having an impairment, noting that Delta Airlines: (1) only disqualified new hires for myopia; (2) retained pilots whose vision deteriorated during their tenure; and (3) Defendant did not question the applicants' ability to obtain employment in the airline industry (in fact, the applicants were working as flight officers for other commercial airlines). The ALJ compared the facts in the instant case to those facts presented in ***Tudyman v. United Airlines***, 608 F. Supp. 739 (D.C. Cal. 1984)(overweight flight attendants).

In sum, the ALJ held that "[m]yopia is simply a commonplace characteristic that does not pose a disadvantage to individuals affected by it in their search for employment. Likewise, even if myopia is considered an impairment, it is not a disability because it does not substantially limit the complainant pilots' employability. As their vision is correctable to 20/20, "neither [applicant is] disqualified from any position except that of a flight officer with [Defendant]." Slip op. at 11-12.

The ARB dismissed the complaint on appeal in ***OFCCP v. Delta Airlines, Inc.***, ARB Case No. 96-088, Case No. 1994-OFC-8 (ARB, Sept. 28, 1999). The ARB noted that Delta Airlines would not hire two pilots who had less than 20/20 vision. Although the complainant pilots were myopic, their vision could be corrected to 20/20 or better with lenses. Citing to ***Sutton v. United Air Lines, Inc.***, 119 S. Ct. 2139 (1999), a case arising under the Americans With Disabilities Act, it was noted that the Court held that a "'determination of whether an individual is disabled should be made with reference to measures that mitigate the individual's impairment, including . . . eyeglasses and contact lenses.'" The ***Sutton*** Court held that, because the position of global airline pilot is a single job, the allegation that the Defendant regards the pilots' poor vision as precluding them from holding a global airline pilot's position does not support a claim that the pilot has a substantially limiting impairment. OFCCP agreed that the ARB should dismiss its complaint based on the indistinguishable holding in ***Sutton***.

[b] Radial keratomy

In ***OFCCP v. United Airlines, Inc.***, ARB Case No. 97-024, Case No. 1994-OFC-1 (ARB, July 25, 2000), a case arising under Section 503(a) of the Rehabilitation Act at 29 U.S.C. § 793(a), the ARB affirmed the ALJ's dismissal of OFCCP's complaint which alleged that an airline pilot was "an individual with a disability" who was discriminated against when the airline prohibited him from flying a 747 commercial aircraft. The pilot had undergone radial keratomy surgery on both eyes, which returned his vision to normal. However, he was disqualified from serving as a pilot, several years later after United Airlines acquired certain routes from PanAm, because of the scarring left by the surgery. OFCCP argued that the pilot was disabled under the Act because his uncorrected vision was so poor as to preclude him from flying a plane. However, the ARB disagreed and stated the following:

> The record in this case shows that even if (the pilot's) allegedly impaired vision had been severe enough to disqualify him from commercial aircraft piloting positions generally, (the pilot) could still have flown other aircraft and served as a pilot instructor.
>
> . . .
>
> (The pilot's) disqualification from a single job cannot be cast into a larger mold by, as OFCCP suggests, called is a disqualification from a profession.

As a result, the ARB concluded that the pilot was not substantially limited in a major life activity. Citing to the Supreme Court's decision in ***Sutton v. United Air Lines, Inc.***, 527 U.S. 471, 477 (1999), the ARB noted that the pilot's impairment "must be judged in its mitigated state," *i.e.* after corrective surgery. The ARB agreed that OFCCP had the burden to establish a *prima facie* case that the pilot's impairment substantially limited his major life activities, which OFCCP failed to do. The ARB found that it was the pilot's scars, and not his myopia, which disqualified him from serving as a pilot for safety reasons. As a result, the ARB dismissed "OFCCP's unexplained position here that there need be no causal connection between the recorded disability and the employer's adverse action" as this untenable position would effectively "prohibit employers from disqualifying individuals based on a non-disabling condition whenever the worker can show he or she had a disability some time in the past." Slip op. at 10.

C. Business necessity for job requirements

1. Defendant's burden to establish

In ***OFCCP v. Central Power & Light Co.***, Case No. 1982-OFC-5 (ALJ, Mar. 30, 1987), if OFCCP demonstrates that Defendant used physical job qualifications that resulted in screening out qualified handicapped individuals, Defendant has the burden of proving that its job qualifications were "directly connected with, and substantially promote business necessity and safe (job) . . . performance." *See also* **Bentivegna v. U.S. Dep't. of Labor**, 694 F.2d 619, 622 (9th Cir. 1982); ***E.E. Black, Ltd. v. Marshall***, 497 F. Supp. 1088, 1103 (D. Hi. 1980) (the regulations place the burden of proof as to business necessity on Defendant). The ALJ further held that Defendant's argument that there was a possibility that persons with radiographic spinal anomalies would develop future chronic back problems was not sufficient to meet its burden of showing that the job qualifications, which rejected all applicants with such conditions, were job related and consistent with business necessity and safe performance.

In ***OFCCP v. Texas Industries, Inc.***, Case No. 1980-OFCCP-28 (Ass't. Sec'y., Jan. 27, 1995), the Assistant Secretary held that, since Defendant admittedly rejected an employee because of her disability, the issue was not whether there was an intent to discriminate, but whether the contractor's qualification standard, which was discriminatory, was justified as being job related and consistent with business necessity and safety. Where Defendant establishes the presence of the likelihood, seriousness and imminence of injury to a sufficient degree, then it has met its burden of proving job relatedness and consistency with business necessity and safe performance.

In ***OFCCP v. Southern Pacific Transportation Co.***, Case No. 1979-OFC-10A (ALJ, Nov. 9, 1982), *remanded on other grounds* (Ass't. Sec'y., Feb. 24, 1994), it was held that a general requirement of the business necessity exception is that a factual basis must exist for believing that generally all or substantially all members of the discriminatee class would be unable to perform the duties. Moreover, the job requirement which the handicapped worker is unable to perform must be of extremely high and crucial importance. The standard for determining the presence of business necessity requires a comparative analysis of the impact on employment opportunities, national productivity, and public safety. Where the public safety risk is very high, the other two considerations must yield; where it is not, they prevail.

If Defendant admits that its decision to terminate the complainant's employment was based on a handicapping condition, Defendant has the burden of proving that its discriminatory action is consistent with business necessity and the safe performance of the duties of the complainant's job. ***OFCCP v. American Commercial Barge Line***, Case No. 1984-OFC-13 (ALJ, Sept. 30, 1986), *rev'd. on other grounds*, (Ass't. Sec'y., Apr. 15, 1992).

Defendant must establish that a substantial correlation exists between safety and its exclusion of the complainant from employment.

In ***OFCCP v. Yellow Freight Systems, Inc.***, Case No. 1982-OFC-2 (ALJ, Sept. 30, 1986), *remanded on other grounds* (Ass't. Sec'y., Oct. 6, 1993), the ALJ noted that the Act does not proscribe pre-employment physical examinations and it does not prohibit the use of the results of such examinations to exclude from employment qualified handicapped individuals. However, he stated that, if physical requirements exclude such persons from employment, these requirements must be consistent with business necessity and safe job performance. Once OFCCP has established a *prima facie* claim of discrimination, then the burden of proof shifts to Defendant to rebut this inference by either (1) establishing that the physical requirement is job related and consistent with business necessity and safe job performance, or (2) demonstrating that the decision was based on prior poor performance.

Under ***Jasany v. U.S. Postal Service***, 755 F.2d 1244 (6th Cir. 1985), once it is established that a worker suffers from an impairment that substantially limits a major life activity, the burden shifts to Defendant to demonstrate that requisite qualifications for the job are job related and required by business necessity, and that reasonable accommodation is not possible. ***OFCCP v. Louisville Gas & Electric Co.***, Case No. 1988-OFC-12 (ALJ, Jan.29, 1990), *aff'd.*, (Ass't. Sec'y., Jan. 14, 1992).

It is Defendant's burden under the regulations to establish the "business necessity" exception to accommodating a qualified handicapped individual. In this vein, the contractor is obligated to have scheduled reviews of job requirements to determine which requirements are necessary for job performance, business necessity, or safe performance of the job. ***E.E. Black, Ltd. v. Marshall***, 497 F. Supp. 1088, 1103 (D. Hi. 1980).

2. Defendant must adequately research employee's condition

[a] Defendant has right to medical records/releases

Defendant had the right to seek more detailed medical records from a manic depressive employee to enable it to make an employment decision consistent with business necessity and the safe performance of the job. ***OFCCP v. American Commercial Barge Line Co.***, Case No. 1984-OFC-13 (Ass't. Sec'y., Apr. 15, 1992).

A contractor may impose "qualification requirements" on employees, even if they tend to screen out qualified handicapped individuals, provided that the requirements are job related and consistent with business necessity and safe performance of the job. Thus, the court held that Defendant did not violate Section 503 by requesting that an employee, who claimed to be epileptic, produce a release from his doctor stating that he could work on dangerous equipment and under dangerous conditions. Defendant had the legal right to demand that complainant meet the job requirements, such as obtaining a release to ensure that he could safely return to the admitted hazardous conditions in the plant. ***Exide Corp. v. Martin***, Civil Action No. 91-242 (E.D. Ky. 1992).

[b] Failure to gather sufficient information

In ***OFCCP v. Louisville Gas & Electric Co.***, Case No. 1988-OFC-12 (ALJ, Jan. 29, 1990), *aff'd.*, (Ass't. Sec'y., Jan. 14, 1992), the Assistant Secretary held that, under ***Jasany v. U.S. Postal Service***, 755 F.2d 1244 (6th Cir. 1985), the burden is on Plaintiff to establish, as part of its *prima facie* case, the existence of an impairment that substantially limits a major life activity. The burden then shifts Defendant to demonstrate that challenged criteria are job related, required by business necessity, and reasonable accommodation is not possible. Under the facts of ***Louisville Gas***, the Assistant Secretary held that Defendant failed to gather sufficient information as required under ***Mantolete v. Bolger***, 767 F.2d 1416 (9th Cir. 1985), to make a reasoned judgment on whether the employee's perceived impairment (lumbar lordosis) prevented him from performing the essential requirements of the job without a reasonable probability of substantial harm to himself or others. Thus, Defendant failed to carry its burden and establish that employee was not a qualified individual with a disability.

3. "Business necessity" established

The business necessity defense was established when Defendant demonstrated that the creation of a suitable accommodation would disrupt normal operations, violate Defendant's collective bargaining agreement, and disrupt its relationship with the union and its employees. ***OFCCP v. American Airlines***, Case No. 1979-OFCCP-2 (ALJ, June 30, 1980), *aff'd.* (Dep'.y Under Sec'y., May 2, 1985).

4. "Business necessity" not established

Individualized inquiry required

In ***Exxon Corp. v. U.S. Dep't. of Labor***, 2002 WL 356517 (N.D. Tex. Mar. 5, 2002) (Memorandum Opinion and Order), the court concluded that Mr. Strawser was not a "disabled individual" under the Rehabilitation Act because OFCCP was collaterally estopped from litigating the issue as EEOC had unsuccessfully litigated the same issue under the Americans With Disabilities Act before the same court in a case involving the same employer and the same allegedly discriminatory policy. However, the holdings of the ALJ and ARB may be instructive. *See* ***OFCCP v. Exxon Corp.***, Case No. 1992-OFC-4 (ALJ, June 15, 1993), *aff'd. in part,* (ARB, Oct. 28, 1996). In ***OFCCP v. Exxon Corp.***, Case No. 1992-OFC-4 (ARB, Oct. 28, 1996), the ARB affirmed the ALJ's finding that the complainant was an individual with a disability because Defendant regarded him as having an impairment which substantially limited a major life activity. The ARB stated that it must be determined whether the worker's "disability" poses a direct threat to property or safety. The phrase "direct threat" has been defined under the American with Disabilities Act ("ADA") to mean a significant risk of substantial harm to health or safety that cannot be eliminated or reduced by reasonable accommodation. Such a determination requires an individualized assessment of the person's present ability to perform the essential function of the job safely. Factors germane to determining whether an individual poses a "direct threat" include the duration of the risk, the nature and severity of the potential harm, the likelihood that the potential harm will occur and the imminence of harm. *See* 29 C.F.R. § 1630.2(r).

According to the ARB, the complainant did not come within the statutory exemption of alcoholics whose current use posed a direct threat, because the record demonstrated that alcohol use or abuse did not affect his employment. Indeed, the record evidenced that Complainant made a strong recovery and his risk of relapse was low. Complainant's records of prior alcohol consumption, of public drunkenness, of adverse marital effects, and diagnosis and history of medical treatment for alcoholism constituted a sufficient record of a substantially limiting impairment to satisfy the definition of individual with a disability.

The ARB overruled the ALJ's conclusion and found Complainant to be an individual with a disability under 29 U.S.C. § 706(8)(B)(ii) in that he has a record of an impairment that substantially limited major life activities other than "working." The ARB further observed that "the nature of the disease of alcoholism requires that there be a continuum of treatment and that the alcoholic be permitted some opportunity for failure in order to come to the acceptance of his disease which is the critical element of his cure." Congress excluded from coverage only those alcoholics whose current use of alcohol prevented them from performing the duties of the job or whose employment, because of current alcohol abuse, posed a direct threat to others. 29 U.S.C. § 706(8)(C)(v).

5. Likelihood and imminence of injury

[a] Generally

To successfully raise a risk of future injury defense under Section 501, Defendant must establish that there is a reasonable probability of substantial harm, not merely an elevated risk of harm. The standard under Section 503 is the same. ***OFCCP v. Keebler Co.***, Case No. 1987-OFC-20 (ALJ, July 20, 1995), *aff'd.* (ARB, Sept. 4, 1996). In ***Keebler***, it was noted that the Secretary of Labor adopted the two-part test for dual motive discharge cases set forth in ***Mt. Healthy City School District v. Doyle***, 429 U.S. 274 (1977). Specifically, once Plaintiff has established that the protected activity played a role in Defendant's adverse decision, the burden shifts to Defendant to persuade the court by a preponderance of the evidence that it would have discharged the plaintiff even if the protected activity had not occurred.

In ***OFCCP v. Central Power & Light Co.***, Case No. 1982-OFC-5 (ALJ, Mar. 30, 1987), Defendant's evidence that there is a possibility that persons with radiographic spinal anomalies will develop future chronic back problems was insufficient to meet its burden of establishing that its job qualifications, which required rejecting all applicants with those conditions, were job related and consistent with business necessity and safe performance.

In ***E.E. Black, Ltd. v. Marshall***, 497 F. Supp. 1088 (D. Hi. 1980), the court held that the possibility of future injury may, in some cases, properly be used to screen out qualified handicapped individuals. However, the fact that a complainant's impairment may impose a risk of worker's compensation claim is not, standing alone, an acceptable justification for imposing a particular job requirement. The court held that consideration of the significance of the worker's condition and the nature of the evidence presented in the administrative proceedings would be required.

[b] Defendant's burden to establish

i. Generally

Under Section 503 of the Rehabilitation Act, Defendant must establish a reasonable probability of substantial harm to establish a business necessity defense. ***OFCCP v. Norfolk and Western Railway Co.***, Case No. 1988-OFC-4 (ALJ,, June 28, 1989), *stipulated dismissal* (ALJ, Nov. 13, 1991). The fact that neither physician who testified could specify how imminent the danger of stroke or congestive heart failure would have been for the complainant, had she been hired, was not dispositive. Rather, the appropriate standard of reasonable probability of substantial harm must be considered in light of the fact that congestive heart failure and stroke are life threatening. In this vein, an employer meets the burden of demonstrating a reasonable probability of substantial harm when evidence is offered that a physician concludes that the complainant was at risk of a stroke or congestive heart attack in the short term. *See also* ***OFCCP v. Texas Industries, Inc.***, Case No. 1980-OFCCP-28 (Sec'y., June 7, 1988) (the fact-finder must determine whether the worker's condition would result in a "reasonably probability of substantial harm"; Defendant's preference is insufficient to carry this burden; work and medical histories must be evaluated in conjunction with physical requirements for the job).

ii. Failure to gather sufficient information

In ***OFCCP v. Louisville Gas & Electric Co.***, Case No. 1988-OFC-12 (ALJ, Jan. 29, 1990), *aff'd.*, (Ass't. Sec'y., Jan. 14, 1992), the ALJ held that Defendant failed to gather sufficient information, as required under ***Mantolete v. Bolger***, 767 F.2d 1416 (9th Cir. 1985), to make a reasoned judgment regarding whether an employee's perceived impairment (lumbar lordosis) prevented him from performing the essential requirements of the job without a reasonable probability of substantial harm to himself or others. Thus, Defendant failed to carry its burden in establishing that the employee was not a qualified handicapped individual. It was further determined that, if Defendant had demonstrated that the employee was not qualified to perform the essential functions of the job without a reasonable probability of substantial harm, then the fact-finder would have been required to determine whether reasonable accommodation could be made, without undue hardship, which would enable the applicant to perform the essential requirements of the job without a reasonable probability of substantial injury.

In ***OFCCP v. Yellow Freight Systems, Inc.***, Case No. 1984-OFC-17 (ALJ, Nov. 6, 1986), *aff'd.* (Ass't. Sec'y., July 27, 1993), the ALJ held that the factors to be considered in determining whether there is a reasonable probability of substantial harm are the likelihood and imminence of injury. This determination should not be based merely on Defendant's subjective evaluation or, except in cases of a most apparent nature, merely on medical reports. Defendant must also consider the individual's work history and comprehensive medical history.

The automatic use of x-ray results to disqualify applicants because of potential back injuries, without sufficient examination of the individuals' actual medical histories and capabilities to perform the job in question, is a violation of Section 503 of the Rehabilitation Act. ***OFCCP v. Texas Utilities Generating Co.***, Case No. 1985-OFC-13 (ALJ, Mar. 2, 1988), *remanded on other grounds* (Ass't. Sec'y., Aug. 25, 1994).

[c] Factors to be considered; individualized consideration required

i. Generally

In ***Exxon Corp. v. U.S. Dep't. of Labor***, 2002 WL 356517 (N.D. Tex. Mar. 5, 2002) (Memorandum Opinion and Order), the court concluded that Mr. Strawser was not a "disabled individual" under the Rehabilitation Act because OFCCP was collaterally estopped from litigating the issue as EEOC had unsuccessfully litigated the same issue under the Americans With Disabilities Act before the same court in a case involving the same employer and the same allegedly discriminatory policy. However, the holdings of the ALJ and ARB may be instructive. *See* ***OFCCP v. Exxon Corp.***, Case No. 1992-OFC-4 (ALJ, June 15, 1993), *aff'd. in part,* (ARB, Oct. 28, 1996).

Pertinent considerations in determining whether there is a "reasonable probability of substantial harm" include the nature, duration and severity of risk as well as the probability that the risk would cause varying degrees of harm. Exxon's categorical exclusion of all individuals treated previously for alcohol abuse does not meet this individualized examination standard. ***OFCCP v. Exxon Corp.***, Case No. 1992-OFC-4 (ARB, Oct. 28, 1996). Because OFCCP established that the complainant, a recovering alcoholic, was a qualified individual with a disability who was transferred because of that disability, Defendant must demonstrate that the worker's continued employment in the designated position would pose a "reasonable probability of substantial harm" and "not merely on an employer's subjective evaluation or, except in cases of a most apparent nature, merely on medical reports." ***Mantolete v. Bolger***, 767 F.2d 1416, 1422-1423 (9th Cir. 1985).

Citing to ***E.E. Black, Ltd. v. Marshall***, 497 F.Supp. 1088, 1103 (D. Hi. 1980) (non-imminent risk of future injury . . . does not make an otherwise capable person incapable"), the ARB held that, absent imminent risk of injury, the only material question is whether the individual is capable of performing the duties of the job. Under the facts of the case before it, the ARB concluded that the complainant would pose an imminent risk only if he currently abused alcohol or if he were at high risk of relapse. Neither of these conditions was established by Defendant. In addition, the ARB reaffirmed the likelihood, imminence, and severity of injury as pertinent considerations for assessing the reasonable probability of substantial harm. The ARB concurred with the ALJ's determination that, in assessing the probability and severity of potential harm, Defendant's "tenuous prediction" of an accident resulting in substantial loss of human life and/or severe environmental damage was contingent upon an emergency and a relapse to drinking occurring simultaneously. As the probability of an emergency and a relapse occurring separately was low, the probability of the two occurring together to result in inappropriate action and catastrophe was "exponentially lower."

Moreover, the ALJ found that the probability of harm was reduced even further if Defendant monitored the complainant's condition through periodic medical examination and random testing. Therefore, in determining whether employment of an individual would pose a reasonable probability of substantial harm, the Rehabilitation Act requires an examination of the *individual's* medical and employment histories. Determinations may not be premised on general medical reports except in cases of the most apparent nature. Thus, substitution of categorical exclusion for individual evaluation requires that all or substantially all individuals with the disability be unable to perform the job safely.

The ARB rejected Defendant's argument that a relapse is almost impossible to predict and concurred with the ALJ, who observed that "[t]he evidence establishes that alcoholics, unlike epileptics and diabetics, experience warning signs before they relapse; that the longer an alcoholic remains sober, the less likely he is to relapse; that job problems are the last to appear when an alcoholic relapses, and thus a progression toward alcoholic drinking can be detected long before any job problems appear." *Id.* at 15. The ARB concurred with the ALJ and held that Exxon's policy of categorical exclusion of all individuals who have had a substance abuse problem from 1800 designated positions, offered a disincentive for "self-identifying" and seeking treatment.

The Board noted that there was no incentive under the policy for individuals who (1) are in current need of rehabilitation, (2) have "self-reformed," or (3) have undergone rehabilitation in the past, to come forward and identify themselves. Moreover, it was noted that the most reliable predictor of how Complainant would perform his job tomorrow was how he performed his job over the past nine years. The ARB held that "categorical exclusion [of all rehabilitated] alcoholics [from positions designated safety-critical] is an expedient means of avoiding risk where individualized assessment would distinguish between those persons who have rehabilitated themselves successfully and those who have not." At bottom, Exxon's "never-ever" policy was based on a judgment that rehabilitated alcoholics were forever disposed to relapse, certainly a "myth, fear or stereotype" associated with alcoholism. In the instant case the reality was the contrary -- for an individual like complainant who maintained sobriety for years, any fear of relapse was not well-grounded. Defendant's "across-the-board policy prohibiting rehabilitated individuals from holding designated position" was "impermissibly inflexible" because it "[did] not differentiate between those who have been successful in rehabilitating themselves and those who have not." It thus violated the Section 503 "mandate of affirmative action and non-discrimination in employment" and, absent application of the policy "on a case-by case basis," Exxon risked future violation.

ii. Risk of higher premiums

In ***E.E. Black, Ltd. v. Marshall***, 497 F. Supp. 1088 (D. Hi. 1980), the court held that the possibility of future injury may, in some cases, properly be used to screen out qualified handicapped individuals. However, the fact that the complainant's impairment may impose the risk of a worker's compensation claim is not, standing alone, an acceptable justification for imposing a particular job requirement. On the other hand, it is noteworthy that, in ***OFCCP v. Shuford Mills Inc.***, Case No. 1980-OFCCP-30 (ALJ, May 26, 1981), *dismissal aff'd. without opinion* (Dep'y. Under Sec'y., Sept. 17, 1985), a complainant, who was fired because he may have exposed Defendant to the risk of higher premiums for worker's compensation insurance if he re-injured himself upon undertaking a more strenuous position, was not discriminated against.

[d] Circumstances at time of decision considered

In determining whether Defendant's decision to reject Complainant was justified because his disability posed a reasonable probability of substantial harm, the court would consider the facts as they existed at the time the decision to reject was made and the reasonableness of the decision in light of the facts. ***OFCCP v. CSX Transportation, Inc.***, Case No. 1988-OFC-24 (Ass't. Sec'y., Oct. 13, 1994).

[e] Complainant's actions

Complainant posed a significant risk in the workplace because, by his own admission and as evidenced by his medical records, the worker *never* maintained proper control of his blood sugar level during the almost twenty years he suffered from diabetes. ***OFCCP v. United Airlines, Inc.***, Case No. 1986-OFC-12 (ALJ, Feb. 3, 1989), *remanded on other grounds* (Ass't. Sec'y., Dec. 22, 1994). The ALJ held that, because Complainant posed a significant risk of injury or harm in the workplace and reasonable accommodation could not eliminate that risk, then he was not "otherwise qualified for the job, and United Airlines was not obligated to place him in the workplace." The ALJ reasoned that, given its hazardous work environment, United's employment policy was reasonably related to maximizing safety in the workplace. The policy did not allow an employee with a significant medical risk of either unconsciousness or decreased consciousness to perform certain critical jobs in the company. Consequently, the ALJ concluded that an insulin dependent diabetic presented a significant risk of safety while working on the airport ramp.

In ***OFCCP v. Norfolk and Western Railway Co.***, Case No. 1990-OFC-8 (ALJ, July 9, 1991), based on credible witness testimony, the ALJ dismissed the complaint because Complainant stated that he used a substitute for his pre-employment medical examination and he intended to injure himself on-the-job in order to collect a large settlement from Defendant. The ALJ concluded that such reasons for dismissal offered by Defendant were not pre-textual and constituted sufficient grounds for dismissal. Therefore, the ALJ concluded that, even if Complainant's eye condition was a factor in his dismissal, Defendant met its burden of showing that it would have dismissed him solely for stating that he (1) had used a substitute for his pre-employment medical examination, (2) intended to injure himself on-the-job in order to collect a large settlement from his employer, and (3) for failing to attend a meeting with his supervisor about the alleged statements.

D. Accommodation

1. Defendant's burden to establish undue hardship

[a] Generally

In ***OFCCP v. American Airlines***, Case No. 1979-OFCCP-2 (Dep'y. Under Sec'y., May 2, 1985), Defendant has the burden of demonstrating that accommodation for a qualified handicapped individual would present an undue hardship on the conduct of its business.

In ***OFCCP v. Ozark Air Lines, Inc.***, Case No. 1980-OFCCP-24 (Dep'y. Under Sec'y., June 13, 1986), the Deputy Under Secretary held that, under 41 CFR § 60-741.6(c)(2),

Defendant has the burden to establish that the handicapped individual's employment would have resulted in harm to himself or others. Moreover, Defendant has the burden to establish that accommodation for the physical or mental limitations of the individual is not reasonable.

Defendant has the burden of demonstrating that accommodation for a qualified handicapped individual would constitute an undue hardship on the conduct of its business. ***OFCCP v. American Airlines***, Case No. 1979-OFCCP-2 (ALJ, June 30, 1980), *aff'd*, (Dep'y. Under Sec'y., May 2, 1985). *See also* ***OFCCP v. Ozark Air Lines, Inc.***, Case No. 1980-OFCCP-24 (Dep'y. Under Sec'y., June 13, 1986).

[b] Must gather information to make determination of reasonable accommodation

i. Generally

In ***OFCCP v. Louisville Gas & Electric Co.***, Case No. 1988-OFC-12 (ALJ, Jan. 29, 1990), *aff'd.*, (Ass't. Sec'y., Jan. 14, 1992), if Defendant proves that the worker is not qualified to perform the essential functions of the job without a reasonable probability of substantial harm, the fact-finder must determine whether reasonable accommodation may be made, without undue hardship, which is sufficient to enable the applicant to perform the essential requirements of the job without a reasonable probability of substantial injury. Evidence that a lifting requirement is essential to the job of janitor is insufficient, standing alone, to demonstrate that Defendant could not reasonably accommodate the employee's perceived back condition.

The obligation to accommodate is an affirmative one and requires an employer to gather information from the applicant and from qualified experts in order to determine what accommodations are necessary; a good faith belief is insufficient. Moreover, Defendant has a duty to suggest reasonable accommodations and to test an applicant's performance with them prior to Defendant's decision not to hire the applicant. Under the facts presented, the Assistant Secretary concluded that Defendant failed to establish that it gathered sufficient information concerning the applicant's perceived handicap (lumbar lordosis) to enable it to make a determination as to reasonable accommodation. In particular, the contractor made no study or attempt to accommodate the applicant and did not consult with a single expert as to the feasibility of reasonably accommodating someone with lumbar lordosis. Defendant's duty under Section 503 is not to eliminate the essential functions of a job in order to accommodate a worker, but Defendant must take steps to reasonably accommodate a handicapped individual so that s/he may perform the essential functions of the job.

In ***OFCCP v. East Kentucky Power Cooperative Inc.***, Case No. 1985-OFC-7 (ALJ, Mar. 17, 1988), the ALJ determined that Defendant failed to gather sufficient information to enable it to make a determination as to reasonable accommodation for the complainant prior to terminating the complainant, where Defendant did not consult experts or heed the expert advice of Complainant's optometrist.

2. Undue hardship

[a] Established

It is unreasonable to expect Defendant to accommodate an individual by assigning him to a specific light duty position, when all employees are rotated on a regular basis among various jobs. ***OFCCP v. Yellow Freight Systems, Inc.***, Case No. 1984-OFC-17 (Ass't. Sec'y., Dec. 22, 1993).

It would be unreasonable to require contractor to provide handicapped employee in senior staff geologist job with training necessary to elevate his skills to an acceptable level, where (1) such training would require years of on-the-job training, (2) Defendant employed only experienced geologists at higher salaries than other employees, and (3) Defendant employed such geologists in only one department. ***OFCCP v. Texas Eastern Transmission Corp.***, Case No. 1988-OFC-30 (ALJ, Apr. 30, 1991). In this vein, it is noted that Defendant has no duty to train or transfer a handicapped employee as an accommodation, where the employee's handicap was not a factor in Defendant's determination that inadequate job performance warranted termination.

Conflict with seniority rules

In ***U.S. Airways, Inc. v. Barnett***, 122 S. Ct. 1516 (2002), the Supreme Court held that, if an employer demonstrates that an employee's requested accommodation conflicts with seniority rules, this generally constitutes sufficient grounds upon which to find that the requested accommodation is unreasonable. However, the Court also stated that an employee may establish the presence of special circumstances which makes an exception to the seniority rule reasonable under particular facts. In the case, a disabled worker, who had suffered a back injury as a cargo handler, was transferred to a physically undemanding mailroom position. However, the worker then lost the job to a more senior employee who "bid" on the job under the company's seniority rules. The Court held that, in determining whether accommodation for an injured worker is reasonable, or does not work an undue hardship on the employer, in a majority of cases "it would not be reasonable . . . to trump the rules of a seniority system." Moreover, the Court noted that this is true regardless of whether the seniority system is "collectively bargained" or whether the system "is unilaterally imposed by management." It reasoned that "to require the typical employer to show more than the existence of a seniority system might well undermine the employees' expectations of consistent, uniform treatment–expectations upon which the seniority system's benefits depend."

As a result, the Court concluded that "the employer's showing of violation of the rules of a seniority system is by itself ordinarily sufficient" to conclude that the accommodation is unreasonable and poses an undue hardship. The Court did leave open the possibility that an injured employee may establish that the requested accommodation is reasonable even though it adversely affects a seniority system. As an example, the Court stated that an employee "might show . . . that the employer, having retained the right to change the seniority system unilaterally, exercises that right fairly frequently, reducing employee expectations that the system will be followed to the point where one more departure, needed to accommodate the individual with a disability, will not likely make a difference."

[b] Not established

In ***OFCCP v. Texas Utilities Generating Co.***, Case No. 1985-OFC-13 (Ass't. Sec'y., Aug. 25, 1994), the Assistant Secretary concluded that Defendant violated Section 503 by failing to make a reasonable accommodation to workers who were, at most, minimally impaired in their ability to lift and who would have required only slight accommodation to perform the jobs.

In ***Exxon Corp. v. U.S. Dep't. of Labor***, 2002 WL 356517 (N.D. Tex. Mar. 5, 2002) (Memorandum Opinion and Order), the court concluded that Mr. Strawser was not a "disabled individual" under the Rehabilitation Act because OFCCP was collaterally estopped from litigating the issue as EEOC had unsuccessfully litigated the same issue under the Americans With Disabilities Act before the same court in a case involving the same employer and the same allegedly discriminatory policy. However, the holdings of the ALJ and ARB may be instructive. *See* ***OFCCP v. Exxon Corp.***, Case No. 1992-OFC-4 (ALJ, June 15, 1993), *aff'd. in part,* (ARB, Oct. 28, 1996). In ***OFCCP v. Exxon Corp.***, Case No. 1992-OFC-4 (ALJ, June 15, 1993), *aff'd.* (ARB, Oct. 28, 1996), the ARB held that, part of establishing discrimination under Section 503, OFCCP must demonstrate that the employee is qualified for a position with Defendant with or without reasonable accommodation. Defendant then has the burden to demonstrate that the accommodation would pose an undue burden on the contractor's business. Assuming that complainant (a recovering alcoholic) needed accommodation to enable him to perform a safety-sensitive job, Defendant could have provided a reasonable accommodation without undue hardship by randomly testing the employee for alcohol use, and by requiring him to continue attending AA meetings.

Other factors which may be considered in determining whether accommodation would present an undue hardship to Defendant included business necessity and financial cost. The ARB held that Exxon's transfer of complainant to a non-safety critical position, pursuant to Exxon's Drug and Alcohol Policy which prohibits any employee who has or had a substance abuse problem from working in a safety designated position, was discrimination, not "accommodation." Exxon regarded Complainant as being disabled whereas, in reality, he was able to perform the job as well as any unimpaired individual with the requisite training and experience. These circumstances "are analogous to capable workers discriminated against because of their skin color or some other vocationally irrelevant characteristics."

The ARB held that the issue of whether the discrimination includes an employer's failure to make reasonable accommodation arises only where the disability "interferes with the individual's ability to perform up to the standards of the workplace . . .." It determined that the key consideration where accommodation may be required is that "each case [must] be individually assessed to determine what type of monitoring would be necessary." As a result, Exxon's policy of blanket exclusion of all individuals who have had a substance abuse problem, from 1800 designated positions, does not achieve this result. Moreover, the Board stated that it is the disabled individual's responsibility to inform his or her employer that accommodation is necessary. The ARB held that, because Exxon was not required to make any modifications or adjustments "in its ordinary work rules, facilities, terms, and conditions of employment to enable complainant to work, . . . [E]xxon was not entitled to choose the means of accommodation, i.e., involuntary transfer, because complainant did not require any accommodation."

Even assuming that accommodation was required, involuntary transfer was not appropriate in this case. Section 503 contemplates accommodation in the particular job held by the employee unless business necessity or financial costs and expenses dictate otherwise. 41 C.F.R. § 60-741.6(d). Section 503 presupposes an interactive process in arriving at suitable accommodation. The ARB agreed with the ALJ that Exxon failed to demonstrate that "accommodation" in the form of testing, supervisor evaluation, and continued Alcoholics Anonymous attendance would constitute an undue hardship. Consequently, complainant would not be subject to transfer since reassignment should be considered only when accommodation in the current assignment would pose undue hardship.

[c] Not at issue; worker capable of performing job without accommodation

Reasonable accommodation is not an issue in determining whether an applicant is a qualified handicapped individual because the applicant (despite having a back impairment) is physically capable of performing the job of cement truck operator without restrictions. ***OFCCP v. Texas Industries, Inc.***, Case No. 1980-OFCCP-28 (Ass't. Sec'y., Jan. 27, 1995).

In ***OFCCP v. Norfolk and Western Railway Co.***, Case No. 1990-OFC-1 (ALJ, June 26, 1991), the ALJ held that, because Defendant failed to demonstrate that employment of a worker with monocular vision would pose a reasonable probability of substantial harm, it was unnecessary to address the issue of accommodation.

[d] Use of transfer as accommodation

i. Generally

In ***OFCCP v. United Parcel Service, Inc.***, Case No. 1987-OFC-17 (Dep'y. Ass't. Sec'y., Nov. 22, 1991), OFCCP failed to sustain its burden for accommodation when it failed to establish that Complainant applied for a transfer to an available position and that contractor rejected her for that position. It is noteworthy that the Deputy Assistant Secretary declined to rule on whether the duty to make reasonable accommodation under Section 503 includes an obligation to transfer or assign a handicapped employee who can no longer perform his or her present job. However, in the event such a duty exists, OFCCP must demonstrate the presence of available jobs into which complainant could transfer. Moreover, assuming OFCCP established that complainant applied for a transfer to an available job and was rejected, OFCCP failed to show that the complainant was rejected because of her handicap, in light of evidence that other employees, who must be presumed not to have been handicapped, had been denied such transfers in the past.

In ***OFCCP v. United Parcel Service, Inc.***, Case No. 1987-OFC-17 (ALJ, Mar. 22, 1989), *rev'd. on other grounds* (Dep'y. Ass't. Sec'y., Nov. 22, 1991), the ALJ held that Defendant has the burden of establishing that a worker's transfer to another position to accommodate his or her impairment would constitute an unreasonable accommodation.

ii. Not constitute accommodation; lower pay

Transferring an asthmatic employee to an alternative position constituted a partial accommodation to her condition, but the concurrent reduction in income was not consistent with reasonable accommodation. ***OFCCP v. Mountain Bell Telephone Co.***, Case No. 1987-OFC-25 (ALJ, Nov. 3, 1989), *remanded on other grounds* (Ass't. Sec'y., Aug. 25, 1994).

E. Employee has duty to mitigate damages

Defendant's burden to establish employee's lack of due diligence

In ***OFCCP v. WMATA***, Case No. 1984-OFC-8 (Ass't. Sec'y., Aug. 23, 1989), *vac'd. on other grounds*, ***WMATA v. DeArment***, 55 EPD 40,507 (D.D.C. 1991), the Assistant Secretary held that it is Defendant's burden to establish that the handicapped worker did not exercise reasonable diligence in finding other suitable employment. Defendant may satisfy that burden only if it demonstrates that (1) substantially equivalent positions were available, and (2) the employee failed to use reasonable care and diligence in seeking such positions.

In ***OFCCP v. Exide Corp.***, Case No. 1984-OFC-11 (Ass't. Sec'y., Apr. 30, 1991), *vac'd. on other grounds*, ***Exide Corp. v. Martin***, Civil Action No. 91-242, (E.D. Ky. 1992), the Assistant Secretary held that it is Defendant's burden to establish that the worker failed to exercise reasonable diligence in mitigation. To meet this burden, Defendant must demonstrate that (1) there were substantially equivalent positions which were available; and (2) the claimant failed to use reasonable care and diligence in seeking such positions.

XI. Retaliation

A. Protected activity, generally

Where the asserted protected activity consists of internal opposition to allegedly unlawful practices, "the employer's right to run his business must be balanced against the rights of the employee to express his grievances and promote his own welfare." ***OFCCP v. The Cleveland Clinic Foundation***, Case No. 1991-OFC-20, slip op. at 4 (ARB, July 17, 1996) (*citing* ***Hochstadt v. Worcester Foundation for Experimental Biology***, 545 F.2d 222, 233 (1st Cir. 1976). Under some circumstances, an employee's means, manner, or conduct in expressing an otherwise protected complaint is so extreme and disruptive as to fall outside the protection of the statute or regulations. The internal complaints in ***The Cleveland Clinic Foundation***, which included writing letters to the employer's Board of Governors alleging racial discrimination and harassment, were not so disruptive or insubordinate to lie outside the protection provisions. *See* ***Dunham v. Brock***, 794 F.2d 1037, 1041 (5th Cir. 1986)(expressing complaint verbally in a loud and abusive manner, which disrupted and workplace and employee's own ability to perform his or her work, did not constitute protected activity); ***EEOC v. Crown Zellerbach Corp.***, 720 F.2d 1008, 1014-16 (9th Cir. 1983) (employee's letter to one of employer's most important customers was a reasonable and protected form of opposition). In ***The Cleveland Clinic Foundation***, the ARB rejected Defendant's argument that the employee's letter was not protected. Defendant alleged the following: (1) the employee persisted in asserting allegations of race discrimination and harassment which were determined to be unfounded; and (2) he made blatantly false and malicious statements regarding his manager which made it impossible for him to function effectively. The ARB noted, to the contrary, that the employee's performance evaluation, issued within days of his suspension, demonstrated that he was fully capable of performing his duties and that his expressions of allegations of discrimination did not interfere with his effective working relationship with his superiors. Any impediment to his effectiveness in performing his job could, according to the ARB, only come from the hostility of his supervisors.

B. Burdens of persuasion and production

1. Generally

To establish a *prima facie* claim of retaliation under the Rehabilitation Act, OFCCP must demonstrate that: (1) the employee engaged in an activity protected by the Act; (2) Defendant acted in a manner which adversely affected the employee; and (3) a casual connection existed between the employee's protected activity and Defendant's adverse employment action. ***OFCCP v. Yellow Freight Systems, Inc.***, Case No. 1982-OFC-2 (ALJ, Sept. 30, 1986), *remanded on other grounds* (Ass't. Sec'y., Oct. 6, 1993). *See also* ***OFCCP v. Keebler Co.***, Case No. 1987-OFC-20 (ALJ, July 20, 1995), *aff'd.* (ARB, Sept. 4, 1996); ***OFCCP v. Yellow Freight Systems, Inc.***, Case No. 1982-OFC-2 (ALJ, Sept. 30, 1986), *remanded on other grounds* (Ass't. Sec'y., Oct. 6, 1993) (the Title VII standard of proof of retaliation is applicable to cases decided under the Rehabilitation Act).

2. Types of protected activity

An employee's letter to Defendant's Board of Governors alleged discriminatory practices and the submission of the letter constituted protected activity such that the employee's termination for the content of that letter constituted direct evidence of retaliation. ***OFCCP v. The Cleveland Clinic Foundation***, Case No. 1991-OFC-20, slip op. at 7 (ARB, July 17, 1996).

Although the anti-retaliation provision of Executive Order 11246 does not include specific language protecting "opposition" to unlawful practices, its language is sufficiently similar to other employee protection statutes administered by the Department of Labor under which the Secretary has held, and courts have affirmed, that internal complaints constitute protected activity. ***OFCCP v. The Cleveland Clinic Foundation***, Case No. 1991-OFC-20, slip op. at 3 (ARB, July 17, 1996).

When a case has been fully tried on the merits, the task of the fact finder is to decide whether the defendant intentionally discriminated against the employee or, in other words, which party's explanation of the employer's motivation it believes. ***OFCCP v. United Parcel Service, Inc.***, Case No. 1987-OFC-17 (Dep'y. Ass't. Sec'y., Nov. 22, 1991). It was determined that, because OFCCP failed to show that the complainant sought to return to her former position after her disability leave or that contractor rejected her for that job, OFCCP failed to establish a *prima facie* case of handicap discrimination. However, assuming that OFCCP did establish a *prima facie* case, the record demonstrated, at most, that there was a serious misunderstanding between the complainant and Defendant regarding how the heavy lifting duties of the job would be met. As a result, OFCCP did not demonstrate by a preponderance of the evidence that the contractor discriminated against Complainant because of her handicap. Moreover, because OFCCP failed to show that Complainant applied for a transfer to an available position and that Defendant rejected her for that position, OFCCP failed to establish burden of proof and production concerning complainant's request for a transfer. Finally, OFCCP failed to establish that Defendant's asserted reason for terminating Complainant -- that she lied in order to obtain additional disability benefits from the company -- was pre-textual, in light of testimony from three officials of the company who testified that the termination decision was made prior to the time Defendant became aware of Complainant's inability to engage in heavy lifting. If Defendant terminated complainant in good faith belief that she acted dishonestly in obtaining disability benefits, then Section 503 of the Rehabilitation Act would not have been violated.

3. Defendant's burden to put forth non-discriminatory reasons for its action

To establish a *prima facie* case of discriminatory discharge, Complainant need only show that he was discharged under circumstances which give rise to unlawful discrimination. ***OFCCP* v. *American Commercial Barge Line Co.***, Case No. 1984-OFC-13 (Ass't. Sec'y., Apr. 15, 1992). OFCCP bears the ultimate burden of persuading the adjudicator that Defendant intentionally discriminated against the worker. In analyzing a discriminatory discharge case, the proper focus of inquiry is Defendant's motivation at the time of the termination decision. In this vein, the Assistant Secretary held that it was error for the ALJ to conclude that a manic depressive employee was discharged because he created a risk of liability under Defendant's view of maritime law; rather, the Assistant Secretary found that the employee was discharged because he failed to provide medical records necessary for Defendant to determine whether he created risk of liability. On the other hand, Defendant met its burden of demonstrating that manic depressive employee's termination was for a non-discriminatory reason, *i.e.*, his failure to release to his employer his psychiatric records held by the VA Hospital. Moreover, it was determined that OFCCP failed to show that manic depressive employee actually and seriously re-applied for an available position after he was terminated. Thus, the fact that Defendant did not re-employ him even after he released his medical records did not establish that the stated reason for discharge (failure to release medical records) was a pretext for discrimination.

4. Dual motives

In ***OFCCP v. Norfolk and Western Railway Co.***, Case No. 1980-OFCCP-14 (Dep'y. Under Sec'y., Dec. 8, 1986), it was held that the burdens of proof set forth in ***Texas Department of Community Affairs v. Burdine***, 450 U.S. 248 (1981), are inapplicable in dual or mixed motive cases. Rather, the burdens of proof to be applied in a dual or mixed motive case are those enunciated in ***Mt. Healthy City School District Board of Education v. Doyle***, 429 U.S. 274 (1976). Under ***Mt. Healthy***, if OFCCP proves by a preponderance of evidence that the protected conduct was a motivating factor in Defendant's action, then Defendant must prove by a preponderance of the evidence that it would have reached the same decision even in the absence of the protected conduct.

When there is an even balance of evidence as to whether the employee was discharged for legitimate or illegitimate reasons, the burdens of proof for a mixed motive case should be applied. The Deputy Under Secretary concluded that, once a plaintiff raises an inference that the protected conduct or condition was a contributing factor in the decision to discharge, the burden of proof shifts to the defendant to demonstrate that it would have reached the same decision, even in the absence of the protected conduct or condition.

Under the dual motive discharge rule, once OFCCP has established a *prima facie* case, Defendant must produce evidence of legitimate non-discriminatory reasons for its adverse action. The trier-of-fact may then conclude that: (1) OFCCP has failed to meet its burden of proving discrimination; (2) the contractor's proffered reasons are pre-textual; or (3) the contractor was motivated by both legitimate and illegitimate reasons. ***OFCCP v. Norfolk and Western Railway Co.***, Case No. 1990-OFC-8 (ALJ, July 9, 1991). Under the facts of the case, the ALJ concluded that, even if the complainant's eye condition was a factor in his dismissal, Defendant met its burden of establishing that it would have dismissed Complainant solely for stating that he had used a substitute for the pre-employment medical examination and that he intended to injure himself on-the-job in order to collect a large settlement from Defendant. The ALJ further noted that Complainant failed to attend a meeting with his supervisor about the alleged statements.

XII. Relief

A. Generally

In ***OFCCP v. Yellow Freight Systems, Inc.***, Case No. 1982-OFC-2 (ALJ, Sept. 30, 1986), *remanded on other grounds*, (Ass't. Sec'y., Oct. 6, 1993), the ALJ held that the remedies of debarment, contract termination, and denial of contract payment are viable methods of relief only when Defendant has not voluntarily chosen to obey the mandates of the Rehabilitation Act. None of these three remedies will advance the employment of handicapped persons. It was further determined that a back pay award is the proper remedy for a complainant who was denied employment.

B. Back wage award

1. Purpose

An award of back pay is designed to restore the injured employee to the position s/he would have been in had the discrimination never occurred. ***Albermade Paper Co. v. Moody***, 422 U.S. 405 (1975).

In ***OFCCP v. American Airlines,*** Case No. 1994-OFC-9 (ALJ, Sept. 19, 1995), Defendant contended that, as in effect at the time of the alleged violations, Section 503 of the Rehabilitation Act of 1973, 29 U.S.C. § 793 (since amended), only mandated affirmative action and did not prohibit discrimination or provide for individual remedies for the victims of discrimination. The ALJ held in his recommended decision that "an affirmative action mandate is broader than a nondiscrimination mandate, that discrimination in hiring practices and decisions is inconsistent with the affirmative action obligation of section 503, and that the affirmative action requirement of section 503 implies an obligation not to discriminate." *See* ***Mantolete v. Bolger***, 767 F.2d 1416, 1422 (9th Cir. 1985); ***Shirley v. Devine***, 670 F.2d 1188, 1201 (D.C. Cir. 1982); ***Fisher v. City of Tucson***, 663 F.2d 861 (9th Cir. 1981)." In addition, the ALJ noted that "[t]he Assistant Secretary has long held that section 503 encompasses the authority to order payment of back wages by contractors who have violated the Act, and that such a remedy is proper because the purpose of the Act is to increase employment opportunities for handicapped individuals by eradicating discrimination and to make victims of such discrimination whole for injustices suffered." *See also* ***OFCCP v. Ozark Airlines, Inc.***, Case No. 1980-OFC-4 (Dep'y. Sec'y., June 13, 1986); ***OFCCP v. Louisville Gas and Electric***, Case No. 1988-OFC-12 (Sec'y., Jan. 14, 1992).

2. May be awarded

[a] Generally

Back pay is an appropriate remedy under the Rehabilitation Act. ***OFCCP v. Texas Industries Inc.***, Case No. 1980-OFCCP-28 (Ass't. Sec'y., June 7, 1988); ***OFCCP v. Texas Utilities Generating Co.***, Case No. 1985-OFC-13 (ALJ, Mar. 2, 1988), *remanded on other grounds*, (Ass't. Sec'y., Aug. 25, 1994); ***OFCCP v. Firestone Tire and Rubber Co.***, Case No. 1980-OFCCP-4 (ALJ, Feb. 6, 1980); ***OFCCP v. Burlington Northern Railroad***, Case No. 1979-OFCCP-23 (ALJ, Feb. 8, 1982) (order approving settlement); ***OFCCP v. Ozark Air Lines, Inc.***, Case No. 1980-OFCCP-24 (ALJ, Dec. 7, 1982), *aff'd.*, (Dep'y. Under Sec'y., June 13, 1986) (back pay is an appropriate remedy since it is acceptable in Title VII and Executive Order 11246 proceedings; the Rehabilitation Act authorizes the Secretary to take such action as the facts and circumstances warrant, and the purpose of the Act is to eradicate discrimination and make victims whole).

Section 503 of the Rehabilitation Act parallels Executive Order 11246 with respect to the agency's authority to order payment of back wages to make victims of discrimination whole. ***OFCCP v. American Airlines, Inc.***, Case No. 1994-OFC-9 (Ass't. Sec'y., Apr. 26, 1996).

Although complainants have no private right of action under Section 503 of the Rehabilitation Act, it does not follow, as Defendant contends, that there is no basis for OFCCP to seek reinstatement or back pay. The regulations may not expressly provide for these remedies, but they do not foreclose them. If Defendant has violated the Act in breach of its contract, the OFCCP is warranted in seeking reinstatement and back pay. ***OFCCP v. Yellow Freight System, Inc.***, Case No. 1979-OFCCP-7 (ALJ, Aug. 26, 1988), *remanded on other grounds*, (Ass't. Sec'y., Aug. 24, 1992). The Assistant Secretary stated that, because the employee who has been the subject of discrimination has no private avenue of recourse under Section 503, a remedial vacuum would exist if OFCCP was barred from seeking back wages, *i.e.*, there would be a wrong without a remedy.

[b] Subject to mitigation

In ***OFCCP v. Louisville Gas & Electric Co.***, Case No. 1988-OFC-12 (ALJ, Jan. 29, 1990), *aff'd.*, (Ass't. Sec'y., Jan. 14, 1992), it was held that the payment of back wages, subject to mitigation, is a type of relief authorized by law. *See also* ***OFCCP v. East Kentucky Power Cooperative, Inc.***, Case No. 1985-OFC-7 (ALJ, Mar. 17, 1988).

In ***OFCCP v. Mt. Bell Telephone Co.***, Case No. 1987-OFC-25 (Ass't. Sec'y., Aug. 25, 1994), the Assistant Secretary held that, in determining whether employment is comparable, the ALJ must examine more than compensation. Considerations such as job duties and responsibilities, promotion potential, working environment, and benefits also may be relevant. Moreover, unless constructively discharged, a complainant is not eligible for post-resignation damages and back pay or for reinstatement. The Assistant Secretary held that a finding of failure to mitigate damages requires proving that an award of back pay or damages should be reduced because of an employee's lack of reasonable diligence in mitigating the damage caused by an unlawful discharge. To comport fully with the "make whole" objective of Section 503, a remedy formula which provides back pay equal to the complaint's projected salary should be adjusted upward to reflect merit pay increases that the complainant reasonably would have received had she continued at commensurate pay under a program to afford her reasonable accommodation. The complainant is also due an award of prejudgment interest.

For further discussion of mitigation of damages under the Rehabilitation Act, *see* Chapter X.

3. Payment not tolled because of delay in adjudication

In ***OFCCP v. Texas Industries, Inc.***, Case No. 1980-OFCCP-28 (Ass't. Sec'y., Jan. 27, 1995), a case involving a seven-year lapse between the ALJ's recommended decision and Assistant Secretary's Final Order, Defendant requested that the back pay award be tolled. The Assistant Secretary reasoned that tolling the back pay period did not accomplish the purpose of the back pay award which was to "make whole" the employee or applicant who suffered economic loss as a result of an employee's illegal discrimination. Consequently, the length of time a Rehabilitation Act case is pending does not relieve a discriminating employer of its obligation to assume the full cost of the back pay due. The cost of delay should not be borne by the employee because the wronged employee is at least as much injured by delay in collecting back pay as is the wrong-doing employer and the employer knowingly created the risk by his own wrong-doing.

4. Not barred by collective bargaining agreement

Collective bargaining agreements do not constitute a bar to back pay, reinstatement, promotion, hiring and award of retroactive seniority. ***OFCCP v. Southern Pacific Transportation Co.***, Case No. 1979-OFC-10A (ALJ, Nov. 9, 1982), *remanded on other grounds*, (Ass't. Sec'y., Feb. 24, 1994).

5. Not offset by unemployment compensation

In ***OFCCP v. Central Power & Light Co.***, Case No. 1982-OFC-5 (ALJ, Mar. 30, 1987), denying back pay to victims of illegal discrimination would frustrate the purpose of the Act, which requires that a discriminatee be made whole. As a result, rejected applicants were awarded back pay less actual earnings on a year-by-year basis, with pre-judgment interest applied at the rate specified in 26 U.S.C. § 6621, and without subtraction of unemployment compensation.

6. Factors to consider in calculating back pay award

Back pay calculations should include performance and attendance bonuses, profit sharing, holiday and vacation pay, pension benefits, and fringe benefits such as health plans, insurance programs, and legal services plans. ***OFCCP v. Ford Motor Co.***, Case No. 1980-OFCCP-12 (ALJ, Mar. 20, 1987). Indeed, it was proper, in the calculation of the complainant's back pay, to compare his quarterly earnings with those of the three workers closest in seniority to him. Complainant had higher seniority that the three other workers such that it was proper to assume he would have made the highest earnings. Appropriate relief should place the rejected applicant in the position he would have been in had he not been the victim of illegal discrimination.

By unpublished decision in ***Lawrence Aviation Industries, Inc. v. Reich***, 182 F.3d

900 (2d Cir. 1999) (unpub.), the court held that female applicants were discriminated against for placement in entry level blue collar jobs. Specifically, the court noted that Lawrence Aviation hired 175 out of 849 male applicants and none of the 28 female applicants. The court disagreed, however, with OFCCP's calculation of the back wages owed because "[t]he agency began with the presumption and women and men would have been hired at the same rate, in the absence of discrimination." The court found that OFCCP calculated the back pay owed based on an average length of employment of 61.29 weeks for male applicants who were laid off, whereas Lawrence Aviation maintained that "the proper measure is the median length of time that successful male applicants remained on the job, whether they left voluntarily . . . or involuntarily as a result of layoffs." The court noted that Lawrence Aviation's method of calculating back pay would result in an average of 12.5 weeks. The court declined to rule on the appropriate method of calculating back pay, but remanded the case to the Secretary of Labor to re-evaluate the evidence presented. The court did, however, approve of accrued interest being assessed on the back pay award.

In ***OFCCP v. Greenwood Mills, Inc.***, Case No. 1989-OFC-39 (ALJ, Feb. 24, 2000), the ALJ was specifically directed to determine a back pay award on remand. Under the facts of the case, Defendant engaged in unlawful discrimination when it hired only one woman, as compared to 30 men, to work in certain laborer positions at "Job Group 8A." The duties involved for Job Group 8A positions included the manual transportation of materials at the plant and cleaning the plant and its machinery. Citing to ***Lawrence Aviation Indust. v. Reich***, 182 F.3d 900 (2d Cir. 1999) (unpub.) and ***Berger v. Iron Workers Reinforced Rodmen, Local 201***, 170 F.3d 1111 (D.C. Cir. 1999), the ALJ held that attrition must be considered in determining the appropriate back wage award. In this vein, he noted that "[t]he employment history of both the female applicants and the 8A hires indicates a substantial likelihood that the female applicants, if hired, would not have remained at Greenwood any longer than the 8A hires." The ALJ then determined that the average tenure for the 8A workers was 3.74 years, which would be factored into the damage award. The ALJ then calculated damages and concluded that the female applicants were entitled to an award of $376,603.46, plus pre-judgment interest.[5]

---

[5] By *Errata Order* dated February 29, 2000, the ALJ stated that he misstated the damage award and noted that it should have been $376,603.46 instead of the total of $345,082.21 set forth in his original decision.

C. Costs incurred by employee as result of adverse action

In ***Exxon Corp. v. U.S. Dep't. of Labor***, 2002 WL 356517 (N.D. Tex. Mar. 5, 2002) (Memorandum Opinion and Order), the court concluded that Mr. Strawser was not a "disabled individual" under the Rehabilitation Act because OFCCP was collaterally estopped from litigating the issue as EEOC had unsuccessfully litigated the same issue under the Americans With Disabilities Act before the same court in a case involving the same employer and the same allegedly discriminatory policy. However, the holdings of the ALJ and ARB may be instructive. *See* ***OFCCP v. Exxon Corp.***, Case No. 1992-OFC-4 (ALJ, June 15, 1993), *aff'd. in part,* (ARB, Oct. 28, 1996). In ***OFCCP v. Exxon Corp.***, Case No. 1992-OFC-4 (ALJ, June 15, 1993), *aff'd.*, (ARB, Oct. 28, 1996), the ALJ held that Defendant was liable for losses incurred by Complainant on the sale of his home, where the sale was the direct result of Defendant's discriminatory actions. Moreover, Defendant was properly held liable for the costs of relocating Complainant to his previous job location, where Defendant violated Section 503 by unlawfully transferring Complainant to another city.

The ARB affirmed the ALJ's recommended remedy that complainant be offered reinstatement to the position of "field foreman at the LaBarge facility. . . . with seniority and the pay he would have received had he not been transferred, and that Exxon reimburse him [consequential damages] for moving costs and the loss realized on the sale of his house." On the other hand, the ARB affirmed the ALJ's rejection of OFCCP's argument for lost wages for his wife, caused by the involuntary transfer.

In ordering Defendant to discontinue its policy of categorical exclusion, the ARB agreed with OFCCP and held that the Rehabilitation Act authorizes the Department of Labor to "take such action" on any complaint of noncompliance "as the facts and circumstances warrant, consistent with the terms of [Defendant's] contract and the laws and regulations applicable thereto." 29 U.S.C. § 793(b). As a result, it was determined that an order directing Exxon to discontinue a policy that violates the affirmative action/nondiscrimination mandate of Section 503 is an "action" which is "consistent with" the Rehabilitation Act.

D. Employee voluntarily leaves work; no relief

An employee who was discriminated against, but left her final work assignment for reasons of personal preference and choice (and not because of constructive discharge) is not entitled to compensation for any period after she left employment. ***OFCCP v. Mountain Bell Telephone Co.***, Case No. 1987-OFC-25 (ALJ, Nov. 3, 1989), *remanded on other grounds*, (Ass't. Sec'y., Aug. 25, 1994).

E. Pre-judgment and post-judgment interest

An award of pre-judgment interest is permitted is discrimination actions. ***OFCCP v. Greenwood Mills, Inc.***, Case No. 1989-OFC-39 (ALJ, Feb. 24, 2000) (citing to ***Lawrence Aviation Indus. v. Reich***, 182 F.3d 900 (2d Cir. 1999)(unpub.)). *See also* ***OFCCP v. Mt. Bell Telephone Co.***, Case No. 1987-OFC-25 (Ass't. Sec'y., Aug. 25, 1994) (a complainant may be awarded pre-judgment interest on a back pay award).

In ***OFCCP v. Ford Motor Co.***, Case No. 1980-OFCCP-12 (ALJ, Mar. 20, 1987), the

ALJ held that pre-judgment interest on back pay award should be assessed to "make Complainant whole." Moreover, Defendant was ordered to pay post-judgment interest-from the date of the original ALJ's decision finding liability on the complainant's back pay award pursuant to 28 U.S.C. § 1961.

F. Compensatory damages not precluded by FECA

In ***Karnes v. Runyon***, 1995 U.S. Dist. LEXIS 19863 (S.D. Ohio 1995), a case involving Title VII and Rehabilitation Act claims, the court followed the decision of the Sixth Circuit in ***DeFord v. Secretary of Labor***, 700 F.2d 281 (6th Cir. 1983) to hold that FECA does not preclude recovery of compensatory damages under 42 U.S.C. § 5851. Specifically, the court found that FECA does not preclude recovery for injuries caused by illegal discrimination under Title VII or the Rehabilitation Act.

G. Violation of conciliation agreement

1. Enforcement by third-party beneficiaries

Not permitted

In ***Dean, et al. v. The Boeing Co.***, 170 L.R.R.M. (BNA) 2318, 88 Fair Empl. Prac. Cas. (BNA) 1791, 2002 WL 1299772 (D. Kan. 2002), the district court held that third-party beneficiaries to a conciliation agreement between the Department of Labor and Boeing-namely women who were subjected to discriminatory practices by Boeing were not authorized under Executive Order 11246 to take enforcement action for an alleged breach or violation of the agreement. Rather, the court stated that the Department of Labor's regulations specifically provide that OFCCP "is responsible for securing government contractor compliance with the provisions mandated by the Executive Order." *See also* ***Brace v. Ohio State Univ.***, 866 F. Supp. 1069, 1073-74 (S.D. Ohio 1994) (in a conciliation agreement based on an alleged violation of Rehabilitation Act rights, recognizing a third-party beneficiary theory would circumvent administrative remedies and would amount to creating a private cause of action where none is authorized).

2. Cancellation of contract

Held not to be proper

In ***OFCCP v. Jacor, Inc.***, Case No. 1995-OFC-17 (ALJ, Nov. 8, 1995), the ALJ concluded that cancellation of existing contracts was not an available remedy under Executive Order 11246 for violation of a general conciliation agreement where there was no evidence regarding a failure to comply with the affirmative action requirements of any specific contract, and the conciliation agreement did not refer to any contracts.

3. Debarment

In ***OFCCP v. Disposable Safety Wear, Inc.***, Case No. 1992-OFC-11 (Sec'y., Sept. 29, 1992), the Secretary concluded that debarment of Defendant for violation of a conciliation agreement was appropriate because, by entering into the conciliation agreement, the contractor had the opportunity to demonstrate compliance for almost four years, yet failed to do so. As a result, the Secretary ordered debarment of Defendant for a period of 90 days based upon its repeated violations of the conciliation agreement. During this period of time, the contractor agreed to correct affirmative action plan violations under the Executive Order 11246, Section 503 of the Rehabilitation Act, and the Vietnam Era Veterans Readjustment Assistance Act. Upon expiration of the 90 days, Defendant could petition for reinstatement in accordance with 41 C.F.R. § 60-1.31.

H. Debarment

1. Generally

In ***OFCCP v. The Cleveland Clinic Foundation***, Case No. 1991-OFC-20, slip op. at 8 (ARB, July 17, 1996), the ARB found that an order requiring the employer to pay back pay with interest was insufficient. The Secretary concluded that the order should have included a provision requiring Defendant to comply with Executive Order 11246 or face debarment from federal contracting. Without inclusion of this provision, the ARB stated that Defendant would have no incentive to comply.

Once a final administrative decision has been issued, the threat of debarment, should contractor fail to comply with the final order, is the established means for obtaining enforcement under Section 503 of the Rehabilitation Act. ***OFCCP v. Louisville Gas & Electric Co.***, Case No. 1988-OFC-12 (Ass't. Sec'y., Jan. 14, 1992).

2. Conduct warranting debarment

[a] Failure to submit written affirmative action program

In ***OFCCP v. Bruce Church, Inc.***, Case No. 1987-OFC-7 (Sec'y., June 30, 1987), the Secretary held that the sanction of debarment is an appropriate remedy for failure to submit a written affirmative action program.

In ***OFCCP v. Disposable Safety Wear, Inc.***, Case No. 1992-OFC-11 (ALJ, Aug. 20, 1992), *rev'd on other grounds* (Sec'y., Sept. 29, 1992), a case arising under Executive Order 11246, Section 503 of the Rehabilitation Act, and Section 402 of the Vietnam Era Veterans' Readjustment Assistance Act, Defendant's violations did not constitute a mere a failure to comply with "paperwork" rules or to file routine reports on time; rather, Defendant's conduct was a deliberative, complete violation of substantive equal employment opportunity law. The personnel data compiled and correlated for an affirmative action plan is not mere paperwork; it was a practical necessity which was needed for self-evaluation by an employer. Because of Defendant's deliberative violations of its affirmative action obligations as well as its violation of a conciliation agreement, the Secretary ordered debarment for a period of 90 days to enable the contractor to correct its violations. Upon expiration of the 90 day period of time, the contractor could petition for reinstatement in accordance with 41 C.F.R. § 60-1.31.

In ***OFCCP v. Goya De Puerto Rico, Inc.***, Case No. 1998-OFC-8 (ALJ, June 22, 1999), *aff'd.*, ARB No. 99-104 (ARB, Mar. 21, 2002), the ALJ concluded that Defendant violated the provisions of Executive Order 11246, the Vietnam Era Veterans' Readjustment Assistance Act of 1974, and Section 503 of the Rehabilitation Act of 1973 for failing to develop and maintain a written affirmative action program. Defendant maintained that it was entitled to an exemption from debarment because (1) the government's business with Defendant was beneficial to the government, (2) it was impossible for Defendant to implement an affirmative action plan because the Puerto Rican population, where Defendant conducted business, was 99.9 percent Hispanic, and (3) debarment would "'mean the closing of many businesses in Puerto Rico.'" The ALJ noted that an exemption from debarment under the Acts and regulations was proper only where national security or special national interests would be affected. The ALJ concluded that Defendant's proffered reasons for failing to implement an affirmative action plan did not rise to the level required to support finding it exempt from debarment.

[b] Denial of access to premises

Defendant was ordered to provide OFCCP with access to its premises for the purpose of conducting compliance reviews. If the University of North Carolina (UNC) failed to comply, then UNC government contracts would be canceled and UNC would be debarred from future government contracts. ***OFCCP v. University of North Carolina***, Case No. 1984-OFC-20 (ALJ, Jan. 23, 1989), *aff'd.*, (Sec'y., Apr. 25, 1989) (order denying stay), *aff'd.*, ***Board of Governors of the University of North Carolina v. U.S. Department of Labor***, 917 F. 2d 812 (4th Cir. 1990), *cert. denied*, 500 U.S. 916 (1991).

[c] Violation of conciliation agreement

In ***OFCCP v. Disposable Safety Wear, Inc.***, Case No. 1992-OFC-11 (Sec'y., Sept. 29, 1992), it was held that the Secretary has authority to order debarment and cancellation of contracts under Executive Order 11246, Section 503 of the Rehabilitation Act, and the Vietnam Veterans' Readjustment Assistance Act. Moreover, it was noted that, although the Secretary's usual practice is to give a contractor a reasonable period of time in which to come into compliance before imposing sanctions, the Secretary has imposed immediate sanctions where the facts are not in dispute and the law is settled. Debarment of Defendant for violation of the conciliation agreement was appropriate because, by entering into the conciliation agreement, Defendant had the opportunity to demonstrate compliance for almost four years, yet failed to do so.

Moreover, it was appropriate to impose sanctions where a clear violation of Executive Order 11246 occurred. The Secretary rejected Defendant's argument that she should not impose the debarment sanction due to possible impact on Defendant's business and the jobs of its current employees. In determining the propriety of the sanctions, the Secretary held that cases arising under the Service Contract Act are not analogous to Executive Order 11246, Section 503 of the Rehabilitation Act, or the Vietnam Era Veterans' Readjustment Assistance Act because of significant differences in those laws regarding the scope of the Secretary's discretion to impose sanctions after a violation has been found. However, the Secretary did note that cases arising under the Fair Labor Standards Act are analogous and it was determined that financial hardship by Defendant caused by an administrative order is not a valid basis on which to deny employees their remedy or to allow a wrong against the public to go uncorrected. In this vein, Defendant bears the burden of establishing that sanctions would so adversely affect its business as to threaten its existence.

The purpose of debarment is to encourage compliance and immediate imposition of sanctions can be an appropriate step in achieving that purpose. Effective enforcement of the laws depends on voluntary compliance and meaningful sanctions when voluntary compliance is not forthcoming. Under the law, the Secretary orders debarment of contractor for a period of 90 days for contractor's repeated violations of a conciliation agreement in which contractor agreed to correct AAP violations under the Executive Order, Section 503 of the Rehabilitation Act, and the VEVRA. After 90 days, contractor may petition for reinstatement in accordance with 41 CFR § 60-1.31.

3. Conduct not warranting debarment automatically

De minimus violation; defendant afforded additional opportunity to comply

In ***OFCCP v. Jacor, Inc.***, Case No. 1995-OFC-17 (Sec'y., Jan. 19, 1996) (interim order), the Secretary addressed the question of "whether a contractor that has exceeded the goals for employment of minorities and has made significant efforts to recruit and employ women construction workers should be debarred and have its current contracts terminated because it has not complied with each and every specification of the regulations." Under the facts presented, the Secretary characterized the complaint as essentially boiling down to whether Defendant should be debarred and have its current contracts cancelled because recruitment letters did not specify the number of workers in particular trades, both journeymen and apprentices, who were being sought at the time the letters were sent.

The Secretary discussed whether debarment and contract cancellation were appropriate, but stopped short of deciding that Defendant would not be debarred and saved from contract cancellation. The Secretary further declined to adopt the ALJ's recommendation to dismiss the case. Rather, the Secretary instructed Defendant "to work with OFCCP to develop affirmative steps to notify recruitment sources of specific vacancies today and as it is awarded contracts for the spring construction season." *See* 41 C.F.R. § 60-4.3(a)7.b. Defendant was ordered to comply with all other affirmative action steps in the regulations and the conciliation agreement, while OFCCP was ordered to file a statement concerning Defendant's compliance and whether it would continue to seek debarment and contract cancellation. The Secretary rejected OFCCP's position that the Executive Order and its implementing regulations permit no flexibility in assessing a contractor's good faith efforts.

To the contrary, the Secretary took into consideration all the other steps taken by Defendant, such as specific requests to unions for women applicants, telephone requests for women to a state employment and training agency and the state Indian Council, and instructions to its supervisors to recruit minorities and women. The Secretary also considered the Defendant's successful efforts to increase employment of minorities and its having substantially exceeded that goal, and the Defendant's current compliance status (the notification of alleged non-compliance was issued in November 1992, but the administrative complaint under the expedited hearing procedure was not issued until August 31, 1995).

Finally, the Secretary considered that the sanction sought by OFCCP (a 180-day debarment and cancellation of existing contracts until Defendant established that it has undertaken efforts to remedy its prior noncompliance and is currently in compliance) would put Defendant out of business. The Secretary stated that he had:

> . . . serious doubt how a contractor that has gone out of business can demonstrate compliance or rectify past noncompliance for the type of violations alleged here. Equally important, it is not clear how putting [the Defendant] out of business will achieve the primary objective of the Executive Order -- increased employment opportunities for minorities and women. Its only result would be to throw [the Defendant's] current employees out of work.

The Secretary distinguished decisions in which the defendants exhibited recalcitrance in attempting to achieve affirmative action goals or ignored the administrative enforcement process.

I. Sanctions

1. Due process required

Sanctions are imposed under each of the contract compliance programs administered by OFCCP only after a finding that a contractor has violated the relevant law and has been given an opportunity to remedy its noncompliance. ***OFCCP v. American Airlines, Inc.***, Case No. 1994-OFC-9 (Ass't. Sec'y., Apr. 26, 1996).

2. Attorney misconduct

There is no provision in Department of Labor regulations governing administrative proceedings under Section 503 of the Rehabilitation Act "[for] an appeal of an ALJ order imposing or denying sanctions for alleged misconduct of an attorney." The only provision for review of ALJ orders in Section 503 cases permits any party to file exceptions to an ALJ recommended decision after the hearing. ***OFCCP v. Mississippi Power Co.***, Case No. 1992-OFC-8 (Ass't. Sec'y., July 19, 1995). The Assistant Secretary held, however, that neither an ALJ nor the Secretary has the authority, absent an explicit grant by statute, to impose the personal sanctions provided for in the Federal Rules of Civil Procedure, *e.g.*, requiring payment of attorneys' fees and costs or holding an individual in contempt for failure to comply with a subpoena. In this vein, it was determined that the ALJ had no authority to issue the sanctions order, rather, his or her authority to regulate discovery and the conduct of parties and their representative is limited to that provided in the regulations. It was noted that debarment could be ordered for refusal to comply with the discovery regulations. *See also* ***OFCCP v. Jacobi-Lewis Co.***, Case No. 1988-OFC-18 (Sec'y., Mar. 2, 1995) (Fed. R. Civ. P. 11 is inapplicable).

J. Equal Access to Justice Act (EAJA) inapplicable

In ***OFCCP v. Jacobi-Lewis Co.***, Case No. 1988-OFC-18 (Sec'y., May 2, 1995), the issue was presented whether, as a condition for dismissal under Rule 41(a)(2) of the

Federal Rules of Civil Procedure, Defendant was entitled to an award of attorneys' fees and costs pursuant under the Equal Access to Justice Act at 5 U.S.C. § 504 (EAJA). The Secretary held that the EAJA does not apply to proceedings under the Rehabilitation Act. In order to apply the EAJA, the statute involved must intend to require full agency adherence to the Administrative Procedure Act (APA) whereas the Rehabilitation Act does not expressly invoke the APA. While the Department regulations provide some of the protections afforded by the APA, there is no indication that the Department intended to be subjected to the entire EAJA. Indeed, the EAJA amounts to a partial waiver of sovereign immunity and renders the United States liable for fees only when the party seeking to obtain them has been subjected by the agency to an "adversary adjudication" and has prevailed against the agency. The Secretary concluded that, absent some other explicit authority for assessing fees against the government, the request for fees must be disallowed.

The ALJ held that, absent a violation of a court order compelling responses to OFCCP's discovery requests and given that American's opposition to the requests is substantially justified, OFCCP's request for an award of expenses and attorney's fees incurred by OFCCP in seeking discovery would be denied. ***OFCCP v. American Airlines, Inc.***, Case No. 1994-OFC-9 (ALJ, Jan. 19, 1995) (discovery order).

XIII. Types of dispositions

A. Consent decree

1. Generally

In ***OFCCP v. American Airlines, Inc.***, Case No. 1994-OFC-9 (ALJ, Aug. 10, 2000), the ALJ issued an *Order Approving Consent Decree* pursuant to 41 C.F.R. § 60-30.13(b) in a case involving alleged violations of Section 503 of the Rehabilitation Act of 1973 at 29 U.S.C. § 793. *See also* ***OFCCP v. Holly Sugar Corp.***, Case No. 1998-OFC-13 (ALJ, Dec. 13, 1999) (a case arising under Executive Order 11246); ***OFCCP v. Wagner Electric Corp.***, Case No. 1980-OFCCP-20 (ALJ, Jan. 21, 1981) (without admitting to violations alleged in the complaint, Defendant agreed to comply with the Rehabilitation Act's affirmative action requirements, pay Complainant, and adjust Complainant's seniority date).

In ***OFCCP v. Beverly Enterprises, Inc.***, ARB Case No. 02-009, 1999-OFC-11 (ARB, Apr. 30, 2002), the Board approved of the parties' consent decree which resolved outstanding issues and permitted OFCCP to conduct compliance reviews of the Defendant's headquarters and nursing homes. One noteworthy paragraph provided the following:

> Enforcement proceedings for violation of this Decree may be initiated at any time after the 20-day period in § 60-33 has elapsed . . . upon filing with the Administrative Review Board a motion for an order of clarification or enforcement and/or sanctions. The Administrative Review Board may, if it deems appropriate, schedule an evidentiary hearing on the motion or remand the matter to the Office of Administrative Law Judges for that purpose. The issues in a hearing on the motion shall relate solely to the issues of the factual and legal claims in the motion.

2. Not subject to ARB review

In ***OFCCP v. Cambridge Wire, Inc.,*** Case No. 1994-OFC-12 (ARB, Nov. 26, 1996), a matter appealed by the union intervenor, the ARB held that, pursuant to 41 C.F.R. § 60-30.13(d), an ALJ's decision on an agreement containing consent findings is the final administrative order of the Department of Labor and is not subject to review by the ARB. In so holding, the ARB rejected the union's argument that the jurisdictional bar applied only to "uncontested contest decrees" and that the case should be remanded for a "fairness hearing" on the union's objections. Slip. op. at 4.

3. May be amended by the ALJ

In ***OFCCP v. SKF USA, Inc.***, ARB Case No. 00-023, 1997-OFC-17 (ARB, Mar. 30, 2001), OFCCP and Defendant submitted consent findings in a case where Defendant failed to hire qualified women applicants for entry-level machine operator positions in violation of Executive Order 11246. The ALJ issued a decision approving of the consent findings and, thereafter, OFCCP learned that one of the individuals named in the consent findings was a man and was not, therefore, entitled to relief. As a result, OFCCP moved that the ALJ amend the consent findings to correct the error.

The ALJ, in turn, denied OFCCP's motion to state that he had no authority to amend the decision approving consent findings. On appeal, the ARB concluded that, pursuant to 41 C.F.R. § 60-13(d), the ALJ's decision based on consent findings constituted the "final administrative order" such that the ARB lacked jurisdiction over the appeal. Although the ARB subsequently dismissed the appeal, it noted the following in a footnote:

> Although we must dismiss this appeal for lack of jurisdiction, we nevertheless feel compelled to point out that an amendment of a Consent Order may not be beyond the ALJ's authority. The fact that there is no Department rule governing the amendment of a Consent Order does not necessarily preclude the parties from obtaining relief from what is an obvious mistake. We note that 41 C.F.R. § 60-30.1 provides, in pertinent part, '[i]n the absence of a specific provision, procedures shall be in accordance with the Federal Rules of Civil Procedure.' Fed.R.Civ.P. 60 permits the court to relieve a party from an order or judgment for, among other things, clerical mistakes, mistakes, or inadvertence.

Slip op. at 2, n. 1.

4. May not be blocked by intervener

It is well-settled that an intervener may not block approval of a proposed consent decree by withholding its consent. ***International Ass'n. of Firefighters v. City of Cleveland***, 478 U.S. 501, 529 (1986) (Title VII discrimination case; an intervener may not block approval of a consent decree but "an intervener is entitled to present evidence and have its objections heard at the hearing on whether to approve a consent decree"); ***Black Firefighters Ass'n. of City of Dallas***, 805 F. Supp. 426, 428 (N.D. Tex. 1992) (Title VII discrimination case).

In ***OFCCP v. U.S. Airways, Inc. and Air Line Pilots' Ass'n., et al***, Case No. 1988-OFC-17 (ALJ, Feb. 14, 2002), the ALJ noted that an intervener generally cannot block a proposed consent decree between the parties to a case. However, the ALJ held that an intervener has the right to be heard regarding its objections to a proposed consent decree. Moreover, under the special circumstances of the case before him, the intervener union had a right to block the consent decree because it violated its collective bargaining agreement with the defendant airline. In particular, OFCCP sought to impose retroactive seniority through the consent decree for an individual, which it alleged was discriminated against by the defendant. The intervener argued that it was improper to approve of a consent decree awarding retroactive seniority because there was no decision on the merits or summary decision wherein the ALJ specifically found that the defendant engaged in discrimination in violation of Executive Order 11246. In support of his holding, the ALJ cited to a number of circuit court cases, including ***United States v. City of Hialeah***, 140 F.3d 968 (11th Cir. 1998) and ***United States v. City of Miami***, 614 F.2d 1322 (5th Cir. 1980), *rev. and rem. in part* 664 F.2d 435 (5th Cir. 1981).

On appeal, in ***OFCCP v. U.S. Airways, Inc. and Air Line Pilots' Ass'n., et al***, ARB Case No. 02-063, 1988-OFC-17 (ARB, Sept. 18, 2002), the Board remanded the case at the request of the parties "to an ALJ for the opportunity to seek entry of a revised Supplemental Consent Decree pursuant to 41 C.F.R. § 60-30.13." The Board further noted that, under 41 C.F.R. § 60-30.13(d), an ALJ's approval of a consent decree constitutes the "final administrative order" and the Secretary of Labor does not have jurisdiction to review the ALJ's decision.

5. Factors to be considered

In ***OFCCP v. Sysco Food Services of Portland, Inc.***, Case No. 1997-OFC-21 (ALJ, Apr. 28, 1998), the ALJ issued a decision and order approving of the parties' consent decree. Citing to ***OFCCP v. Carolina Freight Carriers Corp.***, Case No. 1993-OFC-15 (ALJ, Oct. 20, 1993), ***Williams v. Vukovich***, 720 F.2d 909 (6th Cir. 1983), and ***OFCCP v. Cambridge Wire, Inc.***, Case No. 1994-OFC-12 (ALJ, Dec. 18, 1995), the ALJ noted that there are three steps in considering the adequacy and propriety of a consent decree: (1) the consent decree should be preliminarily approved so long as the compromise embodied within the decree is not illegal or tainted with collusion; (2) the decree should be evaluated to determine whether it is fair, adequate, and reasonable; and (3) the ALJ must consider whether the consent decree is consistent with public interest.

B. Conciliation required under the Rehabilitation Act

1. Generally

In ***OFCCP v. Southern Pacific Transportation Co.***, Case No. 1979-OFC-10A (ALJ, Nov. 9, 1982), *remanded on other grounds*, (Ass't. Sec'y., Feb. 24, 1994), it was held that the regulations at 41 C.F.R. §§ 60-741.26(g)(2) and 60-741.28(a) are mandatory and require that some sort of conciliatory effort be made. There are no rigid guidelines for how to conciliate and the regulations do not demand that mediation be under the guidance of a third party. Rather, the general concept of conciliation appears to contemplate first an investigation of the facts to determine the merits of what violation, if any, has occurred. The agency attempts conciliation by notifying the violator of its findings, conclusions and demands or desires. Next, the agency will communicate to the violator the opportunity to come into compliance with the law voluntarily without litigation and attempt to initiate a dialogue on this subject. The details of the method in each case will depend on the facts. The agency is not required to inform the violator that, if voluntary compliance fails, litigation will follow. To conciliate means to reconcile, compromise, placate, or otherwise satisfy the grievance of the complainant. Consequently, to attempt conciliation means to take some affirmative action or to make some reasonable effort to resolve the differences. The agency's refusal to back down from its position, particularly in the absence of signs of reciprocation, does not prove lack of good faith.

2. Sufficiency of conciliation efforts

In ***OFCCP v. Central Power & Light Co.***, Case No. 1982-OFC-5 (ALJ, Mar. 30, 1987), OFCCP's efforts to conciliate were sufficient even though the meeting to discuss appropriate remedies for Defendant's violations lasted only 15 minutes. The fact that the parties quickly reached an impasse because Defendant refused to consider back pay for rejected applicants does not negate OFCCP's good faith attempt to conciliate. The requirement at 41 C.F.R. § 60-741.26(g)(2), that OFCCP conciliate violations, is not a jurisdictional prerequisite. OFCCP may be granted relief for individuals who were not identified during the investigation nor discussed during conciliation if it is established that these persons are victims of the same improper practices.

Conciliation efforts consisting of several telephone conversations and one face-to-face meeting, though minimal, were sufficient to satisfy the requirements at 41 C.F.R. § 60-741.26(g)(2). ***OFCCP v. East Kentucky Power Cooperative, Inc.***, Case No. 1985-OFC-7 (ALJ, Mar. 21, 1988).

3. Amended complaint; effect on conciliation

In ***OFCCP v. Jefferson County Board of Education***, Case No. 1990-OFC-4 (ALJ, Nov. 21, 1990), the ALJ permitted OFCCP to amend its complaint to broaden time period in which allegations occurred, even though no conciliation occurred with respect to earlier time period. In so holding, the ALJ concluded that the regulations do not require that amendments to complaints be preceded by separate conciliation efforts. However, the ALJ did note that compliance with the regulations governing conciliation might require that further conciliation be undertaken prior to amending a complaint, if the amended complaint asserted an entirely different type of violation from that asserted in the original complaint.

4. Distinction between conciliation and letter of commitment

In ***OFCCP v. First Federal Savings Bank of Indiana***, Case No. 1991-OFC-23 (Sec'y., Oct. 26, 1995), Defendant did not develop a written affirmative action plan on becoming a covered government contractor and did not submit an acceptable affirmative action plan as requested by OFCCP. Defendant corrected the deficiencies in its affirmative action plan before a show cause order was issued. As a result, OFCCP did not seek debarment; rather, it sought an order enjoining future violations and requiring Defendant to submit periodic reports for two years. OFCCP, however, initiated enforcement proceedings because the parties could not agree on the form of a settlement document. Defendant offered to sign a letter of commitment, while OFCCP would only enter into a conciliation agreement. The difference between the two types of documents lies in enforcement; a conciliation agreement does not require a show cause period on the finding of violation before an enforcement action may be commenced whereas a show cause period would be required for a violation of a letter of commitment. The Secretary held that nothing in the regulations give a defendant the right to insist that a settlement take the form of a letter of commitment.

C. Dismissal

1. Upon compliance with consent decree

In ***OFCCP v. The Boeing Co.***, Case No. 1999-OFC-13 (ALJ, Jan. 3, 2000), the ALJ issued an order of dismissal at OFCCP's request where Defendant had complied with the terms of the consent decree.

2. Complaint is moot

In ***OFCCP v. Kaiser Foundation Health Plan of Massachusetts, Inc.***, Case No. 1998-OFC-5 (ALJ, Jan. 26, 2000), the ALJ dismissed the complaint on grounds that the case was moot. The complaint alleged violations of Executive Order 11246 at Kaiser Foundation's Massachusetts operations center for failure to develop a written affirmative action plan. However, Kaiser subsequently closed its Massachusetts operations center which, in turn, rendered the cause of action moot.

3. Settlement

In ***OFCCP v. K. Monkiewicz, Inc.***, Case No. 1981-OFCCP-20 (ALJ, June 30, 1982), *aff'd.*, (Dep'y. Under Sec'y., Sept. 14, 1982), a complaint against Defendant was properly dismissed where the parties reached an agreement in the case. *See also* ***OFCCP v. Wyeth, Inc.***, 2003-OFC-7 (ALJ, June 4, 2004) (the ALJ issued a *Decision and Order Approving Settlement Agreement* pursuant to 41 C.F.R. § 60-30.13(b) and (d)).

4. Factors to be considered

In ruling on a motion to dismiss or for summary judgment based on the timeliness of an action a court must construe the pleadings, affidavits, and record in the light most favorable to OFCCP. ***OFCCP v. CSX Transportation, Inc.***, Case No. 88-OFC-24 (ALJ, Mar. 23, 1990), *rev'd. and remanded on other grounds*, (Ass't. Sec'y., Oct. 13, 1994). Moreover, in order to prevail on a motion to dismiss or motion for summary judgment, there must be an absence of conflicting inferences to be drawn from the subsidiary facts and Defendant must establish beyond a doubt that the plaintiff can prove no set of facts in support of the claim which would justify relief.

5. Types of dismissal

[a] With prejudice

Dismissal with prejudice is a severe sanction, condoned only when the responding party would face dire consequences or substantial legal prejudice. ***OFCCP v. Jacobi-Lewis Co.***, Case No. 1988-OFC-18 (Ass't. Sec'y., May 2, 1995).

[b] Voluntary

In ***OFCCP v. USAir, Inc.,*** Case No. 1995-OFC-3 (Ass't. Sec'y., Sept. 28, 1995), the parties filed a stipulation for voluntary dismissal with the ALJ, who then issued a Recommended Order of Dismissal. The Acting Director of the Office of Administrative Appeals issued a Notice of Case Closing in which he found that the case should be closed pursuant to Fed. R. Civ. P. 41(a)(1)(ii). The regulatory provisions at 41 C.F.R. § 60-30.1 provide that Rule 41 is applicable because "in the absence of a specific provision, procedures shall be in accordance with the Federal Rules of Civil Procedure." The rules at 41 C.F.R. Part 60-741 do not provide for voluntary agreements for dismissal, nor is there such a provision in 41 C.F.R. Part 60-30, which is incorporated in 41 C.F.R. Part 60-741.

Therefore, it was proper to apply Fed.R.Civ.P. 41(a) and permit voluntary dismissal of the complaint. *See also* ***OFCCP v. Jacobi-Lewis Co.***, Case No. 1988-OFC-18 (Ass't. Sec'y., May 2, 1995).

6. Dismissal versus summary judgment

The rules of practice and procedure applicable to Section 503 of the Rehabilitation Act at 41 C.F.R. Part 60-30 do not contain a provision regarding motion to dismiss. Therefore, pursuant to 41 C.F.R. § 60-30.1, Rule 12(b) of the Federal Rules of Civil Procedure is applicable. ***OFCCP v. CSX Transportation, Inc.***, Case No. 1988-OFC-24 (Ass't. Sec'y., Oct. 13, 1994). The Assistant Secretary held that a motion to dismiss for failure to state a claim under Fed.R.Civ.P. 12(b)(6), which relies on facts beyond the complaint, may not be granted. As a result, it was determined that an ALJ's consideration of facts outside of the pleadings as part of his decision to grant a motion to dismiss constituted reversible error. If matters outside the pleadings are presented to support a motion to dismiss under Fed.R.Civ. P. 12(b)(6), and the matters are not excluded by the adjudicator, then the motion shall be treated as one for summary judgment under 41 C.F.R. Part 60-30, which sets forth the specific procedures for such a motion. Summary judgment must be denied where there are outstanding issues of material fact. The duty of an adjudicator in deciding a motion for summary judgment is to determine whether any disputed material facts exist, not to resolve them.

D. Summary judgment

The moving party on a motion for summary judgment has the initial burden of demonstrating the absence of a genuine issue of material fact. ***OFCCP v. Holly Farms Foods, Inc.***, Case No. 1991-OFC-15 (ALJ, Oct. 24, 1991). In the case before him, the ALJ concluded that, because Defendant challenged the handicap status and qualifications of the class members, OFCCP failed to show an absence of genuine issues of material fact and, thus, the motion for summary judgment was denied.

In ***OFCCP v. Graves Truck Lines, Inc***., Case No. 1980-OFCCP-2 (ALJ, Apr. 16, 1980), the ALJ denied a motion for summary judgment because there were genuine issues of material fact in dispute, including whether complainant was a qualified handicapped person and whether accommodating him would have been an unreasonable burden upon Defendant.

In ***OFCCP v. Burlington Northern Railroad***, Case No. 1981-OFCCP-21 (ALJ, Feb. 2, 1982), a motion for summary judgment was denied because there was a material fact in dispute as to whether Defendant was a covered government contractor.

Office of Federal Contract Compliance Programs (OFCCP)

Directives

Office of Federal Contract Compliance Programs (OFCCP)

Renumbered on 9/16/2013 as DIR 1980-01

OFCCP Directive

Transmittal Number: 80-6/EO-1 (Formerly 450a3)
DATE: February 4, 1980
OFCCP ORDER NO.: ADM 80-1/IntAg

MEMORANDUM FOR	**ESA ASSISTANT REGIONAL ADMINISTRATORS FOR OFCCP now known as OFCCP Regional Directors)**
FROM	**WELDON J. ROUGEAU (signed 2-4-80) Director**
SUBJECT	**Interim DOL/DOT Memorandum of Understanding**

The attached "Interim Memorandum of Understanding between the U.S. Department of Labor and the Department of Transportation" was developed in accordance with Policy Issuance 79-78, "Interagency Agreements."

This interim memorandum of understanding provides guidelines for the exchange of information between the Office of Federal Contract Compliance Programs (OFCCP) and the Federal Highway Administration (FHWA); it **does not** delegate authority nor provide for the utilization of the FHWA or any state or local highway entity to act as an agent of OFCCP in the execution of its compliance and enforcement responsibilities under the Executive Order. A final agreement encompassing all components of the Department of Transportation will be developed at a later date.

Please read this MOU carefully. Any questions concerning the application of this specific agreement should be referred to the Branch of Program Policy ____________

Note: This "interim" MOU has never been superseded. Federal Highway Administration Order 4710.8, signed on 2 1 99, confirms that the MOU has never been superseded and that it remains in full force.

INTERIM MEMORANDUM OF UNDERSTANDING BETWEEN THE DEPARTMENT OF LABOR AND THE DEPARTMENT OF TRANSPORTATION

The purpose of this interim memorandum of understanding is to further the objectives of Section 140 of Title 23 of the United States Code and of Section 205 of Executive Order 11246.

Executive Order 11246 prohibits employment discrimination by federal contractors and subcontractors, and federally-assisted construction contractors and subcontractors, and authorizes the Secretary of Labor to administer and enforce the Order. Except for general rulemaking, the Secretary's responsibilities under the Order have been delegated to the Director of the Office of Federal Contract Compliance Programs (OFCCP) (now known as the Deputy Assistant Secretary for Federal Contract Compliance [DAS]).

Section 140 of Title 23 of the United States Code requires the Secretary of Transportation, prior to approving federal-aid highway projects, to receive assurances from each State that employment on such projects will be provided in a non-discriminatory manner. The Federal Highway Administration (FHWA) has been authorized to administer the statute, to oversee the States' actions in fulfilling their assurances, to establish procedures to effectuate the statute, and to maintain a vigorous monitoring and review process to ensure nondiscrimination and affirmative action in federal and federally-assisted highway construction projects.

This interim memorandum of understanding provides that the OFCCP and the FHWA will exchange information, so that the agencies can carry out their responsibilities efficiently and effectively, with as little duplication of effort as possible. The parties to the memorandum agree as follows:

1. The "agencies" referred to in this memorandum are the Office of Federal Contract Compliance Programs (OFCCP) within the Department of Labor, and the Federal Highway Administration (FHWA) within the Department of Transportation.
2. The "appropriate officials" for the DOL/OFCCP are
   a. The Secretary and Under Secretary of Labor;
   b. The Solicitor of Labor;
   c. The Assistant Secretary for Employment Standards;
   d. The Director or Deputy Director of the OFCCP (The official title of the Director of the OFCCP is now the Deputy Assistant Secretary for Federal Contract Compliance [DAS]);
   e. The Associate Solicitor of Labor for Labor Relations and Civil Rights (now known as the Associate Solicitor of Labor for Civil Rights);
   f. Any ESA Assistant Regional Administrator of the OFCCP (now known as OFCCP Regional Director);
   g. Any Regional Solicitor, Associate Regional Solicitor or Regional Attorney; and
   h. Any ESA Area Office Director for OFCCP (now known as District Director or Assistant District Director for OFCCP).
3. The "appropriate officials" for the DOL/FHWA are
   a. The Secretary and Deputy Secretary of Transportation;
   b. The Administrator and Deputy Administrator of the FHWA;
   c. The Directors of Civil Rights for the Department of Transportation and the FHWA; and
   d. Any FHWA Regional Administrator, Division Administrator, or Regional Director of Civil Rights
4. On a quarterly basis, the agencies shall exchange information regarding schedules of review and investigation.
5. An appropriate official for one agency may request permission to inspect and copy any documents pertaining to any contractor or complaint within the jurisdiction of the other agency. The documents referred to in this paragraph include, but are not limited to, the following:
   a. Affirmative Action Programs or contract specifications;
   b. Investigative files;
   c. Conciliation agreements;
   d. Compliance review (evaluation) reports;
   e. Listings of enforcement actions (debarments, suspensions, terminations, **etc**.);
   f. Community data;
   g. Lists of complainants' charge or allegation; and
   h. Copies of judicial or administrative decisions.
6. Whenever an agency receives a request under paragraph (5), and the agency possesses the documents that are the subject of the request, the agency shall make the documents available to be inspected and copied by the requesting officials, or by another person whom the requesting official may designate.
7. An agency receiving a request under paragraph (5) shall respond to the official who made the request, or to another person whom the requesting official may designate, within fourteen days after the request is received; except that documents not immediately available may be provided within forty five days after the request is received.

8. Within thirty days after this memorandum is ratified, the FHWA shall provide the OFCCP with a detailed inventory of the contractor compliance records in its possession.
9. The OFCCP shall rely on the Headquarters or a field office of the FHWA for access to records, reports, or other documents or information in the possession of State highway agencies. The Director (DAS) or Assistant Regional Administrator (Regional Director) for the OFCCP may waive this requirement, but only in cases where the materials are needed immediately and it would cause an unacceptable delay to request them through the FHWA. The official who makes such a waiver shall notify the corresponding official of the FHWA at once. When time permits, the OFCCP shall request such materials through FHWA in writing.
10. Each agency shall notify its field office and other appropriate parties of the content of this memorandum promptly upon its ratification.
11. Each agency shall forward to the other agency, for review, all regulations and other instructions that may be developed to implement this memorandum.
12. Each agency shall periodically review its own implementation of this memorandum.
13. Each agency shall use information obtained under this memorandum only in the performance of its own statutory or administrative function s, and shall not act as the agent of, or on behalf of, the other agency.
14. Within 120 days after this memorandum is ratified, the Department of Transportation and the Department of Labor will develop a similar agreement applicable to all components of the Department of Transportation.

(Signed) Ray Marshall

Ray Marshall,
Secretary of Labor
12-7-79
Date
(Signed) Neil Goldschmidt

Neil Goldschmidt,
Secretary of Transportation
10-26-79
Date

TRANSMITTAL

U.S. DEPARTMENT OF LABOR
Employment Standards Administration
Office of Federal Contract Compliance Programs

Number: 136 Date: May 18, 1990 ADM 90-2/COMPL

1. **SUBJECT:** Establishing Jurisdiction Over an Employer Against Whom a Complaint is Filed

2. **PURPOSE:** To update and replace OFCCP Order No. ADM 83-9/COMPL (formerly OFCCP Order No. 630a4, March 3, 1983, same subject), which established practices and procedures for determining coverage over a contractor against whom a complaint is filed

3. **DISTRIBUTION:** A, B

4. **FILING INSTRUCTIONS:** File in Administrative Binder under COMPL. Remove ADM 83-9/COMPL.

5. **OBSOLETE DATA:** OFCCP Order No. ADM 83-9/COMPL (formerly OFCCP Order No. 630a4, March 3 1983).

(Signed) Cari Dominguez
CARI M. DOMINGUEZ
Director

May 18, 1990
DATE

U.S. DEPARTMENT OF LABOR
EMPLOYMENT STANDARDS ADMINISTRATION
OFFICE OF FEDERAL CONTRACT COMPLIANCE PROGRAMS
WASHINGTON, D.C. 20210

OFCCP Order No. ADM Notice/Other

1. **SUBJECT:** Establishing Jurisdiction Over an Employer Against Whom a Complaint is Filed

2. **PURPOSE:** To update and replace OFCCP Order No. ADM 83-9/COMPL (formerly OFCCP Order No. 630a4, March 3, 1983, same subject), which established practices and procedures for determining coverage over a contractor against whom a complaint is filed. This order reflect changes in practices and procedures since the issuance of ADM 83-9/COMPL.

3. **ORIGINATOR:** Division of Policy, Planning and Review, Branch of Policy

4. **BACKGROUND**: Establishing contract coverage (jurisdiction) over an employer against whom a complaint has been filed is an essential element of the pre-investigation process conducted at the Regional Office (RO). For complaints retained by OFCCP filed under Executive Order 11246, as amended, there must be a contract in excess of $10,000; for complaints filed under Section 503 of the Rehabilitation Act of 1973, as amended, there must be a contract of $2500 or more; and for complaints filed under the Vietnam Era Veterans' Readjustment Assistance Act of 1974, 38 U.S.C. 2012, there must be a contract of $10,000 or more. With regard to all three programs, the action being complained of must have taken place during a period in which there was an active contract of the requisite amount.

   In the past, the OFCCP National Office (NO), through its Branch of Procurement Coordination, provided contract information to the ROs for use in establishing jurisdiction over employers against whom a complaint had been filed. As a result of organizational restructuring at the OFCCP NO, that branch no longer exists. Consequently, the responsibility for determining contract coverage has devolved upon the ROs.

To assist the ROs in determining contract coverage, OFCCP has developed an automated system which provides specific contract information from the Federal Procurement Data System (FPDS). The information available from the automated system is described in detail in OFCCP Order No. ADM 89-3/DEL and the User's Manual attached to the order. This system is the primary source in information for establishing contract coverage by the ROs. In addition, ROs have available EEO-1 data which may help in determining contract coverage.

5. **PROCEDURES:** Regional Offices will document contract coverage in the complaint file before sending the file to a District Office for investigation. Such documentation will be based on the following procedures:

(a) Thoroughly review the FPDS data to determine if the employer is listed as having a contract. The FPDS data contain contract award information for the entire country; therefore, they can also be used to identify establishments of a parent company in other geographical locations which may have contract work. References such as the Directory of Corporate Affiliations can be used to identify other parts of a parent company.

(b) If the FPDS data fail to identify a contract, the EEO-1 data may be useful inasmuch as they reflect what employers have reported on their EEO-1 submission. Check the response on the "contractor status" item in field 25; a "y" indicates that the company or any of its establishments responded affirmatively to the question whether they had a government contract. By itself, this information does not meet the contract coverage requirement of this directive. However, it does provide a rationale for continuing to attempt to identify a specific contract.

(c) Another source of information is Federal contracting agencies which logically might use the employer's product or service. Such agencies should be contacted by telephone for assistance in identifying z contract award.

(d) If none of the above prove successful in identifying a contract, the RD should consider the appropriateness of contacting the complainant to determine if he/she has knowledge of the company's dealings with the Federal government.

(e) As a last resort, after contacting the Division of Program Operations, the employer may be contacted to determine coverage.

(f) If, through the above steps, jurisdiction cannot be established, the complaint will be closed using the appropriate attached letter. If, following closure, the RO learns of coverage, the RD may reopen the complaint, maintaining the original filing date.

6. **ATTACHMENTS:**

1. Letter Closing Section 503 Complaint For Lack of Jurisdiction Over the Employer

2. Letter Closing 38 U.S.C. 2012 Complaint For Lack of Jurisdiction Over the Employer

3. Letter Closing Executive Order Complaint For Lack of Jurisdiction Over the Employer

7. **OBSOLETE DATA:** OFCCP Order No. ADM 83-9/COMPL, formerly OFCCP Order No. 630a4, March 3, 1983.

8. **DISTRIBUTION:** A, B, C

(Signed) Cari Dominguez
CARI M. DOMINGUEZ
Director

May 18, 1990
DATE

TRANSMITTAL

U.S. DEPARTMENT OF LABOR
Employment Standards Administration
Office of Federal Contract
Compliance Programs

Number: 207	Date: DEC 13 1995	ADM Notice/Other

1. SUBJECT: Numerical Goals under Executive Order 11246.

2. PURPOSE: To make minor clarifications in the Notice issued on August 2, 1995, on Numerical Goals under Executive Order 11246.

3. BACKGROUND: On August 2, 1995, the Office of Federal Contract Compliance Programs issued a notice, signed on July 26, 1995, by Deputy Assistant Secretary Shirley J. Wilcher, to reaffirm its longstanding policy that affirmative action program goals under Executive Order 11246 are to be used as a tool to aid in breaking down barriers to equal employment opportunity for women and minorities without impinging upon the rights and expectations of other members of the workforce. Affirmative action program goals are not to be used as quotas which must be achieved through race-based and gender-based preferences.

   Upon issuance of the August 2 Notice questions were raised about whether parts of Sections 4a, 4c and 5 of the Notice reflected a change in OFCCP policy. This revised Notice is being issued to reaffirm that OFCCP's longstanding policy on the appropriate uses of numerical goals in Executive Order 11246 affirmative action programs remains unchanged. Accordingly, Sections 4a, 4c and 5 have been clarified to avoid misunderstanding.

4. OBSOLETE DATA: ADM Notice/Other issued on August 2, 1995, by Transmittal 206.

5. FILING INSTRUCTIONS:

   Holders of ADM and LEG Binders only: File at the end of the "Other" Tab in your Administrative Practices Binder. Remove ADM Notice/Other, issued on August 2, 1995.

   District and Area Offices EOSs and EOAs only: File behind the tab for ADM Directives in your FCCM Binder. Remove ADM Notice/Other, issued on August 2, 1995.

6. DISTRIBUTION: A, B, C electronically

7. EXPIRATION DATE: None

SHIRLEY J. WILCHER
Deputy Assistant Secretary for
Federal Contract Compliance

December 13, 1995
Date

ADM Notice/Other

1. SUBJECT: Numerical Goals under Executive Order 11246.

2. PURPOSE: To reaffirm OFCCP's policy on the use of affirmative action program goals.

3. BACKGROUND: The principles and concepts underlying the current blueprint for affirmative action programs under Executive Order 11246 were originally conceived and successfully implemented in 1961 by Plans for Progress (PfP), a group of 300 leading corporations committed to achieving equal employment opportunity through voluntary affirmative action. Each of these companies adopted a "plan for progress" for the corporation as a whole and for each of its individual establishments. These plans for progress, as a management tool for achieving equal employment opportunity, were the precursors to today's affirmative action programs.

On July 1, 1969, after having successfully tested this model over an eight-year period, PfP merged with the National Alliance of Business, and turned its focus to youth employment. Seven months later, on February 7, 1970, the Office of Federal Contract Compliance incorporated PfP's Guidelines on Affirmative Action as the centerpiece of its affirmative action program regulations applicable to the larger Federal non-construction contractors. These regulations -- 41 CFR Part 60-2 -- and their counterpart for construction industry contractors -- 41 CFR Part 60-4 -- have withstood the test of time as reasonable and successful tools that aid in breaking down barriers to equal employment opportunity for women and minorities without impinging upon the rights and expectations of other members of the workforce.

At the time numerical goals were incorporated into the written affirmative action program regulations, the Office of Federal Contract Compliance recognized that some might misunderstand goals to be quotas which must be achieved through race-based and gender-based preferences. Accordingly, the Office of Federal Contract Compliance squarely addressed these issues in the affirmative action program regulations.

To further clarify and maintain the proper focus of affirmative action in the contract compliance program, OFCCP has periodically issued supplemental guidance and instructions explaining the difference between permissible numerical goals, on the one hand, and unlawful preferences and quotas, on the other.

The earliest and most comprehensive of these instructions was issued in 1973 as a policy statement which also was signed by the Department of Justice, the then United States Civil Service Commission, and the Equal Employment Opportunity Commission.

Despite these longstanding efforts by the Office of Federal Contract Compliance Programs to ensure that numerical objectives under the Executive Order are not confused with unlawful preferences and quotas, criticism that they involve such preferences emerges periodically. This Administrative Notice seeks to help address that criticism and reaffirm the characteristics of affirmative action program goals under the Executive Order.

4. POLICY REAFFIRMATION:

a. The Essence of Affirmative Action Programs: Contractor Self-Evaluation and Self-Correction.

Affirmative action programs (AAPs), as authorized by regulations implementing Executive Order 11246, consist essentially of procedures by which Federal contractors analyze their workforce and evaluate their employment practices for the purpose of identifying and correcting any obstacles to equal employment opportunity. Where the need for corrective action is revealed, the AAP includes outreach and other steps that are precisely tailored to eliminate the barriers disclosed, and numerical goals to measure progress toward achieving that result.

b. Prohibition against Quotas and Preferential Treatment.

The numerical goals component of affirmative action programs is not designed to be, nor may it properly or lawfully be interpreted as, permitting unlawful preferential treatment and quotas with respect to persons of any race, color, religion, sex or national origin. The regulations at 41 CFR 60-2.12(e), 60-2.15 and 60-2.30, specifically prohibit discrimination and the use of goals as quotas.

c. <u>Goals Are Neither Set-asides Nor a Device to Achieve Proportional Representation or Equal Results</u>.

Numerical goals do not create set-asides for specific groups, nor are they designed to achieve proportional representation or equal results. Rather, the goal-setting process in affirmative action planning is used to target and measure the effectiveness of affirmative action efforts to eradicate or prevent barriers to equal employment opportunity. Moreover, the numerical bench marks are realistically established based on the availability of qualified applicants in the job market or qualified candidates in the employer's work force.

d. <u>There is No Requirement, Under the Affirmative Action Component, to Fill any Position on the Basis of Race or Sex</u>.

Goals under Executive Order 11246 do not require that any specific position be filled by a person of a particular race, gender or ethnicity, even where the phenomena of jobs traditionally segregated by race or sex remain substantially in tact. Instead, the requirement is to engage in outreach and other efforts to broaden the pool of qualified candidates to include minorities and women.

e. <u>The Use of Numerical Goals is Consistent with Principles of Merit</u>.

In seeking to achieve its goals, an employer is never required to: 1) hire a person who does not have the qualifications needed to perform the job successfully; 2) hire an unqualified person in preference to another applicant who is qualified; or, 3) hire a less qualified person in preference to a more qualified person. Unlike preferences and quotas, numerical goals recognize that persons are to be judged on individual ability, and are, therefore, consistent with the principles of merit hiring and promotion.

f. <u>Goals May Not Be Treated as a Ceiling or a Floor</u>.

The Executive Order does not require that contractors treat goals as either a ceiling or a floor for the employment of particular groups. Goals establish neither a minimum nor a maximum number of members of a group which must be employed. Either use of a numerical goal would be an impermissible quota.

g. Compliance is Measured by Good Faith Effort.

A contractor's compliance is measured by whether it has made good faith efforts to meet its goals. Failure to meet goals is not a violation of the Executive Order. Therefore, a contractor that has not met its goals will be found in compliance if it has made good faith efforts.

5. IMPLEMENTATION: Whenever evidence is revealed to OFCCP that a contractor has implemented quotas or preferences which are unlawful, it is OFCCP's policy and practice to take quick action to correct the matter, and in the same manner as if the contractor has violated the Executive Order in a different way. This practice will continue.

Compliance officers are instructed to re-emphasize the agency's policy and practice on the use of affirmative action program goals in compliance reviews, technical assistance and other interactions with Federal contractors for the purpose of achieving compliance with the requirements of Executive Order 11246.

Each OFCCP Regional, District and Area Office will be furnished with an information kit containing information of relevance to the Federal EEO contract compliance program. The kit will be made available to members of the press and the general public who wish to be informed about affirmative action and nondiscrimination under Executive Order 11246 and other EEO laws administered by the Office of Federal Contract Compliance Programs.

6. FILING INSTRUCTIONS:

Holders of ADM and LEG Binders only: File at the end of the "Other" Tab in your Administrative Practices Binder. Remove ADM Notice/Other, issued on August 2, 1995.

District and Area Offices EOSs and EOAs only: File behind the tab for ADM Directives in your FCCM Binder. Remove ADM Notice/Other, issued on August 2, 1995.

7. DISTRIBUTION: A, B, C, electronically

8. OBSOLETE DATA: None

9. EXPIRATION DATE: None

DEC 13 1995

SHIRLEY J. WILCHER
Deputy Assistant Secretary for
Federal Contract Compliance

DATE

TRANSMITTAL

U.S. DEPARTMENT OF LABOR
Employment Standards Administration
Office of Federal Contract Compliance Programs
Washington, D.C. 20210

NUMBER: 260 **DATE: September 13, 2002** **ADM Notice/Separate Facility Exemptions/Waivers**

1. **SUBJECT:** Separate Facility Exemptions/Waivers

2. **PURPOSE:** To identify the factors that will be considered by the Deputy Assistant Secretary when deciding whether to grant separate facility exemptions/waivers from the requirements of Executive Order 11246 and the affirmative action provisions of the Vietnam Era Veterans' Readjustment Assistance Act of 1974, and the procedure for considering requests for such exemptions/waivers.

3. **FILING INSTRUCTIONS:**

   Holders of ADM and LEG Binders only: Insert a new tab, "Separate Facility Exemptions/Waivers", immediately after the "SEL" tab in your Administrative Practices Binder, and file this Notice behind that tab.

   District and Area Office CO and EOAs Only: File this notice with the attachment behind the tab for ADM Directives in your FCCM Binder.

4. **OBSOLETE DATA:** None

5. **DISTRIBUTION:** A, B, C

6. **EXPIRATION DATE:** This Notice expires when implemented and may be discarded or retained for reference, at your option.

(signed) 9-13-02

CHARLES E. JAMES, SR. DATE
Deputy Assistant Secretary for
Federal Contract Compliance

EMPLOYMENT STANDARDS ADMINISTRATION
U.S. DEPARTMENT OF LABOR
OFFICE OF FEDERAL CONTRACT
COMPLIANCE PROGRAMS
WASHINGTON, D.C. 20210

ADM Notice/Separate Facility Exemptions/Waivers

1. **SUBJECT:** Separate Facility Exemptions/Waivers

2. **PURPOSE:** To identify the factors that will be considered by the Deputy Assistant Secretary when deciding whether to grant separate facility exemptions/waivers from the requirements of Executive Order 11246 (EO 11246) and the affirmative action provisions the Vietnam Era Veterans' Readjustment Assistance Act of 1974 (VEVRAA), and the procedure for considering requests for such exemptions/waivers.

3. **BACKGROUND:** The regulations implementing Executive Order 11246, and the affirmative action provisions of VEVRAA, provide for an exemption from the requirements of their laws for facilities of a contractor that are not connected to the performance of a Government contract. Specifically, the regulations implementing EO 11246 authorize the Deputy Assistant Secretary to grant an exemption for "any of the prime contractor's or subcontractor's facilities which he finds to be in all respects separate and distinct from activities of the prime contractor or subcontractor related to the performance of the contract or subcontract," provided that there is also a finding that such an exemption "will not interfere with or impede the effectuation of the order." 41 CFR 60-1.5(b)(2).

   Similarly, the regulations implementing the affirmative action provisions of VEVRAA allow the Deputy Assistant Secretary to grant separate facility waivers based on the same general standards. 41 CFR 60-250.4(b)(3).

Under both the regulations implementing EO 11246 and the affirmative action provisions of VEVRAA, the contractor is responsible for providing sufficient information for the Deputy Assistant Secretary to find that: 1) the facility for which an exemption is sought is in all respects separate and distinct from activities of the contractor related to the performance of a Government contract; and 2) such an exemption/waiver will not interfere with or impede the effectuation of EO 11246 or the affirmative action provisions of VEVRAA. This directive identifies the factors that the Deputy Assistant Secretary will consider in deciding whether the contractor has sufficiently demonstrated that it meets the general standards for a separate facility exemption/waiver under EO 11246 and the affirmative action provisions of VEVRAA.

Historically, OFCCP has narrowly interpreted the exemption and waiver provisions and has granted requests for exemptions only in rare and compelling circumstances. OFCCP intends to continue this practice when considering requests for separate facility exemptions/waivers under EO 11246 and the affirmative action provisions of VEVRAA.

4. **POLICY:** The Deputy Assistant Secretary may grant a separate facility exemption/waiver from the requirements of EO 11246 or the affirmative action provisions of VEVRAA, based on a finding that: 1) the facility is in all respects separate and distinct from activities of the contractor related to the performance of its Government contract; and 2) such an exemption/waiver will not interfere with or impede the effectuation of the Order or the statute.

(a) The Deputy Assistant Secretary's finding as to whether the facility for which an exemption/waiver is sought is separate and distinct from the performance of the contractor's Government contracts shall be based upon a consideration of the following factors:

(i) Whether any work at the facility directly or indirectly supports or contributes to the satisfaction of the work performed on a Government contract;

(ii) The extent to which the contractor derives benefits from a Government contract, directly or indirectly, at the facility to be exempted;

(iii) Whether any costs associated with operating the facility are charged to a Government contract;

(iv) Whether working at the facility for which an exemption/waiver is sought is a prerequisite for advancement in job responsibility or pay at facilities connected to a Government contract; and whether working at facilities connected to a Government contract is a prerequisite for advancement in job responsibility or pay at the facility for which an exemption/waiver is sought;

(v) Whether employees who normally work at the facility are required to perform work related to a Government contract at another facility;

(vi) Whether the facility regularly or substantially transfers employees to or from facilities at which a Government contract is performed;

(vii) Such other factors that the Deputy Assistant Secretary deems are necessary or appropriate for considering whether the facility is in all respects separate and distinct from the activities of the contractor related to the performance of a contract.

Other factors could include the number of facilities connected to the contractor's Government contracts and the nature of the contractor's contractual relationship with the Government.

Example: A Government agency seeks to enter into a contract with a company that has several hundred retail stores nationwide. Employees from the company's corporate office would perform the work on the contract and the total costs of the services would not exceed $65,000. The proposed contract would be in effect for a 6-month period. Under the regulations implementing EO 11246, the company would be required to develop and maintain written affirmative action programs for all of its establishments, including its retail stores. The company has requested an exemption from the requirement to develop and maintain written AAPs for its retail stores. In deciding whether the retail stores are separate and distinct from activities related to the proposed Government contract, the Deputy Assistant Secretary considers the total number of establishments connected with the proposed Government contract and nature of the contractual relationship.

(b) The Deputy Assistant Secretary's finding as to whether granting the request for the separate facility exemption/waiver will interfere with or impede the effectuation of EO 11246 or the affirmative action provisions of VEVRAA shall be based upon a consideration of the following factors:

(i) Whether the waiver will be used as a subterfuge to circumvent the contractor's obligations under federal, state, or local equal employment opportunity laws;

(ii) The contractor's record of compliance with Federal, State or local equal employment opportunity laws; and

(iii) Such other factors that the Deputy Assistant Secretary deems are necessary or appropriate for considering whether the granting of the exemption/waiver would interfere with or impede the effectuation of either the Executive Order or the affirmative action provisions of VEVRAA.

5. **PROCEDURES**: A contractor desiring a separate facility waiver/exemption must submit a written request to the Deputy Assistant Secretary. The contractor must reasonably demonstrate that its circumstances meet the standards for a separate facility exemption/waiver. OFCCP will not seek to make unduly burdensome information requests in the process of considering an exemption/waiver request. Contractors seeking such an exemption/waiver must be prepared to submit information and materials in support of the request, and that will allow the agency to understand the rationale for granting its request. Otherwise, OFCCP will deny the request.

OFCCP will act with reasonable promptness in considering a contractor's request for an exemption/waiver. Although no strict deadline can be established for OFCCP's consideration of such requests, in light of their variability, the agency will normally issue a decision within ninety (90) days of the contractor's submission of the necessary information.

The exemption/waiver shall be conditioned upon the contractor promptly notifying OFCCP of significant changed circumstances pertaining to the work at the facility covered by a separate facility exemption/ waiver and the performance of its Government Contracts. Specifically, the contractor shall advise OFCCP of significant changed circumstances relating to the factors enumerated in paragraph 4, above, and considered by the Deputy Assistant Secretary in granting the separate facility exemption/waiver. Based upon the information provided by the contractor or any other relevant information, the Deputy Assistant Secretary will determine whether the separate facility exemption/waiver should continue. The Deputy Assistant Secretary will terminate an exemption/waiver upon sixty (60) days written notice to the contractor, based on a determination that the facility no longer meets the standards for a separate facility exemption/waiver. Once the termination of the exemption/waiver is effective, OFCCP will afford the contractor 120 days to develop affirmative action programs for facilities covered by the terminated exemption.

OFCCP will require the contractor to certify in writing every three years that there has been no changed circumstances affecting the separate facility exemption/waiver.

When a facility covered by a separate facility exemption/waiver gets a Government contract, or performs work that directly contributes to the satisfaction of a Government contract, the exemption/waiver for the facility automatically terminates. The contractor shall notify OFCCP when a facility covered by a separate facility exemption/waiver gets a Government contract or when Government contract work has been shifted to the exempted facility. The contractor will have 120 days from the commencement of the Government contract work at the exempted facility to develop an affirmative action program.

(signed) Charles James — 9-13-02

CHARLES E. JAMES, SR. — DATE
Deputy Assistant Secretary for
Federal Contract Compliance

TRANSMITTAL

U.S. DEPARTMENT OF LABOR
Employment Standards Administration
Office of Federal Contract Compliance Programs

Number: 267 | Date: October 15, 2004 | ADM Notice/Testing

1. **SUBJECT:** Investigative procedures when a test(s) is one cause of adverse impact in hiring.

2. **PURPOSE:** To create an OFCCP investigative procedure to be used when a test(s) is one cause of adverse impact in hiring.

3. **FILING INSTRUCTIONS:**

   Holders of ADM and LEG Binders only: File this Notice with the attachment behind the "Testing" tab in your Administrative Practices Binder.

   District and Area Office EOSs and EOAs only: File this Notice with the attachment behind the tab for ADM Directives in your FCCM Binder.

4. **OBSOLETE DATA:** If there is any conflict between FCCM guidelines or other Notices and the ACM procedures contained in this Notice, these ACM procedures take precedence.

5. **DISTRIBUTION:** A, B (both hard copy and electronically); C (hard copy only).

6. **EXPIRATION DATE:** This directive remains in effect until superseded.

(signed) Charles James — October 15, 2004

CHARLES E. JAMES, SR. — DATE
Deputy Assistant Secretary for
Federal Contract Compliance

EMPLOYMENT STANDARDS ADMINISTRATION
U.S. DEPARTMENT OF LABOR
OFFICE OF FEDERAL CONTRACT
COMPLIANCE PROGRAMS
WASHINGTON, D.C. 20210

ADM Notice/Testing

1. **SUBJECT:** Investigative procedures when a test(s) is one cause of adverse impact in hiring.

2. **PURPOSE:** To create an OFCCP investigative procedure to be used when a test(s) is one cause of adverse impact in hiring.

3. **BACKGROUND:** In the past, OFCCP Compliance Officers have expended great amounts of time and effort, investigating potential systemic hiring discrimination, only to discover after a lengthy investigation, that hiring disparities are caused, in whole or in part, by a test. Tests take many forms, including paper and pencil or electronic question and answer examinations, structured interviews, and assessment centers. When investigating potential hiring discrimination, it is more efficient to determine early in the investigation whether a test is used in the hiring process.

4. **POLICY:** In the interest of Active Case Management, the following procedures will be followed in those cases where there are indicators, from a refined data analysis at the desk audit, that potential systemic hiring discrimination exists:

   a. The Compliance Officer (CO) must call the contractor and inquire as to whether or not the contractor uses a test as one, or more, components of the hiring process for the job(s) in question.

   b. If the answer is no, the CO can move forward utilizing the normal investigative procedures. If the answer is yes, the CO must determine at what point in the hiring process the test is given. If the test is not the final stage of the selection process ("final stage" means that applicants who have taken the test are otherwise qualified for the jobs at issue and are generally hired if they are selected by the test), or if the contractor did not keep data on who took and was selected by the test, then the CO cannot use this Active Case Management procedure, but must conduct a full investigation of the testing issue. If the test is the "final stage" of the process, e.g., all those selected are eligible for hire pending only reference checks, credit checks or physicals and the test takers otherwise possess the qualifications for the position(s) at issue, then the contractor should be requested to submit data, by race, ethnicity, and gender, of all applicants who took the test, and all those selected by the test. The request must be confirmed in writing.

c. When the data is received, the CO must conduct a test of statistical significance to determine whether there is a significantly different rate of selection between the groups compared and the group with the highest selection rate (e.g., women v. men, blacks v. whites).

d. If there is no statistically significant difference in the selection rates among the compared groups then the CO can move forward using the normal investigative procedures. If there is a statistically significant difference in the selection rates between one or more of the compared groups, then the CO must call the contractor to determine if the contractor has a validation study.

e. If the contractor does not have a validation study, then the CO can proceed with the investigation as usual, e.g., refine the data in terms of the qualifications assessment of the candidates, determine how the system works and collect information for the component analysis. If the contractor does have a validation study, the CO must request that the contractor submit a copy of the validation study and confirm the request in writing.

f. The contractor should be advised that the documentation presented must meet the requirements set forth in the Uniform Guidelines on Employee Selection Procedures (UGESP) at 41 CFR 60-3.15 B. criterion-related validity study, C. content validity study, D. construct validity study, E. evidence from other validity studies or F. evidence from cooperative validity studies, as applicable.

g. When the validation study is received, the District Office (DO) must put the case on hold and the Regional Office (RO) must transmit a memorandum to the Director of Operations at the National Office (NO), attention Deputy Director of Operations, requesting the services of the OFCCP testing expert. The case file and the validity study will remain in the DO. No further action on the part of the DO will be necessary until the testing expert has reviewed the validation study.

h. At that point, the case will be active once again, and the DO, with guidance from the RO and the testing expert, will continue with the investigation. There may be a need for additional data gathering before the testing expert can draw any conclusion as to whether or not the test is valid. The CO must secure the data needed by the expert, as well as identifying the components of the entire selection process, and collecting and analyzing data for each component to determine if any other parts of the process, besides the test, have an adverse impact. These testing cases are important to OFCCP's efforts to combat hiring discrimination and the ROs should therefore keep in close contact with the NO to monitor progress.

5. **OBSOLETE DATA:** If there is any conflict between FCCM guidelines or other Notices and the ACM procedures contained in this Notice, these ACM procedures take precedence.

6. **DISTRIBUTION:** A, B (both hard copy and electronically); C (hard copy only).

7. **EXPIRATION DATE:** This directive remains in effect until superseded.

(signed) Charles James — October 15, 2004

CHARLES E. JAMES, SR.
Deputy Assistant Secretary for
Federal Contract Compliance

DATE

TRANSMITTAL

U.S. DEPARTMENT OF LABOR
Employment Standards Administration
Office of Federal Contract Compliance Programs

Number: 279 | Date: May 14, 2008 | ADM Notice/Other

1. **SUBJECT:** Preserving Employment and Personnel Records in Electronic Format.

2. **PURPOSE:** To set forth OFCCP's policy regarding: (1) the use of electronic recordkeeping systems to comply with the record retention regulations; and (2) the destruction of paper originals of personnel and employment records that are otherwise preserved in electronic format.

3. **FILING INSTRUCTIONS:**

   Holders of ADM and LEG Binders only: File this Notice with the attachment behind the "Other" tab in your Administrative Practices Binder.

   District and Area Office EOSs and EOAs only: File this Notice with the attachment behind the tab for ADM Directives in your FCCM Binder.

4. **OBSOLETE DATA:** None.

5. **DISTRIBUTION:** A, B (both hard copy and electronically), and C (hard copy only).

6. **EXPIRATION DATE:** This directive remains in effect until superseded.

Charles E. James, Sr. 5-14-2008

CHARLES E. JAMES, SR. — DATE
Deputy Assistant Secretary for
Federal Contract Compliance

EMPLOYMENT STANDARDS ADMINISTRATION
U.S. DEPARTMENT OF LABOR
OFFICE OF FEDERAL CONTRACT
COMPLIANCE PROGRAMS
WASHINGTON, D.C. 20210

ADM Notice/Other

1. **SUBJECT**: Preserving Employment and Personnel Records in Electronic Format

2. **PURPOSE**: To set forth OFCCP's policy regarding: (1) the use of electronic recordkeeping systems to comply with the record retention regulations; and (2) the destruction of paper originals of personnel and employment records that are otherwise preserved in electronic format.

3. **BACKGROUND**: Section 60-1.12 (a) of the regulations implementing Executive Order 11246 currently requires any personnel or employment record that is made or kept by the contractor to be "preserved" by the contractor for a minimum of two years. However, if the contractor has fewer than 150 employees or does not have a contract of at least $150, 000, § 60-1.12 (a) provides that the record retention period is a minimum of one year. The regulations implementing the Vietnam Era Veterans' Readjustment Assistance Act of 1974, as amended, 38 U.S.C. 4212, and Section 503 of the Rehabilitation Act of 1973, as amended, contain record retention provisions that are similar to § 60-1.12. *See* 41 CFR 60-250.80, 41 CFR 60-300.80, and 41 CFR 60-741.80. The current regulations also require that contractors permit access to their premises so that the OFCCP may inspect and copy their books and records, including computerized records. *See* 41 CFR 60-1.43, 60-250.81, 60-300.81, and 60-741.81.

   Contractors and consultants have asked whether the OFCCP record retention regulations permit the destruction of the paper originals of employment and personnel records when such records are otherwise retained electronically.

   The OFCCP has interpreted the term "preserve" as having its ordinary dictionary meaning, "to keep safe from harm, injury, or destruction." *Webster's Ninth New Collegiate Dictionary*, p. 931 (1984). Historically, the OFCCP has required that records be retained in their original form, and precluded a contractor from destroying the original paper records before the retention period has expired. However, the regulations do not prescribe a particular format in which the records must be preserved.

   The OFCCP record retention provisions contain language similar to that found in the Equal Employment Opportunity Commission's (EEOC) regulations. Significantly, the EEOC addressed whether electronic recordkeeping would satisfy the recordkeeping requirements under Title VII, the ADA, and the ADEA in an Informal Discussion Letter. *See* http://www.eeoc.gov/foia/letters/2006/titlevii_ada_adea_recordkeeping.html. The Informal Discussion letter states in part "nothing in 29 CFR § 1602.14 (Title VII and ADA record keeping) requires preservation of records in paper, rather than electronic, form. However, please make sure that any system adopted by your clients captures and retains all information contained in documents. This would ensure that documents are properly 'preserved' as required by 29 CFR § 1602.14."

In addition, several Government agencies have issued regulations on the use of electronic recordkeeping systems. *See e.g.*, DOL's Employee Benefits Security Administration's(EBSA) regulation at 29 CFR 2520.107-1; the Pension Benefit Guaranty Corporation's (PBGC) regulations at 29 CFR 4000.53 and 4000.54; the Securities and Exchange Commission's regulations at 17 CFR 31.a-2 and 17 CFR 275.204-2; and the Commodities Futures Trading Commission's regulation at 17 CFR 1.31. Generally, these regulations allow paper or non-electronic records to be stored in electronic formats provided certain safeguards are in place to ensure that the electronic storage system is reliable and records stored electronically are complete, accurate, and accessible.

In light of the increasing use of electronic media in all aspects of business administration, and the advances made in the technology used for converting paper documents into electronic formats, the OFCCP believes that it is appropriate to reexamine whether it is permissible for contractors to preserve in an electronic format those personnel and employment records originally created in paper form, and dispose of the paper originals.

4. **POLICY**: The OFCCP regulations at 41 CFR 60-1.12, 60-250.80, 60-300.80 and 60-741.80 require that contractors preserve complete and accurate personnel records. The regulations at 41 CFR 60-1.43, 60-250.81, 60-300.81 and 60-741.81 also require contractors to permit the OFCCP access to their records, including computerized records, for inspection and copying. *See also* 41 CFR 60-1.4(a)(5) and 60-1.20(f). These obligations continue. Contractors may use an electronic recordkeeping system to comply with the record retention requirements. However, if records are maintained electronically, contractors must take care to ensure that the electronic records comply with the record retention and access regulations, i.e., the electronic records are accurate, complete, and accessible to the OFCCP.

A contractor may transfer original paper records to its electronic recordkeeping system, if the medium used accurately reproduces the paper original and would constitute a duplicate or substitute copy of the original paper record under Federal law. In addition, a contractor may dispose of the original paper records any time after they are transferred to its electronic recordkeeping system, except that the original paper record may not be disposed of if the electronic copy would not accurately reproduce the original record. During a compliance evaluation, compliance officers may ask that paper originals stored in electronic format be converted into legible and readable paper copies and provided to OFCCP.

The use of an electronic recordkeeping system does not in any way alter the longstanding requirement that the contractor allow OFCCP to inspect and copy records at the contractor's premises during a compliance evaluation or complaint investigation. Thus, all of the contractor's electronic records must be made readily available for review, and must be readable and capable of being copied by OFCCP.

Compliance officers should consider electronic recordkeeping systems with the following characteristics as complying with record retention regulations:

- the system has reasonable controls to ensure the integrity, accuracy, authenticity, and reliability of the records kept in electronic form;

- the electronic records are maintained in such a manner that they may be readily inspected and/or copied by the OFCCP, as required under the regulations at 41 CFR 60-1.43, 60-250.81, 60-300.81 and 60-741.81 (for example, the recordkeeping system should be capable of retaining, preserving, retrieving and reproducing the electronic records);

- paper originals stored in electronic format are readily convertible into legible and readable paper copy; and

- adequate records management practices are established and implemented (for example, such practices might include labeling electronically maintained or retained records, providing a secure storage environment, creating back-up electronic copies, observing a quality assurance program evidenced by regular evaluations of the electronic recordkeeping system, and retaining paper copies of records that cannot be clearly, accurately or completely transferred to an electronic recordkeeping system).

5. **OBSOLETE DATA:** None.

6. **DISTRIBUTION:** A, B (both hard copy and electronically), and C (hard copy only).

7. **EXPIRATION DATE:** This directive remains in effect until superseded.

Charles E. James Sr. 5-14-2008

CHARLES E. JAMES, SR. DATE
Deputy Assistant Secretary for
Federal Contract Compliance

TRANSMITTAL

U.S. DEPARTMENT OF LABOR
Employment Standards Administration
Office of Federal Contract Compliance Programs

Number: 283	Date: August 14, 2008	ADM Notice/Other

1. **SUBJECT:** Federal contractors' obligation to maintain and analyze the race and ethnicity data of applicants and employees in Affirmative Action Programs prepared in accordance with Executive Order 11246, as amended.

2. **PURPOSE:** To establish field enforcement guidance for evaluating the use of race and ethnicity categories in the Affirmative Action Programs prepared by federal contractors in accordance with Executive Order 11246, as amended

3. **FILING INSTRUCTIONS:**

   Holders of ADM and LEG Binders only: File this Notice with the attachment behind the "Other" tab in your Administrative Practices Binder.

   District and Area Offices:
   File this Notice with the attachment behind the tab for ADM Directives in your FCCM Binder.

4. **OBSOLETE DATA:** None.

5. **DISTRIBUTION:** A, B (both hard copy and electronically); C (hard copy only).

6. **EXPIRATION DATE:** This Directive remains in effect until superseded.

Charles E. James, Sr.
CHARLES E. JAMES, SR.
Deputy Assistant Secretary for
Federal Contract Compliance

August 14, 2008
DATE

EMPLOYMENT STANDARDS ADMINISTRATION
U.S. DEPARTMENT OF LABOR
OFFICE OF FEDERAL CONTRACT COMPLIANCE PROGRAMS
WASHINGTON, DC 20210

ADM NOTICE/OTHER

1. **SUBJECT:** Federal contractors' obligation to maintain and analyze the race and ethnicity data of applicants and employees in Affirmative Action Programs prepared in accordance with Executive Order 11246, as amended.

2. **PURPOSE:** To establish field enforcement guidance for evaluating the use of race and ethnicity categories in the Affirmative Action Programs prepared by federal contractors in accordance with Executive Order 11246, as amended.

3. **BACKGROUND:** Several provisions in the regulations implementing Executive Order 11246, as amended (the "Executive Order"), require federal contractors to maintain and analyze data on the sex, race, and ethnicity of employees and applicants.[1] The Executive Order Affirmative Action Program (AAP) regulations generally require that contractors perform these analyses for minorities in the aggregate, rather than for particular minority groups. Only one provision of the AAP regulations – 41 CFR § 60-2.11 – requires contractors to use specific race and ethnic categories. This section requires contractors to develop an organizational profile reflecting the sex, race, and ethnicity of its incumbents, and indicating the total number of male and female incumbents in each of the following groups: Blacks, Hispanics, Asians/Pacific Islanders, and American Indians/Alaskan Natives. See 41 CFR §§ 60-2.11(b)(3)(iv), 60-2.11(c)(4).[2]

   Under 41 CFR § 60-1.7(a), federal contractors with 50 or more employees, and that meet the following thresholds, must complete and file annually an accurate Standard Form 100 (EEO-1) Report:

   a) have a Government contract, subcontract, or purchase order of $50,000 or more,
   b) serve as a depository of Government funds in any amount, or
   c) are a financial institution that acts as an issuing and paying agent for U.S. savings bonds and savings notes.

   The EEO-1 Report is used by both OFCCP and the United States Equal Employment Opportunity Commission (EEOC) to collect data from private employers and government

---

[1] All references to federal contractors also include covered federal subcontractors. The term "applicant" is intended to refer to both applicants and Internet Applicants as those terms are used in section 60-1.12(c).

[2] See also, 41 CFR § 60-3.4, in which contractors are required to maintain records by "sex, and the following races and ethnic groups: Blacks (Negroes), American Indians (including Alaskan Natives), Asians (including Pacific Islanders), Hispanic (including persons of Mexican, Puerto Rican, Cuban, Central or South American, or other Spanish origin or culture regardless of race), white (Caucasians) other than Hispanic...."

contractors about their minority and female workforce.[3] The agencies also use the EEO-1 Report data to analyze patterns of employment of women and minorities and to support civil rights enforcement.

Since 1977, employers have been required to report data on the EEO-1 Report using five race and ethnic categories, and nine job categories. The race and ethnic categories are:

- Hispanic
- White (not of Hispanic origin)
- Black (not of Hispanic origin)
- Asian or Pacific Islander
- American Indian or Alaskan Native

The job categories are:

- Officials and Managers
- Professionals
- Technicians
- Sales Workers
- Office and Clerical
- Craft Workers (Skilled)
- Operatives (Semi-skilled)
- Laborers (Unskilled)
- Service Workers

In November 2005, the EEOC, after consultation with OFCCP and consideration of extensive public comments, finalized several modifications to the system used by employers to classify, the race, ethnicity, and job categories of their workforce on the EEO-1 Report. The revised EEO-1 Report requires reporting in seven racial and ethnic categories, and subdivides the "Officials and Managers" job category. The chart below outlines these changes:

	OLD EEO-1 REPORT	**NEW EEO-1 REPORT**
Race and Ethnicity	Hispanic	Hispanic or Latino
	White (not of Hispanic origin)	White, not Hispanic or Latino
	Black (not of Hispanic origin)	Black or African-American, not Hispanic or Latino
	Asian or Pacific Islander	Asian, not Hispanic or Latino
		Native Hawaiian or Other Pacific Islander, not Hispanic or Latino
	American Indian or Alaskan Native	American Indian or Alaskan Native, not Hispanic or Latino
		Two or More Races, not Hispanic or Latino.

[3] See 42 U.S.C 2000e-8(c). For more information on who must file the EEO-1 Report, see http://www.eeoc.gov/eeo1survey/whomustfile.html.

Job Categories	Officials and Managers	Executive/Senior Level Officials and Managers
		First/Mid Level Officials and Managers
	Professionals	Professionals
	Technicians	Technicians
	Sales Workers	Sales Workers
	Office and Clerical	Office and Clerical
	Craft Workers (Skilled)	Craft Workers (Skilled)
	Operative (Semi-Skilled)	Operative (Semi-Skilled)
	Laborers	Laborers
	Service Workers	Service Workers

OFCCP's regulations regarding the race, ethnicity, and job categories used by contractors have not changed to reflect the new EEO-1 categories, thus resulting in contractors either maintaining dual data collection systems or delaying implementation awaiting further instructions from OFCCP.

4. **POLICY:** As a matter of enforcement discretion, OFCCP will not cite any contractor for non-compliance with the Executive Order solely because it utilizes the race, ethnicity, or job categories required by the new EEO-1 Report. Further, OFCCP will accept AAPs and supporting records that reflect the race, ethnicity, and job categories outlined in either 41 CFR Part 60-2 or the new EEO-1 Report.

5. **FIELD ENFORCEMENT GUIDANCE:** Compliance Officers should adhere to the following principles when evaluating the use of race and ethnicity categories in the AAPs prepared by federal contractors in accordance with the Executive Order, as amended:

   A. Contractor data tracking responsibilities remain the same.[4] Accordingly, self-identification will remain the preferred method for compiling information about the sex, race or ethnicity of applicants and employees. A contractor's invitation to self-identify race or ethnicity should state that the submission of such information is voluntary. However, contractors may use post-employment records or visual observation when an individual declines to self-identify his or her race or ethnicity.[5]

   B. Until further rules and guidance are provided by OFCCP, contractors should not be cited for noncompliance with the Executive Order if they prepare their AAPs using the revised EEO-1 categories, rather than the race and ethnicity categories listed in §60-2.11 (the original EEO-1 categories). Contractors also should not be cited for continuing to use the racial and ethnic categories provided under OFCCP's current regulations. Regardless of which categories are used, and consistent with the

---

[4] See Contractor Data Tracking Responsibilities Directive, http://www.dol.gov/esa/regs/compliance/ofccp/directives/dir265.htm

[5] Contractors are encouraged to use tear-off sheets, post cards, or short forms to request demographic data.

guidance of the EEOC,[6] Compliance Officers should evaluate whether contractors are: (1) permitting individuals to choose to self-identify as belonging to more than one race; and (2) obtaining this data either by allowing individuals to select more than one of the single race categories or by allowing individuals to select a two or more races category.

C. It is important that contractors be permitted to collect and analyze workforce data in a manner that allows them to meaningfully examine their progress towards equal employment opportunity. Accordingly, nothing in this Directive is intended to prohibit more detailed data collection efforts by contractors. Contractors may, but are not required to, obtain more detailed demographic data from applicants and employees. Some contractors may find such data useful for research or statistical purposes, or for self-monitoring of their equal employment opportunity efforts. For example, some contractors may wish to obtain more detailed demographic data from individuals self-identifying as a single race, such as Asian, while other contractors may wish to obtain more detailed demographic data, including racial data, from those individuals who self-identify as Hispanic or Latino. Still other contractors may wish to collect and analyze more detailed demographic data regarding those individuals who self-identify as belonging to more than one race.

D. Regardless of how detailed the demographic data the contractor collects, it must be maintained in accordance with OFCCP's recordkeeping requirements.

E. Compliance with specific AAP requirements:

1) Workforce Analysis (Organizational Profile 60-2.11): Until further rules and guidance are provided by OFCCP, when developing an organizational profile, as required by § 60-2.11, contractors should not be cited for noncompliance with the Executive Order if they choose to develop such analyses using the revised EEO-1 categories, rather than the race and ethnicity categories listed in §60-2.11 (the original EEO-1 categories). Contractors also are permitted to prepare their AAP using the racial and ethnic categories provided under OFCCP's current regulations.

2) Job Group Analysis (60-2.12): When conducting a job group analysis for affirmative action purposes, small contractors with fewer than 150 employees may prepare the required analysis utilizing the revised EEO-1 Report job categories as job groups. Accordingly, these contractors will generally subdivide the officials and managers AAP job group into two AAP job groups: (1) Executive/Senior Level Officials and Managers and (2) First/Mid Level Officials and Managers. In some circumstances, subdividing the officials and

[6] "Employers may ask employees to specify particular races rather than to check "Two or More Races," but they are not required to do so." http://www.eeoc.gov/eeo1/qanda-implementation.html. The Commission does not require employers to collect and maintain more detailed data than needed to complete the EEO-1 report, although the Commission notes that some employers may find it necessary to do so for research or statistical purposes or for self-monitoring. See 70 Fed. Reg. 71294, 71298 (11/28/05).

managers category may result in job groups with too few incumbents to permit meaningful analyses and goal setting. In these cases, contractors with fewer than 150 employees should combine the Executive/Senior Level Officials and Managers and the First/Mid Level Officials and Managers subcategories when examining potential underutilization.

3) Utilization Analysis (60-2.13 through 60-2.15): Consistent with OFCCP's longstanding policy, all individuals identified as being Hispanic or Latino should continue to be counted as minorities when comparing the percentage of women and minorities in each of a contractor's job groups to the available workforce, as required by §§ 60-2.13, 60-2.14, and 60-2.15, or when examining whether a contractor's employment practices result in disparities in the employment or advancement of minorities, as required by § 60-2.17. If an individual self-identifies as Hispanic or Latino and also selects a race, contractors should continue to identify the individual as being "Hispanic or Latino" when preparing the required AAP analyses. This approach is consistent with the approach adopted by the EEOC for purposes of the revised EEO-1 Report.

   Similarly, contractors should consider all individuals identified as belonging to two or more races as minorities when comparing the percentage of women and minorities in each of their job groups to the available workforce, as required by §§ 60-2.13, 60-2.14 and 2.15, or when examining whether their employment practices result in disparities in the employment or advancement of minorities, as required by § 60-2.17.

4) Placement of Goals (60-2.16): When establishing placement goals pursuant to § 60-2.16, contractors should, in most cases, continue to establish a single goal for all minorities. Where a substantial disparity exists in the utilization of a particular minority group, or in the utilization of men or women of a particular minority group, the contractor may be required to establish separate goals for those groups. Contractors are not expected to set a separate placement goal for individuals identified as belonging to more than one race. If a contractor has established placement goals for particular minority groups and has maintained data regarding the specific races of those individuals identified as belonging to two or more races, the contractor may present such data to OFCCP to demonstrate its good faith efforts in addressing its utilization of particular minority groups.[7]

---

[7] The small number of individuals identified as belonging to more than one race makes it unlikely that many quantitative analyses of a contractor's workforce will reveal a substantial disparity in the utilization of individuals belonging to Two or More Races. In the 2000 Census, 2.4 percent of the total population (or 6.8 million people) identified themselves as belonging to more than one race. See United States Census Bureau, The Two or More Races Population: 2000, Census 2000 Brief, at p. 9 (November 2001), available at http://www.census.gov/prod/2001pubs/c2kbr01-6.pdf. The U.S. Census 2005 American Community Survey Report reported that only 1.9 % of the total U.S. population identified as belonging to the Two or More Races category. See United States Census Bureau, American Community Survey, General Demographic Characteristics: 2005, available at http://factfinder.census.gov/servlet/DTTable?_bm=y&-geo_id=01000US&-ds_name=ACS_2005_EST_G00_&-

5) Additional AAP Requirements (60-2.17): OFCCP's regulations require that a contractor perform in-depth analyses of its total employment process to determine whether and where impediments to equal employment opportunity exist. Section 60-2.17 requires that contractors examine whether their employment practices result in disparities in the employment of minorities in the aggregate.[8] When conducting this analysis, contractors are not required to separately evaluate their employment practices with regard to individuals identified solely as belonging to two or more races. Rather, these individuals should be considered as part of the aggregate group of minorities.

   Some contractors find it useful to conduct the analyses required by § 60-2.17 for particular minority groups, as well as for minorities in the aggregate. Contractors that maintain more detailed information regarding the race and ethnicity of their workforces may choose to reallocate those identified as belonging to two or more races into single race categories for purposes of affirmative action analyses. Contractors electing to do this reallocation may use the allocation rules developed by OMB in its Guidance on Aggregation and Allocation of Data on Race for Use in Civil Rights Monitoring and Enforcement.[9]

6) Support Data (60-2.17(b)(2) and Part 60-3): When evaluating whether a contractor has maintained information on the impact of its selection procedures and conducted an adverse impact analysis under part 60-3, contractors will only be expected to produce analyses relating to the impact on those identified as belonging to one of the single race and ethnic categories. Contractors will not be expected to produce analyses of the impact of employee selection procedures on groups comprised of individuals identified as belonging to more than one race; but contractors may be asked for other employment records they may have relating to such individuals. Such records may include any information regarding the reallocation of individuals identified as belonging to more than one race into single race categories, or records maintained by the contractor that utilize the race and ethnic categories of the new EEO-1 form.

---

mt_name=ACS_2005_EST_G2000_B02001; http://factfinder.census.gov/servlet/ADPTable?_bm=y&-geo_id=01000US&-ds_name=ACS_2005_EST_G00_&-_lang=en&-_caller=geoselect&-format.

[8] Pursuant to section 60-2.17, the contractor must evaluate the following minimum areas: (1) The workforce by organizational unit and job group to determine whether there are problems of minority or female utilization (i.e., employment in the unit or group), or of minority or female distribution (i.e., placement in the different jobs within the unit or group); (2) personnel activity (applicant flow, hires, terminations, promotions, and other personnel actions) to determine whether there are selection disparities; (3) compensation system(s) to determine whether there are sex-, race-, or ethnicity-based disparities; (4) selection, recruitment, referral, and other personnel procedures to determine whether they result in disparities in the employment or advancement of minorities or women; and (5) any other areas that might impact the success of the affirmative action program.

[9] OMB, Bulletin 00-02, Guidance on Aggregation and Allocation of Data on Race for Use in Civil Rights Monitoring and Enforcement (March 9, 2000), available at http://www.whitehouse.gov/omb/bulletins/b00-02.html.

F. Where a contractor has not maintained more detailed demographic information about those individuals identified as belonging to more than one race, Census data, labor market data, and other labor market data may be used to assess a contractor's employment practices. In conducting this analysis, the proportion of individuals identified as belonging to more than one race in the contractor's workforce may be compared with labor force statistics or other data on the percentages of multiple race individuals in the relevant qualified labor force. This data could then be used to estimate single race allocation for those individuals identified as belonging to more than one race when a contractor has not retained such information.

5. **OBSOLETE DATA:** None.

6. **DISTRIBUTION:** A, B (both hard copy and electronically); C (hard copy only).

7. **EXPIRATION DATE:** This Directive remains in effect until superseded.

Charles E. James, Sr. — Aug 14, 2008

CHARLES E. JAMES, SR.
Deputy Assistant Secretary for
Federal Contract Compliance

DATE

TRANSMITTAL **U.S. DEPARTMENT OF LABOR**
Office of Federal Contract Compliance Programs
Washington, D.C. 20210

Number: 290	Date: June 15, 2010	ADM Notice/Other

1. **SUBJECT**: Verification Procedures Under Executive Order 13496, Notification of Employee Rights under Federal Labor Laws, and the Department of Labor's implementing regulations at 29 C.F.R. Part 471.

2. **PURPOSE**: To provide instructions for conducting compliance verification under E.O. 13496 and 29 C.F.R. Part 471 during the onsite phase of a compliance evaluation, or in response to a written complaint of noncompliance.

3. **FILING INSTRUCTIONS**:

   Holders of ADM and LEG Binders only: File this Notice with the attachment behind the "Other" tab in your Administrative Practices Binder. Remove OFCCP Order No. 269, ADM Notice/Other (June 8, 2005) (Executive Order 13201 "Beck" Directive).

   District and Area Office Staff only: File this Notice with the attachment behind the tab for ADM Directives in your FCCM Binder. Remove OFCCP Order No. 269, ADM Notice/Other (June 8, 2005) (Executive Order 13201 "Beck" Directive).

4. **OBSOLETE DATA:** OFCCP Order No. 269, ADM Notice/Other (June 8, 2005) (Executive Order 13201 "Beck" Directive).

5. **DISTRIBUTION**: A, B (both hard copy **and** electronically); C (hard copy only)

6. **EXPIRATION DATE**: This directive remains in effect until superseded or rescinded.

7. **ATTACHMENTS**: 1. Notice of Receipt of E.O. 13496 Complaint; 2. Closure Letter – Complaint (No Findings); 3. Notice of Referral to OLMS - Complaint; 4. E.O. 13496 Technical Assistance Letter; and 5. Text of Executive Order 13496.

Patricia A. Shiu — 6/15/10

PATRICIA A. SHIU — DATE
Director
Office of Federal Contract Compliance Programs

U.S. DEPARTMENT OF LABOR
OFFICE OF FEDERAL CONTRACT COMPLIANCE PROGRAMS
WASHINGTON D.C. 20210

1. **SUBJECT**: Verification Procedures Under Executive Order 13496, Notification of Employee Rights under Federal Labor Laws, and the Department of Labor's implementing regulations at 29 C.F.R. Part 471 (Part 471).

2. **PURPOSE**: To provide instructions for conducting compliance verification with E.O. 13496 and 29 C.F.R. Part 471 during the onsite phase of a compliance evaluation, or in response to a written complaint of noncompliance.

3. **ORIGINATOR:** Division of Policy, Planning and Program Development

4. **BACKGROUND**: Executive Order 13496 (E.O. 13496 or Order) was signed by President Obama on January 30, 2009. 74 FR 6407 (February 4, 2009). The Order requires that notice of employee rights under the National Labor Relations Act (NLRA), 29 U.S.C. 151 *et seq*., be provided to employees of federal contractors and subcontractors, and in Federal contracts, subcontracts and purchase orders. Executive Order 13496 revokes Executive Order 13201, commonly referred to as the "Beck Order."

   Final regulations implementing Executive Order 13496 were published in the Federal Register at 75 FR 28368 (May 20, 2010), and will be located in the Code of Federal Regulations at 29 C.F.R. Part 471. The regulations are also available online at http://www.dol.gov/olms/regs/compliance/EO13496.htm. Effective June 21, 2010, the regulations require Federal departments and agencies to include in their contracts[1] specific provisions requiring contractors, and the subcontractors with whom they do business, to post work place notices informing their employees of their organizing and collective bargaining rights under the NLRA. The text of the required employee notice is provided in Appendix A to the regulations.

   OFCCP shares responsibility with the Office of Labor-Management Standards (OLMS), the primary enforcement agency, for ensuring contractor[2] compliance with E.O. 13496 and Part 471. OFCCP's role is to physically inspect contractor establishments (both supply and service, and construction) where NLRA-covered employees[3] engage in activities relating to performance of the contract, including plants, offices, and work sites, and/or to examine contracts for compliance with the Order's posting and contract clause requirements. OFCCP will also investigate a contractor's compliance with E.O. 13496 in response to a written complaint of the contractor's noncompliance with the Order.

[1] Contract is used in this directive to denote contracts and subcontracts unless otherwise indicated.
[2] Contractor is used in this directive to denote prime contractors and subcontractors unless otherwise indicated.
[3] *Employees* not covered by the NLRA, and therefore not subject to the Order, include those employed: as agricultural laborers; in the domestic service of any family or person at his home; by his or her parent or spouse; as an independent contractor; as a supervisor as defined under the NLRA; by an employer subject to the Railway Labor Act; or by any other person who is not an employer as defined in the NLRA.

5. **POLICY:** This directive transmits procedures for conducting Executive Order 13496 compliance verifications. Such verifications will be conducted by OFCCP compliance officers (COs) as part of the onsite phase of compliance evaluations (including, as appropriate, as part of focused reviews) conducted under Executive Order 11246, Section 503, or VEVRAA.[4]

To meet its responsibilities under the Order and facilitate coordination with OLMS, OFCCP has established procedures for conducting compliance verifications, conciliating compliance problems, and reporting its findings to OLMS. Section A of this directive provides details about the posting and contract clause requirements for non-exempt federal contractors. The directive also provides OFCCP procedures for conducting compliance verifications (Section B), for investigating complaints of contractor noncompliance (Section C), and for providing compliance assistance (Section D). OLMS is responsible for taking any necessary administrative enforcement action and/or imposing any penalties and remedies for noncompliance with E.O. 13496.

A. Executive Order 13496 Requirements

1. Notice Posting Requirement

The notice required by the Order and its implementing regulations contains a description of employee rights under the NLRA, the primary law governing relations between unions and employers in the private sector. The NLRA guarantees the right of employees to organize and to bargain collectively with their employers, to engage in other protected concerted activity with or without a union, or to refrain from all such activity. Generally, the employee notice required by the Order lists employees' rights under the NLRA to form, join and assist a union, and to bargain collectively with their employers. The notice also provides examples of unlawful employer and union conduct that would interfere with these rights. In addition, it indicates how employees can contact the National Labor Relations Board (NLRB), the federal agency that enforces these rights, with questions about the rights, or to file complaints alleging NLRA violations.

Employers exempt from the NLRA, and therefore not subject to the Order, are: the United States or any wholly owned Government corporation; any Federal Reserve Bank; any State or political subdivision thereof; any person subject to the Railway Labor Act; any labor organization (other than when acting as an employer); or anyone acting in the capacity of officer or agent of such labor organization.

Specific types of contracts are also excepted from coverage under the Order. They are: federal-sector collective bargaining agreements; prime contracts that involve purchases below the simplified acquisition threshold, which, as of June 2010, is set at \$100,000; contracts resulting from solicitations issued prior to the June 21, 2010,

[4] OFCCP also has the discretion to conduct compliance verifications in the absence of a compliance evaluation conducted pursuant to E.O. 11246, Section 503 or VEVRAA.

effective date of the regulations; subcontracts below $10,000; contracts for work performed exclusively outside the territorial United States; and any contract subject to an exemption granted by the Director of OLMS. See 29 C.F.R. 471.3.[5]

Non-exempt contractors are required by the Order and regulations to physically post the employee notice. The Department's regulations establish the notice's size, form, and content. The notice must be posted in conspicuous places in and about the contractors' facilities, work sites and offices so that the notice is prominent and readily seen by employees, including, but not limited to, all places where the contractor posts notices to employees regarding the terms and conditions of their employment. The poster must be located to ensure that contract employees covered by the NLRA[6] are able to view the notice. This includes all employees directly involved in working the contract, and those not directly involved but whose activities are contract-related, *i.e.*, the duties of the employee's position include work that contributes to or furthers the performance of the contract, or work whose omission would impede the contract's performance (*e.g.*, maintenance, personnel, repair, etc.). Therefore, a contractor may have to post the notice at more than one of its facilities and in multiple areas of work and activity within individual facilities.

A contractor that customarily posts employee notices about the terms and conditions of employment electronically must also post the required E.O. 13496 notice electronically. Electronic posting requires contractors to post a link to OLMS's website containing the notice where they customarily place other electronic notices to employees about the terms and conditions of employment. The link must be no less prominent than that of other employee notices and must read "Important Notice about Employee Rights to Organize and Bargain Collectively with Their Employers." The electronic posting cannot be used as a substitute for physical posting.

Where a significant portion of a contractor's workforce is not proficient in English, contractors and subcontractors must provide the employee notice in the language(s) spoken by employees. OLMS will provide translations of the employee notice and the link to the Department's website that can be used to comply with the physical and electronic posting requirements. See 29 C.F.R. 471.2(d), (e) and (f).

2. Inclusion of Employee Notice Clause in Contracts and Purchase Orders

All non-exempt federal contracts, subcontracts, and purchase orders resulting from solicitations issued on or after June 21, 2010, must include a clause that sets out the text of the employee notice, and outlines the contractor's posting obligation. It is the responsibility of the contracting agency to ensure that all non-exempt federal

[5] No agency or contractor is permitted to procure supplies and services in a manner designed to avoid applicability of the Order.

[6] *Employees* not covered by the NLRA, and therefore not subject to the Order, include those employed: as agricultural laborers; in the domestic service of any family or person at his home; by his or her parent or spouse; as an independent contractor; as a supervisor as defined under the NLRA; by an employer subject to the Railway Labor Act; or by any other person who is not an employer as defined in the NLRA.

contracts contain the employee notice clause. It is the responsibility of the contractor, unless exempted, to include the employee notice clause in every contract, subcontract and purchase order entered into in connection with its federal contract. The requirements contained in the contract clause are binding on each subcontractor. The employee notice clause does not have to be quoted word for word in every contract and purchase order, and may, instead, be incorporated by reference. To include the clause by reference, the contract or purchase order must cite to "29 CFR Part 471, Appendix A to Subpart A."

B. Compliance Verification Procedures

Executive Order 13496 compliance verification will be conducted as a routine part of the onsite phase of compliance evaluations (including, where appropriate, focused reviews). Provided below are the steps that the CO will take to conduct compliance verification.

1. Contractor Notice of Onsite Evaluation

When an establishment has been scheduled for review and it is determined that an onsite evaluation will be conducted, the CO will notify the contractor that, in addition to other onsite activities, the CO will verify the contractor's compliance with the regulations implementing the Order. During pre-onsite discussions with the contractor (or contractor's representative), the CO will explain that a physical inspection will be conducted and that a sample of contracts/purchase orders will be reviewed. Since written confirmation of an onsite visit is routinely provided to a contractor, the CO will include in this written confirmation his/her discussion with the contractor regarding E.O. 13496 compliance verification.

Prior to the onsite evaluation, the CO will request that the contractor provide for inspection, at a minimum, the last three contracts, subcontracts and/or purchase orders resulting from solicitations issued on or after the Order's June 21, 2010, effective date (*i.e.*, the most recent items subject to the Order).[7] This means, for example, that if a solicitation was issued by an agency on June 1, 2010, the resulting contract (even if executed after June 21, 2010) would not be subject to the Order's requirements. On the other hand, if the solicitation is issued on or after June 21, 2010, any resulting contract is subject to the Order and may be reviewed.

Review of a greater number of contracts and/or purchase orders may be necessary to ensure compliance. The CO should explain to the contractor that additional contracts/purchase orders should be readily available for review upon the CO's request. The CO will select an appropriate sample, as needed. If the documents are not physically maintained at the establishment under review, the CO should make arrangements with the contractor to obtain access to the documents for inspection during the onsite evaluation.

[7] If the contractor has fewer than three contracts, subcontracts and/or purchase orders that are subject to the Order, the CO should review all contracts, subcontracts, and/or purchase orders resulting from solicitations issued on or after the Order's effective date.

2. Onsite Evaluation

During the onsite evaluation, the CO will determine if the contractor has complied with the posting requirement. The notice must be posted in conspicuous places in and about the contractor establishment(s), (*e.g.*, facilities, work sites, plants and offices) where NLRA-covered employees engage in activities relating to the performance of the contract. The CO will conduct a physical inspection of the establishment to determine whether the posted notices are in conspicuous places so that the notice is prominent and readily seen by employees. This will include observation of common work areas, break rooms, personnel offices, etc. If there are specific locations where employee notices are commonly posted, (*e.g.*, employee bulletin boards) the required E.O. 13496 notice must, at a minimum, be posted in these locations. Additionally, during the onsite, the CO will inspect the identified sampling of contracts/purchase orders to determine whether they include the required E.O. 13496 contract clause (*i.e.*, contracts and purchase orders resulting from solicitations entered into on or after June 21, 2010).

Where a contractor customarily posts employee notices about the terms and conditions of employment electronically, the CO will also view the electronic posting, and ensure that its website prominently states, "Important Notice about Employee Rights to Organize and Bargain Collectively with Their Employers," and that there is a link to OLMS's website.

Where a significant portion of a contractor's workforce is not proficient in English, the CO will check to ensure that the poster is provided in the appropriate language.

3. Conciliation

If it is determined that the contractor is not in compliance with the posting requirement or has refused/failed to include the required contract clause in its contracts and purchase orders, the CO will attempt to correct the violation during the onsite evaluation (*e.g.*, OFCCP will provide the posters, and guidance on proper posting and the amendment of contracts/purchase orders to include the required contract clause).[8] OFCCP will make reasonable efforts to obtain compliance through conciliation. If the contractor does not comply with the requirements, the matter should be referred to OLMS for possible enforcement action (see below).

4. Report of Findings

The CO will document the results of his/her findings regarding the contractor's compliance or noncompliance with the Order, as appropriate, on the Standard Compliance Evaluation Report (SCER). Additionally, if there is a finding of noncompliance and conciliation efforts have not resulted in securing corrective action, the noncompliance finding should be noted on the SCER and submitted to the

[8] OFCCP will also provide posters when it conducts compliance assistance. See Section D – Compliance Assistance.

Regional Office. A finding of noncompliance with E.O. 13496 may also exist if a contractor refuses to cooperate or provide access to information needed to verify compliance with the Order, or refuses to allow the necessary physical inspection to be conducted. Such denial of access may warrant enforcement action by OLMS.

5. Closing the Compliance Verification

If compliance verification is conducted as part of a broader compliance evaluation, any findings must be included in the compliance evaluation closure letter. The closure letter must specify that E.O. 13496 compliance verification was conducted. See FCCM Chapter 3 (for supply and service no-violation letters), Chapter 4 (for construction no-violation letters) and Chapter 8 (for violation letters).

If there is not a finding of violation regarding E.O. 13496, or any such finding is corrected prior to the completion of the compliance evaluation, the closure letter will indicate this. A courtesy copy of the closure letter will be sent to OLMS at the following address:

U.S. Department of Labor
Office of Labor-Management Standards
Division of Interpretation and Standards
Room N-5609
200 Constitution Ave NW
Washington, DC, 20210

6. Non-Compliance and Referral to OLMS

If there is a finding of violation of E.O. 13496 that is not corrected, the SCER containing the report of findings will be submitted to the Regional Office. The Regional Office will review the findings of noncompliance, including denial of access findings, and forward the findings to the Director of the Division of Program Operations (DPO), Washington, DC. The Director of OFCCP, or his/her designee, will refer the matter to the Director of OLMS, who may take enforcement action, as appropriate, under 29 C.F.R. 471.13. A letter will be sent to the contractor indicating that OFCCP's findings have been referred to OLMS for possible administrative enforcement action. See Attachment 3 – Notice of Referral to OLMS.

C. Executive Order 13496 Investigation in Response to a Complaint of Noncompliance

OFCCP will conduct a complaint investigation in response to an allegation that the posting and/or contract clause requirement has been violated by a non-exempt contractor. The complaint may be filed directly with OFCCP or transferred to OFCCP from OLMS.

1. Receipt of a Complaint

A written complaint alleging noncompliance with Executive Order 13496 may be filed by an employee with OLMS or OFCCP at 200 Constitution Avenue, NW, Washington, DC 20210, or with any OLMS or OFCCP field office. The date that a complaint is received by any OFCCP or OLMS office will be considered the official receipt date for purposes of complaint processing. Any such complaint received by an OFCCP field office should be immediately forwarded to the appropriate Regional Office (*i.e.*, the office with jurisdiction over the geographic area in which the establishment is located) for processing. NOTE: There is no time frame for when a complaint must be filed.

The Regional Office will record receipt of the complaint as an Executive Order 13496 complaint in OFCCP's Case Management System (CMS). The Regional Office is responsible for conducting the initial review of the complaint to determine its completeness,[9] whether it contains other (non-E.O. 13496) allegations and, if so, how these allegations will be addressed. If the complaint contains allegations over which OFCCP does not have jurisdiction, or which are more appropriately addressed by another agency, the Regional Office will follow established complaint processing procedures with regard to these allegations.

Complaints alleging only noncompliance with Executive Order 13496 will be assigned to a field office for investigation. With respect to a "mixed" complaint, (*i.e.*, containing an allegation of noncompliance with E.O. 13496 and other allegations over which OFCCP has jurisdiction), the Regional Office will assign the complaint to a field office to conduct a compliance investigation under E.O. 13496, and an investigation of the remaining allegations (over which OFCCP has jurisdiction) in accordance with established complaint processing guidelines. (See Federal Contractor Compliance Manual (FCCM) Chapter 6 - Complaint Processing)

2. Notice of Receipt of a Complaint

The Regional Office will provide written notice to the contractor within 10 calendar days of the official receipt date of the complaint. The written notice will specify the allegation(s) of noncompliance with the Order and indicate that an E.O. 13496 complaint investigation will be conducted. The written notice will also indicate that the contractor will be contacted by the field office, and that a copy of the company's employee roster will be requested.[10] The name of the complainant should not be provided in the notice, and must remain confidential throughout the complaint

[9] The complaint must be written and contain the following information: 1) the employee's name, address, and telephone number; 2) the name and address of the contractor alleged to have violated the Executive Order; 3) an identification of the alleged violation and the establishment or construction work site where it is alleged to have occurred; 4) any other pertinent information that will assist in the investigation and resolution of the complaint; and 5) the signature of the employee filing the complaint. If the complaint is only partially complete, the Regional Office should make a reasonable effort to contact the complainant to obtain additional information.

[10] The roster will be used to verify the complainant's employment status.

process. If the complaint is "mixed," OFCCP will determine whether the identity of the complainant must be released in order for the investigation to properly proceed.

3. Time Frame for Completing Complaint Processing

The complaint (whether or not it is "mixed") must be processed and a report of findings rendered within 60 calendar days of the date the field office receives the complaint from the Regional Office. This time frame includes conducting compliance verification and, if applicable, completing the conciliation process. Extension of this time frame may be granted to the investigating field office for good cause shown by the Regional Director.

4. Conducting the Complaint Investigation

If the complaint alleges a failure of the contractor to include the contract clause in specific contracts/purchase orders, or in specific types of contracts/purchase orders, the CO should be sure to include a review of the identified contracts/purchase orders. Similarly, if the complaint alleges a failure to post the required notice in specific break rooms or facilities, or a failure to meet the electronic posting requirements, the CO should include the identified places in his/her establishment inspection and/or inspect the contractor's internal website, as appropriate. The CO assigned to investigate the E.O. 13496 complaint will also conduct compliance verification in accordance with this Directive. See subsections B.1, B.2, and B.3 above.

5. Report of Complaint Findings

a. *E.O. 13496 Complaint Only*

The SCER should be used to record the CO's investigation findings when the complaint only alleges noncompliance with E.O. 13496.[11] The CO should use the findings section of the SCER, and any other relevant SCER sections, to record the CO's findings regarding the contractor's compliance or noncompliance with the requirements of E.O. 13496, a description of conciliation efforts made, corrective action taken, and/or enforcement recommended. The SCER must reflect that the compliance and verification was conducted in response to the receipt of a complaint. The CO will include the complaint (and any attachments) with the SCER as a part of the report of findings.

b. *"Mixed" Complaints*

With "mixed" complaints, the specific findings regarding the E.O. 13496 allegation(s) should be included in the report of findings addressing the other allegations over which OFCCP has jurisdiction. This report will be compiled in accordance with established complaint processing procedures (See FCCM Chapters 6 and 8). Whether there is a finding of compliance or noncompliance with regard to

[11] A Notification of Results of Investigation (NORI) does not have to be completed in addition to the SCER.

E.O. 13496 must be specifically stated in the report of findings, along with a description of conciliation efforts made, corrective action taken, and/or enforcement recommended. If there is a finding of noncompliance with E.O. 13496 and conciliation efforts do not cure the problem, the findings will be submitted to DPO (by the Regional Office) for referral of the matter to OLMS in accordance with subsection B.6 above.

6. Closing the Complaint Investigation

a. *E.O. 13496 Complaint Only*

If there is a finding of compliance, or a finding of noncompliance that has been corrected prior to the completion of the investigation, the CO will issue a closure letter indicating that an E.O. 13496 investigation has been completed, and either that no violation was found, or that appropriate corrective action has been taken. A courtesy copy of the closure letter will be sent to OLMS. See Attachment 2 – Closure Letter (No Findings).

If there is a finding of noncompliance that remains uncorrected after conciliation efforts have been made, the report of findings (SCER) will be submitted to DPO (by the Region) for referral to OLMS. A letter will be mailed to the contractor indicating that OFCCP's findings regarding the allegation have been referred to OLMS for possible administrative enforcement action. See Attachment 3 – Notice of Referral to OLMS.

b. *"Mixed" Complaints*

If the complaint allegations are "mixed," the report of findings and complaint file (case file) must specifically state the E.O. 13496 findings, and the basis for the findings. In this instance, the E.O. 13496 findings will continue to be processed with any other findings in accordance with established complaint processing procedures. If there is a violation of E.O. 13496 and conciliation efforts are not successful, the E.O. 13496 findings will be submitted to DPO (by the Regional Office) for referral to OLMS for possible administrative enforcement action. A copy of the letters referring the matter to OLMS and informing the contractor of the referral should be retained in the case file.

D. Compliance Assistance

During compliance assistance activities, federal contractors should be informed of their E.O. 13496 obligations. OFCCP field offices are responsible for answering inquiries regarding the Order, with assistance from SOL and/or OLMS staff, as appropriate. OFCCP will also distribute E.O. 13496 posters during compliance evaluations, compliance assistance events, and as requested. Information regarding the Order, including the required poster, is available online at http://www.dol.gov/olms/regs/compliance/EO13496.htm and may be downloaded for use by contractors.

In addition, technical assistance regarding the Order should be initiated if a field office receives information[12] that a contractor may not be complying with its E.O. 13496 obligations. The field office should send a technical assistance letter to the head of the contractor establishment and/or its designated representative that outlines the Order's coverage and requirements. The letter should also provide the name and phone number of an OFCCP staff member who can provide additional information regarding the Order to the contractor. See Attachment 4 – E.O. 13496 Technical Assistance Letter.

6. **OBSOLETE DATA:** OFCCP Order No. 269, ADM Notice/Other (June 8, 2005) (Executive Order 13201 "Beck" Directive).

7. **DISTRIBUTION**: A, B (both hard copy **and** electronically); C (hard copy only)

8. **EXPIRATION DATE**: This directive remains in effect until superseded or rescinded.

9. **ATTACHMENTS**: 1. Notice of Receipt of E.O. 13496 Complaint; 2. Closure Letter – Complaint (No Findings); 3. Notice of Referral to OLMS - Complaint; 4. E.O. 13496 Technical Assistance Letter; and 5. Text of Executive Order 13496.

Patricia A. Shiu — 6/15/10

PATRICIA A. SHIU — DATE
Director
Office of Federal Contract Compliance Programs

[12] When a field office receives a written complaint alleging noncompliance with E.O. 13496, it should follow the procedures outlined, above, in section C of this Directive.

ATTACHMENT 1: NOTICE OF RECEIPT OF E.O. 13496 COMPLAINT

(Name of CEO) [*Complaint Number*]
(Title of CEO)
(Company Name)
(Street Address)
(City, State, Zip Code)

Dear (Name of CEO):

On [*date*], the Office of Federal Contract Compliance Programs (OFCCP) received a complaint filed under Executive Order 13496 (E.O. 13496) alleging that (*Name and Location of the Establishment*) is in noncompliance with the Order. The complaint alleges:

☐ failure to post the required employee notice;

☐ failure to comply with electronic posting requirements;

☐ failure to include the required contract clause in its contract; and/or

☐ other (specify)

An investigation of the named establishment will be conducted under E.O. 13496 and the Department of Labor's implementing regulations at 29 C.F.R. Part 471 (Part 471), which require non-exempt federal contractors to provide notice of employee rights under the National Labor Relations Act.

The [*District/Area Office*] will contact the establishment within 5 business days to set a date for the investigation and to request a copy of the company's employee roster to verify the complainant's employment status.

Sincerely,

(Regional Director or designee)

cc: Head of Establishment and/or
Designated Representative

ATTACHMENT 2: CLOSURE LETTER FORMAT FOR EXECUTIVE ORDER 13496 COMPLAINT: NO VIOLATION, OR CORRECTED VIOLATION

(Name of CEO)
(Title of CEO)
(Company Name)
(Street Address)
(City, State, Zip Code)

[*Complaint Number*]

Dear (Name of CEO):

Our recent investigation of your compliance with Executive Order 13496 at (*Name and Location of the Establishment reviewed*) has been completed. The investigation was conducted [*in response to a complaint of noncompliance received on (date)*]. Under Executive Order 13496 and the Department of Labor's implementing regulations at 29 C.F.R. Part 471 (Part 471), non-exempt federal contractors are required to provide notice of employee rights under the National Labor Relations Act (NLRA). [Select either Paragraph 2 or Paragraph 3]

(2) During the investigation, we found no apparent violations of Executive Order 13496 or its implementing regulations. This determination may be modified by the Regional Director, or by the Director of the Office of Federal Compliance Programs (OFCCP), within 45 calendar days of the issuance of this letter. You will be informed if such a modification is made.

[OR]

(3) During the investigation, we identified and resolved the following violation(s): [*identify the specific violation(s) resolved during the investigation/compliance verification*]. It is understood that this/these problem(s) will not recur. This determination may be modified by the Regional Director, or by the Director of the Office of Federal Contract Compliance Programs (OFCCP), within 45 calendar days of the issuance of this letter. You will be informed if such a modification is made.

[Optional] OFCCP sincerely appreciates the cooperation and courtesies extended by you and your staff during the conduct of the complaint investigation.

Sincerely,

(District Director/Assistant District Director)

cc: Head of Establishment and/or
Designated Representative

OLMS

ATTACHMENT 3: FORMAT FOR NOTICE OF REFERRAL TO OLMS - EXECUTIVE ORDER 13496

Certified Mail, Return Receipt Requested

(Name of CEO)
(Title of CEO)
(Company Name)
(Street Address)
(City, State, Zip Code)

[*Complaint Number*]

Dear (Name of CEO):

A recent investigation at (*name and location of the establishment reviewed*) was conducted and a finding of noncompliance was made. This letter is to inform you that the Office of Federal Contract Compliance Programs (OFCCP) is referring its report of findings to the OLMS for possible administrative enforcement action.

The investigation was conducted [*in response to a complaint of noncompliance received on (date)*] under Executive Order 13496 and the Department of Labor's implementing regulations at 29 C.F.R. Part 471, which requires that non-exempt federal contractors provide notice of employee rights under the National Labor-Relations Act (NLRA). During the investigation, the following violations were found [*list Executive Order 13496 violation(s) or denial of access*]. This determination may be modified by the Regional Director, or by the Director of the OFCCP, within 45 calendar days of the issuance of this letter. You will be informed if such a modification is made.

If you have any questions regarding this letter, please contact me at [*contact number*] or [*compliance officer's name*].

Sincerely,

(District Director/Assistant District Director)

cc: Head of Establishment and/or
Designated Representative

ATTACHMENT 4: E.O. 13496 TECHNICAL ASSISTANCE LETTER

(Name of CEO)
(Title of CEO)
(Establishment Name)
(Street Address)
(City, State, Zip Code)

Dear (*Name of Establishment Head/Manager*):

It has been brought to the attention of the U.S. Department of Labor's Office of Federal Contractor Compliance Programs (OFCCP) that your establishment located at [*address of establishment*] may not be aware of certain obligations it may have under federal law. Specifically, Executive Order 13496 (E.O. 13496 or the Order), and the Department of Labor's implementing regulations, 29 C.F.R. Part 471, require that non-exempt federal contractors provide notice to their employees of their rights under the National Labor Relations Act (NLRA) and include contract provisions in all non-exempt subcontracts and purchase orders that require subcontractors to post the same notice to employees.

OFCCP and the Department's Office of Labor-Management Standards (OLMS) are responsible for enforcing the Order and the regulations, with OLMS being the primary enforcement agency. Providing technical assistance to federal contractors regarding the Order is one method we use to ensure contractor compliance. This letter is intended to provide you with such technical assistance and does not constitute a determination of compliance/noncompliance.

E.O. 13496 and its implementing regulations, 29 C.F.R. Part 471, require that non-exempt supply and service and/or construction contractors:

- Physically post the required employee notice in conspicuous places in and about the contractors' facilities, work sites and offices, including where the contractor posts other notices to employees regarding the terms and conditions of their employment;
- In addition to physically posting the notice, if a contractor customarily posts employee notices about the terms and conditions of employment electronically, the contractor must post a link to the OLMS website containing the notice;[♦]
- If a significant portion of a contractor's workforce is not proficient in English, the contractor must provide the employee notice in the language(s) spoken by employees; and,
- All non-exempt federal contracts, subcontracts, and purchase orders must include a prescribed clause that sets out the text of the employee notice, and outlines the contractor's posting obligation. The prescribed contract clause does not have to be quoted verbatim and instead, may be incorporated by reference by citing to "29 CFR Part 471, Appendix A to Subpart A."

[♦] The electronic posting cannot be used as a substitute for physical posting.

If you are unsure whether your company is subject to Executive Order 13496, please be aware that the Order excepts the following employers from coverage: the United States or any wholly owned Government corporation; any Federal Reserve Bank; any State or political subdivision thereof; any person subject to the Railway Labor Act; any labor organization (other than when acting as an employer); or anyone acting in the capacity of officer or agent of such labor organization.

If the company is not an exempt employer, and holds a prime federal contract resulting from a solicitation issued on or after June 21, 2010 that is valued at $100,000 or more, or holds a subcontract as defined in 29 C.F.R. Section 471.1 that is necessary to the performance of a federal contract or subcontract and is valued at $10,000 or more, the establishment may be covered under the Order and its implementing regulations. If your establishment is subject to the Order, it is obligated to comply with its requirements, and may be subject to sanctions and penalties for failure to do so. See 29 C.F.R. Section 471.14 for additional details.

Additional information regarding the Order, including the required poster and implementing regulations, is available online at http://www.dol.gov/olms/regs/compliance/EO13496.htm. The poster may be downloaded for your use free of charge. You may also contact [*District/Area Office contact person and number*] with any questions or concerns that you may have.

Sincerely,

(*District/Area Director or designee*)

cc: *(Name of OLMS representative)*
OLMS

ATTACHMENT 5: EXECUTIVE ORDER 13496

Federal Register / Vol. 74, No. 22 / Wednesday, February 4, 2009 / Presidential Documents **6107**

Executive Order 13496 of January 30, 2009: Notification of Employee Rights Under Federal Labor Laws

By the authority vested in me as President by the Constitution and the laws of the United States of America, including the Federal Property and Administrative Services Act, 40 U.S.C. 101 *et seq*., and in order to ensure the economical and efficient administration and completion of Government contracts, it is hereby ordered that:

Section 1. *Policy*. This order is designed to promote economy and efficiency in Government procurement. When the Federal Government contracts for goods or services, it has a proprietary interest in ensuring that those contracts will be performed by contractors whose work will not be interrupted by labor unrest. The attainment of industrial peace is most easily achieved and workers' productivity is enhanced when workers are well informed of their rights under Federal labor laws, including the National Labor Relations Act (Act), 29 U.S.C. 151 *et seq*. As the Act recognizes, ''encouraging the practice and procedure of collective bargaining and . . . protecting the exercise by workers of full freedom of association, self-organization, and designation of representatives of their own choosing, for the purpose of negotiating the terms and conditions of their employment or other mutual aid or protection'' will ''eliminate the causes of certain substantial obstructions to the free flow of commerce'' and ''mitigate and eliminate these obstructions when they have occurred.'' 29 U.S.C. 151. Relying on contractors whose employees are informed of such rights under Federal labor laws facilitates the efficient and economical completion of the Federal Government's contracts.

Sec. 2. *Contract Clause*. Except in contracts exempted in accordance with section 3 of this order, all Government contracting departments and agencies shall, to the extent consistent with law, include the following provisions in every Government contract, other than collective bargaining agreements as defined in 5 U.S.C. 7103(a)(8) and purchases under the simplified acquisition threshold as defined in the Office of Federal Procurement Policy Act, 41 U.S.C. 403.

''1. During the term of this contract, the contractor agrees to post a notice, of such size and in such form, and containing such content as the Secretary of Labor shall prescribe, in conspicuous places in and about its plants and offices where employees covered by the National Labor Relations Act engage in activities relating to the performance of the contract, including all places where notices to employees are customarily posted both physically and electronically. The notice shall include the information contained in the notice published by the Secretary of Labor in the *Federal Register* (Secretary's Notice).

''2. The contractor will comply with all provisions of the Secretary's Notice, and related rules, regulations, and orders of the Secretary of Labor.

''3. In the event that the contractor does not comply with any of the requirements set forth in paragraphs (1) or (2) above, this contract may be cancelled, terminated, or suspended in whole or in part, and the contractor may be declared ineligible for further Government contracts in accordance with procedures authorized in or adopted pursuant to Executive Order [number as provided by the Federal Register] of [insert new date]. Such other sanctions or remedies may be imposed as are provided in Executive Order [number as provided by the Federal Register] of [insert new date], or by

[6108 Federal Register / Vol. 74, No. 22 / Wednesday, February 4, 2009 / Presidential Documents]

rule, regulation, or order of the Secretary of Labor, or as are otherwise provided by law.

''4. The contractor will include the provisions of paragraphs (1) through (3) above in every subcontract entered into in connection with this contract (unless exempted by rules, regulations, or orders of the Secretary of Labor issued pursuant to section 3 of Executive Order [number as provided by the Federal Register] of [insert new date]) so that such provisions will be binding upon each subcontractor. The contractor will take such action with respect to any such subcontract as may be directed by the Secretary of Labor as a means of enforcing such provisions, including the imposition of sanctions for non-compliance: Provided, however, that if the contractor becomes involved in litigation with a subcontractor, or is threatened with such involvement, as a result of such direction, the contractor may request the United States to enter into such litigation to protect the interests of the United States.''

Sec. 3. *Administration.*

(a) The Secretary of Labor (Secretary) shall be responsible for the administration and enforcement of this order. The Secretary shall adopt such rules and regulations and issue such orders as are necessary and appropriate to achieve the purposes of this order.

(b) Within 120 days of the effective date of this order, the Secretary shall initiate a rulemaking to prescribe the size, form, and content of the notice to be posted by a contractor under paragraph 1 of the contract clause described in section 2 of this order. Such notice shall describe the rights of employees under Federal labor laws, consistent with the policy set forth in section 1 of this order.

(c) Whenever the Secretary finds that an act of Congress, clarification of existing law by the courts or the National Labor Relations Board, or other circumstances make modification of the contractual provisions set out in subsection (a) of this section necessary to achieve the purposes of this order, the Secretary promptly shall issue such rules, regulations, or orders as are needed to cause the substitution or addition of appropriate contractual provisions in Government contracts thereafter entered into.

Sec. 4. *Exemptions.* (a) If the Secretary finds that the application of any of the requirements of this order would not serve the purposes of this order or would impair the ability of the Government to procure goods or services on an economical and efficient basis, the Secretary may exempt a contracting department or agency or group of departments or agencies from the requirements of any or all of the provisions of this order with respect to a particular contract or subcontract or any class of contracts or subcontracts.

(b) The Secretary may, if the Secretary finds that special circumstances require an exemption in order to serve the national interest, exempt a contracting department or agency from the requirements of any or all of the provisions of section 2 of this order with respect to a particular contract or subcontract or class of contracts or subcontracts.

Sec. 5. *Investigation.*

(a) The Secretary may investigate any Government contractor, subcontractor, or vendor to determine whether the contractual provisions required by section 2 of this order have been violated.

Such investigations shall be conducted in accordance with procedures established by the Secretary.

(b) The Secretary shall receive and investigate complaints by employees of a Government contractor or subcontractor, where such complaints allege a failure to perform or a violation of the contractual provisions required by section 2 of this order.

Sec. 6. *Compliance.*

(a) The Secretary, or any agency or officer in the executive branch lawfully designated by rule, regulation, or order of the Secretary, may hold such

[**Federal Register** / Vol. 74, No. 22 / Wednesday, February 4, 2009 / Presidential Documents **6109**]

hearings, public or private, regarding compliance with this order as the Secretary may deem advisable.

(b) The Secretary may hold hearings, or cause hearings to be held, in accordance with subsection (a) of this section, prior to imposing, ordering, or recommending the imposition of sanctions under this order. Neither an order for cancellation, termination, or suspension of any contract or debarment of any contractor from further Government contracts under section 7(b) of this order nor the inclusion of a contractor on a published list of noncomplying contractors under section 7(c) of this order shall be carried out without affording the contractor an opportunity for a hearing.

Sec. 7. *Remedies.* In accordance with such rules, regulations, or orders as the Secretary may issue or adopt, the Secretary may:

(a) after consulting with the contracting department or agency, direct that department or agency to cancel, terminate, suspend, or cause to be cancelled, terminated, or suspended, any contract, or any portion or portions thereof, for failure of the contractor to comply with the contractual provisions required by section 2 of this order;

contracts may be cancelled, terminated, or suspended absolutely, or continuance of contracts may be conditioned upon future compliance: Provided, that before issuing a directive under this subsection, the Secretary shall provide the head of the contracting department or agency an opportunity to offer written objections to the issuance of such a directive, which objections shall include a complete statement of reasons for the objections, among which reasons shall be a finding that completion of the contract is essential to the agency's mission: And provided further, that no directive shall be issued by the Secretary under this subsection so long as the head of the contracting department or agency, or his or her designee, continues to object to the issuance of such directive;

(b) after consulting with each affected contracting department or agency, provide that one or more contracting departments or agencies shall refrain from entering into further contracts, or extensions or other modifications of existing contracts, with any noncomplying contractor, until such contractor has satisfied the Secretary that such contractor has complied with and will carry out the provisions of this order: Provided, that before issuing a directive under this subsection, the Secretary shall provide the head of each contracting department or agency an opportunity to offer written objections to the issuance of such a directive, which objections shall include a complete statement of reasons for the objections, among which reasons shall be a finding that further contracts or extensions or other modifications of existing contracts with the noncomplying contractor are essential to the agency's mission: And provided further, that no directive shall be issued by the Secretary under this subsection so long as the head of a contracting department or agency, or his or her designee, continues to object to the issuance of such directive; and

(c) publish, or cause to be published, the names of contractors that have, in the judgment of the Secretary, failed to comply with the provisions of this order or of related rules, regulations, and orders of the Secretary.

Sec. 8. *Reports.* Whenever the Secretary invokes section 7(a) or 7(b) of this order, the contracting department or agency shall report to the Secretary the results of the action it has taken within such time as the Secretary shall specify.

Sec. 9. *Cooperation.* Each contracting department and agency shall cooperate with the Secretary and provide such information and assistance as the Secretary may require in the performance of the Secretary's functions under this order.

Sec. 10. *Sufficiency of Remedies.* If the Secretary finds that the authority vested in the Secretary by sections 5 through 9 of this order is not sufficient to effectuate the purposes of this order, the Secretary shall develop recommendations on how better to effectuate those purposes.

[**6110 Federal Register** / Vol. 74, No. 22 / Wednesday, February 4, 2009 / Presidential Documents]

Sec. 11. *Delegation.* The Secretary may, in accordance with law, delegate any function or duty of the Secretary under this order to any officer in the Department of Labor or to any other officer in the executive branch of the Government, with the consent of the head of the department or agency in which that officer serves.

Sec. 12. *Implementation.* To the extent permitted by law, the Federal Acquisition Regulatory Council (FAR Council) shall take whatever action is required to implement in the Federal Acquisition Regulation (FAR) the provisions of this order and any related rules, regulations, or orders issued by the Secretary under this order and shall amend the FAR to require each solicitation of offers for a contract to include a provision that implements section 2 of this order.

Sec. 13. *Revocation of Prior Order and Actions.* Executive Order 13201 of February 17, 2001, is revoked. The heads of executive departments and agencies shall, to the extent permitted by law, revoke expeditiously any orders, rules, regulations, guidelines, or policies implementing or enforcing Executive Order 13201.

Sec. 14. *Severability.* If any provision of this order, or the application of such provision to any person or circumstance, is held to be invalid, the remainder of this order and the application of the provisions of such to any person or circumstances shall not be affected thereby.

Sec. 15. *General Provisions.*

(a) Nothing in this order shall be construed to impair or otherwise affect:

(i) authority granted by law to a department, agency, or the head thereof; or

(ii) functions of the Director of the Office of Management and Budget relating to budgetary, administrative, or legislative proposals.

(b) This order shall be implemented consistent with applicable law and subject to the availability of appropriations.

(c) This order is not intended to, and does not, create any right or benefit, substantive or procedural, enforceable at law or in equity by any party against the United States, its departments, agencies, or entities, its officers, employees, or agents, or any other person.

[**Federal Register** / Vol. 74, No. 22 / Wednesday, February 4, 2009 / Presidential Documents **6111**]

Sec. 16. *Effective Date.* This order shall become effective immediately, and shall apply to contracts resulting from solicitations issued on or after the effective date of the rule promulgated by the Secretary pursuant to section 3(b) of this order.

Renumbered on 9/16/2013 as DIR 2011-01

TRANSMITTAL **U.S. DEPARTMENT OF LABOR**
Office of Federal Contract Compliance Programs

Number: 295 Date: December 16, 2010 OFCCP Order No. ADM Notice/Other

---

1. **SUBJECT**: Active Case Enforcement (ACE) procedures.

2. **PURPOSE**: To outline the procedures for conducting Supply & Service (S&S) compliance evaluations under the Active Case Enforcement process.

3. **FILING INSTRUCTIONS**:

   Holders of ADM and LEG Binders only: File this Notice behind the "Other" tab in your Administrative Practices Binder.

   District and Area Office EOSs and EOAs only: File this Notice behind the tab for ADM Directives in your FCCM Binder.

4. **OBSOLETE DATA**: Directive Number 285, issued September 17, 2008. Subject: Active Case Management. Additionally, if there is a conflict between any previous guidance or existing procedures and the ACE procedures outlined in this directive, the ACE procedures will take precedence.

5. **DISTRIBUTION**: A, B (both hard copy and electronically); C (hard copy only)

6. **ATTACHMENTS**: Closure Letter for No Apparent Violations or Technical Violations; and Closure Letter for Substantive Violations.

7. **EXPIRATION DATE**: This directive remains in effect until rescinded or modified.

Patricia A. Shiu 12/16/10

PATRICIA A. SHIU DATE
Director
Office of Federal Contract Compliance Programs

U.S. DEPARTMENT OF LABOR
OFFICE OF FEDERAL CONTRACT COMPLIANCE PROGRAMS
WASHINGTON, D.C. 20210

1. **SUBJECT**: Active Case Enforcement (ACE) procedures.

2. **PURPOSE**: To outline the procedures for conducting Supply & Service (S&S) compliance evaluations under the Active Case Enforcement (ACE) process.

3. **BACKGROUND**: On July 25, 2003, the Active Case Management (ACM) process for conducting S&S compliance evaluations was adopted by the Office of Federal Contract Compliance Programs (OFCCP). The stated purpose of ACM was to concentrate agency resources on identifying and remedying cases of systemic discrimination, thereby enabling the agency to use its resources in a more efficient manner. However, ACM proved to be of limited utility in that it did not allow OFCCP to effectively use all of its investigative tools. OFCCP has therefore rescinded ACM (see Directive 292, dated December 02, 2010) and determined that the ACE process described in this directive will more effectively utilize its resources and strengthen its enforcement efforts.

4. **DEFINITIONS**: To ensure consistency in implementation, the following terms are defined:

   - **Compliance Check** - An investigative procedure that may be used by OFCCP when conducting a compliance evaluation. A compliance check is a determination of whether the contractor has maintained appropriate records consistent with 41 CFR Parts 60-1.12, 60-250.80, 60-300.80, and 60-741.80. See 41 CFR 60-1.20(a)(3), 60-250.60(a)(3), 60-300.60(a)(3), and 60-741.60(a)(3).

   - **Compliance Evaluation** - The investigation and review process used by OFCCP to determine if a federal contractor is complying with the nondiscriminatory and affirmative action employment obligations outlined in 41 CFR Chapter 60. A compliance evaluation consists of any one or any combination of the following investigative procedures: compliance review; offsite review of records; compliance check; or focused review; See 41 CFR 60-1.20(a), 60-250.60(a), 60-300.60(a), and 60-741.60(a).

- **Compliance Review** - The most common investigative procedure that is used by OFCCP when conducting a compliance evaluation. A compliance review is a comprehensive analysis and evaluation of the hiring and employment practices of the contractor, the written affirmative action program (AAP), and the results of the affirmative action efforts undertaken by the contractor. A compliance review may proceed in three stages: desk audit, onsite review and offsite analysis; See 41 CFR 60-1.20(a)(1), 60-250.60(a)(1), 60-300.60(a)(1), and 60-741.60(a)(1).

- **Contractor** - Unless otherwise indicated, a prime contractor or subcontractor.

- **Focused Review** - An investigative procedure that may be used by OFCCP when conducting a compliance evaluation. A focused review is an onsite review that focuses on one or more components of the contractor's organization or one or more aspects of the contractor's employment practices; See 41 CFR § 60-1.20(a)(4), 60-250.60(a)(.4), 60-300.60(a)(4), and 60-741.60(a)(4).

- **Full Desk Audit** - Comprehensive analyses of all of a contractor's written AAPs - Executive Order 11246 (EO 11246), Section 503 of the Rehabilitation Act of 1973 (Section 503) and the Vietnam Era Veterans' Readjustment Assistance Act of 1974 (VEVRAA) - and supporting documentation. These analyses include, but are not limited to, an impact ratio analysis, compensation analysis, and assessment of the reasonableness and acceptability of each AAP.

- **Full Compliance Review** - Implementation of all three stages of a compliance review, i.e., desk audit, onsite, and where necessary, an offsite analysis.

- **Indicator (of discrimination or violation)** - Any one or any group of the following: statistical indicators of possible discrimination, anecdotal evidence to support possible discrimination, patterns of individual discrimination, patterns of systemic discrimination, patterns of major technical violations such as recordkeeping deficiencies or failure to maintain an AAP, and indicators of non-compliance with labor and employment laws administered by other federal agencies that may relate to violations of OFCCP's laws.[1] For example, a contractor with a history of recordkeeping violations under WHD and OSHA may indicate that potential violation of OFCCP's recordkeeping requirements.

- **Offsite Review of Records** - An investigative procedure that may be used by OFCCP when conducting a compliance evaluation. An offsite review of records is an analysis and evaluation of the AAP (or any part thereof) and supporting documentation, and other documents related to the contractor's personnel policies and employment actions that may be relevant to a determination of whether the contractor has complied with the requirements of the EO 11246, Section 503 and VEVRAA and the regulations at 41 CFR Chapter 60;[2] See 41 CFR 60-1.20(a)(2), 60-250.60(a)(2), 60-300.60(a)(2), and 60-741.60(a)(2).

- **Preaward Compliance Evaluation** - A compliance evaluation of any prospective contractor or first-tier subcontractor establishment entering into an S&S contract or subcontract of $10 million or more conducted before the award of the contract to determine the contractor's compliance with EO 11246. A preaward compliance evaluation is conducted unless the OFCCP has evaluated and found the contractor or subcontractor establishment to be in compliance within the past two years. See 41 CFR § 60-1.20(d) and 60-1.29(a).

5. **POLICY**: Effective January 1, 2011, all S&S compliance evaluations scheduled from the Federal Contractor Scheduling System (FCSS) will be processed using the ACE procedures established in this directive. Additionally, if there is a conflict between any previous guidance or existing procedures and the ACE procedures outlined in this directive, the ACE procedures will take precedence.

---

[1] OFCCP currently obtains compliance information from the Equal Employment Opportunity Commission (EEOC), and is in the process of expanding its indicators to include findings of non-compliance with the laws administered by the Department of Labor's Veterans' Employment & Training Services (VETS), Occupational Safety and Health Administration (OSHA) and Wage and Hour Division (WHD).

[2] An offsite review of records is different from the offsite analysis stage of a compliance review. See 41 CFR 60-1.20(a)(1)(iii) and 41 CFR 60-1.20(a)(2).

A. Basic Principles:

1) All S&S contractors selected for review by the FCSS system will be required to submit their AAPs and supporting documentation to OFCCP. See 41 CFR 60-1.20(a), 60-250.60(a), 60-300.60(a), and 60-741.60(a).

2) A full desk audit will be performed in every compliance evaluation to ensure the contractor's compliance with EO 11246, Section 503, and VEVRAA.

3) For quality control purposes, every 25th federal contractor establishment will be selected by FCSS for a full compliance review.[3]

4) Indicators of potential discrimination may be of an individual and/or class (i.e., two or more victims) nature.

5) Whenever an onsite review is conducted, the CO will document the contractor's compliance with Executive Order 13496, which requires notification to employees of their rights under the National Labor Relations Act (NLRA).

6) Contractor establishments that have undergone a compliance evaluation will be excepted from scheduling from the FCSS for another compliance evaluation of any kind for 24 months from the date of closure of the compliance evaluation.

6. **PROCEDURES:** The following procedures apply to scheduling and conducting compliance evaluations of Supply & Service contractors.

A. Scheduling Procedures:

OFCCP will use the FCSS to select Supply & Service contractor establishments for compliance evaluation using administratively neutral selection criteria.

[3] This replaces the quality control measure in the ACM directive that required a full desk audit for every 25th contractor establishment on the FCSS list, and a full compliance review for every 50th contractor establishment on the FCSS list.

Once identified by the FCSS, establishments selected for evaluation will appear on a computer-generated list developed by the OFCCP National Office. This list will designate the contractor establishments that each Regional/District/Area Office is to schedule for a compliance evaluation during the scheduling cycle. Using administratively neutral selection criteria, this list will also designate which investigative procedure (i.e., compliance review; off-site review of records; compliance check; or focused review) will be followed.

The Regional/District/Area Offices are required to schedule the federal contractor establishment identified on the FCSS in strict sequential order.

B. Compliance Evaluation Procedures:

1) **Compliance Review**

When a contractor is designated for a compliance review, OFCCP will take the following steps:

A. Coinciding with the mailing of the scheduling letter, OFCCP will contact the Equal Employment Opportunity Commission (EEOC) and the State and/or Local Fair Employment Practice (FEP) agency to determine the nature, status and outcome of any complaints that have been filed against the contractor at the establishment under review.

B. The CO will conduct a full desk audit in every compliance review and evaluate the contractor's compliance with its obligations under EO 11246, Section 503, and VEVRAA. See 41 CFR Parts 60-1 through 60-50, 60-741, 60-250 and 60-300.

C. The CO will review the contractor's compliance history for the past three years, to assess the contractor's recent compliance history and determine if there are patterns of non-compliance. To do this, the CO will use the OFCCP internal database system, and review any information received from EEOC, State or local FEP, and/or other labor and employment agencies, such as the Department of Labor's Veterans' Employment and Training Service and Wage and Hour Division.

D. The CO will determine whether there are indicators of potential discrimination or violation that will require an onsite investigation. In addition to statistical and anecdotal evidence of discrimination, indicators of potential discrimination/violation also include, but are not limited to: patterns of individual discrimination, patterns of systemic discrimination, patterns of major technical violations such as recordkeeping deficiencies or failure to maintain an AAP, and non-compliance with other labor and employment laws, e.g., wage and hour laws.

E. If the contractor's AAP or supporting document submitted is insufficient to make a compliance determination, the CO may elect to proceed to the onsite.

F. The CO may close the compliance review at the conclusion of the desk audit, if no indicators of potential discrimination/violation are found. However, if the compliance review is designated as the "quality control" review or a focused review, the CO must conduct an onsite review, even in the absence of indicators.

G. If indicators are identified during the desk audit, the CO may conduct an onsite review of the contractor's compliance with all of the laws enforced by OFCCP.

H. An onsite review is not limited to the nature or scope of the indicators that triggered the onsite review.

I. Where an onsite review is conducted, the CO will also document the contractor's compliance with Executive Order 13496.[4]

[4] For more information on E.O. 13496 see Directive Number 290, issued on June 15, 2010. Subject: Verification Procedures Under Executive Order 13496, Notification of Employee Rights under Federal Labor Laws, and the Department of Labor's implementing regulations at 29 C.F.R. Part 471

J. During the desk audit, if minor technical violations are identified and there are no indicators of potential discrimination, the CO should try to remedy the deficiencies at this stage.

K. If the compliance review indicates that there is no potential discrimination or unresolved minor technical violations with EO 11246, Section 503 or VEVRAA the CO will follow established closure procedures and issue the Closure for No Apparent Violations or Technical Violations. See Attachment 1.

L. At the conclusion of an investigation where major technical violations were resolved and/or discrimination was remedied through a conciliation agreement, the CO will issue the appropriate closure document(s), including the Closure Letter for Substantive Violations. See Attachment 2.

M. If the contractor denies OFCCP access or refuses to provide requested information, the CO will follow the show cause notice procedures authorized in 41 CFR 60-1.28; 60-250.64; 60-300.64; 60-741.64, as appropriate.[5]

2) Other Investigative Procedures

Some contractors selected on the FCSS list may be designated for a compliance evaluation that uses an investigative method other than a compliance review. Specifically, OFCCP may designate a contractor for a compliance evaluation using the offsite review of records, compliance check or focused review investigative procedure:

A. All S&S contractors selected for review by the FCSS system will be required to submit their AAPs and supporting documentation to OFCCP for a full desk audit.

B. An offsite review of records, compliance check or focused review, may be expanded to include the use of one or more additional investigative methods, including conducting a full compliance review in

[5] Field offices must obtain approval from the National Office before issuing such a show cause order.

appropriate circumstances, *e.g.*, when indicators of discrimination are found.

C. If there are no indicators found during an offsite review of records, compliance check, or focused review the compliance evaluation may be closed. To close the evaluation the Compliance Officer will issue the Closure Letter for No Apparent Violations or Technical Violations. See Attachment 1.

7. **QUALITY CONTROL**: As a quality control measure to ensure contractor compliance with the laws enforced by OFCCP, a full compliance review - including an onsite review - will be conducted of every 25th contractor establishment. Contractor establishments selected for this quality control compliance review will be selected by the FCSS and provided to OFCCP field offices on their scheduling list.

8. **CASE MANAGEMENT SYSTEM (CMS)**: The Case Management System (CMS) is being revised to incorporate the aforementioned ACE procedures.

PATRICIA A. SHIU
Director
Office of Federal Contract Compliance Programs

12/16/10
DATE

ATTACHMENTS

Attachment 1: Closure Letter for No Apparent Violations or Technical Violations

Name of Establishment CEO
Title of CEO
Establishment Name
Street Address
City, State, Zip

Dear [Name of CEO]:

Our recent evaluation of your equal employment opportunity policies and practices at (Name and Location of the Establishment reviewed) has been completed.

[Select either Paragraph 2 or Paragraphs 3 and 4]

(2)

During the compliance evaluation process we found no apparent violations of Executive Order 11246, as amended, Section 503 of the Rehabilitation Act of 1973, as amended, or the Vietnam Era Veterans' Readjustment Assistance Act of 1974, as amended (38 U.S.C. 4212, or VEVRAA). This determination may be modified by the Regional Director, or by the Director of the Office Federal Contract Compliance Programs, within 45 days of the issuance of this letter.

[OR]

(3) and (4)

During the compliance evaluation process, we identified and resolved the following violation(s): [identify the technical violation(s) resolved during the compliance evaluation, including the appropriate regulatory citation and specific remedy]. It is understood that this/these problem area(s) will not recur.

We found no additional violations of Executive Order 11246, as amended, Section 503 of the Rehabilitation Act of 1973, as amended, or the Vietnam Era Veterans' Readjustment Assistance Act of 1974, as amended (38 U.S.C. 4212, or VEVRAA). This determination may be modified by the Regional Director, or by the Director of the Office Federal Contract Compliance Programs, within 45 days of the issuance of this letter.

[Optional]

The Office of Federal Contract Compliance Programs sincerely appreciates the cooperation and courtesies extended by you and your staff during the conduct of the compliance review.

Sincerely,

(Name of District Director)
District Director

cc: (as appropriate)

Attachment 2: Closure Letter for Substantive Violations

Name of Establishment CEO
Title of CEO
Establishment Name
Street Address
City, State, Zip

Dear [Name of CEO]:

Our recent evaluation of your equal employment opportunity policies and practices at (Name and Location of the Establishment reviewed) has been completed.

Subject to the implementation of commitments detailed in our Conciliation Agreement dated (date), it is the determination of this office that there are no further apparent violations of the requirements of our regulations. This determination may be modified by the Regional Director, or by the Director of the Office of Federal Contract Compliance Programs. However, if neither the Regional Director nor the Director of the Office of Federal Contract Compliance Programs takes action on it within 45 days of my signature on this Agreement, it shall be deemed approved.

This determination does not preclude a future determination of noncompliance based on a finding that the commitments are not sufficient to achieve compliance.

[Optional]
The Office of Federal Contract Compliance Programs sincerely appreciates the cooperation and courtesies extended by you and your staff during the conduct of the compliance review.

Sincerely,

(Name of District Director)
District Director

cc: (as appropriate)

OMB No.:1250-0006
Expires: 04/30/2019

OFCCP

DIRECTIVE (DIR) 2013-01 Revision 1

A Directive (DIR) is intended to provide guidance to OFCCP staff or federal contractors on enforcement and compliance policy or procedures. A DIR does not change the laws and regulations governing OFCCP's programs and does not establish any legally enforceable rights or obligations.

Effective Date: April 28, 2016

1. **SUBJECT:** Functional Affirmative Action Programs (FAAPs).

2. **PURPOSE:** To outline the guidelines for applying for and maintaining Functional Affirmative Action Program (FAAP) Agreements.

3. **REFERENCES**: None

4. **AFFECTED POLICY**: Effective April 28, 2016, Federal contractors and subcontractors seeking an agreement to develop, implement, and maintain FAAPs must follow the procedures outlined in this Directive. Approval of an agreement allowing the use of FAAPs is not automatic; an agreement will be approved only if the OFCCP Director determines that the contractor's overall operational structure, compliance history, and proposed FAAPs meet the criteria set forth in this Directive.

5. **BACKGROUND:** The regulations implementing Executive Order 11246 permit federal supply and service contractors to develop affirmative action programs (AAPs) that are based on a business function or business unit rather than AAPs based on contractor establishments. Specifically, the regulation at 41 CFR 60-2.1(d)(4) provides:

> If a contractor wishes to establish an affirmative action program other than by establishment, the contractor may reach agreement with OFCCP on the development and use of affirmative action programs based on functional or business units. The Deputy Assistant Secretary, or his or her designee, must approve such agreements. Agreements allowing the use of functional or business unit affirmative action programs cannot be construed to limit or restrict how the OFCCP structures its compliance evaluations.

Under the regulation, Federal contractors must have an agreement approved by the OFCCP Director [formerly the Deputy Assistant Secretary] to develop and operate under a FAAP. See example in Attachment A.

On March 21, 2002, OFCCP issued a Directive establishing the procedures for approving contractor requests for agreements to use FAAPs. The 2002 Directive was replaced with Directive 2013-1 issued on December 12, 2012, Subject: Functional Affirmative Action Programs (FAAPs). This Directive supersedes the 2012 Directive.

In the absence of an approved agreement, the regulations require contractors to develop, implement, and maintain a separate AAP for each physical location of an establishment with 50 or more employees.

Any multi-establishment supply and service contractor subject to AAP requirements may request a FAAP agreement that permits the development and use of AAPs based on functional or business units. Some multi-establishment contractors may find it appropriate to develop AAPs based solely on functional or business units, while others may elect to use a combination of both functional units and establishment-based AAPs.

6. **ROLES AND RESPONSIBILITIES**: It is the responsibility of the Division of Program Operations (DPO) to review and recommend approval of contractor requests to develop, implement and maintain FAAPs.

7. **PROCEDURE**: Federal contractors and subcontractors seeking an agreement to develop, implement, and maintain FAAPs must follow the procedures outlined in this Directive.

   a. **DEFINITIONS**: To ensure clarity and consistency in the implementation of the FAAP Program, definitions for commonly used terms in OFCCP programs are provided below:

   Compliance Evaluation – The investigation and review process used by OFCCP to determine if a federal contractor is complying with the nondiscriminatory and affirmative action employment obligations outlined in 41 CFR Chapter 60. A compliance evaluation consists of any one or any combination of the following investigative procedures: compliance review, off-site review of records, compliance check, or focused review. See 41 CFR 60-1.20(a), 60-300.60(a), and 60-741.60(a).

   Compliance Review – A comprehensive analysis of the hiring and employment practices of the contractor, including the contractor's written affirmative action program (AAP), and the results of the affirmative action efforts undertaken by the contractor. A compliance review may proceed in three stages: desk audit, onsite review and offsite analysis. See 41 CFR 60-1.20(a)(1), 60-300.60(a)(1) and 60-741.60(a)(1).

   Establishment - A facility or unit which produces goods or services, such as a factory, office, store, or mine. In most instances, the unit is a physically separate facility at a single location. In appropriate circumstances, OFCCP may consider as an establishment several facilities located at two or more sites when the facilities are in the same labor market or recruiting area. The determination as to whether it is appropriate to group facilities as a single establishment will be made by OFCCP on a case-by-case basis.

Functional or Business Unit - refers to a component within an organization that operates autonomously in the ordinary course of the organization's business. A functional or business unit should also have identifiable personnel practices or transactional activities specific to the functional or business unit (e.g., applicant flow, hires, promotions, compensation determinations, terminations, etc.) that are distinguishable from other parts of the contractor. Functions or business units should be identified and defined based on the organization's existing business operations, personnel practices and management structures.

b. CRITERIA FOR A FUNCTIONAL AAP: To be considered suitable for a FAAP, the functional or business unit must:

i. Currently exist and operate autonomously.

ii. Include at least 50 employees.

iii. Have its own managing official.

iv. Have the ability to track and maintain its own personnel activity.

c. REQUIRED ELEMENTS OF A FUNCTIONAL AAP: All FAAPs must include the required AAP elements outlined in 41 CFR 60-2, Subpart C of 41 CFR 60-300, and Subpart C of 41 CFR 60-741.

d. BASIC PRINCIPLES OF FUNCTIONAL AAP AGREEMENTS:

i. A FAAP agreement will be implemented only after the contractor has received the written approval from the OFCCP Director, or his or her designee.

ii. Applications, modifications, and certifications are not automatic and must be approved by the OFCCP Director, or his or her designee.

iii. OFCCP will consider whether a contractor is currently reporting its compliance under the requirements of a conciliation agreement when determining whether to approve a FAAP agreement.

iv. Notification from OFCCP of receipt of the contractor's request for a FAAP agreement does not constitute approval of the request. The requirement to develop, implement and maintain establishment-based AAPs continues in effect until the contractor receives notice that the FAAP agreement has been approved by the OFCCP Director and the contractor has notified OFCCP that its FAAPs have been implemented.

v. OFCCP will consider EEO violations of the requesting contractor for the past three years from the date of the application, including EEO violations from other local, state and federal government agencies. These findings may impact the approval of the contractor's FAAP agreement request.

vi. A FAAP agreement must cover all employees within the contractor's workforce. However, this does not mean that the entire workforce must be covered by FAAP(s). In some cases, it may be appropriate for a contractor to use both FAAPs and establishment-based AAP(s). For example, a contractor has establishments that are located in Seattle, Denver, and Washington, DC. Each of these establishments includes a Marketing unit and Research functions. The functional AAP agreement might permit the contractor to develop and implement two functional AAPs: one for Marketing and one for Research. The remaining employees in each establishment would be covered in separate establishment-based AAPs and reflected in the FAAP agreement addenda. See Attachment A.

vii. Contractors with approved FAAP agreements must also comply with the affirmative action requirements of Section 503 of the Rehabilitation Act of 1973, as amended (Section 503) and the Vietnam Era Veterans' Readjustment Assistance Act of 1974, as amended (VEVRAA). Contractors must comply with their Section 503 and VEVRAA written affirmative action obligations either by: (a) creating and maintaining Section 503 and VEVRAA FAAPs for the same functional or business units that are covered by their Executive Order 11246 FAAPs; or (b) creating and maintaining establishment-based Section 503 and VEVRAA AAPs for each of its establishments. Contractors must inform OFCCP which method they will use to comply with its Section 503 and VEVRAA affirmative action obligations during the FAAP negotiation or certification process. Under either arrangement, contractors must make their AAPs and/or FAAPs available for review at each of their establishments.

viii. The contractor must demonstrate the ability to efficiently manage and monitor all personnel actions, including recordkeeping and affirmative action responsibilities for all functional or business units regardless of size.

ix. A FAAP agreement will not relieve a contractor of its obligation to comply with OFCCP's regulations at 41 CFR Chapter 60, and OFCCP will not negotiate its procedures for determining compliance with its regulations.

x. A FAAP agreement will not contain provisions limiting access or the manner and means by which compliance evaluations will be initiated or conducted. Such matters are not negotiable.

xi. OFCCP will use the information that the contractor provides in support of its request for a FAAP agreement solely for the purpose of evaluating the request.

xii. Upon request, the contractor must provide OFCCP information about all format(s), including specific electronic formats, in which the contractor maintains its records and other information. The contractor agrees to provide all documents relating to the FAAP agreement, including modifications, updates, and certifications, in any of the formats in which they are maintained, as selected by OFCCP.

xiii. The federal contractor agrees to submit, at a minimum, its personnel activity, *i.e.*, applicant flow, hire, promotion, and termination, and compensation data in a readable and usable electronic format, when so requested during a compliance evaluation. Acceptable formats include MS Excel or MS Access.

xiv. All FAAP agreements will expire three years after the date of approval.

xv. Contractors with approved FAAP agreements will undergo at least one compliance evaluation during the term of their FAAP agreement.

xvi. Only functional units identified in the approved FAAP agreement are covered.

xvii. FAAP units that have undergone a compliance evaluation will be exempt from another evaluation for 24 months from the date of closure of the previous compliance evaluation.

e. **PROCEDURES FOR REQUESTING, UPDATING, MODIFYING OR CERTIFYING A FUNCTIONAL AAP AGREEMENT:** OFCCP desires that the process for approval of a FAAP agreement be simple and fluid. It should be a collaborative effort in which OFCCP and the contractor work together to process the FAAP request in an expeditious manner consistent with OFCCP policies and procedures as noted below.

i. **Requesting a Functional AAP Agreement**:

(1) A contractor requesting a FAAP agreement must submit a written request to the OFCCP Director explaining why it believes that use of FAAP(s) would be most appropriate. This explanation should also describe in detail how the proposed functions correlate to the contractor's specific organizational structure and include a transition plan describing the process and timeframes in which the organization will move from establishment-based AAPs to FAAPs. The request must include the name and contact information for the corporate representative responsible for overseeing the contractor's request for the FAAP agreement.

(2) The request for a FAAP agreement must be received by the OFCCP Director no later than 120 calendar days prior to the expiration of the current corporate headquarters AAP, or within 120 days from the award of the Federal contract if this is a first-time contractor. If this timeframe is not met, the request will be denied. The contractor may resubmit its request prior to its next AAP year.

(3) The contractor must continue to develop, implement and maintain AAPs for each establishment until the FAAP agreement is approved by the OFCCP Director. OFCCP may continue to schedule and conduct establishment-based

compliance evaluations during the approval process.

(4) Contractor establishments scheduled for a compliance evaluation during the FAAP agreement application process, or prior to the implementation of its FAAPs following the approval of a FAAP agreement, will be completed as establishment-based evaluations if the scheduling letter was received by the contractor prior to the FAAP agreement's effective date.[1]

(5) The FAAP Branch will review the application submission and the contractor's rationale for moving from an establishment-based AAP structure to a FAAP structure. Every effort will be made to gather sufficient information regarding the contractor's corporate structure to process the FAAP agreement request. This information enables OFCCP to make informed decisions when evaluating requests for FAAP agreements. Nonetheless, it may be necessary for OFCCP to meet with the contractor to make a final determination on the contractor's request.[2]

(6) OFCCP will also review records of past compliance evaluations of the contractor's establishment(s) and consider whether any past violations have been corrected or continue to be identified as recurring violations during reviews.

(7) Once the federal contractor and OFCCP's FAAP Branch reach an agreement, a copy of the proposed FAAP agreement will be presented to the OFCCP Director for review and approval. Prior to approval, the OFCCP Director may submit questions and comments to the FAAP Branch. If final approval is granted by the OFCCP Director, a copy of the approved agreement will be forwarded to the contractor for signature. If the OFCCP Director rejects the proposed agreement, it will be returned to the FAAP Branch to work with the contractor's representative to address and resolve any concerns about the proposed agreement. After the issues are resolved, the proposed agreement will be resubmitted to the OFCCP Director for re-consideration and approval.

ii. Updating a Functional AAP Agreement:

(1) Contractors are required to report at least annually, 30 calendar days prior to the effective date of its AAP year, any changes to the agreement, including but not limited to change of names of functional units, changes of managing officials or

---

[1] The FAAP agreement becomes effective on the date of the OFCCP Director's final signature. Contractors will have up to 120 days following the effective date of its FAAP agreement to have its FAAPs implemented. The contractor must notify OFCCP when its FAAPs are implemented. Until the contractor has notified OFCCP that its FAAPs have been implemented, compliance evaluations of the contractor will be conducted as establishment-based evaluations.

[2] The FAAP Branch will determine whether it is necessary to conduct a FAAP conference to discuss the application materials. If the FAAP Branch determines that a conference is necessary, the FAAP Branch will discuss with the contractor the most appropriate format for conducting the conference. In addition to face-to-face meetings, alternative formats for conducting the conference include teleconference or web-based conferencing.

contact information, and updated Federal contract information.[3] The employee counts, facility names, and facility addresses included in each functional unit must also be updated. If the contractor is adding new functional units or removing existing functional units, OFCCP will modify the agreement accordingly.

(2) Should the contractor fail to submit an annual update, OFCCP may schedule the contractor for a compliance evaluation.

iii. **Modifying an Approved Functional AAP Agreement**:

(1) When a contractor with an approved FAAP agreement significantly changes its corporate structure so as to alter the functions upon which the original FAAP agreement was based, including but not limited to a merger, acquisition, downsizing or reorganization, the contractor will provide a written explanation of the changes that occurred within 60 calendar days of the effective date of the change(s). This notification will detail how the modified functions or new functions, if any, meet the criteria outlined in Section 7 of this Directive and how the company selected units that would be removed. This explanation should also include the date when the changes will be incorporated into the existing AAP structure. OFCCP will then modify the existing agreement accordingly. In the event of a merger or acquisition, the contractor is required to notify the OFCCP of the name of the newly merged or acquired company. The contractor must also notify OFCCP regarding its plan to incorporate the former company's employees into its AAP structure.

(2) Should the contractor fail to notify OFCCP of any change(s) to its corporate structure that alter the functional or business units covered in its FAAP agreement, OFCCP may terminate the FAAP agreement. If OFCCP terminates the agreement, written notification shall be provided to the contractor. See Section 11 – Termination of a FAAP Agreement.

(3) Any modifications will not extend the three-year term of the FAAP Agreement.

iv. Certifying a Functional AAP Agreement:

(1) The contractor must certify in writing every three years (at least 120 calendar days prior to the expiration of the existing agreement) that there have been no changed circumstances in its business structure affecting the existing FAAP agreement. The certification must include updated information regarding employee counts, facility names, and facility addresses included in each functional unit. If the contractor has undergone changes resulting in the addition or elimination of functional units or establishment-based AAPs, they will be required to submit a written rationale explaining the changes. OFCCP's

[3] Updated contract information is only necessary if the previously provided contract has expired or is no longer applicable.

FAAP Branch will review the information and confirm that the changes meet the criteria outlined in Section 7 of this Directive. OFCCP's FAAP Branch will work closely with the contractor's designated representative to ensure timely and proper processing of the certification request. However, in the event OFCCP is unable to certify the request before the expiration date, the contractor will continue to operate under the existing FAAP agreement until the request has been approved or denied.

(2) The contractor must provide updated information concerning at least one federal contract or subcontract of $50,000 or more, identifying the name of the federal contracting agency, the contract number, the contract period, and the name of the prime contractor if the contractor is a subcontractor.

(3) FAAP agreements that are certified will be re-issued for another three year term after execution of the agreement by the contractor's representative and the OFCCP Director. If OFCCP determines that it will not certify the agreement, OFCCP will provide the contractor with at least 90 calendar days written notification. See Section 11 – Termination of a FAAP Agreement.

(4) During an open compliance evaluation of a functional unit, OFCCP may extend the term of an existing FAAP agreement until the evaluation has been completed, if necessary.

(5) If the contractor fails to certify in writing at least 120 calendar days prior to the expiration of the FAAP agreement that it continues to operate under a functional structure, the said FAAP agreement will expire at the end of the three-year term. The contractor will be required to develop establishment-based AAPs and may be scheduled for compliance evaluations under the Federal Contractor Selection System (FCSS). The certification of an existing FAAP agreement will only be deemed accepted upon the approval and signature of the OFCCP Director.

f. TERMINATION OF A FUNCTIONAL AAP AGREEMENT:

i. Either party may terminate the FAAP agreement upon 90 calendar days written notice. The notice will provide a brief explanation of the reason(s) for the termination and the effective date of the termination.

ii. If a FAAP agreement has been terminated by OFCCP, the contractor may not reapply for a FAAP agreement for a period of three years.

iii. Upon termination of a FAAP agreement, all employees are required to be covered by establishment-based AAPs. The establishment-based AAPs shall be in place no later than 120 days from either OFCCP's or the contractor's notification that the FAAP agreement has been terminated.

iv. OFCCP may terminate a FAAP agreement where the contractor or any of its establishments or functional units has been found in violation of the laws and regulations enforced by OFCCP.

v. OFCCP may also terminate a FAAP agreement where the contractor failed to account for all employees in either a functional or establishment AAP, or notify OFCCP of any modification of its functional units.

8. ATTACHMENTS: A, B, and C.

PATRICIA A. SHIU
Director
Office of Federal Contract Compliance Programs

Note: According to the Paperwork Reduction Act of 1995, an agency may not conduct or sponsor, and a person is not required to respond to, a collection of information unless it displays a valid OMB control number. The valid OMB control number for this information collection is 1250-0006. The time required to complete this information collection is estimated to average 38 hours per response for the initial request of a FAAP agreement, 5.3 hours to modify a FAAP agreement, 5.9 hours to update a FAAP agreement, and 11.1 hours to certify a FAAP agreement. This includes the time for reviewing instructions, searching existing data sources, gathering and maintaining data needed, and completing and reviewing the collection of information. Send any comments concerning this burden estimate or any other aspect of this collection of information, including suggestions for reducing burden to the Office of Federal Contract Compliance Programs, Room C-3325, 200 Constitution Avenue, N.W., Washington, D.C. 20210.

Attachment A

Below are examples of how an establishment-based and functional AAP could be developed. However, developing an AAP is unique and contractors must still provide rationale for forming their AAPs.

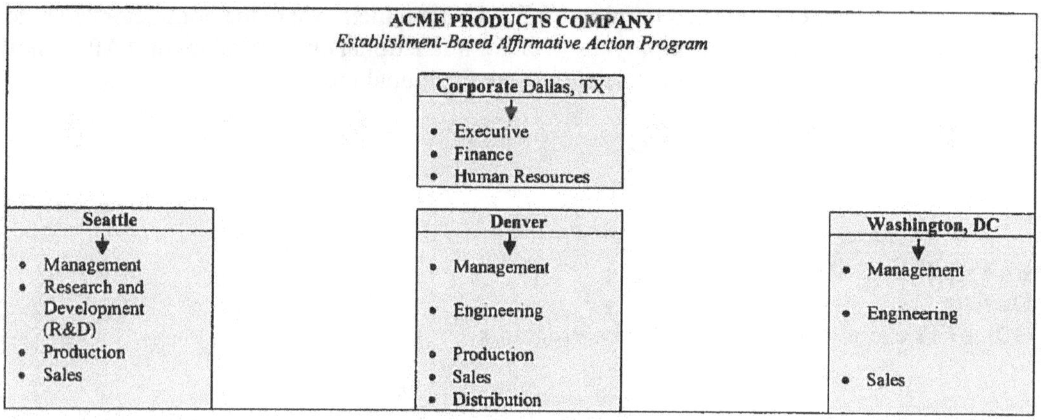

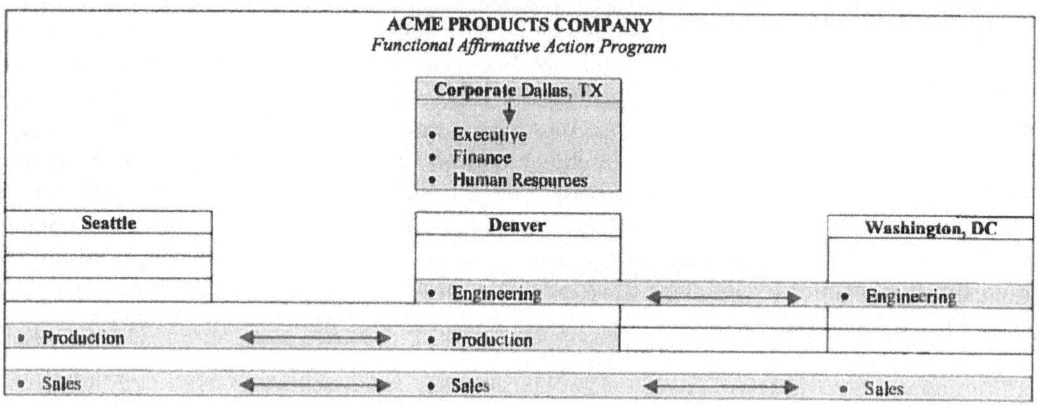

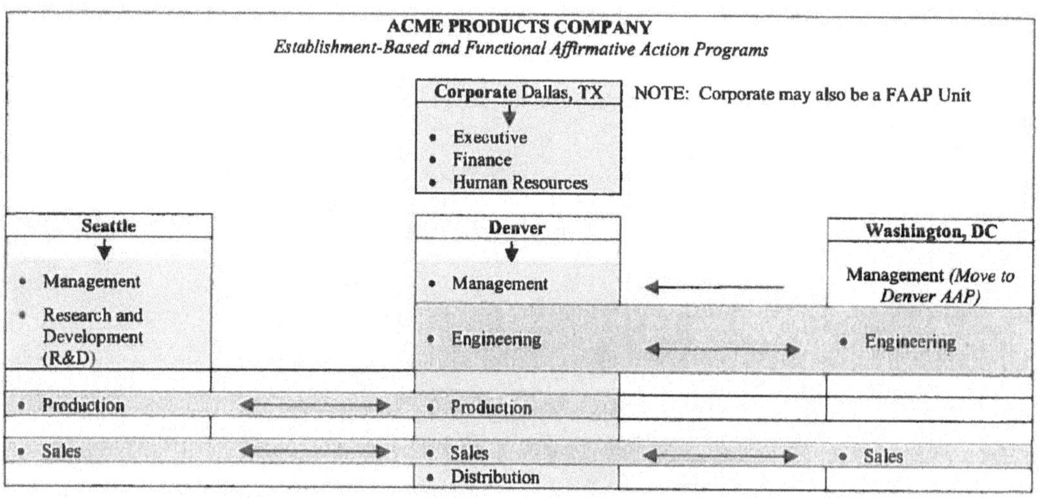

Attachment B

Documentation to Submit with the FAAP Request:

1. A statement that the contractor is a covered federal contractor or subcontractor under 41 CFR 60-1, 60-2, 60-300, and or 60-741, including specific information regarding at least one federal contract or subcontract of $50,000 or more, identifying the name of the federal contracting agency, the contract number, the contract period, and the name of the prime contractor if the contractor is a subcontractor;

2. A copy of the contractor's most recent Consolidated EEO-1 Report;

3. An organizational chart that clearly identifies all of the proposed functional or business units to be covered by the requested FAAP and how they are related to each other within the corporation's overall structure.

4. A narrative description of the "business or function" of each proposed FAAP unit and how it meets the definition of a functional or business unit set forth above;

5. For each proposed functional or business unit provide the company and subsidiary name covered by the FAAP agreement and the street address, total number of employees, and name and address of the managing official;[4]

6. A statement addressing the location, to include city and state, where each proposed FAAP unit will maintain its employee personnel records and applicant processing activities;

7. If the contractor proposes to maintain some establishment-based AAPs, provide a list of the locations with establishment-based AAPs, including for each: the physical address, number of employees, and the phone number of the establishment's managing official, AAP contact and the EEO-1 unit number for each establishment;

8. A statement addressing how the contractor plans to transition from establishment-based AAPs to functional AAPs, including its timeline for completion;

9. The dates of the proposed AAP year for the functional programs; and

10. Copies of personnel policies relevant to evaluating the proposed functions or business units, including organizational and unit-specific policies related to recruitment, hiring, promotion, compensation, and discipline.

[4] Employees who are based remotely should be included in the facility to which they report.

Attachment C

Items to Discuss During the FAAP Negotiation Process:

1. The reporting hierarchy of the functional or business units;
2. Personnel procedures including recruitment; hiring; promotion; compensation; termination; record retention and data analysis as they apply to each functional or business unit, including identification of units that have differing personnel or compensation practices;
3. How the contractor anticipates complying with the affirmative action requirements of Section 503 and VEVRAA, as discussed in Section 7.D.7 of the FAAP Directive;
4. How each functional unit manages its human resources and equal employment opportunity responsibilities; and
5. Any ongoing or past EEO violations from local, state and federal agencies (over the last three years).

DIRECTIVE

U.S. DEPARTMENT OF LABOR
Office of Federal Contract Compliance Programs

Number: 306 Date: January 29, 2013 ADM Notice

1. **SUBJECT:** Complying with Nondiscrimination Provisions: Criminal Record Restrictions and Discrimination Based on Race and National Origin

2. **PURPOSE:** The purpose of this Directive is to provide information to federal contractors and subcontractors and federally-assisted construction contractors and subcontractors (contractors) and to OFCCP personnel about: (1) the circumstances in which exclusions of applicants or employees based on their criminal records may violate existing nondiscrimination obligations; (2) the Training and Employment Guidance Letter (TEGL) 31-11 issued on May 25, 2012 to the American Job Center network and other covered entities in the public workforce system by the Department of Labor's Employment and Training Administration (ETA) and Civil Rights Center (CRC); and (3) the Enforcement Guidance issued by the Equal Employment Opportunity Commission (EEOC) on April 25, 2012.

3. **EFFECTIVE DATE:** This directive is effective immediately.

4. **BACKGROUND:** In recent decades, the number of Americans who have had contact with the criminal justice system has increased exponentially. It is estimated that about one in three adults now has a criminal history record – which often consists of an arrest that did not lead to conviction, a conviction for which the person was not sentenced to a term of incarceration, or a conviction for a non-violent crime.[1] On any given day, about 2.3 million people are incarcerated[2] and each year 700,000 people are released from prison[3] and almost 13 million are admitted to – and released from – local jails.[4]

   Racial and ethnic disparities are reflected in incarceration rates. According to the Pew Center on the States, one in 106 white men, one in 36 Hispanic men, and one in 15 African American men are incarcerated.[5] Additionally, on average, one in 31 adults is under

---

[1] *See* Written Testimony of Amy Solomon, Senior Advisor to the Assistant Attorney General, Office of Justice Programs, U.S. Department of Justice (DOJ), submitted for EEOC Meeting to Examine Arrest and Conviction Records as a Hiring Barrier (July 26, 2011), *available at* http://www.eeoc.gov/eeoc/meetings/7-26-11/solomon.cfm (last accessed January 25, 2013) (citing DOJ Bureau of Justice Statistics data that over 92 million people have a criminal history on file in state criminal history repositories and comparing that to Census data on the number of adults in the U.S.); *see also* Robert Brame, Michael G. Turner, Raymond Paternoster & Shawn D. Bushway, "Cumulative Prevalence of Arrest from Ages 8 to 23 in a National Sample," 129 *Pediatrics* 21-27 (Jan. 1, 20132), *abstract available at* http://pediatrics.aappublications.org/content/129/1/21.abstract (last accessed January 25, 2013).

[2] Lauren E. Glaze, *Correctional Populations in the United States, 2010*, NCJ 236319 (Bureau of Justice Statistics Dec. 2011), *available at* http://www.bjs.gov/content/pub/pdf/cpus10.pdf (last accessed January 25, 2013).

[3] Paul Guerino, Paige M. Harrison & William J. Sabol, *Prisoners in 2010*, NCJ 236096 (Bureau of Justice Statistics Dec. 2011), *available at* http://bjs.ojp.usdoj.gov/content/pub/pdf/p10.pdf (last accessed January 25, 2013).

[4] Todd D. Minton, *Jail Inmates at Midyear 2010 – Statistical*, NCJ 233431 (Bureau of Justice Statistics April 2011), *available at* http://bjs.ojp.usdoj.gov/content/pub/pdf/jim10st.pdf (last accessed January 25, 2013).

[5] The Pew Center on the States, *One in 100: Behind Bars in America 2008* at 6 (2008), *available at* http://www.pewtrusts.org/uploadedFiles/wwwpewtrustsorg/Reports/sentencing_and_corrections/one_in_100.pdf (last accessed January 25, 2013).

correctional control (i.e., probation, parole, or incarceration), including one in 45 white adults, one in 27 Hispanic adults and one in 11 African American adults.[6] Racial and ethnic disparities may also be reflected in other criminal history records. For example, although African Americans constitute approximately 13 percent of the overall population,[7] they account for 28 percent of those arrested[8] and almost 40 percent of the incarcerated population.[9]

In light of these racial and ethnic disparities, contractors should be mindful of federal antidiscrimination laws if they choose to rely on job applicants' criminal history records for purposes of employment decisions. Hiring policies and practices that exclude workers with criminal records may run afoul of such laws, which prohibit intentional discrimination on the basis of race, national origin, or other protected bases, and policies or practices that have a disparate impact on these protected groups and cannot be justified as job related and consistent with business necessity. Policies that exclude people from employment based on the mere existence of a criminal history record and that do not take into account the age and nature of an offense, for example, are likely to unjustifiably restrict the employment opportunities of individuals with conviction histories. Due to racial and ethnic disparities in the criminal justice system, such policies are likely to violate federal antidiscrimination law. Accordingly, contractors should carefully consider their legal obligations before adopting such policies.

5. **POLICY:**

a. EEOC Enforcement Guidance. The EEOC, as the federal agency that administers and enforces Title VII of the Civil Rights Act of 1964, 42 U.S.C. 2000e *et seq.*, issued guidance[10] on the use of arrest and conviction records in employment decisions. This guidance consolidates and updates EEOC's prior guidance regarding the use of criminal records in employment decisions. EEOC is the lead agency for interpreting Title VII, and OFCCP follows Title VII principles in interpreting Executive Order 11246, as amended. Therefore, EEOC's guidance will assist contractors in implementing and reviewing their

---

[6] The Pew Center on the States, *One in 31: The Long Reach of American Corrections* at 5, 7 (2009), *available at* http://www.pewstates.org/uploadedFiles/PCS_Assets/2009/PSPP_1in31_report_FINAL_WEB_3-26-09.pdf (last accessed January 25, 2013).

[7] U.S. Census Bureau, *USA QuickFacts* 2010, *available at* http://quickfacts.census.gov/qfd/states/00000.html (last accessed January 25, 2013).

[8] FBI Uniform Crime Reports 2010, *available at* http://www.fbi.gov/about-us/cjis/ucr/crime-in-the-u.s/2010/crime-in-the-u.s.-2010/tables/table-43 (last accessed January 25, 2013).

[9] William J. Sabol, Todd D. Minton, & Paige M. Harrison, *Prison and Jail Inmates at Midyear 2006*, NCJ 217675 (Bureau of Justice Statistics June 2007), *available at* http://bjs.ojp.usdoj.gov/content/pub/pdf/pjim06.pdf (last accessed January 25, 2013). These racial disparities in the criminal justice system have been attributed primarily to disparate law enforcement practices and sentencing policies. *See, e.g.*, Mark Mauer, *Justice for All? Challenging Racial Disparities in the Criminal Justice System*, 37 Human Rights 4 (A.B.A. Sec. Individual Rights & Responsibilities Fall 2010), *available at* http://www.americanbar.org/publications/human_rights_magazine_home/human_rights_vol37_2010/fall2010/justice_for_all_challenging_racial_disparities_criminal_justice_system.html (last accessed January 25, 2013).

[10] *Enforcement Guidance: Consideration of Arrest and Conviction Records in Employment Decisions Under Title VII of the Civil Rights Act of 1964, as amended*, U.S. Equal Employment Opportunity Commission (April 25, 2012), http://www.eeoc.gov/laws/guidance/upload/arrest_conviction.pdf (last accessed January 25, 2013) (Enforcement Guidance).

employment practices in compliance with the Executive Order. EEOC's guidance applies to all employers that have 15 or more employees.

As described in the Enforcement Guidance, the nondiscrimination principles of Title VII prohibit both "disparate treatment" – intentionally treating members of protected groups differently based on their protected status – and "disparate impact" – the use of policies or practices that are neutral on their face, but have a disproportionate impact on members of protected groups, and are not job-related and consistent with business necessity. Although individuals with criminal history records are not a protected group under the applicable federal laws, antidiscrimination laws may be implicated when criminal records are being considered. For example, studies have shown that employers may treat whites with a criminal record more favorably than similarly-situated African Americans with the same or similar criminal record, which would be a form of disparate treatment.[11] Additionally, OFCCP is aware of job announcements that categorically exclude people who have any kind of conviction or arrest and of contractors that screen out job seekers with criminal records by stating that they will only accept applicants with so-called "clean" criminal records.[12] Due to racial and ethnic disparities reflected in the criminal justice system, these policies or practices will likely have a disparate impact on certain protected groups, in violation of federal law.[13]

The following description, provided in a notice attached to the TEGL, explains these concepts further:

> **"EEOC Information on Employer Consideration of Arrest and Conviction History**
> "Title VII of the Civil Rights Act of 1964 makes it unlawful to discriminate in employment based on race, color, national origin, religion, or sex. This law does not prohibit an employer from requiring applicants to provide information about arrests, convictions or incarceration. But, employers may not treat people with the same criminal records differently because of their race, national origin or another protected characteristic. In addition, unless required by federal law or regulation, employers may not automatically bar everyone with an arrest or conviction record from employment. This is because an automatic bar to hiring everyone with a criminal record is likely to unjustifiably limit the employment opportunities of applicants or workers of certain racial or ethnic groups.

---

[11] *See* 42 U.S.C. 2000e-2(a); Devah Pager, *The Mark of a Criminal Record*, 108 American Journal of Sociology 937, 957-60 (March 2003), *available at* http://www.princeton.edu/~pager/pager_ajs.pdf (last accessed January 25, 2013) *See generally* Devah Pager & Bruce Western, *Race at Work: The Realities of Race and Criminal Record in the NYC Job Market* (NYC Commission on Human Rights 2005), *available at* http://www.nyc.gov/html/cchr/pdf/race_report_web.pdf (last accessed January 25, 2013).

[12] Examples of such job announcements that were recently found posted in One Stop Job Banks included the following criminal record exclusions: "No criminal background"; "Have no criminal history"; "CLEAN criminal background (NO felonies or misdemeanors)."

[13] *See* 42 U.S.C. 2000e-2(k)(1)(A)(i).

> "If an employer's criminal record exclusion policy or practice has a disparate impact on Title VII-protected individuals, it must be job-related and consistent with business necessity….
>
> "Since an arrest alone does not necessarily mean that someone has committed a crime, an employer should not assume that someone who has been arrested, but not convicted, did in fact commit the offense. Instead, the employer should allow the person to explain the circumstances of the arrest to determine whether the conduct underlying the arrest justifies an adverse employment action… For more information: http://www.eeoc.gov/laws/guidance/arrest_conviction.cfm; http://www.eeoc.gov/laws/guidance/qa_arrest_conviction.cfm; http://www.nationalreentryresourcecenter.org/documents/0000/1082/Reentry_Council_Mythbuster_Employment.pdf."

The EEOC explains in its Enforcement Guidance (page 14) that "[t]o establish that a criminal conduct exclusion that has an adverse impact is job related and consistent with business necessity under Title VII, the employer needs to show that the policy operates to effectively link specific criminal conduct, and its dangers, with the risks inherent in the duties of a particular position." The Guidance describes two circumstances in which the Commission believes employers will consistently meet the "job related and consistent with business necessity" defense. First is when the employer validates the criminal conduct exclusion for the position in question in accordance with the Uniform Guidelines on Employee Selection Procedures (UGESP). Second, where validation in accordance with UGESP is not done, the EEOC discusses three factors that provide the starting point for analyzing how specific criminal conduct may be linked to particular positions.[14]

The EEOC explains in its Enforcement Guidance (pages 15-16) the three factors that are relevant to whether a criminal conduct exclusion is "job related and consistent with business necessity" as follows:

i. "The Nature and Gravity of the Offense or Conduct – Careful consideration of the nature and gravity of the offense or conduct is the first step in determining whether a specific crime may be relevant to concerns about risks in a particular position. The nature of the offense or conduct may be assessed with reference to the harm caused by the crime (e.g., theft causes property loss). The legal elements of a crime also may be instructive. For example, a conviction for felony theft may involve deception, threat, or intimidation [citation omitted]. With respect to the gravity of the crime, offenses identified as misdemeanors may be less severe than those identified as felonies.

ii. "The Time That Has Passed Since the Offense, Conduct and/or Completion of the Sentence – Employer policies typically specify the duration of criminal conduct exclusion. The amount of time that has passed since [an employee's or prospective employee's] criminal conduct occurred [is] probative of the risk he

[14] The EEOC describes these factors as the "*Green* factors." See *Green v. Mo. Pac. R.R*, 549 F.2d 1158, 1160 (8th Cir. 1977) (approving employer's use of these factors in making hiring decisions).

pose[s] in the position in question. Whether the duration of an exclusion will be sufficiently tailored to satisfy the business necessity standard will depend on the particular facts and circumstances of each case. Relevant and available information to make this assessment includes, for example, studies demonstrating how much the risk of recidivism declines over a specified time.[15]

iii. "The Nature of the Job Held or Sought – [I]t is important to identify the particular job(s) subject to the exclusion. While a factual inquiry may begin with identifying the job title, it also encompasses the nature of the job's duties (e.g., data entry, lifting boxes), identification of the job's essential functions, the circumstances under which the job is performed (e.g., the level of supervision, oversight, and interaction with co-workers or vulnerable individuals), and the environment in which the job's duties are performed (e.g., out of doors, in a warehouse, in a private home). Linking the criminal conduct to the essential functions of the position in question may assist an employer in demonstrating that its policy or practice is job related and consistent with business necessity because it 'bear[s] a demonstrable relationship to successful performance of the jobs for which it was used'" [citation omitted].

b. Best Practices. The EEOC Enforcement Guidance recommends a number of "best practices" for employers to avoid liability for discrimination based on the use of criminal records in employment. We commend these best practices to contractors. In particular, contractors may consider ensuring that any policies and procedures that screen applicants and employees for criminal conduct require an individualized assessment. Such policies and procedures should be narrowly tailored to the essential job requirements and actual circumstances under which the jobs are performed; to the specific offenses that may demonstrate unfitness for performing such jobs; and to the appropriate duration of exclusions for criminal conduct, based on all available evidence. Like the EEOC, OFCCP recommends that contractors, as a general rule, refrain from inquiring about convictions on job applications.[16] Further, OFCCP

[15] *See, e.g.*, Keith Soothill & Brian Francis, *When Do Ex-Offenders Become Like Non-Offenders?*, 48 HOWARD J. OF CRIM. JUST. 373, 380-81 (2009) (examining conviction data from Britain and Wales, a 2009 study found that the risk of recidivism declined for the groups with prior records and eventually converged within 10 to 15 years with the risk of those of the nonoffending comparison groups); Alfred Blumstein & Kiminori Nakamura, *Redemption in the Presence of Widespread Criminal Background Checks,* 47 CRIMINOLOGY 327 (2009) (concluding that there may be a "point of redemption" (i.e., a point in time where an individual's risk of re-offending or re-arrest is reasonably comparable to individuals with no prior criminal record) for individuals arrested for certain offenses if they remain crime free for a certain number of years); Megan C. Kurlychek, Robert Brame & Shawn D. Bushway, *Enduring Risk? Old Criminal Records and Predictions of Future Criminal Involvement*, 53 CRIME & DELINQUENCY 64 (2007) (analyzing juvenile police contacts and Racine, Wisconsin police contacts for an aggregate of crimes for 670 males born in 1942 and concluding that, after seven years, the risk of a new offense approximates that of a person without a criminal record); Megan C. Kurlychek et al., *Scarlet Letters and Recidivism: Does an Old Criminal Record Predict Future Offending?*, 5 CRIMINOLOGY & PUB. POL'Y 483 (2006) (evaluating juvenile police contacts and arrest dates from Philadelphia police records for an aggregate of crimes for individuals born in 1958, a 2006 study concluded that the risk of recidivism decreases over time and that, six or seven years after an arrest, an individual's risk of re-arrest approximates that of an individual who has never been arrested).

[16] Many contractors are prohibited from inquiring about convictions or arrests on job applications by local law. See National Employment Law Project, *Ban the Box: Major U.S. Cities and Counties Adopt Fair Hiring Policies to*

recommends, if and when contractors make such inquiries, the inquiries are limited to convictions for which exclusion would be job-related for the position in question and consistent with business necessity. Finally, information about applicants' and employees' criminal records should be kept confidential and only used for the purpose for which it was intended.

c. New Procedures Affecting Contractors that Utilize the Federally-Assisted Workforce System. On May 25, 2012, ETA, in conjunction with CRC, issued TEGL 31-11 about the relevance of exclusions based on criminal records to the existing nondiscrimination obligations of public workforce system entities.[17] The TEGL, available at http://wdr.doleta.gov/directives/corr_doc.cfm?DOCN=9230, advises these covered entities to conduct their activities using safeguards to prevent discrimination and promote employment opportunities for formerly-incarcerated individuals and other individuals with criminal records.

Contractors subject to the Vietnam Era Veterans' Readjustment Assistance Act of 1974 (VEVRAA) are required to list all employment openings with "an appropriate local employment service office of the state employment security agency wherein the opening occurs" or "the appropriate employment service delivery system where the opening occurs".[18] Other contractors may also utilize such covered entities to list job openings, screen job-seekers, or receive referrals of qualified applicants. All contractors using covered entities, whether required by VEVRAA to do so or not, can expect that these entities will now follow the procedures, outlined in the TEGL and summarized below, regarding (a) posting of job announcements and (b) screening and referring applicants based on criminal record restrictions:

i. Posting job announcements with American Job Centers.
   - When an employer (including contractors) registers with an American Job Center (or other covered entity) to use the Job Bank, the TEGL requires the covered entity to send the employer a prescribed notice ("Notice #1 for Employers Regarding Job Bank Nondiscrimination and Criminal Record Exclusions"[19]) explaining that the covered entity must comply with federal civil rights laws which, due to the likely adverse impact of criminal record exclusions on protected groups, generally prohibit categorical exclusions of individuals based solely on an arrest or conviction history.
   - Covered entities will be required to use a system (automated or otherwise) for identifying vacancy announcements that include hiring restrictions based on arrest and/or conviction records.

Remove Unfair Barriers to Employment of People with Criminal Records (Feb. 6, 2012), available at nelp.3cdn.net/abddb6b65a14826f92_n5m6bz5bp.pdf (last accessed January 25, 2013).

[17] The "covered entities" to which the TEGL is addressed are the public workforce system and other entities that receive federal financial assistance to operate Job Banks; to help job seekers in locating and obtaining employment; and/or to assist employers by screening and referring qualified applicants. They include the American Job Centers, formerly known as One-Stop Career Centers.

[18] See 41 CFR §60-250.5(a)2 and §60-300.5(a)3.

[19] This and the other required notices are attachments to the TEGL.

- When covered entities identify job postings that exclude individuals based on arrest and/or conviction history, they must provide employers that have posted these vacancy announcements a notice ("Notice #2 for Employers Regarding Job Postings Containing Criminal Record Exclusions") that gives the employer the opportunity to remove or edit the vacancy announcement.

Covered entities may continue to post vacancy announcements containing language excluding candidates based on criminal history only when accompanied by a notice to job seekers ("Notice #3 for Job Seekers to be Attached to Job Postings with Criminal Record Exclusions") explaining that the exclusions in the posting may have an adverse impact on protected groups and informing them that individuals with criminal history records are not prohibited from applying for the posted position.

ii. Screening and referral based on criminal record restrictions.
   - Covered entity staff should refrain from screening and refusing to make referrals because an applicant has a criminal history record. Job seekers who are referred for positions where the job posting takes criminal history into account are to be given a copy of Notice #3 For Job Seekers along with the job announcement.

d. Other Relevant Laws. The Notices attached to the TEGL describe two other federal laws that might affect contractors' employment practices regarding the use of criminal records in making hiring decisions. As described in Notice #1 and Notice #2:

   i. "The Fair Credit Reporting Act (FCRA) imposes a number of obligations on employers that wish to use criminal background checks to screen applicants. This law requires the employer to obtain the applicant's permission before asking a background screening company for a criminal history report, and requires the employer to provide the applicant with a copy of the report and a summary of the applicant's rights before the employer takes an adverse action (such as denying an application for employment) based on information in the criminal history report. For more information: http://www.ftc.gov/bcp/edu/pubs/consumer/credit/cre36.shtm."

   ii. "[T]he Work Opportunity Tax Credit (WOTC) and the Federal Bonding Program (FBP) [are] two incentives to support employers' hiring of individuals with conviction histories. The WOTC provides a credit of 25-40% of first-year wages, or $1,500-$2,400, for employers that hire qualified individuals with felony convictions. For more information: http://www.doleta.gov/wotc. Through the FBP, funded and administered by the U.S. Department of Labor, fidelity insurance bonds are available to reimburse the employer for any loss due to employee theft of money or property, with no employer deductible. For more information: http://www.bonds4jobs.com/index.html."

The TEGL also includes an endnote (Endnote 1) regarding state and local restrictions on employer consideration of arrest and conviction records, as follows:

> "Many states and cities have enacted restrictions on employer consideration of arrest and conviction records. *See, e.g.,* Cal. Lab. Code § 432.7(a); N.Y. Correct. Law §§ 750-755; 18 Pa. Cons. Stat. § 9125; City of Boston Municipal Code 4-7. Covered entities should familiarize themselves with their state and local laws as well. The Department of Labor is aware of the following resources on state and local laws that may be helpful (though the Department cannot guarantee the accuracy of or otherwise endorse these resources): Margaret Colgate Love, *Relief from the Collateral Consequences of a Criminal Conviction: A State-by-State Resource Guide* (June 2008), available at: http://www.sentencingproject.org/detail/publication.cfm?publication_id=115; Selection.com, *State Laws and Their Impact on Use of Criminal Records for Employment Purposes, available at*: www.selection.com/_pdfs/statelaw_criminalchecks.pdf; National Employment Law Project, *Ban the Box: Major U.S. Cities and Counties Adopt Fair Hiring Policies to Remove Unfair Barriers to Employment of People with Criminal Records* (Feb. 6, 2012), available at: nelp.3cdn.net/abddb6b65a14826f92_n5m6bz5bp.pdf."

6. **FILING INSTRUCTIONS:**

Holders of ADM and LEG Binders: File this ADM Notice under the "Other" tab in your Administrative Practices Binder.

District and Area Offices EOSs and EOAs: File this ADM Notice behind the tab for administrative directives in your FCCM Binder.

7. **DISTRIBUTION:** A, B and C electronically.

8. **EXPIRATION DATE:** This directive remains in effect until it is revised or rescinded.

Patricia A. Shiu   1/29/2013

PATRICIA A. SHIU   DATE
Director
Office of Federal Contract Compliance Programs

DIRECTIVE

U.S. DEPARTMENT OF LABOR
Office of Federal Contract Compliance Programs

Number: 307 | Date: February 28, 2013 | ADM Notice/Compensation

1. **SUBJECT**: Procedures for Reviewing Contractor Compensation Systems and Practices

2. **PURPOSE**: To outline the procedures for reviewing contractor compensation systems and practices during a compliance evaluation.

3. **ORIGINATOR**: Division of Program Operations

4. **BACKGROUND**: OFCCP is issuing this Directive in support of its ongoing policy commitment to address pay discrimination by federal contractors and subcontractors. This Directive specifies the procedures OFCCP field investigators use for reviewing contractor compensation systems and practices. It clarifies and improves OFCCP procedures in further support of the agency's efforts to align pay discrimination enforcement with longstanding principles under Title VII of the Civil Rights Act of 1964 (Title VII).

   This Directive is part of a larger assessment of OFCCP's compensation enforcement practices. In 2010, President Obama created the National Equal Pay Task Force, bringing together the Department of Labor (DOL), the Equal Employment Opportunity Commission (EEOC), the Department of Justice, and the Office of Personnel Management to collectively address pay discrimination under their enforcement mandates. The Director of OFCCP, a member of the Task Force, committed OFCCP to review and revise its enforcement guidance and practices to more effectively address compensation discrimination under Executive Order 11246.

   This Directive provides clarity and transparency regarding OFCCP practices for all phases of a compliance review. The Directive sets forth in detail procedures for Compliance Officers (COs) to follow in reviewing contractor compensation systems and practices. In keeping with Title VII principles, COs must be able to use a variety of investigative and analytical tools in conducting evaluations. This Directive provides guidance regarding how to apply OFCCP's case-specific approach to addressing all types of compensation discrimination.

5. **POLICY**: Under Executive Order 11246, as amended, and its implementing regulations, contractors may not discriminate in "rates of pay or other forms of compensation;"[1] and must review and monitor their compensation systems to "determine whether there are

[1] 41 CFR §60-1.4.

gender-, race-, or ethnicity-based disparities."[2] Contractors must maintain records including but not limited to "rates of pay or other terms of compensation."[3] During compliance evaluations, OFCCP requests compensation data and analyzes contractors' compensation systems and practices to determine if discrimination exists and, if so, how to remedy it.

OFCCP enforces Executive Order 11246, including the ban on compensation discrimination, consistent with Title VII's flexible, fact-specific approach to proof. This involves factual investigation, data and legal analyses which allow OFCCP to identify and remedy all forms of compensation discrimination. COs tailor the compensation investigation and analytical procedures to the facts of the case as appropriate under Title VII. This case-by-case approach to compensation discrimination includes the use of a range of investigative and analytical tools. Statistical analyses, such as multiple regression, and non-statistical analyses, such as the use of comparators or cohort analysis, are applied as feasible and appropriate given the factual questions and the available data and evidence. COs seek anecdotal evidence, but will investigate and remedy compensation discrimination regardless of whether individual workers believe they are being underpaid, or whether OFCCP has any anecdotal evidence.

This case-by-case approach is designed to eliminate unnecessary barriers to OFCCP's ability to protect workers from discrimination. It ensures OFCCP fully takes into account explanations or responses from contractors, and that OFCCP conducts an analysis tailored to a contractor's compensation systems and practices. Procedures to facilitate thorough and robust investigations are provided in the sections that follow.

6. **EFFECTIVE DATE**: The investigation procedures established in this Directive apply to all OFCCP reviews scheduled on or after February 28, 2013, and they apply to open reviews to the extent they do not conflict with OFCCP guidance or procedures existing prior to the effective date. Regardless, the 2006 Compensation Standards and Voluntary Guidelines govern determinations regarding the issuance of an NOV for systemic compensation discrimination in any OFCCP review scheduled, opened or otherwise pending on the effective date of this Directive.

7. **DEFINITIONS**: To ensure consistency in implementation, the following terms are defined:

- **Base pay** – Includes only the designated salary or wages for a position or job title. "Non-base pay compensation" also includes all other forms of compensation such as bonuses, commissions, overtime, and perquisites. (See Compensation.)

[2] 41 CFR §60-2.17(b)(3); *see also* 41 CFR §60-2.17(d).

[3] 41 CFR §60-1.12.

- **Cohort Analysis** – A comparison of the treatment of similarly situated individuals or small groups of applicants or employees.

- **Comparators** – Similarly situated employees who are outside of the protected class of the individual to whom they are being compared to determine whether a compensation disparity exists.

- **Compensation** – Includes any payments made to, or on behalf of, an employee as remuneration for employment, including but not limited to salary, wages, overtime pay, shift differentials, commissions, bonuses, vacation and holiday pay, retirement and other benefits, stock options and awards, and profit sharing.

- **Control** – In a statistical analysis of compensation, using controls is a way of accounting for potential explanations of pay differences. For example, controlling for education accounts for the effect of education on any differences in pay.

- **Factors** – Elements which are proposed to explain differences in employee compensation under a contractor's compensation system and practices. Factors may be used as controls in a regression analysis or evaluated in a cohort analysis.

- **Pay Analysis Group** – A group of employees (potentially from multiple job titles, units, categories and/or job groups) who are comparable for purposes of the contractor's pay practices. Regression analysis may be performed on different types of pay analysis groups. A pay analysis group may be limited to a single job or title, or may include multiple distinct units or categories of workers. A pay analysis group may combine employees in different jobs or groups, with statistical controls to ensure that workers are similarly situated.[4]

- **Similarly Situated Employees** – The determination of which employees are similarly situated is case specific. Relevant factors in determining similarity may include tasks performed, skills, effort, level of responsibility, working conditions, job difficulty, minimum qualifications, and other objective factors. Employees are similarly situated where they are comparable on the factors relevant to the investigation, even if they are not comparable on others (see Sections 5 and 6 below).

- **Summary Data** – Compensation data that involves averages or other summaries of worker pay by job title, pay grade, job group, or other category.

- **Systemic Discrimination** – A pattern or practice of discrimination or an identified employment practice with disparate impact. OFCCP defines a systemic discrimination case as meeting one of two criteria: (a) the case addresses a

[4] Statistical testing applied to practices that impact pay such as job assignment may require a different analytic grouping than tests for within job pay differences.

measurable pattern of discrimination (either based on findings from a regression analysis or based on any other appropriate aggregate analysis of compensation data); or (b) the case addresses an identified practice applicable to multiple employees that results in pay discrimination (such as a practice of steering employees who are members of a protected class toward lower paying jobs at hire). There is no specific numeric threshold used to define a systemic case.

8. **PROCEDURES**: When a contractor is scheduled for a compliance evaluation, OFCCP uses the Scheduling Letter to request data and information about the contractor's compensation system and practices. Upon receipt of the data, OFCCP conducts a desk audit. OFCCP may request and review additional compensation data, and conduct an onsite investigation as well as an offsite review of records and data, before making a final determination regarding compliance.[5] During the desk audit and at subsequent stages of the compliance evaluation, the CO should communicate with the contractor, as appropriate, in order to ask clarifying questions about the materials submitted, interpret codes or categories used in the data, identify any missing or incomplete information, and request additional information as needed. The CO should obtain all such information as early in the process as possible.

A. Summary of OFCCP Compensation Investigation Procedures

Below are procedures that the CO follows in reviewing contractor compensation data and information, however it is important to note that the order in which these procedures occur may vary based on the facts and circumstances of each review. At any stage in the process, OFCCP may determine, based on the evidence, that it is appropriate to close the review or may determine that further review is warranted. Generally, the CO:

- Conducts Preliminary Analysis of Summary Data (if necessary or appropriate)
- Conducts an Analysis of Individual Employee-Level Data
- Determines the Approach from a Range of Investigative and Analytical Tools
- Considers All Employment Practices that May Lead to Compensation Disparities
- Develops Pay Analysis Groups
- Investigates Systemic, Small Group and Individual Discrimination

[5] The Paperwork Reduction Act (PRA), 44 U.S.C. Chapter 35, does not apply to this Notice because it does not involve any collection of information subject to the approval of the Office of Management and Budget. To the extent information is collected during the desk audit, it is covered by OFCCP's Scheduling Letter. To the extent information is collected during an OFCCP investigation, it is exempt from the PRA. 5 CFR 1320.4(a)(2) (The PRA does not apply to information collections during an "administrative action, investigation, or audit involving an agency against specific individuals or entities.")

- ➢ Reviews and Tests Factors before Accepting the Factors for Analysis
- ➢ Conducts Onsite Investigation, Offsite Analysis, and Refinement of the Model

Contractors have an opportunity to provide clarification of their submissions and to explain their compensation system and practices. The CO conducts a thorough investigation of all potential compensation discrimination issues and makes a compliance determination.

B. Applying Case-Specific Investigation Protocols

1. Conduct a Preliminary Analysis of Summary Data (if necessary or appropriate)[6]

When OFCCP begins a compliance evaluation with summary compensation data, a CO conducts a preliminary analysis to determine whether to proceed further with the desk audit, including requesting and reviewing individual employee-level data as described in Section 2. A CO may also use the preliminary analysis tools described in this section to assess individual data, by first grouping the data by the contractor's pay ranges or job groups, or may proceed directly to section 2 and analyze the complete individual data. This preliminary analysis, standing alone, is not evidence of discrimination. Results of the preliminary analysis may indicate where further review of compensation data is warranted and assist OFCCP in prioritizing investigative resources.

Prior to conducting a preliminary analysis, the CO reviews the data to make sure it has been provided in the requested format. If a contractor submits summary compensation data based on job groups, titles in those job groups should be consistent with the groupings in the Affirmative Action Plan (AAP). Summary compensation data submitted in a format other than by AAP job group, or the contractor's existing pay grade, level or band system, generally is not acceptable for analysis.

In general, the preliminary analysis assesses quantitative and qualitative factors. Quantitative factors may include:

- The size of the overall average pay difference based on race and gender;
- The size of the largest average pay difference within AAP job groups, or the contactor's existing salary band or pay grade system;
- The number of job groups or grades where average pay differences based on race or gender exceed a certain threshold; or

[6] OFCCP may begin a desk audit with summary compensation data, by pay grades or ranges and by race and gender, at the beginning of a compliance evaluation. When OFCCP receives individual employee-level data at the beginning of a compliance evaluation, a CO may proceed directly to Section 2 or may conduct preliminary analysis of the individual data first.

- The number of employees affected by race-or gender-based average pay differences within job groups or grades.

OFCCP periodically may adjust the size and weight of the factors used for these quantitative comparisons, based on the review of the results of investigations, the results of quality audits, and other factors such as agency resources and priorities.

Qualitative factors may include compliance history, OFCCP or EEOC complaints, anecdotal evidence, potential violations involving other employment practices, or data integrity issues, among others.

Because this preliminary analysis has limited utility for making ultimate determinations of discrimination, OFCCP uses it only to determine whether to continue a compliance evaluation or how to allocate investigative resources. OFCCP does not use preliminary analysis of summary data to limit further compensation data requests or to define the compensation issues OFCCP may pursue in later stages of a compliance evaluation.

After the preliminary analysis, the CO may request that the contractor provide additional information necessary to evaluate compensation issues, including individual compensation data for employees who are covered by the compliance evaluation, other additional data not provided in response to the Scheduling Letter, information regarding the factors used to determine compensation, and information about the contractor's policies and practices related to compensation.

2. Conduct an Analysis of Individual Employee-Level Data

In any case where individual data is provided or requested, the CO uses the data and information in order to understand the contractor's compensation system and practices and to make compliance determinations. The CO may contact the contractor during the initial analysis of the data to ask clarifying questions about the materials submitted, interpret codes or categories used in the data, identify any missing or incomplete information, and request additional information if it is needed.

If complete compensation data and information regarding the contractor's compensation system and practices are not received in response to OFCCP's request, the CO immediately contacts the contractor to secure the information. If the contractor fails to submit requested data or other compensation information in a timely manner, a Show Cause Notice is issued in accordance with OFCCP procedures as specified in the Federal Contract Compliance Manual (FCCM).

Data that the contractor maintains in electronic form must be submitted in a complete, readable and useable electronic form upon request.

After receiving and reviewing the data and information, the CO continues the desk audit applying the investigative framework described below. The CO records all desk audit findings and pending actions to be taken. The results of the desk audit are used to determine whether the evaluation should continue. If at any point during the process of reviewing data and information, the CO determines either that there is evidence of potential compensation discrimination, or that more data or information is needed to make that determination, OFCCP may proceed to an onsite investigation.[7] Closure at desk audit must be consistent with standard OFCCP desk audit procedures.

3. Determine the Approach from a Range of Investigative and Analytical Tools

Investigation of potential compensation discrimination presents complex and nuanced issues. The choice of the best approach for a case depends upon the underlying facts, the available data, and the contractor's compensation system and practices. As such, OFCCP takes a case-by-case approach to analyzing compensation issues.

At the early phase of an evaluation, a CO may conduct a preliminary analysis as described above. As a compliance evaluation moves from the desk audit to an onsite investigation and a final determination regarding compliance, OFCCP reviews and refines the approach in light of information provided by the contractor or developed through the investigation. All final determinations of compliance are based on a rigorous, appropriate and legally sound analysis of the facts and data.

A variety of tools are available for investigating and analyzing compensation issues. There is no single tool that must be used in every case. The use of a particular tool, or combination of tools, depends on the facts of the case. COs determine, in appropriate consultation with their supervisors, OFCCP statistical analysts, and the Regional Solicitors of Labor (RSOL), which investigative or analytical tools are used. Other national office experts and personnel, and the National Office Solicitor of Labor (NSOL), may also be consulted.

In every case there are three key questions to answer:

a. Is there a measurable difference in compensation on the basis of sex, race, or ethnicity?[8]

b. Is the difference in compensation between employees who are comparable under the contractor's wage or salary system?

---

[7] This includes a situation where the compensation information provided at the desk audit does not include individual employee-level data and/or the data is not complete, accurate, readable or useable for analysis.

[8] In situations where there is sufficient data to use regression analysis, a measurable difference generally means a statistically significant difference, two or more standard deviations, consistent with Title VII principles. In the situation of disparities in small group and/or individual compensation, a measurable difference and sufficient evidence will be determined in conformance with Title VII principles (see Section 6 below). Regardless, statistical evidence is not required in all compensation cases; other evidence may be used to evaluate potential discrimination in pay.

c. Is there a legitimate (i.e. nondiscriminatory) explanation for the difference?

Upon finding any compensation disparities (differences), the CO conducts an appropriate factual investigation, and gets assistance with data and legal analyses, to address each of these questions. An investigation may include analysis of workforce data and contractor compensation policies and practices; interviewing personnel and employees; examining payroll and Human Resource Information Systems (HRIS); conducting non-statistical analyses, such as comparative and/or cohort analysis, and statistical analyses, such as regression analysis. Investigations may require consulting with statistical analysts and other experts, and consulting with RSOL and NSOL, as well as examining other relevant information.

4. Consider All Employment Practices that May Lead to Compensation Disparities

In developing an investigation plan at the desk audit phase, and in applying that plan at each step of the compliance evaluation, the CO should examine all employment practices that have the potential to lead to compensation disparities. This covers examination of the compensation system, including base pay and non-base pay data, and other practices as well.

The CO should examine employee access to opportunities affecting compensation, such as: higher paying positions, job classifications, work assignments, training, preferred or higher paid shift work, and other opportunities. The CO should also examine policies and practices that unfairly limit a group's opportunity to earn higher pay, such as "glass ceiling" issues, and access to overtime hours, pay increases, incentive compensation, and higher commission or desired sales territories. The CO may investigate any observed differences in pay, other earnings or benefits, job assignment/placement, training/advancement opportunities, differences in opportunities to increase compensation, or other unexplained differences.

The CO should tailor the approach and tools to be used based on the contractor's compensation practices. Differences may be observed with regard to base pay; job assignment or placement; opportunities to receive training, promotions, and other opportunities for advancement; earnings opportunities; and differences in access to salary increases or add-ons, such as bonuses.

In order to evaluate compensation differences beyond base pay, it may be necessary to make an additional data request regarding the contractor's compensation system and practices or to go onsite.

The CO should consider the nature of the job(s) in question when determining the tools to be used to investigate and analyze the compensation data and information. A commission sales position, for example, is examined differently than an entry-level, hourly rate position. High level professional and managerial positions should be examined to determine if "glass ceiling" issues exist. (See FCCM – Corporate Management Compliance Evaluations.)

The following table contains examples that illustrate differences in employment practices that may lead to compensation disparities warranting review and investigation for potential discrimination:

Type of Difference	Basis for Comparison of Employees	Examples of Differences
Differences in Salary or Hourly Rate	Similar job, different pay	Hispanic customer service agents are paid less than white employees in the same or similar positions due to highly subjective salary system.
Differences in Job Assignment or Placement	Similar qualifications, different job	Women hired into entry-level grocery store positions are disproportionately assigned to the bakery department. Men are assigned to the meat department where pay and promotion opportunities are better.
Differences in Training or Advancement Opportunities	Similar job, different opportunities to increase skills	Employees may participate in a management training program on a recommendation by a manager. Certain managers are referring only white males resulting in disproportionate participation. Resulting promotions to management positions are disproportionately awarded to white males.
Differences in Earnings Opportunities	Similar job, different earnings	African-American sales workers are disproportionately assigned to territories with less potential.
Differences in Access to Increases and Add-Ons	Similar job, different opportunities to increase pay	Female lawyers who get exactly the same base pay as male counterparts earn less on annual bonuses.

5. Develop Pay Analysis Groups

At this stage, the CO has reviewed the data and information submitted by the contractor. The next step in the analysis, if the data allow, is to develop pay analysis groups that are used to test for statistical significance on large groups of employees. The analysis may be based on groups that are larger than individual job titles and AAP job groups. By combining employees into appropriate pay analysis groups, using statistical controls as necessary for title or level, OFCCP is able to more easily identify potential systemic discrimination needing further investigation and potential remedy. Individual or cohort comparisons may be conducted, as warranted, as shown in Section 6. If the data allow, OFCCP analyzes pay disparities based on protected class status that cannot be explained by neutral job-related factors, e.g., identifying potential placement or classification issues for further investigation.

Analytical Model – The CO determines the pay analysis groups to be used in the analytical model, consulting as needed with their supervisors, the statistical analysts and RSOL. (COs may make preliminary determinations that are then refined with the assistance of the statistical analysts and RSOL). A pay analysis group is a group of employees (potentially from multiple job titles, units, categories and/or job groups) who are comparable for purposes of the contractor's pay practices. Regression analysis may be performed on different types of pay analysis groups. A pay analysis group may be limited to a single job or title, or may include multiple distinct units or categories of workers. A pay analysis group may combine employees in different jobs or groups, with statistical controls to ensure that workers are similarly situated. Statistical testing applied to practices that impact pay such as job assignment may require a different analytic grouping than tests for within job pay differences.

OFCCP develops pay analysis groups by considering elements such as: the particular industry, the types of jobs and compensation at issue, the contractor's actual compensation practices, and available data. Compensation practices may differ by role (e.g., executives, managers, supervisors and individual contributors), by level (with higher-level employees tending to receive additional or alternate forms of compensation), by function (such as sales employees who are paid on commission), by unit (department, division, location, etc.) and/or by job classification (exempt or non-exempt, part-time or full-time, bargaining unit, etc.). This information may be found through a review of the contractor's compensation policies or training documents, description of its compensation system or practices, compensation data, records and coding, job descriptions, and interviews. COs may consider other facts relevant to determining groups, such as the ability of workers to rotate or transfer among different positions within a business unit, a common hiring or selection process, a common performance review practice or other common identifiable employment practice related to compensation.

Initially, the CO combines jobs into appropriate larger pay analysis groups, which may include multiple job titles or units, that are comparable for purposes of the contractor's compensation practices. The combination of job titles or jobs is based on what the CO knows of the contractor's compensation system and its practices. Where a combination of job titles or jobs at multiple levels is used, it may be appropriate to statistically control for title and level within the pay analysis group. The size and definition of a group, and whether to include title or level as a control in the analysis, depends on available data and evidence and the compensation practices being analyzed. Reasonable differences may exist among workers in a pay analysis group as long as these differences are properly accounted for in the statistical analysis to be conducted. OFCCP conducts regression analysis on the pay analysis groups to determine whether statistically significant disparities in compensation exist.

The CO also develops pay analysis groups that evaluate broader pay differences based on protected class status that cannot be explained by neutral job-related factors, e.g., assignment, placement or classification issues. Statistical testing for practices that impact compensation such as job assignment may require a different pay analysis group than tests for within job compensation differences.

The analytical model developed by the team (OFCCP investigators, statistical analysts, and RSOL) is used to initially test large pay analysis groups. As the results of the initial analysis and facts warrant, OFCCP refines the analysis, based on pre- or post-onsite information, and OFCCP may conduct subsequent statistical and/or non-statistical tests of smaller groups or individuals.

If possible, the CO develops and applies the model to the data at the desk audit phase, using preliminary determinations regarding appropriate pay analysis groups. If the CO needs more data or information to develop the groups, or conduct or refine the analysis, the CO may proceed to an onsite investigation before performing the analysis. If it is not possible to form pay analysis groups or perform a regression analysis at the desk audit phase, the CO also may use preliminary tests or broad indicators of potential compensation issues at the desk audit to identify pay practices or issues needing further review. As a compliance evaluation moves from a desk audit to an onsite investigation and a final determination regarding compliance, COs review and refine the approach, including the determination of the appropriate pay analysis groups, in light of further information provided by the contractor or developed through the investigation.

6. Investigate Systemic, Small Group and Individual Discrimination

The CO investigates possible systemic, small group and individual compensation discrimination as indicated by the initial analysis of the compensation data and information (see illustration below). Pay analysis groups are developed to examine possible systemic issues. Systemic discrimination may be a pattern or practice of discrimination or an identified employment practice with adverse impact. When the CO completes the analysis of larger pay analysis groups, or in cases where the data are inappropriate or insufficient for regression analysis, the CO may examine the data to address possible compensation discrimination involving specific job titles, particular units or locations.

After analyzing the data for potential discrimination in larger and/or smaller pay analysis groups, the CO may conduct comparative analyses of small groups or individuals to determine if pay disparities exist, and if there is evidence sufficient to support an inference that pay differences are due to discrimination.

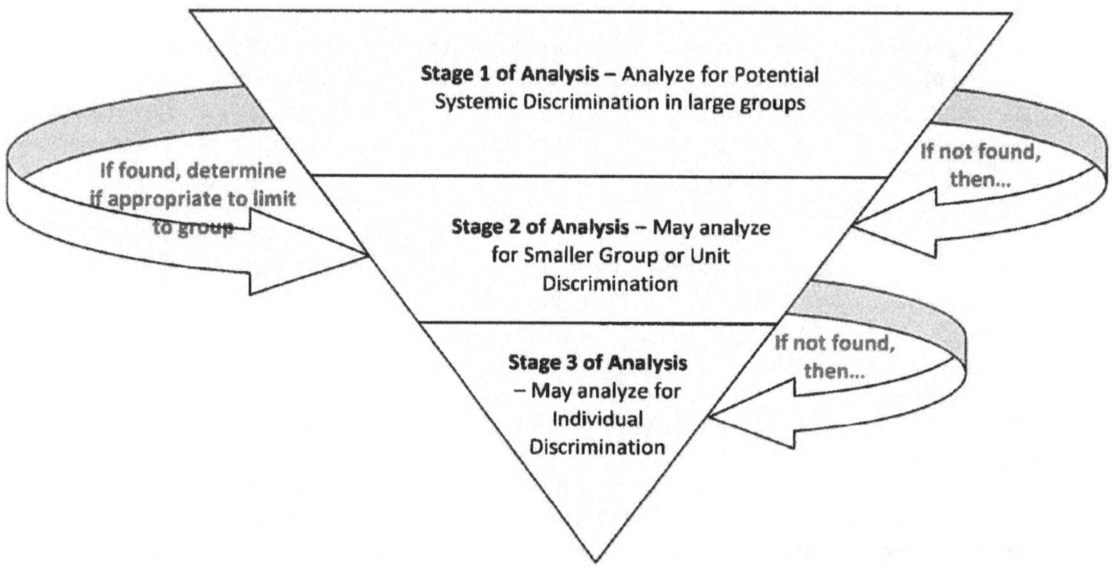

The mere fact that there are pay differences between comparators, without any other evidence of pretext or other indicia of possible discrimination, generally is not sufficient to find a violation of E.O. 11246. Individual or small group pay disparities typically are analyzed under the disparate treatment theory of discrimination.

In conducting a small group or individual analysis, the CO starts by determining if there are similarly situated employees who are comparable to the affected small group or individual. The CO then conducts a comparative analysis, or cohort analysis, to examine the treatment of similarly situated individuals or groups of applicants or employees.

The determination of who is similarly situated is case-specific. Who is similarly situated for purposes of an individual analysis or review of a single specific employment decision may be determined based on different criteria than when conducting a systemic discrimination analysis. For purposes of evaluating compensation differences, employees are similarly situated where it is reasonable to expect they should be receiving equivalent compensation absent discrimination. Relevant factors in determining similarity may include tasks performed, skills, effort, level of responsibility, working conditions, job difficulty, minimum qualifications, and other objective factors. In some cases, employees are similarly situated where they are comparable on some of these factors, even if they are not similar on others. For example, when evaluating a job assignment issue, workers are similarly situated when their qualifications are comparable, but they are assigned to jobs at different levels.

In conducting a comparative analysis, it is also necessary to obtain data and information specific to the individuals or small groups that are being compared. If the contractor has not already provided such information, the CO requests the relevant available information. This information may include applications, personnel files, performance ratings, compensation histories, etc. The CO may determine that an onsite investigation is necessary to fully examine any potential discrimination issue.

7. Review and Test Factors before Accepting the Factors for Analysis

The CO evaluates information from the contractor regarding the factors the contractor considered in making compensation decisions. As in any investigation, the CO must evaluate whether the factors are implemented fairly, consistently applied, and relevant to the contractor's compensation practices before accepting them as appropriate for inclusion in the analytical model and/or comparative analysis. OFCCP considers all relevant factors offered by the contractor to determine whether these factors, in conjunction with other legitimate factors, if any, actually explain pay, are implemented fairly and consistently applied, and whether they should be incorporated into a statistical analysis, on a case by case basis.

A factor is an element that the contractor offers to explain differences in employee compensation under its compensation system and practices. A factor may be a qualification or skill that the worker brings to the position such as education, experience, etc. It may also be an employment element such as position, level or function, tenure in position, performance ratings, etc.

When using factors as controls in a regression analysis, the statistical analyst tests the factors to make certain they are predictive for pay and that the factors are not potentially tainted by discrimination.[9] The statistical analysts and OFCCP investigators work together, and consult with RSOL as needed, to determine what factors to include in the final analytical model. When conducting a comparative analysis, the CO likewise evaluates factors offered by the contractor as to their relevance to compensation and whether they were consistently applied.

In testing the offered factors, the CO first determines if the data are complete and accurate. Second, the CO determines if the factor is relevant to compensation in terms of

[9] Where statistical testing identifies evidence that a factor results in adverse impact, further investigation may be needed to determine whether it is appropriate to incorporate it into the model.

the contractor's policy and how it was applied. Third, the CO determines whether the factor was consistently applied by the contractor. Fourth, the CO determines whether using the factor presents adverse impact issues.

Where identified employment practices such as performance review systems show disparities, COs should proceed to review for potential evidence regarding whether the practices result in disparate treatment or disparate impact – including inquiring about evidence of validation and/or the existence of best practices to reduce adverse impact.[10]

In addition to analyzing data regarding the offered factors, the CO should review policy statements and other documentation addressing how the factors are considered. When conducting an onsite investigation, the CO should conduct interviews with contractor staff and employees to verify how the factors were applied in making compensation decisions, and document the results consistent with the FCCM and other OFCCP procedures.

8. Conduct Onsite Investigation, Offsite Analysis, and Refinement of the Model

Upon completing the previous steps, the OFCCP investigators, statistical analysts, and RSOL decide on a preliminary analytical model having considered all available and relevant information regarding the contractor's compensation system and practices. At this stage, the contractor is given an opportunity to timely provide any additional relevant information to be considered. If that additional information adequately resolves or explains the disparities, consistent with the framework set forth above, the CO concludes the investigation. Otherwise, if an onsite has not yet been conducted, the CO determines whether an onsite is needed.[11]

The CO informs the contractor in writing of the onsite visit. The CO identifies and requests any needed data and information consistent with OFCCP procedures. The CO also discusses the need for interviews with contractor staff members and employees. Any information obtained as a result of the onsite visit and interviews is examined to determine whether the analytical model needs to be refined. For example, data and information obtained during interviews confirms that a factor offered by the contractor to explain a disparity in pay was not consistently applied and resulted in a disparity affecting women. The team refines the model based on the finding that the factor is not a legitimate predictor of pay and should not be incorporated in the statistical analysis.

[10] Relevant questions may include whether rating criteria have been confirmed to be job-related, whether raters are trained and participate in calibration sessions, whether multiple raters are used, whether there is any higher level review of ratings, whether analysis of ratings by race, sex, and ethnicity is done and whether there is an appeals process in place.

[11] The determination of whether an onsite visit will be conducted will be made consistent with the FCCM and other applicable OFCCP procedures (including Directive Number 295, Active Case Enforcement procedures, December 16, 2010).

Refinements to the analytical model and/or determinations of the need to conduct additional comparative analyses are made in accordance with this guidance and Title VII principles. The CO consults with their supervisors, OFCCP statistical analysts and RSOL, as appropriate, before making any refinements to the analytical model to be used. All appropriate analyses are conducted and the findings evaluated.

C. Concluding the Review and Analyses:

Upon completion of the compliance evaluation OFCCP determines whether there are findings of compensation discrimination.

Based on complete and thorough factual investigation and data analysis, and appropriate assistance with legal and statistical analysts from RSOL and National Office statisticians, OFCCP takes the action(s) the findings warrant. The CO evaluates all available evidence before making a determination regarding contractor compliance. Generally, because a compliance evaluation also includes the investigation of other types of possible discrimination (e.g., hiring, terminations, promotions) any findings of compensation discrimination are addressed along with the other findings. Action may include closure of the compensation issue if no violations are found, or issuance of a Notice of Violation (NOV), as appropriate. At this stage of the compliance evaluation, the CO documents all findings.

9. **CONFIDENTIALITY OF INFORMATION**: The Freedom of Information Act (FOIA), 5 U.S.C. 552, applies to all information/data submitted pursuant to this Directive. Upon receipt of a FOIA request, OFCCP evaluates all information submitted by contractors pursuant to the public inspection and disclosure provisions of FOIA and the Department of Labor's implementing regulations at 29 CFR Part 70. OFCCP requires that a contractor affected by a FOIA disclosure request is notified in writing and no decision to disclose information is made until the contractor has an opportunity to submit objections to the release of the information. Moreover, OFCCP does not release data obtained during the course of a compliance evaluation until the investigation, and all subsequent proceedings, if any, are complete.

At 41 CFR § 60-1.20(f), the regulation provides in part that if the contractor is concerned with the confidentiality of information such as lists of employee names, reasons for termination, or pay data, then alphabetic or numeric coding or the use of an index of pay and pay ranges, consistent with the ranges assigned to each job group, are acceptable for purposes of the compliance evaluation. Regardless, the contractor must provide full access to all relevant data pursuant to 41 CFR 1.20(a)(1) and § 60-1.43.

10. **INTERPRETATION**: This Directive does not create new legal rights or requirements or change current legal rights or requirements for contractors. Executive Order 11246, as amended, Section 503 of the Rehabilitation Act of 1973, as amended, the Vietnam Era Veterans' Readjustment Assistance Act of 1974, as amended, OFCCP's regulations at 41

CFR Chapter 60, and applicable case law are the official sources for contractors' compliance responsibilities. Nothing in this Directive is intended to change otherwise applicable laws, regulations or other guidance or to restrict or limit OFCCP's ability to perform compliance reviews, request data, or pursue enforcement of any issue within its jurisdiction. .

11. **FILING INSTRUCTIONS**:

Holders of ADM and LEG Binders: File this Directive in your Administrative Practices Binder.

District and Area Offices EOSs and EOAs: File this Directive behind the tab for ADM Directives in your FCCM Binder.

12. **DISTRIBUTION**: A, B (both hard copy **and** electronically); C (hard copy only).

13. **EXPIRATION DATE**: This Directive remains in effect until OFCCP determines it needs to be revised or rescinded.

14. **SIGNATURE**:

Patricia A. Shiu

PATRICIA A. SHIU
Director
Office of Federal Contract Compliance Programs

DIRECTIVE

U.S. DEPARTMENT OF LABOR
Office of Federal Contract Compliance Programs

Number: 310 Date: July 17, 2013 ADM Notice

1. **SUBJECT:** Calculating Back Pay as a Part of Make-Whole Relief for Victims of Employment Discrimination

2. **PURPOSE:** To provide guidance on calculating back pay as a part of make whole relief for victims of employment discrimination when using formula or individual relief models.

3. **EFFECTIVE DATE:** This directive is effective immediately.

4. **BACKGROUND:** OFCCP seeks back pay to remedy discrimination violations for aggrieved individuals pursuant to Executive Order 11246 (EO 11246), Section 503 of the Rehabilitation Act of 1973, as amended, 29 U.S.C. § 793 (Section 503), and the Vietnam Era Veterans' Readjustment Assistance Act of 1974, as amended, 38 U.S.C. § 4212 (VEVRAA). Upon a finding of discrimination, OFCCP seeks to obtain back pay, in addition to other appropriate make-whole remedies[1], for the victim(s) of the discrimination. Back pay serves to remedy lost earnings that the victim(s) would have received absent the discrimination. There are two distinct models for calculating back pay relief - formula relief and individual relief. This directive explains when each of these models is appropriate to use and the relevant elements, pursuant to each model, when calculating back pay.

   OFCCP follows the principles and case law derived from Title VII of the Civil Rights Act of 1964 (Title VII) in awarding back pay to aggrieved individuals under the laws it enforces. Executive Order 11246's implementing regulations at 41 CFR 60-1.26(a)(2) state in part, "OFCCP may seek back pay and other make whole relief for victims of discrimination identified during a complaint investigation or compliance evaluation." Section 503's implementing regulations at 41 CFR 60-741.65(a)(1), and VEVRAA's implementing regulations at 41 CFR 60-250.65(a)(1) and 60-300.65(a)(1) also provide that OFCCP may seek back pay as part of make whole relief for victims of discrimination. Each of these OFCCP regulations also provides that interest on back pay is calculated from the date of the loss (*i.e.*, the start date of the discriminatory act) and compounded quarterly at

[1] Although not specifically discussed in this Directive, other monetary relief, such as front pay or salary adjustments, may also be available in particular cases. In addition, a wide array of non-monetary relief may be sought by OFCCP for the victims of discrimination, *e.g.*, preferential hiring, preferential promotions, special training programs, reasonable accommodation, systemic injunctive relief, and EEO counseling for supervisors, in addition to awarding back pay.

the percentage rate established by the U.S. Internal Revenue Service (IRS) for the underpayment of taxes.

The U.S. Supreme Court, in *Albemarle Paper Co. v. Moody*, 422 U.S. 405, 418(1975), states that one of the purposes of Title VII is "... to make persons whole for injuries suffered on account of unlawful employment discrimination." The Court also states that" ... given a finding of unlawful discrimination, back pay should be denied only for reasons which, if applied generally, would not frustrate the central statutory purposes of eradicating discrimination throughout the economy and making persons whole for injuries suffered through past discrimination." *Id.* at 421. In light of this standard, back pay is generally sought as a remedy in all cases, both individual and class, where employment discrimination results in a loss of compensation for victims of discrimination.

OFCCP's reliance on Title VII back pay principles has been upheld by the Administrative Review Board (ARB). Specifically, in the EO 11246 case of *OFCCP, U.S. Department of Labor v. Greenwood Mills, Inc.,* ARB Case Nos. 00-044, 01-089, ALJ Case No. 89-OFC-039 (ARB Final Decision and Order December 20, 2002), the ARB held that the covered government contractor discriminated in hiring on the basis of sex, and found that the formula relief model used in Title VII cases was appropriate for computing relief. Following the legal standard set out in *Albemarle,* the ARB found that back pay, as one element of make whole relief, was to be awarded to the victims of discrimination. Similarly, the ARB has applied Title VII back pay principles in the individual relief context. In *OFCCP v. The Cleveland Clinic Foundation*, ARB Case No.1991-OFC-20, ALJ Case No. 91-OFC-20 (ARB Final Decision and Order July 17, 1996) , the ARB held that the contractor discriminated on the basis race, and relied on Title VII principles when awarding back pay to the two victims.

5. DEFINITIONS:

Attrition Rate – The rate at which employees are expected to leave the establishment from one period to the next.

Back Pay – Total lost earnings due to a contractor's discriminatory employment action, practice or procedure. Lost earnings include but are not limited to: compensation or salary, overtime, premium pay and shift differentials, incentive pay, raises, bonuses, lost sales commissions, cost-of-living increases, tips, medical and life insurance, fringe benefits, and pensions, stock awards and options.

Formula Relief – As used in this Directive, a method used in systemic discrimination cases for calculating a total amount of the back pay for an affected class of discrimination victims, that is then divided (pro rata or otherwise) among all the members of that class who are eligible, successfully identified, and agree to participate in the settlement. In appropriate circumstances, formula relief may also be used to assess other types of class relief for discrimination victims.

Individual relief - Also referred to as victim-specific relief, individual relief is the assessment of make-whole relief for identified victim(s) of discrimination on an individualized basis. This method is generally used to calculate back pay in those individual or small group discrimination cases where the victims of discrimination, and the damages they incurred, can be determined with specificity.

Interim Earnings – The amount a victim earns from substitute employment during the liability period. Generally speaking, victims of discrimination who are not current employees (*i.e.*, victims of hiring or termination discrimination) have a duty to use reasonable diligence to seek substitute employment. Under formula relief, back pay awards can be reduced by an appropriate estimate of the amount that could have been earned by the victims of discrimination with reasonable diligence, less expenses reasonably incurred in looking for alternative employment. Under individual relief, back pay awards are reduced by the amount the victim actually earned during the liability period, or by the amount the individual would have earned with reasonable diligence. Under either approach, the contractor has the burden of proof.

Make-Whole Relief - Remedy for discrimination that restores the victim of discrimination to his or her rightful place, *i.e.*, the position, both economically and in terms of employment status, that he/she would have occupied if the discrimination had not taken place. Common elements of make-whole relief include an award of the position the individual was wrongly denied, back pay with interest and retroactive seniority.

Mitigation – Used in cases involving discrimination where the victims are not current employees (*i.e.*, discrimination in hiring or terminations), this refers to the duty of victims to lessen their losses during the liability period. Under the individual relief model, for example, the aggrieved individual must use reasonable diligence to seek alternative employment during the liability period. The earnings from such employment will be deducted from the total amount of back pay awarded to the aggrieved individual (*see* "Interim Earnings," above). Under the formula relief model, mitigation of the amount of losses can be estimated by appropriate evidence of actual or assumed interim earnings to reduce the overall back pay awarded to the class of victims. For example, the contractor may seek to apply a minimum wage rate presumed to have been earned during the liability period to reduce the overall back pay that is awarded to the class of victims, after accounting for an estimated period of unemployment. Mitigation, either for individuals or a class, is an affirmative defense that must be raised and proven by the contractor, not OFCCP.

Pay Additions – Elements of compensation other than salary and wages (e.g. pay from shift differentials, incentive pay, bonuses)

Shortfall – The difference between the actual number of persons in the non-favored group that were selected for the employment opportunity at issue (hires, promotions, etc.) and the number expected to have been selected in proportion to their representation in the pool of qualified candidates, absent discrimination. This concept does not generally apply to compensation discrimination cases,

6. POLICY:

This directive identifies basic principles applicable to the use of the formula and individual relief models for the calculation of back pay as a remedy for discrimination. The directive indicates when it is appropriate to use formula relief or individual relief and the elements that should be considered in making this determination. In each instance, OFCCP makes the decision as to which model is used in determining relief in a specific case, not the contractor. The directive also provides guidance on calculating back pay, including addressing mitigation when raised as a defense by the contractor, depending on the model used.

BASIC PRINCIPLES:

- Generally, in keeping with the *Albemarle* standard, an award of back pay will be sought as a part of the make whole relief awarded to victims of employment discrimination whenever the discrimination results in a loss of compensation or benefits for the aggrieved individual(s).

- Provided that the federal contract is in effect when the discrimination occurred, back pay generally can be obtained for a period up to two (2) years prior to the date of receipt of the scheduling letter (or for a complaint, up to two (2) years prior to the date the complaint is filed). Back pay continues from the date of violation forward until the discriminatory action(s) are stopped by the contractor, or stopped by means of a Conciliation Agreement, Consent Decree, or Final Court/Administrative Order. In any event, back pay calculations will follow longstanding OFCCP principles regarding the circumstances under which discrimination is a continuing violation under the Executive Order (*see* FCCM Chapter 7).

- The elements used to calculate back pay in individual relief cases should not be interchanged with the elements used to calculate back pay in cases utilizing formula relief.

- In hiring and termination discrimination cases, interest on back pay is calculated on the adjusted back pay calculation after mitigation.[2] Interest on the overall back pay award is then compounded on a quarterly basis at the percentage rate established by the IRS for the underpayment of taxes. The current rate may be found at http://www.irs.gov/pub/irs-drop/rr-12-16.pdf.

- Benefits that are a part of the back pay award are not assumed to be subject to mitigation, absent specific evidence the victims of discrimination obtained these benefits.

- A contractor will be in violation of Executive Order 11246 any time it pays wages, benefits, or other compensation that is the result in whole or in part from the application of any discriminatory compensation decision or other practice. This means back pay calculations in compensation cases should remedy any discriminatory pay differences existing during the two years prior to the review forward to the present, or otherwise determined consistent with Title VII principles regarding the so-called Paycheck Rule and continuing violation theory.

7. PROCEDURES:

A. Formula Relief

1. When to Use Formula Relief Model

   The determination of when to use the formula relief model to calculate back pay is made on a case-by-case basis. Formula relief is a way of approximating losses in circumstances in which it is unrealistic to attempt to compute individual losses with accuracy.[3] Circumstances that indicate that formula relief is appropriate include, but are not limited to:

   a. When calculating individual back pay relief for numerous aggrieved individuals is difficult because complete information or documentation (*i.e.*, timecards, payroll records, tax returns) is unavailable or missing;

   b. When using the individual relief model to calculate back pay for each class member will likely cause significant delay or create an undue burden

[2] Because mitigation generally does not apply to cases involving current employees (*e.g.*, compensation discrimination, discrimination in promotions, etc.), back pay is not similarly adjusted before the calculation of interest.

[3] In addition to calculating the total losses for the class, formula principles can be used for distribution of back pay to class members. Under formula relief OFCCP may equally divide the total back pay award among all of the identified class members, which amounts to a pro-rata share of back pay that each class member receives as a remedy. However, OFCCP may also decide to use more individualized calculations for purposes of distribution, as explained in Section 6.A.7 below.

on individual class members to provide documentation to support their compensation and/or interim earnings ;

c. When the number of class members exceeds the number of employment opportunities that are available;

d. When the reconstruction of the employment decision is speculative (*e.g.*, in the instance when there are no lines of progression), which makes it difficult for the CO to determine at what specific stage in the employment process the adverse action actually occurred, or any other situation in which (especially for jobs with few minimum qualifications) it would be impossible to determine which class members would have been hired absent discrimination; and/or

e. When the losses can be calculated on a class-wide basis from available data, as may be the case with compensation issues.

2. <u>Identifying Victims</u>

If the formula relief model will be used to calculate back pay, the class of potential victims must be identified. Having identified a discrimination violation(s), the CO should also identify: (1) the time period (liability period) in which the discrimination occurred; (2) that there was a federal contract/subcontract in effect during the liability period; (3) the nature of the violation(s); and (4) the class of persons (non-favored group(s)) that were discriminated against and entitled to relief. In formula relief cases, OFCCP will include all individuals who meet the case-specific criteria of potential victims, without requiring evidence they were specifically discriminated against. Depending upon the nature of the violation, the employment opportunity that was denied to the class members may have been a position in a specific job, promotion, transfer, etc., or may be a systemic difference in pay for a class or category of employees. Detailed information regarding the position or employment opportunity at issue must be obtained in order to identify the victims and calculate lost earnings.

3. <u>Calculating Lost Earnings</u>

a. General Principles

The next step is to calculate lost earnings. The CO should account for all of the earnings attributable to the employment opportunity at issue. Lost earnings include but are not limited to: wages, salary or other compensation, overtime, premium pay, incentive pay, raises, bonuses, lost sales commissions, cost-of living increases, tips, medical and life insurance, any other fringe benefits, pensions and the value of stock awards or options. This information may be found in payroll records, written policies, manuals,

Internet information about the company, employee handbooks, collective bargaining agreements, and/or obtained during interviews with employees and managers.

When using the formula relief model, the earnings may need to be adjusted or averaged to approximate the loss. For example, in determining overtime hours that may have been worked, an average of overtime hours worked by the employees in the position at issue during the liability period should be used. Similarly, an average of shift differential added to earnings may be applied as a proportional percentage because only a portion of the employees in the position at issue may have received shift differential. Any pay increases or promotions among the comparator class during the time period at issue should also be accounted for. Estimates of the monetary value of benefits can be based on specific data or calculated as a percentage of wages/salary if more specific data is not available or is too cumbersome or complex. To calculate lost benefits, the CO should examine information about when the benefits become effective (*e.g.*, whether there is a waiting period for eligibility) as well as the monetary value of the benefits.

Once the liability period is identified (usually when the scope of the violation is identified), the CO will use this time period for calculating back pay. The CO must determine that the start date for the back pay period is not outside of the contract coverage period. Back pay can be obtained for a period beginning up to two (2) years prior to the date of the scheduling letter. However, the discriminatory act(s) may have taken place less than two years before the scheduling letter is sent. Back pay is due starting from the date of the violation forward until the discriminatory action(s) is ended by the contractor or stopped as a result of a signed Conciliation Agreement, Consent Decree, or Final Court/Administrative Order. Thus, although the start date used in calculating back pay cannot be outside of the federal contract coverage period, the end date used in calculating back pay can be a date beyond the federal contract coverage period.[4]

b. Presumption of Continuous Employment in Hiring Cases

Generally, under Title VII, back pay calculations run from the date of injury until the injury is remedied by the employer either through voluntary action,

[4] If the final resolution takes place after the end of the contract coverage period, back pay for the discrimination that happened during the contract and appropriate interest will continue to accrue until the date of remedy; however there will be no back pay liability for any employment practice occurring after the end date of contract coverage. For example, in a hiring case, the back pay for individuals denied employment during the contract coverage period will continue to run until remedied, but there is no back pay due for jobs denied after the end of contract coverage. In a compensation case, back pay will remedy pay differences existing during the period of coverage, and interest on those losses will continue to accrue until remedy, but back pay will not include the effect of any pay decisions occurring after the end of contract coverage.

settlement or a court judgment. This is consistent with the principle of make-whole relief. In hiring cases, workers are entitled to a presumption of continuous employment that runs through the end date of potential back pay liability. *See EEOC v. Dial Corp.*, 469 F.3d 735 (8th Cir. 2006). However, the presumption may be overcome if the employer provides sufficient evidence that the victims of discrimination would not have worked for this entire period. *OFCCP v. Greenwood Mills,* ARB Nos. 00-044 and 01-089, ALJ No. 1989-OFC-39 (ARB Dec. 20, 2002); *Lawrence Aviation Industries, Inc., v. Reich,* No. 98-6219, 1999 WL 494870, at **1-2 (2d Cir. July 6, 1999).

OFCCP will follow that presumption when considering the expected tenure of workers who were not hired due to discrimination, such as in making calculations of predicted attrition to reduce the total back pay due to a class. A contractor may seek to establish by specific evidence that the presumption should be overcome in a particular case, but the contractor has the burden of proof on this issue.

The accepted practice in systemic cases is to consider the projected effect of attrition on the total losses, without artificially limiting the total liability period. *See Pegues v. Mississippi State Employment Service,* 899 F.2d 1449, 1452 (5th Cir.1990); *United States v. City of New York,* 2012 WL 745560, * 21 (E.D.N.Y. Mar. 8, 2012); *Sledge v. J.P. Stevens & Co.,* 1989 WL 90562, *9 (E.D.N.C Feb. 23, 1989). For example, if data shows that 10% of the workforce left in the first year, and 5% in the second year, a shortfall of 20 would be reduced to 18 at the end of the first year and 17 at the end of the second year for purposes of calculating the lost earnings.

The evidence that a contractor must provide in order to meet its burden of proof and rebut the presumption of continued employment will vary depending on the facts of the specific case. Circumstances that will generally justify overcoming the presumption and limiting or discounting the back pay losses include situations such as:

- a mass work stoppage or layoff that eliminated the positions at issue;
- specific evidence demonstrating that a significant number of affected applicants left the workforce or became ineligible for the positions; or
- Rapid and widespread attrition of actual hires where the presumption would clearly overestimate losses even taking all inferences in favor of the victims of discrimination.

However, even in these cases, OFCCP must investigate the facts asserted by the contractor to determine if it is appropriate to discount back pay losses by projected attrition rates, and will resolve all uncertainties regarding future employment in favor of the victims of discrimination. For instance, in a sex discrimination case, if there is any evidence that a mass layoff or a high attrition rate was motivated by discrimination or the contractor's desire to minimize back pay relief, it would not be appropriate to limit the back pay losses. Similarly, where most workers hired into the position remained employed, overcoming the presumption would be much more difficult than in a case where most workers had left.

OFCCP generally will not accept simple estimates of generalized attrition to limit the back pay liability period until it has investigated the facts behind the data provided and determined that an attrition factor is appropriate. Among the issues compliance officers should consider are:

- For the individuals who were hired for the position in question and subsequently were terminated what was the reason for the termination? If certain individuals were terminated for cause, it may be appropriate to exclude them from the tenure data; otherwise, affected applicants are in effect penalized for the bad actions of someone in the favored group.

- For hired individuals who resigned or were terminated, what is the potential for future employment, rehire, or future increases? If there is evidence that individuals are readily able to return (or, better yet, have returned) to the workplace after a resignation/termination, it may not be appropriate to use attrition data that does not factor in that possibility.

Compliance officers working through these issues are encouraged to reach out to SOL and the National Office Labor Economist early in the process for further guidance on the best approach to take for a given case and how to apply these principles in specific cases.

c. Methods of Calculation

Generally, there are two methods that may be used to structure the back pay calculation for the formula relief method. After the CO determines that the formula relief method is appropriate (see 6.A.1 above), the CO must then determine whether the shortfall or an averaging method will be used.

Shortfall Method: Where job opportunities were at issue, such as hiring, termination, or promotion cases, and the number of victims in the class exceeds the total number of opportunities, the "shortfall vacancies" approach is generally used for computing the amount of back pay attributable to the class. Shortfall is the difference between the actual number of persons in the non-favored group that were selected for the employment opportunity at issue and the number expected to have been selected in proportion to their representation in the pool of qualified candidates, absent discrimination.

Example: 100 individuals apply for one of 20 vacancies for a specific job title. Fifty (50) of the applicants are male and fifty (50) of the applicants are female. All of the applicants meet the required qualifications. However, due to discrimination, 19 of the hires are male, and only 1 is female.

- Expected number of hires: 10 males, 10 females
- Actual number of hires: 19 males, 1 female
- Shortfall: 9 (10 expected female hires minus 1 actual hire)

After calculating the total earnings associated with each position (considering starting pay, hours worked, all increases and pay additions, overtime, benefits, bonuses, or any other applicable aspects of compensation), OFCCP will multiply that amount by the shortfall to generate the back pay losses as a whole. For instance, in the above example, if the lost earnings for each position was $100,000, the monetary relief for the entire class of victims would be $900,000. Shortfall vacancies do not limit the number of individuals entitled to relief.

Averaging Method: The averaging method (formula) may be used in cases where the calculations are based on the number of victims of discrimination, rather than on the number of positions at issue. (*i.e.,* to remedy compensation discrimination, certain types of placement or glass ceiling cases, etc.). The formula should be designed to address the particular violation that was found. For example, if the violation is one of sex segregated departments, the CO may compare the average salary of the men at a given level of seniority to the average salary of the women with the same seniority. The difference in the average salaries defines the measure of back pay to be awarded to each woman in the seniority group.

To remedy compensation violations, it may be appropriate to use the regression model used to establish liability to calculate back pay losses for the class as a whole. In that case, the CO would still use an average or typical estimate of the pay disparities to determine the total losses for the class, but the regression analysis allows OFCCP to use a more sophisticated form of averaging. The National Office Labor Economist and other experts can provide assistance in performing these calculations in particular cases..[5]

Where a contractor has provided only a "snapshot" of compensation data for a single year, losses for prior or subsequent years can be estimated by projecting those differences backward or forward in time, but it is preferable to obtain compensation data for those years and calculate the actual pay differences in each year if possible. Where contractors provide reliable evidence showing

[5] It is generally not appropriate to use individual predicted salaries to establish class-wide losses..

that losses for those years decreased or were eliminated OFCCP will adjust its estimates accordingly.

4. Mitigation (Interim Earnings) as a Defense

   Mitigation refers to the duty of the victim(s) of hiring or termination discrimination to use reasonable diligence to seek alternative employment during the back pay period. Back pay awards can be reduced by the amount the victim(s) could have earned with reasonable diligence (interim earnings), \ less expenses reasonably incurred in looking for alternative employment (*e.g.*, cost to prepare a resume, gas and parking fees incurred when going for an interview). Reasonable diligence does not mean that the victim(s) had to be successful in obtaining other employment, only that he/she is required to make a reasonable effort. Victims are required only to accept employment that is substantially equivalent to or the same as that sought or held with the contractor. It is the contractor's burden to show that with such diligence the victims were reasonably likely to have found comparable employment. The victims need not take any employment position simply to retain their back pay awards. Nor are the victims required to relocate to accept alternative employment.[6]

   The contractor has the burden of proving the amount of interim earnings. In formula relief cases, the average interim earnings provided by the contractor as mitigation should be reviewed by the CO in every case, and accepted in those cases where OFCCP deems the evidence sufficient. The CO should examine the identified source of the interim earnings and the time period identified by the contractor in order to ensure that only appropriate earnings are included in the mitigation computation. Specifically, unemployment, workers compensation, pension, Social Security, and/or other public assistance benefit payments received by the aggrieved individual do not constitute interim earnings and should not be deducted from the aggrieved individual's back pay award. Similarly, employment that is not a substitute for employment with the contractor should not be considered as interim earnings. Such a situation could be a class member that worked both a full-time and part-time job, and could have continued the part-time job even in the absence of the discrimination. Evidence class members could have obtained temporary employment ,without the same benefits or long term prospects as permanent employment, is not evidence that carries the contractor burden on mitigation. Further, OFCCP will generally not rely solely on reported application data such as last known wage, without evidence applicants actually obtained or continued alternate employment at that rate.

[6] Periods when the victim would not have been employed even absent discrimination are excluded from the back pay award (*e.g.*, during periods of incarceration).

Finally, contractors seeking to apply a mitigation rate above minimum wage should provide case-specific evidence that class members obtained or should have obtained higher paying employment with reasonable diligence.

When it is determined that there is sufficient evidence to support mitigation for interim earnings, the back pay computation will include a deduction for the appropriate mitigation wage(s) and time period(s).

5. Unemployment Period

For purposes of making its initial back pay calculations in formula relief hiring cases, OFCCP will assume a period of unemployment for all applicants, regardless of whether they were employed at the time of application, unless there is reliable evidence applicants actually continued employment after applying.[7] Generally, OFCCP will rely on national or state-level data on the average unemployment weeks for workers in the protected group. A common source for this data is the Bureau of Labor Statistic's Current Population Survey available at http://www.bls.gov/cps/tables.htm#charunem. Depending on the facts of the case, OFCCP will choose the unemployment data based on industry, occupation, geography, and/or specific gender or ethnicity groups. Contractors may then attempt to rebut these assumptions with evidence pertaining to applicants' employment, and OFCCP may subsequently amend its back pay calculations depending on the probative weight of this evidence.

Due to the fact that many unemployed persons may not be receiving or eligible for unemployment insurance, OFCCP will not use state unemployment insurance payment data to measure the length of the unemployment period.

6. Computation of Interest

After computing total back pay and deducting appropriate mitigation, the CO must compute interest on the total back pay amount. Once interest is calculated by the CO, then the interest is added to the total back pay amount. The purpose of applying interest on back pay awards is to compensate the victim(s) for the loss of the use of his/her money. Interest on back pay is to be calculated at the same percentage rate as the IRS underpayment formula and is required to be compounded quarterly under the laws OFCCP enforces. (See 41 CFR 60-1.26(a)(2) (EO 11246); 41 CFR 60-250.65(a)(1), and 60-300.65(a)(1) (VEVRAA or Section 4212); and 41 CFR 60-741.65(a)(1) (Section 503)).

[7] Indicators of employment status on applications are not generally sufficient unless specifically and individually verified.

The IRS may adjust this rate on a quarterly basis. The interest rates applicable to various time periods are issued by the IRS and available on the IRS website at http://www.irs.gov/pub/irs-drop/rr-12-16.pdf.

7. Taxes

Generally OFCCP calculates back pay without regard to applicable FICA or other taxes. In OFCCP settlements, contractors are obligated to pay their share of all applicable taxes on the portion of back pay that is calculated and identified as wages, on top of the identified settlement amount. Contractors are obligated to withhold the employee share of Social Security, Medicare and any other applicable taxes, and to provide W-2 forms to each class member indicating taxes paid and withheld. [8] Since employer contributions to most fringe benefits, such as the employer paid portion of health insurance premiums or pension funds, are not taxable (whether retroactive or not), they are not subject to withholding.

Interest included in a settlement, if separately stated, is not subject to deductions for FICA (Social Security and Medicare) or FUTA (unemployment insurance) taxes. Contractors should provide 1099 forms to each class member for any portion of the settlement designated as interest.

COs should work with the Regional Solicitor's office to ensure conciliation agreements handle any tax issues appropriately including accounting for portions subject to W-2 withholding and portions subject to 1099 reporting.

8. Distribution of Remedy

When using the formula approach, the agreed upon remedy is shared by all identified members of the class eligible and agreeing to participate in the settlement. The CO divides the amount of money that represents the group's lost wages among the members of the class either on a pro rata basis or some other equitable basis. The CO, in consultation with his/her supervisor and the National Office Labor Economist, may decide on a method of distribution based upon the facts of the case. It may be appropriate to award back pay in equal amounts to each member of the class of victims or to apportion the back pay award to identified victims or groups of victims depending on the specific factual findings and the type of issues presented. In making this determination, the CO should consider whether there is a factual basis for providing a larger or smaller share to certain individuals as well as the statistical distribution of earnings.

[8] When computing back pay awards, the CO should not offset or deduct for FUTA unless the particular State where the victim was, or would have been employed, requires employers to withhold FUTA taxes from employee wages during the time period for which the back pay is being computed.

For example, where the CO has identified an incumbent class which was denied promotions or assigned to lower paying jobs, a distribution based on the number of months since the denial of the promotion or the number of months in the contractor's workforce might be appropriate.

B. Individual Relief

1. When to Use the Individual Relief Model

The determination of when to use the individual relief model to calculate back pay is made on a case-by-case basis. Generally, OFCCP will use the individual relief model when it has identified a single victim of discrimination, or a small group (*e.g.*, fewer than 5 members in the class). The individual or victim-specific model provides make-whole relief for each identified victim(s) of discrimination. Unlike the formula relief model, the individual relief model is used whenever it is feasible to identify individual victims of discrimination and it is feasible to calculate their individual economic losses. The two models for calculating back pay should not be interchanged. The CO should consider the circumstances that affect the determination to use individual relief, including, but not limited to:

a. The total class size is small (*e.g.*, fewer than 5 members);

b. The liability period is of short duration (*e.g.*, fewer than six months); and/or

c. The economic losses for each individual victim can be traced and supported with documentation.

2. Identifying Victims

Once it has been determined that the individual relief model is to be used to determine monetary relief, the class of individual victims must be identified. Having identified a discrimination violation(s), the CO will have identified the time period (liability period) in which the discrimination occurred, that there was a federal contract/subcontract in effect during the liability period, the nature of the violation, and identified the class of victims (non-favored group) that were discriminated against and entitled to relief. Once the individual victims are appropriately identified as entitled to relief, a precise back pay remedy should be tailored to the situation of each victim.[9]

[9] Although this directive is focused solely on the calculation of back pay only, the CO should also consider all of the different types of harm that the victim has suffered and all of the types of available remedies, including non-monetary relief (*e.g.*, appropriate injunctive relief), in fashioning a complete make-whole remedy.

3. Calculating Lost Earnings

The CO will determine the precise remedy to which each victim is entitled. The CO should gather the information needed to compute each individual's specific economic losses depending on the nature of the violation (*e.g.*, failure to hire, wrongful termination, failure to promote, failure to pay the appropriate salary rate, etc.). This information will include, but is not limited to, wages for the position, appropriate interim raises or step increases in pay, promotion potential (*i.e.*, the earnings associated with all of the promotions the person would have received had the discrimination not occurred), any overtime, any appropriate shift differential, and the value of employee benefits. The CO may obtain this information from a variety of sources, including payroll records, written policies, internet information about the company, employee handbooks, collective bargaining agreements, or during interviews with employees and managers.

One common way to reconstruct the pay a victim of discrimination is due is to identify similarly situated employees/applicants that were not discriminated against (*i.e.*, members of the favored group) for comparison to the affected members of the non-favored group. Proper comparators are those who were hired, promoted, etc., at about the same time the victim(s) of the discrimination should have been hired, promoted, etc., had discrimination not occurred. The CO will then trace the comparators' pay history by examining wage information. If there are gaps in the comparators' employment during the back pay period (*e.g.*, the comparators quit, had a lengthy illness, etc.), a reasonable estimate of the amount of wages the comparators would have made absent the break in service should be made (or, alternatively, if there are no payroll records for a given comparator for a period of time because of illness, it may be appropriate to exclude that comparator for that period of time).

Additionally, to calculate lost benefits to the victim(s), the CO should examine information about when the benefits became effective (*e.g.*, whether there is a waiting period for eligibility) and the monetary value of the benefits. Benefits can be calculated as a monetary figure (*e.g.*, employer contributions into a 401(K) retirement account, plus any interest on those retirement earnings that would have accrued if those contributions were in the employee's 401(K) retirement account); or as a percentage of wages/salary (*e.g.*, 20 percent of total compensation package). This is a fact-specific determination for the CO when applying the appropriate percentage of benefits towards the total back pay amount.

As noted in the discussion regarding formula relief, the CO will use the liability period as the time period for calculating back pay. (See section 6.A.3 above)

4. Mitigation (Interim Earnings) as a Defense in Hiring/Termination Discrimination Cases

Finally, the CO must consider appropriate deductions to the back pay award in anticipation of the contractor raising mitigation as a defense, which can occur under either formula relief or individual relief.

As previously stated, mitigation refers to the duty of victims of hiring or termination discrimination to use reasonable diligence in seeking alternative employment during the back pay period. Back pay awards are reduced by the amount the victim could have earned with reasonable diligence, less expenses reasonably incurred in looking for alternative employment (*e.g.*, cost to prepare a resume, gas and parking fees incurred when going for an interview). The victim is required only to accept employment that is substantially equivalent to or the same as that sought or held with the contractor. It is the contractor's burden to show that with such diligence the victim was reasonably likely to have found comparable employment. The victim need not take any employment position simply to retain his/her back pay award. Nor is the victim required to relocate to accept alternative employment.[10]

The contractor may assert as a defense that the victim failed to take reasonable steps to mitigate back pay losses. The CO must examine this assertion considering that reasonable diligence does not mean the victim had to be successful in obtaining other employment, only that he/she is required to make a reasonable effort. Evidence relevant to the due diligence issue include interview statements by the victim that they applied for jobs, but were unsuccessful, copies of job applications filed with employers, and copies of rejection letters from employers, during the back pay period. If the victim made a reasonable effort to mitigate their losses, but failed to obtain alternate employment, then no deduction should be made to the back pay award. If the individual actually obtained other employment during the liability period (whether or not it was equivalent), than the amount of those interim earnings is deducted from the amount of the back pay award.[11]

[10] Periods when the victim would not have been employed even absent discrimination are excluded from the back pay award (*e.g.*, during periods of incarceration).

[11] If the contractor shows that comparable employment would likely have been obtainable had the victim used reasonable diligence to mitigate their losses, but the victim did not make such a reasonable effort, then the amount of interim earnings that the victim could have earned had the victim used due diligence should be deducted from the back pay award. In this scenario, it is the contractor who must prove the amount of interim earnings that could have been earned.

5. Computation of Interest

Like the formula relief model, the CO must compute interest on the total back pay amount (*i.e.*, total earnings for the liability period, less appropriate deductions and interim earnings). Interest on back pay is to be calculated at the same percentage rate as the IRS underpayment formula and is required to be compounded quarterly under the laws OFCCP enforces. (See 41 CFR 60-1.26(a)(2) (EO 11246); 41 CFR 60-250.65(a)(1), and 60-300.65(a)(1) (VEVRAA or Section 4212); and 41 CFR 60-741.65(a)(1) (Section 503)).

6. Taxes

Contractors are responsible for paying the employer share of applicable taxes on top of any calculated settlement amount, and for providing appropriate tax withholding and reporting as explained above under Formula Relief.

8. **FILING INSTRUCTIONS**:

Holders of ADM and LEG Binders: File this ADM Notice under the "Other" tab in your Administrative Practices Binder.

District and Area Offices EOSs and EOAs: File this ADM Notice behind the tab for administrative directives in your FCCM Binder.

9. **DISTRIBUTION**: Electronically; A, B and C.

10. **EXPIRATION DATE**: This directive remains in effect until it is revised or rescinded.

Patricia A. Shiu

PATRICIA A. SHIU
Director
Office of Federal Contract Compliance Programs

July 17, 2013
DATE

DIRECTIVE (DIR) 2014- 01
Directives (DIRs) provide guidance to OFCCP staff or federal contractors on enforcement and compliance policy or procedures. Directives do not change the laws and regulations governing OFCCP's programs and do not establish any legally enforceable rights or obligations.
Effective Date: May 7, 2014

1. **SUBJECT:** TRICARE Subcontractor Enforcement Activities

2. **PURPOSE:** To establish a five-year moratorium on enforcement of the affirmative obligations required of TRICARE subcontractors and to provide outreach and technical assistance.

3. **REFERENCES:** None.

4. **AFFECTED POLICY:** None.

5. **BACKGROUND:** The Office of Federal Contract Compliance Programs (OFCCP) enforces Executive Order (E.O.) 11246, as amended, Section 503 of the Rehabilitation Act of 1973 (Section 503), as amended, and the Vietnam Era Veterans' Readjustment Assistance Act of 1974 (VEVRAA), as amended. Collectively, these laws prohibit federal contractors and subcontractors from discriminating on the basis of race, color, religion, sex, national origin, and status as a qualified individual with a disability or protected veteran. They also require federal contractors and subcontractors to take affirmative steps to ensure equal employment opportunity in their employment processes. In addition, these laws require that federal contracting agencies include in all covered contracts, and that contractors include in their subcontracts, an equal opportunity clause. For a definition of the terms "government contract," "subcontract," "prime contractor," and "subcontractor" see 41 C.F.R. § 60-1.3 (E.O. 11246); 41 C.F.R. § 60-300.2 (VEVRAA); and 41 C.F.R. § 60-741.2 (Section 503). The authority to administer these laws, and to promulgate these regulations, rests solely with the Secretary of Labor.

   Recent events have brought to OFCCP's attention that there has been a difference in understanding between the Department of Labor and some entities affiliated with the TRICARE community, as to who is a covered subcontractor under the laws enforced by OFCCP. In light of this confusion regarding who is covered and what obligations the TRICARE subcontractor community has under the laws enforced by OFCCP, the agency is issuing this Directive. The Directive establishes a five-year moratorium on enforcement of the affirmative obligations required of all TRICARE subcontractors. During the moratorium period, OFCCP will engage in outreach and technical assistance to provide greater clarity for the TRICARE subcontractor community about their obligations under the laws administered by OFCCP. In addition, the agency will work with other federal agencies to clarify the coverage of health care providers under federal statutes applicable to subcontractors.

6. **ROLES AND RESPONSIBILITIES:** To the extent that there are any open compliance evaluations of TRICARE subcontractors covered by the moratorium as described below in Section (7)(a), OFCCP will administratively close those cases within 30 business days of the effective date of this directive. OFCCP issued its most recent scheduling list on January 24, 2014. Since this moratorium will be implemented subsequent to the issuance of that list and the previous scheduling list, dated March 2013, a TRICARE subcontractor establishment may receive an Office of Management and Budget (OMB)-approved OFCCP scheduling letter requesting an Affirmative Action Program (AAP) and supporting data. Should this occur, the TRICARE subcontractor covered by the moratorium shall send to its local OFCCP office a written request that the compliance evaluation be administratively closed with a copy of its agreement to participate in the TRICARE program. If a TRICARE subcontractor covered by the moratorium has received advance notification of scheduling through an OFCCP Corporate Scheduling Announcement Letter (CSAL), the subcontractor should not contact OFCCP. Instead, the subcontractor should wait to receive the OMB-approved OFCCP scheduling letter before it contacts the local OFCCP office to request that the compliance evaluation be administratively closed. A list of OFCCP's local offices may be found at: *http://www.dol.gov/ofccp/contacts/ofnation2.htm.*

If during the course of his or her work, a Compliance Officer (CO) discovers that a TRICARE subcontractor has inadvertently been scheduled for review during the duration of this moratorium, the CO will administratively close the compliance evaluation through OFCCP's normal administrative closure procedure by submitting a request to the National Office for approval to administratively close the compliance evaluation.

7. **POLICY:** Through the exercise of prosecutorial discretion, over the next five years, OFCCP will limit its enforcement activities of TRICARE subcontractors while it engages in extensive outreach and technical assistance to inform TRICARE participants of their responsibilities under OFCCP's programs. In addition, during this time, OFCCP will work with other federal agencies to clarify the principles governing coverage of health-care providers under federal statutes applicable to contractors and subcontractors.

a. Who Is Covered? The five-year enforcement moratorium applies to all health-care entities that participate in TRICARE as subcontractors under a prime contract between the Department of Defense (DoD) TRICARE Management Activity and one of the prime managed-care contractors, including:
   i. Health-care entities that participate in TRICARE only as subcontractors;
   ii. Health-care entities that participate in TRICARE as subcontractors *and* as subcontractors under any Medicare program;
   iii. Health-care entities that participate in TRICARE as subcontractors *and* as subcontractors under the Federal Employee Health Benefits Program (FEHBP); and
   iv. Health-care entities that participate in TRICARE as subcontractors *and* as subcontractors under any other federal health program.

b. Who is Not Covered? This moratorium does not apply to health-care entities that participate in TRICARE as subcontractors *and* who are holders of prime contracts with an agency of the federal government. Similarly, this moratorium does not extend to TRICARE subcontractors that hold a separate, independent non-health-care-related federal subcontract.

c. Scope of the Enforcement Moratorium: Except for investigation of discrimination complaints, OFCCP is hereby establishing a five-year moratorium on enforcement of all obligations under E.O. 11246, Section 503, and VEVRAA effective from the date of the issuance of this Directive, including enforcement of obligations related to affirmative action programs and recordkeeping, for TRICARE subcontractors as defined in Section 7(a) above. The moratorium does not apply to the processing of complaints of discrimination under 41 CFR 60-1.24; 41 CFR 60-300.61 and 41 CFR 60-741.61. This moratorium does not extend to any obligations a TRICARE subcontractor may have under other federal nondiscrimination laws, including Title VII of the Civil Rights Act of 1964, as amended (42 U.S.C. 2000e *et seq.*) and the Americans with Disabilities Act of 1990, as amended (42 U.S.C. 12101 *et seq.*).

   Upon notice by OFCCP to a TRICARE subcontractor that a complaint of discrimination against the subcontractor has been filed with OFCCP, that subcontractor must retain the following records in its possession until the final disposition of the complaint or any lawsuit or proceeding based on the complaint: 1) personnel or employment records relating to the issues under investigation as a result of the complaint, including all personnel and employment records related to the complainant or other persons alleged to be aggrieved and to all other employees holding or seeking positions similar to that held or sought by the affected individual(s); and 2) all personnel and employment records related to application of the employment practice that is the subject of the complaint, e.g., a pre-employment test or reasonable accommodation practices. Failure to preserve complete and accurate records following the notification that a complaint has been filed will constitute noncompliance with E.O. 11246, Section 503, or VEVRAA, as applicable. Moreover, where the subcontractor has failed to preserve records after notification of a complaint, there may be a presumption that the information destroyed or not preserved would have been unfavorable to the subcontractor. 41 CFR 60-1.12(e); 41 CFR 60-300.80(c); and 41 CFR 60-741.80(c). Further, pursuant to 41 CFR 60-1.43, 41 CFR 60-300.81, and 41 CFR 60-741.81, TRICARE subcontractors must provide OFCCP with access to records and their place of business for the purpose of conducting the complaint investigation, including: inspecting and copying documents, conducting interviews of employees and managers and viewing the workplace.

d. Outreach and Technical Assistance: During the five-year moratorium, OFCCP will provide extensive technical assistance on compliance with the affirmative action obligations under E.O. 11246, Section 503, and VEVRAA. Among other things, OFCCP will:

   i. Provide information, materials, and technical assistance training to TRICARE subcontractors on how to develop cost effective affirmative action plans and recordkeeping and applicant tracking systems;

ii. Conduct regional and national webinars that cover OFCCP's legal authorities, jurisdiction, and federal contractor and subcontractor obligations; and

iii. Convene listening sessions to learn about the unique issues facing TRICARE subcontractors in order to provide relevant and targeted technical assistance under all of OFCCP's legal authorities.

e. Notification of Compliance Assistance Opportunities for TRICARE Subcontractors. If you are a subcontractor under the TRICARE program, please e-mail OFCCP at *OFCCP-Public@dol.gov* to ensure that you receive notification about upcoming technical assistance and training events. In addition, you are encouraged to visit OFCCP's website at *www.dol.gov/ofccp* for additional information about OFCCP, the laws it enforces, technical assistance materials, and upcoming events.

8. ATTACHMENTS: None.

____

Patricia A. Shiu
Director
Office of Federal Contract Compliance Programs

OFFICE OF FEDERAL CONTRACT COMPLIANCE PROGRAMS
OFCCP
U.S. DEPARTMENT OF LABOR

DIRECTIVE (DIR) 2014-02

Directives (DIRs) provide guidance to OFCCP staff or federal contractors on enforcement and compliance policy or procedures. Directives do not change the laws and regulations governing OFCCP's programs and do not establish any legally enforceable rights or obligations.

Effective Date: August 19, 2014

1. SUBJECT: Gender Identity and Sex Discrimination

2. PURPOSE: To clarify that existing agency guidance on discrimination on the basis of sex under Executive Order 11246, as amended, includes discrimination on the bases of gender identity and transgender status.

3. REFERENCES: *Macy v. Holder*, Appeal No. 0120120821, 2012 WL 1435995 (EEOC) (2012), *also available at* http://www.eeoc.gov/decisions/0120120821%20Macy%20v%20DOJ%20ATF.txt (last accessed August 12, 2014), *on remand*, DOJ Final Agency Decision, Agency Complaint No. ATF-2011-00751, DJ No. 187-9-149 (July 8, 2013).

4. AFFECTED POLICY:

   A. 41 CFR § 60-1.1; 60-1.4(a)(1); 60-1.4(b)(1); 60-1.8; 60-1.10; 60-1.20(a); 60-3.1 – 60-3.18; and 60-20.1 – 60-20.6.
   B. Federal Contract Compliance Manual (FCCM) § 1F05; 2H; 2J05; 2L02; 2L03; 3A; 3H03; 3H04; 3I03; 3J; 3L; 6E03; 6E04; 6E06; and 6E10.

5. BACKGROUND: As the Secretary of the U.S. Department of Labor (DOL) has said:

   > Our workforce and our entire economy are strongest when we embrace diversity to its fullest, and that means opening doors of opportunity to everyone and recognizing that the American Dream excludes no one.[1]

   Consistent with this statement, on June 30, 2014, the Secretary announced that DOL is updating its enforcement protocols and nondiscrimination guidance to clarify that DOL provides the full protection of the federal nondiscrimination laws that it enforces to individuals on the bases of gender identity and transgender status. This directive is, therefore, issued to clarify the Office of Federal Contract Compliance Programs' (OFCCP) interpretation of the nondiscrimination obligation.

[1] Secretary Thomas Perez, U.S. Department of Labor, Work in Progress: The Official Blog of the U.S. Department of Labor, Justice and Identity, http://social.dol.gov/blog/justice-and-identity/ (June 30, 2014) (last accessed August 12, 2014).

OFCCP enforces Executive Order 11246, as amended, a law that prohibits federal contractors and subcontractors from discriminating on the basis of race, color, religion, sex, or national origin.[2] OFCCP interprets the nondiscrimination obligations under Executive Order 11246 in accordance with Title VII of the Civil Rights Act of 1964, 42 U.S.C. 2000e *et seq.* (Title VII), which prohibits employers from discriminating on the same protected bases.[3] This means that OFCCP enforces the nondiscrimination obligations under Executive Order 11246 by following Title VII and the case law principles that have developed interpreting that statute. Additionally, since the Equal Employment Opportunity Commission (EEOC) is the lead federal agency responsible for administering and enforcing Title VII, pursuant to Executive Order 12067, OFCCP generally defers to the EEOC's interpretations of Title VII law.

Under current Title VII case law principles, discrimination based on gender identity or transgender status, as defined below, is discrimination based on sex. In its decision in *Macy v. Holder*, 2012 WL 1435995, the EEOC unanimously concluded that discrimination because a person is transgender is sex discrimination in violation of Title VII. The complainant in *Macy,* a transgender woman working as a police detective, alleged that she was denied a job with the Bureau of Alcohol, Tobacco, Firearms and Explosives (ATF) when she informed the ATF that she was in the process of transitioning from male to female. The EEOC concluded that discrimination on these grounds was discrimination "on the basis of sex," citing both the text of Title VII and multiple federal court decisions interpreting the statute.

First, the EEOC identified sex stereotyping as one way in which a transgender employee, job applicant, or former employee[4] could prove sex discrimination. Specifically, disparate treatment of a transgender employee because he or she does not conform to the gender stereotypes associated with his or her biological sex is a form of sex discrimination—a theory frequently upheld by federal courts.[5] The EEOC noted that

---

[2] Executive Order 11246 was amended by Executive Order 13672, effective July 21, 2014, to add sexual orientation and gender identity to the list of categories protected from discrimination. E.O. 13672 will apply to contracts entered into on or after the effective date of the implementing regulations.

[3] *See* OFCCP, FCCM § 2H01 (July 2013), *available at* http://www.dol.gov/ofccp/regs/compliance/fccm/FCCM_FINAL_508c.pdf (last accessed August 12, 2014); *see also OFCCP v. Honeywell*, 77-OFC-3, Sec'y of Labor Dec. and Order on Mediation, June 2, 1993, at 14 and 16 & Sec'y of Labor Dec. and Remand Order, March 2, 1994; *OFCCP v. Illinois Institute of Technology*, 80-OFC-11, Sec'y Final Order, December 23, 1982; *OFCCP v. Firestone*, 80-OFC-15, Sec'y Dec., July 13, 1980, *rev'd on other grounds*, *Firestone v. Marshall*, 507 F. Supp. 1330 (E.D. Tex. 1981).

[4] Hereafter, this Directive uses the term "employee" to refer to applicants for employment and current and former employees.

[5] Among the cases the EEOC relied on were *Glenn v. Brumby*, 663 F.3d 1312 (11th Cir. 2011) (termination of a transgender employee constituted discrimination on the basis of gender non-conformity and sex-stereotyping discrimination under Equal Protection Clause); *Barnes v. City of Cincinnati,* 401 F.3d 729 (6th Cir. 2005) (affirming jury instructions allowing a claim for sex discrimination under Title VII as sex stereotyping in favor of a transgender woman), and *Smith v. City of Salem*, 378 F.3d 566, 574 (6th Cir. 2004) ("discrimination against a plaintiff who is a transsexual – and therefore fails to act and/or identify with his or her gender – is no different from the discrimination directed against [the plaintiff] in *Price Waterhouse* [*v. Hopkins,* 490 U.S. 228 (1989),] who, in sex-stereotypical

Title VII prohibits discrimination based on gender, which "encompasses not only a person's biological sex but also the cultural and social aspects associated with masculinity and femininity." *Macy*, 2012 WL 1435995 at *6.

The EEOC explained that treating a person differently because the person is transgender is by definition sex discrimination because it is "related to the sex of the victim" in violation of Title VII.[6] This is true regardless of whether the discrimination was motivated by sex stereotyping or by some other reason related to the employee's gender identity, such as discomfort with the idea of a transition. The EEOC additionally noted that Ms. Macy would have had a claim of sex discrimination if the employer was willing to hire her when he thought she was a man, but was not willing to hire her once he found out that she was a woman.

The EEOC, therefore, concluded that gender identity and transgender status did not need to be specifically addressed in Title VII in order to be protected bases of discrimination, as they are simply part of the protected category of "sex" under Title VII.[7]

Consistent with *Macy* and the Title VII case law on which it is based, this directive deals with discrimination on the basis of gender identity only as a form of sex discrimination. It does not address gender identity as a stand-alone protected category, which (along with sexual orientation) is the subject of Executive Order 13672. As noted above, Executive Order 13672 amends Executive Order 11246 effective immediately, and will apply to contracts entered into on or after the effective date of the implementing regulations.

---

terms, did not act like a woman"). In addition to these appellate cases, "[t]here has likewise been a steady stream of district court decisions recognizing that discrimination against transsexuals on the basis of sex stereotyping constitutes discrimination because of sex." *Macy*, 2012 WL 1435995 at *9.

[6] *See also Schroer v. Billington*, 577 F. Supp.2d 293, 308 (D. D.C. 2008) (finding the defendant's "refusal to hire Schroer after being advised that she planned to change her anatomical sex by undergoing sex reassignment surgery was *literally* discrimination 'because of . . . sex'") (emphasis in the original).

[7] See also EEOC, "Clarification of processing complaints of transgender individuals added to Title VII/ Section 1614 Claims of Sex Discrimination by LGBT Employees," *available at* http://www.eeoc.gov/federal/directives/lgbt_complaint_processing.cfm (last accessed August 12, 2014). The EEOC's decision also aligns with a number of federal agencies' interpretations of sex discrimination and gender identity under the civil rights statutes that they enforce. See Department of Education, Questions and Answers on Title IX and Sexual Violence (April 29, 2014), *available at* http://www2.ed.gov/about/offices/list/ocr/docs/qa-201404-title-ix.pdf (last accessed August 12, 2014), p. 5 (interpreting Title IX's sex discrimination prohibition as "extend[ing] to claims of discrimination based on gender identity or failure to conform to stereotypical notions of masculinity or femininity"); OPM, "Nondiscrimination Provisions-Proposed Rule," 78 Fed. Reg. 54434 (September 4, 2013) (proposing to amend various nondiscrimination sections appearing in 5 C.F.R. to categorize gender identity discrimination as a form of sex discrimination); Department of Health and Human Services, "Request for Information Regarding Nondiscrimination in Certain Health Programs and Activities," 78 Fed. Reg. 46558, 46559 (August 1, 2013) (including gender identity as "sex discrimination" under Section 1557 of the Affordable Care Act).

6. ROLES AND RESPONSIBILITIES: It is the responsibility of compliance officers (COs) to conduct complaint investigations and compliance evaluations related to transgender status and gender identity in accordance with this directive.

7. POLICY: In accordance with *Macy v. Holder* and the Title VII case law on which it is based, OFCCP continues to fully investigate and seek to remedy instances of sex discrimination that occur because of an employee's gender identity or transgender status. OFCCP continues to accept and investigate individual and systemic complaints alleging sex discrimination against transgender employees. In the case of individual allegations of gender identity discrimination, and pursuant to the Memorandum of Understanding between EEOC and OFCCP,[8] OFCCP will request that it initially retain such complaints to ensure effective enforcement of this Directive. OFCCP continues to seek to remedy any findings of sex discrimination against transgender employees that are discovered by OFCCP compliance officers during scheduled compliance evaluations of federal contractors or subcontractors. When investigating whether a federal contractor or subcontractor discriminated against an employee because of his or her gender identity, the agency continues to adhere to the existing Title VII framework for proving sex discrimination, as outlined in the FCCM.

8. ATTACHMENTS: None.

Patricia A. Shiu
Director
Office of Federal Contract Compliance Programs

[8] **EEOC-OFCCP Memorandum of Understanding, §7(c) (November 9, 2011), *available at* http://www.eeoc.gov/laws/mous/eeoc_ofccp.cfm (last accessed August 12, 2014).**

OFCCP

DIRECTIVE (DIR) 2015-01

A Directive (DIR) is intended to provide guidance to OFCCP staff or federal contractors on enforcement and compliance policy or procedures. A DIR does not change the laws and regulations governing OFCCP's programs and does not establish any legally enforceable rights or obligations.

Effective Date: April 16, 2015

1. **SUBJECT:** Handling individual and systemic sexual orientation and gender identity discrimination complaints.

2. **PURPOSE:** To establish OFCCP's policy on accepting and investigating individual and systemic complaints based on gender identity or sexual orientation.

3. **REFERENCES:**

   A. Executive Order 11246 of September 24, 1965, Equal Employment Opportunity, as amended, at http://www.dol.gov/ofccp/regs/statutes/eo11246.htm (last checked April 3, 2015).

   B. Executive Order 13672 of July 21, 2014, Further Amendments to Executive Order 11478, Equal Employment Opportunity in the Federal Government, and Executive Order 11246, Equal Employment Opportunity, 79 FR 42971 (July 23, 2014).

   C. Implementation of Executive Order 13672 Prohibiting Discrimination Based on Sexual Orientation and Gender Identity by Contractors and Subcontractors, 79 FR 72985 (Dec. 9, 2014).

   D. Processing of Matters, 41 CFR 60-1.24(a).

   E. Gender Identity and Sex Discrimination, DIR. 2014-02 (August 19, 2014), available at http://www.dol.gov/ofccp/regs/compliance/directives/dirindex.htm (last checked April 3, 2015).

   F. Federal Contract Compliance Manual (FCCM) § 6B, Bases of Complaint Allegations, (October 2014).

4. **AFFECTED POLICY:** This directive takes effect on April 16, 2015, and will remain in effect until rescinded by the Director of OFCCP. This supersedes Federal Contract Compliance Manual (FCCM) § 6B (October 2014) and other guidance to the extent that they may be inconsistent with this directive.

5. **BACKGROUND:** OFCCP enforces Executive Order (EO) 11246, as amended, which prohibits federal contractors and subcontractors from discriminating on the basis of race, color, religion, sex, sexual orientation, gender identity, or national origin. OFCCP applies Title VII principles and applicable case law when investigating potential violations of EO 11246. Sexual orientation and gender identity were expressly added to the categories

protected from discrimination under EO 11246 on July 21, 2014, with the signing of EO 13672.[1] The Final Rule implementing EO 13672 became effective on April 8, 2015.[2]

Title VII of the Civil Rights Act of 1964, 42 U.S.C. 2000e et seq. (Title VII), does not expressly cover sexual orientation and gender identity. While violations of EO 11246 may be discovered during compliance evaluations, discrimination based on sexual orientation and gender identity may most often be found through the investigation of discrimination complaints. Therefore, this guidance is issued to clarify that OFCCP will accept and investigate individual and systemic complaints of discrimination based on sexual orientation and gender identity under Executive Order 11246, as amended, applying Title VII principles and case law, as appropriate. A determination about the handling of a complaint, once accepted, is made on a case-by-case basis. These complaints may also contain a Title VII allegation of discrimination based on sex.[3] However, not all courts have conclusively established that sex discrimination is equivalent to discrimination based on sexual orientation or gender identity.[4]

Compliance officers or others responsible for complaint processing usually make referrals of individual complaints to EEOC pursuant to OFCCP's regulation at 41 CFR 60-1.24(a). This provision permits, but does not require, OFCCP to make referrals to EEOC for processing under Title VII. Yet, with the signing of EO 13672, the President gave OFCCP explicit executive authority to ensure that federal contractors and subcontractors treat applicants and employees without regard to their sexual orientation or gender identity.

Considering both the express protections conferred by EO 13672, the authority provided by OFCCP's existing provisions to retain or refer individual complaints, and the protections developed in case law under Title VII sex discrimination theory, OFCCP will continue to coordinate and share information with EEOC to the maximum extent possible to remedy

[1] Executive Order 13672 of July 21, 2014, Further Amendments to Executive Order 11478, Equal Employment Opportunity in the Federal Government, and Executive Order 11246, Equal Employment Opportunity, 79 FR 42971 (July 23, 2014).

[2] On December 9, 2014, OFCCP published the Final Rule in the *Federal Register* revising the regulations to implement EO 13672. *See,* Implementation of Executive Order 13672 Prohibiting Discrimination Based on Sexual Orientation and Gender Identity by Contractors and Subcontractors, 79 FR 72985 (Dec. 9, 2014).

[3] *See,* Gender Identity and Sex Discrimination, DIR. 2014-02 (August 19, 2014). DIR. 2014-02 clarifies OFCCP's policy that discrimination on the basis of sex includes discrimination on the bases of gender identity or transgender status.

[4] Though sexual orientation and gender identity are not explicitly protected by Title VII, EEOC and private litigants continue to develop sex discrimination theory. *Macy v. Holder*, EEOC Appeal No. 0120120821 (April 20, 2012). In *Macy*, the EEOC ruled that discrimination on the basis of gender identity is considered sex discrimination, citing, *inter alia*, *Glenn v. Brumby*, 663 F.3d 1312 (11th Cir. 2011); *Barnes v. City of Cincinnati*, 401 F.3d 729 (6th Cir. 2005); and, *Smith v. City of Salem*, 378 F.3d 566, 574 (6th Cir. 2005). EEOC has also found that federal sector claims by lesbian, gay, and bisexual individuals alleging sex-stereotyping state a sex discrimination claim under Title VII. *Veretto v. U.S. Postal Service*, EEOC Appeal No. 0120110873 (July 1, 2011); *Castello v. U.S. Postal Service*, EEOC Request No. 0520110649 (Dec. 20, 2011). *But see* *Etsitty v. Utah Transit Auth.*, 502 F.3d 1215, 1221 (10th Cir. 2007) (gender identity discrimination not protected by Title VII); *Bibby v. Philadelphia Coca Cola Bottling Co.*, 260 F.3d 257, 260 (3d Cir. 2001) (sexual orientation discrimination not protected by Title VII).

complaints based on sexual orientation and gender identity. Such coordination will be fact-driven and occur on a case-by-case basis. OFCCP will continue to transfer or jointly investigate complaints when OFCCP lacks jurisdiction and in other cases when discrimination is more completely remedied by joint investigation or by EEOC alone.

6. **ROLES AND REPONSIBILITIES:**

A. Regional and Field Managers: It is the responsibility of the appropriate regional and/or field manager(s) to ensure that regional and field staff make decisions about individual complaints and complaint investigations involving allegations of sexual orientation or gender identity discrimination in accordance with the policy stated in this directive.

B. Compliance Officers and Others: It is the responsibility of OFCCP's compliance officers, and employees responsible for complaint processing, to handle individual complaints and complaint investigations involving allegations of sexual orientation and gender identity discrimination in accordance with the policy stated in this directive.

7. **POLICY:** Because of the express prohibitions in EO 11246, as amended by EO 13672, OFCCP will accept and investigate individual and systemic complaints that allege discrimination on the basis of sexual orientation and gender identity against a federal contractor or subcontractor.[5] OFCCP will analyze each complaint to determine whether the alleged discrimination occurred on the basis of sexual orientation or gender identity, as well as on the basis of sex, and will coordinate with, and refer complaints to, EEOC on a case-by-case basis.

8. **ATTACHMENT:** None.

Patricia A. Shiu
Director
Office of Federal Contract Compliance Programs

[5] Under EO 11246, OFCCP has jurisdiction to investigate federal contractors or subcontractors with a contract of $10,000 or greater. For sexual orientation complaints, the contract or subcontract must be entered into or modified on or after April 8, 2015. For gender identity complaints, OFCCP has jurisdiction to accept and investigate complaints even if qualifying new or modified contracts pre-date April 8, 2015, pursuant to DIR. 2014-02.

www.ingramcontent.com/pod-product-compliance
Lightning Source LLC
Chambersburg PA
CBHW061147240926
51846CB00006B/949
* 9 7 8 1 9 3 7 2 9 9 2 6 2 *